The Complete
Wartime Correspondence
of Tsar Nicholas II and the
Empress Alexandra

The Complete Wartime Correspondence of Tsar Nicholas II and the Empress Alexandra

April 1914–March 1917

EDITED BY

Joseph T. Fuhrmann

Documentary Reference Collections

GREENWOOD PRESS
Westport, Connecticut • London

Library of Congress Cataloging-in-Publication Data

Nicholas II, Emperor of Russia, 1868–1918.
   The complete wartime correspondence of Tsar Nicholas II and the
Empress Alexandra : April 1914–March 1917 / edited by Joseph T.
Fuhrmann.
       p.   cm.—(Documentary reference collections)
   Includes bibliographical references and index.
   ISBN 0–313–30511–0 (alk. paper)
      1. Nicholas II, Emperor of Russia, 1868–1918—Correspondence.
2. Alexandra, Empress, consort of Nicholas II, Emperor of Russia,
1872–1918—Correspondence.   3. Russia—Kings and rulers—
Correspondence.   4. Russia—History—Nicholas II, 1894–1917—
Sources.   I. Alexandra, Empress, consort of Nicholas II, Emperor
of Russia, 1872–1918.   II. Fuhrmann, Joseph T., 1940–
III. Title.   IV. Series.
   DK258.N458   1999
   947.08′3′092—dc21   97–18193

British Library Cataloguing in Publication Data is available.

Copyright © 1999 by Joseph T. Fuhrmann

Library of Congress Catalog Card Number: 97–18193
ISBN: 0–313–30511–0

First published in 1999

Greenwood Press, 88 Post Road West, Westport, CT 06881
An imprint of Greenwood Publishing Group, Inc.

Printed in the United States of America

The paper used in this book complies with the
Permanent Paper Standard issued by the National
Information Standards Organization (Z39.48–1984).

10 9 8 7 6 5 4 3 2 1

I dedicate this work to my wife, Mary,

in affection and gratitude

Contents

Introduction

"Once they were published, these letters became the most important historical source for the subject with which they deal, and the main subject of them is the governance of the Russian Empire." [1]

Some people may be surprised to learn that all of the letters and most of the telegrams Nicholas II and the Empress Alexandra exchanged were written in English. But Alexandra was German, not Russian. As was typical of European aristocrats of the day, her studies included French and English. Nicholas knew English, French and German. When the youngsters met in 1884, it was clear that their best common language was English. After "Sunny" married "Nicky"— these were pet names—Alexandra mastered Russian. But in private situations, Nicholas and Alexandra continued to use English. When speaking to one or two of their children, the tsar and his wife used French to monitor the youngster's progress in that language. The family spoke Russian. Significantly, even Alexandra did not care for German; the Romanovs used it only when visiting with the Kaiser or other German dignitaries.

Nicholas was born at Tsarskoe Selo on May 6/18, 1868. [2] Tsarskoe Selo, the "Tsar's Village," was located thirteen miles south of St. Petersburg. It was a residential center for the tsar and other important people. Two royal houses dominated the town, the "Great Catherine Palace" which Empress Elizabeth (reigned, 1740-1762) built in honor of her mother, Catherine I (1725-1727), and the more modest "Alexander Palace" which Catherine II (1762-1796) presented to her favorite grandson, the future Alexander I (1801-1825). [3] Nicholas II's family lived in the west wing of the 100-room Alexander Palace.

Nicholas's father was Alexander III (1881-1894), referred to in the correspondence as "Anpapa." Nicholas's mother was Princess Dagmar of Denmark, known to Russians as Maria Fedorovna. When Nicholas and Alexandra were engaged in 1894, Maria asked her future daughter-in-law to address her as "Motherdear." As we see in the letters and telegrams which follow, Alexandra complied, though the two women never overcame an unusually severe personality clash. Nicholas had two younger brothers who preceded him in death, Alexander (1869-1870) and Georgy (1871-1899). He had two sisters, Kseniya (born in 1875) and Olga (born in 1882), both of whom died in 1960, and a brother, Michael (1878-1918), known in the correspondence as "Misha."

Alexandra was born Alix Victoria Helena Louise Beatrice, Princess of Hesse-Darmstadt, on June 6, 1872. Alix was named in honor of Alice, her mother, who was the third of Queen Victoria's nine children. Alix was close to her grandmother, especially after Alice died at 35 in 1878. Alix was only six years old when the tragedy occurred. Her father, Louis, often visited Queen Victoria with his motherless children. Victoria was especially fond of Alix, who received a good British education. Alix developed an aloof shell after her mother's death. She was henceforth at ease only in situations where she knew she could count upon unquestioned love and acceptance.[4]

Alix first traveled to Russian 1884 for the wedding of her older sister Elizabeth, ("Ella") to Sergei, one of Nicholas's uncles. Nicholas was then 16, Alix was 12. The two young people first met at the wedding. They did not see each over again for five years, until Alix visited Ella in St. Petersburg in 1889. The 21-year old tsarevich[5] entertained his 17-year old guest with particular care and attention. Nicholas and Alix did not meet the following year, 1890, when Alix paid Ella another visit. Even so, Alix thought she was falling in love with Nicholas. Their betrothal came in connection with the marriage of Alix's older brother Ernest, who by now had followed their father as the Grand Duke of Hesse-Darmstadt. Royalty throughout Europe made their way to Coburg for the event in the spring of 1894. Nicholas met Alix at the train station and he proposed the next morning. Alix refused at first because she did not want to abandon her Lutheran faith for the Russian Orthodox Church. But the tsarevich had useful allies in Victoria, the Kaiser and Ella, and they pressed his cause in a variety of ways. Alix accepted, and Nicholas joyfully fired off the news in a telegram to his parents. Whatever their real attitude, Alexander III and Maria Fedorovna wired back congratulations.[6]

Nicholas visited Hesse-Darmstadt again in June 1894. He returned to Russia to find his father in bad health. When Alexander III learned that he was suffering from nephritis, he went to the Crimea for rest and a cure. Nicholas asked Alix to join him at Livadia, and she did, traveling as an ordinary passenger until Nicholas met her at Simferopol. Alexander III suddenly died on November 1, 1894. The late tsar was 49; his son and successor was 26. Before noon of the following day, Alix was officially received into the Russian Orthodox Church as Alexandra Fedorovna. The wedding took place on November 26, 1894, one week after the funeral. At this point, Alexandria began seriously to concentrate on learning the Russian language.

The Emperor Paul (reigned, 1796-1801) so disliked his mother, Catherine the Great, that when he became tsar, he issued an edict concerning succession to the throne which assured that no woman would ever again rule Russia. As an autocrat, Nicholas could, in theory, change the decree, but it had been so sanctioned by time that he refrained from that option. He and Alexandra were consumed by the need to produce a male heir. Their first child was a daughter, Olga, born in November 1895. Tatyana, Maria and Anastasia followed at two year intervals in

1897, 1899 and 1901. Then came a male heir: Aleksei, born on August 12, 1904. Within a few weeks it was clear that the tsarevich suffered from hemophilia. Fearing this would be used to exclude their son from the succession, Nicholas and Alexandra made the critical decision to keep their son's condition a secret. It was widely known that the boy was sickly, and a bout with hemophilia in 1912 was so serious as to force a series of news bulletins to prepare the world for his death. But Aleksei's exact malady remained a secret.

The Siberian peasant, mystic and healer Grigory Rasputin appeared in St. Petersburg in 1905. Impressing and befriending increasingly influential people, he was finally presented to the Royal family in October, at the height of the Revolution of 1905. Rasputin began to serve Aleksei as a healer in 1906. Since the public did not know that Aleksei was a hemophiliac, it did not understand the royal couple's attachment to Rasputin. Rasputin led a scandalous life, he took bribes and consorted with unsavory people. He was boastful and easily drawn into scandalous situations. All this discredited the tsar and his wife, especially now that Russia had entered into an age marked by a legislature (the Duma) and semi-free press. Nicholas knew he had to maneuver through difficult (and ever-changing) currents—and in fact he did this reasonably well as late as the fall of 1915. But Rasputin was a problem that would not vanish.

The public assumed that Alexandra was taken with Rasputin as a holy man. This led to numerous and repeated efforts to prove to the Empress and her husband that Rasputin was corrupt—and a lecher. Nicholas and Alexandra responded to these onslaughts by denying or minimizing the charges against "Our Friend," as he is known in their correspondence. These denials made them seem ignorant, gullible—stupid, even. Ironically, both the emperor and his wife understood what Rasputin was "really like."[7] But what were they to do? Send away the only person who could safeguard their son's life? Candor as to why they needed Rasputin might have strengthened their position, but they had made the decision to keep Aleksei's hemophilia a secret.

Rasputin's behavior gave enemies of the monarchy choice propaganda material, but the actual damage to Nicholas II in this was slight. The situation became more serious when Russia went to war in August 1914. Rasputin was known to be pacifistic, and he predicted that a war with Germany would be a catastrophe for Russia. As his predictions proved correct, *he* was blamed for the difficult situation which descended upon Russia. Rumors held that Rasputin was a spy, a German agent, advocate of a separate peace. The German-born Alexandra was even more vulnerable to such attacks. The shy woman had never been popular with Russians, she had no strong constituencies which would leap to her defense in times of distress. Nicholas II was increasingly seen as a weakling: well-intentioned but so dominated by his wife as to make intentions irrelevant. It was even rumored that Rasputin, not Nicholas, fathered Aleksei.

The Nicky-Sunny Correspondence shows Nicholas's weakness and his wife's overbearing character. Alexandra's letters go beyond expressing opinions and making suggestions. The Empress had an astounding ability to create her own reality. Then she bombarded her husband with letters which sought to pound the same vision into his mind. Alexandra's energy, consistency and conviction are striking. Nicholas simply did not have the energy, focus or self-confidence to resist such onslaughts. Even if he knew his wife was wrong, it was simpler, finally, to let her have her way.

Nicholas's weakness and Alexandra's strength is clearly revealed in the career of the last minister of the interior. "Yesterday I saw a man who pleased me very much," the tsar wrote to Alexandra about Alexander Dmitrievich Protopopov on July 20, 1916.[8] Protopopov was indeed charming, experienced in government, and, at this point, recommended for high office by all sorts of people. Nicholas's instinct was to make the successful businessman his minister of commerce and industry. This was a reasonable idea. If Protopopov subsequently apologized for his performance as minister of the interior, he insisted he would have been successful in a post that involved financial issues.

Protopopov was a pawn in a larger game. Changes on the council of ministers in the summer of 1916 threatened Rasputin. Interior and justice suddenly fell into the hands of Grigory's enemies. The assistant-minister of the interior directed the Okhrana (the secret police) and censorship; it was he who decided how Rasputin would be guarded and how much freedom the press would have to criticize him. The ministry of justice controlled the courts and handled legal charges against Rasputin and his cronies. Either ministry might hurt Rasputin; working together, they could destroy him.

Rasputin was anxious to replace the most dangerous ministers with his allies. This made him receptive to overtures from "Dr. Badmaev," a figure who was well known to the St. Petersburg elite. Badmaev was born Zhamsaran in the Lake Baikal region in 1851. His family was of the Buryat tribe, it became important by serving the interests of Russian expansion in the east. Badmaev eventually settled into the practice of "Tibetan medicine" in an elegant clinic on the outskirts of the capital. Among those who enjoyed Badmaev's herbs, concoctions and "arousing powders" was Vice-President of the Duma, A. D. Protopopov. Protopopov was a landowner (19,600 acres) and cotton manufacturer from Simbirsk. As a member of the Third and Fourth Dumas, Protopopov identified with the "liberal wing" of the moderate conservative Octobrist Party. Syphilis contracted as a guards cadet brought Protopopov to Badmaev's clinic. Protopopov's public behavior grew increasingly erratic in 1915, when he began to show signs of insanity. He lay in Badmaev's clinic for a full six months from late 1915 to early 1916.[9]

Badmaev introduced Rasputin to Protopopov. Both agreed the personable gentleman would be a strong candidate for minister of the interior. He could promote their interests in that post. The Nicky-Sunny Correspondence shows how Protopopov obtained the office. The letters also document Rasputin's skill at manipulating Alexandra, the Empress's ability to bend her husband to her wishes—and the weakness of Nicholas II. The dynamic was that Badmaev gave Rasputin an "idea," he persuaded Alexandra of its validity, she pressured her husband to comply, and if necessary, Alexandra—with Rasputin's help —demolished objections Nicholas might raise. Alexandra behaved in this way even at the point where she must have known that her husband was correct in deciding to fire Protopopov. By then, however, the Empress had formed an emotional attachment to Protopopov which transcended reason.

Rasputin's first task was to persuade Nicholas II not to "waste" Protopopov in the ministry of finance. The incumbent, Prince Vsevolod Shakhavskoi, was already in Rasputin's corner. But Rasputin needed a new minister and assistant-minister of the interior. Protopopov and Paul Kurlov seemed ideal for those positions. Rasputin had known Kurlov since 1908. Kurlov had been assistant-minister of the interior under Stolypin; he was fired for not maintaining the vigilance which might have kept his superior from being assassinated in 1911. During the war, Kurlov directed civilian affairs in the Baltic (he was not entrusted with military responsibilities). He was faulted for his slow response to the German advance, and was forced out of the service on July 29, 1915. Dr. Badmaev and Kurlov then became partners in securing war contracts through Rasputin. Unsavory and disgraced as he might be, Kurlov could bring the expertise to internal affairs which Protopopov lacked. Kurlov's advancement to one of the most sensitive posts in the tsar's government shows how serious the situation had come to be by this time. Nicholas's government was so discredited that able people were no longer willing to serve in it. Kurlov's reputation was so bad that, contrary to law, Nicholas did not publish the decree appointing him to his high office.

"Gregory begs you earnestly to name Protopopov" minister of the interior, Alexandra wrote Nicholas on September 7, 1916.[10] "I don't know him," she continued, "but I believe in our Friend's wisdom & guidance." "You know him [Protopopov] & had such a good impression of him," the Empress further reminded her husband, and "I think you could not do better than name him." Why was Alexandra so convinced of this? She offers one good argument: placing the vice-president of the Duma in a key post might improve relations between the throne and the Duma. Then comes what seems to be the *real* reason: "He likes our Friend since at least 4 years & that says much for a man...." Alexandra reminds the tsar that Rasputin "only want[s] yr. good & [he is a man to] whom God has given more insight, wisdom & enlightenment than all the military put together. His love for you & Russia is so intense & God has sent him to be yr. help & guide & [he] prays so hard for you." Then a final nagging touch. The Empress suggests that Nicholas "write out" a list of subjects he needed to cover with Sturmer when the chairman of the council of ministers would appear at GHQ that Saturday. Then she adds: "no, here[,] I shall write [it] out for you...."

Alexandra wrote two additional letters in the next two days promoting Protopopov's cause. Finally, on September 9, 1916, Nicholas responded in a passage which has been much quoted. "That Protopopov, is I think, a good man, but he is much in affairs with factories etc. ... I must think that question [making him a minister of the interior rather than minister of commerce and industry] over as it takes me quite unexpectedly. Our Friend's ideas about men are sometimes queer, as you know—so one must be careful especially in nominations of high people. ... Is it good to send away both [the minister of the interior and his assistant] at the same time [?] ... All these changes exhaust the head. I find they happen much too often. It is certainly not at all good for the interior of the country because every new man brings changes also into administration. I am sorry my little letter has become so tiresome, but I had to answer your questions."[11]

These were wise words—but Alexandra could not accept them. She reiterated her support for Protopopov in a letter and a telegram of September 10, 1916. Nicholas capitulated that evening. "It will be done," he wired tersely. As a sign of his continuing reservations, however, the tsar appointed Protopopov *acting* minister of the interior.[12] Nicholas immediately saw that Protopopov was a terrible choice as minister of the interior. Indeed, by November 10, 1916, he decided he also had to replace Boris Sturmer (Chairman of the Council of Ministers) and Aleksei Bobrinsky (Minister of Agriculture). This was the tsar's last chance to regain some control over events. Nicholas's problem, as so often in the past, was his wife. Alexandra had never been a very good judge of character. Perhaps the strains of the war accentuated that weakness. Whatever, by now the Empress was surrounded by an amazing gaggle of fools and incompetents, each of whom was skilled in the art of flattering her. None was more accomplished in this task than A. D. Protopopov.

Protopopov was more than a burden to Nicholas II; he threatened the entire tsarist system. The mobs which toppled the government four months later seem to have hated Protopopov even more than "the German woman" or the tsar. Protopopov granted their case when he testified before the Provisional Government's commission which investigated leading figures in the tsarist regime. "My entering the ministry [of the interior] was more than a mistake," he admitted, and "then things happened which led me to misfortune." Protopopov confessed he never even understood the work of the ministry he supposedly led.[13]

Nicholas expected Alexandra to be upset over Protopopov's dismissal, and he could forsee some of the weapons she would use. On November 10, 1916, the tsar referred to "changes wh. are absolutely necessary now." "I am sorry about Prot., a good honest man, but he jumped fr. one idea to another & could not stick to his opinion. I remembered that fr. the very beginning. People said he was not normal some years ago fr. a certain illness (when he went to Badmaev). It is risky leaving the min. of Int.[ernal Affairs] in such hands at such times!" Then a line which has been often quoted: "Only please don't mix in our Friend! It is I who carry the responsibility [and] I want to be free to choose accordingly."[14]

Alexandra fired off two letters and two telegrams in the next two days passionately defending Protopopov. A family visit to GHQ was already planned, and the tsar's loved ones traveled there on November 13, 1916. This—together with at least four telegrams from Rasputin—saved Protopopov. We have no record of what was said back and forth, though—incredibly!—at the end, it was Nicholas who apologized to his noisy manipulative wife: "Forgive me if I have been cross or impatient, sometimes one's temper has to get through!" the tsar wrote on December 4, 1916. In another passage, Nicholas echoed a sentiment Alexandra expressed in a note she left him at her departure: "Yes, these days we spent together, were indeed hard ones—but tis only thanks to you that I stood them more or less calmly. You were so staunch & induring —I admire you more than I can say!"[15]

Alexander Trepov, the new chairman of the council of ministers, was furious to learn Nicholas had changed his mind and was retaining Protopopov. Trepov tried to resign. Failing to get the tsar's agreement to that, Trepov turned to Protopopov and actually persuaded *him* to step down. In vain. The empress had no difficulty in persuading Protopopov to stay. Trepov was fired after 47 days in office. The weak survived; the strong perished.

There is a final, sad note to the Protopopov affair. Alexandra (and Rasputin) know perfectly well the man was worthless as a minister of the interior. By November 1916, hunger stalked Petrograd while food spoiled in the countryside. Russia's railroad system was disintegrating, and the army get top priority in the matter of supplies. Suffering was concentrated in the larger cities. Rasputin and the Empress believed Protopopov's early assurances that he could get food and fuel to Petrograd. But Protopopov was weak and confused, and in office he clearly had no idea of what to do. Protopopov attended few meetings of the council of ministers, but he spent uncounted hours with the Empress extolling the virtues of laissez-faire and the Physiocrats. A skeptical but hopeful tsar did everything he could to grant Protopopov the authority he demanded. This involved transferring the "supply problem" from the ministry of agriculture to interior. But other ministers saw disaster in this; they dared to meet and discuss the matter, and to speak against it by a vote of eight to six. Their act had no legal status, it was simply a message. But Protopopov panicked, he rushed to the Empress and her husband, who then happened to be visiting Tsarskoe Selo. Protopopov tearfully recounted the hostility he faced. Nicholas and Alexandra were stunned at such a reaction to relatively minor opposition! The tsar glanced anxiously at his wife as their visitor sobbed on.   Alexandra smiled; she was quiet—and furious. The Emperor and his wife were "dissatisfied with my indecisiveness," Protopopov later told the investigatory commission.   They insisted "I should stop wavering now that I had obtained the tsar's agreement to direct supply activity."[16] But Protopopov could not act.

Rasputin was astounded when he learned of this meeting. "He himself ran up to me and asked me to give him the rationing question," Rasputin growled, "and when mamasha and papasha agreed, he chickened out. If a minister's a coward, he's out of place."[17] Protopopov remained in office. The people of Petrograd starved and shivered through the winter of 1916-1917. In March, they took revenge.

Russia had four chairmen of the council of ministers, five ministers of the interior, five ministers of agriculture and three ministers of war in the last eighteen months of the tsarist regime. Five other ministries each had five different heads. This was known as " ministerial leapfrog." The historian Michael Florinsky called this chapter an "amazing, extravagant, and pitiful spectacle, and one without parallel in the history of civilized nations.[18]

*   *   *

The Nicky-Sunny Correspondence is the sad chronicle of a weak man with a strong wife. Those who read their letters and telegrams see that their authors were headed for disaster. It is natural to ask questions. Was the fall of the monarchy inevitable? What was the last point at which Nicholas might have saved himself? What would that have required? The tsar and his family seem to have swept along by some terrible force which dictated that they would perish violently, tragically. But that force was within themselves.

Nicholas himself had a sense of how the story would end.

"Do you know on what day my birthday falls?" he asked Stolypin in 1909.

"How could I forget it?" the chairman of the council of ministers replied. "It is May 6."

"What Saint's Day is that?"

"Forgive me, Sire, I'm afraid I've forgotten."

"The patriarch Job."

"Then God be praised!" Stolypin declared. "Your Majesty's reign will end gloriously, for Job, after piously enduring the most cruel tests of his fate, found blessings and rewards showered upon his head!"

"No, no, Peter Arkadievich, believe me! I have presentment—more than a presentment, a secret conviction—that I am destined for terrible trials. But I shall not receive my reward on *this* earth. How often have I not applied to myself the words of Job: *Hardly have I entertained a fear that it comes to pass, and all the evils I foresee descend upon my head.*"[19]

Nicholas and Alexandra faced death nobly. They knew the end was near by the summer of 1918. In a letter smuggled from captivity, the Empress told Anna Vyrubova "We are preparing our souls for the Kingdom of Heaven." Olga relayed the following message from Nicholas in a letter she wrote at Tobol'sk: "Father has forgiven and prays for everyone; he asked to have it passed on to all who have remained loyal to him and to those on whom they might have influence, that they not avenge him; and not avenge themselves, but remember that the evil which is now in the world will become still more powerful, and yet it is not evil which conquers evil, but only love ...."[20]

Nicholas and Alexandra exchanged nearly 1,700 letters and telegrams from April 28, 1914, to March 7, 1917. All of the letters and most of their telegrams are in English, with a considerable use (in descending order) of Russian, French and German words, expressions and phrases. The first stage of my work with the correspondence involved placing on computer disk the texts of Alexandra's letters to Nicholas as published by V. D. Nabokov in Berlin in 1923. I then added the translations of Nicholas's letters and telegrams to Alexandra offered in the Hynes-Vulliamy-Wright volume of 1929. I used A. A. Sergeev's three-volume Russian translation of the correspondence to bridge gaps in the Berlin-London editions. (For full citation, see my Bibliography: Nicholas II and Alexandra Fedorovna, *Perepiska Nikolaia i Aleksandry Romanovykh.*) Finally, I subjected the texts I had so created to a line-by-line check against the originals in GARF, the *Gosudarstvennyi Arkhiv Rossiiskoi Federatsii* (*State Archive of the Russian Federation*), formerly TsGAOR, *Tsentral'nyi Gosudarstvennyi Arkhiv Oktyabr'skoi Revolyutsii* (*Central State Archive of the October Revolution*) during the summers of 1994 and 1995.

Only two of Alexandra's telegrams are in GARF; the archivists believe the other telegrams have been lost. So the empress's telegrams appear here in my translations from A. A. Sergeev's work. This puts me, as an editor, in a strange position. Whereas I mark "sic" the words Alexandra customarily misspells in her letters (e.g., "balkony," "cemetary," "namesday"), these words appear I the telegrams correctly spelled. Alexandra almost certainly misspelled these such in her telegrams, but *sic* is an editorial device whereby the reader is assured that "this is how the text so indicated appears in the original." But since I was forced to work from Russian translations of English telegrams now lost, I cannot give that assurance. Fortunately, the tsar's telegrams offer no particular problems. The English texts appear here as he wrote them, I offer his Russian telegrams in my English translations. Readers interested in the original Russian telegrams may find them in A. A. Sergeev's edition of the Nicky-Sunny correspondence.

The letters and telegrams are published here in the order in which they were written. The first number of each letter or telegram is that assigned by the editor, Joseph T. Fuhrmann. The second number is, in the case of letters, the number the author assigned that letter. Nicholas numbered his letters to his wife through and including his letter of August 25, 1915; the tsar did not number subsequent letters to his wife. Alexandra numbered all of her letters to Nicholas. The first number of each telegram has also been assigned by the editor; the second number is the number assigned by the telegraph dispatch system.

The correspondence of Nicholas and Alexandra is preserved in Fond (Record Group) 640 of GARF, opis' (Series) 1, dela (folders) 102-112, 115, and 1148-1151. The contents of each delo (folder) are as follows:

Fond 640, opis' 1, delo 102, letters of Nicholas II to Alexandra Fedorovna dated 28 April-25 November 1914.

Fond 640, opis' 1, delo 103, telegrams of Nicholas II to Alexandra Fedorovna dated 17 June 1907-19 December 1914.

Fond 640, opis' 1, delo 104, telegrams of Nicholas II to Alexandra Fedorovna dated 23 January-3 December 1915.

Fond 640, opis' 1, delo 105, letters of Nicholas II to Alexandra Fedorovna dated 24 January-26 June 1915.

Fond 640, opis' 1, delo 106, letters of Nicholas II to Alexandra Fedorovna dated 25 August-31 December 1916.

Fond 640, opis' 1, delo 107, telegrams of Nicholas II to Alexandra Fedorovna dated 1 January-30 June 1916.

Fond 640, opis' 1, delo 108, telegrams of Nicholas II to Alexandra Fedorovna dated 1 July-6 March 1917.

Fond 640, opis' 1, delo 109, letters of Nicholas II to Alexandra Fedorovna dated 2 January-31 March 1916.

Fond 640, opis' 1, delo 110, letters of Nicholas II to Alexandra Fedorovna dated 3 April-31 May 1916.

Fond 640, opis' 1, delo 111, letters of Nicholas II to Alexandra Fedorovna dated, 1-30 June 1916.

Fond 640, opis' 1, delo 112, letters of Nicholas II to Alexandra Fedorovna dated 1 July-20 August 1916.

Fond 640, opis' 1, delo 113, typed letters of Nicholas II to Alexandra Fedorovna dated 23 May 1889-16 September 1913.

Fond 640, opis' 1, delo 114, letters of Nicholas II to Alexandra Fedorovna dated 4 September-30 October 1916.

Fond 640, opis' 1, delo 115, letters of Nicholas II to Alexandra Fedorovna dated 1 November 1916-27 February 1917.

Fond (Record Group) 601 is entitled "Imperator Nikolai II°ⁱ. The contents of each of its dela (folders) are as follows:

Fond 601, opis' (Series) 1, delo (folder) 1148, letters of Alexandra Fedorovna to Nicholas II dated 22 June 1899-17 December 1914.

Fond 601, opis' 1, delo 1149, letters of Alexandra Fedorovna to Nicholas II dated 21 January-31 October 1915.

Fond 601, opis' 1, delo 1150, letters of Alexandra Fedorovna to Nicholas II dated 1 November 1915-31 March 1916.

Fond 601, opis' 1, delo 1151, letters of Alexandra Fedorovna to Nicholas II dated 1 April 1916-4 March 1917.

Considerations of space sometimes made it necessary to consolidate small paragraphs in the original texts into larger paragraphs here. In other instances, I divided longer paragraphs in the original into smaller paragraphs. For purposes of citation, I divided larger letters into sections, each marked in brackets by a lowercase letter: "a," "b," "c," etc. If one reads "32c," it means that this document is Number 32, it is divided into paragraphs, and I am referring the reader to the paragraph which has been labelled "c." Nicholas and Alexandra usually placed a cross at the end of their letters. I have not tried to duplicate these notations.

Full footnote citations are given at the ends of the letters or telegrams where they first appear, in most cases. Subsequent references to notes already cited will appear throughout the book, and the reader can refer back to the full citation. In some cases, a footnote number will appear before its full citation in the text, so the reader will need to look ahead in the book to find those full citations.

The Biographical Index of this work gives details concerning the lives of the people who are of importance in the Nicky-Sunny correspondence. Some of these people were important only in this context.

Nicholas and Alexandra used nicknames, irregular spellings and abbreviations to designate many of the people mentioned in their letters and telegrams. These names are marked   <   the first time each appears in a letter or telegram. This mark tells the reader the name in question appears in Appendix I: Name and Term Identifier. This Appendix says, for example, that

Ania< or Anna< was Anna Vyrubova, the empress's closest friend.

Ducky< was Victoria Fedorovna, wife of Kirill.

Kirill<   was g.p. [grand prince] Cyril Vladimirovich, Nicholas's cousin, rear-ad.

etc.

Frequently cited places and terms are also marked, for example:

Znam.<, Znamenia<, Znamenje< was the Znamenskaya church at Tsarskoe Selo.

Coun. of the Em.< refers to the Council of the Empire or "State Council" (gosudarstvennyi sovet); see Footnote 96.

Nicholas and Alexandra sometimes transliterated Russian names into English in ways which were familiar at the time but might confuse modern readers. These translations are also listed in Appendix I. For example:

Galitzin< was Prince N. D. Golitsyn, the last chairman of the Council of Ministers.

Kniajevich< was N. A. Knyazhevich, maj.-gen., cavalry.

The importance of the Nicky-Sunny correspondence is clear. Sir Bernard Pares thought these letters to be the "most important historical source for the subjects with which they deal, and the main subject of them is the governance of the Russian Empire."[21] A complete edition that contains both the original English texts (when possible) and English translations of the remaining material in Russian is timely considering the rising tide of interest in Nicholas II in the West and in Russia.

I wish to thank IREX, the International Research and Exchanges Board, for two generous short-term travel grants, which permitted me to begin my work in Moscow in the summer of 1994 and to finish during the summer of 1995. The University Committee on Institutional Research and Studies of Murray State University was equally generous in supporting my work on the Nicky-Sunny correspondence both in Moscow and in the United States. I am also grateful to the entire staff of GARF for its help and patience with a foreigner, and especially Lyubov' Ivanovna Tyutyutshik, a gracious lady, a fine scholar, and the most capable of archivists. Devin Perkins, Jason Sullivan and Gena Wilson helped prepare the manuscript for publication. These people and organizations have my thanks for helping to improve my work, but only I am responsible for errors and shortcomings which remain.

I dedicate this work to my wife, Mary. Her love, support and patience helped me so much in this and every other enterprise.

NOTES

1. Bernard Pares, *The Fall of the Russian Monarchy, A Study of the Evidence* (New York: Knopf, 1939), p. 249.

2. Peter the Great adopted the Julian calendar, and it remained in use in Russia from 1700 until 1918. The Julian calendar was twelve days behind the Gregorian calendar in the Nineteenth Century, thirteen days in the Twentieth Century. Nicholas and Alexandra dated their letters and telegrams according to the Julian calendar. My dates are likewise "Old Style" (O.S.) unless other-wise noted. "N.S." indicates Gregorian dates.

3. *The Romanov Family Album*, Introductory text by Robert K. Massie, picture research and descriptions by Marilyn Pfeifer Swezey, photographs assembled by Anna Vyrubova (New York: Vendome Press, 1982), p. 12.

4. Robert K. Massie's *Nicholas and Alexandra* (New York: Atheneum, 1968) remains a fine study.

5. The heir to the Russian throne was the *tsesarevich*, his younger brother was the *tsarevich* (plural, *tsarevichi*). In the West, however, the heir was referred to as the "tsarevich," and I have followed that practice. Abroad, the tsar's wife was known as the "tsarina," and I use the word in this manner, too, though actually there is no such Russian word, at least not as applied to this subject. Peter the Great introduced the titles of *emperor* and *empress*, but by Nicholas's time, the titles *tsar* and *tsaritsa* were used alternatively.

6. *Ibid.*, pp. 30-34.

7. Joseph T. Fuhrmann, *Rasputin, A Life* (New York: Praeger, 1990), pp. 25, 51-55, 63, 65-66 etc.

8. See Letter No. 1263.

9. Fuhrmann, *Rasputin*, p. 177.

10. See Letter No. 1380.

11. This is Letter No. 1386, the passage quoted has been slightly edited; cf. the original.

12. See Letter No. 1392. Concerning Protopopov's status as *upravlyayushchii minister*, see Footnote 353.

13. For Protopopov's testimony, see P. E. Shchegolev (ed.), *Padenie tsarskogo rezhima,* I, pp. 140, 161-162, II, pp. 299-300, IV, p. 482 (Moscow and Leningrad, 1924-1927). The "plot" which led to Protopopov's appointment as minister of the interior is reviewed in Fuhrmann, *Rasputin,* pp. 177-180.

14. See Letter No. 1584. See Footnote 305 concerning the "certain illness," syphilis

15. See Letter No. 1597.

16. *Padenie*, I, pp. 77-78.

17. *Ibid.*, II, pp. 67, 439. "Papasha" and "mamasha" are respectful, affectionate peasant names for the tsar and tsaritsa.

18. Michael T. Florinsky, *End of the Russian Empire* (New Haven: Yale, 1931), pp. 64, 86-90.

19. Maurice Paléologue, *An Ambassador's Memoirs*, trans. F. A. Holt (New York: Hippocrene Books, 3rd ed., 1925), I, p. 98.

20. *Romanov Family Album*, p. 126.

21. Pares, *Fall*, p. 249.

The Nicky-Sunny Correspondence

No. 1./ Her No. 232.   Livadia. April 28th 1914.

My sweetest treasure, my very Own one,

   You will read these lines when you get into your bed in a strange place & unknown house. God grant that the journey may be a pleasant & interesting one,
& not too tiring nor too dusty. I am so glad to have the map, as then can follow
you hourly. I shall miss you horribly, but I am glad for you that you will be
away for 2 days & get new impressions & hear nothing of Anias< stories.

   My heart is heavy & sore—must one's kindness & love always be repayed
thus? The black family< & now she [Anna Vyrubova]?[1] One is always told one
can never love enough—here we gave our hearts our home to her, our private life
even—& this is what we have gained! It is difficult not to become bitter—it
seems so cruelly unjust.— May God have mercy & help us, the heart is so heavy!
I am in despair that she gives you worries & disagreeable conversations, no rest
for you either. Well try & forget all these two days. I bless you & cross you &
hold you tightly in my arms— kiss you all over with boundless love & devotion.
I shall be in Church to-morrow morning at 9 & try to go again on Thursday—it
does me good to pray for you when we are separated—cannot get accustomed,
for ever so short, not to have you in the house, tho' I have our 5 treasures[, our
children].—Sleep well my Sunshine, my own precious one & thousand tender
kisses fr. yr. own old   Wify.   [P.S.] God bless & keep you.

   1. Alexandra had recently cooled towards Anna Vyrubova, her closest friend. (See Letter No. 57b
and Fuhrmann, *Rasputin*, pp. 116-117, 126-127, for causes of the rift and the restoration of their
friendship in early 1915.) The "black family" refers to Militsa and Anastasia, daughters of King
Nicholas of Montenegro. Militsa's husband was the tsar's cousin, Peter Nicholaevich; Anastasia's
husband was Peter's brother, Nicholas Nicholaevich, popularly known as "Nicholasha" (the name
could also be spelled in English *Nikolasha*). "Montenegro" means "black mountain"; the swarthy
Montenegrin sisters were known as the "black princesses," the "crows." Nicholas and Alexandra
were once close to the four. Although Alexandra's friendship with the two couples collapsed in
1908, Nicholas maintained good relations with Nicholasha and Peter. Indeed, when the war began,
the tsar unexpectedly made Nicholasha supreme commander of Russian armies in the west.

No. 2/ Telegram 33. Askaniya Nova [on the Crimea]> Livadia. 29 Ap 1914.
4.40> 5.15 p.m.*   To her majesty. Arrived well half an hour before we expected. After Eriklik fine hot weather. Delightful place, such nice comfortable
people. Shall wire more details in the evening. Tender love. Niki

* This indicates the telegram was sent from Askaniya Nova (a private estate on the Crimea) to Livadia. The original telegram states the times as "4 ch. 40 m." and "5 ch. 15 m.," which in English
would read "4 h. 40 min.," "5 h. 15 min." For brevity, I state these times as "4.40," "5.15," which is
consistent with the way Nicholas and Alexandra noted time. In short, this telegram was sent at 4:40
p.m. and arrived at 5:15 p.m.

No. 3/ Telegram 597. Livadia> Askaniya Nova. 29 Ap 1914. 5.39> 6.02 p.m.
To his majesty. Mist on the mountains. Morning dined and went to chapel.
Children and I strolled a bit during the day. Aleksei< is at Massandra. His head
hurts. Miss you. Kiss you passionately. Wish you splendid return trip. God
keep you. Alix

No. 4/ Telegram 37. Askaniya Nova> Livadia. 29 Ap 1914. 8.35> 9.20 p.m.
To her majesty. Thanks for telegram. Saw any amount of interesting animals
[and] birds all living together in freedom. Walked in a lovely park with ponds
full of fish. Drove round the estate through the steppes. Now off to dinner.
Good night to all dears. Niki

No. 5/ Telegram 600. Livadia> Askaniya Nova. 29 Ap 1914. 10.25> 10.42
p.m.   To his majesty. Thank you warmly for two telegrams. Glad it is very
interesting and good. Send wishes for good night and happy trip. Going to
sleep early. Hope to attend Mass again to-morrow morning. Blessings and
greeting from all six.< Alix

No. 6/ Telegram 39. Askaniya Nova> Livadia. 30 Ap 1914. 9.10> 9.55 a.m.
To her majesty. Hope [you] slept well. Today much cooler. After 7.30 drove
about and saw different kinds of cattle. After early luncheon start at 10 on way
back. Looking so forward to this evening. Kiss you and children tenderly. Niki

No. 7/ Radiotelegram in Russian. From Kronstadt. 20 June 1914. 3.15 p.m.
To the empress. Peterhof. English squadron passed [our imperial] yacht exactly
at noon. Very beautiful picture; weather lovely, hot. Will be home for supper.
All embrace [you]. Niki

No. 8/ Her No. 233.   Peterhoff. June 29th 1914.
My Beloved,
    It is very sad not to accompany you—but I thought I would better remain with
the little Ones< quietly here. Heart & soul are ever near you with tenderest love
& passion, all my prayers suround [sic] you—I am therefore glad to [go] at once
to evening service when you leave & to-morrow morning at 9 to Mass. I shall
dine with Ania,< [daughters] Marie & Anastasia & go early to bed. Marie Bary-

atinsky will lunch with us & spend her last afternoon with me.—I do hope you will have a calm sea & enjoy yr. trip wh. will be a rest for you—you need it, as were looking pale to-day.—Shall miss you <u>sorely</u>, my very Own precious One.—Sleep well my treasure,—my bed will be, oh, so empty. God bless & kiss you. Very tenderest kisses fr. yr. own old   Wify.

No. 9/ Her No. 234.   Ts.[arskoe] S[elo]. Sept. 19th 1914.

My own, my very own sweet One,

I am so happy for you that you can at last manage to go, as I know how deeply you have been suffering all this time—yr. restless sleep has been even a proof of it. It was a topic I on purpose did not touch, knowing & perfectly well under-standing your feelings, at the same time realising [sic] that it is better you are not out at the head of the army.—This journey will be a tiny comfort to you, & I trust you will manage to see many troops. I can picture to myself their joy seeing you & all your feelings—alas that I cannot be with you to see it all. It is more than ever hard to bid goodbye to you my Angel—the blank after yr. departure is so intense! Then you, I know, not withstanding all you will have to do, will still miss yr. little family & precious agoo wee one<. He will quickly get better now that our Friend< has seen him & that will be a relief to you. [a]

May the news only be good whilst you are away, as to know you have hard news to bear alone, makes the heart bleed. Looking after the wounded is my consolation & that is why the last morning I even want[ed] to go there, whilst you were receiving, so as to keep my spirits up & not break down before you. To lessen their suffering even in a small way, helps the aching heart. Except all I go through with you & our beloved country & men I suffer for my "small old home" [her native German province of Hesse-Darmstadt] & her troops & Ernie< & Irene< & many a friend in sorrow there—but how many go through the same. And then the shame, the humiliation to think that Germans should behave as they do!—one longs to sink into the ground. But none of such conversation in this letter. I must rejoice with you that you are <u>going</u>, and I do—but yet egoisti-cally I suffer horribly to be separated—we are not accustomed to it & I do so endlessly love my very own precious Boysy dear [Nicholas, her husband]. Soon 20 years that I belong to you & what bliss it has been to be your very own little Wify!—[b]

How nice if you see dear Olga [your sister], it will cheer her up & do you good.—I shall give you a letter & things for the wounded for her. Lovy dear, my telegrams cant be very warm, as they go through so many military hands—but you will read all my love & longing between the lines. Sweety, if in any way you do not feel quite the thing [you] will be sure to call Fedorov,< wont you—& have an eye on Fredericks. My very most earnest prayers will follow <u>you</u> by day and night. I commend you into our Lord's safe keeping—may He guard, guide & lead you & bring you safe & sound back again. I bless you & love you, as man Has rarely been loved before—& kiss every dearly beloved place & press you tenderly to my own heart. For ever yr. very own old <u>Wify</u>.   [P.S.] The Image [icon] will lie this night under my cushion before I give it to you with my fer-vent blessing. [c]

No. 10/ Her No. 235.   Tsarskoe Selo. Sept. 20th 1914.

My own beloved One,

I am resting in bed before dinner, the girls< have gone to church & Baby< is finishing his dinner. He has only slight pains sometimes. Oh my love! It was hard bidding you goodbye & seeing that lonely, pale face with big sad eyes at the waggon-window—my heart cried out, take me with you. If only you had had N.P.S.< or Mordv.< with you, a young loving face near you, you would be less lonely & "feel warmer". [a]

I came home & then broke down, prayed,—then lay down & smoked to get myself into order. When eyes looked more decent I went up to Aleksei & lay for a time near him on the sopha in the dark[;] rest did good, as I was tired out in every sense. At 4¼ I came down to see Lazarev & gave him over the little Image [icon] for the regiment—I did not say it was fr. you, as then you would have to give to all the other newly formed regiments. The girls worked in the stores.[2] At 4½ Tatiana & I received [A. B.] Neidhardt about her committee[3]—the first [meeting] will be in the Winter palace< on Wednesday after a Te Deum, I shall again not assist [i.e., be present]. It is a comfort to set the girls working alone & that they will be known more & learn to be useful. During tea I read reports & then got a letter at last from Victoria,< dated the 1/13 Sep.[4] it has taken long coming by messenger. I copy out what I think may interest you: "We have gone through anxious days during the long retreat of the allied armies in France. Quite between ourselves (so lovy don't tell on better [?]) the French at first left the English army to bear all the brunt of the heavy [G]erman out flanking attack, alone, & if the English troops had been less dogged, not only they but the whole French forces would have been crumpled up. This has now been set right & two French generals who were to blame in the matter, have been deposed by Joffre & replaced by others. One of them had 6 notes from the English Com. in chief [Sir John] French, unopened in his pocket—the other kept sending as answer to an appeal to come on & help, that his horses were too tired. That is past history however, but it has cost the lives & liberty of many good officers & men. Luckily it was kept dark & people here in general dont know about it.— [b]

"The 500,000 recruits asked for are nearly complete & hard at work drilling all day long masses of gentlemen joined the ranks & set a good example. There is a talk of raising a fourther [further] 500,000 including the contingency from the colonies. I am not sure I like the idea of Indian troops coming to fight in Europe, but they are picked regiments & when they served in China & in Egypt kept perfect discipline—so that those who ought to know best are confident they will behave perfectly well no looting or massacring. Their superior officers are all English. Ernies< friend the Maharagah [Maharajah] of Biskanir is coming with his own contingent—last time I saw him was as Ernie's guest at Wolfs-garten.—Georgie< wrote us an account of his share in the naval action off Helgoland[5]. He commands the fore-turret & fired quite a number of shots & his captain says with coolness & good judgement. G.[eorgie]< says that the attempt to destroying the docks of the Kiel Canal (the bridges alone would be little good) by aeroplanes is always in the admiraltys mind—but it is very difficult as all is well defended & one has to wait for a favorable opportunity or the attempt has no chance of success. It is distressing that the only passage into the Baltic for men-of-war, wh. is at all possible of being used, is through the Sound, wh. is not deep enough for battleships or big cruisers. In the North Sea the Germans have strewn mines far out all over the place recklessly endangering neutral trading ships & now that the first strong autumn winds are blowing, they will drift (for they are not anchored) on the Dutch & Norwegien [sic] & Danish shores (some round the German, one must hope)." She [Anna Vyrubova] sends much love.—The sun shone so brightly this afternoon—but not in my room—tea was sad & strange & the armchair looked mournful without my precious <u>One</u> in it. Marie< & Dmitri<[6] dine, so I will stop writing & shut my eyes a little & finish to-night. [c]

Marie & Dmitri were in good spirits, they left at 10 so as to go to Paul.< Baby was restless & only got to sleep after 11, but no strong pain. The girls went to bed, & I to surprise Ania< who lay on her sopha in the big palace<—she has now obliteration of veins, so Princess Gedroytz< had been again to her & told her to keep quiet a few days—she had been by motor to town to see our Friend< & that had tired her leg. I returned at 11 & went to bed. Apparently the engineer-mechanic< is near. My face is tied up, as the teeth, jaw ache a bit; the eyes are sore & swollen still, & the heart yearns after the dearest being on earth who belongs to old Sunny.—Our Friend is happy for your sake that you have gone & was so glad to have seen you yesterday. He always fears Bonheur [Nicholasha<], that is to say, the chalki [crows<] want him to get the P.[etrograd] throne or in Galicia that that is there [their] aim but I said she should quieten him, even out of thanks you would never risk such a thing.[7] Gr.[igory Rasputin] loves you jealously & cant hear N.[icholasha] playing a part.—Xenia< answered my wire—is sad not to have seen you before you left—her train arrived. I miscalculated, Shulenburg< cannot be here before to-morrow afternoon or evening, so I shall only get up for Church, a little later too.—I am sending you 6 little books to give to anybody, perhaps [Generals] Ivanov, Ruzsky or anybody you feel inclined too [to]. Loman invented them. [d]

Those sunny days are to keep the rain & dirt off. Sweetheart I must end now & lay the letter outside, it must leave in the morning at 8½.—Goodbye my joy, my sunshine Nicky beloved treasure. Baby kisses you & wify covers you with the tenderest kisses. God bless & keep & strengthen you. I blessed & kissed your cushion into all I have in thoughts & prayers inseperable [sic]. Your Wify. [P.S.] Remember to say a word to the generals to leave their sori [quarreling]. Messages to all. I hope poor old Freder.< keep us [sic] alright. Mind he eats light food & takes no wine. [e]

2. "Stores" were places where wealthy, charitable Russians accumulated goods to be distributed (free) to the troops.

3. "Her committee" refers to "Tat'yana's Committee," the committee headed by g.p. Tat'yana Nicholaevna. See Footnote 66.

4. The Julian calendar adopted by Peter the Great was thirteen days behind the Gregorian calendar in the twentieth century. I often render dates both "Old Style" (O.S.) and "New Style" (N.S.), as the empress does in this case, e.g., September 1/13, 1914. Nicholas and Alexandra dated their letters and telegrams O.S.

5. The Battle of Heligoland Bight occurred on August 15/28, 1914, off the northwest coast of Germany. It was the first naval battle of the war, and a British victory.

6. Maria Pavlovna ("Marie") and Dmitry Pavlovich Romanov were brother and sister, children of Grand Prince Paul Alexandrovich.

7. "Bonheur" is a sarcastic reference to Grand Duke Nicholas Nicholaevich (Nicholasha), supreme commander and favored by some to replace Nicholas II as tsar. This is the meaning of the reference "... the crows want him to get the P.[etrograd] throne." (See Footnote 1.) This letter shows how Rasputin played upon Alexandra's jealousy and fear of Nicholasha. Alexandra repeatedly tried to undermine Nicholas Nicholaevich, citing Rasputin as an authority. In this—and much else—the emperor ignored his wife's "advice," though for a variety of reasons Nicholas did finally replace his cousin as commander-in-chief in August 1915.

No. 11/ Telegram 173. Tsarskoe Selo> Minsk. 20 Sept 1914. 10.30> 11.00 a.m.   To his majesty. All is well. Nose hurts less. Cold. Crowded. We await wounded. They [the children] write this evening. We kiss you warmly. God keep you. Alix

---

No. 12/ Telegram 1. Novoborisov> Tsarskoe Selo. 21 Sept 1914. 12.58> 2.33 p.m.   To her majesty. Tender thanks for dear letter. Hope [you] slept and feel well. Rainy, cold weather. In thoughts [and] prayers with you and children. How is agoo wee one?<   Loving kisses to all. Niki

---

No. 13/ Telegram 536 in Russian. Stavka> Tsarskoe Selo. 21 Sept 1914. 7.05> 7.15 p.m. To her majesty. Praise be to God Who granted us victory at Suvalki and Maryampol yesterday.[8] Arrived safely. Te Deum just been sung in military church here. Received your wire. Am feeling splendid. Hope all are well. Embrace you warmly. Niki

---

8. "The fighting at Souvalky and Mariampol hardly amounted to a victory. It represented, at best, a partial and local recovery after the crushing defeat of Tannenberg a fortnight previously." Vulliamy, p. 5n.

No. 14/ Telegram 180. Tsarskoe Selo> Stavka. 21 Sept 1914. 9.35 > 10.15 p.m.   To his imperial majesty the emperor. Thank you for both telegrams. Rejoice at victory. Wounded arrived. Worked from four until dinner. Mechanic< arrived. Embrace you warmly. Little one happy. May God keep you. Greetings to all. Alix

---

No. 15/ Her No. 236.   Ts.[arskoe] S[elo]. Sept. 21ˢᵗ 1914.
My very own beloved One,
    What joy to receive your 2 dear telegrams!—thank God for the good [news], such a comfort to receive it upon your arrival [at Stavka]. God bless your presence there! Do so wonder, hope & trust that you will see troops.—Baby< had a rather restless night but no real pain. I went up to kiss him before Church, at 11. Lunched with the girlies< on my sopha, Bekker< arrived. Then lay near Aleksei's< bed for over an hour & then off to the train—not very many wounded. Two officers of one regiment & rota [company] died on the journey & one soldier. Their lungs are much attacked after the rain & having gone through the Nieman in the water. No acquaintances—army regiments—one soldier remembered seeing us at Moscou [sic] this summer at the Khodynka. Paretzky[9] got

worse from his ill heart, overstrain, looks very bad, sunken in face, staring eyes, grey beard—painful impression poor dear—not wounded.—Then we 5 went to Ania< & took tea early there.—At 3 went to our little hospital to put on our chalat & off to the big hospital, where we worked hard. At 5½ I had to return with M. & A. [daughters Marie & Anastasia] as received an otriad [detachment] with Masha Vasilchikov's brother< at the head. Then back to the little hospital, where children were working & I did 3 new officers—then showed Karangozov< & Zhdanov how to really play domino. After dinner & prayers with Baby, went to Ania where the 4 girls already were & saw N.P.< who had dined with her. He felt comforted to see us as very lonely & feels himself so useless. Pr[incess] Ged.< came to see Anias leg wh. I then bandaged & we gave her a cup of tea. Dropped N.P. in the motor near the station. Bright moon, cold <u>night</u>. Baby is sleeping fast. All the little family kiss you ever so tenderly. Miss my Angel quite horribly, & at night whenever woke up tried to be silent not to wake you up. So sad in Church without you near me. Goodbye Sweetheart—my prayers & thoughts follow you everywhere. Bless & kiss you without end, every dearly beloved place. Your own old   Wify. [P.S.] N. Gr. Orlova[10] is going off to morrow to Baranovichi [to] see her husband 2 days. Ania heard from Sashka<—& 2 letters from her brother [S. A. Taneev].—

9. Alexander Nicholaevich Poretsky, lt.-gen., former commander of Izmailovo Life Guard Reg. and the combined guards battalion; died, March 25, 1915.
10. Natalya Grigor'evna Orlova, wife of Maj.-Gen. P. P. Orlov.

No. 16/ Telegram 201. Tsarskoe Selo> Stavka. 22 Sept 1914. 6.15> 6.58 p.m. To his imperial majesty the emperor. Thank you for news through [V. N.] Orlov. [I] Write every day. Marvellous fresh weather. Breakfasted in morning and went to hospital.< Little one< entirely well. Kiss you warmly. Bad headache. God keep you. Alix

---

No. 17/ Telegram 597 in Russian. Stavka> Tsarskoe Selo. 22 Sept 1914. 7.31> 8.15 p.m. To her majesty. Hearty thanks for sweet letter. General Ruzsky briefed me to day. Told much of interest about his celebrated battles in Galicia. Appointed him adjutant-general. Quiet and calm here. Embrace all warmly. Niki

---

No. 18/ His No. 157.   Stavka.[11a] 22 September 1914.
My own beloved darling Wify,
    Loving thanks for the dear letter you gave my man, I read it before going to bed. It was horrid saying good-bye to you & the dear children, though I knew we would be separated for a short time! I slept badly the first night because the engines pushed the train vulgarly at each station. The next day I arrived here at 5.30, it had been raining hard & it was cold. Nikolasha< met me at the station Baranovichi & then we were shunted off into a pretty wood near by not far (5 minutes walk) from his train. The pine wood reminds one very much of Spala; the ground is sandy and not the least damp. On arriving at the Stavka I went to a big wooden church of the zheleznodorozhnaya brigada [Railway Brigade] for a

short te deum [thanksgiving service] officiated by Shavelsky. Here I saw Peti-usha,< Kyrill,< and all Nikolasha's Staff. Some of these gentlemen dined with me & in the evening I had a long and interesting report of Yanushkevich in their train, where naturally as I foresaw the heat was awful. I thought of you—what a luck you were not there! [a]

I insisted that the life they lead here was not to be changed the least since my arrival.This morning at 10, I was present at the usual morning report that N.< receives in a small house just in front of his train—from his two chief aides, Yanushkevich and Danilov. They both do it very clearly & short, they read the reports of the previous day from the commanders of our armies and ask N. for his orders and instructions for the coming operations. We lay on top of big maps full of blue & red lines, numbers, dates, etc. When I come home I will tell you the regime!—Just before luncheon arrived general Ruzskii[,] a pale, thin little man, with his two brand new St. George crosses. I made him general aide de camp for the last victory on our Prussian frontier[8]—the first since his new nomination. He makes a good impression. After lunch a groupe [i.e., a photo-graph] was made with N.'s whole staff. In the morning after the report I went on foot all around our Stavka [headquarters] & past [sic] through the ring of sen-tries and then I came upon a guard of lieb-kazakov [Life-Guard Cossacks] posted not far off in the wood. They spent the night in huts made in the earth—quite cozy & warm. Their duty is to keep a look out for aeroplanes! Splendid smiling men with bunches of hair sticking out from beneath their caps! The whole regiment is quartered quite near to the church in the small wood houses of the railway brigade.— [b]

Gen. Ivanov is gone to Varsovie [Warsaw] and will be back at Kholm on Wednesday, so I remain here one day longer, without changing the rest of my program. I leave this place to-morrow night and arrive at Rovno in the morning of Wednesday, I remain there till 1. o'clock & start for Kholm where I shall be about 6. in the evening. Thursday morning at Belostok—if it is possible I will pay an unexpected visit to Osovets. I only am not certain about Grodno[,] that is to say I do not know whether I shall stop there—I fear all the troops have left for the frontier. I took a good walk with Drenteln in the wood and upon returning to the train I found with joy the fat packet with your letter & the 6 little books. Best thanks, sweet love, for your precious lines. How interesting the part of Victoria's< letter you kindly copied out for me. I have heard about the difficul-ties in the beginning of the war between the english and the french from Benk-endorff's telegrams[11b] some time ago. Both the foreign attaches here—have left a few days ago for Varsovie, so this time I won't see them. It is difficult to believe a great war is raging not so far away, everything looks so peaceful & calm. The life one leads here reminds one more of old days when we lived like this during the maneuvers; the only difference is that now there are <u>no troops</u> at all in the neighbourhood! Lovy-mine, I miss you so awfully much, because I am so free now & have time to think of my Wify & family. Strange but true! I hope you are not feeling rotten pain in the jaw and do not overtire yourself. God grant that agoo wee one< may be quite well when I return. I bless you & kiss your precious face ever so tenderly[,] also all the dear children. Thank the girls for their dear letters. Good-night my own sweet Sunny. Ever your own old huzy Nicky. [P.S.] Give my love to Ania.< [c]

11a. Letter No. 18 was written from "Stavka [GHQ] of the High Command, the New Imperial Train." Letters No. 21 and 50 were written from the "Stavka of the High Command." Beginning with Letter No. 65, Nicholas writes simply "Stavka."
11b. Alexander Constantinovich Benckendorff was the Russian ambassador to London from January 1902 to July 1916.

No. 19/ Her No. 237.   Ts.[arskoe] S[elo]. Sept. 23rd 1914.
My own beloved Darling,
   I was so sorry not to be able to write to you yesterday, but my head ached hideously & I lay all the evening in the dark. In the morning we went to the Grotto church for half of the service & it was lovely; I had been before to see Baby!< Then we fetched the Pr. G.< at Anias.< My head already ached & I cant take any medecins [sic] now, neither for the heart. We worked from 10-1, as there was an operation wh. lasted long. After luncheon I had Shulenburg who left again to-day, as Rennenkampf told him to hurry back. Then I came up to kiss Baby & went down & lay on my bed till tea-time, after wh. I received Sandra Schuvalov's< otriad [detachment], after wh. to bed with a splitting headache. Ania was offended I did not go to her, but she had lots of guests, & our Friend< for three hours. The night was not famous & I feel my head all day—heart enlarged—generally I take drops 3 or 4 times a day, as otherwise I could not keep up, & now I cant these days. I read doklady [reports] in bed & got on to the sopha for luncheon. Then received the couple Rebinder< from Kharkhov (they have my stores there² & she had come from Vilna where she had been to bid goodbye to her brother Kutaissov<). He showed her the Image [icon] I had sent the battery from Baby & it looked already quite used—it seems they daily have it out for prayers & before every battle they pray before it—so touching. [a]
   Then I came to Baby & lay near him in the half dark whilst Vlad. Nik.< was reading to him, now they are playing together, the girls too, we have had tea up here too. The weather is bright, in the night almost frost.—Thank God the news continues being good & the Prussians retire. The mud hunted them away. Mekk< writes that there are a good many cases of cholera & dissentry [sic] in Lvov but they are taking sanitary measures.—There have been difficult moments there, according to the papers; but I trust there wont be anything serious—one cannot trust those Poles—after all we are their enemies & the catholics must hate us. I shall finish in the evening, cant write much at a time. Sweet Angel, soul & heart are ever with you. [b]
   I am writing on Anastasias paper. Baby kisses you very much—he has no pains at all, lies, because the knee is still swollen, do hope he can be up then by your return.—I got a letter from old M-me Orlova, to whom [her grandson] Ivan< wrote that he wants to continue the military service after war—he told me as much too—he is Flyer Orlov, 20th Corps, active Army—he received the St. George's cross, has the right to another decoration, but perhaps he might receive the grade of praporshchik (or podporouchik).¹² He did his "reconnoitring [sic] under heavy fire of the enemy"—one day he flew alone particularly high up &

the cold was so intense, he did not know what to do—the hands freezing—machine stopped working—he did not care what would become of him, so numbed he felt—then he began praying & all of a sudden the machine went off working again alright. When it pours they cannot fly so sleep & sleep. Plucky boy to fly so often alone—what nerves one needs; indeed his father would have been proud of him therefore the Grandmama asks for him.—

I write abominably to-day, but my brain is tired & heavy.—Oh my sweetheart, what an <u>intense</u> joy it was when your precious letter was brought to me, & I thank you for it from all my heart. It was good of you writing—I read parts of it to the girls & Ania, who had been permitted to come to dinner & remained till 10½. How interesting it must all have been.—Ruzsky< for sure was deeply moved that you made him general a.d.c. Wont agoo wee one< be happy you wrote! He has no more pain, thank God. You are probably now off in the train again—but how short you remain with [your sister] Olga. What a recompense to the brave garrison of Osovets if you go there;—perhaps Grodno, if some troops are still resting there.—Shulenburg saw the lancers, their horses are completely done up, the backs sore to blood—hours in the saddle—& their legs quite weak. As the train stood near Vilna several of the officers came & slept change about several hours on his bed, & they enjoyed this luxury of a train-bed even, & to find a real W.C. was exquisite joy to them—[D. M.] Knyazhevich< did not want to come out any more he was so comfortable there! (this Sh.'s< wife [is] related to Ania).

And beloved huzy misses his little Wify? And do I not you too! But I have the nice family to cheer me up.—Do you go into my compartment sometimes? Please give Fred.< many kind messages. Have you spoken to Fedorov< about the military students & Drs? No telegram from you to-day, that means that you did nothing in particular, I suppose.— Now my own sweetest one my Nicky dear, I must be trying to sleep & lay this letter out to be taken at 8½. I had no more ink in my pen, so had to take another. Goodbye, my Angel, God bless & protect you & bring you safe & sound back again. Every possible tender kiss & caress fr. yr. fondly loving & truly devoted little Wify. Alix. [P.S.] Ania thanks for your message & sends much love.— [c]

12. A "praporshchik" was an army ensign, a "podporuchik" was the next highest rank, second-lieutenant.

No. 20/ Telegram 207. Tsarskoe Selo> Stavka. 23 Sept 1914. 9.51> 10.25 p.m. To his imperial majesty the emperor. To-day better. Stayed home. Nose stopped hurting. [Daughter] Olga at conference. Weather clear, fresh. Warmly embrace you. May the Lord keep you. Alix.

No. 21/ His No. 158.   Stavka.[11a] 23rd Sept. 1914.
My own beloved Wify,

Tender thanks for your dear letter, & for the one you, the girls, Ania and N.P.< wrote all together. Your lines are always so deep & when I read them over their sense goes straight to the heart & my eyes are often moist. It is hard to be separated for even a few days, but such letters as yours are such a consolation, that it is worth the while to be apart. To-day it is pouring—of course I went out walking with Dr. F.[edorov] which did me much good! This night poor old Fredericks had a small repetition of what happened to him in town lately—a tiny blood-spitting. Now he feels better, but [Doctors] Fedorov and Malama both insist he must remain quiet & not be shaken for 24 hours. It will be very difficult to make him obey them. They propose that he remain here & not go with me to Rovno, but that he can catch my train at Belostok in two days—Thursday. It is so complicated having the old man in these circumstances, because it is a constant worry for me & puts him in a troublesome position towards everybody. [a]

I am just feeling so well again & assure you, that these days I feel rested—especially on account of the good news. Alas! Nikolasha<, as I was afraid, will not let me go to Osovets, which is insupportable, as now I won't see any troops which have recently fought! At Vilno I think of visiting two hospitals—a military one & of the Red Cross;—but that is not only what I came here for! Among the rewards that I approved today—gen. Ivanov presented Keller< to the order of st. george. I am so happy for him. So to-morrow atlast [sic] I shall see [my sister] Olga & remain at Rovno the whole morning. Now I must end as the messenger has to leave. Good-bye my sweet beloved Sunny. God bless & protect you & the dear children. I kiss you & them tenderly. Ever your very own huzy Nicky. [b]

No. 22/ Telegram 209. Tsarskoe Selo> Rovno. 24 Sept 1914. 9.46> 10.25 a.m. To his majesty. Heartfelt thanks for dear telegram. Terribly glad to receive it. All warmly kiss you and dear Olga[, your sister]. Glad you are together. Wonderful weather. God keep you. Alix

---

No. 23/ Telegram 2579 in Russian. Brest> Tsarskoe Selo. 24 Sept 1914. 6.10> 6.56 p.m.   To her majesty. Very grateful for news. So glad to see [my sister] Olga in Rovno. Inspected her hospital and the local one. Not many wounded left. Weather cold, bad. Embrace all warmly. Niki

---

No. 24/ Her No. 238.   Ts.[arskoe] S[elo]. Sept. 24th 1914.
My beloved Darling,
From all my heart I thank you for your sweet letter. Your tender words touched me deeply & warmed my lonely heart. I am deeply disappointed for you that one advises you not to go to the fortress—it would have been a real recompense to those wonderfully brave men. One says Ducky< went there for the thanksgiving Te Deum & that she heard the cannons firing in the distance.—At Vilna there are many troops resting as the horses are so worn out, I hope you can see them. [Your sister] Olga wrote such a happy telegram after having seen you—dear child, she does work so bravely, & how many grateful hearts will carry home pictures of her bright sweet being into the ranks again & others home into their villages & her being your Sister will make the link yet stronger

between you & the people.—I read such a pretty article out of an English paper—they praise our soldiers so much & say that their deep religiousness & veneration for their peace-loving monarch makes them fight so well & for a holy
cause.—How utterly shameful that the Germans have shut the little Grandduch-
ess [Maria-Adelaida] of Luxembourg in a castle near Nurnberg—such an insult!—

Fancy only I got a little letter from Gretchen[13] without signature or beginning,
written in English & sent from England & the adress [sic] written in another
handwriting—I cannot imagine how she got it sent.—Ania's< leg is much better
to-day, & I see she intends to be up for your return—I wish she had been well
now & the leg next week bad, then we should have had some nice quiet evenings cosily to ourselves.—We only went at 11 to the hospital,< fetched the Pss.<
at Anias. We assisted at 2 operations—she did them sitting, so as that I could
give her the instruments sitting too. The one man was too amusing when he
came to himself again in bed—he began singing away at the top of his voice &
very well, & conducting with his hand, upon wh. I concluded he was a "Za-
pievola"[14]—& so he was most cheery & said he hoped he had not used rude language—he wishes to be a hero & soon go back again to the war as soon as his
foot heals up again.—The other one smiled mischivously [sic] & said [Alexandra
wrote the following quote in Russian]: "I was far, far away, I walked &
walked,—it was nice over there. Almighty God, we were all together you don't
know where I have been!" & thanking God & praising him—he must have seen
wonderful sights whilst one was extricating the ball out of his shoulder. She did
not let me bind up anyone, so as to keep quiet, as felt my head & heart. [a]

After luncheon I lay in Babys< room till 5, M. G.[illiard]< read to him & I
think I took a short nap. Then Aleksei read 5 lines in French aloud, quite nicely.
Then I received Uncle Mekk< after wh. [I] flew for a half an hour with [daugh-
ter] Olga to Anias house, as our Friend< spent the afternoon with her & wanted
to see me. He asked after you & hoped you would go to the fortress.—Then we
had our lecture with Pss. G.—After dinner the girls went to Ania where N.P.<
was, & I followed after prayers. We worked, she glued & he smoked. She is
not over amiable these days & only thinks of herself & her comfort & makes
others crawl under the table to arrange her leg on lots of cushions, & does not
trouble her head whether others sit comfortably—spoilt & badly brought up. She
has lots of people coming to see her all day long, so she has no time to be lonely,
tho' when you return she will groan that she was wretched the whole time.—She
is surrounded by several big photos of you enlarged ones of hers—in every corner & heaps of small ones.—We dropped N.P. near the station & were home at
11.—I wanted to go to Church every day & only got there once, such a pitty [sic],
as it is such a help when the heart feels sad. We always place candles before we
go to the hospital & I like to pray for God & the holy Virgin to bless the work of
our hands & to let them bring healing to the ill.—I am so glad you are feeling
better again, such a journey is beneficient [sic], as still you feel yourself nearer
to all & could see the chiefs & hear all from them directly & tell them your
ideas.— [b]

What joy for Keller—he really has deserved his cross & now he has repayed us
for everything, it was his ardent wish all these years.—How dead-tired the

French & English troops must be, fighting without ceasing for 20 days or more.—And we have the big guns from Koenigsberg against us. To-day [Fat] Orlov< sent no news, so I suppose nothing in particular has occurred.—To be away from all the petty talks must do you good—here there are such rumours always, & generally without foundation.—Poor old Fredericks, the other one, had died. How sad our poor old one got worse again[15]—I was so afraid it might happen again when out with you, & it would have been more delicate had he remained behind—but he is so deeply devoted to you, that he could not bear the idea of your going alone. I fear we shall not keep him long amongst us, his time is near at hand—what a loss it will be—there are no more such types to be found & such an honest friend is difficult to replace. Sweetheart, I hope you sleep better now, I cannot say that of myself, the brain seems to be working all the time & never wanting to rest. Hundreds of ideas & combinations come bothering one.—I reread your dear letters several times & try to think its Lovy speaking to me. Somehow we see so little of each other, you are so much occupied & one does not like to bother with questions when you are tired after your doklady [reports] & then we are never alone together.—But now I must try & get to sleep, so as to feel stronger to morrow & be of more use—I thought I should should [sic] do so much when you were away, & Bekker< spoilt all my plans & good intentions.—Sleep well wee One, holy Angels guard your slumber & Wify's prayers & love suround [sic] you with deep devotion & love. [c]

25-th. Good morning my treasure. To-day the Feldjeger fetches the letter later so I can write still a little. This may be the last letter if Fredericks[15] is right, that you are returning to-morrow, but it seems to me you wont, as you are sure to be seeing the hussars, lancers, artillery & other troops resting at Vilna. There were 2 degrees of frost this night—now there is again glorious sunshine.—We shall be at 11 at the hospital, I still cannot take medicins [sic] wh. is a great nuisance, as my head daily aches tho' not very strongly & I feel my heart, tho' it is not enlarged, but I must keep still rather quiet to-day. I have not been for a real airing since you left.—Sergei< is a little better—Pss. Orlov< too feels quite alright, only weak.—Baby slept & feels well. One continues speaking of that property in the Baltic provinces where the place is marked white & a hydroplane rested upon their lake there—as tho' officers, ours, had dressed in plain clothes & seen it—nobody is allowed to go there.—I do wish one could have it seriously enquired into.—There are so many spies everywhere that it may be true, but it would be very sad, as there are still many very loyal subjects in the Baltic provinces. [d]

This miserable war, when will it ever end. [Kaiser] William, I feel sure must at times pass through hideous moments of despair, when he grasps that it was he, & especially his antirussian set, wh. began the war & is dragging his country into ruin. All those little states, for years they will continue suffering from the after-effects. It makes my heart bleed when I think how hard Papa< & Ernie< struggled to bring our little country [the German state of Hesse-Darmstadt] to its present state of prosperity in every sense.—With God's help here all will go well & end gloriously, & it has lifted up spirits, cleansed the many stagnant minds, brought unity in feelings & is a "healthy war" in the moral sense. Only one thing I long that our troops should behave examplarily [sic] in every sense, &

not rob & pillage—leave that horror to the Prussian troops. It is demoralising [sic], & then one looses [sic] the real control over the men—they fight for personal gain & not for the country's glory, when they reach the stage of highway robbers.—No reason to follow bad examples—the rearguard, "obozy" [transport units] are the curse in this case all speak in despair of them, nobody to hold them in hand.—There are always ugly sides & beautiful ones to everything, & so is it here.—Such a war ought to cleanse the spirits & not defile them, is it not so?—Some regiments are very severe I know & try to keep order—but a word from above would do no harm, this is my very own idea, Darling, because I want the name of our russian troops to be remembered hereafter in the countries with awe & respect—& admiration. Here people do not ever quite grasp the idea that other peoples property is sacred, & not to be touched—victory does not mean pillage.—Let the priests in the regiments say a word to the men too on this topic.—Now I am bothering you with things that do not concern me, but only out of love for your soldiers & their reputation.[16]

Sweetest treasure, I must be ending now, & get up. All my prayers & tenderest thoughts follow you; may God give you courage, strength, & patience,—faith you have more than ever & it is this wh. keeps you up—yes prayers & implici[t] trust in God's mercy alone, give one strength to bear all. And our Friend helps you carry yr. heavy cross & great responsabilities [sic]—& all will come right, as the right is on our side. I bless you, kiss your precious face, sweet neck & dear loving handies with all the fervour of a great loving heart. How lovely to have you soon back again. Your very own old   Wify. [e]

13. Reference is apparently to Margarita Fabritse, a friend of the empress who lived in Germany.
14. A "zapevala" is the leader of a choir.
15. Reference to "the other one" is probably to a recently deceased cousin of "our poor old" Count Vladimir Borisovich Fredericks, the elderly Minister of the Imperial Court and Appanages who appears so often in this correspondence. The latter did (as predicted) get "worse again," though he did not die until 1927.
16. This was Alexandra's first attempt in these letters to meddle in state and military affairs. Cf. Letter No. 43a.

No. 25/ Telegram 970 in Russian. Grodno Railway Station> Tsarskoe Selo. 25 Sept 1914. 12.45> 1.26 p.m. To her majesty. Stopped in Belostok all the same and visited Osovets; found garrison looking very well. Many projectiles fell into fortress, the craters they made are evident. Today will inspect hospitals in Vilno. To-morrow morning, God willing, we will see each other. Hope all are well. Tenderly embrace [all]. Niki

No. 26/ Telegram 224. Tsarskoe Selo> Vilno. 25 Sept 1914. 2.30> 3.10 p.m. To his majesty. Tenderly thank you for news in dear letter. Terribly glad you were in Osovets and saw brave garrison. Wonderful weather, two degrees of frost last night. All well, warmly embrace you, glad to see you soon. Alix

No. 27/ Her No. 239.   Ts.[arskoe] S[elo]. Oct. 20th 1914.
My love of loves, my very own One,

Again the hour of separation is approaching & the heart aches with pain. But I am glad for you that you will get away, see other things & feel nearer to the troops. I hope you can manage to see more this time. We shall eagerly await your telegrams. When answering to the Stavka I feel shy because I am sure—lots of officers read the telegrams & then one cannot write as warmly as one would wish to. That N.P.< is with you this time, is a comfort to me—you will feel less lonely as he is bit of us all & you understand many looks & things together which warm one up, & he is intensely grateful & rejoicing to go with you, as he feels so useless in town,< with all the comrades out at the war.—Thank God you can go away feeling quiet about Baby sweet<—if there should be anything the matter, I shall write "rutchka"< [with a little pen], all in the diminutive, then you will know I write about agoowee one.[17a]—Oh, how I shall miss you! I feel so low these days already & the heart so heavy! Its a shame as hundreds are rejoicing to see you soon—but when one loves as I do—one cannot but yearn for ones treasure. [a]

Twenty years to-morrow that you reign & that I became orthodox. How the years have flown, how much we have lived through together! Forgive my writing in pencil, but I am on the sopha & you are confessing [sic] still. Once more forgive your Sunny if in any way she has grieved or displeased you, & believe it never was willingly done.[19]—Thank God we shall have the blessing of Holy Communion together to-morrow—it will give strength & peace.[17b] May God give us success on shore & at sea—our fleet be blessed! —Oh my love, if you want me to meet you, send for me & O. & T. [daughters Olga and Tatyana]—Somehow we see so little of each other & there is so much one longs to talk over & ask about, & at night we are tired out & in the morning are hurrying. I shall finish this in the morning.

21-st. How lovely it was to go to Holy Communion together on this day! & the glorious sunshine—may it accompany on yr. journey in every sense. My prayers & thoughts & very, very tenderest love will follow you all the way. Sweetest of loves, God bless & protect you & the Holy Virgin guard you from all harm! My tenderest blessing. Without end I kiss you & press you to my heart with boundless love & fondness. Ever, Nicky Mine, yr. very own little   Wify. [P.S.] I copy out Gr.'s< telegr. for you to remember. [The following quote is in Russian.] "Having been administered the sacred mysteries at the communion cup, beseeching Christ, tasting of His body & blood, there was a spiritual vision of Heavenly Beautiful rejoining. Grant that the Heavenly Power be with you on the road, that angels be in the ranks of our warriors for the salvation of our steadfast heroes with joy and victory." Bless you. Love you. Long for you. [b]

17a. "Rutchka" ("ruchka") means "little pen." The empress seems to be saying that she will tell her husband of their son's hemophiliac attacks by using some type of a code, perhaps something involving diminutives. Russians knew Aleksei was not well; official bulletins admitted he almost died at Spala in 1912. But Nicholas and Alexandra kept his exact malady a secret, fearing that knowledge that Aleksei was a hemophiliac would be used to exclude him from the throne. The empress suspected the communications she and her husband exchanged were scrutinized —hence the need for a code. Actually, the royal correspondence does not *appear* to employ cryptic communications indicating hemophilia, but see No. 806.

17b. The empress is referring to herself and Nicholas. The first sentence of this letter indicates it was written before Nicholas's departure, as do other passages. Cf. Letter No. 30b, in which she reiterates: "What a blessing we took Holy Communion before you left...." Apparently, Nicholas left for Stavka on 21 October.

No. 28/ Telegram 24 in Russian. Povinka> Tsarskoe Selo. 21 Oct 1914. 4.08> 5.50 p.m. To her majesty. Warmly thank you for all your letters. Sad, lonely, at last station strolled with N.P.< at night. Tenderly embrace [you]. Niki

---

No. 29/ Telegram 340. Tsarskoe Selo> Vitebsk. 21 Oct 1914. 6.50> 8.10 p.m. To his majesty. Gladdened by your telegram. Many seriously wounded arrived. Kazanisha [a pet?] is in your armchair. Ortipo [a dog] visited wounded with us. Agoowee one< riding in car. We greet [you]. Sleep well. Sad. Kiss [you] tenderly. God keep you. Alix

---

No. 30/ Her No. 240.   Tsarskoe Selo. Oct. 21st 1914.
My own sweet Love,

It was such an unexpected joy to get your dear telegram & I thank you for it with all my heart. Thats nice that you & N.P.< took a turn [walk] at one of the little stations, it will have freshened you up.—I felt so sad seeing yr. lonely figure standing at the door—it seems so unnatural your going off all alone—everything is queer without you, our centre, our sunshine. I gulped down my tears & hurried off to the hospital< & worked hard for two hours. Very bad wounds; for the first time I shaved one of the soldiers legs near and round the wound—I worked all alone to-day, without a sister [nurse] or Dr.—only the Princess< came to see each man & to [see] what was the matter with him & I asked her if it was right what I intended doing—tiresome M-lle Annenkov[18] gave me the things I asked for. Then we went back to our little hospital< & sat in the different rooms with the officers. From there we went & looked at the little Peshcherny Khram [Chapel]< under the old Palace Hospital< once—in Catherin[e the Great]'s time there was a Church there. This has been done in remembrance of the 300 years Jubilee[18]—it is quite charming all chosen by Vilchkovsky,< purest & ancient Byzantine style, absolutely correct—you must see it. The consecration will be on Sunday at 10, & we shall get our officers & men who are able to move, to come to it. There are tables with the names of those wounded who have died in all our hospitals of Ts.[arskoe] S.[elo], & those officers too who received St. George's crosses or the gold arms. After tea we went to M. & A.'s [daughters Marie and Anastasia] hospital—they have several very gravely wounded men. Upstairs are 4 officers in most cosy rooms.—Then I received 3 officers who return to the A.[ctive] Army—one lay in our hospital & the other 2 in my redcross station here; then I rested. Baby< said his prayers down here, as I was too tired to go up. Now O. & T. [daughters Olga and Tatiana] are at Olga's Committee[3]—before that Tatiana received [A. B.] Neidhardt alone for half an hour with his doklad [report]—its so good for the girls & they learn to become independent & it will develop them much more having to think & speak for themselves, without my constant aid. [a]

I long for news from the Black Sea—God grant our fleet may have success! I suppose they give no news, so as the enemy should not know their whereabouts by wireless telegraphy.—It is very cold again to-night. I wonder whether you are playing domino? Oh, my love, how lonely it is without you! What a blessing we took Holy Communion before you left—it gave strength & peace. What a great thing it is to be able to take holy Sacrement [sic] at such moments & one longs to help others to also remember that God gave this blessing for all—not as a thing that must be done obligatorily once a year in lent—but whenever the soul thirsts for it & needs strength! When I get hold of people alone who I know suffer much—I always touch this subject & with God's help have many a time succeeded in making them understand that it is a possible & good thing to do & it brings relief & peace to many a weary heart. With one of our officers I also spoke & he agreed & was so happy & courageous afterwards & bore his pains far better. It seems to me this is one of the chief dutys of us women to try & bring people more to God, to make them realise that He is more attainable & near to us & waiting for our love & trust to turn to Him. Shyness keeps many away & false pride—therefore one must help them break this wall.—I just told the Priest [A. P. Vasil'ev?] last night that I find the clergy ought to speak more with the wounded in this way—quite simply & straight out, not sermonlike. Their souls are like children & only at times need a little guiding. With the officers its far more difficult as a rule. [b]

22-nd. Goodmorning my treasure. I prayed so much for you in the little Church this morning—I came for the last 20 min. It was so sad kneeling there all alone without my treasure, that I could not help crying. But then I thought of how glad you must be to get nearer to the front & how eagerly the wounded will have awaited your arrival this morning at Minsk. We bound up the officers from 10-11 & then went to the big hospital< for three operations— serious ones rather, 3 fingers were taken off as bloodpoisoning had set in, & they were quite rotten. Another had an "oskolok" [fragment] taken out of his—another lots of fragments (bones) out of his leg. I went through several wards. Service was going on in the big hospital-church & we just knelt down on the top balkony [sic] during the prayer to the Kaz[an] Virgin's Image [Icon]. Your Rifles feel sad with you away.—Now I must be off to my supply train No. 4. Goodbye my Nicky love, I bless & kiss you over & over again. Slept badly, kissed your cushion & thought much of you. Ever your very own little Wify. [P.S.] I bow to all & especially to N.P.< whom I am glad you have with you—more warmth near you. [c]

---

18. This nurse was probably fraulein Maria Michaelovna or her sister Vera. Concerning the 1913 Jubilee, see Footnote 65. "Olga's committee" refers to their daughter's committee; see Footnote 3.

No. 31/ Telegram 700 in Russian. Stavka> Tsarskoe Selo. 22 Oct 1914. 7.08> 7.38 p.m. To her majesty. Arrived safely. This morning inspected two hospitals in Minsk; found them in splendid order. Not cold. Foggy. In thoughts I am with you all. Tenderly embrace [you]. Niki

---

No. 32/ Her No. 241.   Tsarskoe Selo. Oct. 22nd 1914.
My own beloved One.

It is 7 o'clock & as yet no news from you. Well, I went to see my supply-train No. 4 with Mekk<—they leave to-night for Radom. I think & from there Mekk will go to see Nikolasha,< as he must ask him some questions. He told me pri-

vately from Ella< that she wants to go & see my store[2] at Lvov, without anybody knowing about it—she will come here so as that the Moscou [sic] public
should know nothing, the first days of November. We envy her & Ducky< fearfully—but still hope you will send for us to meet you. It will be hard leaving
Baby,< whom I have never been long away from, but whilst he is well & M. &
A. [younger daughters Marie and Anastasia] are there to keep him company, I
could get away. Of course I should like it to be a useful journey—best if I could
have gone with my train, one of the sanitary ones[19]—out to their destination to
see how they take in the wounded & bring them back again & look after them.
Or meet you in Grodno, Vilna, Bielostok where there are hospitals. But that I all
leave in your hands, you will tell me what to do, where to meet you—or to
Rovno & Kharkov—whatever suits you[20]—the less one knows I come, the better.—I received Shulenburg who leaves to-morrow, (my train which Loman &
Co.< arrange) leaves the 1-st I think. Then we had the P-ss.< for our lecture. We
have finished a full surgical course, with more things than usual, & now shall go
through anatomy & interior illnesses as its good to know that all for the girls
too.— [a]

I have been sorting out warm things for the wounded returning home—& going
back to the army again. Ressin< has been to me & we have settled to go to Luga
to-morrow afternoon to my "Svietelka" [attic]. It was a country-house [dacha]
given to Aleksei which I took & arranged as a "depend[e]nce of my school of
popular art",—the girls work, make carpets there & teach the village women how
to make them—then they get their cows & poultry & vegetables, & will be taught
housekeeping. Now they have arranged 20 beds & look after the wounded.—We
have to take a short train, as the ordinary ones go slower & at inconvenient
hours—Ania,< Nastinka,< & Ressin will accompany us three—nobody is to know
anything about it. M-elle Schneider< only knows A.[nna Vyrubova] &
N.[astinka<] are coming,—otherwise she might just be away.—We shall take
simple cabs & go in our nurses' dresses to attract less attention & as its a hospital
we visit.—M-me Becker< is a bore, should be much freer without her.—How vile
one having thrown bombs from aeroplans [sic] onto King Albert's Villa in wh.
he just now lives—thank God no harm was done but I have never known one
trying to kill a sovereign because he is ones enemy during the war!—I must rest a
¼ of an hour before dinner with shut eyes—shall continue to-night.— [b]

What good news! Sandomir ours again & masses of prisoners heavy guns and
quickfiring ones—yr journey has brought blessings & good luck again.—Baby
love< came down to say prayers again, as I felt so tired in every sense. My Image [icon] was in Church this morning & hangs now in its place again.—It is
warmer this evening so I have opened the window.—Ania is in splendid spirits &
enjoys her young operated friend—she brought him yr "Skopin S." to read.—Ago
wee one< wrote out for me during dinner on the menu j'ai, tu as etc. so nicely;
how you must miss the little man! Such a blessing when he is well!! I gave my
good night kiss to your cushion & longed to have you near me—in thoughts I see
you lying in your compartment, bend over you, bless you & gently kiss your
sweet face all over.—oh, my Darling, how intensely dear you are to me!—could I
but help you carrying your heavy burdens, there are so many that weigh upon
you! But I am sure all looks & feels different now you are out there, it will

freshen you up, & you will hear lots of interesting things.—What is our blacksea fleet doing? The wife of my former Crimean M. Lichachev[21] wrote to Ania from Hotel Kist, that a shell had burst quite near on the place there. She pretends the German ship got one shot from us, but that he was not blown up by our mines, over wh.[ich] she went, because Eberh.< had them (how does one say it?) ausgeschaltet,[22] I can't find the word, my brain is cretinised. Probably our squadron was intending to go out, she said they were heating the boilers when the shots flew—well, this is lady's talk, may or may not be true. I enclose a telegram fr. Keller sent through [Gen. N. I.] Ivanov to Fredericks< for me—an answer to mine probably of congratulations for his St. Georges Cross.—In what a state of nervousness Botkin must be, now that Sandomir is taken;—wonder whether his poor son is yet alive.—Ania sends you rusks, a letter & newspapers open.—I shall have no time to write to-morrow in the day, as we go for half an hour to Church, then to the hospital,< & at 1½ to Luga, back by 7—shall lie in the train, takes 2 hours there & 2 back.— Goodnight my sunshine, my very Own one, sleep well, holy Angels guard your bed & the blessed Virgin keeps watch over you. My very tenderest thoughts & prayers hover ever around you— yearning & longing, feeling your moments of loneliness accutely. Bless you. [c]
23-rd. Good morning Lovy-mine! Bright & sunny! We had little to do this morning & so I sat nearly all the time & did not get tired.—We went a moment to M-me Levitsky[23] to see her 18 wounded, all our old friends. Now we must eat & fly—too bad, C-ss Adlerberg[24] has found out we go & wants to come—but I have told Iza< to answer that she knows nothing & once I say nothing, it means I wish it to be kept secret, so as better to see things than when all is prepared.—Goodbye Sweetheart, I bless & kiss you over & over again. Your very own Wify. [P.S.] My love to N.P.< to whom we send this card.— [d]

19. Sanitary trains provided delousing and baths to troops in the trenches. Some also provided a hot meal, reading materials, etc.

20. The empress's tone is differential, yet it seems in some way she is testing her husband. He will decide where they meet, but did he wish her to make a trip at all? Compare this with Letter No. 43 below, dated only three days later.

21. M-me Likhachev was the wife of a former officer in Alexandra's Crimean cavalry regiment.

22. "Ausgeschaltet" is German for to "turn off" lights, machinery, etc. Apparently these Russian mines were activated by the vibrations of ship engines, and the German ship in question survived because the triggering devices of the mines were turned off.

23. Reference here is apparently to Olga Pavlovna Levitskaya, a physician in the order of Red Cross nurses headed by Alexandra's sister Elizabeth ("Ella").

24. Catherine Nicholaevna Adlerberg, countess, former lady-in-waiting, wife of Count A. V. Adlerberg.

No. 33/ Telegram 348. Tsarskoe Selo> Stavka. 22 Oct 1914. 8.55> 9.22 p.m. To his majesty. Thank you for news. All is well. Were in Peshcherny Chapel<, worked in hospital.< Tell Sukhomlinov [daughters] Olga and Tatyana [are] delighted with their trains. Was in my train-store[2] which this evening goes with Mekk< to Radom. Weather good, I am sad. Warmly kiss you. We wrote. God keep you. Alix

No. 34/ Telegram 352. Tsarskoe Selo> Stavka. 23 Oct 1914. 10.56> 11.20
a.m. To his majesty. Terribly delighted by good news. All thoughts with you.
Marvellous weather. [We] are going to hospital.< [We] will write. [We]
warmly embrace [you]. Alix

No. 35/ Telegram 734. Stavka> Tsarskoe Selo. 23 Oct 1914. 12.32> 1.19 p.m.
To her majesty. Fondest thanks for news. Weather milder than at home. Absence of snow. Petia< is here. Has become much calmer since he was under
heavy fire in Galicia. He and Kostia's boys< eat with me. Tender love. Niki

---

No. 36/ Telegram 750 in Russian. Stavka> Tsarskoe Selo. 23 Oct 1914. 6.10>
6.51 p.m. To her majesty. Joyful news received that Austrian army is in full
retreat from Sanok. Now going to Te Deum. Warmly embrace [you]. Niki

---

No. 37 / Telegram 358. Tsarskoe Selo> Stavka. 23 Oct 1914. 8.46> 9.25 p.m.
To his majesty. Thank you for two telegrams. Thank God for everything. Just
returned from Luga, visited three hospitals. Travelled quite successfully by cab
with Ania,< Nastenka< and Ressin,< greeted the family. God keep you. All
warmly embrace you. Alix

No. 38/ Her No. 212.   Tsarskoe Selo. Oct. 23rd 1914.
My sweetest Love,
    Thank God for the good news that the Austrian army is in full retreat from the
river San, & what good news in Turkey– Endigarov< is wild with joy & my
Crimeans.<–I beg your pardon for having forgotten to send Ania's< rusks, but I
had to seal up my letter in such a hurry before we left, that I forgot sending
them, but shall forward them to-morrow. Our expedition to Luga was most successful. When we arrived at the station we were met by old M-lle Sheremet.[25]
(sister of M-me Timashev) who told me that there were two hospitals, & she
thought I had come on purpose–so I told her we should go there after the
Svietelka.[26] We went off in three cabs, with the chief of police in front in a
charming cart. The 3 hospitals were very far from each other, but we enjoyed
the primitive drive through the streets & sandy roads into the pinewood–quite
near the place where we took a walk then near a lake years ago. M-lle Schnei-
der< got an awful shock when she saw us, as she never received Ania's telegram,
and laughed nervously, excitedly the whole 20 m. we were there. 20 men lie in
the little country house–they had been wounded near Suvalki end of Sept., but
light wounds–they were evacuated from Grodno. They all came by the same
train, 80 men on the whole, mostly regiments from the Caucasus. One Eriva-
nets< who had seen us at Livadia.<–One Timashev daughter was in one hospital
as nurse and a younger sister [of] M-lle Sheremeteva[25] at the head of another
near the Artillery barracks.–Friede[27] I suddenly discovered there. Many of the
men were soon going off again to the army. They have a Kitchen at the station
since 2 months & not one sanitary or military train[19] has stopped there. On our
way back we took tea. We knitted a lot & Ressin< kept us company.–The
weather was fine & not too cold. [a]

It is nearly 1. I think I ought to try & sleep—I had very little sleep these nights, tho' I kept the window open till 3 o'clock in the night.—Baby sweet< motored in the garden, M. & A. [daughters Marie and Anastasia] drove with Isa<, went to their hospital & then worked in the store.[2] I received Alia< who accompanys her husband on Sunday till where Misha< is.—Goodnight my Sunshine<, my huzy sweet, sleep peacefully & feel wify's presence ever near you full of love.

24-th. I must finish my letter, then lunch, change & be off to town< to my store[2] & if headache not much worse, then to my Krestov[skaya, i.e., Red Cross] Station.—We worked all the morning & were very sad to bid goodbye to my 5 Crimeans,< & lancer Ellis[28] who are off with 3 others in a waggon with a nurse & 1 sanitary[19] to Simferopol & Kutchuk-Lambat.—M-me Muftizade returned from the Crimea and brought me roses & apples.—God bless you my Angel love. I kiss you ever so tenderly, your very own Sunny. [P.S.] Thank God my Alexander squadron [see Letter No. 39] has turned up. I was so anxious about them. Our love to N.P.< [b]

25. Anastasia Sergeevna Sheremeteva, daughter of Egermeister S. S. Sheremetev. The younger sister mentioned here was Vera.
26. "Svietelka" is explained in Letter No. 32b.
27. Evidently Alexander Alekseevich Fride, an officer in the lst Life Guard artillery brigade.
28. An officer in Alexandra's Life Guard lancer regiment.

No. 39/ Telegram 766 in Russian. Stavka> Tsarskoe Selo. 24 Oct 1914. 8.44> 9.12 a.m. To her majesty. Heartfelt thanks to you and children for letters. Very glad you went to Luga. Yesterday your squadron of Alexandrine hussars joined our troops after four-week absence in enemy's extreme rear with very few losses. Embrace all tenderly. Nicholas

---

No. 40/ Telegram 360. Tsarskoe Selo> Stavka. 24 Oct 1914. 5.53> 6.30 p.m. To his majesty. Warm thank you for telegram. Terribly glad that Alexander squadron returned. Were at store and Church of the Exaltation of the Cross Monastery. Clear weather. All well. Warmly kiss you. God keep you. Alix

---

No. 41/ Her No. 243.   Tsarskoe Selo. Oct. 24th 1914.
My own precious Darling,

Well we got through everything alright in town.< [Daughter] Tatiana had her Committee wh. lasted 1½ hour; she joined us at my Krestov. [Red Cross] Station, where I went with [daughter] Olga after the supply store. Lots of people were working in the Winter Palace and many came to fetch work and others to bring back their finished things. I saw the wife of a Dr. there, who just had a letter from her husband from Kovel, where he is in a military hospital, where they have very little linnen [sic] & nothing to dress the men in, when they leave the hospital. So I quickly told them to put lots of linnen & warm undergarments to send to Kovel & a biggish Image of Christ painted on linnen (& brought as a gift to the store) as its a little Jewish town & they have no Image in their hospital wh is in barracks. I wonder how you spend your days & evenings & what your plans are. Our Friend< was very pleased we went to Luga & in sisters [nurses'] dresses & wants me to go about more & not wait for yr return to go to Pskov, so I shall spin off again, only this time must tell the Governor I suppose, as its a bigger town—but that makes it always shyer work. I shall take then linnen with me to the military hospital which Marie< said needed things, or send it after.—There were many wounded at the [Red Cross] Station to-day, one officer had been 4 days in [your sister] Olga's hospital & said there was not such a second sister. Some men had very serious wounds. They had mostly been wounded near Suvalki, or been lying since some time at Dvinsk.— [a]

We read the description of yr visit to Minsk in the papers; I received a wire from the Governor thanking for the Images [icons] & gospels you had left there from me.—Now I must try & sleep, which I do very badly all these nights—cannot get off to sleep before 3 or 4. Goodnight my Sunshine, I bless & kiss you as tenderly & lovingly as is only possible.—

25-th. Goodmorning my love! I slept much better this night, only need to begin more heartdrops I feel, as chest & head ache. Thermometer is on zero this morning.—Ania< is in excellent spirits this time.—Our Friend intends leaving for [his] home [in Siberia] about the 5-th & wishes to come to us this evening. Paul< has asked to take tea & Fred.<[15] to see me, so we will lunch & then we have to go to the consecration of the hospital in the Mixed Regiment, wh. has got already wounded out of M. & A.'s [daughters Maria and Anastasia's] hospital, who were already better & had to leave to give place for severely wounded.—Now must get up & dress for the hospital<—& place candles at Znam.< before [arriving at the hospital]. God bless & keep you, my Treasure. Have no time for more. Kisses without end. Ever your own old   Wify.   [P.S.] The girls kiss you fondly.—Our love to N.P.< [b]

No. 42/ Telegram 796 in Russian. Stavka> Tsarskoe Selo. 25 Oct 1914. 11.05> 11.45 a.m. To her majesty. Thank you very much for letter and magazine.Yesterday watched with pleasure the regiment of Hussars and their quarters. Today inspecting two hospitals with wounded and the cavalry guard. Unfortunately had no time to write. Am going for 24 hours to Kholm and Sedlets. Returning on morning 27th. Hope you are well. Embrace all tenderly. Niki

---

No. 43/ Her No. 244.   Tsarskoe Selo. Oct. 25th 1914.
My own sweet Treasure,

Now you are off to Kholm & that will be nice & remind you of ten years ago. Loving thanks for your telegram—it was surely pleasant seeing your dear hussars, & the G. à Cheval [Horse Guard] in Reval.—After the hospital< this morning we went into 2 private houses to see the wounded—always old patients of ours. Fredericks[15] came to luncheon, really he had nothing to tell, brought several telegrams to show & looked pretty well. At ¼ to 2 we were at the barracks of the Mixed Regiment looked at the hospital arranged & had a Te Deum & blessed the rooms—the men looked very contented & the sun shone brightly upon them. From there we went to Pavlovsk, picked up Mavra< who showed us over four hospitals.—Paul< came to tea. He longs to go to the war, & so I am writing this to you with his knowledge, so as for you to think it over before you meet him again. All along he hoped you would take, but now he sees there is little chance, & to remain at home doing nothing drives him to exasperation. He would not like to go to Ruzsky's< staff as would be inconvenient, but if he might begin by going out to his former comrade Bezobrazov he would be delighted. Wont you speak this question over with Nikolasha?<⁻

Then we went to the evening service in the new Peshcherny Chapel under the existing one in the big Palace hospital.< There was a Church there in Catherin[e]'s time; after that we sat with our wounded; Many of them & all the nurses & ladies had been in Church. Gogoberidze< the Erivanets< had just arrived.—Our Friend< came for an hour in the evening; he will await yr return & then go off for a little [visit] home[, to Siberia].—He had seen M-me Muftizade who is in an awful state, & Ania was with her—it seems Lavrinovsky< is ruining everything—sending off good Tartars to Turky [sic] & most unjust to all—so that they begged her to come to their Valideh [realm] to pour out their complaints, as they are truly devoted subjects. They would like [N. A.] Knyazhevich to replace Lavr. and our Friend wishes me quickly to speak to Maklakov,< as he says one must not waste time until your return. So I shall send for him, pardon my mixing in what does not concern me, but its for the good of the Crimea & then Maklakov can at once write a report to you to sign—if you cannot let Knyazhevich leave the army now (tho' I think he would be of more use in the Crimea) then another must be found. I shall tell Maklakov that you & I spoke about Lavr. already. He seems to be most brutal to the Tartars & its certainly not the moment when we have war with Turky to behave like that. Please don't be angry with me, & give me some sort of an answer by wire—that you "approve", or "regret" my mixing in—& whether you think Kn. a good candidate, it will quieten me;[29] & I shall know how to speak to Masha Muftizade.—You remember he was angry she wished to see me about sending things to the regiment, that Tartars must not show themselves in their dresses before us, & so on offending them constantly. He may do better in another government [gubernaya]; I know Apraksin< is of the same opinion, & was deeply grieved by the change he found.—Its nearly one, must try & sleep. I saw Alia< & husband at 10½, he joins Khan< & Misha. [a]

26-th. We just returned from 2 hospitals, where saw wounded officers & the old Priest of your rifles from here, who got overtired & was sent back.—I enclose a letter fr [your sister] Olga for you to read (privately) & if you see her, can you give it back to her. I got another sweet letter from her to-day, so full of love, Dear Child, she does work so hard. Now, Loman's train ([which bears] my name) will only be ready later, am so sorry. Wonder whether you will send for us anywhere, or whether we can get into Shulenburg's train, think he must return soon.—The weather is mild to-day & its gently snowing. Baby motored then made a fire wh he enjoyed.—The Children told you probably all about the Consecration of the Church (you must see it) & that we visited our officers afterwards. Igor< gave me news you had seen him.— Thank God all goes so well in Turky—would that our fleet could have success.—I received M-me Knyazhevich[30] ([wife of the] lancer) who offered me money for 10 beds from my lancer ladies—& through her husband I got money from all the squadrons & shall get monthly too, to keep up 6 beds—too touching.—Then M-me Dedyulin< came to thank for my note & you for the telegram wh came so unexpected & touched her very deeply.— Must end now my treasure. Goodbye & God bless you, sweetest, deeply missed one. I cover your precious face with tender kisses. Ever yr very own wife. Alix. [P.S.] Our love to N.P.< [b]

29. This letter is filled with the type of behavior that in time, would discredit Nicholas and help foster his downfall. Alexandra knew it was inappropriate for her to meddle in state affairs; she apologizes while justifying it; she presents her husband with an accomplished fact, hoping to be assured he was not "angry" with her. The letter documents Rasputin pressuring a minister through the empress. For the first time, Alexandra seeks to empty and fill a political office, etc.

30. Lidiya Afanas'evna, wife of D. M. Knyazhevich.

No. 44/ Telegram 3663. Brest> Tsarskoe Selo. 26 Oct 1914. 5.14> 6.03 p.m. To her majesty. Spent morning in Kholm, went to Mass and inspected large Red Cross hospital. We passed Vlodava. Weather calm, warm. Embrace you and children warmly. Niki.

No. 45/ Telegram 370. Tsarskoe Selo> Sedlets. 26 Oct 1914. 8.30> 9.30 p.m. To his majesty. Warmly thank you for telegram. [We] attended dedication of a church, visited three hospitals, are well, warm, damp weather hangs on. [We] all embrace you warmly [and] write every day. May God keep you. Heartfelt greetings to all. Alix.

No. 46/ Her No. 245.   Tsarskoe Selo. Oct. 26th 1914.
My very own precious One,
    I fear my letters are somewhat dull, because my heart & brain are somewhat tired & I have always the same thing to tell you. Well, this afternoon I wrote what we did. After tea we went with Aleksei< & Ania< to the hospital< & sat there for an hour & a half—several officers had gone to town< as they did not know we would come.—Just this minute Tudels< brought me a wire from Botkin,< thank God he has news that his son recovered very well & was well looked after, but taken [as a prisoner of war] to Budapest Oct. 1-st—Botkin returns here over Kholm.—How nice that you were there for Church; do so wonder, whether you can get for a peep to Lublin or anywhere else to see some troops.—I am so glad it has been settled by the Princess< & Zeidler< that Shesterikov & Rudnev[31] need not be operated, one can leave the bullets in them—its safer as they sit very deep in, & cause no pain. Both are enchanted, walk about again & went to the Consecration of the little Church this morning.—Kulinev we found less well, grown pale & suffers more from his head, poor boy. Young Krusenstern returned to his regiment. Genig lies in the red cross station; he is also contusioned in the head, lies with dark spectacles in a half dark-room.[a]
    The Erivanets< Gogoberidize< has come to us now.—Baby< says his prayers of an evening down here, so as for me not to go up, as I do much now & feel my heart needs caring after. At last, the eng.-mech.< left me. To-day, an endless visit. To-morrow its a week we parted, & the longing that fills my heart is great. I miss my angel terribly, but get strength by remembering the joy of all who see you & your contentment at being out there. Do you play domino of an evening I wonder? We intend going to Georgi< to-morrow to see his wounded, he only knows the big girls< go, about myself I did not say—then I shall ask to see Ser-

gei< a minute—& go to some smaller hospitals. Now, after blessing & kissing you fondly in thought, I must put out my lamp & get to sleep—am very tired.

27-th. I am so glad you are contented with your expedition.—We have had a busy day—3 operations this morning, & difficult ones too, so had no time to be with ours in the little house, this afternoon were in town<—went to Georgi<—the wounded lie in the big room & looked contented. Sat with Sergei<—find him much changed, greyish complexion, not thin face, eyes strange—is a little bit better, had been very bad; saw old Zander[32] there. Then went to the Palace Hospital< where wounded (& usual ill) lie—found Mr. Stuart there, lies there since 6 weeks, had typhoid.—Then off to the Constantin[e] School< on the Fontanka [Boulevard]. There 35 men some Izmailov officers.<—Am tired, have Taneev< at 6, & Svechin< with report at 6½.—Miss you always, my Sunshine, think of you with yearning love.—God bless & protect you, Nicky dear, big agoowee one. I kiss you over & over again. Ever your very own Wife   Sunny.   [P.S.] All the girls send you lots of love. We also send our love to N. P.< [b]

31. Alexandra Fedorovna mentions six wounded soldiers in this letter. The first was probably Georgy Alexandrovich Shesterikov, an officer in the Life Guard infantry regiment. "Kulinev" was probably Leonid Ivanovich Kul'nev, officer of the Royal Family's 4th Rifle regiment. The fifth, "Krusenstern," was probably Constantine Akselevich Kruzenshtern, officer of the Semenovsky Life Guard regiment.

32. Doctor Alexander Lvov'ich Zander, physician-in-ordinary to the imperial court, held the service rank of t.s.

No. 47/ Telegram 849 in Russian.   Stavka> Tsarskoe Selo.   27 Oct 1914. 11.04> 11.20 a.m.   To her majesty. Thank you very much for letter which arrived during my return here to-day. Remain satisfied with trip. Fog, damp. Will write. Unfortunately, could not do so earlier. Thank Aleksei for letter. Embrace all warmly. Niki.

No. 48/ Telegram 373. Tsarskoe Selo> Stavka. 27 Oct 1914. 5.44> 6.18 p.m. To his majesty. Am happy you are satisfied with trip. Were at hospitals at Constantine School,< at Palace< and Georgi's.< Visited Sergei.< He is a bit better but looks bad. [We] warmly embrace [you]. May God keep you. Alix.

No. 49/ Her No. 246.   Tsarskoe Selo. Oct. 27th 1914.
My own sweetest Nicky dear,

I have come earlier to bed, as am very tired—it was a busy day, & when the girls went to bed at 11, I also said goodnight to Ania,< her humour towards me has been not amiable this morning—what one would call rude & this evening she came lots later than she had asked to come & was queer with me. She flirts hard with the young Ukrainian—misses & longs for you—at times is colossaly gay;—she went with a whole party of our wounded to town< (by chance), & amused herself immensely in the train—she must play a part & speak afterwards of herself the whole time & their remarks about her. At the beginning she was daily asking for more operations, & now they bore her, as they take her away from her young friend, tho' she goes to him every afternoon & in evening again. Its naughty my grumbling about her, but you know how aggravating she can be.

You will see when we return how she will tell you how terribly she suffered without you, tho' she thoroughly enjoys being alone with her friend, turning his head, & not so as to forget you a bit. Be nice & firm when you return & don't allow her foot-game etc. Otherwise she gets worse after—she always needs cooling down. [a]

Her Father [A. S. Taneev] came with a report to me, then Svechin< about more motors he has got for our trains.—How is the news to-day, I wonder—she says our Friend< is rather anxious—perhaps to-morrow He will see all better again, & pray all the more for success. My Becker[33] wired from Varsovie [Warsaw] telling about my squadrons 5 weeks amongst the enemy. They lost 1 officer & 23 men. I always kiss & bless your cushion in the evening & long for my Lovy. I quite understand you had no time for writing & was grateful for your daily telegrams—& I know you think of me, & that you are occupied all day long. Dearest Treasure, this is my 7-th letter, I hope you get them alright.—Does N.P.< photograph? He took his apparatus I think with him.—We had a letter from Keller again.—Css. Carlow's< second daughter Merica< is engaged to a C.[hevalier] Orzhevsky,[34] who is only 22—the mother is not contented.—I saw in the papers that Greek Georgie & wife< have left for Greece from Copenhagen via Germany, France & Italy—I am astonished one has let them through.—What is Eberhardt< doing? They have been bombarding Poti.— [b]

Oh this miserable war! At moments one cannot hear it any more, the misery & bloodshed break one's heart; faith, hope & trust in God's infinite justice & mercy keep one up.—In France things go very slowly—but when I hear of success & that the Germans have great losses, I get such pang in the heart, thinking of Ernie< & his troops & the many known names. All over the world losses! Well, some good must come out of it, & they wont all have shed their blood in vain. Life is difficult to understand—"It must be so—have patience", thats all one can say.—One does so long for quiet, happy times again! But we shall have long to wait before regaining peace in every way. It is not right to be depressed but there are moments the load is so heavy & weighs on the whole country & you have to carry the brunt of it all. I long to lessen your weight, to help you carry it—to stroke your brow, press you to myself. But we show nothing of what we feel when together, which happens so rarely—each keeps up for the others sake & suffers in silence—but I long often to hold you tight in my arms & let you rest your weary head upon my old breast. We have lived through so much together in these 20 years—& without words have understood each other. My brave Boy, God help you, give strength & wisdom, comfort & success. Sleep well, God bless you—holy Angels & Wify's prayers guard your slumber. [c]

28-th. Good morning Darling! I slept very badly, only got off after 4 & then constantly woke up again, so tiresome, just when one needs a good rest. Its warmer to-day & grey weather.—Just before going to the hospital< received your beloved letter—it was sweet of you to have rejoiced my heart like that—& I thank you from all my loving heart.—Certainly we shall come with greatest pleasure & let Voeikov< arrange all & say exactly, when to meet you—perhaps we can stop on the way out & see some hospital at Dvinsk or so—I have sent for Ressin< to talk all over.—We shall then go off to Pskov to-morrow, sleep this night in the train, & be back to-morrow for dinner. Probably Babys train will arrive Thursday.—We saw Marie's [train]< at Alex. station—the most were wounded in the legs—came from Varsovie [Warsaw] hospitals & Grodno.— [d]

We are going to another hospital now directly.—I think, if its possible to stop perhaps at Dvinsk on the way to you, if there is time. R.[ostovtsev?] is finding out about the hospitals (privately) —there we shall go as sisters [nurses] (our Friend< likes us to) & to-morrow also. But being with you at Grodno we shall dress otherwise, not to make you shy driving with a nurse.—M.[aklakov] is coming at 9, & I shall tell him also your wish about Lavr.[inovsky].[35] Feeling myself a wound-up mashine [sic] which needs medicins [sic] to keep her up—seeing you, will help mightily. I think of bringing Ania & Iza< & O. Evg.< & perhaps one maid for the 2 girls & me, & one for the ladies (to meet you)—the less people the better & to hang less on to your train afterwards.—Its best taking Ressin I think, as a military man.—Now must end. Blessings & kisses without end. The joy of seeing you will be intense—but hard leaving my Sunbeam<.— Instead of Pskov, perhaps we might stop with you still in some other town.—I bless you over & over again—a whole week already to-day! Work is the only remedy.— Ever your very own old Sunny. [P.S.] Love to N.P.< [e]

33. Possibly V. V. Bakherakht, former Russian envoy to Vienna.

34. Aleksei Vladimirovich Orzhevsky, cornet in the Dowager Empress Maria Fedorovna's guards cavalry regiment; during the war transferred to Preobrazhensky Life Guard regiment; killed in 1915.

35. Alexandra wanted N. N. Lavrinovsky removed as governor of Tavrida, and Nicholas II had obviously decided to do this. (See Letter No. 43a.) Maklakov, as minister of internal affairs, assigned governors. Maklakov had been governor of Chernigov; after removing Lavrinovsky as governor of Tavrida, Maklakov sent him as governor to Chernigov.

No. 50/ His No. 159.   Stavka.[11a] 27 October 1914.

My beloved darling Sunny,

At last I can write a few lines to thank you for your sweet letters, the sight of wh. make my old heart jump for joy when I see them lying on my table. The first days here I had to see gen Panteleev—about Samsonov's sad story, then old Troitskii,[36] who is going to Kiev to put order there, then Pr.[ince] Shcherbatov< about the question of our horses. I found old Petiusha< here fresh fr. Lvov & a battle where Radko Dmitriev took him. They were for three hours under fire of the austrian heavy artil.[lery]. It seems from the other's telegr. that Petya behaved very cooly & he asked to give him a reward; so I gave him the Georgievskoe oruzhie [Order of St. George], wh. made him half wild. He did not expect that. Now he caught cold & is shut up in an empty barrack near the train. On the whole we all think that he has become much less excited than he used to be probably after being under fire. The whole of Saturday I had the joy of spending with Misha,< who was his old self and such a dear again! We went to vsepoluchanie [vespers] together & separated after dinner. Both afternoons I spent with the garde à cheval [Cavalry Guards] & with my huzards [Hussars]. I talked with the officers & then with the men & afterwards went to look at their stables. The g. á ch. horses are nearly alright, but the huzard have got till now a pitiable look. They all say that curiously enough the german horses wh. they took, stand the hard work much less than our's. [a]

Now about my program. Wednesday I shall spend at Rovno. Thursday Lyublin and Ivangorod and the battlefield outside (Kozenitsy)—then Saturday at Grodno. If you came there to meet me it would be delightful. I spoke to Voeikov< and all the arrangements shall be made. I had thought of spending the whole of Saturday at Grodno (hospitals & fortress) & of arriving at Pskov Sunday morning. Mass in a church & then a hospital< and be home for dinner. But if you go there alone then Pskov drops out. Now my sweetest Wify I must close this letter. I do hope you are feeling strong & well again. I kiss you & the beloved children tenderly. God bless you. Ever your own old   Niki [b]

36. Alexander Il'ich Panteleev was a cavalry general, member of the State Council, former commander of the gendarmes and governor of Irkutsk. See Samsonov in the Biographical Index.

No. 51/ Telegram 883.   Stavka> Tsarskoe Selo.   28 Oct 1914.   11.55 a.m.> 1.32 p.m.   To her majesty.   Loving thanks for letter and news. [You] can certainly see M[aklakov,] agree entirely upon question of changing governor in the south.[35] Wrote to you yester-day about my plans. I arrive at Grodno the 1 November in the morning [and] remain there the whole day.   Would you like to meet me at that place? I spend the day of to-morrow at Rovno then two days at the fortress. I am longing to see you. Tender love.   Niki.

No. 52/ Telegram 378.   Tsarskoe Selo> Stavka.   28 Oct 1914.   3.12> 3.43 p.m. To his majesty. Thank you heardily for precious letter and telegram with good news we will see each other Saturday. Resin< sent Voeikov< cyphered telegram concerning arrangements.   Many hospitals in fortress.   You will see my supply-train No. 4 which will bring a mass of things there.   We will get ready to-morrow to go to P[skov].   This morning visited the wounded in Marie's train.< To-day rainy.   Bless and kiss [you].   Alix

No. 53/ Telegram 535 in Russian.   Army in the Field> Tsarskoe Selo.   29 Oct 1914.   2.20> 6.48 p.m.   To her majesty.   Very glad to be here again and to see [my sister] Olga.   Was at her hospital, now going to military hospitals.   Weather splendid, warm.   Staying till evening. Thank you for letter, warmly embrace [you].   Niki.

No. 54/ Telegram 785.   Luga, Southwest Sector> Rovno.   29 Oct 1914.   7.25> 7.20 p.m.   To his majesty.   Were in Pskov from 9 to 1.   Saw [our daughter] Marie's hospitals,< Red Cross's modern school, two [hospitals?] in barracks of Irkutsk regiment.   Were in cathedral. Marvellous sunny day.   By chance visited Sukhomlinov's coach. Tired. Am repeating lectures of Princess [Gedroits for volunteer nurses]. Could we not go together on return trip to Dvinsk?   [We] warmly kiss you and [your sister] Olga.   Alix

No. 55/ Telegram 126 in Russian.   Ivangorod Fortress> Tsarskoe Selo.   30 Oct 1914.   7.30> 9.12 p.m.   To her majesty.   Many thanks for letter of 28th.   This morning inspected 3 hospitals in Lyublin.   Were in good order.   Found much of interest here, will tell you at our meeting. Saw many soldiers and sailors I know. So glad to find them here. Weather quite warm. To-morrow will drive around battlefields. Said we will stop in D[vinsk]. Embrace all warmly. Nicholas

---

No. 56/ Telegram 859. Luga train station> Ivangorod. 31 Oct 1914. 7.50. To his majesty. Travelled well. Bandaged in the morning, received many during the day. Very tired. [We] are happy about to-morrow's meeting. [We] warmly kiss [you]. Little ones also stay here. May God keep you. Alix

---

No. 57/ Her No. 247.   Tsarskoe Selo. Nov. 17th 1914.
My own beloved One,
    The train will be carrying you far away from us when you read these lines. Once more the hour of separation has come—& always equally hard to bear.—The loneliness when you are gone, tho' I have our precious Children, is intense—a bit of my life gone—we make one. God bless & protect you on your journey & may you have good impressions & shed joy around you & bring strength & consolation to the suffering! You always bring revival as our Friend< says. I am glad his telegram came, comforting to know His prayers follow you. Its good you can have a thorough talk with N.< & tell him your opinion of some people & give him some ideas. May again your presence there bring goodluck to our brave troops!— [a]
    Our work in the hospital< is my consolation & the visiting the specially suffering ones in the Big Palace<.—I only dread Ania's< humour—last time our Friend< was there, once a bad leg, & then her little friend. Lets hope she will hold herself in hand. I take all much cooler now & don't worry over her rudenesses & moods like formerly—a break came through her behaviour & works in the Crimea—we are friends & I am very fond of her & always shall be, but something has gone, a link broken by her behaviour towards us both—she can never be as near to me as she was.—One tries to hide one's sorrow & not pride with it—after all its harder for me than her, tho' she does not agree as you are all to her & I have the children—but she has me whom she says she loves.—Its not worth while speaking about this, & it is not interesting to you at all. It will be a joy to go & meet you, tho' I hate leaving Baby< & the girlies.< And I shall be so shy on the journey—I have never been alone to any big town—I hope I shall do all properly & your wife wont make a mess of herself.— Lovy my dear, huzy my very, very own—20 years my own sweet treasure—farewell & God bless & protect you & keep you from all harm. My light & sunshine, my very life & being. For all your love be blessed, for all your tenderness be thanked. I bless you, kiss you all over & gently press you to my deeply loving old heart. Ever, Nicky my Own, your very own   Wify   [P.S.] I am so glad N.P.< accompanies you, it makes me quieter knowing him near you and for him its such a colossal joy.— Our last night together, its horribly lonely without you—and so silent—nobody lives in this story. Holy Angels guard you and the Sweet Virgin spread her mantle of love around you.— Sunny. [b]

No. 58/ Her No. 248.   Tsarskoe Selo. Nov. 18th 1914.
My own beloved One,

   As a Feldjeger leaves this evening, I profit to write & tell you how we spent
the morning. Such pain fills the heart without my Sweetheart being here—so
hard to see you having [to be] all alone.—We went straight to the hospital< after
Fredericks had given me a paper to sign at the station. We had a good deal to
do, but I sat long whilst the children worked. A.[nna Vyrubova] was in a stupid,
unamiable mood. She went off earlier to see Alia< who arrives, & will only
come back at 9 & not to our lecture. She never asked what I would do—once
you are not there, she is glad to get out of the house. Its no good running away
from ones sorrow. But I am glad to see less of her when she is unamiable. [a]

   What dirty weather! I am going to the Children's hospital & then to the big
palace<. [Daughters] Marie & Olga go rushing about the room, Tatiana has a
lesson, Anastasia sits with her—Baby< is going out after resting. The Governor
calls me quickly.—I just received M-me Muftizade< & then the business manager of my Tsarskoe Selo red cross of Suvalki. He has come to fetch things &
ask for 2 motors. Beloved One, my very own Huzy dear—me wants [to] kiss you,
to cudle [sic] close & feel comfy. Now the children call me to the hospital, so I
must be off. The man goes at 5. Goodbye lovy mine, God bless & keep you
now & evermore. All the children kiss you tenderly. Ever your very own
Wify [b]

No. 59/ His No. 160.   In the train. Nov. 18th 1914.
My own beloved Sunny and darling Wify,

   We have finished luncheon & I have read through your sweet tender letter—with moist eyes. This time I managed to keep myself in hand the moment
of parting, but it was a hard struggle! The weather is dull and it is raining hard,
very little snow left. When we left I paid a visit to the gentlemen [of my suite]
& looked into each compartment. This morning, among the Min.[ister] of War's
papers, I found a signed one concerning to Rennenkampf—he is to leave his
army.³⁷ I do not know who Nik.[olasha<] thinks of in his place. If only we
could have travelled all this journey together—what joy and comfort it would
have been. Lovey mine, I miss you horribly, much more than my tongue can tell
it you. Every day a messenger will leave with papers for town<; I shall try &
write often as to my surprise I can write while the train is moving. My hanging
bar proved to be very practical and useful! I hung on it and chined lots before
eating. It is really good for one in train and shakes the blood & the whole system up! I love the pretty frame you gave me, it lies before me on the table, for
safety sake, else a sharp knock might break the nice stone. All the miniatures
are good except [daughter] Marie's. I am sure that everybody will appreciate it.
It is such joy & comfort to see you well & doing so much work for the wounded.
As our Friend< said, it is God's mercy, that at such a time you should be able to
do & to stand such a lot. Believe me, my sweet love, do not fear, but be more
sure of yourself, when you are alone, and everything will go off smoothly &
successfully. Now God bless you own Wify-dear. I kiss you and the children
tenderly. Keep well & try not to think you are lonely! Ever your own huzy
Niki

37. Paul Karlovich Rennenkampf (1854-1918) distinguished himself during the Russo-Japanese War. His failure to counterattack after the failed German assault on his First Army at Gumbinnen (August 20, 1914) made him seem responsible for the Russian debacle at Tannenberg (August 26-30, 1914). The Germans then defeated him at the First Battle of the Masurian Lakes (September 9-14, 1914). Nicholas wrote this letter after another defeat at Lodz (November 25, 1914), when the ever-timid Rennenkampf permitted the German XXV Reserve (!) Corps, almost encircled, to escape. Rennenkampf deserted his army, was accused of treachery and dismissed, probably *via* the "paper" the tsar mentions in this letter. Rennenkampf was subsequently made a scapegoat for Russian difficulties in the early months of the war. Rennenkampf was shot by the Bolsheviks at Taganrog for refusing to serve in the Red Army.

No. 60/ Telegram 298 in Russian. Sushchevo> Tsarskoe Selo. 18 Nov 1914. 6.11> 6.51 p.m. To the empress. In thoughts with you all, sent letter, hope you are not tired. Good night, embrace you warmly. Niki

---

No. 61/ Telegram 170. From Tsarskoe Selo> Vitebsk. 18 Nov 1914. To be dispatched after departure of imperial train. To his Majesty. Thank you for telegram. Sent letter. Am tired, we worked this morning, received during the day. Were with children at the hospital< and the Big Palace<, terribly crowded with newly wounded. Lectures there. Sleep well. God keep you. All warmly kiss you. Miss [you] very much. Alix.

No. 62/ Her No. 249.   Tsarskoe Selo. Nov. 19th 1914.
My very own beloved One,

Your letter was such an intense joy, consolation to me, God bless you for it & a thousand tender thanks. I love to read all the dear things you say, it warms me up because I cannot help feeling yr absence greatly, the "thing" is missing in all the life of my home. I lunch now always on the sopha when we are alone. How lucky one has taken Rennenkampf[37] away before you came, I am glad may they only find a good one instead—it wont be Mischenko< by any chance? He is so loved by the troops & a clever head, is he not?—One says the blue curassiers are enchanted to have my [E. C.] Arseniev< & well they may be.—Really it was an excellent idea yr arranging yr stick for gymnastics—good exercise when you will be shut up for so long, except standing in hospitals wh. is horribly tiring.—At 9 [our children] Olga, Anastasia, Baby< & I went off to his train. We have very heavy wounded this time, the train was at Sukhachev, 6 versts from the battle, & the windows shook from the artillery. Aeroplanes were flying there & over Varsovie [Warsaw]. Shulenburg says that the 13th & 14th Sib.[erian Infantry Regiments] were hideously afraid of all & thought God was with the Germans, not grasping what the aeropl. were & so on, & one could not get them to advance—all new troops, & not real Siberians. They have discovered our 6 motors of his train, wh. had disappeared since the 1-st—they are at Lodz only cant get away, otherwise may be taken, but they do still bring wounded. Lots came on foot now so have their lungs in a precarious state. Yagmin arrived (Nizhegorodsky<) I get no news—in town< one says it was bad yesterday—in the papers lots [of spaces] are white, not printed [because the material was deleted by the censors];—probably we retreated near Sukhachev. Some of these wounded had been taken by the Germans & then ours got them after 4 days back again. Dear me what wretched wounds, I fear some are doomed men;—but I am glad we have them & can at least do all in our power to help them.—I ought to have gone now to see the rest, but am too awfully tired, as we had 2 operations besides, & at 4, I must go to the big palace<, as I want the P-ss< also to have a look at the poor boy, & an officer of the 2-nd rifles whose legs are already getting quite <u>dark</u> & one fears an amputation may be necessary.—I was with the boy yesterday during his dressing awful to see, & he clung to me & kept quiet, poor child.—We have some heavy cases in the big Palace<.—[a]

It was grey & <u>rainy</u> yesterday & warm, this morning the sun shone, but its grey. A.[nna Vyrubova] has gone for a walk & then will come to me—she was in a disagreable [sic] mood the whole evening, so I went to bed at 11—this morning she continued, but we succeeded in breaking her. Its doubly painful when one feels sad, & she pretends being the "chief mourner" before others. I keep up & talk—& she might do the same. She continues asking about the Feld-jeger, I suppose intends writing—whether you have allowed it —I do not know.—[Daughters] Olga & Tatiana have gone to town< to receive donations in the Winter-palace.—Boris< is at Varsovie [Warsaw] for a week, Shulenburg took him to wash & clean up, as he has the itch—well Miechen< is in good time.—Yesterday we went also to the Children's hospital—sat with Nikolaev[38] & Lazarev.—A Volynets officer [from Volhynia] lay in the train to-day—they have only 12 officers in the regiment & few men left.—The Children all kiss you fondly, daily one of them will write, [daughter] Marie has begun now.—Please give N.P.< my love.—Did you hear whether Giants [this was a special unit] are wounded, there are such rumors from town<.—Oh yes, it would indeed have been lovely to have gone together, but I think yr journey to the Causasus at such a time, is better undertaken alone—there are moments when we women must not exist.—Yes, God has helped me with my health & I keep up—tho' at times am simply deadtired—the heart aches & is enlarged—but my will is firm—anything only not to think.— My Sweetheart, my very own Treasure, I must end now, the messenger leaves earlier to-day. —When you return, you must give me my letters to number, as I have no idea of how many I have written. Once more, endless thanks for yr dear letter, wh. is very well written tho' the train moved.—I press you to my yearning breast, kiss all the dear places I so tenderly love. God bless you & guard you from all ill! Ever Nicky my Angel, my own treasure, my Sun-shine, my life— yr very own old   Wify.   [P.S.] Messages to Dm. Shereme-tiev.< [b]

---

38. Stepan Leonidovich Nikolaev was a former officer of Alexandra Fedorovna's Crimean cavalry regiment, later of the 4th Kharkov lancer regiment.

No. 63/ Telegram [unnumbered]. Tsarskoe Selo> Stavka. 19 Nov 1914. 2.14> 2.53 p.m.   To his majesty.   Unspeakably happy with your dear letter, so com-forting.   Worked a lot.   Visited Aleksei's train which came from Sukhamev. Mass of wounded, many with very serious wounds.   Girls< went to Winter Pal-ace,< I to Big [Palace] to be present at bandaging of new officers.   Tired, but God helps.   Am sending letter.   [We] all tenderly kiss [you].   May God bless you.   Would like to know what is new.   Alix

No. 64/ Telegram 441 in Russian. Stavka> Tsarskoe Selo. 19 Nov 1914. 2.55>
3.20 p.m. To her majesty. Arrived well, thanks for letter and telegram. The
weather is as yesterday, without frost. Kirill< and Dmitry< here at present.
Warmly embrace you and children. Niki

No. 65/ His No. 161.   Stavka.[11a] Nov. 19. 1914.
My own precious Wify,
   Thank you tenderly for your sweet letter (the second) wh. came to-day in the
afternoon. I arrived punctually at 12.30. N.< met me at the big station outside
the wood. He looks well and quiet, though he went through atrocious moments,
rather days, when the germans were coming in deeper & deeper! The one great
serious difficulty for our armies is this—we are again running short of our artillery ammunition. Therefore during battle our troops have to be careful & economical, which means that the whole weight of the fighting lies upon the infantry—therefore the losses have at once become enormous. Some army corps have
become divisions, brigades melted into regiments etc. The popolnenie [rein-
forcements] arrive well, but the half has no rifles, as the troops lose such a
quantity of arms. There is no one to pick them up on the battlefields! It appears
that the germans are pulling the austrians up, higher north; several of their corps
are fighting on our ground as if they have come in from Thorn. And their troops
are all commanded by prussian generals. One says that the austr. prisoners swear
at their allies for that. Petiusha< is again here and feels well. I also saw Kiril,<
Dmitri<—and Ioanchik,< who asked me in case he is killed, to name our
[daughter] Olga president of the com.[mittee] for the construction of the large
cathedral! The four foreign generals dined with me, talked with them in the
evening. They have been much about Sukhachev, Seradz, Lodz etc. where now
fighting is so strong. To-day there have not been any details from the front.— My
beloved little Sunny, me loves you with an unceasing love; as you see, I might
call it un "puits d'amour"—after 20 years. God bless you, my darling. May he
watch over you and the children! I kiss you all very tenderly. Your own Niki·

No. 66/ Her No. 250.   Tsarskoe Selo. Nov. 20th 1914.
My own beloved Nicky dear,
   There is a belated gnat flying round my head whilst I am writing to you.—Well,
I went to the big Palace< to that poor boy's dressing, & somehow it seems to me
as tho' the border of the great bedsore wound were getting firmer—the P-ss< did
not find the tissue too dead looking. She looked at the rifle[man]'s leg & finds
one ought at once to take off before it is too late, & it must be done very high.
Vlad. Nikol.< & [Doctor Alexander Alexandrovich] Eberman find one must first
try another operation of the veins aneurism [sic] & if that does not help, then
take the leg off. His family want some celebrity to consult—but all are away
except Zeidler<, who could not come before Friday. I am going to have a talk
still with Vlad. Nik.—The evening I read Rost.'s< papers till 10 o'clock. Before
dinner I received M-me Zizi< & then I got a nap. Ania< wants us to go off to
Kovno, as we cannot menage [sic] the Sanitary train this time, to our regret, &
Voeikov's< joy. But that means also Vilna. I cant pass without stopping there.

The children like that idea, as hope to see our "friends"—she says there are heaps of wounded there. Ella< arrived Monday—really don't know what to do—wish you were here to ask & this letter will reach you only Saturday at earliest, & then we ought to be off. I shall think it over still. Am so tired & don't much care to go off now, & then here is much work & our Children, whom I must leave on the first. But perhaps it would be good to go there. Ania wants change & "Dr. Armia" [Dr. Army] as she always says. Dearest Beloved—I kiss yr. cushion morn & evening & bless it & long for its treasured master.—I enclose a postcard of us at Dvinsk. I think it might amuse you to have for yr. album. [a]

Its quite mild weather to-day. Baby< is going in his motor & then [daughter] Olga who is now walking with Ania, will take him to the big palace< to see the officers, who are impatient for him. I am too tired to go & we have at 5¼ an amputation (instead of lecture) in the big hospital. This morning we were present (I help as always, giving the instruments & Olga threaded the needles) at our first big amputation (whole arm was cut off) then we all had dressings (in our small hospital) very serious ones in the big hospital.—I had wretched fellows with awful wounds[—]scarcely a "man" any more, so shot to pieces, perhaps it must be cut off as so black, but hope to save it—terrible to look at. I washed & cleaned, & painted with iodine & smeared with vaseline & tied them up & bandaged all up—it went quite well & I felt happier to do the things gently myself under the guidance of a Dr.—I did three such—& one had a little tube in it. Ones heart bleeds for them—I wont describe any more details, as its so sad, but being a wife & mother I feel for them quite particulary—a young nurse (girl) I sent out of the room—M-lle Annenkov[16] is already older—the young doctor so kind— [b]

Ania looked on so cooly, quite hardened already, as she says—she astonishes me with her ways constantly—nothing of the loving gently woman like our girlies<—she ties them up roughly when they bore her, goes away when she has had enough—& when little to do, grumbles. Iedigarov< noticed that they already bore her—& she fidgets & hurrys one.—I am disappointed in her—must always have something new like Olga Evg.< At 4 she goes off to her sister [Alia<] instead of coming to the amputation, once we go—she might have spent the evening at her sister. P-ss. Gedroitz< said to me she soon noticed how Ania does not care doing or knowing things a fond & she feared we might be so, but is grateful its not the case & that we do all thoroughly. Its not a play—she wanted & fidgeted for the cross, now she has it, her interest has greatly slakened [sic]—whereas we feel now doubly the responsability [sic] & seriousness of it all & want to give out all we can to all the poor wounded, with slight or serious wounds, equally lovingly. [Daughter] Marie saw an officer of her regiment. You will give N.P.< our love please, & tell him the news we give you, as all we do interests him. My nose is full of hideous smells from those blood-poisoning wounds.—One of the officers in the big palace< showed me German fabricated dum-dums, very long, [at this point in the middle of her letter the empress sketches the bullet she is describing] narrow at the tip, red copper like things.—Me misses you, me wants a kiss badly. Lovy my child, I long for you, think & pray for you incessantly. Sweetest One, goodbye now & God bless & protect you. I press you tenderly to my heart, kissing you fondly, & remain forever your deeply loving own old wify   Sunny.   [P.S.] The Children all kiss you. [c]

No. 67/ Telegram 174. Tsarskoe Selo> Smolensk. 20 Nov 1914. 3.10> 3.35 p.m. [To his majesty] [My] tender thoughts follow you, [I] remember our visit together to Smolensk. Mild weather. Resting now after hard work in hospital,< departure of badly wounded, amputation of arms. Another arm amputation after 5. [Daughter] Tatiana has [meeting of her] committee[66] in town.< [Children] Olga and Aleksei are at Big Palace.< [I] write every day. [We] warmly embrace all, kiss and pray for you.   Alix

No. 68/ Telegram 1 in Russian. Dorogobuzh> Tsarskoe Selo. 20 Nov 1914. 9.10> 10.40 p.m.   To her majesty. Thank you for telegram. In Smolensk I thought of our visit in 1912. Visited four hospitals there. All in excellent order. Warm, quiet [weather]. Am with you in thoughts. Warmly embrace all. Niki

No. 69/ Telegram 177. Tsarskoe Selo> Kaluga. 20-21 Nov 1914. 10.05 p.m.> 12.13 a.m.   To his majesty. Kaluga. What news from Stavka? Have not heard anything since you left. Mild weather. Three sisters [i.e., nurses] leave this evening. Where did Oleg K.[39] die and where are the sailors? We return Sunday. All warmly kiss and embrace [you]. Follow you in thoughts on your interesting trip. Alix

39. The reference is to Prince Oleg Constantinovich, one of the four sons of Grand Prince Constantine Constantinovich.

No. 70/ Her No. 251.   Tsarskoe Selo. Nov. 21st 1914.
My Lovebird,
    I don't want the Feldjeger to leave to-morrow without a letter from me. This is the wire I just received from our Friend<: "When you comfort the wounded, God makes His name famous through your gentleness & glorious work." [The quote is in Russian] So touching & must give me strength to get over my shyness.—Its sad leaving the wee ones<!—Iza< suddenly had [a temperature of] 38 & pains in her inside, so Vlad. Nik.< wont let her go. Fullspeed we telephoned to Nastinka< to get ready & come. We are taking parcels & letters from all the naval wives for Kovno. We are eating, & the Children chattering like waterfalls, which makes it somewhat difficult to write.—Now Light of my life, farewell. God bless & protect you & keep you from all harm. I do not know when & where this letter will reach you.—Blessings without end & fondest kisses from us all. Your very own   Sunny.   [P.S.] We all send messages to N.P.<—& Dm. Sherem.<

No. 71/ Telegram 290. Tula> Tsarskoe Selo. 21 Nov 1914. 4.30> 5.25 p.m. To her majesty. Tender thanks for two dear letters. Advise you if feel well to go to K[ovno] and V[ilno]. This morning after church visited a munitions factory, so interesting, ten thousand workers. Now off to the hospitals, there are about 40 here. No time for writing. Tender love and kisses to all. Niki

No. 72/ Her No. 252.   Tsarskoe Selo. Nov. 21ˢᵗ 1914.
My own beloved Treasure,
    Its nice that we were together at Smolensk 2 years ago with Keller so I can imagine where you were. Aleksei's "obshchina" [committee][40] wired to me after you had been there to see them. I remember them giving Baby< an Image [icon] at that famous tea there.—Still no news of the war through fat Orlov< since you left. One whispers that Joachim[41] has been taken by our troops—if so, where has he been sent to, I wonder. If true, one might have let Dona< know through Vicky of Sweden< that he is safe & sound (not saying where) but you know better, its not for me to advise you, its only a mother pittying [sic] another mother.—[a]
    I remained at home in the afternoon yesterday, & lay in bed before dinner, being dead-tired. The girls went to the hospital< instead of me. After dinner I received Shulenburg rather long; he leaves Saturday again. The bombs were being thrown daily over Varsovie [Warsaw] & everywhere & at night. Baby's train stuck an hour & ½ on the bridge (full of wounded, over 600) & could not get into the station (coming from Praga) on account of the other trains, & he feared every minute that they would be blown up.—Then I received Ressin<—quick man—in an hour he settled all the plans, & we leave this evening at 9, reach Vilna Saturday morning at 10.15-1.—Then continue to Kovno 2.50-6, back to Ts.[arskoe] S.[elo] Sunday morning at 9. Ressin only lets the Gov. of Vilna know, because of motors or carriages & he is not to tell on—from there he will let the Gov. at Kovno know (or its the same man). Ania< has telephoned privately to Rodionov—I hope we may catch a glimpse of them some-where.—A.[nna Vyrubova] is very proud she kept me from going to the hospital as tiring—but its her doing this expedition which is tiring—2 nights in the train & 2 towns to visit hospitals—if we see the dear sailors, it will be a recompense.—I am glad we can manage it so quickly & wont be long away from the Children. [b]
    Excuse this dirty page, but I am quite ramolie< & my head is weak, I even asked for a little wine. 100 questions, papers— beginning by Vilchkovsky< in the hospital<, every morning questions to answer, resolutions to be taken & so on—& my brain is not as strong or fresh as it was before my heart got so bad all these years. I understand what you feel like of a morning when one after the other come bothering you with questions!—At the hospital I received a "Khan-sha" who gave M-me Mdivani motors[42] & was going to send an unit for the Caucasian troops on the German frontier—now she asked my permission to change, & have it in the Caucasus where sanitary help is yet more deficient.—
    I could not get to sleep this night, so at 2 wrote to Ania to tell her to let the naval wives know there is an occasion safely to forward letters or packets—then I sorted out booklets, gospels (1 Apostel[43]), prayers to take for the sailors, goodies & sugared fruits for the officers—perhaps shall find still warm things to add.—For your second dear letter, thanks without end. It was a joy to receive it, sweetheart. It is such anguish to think of our tremendous losses; several

wounded officers, who left us a month ago, have returned again wounded. Would to God this hideous war could end quicker, but one sees no prospect of it for long. Of course the Austrians are furious being led by Prussians, who knows whether they wont be having stories still amongst each other.—I received letters from Thora[44], A.[unt] Helene[45]< & A.[unt] Beatrice,[46] all send you much love & feel for you deeply. They write the same about their wounded & prisoners, the same lies have been told them too. They say the hatred towards England is the greatest. According to the telegrams Georgie [King George V] is in France seeing his wounded.—Our Friend< hopes you wont remain too long away so far.—I send you papers & a letter from Ania.—Perhaps you will mention in your telegram, that you thank [her] for papers & letter & send messages. I hope her letters are not the old oily style again.— [c]

Very mild weather. At 9½ we went to the end of mass in the Peshcherny Chapel—then to our hospital where I had heaps to do, the girls nothing & then to an operation in the big hospital. And we showed our officers to Zeidler< to ask advice.—[Daughters] Olga & Tatiana went in despair to town< to a concert in the Circus for Olga's committee—without her knowledge one had invited all the ministers & Ambassadors, so she was obliged to go. M-me Zizi<, Isa< & Nastinka< accompanied them, & I asked Georgi< to go too & help them,—he at once agreed to go—kind fellow.—I must write still to [your sister] Olga with the eatables I send her. Her friend has gone there for short, as he is unwell, like Boris< with the itch, & needs a good cleaning.—A.[nna Vyrubova] says she has looked through the newspaper & its very dull, she begs pardon for sending it, she thought it was a nice one. Just back from the Big Palace< & dressings I looked at, & sat with officers. Now Malama comes to tea to say quite goodbye. Goodbye my angel huzzy. God bless & protect you! 1000 fond kisses from your own old   Wify.   [P.S.] The Children all kiss you. We all send heaps of messages to N.P.<—Long for you! [d]

40. "Aleksei's committee" refers to a committee whose titular head was the tsarevich Alexis.

41. Joachim was a son of Kaiser Wilhelm II and an officer in the 14th German Hussar regiment.

42. M-me. Mdivani was the wife of Z. A. Mdivani, commander of the 13th Erivan Life Guard regiment (1912-June 1915). The "Khansha" was apparently a lady from the Caucasus who earlier had given M-me. Mdivani automobiles and who now wanted to send an automobile unit to Caucasian troops on the German frontier, though as the empress notes, the unnamed benefactor altered these plans.

43. An *Apostol* contains the Gospels and apostolic letters.

44. "Thora" was Victoria, the princess of Schleswig-Holstein, cousin of Alexandra Fedorovna.

45. "Helene" probably refers to Elena Petrovna, born a Serbian princess, married to Prince Ioann Constantinovich.

46. Aunt Beatrice was a daughter of Queen Victoria, aunt of Alexandra Fedorovna and the Princess of Battenburg.

No. 73/ Telegram 321. Kovno> Sazhnoe. 22 Nov 1914. 4.35> 9.40 p.m. To his majesty. Sazhnoe. [We] travel well. [I] slept badly. At Vilna visited relics and the Ostrobramskaya Image [Icon].[47] Inspected hospital and female gymnasium [school], court and officers' hospitals. Met Voronov. Inspected 2 completely overcrowded sanitary trains. Warmly embrace and kiss [you]. Alix

47. The Ostrobramskaya Icon in Vil'no was famous for its miracle-working properties.

No. 74/ Telegram 00315. Vilna> Sazhnoe. 22 Nov 1914. 8.40> 10.15 p.m.
To his majesty. Sazhnoe. In Kovno visited cathedral, four hospitals. Comman-
dant is renowned. Leaving at station [we saw military] companies departing.
Shirinsky-[Shikhmatov], Butakov, Nolde, Shchepotev, Zimonin[48] [are here].
The rest are on expedition. Good weather. In Landvornovo will see a sanitary
center. [We] warmly embrace [you]. Greetings to all. Alix

48. See Shirinsky-Shikhmatov and Butakov in the Biographical Index. Baron Nol'de, Shchepot'ev
and Zimonin were officers in the guards ship's company; see also Letter 76b.

No. 75/ Telegram 192. Tsarskoe Selo> Kharkov. 23 Nov 1914. 12.33> 2.22 p.m.
To his majesty. Returned successfully. Visited militia sanitary train on way last
night, wounded delighted to see us, not angry to be awakened for visit. Not going to church because very tired and besides should inspect my train arriving
after lunch. [Daughter] Olga sledging. Expect Ella< to-morrow. Little ones are
well, [we] all miss you very much. All warmly kiss and bless [you]. Alix.

No. 76. Her No. 253.   Tsarskoe Selo. Nov. 23rd 1914. Sunday.
My own beloved Darling.
     We returned here safely at 9¼, found the little ones well & cheery. The girls<
have gone to Church—I am resting, as very tired, slept so badly both nights in the
train—this last we tore simply, so as to catch up an hour. Well, I shall try to begin from the beginning.—We left here at 9, sat talking till 10, & then got into our
beds. Looked out at Pskov & saw a sanitary train standing—later one said we
passed also my train, which reaches here to-day at 12½. Arrived at Vilna at
10¼—Governor & military, red cross officials at the station, I cought [sic] sight
of 2 sanitary trains, so at once went through them, quite nicely kept for simple
ones—some very grave cases, but all cheery, came straight from battle. Looked
at the feeding station & ambulatory.—From there in shut motors driven (I was
just interrupted—Mitia Den< came to say goodbye) to the Cathedral where the 3
Saints lie, then to the Image [Icon] of the Virgin, (the climb nearly killed
me)—lovely face the Image has (a pitty [sic] one cannot kiss it)! Then to the
Polish Palace hospital—an immense hall with beds, & on the scene the worst
cases & on the gallery above officers—heaps of air & cleanly kept. Everywhere
in both towns one kindly carried me up the stairs which were very steep. Everywhere I gave Images & the girls too.—Then to the hospital of the red cross in
the   Girls   gymnasium,   where   you   found   the   nurses   pretty—lots   of
wounded—Verevkin's both daughters as nurses. His wife could not show herself, as their little boy has a contagious illness; his aids wife replaced her. No
acquaintances anywhere. The nurses sang the hymn, as we put on our cloaks;
the Polish ladies do not kiss the hand. [a]
     Then off to a small hospital for officers (where Malama & Ellis[49] had layn
[sic] before). There one officer told Ania< he had seen me 20 years ago at Simferopol, had followed our carriage on a bicycle & I had reached him out an apple
(I remember that episode very well) such a pitty he did not tell me! I remember

his young face 20 years ago, so could not recognise [sic] him [now].[50]—From there back to the station we could not go to more, as the 2 sanitary trains had taken time. Valuev< wanted me to see their hospital in the woods, but it was too late. Artsimovitch[51] turned up at the station thinking I would go to a hospital where sisters [i.e., nurses] from his government [gubernaya] were. I lunched & dined always on my bed. At Kovno the charming commandant of the fortress (no Governor counts there now, as it is the active front) & military authocraties [sic], some officers, Shirinsky, [Butakov, Nolde (with a beard)] & Shchepotev stood there too. The others had been just sent out to town expeditions, close to Thorn to blow up a bridge & the other place I forget, such a pitty [sic] to have missed them. Voronov, we passed at Vilna in the street. Again off in motors, flying along to the Cathedral (from Vilna we let know we were coming)—carpet on the stairs, trees in pots out, all electric lamps burning in the Cathedral, & the Bishop met us with a long speech. Short Te Deum, kissed the miraculous Image of the Virgin & he gave me one of St. Peter & St. Paul, after whom the Church is named—he spoke touchingly of us "the sisters of mercy" & called wify a new name, "the mother of mercy". [b]

Then to the red cross, simple sisters, skyblue cotton dresses— the eldest sister, a lady just come there, spoke to me in English, had been a sister 10 years ago & seen me there, as my old friend Kireev had asked me to receive her. Then to another little wing of the hospital in another street. Then to a big hospital about 300 in the bank—looked so strange to see the wounded amongst such surrounding of a former bank. One lancer of mine was there. Then we went to the big military hospital, tiny service & wee speech. Lots of wounded & 2 rooms with Germans, talked to some. From there to the station, on the platform stood the [military] companies (I had begged for them, I must confess), so difficult to recognise them, & not many acquaintances, you saw them. Zimonin[49] looked a dear. The boatswain of the [ship] Peterhof with the St. George's cross—all well, Shirinsky[49] too looks well. The Commandant is such a nice simple kind, not fussy man. Begged me to send still 3000 Images or bibles. He blessed us when the train left, touching man—to be cheered by our sailors at a fortress-station, they dressed as soldiers, we as nurses, who would have thought that possible a few months ago. At Landvarovo we stopped & looked at the feeding station & barracks hospital at station & service in wee Church. Some heavy cases. The Livland committee—(Pss. Shetvertinskaya[52] at the head, her property is close by), the daughter as nurse.—At 2 we stopped at a station, I discovered a sanitary train & out we flew, climbed into the boxcars. 12 men lying comfortably, drinking tea, by the light of a candle—saw all & gave Images—400. An ill Priest too was there— Zemsky [i.e., a militia] train, 2 sisters (not dressed as such) 2 brothers of mercy [i.e., male nurses], 2 doctors & many sanitaries. I begged pardon for waking them up, they thanked us for coming, were delighted, cheery, smiling & eager faces. So we were an hour late & cought [sic] it up in the night, so that I was rocked to & fro, & feared we should capsize.—So now I saw Trina,< after which must meet my Sanitary train. Ella< arrives to morrow evening. God bless & protect you!—no news from you since Friday. Very tenderest, fondest kisses from your very own old wify   Sunny. [P.S.] Victoria< sends love, living [at] Kent House Isle of Wight. Messages to N.P.< [c]

49. Ellis was an officer in Alexandra Fedorovna's Life Guard lancer regiment.
50. Alexandra recalls her arrival in Russia in October 1894. Nicholas realized his father, Tsar Alexander III, was dying, and he asked his fiancé to come to his side to share the ordeal. Alexandra travelled, unaccompanied and unnoted, from Germany to the Crimea, where Nicholas met her at Simferopol. The young couple rode in an open carriage to the royal residence at Livadia. They enjoyed great public affection during the four-hour drive, their carriage was filled with flowers and fruit by the time it arrived at its destination. See Massie, *Nicholas and Alexandra*, pp. 39-40.
51. Michael Viktorovich Artsimovich, shtalm., d.s.s., was the governor of Vitebsk.
52. Probably Leonilla Stanislavovna Svyatopolk-Chetvertinskaya.

No. 77/ Telegram 323. Kharkov> Tsarskoe Selo. 23 Nov 1914. 2.54> 3.35 p.m. To her majesty. Tender thanks [for] dear letter. Yesterday's papers hope arrived well. Saw lots of hospitals but had no time to see C.[ount] Keller's son. Such a touching reception. Leave at 4 o for Ekaterinodar. Loving kisses to you and children. Niki

---

No. 78/ Telegram 204. Tsarskoe Selo> Ekaterinodar. 24 Nov 1914. 2.20> 3.39 p.m. To his majesty. Thank you for last evening's telegram. Cloudy weather, warm. Were at four operations. Petia< had tea last evening, Sashka< to-day. Service at four for our three Nizhegorodskie.< My train brought my two very badly wounded Crimeans we saw in in [sic] Dvinsk. [They] just arrived, am tired, warmly embrace [you]. Alix

---

No. 79/ Her No. 254.   Tsarskoe Selo. Nov. 24th 1914.
My very own beloved One,
    I am so glad you had such a touching reception at Kharkov—it must have done you good & cheered you up. The news from out there make one so anxious—I don't listen to the gossip of town< which makes one otherwise quite nervous, but only believe what Nikolasha< lets know. Nevertheless I begged A.[nia]< to wire to our Friend< that things are very serious & we beg for his prayers. Yes, its a strong enemy we have facing us & a stubborn one.— Sashka< is coming to us to tea, on his way to the Caucasus—one says he married an actress & therefore leaves the regiment, he denied it to Ania & said it was his bad health which obliged him to ask for leave & he wanted to see his parents.—Malama took tea before leaving too.—Ella< arrives this evening.—We had 4 operations this morning in the big hospital & then officers dressings—My 2 Crimeans from Dvinsk arrived—they happily look better than they did then.—Almost daily I receive officers returning to the army or leaving to continue a restcure in their family.—Now we have placed officers in the big palace< on the opposite side too; General Tancray (the father of mine [i.e., the father of a patient of mine]) lies there too.—I am going off to see them at 4, the poor little fellow with the terrible wound always begs me to come. [a]
    The weather is grey & dull.—Do you ever manage to get a run at the stations?— Fredericks< was again ill two night ago & spat blood—so he is kept in bed—poor old man, it is so hard for him—& he suffers morally terribly.—Masses of your Mamas 11th Siberian regiment came in my train, 7 of her officers lie here in different trains.—Yesterday we received three Pavlovtsi [members of the Pavlovsky Life Guard regiment] to congratulate us on their feast-day, & Boris< wired

from Varsovie [Warsaw] in the Ataman's name.—Petia< looks alright, told us a lot, smelt of garlic, as he has injections of arsenic made him.—The Children are well & cheery.—Such a pitty [sic] I cannot get off now in a sanitary train! I long to be nearer the front, as you are so far away—that they should feel our proximity & gain courage.—A.[unt] Eugenie[53] has 100 wounded in the hall & adjoining room.— I do so long for you, my treasure—to-morrow a week that you left us—heart & soul are ever near you. I kiss you as tenderly as I only can & hold you tightly in my arms. God bless & strengthen you & give consolation & trust!—Ever, Nicky my own, your very own deeply loving old Wify Alix. [P.S.] Wonder whether you saw my supply store at K.[har'kov]: the Gov. is on bad terms with the Rebinders & so does not give a penny to my store, alas!—Please, give N.P.< our best love.—The Children kiss you 1000 times. I wonder where this letter will reach you! [b]

53. Eugenia Maximilianovna, born the Duchess of Lichtenberg, wife of Prince Alexander Petrovich Ol'denburg.

No. 80/ Telegram 28 in Russian. Sdanichnaya> Tsarskoe Selo. 24 Nov 1914. 5.55 p.m.> 7.33 p.m. To her majesty. Spent three happy hours at Ekaterinodar. Thank you for telegram. Greeted [my sister] Olga for you all. Embrace you all warmly. Niki

---

No. 81/ Telegram 212. Tsarskoe Selo> Khachmas. 25 Nov 1914. 2.37> 5.30 p.m. To his majesty. All well. Ella< arrived. Everything she says is quite interesting. Strongly impressed by fact that all are working so much. Gray weather. Very busy. [I] write every day. Feat of hussars remarkable. Poor Lopukhin died of wounds. [We] warmly kiss [you]. Greetings. Alix

---

No. 82/ Her No. 255.   Tsarskoe Selo. Nov. 25th 1914.
My own beloved One,
   In great haste a few lines. We were occupied all morning— during an operation a soldier died—it was too sad!—the first time it had happened to the Pr[incess]< & she has done 1000 of operations already: Hemorrhage. All behaved well, none lost their head—& the girlies< were brave—they & Ania< had never seen a death. But he died in a minute—it made us all so sad as you can imagine—how near death always is! We continued another operation. To-morrow we have the same one again & [it] may end fatally too, but God grant not, but one must try & save the man. Ella< came for luncheon, remains still to-morrow. We had her report & the 2 Mekk's,< Rost.< & Apraksin<—for 2 hours, that is why I had no time to write a real letter. Edigarov< dined cosily with us yesterday, he leaves in a day or 2 & has left the hospital already—fancy my having had courage to invite him—he was a dear & so simple.— Weather very mild.—Must end, man waits, others drinking tea around.— Blessings & very fondest kisses from your own old   Sunny.   [P.S.] Remember me to Vorontsov[-Dashkov, the old Count<] & N.P.< Ella & Children kiss you. Ella says General Schwarts adores you.

No. 83/ Telegram 131 in Russian. Derbent> Tsarskoe Selo.   25 Nov 1914.
5.05> 5.57 p.m. To her majesty. Are travelling splendidly, this is a marvellous
day, absolutely warm. Sent a letter. In thoughts am with you. Warmly embrace
[you]. Niki

No. 84/ His No. 162.   In the train. Nov. 25 1914.
My beloved Sunny-darling,
   It seems a long time since we separated. Two days ago I got your last letter
from Kharkov with our group [photograph] made at Dvinsk. To-day is my first
free day. We are travelling through a beautiful country, new to me, with the
beautiful high mountains on one side & steppes on the other. Since yesterday it
is much warmer and to-day it is glorious weather. I sat a long time next to the
open door of the carriage and breathed with delight the fresh warm air. At every
station the platform is crammed full of people, especially children, thousands of
them—so nice they look with tiny "papachi" [fur caps] on their heads. Certainly
in each town the receptions were touchingly warm. But yesterday at Ekaterinodar, the capital of the Kuban voisko [province], there was another & better impression, something so homely, like on board [ship?], on account of the masses
of old friends and the acquainted [familiar] faces of cossacks, who I remember
since my childhood in the convoy. I drove of course in my motor with the
ataman [hetman] gen. Babych[54] & saw several hospitals, excellent ones, with
wounded of the caucasian army. Some poor fellows with frozen feet. The train
shakes abominably so excuse my writing. [a]
   After hospitals I went for a minute at the Kuban zhensky [Female] Institut & a
large sirotsky priyut [orphanage] from the last war, only girls of cossacks[—]so
nice—real military discipline, they look healthy and natural, some very pretty
faces. N.P.< and I were contented with what we saw.—Just finished luncheon.
Quite hot in the train. We are running along the coast of the Caspian Sea, so
resting for the eyes to look at the blue distance, it reminded me of our Black Sea
and makes me feel sad. The hills are not far, gloriously lit up by the sun. Too
tiresome, why are we not together? After all—travelling here one is infinitely
further off the seat the war than being at Kovno or Grodno. N.P. and I are very
glad you went there and saw our friends! I shall send you this letter with a messenger from Derbent.   Peter the Gr.[eat] of course took that old place in
1724—can't remember where the keys are kept—I know they must be in one of
the palace churches because I have seen them, but am not sure where? [b]
   Tell [our daughter] Olga I thought much about her yesterday in the Kubanskaya oblast [province]! Splendid rich country that of the cossacks, lots of fruit
gardens, they are becoming prosperous and above all that tremendous <u>incon-
ceivable</u> quantity of tiny children[.] Baby's future subjects! All that makes one
overjoyed with faith in God's mercy[,] I may trust & look forward with calm to
what is in store for Russia! This second a telegram fr. our Friend< was brought
to me at a small station where I took a run. I think it a most comforting one! By
the way, I forgot to explain why my program was a bit changed? When we were
at the Stavka old C.[ount] Worontz. [Vorontsov-Dashkov] wired to ask me
whether I would not visit both cossack provinces & the two principal towns. As
we had some free time taken from the whole of the journey—Voeikov promptly

arranged it and so enabled me an opportunity to see more useful and necessary places— Ekaterinodar & on my way back north[,] Vladikavkaz —[center of the] Tersky voiska [host, army]. The days of my visit to Tula, Orel, Kursk & Kharkov I was too busy and half cretinized to be able to write to you and even to telegraph to you as you must have remarked! Therefore to-day is a real rest to all of us; the gentlemen being also as tired as me. But I repeat once more, all our impressions are lovely. What the whole country is doing & will do to the end of this war—is quite remarquable [sic] and enormous. I have seen some of this work with my own eyes—even Fedorov fr. the special medical point of view is quite surprised. Now lovy-mine I must end. I kiss you and the dear children fondly & tenderly. Me longs for you & wants you so!! God bless & protect you! Ever your very own huzy Niki. [P.S.] N.P. thanks you. [c]

---

54. Michael Pavlovich Babych, infantry general, nachal'nik of Kuban oblast' and nakaznyi ataman of the Kuban Cossack Host.

No. 85/ Telegram 221. Tsarskoe Selo> Tiflis. 26 Nov 1914. 1.12> 4.15 p.m. To his majesty. Tiflis. Warmly congratulate you on great [St. George's] feast. Attended mass with wounded, worked all morning, later attended requiem for Nizhegorodtsy< in new Peshchernyi chapel<, [another, regular] service there to-morrow. Ella< leaves for Moscow this evening. Compliments to count and countess [Vorontsov-Dashkov]. Bless and kiss [you]. We miss [you] very much. Alix

---

No. 86/ Her No. 256.   Tsarskoe Selo. Nov. 26th 1914.
My very own precious One.

I congratulate you with the St. George's feast—what a quantity of new cava-liers-heroes we have now! But ah me, what heartrending losses, if one can be-lieve what town< says. Ambrazantsev[55] is killed, Mme Knorring (his great friend, nee Heyden) got the news. One says terrible losses in the hussars, but I cannot trust to it being true. But I have no right to fill your ears with "les on dit" ["what one says"], I pray they may not be true. Well, we all knew that such a war would be the bloodiest & most awful one ever known, & so it has turned out to be the case, & one yearns over the heroic victims martyrs for their cause!—A.[nia]< has twice been to see Sashka<, I told her it was very wrong, but she does not heed me in the least. Ella< went in the afternoon with [our daugh-ter] Olga & me to the big palace< & she spoke to all the wounded; one of them was wounded last war & lay at Moscou [sic], & remembers her having come to see him. Its difficult finding time to write these two days whilst she is here.—[a]

Sweet Treasure, its ages since you left & me longs for "Agoobigweeone".< We went to early mass in the Peshch[erny] Chapel & from there Ella went to town till 3—& we till 1 to the little hospital—a small operation & 19 dressings, people I mean, as some had many wounds to be seen after.—Very warm again.—At 4 I am going to the big palace,< because they daily wait for the motor & are disappointed if we dont go, which happens rarely & the little boy begged me to come earlier to-day.—I feel my letters are very dull, but am ramolie< & thoughts wont come. The heart is full of love & boundless tenderness for you. I

eagerly await your promised letter, long to know more about you & how you
spend the time in the train after all receptions & inspections.—I hope you have
fine weather & lots of sun, here its so grey & wet. Have not been out since you
left only in shut motors. My Angel good-bye now & God bless you. May St.
George bring special blessings & victories to our troops!—The Children & I kiss
you ever so tenderly.—Count [N. E.] Nirod is just coming to speak about the
Xmaspresents for the troops. Ania sends you a funny newspaper. Fondest
kisses, Nicky love, from your very own   Wify. [P.S.] The Children & I send
N.P.< many messages. Well, the Xmas presents cannot be got in time, so we
shall do it for Easter—then 10 years ago for 300,000 it took from 3-4 months
collecting & now its much more needed.— [b]

55. This was Ivan Alekseevich Ambrazantsev-Nechaev, colonel in the Preobrazhensky Life Guard
Reg., killed November 1914.

No. 87/ Telegram 2317. Tiflis> Tsarskoe Selo. 26 Nov 1914. 2.05> 3.28 p.m.
To her majesty. Arrived safely, grand reception, beautiful weather. Old Count
[Vorontsov-Dashkov] not quite well today. Shall visit some hospitals, awful pity
you are not here. Tender love to you, Ella,< children. Niki

No. 88/ Telegram 243. Tsarskoe Selo> Tiflis. 27 Nov 1914. 2.00> 2.50 p.m.
To his majesty. Warm, raining. Worked all morning. Going to service for Nizhegorodtsy.< Congratulate you on festival of glorious regiment. Tenderest
blessings & greetings. Ambrazantsev[55] is dead. Three hussars slightly contusioned. Alix

No. 89/ Her No. 257.   Ts.[arskoe] S[elo]. Nov. 27. 1914.
My own beloved One,
    In great haste a few lines—we are at once off to the mass for & with the Nizhe-
gorodtsy,< our wounded & other officers, General Bagration, old Navruzov[56] &
ladies of the regiment. Worked the whole morning & had a big operation. At
9½ had a mass at Znamensky church, as its the feast of the Church's Image. Its
pouring & very dark. All of us are well. We are taking all 5 children to Church
as Baby< is inscribed into the regiment.— Well, all went off well. From there
we went to big palace< to all the wounded—they wait for the motor daily, so
there is no way of keeping away. I find the young boy gradually getting worse,
the temp. is slowly falling, but the pulse remains far too quick, in the evenings
he is off of his head & so weak. The wound is much cleaner, but the smell they
say is quite awful. He will pass away gradually—I only hope not whilst we are
away. Then we went to the one house of my red cross obshchina [unit].—Now
have drunk tea & Goremykin waits & then the P-ss.< Can't write any more.
Blessings & kisses without end. Ever Sweetheart, your very own   Sunny.
[P.S.] Its pouring hard.

56. I have not been able to identify which "General Bagration" is indicated here. (See the Biographical Index for several possibilities.) "Old Navruzov" was Kirim Bek Navruzov, commander of
the court grenadier company; not to be confused with the more frequently mentioned Teimur Bek
Navruzov, cavalry captain first grade of the Emperor's 17th Nizhegorodsky Dragoon Reg.

No. 90/ Telegram 2494. Tiflis> Tsarskoe Selo. 27/28 Nov 1914. 10.05 p.m.>
1.22 a.m. To her majesty. Loving thanks [for] dear letter with Marie's and Aleksei's in it. Count and Countess [Vorontsov-Dashkov] very touched by your message. In the morning huge reception, saw two young officers [from the] Nizhegorodskie< wounded. Thank you for congratulation. In two days saw over thousand wounded. Please distribute to seriously wounded medals in my name. Am tired but very happy with what I see and hear. Tenderest love to you and children. Niki

No. 91/ Telegram 250. Tsarskoe Selo> Tiflis. 28 Nov 1914. 2.02> 3.05 p.m.
To his majesty. Thank you for dear telegram. Happy you gathered good impressions. Hope you will receive my letters neatly. Several operations at the hospital<, heaps of work. Now I should go to town< to visit Pokrovskaya committee hospitals organized by Buchanan< and my store, then to tea at Anichkov<. Zilotti suddenly died. Baka Baryatinsky gravely ill. Bless you, warmly embrace you. Alix

No. 92/ Her No. 258.   Tsarskoe Selo. Nov. 28th 1914.
My very own precious One,
   I could not manage to write to you by to-day's messenger, I had such a lot to
do. We were at the hospital< all the morning & as usual Vilchkovsky's< Committee on Vas[il'ev] Island. The 3 Buchanans< & some more English of the committee & nurses received us. A big ward for officers & a nice saloon for them with chintz & 3 rooms for men, quite simple & nice. Then we went through the wards & saw more wounded, & in the yard there was a big building belonging to the Committee of the City Hospital—in the upper story were 130 wounded.—From there we rushed to my store—masses of ladies working I am glad to see & heaps of things prepared. Then to Anichkov< to tea;—Mother dear< looks well, I think my journeys alone astonish her.—but I feel its the time to do such things, God has given me better health & I find that we women must all, big & small, do everything we can for our touchingly brave wounded. At times I feel I cant any more & fill myself with heart-drops & it goes again—& our Friend< wishes me besides to go, & so I must swallow my shyness. The girls help me. Then we came home I lay & read heaps of papers from Rost.<—Lovy dear, I hope you wont be displeased at Fred.'s< telegram to Voeikov<, we spoke it over by telephone, as he may not go out yet. You see its a national thing—this exhibition with trophies of the war, & so its better the entry should be gratis—one can stand collection boxes near the door, then it obliges nobody to pay. I do not wish Sukhomlinov harm, on the contrary, but his wife is really most "mauvais genre" [of an evil type] & has made every body, the military especially, angry with her as she "put me in" with her collect[ion of money] on the 26-th. The day was alright & that singers wished to sing gratis in restaurants so as to get money for her store. And I allowed it. To my horror I saw the anouncement [sic] in the papers, that in all the restaurants & cabarets (of bad reputation) drinks would be sold for the profit of her branch store (my name in big letters) till 3 in the morning (now all restaurants are closed at 12) & that

Tango & other dances would be danced for her profit. It made a shocking impression—you forbid (thank Heaven) wine—& I, so to speak, encourage it for the store, horrid & with right all are furious, the wounded too.— And the ministers & aides de camp were asked [i.e., asked] Obolensky< to order the rest to be closed at 12 except the decent ones. [a]

The fool harms her husband & breaks her neck.—She receives money & things in my name & gives it out in hers—she is a common woman, & vulgar soul, therefore such things happen, tho' she works hard & does much good—but she is harming him very much, as he is her blind slave—& all see this—I wish one could warn him to keep her in hand. When Rost.< told them my displeasure, he [her husband, General Sukhomlinov] was in despair, & asked whether she ought to close her store, so Rost. said of course not, that I know the good she does, only here acted most wrongly.—Enough of this, only I want you to know the story, as there were strong articals [sic] in the papers about it.—Therefore another collect[ion] for her now would make things worse. One wished my store to collect at Xmas, & I declined the project, one cannot go on begging incessantly, its not pretty.—The Commander of my 21-st Siberian regiment arrived to-day—happily his wounds are but slight.—Now I must get to sleep, its 1 o'clock. For the first time 2 degrees of frost to-day.—

29-th. How Can I thank you enough for your sweetest letter of the 25-th which I received this morning? We follow with interest all you are doing—it must be a great consolation to see these masses of devoted happy subjects! I am glad you managed to go to yet two other towns where the cossacks are.—We went to the local hospital & there I gave 4 medals to amputated soldiers—there were no very heavy cases otherwise.—Then we went to the big palace< to see all our wounded—they are already sorrowing that they wont see us so long.—This morning both Nizhegorodtsy, [Teimur Bek] Navruzov and Yagmin were operated—so we want to peep in this evening & see how they feel. They were mad with joy over your telegr. which they read in the papers—that you called them "incomparable" is the greatest recompense, as such a word was never used before.—Knyazhevich< comes this evening about affairs.—Are going to Church, so must end, & want to rest before.—Very tenderest blessings & kisses, Nicky mine, from your very own Wify. [P.S.] Our love to N.P.<—glad, you two sinners had pretty faces to look at—I see more other parts of the body, less ideal ones!! [b]

No. 93/ Telegram 2588. Tiflis> Tsarskoe Selo. 28 Nov 1914. 7.25> 8.27 p.m. To her majesty. Loving thanks for dear letter about your splendid journey to Vilno and Kovno. Visited educational places all day long. Countess [Vorontsov-Dashkov] showed me your store here in house. Saw not less than 200 ladies and women at work. Was much cretinized. Tea with nobility, many pretty faces, was cretinized. All impressions excellent. All have been hoping to see you and children for some time. [I] warmly kiss all six of you. Niki

---

No. 94/ Telegram 254. Tsarskoe Selo> Tiflis. 29 Nov 1914. 2.24> 3.19 p.m. To his majesty. Warmly thank you for dear letter, madly glad to receive it. What a delightful trip. Thanks be to God, all these people were able to see you.

Sad I was not with you, we will hope next time it will be possible to travel together. Worked all morning. Presented several medals at local hospital. At Tsarskoe [Selo hospital] they need me only for seriously wounded. We all kiss and
bless [you]. Greetings to old couple [Vorontsov-Dashkov]. Nizhegorodtsy< in
rapture from your telegram. Alix

No. 95/ Telegram 2692. Tiflis> Tsarskoe Selo. 29 Nov 1914. 3.00> 6.10 p.m.
To her majesty. Loving thanks for dear letter, also [to our children] Olga and
Aleksei for theirs. Ideal warm weather. After large reception of deputations this
morning [I] went to girl school for daughters of the clergy, then to military
school. Received people after lunch, walked here in the charming garden. Now
off to tea at town. Shall leave in the evening for Kars. Tender kisses to all. Niki

---

No. 96/ Telegram 264. Tsarskoe Selo> Kars. 1 Dec 1914. 2.50> 3.50 To his
majesty. Thank you for telegram. Just returned from hospital< after early dinner. [Son] Aleksei was present during bandaging. Next we go to Big Palace<
and Invalides [home for invalid soldiers]. Baka Baryatinsky died. [We] warmly
kiss [you]. Alix

No. 97/ Telegram 511. Kars< Tsarskoe Selo. 30 Nov 1915. 4.35< 6.15 p.m.
To her majesty. Arrived this morning into real winter. Luckily not cold, 4 degrees. Had mass in an ancient church, now garrison one. Saw lots at [of] troops,
very few wounded. Motored all over the fortress; very interesting but thick fog
prevented from seeing far. Loving kisses to all. Niki

No. 98/ Her No. 259   Tsarskoe Selo. Dec. 1st. 1914.
My own beloved One,
   This is my last letter to you before we meet—God grant in 6 days. To-morrow
its two weeks since you left & I have missed my Sweetheart more than I can
say. The joy to meet will be intense, only the pain to leave the little Ones for a
whole week is great—I cant get accustomed to seperations [sic]—sweet
Agooweeone,.—Thank God he is well that is my consolation.—Oh I am so
tired—so much to do & people to see the last days, therefore I could not write
yesterday.—Then I went to the local hospital on Saturday, yesterday to the Invalides [home for invalid soldiers], to-day to our big hospital (took Aleksei) &
gave medals in your name—they were so happy & grateful poor miserable fellows.—We shall miss our sick & they were sad to bid us goodbye.—Petia<
lunched, & yesterday Paul< took tea—he yearns for a nomination. Rostof.<
comes now, I want to find out why Maklakov< wont allow the Americans to see
how our prisoners are kept—they [these American observers] have been sent to
Germany to see. France & England, & I find it wrong one does not show ours—
Cannot write any more. Blessings—kisses without end.—Ever, Nicky love,
your very own deeply loving old   Sunny. [P.S.] Our Friend wired [the following quote is in Russian]: "Be crowned with earthly happiness, the heavenly
wreaths follow you."

No. 99/ Telegram 3 in Russian. Sarykamysh Railway. 1 Dec 1914. 9.10>
10.25 a.m. To her majesty. Tenderly thank you and [daughter] Tatiana for letter. Only just arrived and see at station, to my joy, my company of Kabardinsky
Regiment. Warmly embrace you. Niki

No. 100/ Telegram 5. Tsarskoe Selo> Kars. 1 Dec 1914. 2.40> 4.05 p.m. To
his majesty. Heartily thank you. Worked, gave medals in your name. We will
arrive [at] 7.30. Sad to leave little ones. All are well. [I] warmly kiss [you]. God
keep you. Alix

No. 101/ Telegram 43 in Russian. Kars> Tsarskoe Selo. 1 Dec 1914. 8.20>
10.08 p.m. To her majesty. Spent an ever-memorable day. Drove from
Sarykamysh in car to Medginghert, right on frontier. There were gathered all
lower rank of all parts of Caucasian Army who most distinguished themselves,
about 1,200 men. Distributed St. George crosses and medals. They came straight
from front lines, had excellent sunburnt appearance. Weather warm there last
few days. Young Gandurin recovered and returns to his regiment in three days.
Exceedingly glad to see glorious Kabardintsy [Regiment]. Road to frontier excellent. Passed over two beautiful mountains covered with woods. Now returning. Tenderly embrace all. Niki

No. 102/ Telegram 544. Moscow> Alzhikabul. 2 Dec 1914. 1.20> 3.08 p.m.
To his majesty. Were at two hospitals of Iversk [Order of Sisters, i.e., Nurses],
saw wives of reservists working at governor's house. Later to-day will go to
other hospitals and to Ella< for tea. Cold, rain and snow falling. Sad without you
and little ones. Gladdened by your telegram. [We] warmly embrace [you]. Alix

No. 103/ Telegram 6 in Russian. Kyurdamir> Moscow. 2 Dec 1914. 2.25>
4.10 p.m. To her majesty. Moscow. Tenderly thank you for two letters,
[daughter] Tatiana also. In morning we descended from mountains and it became warmer again. Hope you are not tiring yourself in hospitals. Tenderly embrace all four [of you]. Niki

No. 104/ Telegram 19 in Russian. Derbent> Moscow. 3 Dec 1914. 2.20> 4.15
p.m. To her majesty. Tenderly thank you and [daughter] Olga for dear letters.
Today is free day. Now going for walk along Caspian Sea, to-morrow morning
to Vladikavkaz. Weather warm, damp. Warmly embrace you [all]. Niki

No. 105/ Telegram 3144. Moscow> Manas. 3 Dec 1914. 2.35 p.m. Were at
mass in side-chapel of Uspensky Cathedral, at Romanov hospital, city distribution center, sanitary train. Snow blizzard. We now go to Poteshnyi palace, my
store, theater hospital, Lakhtin's hospital. Tea with Ella.> [We] warmly kiss
[you]. Alix

No. 106/ Telegram 13 in Russian. Skuratovo> Prokhladnavya. 4 Dec 1914.
1.25 p.m. To his majesty. Visited three hospitals at cathedral. Marvellous, clear

day. Deputation at station at departure[–]one of our wounded officers. Very touching. All embrace [you] warmly. Alix

No. 107/ Telegram 1 in Russian. Prokhladnaya> Orel. 4 Dec 1914. 4.05> 4.34 p.m. To her majesty. Orel. Very satisfied with time [and] inspections at Vladikavkaz. Weather was marvellous. Hope you are not very tired. Embrace all three of you warmly. Niki

No. 108/ Telegram 68 in Russian. Novocherkassk> Sazhnoe. To her majesty. Sazhnoe. Thank you very much for last letter. Glad to visit the Don. Very pleased with reception. Were at many hospitals. Leaving at 7 o'clock in evening. Happy to meet you to-morrow. Tenderly embrace you and children. Niki

No. 109/ Telegram 121. Kharkov train station> Zverevo. 5 Dec 1914. 5.54> 8.45 p.m. To his majesty. Heartfelt thanks for telegram. In Kursk visited cathedral church, three hospitals. Now leaving for store and hospitals. We leave to-morrow at 9 without retinue for service at [Church of] St. Iosaf. We are very tired. Impatiently await to-morrow's meeting. Tender wishes, blessings and kisses. Alix

No. 110/ Telegram 3. Sazhnoe, Kursk gubernaya> Saguny. 5-6 Dec 1914. 10.36> 1.20 a.m. To his imperial majesty, the emperor. Mama, the Voznesenets and the Elisavetgradets [the emperor's daughters Tatiana and Olga were the titular commanders of, respectively, the Voznesensky and Elisavetgradsky Regiments] warmly kiss [you] and congratulate you on [this] festival. We will be glad to see you, papa-dear. Were at St. Iosaf['s Church] where we prayed for you very well. [Unsigned]

No. 111/ Her No. 260.   Moscou [sic]. Dec. 12th 1914.
My beloved Angel,
Once more we separate, but God grant shall meet again in 5 days.—I want to remind you to speak to Nikolasha< about alowing [sic] officers to go on leave home to be treated & not to have them kept in towns, where by chance the sanitary train has brought them. They will recover far quicker if can be near their families & some must finish their cures in the south to get their strength back, especially those wounded through the chest.—I am glad you will get one days rest in the train & being at the Stavka will freshen you up after these awful fatigues & endless receptions. One consolation, you have made 1000 wounded endlessly happy.—I shall try & keep a little quiet these days, more or less—as M-me B.< will be coming & the heart has been much enlarged these days.— Lovy dear, why don't you nominate Groten for your hussars, they sorely are in need of a real commander. Goodbye my treasure & sleep well, shall miss you horribly again. God bless & keep you!—If you can, speak with Voeikov & Benk.< about the Xmas-trees, for the wounded, & I shall to Vil'chkovsky.< Press you to my heart & kiss you ever & ever again with deepest tenderness.

Ever yr. very own <u>Wify</u>. [P.S.] In my glass cupboard over the writing table [in your railway carriage] are candles [hemorrhoid medicine] in case you need any.

No. 112/ Telegram 50. Tsarskoe Selo> Novoborisov. 13 Dec 1914. 12.10> 1.16 p. m. To his majesty. Arrived safely. Nose better. [Daughter] Marie has [a temperature of] 39. Probably caught cold. Very tired. Sad to be so far away. [I] warmly kiss [you]. Greetings to all. May God keep you. Alix

No. 113/ Telegram 3 in Russian. Novoborisov> Tsarskoe Selo. 13 Dec 1914. 5.15> 7.35 p. m. To her majesty. Today saw group of recovered wounded who will return to army. Clear, 4 degrees of frost without snow. Thanks for letters. Tenderly embrace all. Niki

No. 114/ Telegram 259. Stavka> Tsarskoe Selo. 13 Dec 1914. 11.05> 11.45 p.m. To her majesty. Arrived safely. Thanks for news. Please do not get tired. Tender love to all. Niki

No. 115/ Telegram 51. Tsarskoe Selo> Stavka 14 Dec 1914. 11.04> 11.50 a.m. To his majesty. Glad you arrived successfully. [Daughter] Marie better. [She has] Tonsillitis. Sunbeam< slept marvellously. Daughters went to hospitals yesterday. [My] heart much enlarged. Need to rest. So far feel terribly tired. Miechen< has influenza. 4 degrees [temperature outside to-day]. Girls sledging. What news? I warmly embrace [you]. Alix

No. 116/ Her No. 261.   Tsarskoe Selo. Dec. 14th 1914.
My very own beloved One,
    A Feldjeger is leaving, so I hasten to send you a few lines. Agooweeone's< foot is really alright, only hurts him to put it down, so he prefers not using it & for prudence's sake keeps on the sopha.[57] [Daughter] Marie's angina is better, she slept well & has 37 [degrees temperature], [daughter] Tatiana has Mme Becker,< so only gets up for luncheon. Botkin has put me to bed as heart still very much enlarged & aches & I cannot take medicins [sic]; & feel still horribly tired & achy all over. Yesterday remained on the sopha, except when went up to Marie & Baby. < Alia< came to me for half an hour in the evening as feels sad & lonely without her husband—she spent the night at Anias.< The girls< went to the hospitals after luncheon & sledgeing—& in the evening. To-day they will go again, & to-morrow begin their work there.—I cant, alas, as yet & am very sorry about it, as it helps me morally.—Our Friend< arrives to-morrow & says we shall have better news from the war—Ania goes to meet him in town<. Miechen< is in town laid up with influenza; Paul< one says, neither well [i.e., people say that neither Paul nor his wife Miechen are well].— [a]
    A.[nia] received 2 letters from Tchakhov [Chakhov], 2 from [I]edigaroff & Malama so touching all of them—I begged them always to give us news through A. I shall see Afrosimov to-morrow he leaves back to the regiment wh soon goes to the Stavka & longs to see its beloved chef (& family) there. Won't you speak about Kirill< to Nikolasha<? & them tell yr Mama [Maria Fedorovna]; it

wld. really be good to settle all, & now during the war its easiest being done.—Where are all the sailors now united?—Poor Botkin continues being in great anguish about his eldest son—always hopes still that he may be alive. One says the sister (ladies) in the "otriad" of Sandra Shuvalov have received medals on St. Georges ribbons, as were working under fire, taking out wounded, I think.—Sunbeam< has just gone out in the donkey sledge—he kisses you—he can put the foot down but prefers being careful so as to be soon quite alright again.—How horrid it was saying goodbye to you in Moscou [sic], seeing you stand there amongst heaps of people (all so unlike you in every respect! P & I had to bow & look at them too & smile & could not keep my eyes fixed on you, as should hae wished to.—you know before our arrival to Moscou, three military hospitals with German & Austrian wounded were cleared out to Kazan—I read the description of a young gentleman (Russian) who took them—many half dying who died on the road & never should have been moved with fearful wounds, smelling poisonously, not having been bandaged for several days–& just during their Xmas being tortured like that in no lovely sanitary trains. From one hospital they were sent even without a Dr. to bring them, only sanitaries.—I have sent the letter to Ella< to enquire into this & make a good row, its hideous & to me utterly incomprehensible. At Petrograd one says scarcely a vacant bed. Babys train arrives from Varshava [Warsaw] to-day—Loman found no wounded there, so has gone to look for them elsewhere. Does that mean all is quiter these days (their Xmas & we like Christians don't profit) & therefore less losses? One longs to know something clearer.—Must stop now as my head aches yet fr. the cold, tho' the nose no longer runs.— [b]

Sashka< has returned fr. the Caucasus again, one says.—Its so lonely here without you my Treasure, tenderly, beloved Ones, always expect the door to open & see you enter from yr. walk. Its gently snowing. Give our love to N.P.<, so happy he is with you.—The Children kiss you endlessly & so does your wify. I hope you feel more rested now.—One says the Synod< gave an order there should be no Xmas tree—I am going to find out the truth about it & then make a row, its no concern of theirs nor the Churches, why take away a pleasure fr. the wounded & children, because it originally came from Germany—the narrow-mindedness is too colossal.—I say Olga Evg.< she has quite broken down after her brother's death, the nerves have given way & phisically [sic] her strength fails her, wretched soul—so she needs a month's good rest & hopes then to set to work again.—God bless & keep you my very own precious Nicky dear, I kiss you & press you lovingly to my old heart, & gently stroke yr. weary brow. Ever is true that little Aleksei Orlov is wounded? It may be again gossip—I do not know where the regiment is, & why one is at the General Quarter [Stavka] now.—wont you ask Shavelsky< to send out the priest in the regiments more Saint Sacraments & wine, so as that more can take Holy Communion—I send what I can with our store trains,–Ella< too.— [c]

---

57.   Alexandra refers to Aleksei's difficulty in walking, probably after a recent bout with hemophilia.

No. 117/ Telegram 286. Stavka> Tsarskoe Selo. 14 Dec 1914. 10.10> 11.20 p.m. To her majesty. Thanks [for] telegram. To day no news as quiet nearly on whole front. Took a long walk, feel also tired from Moscow. Night, night, sleep well. Tender kisses. Niki

---

No. 118/ Telegram 60. Tsarskoe Selo> Stavka. 15 Dec 1914. 10.56> 11.22 a.m. To his majesty. Stavka. Thanks for telegram. [Daughter] Marie recovered. [My] heart still quite enlarged, head hurts, am not moving about. News: Botkin's son, not wanting to surrender, was killed. Children went to work at hospital.< Sent letter yesterday. Bless and tenderly embrace [you]. Four degrees. Alix

---

No. 119/ Her No. 262.   Tsarskoe Selo. Dec. 15th 1914.
My beloved Darling,

Fredericks< let me know that you are only returning on Friday as are going to see the troops—I am delighted for you & them, a great consolation for you all & will give them now strength. And this morning Zelenetske< let me know & then Kiryll< wired from town, that our dear Butakov had been killed—it is too sad, that kind good man, loved by all. How wretched his little wife will be! She who is only one bit of nerves already. Another one of our yacht friends gone already, how many more will this terrible war yet claim!—And now Botkin got the news from the regiment that his son was killed as he would not surrender—a German officer, prisoner told the news; poor man is quite broken down.—I saw Afrosimov who soon returns to the front, but I think its too soon, he was contusioned long ago & one sees his eye blinks & he suffers from giddyness.

The Children< began their work to-day & had heavy cases. My heart is still enlarged & aches, as does my head & feel so giddy—I had to come over onto the sopha as Aunt Olga< comes at 4½.—Marie< & Dmitri< wished to come to dinner, but I cant have them, feel too rotten still.—[Daughter] Marie has not yet come down as her throat is not quite in order, temp. normal. Baby< goes out twice daily in his little donkey-sledge. I have much to do thinking over Xmas-presents for the wounded & its difficult when one feels rotten.—I am glad you get a walk, it will have done you good. [a]

Ella< wrote in despair, trying to get to the bottom of the things about the trains & hospitals—she believes the orders came from Petrograd. Often the orders from there are very cruel towards the wounded in the military hospitals. When she know all, she will write to Alek<.—In town< there are scarcely any vacancies, don't know where I shall send my trains if they don't give me Finland.—Bright sunny day. He [Rasputin] must have arrived, A.[nia]< has gone to meet him, I only saw her a second, she was with the Children in the hospital< & then lunched with them. [Daughters] Olga & Anastasia are sledging with Isa<, Tatiana has lessons—Shura is reading aloud to Marie. Baby left & I feel bad. Precious one, its lonely without you, but am glad for your sake that you are out & will see the troops.—I want so much to go to Holy Communion this lent, if I can manage with my health.—My precious one. Goodbye now & God bless—& protect you & keep you from all harm! I press you to my heart & kiss you over & over again with gentle tenderness. Ever yr very own <u>Wify</u>. [P.S.] Give my love to N.P.< He will be sad about Butakov.

Make Fedorov< go unexpected to small hospitals & poke his nose everywhere.
[b]

No. 120/ Telegram 228. Stavka> Tsarskoe Selo. 15 Dec 1914. 3.21> 4.00 p.m.
To her majesty. Thanks [for] telegram, so sorry for poor Botkin. Here one knows nothing. Guards Infantry Regiments are called back so [I] want to see them. That will take two days. Hope you don't mind my returning Friday evening. Tender love. Niki

---

No. 121/ Telegram 68. Tsarskoe Selo> Stavka. 15 Dec 1914. 6.30> 7.25 p.m.
To his majesty. Thank you for telegram. Completely understand you [must] stay to see troops—am glad you and they will have this pleasure. Aunt Olga< had tea with us. She kisses you. All saddened by death of poor Butakov. [I] write every day. [I] bless and kiss you. Alix

---

No. 122/ Telegram 303. Stavka> Tsarkoe Selo. 16 Dec 1914. 12.43> 1.20 p.m.
To her majesty. Warmest thanks for precious scented letter and [to daughter] Marie also. Here all quiet. Good news. Inspected yesterday new 53rd Don Cossack Regiment commanded by Zvegintsev. A. Orlov not wounded. Sorry about Butakov. Loving kisses. Niki

---

No. 123/ Her No. 263.   Tsarkoe Selo. Dec. 16th 1914.
My own beloved One,
    A glorious, sunny day. The girls< are in the hospital,< Baby< has just gone out, [daughter] Anastasia has a lesson & [daughter] Marie has not yet been let come down.—I slept badly & feel giddy & rotten, tho' just now the heart is not enlarged—am to keep lying as much as possible, so shall only go over onto the sopha after luncheon, like yesterday. A.[unt] Olga< took tea with me & was very sweet & dear—kisses you.—Have been reading through lots of papers & feel quite idiotical.—Here am I on the sopha, had Vil'chkovsky< with a report, heaps of questions as he tells me everything of the evacuation committee o Ts.[arkoe] S[elo]. Wh. He is at the head of—then questions about Xmas-trees.—Mavra< sent you a letter of Onor< to Vicky of Sweden<, to give over her love to us & say that Ernie< came for quite short after 3 months, that he left again & is well.—I enclose a letter of Keller—as it will interest you to see what he says—happily he seems not badly wounded. From my store trains good news & begging always for more things, as the troops know them already, & when in need, turn up.—Glad my letter smelt nicely, when you got it, it was to remind you quite especially of your very own wify, who misses you awfully.—At last Xenia< is out of quarantine she let know.—
    I feel still not famous, such a nuisance not to work, but I go on with my brain doing business.—I have nothing interesting to tell you, alas. Long for news of the war—so anxious.—It seems masses of sanitary trains were sent here to town< instead of Moscou [sic], whilst we were there & there are no more vacancies at Petrograd. There is something wrong about this evacuation question, Ella< is trying to clear it up on her side.—Loman has not returned, as

thank God there are few wounded at the present moment.—The Children kiss you very tenderly, Wify clasps you fondly to her lonely heart, & blesses you with fervour. Ever yr. own old <u>Sunny</u>. [P.S.] Messages to N.P.< please & the little Admiral<.—I spoke a second to Gr. By telephone, sends [the following message in Russian]. "Fortitude of spirit,—will soon come to you, will discuss everything".

No. 124/ Telegram 83. Tsarskoe Selo> Brest. 16 Dec 1914. 9.35> 10.14 p.m. Tenderly thank you for telegrams. Sleep peacefully. [The people] want you [to be a]. "fortress of the spirit". [A message from Rasputin.] Girls< and Xeniya< go to funeral of poor Butakov to-morrow morning and will lunch at Anichkov.< [They] have to amputate Shevich's leg above the knee, temperature 40, pulse 150, he is very sick, [I] am terribly worried. Olga has committee. I was on sopha, now lying again because head is going around. Hope you will see dear troops to-morrow. Kiss [you], wish [you] happiness. Alix

---

No. 125/ Telegram 321. Stavka> Tsarskoe Selo. 16 Dec 1914. 7.40> 8.15 p.m. To her majesty. Loving thanks [for] beloved letter. Now at 9.30 to morrow hope to see First Infantry Division in the morning and our rifles in the afternoon. Cold bitter wind. Tender kisses to all. Niki

---

No. 126/ Her No. 264.   Tsarskoe Selo. Dec. 17th 1914.
My own precious One,
    This will probably be my last letter, if you return on Friday. Now you are with the troops—what a joy for you & them—tho' painful to see masses of known faces missing. The Children are working & then go to Anichkov< to luncheon before receiving donations in the Winter Palace. The train with poor Butakov's body is 24 hours late, so the funeral can only be to-morrow morning. I scarcely slept a wink this night, perhaps from 4-5 & 6-7. The rest of the time could not, & in despair kept always looking at the watch, hundred[s] of sad thoughts coursed through my tired brain & gave it no rest. The heart again enlarged this morning— to-morrow hope to rebegin my medicines again, then I shall get quicker right again.—6 degrees this morning—[Daughter] Olga walks through the garden to Znamenia< & fr. there on foot to the hospital<. [Daughter] Tatiana follows in a motor after her lesson, Olga feels the better for air & short exercise in the morning.—Sonia[58] sat with me yesterday & chattered a lot whilst I lay on the sopha & threaded Images [icons].—Ania's< brother [S. A. Taneev] returns to-morrow, so he asked to see me a minute at 4.—Anastasia & Ania have gone for a turn, they say its beastly cold & windy; Baby's< foot hurts a wee bit, [daughter] Marie is coming down at last. Thoughts so much with you—what joy to see the dear brave troops.—This morning our Friend< told her by telephone that He is a little more quiet about the news.—The papers say we took German quickfiring guns at Inovladtsy—it does indeed seem strange!—Excuse a mighty dull letter, but feel quite cretinised & good for nothing.—Just a wee bit of scent again to remind you quite particularly of your Wify, who is impatiently awaiting yr. return. You remember I left candles [hemorrhoid medicine] for you in my

compartment in the glass cupbord [sic] over my writing-table [in the railway carriage]. Now my sweet Treasure goodbye & God bless & protect you. I kiss you ever so tenderly & bless you. Ever my Nicky yr. very. own tenderly loving Sunny. [P.S.] Ania kisses yr. hand. All the Children kiss you.

58. Probably the empress's friend Julia Dehn or her lady-in-waiting, Princess Sophia Ivanovna Dzhambakurian-Orbeliani.

No. 127/ Telegram 227 in Russian. Garvolin> Tsarskoe Selo. 17 Dec 1914. 12.27> 2.27 p.m. To her majesty. This morning saw First Division and a company of Her Majesty's Guards Equipage<. Wonderful, healthy, cheery appearance. Warm weather here. Will send news this evening. Niki

No. 128/ Telegram 85 in Russian. Tsarskoe Selo> Sedlets. 17 Dec 1914. 2.00> 6.20 p.m. To his majesty. Am thinking of your happiness at meeting dear troops. Strong wind, cold. Older [daughters] at Anichkov<. [Daughter] Marie came down[stairs]. Aleksei sleighing. Anastasia and Ania< strolling; they kiss [you]. Not feeling very famous. Heart still enlarged, head going around, hardly slept. May God keep you. Butakov['s body] arrives only to-morrow. Tenderly kiss you. Alix

No. 129/ Telegram 633 in Russian. Sedlets> Tsarskoe Selo. 17 Dec 1914. 7.25> 8.42 p.m. To her majesty. Thank you for telegram. Delighted with rifles and [M. N.] Grabbe's Cossacks. Weather absolutely spring like. Am in a gay mood. Good-night. Niki

No. 130/ Telegram 86. Tsarskoe Selo> Brest-Litovsk. 18 Dec 1914. 1.15> 2.03 p.m. Am happy [you] are satisfied with dear rifles. [Daughters] Olga and Tatiana went to Butakov's funeral. [They] are lunching at Anichkov<, inspecting hospital. Snow, wind. Heart still much enlarged. General state not good. We warmly kiss [you]. Alix

No. 131/ Telegram 91. Tsarskoe Selo> Orsha train station. 18 Dec 1914. 6.31 p.m.> 2.00 a.m. To his majesty. Children returned from town<. Shevich died. Valya< and I ordered Christmas presents for wounded. Report by Vil'chkovsky<. Feel bad. Please ask N.P.< if he received my telegram about Butakov and two telegrams on Tuesday from cow<. She [Anna Vyrubova] thanks [him] for to-day's telegram and 2 letters [of] to-day and Tuesday. Not possible to answer because she does not know address. Her brother [S. A. Taneev]'s engagement announced. [I] kiss and bless [you]. Sleep well. Alix

No. 132/ Telegram 283 in Russian. Stolbtsy Al train station> Tsarskoe Selo. 18 Dec 1914. 9.50> 11.10 p.m. To her majesty. Many thanks for two letters, also to [daughters] Tatiana and Olga. Today saw Moscow, Pavlovsk and Ataman Regiments. Was warm. We are returning home. So glad to be with all to-morrow night. Tenderly embrace [you]. Niki

No. 133/ Telegram 81 in Russian. Novosokolnikovo train station> Tsarskoe
Selo. 19 Dec 1914. 12.00> 12.48 p.m. To her majesty. N.P.< received your
telegram, did not receive A.[nia]'s letter. Weather warm. Happy to return
[home]. Warmly embrace [you]. Niki

No. 134/ Telegram 94 in Russian. Tsarskoe Selo> Peredol'skaya. 19 Dec 1914.
3.45> 4.28 p.m. To his majesty. Fondest thanks for telegram. [We] are happy
to meet soon, sorry [I] cannot be at station because still feel bad, and heart enlarged, but [I sent] him [N. P. Sablin] two telegrams, not letters. All warmly kiss
[you]. Alix

No. 135/ Her No. 265.   Tsarskoe Selo. 21 Yanv. [Jan.] 1915.
My very own beloved One,
    Once more I pen a letter to you wh. you will read when the train carries you
away from us to-morrow. It's not for long, & yet it is painful, but I wont grumble, knowing it brings you comfort & a change & others intense joys.—I hope
that Baby's< leg will be alright again by yr. return—it looks like it did in Peterhof
& then alas it lasted long. I shall always give you news about the pozhka [little
toot, our son, Aleksei] & about Ania<,—[referring to her as] either "A." or the
"invalid." Perhaps you will think some times in yr. telegram to me to ask after
her health, it will touch her as she will miss yr. visits sorely.[59]
    I shall try & go to the hospital< to-morrow morning, as I get up to go to
Church with you & see you off, hate that moment & can never get accustomed
to it.— Darling, you will think of speaking about the officers of the different
regiments, that they should not loose [sic] their places & speak over those different questions with Nikolasha<; perhaps you wish to mention the Manifest[o]
to him. [See Letter No. 136a below.] If you want to do another kind act, telegraph once to Fredericks<, or tell Voeikov< who wires to him daily, to give a
message fr you. In prayers & thoughts I shall accompany you, alas not in reality—feel my presence & incessant love hovering around you, tender & caressing.
Goodbye, Sweetheart, treasure of my soul, God bless & protect you & bring you
safe & sound back again. I kiss you fervently & remain, huzy dear, yr. very own
old wify   Alix.   [P.S.] In the glass cupboard in my compartment [in your railway carriage] you will find candles [i.e., hemorrhoid medicine], in case you
need any; think I am lying there at night & then you wont feel so lonely.—

59. On January 15, 1915, Anna Vyrubova was victim of a train wreck. Her shoulder was dislo-
cated, both legs were shattered, her head and spine suffered major blows. Gedroits and other physicians did not expect her to live. When Rasputin learned of the tragedy on January 16, he rushed to
Anna's bedside and prayed intensely. To the amazement of her doctors, Vyrubova was able to un-
dergo surgery on January 17. She remained a cripple, walking (as she later wrote) "slowly and with
the aid of a stout stick." The ordeal restored the friendship between Alexandra and Anna which had
been impaired at the time the war began. (See Letter No. 1.) Indeed, Vyrubova now enjoyed un-
precedented influence with Alexandra and the tsar. Anna henceforth used the royal "we." "'We do
not permit' or 'We do not agree'—meaning Nicholas II, Alexandra Fedorovna—and herself." (See
Fuhrmann, Rasputin, pp. 126-127, and Padenie, IV, pp. 324-325, also Letters No. 139 and 151a.)
Even so, No. 156b shows the empress yet harboring negative feelings towards Anna, while No. 572e
finds Alexandra carping at Vyrubova's new political role.

No. 136/ Her No. 266.   Tsarskoe Selo. Jan. 22, 1915.
My beloved one,
   I have just heard that a Feldjeger leaves, so hasten to send a few lines. Baby<
spent the day alright & has no fever, now he begins to complain a little of his leg
& dreads the night.—From the station I went to him till 11 & then to hospital<, to
1 [o'clock], sat with Ania< who is alright—she begs me to tell you what she forgot giving over to you yesterday fr. our Friend<, that you must be sure not once
to mention the name of the commander in Chief, [Nicholasha<] in your manifest[o]—it must solely come fr you to the people.—Then I went to see the wound
of our praporshchik [lieutenant]—awful, bones quite smashed, he suffered hideously during the bandaging but did not say a word, only got pale & perspiration
ran down his face & body.—In each ward I photographed the officers.   After
luncheon I received Gogoberidze who came to say goodbye & then I rested &
got a wee nap, after wh. I went up to Aleksei<, read to him, played together &
then had tea near his bed.   I remain at home this evening, enough for one day.—
Sweet treasure, I am writing in bed, after 6—the room looks big & empty, as the
tree has been taken away.   Sad without you, my Angel & seeing you leave was
nasty.   Tell Fedorov I have told Vil'chk<.—to find out whether General Marti-
nov< would like to lie in the big place< as he wont be able to move for very
long—& here we can get him out fine days into the garden in his bed even—I
want to let the sick lie out, I think it will do them much good.   Now the man
waits, so I must end.—I miss you & love you, my own Nicky dear.   Sleep well.
God bless & keep you.   1000 kisses fr. then Children & fr. old <u>Wify</u>.   [P.S.]
Baby kisses you very much. He did not complain in the daytime.

No. 137/ Telegram 324 in Russian.   Tsarskoe Selo> Orsha station. 22-23 Jan
1915. 9.40 p.m.> 12.15 a.m. To his majesty. Morning was at hospital<. She
[Anna Vyrubova] is better. [I] laid upstairs during day and drank tea there. Day
was peaceful, now am hurting a bit. Have written. [We] all kiss [you] warmly.
Children at hospital<. Sleep well. May God keep you. [We] miss you. Alix

No. 138/ Telegram 2187.   Vitebsk> Tsarskoe Selo.   22-23 Jan 1915.   11.10
p.m.> 1.38 a.m. To her majesty. Tender thanks [for] dear letter. Weather bright.
Walked several times. Feel lonely. Hope wee one< better. Loving kisses to all.
Niki

No. 139/ Telegram 325. Tsarskoe Selo> Stavka. 23 Jan 1915.   10.17> 11.15
a.m. To his majesty. Heartily thank you for telegram. Little one< again spent
night poorly. [His] leg hurts terribly. She [Ania]< spent night better. Temperature rose again because [her] active pulmonary tuberculosis continues. We operate on Kobylin. Sunny weather, 13 degrees. Lonely. [We] tenderly embrace and
bless [you.] Alix

No. 140/ Her No. 267.   Tsarskoe Selo. Jan. 23, 1915.
My own beloved Nicky dear,

I am lying on the sopha next to Baby's< bed in the sunny corner room—he is playing with Mr. Gill[i]ard. Benkendorff came to me & before that M-me Sca-lon (Khomiakova)—she told me how much one needs sisters out in the front fly-ing-detachment as the poor wounded are often very badly cared for, having no real doctors & no means of sending off their wounded—its all well arranged to the east & north, but in Galicia & the X. armycorps much ought yet to be done.[60] This morning I sat with Baby. He had not had a famous night—slept fr. 11-12 then woke up constantly, not fr. very great pain happily. So I had sat with him in the evening—whilst the girls< were in the hospital<, Isa< came to me. In the morning I gave instruments during the operation, & felt happy to be at work again, then I watched the girls a little at work, after which I sat with Ania<—met her brother [S. A. Taneev] & nice looking bride there. The sun is shining brightly, so I have sent the girls for an hour's walk.—

According to the agency telegrams, such a heavy fighting has begun again,[60] & I had so much hoped there would have been a little quiet. Ania had slept better, [she had a temperature of] 38.2 yesterday evening, this morning 37.8—but that does not matter, she hopes you will give over the news of her health to N.P.<—I think you both must be glad to hear no more grumbling. Sweetest one I miss you very much & long for your tender love. Its so silent & empty without you. The children have lessons or are in hospitals, I have lots of papers fr. Rostovt-sev< to finish.—Forgive a dull letter, but my brain is tired.—Baby kisses you many times, but wify yet much more.—Goodbye & God bless you my treasure, my sweetest one—my tenderest thoughts suround [sic] you. I am glad you got a little airing at the stations.—I bless you & kiss you, & remain Y. very own old Sunny. [P.S.] Give my love to N.P. & Mordvinov. If there is any interesting news, do tell fat Orloff< to let me know, please.

No. 141/ Telegram 492. Stavka> Tsarskoe Selo. 23 Jan 1915. 3.10> 4.20 p.m. To her majesty. Fondest thanks [for] two telegrams. Here everything good.[60] Same weather as with us. Give her my love. Kiss you and children very fondly. Niki

60. All was not "well" for the Russians. Perhaps Nicholas was shielding his wife from reality, perhaps he feared she would share the truth with such talkative friends as Rasputin. (Censorship, of course, controlled what the general public knew of military developments.) Whatever, in January 1915, the Germans and Austrians launched a major offensive, hoping to take Russia out of the war. A feint near Warsaw was followed by a German assault in a blinding snowstorm against the Russian 10th Army. The Russian 20th Corps fought a holding action before it surrendered (Feb. 8/21), per-mitting the other three corps to escape. Hindenburg took 100,000 prisoners and inflicted 200,000 casualties. But the Russian army, reinforced, was still in action. The 70-mile German advance was halted when the newly formed Russian 12th Army counterattacked on Feb. 9/22. A strong thrust in the south halted the Austrian drive to relieve Peremyshl', where the Russians continued to hold a large Austrian garrison under siege. (Dupuy and Dupuy, *Encyclopedia*, p. 950) Peremyshl' surren-dered to the Russians on March 9/22, 1915.

No. 142/ Telegram 327. Tsarskoe Selo> Stavka. 21 Jan 1915. 10.30 a.m.> 12.35 p.m. To his majesty. Heartfelt thanks for dear telegram. Little one slept much better and is merry. She [Anna Vyrubova] likewise. Clear, sunny day, cold. At 11 leave for hospital<. Georgi< comes for lunch because to-morrow he goes to Xenia's< estate. We all embrace and tenderly kiss [you]. Alix

No. 143/ Her No. 268.   Tsarskoe Selo. Yanv. [Jan.] 24. 1915.
My beloved Darling,
    A glorious sunny morning again—I have to keep the white curtain down, as the sun shines into my eyes as I lie. Baby< slept well, thank God, woke up 5 times, but soon went to sleep again, & is merry. Ania< slept also with interruptions, [she now has a temperature of] 37.4, yesterday evening 38.6. The girls< were in the hospital< in the evening, but she was sleepy so did not keep them. I go earlier to bed now, as got up earlier too, on account of Aleksei< & the hospital<. —Now I am next to Baby's bed again—I had an endless report with Rostovtsev<. Then Isa< with affairs, & before that Georgi< lunched.—In the morning I made two bandages & sat with Ania who finds an hour always too little & wants me in the evening, but I remained because of Baby & that she understood—besides I have been feeling so tired of an evening.—Only seeing suffering makes a bit weary.—Such sunny weather! Voeikov< wired to Fred.< you have it too, thats nice. I am sure Vesselkin< tells you lots of interesting things. I sent you a letter fr. Ella< wh. I got.—Baby is better & wishes me to tell you so; the dogs romp in the room.
    Several of our officers are off to the Crimea to get stronger. The children< walked & are off to the big place<; [Daughter] Marie stands at the door & alas! picks her nose. Vlad. Nik.< & Baby are playing cards until I finish. I feel my letters are mighty dull, but I hear nothing worth reporting. My train arrives now.—My treasure! I miss you so much! But I hope you can get some good walks to brace you up, give apetite [sic] & sleep.—I went into Znamensky church< a moment before this [trip to the] hospital & placed a candle for you, huzy mine.— Are you really having the dull [Gen. N. N.] Shipov for yr. hussars? My ex-Shipov [Gen. P. D. Shipov] has received the St. George's Cross—Sandra P.< telephoned to [daughter] Tatiana to share the news with us.—All the children kiss you ever so tenderly—I enclose letters fr [daughter and son] Olga & Aleksei, our love to N.P.< & Mordvinov. Goodbye my very Own, God bless & protect you—Ever yr. very own   Sunny.

No. 144/ His No. 163.   Stavka. Jan. 24, 1915
My Own Beloved Sunny,
    Both your dear letters touched me, deeply, tender thanks for them. It was hard leaving you & the children this time on account of wee one's< leg. I am also afraid it may last long! Please do not get tired now that you must be often upstairs with him—except going to the hospital<. Our journey was pleasant & calm. It is such a luck that all the gentlemen have become accustomed to each other & there are no stories! In the evening we played with Mama's [Maria Fedorovna's] new dominoes and listened to Voeikov or Fedorov< reading Ania's< funny book here. I found Nikolasha's< staff in very good spirits. I am very glad to meet old Ivanov, who came for affairs for one day; luckily he grumbled less than usual. He begs you to send him your photo. Please do so—that will also calm the good old man. Kyrill< and Petia< are [here]; the latter will remain

under N.'s< orders. I was also glad to see dear fat Veselkin; he took tea and dined and amid serious & interesting things told us stories that sent every one into fits of laughter. It is now the seventh time he travelled by the Danube to Serbia with his Supply Expedition. The risks become greater, as the Austrians are trying to do all in their power to blow up our steamers. God grant they may be spared! As it happened each time when I arrived here, the first day is a very busy one, except for a good walk in the afternoon I had to receive people till the evening. Now, good bye, my darling little Wify. God bless you and the children. I kiss you and them very tenderly. Give my love to A[nia]. Ever your very own huzy Niki

No. 145/ Telegram 524. Stavka> Tsarskoe Selo. 24 Jan 1915. 4.55> 5.28 p.m. To her majesty. Fondest thanks [for] dear letter. The two thank you for compliments. Cold, fine, windy. Saw to day Engalychev, gov[ernor]-gen[.of Warsaw]. His first steps successful. Have written. Blessings [and] tender kisses to all. Niki

No. 146/ Telegram 332. Tsarskoe Selo> Stavka. 25 Jan 1915. 10.48> 12.32 p.m. To his majesty. Terribly gladdened by your dear letter—thank you from my heart. Sunny, very cold. [We] are leaving for wedding of a wounded officer. Little one< feels much better, slept well. His leg does not hurt. In the evening [Aleksei's temperature was] above 38, almost normal this morning. All embrace and kiss [you]. Sending photo to old I[vanov]. Alix

No. 147/ Her No. 269.   Tsarskoe Selo. Jan. 25th 1915.
My very beloved One,
    Again a gloriously sunny morning, 10 degrees. Only got to sleep after 4 & then woke up still several times. Ania< had last night [a temperature of] 38.8, [her] leg hurt—[she] slept better, this morning 37.3. Now she suddenly likes the sister Shevtchuk & wants her in the room at night to send her to sleep, so they sat in the other ward. Baby sweet< was quite cheery yesterday & asleep before 10.—Motherdear< feels depressed getting no news of the war since you left.— Such intense joy, I received yr. yesterdays' precious letter, thank you for it with all my loving heart.—Don't be anxious about me, I am very careful & my heart is behaving very well these days, so that Botkin only comes in the morning. Fancy, I just heard that M-me Purtseladze< received a letter fr her husband fr. Germany—thank God he was not killed—she adores him so, poor little woman—I can imagine how interesting Vesselkin< was—God grant his expeditions further success. So Petiusha< remains with N.<[—]lets hope he will use him thoroughly & send him about to wake him up.—Yes, its lucky your people get on well together, it makes all the difference—I shall tell Ania her book has such success. Were at the wedding [of Anna's brother, S. A. Taneev]— sat with Ania (who sends this note) fr 1-2 & then again— & then to the big palace<. I send you our very tenderest love, kisses & blessings, my one & all, my muchly missed treasure.— Ever yr. very own Sunny. [P.S.] Messages to N.P.< and M.<

No. 148/ Telegram 546. Stavka> Tsarskoe Selo. 25 Jan 1915. 5.00> 5.22 p.m.
To her majesty. Tender thanks for letter and telegram. To day after church gave
decorations and crosses to officers and men of my Cossack Red [i.e., composite]
Regiment. Had no time to write to day. Warmer but windy. Loving kisses to all.
Niki

No. 149/ Telegram 333. Tsarskoe Selo> Stavka. 25 Jan 1915. 7.39> 9.20 p.m.
To his majesty. Tenderly thank you for telegram. Aleksei twice going about in
his little sledge and is very happy with it. Were at our hospital, then wedding
and [after that to the] hospital at Big Palace<. Wish you a successful trip. All
embrace and kiss [you]. Alix

No. 150/ Telegram 339. Tsarskoe Selo> Rovno. 26 Jan 1915. 10.05> 10.54
a.m. To his majesty. Warmly embrace you and dear Olga [your sister]. For the
first time to-night he [Aleksei] slept totally well. Wonderful, sunny weather
continues. Her [Anna Vyrubova's] temperature fell, of course she feels fairly
weak. Boris< lunched with us. [We] all tenderly kiss [you]. Alix

---

No. 151/ Her No. 270.   Tsarskoe Selo. Jan. 26th 1915.
My own beloved One,
    How happy [your sister] Olga must be to have you with her to-day a sunny day
& recompense for her hard work.—Fredericks sends me the copies of Voeikov's<
telegrams, so I got the news of all you do, & whom you see.—This morning I
went to Znamenia< & the hospital<, dressed several wounds & sat a little with
Ania<. She had the coiffeur [hairdresser] so as to get her hair untangled,
to-morrow he will come again & clean it. Zina< is again ill, so nobody can do it
well. She looks alright, complains only always about the right leg. Longs to go
over to her house, & if the temp. gets quite normal, the Pss.< has nothing against
it.—How tiring it will be for us!—but lovy, fr the very first you must then tell her
that you cannot come so often, it takes too much time—because if now not firm,
we shall be having stories & love-scenes & rows like in the Crimea now, on
account of being helpless she hopes to gain more caresses & old time back
again—you keep fr. the first all in its limits as you did now—so as that this accident[60] should be profitable & with peaceful results. She is much better, morally,
now.— [a]
    I have heaps of petitions our Friend< brought her for you.—Here I enclose the
telegr. you received before leaving.—Fat Orloff< might find out through Buchanan what sort of a man this son of Steads[61] is.—Boris< came here for 3 days
to fetch Miechen<—she cannot come to see me as she has not yet been out &
there in Varsovie [Warsaw] the warm air is to her good. She goes to see her
hospital & train & motors. Its a great pitty [sic], as the Poles neither care for the
way in wh. she invites herself to their houses to meals—its so tactless of her arranging a second Paris.[61]—Tatiana K.< received the St. George's medal for having been under fire, soi disant [self-styled], in her motor, when she went to bring
presents to the Erivantsy<—the General there gave it to her—that's not right, it
makes the order too cheap—if a bomb, a shell burst near the motor & you are

simply driving by chance with presents, not working under fire, you get it—&
others who work for months, as [your sister] Olga, quietly in one place, & therefore have by chance not got under fire, won't receive it.—Next Miechen will be
returning with it, you will see—then Helene<[61] & Marie< deserve it much more
for their work in Prussia at the beginning of the war. [b]

Baby< was out twice again & has rosy cheeks & does not complain of his leg
nor of his arm—but he lies in bed. We take tea there, wh. is cosy & not so sad as
down in my mauve room without you. One misses you dreadfully my love, have
such bad nights—get to sleep only after 4 these three nights & wake constantly
again, but the heart is keeping decent for the present. Just got yr. telegram from
Rovno & rejoice for you both Dears[61]—I hope all will go off well at Kiev. Precious one, my tenderest thought[s] always suround [sic] you longingly, lovingly
& I rejoice for those that see you & to whom you bring new energy & courage.
You brighten up all always by your serenity.[62] Lets hope you will have daily
warmer, sunnier weather & will return browner than you went.— Please, give
kindest messages from us all to N.P.< & M.<—Do you sit sometimes in my
compartment [sic]? Now I must give my letter out, as the man has to take it to
town<,—& then I shall get a little rest before dinner. Do not worry, that you
have no time for writing, I understand it perfectly well, & not for a moment am
hurt—Goodbye my precious One, I bless you & kiss you over & over again—ever
so tenderly, all the favourite places.—Ever yr. very own Wify. [c]

61. The reference to "son of Steads" apparently involved a then-prominant British journalist. A
"second Paris": the empress is saying it was unreasonable for Miechen to expect the Poles to offer
her entertainment only slightly less exciting than what one would expect in Paris. "Helene" was
probably Elena Vladimirovna, wife of Greek Prince Nicholas. The "telegram from Rovno" is No.
152; "both dears" were Nicholas II and his sister, Olga.
62. Many observers commented on this quality of the emperor—and strangely opposite character-
istics in his wife. Maria Pavlovna, for example, often observed both when they visited hospitals.
Alexandra sympathized with the men, she spoke Russian "almost without any foreign accent." Even
so, Maria noticed the "men did not appear to understand her." Something "eluding definition" kept
Alexandra from "comforting the person she addressed." Her words were "distant and inscrutable,"
soldiers "watched her move about the ward with eyes that were anxious and frightened." Nicholas II
was "quite different." He possessed "real simplicity and exceptional charm," he created "a special
atmosphere, grave yet uplifted." Although short, "he always seemed taller than anyone else in the
room"; his grey, luminous eyes "radiated life and warmth and established in the person addressed an
almost mystic sense of contact." Often, as the emperor moved to speak with the man in the next bed,
the soldier he was leaving shut his eyes "as if to retain his image in complete and blistful beatitude."
(Marie, *Education of a Princess*, pp. 194-195.)

No. 152/ Telegram 105. Rovno> Tsarskoe Selo. 26 Jan 1915. 3.22> 5.05 p.m.
To her majesty. Delighted to be together. Saw [my sister] Olga's hospital. 220
wounded. Also glorious sunny weather. Shall take a walk outside the town.
Fondest love from both [of us] to you and the children. Niki.

No. 153/ His No. 164.   Rovno Jan. 26, 1915.
My Dear Beloved Wify,
Many tender thanks for your sweet letters. I was so sorry not to have written
yesterday, but I had endless receptions. In Baranovichi, after church, Crosses of
St. George were distributed among my black, handsome Cossacks—many of

whom have speared or cut down some of the enemy. I paid a visit to Nikolasha<
& looked through his new railw[ay] carriage, most comfortable & practical, but
a heat not to be stood for more than half an hour. We had a very good talk about
several important questions, & am glad, completely agreed upon those we have
touched. I must say when he is alone and in a quiet mood he is sound—I mean,
he judges rightly. Everybody remarks great change in him since the war. Life in
that solitary place wh he calls his skit [hermitage], & feeling that crushing responsibility on his shoulders—must leave a deep impression upon his soul, & it
is also a podvig [heroic deed] if you like.

I arrived here this morning, & was met by [sister] Olga dear & a few people.
She looks & feels quite well & fresh again. We drove in my motor to her hospital. After visiting the wounded, I went to her room where we sat a while &
then returned to the train. Lunched— then sat together. The weather being perfect
she proposed to take a walk. We drove out of town, got out on a high slope &
walked back by another road through a pretty wood. Mordv.<, Drent.< & N.P.<
walked with us & we all enjoyed it thoroughly. Now we two are busy writing to
you in my compartment, sitting cosily together. My train leaves at 7.0. Fancy, I
just got a telegram fr [the governor of Yalta, Ivan Antonovich] Dumbadze that
beastly Breslau[63] has sent about 40 [rounds] at Yalta & has rather spoiled the
"Russia" Hotel. Swines! Now, good-bye & God bless you & the dear children.
Thank them for their letters. With tender love ever my Treasure your own old
Niki

63. The German battle cruiser *Goeben* and the light cruiser *Breslau* shelled Algerian ports when
war with France broke out, then reached Turkey before hostilities with Great Britain began. These
ships gave the Turks naval supremacy in the Black Sea and encouraged them to enter the war on
Germany's side. Turkey began her war against Russia by shelling Odessa, Sevastopol' and Theodosia
without warning on October 16/29, 1914. Von Souchon now commanded the Turkish fleet. Turkey's alignment with the Central Powers closed the Black Sea to the Entente and cut the best link
between Russia and her allies. (Dupuy and Dupuy, *Encyclopedia*, pp. 944, 946.) The *Goeben* and
Breslau shelled Yalta on Jan. 26/ Feb. 8, 1915—as noted here.

No. 154/ Telegram 344. Tsarskoe Selo> Kiev. 27 Jan 1915. 10.34> 11.15 a.m.
Sunny morning. Glad you spent day with [your sister] Olga. What a disgrace
they bombed Yalta, sheer malice. Thanks be to God none suffered, but what a
fright must have been caused by those bombs.[63] He [son Aleksei] is now dressed
and will lunch with us. Her [Anna Vyrubova's] phlebitis causes her much suffering. We tenderly embrace and kiss [you]. Alix.

No. 155/ Telegram 3881. Kiev> Tsarskoe Selo. 27 Jan 1915. 2.56> 3.50 p.m.
To her majesty. Fondest thanks [for] letter. Saw both sisters' [Xenia and Olga?]
charming hospital and then nobility's for 85 officers. Lovely frosty weather.
Very warm reception. Tender kisses to all and A[nia]<. Niki

No. 156/ Her No. 271.   Tsarskoe Selo. Jan. 27th 1915.
My own beloved Nicky,
I just received yr. wire from Kiev, am sure it is a tiring day you are hav-
ing.—How disgusting the Breslau having shelled Jalta—only out of spite —thank

God no victims! I am sure you will long to fly off by motor to see the damage done.[63]—The fighting is strong again at the front & heavy losses on all sides;—these dum-dums are infernal!—I saw Betsy Shuvaloff<, who is arranging a front detachment for Galicia,—she is still full of your visit to her hospital & the joy it brought to all hearts.— [a]

We had an operation this morning—rather long but went off well.—Ania< gets on alright tho' her right leg aches, but the temp. is nearly normal in the evening. Only speaks again of getting into her house. I foresee my life then! Yesterday evening I went as an exception to her, & so, as to sit with the officers a tiny bit afterwards, as I find her stomach & legs colossal (& most unapetising [sic])—her face is rosy, but the cheeks less fat & shades under her eyes. She has lots of guests; but dear me—how far away she has sliped [sic] from me since her hideous behavior, especially autumn winter, spring of 1914—things never can be the same to me again—she broke that intimate link gently during the last four years—cannot be at my ease with her as before—tho' she says she loves me so, I know its much less than before & all is consecrated [concentrated?] in her own self—& you. Let us be careful when you return. How I wish one could sink that odious little Breslau![63]— [b]

The weather continues being glorious. Baby< is daily better, lunched with us & will come down to tea, now he has a French lesson, so I came down again. —Two more of my Siberians arrived, nice officers.—Have no answer fr. Martinov<.—Give my love to N.P.< Ania got his wire fr. the Stavka but dawdled about answering. Shall give her over yr. love. Girls committee this evening.—I slept 3 hours from after 4½ till 7½ this night, so tiresome I cannot get to sleep early.—Must end now, Treasure, my sunshine, my life, my Love—I kiss & bless you.—Ever yr. very own   Sunny.   [P.S.] Baby wishes us to come up to tea. Think of me at Sebastopol & all known places.—Feel Jalta will tempt you—don't mind on our account being a day late. [c]

No. 157/ Telegram 347. Tsarskoe Selo> Poltava. 28 Jan 1915. 10.15> 10.55 a.m. Wonderful, sunny weather. All are well. We await [daughter] Marie's train, many wounded. I fear you will see that disgusting F[eofan].[64] Girls< go to town to-day. We all warmly embrace and kiss you. I write every day. Alix

64. In 1902, Feofan was the royal family's confessor and inspector of the St. Petersburg Seminary. Church leaders in Kazan told Feofan about Grigory Rasputin, a "holy man" who appeared in the city. Feofan brought the peasant to Petrograd, thinking he might contribute to the religious revival under way among the lower classes. Feofan introduced Rasputin to important people such as Nicholasha<, who in turn presented Grigory to Nicholas and Alexandra. Feofan eventually concluded that Rasputin was a false holy man and dangerous, and he supported the campaign of the "Black sisters"< to discredit Grigory and force his return to Siberia in 1910. As punishment, Feofan was sent to the Crimean diocese of Tavrida and Simferopol', an assignment which approached a death sentence for one susceptible (as he was) to tuberculosis. In 1912 Nicholas and Alexandra planned a visit to the Crimea, but did not want to be "welcomed" by the local bishop, Feofan—so he was transferred to Astrakhan. In 1913 Feofan was partially "rehabilitated" and assigned to Poltava. This telegram shows Alexandra was still angry with this enemy of her "Friend," and she regretted her husband would have to see Feofan on his visit.

No. 158/ Telegram 1. Poltava> Tsarskoe Selo. 28 Jan 1915. 1.28> 2.25 p.m.
To her majesty. Loving thanks to you and dear children for letters. Yesterday
and to day most successful. Am delighted with both towns. Cold, windy. My
gentlemen [i.e., the members of my suite] thank you. Tender kisses. Niki

---

No. 159/ Her No. 272.   Tsarskoe Selo. Jan. 28th 1915.

My beloved One,

   Such loving thanks for yr. dear telegram. Voeikov's< to Fredricks I read with
great interest as they tell in detail where you have been. How tired you must be
after all you did at Kiev, but what a sunny remembrance you leave with all!—you
our Sunshine, Baby< our Sunbeam!< I was just now in the big palace< with
[daughters] Marie & Anastasia, 2 of my Siberians arrived there & 2 in our hos-
pital<, then an officer of the 2-nd Siberian regiment (comrade of Matsnev) with
an amputated leg & a priest of the 4-th S. regiment wounded in the soft part of
his leg, made a charming impression & spoke of the men, with such love &
deepest admiration.—In the morning I made three dressings. A little Crimean,
whom I received in autumn after his promotion, is wounded in the arm—already
in the Carpathian hills.—Ania's< lungs are quite alright again, but she is weak &
giddy, so is to be fed every two hours. I fed her personally, & she ate a good
luncheon, more than I eat.—I read two short stories of Saints to her & I think it
was good & has left her something to think over, & not only of herself, wh. is
my aim with her.—The big girls< went to town to Css. Carlov's< small hospital
in her house & to the Winter Palace< to receive donations.—Baby has his lessons, goes out in the donkey sledge twice a day; he says your tower has dwindled somewhat. We take tea in this room, he likes it, & I am glad not to have it
here without you.—Some regiments get their rewards awfully slowly, how I wish
one could hurry it up!—And they do complain so, Vil'chkovsky< said about
those 6 weeks as they loose [sic] so much & it makes them bitter, because if
they go back too soon, they quite loose [sic] their health & if they remain over
their term of 6 weeks, they loose so much.— [a]

   Nikolasha's< long telegram fills one's heart with admiration & deepest emotion—what bravery to withstand 22 attacks in one day! Really saints & heros
[sic] all of them. But what ghastly losses the Germans have & they don't seem
to care.—Thanks so much for letting me get these telegrams.—One says Rodzianko's speech was splendid, especially the end, I have not had time to read it
yet.—Isa's< mother comes to me this afternoon, as she is going to Denmark, tho'
her husband [Baron K. K. Buxhoeveden] does not want her [to do that].—What
do you think Madeline< told me, fr. people she knows, whose acquaintances
returned just now [to Russia] fr. Jena, where they had lived several years? At
the frontier one undressed the couple in separate rooms & then searched their
b[ehinds?] to see whether they had hidden any gold there. Too shameful &
mad!—In the goldmines, niggers hide away gold there, but you see Europeans
doing such a thing—ridiculous if not so degrading! —I daily place my candles at
Znamenia<.—Yesterday I was in bed at 11¼ & got to sleep after 2—slept til 8
with interruptions—an Orenburg shawl on my head helped me to get to
sleep—but waiting so long for sleep is a wee bit dull, but not to be complained of
as have no pains.—Thank God my heart keeps decent & I can do more again

with care.—[Daughter] Marie has a bad finger since several days, so Vlad. Nik.<
cut it to-day in my room—she was very good about it & did not move—those
things hurt—it reminded me of Pss. Gedroits whose 2 fingers I had to cut & ban-
dage & the officers looked on through the door.—Sweet Manny mine, beloved
One, huzy my very own Treasure, goodbye. God bless & protect you! I kiss you
ever so tenderly & fondly & bless you, yr. own old   Sunny. [P.S.] You will
receive this already on yr. homeward journey.—Many messages to N.P.< &
Mordv.< Glorious, sunny weather continues.—Goodbye wee one, me's awaiting
you with open, loving arms! I enclose a letter fr. Marie. [b]

No. 160/ Telegram 333. Tsarskoe Selo> Sevastopol. 29 Jan 1915. 9.52> 11.55
a.m. To his majesty. In thoughts am with you on the way to Sevastopol with
which so many memories are connected. Clear, sunny day, 13 degrees frost.
Ania's< lungs are alright [though] now she has functional lung inflamation [sic]
so that her temperature is again slightly elevated, [she is] in depressed mood,
capricious. Operation this morning, then to lunch with Fredericks and Emma<.
Tenderly kiss [you]. Greetings to everyone from everyone. Alix

No. 161/ Telegram 520. Sevastopol> Tsarskoe Selo. 29 Jan 1915.   10.50>
12.10 a.m. To her majesty. Just arrived. 2 degr[ees] of warmth. Lots of snow.
Fleet just returned yesterday. Shall visit them now. Loving kisses. Niki

No. 162/ Telegram 354. Tsarskoe Selo> Sevastopol. 29 Jan 1915. 3.10> 4.00
p.m. To his majesty. Thank you heartily for unexpected treasured letter and
telegram. What joy you are able to see dear fleet! My tender thoughts are with
you. Troitsky's operation went well. Warmly embrace [you]. Fredericks and
Emma< had lunch. Both feel better. Alix

No. 163/ Telegram 528. Sevastopol> Tsarskoe Selo. 29 Jan 1915. 5.15> 6.20
p.m. To her majesty. Thanks for telegram. So happy to be here and to be able
to thank all them who work and serve so hard. Before lunch went on board the
Eustaphia and *Kagula* and to the naval hospital. Only four wounded sailors remained. In the afternoon I saw the young sailors and went though the barracks
of naval cadet school. Excellent impression in general. Fine mild, calm weather.
Tender kisses and love. Niki

No. 164/ Her No. 273.   Tsarskoe Selo. Jan. 29th 1915.
My own beloved One,
   Loving thanks for two dear telegrams. I can imagine how emotioning it was
going on board our dear ships, & how your precious presence will have given
them new courage for their difficult work. How one longs for them quickly to
get hold of the Breslau[63] before she does any more harm! How lucky there were
only so few wounded still in the hospital!—Over & over I thank you for your
dearest letter from Rovno—it came as a very great & most pleasant surprise
whilst I was still in bed. Fancy [your sister] Olga going to be the eldest sister

now of the red Cross obshchina [community] out there—with God's help I am
sure she will manage well.—

Petia< has turned up & comes to-morrow to luncheon. I shall be having to see
his mad father, as I sent Loman twice to him with questions about our trains, &
he received before others & screamed at him & insulted him & understood everything wrong, tho' he had the paper wh. I had seen before he got it. He is so
impossible rushing about the room, giving others no time to speak & screaming
at all.—This night I went to sleep after 4½ & woke up early again—such dull
nights! Then we had Troitsky's Operation, it went off well, thank God—hernial
rupture & then I had to do several pensements [slings], so scarcely saw Ania<.
Our Fr.[iend]< came there, as He wanted to see me a second.— Fredericks &
Emma< lunched, I photographed them. [Daughters] Olga & Tatiana only returned near 2, they had so much to do. In the afternoon I rested & slept half an
hour. Then we took tea with [son] Aleksei upstairs, then I saw Loman,—
Vil'chkovsky's< doklad [report] is always at the hospital<.—Baby< stands—& I
hope, by the time you return, that he will be able to walk again. [Daughter]
Marie's finger is not yet right.—Ania is better, but the humour not famous— I fed
her, so she ate alright & she sleeps quite decently now.—The most of the
wounded I could not see to-day, there was no time.—I am so glad you had good
talks with N.< Freder.< is rather in despair (rightly) about many orders he gives
unwisely & wh. only aggravate, & things one had better not discuss now—others
influence him & he tries to play your part wh. is far from right— except in military matters—& ought to be put a stop to—one has no right before God & man to
usurp your rights as he does—he can make the mess & later you will have great
difficulty in mending matters. Me it hurts very much. One has no right to profit
of one's unusually great rights as he does. [a]

The weather continues being glorious, but I cannot venture out into the garden.—Do you remember one of our first wounded officers Strashkevich who had
his head tied up & spoke so long to you, until you felt quite faint! Well poor
man, he returned to his regiment & has been killed. Sad for his poor family —he
served in a bank.—I said to Loman that some of the wounded might also come
with us to Church & take Communion with us—it would be such a consolation
for them, & I hope you do not object. Loman will speak with Vil'chkovsky<, &
you can warn Voeikov<, if you don't forget.—How the "noises" this night will
remind you of the Yacht—that clang clang of Sebastopol. Sweetheart, what joy
to have you back in four days! Now I must send off my letter. Good-bye & God
bless & protect you my dearest darling Treasure. I kiss you ever so tenderly &
hold you tight in my loving old arms. Ever, Lovy, yr. very own   Wify. [b]

No. 165/ Telegram 358. Tsarskoe Selo> Sevastopol. 30 Jan 1915. 10.52 a.m.>
12.06 p.m. To his majesty. Thank you heartily for dear telegram. Glad your
impressions are good and that you were able to thank everyone. Leaving now for
hospital<. Petia< lunched with us. First day without snow. All are well. Warmly
embrace and kiss [you] without end. Alix

No. 166/ Telegram 554. Sevastopol> Tsarskoe Selo. 30 Jan 1915. 1.12> 2.40
p.m. To her majesty. Visited all the fortifications and batteries of the northern

side. Saw a few wounded who have recovered. Miss you awfully here. Tender
love. Niki

No. 167/ Telegram 361. Tsarskoe Selo> Dzhamkoi. 30 Jan 1915. 4.25> 8.00
p.m. To his majesty. Thank you tenderly for telegram. Sad we are not together.
Am certain [your] impressions are delightful. We all tenderly kiss and wish
[you] a happy trip. Petia< is having lunch, has a headache. [Dr.] Karpinsky
thinks this is from contusion. Alek< has a pekhenschuss [stiff back][so] that he
cannot come. Big girls< again in town<. Blessings without end. Alix

---

No. 168/ Telegram 572. Sevastopol> Tsarskoe Selo. 30 Jan 1915. 8.25> 9.15
p.m. To her majesty. Fondest thanks for letter. motored along the southern
batteries by car, some of which I saw in 1913.[65] In town saw some wounded
officers and men from the army sent here for a cure. Beautiful day. Am leaving
now. Good night and Tender blessings. Niki

---

65. Nicholas and Alexandra toured the empire during the tercentenary of the Romanov dynasty in
1913. The trip was not a public relations success, though the tsar and his wife insisted on viewing it
in that light. See Fuhrmann, *Rasputin*, pp. 99-101.

No. 169/ Her No. 274.   Tsarskoe Selo. Jan. 30th 1915.
My own beloved One,
    This is probably my last letter to you. So interesting all the news of Sebas-
topol, I regret not being with you. How interesting all you saw, you will have a
lot to tell us. Thank God so few wounded. But it must have seemed to you like
a dream going out in the steam-launch round the squadron—& so emotioning!
—God bless the dears & may he give them success! The darkness at night must
be rather uncanny I should say.—Alas! the news fr. East Prussia are not so good
& we have had to go back for a second time—well we shall have all our forces
stronger together then[60]—I just read a very interesting letter Sonia< received fr.
Lindenbaum [an officer of the Korotoyaksky Infantry Regiment], thanking for
the things we sent. He loves his regiment wh only exists half a year— Korotoyaksky, I think; he was in [East] Prussia, & wrote the 22-d whilst battles were
going on.—Nikolasha< sent Petia< here to look after his leg— [Dr.] Karpinsky
thinks it has been contusioned & so must be treated according[ly]; but Petia
cannot imagine when it happened as he felt no pain for ages.—Alek< has a stiff
back & so could not come & sent Petia with papers, & I gave him mine, &
Vil'chkovsky< to help him explain all.—Then I had Rost.< & B.[aron] Witte
about Xenia's committee.[66] In the morning I came to a Te Deum before the Image [icon] at Znam.[enia Church]< wh. was nice—then I did several dressings &
sat with Ania<—our Friend's girls< came there to see us. Her [Ania's] throat is
much better, 37.1 [temperature]—but last night 38.5—dont know why. I did not
go, as too tired.—She speaks in an extinguished voice & is dull poor soul,
scarcely opened her mouth, except to eat, wh. she did well. Her poor back is
sore again from lying. To-day its 4 weeks [since the accident which crippled
Anna Vyrubova; see Footnote 48].—I must go this evening, as did not see all the
wounded. To-morrow we have an operation. No sun to-day for the first

time.—Now goodbye & God bless you my Sunshine. I kiss you very tenderly & lovingly, longingly, Ever yr. own old   Wify.

66. Prominent Russians sponsored charitable committees during World War I. Many were titular "heads," others—such as Alexandra's daughters—were deeply involved in the work of "their" committees. The tsar's sister Kseniya headed "Xenia's Committee," referred to here. G. G. von Witte was an example of those who administered these committees. Witte, an official in the ministry of internal affairs, directed the Supreme Council to Aid Russian POW Families. He was also a member of the committee chaired by Nicholas II's daughter Tatiana, the Romanov committee, and other committees.

No. 170/ Telegram 363. Tsarskoe Selo> Ekaterinoslav. 31 Jan 1915. 10.09> 10.35 a.m. To his majesty. 5 degrees. Snowing. Xenia< and Ducky< will have lunch. Operation in morning. Children walk every day. A.[nia]< had a temperature of 38.5 degrees] last night. [They] still don't know why. I think they will have to probe inside her. Are happy to see you soon. God keep you. [We] kiss you warmly. Alix.

No. 171/ Telegram 1 in Russian. Ekaterinoslav> Tsarskoe Selo. 31 Jan 1915. 3.00> 3.29 p.m. To her majesty. Thank you heartily for dear letter and two telegrams. Very pleased with warm reception. Inspected two splendid hospitals. Weather still, sunny. Today will inspect Bryansky armour factory. Embrace all warmly. Nicholas.

No. 172/ Her No. 275.   Tsarskoe Selo. Jan. 31st 1915.
My beloved One,
    This is [daughter] Marie's paper, because I am beginning on Baby's< sopha & did not bring up my thing for writing.—Just received yr. dear telegram fr. Ekaterinoslav. I had quite forgotten that you were stopping there. Can imagine how interesting the iron plate factory must be—& yr. visit will encourage all to work quicker. The operation went off alright this morning.—The officer Kubatov[67] has invented a machine gun, wh. he watched being made at Tula & the navy has ordered. In the afternoon we went to the big palace< & sat sometime with my Rifles, 2 fr. our hospital< had also come to see them. Xenia< & Ducky< lunched—both are well. At 6 I received M-elle Rosenbach, who has the Invalid house.[67]—I said goodbye to 5 officers who are going back to the war—amongst them Shchevich.[67] He was sad not to be able to await yr return —he leaves to-morrow, as otherwise fears loosing [sic] the regiment. Zeidler< said he might leave, but he has not even tried to ride & his foot will always I am sure remain weak, as the sinews were torn—jumping off his horse will always be risky & walking on enemi [sic] ground—his foot is tightly bandaged. But he felt tho' ashamed to remain here any longer.—Its much milder to-day & snowed hard this morning. Baby & Vl. Nik.< are dining [while our daughters] O.[lga] & A.[nastasia] are shooting [target] soldiers. Ania< is impatiently awaiting yr. return. She has grown really much thinner, & as she sits better one notices it more.—Now my very own one I must end, as the messenger leaves early. Goodbye & God bless you beloved Nicky dear, such joy to think that in two days you

will be here. I kiss you over & over again & remain yr. very loving Sunny.
[P.S.] You understand I can't come so early to the station?

67. Nicholas Ivanovich Kubat'ev was an officer of Alexandra's 21st E. Siberian Rifle Reg. Lidya
Nicholaevna Rozenbach was the daughter of Adj.-Gen. N. A. Rozenbach and one of Alexandra's
ladies-in-waiting. See the Biographical Index for details about Maj.-Gen. Georgy Ivanovich Shevich,
then commander of the Life Guards Hussar Reg.

No. 173/ Telegram 1. Tsarskoe Selo> Tula. 1 Feb 1915. 11.30 a.m.> 12.27
p.m. To his majesty. All are well. Warm weather. Are going to dine. A.[nia]<
has normal temperature this morning. Thank you for yesterday's telegram. [We]
kiss [you] tenderly. Are happy to see you soon. May God keep you. Alix

No. 174/ Telegram 1 in Russian. Lopasnya> Tsarskoe Selo. 1 Feb 1915. 4.20>
5.55 p.m. To her majesty. Heartily thank you for two letters and news. Weather
mild; thawing. All send greetings and N.P.< and M.< thanks. Happy to see you
to-morrow. Embrace you and children. Niki

No. 175/ Telegram 569. Helsingfors> Tsarskoe Selo. 25 Feb 1915. 1.47 p.m.>
2.09 p.m. To her majesty. Travelled most comfortably. Much warmer—3 degrees. Saw all the ships, lots of friends, in very high spirits. Excellent impression. Fondest love. Niki.

No. 176/ Telegram 12040. Tsarskoe Selo> Helsingfors. 27 Feb 1915. 2.22
p.m.> 4.15 p.m. All well. Wonderful, sunny day. Going now ... to Vorontsov's
home, then to Supreme Council[68] and store<. Assisted in Badovsky's operation.
Am with you in thoughts and prayers. Hope all is going successfully. Tenderly
kiss and bless [you]. Alix

68. The ellipsis in Sergeev's edition of this telegram claims the passage deleted is an "unintelligi-
ble expression." "Vorontsov" is presumably Col. Alexander Illarionovich Vorontsov-Dashkov or his
brother Illarion, also a colonel of the Hussar Life Guards Reg. The "Supreme Council" was perhaps
a meeting of the Council headed by G. G. von Witte. (See Footnote 66.)

No. 177/ Her No. 276.   Tsarskoe Selo. Feb. 27th 1915.
My very own deeply beloved One,
    God bless you quite particularly on this journey, & give you the possibility of
seeing our brave troops nearer! Your presence will give them new force &
courage & be such a recompense to them & consolation to you. The Stavka is
not the thing—you are for the troops, when & where possible—& our Friend's<
blessing & prayers will help. Such a comfort for me that you saw Him & were
blessed by Him this evening! Sad I cant follow you out there—but I have the
little ones to look after. I shall be good & go once to town< before M-me. B.<
comes & visit some hospital, as they are impatiently awaiting us there.—My Angel sweet[,] me no likes saying goodbye—but I wont be selfish—they need you &
you must have a change. My work & prayer must help me over the separation—the nights are so lonely—& yet you are far lonelier, poor
agooweeone<!—Goodbye Lovy, I bless you—& kiss you without end, love you

more than word can say. All my soul will follow & suround [sic] you every-where.—I press you tenderly to my old loving heart & remain yr. very own Wify. [P.S.] Oh such pain saying goodbye! Feel so sad to-night—me does love you so intensely. God be with you!—

No. 178/ His No. 165.   [No place.] Feb. 28th 1915.
My own beloved Darling,

Though it very sad of course of [sic] leaving you & the dear children—this time I start with <u>such</u> calm peace in the soul which even astonishes me. Does it come from having talked with our Friend< last night, or is it the paper that Bu-chanan gave me, [S. Yu.] Witte's death, or perhaps a feeling of something good going to happen at the war—I cannot say, but a real Easter comfort is rooted in my heart. I wish I could have left it [with] you.—I was so happy to have spent two days at home—perhaps you noticed it, but I am stupid, & never say what I feel. Such a nuisance to be always so occupied & never to sit quietly together & talk! In the afternoon I can never remain at home, such a yearning of getting into the fresh air—& so all the free hours pass & the old couple is very rarely together. Especially now when A[nia]<. is not well & cannot come to our house. Do not overtire yourself, my love, think of your health, make the girls work for you sometimes. God bless you & them! With tenderest love & kisses, ever your own old endlessly loving old huzy. <u>Nicky</u>. [P.S.] I will always let you know where I am going.

No. 179/ Her No. 277.   Tsarskoe Selo. Feb. 28th 1915.
My very own One,

It was sad seeing you go off in the train all alone, & my heart ached.—Well I went straight to Ania< for 10 minutes & then we worked in the hospital< till 1. After luncheon we received 6 officers who return to the army—those wh. we had sent to the Crimea look splendid, round & brown.—Then Ioanchik< called [our daughter] Olga to the telephone to tell her, that poor Struve is killed—he is aw-fully sad, because he was his great friend. He told J. that if he should fall in war, he was to be sure to tell you, that he had <u>never once</u> taken off his achselbant [aiguillette] since you gave them to him—poor, kind, cheery, handsome boy! His body is being brought back. Then I went to the big palace< & sat for some time with the worst, I took the lovely postcards of Livadia< to show & they were greatly admired—then the Children joined me & we went through all the wards.—I shall go for a little to church, it does one good; that & work, looking after those brave fellows, are one comfort. In the evening we shall go to Ania—she finds I am too little with her, wants me to sit longer, (& alone) but we have not much to speak of—with the wounded one always can.—My Angel, I must finish because the messenger has to leave.—I bless & kiss you over & over again, my Nicky dear—a lonely night awaits us. Ever yr. very own <u>Wify</u>. [P.S.] The Children kiss you very much. Hope tiny Admiral [C. D. Nilov] "behaves" himself.—

No. 180/ Telegram 1. Tsarskoe Selo> Stavka. 1 Mar 1915. 11.12 a.m.> 12.20
p.m. To his majesty. Extremely rejoiced at unexpected letter. Tenderly thank
[you]. Baby< takes great pleasure bathing in your pool. We all watched him.
Mild weather. We spent evening with her [Anna Vyrubova]. We go to church
before our hospital<. Poor Struve killed. Ioanchik< in despair. We miss [you]
terribly. Tenderly bless & kiss [you]. Alix

No. 181/ Her No. 278.   Tsarskoe Selo. March 1st 1915.
My very own Huzy dear,
   What an unexpected joy yr. precious letter was, thank you for it from all my
loving old heart. Yes, lovy mine, I saw you were happy to be home these 2 days
again & I too regret that we cannot be more together now that A.[nia]< is not in
the house. It reminds one of bygone evenings–so peaceful & calm, & no one's
moods to bother & make one nervous.–I went to Church last night at 7, the cossacks sang well & it was soothing & I thought & prayed much for my Nicky
dear–I always think you are standing near me there.–Baby< madly enjoyed yr.
bath, & made us all come & look on at his pranks on the water. All the daughters beg too for the same treat some evening–may they?–Then we went to Ania,
I worked, [daughters] Olga glued her Album, Tatiana worked– M.[arie] &
A.[nastasia] went home after 10 & we remained till 11. I went into the room
where the Strannitsa (blind) was with her lantern–we talked together & then she
said her prayer.[69] The Com.[mittee] of the O.[sovets] fortress Shulman< knew
us when he was at Kronstadt to put order there & then at Sebastopol he commanded the Brest regiment, wh. behaved so well during the stories–I remember
his face very well.–After luncheon shall finish–now must dress. [Our dog] Ortipo has been rushing all over my bed like mad & crushed Vil'chkovsky's< doklady [reports] I was reading.–The weather is quite mild, zero.–I had Olga E.< to
say goodbye, she leaves for a quiet sanatorium near Moscou [sic] for 2 months.
Then we went to the cemetry [cemetery], as I had long not been there, & then on
to our little hospital & the big palace<. Upon our return found your dear telegram for wh. tenderest thanks.–We all kiss & bless you over & over again. Our
love to N.P.–Ever my Treasure, yr. very own Wify who misses her sweet heart
very much.

69. A strannitsa (pl. strannitsy) was a female pilgrim; her male counterpart was a strannik (pl.
stranniki). It was not an office in the Russian Church but a self-proclaimed vocation recognized by
the masses. Strannitsy and stranniki were simple, devout people who wandered, exchanging counsel
and prayer for food and lodging. Nicholas and Alexandra were partial to such holy people, especially
if they were of peasant background, which was usually the case.

No. 182/ Telegram 9. Stavka> Tsarskoe Selo. 1 Mar 1915. 2.41 p.m.> 3.20
p.m. To her majesty. Fondest thanks for letter and telegram. Terribly sorry
about poor Struve. Weather here very mild, practically no snow. News from
everywhere good.[70] Georgi< here and very busy. Warmly kiss you and children.
Niki

70. The German offensive registered initial successes, though the Austrian attack proceeded with more difficulty. The Russians resisted fiercely, retreated and often counter-attacked. Although Nicholas's armies had lost the initiative, much of the news for them was indeed—if briefly—"good."

No. 183/ Telegram 2. Tsarskoe Selo> Stavka. 2 Mar 1915. 9.35> 10.25 a.m. To his majesty. Hearty thanks for dear telegram. [We] spent evening with her [Anna Vyrubova]. Leaving to inspect my train<, then as usual to hospital<. [We] tenderly embrace and kiss [you]. In thoughts always together. Alix

---

No. 184/ Her No. 279.   Tsarskoe Selo. March 2nd 1915.
My beloved One,
   Such a sunny day! Baby< went in the garden, he feels well, tho' has again a little water in the knee. The girls< drove & then joined me in the big Palace<. We inspected the sanitary train [No.] 66, its an endlessly long one, but well arranged—it belongs to the Ts.[arskoe] S.[elo] district. In the morning we had a hernial rupture operation of a soldier. Yesterday evening we were with Ania< —Shvedov & Zabor< too.[71]—I got a letter fr. Ella's< Countess Olsofieff—she has been placed at the head of 16 Comit'és de bienfaisance des 22 hospitaux militaires de Moscou. They need money, so she asks whether she might get the big theatre for a big representation May 23-rd—(second Easter holiday) she thinks they might gain about 20,000 [rubles] (I doubt) for those hospitals. They give them things the ministery [sic] (military) cannot give them.[66] If you agree, then I shall tell Fredericks & he can send you the official paper.—On the affiches [placards] they will print that the theatre has been given by a special grace of yours.—The idea of going to town< to a hospital is rather awful, but still I know I must go, so to-morrow afternoon we shall be off. In the morning Karangosov's< appendicitis will be cut off.—How glad I am you get yr. walks daily.—God grant you will really be able to see lots & have talks out there with the Generals.—I have told Vil'chkovsky< to send fat Orloff< a printed paper one of the wounded received from his chief—far too hard orders & absolutely unjust & cruel—if an officer does not return at the time mentioned he must be disciplinied [sic] [and] punished etc. I cant write it, the paper will tell you all. One comes to the conclusion that those that are wounded are doubly badly treated—better keep behind or hide away to remain untouched & I find it most unfair—& I dont believe its everywhere the same, but in some armies.—Forgive me bothering you my Love, but you can help out there, & one does not want bitterness setting in their poor hearts.—Must end.—Blessings & kisses without end. Ever yr. own Sunny.

71. A. K. Shvedov was also called "Shurik." Viktor Erastovich Zborovsky was a *sotnik* in His Majesty's convoy.

No. 185/ Telegram 15. Stavka> Tsarskoe Selo. 2 Mar 1915. 12.28> 1.00 p.m. To her majesty. Fondest thanks for dear letter and news. Warm but grey. Have lots to do and to talk about. Manage to take usual long walks after lunch. Shall write. Tender love to all. Niki

---

No. 186/ Her No. 280.   Tsarskoe Selo. March 2nd 1915.

My own sweet one,

I am beginning my letter this evening, as I want to talk to you. Wify feels hideously sad! My poor wounded friend has gone! [The officer's name, Grobov, is given in No. 188.] God has taken him quietly & peacefully to Himself. I was as usual with him in the morning & more than an hour in the afternoon. He talked a lot—in a wisper [sic] always—all about his service in the Caucasus—awfully interesting & so bright, with his big shiny eyes. I rested before dinner & was haunted with the feeling that he might suddenly get very bad in the night & one would not call me & so on—so that when the eldest nurse called one of the girls to the telephone—I told them that I knew what had happened & flew myself to hear the sad news. After T., M. & A. [daughters Tatiana, Maria and Anastasia] had gone off to Ania<, (to see Ania's sister in law< & Olga Voronov<) [daughter] Olga & I went to the big palace< to see him. He lay there so peacefully, covered under my flowers I daily brought him, with his lovely smile—the forehead yet quite warm. I cant get quiet—so sent Olga to them & came home with my tears. The elder sister [nurse] cannot either realise it—he was quite calm, cheery, said felt a wee bit not comfy, & when the sister, 10 m. after she had gone away, came in, found him with staring eyes, quite blue, breathed twice—& all was over—peaceful to the end. Never did he complain, never asked for anything, sweetness itself as she says—all loved him—& that shining smile.—You, Lovy mine, can understand what that is, when daily one has been there, thinking only of giving him pleasure—& suddenly—finished. And after our Friend< spoke of him, do you remember, & that "he will not soon leave you" I was sure he would recover, tho' very slowly. And he longed to get back to his regiment—was presented [recommended] for golden sword & St. G.[eorge] Cross & higher rank.—Forgive my writing so much about him, but going there, & all that, had been a help, with you away & I felt God let me bring him a little sunshine in his loneliness. Such is life! Another brave soul left this world to be added to the shining stars above.—And how much sorrow all around—thank God that we have the possibility of at least making some comfortable in their suffering & can give them a feeling of homeliness in their loneliness. One longs to warm & help them, brave creatures & to replace their dear ones who cant come.—It must not make you sad what I wrote, only I could not bear it any longer—I had to speak myself out. [a]

Benkendorff has asked to accompany us to town to-morrow, so I had to say yes, tho' I had only thought of taking Ressin< & Isa<.—Baby dear's< leg is better—he sledged to Pavlovsk to-day, Nagorny< & the man of the donkey sledge worked alone at the hill.— If by any chance you ever happen to be near one of my train stores (of wh. I have 5 in all directions), it wld. be very dear if you could peep in, or see the com.[mander] of the train & thank him for his work—they honestly are splendid workers & constantly have been under fire—I am writing to you now in bed, I am lying since an hour already, but cant get to sleep, nor calm myself, so it does me good talking to you. I have blessed & kissed your dear cushion as always.—One says Struve is going to be buried in his country place.—To-morrow we receive 6 officers going back to the war, two of my Siberians<, Vykrestov[72] & the Dr. Menshutkin—& Kratt for the second time, God grant he may not be wounded again. First time the right arm—the next time left arm & through the lungs—the Crimea did him no end of good.—The Nizhe-gorodtsy< are wondering whether their division won't be sent back again, as they have nothing to do now.—Shulman thinks of his Osovets [Fortress] with anguish & longing—this time the shots are bigger & have done more harm—all the officers houses are already quite ruined.—One does so long for detailed news. I heard Amilachvari[72] is wounded, but slightly only.—Igor< has gone to the regiment, tho' the Drs. found him not well enough to leave.—Now I must try and sleep, as to-morrow will be a tiring day—but I don't feel like it. You sleep well my treasure, I kiss & bless you.

March 3-rd. We have just returned from town—were in M.[arie] & A.[nastasia]'s hospital in the new building of the Institute of Rukhlov's<. Zeidler< showed us over all the wards 180 men—& in another building 30 officers. Karangozov's< operation went off well—he had a rotten appendicitis & the operation was done just in time. At 12½ we went to the funeral service in the little hospital Church below, where the poor officer's coffin stands—so sad no relations there—so lonely somehow.—Its snowing hard.—Must end. God bless & protect you—kisses without end, my treasure. Ever yr. very own Wify. [P.S.] Messages to N.P. [b]

---

72. Nicholas Grigor'evich Vykrestov, lt.-col. in Her Majesty's 21st E. Siberian Rifle Reg., was killed in battle. "Amilachvari" was Prince Alexander Amilakhvari, Tatar cavalry capt. 2nd grade.

No. 187/ His No. 166.   Stavka. The New imperial train.
My Tenderly Beloved,   March 2nd 1915.

I thank you so fondly for two dear letters. Whenever I see an envelope with your firm writing on it, my heart leaps several times & I shut myself up and read, or rather devour it up! Of course the girls< may bathe in my swimming-basin; I am glad Tiny< enjoyed himself; I told the rascal to write to me about it all! Now I am here for the seventh time—I think! At the front all is pretty well.[70] N.< is in good spirits and as usual wants rifles and ammunition. The question of our coal supplies for the railroads & fabrics [factories] is a precari-ous nature, so I have asked Rukhlov to take it all in his hands. Think only if our war material fabrication stopped & that on account of lack of coal or rather from not getting enough of it out of our coal mines in the south! I feel confident that energetic measures will pull us out of these difficulties.

I found Georgi< looking very well & so brown; he told me lots of interesting things, wh he will repeat to you later. Petiusha< is here & has recovered. I heard from him that [his son] Roman has had typhoid, but is much better. Good old, Pau, the French general, arrived today from Galacia—overjoyed with his trip & of having been under Austrian fire. Sazonov also came this morning, so they all lunched with me. To-morrow will arrive Paléologue, who has to bring France's official answer about Constantinople & also her wishes in Turkey's spoil.[73] [a]

3 March. During the day we had long conversations—N.<, Sazonov, Yanush-kevich and I—which ended with mutual satisfaction. There are so many ques-tions that it is impossible to finish them off in one day. My plans are not yet settled. N. would not hear about my going towards Lomzha the first day. He says the German aeroplanes are flying over our troops there, to find out our re-serves, that all the roads are blocked up with transports & carriages etc. and that

for these reasons he advised General Pau not to go in that direction.[70] I will see what to do! I have sent Dzhunkovsky to look about there & he as a practical man will be able to judge if that expedition is possible. The news from everywhere are quite good. Little Osovets is holding out satisfactorily against the bombardment, whatever is damaged by day is repaired by night & the garrison is in excellent spirits and strong enough. I have sent them my thanks. This time the Germans are further away [from their objective] than they were the first time in September.[70] [b]

Yesterday N. brought me a report of Ivanov from Brusilov & your Khan-Nakhichevansky< about Misha's< division's excellent conduct in the battles in February, when they were attacked by two Austrian divisions in the Carpathians. The Caucasians not only repulsed the enemy but attacked them & were the first to enter into Stanislavov, Misha being himself the whole [time] in the firing lines. They all beg me to give him the St. George's Cross, wh I am going to do. N. is sending one of his a.d.c. this evening with my letter and the order to Misha; I am happy for him because I think this military reward really is deserved by him this time & it will show that he is, in the end, treated like the others, and that for doing well his duty he gets also recompensed!—The little admiral< behaves very well and often during our evening of domino game makes us laugh by his witty remarks about Tatishchev and Svechin, who both bore him with their endless talks. It is true the latter loves to tell tiresome anecdotes, with French phrases, when we breakfast or have tea and he begins to drive all of us to distraction. The Admiral has become great friends with Fed.[orov], and they speak about strategical questions. Well, I have talked enough rubbish. Forgive me, my darling Wify. God bless you and the dear children. I kiss you all tenderly. Always your own old devoted huzy   Nicky. [c]

73. Imperialist designs did not figure in the outbreak of World War I, but they became visibly important as the conflict progressed. At this point, Nicholas II was pressuring France to recognize Russia's designs against Turkey. Nicholas, his foreign minister (Sazonov) and the French ambassador (Paléologue) were about to meet to discuss the question. In March-April 1915, Sazonov secured Anglo-French recognition of Russian sovereignty over Constantinople, the Bosporus and the Dardanelles. Russia promised to keep the Straits open to commerce and to make Constantinople a "free port." The French agreed while speaking of the possibility that the area might finally be neutralized. The "Straits Agreement" was secret, though its terms were widely suspected. Trepov, as the new chairman of the council of ministers, first confirmed the accords in his inaugural speech to the Duma on November 19, 1916. See Oldenburg, *Last Tsar*, IV: 89, 106, 182n, 184n.

No. 188/ Telegram 5. Tsarskoe Selo> Stavka. 3 Mar 1915. 2.04> 3.17 p.m. To his majesty. Warm, snowing. [We] are leaving for town<, to hospital<. My poor wounded officer Grobov unexpectedly died last night. Very sad. He was so lively all these days. Embrace and kiss [you]. Will write. Alix

No. 189/ Telegram 35. Stavka> Tsarskoe Selo. 3 Mar 1915. 4.46> 5.20 p.m. To her majesty. Fondest thanks [for] dear letters from you and the children. Have been occupied the whole evening with reading and writing. Filthy, wet, windy weather. Good news from all parts. Kiss you all lovingly. Niki

No. 190/ Telegram 11. Tsarskoe Selo> Stavka. 4 Mar 1915. 10.50> 11.30 a.m.
To his majesty. All went well in town<. Were at Rukhlov's< hospital, 180 soldiers, 30 officers—in evening in hospital< with Ania<. Laid down because heart
felt bad. What disappointment, could not work but had to lie down. Mild
weather. Tiny's< leg almost well and does not bother him at all. Girls< leaving
for town. [Daughter] Olga has a benefit, Tatiana committee [meeting]. [We]
bless and kiss [you]. Alix

No. 191/ Telegram 53. Stavka> Tsarskoe Selo. 4 Mar 1915. 11.36 a.m.> 12.15
p.m. To her majesty. I am short of writing paper. Could you send me mine in
blue box on shelf opposite first window. I stupidly forgot. Everything good, bad
weather, snowstorm, tender kisses. Niki

No. 192/ Telegram 13. Tsarskoe Selo> Stavka. 4 Mar 1915. 1.17> 2.20 p.m.
To his majesty. Heartily thank you for letter and telegram. Am sending the paper. Sunny, not much snow. All tenderly embrace and kiss [you]. Alix

No. 193/ Her No. 281.   Tsarskoe Selo. March 4th 1915.
My own beloved Darling,
   With what joy I received yr. dear letter, thanks over & over for it! I have read
it already twice over & kissed it several times.—How tired all those complicated
talks must make you! God grant the coal question may soon be settled satisfactorily & the guns too. But they too must soon be running short of everything.—About Misha< I am so happy do write it to Motherdear<, it will do her
good to know it. I am sure this war will make more of a man of him—could one
but get her out of his reach! Her dictating influence is so bad for him.—I shall
tell the children< to fetch your paper & send it with this letter—Baby< has written in French, I told him to do so & he writes more naturally than with Peter
Vas.< His [Aleksei's] leg is almost alright, does not limp—the right hand is bandaged as rather swollen, so wont be able to write probably a few days. But he
goes out twice daily.—The four girls< are going to town<—Tatiana has her committee,[66] M.[arie] & A.[nastasia] will look on whilst Olga receives money &
then they will all go to Marie[74]—the little ones have never seen her rooms. [a]
   Botkin has put me to bed, heart a good deal enlarged & have rather a cough—I
felt rotten, in every respect, these days & now M-me Becker< arrived & prevents me from taking my drops.—Am glad I managed the hospital in town yesterday—we did it quickly 1 hour & ¼ & one carried me up the stairs—the 4 girls
helped giving the Images [icons] & talking, & Ressin< arranged those well
enough to be stood in a row in the corridor—tell this to N.P.< as he thought I
wld. overtire myself in town—its the strain of these weeks, 2 a day to Ania<,
who never finds it enough, wrote now she had wanted to see me more to talk
(have nothing to say, hear only sad things), Nini< brightens her far more up with
her "bavardage" [chatter] & gossip & to read to her—have a cough these days, so
could not. And she cant understand this death [of Grabov, see Letters No. 186a
and 188] having upset me so—Zizi< does, wrote so kindly.—I cannot do a thing
by halves & I saw his joy when I came twice daily—& he all alone, others were

not at in—he had no family here.— She grudges me to the others, I feel, & they so touchingly always ask me not to tire myself—"you are only one for us, we are many".—He told me too still the last afternoon that I overtire myself—so on—awfully kind—so how cannot I try & give them everything of warmth & love—they suffer so & are unspoiled—she has all, tho' of course her leg is a great worry to her & does not grow a bit together yet—the Pss.< looked yesterday. But A.[nia] one never can satisfy & that is the most tiring, & she does not understand Botkin's hints at all about me.— [b]

The sun is shining & its snowing a little.—I got nurse Lyubushcha (the eldest sister [senior nurse] of big Palace<) to come & sit with me for half an hour, she is cosy, told me about the wounded & more details about the other. To-morrow one buries him [Grobov] —our Friend< wrote me a touching little letter about this death.—I can imagine Svetchin< makes you wild—me he drove to distraction a few days ago in the Crimea with these half French anecdotes—one says he is the son of old Galkin-Vrassky.—Send him about to look at motors or hospitals close by.—Now I wonder what you will do—dont tell where you intend going, then you can get through unawares & I am sure, he knows far less where you can go, then when you are nearer out there already in the train.— To-morrow is N. [Uncle] Willy's< death day—2 years! My precious one, my muchly missed one, I must end now.— God bless & protect you & keep you safe from all harm. I kiss you over & over again with deepest tenderness. Ever yr. very own wify Sunny. [P.S.] I bow to yr. people.— [c]

74. Reference is probably to Maria Pavlovna (the younger) or to Maria Vladimirovna Baryatinskaya.

No. 194/ Telegram 56. Stavka> Tsarskoe Selo. 4 Mar 1915. 4.12> 4.40 p.m. To her majesty. Tender thanks [for] letter [and] two telegrams. On [sic] despair you feel tired. So sorry about your poor wounded officer. Understand you perfectly. Kiss all lovingly. Niki

---

No. 195/ Telegram 15. Tsarskoe Selo> Stavka. 5 Mar 1915. 10.30> 11.15 a.m. To his majesty. Heart better but still weakness. I am tired and for that reason still lying down. Children leaving for hospital<, then to town< for Olga's committee.[66] Hope news everywhere is good.[70] I warmly embrace and kiss you. Alix

---

No. 196/ Her No. 282.   Tsarskoe Selo. March 5th 1915.
My very own beloved One,

I enclose a paper fr. Ella< wh. you can send to Mamantov, or fat Orloff< & then a letter from Ania<. She is very put out, that I do not go to her again, but B.< keeps me again in bed till dinner, like yesterday. The heart is not enlarged this morning, but I feel still rotten & weak & sad—when the health breaks down its more difficult to hold oneself in hands. Now he [Grobov, the officer referred to in Nos. 186a, 188, 193b,c, 194, 198, 200b] is being buried. I dont know whether they will leave him here or not, because the regiment intends burying all the officers after the war in the Caucasus,—they have marked the graves every where—but some died in Germany. I got a telegr. fr. my Veselovsky< that they had all just enjoyed the bania [bath] train & clean linen & are off to the okopi [trenches].—

Then I got a doklad [report] (according to my wish) from him. He returned Feb. 15-th. But of the heaps who are to receive decorations, only one Pr.[ince] Gantimurov got the [St.] Georg.[e] Sword as yet—he himself is not presented to anything, as in the absence of his chiefs who commanded over [him]; the Divisionary General von Gennings was dismissed from his post, and the Brigadier-Gen. Bykov is taken prisoner. A terrible worry & sorrow is that they have no flag, they entreat you to give them a new one, representations regarding this have already been made to the War-Minister [Sukhomlinov] by the commander-in-chief [Nikolasha<] on February 7, under No. 9850. Their losses were quite colossal, 4 times the reg. has been filled up again, during the battles above vil.[lage of] B.,—but I better write this on an extra paper, instead of filling up my letter with it; I shall copy out bits for you.—My Image [icon] reached them just after [the] 30-th, their Lieut. Colonel Sergeev<, burned their flag. After he was wounded then, the chief of the supply service took the regiment & during 3 months did all splendidly.—I fear this letter is mighty dull.—Have let off Madelaine< for the day to town—6 weeks Tudels< has not turned up. Sunny [day] again.—[a]

I had Isa< for affairs—& then Sonia<.—Just got yr. dear telegram. Ania wrote that Fred.< is intensely happy over your letter, of course she envies him. Perhaps you will put in your telegram to me that you thank for inclosed letter & send love or messages.—she said I was to burn hers if I thought you would be angry—how can I know. I answered her that I would send it, so I hope she does not bother you with it—she can not grasp that her letters are of little interest to you, as they mean so much to her.—I have send the little ones to her—she wanted them in the evening; but they said they wished to remain with me then, as don't see them all day.—Dont you tell N.< & go off where it suits you & where nobody can expect you—of course he will try to keep you back, because one won't let him move—but if you go, I know that God will hold you in safe keeping & you & the troops will feel comforted. Now my very own Sunshine my treasure beloved, I will close my letter. God bless & protect you now & ever, I cover your dear face with tenderest kisses, & remain, Ever yr. very own   Wify. [P.S.] I wish I were near you as I am sure you go through many difficult moments, not knowing who speaks the exact truth, who is partial & so on—& personal offenses etc., which ought not to exist at such a time, just show themselves, alas, now in the rear, I fear.—Where are our dear sailors? What are they doing & is Kirill< with them? [b]

No. 197/ Telegram 68. Stavka> Tsarskoe Selo. 5 Mar 1915. 2.17> 2.40 p.m. To her majesty. Tenderest thanks for dear letter and paper. Am pleased with Baby's letter in French. Hope you really feel better. News good. [I will] remain still a few days here. Weather better but windy. Fondest kisses to all. Niki

---

No. 198/ His No. 167.   Stavka. March 5th 1915.
My Own love bird, Sunny,

Tender thanks for your long precious letter. I so well understand your grief about the poor fellow's [Grobov] sad death, with nobody of his own near him! Truly, it is really better to be killed at once—like Struve—because death in action comes in presence of a whole unit or regiment and gets written down in history! To day the weather is fine, but frosty & lots of snow. The sun shines so prettily through the trees in front of my window. We have just returned from our after-noon walk. The roads in the fields are abominably slippery and my gentlemen fall down occasionally. Some days ago Sazonov fell going from train to his carriage, & hurt foot & nose. Yesterday Drentel'n slipped on the same spot & tore the sinews of his ankle; he has to lie, and Fedorov looks after him. To-day, [M. N.] Grabbe fell down during our walk, he is alright; and towards the end he went through some ice in a ditch but also without any harm. You can see from this that we spend our time quietly & with no incident of great importance. In the morning I spend an hour or an hour and a half with N.< and the two generals of the staff.

I see much of Georgi< often—he is wonderfully changed to his advantage, every one who sees him find the same, since he has been in Caucasus! Having found out how well my plastuni[75] (my special weakness) have behaved down there, I have named myself chief of the 6th Kuban plast. battalion, and him—Georgi—the same of the 4th Kuban plast. bat., because he was in their trenches— grand isn't it? Tell Olga about it. All those splendid men leave Batum in a few days for Sevastopol, to be ready for the final expedition.[75] Now lovy-mine I must close. God bless you & the dear children! I kiss you tenderly & lovingly & remain, sweet darling, ever your own old huzy   Nicky.

75. A *plastun* was a dismounted Cossack. The "plastuni battalions" were Kuban Cossack units "consisting of picked marksmen. They were originally attached to the various infantry units of the Black Sea forces, but in 1870 they were formed into independent battalions—six battalions in peace time and sixteen in war." (Vulliamy, p. 35n) Vulliamy also notes that the "final expedition" men-tioned here was to have been a drive against Constantinople, "the fulfillment of the long cherished hopes of Russian imperialism."

No. 199/ Telegram 20. Tsarskoe Selo> Stavka. 6 Mar 1915. 12.00> 12.45 p.m. To his majesty. Your dear letter was such an unexpected joy! Endless thanks. 12 degrees of frost, very sunny. Am still lying down all the time because heart enlarged and feel weary. Your loving words are such comfort. All tenderly em-brace and kiss you. Alix

No. 200/ Her No. 283.   Tsarskoe Selo. March 6th 1915.
My very own Sweetheart,
    A bright sunny day again, but 12° of frost. This morning the heart is not en-larged, but it has slipped to the right, so the feeling is the same.—Yesterday eve-ning it was again enlarged. I get over onto the sopha for dinner till 10½ or 11. Feel still so weak. A.[nia]< fidgets for me to come to her but Botkin is going there, so as to tell her, that I cannot yet, & need quiet still some days. Thank God, the wounded officers in both hospitals are pretty well, so that I am not ab-solutely necessary this moment & the girls< were at soldiers' operations again

yesterday. They so touchingly ask after me through the girls, Zizi< or Botkin. I miss my work, & all the more so that you, my Angel, are not here.

Do so wonder where & when you will be able to move on—standing so long at the Headquarters must be rather despairing.— Lovy dear, people want to send gospels to our prisoners, prayerbooks they (the Germans) do not allow to be forwarded to Germany—Loman has 10,000—may they be sent with an inscription that they come from me, or better not, kindly answer by wire "gospels yes—or not", then I will understand how to have them sent.—Sonia< sat with me yesterday afternoon ¾ of an hour, shall ask M-me. Zizi< to-day, as children must go out & to hospitals.— Please give the enclosed letter to N.P.< through your man, it's one from O, T [daughters Olga and Tatyana] & me together.— My lancer Apukhtin is for the moment commanding an infantry regiment (forget which), because only a captain was left eldest there.—Just got your precious letter—such an unexpected intense joy, thanks ever so tenderly! Warm words comfort my tired heart.—That is nice your having named yourself "chief" & Georgi too—with what force & cheer those brave "Plastuni" will now be off[75]—God bless their voyage & give them success.— [a]

Your walks are surely refreshing, & the different falls must cheer up the monotony (when not too painful).—Lovy mine, your letters are just as a ray of Sunshine to me! Yesterday they buried the poor fellow [Grobov] & sister Liubusha [the senior nurse, Lyubushchina] said he had still his happy smile —only a little changed in colour, but the expression we knew so well, had not faded. Always a smile, & he told her he was so happy & wanted nothing more —shining eyes which struck all & after a life of ups & downs, a romance of changes, thank God he was happy with us.—How many "plastuni" regiments go? as I might send them quickly Images [icons][75]—how many officers in each regiment? Make Drentel'n cypher [sic] the wire through Kira< to me, please. —Ania's Mother [Nadezhda Taneeva] was very ill with a colossal attack of stones in the liver, but is now better—another such strong attack, our Friend< said, would be her end.—Again she [Anna Vyrubova] fidgets I am to telephone & come in the evening, when we daily explain I can't yet; so tiresome of her, & heaps of letters every day!—its not my fault, & I must get quite right & only by quiet lying (as can't yet take medicine) can help me— She only thinks of herself & is angry I am so much with the wounded—they do me good & their gratitude gives me strength—whereas with her, who complains about her leg always, it's more tiring—one gives out so much of oneself, moral & physical all day, that in the evening little is left.— [b]

Got again a loving letter from our Friend, wants me to go out in the sun, says it will do me good (morally) more than lying. But its very cold, I have a cough, the cold I keep down, then feverish again & so weak & tired.—Got a wire from my Tuchkov from Lvov (Lemberg) supply train who arranged (have 4) a flying one so as to help more, it will become our 5-th. [The following quote is in Russian.] "The flying train finished its 2-nd trip by touring the region of the Stry, Skole and Vygoda, some military units and sanitary sections received their supplies in the neighbourhood of the front positions of Tukhli, Libokhori and Kozyuvki, at the same time distributing gifts and images (from me). The attentions bestowed by Y[our] M[ajesty] everywhere provoked the sinc[erest] enthusiasm and limitless joy. On the return trip the empty cars furnished with portable stores carried from Vygoda about 200 wounded, the evacuation of whom considerably lightened the task of the hospital, etc." So the nearer these little trains go in [i.e., to the] front, the better it is—[Uncle] Mekk< is a wee genius, inventing & setting all this going—all he does is really well & quickly done & he had the chance of getting good gentlemen for these supply trains.—Zizi< sat an hour & was very dear. The girls walked & now have gone to the big palace<.—

A man leaves for [your sister] Olga, so must send her a line.—Please tell Drentel'n that we send messages & hope his leg is better. Bow to [M. N.] Grabbe, N.P.< & wee [i.e., the little] Admiral< & my friend Fedor[ov]. Good-bye now, my own precious one, my huzy dear, my sweet Sunshine, I cover you with very tenderest kisses, Baby< too. The girls are wild that they may bathe in your bath. God bless & protect you & keep you from all harm!—prayers & thoughts are ever with you. Ever your own   Sunny. [c]

No. 201/ Telegram 79. Stavka> Tsarskoe Selo. 6 Mar 1915. 1.54> 2.20 p.m. To her majesty. Loving thanks [for] dearest letter with note about your 21st Regiment. Thank her [see Letter No. 196a] and give my love. Lovely, frosty weather. Hope heart better. You must take care of yourself. Tenderest love and kisses. Niki

---

No. 202/ Telegram 26. Tsarskoje Selo> Stavka. 7 Mar 1915. 11.13 a.m.> 12.24 p.m. To his majesty. Still lying down upstairs because heart very enlarged towards evening and felt completely tired and weary. Girls< in extreme rapture over swimming-bath. Cold and overcast. All embrace and kiss [you]. Alix

---

No. 203/ Her No. 284   Tsarskoe Selo. March 7ᵗʰ 1915.
My own beloved One,

A week to-day you left us—it seems much longer. Your telegrams & precious letters are such a comfort & I constantly read them.—You see I am looking after my tired old self, & to-day again only get up for 8. Ania< won't understand it, the Dr., children & I explain it to her, & yet every day 5 letters & begging me to come— she knows I lie in bed, & yet pretends to be astonished at it—so selfish. She knows I never miss going to her when I only can, & dead tired too she still grumbles why I went twice daily to an unknown officer & does not heed Botkin's remark, that he needed me & that she always has guests all day long almost. My visits to her are as a duty she finds (I think) & therefore even often does not seem to appreciate them, whereas the others thank for every second given to them. It is quite good she does not see me some days—tho' last night 6-th letter complained she had had no good-night kisses nor blessings for so long. If she would kindly once remember who I happen to be, then she might learn to understand that I have other duties except her.—100 times I told her about you too, who you are, and that an E.[mperor] never goes daily to a sick person—what would one think otherwise, & that you have your country first of all to think of, & then get tired from work, & need air & its good you should be with Baby< out, etc. It is like speaking to a stone—she won't understand, because she goes before everybody.—She offers to invite officers in the evening for the children<, thinking to get me like that, but they answered that they wished to remain with me, as its only time we are quietly together. We have too much spoiled her—but I honestly find, as a daughter of our friends [i.e., a spiritual daughter of Rasputin], she ought to grasp things better & the illness[59] ought to have changed her. Now enough about her, it's dull—it has stopped worrying me as it used to, & only aggravates one, because of the selfishness.

It's cold, grey & snowing.—The girls wildly enjoyed your swimming bath—first the 2 little ones [Maria and Anastasia] & then the eldest [Olga]—I could not go.—I slept badly & feel weak & tired—so far the heart is not enlarged, it becomes so every afternoon—so I think I won't see anybody & remain completely quiet, then it may behave itself!—Had heaps of papers to read this morning from Rostovtsev etc.. Shulman< was so grateful to hear about Osovetz, I told the children to tell him.—Baby's "Moscouits" [Muscovite Regiment] are not far from there. Galfter wrote. Hope Drenteln's leg is better, bow to him & N.P.< Goodbye & God bless & protect you my precious Angel. Kisses without end from your own wify Alix.

No. 204/ Telegram 84. Stavka> Tsarskoe Selo. 7 Mar 1915. 5.00> 5.52 p.m. To her majesty. Tender thanks for dear letter No. 283.[76] Gospels, yes. Shall let you know about plastuni.[75] Gentlemen [of my suite] all thank you. To day warm, thawing. Fondest love and kisses to all. Niki.

76. This letter from Alexandra was dated March 6, so it appears that the tsar enjoyed next-day delivery.

No. 205/ His No. 168   Stavka. March 7th 1915.
My own beloved Sunny,

I thank you ever so much for your dear letter N[o.] 282, & am angry with myself for not writing to you every day, as I intended. The messenger has to leave the train for the station at 6.30, so I must always hurry up with my papers. And when I am occupied with the morning usual reports there hardly remains any time for writing letters before luncheon. We all here are astonished how quickly the time passes. It was useful my remaining here longer, as we had lots of serious & urgent questions to discuss—and if I were away it would have any amount of time & telegrams sent to & fro.

You seem to think that N.< keeps me back for the pleasure of not allowing me move & see the troops—but really it is not quite so. A fortnight ago, when he wrote to me to come—he told me that I might have easily visited three army corps, because they were massed together in the rear. Since then much has changed & they have all been sent to the front lines,[60] which is true, I get the proof every morning during the reports. Even General Pau was not allowed to go to Lomzha (my place). He only went through Varsovie [Warsaw] to Bzura & Ravka, where at the moment it is quiet. Yesterday I motored out for 24 versts [15.9 miles] & walked in a pretty wood & though the camp of the 4th Army Corps—the place is called Skobelevsky Camp. The little huts in wh. officers live bear their names surrounded by little gardens with benches, gymnastic & different amusements for children. I thought with anguish of those who probably shall never again return here! It was bitterly cold driving in an open motor, but we were warmly clad. Today it is thawing. Chemodurov got for me these postcards here at the post. Give A.[nia]< my love and tell her I liked the verses she copied out for me. I hope you are feeling better lovy-mine, my Wify-dear. God bless you & the children. Am always in prayers & thoughts with you. With fondest love ever your own Nicky.

No. 206/ Telegram 35. Tsarskoe Selo> Stavka. 8 Mar 1915. 11.08> 11.50 a.m. To his majesty. Cold and sunny morning. Girls< went to church. No change in my health. [I] bless and kiss [you]. Alix

---

No. 207/ Her No. 285.   Tsarskoe Selo. March 8th 1915.
My own beloved One,
    I hope you get my letters regularly, I write & number them daily, also in my little lilac book.—Forgive my bothering you, by sending a petition, but one would like to help those poor people—I think it's the second time they write—kindly put a decision & send it to the minister of Justice [S. G. Shcheglovitov].—I copied out a telegram it might amuse you to read, thanking our store for presents; I don't need it returned. Then a note from [daughter] Marie to Drentel'n. What a good thing Memel has been taken,[92] they did not expect this, I am sure, & it will be a good lesson to them. And everywhere the news, thank God, seem good, I have time to read up all now, lying in bed.—I am going over onto the sopha for [until] 4½ [o'clock] already, bit by bit a little more [regular activity], tho' every evening the heart is enlarged, & every day Ania< asks me to come.—Glorious sunshine but very cold, they say. Ducky< had a correspondant [sic] with her, & he wrote most interesting all she had done at Prasnish—she really does a lot with her unit, & is really under fire. Miechen< promenades with her decoration to all exhibitions[,] etc; you ought to find out really how she got it, & that such things don't happen again, & Tatiana [K.]< neither. [See Letter No. 151b] Ducky deserves it certainly.—How sad the losses of the "Bouvet", "Irresistible" & "Ocean", so hideous to be sunk by floating mines & so rapidly too—not as tho' in battle.[77] I had a letter from Victoria< from Kent House—nothing new in it. Have, alas, nothing interesting to tell you. The children< are lunching next door & making an unearthly noise.— [a]
    What joy sweetheart to have got another letter from you—it was just brought to me, & the nice postcards & the children's cards—we all thank over & over again & are very deeply touched you find time to write to us.—I see now why you did not go more forward [see Letter No. 205], but surely you could go still to some place before returning, it would do you good & cheer the others up— anywhere. That drive must have been nice, but I understand the sad impression of those empty houses, probably many of them never to be inhabited by the same people again. Such is life—such a tragedy! Did Sergei L.[78] make a better impression upon you, less sure of himself & simpler? I at once sent Ania your message, it will have given her pleasure. She probably thinks that she alone is lonely without you.—Ah, she is greatly mistaken! But I know it's right you should be there & the change is good for you. only I should have wished more people to have

profited & seen you.—I suppose you had service to-day.—The children went this morning. Just heard Irene [Yusupova] had a daughter (thought it would be a girl) glad it's over, poor Xenia< worried about it all along.—It would have seemed more natural, had I heard that Xenia herself had borne a Baby.—Such sunshine! The girls< drove, now have gone to my red cross community, then to Ania & after tea the eldest go to Tatiana [K].< Aleksei has three of Xenia's boys.[79] I am going to be up by ¼ to 5.—Goodbye my Sunshine—don't worry if you can't write daily, you have much to do, & must have a little quiet too—& letter-writing takes you so much time. God bless you, Nicky treasure, my very own huzy, I kiss & bless you & love you without ceasing. Ever yr very own wify   Alix. [b]

77. The empress refers here to the "Dardanelles Operation" of February 6/19-March 5/18, 1915. The Entente hoped to force a naval passage through the Dardanelles, capture Constantinople, take Turkey out of the war, and establish a secure supply route to Russia. The Anglo-French fleet had initial success, but Turkish minefields proved effective. The French lost the battleship *Bouvet*, followed by H.M.S. *Irresistible* and *Ocean*. Other ships were damaged. Shaken, the fleet commander withdrew just when (many now think) the battered Turkish defenses were about to crumble. The British attempted an unsuccessful amphibious landing a month later.

78. Prince Serge Georgievich Romanovsky, duke of Leuchtenberg, a.d.c., senior naval lt.

79. These were Dmitri, Rostislav and Nikita, children of Nicholas's younger sister Xenia< and g.p. Alexander Michaelovich.

No. 208/ Telegram 36. Tsarskoe Selo> Stavka. 8 Mar 1915. 2.28> 4.05 p.m. To his majesty. Your dear letters were such joy! All thank [you] warmly. Irene [Yusupova] had a girl. [I] tenderly embrace [you]. Alix

No. 209/ Telegram 103. Stavka> Tsarskoe Selo. 8 Mar 1915. 6.15> 7.07 p.m. To her majesty. Fondest thanks for letter, deliciously smelling lilies and two telegrams. Very glad about Irina. From everywhere good news.[70] Leave Tuesday, shall be home Wednesday morning. Tender kisses. Give her [Anna Vyrubova] my love. Niki

No. 210/ Telegram 44. Tsarskoe Selo> Stavka. 9 Mar 1915. 10.23> 11.51 a.m. To his majesty. Irene feels and sleeps well— little Irene also. Cold, sunny. Feel better today because am still lying down. All day we worked hard preparing for Wednesday. All embrace and kiss [you]. Alix

No. 211/ Telegram 126 in Russian. Stavka> Tsarskoe Selo. 9 Mar 1915. 12.00> 12.15 p.m. To her majesty. Peremyshl taken.[80] Thanks be to God. Niki

80. Peremyshl' surrendered on March 9/22, 1915 after a siege of 194 days. The Russians took 110,000 Austrian prisoners and 700 heavy guns. Nicholas's troops also crossed the Prussian border and launched successful raids against Memel and Tauroggen, cities the Germans had captured in February 1915. All this boosted Entente morale. But the Russian drive through the Carpathians, despite early successes, was checked by a German-Austrian force on April 12/25, 1915. Even so, the tsar was receiving good news for a time.

No. 212/ Telegram 46. Tsarskoe Selo> Stavka. 9 Mar 1915. 12.58> 2.05 p.m. To his majesty. Thanks be to God, what joy and divine mercy! Just received a letter from [your sister] Olga, she is satisfied with her visit to Lvov. We all kiss and embrace [you]. Give my greetings and congratulations to Nikolasha. Alix

---

No. 213/ Her No. 286.   Tsarskoe Selo. March 9th 1915.
My Huzy sweet Angel,
    What happiness to know that the day after to-morrow I shall be holding you tight in my arms again, listening to your dear voice & looking into your beloved eyes. Only for you I regret, that you won't have seen anything. If I could only be decent by the time you return. This night I only got to sleep after 5, felt such pressure on the heart, & the heart rather much enlarged. Yesterday it kept normal, & I was also from 5-6 on the sofa & 8-11—Irene [Yusupova] & [her new] Baby are well—she suffered a good deal, but was brave—she likes her name, & so wished the child to be called by it, funny little thing.—Dmitri, Rostislav & Nikita came to Aleksei, & the latter dined with us.[79]—It is cold, but bright sunshine.—I enclose a letter from Masha<, (from Austria) wh she was asked to write to you, for peace's sake. I never answer her letters, of course, now; then a letter from Ania<;—I don't know whether you agree to her writing, but I can't say no, once she asks me, & better like this than through the servants.[81] She [Ania] sent for Kondrateff yesterday— so foolish to get the servants to talk to—in the hospital she already wanted to see them—only to make a fuss—it's not quite ladylike, I must honestly say. Now she will be sending for your men, & that will be quite improper;—why can't she then sooner ask, after the poor wounded she knows, & with whom she won't have anything to do!—
    Just got your telegram, it came in 15 min; thank God Przemysl [Peremyshl'] taken, congratulate you with all my loving heart—this is good—what joy for our beloved troops! They did have a long time of it, & honestly speaking I am glad for the poor garrison & people who must have almost been dying of hunger. Now we shall have those army corps free to throw over to more weak places. I am too happy for you!—[See No. 211] From [your sister] Olga good news, likes Lvov (Lemberg), she feels sad Misha< is with wife[82] there & she has never seen him for 4 years. Now goodbye my treasure, I bless & kiss you over & over again—your very own   Sunny.

---

81. This is the first reference in the Nicky-Sunny correspondence to a separate peace. Alexandra & "Masha"—Maria Alexandrovna Vasil'chikova—were old friends. Vasil'chikova was living in Vienna when the war broke out. She returned to Russia in the late fall of 1915 with letters to open negotiations for a separate peace between Russia and the Central Powers. Although the enemy hoped the German-born Alexandra would favor such a project, she was entirely pro-Russian and committed to victory. She refused to see Masha and ignored her communications. ("I never answer her letters, of course, now.") Masha then turned to Anna Vyrubova, giving her a letter "for peace's sake." Alexandra obviously feared the well-intentioned but naive Vyrubova might reply; she also knew Anna's servants would soon be gossiping about the compromising situation. Alexandra referred the problem to her husband, who also received a letter from Masha, as did his foreign minister, Sazonov. Later peace feelers came to Alexandra through German contacts. The first recorded in this correspondence involved her brother Ernie. (See Letter No. 268b.) Alexandra refused to believe Masha was a traitor, though Letter 336c indicates Vasil'chikova actually spied upon the royal family in the Alexander Palace from her own nearby home at Tsarskoe Selo. Masha was exiled to her estate in

the provinces until the end of the war. She was also deprived of her rank of *fraulein* of the Russian court on January 1, 1916. (Buxhoeveden, *Life and Tragedy*, pp. 225-226.)

82. Russian law held members of the imperial family to a standard of marital behavior which exceeded that of commoners. It fell to the tsar to enforce these rules. The scandalous relationship of Nicholas's brother Michael ("Misha") with Countess Natalya Sergeevna Cheremetevskaya caused stress within the Romanov family. Natalya was a commoner and twice divorced. Michael fell in love with her and requested Nicholas's permission to marry Natalya in 1906. Nicholas refused, so Michael and Natalya went abroad. They had a son in 1910, and in 1912 they were married in an Orthodox Church in Vienna. Confronted with this *fait accompli*, Nicholas recognized the marriage and granted Natalya the title *Countess Brasova*. Neither Nicholas nor Alexandra received the countess, though they maintained relations with Misha. (See Massie, *Nicholas and Alexandra*, pp. 232-235.) Michael had been close to his sister Olga; but as we see here, Olga had not seen him for four years. Olga could now visit Misha at Lvov, but had no plans to do so since she would also see her unwanted sister-in-law. For Alexandra's attitude towards Brasova, see Letter No. 419b.

No. 214/ His No. 169.   Stavka. March 9th 1915.
My own beloved Sunny,

How can I thank you enough for your two dear letters & for the lilies? I poke my nose into them & have often kissed them, I hope on the places wh. your sweet lips have touched. They stand night and day on my table; when the gentlemen pass my door I let them smell the flowers! God grant I shall be back on the 11th—probably at 10 o'clock in the morning. What joy to be once more in one's nest—cozily & tightly (in all senses) together!! Just at this very minute, 11.30, Nikolasha< rushed into my carriage, out of breath and with tears in his eyes, & announced the fall of Peremyshl'. Thank God! Since two days we were all waiting the news with hope & anguish. The fall of that fortress has an enormous moral & military importance. After several wearying months, this news strikes one as a sudden ray of bright sunshine, & just the first day of spring![80]

I began my letter quietly, but now all my thoughts are topsy turvy in my head, so please excuse the second part of my letter. Oh! Lovy-mine one is so deeply happy with this good news, and so grateful to God for His mercy! I have ordered a thanksgiving service to be sung at 2 o'clock in the church here, where I have been also on previous occasions for thanksgiving prayers last year! Yesterday I motored to the same fine wood near the Skobelevsky Camp & took a good walk on the other side of the high road—it was warm and thawing hard! Since Drent.< hurt his ankle [A. N.] Grabbe took his place for our domino. The little admiral< and he are so funny together & send N.P.< & me into fits of laughter. I am going to send Grabbe to the army at Peremyshl' with lots of decorations & my thanks to officers and men. 3 o'clock just back from church, crammed full of officers & my splendid cossacks— beaming faces! Shavel'sky said a touching word. Everybody has an Easter feeling! Now well, good-bye, my own treasure, my Sunny! God bless you & the dear children! Awfully happy to return home. With fondest love & passionate kisses ever your own old huzy Nicky.

No. 215/ Telegram 50. Tsarskoe Selo> Stavka. 10 Mar 1915. 10.47> 11.02 a.m. To his majesty. Profoundly touched. Thanks for dear letter. Can well imagine universal rapture and thanksgiving! Good you are still there and were present at [thanksgiving] service. Snowing heavily. Heart a bit better this morning. [I] kiss [you]. Have a good trip. Alix

No. 216/ Telegram 157. Stavka> Tsarskoe Selo. 10 Mar 1915. 11.48 a.m.>
12.45 p.m. To her majesty. Forgot to thank you yesterday for dear letter, as was
so excited about happy news. Amount of prisoners there colossal.[80] Fine sunny
weather. Leave at 3 o'clock. Tender kisses. Niki

No. 217/ Telegram 167. Stavka> Tsarskoe Selo. 10 Mar 1915. 2.12> 3.00 p.m.
To her majesty. Fondest thanks for dear letter and to the children also for their
[letters]. Hope heart better. Leave in one hour. Kiss tenderly all. Niki

---

No. 218/ Her No. 287.   Tsarskoe Selo. April 4th 1915.
My very own Treasure,
    Once more you are leaving us, & I think with gladness, because the life you
had here, all excepting the work in the garden—is more than trying & tiring. We
have seen next to nothing of each other through my having been lain up. Full
many a thing have I not had time to ask, & when together only late in the evening, half the thoughts have flown away again. God bless your journey my beloved One, & may it again bring success & encouragement to our troops! You
will see a bit more I hope before you get to the Headquarters & should Niko-
lasha< say any thing to Voeikov in form of a complaint, have it at once stopped
& show that you are the master. Forgive me, precious One, but you know you
are too kind & gentle—sometimes a good loud voice can do wonders, & a severe
look—do my love, be more decided & sure of yourself—you know perfectly well
what is right, & when you do not agree & are right, bring your opinion to the
front & let it weigh against the rest. They must remember more who you are &
that first they must turn to you.
    Your being charms every single one, but I want you to hold them by your
brain & experience. Though N.< is so highly placed, yet you are above him. The
same thing shocked our Friend,< as me too, that N. words his telegrams, answers to governors, etc. in your style—his ought to be more simple & humble &
other things.—You think me a medlesome [sic] bore, but a woman feels & sees
things sometimes clearer than my too humble sweetheart. Humility is God's
greatest gift—but a Sovereign needs to show his will more often. Be more sure
of yourself and go ahead—never fear, you won't say too much. [a]
    Dear old Fredericks, may all go well with him—I feel he goes for your cause as
he alone can allow himself to say anything to N. [A. N.] Grabbe will amuse you
at domino & when N.P.< is with you, I feel always quiet, as he is quite our own
& nearer to you than the rest, & is young & not as heavy as Dmitri Sh.< —That
reminds me, what about Dmitri P.< is he ever going to stick here? Look what a
letter, but it seems I have not talked to you simply for ages (& Ania< imagines
hourly we do)! Perhaps you can find time to go to one of the hospitals at Belostok as very many wounded pass there? And see that Fred.< does not insist
upon accompanying you upon bad roads, Fed.< must keep a severe watch over
him.—How lonely it will be without you, my Sunshine! Tho' I have the children—but lying without work now is difficult & I long to get back to the hospi-
tal<. To-morrow the Dr. wont come, (unless I should feel worse) as he wishes to
be at the funeral of a friend of his.—It's a rest not seeing poor Ania & hearing her
grumbling. You open the windows nicely in my compartment then yours won't

be so stuffy.—Sweetheart, you will find some flowers (kissed by me) upon your writing table, it cheers up the compartment. Goodbye & God bless you, Lovy my very Own dear One—I press you tenderly to my heart & kiss you all over & hold you tight, oh so tight. Ever yr. very own wify. Alix. [b]

No. 219/ Telegram 23. From Luga to Tsarskoe Selo. 4 April 1915. 4.45> 5.21 p.m. To her majesty. Tender thanks [for] dear letter. Have changed beginning of program, am going first to the Stavka, and then to both other places which I wrote down in your note book.[83] Feel lonely. Loving kisses to all. Niki

---

83. Russia's military situation had apparently improved at this time. The Germans were stopped in Poland while Russian armies in the south advanced into most of Galicia and Bukhovina. Italy was about to enter the war; this new front would further vex Austria. (See Footnote 104.) Russia was contemplating an invasion of Hungary which might turn the Magyars against Austria. Flushed with success, Nicholas II decided to inspect the newly gained territory. Rasputin advised the tsar against such premature self-congratulation, as did Alexandra, though she seemed more concerned for her husband's safety than the possibility that his trip might backfire. (See Letters No. 227b and 231.) The emperor visited L'vov on April 9/22 and Peremyshl' on April 10-11/23-24, 1915. Then came a German-Austrian counterattack seven days later. The Russians lost everything they had gained—and more. Nicholas looked foolish for his "triumphal receptions" at Peremyshl' and L'vov.

No. 220/ Her No. 288.   Ts.[arskoe] S[elo]. April 4th 1915.
My Own precious One,
   A Feldjeger leaves this evening at 5, so I must write to you, tho' have no news to give. Thanks sweety for sending Baby< back to rest with me, so I had to keep my tears back, not to grieve him—I got back into bed & he lies for half an hour near me. Then the girls returned.—It is so hard every time—it wrenches at one's heart & leaves such an ache & endless longing—Ortipo [the dog] too feels sad, & jumps up at every sound & watches for you. Yes Deary, when one really loves —one indeed loves! Dreary weather too. I am looking through masses of post-cards from soldiers.— Ania< sent me lovely red roses as goodbye from N.P.< —they stand near my bed & smell too divinely, do thank him for his awfully kind thought & that I was very sad not have been able to say goodbye to him. She gave him a letter for you, as wrote it late & he went straight to church from her. All the girls< have gone to M. & A.'s hospital to the concert arranged by Marie's friend D. [Mariana von Derfel'den]—Baby was going to play near the white tower with D.'s children.—Each child brought me your message—ah lovy mine, I cry now like a big baby—& see your sweet, sad eyes, so full of love before me.—Keep well, my treasure—wify is ever near you in thoughts & prayers. 1000 kisses. God bless & protect you & keep you from all harm. Ever yr. very own old Sunny.
   The temp. is rising again over 37 & I feel my enlarged heart.— Bow to all & tell "the old Man who wont feel old" [Fredericks] that I hope he will behave himself nicely, otherwise I shall appear to him. Sit [a] shorter [time] at table, it is tiring & the air gets too stuffy & see that he smokes less & has his compart-ments well aired when he is not in there. I shall be careful Deary, I promise you—because I really feel still rather rotten & weak. Everything that a tender heart can wish you, I send for my love.

No. 221/ Telegram 56. Stavka> Tsarskoe Selo. 5 April 1915. 10.07> 10.25 a.m. To her majesty. Arrived at 9 o'clock, fine cold day, snowed in the night. Shall let you know later what my plans are. Hopeful [you feel] better and slept well. Tender kisses. Niki

No. 222/ Telegram 20 in Russian. Tsarskoe Selo> Stavka. 5 April 1915. 10.10> 10.45 a.m. To his majesty. Was happy to receive telegram yesterday. Marvellous weather, slept well, feel wonderful, in evening my temperature fell again. Lie a bit on the couch during day. Sad, empty—we all kiss [you] warmly. God keep you. Alix

No. 223/ Her No. 289.   Ts.[arskoe] S[elo]. April 5th 1915.
My own huzy darling,
    Just got your telegram. This is wonderful. You left at 2 & arrived at 9. When you leave at 10 you reach there only at 12! Bright, sunny weather, I hear the birdies chirping away. Wonder why you changed your plans.—The girls< have just gone to church; baby< moves the arms better, tho' water in the elboes [sic] still he says. Yesterday he went with Vl. Nik.< to Ania<, & she was mad with joy, he goes again to-day to see Rodionov & Kozhevnikov. Now she has Vl. Nik. to show how to electrify her leg—every day a new Doctor. [Daughters] Tatiana & Anastasia were there in the day & found our Friend< with her. He said the old story that she cries & sorrows as gets so few caresses. So Tatiana was much surprised & He answered that she receives many, only to her they seem few. Her humour seems not famous (the chief mourner) & notes cold, so mine too.—
    I did sleep alright [sic], as so awfully tired—but feel the same so far. Yesterday again 37.3, this morning 36.7, & morning's headache—the empty cushion beside me makes me, oh so sad! Dear sweet One, how is all arranging itself? You will let me have telegrams through fat Orloff< when there are news, won't you?—Spent the evening lying quietly & the girls each reading a book. [Daughters] Olga & Tatiana went for ½ an hour to the hospital to see how all were.—I hear Shot barking before the house.—I send you your Image [icon] from our Friend of St. John the Warrior, wh. I forgot to give yesterday morning. I have been rereading what our Friend wrote when he was at Constantinople, it is doubly interesting now—quite short impressions.[84] Oh, what a day when mass will again be served at St. Sophie. Only give orders that nothing should be destroyed or spoiled belonging to the mahomedans [sic], they can use all again for their religion, as we are Christians & not barbarians, thank God! How one would love to be there at such a moment! The amount of churches everywhere used or destroyed by the Turks is awful—because the Greeks were not worthy to officiate & have such temples. May the Orthodox Church be more worthy now & be purified again. This war can mean so colossaly much in the moral regeneration of our Country & Church—only to find the men to fulfill all your orders & to help you, in all your immense tasks! [a]
    Here I am back again—lay two hours on the sopha, had M-me. Zizi< half an hour with petitions—feel rottenly weak & tired & she did not approve of my

looks.—My dear, Ania has been wheeled by Zhuk [a servant] as far as Voeikov's< house, Dr. Korenev near her & was not a bit tired—now to-morrow she wants to come to me! Oh dear, & I was so glad that for a long time we should not have her in the house, I am selfish after 9 years, & want you to my-self at last & this means, she is preparing to invade upon us often when you re-turn or she will beg to be wheeled in the garden, as the park is shut (so as to meet you) & I wont be there to disturb. Shall give Putyatin< the order to let her in to the big park, her chair wont spoil the roads.—I should never have ventured out—what a sight! Covered by a shuba [fur coat] & shawl on her head—I said better a tennis cap & her hair plaited tidily will strike less! The man [Dr. Ko-renev] is needed in the Fed[orov] hospital & she uses him constantly. I told her to go to Znamenia< before coming to me—I foresee lots of bother with her; all hysteria! Pretends to faint when one pushes the bed, but can be banged about in the streets in a chair.

The children< went out before one, & I shant see them till 5 for quite short, then they go off to Ania to see our officers, Baby after his dinner. I was up fr. 1-3.—Fancy your having had snow in the night! Sweetest treasure—how I miss you! Long & lonely days—so when head aches less copy out things of our friends, & then the time passes quicker. Please give my love to N.P.< & [A. N.] Grabbe. What a lot of prisoners we have taken again! Now this must go.—Goodbye, Nicky love, I bless & kiss you over & over again with all the tenderness of wh. I am capable. Ever yr. very own old <u>Wify</u>. [b]

84. Alexandra refers to a book just published under Rasputin's name, a collection of pious reflec-tions based on his pilgrimage to Jerusalem during Lent 1911. Alexandra paid a large sum of money to have this book printed in a lavish edition. (See Fuhrmann, *Rasputin*, pp. 67-70) Nicholas wanted plans for his trip to Galicia kept secret, but apparently Alexandra told Rasputin *via* Vyrubova so that Rasputin could pray for the undertaking. Alexandra committed a similar indiscretion in November 1915 (see Letter No. 573f) so that Rasputin could pray for the success of that trip.

No. 224/ Telegram 65. Stavka> Tsarskoe Selo. 5 April 1915. 6.01> 6.20 p.m. To her majesty. Fondest thanks for dear letter with violet and telegram. Every-thing good. Remain here a few days, shall explain by letter my plans. Loving kisses. Niki

---

No. 225/ His No. 170.   Stavka. April 5th 1915.
My own beloved Sunny,

I thank you from the depth of my loving old heart for your two sweet letters, the telegram & lilies, that touched me so! I felt very sad & low, leaving you not quite well yet & was in that mood until I went to bed. Already on my way here, Voeikov informed me that it would be better to turn off from Vilno, as the Ger-man aeroplanes were dropping bombs on the line & trains [were] passing Be-lostok and that Ge[neral] Alekseev was not at Sedlets! So we arrived here this morning at 9 o'clock. I had a long talk with N.,< then the normal doklad [re-port], & church. He proposed me soon to go to Lvov & Peremyshl', as later some measures will have to be introduced in Galicia. The same Bobrinsky told me a few days ago. N. will accompany me, as it will be my first visit of a con-quered country. Naturally it must be quite short this time as the railway there is

overladen by traffic. After that I shall see Ivanov & Alekseev and then continue ·
my trip to the south. The dates I cannot fix yet, but of course shall always let
you know in time!

It is rather interesting or out of the common to spend a few days like that.
Petiusha< & Petia< are here, both well. Old Fredericksy just now has his talk
with N. At dinner I will be able to judge by their expressions how that talk went
off. I took a good walk with my people, the wind blew hard, but the sun very
warm. The snow that fell this night has disappeared, little birds sang galily [sic]
in the wood and my Life Guard Cossacks were practising [sic] with their machine-guns, making a frightful row. I came up to them on my way home and
watched them. Now, lovy mine, I must end. The man leaves directly at 6.30. I
kiss you my darling Wify & the children very tenderly & remain ever your own
devoted huzy Nicky. [P.S.] God bless you!

No. 226/ Telegram 23. Tsarskoe Selo> Stavka. 6 April 1915. 10.49> 11.47
a.m. To his majesty. Thank you heartily for dear telegrams. Splendid, sunny day.
Slept poorly, still completely weak. Children all well. [We] tenderly embrace
and kiss [you]. Just received your precious letter, thank you heartily. Alix

No. 227/ Her No. 290.   Ts.[arskoe] S[elo]. April 6th 1915.
My own beloved Darling,

Ever such tender thanks for yr. precious letter, I just received. It is such an
intense joy to hear from you, Sweetheart & comfort, as I miss you awfully!—So
that is why you did not travel as intended! But the idea of [you going to]
L.[vov] & P.[eremyshl'] already now, makes me anxious, is it not too soon, as
all the spirits are not much for Russia—in the country, yes, but not at L.[,] I
fear.[83]— Well, I shall ask our Friend< to quite particularly pray for you
there—but, forgive my saying so—its not for N.< to accompany you—you must be
the chief one, the first time you go. You find me an old goose, no doubt, but if
others wont think of such things, I must. He must remain & work as
usual—really don't take him, as the hate against him must be great there & to see
you alone will rejoice those hearts that go out to you in love & gratitude.—

Such sunshine! The little girlies< drove between their lessons— & I am going
to have Ania's< visit!! The Dr. lets me get up more, only to lie when the temp.
rises, heart nearly normal, but feel horribly weak yet, & my voice like
Miechens< when she is tired.—One just brought me an endless letter fr. the
Countess Hohenfelsen<—I send it to you to read through in a free moment, &
then return it to me. Only speak to Fredericksy about it. Certainly not on my
namesday [sic] or birthday as she wishes—but all can be alright [sic] in her wish,
excepting the "Princess", that is vulgar to ask for. You see it will sound well
when one announces them together, almost as V. K. [Velikaya Knyaginya, i.e.,
grand princess]. Only what reason to Misha< later [i.e., what precedent will this
establish if Misha presses a similar case later?—see Footnote 82]—both had children before, whilst married to another man, tho' no, Misha's wife was already
divorced. And she forgets this eldest son—if one acknowledges the marriage fr.
the year 1904, this Son, clear to all, was an illegal child—for them I don't mind,
let them openly carry their sin—but the boy? You speak it over with the old man
[Fredericks], those things he understands, & tell him what yr. Mamma said

when you mentioned it to her. Now perhaps people will pay less attention.—My love to N.P.< & tell him the roses are still quite fresh.— [a]

Here I am back into bed again, was 3 hours on the sopha—so stupidly weak & tired. Well, Ania came, & she has invited herself to luncheon one of these days. Looks very well, but did not seem so overjoyed to see me, nor that had not seen me for a week, no complaint, thank goodness—but those hard eyes again wh., she so often has now.—The Children< are out, Baby's< arms are better, so he could write to you Sweetheart.—Mary Wassiltshikov's son-in-law Shcherbatov (ex naval officer) died suddenly yesterday. He had recovered from typhoid & was taking tea with his wife, nice Sonia, when suddenly died from a failure of the heart—poor young widow! You remember her last baby was born the day of Ducky's< gardenparty for the English naval officers—the grandmother came straight there. I wonder how Fr.[ederick's] conversation with N.< went off. Our Friend is glad for the old man's sake that he went, as it gave such intense pleasure, & perhaps its the last time he can accompany you on such a journey—well, as long as he is prudent.— Have been choosing, as yearly, summer stuffs for my ladies & the maids & housemaids.—Au fond, our Friend wld. have found it better you had gone after the war to the conquered country, I only just mention this like that.—The man is waiting for my letter.— Beloved Nicky, my very, very own treasure, I bless & cover yr. sweet face & lovely big eyes with the tenderest of kisses, ever yr. very own   Sunny. [b]

No. 228/ Telegram 84. Stavka> Tsarskoe Selo. 6 April 1915. 2.16> 2.46 p.m. To her majesty. Tender thanks for dear letter and telegram, also thank [daughter] Marie. Nothing particular as news. Saw Engalychev. Weather much better and warmer. Fondest kisses. Niki

---

No. 229/ His No. 171.   Stavka. April 6th 1915.
My own precious Sunny,

So many loving thanks for your sweet letter, that came already in the morning. Yes, it is curious—leaving at 2 o'clock by the Warsaw line, one arrives here at 9 o'clock in the morning; whereas, leaving at 10 o'clock in the morning one gets here only at about 12 by the Vindavo-Rybinsky railway, which is a bad line and the trains move slower on it. Yesterday, after long deliberations, it has been decided that we leave the Stavka on Wednesday night & arrive at the old frontier station of Brody on Thursday morning. From there, N.<, I and some of our suite go by motor to Lvov, & the rest with Fred.< going by train. Like that we will follow the road taken in August by our Third Army, & see the battlefields. Spend the night at Lvov & on Friday go by rail through Sambor, where Brusilov is, to Peremyshl'.[83]—Shall spend the night there & come back the same route. I will be able to catch up somewhere between those two places the 3rd Caucasian Corps, which is being concentrated in reserve. Fancy what a joy if that really happens! All these changes will add one more day to my entire trip, wh. I hope my Wify will not mind too much!

I am glad to see Olga dear [my sister]. Today the weather is really very fine & warm. We took a good walk across the fields & got into the middle of a stinking bog. There were funny scenes that happened, especially when Grabbe, with his petticoats tugged up, was trying his best to get out of the deep dirt! He came back in a nice state as you can imagine. Now my love bird I must end, the messenger has to leave. We are all going to the cinematograph. God bless you & the dear children! Ever my beloved one your own huzy Niki.

No. 230/ Telegram 27. Tsarskoe Selo> Stavka. 7 April 1915. 10.26> 11.15 a.m. To his majesty. Thank you heartily for priceless letter. Feel the same. Weather today grey. I embrace and kiss [you]. Alix

---

No. 231/ Her No. 291.   Tsarskoe Selo. April 7th 1915.
My very own sweet One,
   Every possible tender wish for to-morrow. The first time in 21 years we dont spend this anniversary[85] together.—How vividly one remembers all! Ah my beloved Boy, what happiness & love you have given me all these years—God verily richly blessed our married life. For all your wify thanks you from the depths of her loving heart. May God Almighty make me a worthy helpmate of yours, my own sweet treasure, my sunshine.   Sunbeam's< Father!— Tudels< just brought me your dear letter, & I thank you for it with all my heart—such joy when I receive it, & many a time it is reread. I can imagine what a funny sight [A. N.] Grabbe sticking in the bogg [sic], must have been; those walks I am sure do all no end of good.—How interesting all you are going to do! When A.[nia]< told Him [Rasputin] in secret, because I want His special prayers for you,[74] he curiously enough said the same as me; that on the whole it does not please Him[. The following quote is in Russian.] "God will help; but it is (too early) to go now, he will not observe anything, will not see his people, it is interesting, but better after the war."—
   [Rasputin d]oes not like N.< going with you, finds everywhere better alone—& to this end I fully agree. Well now all is settled, I hope it will be a success, & especially that you will see all the troops you hope to, it will be a joy to you, & recompense to them. God bless & guard this voyage of yours.[84] Probably you will see both Xenia< & [your other sister] Olga & Sandro<. In case you see a sister [nurse] all in black anywhere, its M-me. Gartwig (von Wiesen)—she is at the head of my stores< & often at the station.—I am feeling much the same, 37.2 [degrees temperature] in the evening, 36.6 this morning—a little redness is still there.—I am glad you send Fred.< by rail to L[vov].—Grey, rainy morning rather.— My letters are so dull, have only report[s] to read & that is all, seeing people tires me too much, tho' I long for a glimpse of Koj.<, Rod.< & Kubl.< who will be at Anias from 3-4, they leave this evening for O. Tell Fred.< I send him my love & beg of him to be very good & prudent, & to remember he is no longer a wild young cornet!—I send you some lilies of the valley, I kissed, & wh. are to perfume yr. little compartment. The note for Olga yr. man can send her at Lvov, as you wont have time to think about it. I saw Rod.< & Kubl.< both look well & brown—longing I think to go with the Plastuny special force[75] & not only for the end (they are to be spared one says) but this they did not tell me. Now all & Baby< take tea at Anias. She came this morning. My blessings, tenderest prayers suround [sic] you. 1000 of kisses. Ever yr. old Wify.   [P.S.] Of course I understand if you are a day or two later back [home]. You also may like a fly

[quick trip] to Livadia!—All the children kiss you—they & I send love to N.P.<—Have sent Ropsha strawberries.

No. 232/ Telegram 112. Stavka> Tsarskoe Selo. 7 April 1915. 7.20> 7.50 p.m. To her majesty. Fondest thanks [for] dear letter, also [daughter] Olga and [son] Aleksei. Heavenly weather. Very occupied [in the] morning. Motored to our wood, lovely air. Hope [you] are better. Tender love. Niki

No. 233/ His No. 172.   Stavka. April 7th 1915.
My own beloved Sunny,
     I thank you heartily for your dear letter & send you the Countess's letter back. I think there is no difficulty about that question—a little goodwill on our side and the thing shall be done, and we shall have one worry less in life. I will certainly speak about it with the old man [Fredericks]. Today my morning was a busy one—after the report I received Grunwald, who comes fr Vilno where he visited all the hospitals, and then Engalychev. Also our Vielopolsky [see No. 1255], who looks like a king who has lost his kingdom! They all lunched. N.< was receiving the Belgian Mission & entertained them in his train. Darling mine, I am not of your opinion that N. ought to remain here when I go to Galacia. On the contrary, just because it is a conquered province that the Commander in Chief must accompany me. I think that all my people find this right. He accompanies me not I in his suite. As I wrote yesterday, I hope to see the 2nd Caucasian Corps near Sambor, and to be not far away from the 8th Army of Brusilov. Except in the Caucasus, last year, I have not had the chance of being near the troops which have been victorious fr. the very beginning of the war! Today we motored along the beautiful road we know & went further on in a lovely wood. It was simply hot & we found some flowers—This is one of them!—Tomorrow is our engagement day,[85] how many peaceful remembrances! God bless you, my treasure, & the children & thank [our children] Olga and Aleksei for their letters. I kiss you all tenderly, & remain ever your own old huzy   Nicky. [P.S.] Give A.[nia]< my love.

85. Nicholas and Alexandra were engaged at Coburg on April 8/21, 1894. Three years later, while a prisoner in Tobol'sk, Nicholas again noted this anniversary in his diary. (Vulliamy, p. 45n)

No. 234/ Telegram 29. Tsarskoe Selo> Stavka. 8 April 1915. 10.02> 10.59 a.m. To his majesty. My tenderest thoughts and feelings of deepest devotion are with you on this dear anniversary. Am sad we will not spend it together. Bright, sunny day. Slept well, still very weak. Still redness in throat, temperature lower. Lay on sopha four hours last evening. All six< tenderly kiss [you]. Alix

No. 235/ Telegram 32. Tsarskoe Selo> Stavka. 8 April 1915. 10.35> 11.45 a.m. To his majesty. How to thank you for dear letter and wonderful little cross! This completely unexpected surprise touched me terribly. All children healthy. Sonia< too. First time was able to lie on balcony since it is very warm. All embrace [you]. With you in thoughts. Greetings to all. Alix

No. 236/ Her No. 292.   Tsarskoe Selo. April 8th 1915.
My very own beloved Husband,

Tenderly do my prayers & grateful thoughts full of very deepest love linger around you this dear anniversary![85] How the years go by! 21 years already! You know I have kept the grey princesse dress I wore that morning? And shall wear yr. dear brooch. Dear me, how much we have lived through together in these years—heavy trials everywhere, but at home in our nest, bright sunshine! I send you in remembrance an Image [Icon] of St. Simeon of V.—leave it for always as a guardian angel in your compartment—you will like the smell of the wood.—Such a sunny day!—Poor M-me. Vil'chkovsky< is going to have her apendicitis [sic] cut out—she lies in our little room, where Ania< was the first night. They say she looks so clean & apetising [sic] in white & lace with pretty ribbons in jacket & hair—[Kirim Bek] Navruzov who is there again—comes & looks after her, writes down her temp. & is most touching with her—am in despair not to be with her.—Lovy mine, how can I thank you enough for that ideally lovely cross? You do spoil me, I never for a second imagined you would think of giving me anything. How lovely it is! Shall wear it to-day—just what I like, & this one we had not seen. And yr. note & the dear letter—all came together after the Dr. He lets me go on the balkony [sic], so I shall get Ania to come out there.—I see now why you take N.< with you, thanks for explaining deary. The sweet flower has gone into my gospel—we used to pick those flowers in spring on the meadow at Wolfsgarten, before the big house always.—Am sure you will all return nicely bronzed.—My throat is almost in order, heart still not yet quite normal, tho' I take my drops & keep so quiet. [a]

I hear the Churchbells ring, & long to go to Znamenia< & pray there for you—well my candle burns here too for you, my very own treasure. I am finishing my letter to you on the sopha. The big girls< are in town, the little ones< walked, then went to their hospital & now have lessons, Baby< is in the garden. I lay for ¾ of an hour on the balkony [sic]—quite strange to be out, as it happens so rarely I get into the fresh air. The little birdies were singing away— all nature awakening & praising the Lord! Doubly it makes one feel the misery of war & bloodshed—but as after winter cometh summer, so after suffering & strife, may peace & consolation find their place in this world & all hatred cease & our beloved country develop into beauty in every sense of the word. It is a new birth—a new beginning, a "Läuterung" & cleansing of minds and souls— only to lead them aright and guide them straight. So much to do, may all work bravely hand in hand, helping instead of hindering work for one great cause & not for personal success & fame.

Just got your dear telegram, for wh. a tender kiss.—Mme Vil'chkovsky's operation went off alright [sic].—My stupid temp. is now already 37.1, but I think that does not matter.—I wear your cross on my grey teagown & it looks too lovely—yr. dear brooch of 21 years ago I have also got on.—Sweet treasure I must end now. God bless & guard you on yr. journey. You will no doubt receive this letter in Lvov. Give my love to [your sisters] Xenia<, Olga & Sandro<. I send you a wee photo I took of agooweeone< on board last year. A fond blessing & thousands of very tenderest kisses, ever, Nicky sweet, yr. own old <u>Wify</u>. [b]

No. 237/ Telegram 139. Stavka> Tsarskoe Selo. 8 April 1915. 2.35> 3.45 p.m. To her majesty. Tender thanks [for] letter, telegrams, lilies. In prayers and thoughts more than ever with you. Lovely warm day. Hope [you] feel better. Loving kisses to you and children. Niki

No. 238/ His No. 173.   Stavka. April 8th 1915.
My own precious Darling,
   Fondest loving thanks for your dear letter so full of sweet words & for two telegrams. Have not also I thought of & of this day 21 years ago?[85] I wish you health & everything that a deeply loving heart can wish, and thank you on my knees for all your love, affection, friendship & patience you have shown these long years of our married life! The weather today reminds of that day at Co-burg—It is sad not to be together! Nobody knew it was our engagement day—curious how people quickly forgot—tho' it means nothing to them. Krivoshein has arrived to explain to N.< before me different ideas about meas-ures that might be taken in order to reward officers and men, leaving the army at the end of the war; those who have distinguished themselves, who are mutilated & in general all the wounded! Many good ideas wh[ich] I shall explain to you at home. I forgot their families [i.e., family names] of course. Today I had no time to write to you before the messenger's departure, as I had to hurry with my nor-mal papers. I shall send this letter to-morrow from the border station Brody. I am afraid I won't have time to write from Galicia, but shall do so from the south later. In the afternoon I motored along our old road till a small town Slonim in the province of Grodno. It was simply extraordinarily warm and lovely the smell of the pine forest—one felt soft & weak, etc! I send you Ella's< telegram in cipher—cannot imagine what she wants? [P.S.] Brody, April 9th. Here I am on ex-Austrian soil. Lovely hot weather. Had the report in N.'s train next to mine & after lunch leave for Lvov by motor. God bless my precious Sunny. I kiss you and the children very very tenderly! Ever your very own huzy Nicky

No. 239/ Telegram 39. Tsarskoe Selo> Lvov. 9 April 1915. 11.06 a.m.> 1.05 p.m. To his majesty. My tender thoughts and prayers accompany you. And blessings upon the gentlemen with you! Spent the day on the balcony, tempera-ture fell last night, heart still greatly enlarged. Morning was clear, now overcast. I kiss [you] tenderly. Greetings to [your] sisters. Children well. Alix

No. 240/ Telegram 4 in Russian. Brody> Tsarskoe Selo. 9 April 1915. 11.55 a.m.> 1.05 p.m. To her majesty. Arrived at 10 o'clock, weather marvellous. Leaving for Lvov at 1 o'clock. Sent letter from here. Tenderly embrace [you]. Niki

No. 241/ Her No. 293.   Ts.[arskoe] S[elo]. April 9th 1915.
My own Sweetheart,
   Such a sunny morning again. Slept badly, heart more enlarged. Yesterday at 6 temp. 37.3, at 11—37.2. This morning 36.5;—such an infection generally acts upon a not strong heart, & as mine was again so tired, of course I feel it more.

Botkin turned up to my surprise, to-morrow [Dr.] Sirotinin comes for the last time.—I send you a French letter from Aleksei, & one from Anastasia.—I wore yr. lovely cross the evening in bed still.—My thoughts are the whole time with you, & I keep wondering what you are doing & how getting along. What an interesting journey. Hope somebody will photograph. Had news fr. my flying stores train No. 5, that Brusilov inspected it, & was very contended with the help it gives—they bring out presents, medicaments [sic], linnen [sic], boots, & return with wounded. The bigger ones have the kitchen & Priest;—all this is thanks to little [N. K. von] Mekk.—

It grew so dark & now there has been a good downpour & more to follow, so I wont go on the balkony [sic] & its windy besides— Ania< still intends coming, tho' I strongly advised her not to—why get wet & have Juk [Zhuk, a servant] soaked, (only so as to come to me) its selfish & foolish, she might as well be a day without seeing me, but she wants more, says an hour is too little already. But I want little at a time, as get so tired still.—Fond thanks for yr. letter from Brody. How glad I am you have fine weather. Our Friend< blesses your journey.—I keep thinking of you the whole time. It got fine this afternoon, but I was too tired to go out. Received Khlebnikov, my exlancer who has civil service in the Crimea because of his health, but whom I helped to get into the regiment as soon as the war began (he looks & feels flourishing)— told me about the lost platoon of the 6-th squadron. 10 men ran away & got back to the regiment after wandering about in the forests & dressed as peasants. Then Apraksin came, whom I had not seen for four months.—Ania sat for an hour. Now she has our Friend & the girls<, after walking & driving have gone to the big Palace; Baby< is in the garden. I wear your ideal cross. God's blessing be upon you, guard & guide you. Very fondest kisses fr. yr. very own <u>Wify</u>. [P.S.] My love to the old man [Fredericks] & to N.P.< & give him news of my health.—Just now 37.1 again.

No. 242/ Telegram 5. Lvov at the headquarters of the Governor General> Tsarskoe Selo. 9 April 1915. 8.27 p.m.> 9.31 p.m. To her majesty. Thanks for news. Am full of deepest impressions, interesting road, lots of graves of our soldiers here. Touching reception. Saw [my sisters] Xenia and Olga in her hospital. Summer weather. Tender kisses. Niki

No. 243/ Telegram 42. Tsarskoe Selo> Sambor. 10 April 1915. 10.34> 11.20 a.m. Active Army. To his imperial majesty. Thank you warmly for dear telegram. I can imagine how keenly interesting your trip must be. God bless and keep you! [My] health still not at all impressive. Trying to lie out on balcony. I embrace [you], happy you are satisfied. All six of us kiss you. Alix

No. 244/ Her No. 294.   Ts.[arskoe] S[elo]. April 10th 1915.
My very own Treasure,

I wonder when and where this letter will reach you. Such fond thanks for yesterday evening's telegram. Indeed your journey must be very interesting—& so emotioning seeing all those dear graves of our brave heroes. Wont you just have a lot to tell us upon your return! Difficult writing yr. diary, I am sure, when there are so many different impressions. How happy Olga [your] dear [sister] will be to see you—Xenia< wired upon yr. arrival so kindly.—Wonder whether you took Shavel'sky with you.—Ania< gave over what you telegraphed to our Friend<, He blesses you & is so glad you are happy.—This morning the weather is going to be finer, I think, then can lie out. Heart still enlarged, temp. rose to 37.2—now 36.5, & still so weak, they are going to give me iron to take.—Gr.< is rather disturbed about the "meat" stories, the merchants wont lessen the price tho' the government wished it, & there has been a sort of meatstrike one says. One of the ministers he thought, ought to send for a few of the chief merchants & explain it to them, that it is wrong at such a grave moment, during war to highten [sic] the prizes [prices], & make them feel ashamed of themselves. Have read through the papers & found nothing of interest.—[Daughter] Marie is going to the cemetry [sic] to lay flowers on poor Grabovoy's [Grobov's] grave, 40 days to-day! So the time flies by.—M-me. Vil'chkov.< is getting on nicely. I saw Aleinikov (& wife) 5 months he lay in the big palace<—he longs to continue serving, only his arm aches still so (right to the top the right one is off) & he has to take mudbaths. Then Kobiev who goes back to his regiment, & then Grunwald with messages fr. you, Sweetheart. I lay half an hour on the balkony [sic], quite mild.— Now Ania is coming, so goodbye & God bless you! I cover yr. sweet face with tenderest kisses, Nicky love, & remain ever yr. very own Sunny.

No. 245/ Telegram 490 in Russian. Telegraph Office 152> Tsarskoe Selo. 10 April 1915. 8.25 p.m.> 9.39 p.m. To her majesty. Arrived safely in Khyrov via Sambor. Saw wonderful Caucasian Corps. Area delightful. Weather summerlike. Deepest and most joyful impressions. Warmly embrace [you]. Niki

No. 246/ Telegram 510 in Russian. Telegraph Office 152> Tsarskoe Selo. 11 April 1915. To her majesty. Last night received ikon, letter and photograph. Very grateful. Going to inspect fortifications. After lunch back to Lvov, from there in evening to Brody. Weather splendid. Everything budding. Tenderly embrace [you]. Niki

No. 247/ Telegram 45. Tsarskoe Selo> Przemysl. 11 April 1915. 10.50> 11.20 a.m. To his majesty. Gladdened by telegram. Happy all goes well. Grey weather. [My] health not at all impressive. Children healthy. We tenderly embrace [you]. God keep you. Alix

No. 248/ Her No. 295.   Ts.[arskoe] S[elo]. April 11th 1915.
My very own Darling,
   Your dear telegram yesterday made us all so happy.—Thank God, that you have such beautiful impressions—that you could see the Caucas.[ian] corps & that summer weather blesses your journey. —In the papers I read Fred.< short telegram fr. Lvov, telling about the Cathedral, peasants etc. dinner, and nomination of [G. A.] Bobr.[rinsky]. into yr. suite—what great historical moments. Our

Friend< is delighted and bless you.—Now I have read in the Novoe Vremia [newspaper *New Times*] all about you, & feel so touched & proud for my Sweetheart. And your few words on the balkony [sic]—just the thing! God bless & unite in the fully deep, historical & religious sense of the word, these Slavonic Countries to their old Mother Russia! All comes in its right time & now we are strong enough to uphold them, before we should not have been able to. Nevertheless we must in the "interior" become yet stronger & more united in every way, so as to govern stronger & with more authority.—Wont E.[mperor] N.[icholas] I be glad! He sees his greatgrandson reconquering those provinces of the long bygone—& the revenge for Austria's treachery towards him. And you have personally conquered thousands of hearts. I feel, by your sweet, gentle, humble being & shining, pure eyes—each conquers with what God endows him—each in his way. God bless yr. journey on! I am sure it will revive the strength of our troops—if they need this. I am glad [your sisters] Xenia< & Olga saw this great moment!—How nice you went to Olga's hospital—a recompense for her infatigable [sic] work!—[a]

This moment got yr. wire fr. Perem.[yshl'] & plans for to-day—& now yr. sweet letter fr. the 8-th, for wh. 1000 of tender thanks; such joy to get a letter from you, love them so!!—Here is Ella's< telegram unciphered; I return it, in case you wish to mention anything about it, or find out from the railway officials, whether true.—Had masses of reports to read through, & now must get up & finish later on.—I received an awfully touching telegram from Babys' Georgian regiment Akhmisury [Otkhmezuri] arrived back & told them he had seen you, & gave over our messages—& thanking for my looking after their officers etc.— Mme Zizi< came after luncheon with papers—then my Siberian Geleznoi [P. V. Zheleznykh] to say goodbye. Then I lay on the balkony ¾ of an hour, & the eldest sister (Liubusha) [Lyubushchina, the senior nurse] of the big Palace<, sat with me. Ania< came from 12-1 as usual.—My train No. 66 has just been to Brody to fetch wounded —lots of men, over 400, but only two officers.—Goodbye Lovy mine—I do so wonder where you are going to see Ivanov and Alekseev< & can you get at them this time.—Goodbye & God bless and keep you. Very tenderest kisses fr. yr. very own old   Wify. [P.S.] The Children all kiss you, & with me send love to the old man [Fredericks] & N.P.<— [b]

No. 249/ Her. No. 296   Ts.[arskoe] S[elo]. April 12th 1915.
Beloved One,

I wonder where you are? Xenia< wired that you had dined together before leaving. Must have a look at the papers. Till now I go to bed at 6 & dont get up any more, & am up from 12-6.—The Children< have gone to Church. Baby's< foot is not quite the thing, so he is carried & drives, but does not suffer—he played "Colorito" on my bed this morning before his walk.—The weather is very sunny, tho' at times dark clouds hide all—hope to lie out again. Take lots of iron & arsenic & heartdrops & feel a little stronger now at last.—We saw dear little Madame Purtseladze & her adorable baby boy yesterday—brave little soul!—She gets letters fr. him [her husband], but does not know whether he is severely wounded & how treated, that he dare not write—but thank God he is alive.—2 hours I lay on the balkony [sic], & Ania< kept me company—Baby drove about in his motor & then in a little carriage. I received my [D. M.] Knyazhevich<, who intends going back to the lancers—over the Headquarter[s]—but poor man doubts he can continue commanding the regiment, as fears he cannot ride on account of his kidneys—if so, he will return & seek some other service, as finds it dishonest towards the regiment.—Precious mine, quite spring, so lovely.—I bless you & kiss you without end from the full depth of my great love. Goodbye Sweetheart. Ever yr. very own old   Sunny. [P.S.] About 16 lancers have es-caped—2 got on German officers['] horses & flew back—they had been well treated. Many messages to the old man [Fredericks], the little Admiral<, [A. N.] Grabbe & N.P.<—The Children all kiss you tenderly.—Miss you sorely, precious Sunshine of our little home!—Is it true Mdivani receives another nomination, & who is his successor?—

No. 250/ Telegram 12. Brody> Tsarskoe Selo. 12 April 1915. 1.55> 5.15 p.m. To her majesty. On arriving here last night found two dear letters. Tender thanks. Leaving directly for the south under brightest impressions. Summer weather. Loving kisses. Niki

No. 251/ Telegram 51. Tsarskoe Selo> Krasilov. 12 April 1915. 5.28> 7.12 p.m. To his majesty. Wonderful weather. Lay two hours on balcony. Children sledged and then visited three hospitals. Aleksei drove around in his car. Feel better. God keep you. Alix.

No. 252/ His No. 174.   The New Imperial Train. Proskurov.
My own precious Darling,   April 12th 1915.
    First of all tenderest thanks for two dear letters and image [Icon] of St. Simeon Verkh.[otur'e] & Baby's photo wh. alas! I dropped out of the box & smashed the glass [in which the photographs were framed]. That happened at Przemysl! Well—how difficult it is to describe quickly all I have seen or rather lived through during the last three days! April 9th I arrived in Brody across the old frontier. N.< was already there with his staff. After the report I finished my last letter & papers, lunched and started by with N. It was hot & windy, our own dust covering us like a white sheet; you cannot imagine what we looked like. Stopped and got out twice to look at the position of our troops and those of the Austrians during the first great battles in August last year. Lots of crosses on the common [fraternal] graves & on solitary ones. Astonishing what long marches our army did then fighting every day! At about 5.30 having cleaned ourselves a bit—[G. A.] Bobrinsky met us on a hill and we drove down straight into Lvov. Very pretty town, reminds one in smell of Varsovie [Warsaw], lots of gardens and monuments, full of troops and Russians! The first thing I did was go to an enormous riding school, which has been converted into our church, and can hold 10,000 men; there behind a guard of honor I saw my two sisters [Xenia and Olga]. Then I drove to Olga's hospital, not many wounded now, saw Tat. Andr. [Gromova] and other acquaintances from Rovno, doctors, sisters [i.e., nurses], and so forth—and just before sunset arrived to the Gov[ernor]-Gen[eral's] palace. A squadron of my Life Guard Cossacks was drawn up in front. Bobrinsky put

me into one of his rooms, not pretty and not comfortable—a sort of heavy station-like style with no door, except at the bedroom. I slept in old Franz Joseph's bed if you please. [a]

April 10th I left Lvov by rail in Austrian carriages and arrived at Sambor at 1 o['clock]; was met by Brusilov & to my enormous surprise, by the honor guard of my splendid rifles of the 16th Odessa Regiment. The company was commanded by my friend the feldfebel, as all the officers were wounded and the captain killed. When they marched past the band played the march we all liked so much in Livadia, and I could not keep my tears back. Drove to Brusilov's house; he presented the whole of his Staff to me, and then we lunched. After that back to the train and at 4 o. arrived at Kharkov so prettily situated among the hills. There, on a large field, was drawn up the mass of troops of the 3rd Caucasian Corps. Such splendid regiments, my Shirvantsi & Alekseev's Salyantsi among them. I recognised [sic] only one officer and one ensign [petty officer]. They had only arrived a day or two before from Osovets & were pleased to see the hills and be in a warmer climate. I walked along the three long lines on a ploughed field & nearly fell several times, it was very uneven & [I] had to think of Dmitry! As there was little time left, I passed the [remaining] troops in a motor to thank them for their fine service. We were awfully tossed about N and I. I got back to the train completely hoarse, but so pleased & happy to have seen them. An hour later we arrived in Przemysl. [b]

A small town with narrow streets and grey dull houses, full of troops and of Orenburg Cossacks. N. and I and some of the gentlemen [of the suite] lived in a small house, rather clean, whose owner fled before the fall. The place is surrounded by hills & looks very pretty. We dined in the garrison club where everything remained untouched. Slept badly. April 11th got up early and drove out with all the lot of us to look at the fortifications. Very interesting colossal works & awfully well fortified, not an inch of earth remained untouched. Such pretty views fr the forts, all covered with grass and fresh flowers. I send you one I dug up with [A. N.] Grabbe's dagger. At 12 returned to town, lunched in the club & drove by another road to Lvov through Radymno & Yavorov, again along battlefields in September. The weather was beautiful the whole time. Xenia and Olga came to me before dinner. Left Lvov at 9.30 by rail & arrived at Brody at 12.30 in the night. Got there into our own train. Today got up late, had the usual report & left N. at 2. Forgive me for this short dry account but have no time left. God bless you, my beloved Sunny, and the children. I kiss you all tenderly. Ever your own old huzy Nicky. [c]

No. 253/ Telegram 2194 in Russian. Proskurov> Tsarskoe Selo. 13 April 1915. 9.31> 10.15 a.m. To her majesty. Thank you for telegram. Glad your health is better. Going now to Kamenets-Podolsk for inspection of Trans-Amur border guards. Weather is remarkable. To-morrow Odessa. Tenderly embrace [you]. Niki

---

No. 254/ Telegram 53 in Russian. Tsarskoe Selo> Kamenets- Podolsk. 13 April 1915. 11.20 a.m.> 12.01 p.m. From my soul I thank you for news. Terribly glad you are seeing glorious Trans-Amur border guards. Wonderful weather.

Children< eating upstairs. I will be on balcony. Health improving, more strength. We embrace [you] warmly. God bless you. Alix.

No. 255/ Her No. 297.   Tsarskoe Selo. April 13th 1915.
My very own Life,
   Such a glorious, sunny morning! Yesterday I lay two hours out—shall lie out at 12 & 1 think after luncheon again.—The heart is not enlarged, the air & medicins [sic] are helping & I decidedly am feeling better & stronger, thank goodness.—To-morrow 6 weeks I worked last in the hospital<.—The Commander of Baby's< Georgians [14th Georgian Reg.] sat with me for half an hour yesterday—such a nice man. Was before in the General staff, over the frontier guards in the Caucasus, singing highly the praises of his regiment & of poor Grabovoy [Grobov]—seems Mistchenko mentioned the young man in 2 of his orders (he was to get the St. George's cross & sword,—the Commander presented [i.e., recommended] him for both)—I got onto the sopha for dinner & remained till 1.—Fancy only, there was a youngster in Olga Orlov's hospital Shvedov with the St. George's cross—there was something at the end louche [equivocal] about him, how cld. a Volunteer have an officer's cross, & to me he said he had never been a Volunteer quite a boy to look at—he left—one found german chiffres [codes] on his table—& now I hear he has been hung! Too horrid—& he begged for our signed photos. I remember;—how could one have got hold of such a mere chap! Baby just brought one of those German arrows one drops fr. aeroplans [sic]—how hideously sharp—Romanovsky brought it (is he a flier?) & asked for Baby's card—the aeroplan [sic] lies somewhere out here, Baby forgot fr. where it was brought. [a]
   So now you are off to the south—did not get hold of your Generals? To-day perhaps in Odessa already—how brown you will get—I whisper a wish of Kirylls<, wh. he told N.P.< who repeated it, en passant to Ania< (because thought he could not tell you)—that he hoped you would take him to Sebastopol & Nikolaev —I only mention it like that, because I don't think you have any place for him. Our dear sailors, how glad I am you will see them.—Now you will find out how many plastuni battalions[75] & then I can send Images [icons]. Our Friend< is glad you left for the south. He has been praying so hard all these nights, scarcely sleeping—was so anxious for you—any rotten vicious jew might have made a scandal. Just got yr. wire fr. Proskurovo that is nice that you will see the Zaamursky frontier guards at Kamenets-Podolsk! Really, this journey at last gives you more to see & brings you into contact with the troops. I love to know you do and see unexpected things, not everything wh. is planned & marked out before—a la lettre—spontanious [sic] things (when possible) are more interesting.—What a lot you will have to write in your diary & only during stoppages!—We only remained half an hour on the balkony [sic], it got too windy & fresh. Received two officers after luncheon then Isa<, after wh. Sonia< over an hour, then Mme Zizi< & at 4½ [Teimur Bek] Navruzov, as want so much to see him again.—I hope the rest of your journey will go off alright [sic]. Goodbye & God bless & keep you, my Angel. I cover yr. dear face with kisses, & remain yr. ever very fondly loving old wife Alix. [P.S.] Bow to yr. Gentlemen. On the 16-th is N.P.'s< birthday. Ask N.P. whether Nik. Iv. Tchagin [Chagin] who died,

was brother of Ivan Ivanovich (General of Infantry) it says in Petrograd. I only know he had a brother in Moscou & one who died—an architect.[b]

No. 256/ Telegram 1 in Russian. Zhmerinka> Tsarskoe Selo. 13 April 1915. 9.30> 10.30 p.m. To her majesty. Thank you for telegram. I saw the splendid Trans-Amur border guards and your Crimeans. [They are] in beautiful condition. They asked me to give their greetings to their chief [i.e., you, as empress, their titular commander]. Was very glad to come across them here by chance. Warmly embrace [you]. Niki

No. 257/ Telegram 53. Tsarskoe Selo> Odessa. 14 April 1915. 11.32 a.m.> 1.30 p.m. To his majesty. Odessa. Very glad you saw my Crimeans. What a happy unexpected thing for them! Am envious that today you saw our dear friends and my glorious giants. Are you bringing Kirill< along to other 2 places? Cold, rain mixed with snow, hence I am not able to lie on balcony today. Feel better. In evening girls< went for drive. [We] all embrace and kiss [you]. Alix

No. 258/ Her No. 298.   Tsarskoe Selo. April 14ᵗʰ 1915.
My own beloved One,
    Fancy only, it is snowing slightly & a strong wind! Thanks so much for yr. dear telegram. That was a surprise you saw my Crimeans, am so glad & shall eagerly await news about them & why they were there—what joy for them!—Poor Ania< has got again flebitis [sic] in her right leg & strong pain, so one has to stop massage, & she must not walk—but may be wheeled out, as the air is good for her—poor girl, she now really is good & takes all patiently & just as one was hoping to take off the plaster of Paris (gypsum). Yesterday morning for the first time she walked alone on her crutches to the dining room without being held. Awful bad luck!—[Teimur Bek] Navruzov sat half an hour with me yesterday & was sweet;—to-day Pr.[ince] Gelovani will come, as I only saw him once en passant & it does one good seeing them—freshens one up. Am feeling better & shall put on my stays for the first time.—Well, Ania came for 2 hours & now Pr. Gelovani comes to me, [our daughter] Tatiana arranged this. Very windy, but sunny.—All my love & tenderest thoughts follow you. God bless & protect you, my Sunshine. Fondest kisses fr. yr. very own old Sunny. [P.S.] Bow to all.—[The following appears on a separate card fragment.] I send you some lilies of the valley to stand on yr. writing table—there are glasses one always brought for my flowers; I have kissed the sweet flowers & you kiss them too.

No. 259/ Telegram 227. Razdel'naya> Tsarskoe Selo. 14 April 1915. 5.00> 5.56 p.m. To her majesty. Tender thanks [for] letter. Today went to our beauties [fine fellows] at Odessa at a large review. Went to two hospitals. Lovely summer weather. Kirill< goes to both other places. Loving kisses. Niki

No. 260/ Telegram 260. Tsarskoe Selo> Nicholaev. 15 April 1915. 11.25 [a.m.]> 1.45 [p.m.]. To his majesty. Cold, windy, ice beginning to break up on

[Lake] Ladoga. I have three reports. For first time today am going to her [Anna Vyrubova] since I feel significantly stronger and in my opinion it is better that she not move about since she has flebitis [sic] again in right leg. How vexing. Glad you saw our beauties [see Letter No. 259]. God bless your journey. We all kiss [you]. Older girls< going to town<. Alix

---

No. 261/ Her No. 299.   Tsarskoe Selo. April 15th 1915.
My own beloved Treasure,
    A windy, cold day—there was frost in the night, the Ladoga ice is passing, so shall not be able to lie out again. Temp. 37.2 again yesterday evening, but that means nothing, am feeling decidedly stronger, so will go to Ania< this afternoon & meet our Friend< there, who wishes to see me. At 11½ I have Vil'ch.< with a report wh. is sure to last an hour—then Shulenburg with his papers at 12½; & at 2 Witte with his affairs, sent by Rauchfuss.—Yesterday Gelovani sat 1/2 an hour with me, spoke much about the regiment.—You must have felt very tired at Odessa doing so much in such a short time And our dear sailors! & 2 hospitals, that is nice indeed & will have rejoiced all hearts.—
    I wonder, what that woman's legion wh. is being formed in Kiev is? If only to be as in England, to carry out the wounded & help them like sanitaries, then it can be alright [sic]—but I should personally not have allowed women to go out there "en masse"—the sister's [nurse's] dress is still a protection & they hold themselves otherwise—but these will be what? Unless in very severe hands, well watched they may do very different things. A few of them with sanitary detachements [sic] cld. be good, but as a band—no—that is not their place—let them nurse out there, from nurses detachements. There is an English lady who does wonders in Belgium in her warkit [i.e., protective military jacket] & short skirts—rides & picks up wounded, flies about to get vehicles to transport them to the nearest hospital, binds up their wounds—& once even read the prayers over the grave of a young English officer who died in a garret in a Belgium town taken by the Germans, & one dared not have a regular funeral.—Our women are less well educated & have no discipline so I don't know how they will manage "en masse"—wonder who allows them to form themselves.— [a]
    I think you may get these lines before leaving Sebastopol—the dear black sea! And the fruit trees all in blossom—a flying visit to Livadia & Jalta would be lovely, I am sure!—Ania's leg is not at all good, such red spots—fear this flebitis [sic] can last some time! Her Mother [Nadezhda Taneeva] too is again ill, & Alia< & the [i.e., Alia's] Children.—Well, that was a surprise yr. precious letter & the dear little flower, thanks ever so much. Too interesting all your journey, everything you wrote—one sees it all before one. From [your sister] Olga I also got a letter with her impressions —how happy she was to see you!— It is so cold! And the wind howls down the chimn[e]y—Baby< drove in the morning & will now again. His motor has a stronger mashine [sic] & so goes very quickly—Mr. Gill[i]ard & Der.< follow him in a big one.—Precious One, I suppose you are at Nikolajev now— interesting all you will see, & give the men energy to build on quickly & get our ships done.[86]—Goodbye, my own huzy love, God bless & protect you, I kiss ever so tenderly & with deepest devotion. Ever yr. very own old Wify.   [P.S.] Messages to Fred.< and N.P.< [b]

86. Although the Russian Black Sea fleet was made up of obsolete ships at the outbreak of the war, three modern dreadnoughts were under construction in Odessa at this time.

No. 262/ Telegram 344. Nicholaev> Tsarskoe Selo. 15 April 1915. 3.10> 4.18 p.m. To her majesty. Loving thanks for news. Saw our new ships and went through splendid dockyards. After lunch continue my visit to other ship building and ammunition factories. Awfully interesting. Cold, windy. Leave at 6 for dear Sevastopol. Tender kisses. Niki

No. 263/ Telegram 56. Tsarskoe Selo> Kutsovka. 15 April 1915. 6.20> 10.00 p.m. To his majesty. From all my heart thank you for dear telegram and very interesting letter. Very touched by dear flowers. Cold, windy. Was at Znamenie< and at Ania's< for first time. How wonderful you were able to see so much today! [We] embrace and kiss [you]. Alix

No. 264/ Telegram 59. Tsarskoe Selo> Dzhankoi. 16 April 1915. 11.02 a.m.> 12.30 p.m. To his majesty. My tender thoughts accompany you to dear Sebastopol and among your beloved armies. Wind and cold for a third day. Have not gone out because heart again a bit enlarged. God bless you! We all warmly kiss [you]. Bow to all. Alix

No. 265/ Her No. 300.   Tsarskoe Selo. April 16th 1915.
My Sweetheart,
    I have just been eating up the newspapers with Freder.< long telegrams about your journey. You have done & seen a lot, I am delighted—& been to hospitals too. Some of our wounded officers are now at Odessa & will surely have seen you there. But you must be very tired. Pitty [sic] you cannot have one quiet day's rest in the South, to have quietly enjoyed the sunshine & flowers. Life once back here is so awfully tiring & fidgety for you always, my poor treasure. I want the weather to get again warm & nice for yr. return & Baby's< foot. He is very careful with it I think on purpose. This morning he is out driving with Mr. Gibbs.—I had hoped to go to our hospital< to sit a bit there but the heart is again a little enlarged, so have to remain at home.—Our Friend< was not long at Anias< yesterday, but very dear. Asked lots about you.—To-day receive three officers returning to the war, yr. Kobilin too, & then Danini & two others, whom I sent to Evpatoria to choose a sanatorium. We have taken one for a year—the money you gave me covers the expenses. There are mud, sea, sun, sandbaths there, a Zanderroom, electricity, watercures, garden & plage [i.e., a beach] close by—170 people, & in winter 75—its splendid. Duvan, who has built a theatre, streets etc. there, I am going to ask to be the Burser. [N. A.] Knyazhevich thinks he may help materially then too.—Xenia< has returned one says.—How glad you will be to see your plastuni[75] to-day.—Well, my treasure, I must say goodbye now. God bless & protect you. I kiss you over & over again with tenderness, & remain yr. ever fondly loving old Wify. [P.S.] How is Fred.< I wonder! Bow to him & N.P.<

No. 266/ Telegram 418. Sevastopol> Tsarskoe Selo. 16 April 1915. 7.10> 8.47 p.m. To her majesty. Arrived well. Same cold weather 6 degr[ees]. Tender thanks [for] dear letter [and] two telegrams. Happy are feeling better. Sad not to be together. Fondest kisses. Niki

---

No. 267/ Telegram 63. Tsarskoe Selo> Sevastopol. 17 April 1915. 10.12 a.m.> 12.40 p.m. To his majesty. Marvellous weather. Will lie on balcony—heart still enlarged. Yesterday evening terrible explosion in Okhto mill section—all buildings destroyed. Number of fatalities still unknown because so many fled their dwellings. Said here that in one house glass shattered [though] in Petrograd many did not notice. [We] embrace and kiss [you]. Alix

---

No. 268/ Her No. 310.   Tsarskoe Selo. April 17th 1915.
My own sweetest One,
   Bright, sunny but cold, lay an hour on the balkony [sic] & found it rather too fresh.—Yesterday Paul< came to tea. He told me he had just received a letter from Marie<, telling him about your talk in the train concerning Dmitri<. So he sent for the boy last night and was going to have a serious talk with him. He too is greatly shocked at the way the boy goes on in town etc.—In the evening at 8.20 there was this explosion—I send you Obolensky's paper. Now I have had telephoned to Sergei< for news—one says 150 severely wounded—how many killed one cannot say, as one collects the bits—when the remaining people are assembled together, then they will know who is missing. Some parts in town & streets heard absolutely nothing—here some felt it very strongly, so that they thought it had occured [sic] at Tsarskoe [Selo]. Thank God its not the powder-magazine as one at first had said.— [a]
   I had a long, dear letter fr. Erni<—I will show it you upon your return. He says that "if there is someone who understands him (you) & knows what he is going through, it is me". He kisses you tenderly. He longs for a way out of this dilema [sic], that someone ought to begin to make a bridge for discussion.[81] So he had an idea of quite privately sending a man of confidence to Stockholm, who should meet a gentlemen [gentleman] sent by you (privately) that they could help disperse many momentary difficulties. He had this idea, as in Germany there is no real hatred against Russia. So he sent a gentlemen to be there on the 28th—(that is 2 days ago & I only heard to-day) & can only spare him a week. So I at once wrote an answer (all through Daisy<) & sent it [i.e., informed] the gentlemen, telling him you are not yet back, so he better not wait— & that tho' one longs for peace, the time has not yet come.—I wanted to get all done before you return, as I know it would be unpleasant for you. W[ilhelm II, the kaiser?]. knows of course absolutely nothing about this.—He says they stand as a firm wall in France, & that his friends tell him, in the North & Carpathians too. They think they have 500.000 of our prisoners.—The whole letter is very dear & loving;—I was intensely grateful to get it, tho' of course the question of the gentleman waiting there & you away, was complicated;—& E.[rni] will be disappointed.—My heart is again enlarged, so I don't leave the house. Lilly D.< is coming to me for half an hour.—I do hope you have warmer weather to-day, Sebastopol is not amiable both times.—Xenia< is coming to-morrow to lunch-

eon. Ania< sat with me this morning for an hour.—2 Girls are riding & 2 driving—Aleksei< out in his motor.—I wonder whether you return 21-st or 22-d.
Ressin< has gone to town to see the place & bring me details, as I should like to
help the poor sufferers.—Now Lovebird, I must end, as I have to write for the
English messenger & to [your] sister Olga.—God bless & protect you. I kiss you
over & over again in tenderest love, ever, Nicky dear, yr. old   Sunny. [b]

No. 269/ Telegram 2. Sevastopol> Tsarskoe Selo. 17 April 1915. 4.50> 6.15
p.m. To her majesty. Hearty thanks [for] dear letter and telegram. This morning
heard about sad accident [and] explosion. Today lovely weather, but not hot.
Went round the ships and on board some. Visited hospital ship. Now am going
to inspect my plastuni[75] on the pier before the train. To-morrow review of all the
rest. Tender kisses. Niki

No. 270/ Telegram 67. Tsarskoe Selo> Sevastopol. 17 April 1915. 8.35> 10.45
p.m. To his majesty. Very happy all goes well. In thoughts are together. Am
lying on balcony, clear but cold. Thinking of the 200 victims [of the explosion,
see Letters No. 267, 268a], 75 corpses found so far. Alek< assisted all night.
Ressin< was also there. Apparently done by evil design, otherwise would have
been only fire without explosion. I bless and kiss [you]. Bow to old man
[Fredericks]. Sleep peacefully. Alix

No. 271/ His No. 175.   Sevastopol. 18 April 1915.
My own beloved Sunny,
    I thank you from all my heart for your sweet letters that give me such comfort
and joy—in my solitude after all. Though wherever I go this time, I am surrounded by members of the family—in Galicia, at Odessa & here. This will
probably be my last letter. My visit to Kamenets-Podolsk pleased me enormously. The town is quite pretty and I have simply lost my head over the
Trans-Amur men and your delightful Crimeans. The former, having just arrived
from Kharbin, look splendid & as well equipped & tidy as guards regiments.
The Tartars have rested, & they all smiled broadly when I passed them. It did
not strike me they had few officers. The next day Odessa was over enthusiastic,
perfect order in the streets. Our beauties of the Guards Equipage< were more
impossing [sic] than ever—that mass of magnificent men. I had to tell them a
few warm words & decorate 20 of them. By the side of them stood a new Caucasian Regiment I had not seen at Kars—the 9th Caucasian Rifle Regiment—they
were fighting the Turks then & lost about 600 men [and] 14 officers. But are
filled up again. Except their [sic] were at the review the 53rd and 54th Don
Regiments. The 53rd was at the Stavka last year. The next day at Nicholaev the
weather suddenly became awfully cold. It is too long to describe all I saw
there—it was wonderfully interesting & comforting to see what our people are
capable of when they set to work in earnest: 3 dreadnoughts, 4 cruisers, 9 destroyers, and a lot of large submarines, railway engines, carriages, turbines and
shrapnels, shrapnels without end! Yesterday I was happy to find the fleet here.
In the afternoon I toyed with my 6th Battalion of plastuni,[75] on the pier and to-

morrow shall review the whole lot of them at their camp. I love this place—God bless you, my precious Wify & the children. I kiss you lovingly. Ever your own huzy   Nicky.

No. 272/ Telegram 72. Tsarskoe Selo> Sevastopol. 18 April 1915. 10.55> 11.50 a.m. To his majesty. Xenia< and Irina [Yusupova] are lunching with us. Overcast, grey, 5 degrees. Am sending money to most unfortunate victims [of the explosion, see Letters No. 267, 268a, 270 above] and images [icons] to wounded houses in various hospitals. Would like to know who you will still see today. Bless and kiss [you]. Wish you a happy journey. Alix

---

No. 273/ Her No. 302.   Tsarskoe Selo. April 18th 1915.
My own sweet precious One,
   A grey, cold, damp morning—the barometer must have fallen, feel such a pressure on my chest.—Yesterday evening Hagentorn took off Ania's< gypsum from round her stomach, so that she is enchanted, can sit straight, & back no longer aches. Then she managed to lift her left foot, for the first time since 3 months, wh. shows that the bone is growing together. The flebitis in the other leg is very strong—so massage cannot be done on either leg, wh. is a pitty [sic]. She lies on the sopha & looks less of an invalid; she comes to me, as I remain at home on account of my heart.—This morning I receive [Uncle] Mekk—he will, entre autre, tell me about Lvov, where he saw you in Church. My little flying stores trains have hard & useful work in the Carpathans [sic], & our mules carry the things in the mountains—hard fighting, ones heart aches,— & in the North too again. There, the kind sun is peeping out. Yr. little plant stands on the piano & I like looking at it—reminds me of the Rosenau 21 years ago!! [a]
   Our Friend< says if it gets more known that that catastrophy [sic] happened from an attempt to set fire, the hatred towards Germany will be great.[87]—(Hang those aeroplans [sic] in the Carpathans [sic] now too?) I am going to send money to the poorest families & Images [icons] to the wounded.—[Daughter] Olga wrote you the details [of the explosion]; & I suppose others do officially, so I wont any more.—My temp. rose to 37.3 in the evening & this morning 37; heart just now not enlarged.—Shall finish this in the afternoon, Xenia< & Irina [Yusupova] lunch with us,—& perhaps I may find something more interesting to tell you by then. Well, now they have gone, Irina looked pretty, only much too thin.—It seems there was a fire in Ania's house, the little blind woman's candle fell down & things took fire, so the floor in the back room burned a little & two boxes with books, Ania got a nice fright—bad luck always.—Now goodbye & God bless you—soon, soon I shall have you back, what joy!! 1000 fond kisses. Ever yr. old Wify. [b]

---

87. Reference is to the explosion in Petrograd on April 17, 1915, discussed in Letters No. 267, 268a, 270, 272.

No. 274/ Telegram 3. Sevastopol> Tsarskoe Selo. 18 April 1915. 1.08> 2.50 p.m. To his majesty. Tender thanks [for] dear letter [and] telegram. Just had review of all the 11 battalions of plastuni.[75] Interesting, pretty unique sight.

Have named [our son] Aleksei chef of 3rd Bat[talion]. Please telegraph in his name to them. Loving kisses. Niki

---

No. 275/ Telegram 510. Sevastopol> Tsarskoe Selo. 18 April 1915. 2.30> 4.07 p.m. To her majesty. Send thirteen thousand images [icons]. Am going to motor out beyond Baidari. Tender love. Niki.

No. 276/ Telegram 75. Tsarskoe Selo> Sevastopol. 18 April 1915. 5.42> 7.40 p.m. To his majesty. Thank you heartily for two dear telegrams. Very happy at Baby's< appointment, sending telegram. Hope you travelled well by car on that wonderful road. Sunny but cold. Xenia< and Irene [Yusupova] had lunch. We embrace and kiss [you]. Alix.

No. 277/ Her No. 303.   Tsarskoe Selo. April 19th 1915.
My own darling Huzy dear,
    Such a gloriously sunny morning! Shall lie out on the balkony [sic] at last again. Yesterday M-me. Janov sent us flowers from beloved Livadia—glycinias, golden rain-drops, lilac iris wh. have opened this morning, lilac & red Italians anemonies [sic] wh. I used to paint & now want to again—Judas tree little branches, one pioni & tulips. To see them in ones vases makes me quite melancholy. Does it not seem strange, hatred & bloodshed & all the horrors of war—& there simply Paradise, sunshine & flowers and peace—such a mercy but such a contrast. Do hope you managed to get a nice drive beyond Baidary. Well, Baby< & I went at 11½ to Church, & came just during the Credo—so nice being in Church again, but missed you, my Angel, awfully—& was tired & felt my heart.—Blind Anisia< took holy Communion—she upset the lantern in Ania's< house & set the room on fire. After luncheon I lay knitting for an hour on the balkony, but the sun had gone & it was cold. Ania sat with me from 1½-3¼.—Such tender thanks for the divine lilacs—such perfume!
    Thanks over & over again from us all—I gave Ania some too.—The Children are giving medals in a hospital (with Drenteln) & then they & Baby go to Ania to meet the 2 cossacks & [daughter] Marie's friend.—How dear you named Baby chef of one of those splendid battalions, ["Old Count"] Vorontsov< sent me a delighted telegram. Eagerly awaiting your return—lonely without you, my Sweetheart; & you will have such a lot to tell.—Schwibzik [daughter Maria] is sleeping near me. Now Goodbye, my very Own, God bless & protect you & bring you safely home to us. Very fondest kisses fr. yr. own Sunny. [P.S.] Messages to everybody!

No. 278/ Telegram 3. Likhachevo South> Tsarskoe Selo. 19 April 1915. 2.10> 3.19 p.m. To her majesty. Fondest thanks [for] letter No. 301. Also thank all the children. Heavenly weather. Went yesterday half way to Yalta, saw big landslip there. Much fresher. Old man [Fredericks] well, [sends his] thanks. Shall stop at Borki. Tender love. How is her [Anna Vyrubova's] leg? Niki[88a]

88a. Vulliamy notes that on this day von Mackensen broke through the Russian front on the middle Dunaets. The Russian army was in severe crisis for the next two months. "But here again, as at the time of the Masurian battles [in August 1914], the Tsar makes no comment on the disastrous course of events. It is inconceivable that he was not informed." (pp. 51-52n) See Footnote 88b.

No. 279/ Telegram 77. Tsarskoe Selo> Dergachi. 19 April 1915. 3.45> 4.10 p.m. To his majesty. Was briefly in church. During day lay on sopha on balcony. Was cold. Thank you passionately for wonderful lilac. We all embrace you warmly. Alix

No. 280/ [This is a note.] Sazhnoe. April 19th 1915. My Love, These photographs were taken in Sevastopol when I was playing about with my plastuni.[75] You will return them to me, will you not, when I return? Heat in train is terrible—22 degrees. Love you passionately and kiss you. Your Niki

No. 281/ Telegram 605. Tsarskoe Selo. 19 April 1915. 9.39> 10.30 p.m. To her majesty. Arrive home Wednesday early morning. Now cooler. Good night. Loving kisses. Niki

No. 282/ Telegram 81. Tsarskoe Selo> Bezhnitsa. 20 April 1915. 10.45 a.m.> 12.00 p.m. To his majesty. Bezhnitsa. Terribly happy and thank you for dear letter. All very interesting. Snowed heavily last night, everything still covered with a white shroud, gives off strong heat in the sun. She [Anna Vyrubova] thanks you very much, [her] flebitis [sic] is a bit better. Thousand thanks for dear flowers. They make me remember my home places [on the Crimea, see Letter No. 283a]. All embrace and kiss [you]. Alix

No. 283/ Her No. 304.   Ts.[arskoe] S[elo]. April 20th 1915.
My own beloved Darling,
    This is my last letter to you. For your precious & unexpected one & lovely flowers, tenderest thanks. One feels homesick for the beautiful Crimea—our earthly Paradise in spring!—All you write is so interesting—what a lot you have done!—must be tired I am sure, dear precious One, Huzy mine! Yes, my heart, I know you are lonely, and that makes me always so sad, that Sunbeam< is not old enough to accompany you everywhere. The family is alright [sic], but none of them are near to you,—or really understand you.—What a jubilation when you return!—Ania's Aunt< returned full haste from Mitave, & the Governor with all the documents—a panic—the Germans coming! No troops of ours!—German scouts I think near Libau—I feel sure they want to make a landing with their heaps of sailors (doing nothing) & other troops, to push down from there towards Varsovie [Warsaw] from the back, or along the coast, to get the Germans [i.e., the tsar's subjects of German extraction] onto their side—that has all along been in my head since autumn.—Our Friend< finds them awfully slie [sic]—looks at all seriously, but says God will help.—My humble opinion. why does one not get some cossack regiments along the coast, or our cavalry a little bit up more towards Libau, to keep them fr. ruining everything & finding basis for settling down with their devilish aeroplans [sic]? We dont want them ruining our towns, not to say killing innocent people. [a]

Baby< enjoyed himself at Ania's< yesterday.—To-day the young couple Voronov are coming to us to tea, they have come for a few days from Odessa. I receive 7 officers returning, amongst others the General, Commander of Baby's Georgians, then priest fr. the [royal yacht] Standart to say goodbye before leaving & Benkendorff<, & then Ania. I went for ¾ of an hour at last to the hospital<. Gogoberidze suddenly appeared to our surprise, he was only a month in the regiment & then went to Batum as was quite ill—now he looks brown as a nut—he returns to the regiment in a few days.—It rained again, so I shall not lie out.—Sweetest one, I have got to see all those people now, so cannot write any more. The Children all and I kiss you ever so tenderly and warmly, beloved One.—God grant in two days I shall have you back again in my longing arms.—The Children< go to an exhibition to-morrow and then take tea at Anichkov<. God bless & keep you. Ever yr. very own tenderly loving old wife Alix. [b]

No. 284/ Telegram 877. Orel> Tsarskoe Selo. 20 April 1915. 11.09 p.m.> 12.15 a.m. To her majesty. Tender thanks [for] dear letter. Had a very interesting and full day at the Bryansky factory. Terribly hot in the morning. After storm and rain now only 6 deg[rees]. See Ella< to-morrow morning. Fondest kisses. Niki

---

No. 285/ Telegram 84. Tsarskoe Selo> Tver. 21 April 1915. 10.36> 11.12 a.m. To his majesty. Thank you warmly for telegram, marvellous photographs and note. Cold here, sometimes sun shows itself. Children< going to town. We embrace and tenderly kiss [you]. We rejoice at to-morrow's day. Alix

---

No. 286/ Telegram 430. Tver> Tsarskoe Selo. 21 April 1915. 2.15> 3.26 p.m. To her majesty. Loving thanks [for] last letter. Saw Ella< 10 minutes. Now off to town< here till evening. Icy cold weather. So happy to be back to-morrow. Fondest kisses. Niki

---

No. 287/ Her No. 305   Ts.[arskoe] S[elo]. May 4th 1915.
My own sweetest of Sweets,
    You will read these lines before going to bed—remember Wify will be praying & thinking of you, oh so much, & miss you quite terribly. So sad we shall not spend your dear birthday together—the first time! May God bless you richly, give you strength and wisdom, consolation, health, peace of mind to continue bravely bearing your heavy crown!—ah it is not an easy nor light cross He has placed upon yr. shoulders—would that I could help you carrying, in prayers & thoughts I ever do. I yearn to lessen yr. burden!—so much you have had to suffer in those 20 years—& you were borne [sic] on the [names]day of the longsuffering Job too, my poor Sweetheart. But God will help, I feel sure, but still much heartache, anxiety, & hard work have to be got through bravely, with resignation & trust in God's mercy, and unfathomable wisdom. Hard not to be able to give you a birthday tender kiss & blessing!—One gets at times so tired from suffering & anxiety & yearns for peace—oh when will it come I wonder? How many more

months of bloodshed & misery! Sun comes after rain—& so our beloved country will see its golden days of prosperity after her earth is sodden with blood & tears—God is not unjust & I place all my trust in Him unwaveringly—but its such pain to see all the misery—to know not all work as they ought to, that petty personalities spoil often the great cause for wh. they ought to work in unisson [sic]! Be firm, Lovy mine, show yr. own mind, let others feel you know what you wish. Remember you are the Emperor, & that others dare not take so much upon themselves—beginning by a mere detail, as the Nositz [G. I. Nostits] story—he is in yr. suite & therefore N.< has absolutely no right to give orders without asking your permission first. [a]

If you did such a thing with one of his aide de camps without warning him, wld. he not set up a row & play the offended, etc. & without being sure, one cannot ruin a man's career like that.—Then, Deary, if a new Com.[mander] of the Nizhegorodtsy< is to be named, wont you propose Jagmin?< I meddle in things not concerning me—but its only a hint,—(& its your own regiment, so you can order whom you wish there). See that the story of the Jews is carefully done, without unnecessary rows, not to provoke disturbances over the country.—Dont let one coax you into unnecessary nominations & rewards for the 6-th—many months are yet before us!—You cant fly off to Cholm [Kholm] to see Ivanov or stop on the way to see soldiers waiting to be sent to refill the regiments? One longs that each of yr. journeys should not only be the joy for the Headquarters (without troops)—but for the soldiers, or wounded, more need strength from you & it does you good too. Do what you wish & not the Generals—yr. presence gives strength everywhere.— [Not signed] [b]

No. 288/ Telegram 22. Tsarskoe Selo> Vilno. 5 May 1915. 9.35> 10.29 a.m. To his majesty. 10 degrees, overcast. Very lonely. Leaving now for hospital<. My tenderest thoughts and prayers accompany you. We kiss you warmly. Alix

No. 289/ Telegram 0095. Vilna> Tsarskoe Selo. 5 May 1915. 11.55 a.m.> 12.53 p.m. To her majesty. Loving thanks [for] dear letter. Weather fine, much warmer. Thoughts constantly with you. Tender kisses. Niki

No. 290/ Her No. 306.   Tsarskoe S[elo]. May 5th 1915.
My own beloved One,

I send you my very tenderest goodwishes & blessings for yr. dear birthday. God Almighty take you quite particularly into His holy keeping.—I hope the candlesticks & magnifying glass will be useful for the train—I could not find anything else suitable, alas. —Ania< sends you the enclosed card.—This morning I went to Znamenje<, then to her for half an hour. At 10 to the hospital, operation & dressings—no time to write details. Got back at 1¼— left at 2 for town<. Xenia< & Georgi< were also at the committee —lasted an hour & 20 m. then went to stores got home at 5½—now must receive peasants from Duderhof & Kolpino with money. The Feldjeger must leave at 6.—Sunny, but cold. Am ramolie<, so cannot write much & awful hurry.—Slept badly—so lonely.—My

Angel Darling, I kiss & bless you without end—awfully sad not to spend dear
6-th together. Goodbye my love, my huzy sweet. Ever yr. own old   Sunny.

No. 291/ Telegram 48. Stavka> Tsarskoe Selo. 5 May 1915. 6.00> 6.20 p.m.
To her majesty. Just arrived well. Lovely weather, woods quite green, delicious
smell. Now off to church. Thanks for telegram. Tender love. Niki

No. 292/ Telegram 40. Tsarskoe Selo> Stavka. 5 May 1915. 6.18> 6.45 p.m.
To his majesty. Tenderly thank you for dear telegram. Attended committee,
then store<, now receiving peasants. [See Letter No. 290.] Fresh, sunny. Darling, we all convey our best wishes on to-morrow's event [your birthday]. In her
telegram Ella< asked us to convey her warm congratulations. We kiss [you]
warmly. Alix

No. 293/ Telegram 29. Tsarskoe Selo> Stavka. 6 May 1915. 7.55> 9.20 a.m.
To his majesty. Best wishes on this dear day [your birthday]. I kiss [you]
warmly. All tenderly embrace [you]. God help you in everything! Alix

No. 294/ Telegram 57. Stavka> Tsarskoe Selo. 6 May 1915. 9.45> 10.53 a.m.
To her majesty. So touched by charming presents and good wishes [on my
birthday to-day]. Sad not together. Thank Ella<. Kiss you and dear children
lovingly. Niki

No. 295/ Her No. 307.   Ts.[arskoe] S[elo]. May 6th 1915.
My very own precious One,
   Many happy returns of this dear day. God grant you many spend it next year
in peace & joy, & the nightmare of this war be over! I cover you with tender
kisses—alas, only in thoughts—& pray God to protect & quite particularly bless
you for all your undertakings. Such a sunny morning—(tho' fresh) may it be a
good omen!—Our Friend's< lovely telegram will have given you pleasure—shall I
thank him for you? And for Ania's< card, wire me a message to give over to
her.—We sat with her in the evening as she had spent a lonely day, by chance
nobody, except mother & son Karangozov came to see her.—We had a tiring
day, so I did not take [daughter] Olga to town<, because of her cold & Becker's<
visit; [daughter] Tatiana replaced her at the Committee. At the stores Marie
Bariatinsky< & Olga [Baryatinskaya] were making stockings, the same as they
had been doing at Moscou [sic] so far.—[a]
   Everybody asks for news—I have none to give—but the heart is heavy—through
["Uncle"] Mekk's telegrams one sees the movements more or less.—[Teimur
Bek] Navrusov spoke with us by telephone, the sinner only leaves to-night—as
he said to me, he had "fasted" for six months, now he must enjoy town. I called
him a hulligan [sic], wh. he did not approve of,—too bad, he says my health is
better now, because he has been drinking for my health.   I told him Pss.
Gedroits< who is very fond of him, calls him our enfant terrible; then I spoke
with Amilakhvari [72] by telephone, & he will come to say goodbye to-day.—[G.
A.] Bobrinsky has left full speed to Lvov. They sang beautifully in Church. We

had all my ladies, Benkend.< & Ressin< to lunch, then I received Kochubey, [N. A.] Knyazhevich, Amilakhvari then went to Ania & read to her, after wh. to the big palace for 10 m. Now Xenia< & Paul< come to tea, so must end,—always a hurry. Blessings & kisses without end—no news, so anxious. Sweetheart, yr. very own, longing for you Wify. [b]

No. 296/ Telegram 71. Stavka> Tsarskoe Selo. 6 May 1915. 1.06> 1.54 p.m. To her majesty. Tender, loving thanks once more for good wishes. Please thank our Friend< for his touching words. After great heat and shower in the night now much cooler. Kisses Niki

No. 297/ Telegram 44. Tsarskoe Selo> Stavka. 7 May 1915. 10.50> 11.15 a.m. To his majesty. Warm, clear sun. Leaving for the hospital< with tender thoughts of you. What is new? I know nothing since you left—only the newspapers.[83] All tenderly kiss you. Tatiana's committee at 4. Alix

No. 298/ Her No. 308.   Ts.[arskoe] S[elo]. May 7th 1915. My very own Angel,
   Again I write in full haste, no quiet time.—Yesterday evening were at Ania's<, Raftopolo, Karangazov, Vachnadze were there.   Slept not famously—heart heavy of anxiety, hate not being with you when trying times.—This morning after Znamenje< peeped in to Anias, her sweet nieces & Alia< overnighted in her house so as to get good air.—Then we had an operation—anxious one, serious case—& worked till after 1. Before 2 said goodbye to Karangozov & Gordinsky, then Tatiana's committee—big group 2¼ to 4. Went to A.[nia] till 5, saw our Friend< there—thinks much of you, prays, "we sat and talked together,—and still God will help." Its horrid not being with you at a time so full of heartache & anxiety!—would to God I could be of help to you!—one comfort N.P.< is near you & then I am quieter—a natural, warm heart & kind look helps when worries fill the soul; not a fat O.< or Drent.<   As the Cossacks begged everytime so much, have said two or 1 officer may come with us.—Fear it will be very official still, but our Fr. wants me to go on such journeys.— Treasure of my soul, Angel beloved, God help you, console & strengthen & help our brave heroes.—I kiss you over & over again & bless you without end. Must finish. Ever yr. very own Wify

No. 299/ Telegram 130. Stavka> Tsarskoe Selo. 7 May 1915. 2.55> 3.30 p.m. To her majesty. Tender thanks you [for] dear letter. Tell her [Anna Vyrubova (that) I] was touched by note. News not satisfactory.[88b] Wish you lucky journey, hope won't be tiring. Fondest kisses. Niki

88b. Nicholas finally admits the news was bad. (Cf. Footnote 88a.) It is difficult to know what the tsar had in mind when, on May 8, 9 and 11 he wrote that the situation was "slightly improved." (See Nos. 302, 306, 311.) He might have been referring to local Russian counterattacks; perhaps he was seeking to reassure his wife. The fact is the Germans were on the offensive and doing well.

No. 300/ Telegram 48. Tsarskoe Selo> Stavka. 7 May 1915. [Sent,] 6.15 p.m.
Warmly thank you for letter. In heart and spirit am with you, my dear. God help
us—he will help and bring us success, am sure of that. Weary day. Operation,
committee. Clear day. Am sorry to abandon my ... [ellipsis in original]. All embrace and kiss [you] warmly. Alix

No. 301/ Telegram 1381. Vitebsk> Stavka. 8 May 1915. 9.52> 11.40 a.m. To
his majesty. We arrived here safely. Clear, sunny day, more green [spring
growth]. Did not sleep well. We all kiss you warmly. [Things] weigh heavily on
my heart, I share your anxiety. God bless and help you. Alix

No. 302/ Telegram 151. Stavka> Vitebsk. 8/V - 1915. 2.56> 4.07 p.m. To her
majesty. Many thanks [for] letter and telegram. Hope not too tired today. A ray
of light among the news.[88b] Think it better to remain here a few days longer till
affairs become clear. Am sure you understand. Warm but grey. Tender kisses
and love to O[lga] and T[at'yana]. Niki

No. 303/ Her No. 309.   Vitebsk. 8 May 1915.
My beloved One,
    Artsimovitch[61] will meet you at Dvinsk to-morrow, and has proposed to bring
you a letter. But I have the feeling that if the news continue not being good, that
you will probably be remaining on still at the Headquarters. [88b] Such splendid
weather & all quite green, a great difference after Tsarskoe [Selo]!—So far all
has gone beautifully & we are having three hours rest, wh. is splendid, as my
back aches a lot.—We went to the Cathedral, a Te Deum of 5 minutes, the
Bishop Cyrill [sic] seemed ramoli<, I must say. Then went to 4 hospitals, the
sisters of my Krestovozdvizhensky Community work in one since August—in
another, sisters & Drs. from Tashkent—everywhere good air, clean & nice; & not
fussy. A group [photograph] was taken of us with masses of wounded in a garden. Masses of Jews, & trains arrive with them from Curland— painful sight
with all their packages & wee children.[89] [a]
    The town is pretty when one crosses the river. The Children< had the Gover-
nor & Mezentsev to luncheon & then the latter came & sat with me—such a nice
man & works well one sees. Now we shall be going to one of his stores & to
three hospitals & to the Palace where the Gov. lives as there is a store under my
protection there. We leave again at 7. I did not sleep very well. Wonder what
news, feel so anxious far from you.—Now my Lovy, Goodbye & God bless you.
I kiss you from the depths of my loving heart. Ever yr. very own old Wify.
The girls kiss you. [b]
    I got your wire, that you have put off yr. journey, wh. is more than compre-
hensible—easier to be nearer these trying days—would to God that that "ray of
light" [see Letter No. 302] might brighten into sunshine—one yearns for success!—& now Essen's death, the one that the German's[sic] feared has died! Ah,
what trials God sends!—whom do you name in his place I wonder, who has the
same energy as he for the time of war? I hate not being near you, knowing your
suffering! But God Almighty will help, all our losses wont be in vain, all our

prayers must be heard, no matter how hard it is now—but being far away, with scarce news is trying & yet you cannot get nearer. Sweet one, I know yr. faith & trust in God.—St. Nicolas feast to-morrow may that holy Saint intercede for our brave, struggling troops!— [c]

I had my wish & saw a sanitary train wh. brought fresh wounded of four days ago, of the sixth infantry division the Muromtsevsky and Nizovski. There were no very severe cases, thank God, tho' bad wounds, to many I said I should tell you I had seen them & their faces lit up.—We went over my store of the red cross wh. Mesentsev has, still 3 hospitals & the stores in the Governor's palace & took a cup of coffee wh. gave one new strength. My back hurts aw-fully—kidneys, I think crystals again wh. always cause pain. The pavement vile, glad, had our motors. Ortipo [our pet dog] climb[s] onto my lap, have sent her off several times without success—so yet more difficult writing on the top of her back in a shaking train. All the convalescents stood near the station when we returned, & schoolchildren. Glorious sunset—quite summer— such dust. Shall finish this at Tsarskoje [Selo] to-morrow. [d]

May 9-th. We got her[e] alright [sic], the Pavlovsk line, as near Gatchina their [sic] had been an explosion on the train going with ammunitions—such a hor-ror!—12 waggons [sic] they managed to save—one sees it was done on purpose; just what one so soreley [sic] needs, it does seem cruel!—The little ones met us at the station. Worked as usual in the hospital<, was at Ania's<, placed candles in Church. After lunch received Apraksin<, Hartman the Com.[mander] of the Erivantsi & a wounded officer.—Yr. Taube lies still at Lomzha & one was obliged, alas, to amputate his leg above the knee. Now I have got Ania coming, Sonia< lunched with us—one says news a wee bit better?—The a.d.c. of the blue curassiers brought us flowers—they love Arseniev & highly appreciate him.—The wife of one of the Georgian officers is coming to me as its their feast—& later I want to take flowers to Grabovoy's [Grobov's] grave. God bless you my Sun-shine I cover yr. sweet face with kisses—Ever yr. very own   Sunny   [P.S.] I have got hold of a rotten pen. Hope to go to Church—sad to-morrow's great feast not together.— Bow to all yr. people. [e]

89. The German advance caused refugees to flood into the capital. Chief of Staff Yanushkevich added to the pain by ordering an evacuation of Jews from Galicia and adjacent territories. Russians believed Jews were pro-Austrian. Oldenburg thought some transmitted information "with signals or by greeting the advancing foe with ready information on the number and weapons of the Russian troops." Yet he insists an "indiscriminate condemnation" of the entire population was "unfounded." Hundreds of thousands of these wretched people were driven deep into Russia. They became a "breeding ground first of panic and plague and then of a smoldering hatred for the state." (Olden-burg, Last Tsar, IV, 30, 33. See also Lincoln, Passage, pp. 139-143.)

No. 304/ Telegram 6. Vitebsk> Stavka. 8 May 1915. [Sent,] 8.05 p.m. To his majesty. Were in cathedral and four hospitals. Then rested several hours be-cause we were tired. Governor Mezentsov lunched with children<. Then again several hospitals, governor's house. Just received your telegram. Was certain yo ir plan was exactly that. Understand you completely. Thanks be to God—news better. Very saddened by Essen's death, this is a great loss. We embrace and kiss you. Alix

No. 305/ Telegram 57. Tsarskoe Selo> Stavka. 9 May 1915. 10.20> 11.05 a.m.
To his majesty. Arrived safely. I am not very tired. Wonderful weather. We are
leaving for hospital<. Little ones< healthy. My tenderest thoughts are with you.
Strongly believe news will be better.[88b] All embrace and kiss you. Alix

No. 306/ Telegram 180. Stavka> Tsarskoe Selo. 9 May 1915. 2.53> 3.43 p.m.
To her majesty. Happy to know you are back. Best thanks for news. Situation a
little better.[88b] Also very fine weather at last. Please thank the three youngest for
letters. Tender love Nikolai

No. 307/ Telegram 69. Tsarskoe Selo> Stavka. 10 May 1915. 1.16> 1.40 p.m.
To his majesty. Bright, sunny day. Just returned from church. My tenderest
prayers and thoughts surround you. God help. All kiss [you] tenderly. Alix

No. 308/ Telegram 203. Stavka> Tsarskoe Selo. 10 May 1915. 2.45> 3.02
p.m. To her majesty. Loving thanks [for] dear letter and news. News better
thank God.[88b] Weather not too hot. Sorry are not together. Fondest love. Old
man [Fredericks] begs to be remembered. Niki

No. 309/ Her No. 310.   Ts.[arskoe] S[elo]. May 10th 1915.
My own precious One,
    A lovely, warm, sunny morning; yesterday too it was fine, but so cold lying on
the balkony [sic] after the summerweather at Vitebsk. Our Church is so prettily
decorated in green—do you remember last year at Livadia how lovely our little
Church was—& once this day on board in Finland too? Dear me, how much has
happened since the peaceful, homely life in the fjords! Edigarov< writes that
they have 35 degrees of warmth.—[Your sister] Olga wrote that all their
wounded had to be sent off in full speed with deep sorrow on both sides—the
very worse were transferred to another hospital wh. must remain. God grant still
L.['vov] & P.[rzemysl'] wont be taken[90] & that these great feastdays may bring
us luck! This journey of yours [means] I get no telegrams alas, & so have to
hunt in the papers for news—one lives through a time of grave anxiety—so I am
glad you are not here, where everything is taken in a different tone, except by
the wounded, who understand all much more normally. [a]
    Drive with A.[nia<] to Pavlovsk—my first drive since autumn— lovely, only
one feels so sad at heart—& my back aches awfully since 3 days—then remained
on the balkony [sic] & we are drinking tea there too. Thanks for yr. telegram
Deary,—thank God the news are better.[88b] I saw 3 of Olga's ladies, its the regiment's feast, then Kostia< & Commander of Izmail.[ovo] reg.—Sister Ivanova
(Sonia's Aunt) fr. Varsovie [Warsaw]—interesting all she told about the hospitals
there.—Tiechen [Elena Georgievna] heard through the Pss. Oginsky & told
Mavra to tell me, that the prisoners (wounded) catholics are allowed to confess
to Priests (Vilna) but not have holy Communion—thats quite wrong, but is Tumanov's order—if they are afraid of the Priests, then why allow confession? —I
suppose those are Bavarians, I don't know how the protestants are treated—can
you speak to somebody to enquire into this? Thank old man [Fredericks] & bow

fr. me, & bow to N.P.<— A.[nia] sends her love & kisses yr. hand.—Blessings & kisses without end, beloved One. Ever yr. very, very own Wify. [b]

90. The enemy recaptured Peremyshl' (also Przemysl) on May 21/June 3, 1915, L'vov on June 9/22, 1915.

No. 310/ Telegram 73. Tsarskoe Selo> Stavka. 11 May 1915. 9.16> 10.45 a.m. To his majesty. Only 10 degrees and overcast. Attended early mass in church on lower [floor] of our hospital<, then worked. All my tenderest thoughts are with you. I kiss and embrace you. Greetings to old man [Fredericks]. Alix

No. 311/ Telegram 225. Stavka> Tsarskoe Selo. 11 May 1915. 2.32> 3.21 p.m. To her majesty. Loving thanks for dear letter. Have written. Today very warm, even close air. News all right.[88b] Old man [Fredericks] thanks. Tender kisses. Niki

No. 312/ Her No. 311.   Tsarskoe Selo. May 11th 1915.
My own precious Nicky,
    Again quite fresh and grey, & in the night only one degree— extraordinary for the month of May.—We spent the evening at Ania's< yesterday, some officers were invited 8-10½ & they played games—Aleksei came fr. 8 to 9¼ & enjoyed himself greatly; I knitted. She gave me the letters fr. the wretched Nostits couple to read—it seems this hideous intrigue was written to her relations to America, by a Gentleman of the American embassy, instigated by her enemies—the Ambassador is a friend of theirs. She thinks it is all done by M-me. Artsimovich (an American by birth) a story of jealousy. But it was sad to read their despairing letters of lives ruined—but I feel sure you will see that this story is cleared up satisfactorily & justice done them. I care for neither, but the whole thing is a crying shame & N.< had no right to act as he did with a member of your Suite, without asking first your permission—so easy to ruin a reputation & more than difficult to reestablish it.—I must dress now.—I ordered service at 9½ in the Peshch.[erni] chapel of the Dv. [court] hospital, so that we can work at once in the hospital when mass is over. My heart keeps decent (drops always) but back aches very strongly—for sure kidneys. [a]
    I had Engalichev< to-day & he told me many interesting things.— Went to the big palace< & then lay on the balkony [sic] reading to Ania, tho' cold. Our Friend< saw Bark for 2 hours & they talked well together.—God be thanked that the news is better, may it only continue thus! What joy, you are writing to me! To-day its a week you left us.—The Children all kiss you & so do I, my lovebird. Send blessings without end. Ever, huzy love, yr. very own old Sunny. [P.S.] Bow to old man [Fredericks] & N.P.< [b]

No. 313/ His No. 176.   Stavka. May 11th 1915.
My Own Dear Love,
    Today it is exactly a week that I left. I am so sorry not to have written to you since then. But somehow it happens to me to be occupied here like at home. The morning doklady [reports] were long, as you may imagine, then church

nearly every day, conversations without end, etc. All this took up nearly all my time, except half of the afternoon, wh was filled up by the useful constitutions. The result—a headache or complete ramolishment in the evening. But that is past & now everything's become better & normal, as it used to be. [a]

When I arrived the prevailing feeling here was a depressed & low on[e]. In a halfhour's talk, N.< explained the whole situation very clearly. Ivanov's Chief of the Staff, poor Gen Dragomirov, went off his head & began telling right & left that it was necessary to retreat to Kiev.[83] Such talks coming from the top, of course acted strongly on the minds of the commanding generals, and coupled with the tremendous German attacks & our terrible losses, brought them to the conclusion that nothing remained for them but to retreat. Since January N. gave strict orders to all of them to fortify strong positions in the rear. This was not done. Therefore, Radko-Dmitriev has to leave his army; while Lesh being named as his successor. Dragomirov was replaced by Gen. Savvich, an excellent man who came with his Siberian corps from Vladivostok. Ivanov gave orders to evacuate even Przemysl! I felt that all along, before N. told me about it. But now, after the nomination of Savvich, thank God, thanks also to his [Savvich's] strong & calm will & clear head, the generals' mood has changed. N. sent Gen. Danilov who came back yesterday, perfectly calmed by what he has seen and heard. The moral state of our troops is splendid, as usual; but the only thing which causes anxiety, as in the past, is the lack of ammunition.[91] [b]

Fancy, that has also happened to the Germans down there, according to what their prisoners tell our officers—namely that their attacks had to be stopped owing to their ammunition running short & also on account of their enormous losses. N. is very pleased with Gen. Alekseev, my squinting friend, and finds him the right man in the right place! Now you can judge whether I was to leave this place under such difficult circumstances? It would have seemed that I wished to avoid remaining with the army during serious moments. Poor N. cried in my cabin when he had explained all this & even asked me whether I was not thinking of replacing him by any other more capable man. He was not in the least excited; I felt he meant what he had said. He thanked me over & over for remaining here longer, because my presence calmed him personally. [c]

There! I had to explain all this to you, my Treasure. Now my conscience feels clear. I hope to come back on the morning of the 14th—again, if all goes smoothly. Adm. Essen's sudden death is a heavy loss to the country! Adm. Kanin, who he put very high, shall be named in Essen's place. The weather has become glorious since four days. The woods smells too delicious & the birdies sing so loud. It is a real country idyll—if it were not during war. I motor about & look at new places, get out & walk a good deal. I send you this telegram of N. wh. only came this morning. I am delighted for your regiment, of course Bat. [?] shall get his cross! I have to end. God bless you my darling Sunny and the dear children. Give A.[nia]< my love. With tender kisses I remain ever your own loving huzy. Nicky. [d]

___

91. The German-Austrian attack found Russians suffering a continuation of the shortage of rifles and artillery Nicholas referred to in Letter No. 187a. One Russian army corps had four heavy guns *versus* 200 comparable weapons directed against it. The four Russian guns were limited to 10 shells per gun per day. German guns were firing 700,000 shells in a few hours; Russian factories then

needed six months to produce the same ordnance. (Oldenburg, *Last Tsar*, IV, pp. 27-31, 67) Responsibility for this incredible situation fell squarely on Minister of War Sukhomlinov.

No. 314/ Telegram 77. Tsarskoe Selo> Stavka. 12 May 1915. 9.50> 10.35 a.m. To his majesty. Sunny but windy. Leaving for work. Spent last evening peacefully at home. Many new wounded. All tenderly embrace and kiss you. Alix

---

No. 315/ Her No. 312.   Ts.[arskoe] S[elo]. May 12th 1915.
My own beloved One,
   When we returned from the hospital I found your beloved letter, & thank you for it from the depths of my loving heart. <u>Such</u> joy to hear from you, Sweetheart! Thanks so much for all details, I was so longing to get real, exact news from you. How hard those days were, & I not near you & such hard work, much to do! Thank God that all is better now & may Italy draw some of the troops away.[92] I remember Savvich, did he not come to the Crimea? The new Admiral's face I don't remember, he is [M. P. Sablin,] a cousin of N.P.<—Have the Eriv.< & all the Caucasian division been sent to the Carpathans [sic], or is it not true? They were asking me again.—Engal.< said one expects the next heavy battles will be near Varsovie [Warsaw],[83] but he finds our 2 Generals (don't remember the name) weak & not the types to meet heavy attacks. He told N.< & Yanushk.[evich] so. [a]
   Am so glad about the paper you sent of my Crimeans<—they are then again in another division.—My Alexand.< have also been doing well near Shavli. Wonder how my [D. M.] Knyazhevich's health is, have no news since he left.—Just now received 11 officers—the most going off to Evpatoria—that law of 8 or 9 months is fearfully hard—we have some with broken limbs wh. can be healed only after a year, impossible before, but then alright [sic] for service—& as they cannot possibly now return to their regiments, they loose [sic] their pay—& some are so poor, have no fortune of their own—it does seem unjust. Crippled, not always for life, but for a time, doing their duty bravely, wounded & then left like beggars—their moral sufferings becomes so great. Others hasten back too early, only not to loose all & may completely loose their health fr. that. Certainly some types (few) must be hurried off to their regiments because are fit for work already.—Its all complicated. My back still aches & now higher up, a sort of Hexenschuss [lumbago] wh. makes many movements very painful—still I managed to do my works. Now I shall lie on the balkony [sic] & read to Ania<, as driving been shaken [i.e., the shaking of an automobile], makes the back worse.—What joy if we meet really on Thursday! Goodbye my Love, God bless & keep you from all harm! Ever such tender kisses from us all. Yr. very Own. [unsigned] [b]

---

92. Italy was an ally of Germany and Austria-Hungary when the war broke out. Italy proclaimed neutrality on the grounds that the Triple Alliance was a *defensive* pact invalidated by the offensive actions of Germany and Austria. Actually, the Italian government bargained with both sides, intending to enter the conflict on whichever side promised greater spoils. Germany was handicapped in this by the fact that Italy's ambitions centered on areas held by Austria-Hungary. Italy finally declared war on Austria on May 10/23, 1915. As the empress indicates, Russia hoped the initial Italian offensive against Gorizia and Trieste would draw Austrian divisions from the eastern front.

But the Austrians held a strategic advantage on her border with Italy, the smallish Italian army was not ready for war—and the Italians did little to satisfy the hopes of her weary allies.

No. 316/ Telegram 256. Stavka> Tsarskoe Selo. 12 May 1915. 7.51> 8.10 p.m. To the empress. Fondest thanks [for] news and dear letter. Divine weather, lilacs are out. Leave to-morrow at 2,0. Tender kisses. Niki

---

No. 317/ Telegram 79. Tsarskoe Selo> Stavka. 12 May 1915. 9.10> 9.35 p.m. To his majesty. Hearty thanks for dear letter and telegram. Such joy. Wonderful weather. Am lying on balcony. All kiss you. Sleep well. Alix

---

No. 318/ Telegram 265. Stavka> Tsarskoe Selo. 13 May 1915. 12.51> 1.12 p.m. To her majesty. Tender thanks [for] dear letter. Took my last walk. Very warm. Leave after lunch. Happy to return. Fondest kisses. Niki

---

No. 319/ Telegram 81. Tsarskoe Selo> Lida. 13 May 1915. 2.18> 3.49 p.m. To his majesty. Thank you for telegram; am terribly glad to see you soon; we worked in hospital<, now arriving [home]. [We] warmly embrace [you], wish [you] a good trip. May God keep you. Alix

---

No. 320/ Her No. 313.   Ts.[arskoe] S[elo]. June 10th 1915.
My very own precious One,
    It is with a heavy heart I let you leave this time—everything is so serious & just now particularly painful & I long to be with you, to share your worries & anxieties. You bear all so bravely & by yourself!—let me help you my Treasure. Surely there is some way in wh. a woman can be of help & use. I do so yearn to make it easier for you & the ministers all squabbling amongst each other at a time, when all ought to work together & forget their personal offenses—have as aim the welfare of their Sovereign & Country—it makes me rage. In other words its treachery, because people know it, they feel the government in discord & then the left profit by it. If you could only be severe, my Love, it is so necessary, they must hear your voice & see displeasure in yr. eyes; they are too much accustomed to your gentle, forgiving kindness. [a]
    Sometimes a word gently spoken carries far—but at a time, such as we are now living through, one needs to hear your voice uplifted in protest & reprimand [sic] when they continue not obeying yr. orders, when they dawdle in carrying them out. They must learn to tremble before you—you remember Mr. Ph.< & Gr.< say the same thing too. [See No. 343e.] You must simply order things to be done, not asking if they are possible (you will never ask anything unreasonable or a folly)—for instance, order as in France (a Republic) other fabrics [factories] to make shells, cartridges (if guns & rifles too complicated)—let the big fabrics [factories] send teacher[s to the smaller factories]—where there is a will there is a way & they must all realise that you insist upon yr. wish being speedily fulfilled. It is for them to find the people, the fabricants [factory workers], to settle all going, let them go about & see to the work being done, themselves. You know how talented our people are, how gifted—only lazy & without initia-

tive, start them going, & they can do anything, only dont ask, but order straight off, be energetic for yr. country's sake! [b]

The same about the question wh. our Friend< takes so to heart & wh. is the most serious of all, for internal peace's sake—the not calling in the Second class[93]—if the order has been given, you tell N.< that you insist upon its counterordering—by your name to wait, the kind act must come fr. you—dont listen to any excuses—(am sure it was unintentionally done out of not having knowledge of the country). Therefore our Friend dreads yr. being at the Headquarters as all come round with their own explanations & involuntarily you give in to them, when yr. own feeling has been the right one, but did not suit theirs. Remember you have reigned long, have far more experience than they—N. has only the army to think of & success—you carry the internal responsabilities [sic] on for years—if he makes faults (after the war he is nobody), but you have to set all straight. No, hearken unto our Friend, believe Him, He has yr. interest & Russia's at heart—it is not for nothing God sent Him to us—only we must pay more attention to what He says—His words are not lightly spoken—& the gravity of having not only His prayers, but His advise [sic]—is great. The Ministers did not think of telling you that this measure is a fatal one but He did. [c]

How hard it is not to be with you, to talk over all quietly & to help you being firm! Shall follow & be near you in thoughts & prayers all the time. May God bless & protect you, my brave, patient, humble one! I cover yr. sweet face with endless, tender kisses,—love you beyond words, my own, very own Sunshine & joy.—I bless you.—Sad not to pray together, but Botk.[in] finds wiser my remaining quiet, so as soon to be quite alright [sic] again. Yr. own Wify [P.S.] Our Marie will be 16 on the 14-th, so [I plan to] give her diamond-necklace fr. us, like the other two [older daughters] got. [d]

---

93. Russia, like other countries, divided her conscript population into "classes." By June 1915, at least 3,800,000 Russians were killed, wounded, taken prisoner or missing in action. The government was then ready to call up the "second class," untrained men ages 21-43. This had happened only in 1812 and 1854—such talk indicated an emergency. But some objected that the call would deprive factories and farms of critical manpower while the army might be unable to use so many conscripts. Letter 323b suggests Rasputin helped influence Alexandra against this admittedly unwise policy. See also Letters No. 329d and 1295f.

No. 321/ Telegram 15 in Russian. Peredolskaya> Tsarskoe Selo. 11 June 1915. 7.15> 8.10 p.m. To her majesty. It has become very hot in the coach, am with you [all] in thoughts, thank you for letter, I embrace [you]. Niki

---

No. 322/ Telegram 89. Tsarskoe Selo> capital of Minsk gubernaya. 11 June 1915. To his majesty. Tenderly thank you for last evening's dear telegram. Miss [you] terribly, so sad, weather marvellous, we dined on the balcony and will also have lunch there. Feel better but not very well. We all tenderly kiss you. God help you so that news will become better! Alix

---

No. 323/ Her No. 314.   Tsarskoe Selo. June 11th 1915.
My very own precious One,

All my tenderest thoughts surround you in love and longing. It was a lovely surprise, when you suddenly turned up again—I had been praying & crying & feeling wretched. You don't know how hard it is being without you & how terribly I always miss you! Your dear telegram was such a consolation, as I felt very low & Ania's< odious humor towards me (not to the Children) did anything but enliven my afternoon & evening.—We dined out & took tea on the balkony [sic]—this morning its glorious again—I am still in bed, resting you see, as heart not quite the thing, tho' not enlarged—I have been sorting out photos to be glued into albums for the exhibition-bazar [sic] here.—Fancy, big Marie Baryat.'s< husband died from a stroke on the 9-th at Berezhany in a property named Rai—one carries his body to Tarnopol. He was commissioner of the red cross at the 11-th Army, can imagine Marie & Olga's despair, as they loved so their brother Ivan. Then the old C.[ount] Olsuf'ev has died—they lived as turtledoves, she will be brokenhearted.—One hears of nothing but deaths it seems to me.—Fancy, what I did last night in bed? I fished out yr. old letters & read through many of them, & those few before we were engaged— & all yr. words of intense love & tenderness warmed up my aching heart, & it seemed to me, as tho' I heard you speaking. [a]

I numbered yours, the last 176 fr. the Head-Quarters. You number my yesterdays please, 313—I hope my letter did not displease you[94] but I am haunted by our Friend's< wish & know it will be fatal for us & the country is not fulfilled. He means what He says, when speaks so seriously—He was much against yr. going to L.['vov] & P.[rzemysl']—it was too soon, we see it now[83] —was much against the war[95] —was against the people of the Duma coming [into session in January 1915], an ugly act of Rodz.< & the speeches ought not to have been printed (I find).[96] Please, my Angel, make N.< see with your eyes—dont give in to any of the 2-nd class being taken—put it off as long as only possible—they have to work in the fields, fabrics [factories], on steamers etc.;[93] rather take the recroutes [sic] for next year now—please listen to His [Rasputin's] advise [sic] when spoken so gravely & wh. gave Him sleepless nights!—one fault & we shall all have to pay for it.—I wonder what humour you found at the Head-Quarters & whether the heat is very great.— [b]

Felix [Yusupov the Younger] told Ania that one threw (then) stones at Ella's< carriage & spat at her, but she did not wish to speak to us about it—they feared disorders these days again[97] —don't know why.—The big girls< are in the hospital, yesterday all 4 worked in the stores—bandages—& later went to Irina [wife of Felix Yusupov the younger].—How do you feel, my Love, your beloved sad eyes haunt me still. Dear Olga [your sister] wrote a sweet letter & kisses you & asks sweetly how you bear all, tho' she knows you will always wear a cheery face & carry all hidden inside. I fear often for yr. poor heart—it was so much to bear—speak out to yr. old wify—bride of the bygone—share all with me, it may make it easier—tho' sometimes one has more strength carrying alone, not letting oneself get soft—the phisical [sic] heart get[s] so bad from it, I know it but too well. Lovebird, I kiss you without end, bless you, cover yr. precious face with kisses & long to let you dear head rest upon my old breast, so full of unutterable love & devotion. Ever yr. own old   Alix.   [P.S.]   My love to the old man [Fredericks] & N.P.<   I receive M-me, Hartwig, Rauchfuss, the 4 Trepov daughters (2 married). Remember to speak about the wounded officers being allowed to finish their cures at home before returning for 2, 3 or 4 time[s] to battle, its cruel & unjust otherwise, N. must give Alek< the order.

94. Alexandra often gave her husband a letter to read as he returned to Stavka; such was apparently the case with this scolding epistle. Nicholas's reply (No. 321) suggests displeasure: the telegram is brief, we learn it "has become very hot in the coach." The emperor thanks his wife for her message but does not say, as was habitual, that he embraces her "tenderly," etc. The well-bred Nicholas II indicated negative feelings through such small gestures.

95. Alexandra touched on sensitive issues in this passage. Rasputin had opposed war, he warned Nicholas it would bring the end of the dynasty. Military developments at this point seemed to confirm Rasputin's foreboding. Although the tsar's armies took Galicia in March, the German-Austrian counterattack recaptured lost ground—and more. After the Russians abandoned Warsaw (July 26/August 7), their entire front fell into disarray. By September 6/19, the Germans occupied Vil'no and celebrated an advance of 300 miles. Nicholasha was a master of retreat, however, and most of his army escaped. The fall rains of 1915 turned the roads to mud and halted the German advance. "By year's end the Eastern Front was a line running north and south from Riga on the Baltic to the eastern end of the Carpathians." (Dupuy and Dupuy, *Encyclopedia*, p. 952.) In 1914, the Germans massed enormous forces against France, yet failed to take her out of the war. This scenario was replayed in early 1915 against Russia—and with the same lack of success.

96. Russia's legislature consisted of the Duma (lower house) and State Council (upper house). The Duma was elected for five-year terms by indirect vote weighted in favor of the propertied classes. The tsar appointed half of the State Council for one-year terms; the others were elected to five-year terms by such corporate bodies as the clergy, businessmen, zemstvoes (local representative assemblies), Polish landowners, etc. Laws had to be approved by the Duma, the State Council and the tsar, who also had the power to convene and recess the Duma. Nicholas called the Duma into a one-day session on July 26/ August 1, 1914 to approve war credits. It also met for three days in late-January 1915. The Duma became increasingly critical of the government in the wake of Russian defeats and shortages. From the outset, the Duma had been an unwilling concession from the throne to bring the Revolution of 1905 to an end. Nicholas always regretted this decision. He would have liked to use the war as a pretext to reduce the powers of the Duma or abolish it altogether.

In this letter we see the empress was critical of Michael Rodzyanko, member of the moderate-conservative Octobrist Party and President of the Duma. Rodzyanko was a monarchist; he loved the tsar and hoped to persuade Nicholas II to work with the Duma. Rodzyanko enlisted deputies to work with the "War Industries Committees" organized independently of the government to harness Russian industry. Rodzyanko also hoped for a "ministry of public confidence," an arrangement whereby the ministers would be responsible to the Duma as well as the tsar. The ministers would work with War Industries Committees to organize the nation for victory. But Nicholas saw all these moves as threats to his authority. He resented Rodzyanko's well-intentioned efforts. Even so, military setbacks forced the tsar to compromise. As the letters show, in a few days Nicholas went against his wife's wishes and dismissed his most unpopular ministers, replacing them with men who enjoyed the respect of the Duma and educated Russian "society." Nicholas even agreed to reconvene the Duma on July 19/August 1, 1915.

97. Moscow responded to German advances with anti-German riots on May 27-29/ June 10-12, 1915. People with German surnames were beaten and killed, and their property was plundered while the police stood by. As we see in this letter, Alexandra's sister Elizabeth, a German, was threatened, though not harmed. Felix Yusupov (the Elder) was governor of Moscow. When he finally acted, he put the disorders down with incredible severity. Nicholas dismissed Yusupov for his inept handling of this crisis. See de Jonge, *Life and Times of Grigorii Rasputin*, pp. 304-308

No. 324/ Telegram 164. Stavka> Tsarskoe Selo. 11 June 1915. 6.19> 6.28 p.m. To her majesty. Arrived well. Very warm showers on the way. Thanks for news. Nothing particularly bad [to report]. Hope you will soon feel quite strong. Tender love. Niki

No. 325/ Her No. 315.   Tsarskoe Selo. June 12th 1915.

My very own precious One,

With such anxiety I wait for news & eagerly read the morning papers so as to know what happens!— Glorious weather again—yesterday during dinner (on the balcony [sic]) there was a colossal downpour, seems it must daily rain, personally I have nothing against it, as always dread the heat & yesterday it was very hot & Ania's< temper beastly, wh. did not make me feel better— grumbling against everybody & everything & strong hidden pricks at you & me.—This afternoon I may drive & to-morrow I hope to go (after a week's absence) to the hospital,< as one of the officers must have his apendicitis cut off.—Dmitri< had his leg put in plaster of Paris Gypsum & to-day they are going to look with Rontgen-rays to see whether the leg is really broken, crushed or strained—what bad luck always! [a]

Sweet one, please remember the question about the Tobolsk Tatars to be called in—they are splendid, devoted fellows & no doubt would go with joy & pride.—I found a paper of old Marie Fed. [Maria Fedorovna, the wife of Emperor Paul] you once bought me, & as it is funny, I send it to you.—I saw Mme Hartwig yesterday—she told me many interesting things when they left Lvov—& sad impressions of soldiers being depressed & saying that they wont return to fight the enemy with empty fists—the rage of the officers against Sukhomlinov is quite colossal—poor man—his very name they loathe & yearn for him to be sent away—well for his sake too, before any scandle [sic] arises, it would be better to do so. It is his adventurer wife who has completely ruined his reputation—because of her bribes he suffers & so on;—one says it is his fault there is no ammunition wh. is our curse now etc.[98] I tell you this to show you what impressions she brought back.— [b]

How one craves for a miracle to bring success, that ammunition & rifles should do double work!—Wonder how the spirit in the Head-Quarters is?—Would to God N.< were another man & had not turned against a man of Gods [i.e., Grigory Rasputin], that always brings bad luck to their work & those women [his wife Anastasia and her sister Militsa] wont let him change; he received decorations without end & thanks for all—but too early—its pain to think he got so much & nearly all has been retaken. But God Almighty will help & better days will come, I feel convinced. Such trials for you to bear my own Sunshine! I long to be with you, to know how you are feeling morally—brave & calm as usual, the pain hidden away as usual? God help you my very own sweet Sufferer & give you strength, trust & courage! Yr. reign has been one of sore trials, but the recompense must come some day, God is just.—The little birdies are singing away so cheerily & a soft breeze comes in by the window. When I finish my letter, I shall get up;—these quiet days have done my heart good. [c]

Give many kind messages to the old man [Fredericks] & N.P.< I am glad the latter is near you, I feel a warm heart with you & that makes me quieter for your sweet sake.—Try & write a wee word for [our daughter] Marie, her 16th birthday being on Sunday.— [Daughter] Tatiana went for a ride yesterday, I encouraged her, the others were of course too lazy & went to the Nurse's school to play with the babies.—A Pr. Galitsine [Prince Golitsyn] Serg. Mikh. died at Lausanne—I suppose its the man of many wives.—Now my own Nicky darling, I must say goodbye. I regret having nothing of interest to tell you. The 4 [D. F.]

Trepov daughters beg to thank you ever so deeply for having permitted their mother to be buried next to their Father—they saw his coffin, still quite intact.—Blessings without end be yours, my Love, I cover yr. sweet face with kisses, & remain ever yr. very own Sunny. [d]

98. Alexander Guchkov was a daring adventurer who fought in wars in Europe, Africa, and Asia. In 1905 he advised Nicholas to pacify the moderates by offering the nation a Duma. Guchkov helped establish the "Octobrists," a moderate conservative party which hoped to adapt the monarchy to new, constitutional conditions. As president of the Duma in 1910, Guchkov reported directly to the tsar. He hoped to act as a broker between the throne and the Duma. But Nicholas disliked the Duma and those associated with its creation. Once Guchkov realized this, he turned on the tsar and worked to ruin his reign. Rodzyanko also sought a mediator's role with the same lack of success—though personally the tsar and Rodzyanko liked each other. (See Footnote 96.) Polivanov had ties to Guchkov; this offended Nicholas. But as Sukhomlinov's assistant, Polivanov deserved credit for most of the war ministry's accomplishments since August 1914. Polivanov was the logical choice to succeed Sukhomlinov, and Nicholas showed a rare ability (for him) to overlook past injuries and select the best man for this important post.

No. 326/ Telegram 286. Stavka> Tsarskoe Selo. 12 June 1915. 11.58 a.m.> 12.36 p.m. To her majesty. Fondest thanks [for] dear letter, also to [daughter] Olga for hers. After rainy night grey, warm weather. Lots to do but shall try and write. Loving kisses. Niki

No. 327/ Telegram 98. Tsarskoe Selo> Stavka. 12 June 1915. 1.29> 2.45 p.m. To his majesty. Heartfelt thanks for yesterday's and today's telegrams. Marvellous weather. We are dining on balcony. Feel better. Later we go for drive. We tenderly embrace and kiss you. What news? Alix

No. 328/ His No. 177.   Stavka. June 12th 1915.
My own beloved Wify,
   Thank you ever so much for your two dear letters; they refreshed me. This time I left with a very heavy heart. Thought over those difficult questions— changing ministers, about the Duma, the 2nd razryad [class], etc. On my arrival, I found N.< serious, but quite calm. We at once began speaking the latter question. He told me he understood the gravity & that he had a letter from Goremykin on the subject. Everything in one's power shall be done to put it off. I asked him who he would recommend in place of Sukhomlinov's<. He answered—Polivanov. After having looked through many names of Generals—I came to the conclusion that, for the moment he might be the right man. So he was sent for & arrived this afternoon. I spoke to him quite frankly & told him why I was displeased with him before (A. Goutchkov etc.)[98] He said he knew it & bore that burden of my displeasure for 3 years. He lost his only son in this war & has helped Alek< very much & in a good way. So I hope his nomination will be a successful one.
   Today I saw Krivoshein too & had a long talk; he was less excited & therefore more reasonable. I have sent for Goremykin & a few of the older Ministers & to-morrow we shall discuss some of these questions & leave nothing unsaid. Yes, my sweet one, I begin to feel my old heart. The first time it was in August last, after [the] Samsonov disaster [at the Battle of Tannenburg in August 1914],

and now again—so heavy on the left side when I breathe! Well what is to be done! Alas! I must end now, they are all collecting for dinner near the big tent. God bless you, my Treasure, my comfort & happiness. I kiss you all fondly. Ever your own huzy. Nicky .[P.S.] Divine weather. [b]

No. 329/ Her No. 316.   Tsarskoe Selo. June 12th 1915.
My very Own,
    I begin my letter still to-night, as to-morrow morning I hope to go to the hospital< & shall have less time for writing. Ania< & I took a nice drive to Pavlovsk this afternoon—in the shade it was quite cool; we lunched & took tea on the balkony [sic], but in the evening it got too fresh to sit out. From 9½-11½ we were at Anias, I worked on the sopha, the 3 girls & officers played games. I am tired after my first outing.—My Lvov store is now at Rovno near the station for the time—God grant we shant be driven back fr. there too.—That we had to leave that town [Lvov] is hard, but still it was not quite ours yet—nevertheless its sad to have fallen into other hands—[Kaiser] William will now be sleeping in old Fr.[anz] J[oseph]'s bed wh. you occupied one night—I don't like that, its humiliating,[90]—but that one can bear—but to think that once more the same battle-fields may be strewn with the bodies of our brave men—thats heartrending. But I ought not to speak to you in this tone, you have enough sorrow—my letters must be cheery ones, but its a bit difficult when heart & soul are sad. I hope to see our Friend< a moment in the morning at Anias to bid Him goodbye— that will do me good. Serge Tan.[eev] was to leave to-night over Kiev but got a telegram that the Akhtirtsy are being sent elsewhere & he must leave to-morrow. I wonder what new combination.— How one wishes Alekseev had remained with Ivanov, things might have gone better—Dragomirov set all going wrong. [a]
    One prays & prays & yet never enough—the Schadenfreude [one who delights in others' misfortunes] of Germany makes my blood boil. God must surely hearken unto our supplications & send some success at least;—now shall be having them turn towards Varsovie [Warsaw] & many troops are near Shavli, oh God, what a hideous war![95]   Sweet, brave Soul how I wish one could rejoice your poor, tortured heart with something bright & hopeful! I long to hold you tightly clasped in my arms, with yr. sweet head resting upon my shoulder—then I could cover Lovy's face & eyes with kisses & murmer [sic] soft words of love. I kiss your cushion at nights, thats all I have—& bless it.—Now I must go to sleep. Rest well, my treasure, I bless & kiss you ever so fondly & gently stroke your dear brow. [b]
June 13-th. How can I thank you enough for your beloved letter, I received upon our return from the hospital. Such an intense joy hearing from you, my Angel, thanks thousands of times! But I am sad your dear heart does not feel right, please let Botkin see you upon yr. return as he can give you drops to take from time to time when you have pains. I feel so awfully for those who have anything with the heart, suffering from it myself for so many years. Hiding ones sorrow, swallowing all, makes it so bad & it gets [one] besides phisically [sic] tired—your eyes seemed like it at times. Only always tell it me, as I have after all enough experience with heart complain[t]s & I can perhaps help you. Speak

about all to me, talk it out, cry even, it makes it phisically too, easier sometimes. [c]

Thank God N.< understood about the second class.[93] —Forgive me, but I don't like the choice of [Polivanov as] Minister of war—you remember how you were against him, & surely rightly & N. too I fancy. He works with Xenia< too—but is he a man in whom one can have any confidence, can he be trusted? How I wish I were with you & could hear all yr. reasons for choosing him! I dread N.'s nominations, N. is far from clever, obstinate & led by others—God grant I am mistaken & this choice may be blest —but I like a crow, croak over it rather. Can the man have changed so much? Has he dropped Guchkov[98] —is he not our Friend's< enemy, as that brings bad luck. Make dear old Goremykin thoroughly speak with him, morally influence him. Oh may these 2 new ministers be the right men in the right place, ones heart is so full of anxiety & one yearns for union amongst the ministers, success.[99] Lovy mine, tell them upon their return from the Headquarters to ask & see me, one after the other, & I shall pray hard & try my utmost to be of real use to you. Its horrid not helping & letting you have all the hard work to do.— [d]

Our Friend dined (I think) with Shakhovskoi again & likes him—He can influence him for the good. Fancy how strange! Schcherbatov wrote a most amiable letter to Andronnikov (after having spoken against him to you).—There is another minister I don't like in his place, Shcheglovitov,< (to speak to pleasant [sic]) he does not heed to your orders, & whenever a petition comes wh. he thinks our Friend brought, he wont do it & not long ago tore one of yours through again. Verevkin his aid (Gr.'s friend) told this—& I have noticed that he rarely does what one asks—like Timiryasev obstinate & "by the letter" not by the soul. Its right to be severe— but one might be more just than he is & kinder to the small people, more lenient.—Our apendicitis [sic] operation went off well; saw the new officers—the poor boy with tetanos [i.e., tetanus or lockjaw] is a little better—more helpful. [e]

Such fine weather, am lying on the balkony [sic] & the birdies are chirruping away so gaily.—A.[nia<] just sat with me, she saw Gr.< this morning, he slept better for the first time since 5 nights & says its a little better at war. He begs you most incessantly to order quickly that on one day all over the country there should be a church procession to ask for victory, God will sooner hear if all turn to Him—please give the order, any day you choose now that it should be done—send yr. order (I think) by wire (open that all can read it) to Sabler[99] that this is yr. wish—now is Petr[ovski] Lent, so it is yet more apropriate [sic], & it will lift the spirit up, & be a consolation to the brave one's [sic] fighting—& tell the same thing to Shavel'sky Deary—please Darling, & just that its to be an order from you, not from the Synod. [See Letter No. 338b] I could not see Him [Rasputin] to-day—hope to-morrow.[f]

A.[nia], Alia< & Nini< have gone by motor to Krasnoe to talk with Groten. Now I must quickly send off this letter. Marie Bariatinsky dines with us & leaves to-morrow with Olga [her sister-in-law] for Kiev I think.—God bless & protect you!—heart & soul with you, prayers without end surround you. Feel sad & low-spirited, hate being separated fr. you, all the more so when you have so many worries. But God will help & if these church processions are done, am sure He will hearken unto all prayers of your faithful people. God guard & guide you, you my very own Love. If you have any question for our Fr. write at once. I cover you with fondest kisses. Ever yr. own old <u>Wify</u>. [P.S.] Love to old man [Fredericks] & N.P.< [g]

99. Nicholas made Ivan Goremykin—an arch-monarchist who would faithfully execute orders—chairman of the council of ministers in January 1914. By August 1915, none of the ministers wanted to serve any longer under him. [See Letter No. 331d.] But Nicholas trusted Goremykin and retained him until January 1916. The tsar dismissed four other (unpopular) ministers in the "purge" of June 1915. The "2 new ministers" Alexandra mentions were Alexander Polivanov and Prince Nicholas Shcherbatov. They replaced Sukhomlinov (minister of war) and Maklakov (internal affairs). Alexandra conceded (Letter No. 325b) that Sukhomlinov was despised and had to go. But she did not like the new appointees. Alexander Samarin replaced Vladimir Sabler as Director of the Holy Synod, while Alexander Khvostov followed Ivan Shcheglovitov as minister of justice. Sabler was unpopular because of his German surname and an (undeserved) reputation of being a toady of Rasputin. With these changes, the council contained some extremely able men.

No. 330/ Telegram 102. Tsarskoe Selo> Stavka. 13 June 1915. 10.10> 11.05 a.m. To his majesty. Beautiful weather. We are leaving again for the hospital.< Feel better at last. We tenderly embrace and kiss [you]. Today I inspect English automobiles. Greetings to old man [Fredericks]. Alix

No. 331/ Telegram 103. Tsarskoe Selo> Stavka. 13 June 1915. 2.32> 3.31 p.m. To his majesty. Inexpressible thanks for dear telegram. Am sorry you did not find any one else.[99] [We] are having lunch on balcony. Operation went well. Very melancholy. Sad I am not with you at such a time. God bless and help you. All warmly embrace and kiss [you]. Alix

No. 332/ Telegram 196. Stavka> Tsarskoe Selo. 13 June 1915. 6.45> 7.05 p.m. To her majesty. Fondest thanks [for] beloved letter, also [our children] Tatiana and Aleksei. Have written to Marie for her birthday. Divine weather. News not so bad.[88] Very occupied day. Tender kisses. Niki

No. 333/ Her No. 317.   Ts.[arskoe] S[elo]. June 14th 1915.
My own beloved One,
    I congratulate you with all my loving heart for our big [daughter] Marie's 16-th birthday. What a cold, rainy summer it was when she was borne [sic]—3 weeks I had daily pains until she turned up. Pitty [sic] you are not here. She enjoyed all her presents, I gave her her [sic] first ring from us made out of one of my Buchara [Bukhara] diamonds. She is so cheery & gay to-day. I am writing on the balkony [sic], we have just finished luncheon after we had been to Church. Baby< is going to Peterhof for the afternoon & later to Ania.< Such lovely weather & the wind keeps it from being too hot—but the evenings are fresh. Marie Bariatinsky dined with us & remained till 10½ & then I went to bed as had a headache. The girls had a repetition [rehearsal] in the "little house" [of Anna Vyrubova?].— [a]
    Beloved one, all my thoughts & prayers are with you the whole time & so much sorrow and anxiety fills the heart!—I hope you will say about the church processions. [See Letter No. 338b.] Old Fred.< of course made a confusion &

gived [sic] O. Evg.< [a gift based] on her money she got as my lady, not her Father's pension (wh. was much less) & she asked for. She feels quite confused at. yr. great kindness.—Yesterday I looked at the 10 English motors— quite splendid, much better than ours, for four [wounded occupants] lying & a sister or sanitary can sit inside with them & always hot water to be had for them—they hope to get yet 20 more for us, yr. Mama [Maria Fedorovna] & me together. As soon as she has seen these, they ought to be sent off I find at once where the cavalry is most in need of them now, I don't know where, perhaps you could ask, & then I can hint it to Motherdear<. She is now at Elagin<. Paul< comes to tea & then the children go to Ania, perhaps I too for a bit if not too tired. I see our Friend< this evening or to-morrow morning. We are going out driving this afternoon, A.[nia] & I; the girls< will follow in two small carriages. Now I must end dear Love. How I long to know how the news really are, such anxiety fills the soul!—Goodbye Nicky mine, my very, very own. God bless & protect you! I cover your precious face with kisses. Ever yr. very own Sunny. [b]

No. 334/ Telegram 217. Stavka> Tsarskoe Selo. 14 June 1915. 12.47> 1.55 p.m. To her majesty. Tender thanks for dearest letter and best wishes for Marie's birthday. Just back from church. After lunch council of ministers. Divine weather and cool nights. Fondest kisses. Niki

---

No. 335/ Telegram 105. Tsarskoe Selo> Stavka. 14 June 1915. 1.16 p.m.> 1.57 p.m. To his majesty. Tenderly congratulate you on birthday of our older daughter [Marie]. Clear, cool, windy. Are having lunch on balcony. I went to church. Think of and pray for you. All warmly kiss [you]. God bless you. Alix

---

No. 336/ Her No. 318.   Ts.[arskoe] S[elo]. June 14th 1915.
My own beloved Nicky,
    So many thanks for yr. dear telegram! Poor Darling, even on Sunday a council of ministers!—We had a nice drive to Pavlovsk, coming back, little Georgi on his small motor (like Aleksei's) flew into our carriage, but luckily he did not upset & his machine was not spoiled.—Paul< came to tea & remained 1 & ¾ hours, he was very nice & spoke honestly & simply, meaning well, not wishing to meddle with what does not concern him, only asking all sorts of things wh. I now repeat to you, with his knowledge. Well, to begin with, Paléolog[ue] dined with him a few days ago & then they had a long private talk & the latter tried to find out from him, very cleverly, whether he knew if you had any ideas about forming a seperate [sic] peace with Germany, as he heard such things being spoken about here, & as tho' in France one had got wind of it—& that there they intend fighting to the very end. Paul answered that he was convinced it was not true, all the more, as at the outset of the war we & our allies had settled, that peace could be concluded together on no account seperately [sic]. Then I told Paul that you had heard the same rumour about France; & he crossed himself when I said you were not dreaming of peace & knew it would mean revolution here & therefore the Germans are trying to egg it on. He said he had heard even

the Germans had conditions posed to us.—I warned him he wld. next hear, that I am wishing peace to be concluded.[81] [a]

Then he asked me whether it was true that Shcheglovitov< was being changed & that rotten Manukhin named in his place—I said I knew nothing, wh. is the truth, & neither why Shchegl. has chosen the moment now to go to the Solov.[etsky] convent. Then he mentioned another thing to me wh. tho' painful its better to warn you about—namely, that since 6 months one speaks of a spy being at the Headquarters & when I asked the name, he said Gen. Danilov (the black one)[see No. 892], that from many sides one had told him this "feeling" & that now in the army one speaks about it. Lovy mine, Voeikov< is sly & clever, talk to him about this, & let him slyly & cleverly try & have an eye upon the man & his doings—why not have him watched—of course as Paul says one has the spy mania now, but as things are at once known abroad wh. only very wellinitiated people at the Headquarters can know, this strong doubt has arisen, & Paul thought it honest to ask me whether you had ever mentioned this to me—I said no.—Only dont mention it to Nikolasha< before you have taken information, as he can spoil all by his excited way & tell the man straight out or disbelieve all. But I think, it would only be right, tho' the man may seem perfectly charming & honest, to have him watched. Whilst you are there the yellow [?] men & others can use eyes & ears & watch his telegrams & the people he sees etc. One pretends as tho' he often receives big sums. I only tell you all this, knowing nothing whether there is any foundation in it, only better to warn you. Many dislike the Headquarters & have an uncomfortable feeling there & as, alas, we have had spies & also innocent people accused by Nik.[olasha], now you can find out carefully, please.—Paul says Shcherbatov's< nomination was hailed with delight; he does not know him.—Forgive my bothering you so, poor weary Sweetheart, but one longs to be of help & perhaps I can be of some use giving over such messages.— [b]

Mary Vassiltchikov< & family live in the green corner house & fr. her window she watches like a cat all the people, that go in & out of our house & makes her remarks. She drove Isa< wild asking why the children one day went out of one gate on foot & next time on bicycles, why an officer comes with a portfolio in the morning in one uniform & differently dressed in the evening— told Cess. [G. E.] Fred.[ericks] that she saw Gr.< driving in—(odious). So to punish her, we went to A.[nia] this evening by a round about way, so she did not see us pass out. He [Rasputin] was with us fr. 10-11½ in her house—I send you a stick (fish holding a bird), wh. was sent to Him fr. New Athos< to give to you—he used it first & now sends it to you as a blessing—if you can sometimes use it, wld. be nice & to have it in yr. compartment near the one Mr. Ph.< touched, is nice too. He spoke much & beautifully—& what a Russian Emperor is, tho' other Sovereigns are anointed & crowned, only the Russian one is a real Anointed since 300 years. Says you will save your reign by not calling out the 2nd class now[93] —says Shakhovskoi was delighted you spoke about it, because the ministers agreed, but had you not begun [to discuss the issue], they did not intend speaking. Finds, you ought to order fabricks [factories] to make Ammunition, simply you to give the order even choose wh. fabrick, if they show you the list of them, instead of giving the order over through commissions wh. talk for weeks &

never can make up their minds. Be more autocratic my very own Sweetheart, show your mind.— [c]

The exhibition-bazar [sic] began to-day in the big Palace<, on the terrace—not very big (have not yet been there) & our works are already bought up, it's true we had not done very much & we shall continue working & sending things there; they sold over 2100 entrance tickets at 10 kop.[ecks], soldiers (wounded) need not pay, as they must go & see what works please them & wh. they can make. I gave a few of our vases & two cups, as they always attract people. Tell the old man [Fredericks] I saw his family a moment yesterday, when I went to fetch Ania at Ninis<, & found the three ladies looking well. Tell Voeikov, that I find his cabinet quite charming (happily not smelling of cigars). Now I must go to sleep & finish to-morrow. So fresh, we dined out & there were only 9 degrees. Baby< enjoyed Peterhof & then the games with the officers. Dmitri< is better & hopes to leave on Thursday, if even on crutches—is in despair to have remained behind. The last Dolgoruky, Aleksei died in London.—Sleep peacefully & rest well, my treasure—I have blessed & kissed your cushion, as alas! have not you here to tenderly caress & codle [sic]. Goodnight my Angel! [d]

June 15-th. Very fine again, am writing on the balkony [sic], we have lunched, then I must receive some officers & hereafter go to Mavra<. We photographed at the hospital in the garden & sat on the balkony after we had finished everything.—Do so long for news.—Wonder how long you will remain away. Ania has gone for the first time to town by motor to her Parents, as her Mother [Nadezhda Taneeva] is ill, & then to our Friend<.—Now goodbye my very own, longed for Treasure, my Sweetheart, I kiss you ever so fondly & pray God to bless, protect & guide you. Yr. own old   Wify. [P.S.] Have you the patience to read such long letters? [e]

No. 337/ Telegram 136. Tsarskoe Selo> Stavka. 15 June 1915. 2.18> 2.36 p.m. To his majesty. Are all having lunch on balcony and send you our tender kisses. We worked at hospital. Are leaving for Mavra<. All are healthy and embrace [you]. In thoughts ever together. Alix

---

No. 338/ His No. 178.   Stavka. June 15th 1915.
My Beloved, Darling Sunny,

Most tender thanks for your two dear letters. I had not a minute to write yesterday, as was heavily occupied all day. It was [our daughter] Marie's birthday, & I was happy to go church in the morning. I spoke to Shavel'sky about the krestny khodov [procession of the Cross] all over Russia. He found it very right & proposed to do on the 8 July, the day of the Mother of God of Kazan, wh is feasted everywhere. He sends you his deep respects. During our talks he mentioned Sabler's name & said how necessary it is to change him. It is curious how all understand it & want a pure, religious & well intentioned man in his place. Old Gorem.[ykin], and Krivoshein and Shcherbatov all told me here the same thing & they find Samarin the best. I remember now that Stolypin wanted to have him some six [years ago] & with my permission spoke to him, but he refused. I allowed Gorem to send for him & propose him that place. I am sure that will not please you, because he comes from Moscow, but the changes must happen now & one must choose a man whose name is known in the whole country & who is unanimously estimated. With such people in the government one can work & they will all stick together [i.e., work in harmony]—that is quite sure. [a]

The sitting yesterday took place luckily in the big tent & lasted fr 2.0 till 5.0. I felt rather tired, but they all and N.< were extremely pleased. Old Gor. said that sitting was more productive than their usual three months! In my next letter I shall give you some details of it—today I have no time. My papers are neglected, & I must look to them. I miss you too quite especially in these days my Sunbeam! God bless you! I kiss you and the dear children very tenderly. Ever your own huzy Niki. [b]

No. 339/ Telegram 240. Stavka> Tsarskoe Selo. 15 June 1915. 7.27> 7.46 p.m. To her majesty. Thousand thanks for dear letter. Have written. Lovely weather. Took a nice motor drive and a walk. Fond kisses. Niki

---

No. 340/ Her No. 319.   Ts.[arskoe] S[elo]. June 15ᵗʰ 1915.
My own beloved One,

Before going to sleep, I begin my letter to you. Thanks for yr. wire, I received during dinner—we dined in, as there were only 9 degrees & I suppose there is nothing particular to tell. When you are not there, one gets no direct news & feels lost. I am eagerly awaiting your promised letter.—Town< is so full of gossip, as tho' all the ministers were being changed—Krivoshein first minister, Manukhin instead of Shcheglovitov, Guchkov as aide to Polivanov & so on & our Friend<, to whom A.[nia]< went to bid goodbye, was most anxious to know what was true. (As though also Samarin instead of Sabler, whom it is better not to change before one has a very good one to replace him, certainly Samarin wld. go against our Friend & stick up for the Bishops we dislike—he is so terribly Moscovite & narrowminded.) Well, A.[nia] answered that I knew nothing. He [Rasputin] gave over this message for you, that you are to pay less attention to what people will say to you, not let yourself be influenced by them but use yr. own instinct & go by that, to be more sure of yourself & not listen too much nor give in to others, who know less than you. The times are so serious & grave, that all your own personal wisdom is needed & yr. soul must guide you. He regrets you did not speak to Him more about all you think & were intending to do & speak about with yr. ministers & the changes you were thinking of making. He prays so hard for you and Russia & can help more when you speak to Him frankly.—I suffer hideously being away from you. 20 years we shared all together, & now grave things are passing, I do not know your thoughts nor decisions, & its such pain. God help & guide you aright, my own sweet Darling!— [a]

I too am much quieter when you are here—I dread their profiting of yr. kind heart & making you do things, wh., when calmly thought over here, you wld. perhaps do otherwise. I went to Mavra< for an hour, she is calm & brave—Tatiana [K.<] looks awful & yet thinner & greener.—How too horribly sad that accident is that occured [sic] to the young couple Kazbenk! They were going at a terrific speed in their motor & flew against a Schlagbaum [a swinging-gate barrier placed at roads and railway crossings], wh. they did not see was closed. He was killed on the spot & she has her arm broken, at first they said her both legs & head, but now one says only the arm & not so bad & one has not told her about her husband. The wretched Father has now lost his third son—ghastly!— [b]

We went to the exhibition-bazar [sic]—very nice works made by the wounded were shown & I hope it will prove useful & encourage all learning some handi-craft.—My head ached again rather, so I better try & sleep now—it is 12½. All my prayers & tenderest thoughts surround you in deepest love & compassion. Oh, how I long to help you & give you faith in yourself.—How long do you re-main still? Sleep well & peacefully, holy Angels guard yr. slumber. [c]

June 16-th. Just received yr. precious letter, for wh. heartfelt thanks. Glad you were contented with the work & sitting. Yes, Lovy, about Samarin I am much more than sad, simply in despair, just one of Ella's< not good, very biggoted [sic] clique, bosom friend of Sophie Iv. Tiutchev and that bishop Trifon. I have strong reason to dislike him, as he always spoke & now speaks in the army against our Friend—now we shall have stories against our Friend beginning & all will go badly. I hope heart & soul he wont accept—that means Ella's influence & worries fr. morn to night, & he against us, once against Gr.< & so awfully nar-rowminded a real Moscou [sic] type—head without soul. My heart feels like lead, 1000 times better Sabler a few months still than Samarin! Have the church procession now, don't go putting it off, Lovy, listen to me, its serious, have it quicker done, now is lent, therefore more appropriate, cho[o]se Peter & Paul day, but now soon. [See Letter No. 338b.] Oh, why are we not together to speak over all together & to help prevent things wh. I know ought not to be. Its not my brain wh. is clever, but I listen to my soul & I wish you would too my own sweetest One.—I don't want to croak, but I only say all straight out to you.—Goodbye my own & all, God bless & help you—I kiss you without end. Ever yr. own sad Wify. [d]

No. 341/ Telegram 251. Stavka> Tsarskoe Selo. 16 June 1915. 3.10> 3.28 p.m. To her majesty. Loving thanks for letter, also to Marie and Aleksei. Great heat but not stuffy. Nothing new, but they are always pressing on in some places.[88] Tender kisses. Niki

---

No. 342/ Telegram 142. Tsarskoe Selo> Stavka. 16 June 1915. 4.13> 4.45 p.m. To his majesty. Heartily thank you for precious letter. Difficult not to be together at such a time. God help you. Weather clear. We all kiss [you]. Alix

---

No. 343/ Her No. 320.   Ts.[arskoe] S[elo]. June 16th 1915.
My beloved One,

Just a few words before the night. Your sweet smelling jasmin I put in my gospel—it reminded me of Peterhof. Its not like summer not being there. We dined out this evening, but came in after 9 as it was damp. The afternoon I re-mained on the balcony [sic]—I wanted to go to Church in the evening, but felt too tired. The heart is, oh. so heavy & sad!—I always remember what our

Friend< says & how often we do not enough heed His words! He was so much
against yr. going to the Headquarters, because people get round you there &
make you do things, wh. would have been better not done—here the atmosphere
in your own house is a healthier one & you would see things more rightly—if
only you would come back quicker. I am not speaking because of a selfish
feeling, but that here I feel quieter about you & there am in a constant dread
what one is concocting—you see, I have absolutely no faith in N.<— know him to
[be] far fr. clever & having gone against a Man of God's, his work cant be
blessed, nor his advice be good.—When Gr.< heard in town< yesterday before
He left, that Samarin was named, already then people knew it—He was in utter
despair, as He, the last evening here, a week ago to-day, begged you not to
change him Sabler just now, but that soon one might perhaps find the right
man—& now the Moscou [sic] set will be like a spiders net around us, our
Friend's enemies are ours, & Shch.[erbatov]< will make one with them, I feel
sure. I beg your pardon for writing all this, but I am so wretched ever since I
heard it & cant get calm—I see now why Gr. did not wish you to go there—here I
might have helped you. People are affraid [sic] of my influence, Gr. said it (not
to me) & Voeikov, because they know I have a strong will & sooner see through
them & help you being firm. I should have left nothing untried to dissuade you,
had you been here, & I think God would have helped me & you would have
remembered our Friend's words. When He says not to do a thing & one doesnt
listen, one sees ones fault always afterwards. Only if he does accept, N. will try
& get round him too against our Fr. thats N.'s campaign. [a]

I entreat you, at the first talk with S.[amarin] & when you see him, to speak
very firmly—do my Love, for Russia's sake—Russia will not be blessed if her
Sovereign lets a man of God's sent to help him—be persecuted, I am sure. Tell
him severely, with a strong & decided voice, that you forbid any intrigues
against our Friend or talks about Him, or the slightest persecution, otherwise you
will not keep him. That a true Servant dare not go against a man his Sovereign
respects & venerates. [b]

You know the bad part Moscou [sic] plays, tell it him all, his bosom friend S.
I. Tiutchev< spreads lies about the children, repeat this & that her poisenous
[sic] untruths did much harm & you will not allow a repetition of it. [100] Do not
laugh at me, if you know the tears I have cried to-day, you would understand the
gravity of it all. Its not woman's nonsense—but straight forward truth—I adore
you far too deeply to tire you at such a time with [a] letter like this one, if it were
not that soul & heart prompt me. We women have the instinct of the right
sometimes Deary, & you know my love for yr. country wh. has become mine.
You know what this war is to me in every sense—& that the man of God's who
prays incessantly for you, might be in danger again of persecution—that God
would not forgive us our weakness & sin in not protecting Him.—You know N's
hatred for Grig.< is intense. Speak once to Voeikov, Deary, he understands such
things because he is honestly devoted to you. [c]

S.[amarin] is a very conceited man, in summer I had occasion to see it, when I
had that talk with him about the evacuation question—Rostov.< & I carried off a
most unpleasant impression of his selfsufficiency—blind adoration of Moscou
[sic] & looking down upon Petersburg. The tone in wh. he spoke shocked

Rost.< greatly. That showed me him in another light, & I realised [sic] how unpleasant it wld. be to have to do with him.—When one proposed him for Aleksei before, I unhesitatingly said no;[101] for nothing such a narrowminded man. Our Church just needs the contrary—soul & not brain.—God Almighty may He help & put things aright, & hear our prayers and give you at last more confidence in yr. own wisdom! not listening to others, but to our Friend & yr. soul. Once more excuse this letter written with an aching heart & smarting eyes. Nothing is trivial now—all is grave. I venerate & love old Goremykin had I seen him, I know how I should have spoken—he is so franck [sic] with our Friend[102] & does not grasp, that S.[amarin] is your enemy if he goes & speaks against Gr.— [d]

I am sure your dear heart aches more, is enlarged & needs drops. Please deary, walk less—I ruined mine walking at the shooting & in Finland before speaking to the Drs. & suffering mad pain, want of air, heartbeating. Take care of yourself— agoo wee one< I hate being away fr. you, its my greatest punishment at this time especially—our first Friend [Mr. Philippe] gave me that Image [icon] with the bell to warn me against those, that are not right & it will keep them fr. approaching, I shall feel it & thus guard you from them.[103]—Even the family [i.e., Nicholas's relatives] feel this & therefore try & get at you alone, when they know its something not right & I wont approve of. Its none of my doing, God wishes your poor wify to be your help, Gr. always says so & Mr. Ph.< too—& I might warn you in time if I knew things. Well, now I can only pray & suffer. I press you tightly to my heart, gently stroke your brow, press my lips upon yr. eyes & mouth, kiss with love those dear hands wh. always are pulled away. I love you, love you & want yr. good, happiness & blessing. Sleep well & calmy—I must try & sleep too, its nearly one oclock. [e]

My train brought many wounded—Babys< has fetched a lot from Varsovie [Warsaw] where they empty out the hospitals. Oh God help!—Lovy, remember, quicker the church procession, now during lent is just the most propicious [sic] moment, & absolutely from you, not by the new Chief Procurator of the Synod [see No. 338b] —I hope to go to holy Communion this lent, if B.< does not prevent me.—Reading this letter you will say—one sees she is Ella's< sister. But I cant put all in three words, I need heaps of pages to pour all out & poor Sunshine has to read this long yarn—but Sweetheart knows & loves his very own old wife. [f]

The boys from the college come & make bandages every morning at our stores here from 10-12½ & now will make the newest masks wh. are far more complicated but can be used often.—Our little officer with tetanos [i.e., tetanus or lockjaw] is recovering, looks decidedly better—his parents we sent for fr. the Caucasus & they live also under the colonnades—we have such a lot living there now.—The exhibition-bazar [sic] goes very well, the first day there were over 2000, yesterday 800—our things are bought before they appear —beforehand already people write down for them & we manage to work a cushion or cover each, daily.—Tatiana rode this evening 5½-7—the others acted at Anias<—the latter sends you the enclosed card she bought to-day at our exhibition—tell me to thank her.— Poor Mitia Den< is quite bad again & cannot walk at all, Sonia

[Dehn] is going to take him near Odessa, [to the town of] Liman for a cure—so sad.— [g]

June 17-th, Good morning, my Pet. Slept badly & heart enlarged, so lie the morning on bed & balkony [sic]—alas, no hospital, head too rather achy again. Churchbells ringing.—Shall finish [this letter] after luncheon. Big girls< go to town<, [daughter] Olga receives money then go to a hospital & tea at Elagin<. It is very hot & heavy air, but a colossal wind on the balkony, probably a thunderstorm in the air & that makes it difficult to breathe. I brought out roses, lilies of the valley & sweet peas to enjoy their perfume. I embroider all day for our exhibition-bazar. [h]

Ah my Boy, my Boy, how I wish we were together—one is so tired at times, so weary from pain & anxiety—nigh upon 11 months—but then it was only the war, & now the interior questions wh. absorb one & the bad luck at the war, but God will help, when all seems blackest, I am sure better, sunnier days will come. May the ministers only seriously work together fulfill your wishes & orders, & not their own—harmony under your guidance. Think more of Gr. Sweetheart, before every difficult moment, ask Him to intercede before God to guide you aright.— [i]

A few days ago I wrote to you about Paul's conversation, to-day the Css. H.[ohenfelsen, Princess Paley] sends me Paléologue's answer. "Les impressions que S. A. S. le Gr. D. a rapportées de son entretien & que vous voulez bien me communiquer de sa part me touchent vivment. Elles confirment avec toute l'autorité possible, ce dont j'étais moralement certain, ce dont je n'ai jamais douté, ce dont je me suis toujours porté garant envers mon Gouvernement. A un pessimiste qui essayait recémment d'ébranler ma foi, j'ai répondu. "Ma conviction est d'autant plus forte qu'elle ne repose sur aucune promesse, sur aucun engagement. Dans les rares occasions, ou ces graves sujets ont été abordés devant moi, on ne m'a rien promis, on ne s'est engagé a rien; parceque toute assurance positive eut été superflue; parceque l'on se sentait compris, comme j'ose esperer avoir été compris moi-même. A certaines minutes solennelles, il y a des sincérités d'accent, des droitures de regard, où toute une conscience se révèle & qui valent tous les serments".—Je n'en attache pas moins un très-haut prix au témoignage direct qui me vient de S. A. S. le Gr. D. Ma certitude personnelle n'en avait pas besoin. Mais, si je rencontre encore des incrédules, j'aurai désormais le droit de leur dire, non plus seulement: "Je crois, mais je sais".[104]— [j]

This was about the question of a separate peace negociation [sic]. Have you spoken to Voeikov about Danilov[see No. 892], please do so—only not to fat Orlov<, who is N.['s] colossal friend—they correspond the whole time when you are here, V.[oeikov] knows it. That can mean no good. He grudges no doubt about Gr.'s visits to our house, & therefore wants you away from him, at the Head-Quarters. If they only knew how they harm instead of helping you, blind people with their hatred against Gr.! You remember dans "Les Amis de Dieu" it says, a country cannot be lost whose Sovereign is guided by a man of God's. Oh let Him guide you more! [k]

Dmitri< is feeling better, tho' his leg hurts him still.—The poor little Kazenbek one answered, does not suffer from her broken arm too much, but is I think in a rather dazed state, therefore one has not yet told her about her husband's death.

How full of life they were when N.P.< was at their Wedding!—Now this letter has volumes & will bore you to read, so I better end it. God bless & protect you & keep you from all harm, give you strength, courage & consolation in all trying moments! Am in thoughts living with you my Love, my one & all. I cover you with kisses & remain ever yr. tenderly & deeply loving old <u>Sunny</u>. [P.S.] All the Children kiss you.—Many messages to the old man [Fredericks] & N.P.—Khan Nahitchev.[anski]< comes to say goodbye to-morrow.— [l]

100. Sophia Tyutcheva was granddaughter of the poet Fedor Tyutchev. As governess of the royal children, she was offended at Rasputin's access to the family's living quarters. Alexandra and the tsar ignored her complaints. Tyutcheva then turned to Feofan and the "black princesses"< and partici-pated in their futile public campaign of 1910 to discredit Rasputin and oust him from the palace. Tyutcheva was dismissed and remained a vocal critic of Rasputin.

101. Moscow aristocrats were devoted to Nicholas II, but they considered the capital's nobles to be bureaucrats, intriguers, sycophants, etc. Moscow nobles viewed themselves as pious, dedicated to public service, the "Old Russia," etc. Alexander Samarin, member of the illustrious Slavophile fam-ily, was elected marshal of the Moscow nobility in 1908 at the age of 31. Wealthy, educated and extremely conservative, Samarin was a distinguished man who enjoyed the goodwill of many liber-als, even. Nicholas shared his wife's distrust of "Moscow," but he liked Samarin, and in 1909 of-fered him the directorship of the Holy Synod. Samarin was interested in church reform, but he re-fused—in part because of Rasputin's growing influence. Given the crisis of June 1915, Nicholas brought Samarin to Stavka and after lengthy discussions persuaded him to accept the position. It is unlikely that Nicholas promised to discipline Rasputin, but many concluded Samarin's appointment indicated this—which was one reason it was popular. Alexandra's letter suggests someone had once been interested in making Samarin tutor of her children. Was this person Nicholas himself?

102. Many conservatives, even, deplored Goremykin's age (he turned 76 in 1915), his devotion to an earlier view of autocracy, and subservience to the tsar. Nicholas and Alexandra, on the other hand, considered Goremykin to be wise and seasoned. As an experienced bureaucrat, Goremykin knew how to deal with Rasputin. Goremykin did not grant "favors" he considered unjustified, but he received the peasant and was cordial; this meant much to Rasputin and Alexandra. Goremykin knew his limitations and was anxious to retire. Incredibly, when this finally happened in January 1916, the appointment went to Boris Sturmer, another old man but one with less experience, ability and honor than Ivan Logginovich Goremykin.

103. This is a frequently quoted passage from the Nicky-Sunny Correspondence; it is a devastating commentary on the empress.

104. "The impressions which S. A. S. [his highness] the grand prince [Paul Alexandrovich, the emperor's uncle] gained from your conversation and which you so kindly conveyed in his name have deeply moved me. They confirm with all possible authority that of which I was certain and never doubted and have always affirmed before my government. To a pessimist who sought the other day to shake my faith, I replied that my confidence [in our Russian ally] is so firm that it rests neither on a particular promise or obligation. On the rare occasions when those serious questions [of loyalty to the alliance] were examined in my presence, they [our Russian allies] promised me nothing and were in no way obligated as any positive assurance was superfluous for my interlocutors, feeling as they did that I understood them in the same way I would hope for them to understand me. At certain solemn moments there was such a sincere tone, such a direct gaze indicating conscience and [these] were worth all the oaths [in the world]. Nevertheless, I assign a very high value to direct evidence coming from S. A. S. [his highness] the grand prince. This was in no way necessary for my personal conviction. But should I yet encounter disbelievers, henceforth I have the right to say. 'I not only believe, I know.'"

No. 344/ Telegram 146. Tsarskoe Selo> Stavka. 17 June 1915. 2.45> 3.52 p.m. To his majesty. Hot, stuffy, windy; am lying on balcony. Heart enlarged so remain at home. Big girls< went to town<. Warmly embrace, kiss and think about you without end. What news? Alix

No. 345/ His No. 179.   Stavka. June 16ᵗʰ 1915.
My own beloved Sunny,

Tender thanks for your dear long letter in which you give me [an] account of your conversation with Paul<. Your answers were perfectly correct about the question of peace. This is precisely the main point of my rescript to old Goremykin, wh[ich] is going to appear. What concerns Danilov—I think the idea of him being a spy not worth a straw.[See No. 892] I also know he is disliked even hated in the army, beginning from Ivanov down to the last officer. He has got an awful character & is very cutting with his juniors. N.< knows this & from time to time puts him into his place; but he finds it impossible to replace him after 11 month's hard work—so well the man know his duty. Even Krivoshein spoke to me upon this subject—he finds, for inst[ance] N. ought to make changes in his staff & choose other men in Yanushk[evich] and Danilov's place. I advised to tell it N., which he did—of course fr[om] his own personal point of view, naturally. Later he told me that N. had evidently been displeased by his frankness. [a]

Our sitting [of ministers], the other day concerned three questions: the treatment of German and Austrian subjects still living in Russia, of the military prisoners, the wording of the above-mentioned rescript & lastly about the soldiers of the Second Category.⁹³ When I said I wished the class of 1917 to be called in all the ministers made a sigh of relief. N. gave in at once. Yanushk[evich] begged only to be allowed to work out preparatory measures only in case of emergency. Naturally if the war lasted a year longer, one would be forced to call in some of the younger men of the Second Category, but now that falls off. Yusupov [the Elder], who I sent for, was present at the council for the first question; we put the damper on him & gave him a few clear instructions. ¹⁰⁵ There were some funny moments while he read his report about the Moscow riots—as he got excited & shook his fists & thumped them on the table. I hope to motor to Belovezh for a whole day soon & to do it all of a sudden. The old man [Fredericks] & Voeik.[ov] thank you very much. Now I must stop. God bless you my darling Wify. I kiss you and the dear children ever so tenderly. Your own Nicky. [b]

---

105. F. F. Yusupov (the Elder), governor of Moscow, was criticized first for permitting the anti-German riots of May 27-29 (O.S.), 1915, then for the degree of force he used to restore peace. See Footnote 97 and de Jonge, *Life and Times of Rasputin*, p. 308.

No. 346/ Telegram 147. Tsarskoe Selo> Stavka. 17 June 1915. 5.38> 6.15 p.m. To his majesty. Your dear letter arrived just as I sent mine. Think a lot about you. God help you! Very hot. All kiss [you] warmly. Sleep peacefully. Alix

---

No. 347/ Her No. 321.   Tsarskoe S[elo]. June 17ᵗʰ 1915.
My very own Darling,

I had just finished my letter, when yr. dear one was brought to me—thanks ever so tenderly for it. You don't know the joy yr. letters give me, as I know you have little time for writing & are so tired. Wify ought to send you bright & cheery letters, but its difficult, as am feeling more than lowspirited & depressed these days —so many things worry me! Now the Duma is to come together in August, & our Friend< begged you several times to do it as late as possible & not now, as they ought all to be working in their places [i.e., at home]—& here they will try to mix in & speak about things that do not concern them. Never forget that you are & must remain authocratic [sic] Emperor!—we are not ready for a constitutional government, N.'s< fault & Wittes it was that the Duma exists, & it has caused you more worry than joy.[106] Oh I do not like N. having anything to do with these big sittings wh. concern interior questions!—He understands our country so little & imposes upon the ministers by his loud voice & gesticulations. I can go wild at times at his false position. [a]

Why did the ministers ask that [your earlier decision to convene the Duma at a later date] to be changed? That [support of your earlier decision] was their first duty. He has no right to meddle in other affairs & one ought to set ones fault to rights & give him only all the military things—like French & Geoffre [Joffre]. Nobody knows who is the Emperor now—you have to run to the Head-Quarters & assemble yr. ministers there, as tho' you could not have them alone here like last Wednesday. It is as tho' N. settles all, makes the choices & changes—it makes me utterly wretched. He did not like Kriv.< speaking about Danilov[See No. 892] & the man did his duty—there must be a reason, except his bad character, that the whole army & old Ivanov hate him—all say he holds N. & the other Grand Dukes completely in hand. Forgive my writing all this, but I feel so utterly miserable, & as tho' all were giving you wrong advises [sic] & profitting [sic] of your kindness. Hang the Head-Quarters[,] no good broods there. Thank God you may get a good day at Belovezh in God's glorious nature, away from intrigues—could you fly off another day to Ivanov, another somewhere where the troops are, not to the guard again but where others are massed together waiting. You are remaining still long away, Gr.< begged not—once all goes against His wishes my heart bleeds in anguish & fright;—Oh, to keep & protect you from more worries & miserys [sic], one has enough more than the heart can bear—one longs to go to sleep for a long rest.— [b]

Lovy, wont you write to poor old Gen. Kazbek who has now lost his third son, it would be a true consolation to the poor old Father.— The heat is colossal to-day & the air heavy & sultry & the wind very strong, the curtains on the balkony [sic] went flying about.—Daisy< heard fr. Vicky of S.[weden]< from Karlsruhe, that when the French threw bombs onto the palace—they all fled into the cellars in the morning at 5. Sad, just their palace, next will be ours at Mainz & the splendid old museum; each country by turn.— Ivan Orlov has to fly daily for a week over Libau I am so glad you spoke about all helping, working to prepare ammunition etc. in yr. rescript—now at last they must do it.—Do my long, grumbling letters not aggravate you, poor wee One? But I only mean all for yr. good & write fr. the depths of a very suffering, tormented heart.— [c]

My lancer [D. M.] Kniazh.[evich] has come for 2 days & I shall see him to-morrow, also make Pr. Shcherbatov's acquaintance.— N.P.< must be very unhappy about poor Kasbek [Kazbek]. Dear me, what an amount of misery on all sides! When will once again peace & happiness reign in the world?— The nice, young, pretty Kalzanova [Olga Kolzakova] who works with us in the hospital always, has to leave for 2 months—she overworked herself, & her always ailing

heart has become so bad that one has sent her to the country & thence to Livadia. Kind Heyden gave the "Strela" to-day to take Mme Taneeva< to Peterhof
as she is too ill to go by motor or rail. Our Friend said they were not to go there
this summer, but they could not bear the air any longer in town<, poor woman
suffers so hideously fr. stones in the liver & now I think she has jaundice. As
Ania< can bear the motor, she will go there to-morrow after luncheon & return
on Friday, as its wiser to stop the night there.—Do you think you could tell me
where my Crimean's are now—I heard as tho' one had sent them fr. the
Bukhovina elsewhere.—Such grateful thanks for dear telegram, have at once
asked Goremykin to come to-morrow, Thursday, & shall be happy to listen to
the dear old man, & to him I can speak quite frankly, I know him ever since I
married & he is so utterly devoted to you & will understand me. Such a downpour suddenly at 9 & twice very distant thunder, now its raining steadily for four
hours—it will refreshen the air wh. was so close all day. Gr. telegraphed to
A.[nia] from Vyatka. "I travel quietly, sleep, God will help, kiss all." Good-
night wee One, sleep peacefully—holy Angels guard your slumber and loving
Wify's earnest prayers for her very own precious sunny, big eyed Darling. [d, e,
f]

18-th. Good morning my Treasure—no sun, grey, rained a little, warm hot &
heavy thunderstorming air—heart sill enlarged, so remain again quiet, shall go
over the balcony towards 12 like yesterday. I have told them to put electric
strings wires, then we can have lamps & spend the evenings out, when it is
warm.—Think of us at Belovezh! Such remembrances of many years ago when
we were younger & went about together—& of the last awful time [at Spala, in
1912?], when poor suffering Baby< lay hours on my bed & my heart also was
bad—remembrances of pain & anguish—you all away—the days endless & full of
suffering.—My name you will find on the bedroom window leading out onto the
balkony under my initials in wire covering the windowpane.—[g]

Lovy, I saw my [D. M.] Kniazhewitch & we spoke about Maslov. In Aug. it
will be 25 years that he is in the regiment—he managed very well indeed whilst
the commander was ill, yet there are many questions difficult to him & if he got
another regiment, he wld. loose [sic] the lancer uniform & probably not be a
very perfect commander. He feels sticking in the regiment, that he keeps others
fr. advancing. Could you not have made him your aide-de-camp it would have
been a kindness, as he is such a really honest & good fellow; only then better
sooner—Kniazh. has kept the papers back all along, about whether he should
accept a regiment—this wld. enable him to stay on without harming anybody.
There are lots of old Colonels in the Chev.[alier] G.[uards] regiment, they manage it somehow.[107] [h]

I saw Pr.[ince] Shcherbatov who made me a pleasant impression, as far as I
can judge after one talk.[108]—The girls have gone to the Invalid hospital—& Ania
to Peterhof, so am alone. Am surrounded by masses of roses (just sent fr. Peterhof) & sweetpeas—the smell is a dream, wish I could send them to you.—Just got
yr. sweet telegr. for wh. thanks; thank heavens you feel better; only don't overdo
things by walking too much, its never advisable when the heart is not quite in
order, too much of a strain at a time, phisical [sic] & moral.—Must send this off.
Saw in the papers our torpedoboats acted well.—Goodbye & God bless you, be-

loved Sunshine, caress & kiss with unboundless love & tenderness. Ever, Nicky mine, yr. very own wify   Sunny. [i]

106. During the October 1905 general strike, Witte, Nicholasha< and others advised Nicholas II that he must proclaim a military dictatorship (in which case they would resign) or grant a legislative Duma. Nicholas did the latter in the "October Manifesto," which reconciled liberals and moderates to the government. Even so, Nicholas remained devoted to autocracy, he regretted this "moment of weakness," he blamed his advisors for this "false move." Alexandra played to that sentiment in this letter. But Nicholas had a keener sense than his wife of how to govern Russia. In his June 1915 campaign to pacify his critics, the tsar fired four unpopular ministers and, as we see here, announced that the Duma, long in recess, would meet in August 1915.
107. Russia, like other countries, began the First World War with a number of incompetent senior officers who had attained high rank through favoritism, seniority, etc. Many claimed special treatment because of age. Alexandra refers to such examples of this group as Maj.-Gen. M. E. Maslov, commander of Her Majesty's Life Guards Lancer Regiment, and "lots of old Colonels" in other guards cavalry units. Some of the latter found non-combat sinecures. In Maslov's case, Alexandra hopes he will be "kicked upstairs" by being made an aide-de-camp to her husband.
108. Prince Nicholas Shcherbatov, the new minister of internal affairs, visited the empress in an effort to win her support. Despite the good initial impression noted here, this did not occur. Shcherbatov was conservative and devoted to his tsar; he was also a foe of Rasputin. The prince relaxed censorship, which was under his ministry. Russian newspapers were now forbidden only to make direct references to Rasputin's relations with the royal family. This culminated in a press campaign against Rasputin in August 1915. (See Fuhrmann, *Rasputin*, p. 131.) Shcherbatov, like Samarin, offended Nicholas and Alexandra in a variety of ways, and within a few weeks, both were dismissed from the council of ministers.

No. 348/ Telegram 270. Stavka> Tsarskoe Selo. 17 June 1915. 7.22> 7.56 p.m. To her majesty. So thankful [for] dear letter and two telegrams. Also [our children] Tatiana and Aleksei. Also very hot and windy. 22 degr[ees] in our carriages. Please do not worry try and see Goremykin, who will quieten you.[102] Fondest kisses to all. Niki

No. 349/ Telegram 153. Tsarskoe Selo> Stavka. 18 June 1915. 11.37 a.m.> 12.47 p.m. To his majesty. Hot, stuffy, am lying on balcony. Still do not feel very good. Will see old man [Goremykin] today. Warmly embrace [you]. In thoughts always together. Alix

No. 350/ Telegram 278. Stavka> Tsarskoe Selo. 18 June 1915. 12.41> 12.58 p.m. To her majesty. Tender thanks [for] long letter, also [daughter] Olga and A[nia].< Tremendous heat, very dry. Feeling better, hope you also. Loving kisses. Niki

No. 351/ Telegram 155. Tsarskoe Selo> Stavka. 18 June 1915. 8.25> 9.05 p.m. To his majesty. Saw dear old man [Goremykin]. Interesting conversation. He said everything I myself think. Believe you received his letter today. Would be very good if you understood what I wrote. Wonderful weather, though quite hot. [Spent] entire day on balcony, also dined there. Sleep well. Kiss [you]. God bless, keep and guide you. Alix.

No. 352/ Her No. 322.   Tsarskoe Selo. June 18th 1915.

My own Darling,

Real summer weather[—]very hot in the daytime, & in the evening delicious; I hope to-morrow the lamps will be ready, then we can sit out longer, if not eaten up by gnats. The girls motored after dinner, before that they went to see Tatiana<.—Dear old Goremykin sat for an hour with me & I think we touched many questions. God grant him life!—I asked about Polivanov, he said when one proposed him for Varsovie [Warsaw], N.< made an awful grimace & now at once proposed him, & when G.[oremykin] asked him why he mentions his name now, he answered that he had changed his opinion. He told me what Samarin said to him & what he hadn't written to you, I told him my opinion about him & Shcheglovit.< & then he pleasantly surprised me by saying that you had told him yr. intention to change him—he thinks [A. A.] Khvostov will be a good choice.—He sees & understands all so clearly, that its a pleasure speaking to him—we spoke about the question of the Germans & Jews & the wrong way all had been managed & orders given by generals & Nikolasha<. The way they have treated Ekesparre for instance.—I wish others had his sound mind.—Am very tired, so will end & try to sleep. God bless yr. slumber.—[a]

19-th. Goodmorning my Treasure. Lovely weather again, such a Godsend after the late summer & much rain. The "Enginaer [sic] Mechanic"< has come to me, & I should like to send him flying.—I wonder what news from the war, one hears so little. Our steady retreat will in the long run make the line very long & complicated for them & that be our gain, I hope.[95] How about Varsovie? The hospitals are being emptied out & even some quite evacuated—is that only as an extreme precaution, because surely in months one has had time to well fortify the town; they seem to be rebeginning their autumn move, only now they will bring their very best troops & it will be easier, as they know the ground by heart.[109] My dear Siberians with their comrades will have the mass coming in upon them—& may they once more save Varsovie. All lies in God's hands—& as long as we can drag on till sufficient amunition [sic] comes & then fall upon them with full force. Only the perpetual great losses make the heart very heavy—they go as martyrs straight to their heavenly home, its true, but still its ever so hard.— [b]

Pay attention to Baby's< signature in his letter—its his own invention & it seems his mood at his lesson this morning was somewhat wild, & he only got 3.—The girls have some of their lessons on the balkony [sic].—Benkendorf< suddenly had a fainting fit in town & hurt himself when he fell—they say it may be fr. his stomach, but I fear worse things—we shall see what the Drs. say this morning. It would be a loss, as he is far more worth than Valia<—& one of the old style still wh. now, alas, no longer exist.—I have an immense bunch of jasmin[e] standing near me on the balkony [sic] Mme Vil'tchk.< picked it in the hospital garden.—Goodbye Sweetheart, my light, my joy. I bless, & kiss you incessantly with deepest love. Ever yr. very own   Wify. [c]

---

109. The Russians abandoned Warsaw after a battle which lasted from July 23/August 4 to July 26/August 7, 1915. See Footnote 95.

No. 353/ Telegram 297. Stavka> Tsarskoe Selo. 19 June 1915. 2.43> 3.22 p.m.
To her majesty. Fond thanks for dear letter, also [daughter] Anastasia. This
evening arrives S.[amarin]. Lovely hot weather. Hope feel strong and calm.
Tender love. Niki

No. 354/ His No. 180.   Stavka. June 19th 1915.
My own darling Sunny,

I beg your pardon for sending you the empty bottle of cascara, but I am in
need of some more. I put inside the end of my candle—give it to Aleksei for his
collection. I thank you so much for your dear letters, for all your devotion &
love you show me. It gives me strength. Bless you my beloved One. It is too
hot to write about such serious questions. I am glad you saw the old man
[Goremykin]. Has he calmed you? I send you a tiny photo that Dzhunk.< made
here the last time. I have decided to leave on Tuesday, therefore God grant we
shall meet on Wednesday at last. [a]

Now the guards and other troops are being brought over towards Kholm and
Lyublin because it is in that direction the Germans are pressing. This is the reason why I remain here until the concentration [of troops] is over. I am feeling
allright again—I simply had a drachenschuss [lumbago] in the left side of my
back which hurt me whenever I wanted to take a full breath; it hurt especially by
night, but now it's quite gone. On account of the heat we take long motor drives
& walk very little. We chose new roads, & go around the neighbourhood after
the map. Often there happen mistakes, as the maps are old, made 18 years ago;
there are new villages and some woods gone which changes the map! Sometimes horses fly off with the carts we meet—then we stop and send the chauf-
feurs to their rescue. On Monday I hope to run over to Belovezh. It is good you
saw Shcherbatov; try and see now Gen. Polivanov & be frank with him. Now
the messenger has to leave. God bless you my own Wify, my Treasure! I kiss
you and the dear children most tenderly. Ever your own huzy Nicky. [P.S.]
Give her [Anna Vyrubova] my love. [b]

No. 355/ Telegram 158. Tsarskoe Selo> Stavka. 19 June 1915. 9.53> 10.15
p.m. To his majesty. Second half of day and wind blows on balcony. Wonderful weather. Feel more peaceful but very weak. Children healthy and merry. All
embrace you. Sleep well. God bless you. Alix

No. 356/ Her No. 323.   Ts.[arskoe] S[elo]. June 20th 1915.
My beloved Nicky dear,

All my thoughts are ever near you in tender love & loneliness. I hear the
churchbells & long to go and pray for you there, but the heart is again enlarged,
so must keep quiet. Weather again splendid. Our corner on the balcony [sic] is
so cosy & pretty in the evening with two lamps, we sat out till after 11.—Ania<
saw the [yacht] "Alexandrie," [and the] "Dozorny," "Razvedchik," & "Rabotnik"
[—other ships—]from far—lots of public, music, everything looking lovely. It
seems sad & strange for the first time since 20 years not to go there—but here

there is more work to do & to run over fr. Peterhof constantly, I could not have managed. Then people can be sent for & got at quicker when one needs them. [a]

Do so wonder what you settled with Samarin, whether you let him off–if so, then don't hurry getting another [director of the Holy Synod] & lets talk it quietly over here. I told the old man all, & I think he understood me, tho' being very religious he personally knows little about Church affairs (Goremykin). This wire A.[nia] got to-day from our Friend< from Tiumen. [The following quote is in Russian.] "Encountered singers, we sang in praise of Easter, the abbot was jubilant, remember it's Easter, suddenly a telegram reaches me that my son is being drafted, I said in my heart, am I like Abraham, of ages past, having one son and supporter, I hope he will be allowed to rule under me as with the ancient tsars." Beloved One, what can one do for him, whom does it concern–his only son ought not to be taken. Cannot Voeikov< write to the local military chief, I think it concerns him–will you say, please. [110]– [b]

The train with your Feldjeger is 8 hours late, so shall only get your letter at 7. This moment Varnava telegraphs to me [in Russian] fr. Kurgan. "Our own empress, the 17-th on the day of the Saint Tikhon the Miracle Worker, during the procession around the church in the village of Barabinsk, there suddenly appeared on the sky a cross, which was seen altogether for 15 minutes, and as the Holy Church is praying 'the Cross of the Czar is the support of the kingdom of the believers.' I felicitate you with this vision and believe that God sent this vision and sign in order to uphold visibly with love his devoted ones. I pray for all of you." God grant it may be a good sign, crosses are not always. [111] –Benkendorff< came to me, he looks alright [sic], feels only a bit weak still.–He said Valia< had written that you were perhaps returning [on] the 24-th–is it really true? What joy to have you safely back again.–I bless & kiss you with all the strength of my great love. Ever, Sweetheart, yr. very own Sunny. [c]

---

110. News about the drafting of Dmitry Rasputin, "Our Friend's" only son, was an invitation for the tsar to spare the young man. The grounds for this might have been that Dmitry lived with his mother on the family farm in Siberia. (Dmitry's two sisters lived with their father in Petrograd.) Deferments had been granted to only sons who were their families' main source of support in 1914. This was abolished as it became clear the war would be long and more soldiers were needed. As we see in Letter No. 453b, Nicholas refused to extend partiality to young Rasputin. Anna Vyrubova used her influence to have him assigned to medical service. "Rumors of this favoritism reinforced the notion that Rasputin was the real power in Russia, and the empress's lover." (Fuhrmann, *Rasputin*, p. 191)

111. Like Rasputin, the peasant Varnava was crude, semi-literate, and given to a scandalous life. With Rasputin's support, Varnava became bishop of Tobol'sk and Siberia in November 1913. Varnava protected Rasputin within Grigory's native (Siberian) diocese. He was also a rival for the attentions of the royal family. But Varnava was less adept in handling the empress, as we see here from her ambivalent reaction to this "miraculous sign."

No. 357/ Telegram 324. Stavka> Tsarskoe Selo. 20 June 1915. 2.30> 3.00 p.m. To her majesty. Loving thanks for dear letter, also [daughter and son] Marie and Aleksei. Colossal heat. Saw Samarin, who accepted but asked nomination to be in a fortnight. [112] Fond kisses to all. Niki

112. Rasputin visited Moscow in March 1915 to pray at holy places. The object of this publicized trip was to strengthen Grigory's credentials as a "man of God." Devotions done, Rasputin got drunk in a gypsy restaurant and dropped his pants to prove he was *the* renowned Rasputin. Rasputin actually claimed intimacy with the empress! Uncertain of how to proceed, the Moscow police telephoned Vladimir Dzhunkovsky, who, as assistant-minister of internal affairs, headed the police. Dzhunkovsky had Rasputin arrested. Nicholas ordered Dzhunkovsky to investigate the episode and present a "paper," a report. Alexandra blamed Dzhunkovsky for the scandal; the tsar was angry with Rasputin. Alexandra henceforth urged her husband to "get rid of Dzhunkovsky." His dismissal on August 15, 1915, seemed further proof of Rasputin's unlimited power. Actually, Rasputin had little or nothing to do with this and related changes in the ministry. Nicholas was not so much offended at the report—he had ordered it—as by the fact that Dzhunkovsky leaked it, hoping to shake Rasputin's position and see him ousted from the capital. The tsar rewarded Dzhunkovsky with appointments closer to his military interests and continued to treat him as a friend. (See Fuhrmann, *Rasputin*, pp. 119-121, 143, 145, 240-241 n. 17.) Dzhunkovsky had served in the Preobrazhensky Guards Regiment, hence the empress supposed—no doubt correctly—that a "clique" within this unit sympathized with Dzhunkovsky.

No. 358/ Telegram 162. Tsarskoe Selo> Stavka. 20 June 1915. 5.21> 5.54 p.m. To his majesty. Lying on balcony, splendid weather, hot but light breeze. Irina and Felix [Yusupov] coming for tea. Greetings from all, lovy. Would like to know the news. [Daughter] Tatiana riding, others at store<. Thanks for telegram. Sad that he agreed [see No. 357], very uneasy. Alix

---

No. 359/ Telegram 166. Tsarskoe Selo> Stavka. 21 June 1915. 11.08> 11.47 a.m. To his majesty. Tenderly thank you for dear letter received yesterday evening. Ideal weather, gentle breeze, nightingale singing. Heart better this morning but don't feel very good—am aching. Bless and kiss you. Alix.

No. 360/ Her No. 324.   Ts.[arskoe] S[elo]. June 21st 1915.
My sweetest One,

Ever such fond thanks for your dear letter, I received yesterday before dinner—Baby< thanks [you] for the candlestump. I gave yr. man an extra candle on the way. Here I return your cascara [See No. 354a]. I am so glad yr. Drachenschuss [lumbago] is better, I have it continually & generally fr. a false movement & the left side, wh. makes the heart worse.—To-day my heart is not enlarged, but I keep quiet. Kostia< (to say goodbye) & Tatiana [K.<?] come to tea before the Children go to Ania's< to play—Baby has gone to Ropsha before for a few hours—he enjoys these expeditions.   Such air, quite divine & delicious breeze & birdies singing away so brightly.—Shall think of you so much to-morrow & hope you will enjoy our dear Belovezh.—Yesterday evening we went to Anias<, there were the 2 Grabbes, Nini<, Emma<, Alia<, Kussov of the Mosc.[ow] Drag.[oon] Regiment (ex-"Nizhegorodtsi")—the first time I saw him & we were quite at home together as tho' we had known each other for years—I lay working on the sopha & he quite close chatting away busily. I am going to invite him here too once, so nice to speak [to him] about all our wounded friends.— [a]

I congratulate you with yr. Curassiers' feast—little Vick came with a bouquet of yellow roses in the regiments name, so touching.—The giving over of Mme Souchomlinov's< (my stores) to me is going alright [sic] & with tact luckily—because I dont want them to suffer in this, as she really did a lot of good.—Just got a telegram from Romanovsky (why he signs G. M. Romanov I can't think), that he leaves the 20-th Gal.[ician] Regiment has a nomination in the Staff of the Army. I suppose this is my last letter to you, unless I hear a man goes to meet you.—What joy to have you back again! You precious One, Wify is lonely & has a heavy heart.— S.[amarin]'s nomination makes me sad, can't help it as he is an enemy of our Friend< & that is the worst thing there can be, now more than ever. Blessings & kisses without end & such love, love! Ever my Nicky yr. very own old Sunny. [b]

No. 361/ Telegram 339. Stavka> Tsarskoe Selo. 21 June 1915. 9.59> 10.19 p.m. To her majesty. Many thanks [for] dear letter and telegram. Had no time to write. Go to-morrow for whole day to Belovezh. Think adviseable [sic] for me to remain here a little longer for military reasons.[109] Tender kisses sleep well. Niki.

No. 362/ Telegram 170. Tsarskoe Selo> Stavka. 21 June 1915. 11.35> 11.59 p.m. To his majesty. Warmly thank you for priceless telegram. Hope to-morrow will be good, remember us to everyone. Sad that [your] return is postponed but fully understand you have serious reasons. Tenderly kiss [you]. May Lord bless you. Alix

---

No. 363/ Her No. 325.   Ts.[arskoe] S[elo]. June 22nd 1915.
My own beloved One,
   I wonder how you got to Belovezh & whether the weather is as beautiful as here.—So you have put off your return back—well, nothing is to be done;—if you could at least profit & see some troops. Cant you flie [sic] off again, as tho' to Belovezh but go another way, without telling anybody.—Nikolasha< need neither know, nor my enemy Dzhunk.< Ah dear, he is not an honest man, he has shown that vile, filthy paper (against our Friend<) to Dmitri< who repeated all to Paul< & he to Alia<. Such a sin, & as tho' you had said to him, that you have had enough of these dirty stories & wish him to be severely punished.[112] You see how he turns your words & orders round—the slanderers were to be punished & not he—& that at the Headquarters one wants him to be got rid of (this I believe)—ah, its so vile—always liars, enemies—I long knew Dzh.< hates Gr.< & that the "Preobrazhensky" clique therefore dislikes me,[112] as through me & Ania< he [Rasputin] comes to the house. In winter Dzh.< showed this paper to Voeik.< asking him to give it over to you & he refused doing anything so disgusting, thats why he hates Voeik.< & sticks with Drentel'n.—I am sorry to say these things, but they are bitter truth, & now Samarin added to the lot—no good can come out of it. [a, b, c]
   If we let our Friend be persecuted we & our country shall suffer for it—once a year ago one [Chionya Guseva] tried to kill him & one has slandered him enough. As if they would not have called the police straight in to catch him [i.e., her] in the act [in Pokrovskoe on June 28, 1914]—such a horror! Speak, please to Voeikov about it, I wish him to know Dzhunk.'s< behaviour & false using of yr. words. Voeikov [is] not a fool, without mentioning names can find out more

about it. It dare not be spoken about!   I don't know how Shcherb.< will act—probably also against our Fr. therefore against us.—And the Duma dare not broach this subject when they meet—Loman says they will, so as to force one to get rid of Gr. & A.[nia], I am so weary, such heartache & pain fr. all this—the idea of dirt being again spread about one we venerate is more than horrible. [d]

Ah my Love, when at last will you thump with your hand upon the table & scream at Dzh.< & others when they act wrongly?—one does not fear you—& one must—they must be frightened of you, otherwise all sit upon us, & its enough Deary—don't let me speak in vain. If Dzh.< is with you, call him, tell him you know (no names) he has shown that paper in town & that you order him to tear it up & not to dare to speak of Gr. as he does & that he acts as a traitor & not as a devoted subject, who ought to stand up for the Friends of his Sovereign, as one does in every other country.   Oh my Boy, make one tremble before you—to love you is not enough, one must be affraid [sic] of hurting, displeasing you! You are always too kind & all profit. It cannot go on like that Deary, believe me once, its honest truth I speak. All, who really love you, long that you should be more decided & show your displeasure stronger, be more severe—things cant go well so. If your Ministers feared you, all would be better. The old man, Gorem.< also finds you ought to be more sure of yourself & energetically speak, & show more strongly when you are displeased.—How much one hears complaints against the Headquarters, these surrounding Nikolasha<. [e]

Now another affair—don't know how to explain it well, wont mention names, so as that nobody should suffer.—The "Erivantsi" [men of the 13th Erivan Life Guards Grenadier Regiment] are perfect—where there is a difficult place—one sends them & keeps them to the last, as one is so sure of them. Now one intends taking of their own officers & putting them into other regiments to make those better. This is quite wrong & breaks their hearts. If you take their old ones away, then the regiment will no longer be what it was. They have lost enough killed, wounded (made prisoners) & cannot spare their own. Please do not let the regiment thus be ruined, & leave those officers, they love their regiment & keep up its fame. One does it with other officers of the 2-nd Brigade & they fear their turn is coming too & it worries the Commander & all—but they dare not say anything, have no right—therefore they want their chief [you, the tsar] to know it, & not to allow their Veteran officers to be taken fr. them into other regiments. [The following quote is in Russian.] "We shall be able to stand up for the country's cause in the ranks of our own regiments, we will not waver about sacrificing our lives for it. This is so urgent a situation that one must hurry if our own nest is not to be broken up. I think that the regiment has some right to claim such attention (not like the others), for its fighting service in the past, and as to the present, the order to the Division is eloquent enough. All the brunt of the rearguard battles, from the 31-st of May to the 6-th of June were carried by its shoulders, which has been recognized at the top." Only do not let N.< or others guess that the regiment asks this, otherwise they will suffer for it.—Do try & do something & give me an answer, they are very anxious—one sent a delightful pettyoffice[r] fr. there with a letter here. Must end, man waits. Blessings &

kisses without end fr. own   Wify.   [P.S.] Ania kisses your hand.—Excuse
beastly dull letter. [f]

No. 364/ Telegram 76 in Russian. Belovezh> Tsarskoe Selo. 22 June 1915.
4.00> 5.00 p.m. To her majesty. Arrived here very well. Remember and think
of [you] all. Forest is so beautiful. Warmly embrace [you]. Niki

---

No. 365/ Telegram 173. Tsarskoe Selo> Stavka. 22 June 1915. 8.28> 9.34 p.m.
To his majesty. Much gladdened by telegram from dear Belovezh. Glad you
visited there. Sat in hospital garden in morning. Rested on balcony during day.
Tenderly kiss [you]. God bless you. Alix

No. 366/ Her No. 326.   Ts.[arskoe] S[elo]. June 22nd 1915.
My very own beloved One,
    The letter I wrote in such haste to-day, I fear will have caused you little
pleasure & I regret, that I had no time to add nothing nice. It was a joy to get
your telegram from Belovezh—I am sure it did you good seeing the splendid
forest—but yet a sad feeling seeing the old places & realising [sic] that now a
terrible war is raging not so very far off from that peaceful place.—This morning
I went in my "droshki" with Aleksei to our hospital & we remained there over
two hours. Spoke to the wounded, sat in the hospital embroidering & then in the
garden whilst the others played croquet. But my heart felt bad & ached so—too
early probably for such a visit yet—but I was so glad to see them all. Kolenkin
turned up after commanding the "Alexandr."< only a month, he had to come
away because of terrible abscesses in the ear—they burst the drum of the ear too,
so he hears nothing on the left ear, poor fellow.— [a, b]
    I had Rostovtsev< for an hour & a half talking over the store< of Mme
Sukhomlinov—all is arranging itself satisfactorily & without any scandal.—To-morrow I shall receive Polivanov—Shcherbatov< leaves very great
freedom to the press—Maklakov [his predecessor as minister of internal affairs]
was far severer, but now the result is one speaks & gets too excited about the
Duma wh. is not a good thing.[102] — One longs sometimes to go to sleep & to
awake when all will be over & peace [will] once more reign everywhere— external & internal. —Everywhere Samarin's name is already mentioned—so disagreeable before his nomination comes out—how that fills me, with deepest anxiety. I
fear I aggravate you by all I write, but its only honestly & well meant, Sweetheart—others will never say anything, so old wify writes her opinion frankly,
when she feels its right to do so. One longs to help keeping of[f] any disaster,
but often ones words, alas, come too late, when already nothing can be done.
Now I must try & sleep, its late.   God bless yr. slumber, send you rest &
strength, courage & energy, calm and wisdom.— [c, d]
    June 23-rd.   Just got the report of my "Alex.[androvtsy]" you kindly sent
me—thanks Deary, even an envelope is a nice thing to receive with sweet handwriting upon it.—I remain quiet to-day, as heart again enlarged, pulse rather
weak & head aches. Am lying on the balcony [sic]—all are out & away & Ania<
gone to Peterhof. I enclose a letter from Victoria< wh. you may like to read.

Css. Hohenfelsen wrote to A.[nia] asking, whether she thinks we & the children would have accepted a luncheon at their house after Church—on Paul's< names-day [sic], with the people living in their house & whomsoever we wld. wish. I told her to answer (this was to be found out in case of a refusal, so that it should not follow upon a regular invitation), that I do not know when you return & my heart troubling me again it is doubtful I could sit at big luncheon. So foolish & tactless to ask. If we liked we might call upon him to congratulate— but not like this, with Babake [Mariana Ericovna von Derfel'den] & Olga Kreuts [Kreits], & the Countess [Princess Paley]! Sweetheart, me is so lonely without you, agoo wee one!—Goodbye Lovebird, I bless & kiss you with fervour & great love.—Hope so much to go Friday morning to Holy Communion, if [I prove to be] well enough, otherwise one of the last days of this Lent.—Wonder what you have settled for the day of the cross, hope you have said its to be done by your order. [See Letter No. 338b.]—God bless & protect you, I cover you with kisses. Ever yr. own old Sunny. [P.S.] Love to old Man [Fredericks] & N.P.<—[e]

No. 367/ Telegram 176. Tsarskoe Selo> Stavka. 23 June 1915. 11.34 a.m.> 12.10 p.m. To his majesty. In thoughts am with you, because of heart do not feel very well. Marvellous weather, light breeze continually. Hope you will return safely. Would like to know what is new. All embrace and kiss [you]. Toria's< birthday today, will telegraph her. Alix

---

No. 368/ Telegram 370. Stavka> Tsarskoe Selo. 23 June 1915. 3.00> 3.40 p.m. To her majesty. Best thanks [for] dear letter. Enjoyed my yesterday's trip enormously Writing about it. Got back at 11 of the evening. Weather divine. Remembered her [Toria's]< birthday and wired. Fondest kisses to all. Niki

---

No. 369/ His No. 181.   Stavka. June 23rd 1915.
My sweet Wify-dear.

So many thanks for your dear letters. Yesterday I really enjoyed myself in Belovezh. It was too strange to be there alone, without you and the children. I felt lost and sad but yet pleased to see the house & our nice rooms & to forget the present & to live through the days which have passed. But the night before starting I spent in anguish. The moment I finished playing domino N.< appeared and showed a telegr[am] he had just gotten from Gen. Alekseev, in wh[ich] it was said the Germans had torn through our lines and were marching deep into our rear.[99] N. left in his train at once & promised to wire in the morning from Sedlets. Of course, I could not start for Belovezh as had intended at 10.0. All my people felt very low, except Voeikov, because they did not know what was the reason of N.['s] sudden departure. At last at 11.40 a good telegr[am] came, fr. him saying that the prorich [breach] was stopped by a vigorous counter-attack by three of our regiments & that the enemy had been repulsed with heavy losses. So at 12.o with a light heart off I flew with, the old man [Fredericks] & all my gentlemen. The road till Belovezh is 183 versts [121.3 miles], & very good & smooth. Three towns lie on one's way—Slonim, Ruzhany & Pruzhany. I arrived at our house at 3.20 the others each five minutes later owing to the terrific dust.

A cold lunch we eat [sic] in the dining-hall, & then I showed the gentlemen all our rooms & the children's. Then we drove to the preserve because all wanted to see the wild bison & other animals. We were lucky enough to meet a large herd of bizons, who looked at us very quietly. [a, b]

We drove on through the wood along those excellent grass road & worked our way on to the high road near the end of the poushcha [woods]. The weather was perfect, but everything is so dry this year, even the bogs have disappeared, there was a thick dust even in the wood, all those who followed were quite black in there [sic] faces [and] hardly to be recognized. The little admiral especially<. The intendant of Bel.[ovezh] is new[—]he is called Lvov, a fat man, who is a cousin of the admiral. The old priest died and also tiny, Neverli, wh[om] I did not know. His successor is Bark, cousin of the minister, who has served here for 20 years as forester—an energetic man, who thoroughly knows the forest & the game. On the way back the tyres of all the motors began to breaking—my motor three times, owing to the heat during the day & to lots of nails lying about. These stoppings were quite opportune, they gave one the possibility of getting out to unstretch one's legs. The evening & night became beautifully fresh & the air in the woods so deliciously perfumed. [c]

We arrived here at 10.45 the very moment when N.'s train was slowly steaming to its place. After a talk with him I had supper with my people & went immediately to bed. He told me that on the whole the situation had not become worse yesterday & it would improve if the Germans do not press us at that same place for a few days. In this case we would have time to collect enough troops (fresh ones) to try & stop them. But again that damned question of lack of artillery ammunition & of rifles—puts a stop to an energetic movement forwards, because after three days serious fighting it may become exhausted (ammunition). Having no new rifles it is impossible to fill up the losses of men & the army is now a little bit stronger than in time of peace. It ought to be & was in the beginning three times stronger! Such is the situation we are in for the moment. If there were no battles for a month our case would be much better! Of course, this is only for you to know, please don't speak about it, my darling. This letter has become rather long & one has no more time. God bless you my beloved Sunny! I kiss you and the children very very tenderly. May you feel strong & well again! Ever your own huzy. Nicky. [d]

No. 370/ Telegram 185. Tsarskoe Selo> Stavka. 24 June 1915. 4.28> 5.05 p.m. Endless thanks for dear letter only just received. Share all your thoughts and prayers; am always with you. Lying on balcony. Splendid weather. Serge< and Petia< are coming for tea. All warmly kiss [you]. Alix

No. 371/ Her No. 327.   Ts.[arskoe] S[elo]. June 24th 1915.
My beloved Nicky dear,

Again a splendid day. Slept little this night & at 3 looked out of the window of my mauve room. A glorious morning, one felt the sun behind the trees, a soft haze over all, such calm—the swans swimming on the pond, steam rising from the grass—oh so beautiful, I longed to be well & go for a long, long walk as in bygone days.—Sergei M.< comes to tea, it seems he is quite well again & Petia.<

Saw Polivanov yesterday—don't honestly ever care for the man—something ag-gravating about him, cant explain what—preferred Sukhomlinov, tho' this one is cleverer, but doubt whether as devoted. Sukhomlinov has made the great mis-take of showing your private letter to him, right & left, & others have copies of it. Fred.< ought to write him a word of reprimand. I understand he did it to show how kind you are to him to the end —but others need not know the reasons he left, except that he told an untruth at the famous sitting at Peterhof, when he said that we were ready & had enough to hold out, when we had not sufficient ammunition—this is his only very great fault, the bribe of his wife the rest.[113] Now others can think that public opinion is enough to clear out our Friend< etc. a dangerous thing before the Duma. [a, b]

You cannot imagine the cruel suffering of not being with you—I know I could help & guard off things sometimes & here I am, eating out my heart fr. [a]far, feeling my inability of being any use, only writing disagreeable letters to you, my Love.—From the outset Gorem.[ykin] must speak to Samar.[in] & Shcherb.[atov] how they have to behave about our Friend, to prevent any cal-umnies & stories.—Alas, have nothing cheerful or interesting to tell you. Spent day & evening on balkony [sic], to-day too as don't feel well, tho' heart not yet enlarged & can begin my medicins [sic] again. Eagerly awaiting yr. letter about Bielovezh.— [c]

Its true one is completely evacuating Varsovie [Warsaw]? (for prudence sake!)[109] —Hope to go to holy Communion, depends upon health, wh.[ich] day, think Sunday at early mass downstairs with A.[nia];< when do you return? to-day two weeks—seems at least a month—(& our Friend begged for quite short [stay on your part at Stavka], knowing things wld. not be as they ought if one kept you & profitted of your kindness).—Are you going off unaware [i.e., on a surprise visit] to Belostok or Kholm to see the troops? Do show yourself there before returning—give them & yourself the joy. The Active Army is not tho' Headquarters thank God—surely you can see some troops. Voeikov can arrange all (not Dzhunk.<), nobody need know, only then it will succeed—say you are going off again for a trip;—had I been there, I should have helped you going off—Sweetheart needs pushing always & to be reminded that he is the Emperor & can do whatsoever pleases him—you never profit of this—you must show you have a way & will of yr. own, & are not lead by N.< & his staff, who direct yr. movements & whose permission you have to ask before going anywhere. No, go alone, without N., by yr. very own self, bring the blessing of yr. presence to them—don't say you bring bad luck [118]—at Lemberg & Przmysl it happened, be-cause our Friend knew & told you it was too early, but you listened instead to the Headquarters. [d]

Forgive my speaking so straightforwardly, but I suffer too much—I know you—& Nikolasha—[and I say you should] go to the troops, say not a word to N.; you have false scruples when you say its not honest not telling him—since when is he your mentor, & in what way do you disturb him? Let at last one see that you do after yr. own head, wh. is worth all theirs put together. Go Lovy—cheer up Ivanov too—such heavy battles are coming—bless the troops by your precious Being, in their name I beseech you to go —give them the spiritual rise, show them for whom they are fighting & dying —not for Nikolasha, but for you! 1000[s] have never seen you & yearn for a look of yr. beautiful, pure eyes. Such masses have moved down—one can't lie to you, that none are to be got at. Only if you say it to Nikolasha the spies that are at the Headquarters— who?—will at once let the Germans know & then their aeroplans [sic] will set to work [to kill you]. But 3 simple motors otherwise wont be seen, only wire to me something that I can understand & let our Friend know to pray for you. Say like that ["]going to-morrow again for an expedition["]—please Lovebird. Trust me, I mean yr. good—you always need encouraging & remember, not a word to Nikolasha let him think you go anywhere, Belovezh or wheresoever it pleases you. Its a false Headquarter[s] wh. keeps you away, instead of encouraging you to go. But the soldiers must see you, they need you, not the Headquarters, they want you & you them. Now goodbye my Sunshine, kisses & blessings without end.   Ever yr. very own   Sunny. [e]

113. Nicholas liked Sukhomlinov and dismissed him in June 1915 in a letter filled with gratitude and praise. Apparently Sukhomlinov was showing this letter to people. Madame Sukhomlinov was 35 years old, her husband was 67; she led an extravagant life and was accused of various malfeasances, including taking bribes. See Massie, *Nicholas and Alexandra*, pp. 271-273.

No. 372/ Telegram 388. Stavka> Tsarskoe Selo. 24 June 1915. 9.42> 10.10 p.m. To her majesty. Ever so many thanks for dear letters and [daughter] Marie's which came at 9 instead of in the morning. Divine weather. Bathed in a small river in my favourite wood. Tender kisses, sleep well. Niki

No. 373/ Her No. 328.   Ts.[arskoe] S[elo]. June 25th 1915.
My Sweetheart,
    I thank you ever so fondly for yr. dear, long letter I was overjoyed to receive. How nice that yr. expedition was so successful—tho' you were lonely without yr. "Benoitons" [apparently a code name] to keep you company. I never knew that Neverle had died, good old man!—What luck you saw the Moose & could drive through the thick woods.—Ah my love! What anguish you must have gone through when Nikolasha< got that bad news. Here I hear nothing & live in anguish & suspension, yearning to know what is going on out there. God will help, only we shall have still much misery & heartache I fear. That ammunition question can turn ones hair grey.—Deary, I heard that the horrid Rodzianko & others went to Goremykin to beg the Duma to be at once called together—oh please dont, its not their bussiness [sic], they want to discuss things not concerning them & bring more discontent—they must be kept away—I assure you only harm will arise—they speak too much. Russia, thank God, is not a constitutional country, tho' those creatures try to play a part & meddle in affairs they dare not. Do not allow them to press upon you—its fright if one gives in & their heads will go up.— [a, b]
    You know Guchkov< is still Polivanov's friend—that was the reason there, that P.[olivanov] & Sukh.[omlinov] went apart. I dont like his choice—I loathe yr. being at the Headquarters and many others too, as its not seeing soldiers, but listening to N.'s< advice, wh. is not good & cannot be—he has no right to act as he does, mixing in your concerns. All are shocked that the ministers go with

report[s] to him, as tho' he were now the Sovereign. Ah my Nicky, things are not as they ought to be, & therefore N. keeps you near, to have a hold over you with his ideas & bad councels [sic]. Wont you yet believe me, my Boy? Cant you realise that a man who turned simple traitor to a man of Gods [i.e., Rasputin], cannot be blest, nor his actions be good—well, if he must remain at the head of the army there is nothing to be done, & all bad success will fall upon his head—but interior mistakes will be told home upon you, as who inside the country can think that he reigns besides you. Its so utterly false & wrong.—I fear I anger & trouble you by my letters—but I am alone in my misery & anxiety & I cant swallow what I think my honest duty to tell you.— [c]

Yesterday evening I invited Kussov< (ex Nizhegor.<) of the Moscou [sic] reg. from Tver—& I was struck how exactly he spoke as I think, & he does not know me, only second time we have met —so how many others must judge like him. He was 3 days at the Headquarters & did not carry away a pleasant impression, neither do Voeikov & N.P.<, who are the most devoted to you.— Remember our Friend< begged you not to remain long [at Stavka]—He sees & knows N.< through & through & your too soft & kind heart.—I here, incapable of helping, have rarely gone through such a time of wretchedness—feeling & realising things are not done as they should be,—& helpless to be of use—its bitterly hard; & they, N. knows my will, & fears my influence (guided by Gregory<) upon you; its all so clear.—Well, I must not tire you any longer, only I want my conscience to [be] clear, whatever happens.—Is it true Yusupov [the Elder] has had the half of his duties taken fr. him, so that he plays a secondary part?[114] — [d]

Sergei< does not look famous—we touched no subjects—he is going to ask permission to go on Saturday to the Headquarters. Petia< full of secrets & his "heart".—How nice you could bathe, so refreshing. Here the heat is not great, always a breeze & ideal on the balkony [sic]—don't feel well enough to drive. Paul< has invited himself to tea. Girls< are in hospital, lessons.—Please answer me, are the cross Processions going to be on the 29th, as such a great holiday & the end of lent? Excuse bothering you again, but so eager to know, as hear nothing. [See No. 338b.] —To-day I receive the Gentlemen of my committee for our prisoners in Germany & an American (of the young Christian's men's association like our "Mayak") who undertakes to bring all our things personally to the prisons. He has travelled & photogr. in many places, especially Siberia, where we keep our prisoners & wh. are well arranged, those he will exhibit in Germany, hoping it will help ours in return.—What answer about the "Erivantsi"?< [See No. 363f.] Now goodbye, my very own tenderly beloved one. I cover you with kisses & ask God's blessing upon you.—Ever yr. own old Wify. [e]

---

114. Prince Felix Yusupov (the Elder) was dismissed as governor of Moscow. This apparently began his son's disillusionment with the royal family. The younger Yusupov concluded Rasputin was a poisonous influence and, given the tsar's refusal to part with Grigory, only Rasputin's murder would save the dynasty and Russia. See Yusupov, *Lost Splendor*, pp. 183-185.

No. 374/ Telegram 194. Tsarskoe Selo> Stavka. 25 June 1915. 7.05> 7.40 p.m. To his majesty. Paul< had tea with us. Very good weather. Spent entire day on balcony because do not feel very good. Children healthy. We embrace and kiss [you]. Alix.

No. 375/ Telegram 405. Stavka> Tsarskoe Selo. 25 June 1915. 10.11> 10.33 p.m. To her majesty. Many thanks [for] dear letter, also [daughter] Tatiana today. Stiffling [sic] heat. Hope to be back Sunday afternoon. News better. Fondest kisses. Niki

No. 376/ Her No. 329.   Ts.[arskoe] S[elo]. June 25th 1915.
My very Own!
   Oh, what joy, if you really return on Sunday & the news are better! I was just so miserable, as had a telegram fr. the com.[mander] of my Siberian regiment that they had very heavy losses in the night 23-24 fr. 10-3—& I wondered what great battle was going on—because the wire came from a new place.—Well I saw that American fr. the young Men's Christian Association & was deeply interested by all he told me of our prisoners there & their[s] here. I enclose his letter wh. he is also going to have printed & shown in Germany (& photos, wh. show our excellent barracks). He intends only telling the good on either side & not the bad things, & hopes thus to make all sides work humanely. This evening I got a letter fr. Vicky< wh. I send you with Max['s]< letters (I fear I worry you, but you are free'er of an evening there than here[—]please read it & you may like to mention some things there). I have let the American who leaves for Germany to-morrow know that I wish him to send the papers to Max< & to go & see him & tell him all, so as to rectify all their false impressions upon the way we keep our prisoners. [a, b]
   I never heard about so many illnesses in Russia.—I think he said (the American) that 4000 had died at Cassel from spotted typhus, awful!—Chiefly read Max' English paper, & in Vickys fr. Max you will see our paper wh. my Dear is idiotically worded & without any explication—& abominable German. "Es ist befohlen die 10 ersten deutschen Kriegsgfangenen—als Erfolg (all wrong) der mörderischen Thaten, die sich einige deutsche Truppen erlauben, zu erschiessen." One might have written it in decent German; explaining that in the spot where one finds a [Russian] man had been tortured one will shoot 10 [enemy] men just taken. Its badly written—Erfolg (means result—success) one says als Folge, but even that sounds wrong. Let it be decently worded in proper, grammatical German & more explanitarily written. [c]
   Then its not meant every time to shoot men down, you never meant that, its all wrong, somehow & therefore they dont understand what one means.—Please dont mention fr. where the letters came, except to Nikolasha< about Max, as he looks after our prisoners;—& they sent the letters through a Swede to Ania<, not to a lady in waiting on purpose—nobody is to know about this, not even their embassy—don't know why this fright. I wired openly to Vicky that I thank her for her letter & beg her to thank Max fr. me for all he does for our prisoners & that he is to rest assured that one does ones best for their prisoners here. I don't compromise myself in that—I don't do anything personally & as I intend doing all for our prisoners & this American will take our things there & tell as where

& what is needed & will help as much as he can.—Please, return the papers, or bring them on Sunday, if you really come then.— [d]

I had Paul< to tea & we chatted a lot. He asked whether Sergei< would be relieved of his post [as inspector general of artillery] as all are so much against him, right or wrong—& Kch.[115] is mixed up again—she behaved like Mme Sukh.[omlinov] it seams with bribes & the Artillery orders—one hears it fr. many sides. Only he reminded me, that it must be by your command, not Nikolasha's as you can only give such an order, (or hint to ask for his resignation) to a Grd. [Grand] Duke who is no boy, as you are his Chief & not Nikolasha, that wld. make the family very displeased. He is so devoted, Paul, & putting his personal dislike to Nikolasha aside,—finds too that people cannot understand his position, a sort of second Emperor, mixing into everything. How many (& our Friend<) say the same thing.—Then I enclose a letter fr. Count Pahlen, rectifying himself—Goremykin (or Shcherbatov<) also found one had acted wrongly towards him (I think Goremykin told me;—the paper Mavra< gave me).—Look through it Deary & forgive me bothering you again.—You will "hang her" when you get such long epistles from me—but I must write all.—I did not see the Siberian soldier, Petia< let me know one forbade him coming to me, because he had run away from Germany—I dont understand the logic, do you?— [e, f]

26-th. Then this will be my last letter to you, fear even it many not reach you before you leave, as trains so slow.—Heart enlarged so cant go to Church, hope still for to-morrow evening, so as to go Sunday at 8 or 9 to mass & holy Communion in the little Church below with Ania. Sweety, from heart & soul I beg your tender forgiveness for any word or action of mine wh. may have hurt or grieved you; & believe it was not intentional. Am longing for this moment, to get strength & help. Am not without courage, Lovy, oh no, only such pain in heart & soul from so much sorrow all around & misery at not being able to help.—There must be woods burning, smells strong since yesterday; & to-day very warm but no sun—shall lie out as usual if no rain.—Fear can't meet you at station, as Church will already be a great exertion & do feel so rotten still! What intense happiness to having you back soon—but I still tremble it may not be—God give success to our troops that you can leave there with a calmer heart. Wonder if you can manage to see troops on yr. return route.—[Your sister] Xenia has announced herself to tea after her lunch at Irina [Yusupova]'s—am so glad to see her at last again. Another "Erivan" officer had been brought to our hospital—what answer to their demand, I wonder? [See No. 363f.] Goodbye, my own beloved One, my Nicky sweet. God bless & protect you & bring you safely home again into the loving arms of your Children & your yearning old Wify. [P.S.] Baby< & I are going to see Galfter & then 3 wounded of[ficers].—Miss my hospital & feel sad not to be able to work & look after our dear wounded. Love to old Man [Fred.], Dmitri Sh.< & N.P.< [g, h]

---

115. The empress speaks of the famed Russian-Polish ballerina Mathilde Kschessinska. Nicholas had a lengthy affair with her before he met Alexandra. He confessed this to Alix before they were married, and was forgiven. See Massie, *Nicholas and Alexandra*, pp. 19-20, 23, 25, 36-37, etc.

No. 377/ Telegram 197. Tsarskoe Selo> Stavka. 26 June 1915. 11.45 a.m.>
12.22 p.m. To his majesty. Such joy that your arrival is possible on Sunday and
that the news is better! With God's help things are getting better. Do not feel
especially good today. Very warm but no sun. Think they are burning wood
somewhere. Has smelled of smoke for two days now. All kiss [you] warmly.
Hope you received my letter yesterday before dinner. We embrace and kiss
[you]. Alix

No. 378/ Telegram 421. Stavka> Tsarskoe Selo. 26 June 1915. 3.28> 4.30
p.m. To her majesty. Loving thanks [for] dear letter and Aleksei too. Refreshing thunderstorm during lunch. Procession of the Cross [scheduled] on July 8.
Unspeakably happy to leave to-morrow. Tender kisses. Niki

No. 379/ His No. 182.   Stavka. June 26ᵗʰ 1915.
My Precious Sunny,
    Tender thanks for three dear letters. I could not write before, as was very busy
with my rotten papers which came at extraordinary hours of the day. This happened because so many military trains were going down fr Vilna & Belostok.
Yesterday I had the joy of seeing the 6th Squadron of my Hussars passing the
station. The train stopped for 15 min[utes,] all the men got out—the flag also. I
saw them climb in again & leave cheering, gaily. Such a joy and refreshing
feeling! The dragoons also passed here, but your lancers went by another line.
Sorry not to have seen them.—I quite agree with you, my darling—that the prin-
ciple thing for me is to see the troops. I have often spoken to Voeikov about
it—it is most difficult to arrange practically fr here. From Belovezh, certainly
easier. But when not being here [i.e., there] I don't know where what troops are,
and as those behind the front line are always moving up & down it is difficult to
find them. Moving in the train now is out of the question. It is like an impasses,
as the French say! [a]
    Thank you so much for sending Victoria's< letter—she always writes so posi-
tively and clearly. During lunch to day a thunder storm passed, the downpour
was strong & lasted for an hour. It refreshed the air deliciously, bringing the
temperature fr 23 down to 15 degrees. This is my last letter to you Lovebird—I
am really happy to come home again to my own family! I kiss you most tenderly, also the dear children. I hope to be back on Saturday at 5.o afternoon.
God bless you my beloved darling Wify. Ever your own old huzy. Nicky [b]

No. 380/ Telegram 206. Tsarskoe Selo> Stavka. 27 June 1915. 10.52> 11.20
a.m. To his majesty. Wish you a happy trip. Await your arrival with interest.
Hope you received my letter yesterday evening. Wonderful day, rained and air
became fresher. [I] am not able to go to church because heart still quite enlarged
and do not feel good. Bless and kiss [you]. Alix

No. 381/ Telegram 432. Stavka> Tsarskoe Selo. 27 June 1915. 2.08> 2.37 p.m.
To her majesty. Fondest thanks [for] dear letter with papers, also [daughter and

son] Olga and Aleksei. Leaving now under good impression. News thank God, decidedly better.[116] Hope you will feel better. Tender kisses. Niki

116. The Russian armies had regrouped and were optimistic about holding the Germans on the line established at this point. But the Russians were forced to resume their retreat until September, when heavy rain halted the German advance. See Letter 420c.

No. 382/ Telegram 210. Tsarskoe Selo> Orsha train station. 27 June 1915. 8.22> 10.50 p.m. Terribly gladdened by dear letter and telegram. Thanks be to God news better. Glad to see you to-morrow. Sleep well. God keep you. We kiss [you] warmly. Alix

No. 383/ Her No. 330.   Tsarskoe Selo. Aug. 22nd 1915.
My very own beloved One,
   I cannot find words to express all I want to—my heart is far too full. I only long to hold you tight in my arms & whisper words of intense love, courage, strength & endless blessings.   More than hard to let you go alone, so completely alone—but God is very near to you, more then ever. You have fought this great fight for your country & throne—alone & with bravery & decision. Never have they seen such firmness in you before & it cannot remain without good fruit. Do not fear for what remains behind—one must be severe & stop all at once. Lovy, I am here, dont laugh at silly old wify, but she has "trousers" on unseen [see No. 383b], & I can get the old man [Goremykin] to come & keep him up to be energetic—whenever I can be of the smallest use, tell me what to do—use me—at such a time God will give me the strength to help you—because our souls are fighting for the right against the evil. It is all much deeper than appears to the eye—we, who have been taught to look at all from another side, see what the struggle here really is & means—you showing your mastery, proving yourself the Autocrat without wh. Russia cannot exist. Had you given in now in these different questions, they would have dragged out yet more of you. [a, b]
   Being firm is the only saving—I know what it costs you, & have & do suffer hideously for you, forgive me, I beseech you, my Angel, for having left you no peace & worried you so much—but I too well know yr. marvelously gentle character—& you had to shake it off this time, had to win your fight alone against all. It will be a glorious page in yr. reign & Russian history the story of these weeks & days—& God, who is just & near you—will save your country & throne through your firmness. A harder battle has rarely been faught [sic], than yours & it will be crowned with success, only believe this.   Yr. faith has been tried—your trust—& you remained firm as a rock, for that you will be blessed. God anointed you at your coronation, he placed you where you stand & you have done your duty, be sure, quite sure of this & He forsaketh not His anointed. Our Friend's< prayers arise night & day for you to Heaven & God will hear them. [c]
   Those who fear & cannot understand your actions, will be brought by events to realise your great wisdom. It is the beginning of the glory of yr. reign, He [Rasputin] said so & I absolutely believe it. Your Sun is rising—& to-day it shines so brightly. And so will you charm all those great blunderers, cowards,

lead astray, noisy, blind, narrowminded & (dishonest false) beings, this morning. And your Sunbeam< will appear to help you, your very own Child—won't
that touch those hearts & make them realise what you are doing, & what they
dared to wish to do, to shake your throne, to frighten you with internal black
forebodings—only a bit of success out there & they will change. They [our soldiers at the end of the war] will disperse home into clean air & their minds will
be purified & they carry the picture of you & yr. Son in their hearts with them. I
do hope Gorem will agree to yr. choice of [A. N.] Khvostov—you need an energetic minister of the interior—should he be the wrong man, he can later be
changed—no harm in that, at such times—but if energetic he may help splendidly
& then the old man [Goremykin] does not matter. If you take him, then only
wire to me "tail (Khvostov) alright [sic]" & I shall understand.[117]—[d, e]

Let no talks worry you—am glad Dmitri< wont be there now—snap up Voeikov
if he is stupid—am sure he is affraid [sic] meeting people there who may think he
was against N.< & Orlov & to smoothe things, he begs you for N.—that would
be the greatest fault & undo all you have so courageously done & the great internal fight[118] would have been for nothing. Too kind, don't be, I mean not specially, as otherwise it would be dishonest, as still there have been things you
were discontented with him about. Remind others about Misha, [that he is] the
Emperor's brother[,] & then there is war there too. All is for the good, as our
Friend says, the worst is over.—Now you speak to the Minister of war & he will
take energetic measures, as soon as needed—but Khvostov, will see to that too if
you name him.—When you leave, shall wire to Friend to-night through Ania—&
He will particularly think of you. Only get Nikolasha's nomination quicker
done—no dawdling, its bad for the cause & for Alekseev too—& a settled thing
quieten[s] minds even if against their wish, sooner than that waiting & uncer-
tainty & trying to influence you—it tires out ones heart. [f, g]

I feel completely done up & only keep myself going with force—they shall not
think that I am downhearted or frightened —but confident & calm.—Joy we went
to those holy places together—for sure yr. dear Father [Alexander III] quite particularly prays for you. Give me some news as soon as you can—now am affraid
[sic] for the moment N.P.< wiring to Ania until am sure nobody watches [their
correspondence] again. Tell me the impression, if you can. Be firm to the end,
let me be sure of that otherwise shall get quite ill from anxiety. Bitter pain not
to be with you—know what you feel, & the meeting with N. wont be agreeable—you did trust him & now you know, what months ago our Friend said, that
he was acting wrongly towards you & your country & wife—its not the people
who would do harm to your people, but Nikolasha & set [made up of] Guchkov,
Rodzianko, Samarin etc. [h]

Lovy, if you hear I am not so well, don't be anxious, I have suffered so terribly, & phisically overtired myself these 2 days, & morally worried (& worry
still till all is done at the Headquarters & Nikolasha< gone) only then shall I feel
calm—near you all is well—when out of sight others at once profit—you see they
are affraid [sic] of me & so come to you when alone—they know I have a will of
my own when I feel I am in the right—& you are now—we know it, so you make
them tremble before your courage & will. God is with you & our Friend for
you—all is well—& later all will thank you for having saved your country. Don't

doubt—believe, & all will be well & the army is everything—a few strikes nothing, in camparison [sic], as can & shall be suppressed. The left are furious because all slips through their hands & their cards are clear to us & the game they
wished to use Nikolasha for—even Shvedov knows it fr. there. [i]

Now goodnight lovy, go straight to bed without [taking] tea with the rest &
[having to see] their long faces. Sleep long & well, you need rest after this
strain & your heart needs calm hours.—God Almighty bless your undertaking,
His holy Angels guard & guide you & bless the work of your hands.—Please
give this little Image [Icon] of St. John the Warrior to Alekseev with my blessing & fervent wishes. You have my Image I blessed you with last year—I give
no other as that carries my blessing & you have Gregory's St. Nicolas [sic] to
guard & guide you. I always place a candle before St. Nicolas at Znamenje< for
you—& shall do, so to-morrow at 3 o'clock & before the Virgin. You will feel
my soul near you. I clasp you tenderly to my heart, kiss and caress you without
end—want to show you all the intense love I have for you, warm, cheer, console,
strengthen you, & make you sure of yourself. Sleep well my Sunshine, Russia's
Saviour[.] Remember last night, how tenderly we clung together. I shall yearn
for yr. caresses—I never can have enough of them. And I still have the children,
& you are all alone. Another time I must give you Baby< for a bit [i.e., Aleksei
should visit you at Stavka] to cheer you up.—I kiss you without end & bless you.
Holy Angels guard your slumber—I am near & with you for ever & ever & none
shall seperate [sic] us.—Yr. very own wife   <u>Sunny</u>. [j, k]

117. Aleksei Nicholaevich Khvostov (1872-1918) was a rightist member of the Fourth Duma,
which was in session at the time this letter was written. Nicholas considered making Khvostov
minister of the interior in 1911. Khvostov's uncle, Alexander Khvostov (then assistant-minister of
justice), conceded that his nephew was able, but he warned the tsar that the young man was also
greedy and corrupt. V. N. Kokovtsov was becoming chairman of the council of ministers at this
time. He likewise opposed A. N. Khvostov; the tsar let Kokovtsov have his choice of minister of
the interior: A. A. Makarov. But Nicholas continued to be interested in Khvostov. In August 1915,
A. N. Khvostov learned Shcherbatov was on the way out as minister of the interior. Khvostov
formed an alliance with Prince Michael Andronnikov to install himself in Shcherbatov's place. The
empress had not met A. N. Khvostov, yet on the strength of what she was *hearing* about him—and it
could not have been entirely favorable—she hoped Khvostov would be made minister of the interior:
"[S]hould he be the wrong man, he can later be changed—no harm in that, at such times [!]" In this
letter Alexandra hints that Goremykin might not want Khvostov. Alexandra was correct, and Goremykin blocked Khvostov's appointment. (See Letter No. 384e.) A. N. Khvostov finally became
minister of the interior. The appointment was a disaster; it marked a new stage in the crisis which
ended in the overthrow of Nicholas's government. "Khvost" in Russian means "tail," hence Alexandra's pun: "wire to me 'tail (Khvostov) alright' & I shall understand." Actually, A. N. Khvostov was
not shaped like a tail. In the words of one contemporary, "he was repulsively fat and singularly
ingratiating." (Fuhrmann, *Rasputin*, pp. 72-73, 143-144, etc.)

118. The "great internal fight" was between Nicholas and his wife. Although Alexandra thought it
good for the tsar to visit his troops, she and Rasputin opposed his lengthy stays at Stavka (Letters
No. 320c, 343a, 371d) since influences there (apparently) caused Nicholas to make what they
thought were "unwise" decisions. The military situation by August 1915 changed the empress's
thinking. Alexandra now urged her husband to fire Nicholasha and assume personal command of
Russian armies in the west. (Actual conduct of the war would be in the hands of the new chief of
staff, Gen. Michael Alekseev.) Nicholas was not easily won to this plan. If it reflected his own
desires, he realized it would stir controversy since Nicholasha was popular. The tsar, by contrast, had
a reputation for bringing bad luck. (The empress admits this in Letter No. 371d.) Rasputin was in
Siberia as Nicholas and Alexandra debated these changes. Alexandra called Rasputin back to the
capital to support her position. (Fuhrmann, *Rasputin*, pp. 132-133) Alexandra prevailed. Nicholas

returned to Stavka on August 22/ September 1, 1915, ready to announce changes would stun Russia and her allies. See Letter No. 1311a for later comments from Nicholas on his decision to assume the supreme command.

No. 384/ Her No. 331.   Tsarskoe Selo. Aug. 23rd 1915.
My very own priceless one,

All my thoughts & prayers surround you in tenderest love. Such calm filled my soul (tho' terribly sad) when I saw you leave in peace and serene. Your face had such a lovely expression, like when our Friend< left. God verily will bless you and your undertakings after this moral victory. Wonder how you slept—I went straight to bed, lovely, 13 degr.[ees] that I drove 20 m. with the three big girls< in a half open motor. This morning it is very damp, grey & drizzling.— A.[nia] said Nini told her, that fat O.[119] took it very decently, thats all I know about him, that Emma cried as she was fond of him [Nicholasha?], & Nini feared it was an intrigue of her husbands', but A.[nia] quietened her.— [a, b]

Whilst Mitia Den< is with you, he might also do duty, when there is no walking about to be done. Oh how I should love to see how you do all, altogether I should like a concealing-fairy-cap to peep into many a house & see the faces!!!—Baby< enjoyed himself very much in the "little house" with Irina Tolstoy & Rita Khitrovo<, they played games together.—I went with [daughter] Marie to the Cath.[erine] S.[obor, i.e., Cathedral] to mass, so nice, & from there at 12 to our hospital to sit with our wounded. Then we lunched upstairs in the corner room & remained there till 6. Baby dear's left arm hurts & is very swollen, hurt fr. time to time in the night & to-day—the old thing, but he has not had it very long, thank God. Mr. Gill[i]ard read aloud & then showed us the magic lantern. I received 7 wounded; & Ordin. A.[nia] was at Peterhof a few hours. Out such a frizzle. I see nothing had appeared yet in the papers [about the change in command], so suppose you intend telling it be known to-morrow when N. leaves [for his new assignment as viceroy of the Caucasus].—I wonder.—Did you appreciate Volodia [Trubetskoi]'s success in the black sea? [c, d]

I got a charming letter fr. Nicolai [Michaelovich] about yr. having taken over the command & shall send it you to-morrow —this evening I must answer it.—Ania sends her love & kisses yr. hand & is always thinking of you.—We all send our love to N.P.< God bless & protect you my Treasure—miss you very, very much, as you know cannot be otherwise; press you tenderly to my heart & cover you with caresses & kisses. I bless you & pray for God's help. Ever yr. old   Wify. [e]

Ella's< prayers are with you—she is going for these last days to Optin convent. This is just about another injustice Taube, Pss Gedroits< & our young Dr. back fr. the war were telling me. It has just come out, that henceforth the Drs. are only to get 3 military rewards, wh. is unfair, as they expose themselves continually to danger—& till now masses received rewards. Taube found quite wrong, people fr. the ordnance who sit behind in the rear should receive the same, as those under fire. The Drs. & sanitaries do marvels, are constantly killed—whilst the soldiers have to lie flat, these walk upright carrying out the wounded.— My little Dr. Mat[y]ushkin of the 21 S[iberian]. r.[ifle] Regiment has again been commanding a company.—One cannot recompense those enough, that work under fire.—One of your young curassiers was wounded by an officer, a quite young boy something like Minkwitz, Hessian reserve reg., such pain to hear that.—Am sure shall hear much now, hoping that I will repeat all to you.— Longing for news from you & the war. God help you.—This is gossip. [f, g]

Aug. 24 1915. Only one word, one says, that on Wednesday in the Duma all parties are going to address themselves to you to ask you to change the old Man [Goremykin, chairman of the council of ministers]. I hope still, that when at last the change is made officially known things may get right, if not, I fear the old man cannot continue working when all are against him. He will never dare ask to leave, he said, but, alas, I don't know how things will work. To-day he sees all the ministers & intends speaking firmer to them, it can finish him off poor dear, honest Soul.—And whom to take at such a moment firm enough? Minister of war [Polivanov], so as to punish them for (don't at all like the idea) a short time, as he understands nothing of interior questions, but will look like dictator ship. How is Kharitonov? I don't know. But better to wait still. They of course aim at Rodz.<, wh. wld. be the ruin & spoil all you have done & never to be trusted—but Guchkov< is behind Poliv.[anov] & you have no minister of the Interior yet [to replace the incumbent, Prince Shcherbatov, now in disfavor].—Forgive bothering you, but its only a rumour, wiser to know.— [h, i]

119. Prince V. N. Orlov ("Fat Orlov") was at Stavka as director of Nicholas II's infantry chancellery. Orlov accompanied Nicholasha to the Caucasus as his director of civilian affairs.

No. 385/ Telegram 1. Vitebsk> Tsarskoe Selo. 23 August 1915. 12.15> 12.45 p.m. To her majesty. Tenderest thanks [for] dear letter, also children. Slept well, feel strong and decided. Hope you are calm and not too tired. Shall telegraph this evening when all is over.[120] Blessings and endless love. Niki

120. Nicholas decided to inform Nicholasha< in person of his decision to replace him as commander of the Russian armies. Nicholasha was "promoted" to viceroy of the Caucasus, which meant he commanded Russian armies facing the Turks.

No. 386/ Telegram 180 in Russian. Tsarskoe Selo> Stavka. 23 Aug 1915. 1.29> 4.00 p.m. To his majesty. Warmly thank you for telegram. [I am] peaceful. Attended church with [son] Aleksei. All six< [of us are] now having lunch on balcony. Summer day. Will see old man [Goremykin] at 5 o'clock. Miss you but glad all is well. Father [A. P. Vasil'ev] delivered a splendid sermon. Thoughts [and] especially prayers surround you. We warmly kiss you. Alix

No. 387/ Telegram 01. Imperial Stavka> Tsarskoe Selo. 23 Aug 1915. 7.39> 8.39 p.m. To her majesty. Thanks for news. Meeting [with Nicholasha<] went off marvellously and simply. He leaves after to-morrow but change has already taken place today. Now all is done. Kiss you [and] children tenderly. Niki

No. 388/ Telegram 183. Tsarskoe Selo> Stavka. 23 Aug 1915. 9.30> 10.25 p.m. To his majesty. God bless you and your manly decision, my beloved. Thank the Lord all went well. We "all" kiss you. Have written. Sleep well and

peacefully. Very touched by first telegram in my name from Imperial Stavka.[121]
Alix

---

121. When Nicholasha< was at the helm, headquarters was known as "Stavka verkhovnago glav-
nago" (headquarters of the supreme command). After the emperor assumed command, headquarters
was formally known as "Tsarskaya Stavka," "Imperial Stavka" or "the Tsar's Stavka." (Note the
address of No. 387). Actually, this and most subsequent telegrams were still simply addressed to and
from "Stavka." The advance of German armies in Poland forced the Russians to move Stavka from
Baranovichi shortly before this time. Stavka was now located 180 miles to the southwest, at
Mogilev, on the banks of the Dnieper in Belorussia.

No. 389/ Her No. 332.   Ts.[arskoe] S[elo]. 24 Aug. 1915.
My own beloved One,
    Thank God all is done & that the meeting went off so well—such a relief.
Bless you my Angel & your brave undertaking & crown it with success & victory, interior & exterior. So emotioning Telegram 01 Imper-H. [121] —I have kept
the envelope too as remembrance of that memorable day; Babykins< is so
happy, & interested in all, Ania< too at once crossed herself & I directly called
Nini< to the telephone to quieten her, that all went off well, she had her Mother
& Emma< with her, & I knew it would soothe them. The evening was so dead-
beat & very lonely. Dear Girlies< proposed to sleep by turn in the room next
door, as I am all alone on this floor—but I begged them not to, am quite accustomed to it & don't mind. I feel you near me, bless & kiss your cushion. Slept
midling. Such a sunny morning—the three girls went at 9 to Church, as Olga &
Tatiana wish to work in the hospital till 12½.— Wonder how the spirits around
you are—your peace must spread itself upon them. [a]
    I had a talk with N.P.< & begged him not to heed to Voeikov's< varying
moods.—The whole time those odious trains make a noise to-day, the wind
comes from that side, but to me it seems that that big new chimney (where the
electric mashenes [sic] are) makes the same noise, as it continues since a long
time with intervals.—The Churchbells are ringing, I love the sound, with the
windows open; I shall go at 11, as till now, tho' the heart & chest ache, it is not
enlarged & I take many drops. The body feels very beaten & achy. Have got
Botkin to allow Anastasia to sit in the sun on the balkony [sic], where there are
20 degrees, it can only do the child good. It is 10 & Baby< has not yet turned
up, took a good sleep no doubt. Such peace in the soul after those anxious
days—& may you continue feeling the same.—If you have the occasion, give
N.P. our love & give him news as I don't let A.[nia]< wire now for a time, after
one was so nasty & she gave him news of my health always.— I hope old Fred.<
is not too gaga [senile] & wont beg for field-marshal etc., wh. can only be given
after the war, if at all.— Remember to comb your hair before all difficult talks &
decisions, the little comb will bring its help. Dont you feel calm now that you
have become "sure of yourself"—its not pride or conceit—but sent by God & it
will help you in the future & give strength to the others to fulfil your orders.
Have let the old man< know, that I want to see him to-day, & he is to choose the
hours. [b, c]
    Well, Deary, I just had the old man for half an hour. He was so glad to get
your message, that you left quiet & calmly & Frederick's letter (I did not know

he had written). But shocked & horrified with the ministers letter, written by Samarin he says.[122] Finds no words for their behaviour & says how awfully difficult it is for him to preside, knowing they all go against him & his ideas, but he wld. never think of asking to leave, as he knows you would tell him if it were yr. wish. He has to see them to-morrow & will mention what he thinks about this letter, wh. is so false & untrue in saying "all Russia" & so forth—I begged him to be as energetic as possible. He will also talk before with the minister of war [Polivanov], to know what you told him. About [A. N.] Khvostov he says better not [appoint him minister of the interior], it is he who spoke in the Duma against the government & Germans (is a nephew of the minister of justice), finds him trop leger [light-headed], probably not quite sure person in some respects.[123] He will think over names and send or bring me a list for you of people he thinks might do.—Finds certainly Shcherbatov< [the current minister] cannot remain, already that he took no hold on the press is a sign what an incapable person he is for that place.[108]—He says, he would not be astonished, if Shch & Sazonov asked to be released from their places, wh. they have no right to [do][119] —Sazonov goes about crying (the fool) & [claims] I said I was convinced, that our allies will immensely appreciate yr. action [i.e., dismissing Nikolasha< and taking up residence at Stavka], with wh. he agreed too.—[d, e] I told him to look at all as a miasm [sic] of St. P[etersburg] & Moscou [sic] & that all need a good airing to see all with fresh eyes & hear no gossip fr. morn to night.—He says, the Duma cannot be dispersed before the end of the week as they have not finished their work—he & others especially fear the left may out-pass [i.e., bypass] the Duma—I begged him not to worry about it, that I am con-vinced its not so serious & more talking than anything else & that they wanted to frighten you & now that you have shown a strong will of your own, they will shut up. It seems Sazonov called them all together yesterday—fools. I told him that the ministers were all des poltrons [cowards] & he agreed—thinks Polivanov will work well. Poor man, it hurt him reading all the heresies of those, who signed against him[119] & I was so pained for him. He so rightly says, each must honestly tell you his opinion, but when you have said yr. wish, all must fulfill it & forget their own desires, [but] they [the ministers] don't agree, neither did poor Serge!<—I tried to cheer him up, & a wee bit I think I did, as I showed him how little serious, au fond, all this empty noise is. Now the Germans & Austri-ans have to occupy [our] minds & all & nothing else—& a good minister of the interior will keep order.—He says, in town< good mood & quiet after yr. speech & reception—& so it will be, I told him what our Friend said.—He begged me to see Krupensky [a sympathetic member of Fourth Duma] to hear, what he has to say about the Duma, as he knows everybody—do you agree, then I certainly will, & without any noise. Only wire "agree".—I told him Ivanov also begged you to come, through me.—[f, g]

Finds the more you show yr. energy, the better, to wh. I agreed, & he also found the idea good, that you should send your eyes [inspectors] to the fabrics [factories], even if the suite don't understand much, but to show they come from you is good—not only the Duma who looks after all.—I went with Baby to Church & prayed so fervently for you. The Priest spoke beautifully & I only regretted the ministers were not there to hear it & the men listened with deepest interest. What this 3 days lent means—& how all must cling & work together around you & so on, beautiful & so true & all ought to have heard it.—[Daughter] Anastasia remained out till 4—& I writing on the balcony. Baby returned fr. Peterhof & has gone to Ania, where [our daughters] Olga, Tatiana & Maria are.—Here is a letter from old Damansky, he left it at Ania's when she was out—he came with his old sister half paralised [sic] & scarcely able to speak—am so pleased you gave that honest man this happiness, it will console him in his sorrow.— [h, i]

I copy out 2 telegrams from our Friend. If you have an occasion, show them to N.P.—one must keep him up more about our Friend, as in town he hears too much against him, & begins to heed less to His telegrams. Gorem[ykin] asked whether you would be back this week (to disperse the Duma then) I said you could not possibly yet tell.—The Children & I went to Znamenje< at 3¼ & I placed a very big candle, wh. will burn very long & carry my prayers to God's throne for you & before the Virgin & St. Nicolas [sic].—Now, my love, I must end.—God bless & protect you & help you & all you undertake. Kisses without end on all dear places, for ever yr. very own trusting proud Wify. [j, k]

Only a word en passant, Alia's< husband returned & each time speaks against Brussilov< as does also Keller—you [should] enquire [into] other opinions about him still.—The Headquarters has given the order, that all officers with German names serving in the staffs are to be sent out to the army, so Alia's husband too, tho' Pistolkors is a Swedish name & more devoted servant you scarcely have. According to me, it is again wrongly done—gently ought to have been told to hint to those to go back to their regiments, that they want others [at Stavka] & these are to have their turn to fight. All is done so clumsily. I shall write to you always all I hear, (if think right) as may be of use to you to know now & to prevent injustices—can imagine what Kussov< will write, so as to help the good cause. Now I must lie down, as very tired—am feeling better & spirits up & full of trust, courage & hope—& pride in my Sweetheart. God bless, guard & guide you.—Hope Voeik[ov] did not tell you the rot he told A.[nia:] he wld. beg you to make N< give his word of honour not to stop at Moscou—coward Voeikov, & fool, as tho' you were jealous or frightened—I assure you I long to show my immortal trousers [see Letter No. 383b] to those poltrons [cowards]. If Paul< should ask to see me, can I tell him that you wish to take him next time. It will touch him & change his thoughts into the right current; he is sure to come—wire about Krupensky agree or don't agree I shall understand—tell Paul, or don't tell Paul.—Smell the letter. [l, m]

122. The ministers fell into an uproar when, at their meeting on August 19/ September 1, 1915, they learned of the tsar's decision to dismiss Nicholasha and assume command at Stavka. The ministers not only despaired of Russia losing a talented commander. They also realized that with the tsar at Headquarters, Alexandra (and Rasputin) would wield greater influence in Petrograd. The ministers met with Nicholas on August 20, 1915, and pleaded with him to not take this step. When the tsar stood firm, the ministers then asked Samarin to draft a letter stating their desire to resign should their advice be disregarded. Goremykin was also criticized. Ten of the thirteen ministers signed or verbally endorsed the letter. Nicholas and Alexandra were correct on one point: Russian ministers did not have the "right" to act collectively, each minister was individually responsible to the emperor. Goremykin was sly in affecting surprise when Alexandra told him of the ministers' letter. Goremykin had been attending these "emergency" meetings of the ministers, he admitted to his outraged col-

leagues—though not to Alexandra or the tsar—that Nicholas was mistaken in dismissing Nicholasha, assuming command, etc. (Pares, *Fall*, pp. 264-271; the letter is on page 270.)

123. A. N. Khvostov gave a fiery speech in the Duma in August 1915, blaming Russia's economic problems on German capital, which he charged was powerful even during the war. Khvostov promised his next speech would address German ownership of Russia's electrical industry. This threatened Andronnikov's own investments and caused him to approach the ambitious demagogue, thinking that bringing him into an alliance was the best way to control him. (Fuhrmann, *Rasputin*, p. 144)

No. 390/ Telegram 186. Tsarskoe Selo> Stavka. 24 Aug 1915. 3.06> 4.02 p.m. To his majesty. Tenderly thinking of you. Overcast, rain. Lunched and now to hospital<. We all warmly kiss and bless you. Hope all is going well. What news? Alix

No. 391/ Telegram 04. Stavka> Tsarskoe Selo. 24 Aug 1915. 7.35> 8.36 p.m. To her majesty. Many loving thanks for news. Have signed the papers about military nominations yesterday. Began my work with Alekseev, who thanks you for image [icon]. Town [of Mogilev is] well situated near the river.[122] Motored and walked. Weather divine. Feel pleased and calm. Kiss you children [and] "all" tenderly. Niki

No. 392/ Telegram 188. Tsarskoe Selo> Stavka. 25 Aug 1915. 11.05> 11.58 a.m. To his majesty. Rain, dark, going to dinner and hospital<. When will change [in command] be published? Have you received both of my letters? Spent night not especially well because arm hurts. All tenderly kiss you. Alix

No. 393/ Her No. 333.   Ts.[arskoe] S[elo]. Aug. 25th 1915.
My own Sweetheart,

Thanks for your dear telegram, Lovy. I am glad the country near Mogilev is pretty—Zlebov always said it was very picturesque—but that was natural, as he was born there. But still I suppose you will choose a nearer place, so as that you can quicker & easier move about. When do my letters reach you? I give them out at 8 & they leave town< at 11 at night.—Am anxiously awaiting when the change [in command] will be made public. It is pouring again & quite dark.—Baby's< night was not famous, slept little, but pain not too strong. Olga & Tatiana sat with him fr. 11½-12½ & they kept him cheery.—In the papers, there was an article as tho' people, 2 men & a woman had been cought [sic] near Varsovie [Warsaw], who were going to make an attempt upon Nikolasha's life—people say Suvorin invented it to be more interesting (the censor told A.[nia]< those were "canards"). A month ago all the redacteurs [editors] from St. Pbg. were at the H. Q., & Yanushkevich< gave them his instructions,—this the military censor, under Frolov told A.[nia]—Samarin seems to be continuing to speak against me, well all the better, he too will fall into the pit he is digging for me. Those things dont touch me one atom & leave me personally cold, as my conscience is clear & Russia does not share his opinions—but I am angry, because it indirectly touches you. We shall hunt for a successor [to Samarin as director of the Holy Synod].— [a, b]

How do you find work with Alekseev? Pleasant & quick I am sure. Have no particular news; only [V. V.] Mekk let me know that my central stores< (Lvov,

Kovno) fr. Proskurov will probably have to move in 5 weeks to Poltava—I cannot grasp why, & hope it will not be necessary. [Daughter] Marie's ladies fr. Jitomir [Zhitomir] ask if one has to evacuate that town, where her hospital is to move to—all this is a bit early to decide, I think.—How very sad Molostvov's death is, I hear you have made [A. S.] Velepolsky your a.d.c.,—I suppose Voeikov< begged for him—he is not a very sympathetic man & such a "saloon" fellow. I suppose his health obliges him to leave the regiment & therefore you take him—but the Suite ought not to be a place like the honor.[ary] curator, where one pokes people into it. I alas, begged for my Maslov, but he had commanded the reg. for several months at the war already. Vel. is Olga O's< sweetheart (a great secret she had to make a fausse couche [abortion] fr. him a few years ago) he was not nice to her after—not a famous type, but Voeikov's friend, so suppose good officer.[124] – [c]

The enclosed picture is for N.P.<—Is not this ugly, again somebody wishing to be nasty to N.P., so you better tell Fred.< to have printed (privately not fr. his name) that there wont be a lieutenant as you have now the big chancellry & Dr.< & Kira< remain on; it comes I am sure fr. the same source as the story of the telegr. then at the H. Q. I fastened so, for you to show Voeikov as easy to slip out—one need only let the military censor Vissarionov know what to write, as he is Frolov's chief censor & a good man;—its Suvorin's doing, last night & this morning.—So anxious no telegram yet cannot imagine why the change has not been officially announced, it would have cleared & uplifted the minds & quicker have changed the current of thoughts in the Duma. I thought to-day was already the longest [day, i.e., the last day] to wait as N. leaves—now yr. yesterday's wire was fr. H.Q.,—on Sunday evening Imp. H. Q., it sounded so nice & promising.[122] [d]

These are fasting days approaching fr. to-morrow on, so the news ought to have come before & the Te Deum, its a mistake all falling together, was necessary beforehand, forgive my saying this—who again begged you put off the official anouncement [sic], did wrong—no harm N. being there, as it will be known you were working already with Alekseev. It was a bad council—how against it one party is, one sees it by this. The quicker officially known, the calmer all spirits, all get nervous awaiting the news wh. never comes—its never good such a situation & false—& only cowards can have proposed it to you, as Voeikov & Fred. they think of N. before you—its wrong being kept secret, none think of the troops who are yearning for the good news—I see my black trousers [see Letter 383b] are needed at the H. Q., too bad, idiots—& such perfection the jubilation & then fasting to pray for your success—& Tuesday passes & nothing; out of despair I wired this morning early, but got no answer & its already 7 o'clock.—[Daughters] Marie, A.[nastasia] & I went to Cath.[erine] C.[athedral] again & then to the hospital<, where I talked with the wounded. We lunched upstairs & will dine there too. The rain & darkness make one quite ramolie<. Baby has much less pain & slept in the morning. Helene< & [her son] Vsevolod [Ivanovich] came to tea & then I received my lancer Toll< with more photos. He says [D. M.] Knyazhevich entreats to receive our brigade instead of Shevich. Then I sent for the Commandant Ossipov to speak about the cemetry [sic] & Church I build for the dead of this war in our hospitals, to clear up that question.—Mme Lopukhin, wife of the Vologda gov. wrote to me, because her husbands heart is so much worse again. [Drs.] Botk.[in] & Sirotinin find too that his health cannot stand the strain of work he has. If you made him Senator, he could serve there & it would be a rest for a time,[125] & perhaps later cld. get more to do if heart improves. He has served 25 years. It would be good if you could have this done.— [e, f]

My Sunshine, I miss so very much, but am glad you are away.—You can let yr. ministers come by turn with their report[s] —it will freshen them up too. I hope you sleep well.—Don't forget to wire to Georgie [King George V] etc. when at last all is official [concerning the change in command]. Goodbye my treasure, I bless & kiss you without end, every precious, dearly beloved place. Ever, Nicky mine, yr. very own old   Wify.   [P.S.] The stories about [Bishop] Varnava, a monk fr. there [Tobol'sk, headquarters of the diocese] came to let me know, are untrue. Samarin wants to get rid of him.—[N. A.] Ordovsky[-Tanaevsky] is the name our Friend wld. like as gov.[ernor of Tobol'sk, Rasputin's native province in Siberia], he is the president of the Etchequer [sic] chamber at Perm. You remember he gave you a book he wrote about Tcherdyn where a Romanov is buried & one considers him a saint. [g, h]

124. For the image of a "good officer" in the pre-war army see John Bushnell, "The Tsarist Officer Corps, 1881-1914. Customs, Duties, Inefficiency," *The American Historical Review*, vol. 86, number 4 (October 1981), pp. 753-780. Voeikov was typical of this breed, most of whom were killed in the first months of the war.

125. The Senate was the highest court in the Russian legal system. It also enforced legality throughout the government and formed commissions to investigate controversial legal matters, which the Senate then decided as a body. The tsar appointed senators. For lawyers it was an honor. Disgraced officials, on the other hand, were "promoted" to the Senate from responsible political posts; Beletsky and Klimovich are examples who appear in this correspondence. Such senators might or might not help with the Senate's work; for the latter, being a "senator" simply brought a salary and privileges. The State Council was another dumping ground for "retired" officials who could be counted upon to vote as the tsar wished. Oldenburg, *Last Tsar*, IV, p. 22. Lieven, *Russian Rulers*, pp. 75, 137-138, 179.

No. 394/ Telegram 013. Imperial Stavka> Tsarskoe Selo. 25 Aug 1915. 7.00> 8.18 p.m. To her majesty. Loving thanks [for] dear letter. Am awaiting the next one This evening because all the trains get with difficulty through. At 6 o'clock saw departure N.< [from Stavka for the Caucasus] off under best impression. Nothing particular among news. Weather colder. Kiss everybody tenderly. Niki

No. 395. [The tsar does not number his letters from this point]

Stavka. Aug. 25th 1915.

My own beloved, Darling Sunny,

Thank God it is all over and here I am with this new heavy responsibility on my shoulders! But God's will be fulfilled—I feel so calm, A sort of feeling after the Holy Communion! The whole morning of that memorable day Aug 23, while coming here, I prayed much & read your first letter over & over again. The nearer the moment of our meeting approached the more peaceful felt my soul. N.< came in with a good cheery smile simply asked for my order when he was to leave. I answered, in the same manner, that he could remain for two days; then we spoke about questions concerning the milit[ary] operations, about some generals and that was all. The following days at luncheon & dinner he was very talkative & in a good humour that we all have rarely seen him in for many a month. Pet.[ia]< also, but his a.d.c.s were black in their expressions—it was even funny. I must do justice to my gentlemen, beginning by old Fr.<—they behaved well & I did not hear any discordant note, not one word to snap at. [a, b]

Of course, while N. was here I asked him to be present both mornings at the doklad [report]. Alekseev does it so well. He was most touched by the little image [icon] & blessing you sent through me. N. repeated to me that he leaves this place with a quiet feeling knowing I have such a help as Alekseev under me. We spoke much about the Caucasus, he likes it & interests himself in the people & fine nature, but he begs to remain long after the end of the war. He put on at once a fine old Circassian sword, a pr[esent] [G. D.] Shervashidze had given him years ago & is going to wear it the whole time. He thinks he will remain at Pershino for 12 days and then start straight for Tiflis meeting the old Count V.< at Rostov-on-Don. The whole collection of black women< join him from Kiev at his estate & start altogether! Now begins a new clean page, and what will be written on it only God Almighty knows? I signed my first prikaz [order] & added a few words with a rather trembling hand! We have just finished our evening meal & after that I had a long talk with Laguiche & then with Gen. [Hanbury-]Williams. Georgie [King George V] and [Albert I] King of the Belgians have both answered my telegrams in which I announced this change with us—so quick! [c, d]

I am delighted you spoke and soothed dear old Gor.[emykin]. Please tell him next time that as soon as the St.[ate] Council & Duma have finished their work—they must be closed, quite the same whether I am back or still here! Why not see Krupensky?— he is a trustworthy man & can tell you perhaps things worth hearing. [See Letter No. 384g,m.] Fancy, my Wify, helping Huzy when he is away![126] What a pity you did not perform that duty long ago, or at least now during the war! Nothing gives me more pleasure than to feel proud of you, as I have all these last months when you worried me thoughly [sic] to be firm & stick to my opinion. We just finished playing domino when I got a telegram through Alekseev from Ivanov, who announced that today our 11th Army (Shcherbachev's) in Galicia attacked two German divisions (the 3rd Guard & 48th Infantry) with the result that over 150 off[icers] and 7000 men, 30 guns & many machine guns were taken![127]   And this happened directly after our troops had heard about my taking over the leadership. This is realy [sic] God's mercy, and such a quick one! Now I must end, it is late & I must go to bed! God bless you, my beloved treasure, my Sunbeam. I kiss you and the dear children very tenderly. Ever your own old huzy Nicky. [P.S.] Give A.[nna Vyrubova] my fond love. [e, f, g]

126. With Nicholas at Stavka, the ministers expected Alexandra to emerge as a "co-tsar"—which was one reason they objected to the plan. And yet it was apparently only at this moment that Nicholas asked his wife to "help" him; following letters suggest she did not immediately accept the challenge. Nicholas was still popular with the army. Taking command briefly lifted spirits at the front; his appearances elicited enthusiasm among the troops. It also reassured the allies that Russia was

committed to victory. Alekseev was a competent replacement for Nicholasha now that his masterful "long retreat" was successfully concluded. Nicholas did not meddle in military operations. Dispatching Nicholasha to the Caucasus removed what Alexandra considered a political threat, though in truth the grand prince was entirely loyal to his cousin, the tsar.

127. The Russian counterattack in Galicia on the Sereth was briefly successful; the tsar's armies took 8,000 prisoners. But the German-Austrian armies quickly regained the initiative. Russia suffered over 2,000,000 casualties on this front in 1915, of whom about half were taken prisoner. German-Austrian casualties exceeded one million. See Footnotes 107 and 111. (Vulliamy, p. 72n. Dupuy and Dupuy, *Encyclopedia*, p. 952)

No. 396/ Telegram 1478. Tsarskoe Selo> Stavka. 26 Aug 1915. 10.45 a.m.> 1.14 p.m. To his majesty. We "all" embrace [you] and send best wishes. Now leaving for church to pray for you with all our heart and soul, for our heroes and dear country. Much colder but clearer. Spent the night well. Thousand kisses. Alix

---

No. 397/ Telegram 015. Imperial Stavka> Tsarskoe Selo. 26 Aug 1915. 10.09 a.m.> 12.05 p.m. To her majesty. Tender thanks for letter No. 332. Last evening late got a telegram from Ivanov about a fine success of our army in Galicia where two German divisions lost over 150 officers and 7000 men prisoners with 30 guns taken by us. This happened directly after my nomination was announced. Thank God such a comfort. Loving kisses. Niki

---

No. 398/ Telegram 197. Tsarskoe Selo> Stavka. 26 Aug 1915. 2.53> 4.01 p.m. To his majesty. Terribly happy over good news from Ivanov. Wonderful beginning! Attended church for mass and Te Deum. Priest [Father Vasil'ev] delivered wonderful sermon. Older girls< went to town< and will have tea at Elagin<. We tenderly bless and kiss [you]. Alix

---

No. 399/ Her No. 334.   Ts.[arskoe] S[elo]. Aug. 26[th] 1915.
My very own Sweetheart,

I am writing in the corner room upstairs. Mr. Gill[i]ard is reading aloud to Aleksei. [Daughters] Olga & Tatiana are in town< this afternoon. Oh Lovy, it was beautiful–to read the news in the papers this morning & my heart rejoyced [sic] more then I can say. [Daughter] Marie & I went to mass in the upper church, Anastasia came to the Te Deum. The priest [Father Vasil'ev] spoke beautifully, I wish a good big crowd in town had heard him, it would have done them no end of good, as he touched the inner currents so well. With heart & soul I prayed for you my treasure. It lasted fr. 10½-12½. Then we went to Ania< to meet her dear big Lili< returning from church. She had been hunting for her mother whose husband has been killed & she was looking for his body. She could no more get to Brest, the Germans were at 18 versty [11.9 miles] fr. where she was. Fancy, Mishchenko asked her to lunch–she amongst 50 officers. She spent the night at Anias & leaves again to join her Boy [Titi<]; she has no news from her husband[, Karl von Dehn]. We lunched, took tea & shall dine here. I went for a short turn in a half opened motor with Ania & Marie to get a little air–quite like September.–Kostia< comes at 6 & then I go to church–a consolation to be in church & pray with all together, for my huzy.–And Ivanov's good news was indeed a blessing for the beginning of your great work. God help you, Sweetheart. All seems small now, such joy reigns in my soul.—[a]

I have had no news from the old man [Goremykin] since Sunday.—Samarin goes on speaking against me—hope to get you a list of names & trust can find a suitable successor [as director of the Holy Synod] before he can do any more harm.—How are the foreigners [at Stavka]? I see Buchanan to-morrow, as he brings me again over 100,000 p.[ounds?][128] from England. I got a letter from M-me Baharacht, who begs her husband should not be sent away till after the end of the war. He is of limit of age, but he does a lot at Bern [as a diplomat, see Biographical Index] for the Russians & tries his best—perhaps you will remember when his name may be mentioned by Sazonov.—The gramophon [sic] is playing in the bedroom for Marie & Anastasia.—Baby slept on the whole 9 hours—with interruptions—is cheery & suffers little. I told Fred.<. it was unnecessary to arrange anything for the wounded at present at Livadia, as there are still very many empty places at Yalta—& now fr. all the sides fr. the Crimea one tells me all is being arranged.—Do ask Fred. why?—as I do not find it as yet necessary; perhaps later—soon my sanatorium, the military one, & the Livadia hosp. will be ready—enough for the present. [unsigned] [b]

128. Was this part of the "Romanov fortune" supposedly deposited in the Bank of England and other European banks? The various people claiming to be Anastasia or her siblings were often, no doubt, parties to conspiracies that hoped to tap this supposed wealth. It seems the Romanovs liquidated their foreign assets to finance wartime charities, as apparently we see Alexandra doing here. See Fuhrmann, *Rasputin*, p. 240 note 5.

No. 400/ Telegram 207. Tsarskoe Selo> Stavka. 27 Aug 1915. 4.20> 5.15 p.m.
To his majesty. Am thirsting to have news. Cold but very sunny. Went to our church at hospital<—Te Deum there. Now going to walk. Paul< coming for tea. We tenderly embrace and kiss [you]. Always together in thoughts. Alix

---

No. 401/ Her No. 335.   Tsarskoe Selo. Aug. 27th 1915.
My very own beloved One,

I wonder whether you get my letters every day—pitty [sic] so far away & all the trains passing now stop the movement.—Again only 8 degrees, but the sun seems to wish to appear. Do you get a walk daily, or are you too much occupied? Baby< slept very well, woke up only twice for a moment, & the arm aches much less I am happy to say; no bruise is visible, only swollen, so I think he might be dressed to-day. When he is not well I see much more of him, wh. is a treat (if he does not suffer, as that is worse than anything). [Daughters] Olga & Tatiana returned after 7 from town<, so I went with Marie to the lower church 6½-8. This morning I go with the two little ones upstairs at 10½, as the others have Church before 9 below. My fasting consists now of not smoking, as I fast since the beginning of the war, & I love being in Church. I do want to go to Holy Communion & the Priest [Father Vasil'ev] agrees, never finds it too early to go again & it gives strength—shall see. Those soldiers that care, will also go.—Saturday is the anniversary of our store!<—Css. Grabbe told Ania< yesterday, that [V. N.] Orlov & wife were raging in town, at being sent away, turned out—wh. shocked others—he told her too that N.P.< was going to replace him (I was sure he had had it put into the papers) an ugly trick, after his wife having begged N.P. to come & talked with him—such are people. Many are glad, who knew his dirty money affairs & the way he allowed himself to speak about me.—Will you find time to scrawl a line once? We get no news, as I told N.P. better not to wire nor write for the present, after that ugly story at the H.Q. [a, b]

Wonder what news. You will let them send me telegr. again, wont you, Deary.—Baby dear is up & half dressed, lunched at table with us & had the little boys to play with. He would not go out, said he did not feel strong enough, but would to-morrow—he did not write yet, because he could not hold the paper with his left hand. We dine up there again—its cosy & not so lonely as down here without you. Well, this morning I went with the two youngest at 10½ to mass & Te Deum with lovely prayers for you to the Virgin & St. Serafim—from there we went to our hospital, all were off to the Te Deum in the little grotto church there so we went again—& now at 6½ to evening service. I hope very much to go to holy Communion on Saturday, I think many soldiers go too, so Sweetheart please forgive yr. little wify if in any way I grieved or hurt you,[129] & for having bored you so much these trying weeks. I shall wire if sure I go, & you pray for me then, as I for you—its for you somehow this fasting, church, daily Te Deum, & so Holy Communion will be a special blessing & I shall feel you one with me, my dearly beloved Angel, very, very own Huzy. [c]

Here I enclose a pretty telegr. fr. Volodia [Trubetskoi] I want you to read.—Paul< came to tea, very quiet & nice. About himself he spoke, & I said what we had spoken about, that you hoped taking him or sending him about. He wants in no way to be pushy or forward, but longs to serve you, wont bother you with a letter, asks me to give all this over to you. Or if you wld. send him to some armycorps under a good general—[he is] ready for anything & full of good intentions. Wont you think it over & speak with Alekseev & then let me know please.—We spoke about Dmitri<, dont repeat it to him— it worries him [Paul, Dmitri's father,] awfully & he is so displeased, that he stuck for ever in the H.Q., finds he ought absolutely not to stay there, as its very bad for him, spoils him & he thinks himself then a very necessary personage. Paul was greatly discontented that he came now & sorry you did not shut him up quicker, instead of allowing him to try & mix up in things about wh. he understands nothing.—Best if he [Dmitri] returned into the regiment wh. uniform he has the honour to wear & in wh. he serves. In speaking about the G. à Cheval [the cavalry guards], Paul said that he found a new commander ought to be named, this ones wound does not heal, he has received everything, done all he could & the regiment cannot get along with only youngsters & no real Commander—as he says any good one fr. the war, no matter who he is, only that he should be good, so you will perhaps also talk this over (not with Dmitri) with Alekseev. [d, e]

Buchanan brought me over 100.000 p.[ounds?] again,[128] he wishes you also every success! Cannot bear town< any more. Says what difficulty to get wood, & he wants to get his provisions now already & is waiting since 2 months & now hears it wont come. One ought to get a good stock beforehand, as with these masses of refugees who will be hungry & freezing. Oh, what misery they go through, masses die on the way & get lost & one picks up stray children everywhere.[89] Now must be off. I bless & kiss you a 1000 times very, very ten-

derly, with yearning love. Ever yr. own old Alix.   [P.S.] Wont the Duma be
shut at last— why need you be here for that? How the fools speak against the
military censors, shows how necessary [to control the Duma]. All our love to
N.P. [f]

No. 402/ Telegram 144. Stavka> Tsarskoe Selo. 27 Aug 1915. 6.55> 7.50 p.m.
To her majesty. Tender thanks [for] letter and messages. Owing to dampness in
the wood where stood the train I have settled here in governor's house. The staff
is close which makes it all the more convenient. All are pleased with this arrangement. Cool, rainy weather. Hope all are well. Loving kisses. Niki

---

No. 403/ Telegram 208. Tsarskoe Selo> Stavka. 27 Aug 1915. 9.49> 10.43
p.m. To his majesty. Terribly gladdened by dear letter, warmly thank you,
sweetheart, also for telegram. All are well. Warm summer day. We attended
church. Having lunch in nursery. We warmly embrace and kiss [you]. Alix

---

No. 404.   Mogilev. Aug. 27th 1915.
My darling precious Sunny,
    Many loving thanks for your dear 2 sweet letters. They take such a time to
reach one, the trains go very inexactly on account of the colossal work the lines
have to do. That is one of our greatest difficulties from the military point of
view. Troops, war material, supplies going in one direction, the evacuation especially these miserable bezentsy [refugees] coming from the opposite direction!
There is no stopping those poor people fr[om] leaving their homes in front of the
advancing enemy, because nobody wants to risk remaining in the hands of the
Germans or Austrians. Those who find no place in trains, walk or drive along
the roads, the weather becoming cold makes this pilgrimage awfully trying,
children suffer very much, & unluckily many of them, die on the way.[89] [a]
    All the local authorities and members of different committees work & do all
they can—I know this; but they frankly acknowledge that they cannot [do] all. It
is a sickening idea what unexpected sufferings the war has brought except the
usual misery it always brings! And yet that must all finish one day!!! I cannot
say how pleased I am with Gen. Alekseev. What a conscientious, clever &
modest man he is & what a worker! His reports are of a different style to those I
was present at before. He works alone, but has got two little generals— Pustovoitenko and Borisov, who have been with him since years and who help only in
details or in secondary questions. But I am afraid that I bore you with this dry
topic. Thanks for sending me N.'s< letter—I think he is sincere & means what he
wrote. It is nonetheless very curious, as it shows that sometimes he has got his
own opinion, independently of what other people around him think. I am so glad
about the exploits of Vol[odia] Troub.[etskoi], the man certainly deserves to
receive the St. George cross, wh I hope he will soon get. I see Mitia Dehn every
day now. He looks quite well, walks decently, but has nothing to do, & bored to
distraction after his busy years in the Black Sea. He wants to have some work
near us. So the old man [Fredericks] proposed whether he would not do at the

head of our garage instead of fat Orloff?< What do you think of this idea? I find it a good one. [b, c, d]

The little wood in which stood our train is very cozy, but owing to the rains it became damp, also in the cars; therefore to be near my staff & to live in a house I found it better & more simple to come over to town [Mogilev]. The building is old, but quite comfortable, with a little garden & charming view on the Dnieper and distant country—in fact like Kiev in small. The foreigners used to be invited by N. to the meals, so I intend continuing that habit. In all we are 20 at table in a spacious dining-room. The last two mornings, when I came to town, I received before the reports—the nobility & the highest people of the [local] administration. Now the official side of my stay is over. I have been out motoring twice on the other side of the river—a pretty woody sympathetic country & beautiful high roads. Dmitry's< bad mood has gone completely, I mean the one I saw in that day at Tsarskoe [Selo]. Now he does duty changing with N.P.< & Dm. Sherem.< He asked me to give you many messages—he is his old self again. I fast these three days & shall try and go to church before Sunday. Good-bye, my sweetest Wify, my Sunbeam. I kiss you and the dearest children. God bless you! Ever your own old huzy. Nicky. [P.S.] your sweet letter No. 334 just arrived. Thousand of thanks. Glad you are calm! [e]

No. 405/ Telegram 211. Tsarskoe Selo> Stavka. 28 Aug 1915. 2.28> 3.03 p.m. To his majesty. Wonderful summer weather. Attended church at the hospital<. Hope to-morrow morning to take communion with [daughters] Marie and Anastasia—I ask forgiveness [of you].[129] Am going to confession at 9½. Always with you in thoughts. Aleksei [has been] outside all day. I bless and kiss [you]. Will see old man [Goremykin] this evening. Alix

129. At this time it was a custom in the Russian Orthodox Church during important fasts to ask family members, friends and associates to forgive sins inflicted since the last time pardon was sought. Such forgiveness might also be sought at difficult or solemn moments, as we see in Letters No. 650c, 652, 653. It is interesting to note that Alexandra often asks Nicholas to forgive her, but never once, in the correspondence, does he make that request of her.

No. 406/ Her No. 336.   Tsarskoe Selo. Aug. 28th 1915.
My beloved Nicky dear,

How can I thank you enough for your very precious letter wh. came as a most welcome surprise. I have reread it already several times & kissed the dear handwriting. You wrote the 25-th & I got it 27-th before dinner.—All interested us immensely, the children & A.[nia]< eagerly listened to some parts I read aloud—& to feel that you are at peace fills our hearts with joyful gratitude. God sent you the recompense of your great undertaking—yes, a new responsibility, but one particularly dear to yr. heart, as you love all that is military & understand it. And having shown such firmness must bring blessings & success. Those that were so frightened at this change & all that nonsense [sic], see how calmy & naturally all took place, & have grown quieter. [a]

I shall see the old man [Goremykin] & hear what he has to tell. The P.[etrograd] Municipal Council needs smacking, what right have they to imitate Moscou [sic]?[130] Guchkov< again at the bottom of this & the telegr. you

got—would they but mind their own business, look after their wounded, fugitives, fuel, food & so forth—they need a sharp answer, to mind their own business & look after the sufferers of the war—nobody needs their opinion, cant they
see to their canalisation [sewerage] first. I shall tell that [to] the old man—I have
no patience with these meddlesome chatterboxes. Oh Sweetheart, I am so
touched you want my help [see Letter No. 395e], I am always ready to do anything for you, only never liked mixing up without being asked—only here I felt
too much was at stake. [b, c]

Such glorious sunshine & 18 [degrees] in the sun & cool breeze—curious
weather this summer. Certainly, its wiser you have settled down in the Governor's house if its damp for everybody in the woods—& here you have the staff
close by, but still a bore being in town [Mogilev] for you. Wont you come
nearer [i.e., move Stavka nearer to Petrograd] as V.[oeikov] proposed, then you
can be up & done here if necessary & get yr. ministers to come—this [Mogilev]
is yet further [from Petrograd] than Baranovitchi is it not? & there you could
reach Pskov & sooner get at the troops. [See Letter No. 420b.]—We all go to
Church again, the big ones< early, we at 10½ & then to the hospital< if the
priest [Vasil'ev] wont speak again, he held a sermon yesterday evening & again
a good one. Then at 2 we go to the christening of Underlieuten.[ant] Cobb's
[Kobb's] child, I christened his first child last autumn (he was our wounded &
then served in Marie's train) so Marie & Jakovlev< (ex lancer, com.[mander] of
her train) christen the boy in the lower Hospital church. Georgi< met the train &
gave the sisters [i.e., nurses] medals—I am sure Shulenb[urg] will be in despair,
as they were also under fire last year.—Then we shall drive & peep into the little
house, as our Friend's wife< will be there with the girls whom she has brought
for their lessons. Then Shulenburg at 5¾—Church—7¾ Goremyk.[in] before he
has a sitting [i.e., reception of people having business with the chairman of the
council of ministers]. We have got 3 of [daughter] Tatiana's lancers in our hospital & a fourth lies in the big palace<—there are 25 vacant places there, happily
again.—I enclose a letter of C.[ountess] Kellers you may like to read, as it shows
his [her husband's] way of looking at things, sound & simple as the most who
are not in St. P.[etersburg] & Moscou [sic]. He did not know of the change at
the H. Q. then. To-day he returns to the army—I fear too early—but certainly he
is needed there.—Rumours say the Novik [a cruiser in the Baltic fleet] had a battle & successful, but I do not know what is the truth about it. [d, e, f]

I hope I don't make you wild with my cuttings—is this naval news true or not?
I cut it out.—We had a lovely drive, divine weather & ones souls singing, surely
it means good news.—In the village of the Pavlovsk farm we stopped at a shop &
bought two big flasks with strawberry-jam & redberries then met a man with
mushrooms & we bought them [for] Ania —we drove along the border of Pavlovsk park—such weather is a real treat, & we are having tea on the balkony
[sic]—& miss you, my very own Angel, to make it perfect.—Gr. [Rasputin]'s
wife< sends you her love & asks Archangel Michael to be with you—says he
[her husband] had no peace & worried fearfully till you left. He finds it would
be good the people be let out of prisons & sent to the war, there are a category, I
am sure, of harmless ones sitting, whose moral saving it would be to go; I can
hint it to the old man [Goremykin] to think over—[a policy similar to this was

actually adopted in February 1916] he comes at ¼ to 8 so I must send my letter off before.—His governor [i.e., the governor of Tobol'sk] has quite changed towards Him [Rasputin] (has returned you [?]), he says will have our Friend stopped as soon as he leaves [for Petrograd]. You see, that others have given him [the governor] this order—more than wrong & shameful. [g]

There is confession in common, so the priest asked us to come to it in the upper Church, as lots of soldiers are going & to-morrow morning too with all upstairs. All the Children & Baby< will come too—oh, how I wish you could have been there too—but I know you will be in hearts & thoughts. Once more forgive me, my Sunshine.[129] God bless & protect you & keep you fr. all harm & help you in everything. To-morrow the day of the stone [see Letter No. 413d]! I kiss you without end with deepest love & devotion. Ever yr. very own <u>Wify</u>. [P.S.] Baby hopes to write to-morrow, he is thin & pale, been out all day. Slept till 10.15 this morning, very cheery & happy to go with us to holy Communion. Such a nice photo you bathing. A few words for you fr. A.[nia] & from me for N.P.< [h]

130. The Moscow city duma had just telegraphed Nicholas a "humble petition" concerning problems of the moment. (Note to A. A. Sergeev's edition of the *Perepiska*, III, p. 276n)

No. 407/ Telegram 154. Stavka> Tsarskoe Selo. 28 Aug 1915. 6.17> 7.05 p.m. To her majesty. Bless you my darling so glad you go again to holy communion. Now off to church, to-morrow also. Saw this morning our splendid Cossacks from Pavlovsk, they are going there. Told the commander to present himself to you. Weather mild, sunny. Tenderest love to all. Niki

---

No. 408/ Telegram 214. Tsarskoe Selo> Stavka. 28 Aug 1915. 9.20> 10.43 p.m. To her majesty. Just returned from general confession. Was splendid. Very strong impression. We all proceeded to make confession and "all" ask your forgiveness.[129] Thank you for dear telegram. Will be glad to see commander. [See Letter No. 407.] Saw old man<. He returns to-morrow, will be with you Sunday. We embrace and kiss you. Alix

---

No. 409/ Her No. 337.   Tsarskoe Selo. Aug. 28th 1915.
Beloved One,

I just saw the old man [Goremykin], he must see you, so will leave to-morrow. He has thought about a minister of the Interior, he finds no one except perhaps [A. B.] Neidhardt & I think he would not be bad (Papa [A. S.] Taneev mentioned him too)—of Tatiana's committee, he is a splendid worker, has shown it now, most clear-headed energetic—that he is snob, cant be helped, his "grandness" may be effective towards the Duma—then you know him well, can speak as you like with him, you need not se gener [be restrained] with him—hope he is only not in the Dzhunk.[ovsky]-Drent.[el'n] set. I think he wld. hold the other ministers in hand & thus help the old man. He finds it almost impossible to work with the ministers who wont agree with him, but also finds like us, that now he ought not to be sent away because they wish it—& once one gives in they will become worse—if you wish, then of your own accord a little later. You are

Autocrat & they dare not forget it. He says alright shutting Duma, but Sunday holiday, so better Tuesday, he sees you before. Finds ministers, worse than Duma. Infections about censure—one allows rot to be printed, also says "canards" about the 2 attempts against Nikolasha<. Finds Schcherbatov< is impossible to keep, better quick to change him. I think Neidhardt would be possible to trust—his rather [G]erman name I dont think would matter, as one praises him everywhere about Tatianas committee. Cons. de l'Emp. [the State Council] can finish the question about refugees. Will do dear old Goremyk. [so much] good to see you—he is such a dear. Just back fr. confession in Common—most emotioning, touching & all prayed so, so hard for you—Must quickly sent this off. Blessings kisses without end—pray incessantly for you—such a joy in one's soul all these days—one feels God near you my Sweetheart. Ever Y. very own Sunny.

No. 410/ Telegram 155. Stavka> Tsarskoe Selo. 29 Aug 1915. 9.32 a.m.> 10.10 a.m. To her majesty. In prayers [and] thoughts [am] with you darling and all. Glad you had this comfort. Tender kisses. Niki

---

No. 411/ Telegram 218. Tsarskoe Selo> Stavka. 29 Aug 1915. 11.32 a.m.> 12.37 p.m. To his majesty. We all thank you from our hearts for your telegram. Spirits are with you and we are sad you are not with us. Was so splendid[—]wonderful sunny day. [We] are drinking tea on balcony, then [I] go to hospital<. [We] "all" kiss [you], greetings to all from all. Alix

---

No. 412/ Telegram 232. Tsarskoe Selo> Stavka. 29 Aug 1915. 7.59> 8.53 p.m. Terribly thankful for your dear, interesting letter. Splendid weather. We walked. Warm, sunny. Do not take any final [step] concerning "Tail,"< if possible, until my letter of to-morrow. What news? We send tenderest kisses and blessings. Alix

---

No. 413/ Her No. 338.   Tsarskoe Selo. Aug. 29th 1915.
My own beloved One,
   One just now brought me your sweet letter of the 27-th. I thank you for it with all my heart, sweetest Pet. It is such a comfort to know that you are contented with Alekseev & find work with him easy. Is Dragomirov going to be his help [assistant]? A man may fall ill & its safer [to have on hand] one who knows the affairs a little—wont it be easier if you come nearer—where there are more railway lines.—Mogilev is so far & with all the crowded trains passing. One ought really to do something more for the refugees— more food stations & flying hospitals—masses of children are homeless on the highroad & others die—all returning from the war —one says its bitterly painful to see.[89] The government is working out questions for the fugitives after the war, but its more necessary to think of them.—But God grant soon the enemy wont any more advance & then all will go on smoother. The news is most consoling wh. I read in the papers & much better edited, one feels another person writes it.—But [Our] Friend< finds more fabrics [factories] ought to make amunitions [sic], where goodies [candy]

are made too.—I love all the news you give, the children & A.[nia]< listen with deepest interest, as we live with you, for you from far. [a]

Let M. Den< be at the head of the garage [see Letter No. 404d] for the moment, perhaps one can get him a place later in the navy again, as he loves & understands the work. Yes, do invite the foreigners [see 404e], its far more interesting with them & one finds more topics for talking. I am glad Dmitry< is alright—give him my love—but remember he ought not to remain there, its bad for him, of your own accord let him go, its unhealthy doing nothing, when all are at the war, & now he lives in gossip & plays a part. Only dont say Paul< and I think so. Paul begs you to be more severe with him, as he gets spoilt & imagines he can give you advice.— Bless you Sweetheart for fasting. Perhaps you better give Samarin the short order that you wish Bishop Varnava to chant the laudation of St. John Maximovich[131] because Samarin intends getting rid of him [Varnava], because we like him & he is good to Gr.<—We must clear out S.[amarin]. & the sooner the better he wont be quiet till he gets me & our Friend< & A.[nia]< in a mess—its so wicked & hideously unpatriotic & narrow-minded, but I knew it would be so & therefore they begged you to name & I wrote in such dispair [sic] to you.[132] [b, c]

Poor Markosov< has returned I must try & see him. It was lovely in church, only two hours, masses went to Holy Communion, every sort of person, lots of soldiers, 3 cossacks, Zizi<, Isa<, Sonia<, Ania, M-me Dedyulin & sister, Baby's< friend Irina [T.<], Jonk [Zhuk<], Shah Bagov [Shakh-Bagov], Kunov, Tchebytarev, Russin<, Perepelitsa, Kondratiev etc. We went below to kiss the images [icons] before service, upstairs the children found too shy work [i.e., the children were too shy to do this]. Then we got your telegram to rejoice us & feel you with us the whole time—missed you awfully & still felt your sunny presence. Breakfast, luncheon (with Isa & Zizi) & tea on balkony [sic]. I made the dressings in the hospital, felt so energetic & full of inner joy.—Drove to Pavlovsk. Baby alright, cought [sic] wasps again. Vict. Erast.[72] left to day for Mogilev. We are not going to church this evening, as are tired, the services twice dayly these four days were very long, but so lovely. The day of our stone [reference is probably to a piece of jewelry] to-day!— [d]

I saw M-me Paretski [Poretskaya] & she spoke much of you—she goes over to town< for winter again—I gave her our groop [group photograph?] & said I shall ask you to sign it when you return. Have you any ideas of your plans? This evening is a week you left—& how different are the feelings since—peace, trust & the "new fresh pure beginning." That reminds me, wont you have the com.[mander] of [the] Kovno [Fortress] Grigoriev quicker judged— it makes a very bad impression his wandering about like that, when one knows he gave up & left the fortress. (Shulenburg hints this to me & another thing about the Semenovtsy [Guards Regiment]—a sure thing, not gossip, Ussov [Usov], whom he can trust, told it him with tears—they simply bolted [i.e., fled] & therefore the Preobr.[azhensky Guards Regiment] lost so many. Do find them a good brave commander.) I hope, you do not mind my telling you all these things, they may be of use—you can have it found out & altogether make a clearing. [e]

Many splendid, brave youngsters received no rewards—& high placed ones—having got [i.e., are the ones who did get] the decorations. As Aleks.[eev]

cannot possibly do all, my weak brain imagines, some special people might see to this, to look through the immense lists & watch that injustices are not done.—In case (as I dont a bit know whether you approve of [A. B.] Neidhardt) you name him [to replace Shcherbatov as minister of the interior] & he presents himself, have a strong & frank talk with him—see that he does not go Dzhunk.< line. Put the position of our Friend clear to him from the outset, he dare not act like Shcherb.< & Sam[arin]. Make him understand that he acts straight against us in persecuting [Rasputin] & allowing him to be evil written about or spoken of. You can catch him by his amour propre. And forbid the continuing of cutting down the Barons mercilessly, have you remembered about dispersing the Lett. bands amongst the regiments? Is nice Dimka [D. B. Golitsyn] with you? I am going to see Maximov[ich] who returned from Moskou [sic]. Sweety, remember to use the suite [for inspectors] (other pen dried up) to be sent to the different fabrics [factories] in your name—please do it, it will have an excellent effect & show you watch all & not only the Duma pokes her nose into all—make a careful choice. [f, g]

Beloved, A.[nia] just saw Andr.[onnikov] & [A. N.] Khvostov & the latter made her an excellent impression (the old man [Goremykin] is against him, I not knowing him, dont know what to say.) He is most devoted to you, spoke gently & well about our Friend to her, related that to morrow has to be a question about Gr.< in the Duma one asked for Khovst.'s signature, but he refused & said that if they picked up that question, amnestie [sic] would not be given—they reasoned & abolished again asking about him. He related awful horrors about Guchk.<, was at Gorem.< to-day, spoke about you, that by taking the army you saved yourself. Khvost. took the question about German over powering influence & dearth of meat,[120] so as the left[ist] ones [members of the Duma] wld. not take it—now [that] the right[ist] ones have this question it is safe—she feels taken by him & has good impression. Gorem. wanted to present Kryzhanovsky but I said you would never agree. Do talk him over except Neidhardt—I did not see his article then—I mean his speech of the Duma its difficult to advise. Are others against him, or only the old man, as he [Goremykin] hates all the Duma. Awfully difficult for you to decide again, poor Treasure—I cant say as I dont know the man. She had a very good impression indeed. Talk him over with Gorem. [h]

Now I must send this off. Hope you will clear out the Duma, only who can close it, if the old man [Goremykin] is affraid [sic] of being insulted. I long to thrash nearly all the ministers & quickly clear away Shcherb.< & Sam.[arin] back to his serious evacuation questions—you see the metrop.[olitan, Vladimir] is against him. I hope to send you a list of names to-morrow for choice of decent people. Goodbye, Lovy, God bless & protect you, I kiss you without end & press you to my breast with infinite tenderness. Ever, Nicky mine, your very, very own Wify. [P.S.] Love to old man [Fredericks] & N.P.< Excuse rotten writing, but am in a great hurry & pen not famous.—If you could find a place for Paul< out at the front, wld. he really a good thing & would not fidget you, under a real good clever general. Is Bezobrazov's story [problem] cleared up? [i]

---

131. Under Samarin, the Holy Synod denied Varnava's petition to canonize John Maximovich, a "holy man" buried at the cathedral in Tobol'sk. Varnava and Rasputin were determined to proceed,

Nicholas and Alexandra supported their friends—with disastrous consequences for the authority and stability of the Russian Orthodox Church. See Fuhrmann, *Rasputin*, pp. 128-139.

132. "Raising a question" was done by voting an *interpellation*. The State Council or Duma did this if 30 members signed a complaint which was forwarded to the appropriate minister who had a month to study the issue, take remedial action, express opinions, etc. The house voting the interpellation could then debate the issue. Ministers were not required to attend debates or answer questions, but newspaper coverage and the need to work with the Duma often produced positive responses. A. N. Khvostov was apparently asked to sign this interpellation concerning Rasputin, but, currying favor as he was at this point, he refused.

No. 414/ Her No. 339.   Tsarskoe Selo. Aug. 30th 1915.
My own beloved Darling,

Again a lovely sunny morning with a fresh breeze—one appreciates the bright weather so much after the grey weather we had & darkness. With eagerness I throw myself every morning upon the Novoe Vremia<, & thank God every day good things are to be read about our brave troops—such consolation, ever since you came God really sent His blessing through you to the troops & one sees with what new energy they fight.—Could one but say the same thing about the interior questions. Guchkov< ought to be got rid of, only how is the question, war-time—is there nothing one could hook on to have him shut up. He hunts after anarchy & against our dynasty, wh. our Friend< said God would protect—but its loathsome to see his game, his speeches & underhand work. On Thursday their questions in the Duma are coming out, luckily a week late—could one not shut it before—only dont change the old man [Goremykin] now, [do so] later when it pleases you, Gorem. agrees to this, [as do] Andron.[nikov] & [A. N.] Khvostov—that it would be playing into their hands. They [the Duma and its supporters] cannot get over yr. firmness, as had sworn they would not let you go [to assume command at Stavka]—now you keep on in this spirit. You are still as full of energy & firmness, tell me Lovy? [a]

Its horrid not being with you. Have so many questions to ask & things to say & alas, we have no cypher [sic] together¹³³—cannot through Drent.< & by telegraph do not dare either—as others watch them—am sure the ministers who are badly intentioned towards me, will keep an eye upon me, & then that makes one nervous what to write.—We went to Church & then had luncheon on the balkony [sic], Sonia< too.—I received 5 of my Alexandr.< as its their visit. —Then Maximovich & we had a long talk about everything—he was glad to see my spirits up & my energy & I begged him also to pay attention, & when he hears things that are not nice, to stop & to pay attention at the club—he has not been there for 5 months; when he is there of course nobody ventures to say anything, but he has been told, that not nice talkings were going on there & will pay attention—the same Css. Fred.< told him about ["Fat"] Orlov who before him neither dares say anything incorrect. O. now spreads that our Friend had him sent away—others say he lives at T.[sarskoe] S.[elo], as before they said we had [my brother] Ernie here. [b]

I saw Mme Ridiger, the widow of one of the Georgian officers, he is buried at Bromberg—I have asked her to look after my Sanatorium at Massandra. Here is wire A.[nia]< got from our Friend just now.—"On the first news of the Ratniki being called, inquire carefully when our (his) government is to go. Gods will, those are the last crumbs of the whole. Gracious St. Nicolas [sic], may he work miracles."—Can you find out when those of his government (Tobolsk) are taken & let me at once know.—I suppose in yr. staff all is marked down exactly. Does it mean his boy, but he is not a ratnik. So strange, when Praskovia left, He [Rasputin] said she would not see her boy again.[134] Please, answer more quickly. [c]

Maksim.< found hospitals in good order, but the atmosphere needing a strong hand to keep order—he finds Yussupov [the Elder] ought to go back again [i.e., return as governor of Moscow] & not stick here, with wh. I agree.—[105] Botkin told me, as Gardinsky [Gordinsky] (Ania's friend) was returning fr. the south, where he had been to see his mother, in the train he heard two gentlemen speaking nasty about me & he at once smacked them in the face & said they could complain if they liked but he had done his duty & would do it to all who allowed themselves to speak so. Of course they shut up.—Just energy & courage are needed, & all goes well.— Am anxious, no wire from you, [wonder] whether you got my telegram last night about the Tail—Khvostov[135]—he made such an excellent impression upon her, & I should like you to have read my letter before settling with Gorem. [to discuss who would be suitable as new minister of the interior;] & did you get both letters on Saturday.—You are too far away, one cant get at you quickly. —Only quickly shut the Duma before their "question" can come out.[132] Continue being energetic. Maksim.< was delighted. To Botk.[in] I told a lot to make him understand things, as he is not always as I should wish—he saw I know all & could make him understand things he was unclear about. I talk away, its necessary to shake all up & show them how to think & act.— [d, e]

Can you give, or send through yr. man the enclosed letter to N.P.<—not through Dmitri< only—as he wld. make remarks that we write. It will amuse you how Anastasia writes to him.—I enclose a petition from our Friend, you write your decision upon it, I think it certainly might be done.—Aeroplans [sic] are flying overhead, I am in bed, resting before dinner.—If there is anything interesting, can yr. Mama [Maria Fedorovna] & I get the news in the evening as its long waiting till the next morning.—Now must end. Goodbye & God bless you my Beloved, my Sunshine, my life. Miss you greatly. Kiss you over & over again. Ever yr. very own wify   Alix. [P.S.] Bow to old man [Fredericks].—It seems la Guiche when here shortly, spoke against N.< being changed, in the club (Sandro L.[euchtenberg] heard it) so be a little careful what sort of man he is.—All look upon yr. new work as a great exploit. A. kisses you very tenderly. Please quickly give me an answer. [f]

133. The sense is probably, "we have no code to use to keep our letters confidential." The empress had once been friendly to A. A. Drentel'n, Nicholas's aide-de-camp. She now regarded him as an enemy. Part of an a.d.c.'s duties involved handling correspondence, so Alexandra assumed Drentel'n read her husband's letters and telegrams. She thinks Drentel'n (and/or others) might brief the ministers on subjects of interest. Drentel'n was removed from his post in September 1915 and made commander of the Preobrazhensky Life Guards Regiment. On the matter of spying, note that later in this letter Alexandra refers to one of *her* informants, Gen. Maximovich.

134. Praskovaya Rasputina and her husband were wondering when their son Dmitry and others from their "government" (*gubernaya*) of Tobol'sk were leaving for basic training. Alexandra passes the question on to her husband. The Rasputins thought Dmitry was a *ratnik*, an obsolete term denot-

ing a man eligible to bear arms who had not yet gone through training. Alexandra uses the term, then realizes it was not quite correct, or at least not in current use.
    135. See Letters No. 412 and 413h.

No. 415/ Telegram 343. Tsarskoe Selo> Stavka. 30 Aug 1915. 5.25> 6.23 p.m. To his majesty. [We] were at hospital of Bolshoi Dvorets [Grand Court]. Earlier we hurridly [sic] visited my train. Were at church, took a drive. Bright sun, very fresh but are having lunch and drinking tea on balcony. Hope you received my two letters and yesterday's evening telegram. With you in prayers and thoughts. [We] kiss you tenderly. Alix

No. 416/ Telegram 162. Stavka> Tsarskoe Selo. 30 Aug 1915. 6.45> 7.40 p.m. To her majesty. Loving thanks for two dear letters received last night. [I] saw old man [Goremykin] spoke much, but [I] put off final decision [see Letter No. 419a] until I return. To my joy to day Keller suddenly appeared looks well goes back to the front. Gave him messages from you. Delicious weather. Tender kisses to all. Niki

No. 417/ Telegram 254. Tsarskoe Selo> Stavka. 31 Aug 1915. 2.08> 2.44 p.m. To his majesty. Marvellous sun. [We] are lunching on balcony. [I] was at Red Cross, also saw Groten, he seemed healthy only quite pale. Then our hospital. Are leaving for drive. [I] pray and think about you. All tenderly kiss [you]. Alix

No. 418/ Telegram 169. Stavka> Tsarskoe Selo. 31 Aug 1915. 2.48> 3.10 p.m. To her majesty. Received all your letters, tender thanks was much occupied these days, therefore could not write. Thank the girls for their letters. Lovely weather, better for us if it rained more [and thus slowed the advance of German army]. Kisses to all. Niki

No. 419/ Her No. 340.   Tsarskoe Selo. Aug. 31st 1915.
My sweet Beloved,
    Again a sunny day—I find the weather ideal, but Olga freezes, its true, the "fond de l'air" is fresh.—I am glad you had a good talk with the old one as our Friend< calls Gorem.<—what you mention as having put off till your return, I suppose means the change of the Minister of the Interior—how good if you could see [A. N.] Khvostov & have a real talk with him & see whether he would make the same favorable, honest, loyal, energetic opinion on you as upon A.[nia]<—But the Duma, I hope will at once be closed. [a]
    Paul< is not well, suffers, has fever, a colique [sic] wh. he has not had for many months, so is in bed—besides he is worried about D.< If I could get some sort of an answer about himself, if you can make use of him at the front or H.Q. & whether you are not sending D. to his regiment—I could go & tell him this.—Wont you send for Misha< to stay a bit with you before he returns, would be so nice & homely for you, & good to get him away from her[82] & yr. brother is the one to be with you. I am sure, you feel more lonely since you left the train—alone in a house for breakfast & tea must be sad. Will you come nearer? [I.e., will you move Stavka closer to Tsarskoe Selo?]—And when about do you

think of returning for a few days—difficult to say no doubt, but I meant on account of changing Stchjerbatchev [Shcherbatov, minister of the interior] & "[s]macking" [disciplining] the Ministers, whose behaviour to the old man [Goremykin] & cowardice, disgust me.—I went this morning to Znam.< with my candels [sic], there I picked up A.[nia] & we went to the red Cross. She sat for an hour with her friend whilst I went over both houses. The joy of the officers, that you have taken over the command, is colossal, & surety of success. Groten looks well but pale. Then I went to our hospital & sat in the different wards. After lunch I received, then went to A.'s< to see Alia's< husband who leaves for the war again to-morrow, & she with her Children to town. We took a nice drive—lunched & had tea on the balkony [sic]. Now Baby< has begged me to take him to Anias to see Irina T.< & Rita H.<, but I wont remain there & shall finish this when I return. Well, I sat there 20 m. & then I went to pray & place candles for you my Treasure, my own sweet Sunshine. "One says" you are returning on the 4-th for a committee of ministers?! Aeroplans [sic] are flying again overhead with much noise.—Baby has written his letter quite by himself, only asked Peter Vass.< when not sure about the spelling. Gr.s wife< has quickly left, hoping to see her Son [Dmitry Rasputin, she is] still so anxious for Gr.'s life now.—Goodbye my Angel. God bless, protect you & help you in all. Very tenderest kisses Nicky love, fr. yr. own old   Sunny. [P.S.] How nice that you saw Keller, such a comfort to him I am sure. [b, c]

No. 420.   Mogilev. 31 August 1915.
My Precious darling Wify,

I thank you ever so much for your dear letters! In my loneliness they are my sole comfort and I wait for their arrival impatiently, but never know when they may come! During the fasting days I was every day in church either in the morning or in the evening & except that I was busy with Alekseev—so I had little time to write, letters, yes of course & my usual papers too I forgot. I get out here only once in the afternoon, though there is a tiny garden belonging to the governor's house, very sunny and prettily situated. What do the children say to my living in the governor's house? He is an excellent clever and energetic man, his name is not pretty—Pil'ts; that is why there is an abundance of mushrooms around the place! ["Pilz" is German for *mushroom*.] We eat them every day & the foreigners begin to like them, especially the Japanese general. [a]

Sandro [Leuchtenberg] spent two days here. He made a doklad [report] & after that we had a long & interesting talk. He is very happy with the change [whereby the tsar replaced Nicholasha< as supreme commander] told me much the same what Nikolai M.< wrote to you, & was astonished that I stood so long the false position! Now he is off to Smolensk. Kirill< arrived here yesterday. I was so glad to have seen good Keller, who suddenly appeared & left the same evening to his cavalry corps. Unfortunately I had no time to speak longer to him as old Gorem.< arrived the same morning—it being Sunday. I received the old man [Goremykin] after lunch, but at least spoke with K.[eller] accross [sic] the table, everyone listened to the interesting things he was narrating. He asked to convey to you his deepest respects & thanks. I am glad Alekseev has also a high opinion about him. I see that you find Mogilev is too far from home. [See Letter

No. 406d.] If you remember, I also thought so before coming here; but now it seems to me a most suitable place. It lies in the centre behind our whole front & out of the great movement of troops, etc. It is not farther than Vilna from Tsarskoe Selo [Stavka's location before the retreat of 1915] & when the railway lines begin working normally once more it wont seem far at all. Now a few words concerning the military situation.—it is threatening towards Dvinsk and Vilna, serious in the middle towards Baranovichi and good in the south (Gen. Ivanov) where our success continues. The seriousness lies in the frightfully weak state of our regiments, less than one quarter of complement; before a month they cannot be filled up because the recruits wont be ready & there are so few rifles. And fighting goes on and with it the losses too! Nevertheless strong efforts are being made to bring as much reserves as is possible from other places up to Dvinsk to keep the enemy back fr. that place. But here again our overworked railway lines cannot be relied upon as before. This concentration will be ended, only on Sep. 10th or 12th if, God forbid, the enemy does not get there before. That is also the reason why I cannot venture coming home until these dates! Please, lovy mine don't mention these details to anybody, I only wrote them down for you. [c]

Just this very minute Katov brought me your sweet letter No. 339, with the other for N.P.< Be perfectly quiet & sure about me, my darling Sunny. My will is firm & my brains sounder than they were before I was leaving. We spoke well and to the end with old Gor.<; you will probably see him on Thursday when the Duma is going to be shut up! He can repeat to you our conversation—but I quite forgot to mention [A. N.] Khvostov's name. It is better to leave these questions till I return. Your dear flowers, you gave me in the train, are still on the table before me—they are only a bit faded. Touching is it not? I shall finish this letter to-morrow. Good-night my sweet love-bird. [d]

September 1. It is a heavenly day. The whole morning, fr 10.30 till 12.30 I sat in the Staff near the open window as usual & worked with my Gen. Alekseev and in the beginning with Gen. Pustovoitenko too. Yesterday we made a charming excursion, crossed the Dnieper in a ferry-boat with our motors & came back from another direction. The country and the views are quite delightful & so calming for the soul. God bless you my beloved One & the children. I kiss you and them ever so fondly. Ania< too. for ever your own old huzy Nicky. [e]

No. 421/ Telegram 1. Tsarskoe Selo> Stavka. 1 Sept 1915. 2.05> 3.07 p.m. To his majesty. Operation went well. Perfect weather. Are going for a drive. [Daughter] Tatiana enraptured and thanks [you] for telegram. All is well. Always together in prayers and thoughts. [We] tenderly kiss [you]. Greetings to Kirill< and Dmitry<. Alik

No. 422/ Her No. 341.   Tsarskoe Selo. Sept. 1st 1915.
My own sweet Nicky dear,

Grey and dark & I am writing by lamp light. Slept badly.—Looked through the papers—what terrible hard work for our troops, such concentrated strength against us—but God will help on! It is pleasure to read how much clearer better the news is written now & it strikes all—it explains everything easier.—Is the Duma being closed? Every day articles, that its impossible one will send it away when so much needed etc. but you see the papers too—high time 2 weeks ago to have closed it.—But they do go on persecuting the German names, Shcherbatov, who told me he would be just and not harm them, now bows down to the wishes of the Duma, clears away all German names.—poor Gilhen [Kil'khen] hunted away one, two, three from Bessarabia, he came crying to old Mme Orlov<. Really he is a mad coward—all those honest people, completely Russian besides—kicked out—why, Lovy, did you give the sanction? Change him quicker, one only gains enemies instead of loyal subjects—the mess he makes in a day will take years to correct. [a, b]

A.[nia]< got a charming telegram from Kussov< [who was] intensely happy having heard the news about you [replacing Nicholasha as supreme commander].—She saw Bezak [a member of the Duma] at Nini's, & he spoke splendidly, enchanted that Dg.[,] Orl. & Nik.[136] have left & Nikolai [Vasil'evich] agrees too, says it right & left, & spoke so well about Goremykin.—One says the prorogation of the Duma [will be] till Oct. 15, pitty [sic] date is fixed so early again, but thank goodness it now dispersed—only one must work firmly now to prevent them doing harm when they return. [A royal decree of September 3, 1915, recessed the Duma until November 1915.] The press must really be taken better in hand—they intend launching forth things soon against Ania—that means me again, our Friend< was for me too, so A. sent a letter she received to Voeikov to-day, that he must insist Frolov should forbid any articles about our Friend or A. being written, they have the military power & its easy for them—Voeik.< must take it upon himself, yr. name has not got to be mentioned—in his place, V.< has to guard our lives & anything that harms us, & these articles are against us; nothing at all to be afraid of, only very energetic measures must be taken—you have shown yr. will & no slacking in any direction—once begun its easy to continue.— [c]

The operation went off well & then I did some dressing. Little Ivan Orlov was very interesting, he has 3 St. George's crosses [and] is presented to [recommended for?] the officers cross & has St. Stanislav with Swords. He was a little contusioned & two men killed, bombs were thrown on his mashene [sic], when it was on the ground. He has come for another. Throws bombs & arrows & papers warning them.—[D. M.] Knyazhevich came for a few days—looks well.— Then we drove, became sunny & nice. Met Baby in Pavlovsk park in his big motor with the boys.—Thats nice Kirill< is now too at the H.Q., can have good talks with him. Egg him on to get rid of Nik. Vass. [see Letter No. 422c]. I shall go with the big girls< to town< to-morrow to see our wounded, who returned from Germany, & then to tea to Elagin<, & hope to place a candle at the Saviour Church for you.—We were yesterday evening at Anias to [with] Shurik< & Yusik<.—I have nothing interesting to tell you my Sweetheart. God bless & protect you & help you in your very hard work & send force & success to our troops! A thousand kisses, Nicky mine, fr. yr. very own deeply loving old Wify. [d, e]

Our Friend is in despair his boy has to go to the war,—the only boy, who looks after all when he is away.[134]—Fat Orlov< says he has been told not to leave before you return & he still hopes to remain.—His amour propre is hideously wounded—forgets all he has said & done no doubt, & all his dirty money affairs.—Zinaida [Yusupova] one says rages, that the 3[136] have left, & in the next room Papa Felix [Yusupov the Elder, her husband] tells Bezak he is delighted they have gone! Tell the old man [Fredericks] I saw his wife & 2 daughters at the door & they look well & have left for Siverskaya.— [f]

---

136. V. F. Dzhunkovsky, V. N. ("Fat") Orlov and Nicholasha.

No. 423/ Telegram 3. Stavka> Tsarskoe Selo. 2 Sept 1915. 9.38> 10.52 p.m. To her majesty. Tender thanks for dear letter and for [daughter] Marie's. Kirill< and Dmitry< thank [you] very much. Motored far away today, delightful country and weather. Loving kisses to all. Niki

---

No. 424/ Telegram 8. Stavka> Tsarskoe Selo. 2 Sept 1915. 2.50> 3.15 p.m. To her majesty. Tenderest thanks [for] dear letter, also [son] Aleksei and [daughter] Anastasia. News on the whole better. Summer weather. Thoughts always near you. Kiss all fondly. Niki

---

No. 425/ Telegram 8. Tsarskoe Selo> Stavka. 2 Sept 1915. 3.15> 4.00 p.m. To his majesty. Just received dear letter for which warmly thank [you]. Inexpressibly happy over news. Clear [weather]. [We] are having lunch on balcony, then going to town< to see our latest party of wounded from Germany and to tea at Elagin<. All tenderly embrace and kiss you. [We] are taking her [Ania>] on the train for the first time since the accident.[58] Alix

---

No. 426/ Her No. 342.   Tsarskoe Selo. Sept. 2nd 1915.
My Own beloved One,
   Such a glorious sunny morning, both windows were wide open all the night & now too. I have new ink now, it seems the other is at an end now, it was not Russian.—It always grieves me to see how bad things one makes here, all comes from abroad, the very simplest things, as nails for instance, wool for knitting, knittingneedles in metal & any amount of necessary things. God grant, that after this terrible war is ended, one can get the fabrics [factories] to make leather things, & prepare the fur themselves—such an immense country dependant [sic] upon others. Young Derfel'den (the brother of the G. à cheval [guards cavalryman] you know), Paul's< son in law[,] returned with G. Kaufmann; the administration [equipment?] sent from France, he says, was without the key, so that they are no good & must be arranged here, wh. will take very long, the French say we must do it,—the boy wired to France & got that answer. [a]
   Sandro [Leuchtenberg] wrote such a contented letter to Olga after having seen you on his first report with you. Was at first too anxious & I think against you taking over the command & now sees with other eyes. N.P.< wrote a charming letter to A.[nia]< & it was agreable [sic] to see how he has grasped all, as one has frightened him too, tho' he held his tongue till now about it, he marveled at you having gone against everybody & [as] it has proved itself you were wise & right, his spirits are up again. Certainly being away fr. Petr.[ograd] & Moscou [sic] is the best thing, pure air, other scenery, no vile gossip.—In town< one says

you return on Saturday?—We go to town (an aeroplane is passing, for the first time in the morning)—I want to see our poor fellows who came back from Germany & then we take tea at Elagin< at 4½.—One says Paul keeps to his room & is in an awfull [sic] state. His boy [see No. 427a] leaves & only longs to be with you or in the army, & now is frightened you will sent for him & he is just feeling ill, so his humour is most depressing. I thought I would look in & cheer him up only I wish I had some sort of an answer for him. The photos Hahn did of Baby< were not successes, & the idiot did him sitting on the Balkony [sic] as tho' he had a bad leg, I have forbidden it to be sold & shall have him done again. Lovebird, good news again, thank God. One terrible hard fighting, they push on, but constantly [are] beaten back again.—Now the members of the Duma want to meet in Moscow to talk over everything when their work here is closed—one ought energetically to forbid it, it will only bring great troubles.—If they do that—one ought to say, that the Duma will then not be reopened till much late—threaten them, as they try to the ministers—& the gouvernement [sic]. Moscow will be worse than here, one must be severe—oh, could one not hang Guchkov? [b, c]

You can not imagine what a joyful surprise it was to receive your sweet letter. I perfectly well understand how difficult it is for you to find time for writing therefore it touches me deeply, Sweetheart.—That is a name Piltz!—but at least the mushrooms are agreable [sic] to eat.—Now I understand you find Moghilev alright & that it does not disturb there. Just got your wire.—Thank God, news on the whole better, one feels so anxious their trying to cut off Vilna, but perhaps we can catch them in a trap, & then Baranovichi—strange [that the Germans are moving] towards that place now—there too military people think in two weeks time it will be better. With much skill [D. M.] Knyazhevich finds the losses might be less, as where the heavy firing goes on, one must quickly go under their range, as they are [set] for great distances & cannot change quickly. The mans [men?] now are of a far less good cathegory [sic]. We just met a train going out & they waved their caps to us as we waved to them. Those heavy losses are hard —but theirs are yet worse. Of course, you are more needed there now & Motherdear< understands it perfectly. Its good you get out of an afternoon. [d]

We had divine weather to-day, like summer. I went with A. in my droshka to the cemetry [sic], as I wanted to put flowers on the grave of the Georg.[ian] officers, who died 6 months ago to-day in the big palace<—& then took her [Anna Vyrubova] to [A. A.] Orlov's grave, where she has not been since her accident. Then to Znamenia[.]< I remained through half a mass & then to our hospital, where I sat with our wounded. Luncheon on the balkony, then Baby was photographed on the grass. Then at 2½ off to town to the Hospital of Hel. P.< to see our prisoners back from Germany & Austria—the last arrived this month. Your Mamma [Maria Fedorovna] had been there this morning. We saw several hundreds & 70 from another hospital, because they cried so [i.e., because] she had not seen them. They did not look too bad on the whole, several poor blinds, lots without legs & arms—two with galloping consumption, alas; & the joy to be back.—I told them I should write to you, that I had seen them. Then to Elagin<—Fedor has grown so thin, that I at first took him for Andryusha[137] & very weak. Irina [Yusupova] is in bed in the Crimea, also ill with the stomack

[sic].—Motherdear looks well, [your sister] Xenia< fidgets, knowing the children not well & separated. Fedor, Nikita, Rostislav and Vassya are here, the other three[138] in the Crimea.—[e]

I do wish Yussupov wld. go back [as governor] to Moskou, [his wife] Zinaida I believe keeps him from fright [i.e., from being unstable].—Masses of movement in town, one gets quite giddy. I feel tired. At Elagin, our runner Vakhtin & your Mama's runner (ex sailor) carried me up on their hands.—Lovely air, window wide open. We always dine in the play room, but to-day I prefer remaining down as am tired & limbs ache. Think incessantly of you my Angel, pray heart & soul for you & miss you more than I can say—but happy you are out there & know at last all.—Now goodbye, Lovy mine, the man must leave. God bless & protect you! I kiss every dear spot over & over again & hold you tight in my arms. Ever you own very own wify. Alix. [P.S.] I receive Kulomsin<, Ignatiev to-morrow & your Eristov lunches with us.—Dona [Augusta-Victoria, wife of Kaiser Wilhelm II] received our 3 Russian nurses & Motherdear said she would not [receive?] the Germans [nurses] & now she feels, she must & fears being rude to them. Miechen< & Mara< could not in consequence, but then they too will. Now, if they ask me, what shall I answer. Every kindness shown them will make them sooner ready to be kind to ours & they would never understand, if I dont see them if they ask;—& here [in Russia] one will no doubt rage against me. The red cross nurses make a difference, it seems to me. What do you think, tell me Sweetheart, please; I find, I might, as they are women, & I know Ernie< will or Onor< [his wife will] see ours, & Grd. Dchs. of Baden[139] for sure.—How this new ink stinks, shall scent the letter again. [f, g]

137. Andrew Alexandrovich ("Andriusha") was the elder son of g.p. Alexander Michaelovich; Fedor was his brother.

138. These were the sons of the tsar's older sister Kseniya and her husband, Alexander Michaelovich ("Sandro").

139. Reference is to Maria Maximilianovna ("Aunt Maroussa"). She was a Russian, a Romanov, the grand duchess of Luxembourg, and, as the wife of Prince Wilhelm of Baden, the princess of Baden.

No. 427/ Her No. 343.   Tsarskoe Selo. Sept. 3rd 1915.
My own beloved Nicky dear,

Grey weather. Looking through the papers I saw that Litke [C. N. Lutke] has been killed—how sad, he was one of the last who had not once been wounded, & such a good officer. Dear me, what losses, ones heart bleeds—but our Friend< says they are torches burning before God's throne, & that is lovely. A beautiful death for Sovereign & country. One must not think too much about that, otherwise it [is] too heartrending.—Paul's Boy [Prince Paley] left yesterday evening after having taken Holy Communion in the morning. Now her [Princess Paley's] both sons are in the war, poor woman & this one is such a marvelously gifted boy, wh. makes one more anxious—he is sooner ready to be taken from this world of pain.[140]—Wont you get Yussupov [the Elder] & give him instructions & send him off quicker to Moscou [sic], its very wrong his sitting here at such a time when his presence can be needed any moment—she [his wife Zinaida, see Letter No. 426f] keeps him. [a]

But one must have an eye on Moscou & prepare beforehand & be in harmony with the military, otherwise disorders will again arise. Stcherbatchev being a nullity, not to say worse, wont help when disorders occur, I am sure. Only quicker to get rid of him & for you to get a look a [A. N.] Khvostov, whether he would suit you, or [A. B.] Neidhardt.—(who is such a pedant)! Thank God, you continue feeling energetic—let one feel it in everything & in all yr. orders here in this horrid rear.—We take tea at Miechens<. Here are the names of Maria Plaoutin's [Plautina] sons—she entreats to get news of them—can somebody in yr. staff, or Drenteln try to find out their whereabouts?—Well, I placed my candles as usual, ran in to kiss A.[nia]< as she was off to Peterhof—then hospital, operation. Your Eristov lunched with us, has grown older, limps a little, was wounded in the leg & lay at Kiev,—would not follow hospital regime and headed for us. Then I received Ignatiev (ministers) & talked long with him about everything & gave him my opinion about all, they shall hear my opinion of them & the Duma. I spoke of the old man [Goremykin], of their ugly behavior towards him, & turned to him as a former Preobr.,< what would one do to officers who go behind their commanders back & complain against him & hinder & wont work with him—one sends them flying—he agreed. As he is a good man I know, I launched forth & he I think understood some things more rightly afterwards.—Then I had Css. Adlerberg; after wh. we made bandages in the stores. [b, c]

O., T. [daughters Olga, Tatiana] & I took tea at Miechen, Ducky< came too, looking old, & ugly even, had a headache & felt cold & was badly coiffee [coiffeured].—We spoke much & they looked at things as one ought to; also angry at the fright & cowardice & that none will take any responsability [sic] upon themselves. [She was f]urious against the Nov. Vremia<, finds one ought to take strong measures against Suvorin. Miechen knows that a correspondence goes on between Militsa< & Suvorin, make the police clear this up, it becomes treachery. I send you a cutting about Hermogens [Bishop Hermogen]—again Nikolasha< gave orders about him, it only concerned the Synod & you—what right had he to allow him to go to Moscou—you & Fredericks ought to wire to Samarin that you wish him to be sent straight on to Nicolo Ugretsk—as remaining with Vostorgov, they will again cook [up trouble] against our Friend & me.[141] Please order Fred.< to wire this.—I hope they wont make any story to Varnava; you are Lord & Master in Russia, Autocrat remember that.—Then I saw Gen. Shulmann of Osovets—his health is still not yet good, so he cannot yet go to the army.—Uncle Mekk< was long with me & we talked a lot about affairs—& then about all the rest. He finds Jussupov [the Elder Count Yusupov] no good. Miechen said Felix [the Younger Count Yusupov] told him his Father had sent in his demission [request for retirement] & got no answer.— Big strikes in town. God grant Ruzsky's< order will be fulfilled energetically.—[N. K. von] Mekk is also very much against [N. I.] Guchkov—he says the other brother [A. I. Guchkov] also talks too much. Lovy, have that assembly in Moscou[144] forbidden, its impossible, will be worse than the Duma & there will be endless rows.— [d, e]

Another thing to think seriously about is the question of wood—there wont be any fuel & little meat & in consequence can have stories & riots. Mekks railway gives heaps of wood to the town of Moscou, but its not enough & one does not think seriously enough about this.—Forgive my bothering you Sweetheart, but I try to collect what I think may be of use to you.—Remember about Suvorin's articles wh. must be watched & damped.—A great misfortune, one cannot get the refugees to work, they wont & thats bad, they expect one to do everything for them & give & do nothing in exchange.—Now this must go. The Image [icon] is fr. Igumen Serafim (fr. whom St. Seraphim came, wh. you held in your hand). The goodies, toffee is from Ania.—Weather grey & only 8 degr. Lovy, please send of your suite to the different manufactures, fabricks [factories] to inspect them—your eye—even if they do not understand much, still the people will feel you are watching them, whether they are fulfilling your orders conscientiously—please dear.—Many a tender kiss, fervent prayer & blessing huzy mine, fr. yr. very own old   Sunny. [P.S.] God will help—be firm & energetic—right & left, shake & wake all up, & smack firmly when necessary. One must not only love you, but be afraid of you, then all will go well.—Is it true nice Dimka [D. B. Golitsyn] also goes to Tiflis—a whole suite of yours follow, thats too much, & you need him with the foreigners & for sending about. All the children kiss you.— [f, g]

140. Reference is to Prince Paley, son of g.p. Paul Alexandrovich and his morganatic spouse, Olga Pistol'kors, who received from Nicholas II the title "Countess" Paley.
141. Concerning Vostorgov, see Fuhrmann, *Rasputin*, pp. 157, 218.

No. 428/ Telegram 14. Stavka> Tsarskoe Selo. 3 Sept 1915. 7.14> 7.38 p.m. To her majesty. Fondest thanks [for] dear letter and for [daughter] Olga's. Hope not tired yourself from all you are doing. I feel well and unflinching. Boris< arrived, sent by commander of guards with report about their losses. Loving kisses to all. Niki

No. 429/ Telegram 12. Tsarskoe Selo> Stavka. 3 Sept 1915. 8.14> 9.10 p.m. To his majesty. Heartily thank you for telegram. Overcast and cold. Was at hospital, your Eristov lunched with us. Then received, report, tea with Miechen< where saw Ducky<. Again received. Large strike in town<. [We] embrace and kiss you. God helps us in everything. Sleep peacefully. Alix.

No. 430/ Her No. 344.   Tsarskoe Selo. Sept. 4th 1915.
My very own Sweetheart,
    I have remained in bed this morning, feeling deadtired, & having slept badly. My brain continued working & talking—I had spoken so much yesterday & always upon the same subject until I became cretinized; & this morning I continued to Botkin, as its good for him & helps him put his thoughts to right, as they also did not grasp things as they were. One has to be the medicine to the muddled minds after the microbes from town<—ouff! She [Ania<] got his [Rasputin's] telegram yesterday, perhaps you will copy it out & mark the date Sept. 3-rd on the paper I gave you when you left with his telegr. written down. [The following quote is in Russian.] "Remember the promise of the meeting, this was the Lord showing the banner of victory, the children or those near to the heart

should say, set us go along the ladder of the banner, our spirit has nothing to fear." [a]

And your spirit is up[−]so is mine & I feel enterprising & ready to talk away. It must be alright & will be—only patience & trust in God. Certainly our losses are colossal, the guard has dwindled away, but the spirits are unflinchingly brave. All that is easier to hear than the rottenness here. I know nothing about the strikes as the papers (luckily) don't say a word about them.—Ania sends her love—wont you wire to me to, "thank for letters, Image [icon], toffee"—it would make her happy. Aunt Olga< was suddenly announced to me yesterday evening at 10½—my heart nearly stood still, I thought already one of the boys was killed—thank God it was nothing, she only wanted to know whether I knew what was going on in town< & then I had to let forth again, for the fourth time in one day, & put things clearer to her, as she could not grasp some things & did not know what to believe. She was very sweet, dear Woman. Here is a paper for Alekseev, you will remember the same officer asked some time ago about forming a legion; well, you will think about it—perhaps it would do no harm to form it & keep it in reserve in case of disorders or let it replace another regiment wh. might come more back as a rest.—The legion of Letts, are you having it disbanded into other existing regiments, as you had intended & wh. would be safer in all respects & more correct. The Children have begun their winter-lessons, Marie & Anastasia are not contented, but Baby< does not mind & is ready for more, so I said the lessons were to last all 50 instead of 40 minutes, as now, thank God, he is so much stronger.—All day long letters & telegrams come—but its yours I await all day with intense longing. [b, c]

Eristov asked why we do not have a telephone leading ingeniously from your room to mine like N.< and [his wife] S.< had in Kiev. This would be delightful as you would be able to tell me good things or ask any question. But this would be useful for you and we would try to not bother you since I know you don't like to talk. This would be exclusively our private wire and we would be able to talk without the danger that someone or other would overhear. This would be advantageous in a certain type of extreme situation. How gratifying it would be to hear your tender voice! Some member of your suite could come on in case you were not there. If need be talk the matter over with Voeikov if you would let us do this.—Now I must place my candles at Znamenie<, and then get out. I expect Mitia Den< for lunch, then I receive the commander of the Sib.[erian] Cos.[sack] regiment from Imperial Stavka, senator Pr.[ince] Golitsyn concerning affairs of the military-prisoners, Zeime from my sanitary-train, Kharten [E. O. von Harten], com.[mander] Tverts.[y, of Tver Regiment]—And so it is every day! If it rains, I will go outside. I want to go to Church this evening.—Ania sends you her fondest love. [The weather g]ot finer after luncheon & we drove. The girls had a concert.—So anxious for news.—Kiss you endlessly, my love & long for you. When you come, I suppose it will only be for a few days?—Have nothing interesting to tell you, alas. All my thoughts incessantly with you. Send you some flowers, cut the stalks a little, then they will last longer. God bless you! Always your old Wify. [P.S.] Love to Kirill<, Dmitry< & Boris. [d, e]

No. 431/ Telegram 21. Tsarskoe Selo> Stavka. 4 Sept 1915. 6.07> 6.30 p.m.
To his majesty. Rainy day though clear. Went for a walk. Laid down in the
morning since I was tired. Now [we] go to Church. In thoughts always together.
[We] embrace and kiss you. Alix

No. 432/ Telegram 21. Stavka> Tsarskoe Selo. 4 Sept 1915. 6.46> 8.14 p.m.
To her majesty. Best thanks for [your] dear letter and [letter from daughter]
Tatiana. Have said [made arrangements] about motor car for Ella<. She will get
it in a week. After rain cooler. Many messages to you from cousins here. Tender
kisses to all. Niki

No. 433   Mogilev. Sept 4. 1915.
My Own Darling,
    I kiss you over & over for your beloved letters; the two last ones smelt deli-
cious of your scent, wh even went through the envelope in the shape of a greasy
spot! Tell Paul<, when you see him that I intend sending him to the armies later.
Georgi< is passing now from one army to another. He wired that on September
1 Lida & station were bombarded by a Zepp.[elin] and aeroplanes and that about
20 people were killed! Boris< arrived yesterday with interesting papers for me
fr Gen. Olokhov—Bezobrazov's successor. It is agreeable to hear such praises of
Bor[is] from all sides & how he is loved not only by his own regiment but also
by others. I have got an idea of naming him pokhodnyi ataman [field hetman] in
the place of the excellent Gen. Pokotilo who has gone back again to the Don a
fortnight ago. I am sure you will ask me why not Misha<? But I will try & get
him near me and then one see, perhaps he might get the command of
Khan-[Gussein] Nakhichevansky's Cavalry Corps. [a]
    A few days ago I got Yusupov's petition to leave Moscow, and I consented,
the more so as the very energetic and good Gen. Mrozovsky has just been
named Command.[ant] of the troops of the Moscow mil.[itary] district. He
commanded there & at the [outbreak of the] war the grenadier corps, knows the
town and will prove his worth, I hope, when the moment comes. You ask me
about the reception of the 3 German nurses. I think, certainly yes— especially if
Mama is receiving them. Those sort of things seem here much simpler and
clearer! My lovebird, me wants you so at times & me feels so lonely!!! The
Germans are pouring in an empty space between our troops at Dvinsk & the
others near Vilna and this preoccupies Alekseev, as information and more details are lacking. Their cavalry patrols with infantry behind—have reached the
railway line near Polotsk! This movement upsets our plans of bringing quicker
up our reserves to the two mentioned towns. It is despairing not to be able to
move & concentrate troops as fast as one would like to. [b, c]
    He (Aleks.[eev]) told me today he finds it necessary to change the quarters for
the Stavka and thinks that Kaluga perhaps might do. This makes me very sad,
because again I will feel further away from the army. He sent somebody &
Voeikov also to choose a suitable place. Perhaps he is right, but the idea displeases me greatly! If God sent us a new blessing & we could stop that invasion
of the enemy—then of course the Stavka might remain at Mogilev, which is
comfortable and suitable—every thing is close & near at hand here. My friend,

gen. [Hanbury-]Williams, showed me a telegram about the safe arrival of two new submarines in the Baltic. Now there are five English boats with our fleet. That is the result of my telegram to Georgie [King George V] if you remember—wh. I sent him before I left. Have you seen in the newspapers the speeches by Kitchener and Lloyd George on the war, and on the part played in it by Russia? It is very true. If only God would grant that they and the French began [an offensive] now—it is long overdue! [d, e]

This minute I got your dear letter with two small paper-cuttings & [daughter] Marie's letter. Thank you from my heart for all you write and also for the box with goodies, wh are excellent. To-morrow I see Shcherbatov who comes also [with] Polivanov. Dimka Golytsin begged to go later to Tiflis—he can be good help to Nikol.[asha]< as he knows the society & people so well—so I allowed him to follow N.< Better he is surrounded by good people! Now I must end as it is late. Good-night, sleep well, my precious little Wify. [f]

Sept 5. Good morning my beloved Sunny. It is grey & cold and looks like rain. I have to receive two deputations & then off to my usual doklad [report]. Today is Ella's< namesday [sic]. God bless you, my precious Wify & the children. I kiss you all very tenderly. Ever your own old huzy Nicky. [P.S.] Please give A.[nia] this little letter. [g]

No. 434/ Telegram 37. Tsarskoe Selo> Stavka. 5 Sept 1915. 6.25> 7.23 p.m. To his majesty. Was in town< at various places to see refugees. Please sternly prohibit their names being mentioned in newspapers. Tell this to Shch.< Massalov [Mosolov] spoke with him [Shcherbatov] today concerning the command of your old count [Yusupov], but I ask you to tell him [Shcherbatov] this quite firmly. Everything comes from Moscou [sic]. Nini's< husband knows about all this, will take measures at proper time to stop attacks on [Our] Friend<. We all kiss you.   Alix

---

No. 435/ Her No. 345.   Tsarskoe Selo. Sept. 5th 1915.
My own beloved Darling,

Grey weather. Again Ivanov & S.[outhern] army had success—but how hard it is to the north—but God will help, I am sure. Are we getting over more troops there? The misery of having so few railway lines!—I have nothing of interest to tell you, was yesterday in our lower church fr. 6½-8 & prayed much for you, my Treasure; the evening we spent knitting as usual & soon after 11 to bed.—I must get up & have my hair done before Botkin, as have sent for Rostovtsev at 10 o'clock.—Me kisses you.—Well I had Rostovtsev & told him we were going to town< & he was to meet us at the station with Apraksin, [A. B.] Neidhardt, [I. I.] Tolstoy, [A. N.] Obolensky & so it was at 3 (& M.[itia] D.[ehn] with the motors met us) & at the station R.[ostovtsev] told them I wished to go & see the refugees. So we went, quite unexpectedly to different, 5 places to see them, a nighthouse wh. stands empty near the Narva gate (as people dont drink & so can find where to sleep)—& there women & children sleep in two lageryakh [i.e., camps, groups],— next a house where the men are. Many were out looking for work. Then the place they are first brought to, bathed, fed—written down & looked at by the Dr. Then another place, former chocolate fabric [factory], where women

& children sleep, all kissed my hands, but many could not speak being Letts, Poles. But they did not look too bad nor too dirty. The worst is to find them work when they have many children. There is an excellent new wooden building with large kitchen, dining passage, baths & sleeping rooms, built in 3 weeks near Packhouses & where the trains can be brought straight.—But now I am tired & cant go to Church.—[a, b]

I wonder if you understood my telegram, written in Ella's< style rather—but A.[nia]< begged me do it quickly as Massalov [Mosolov] spoke to her by telephone & said Shcherbatov would see you to-day.—The papers intend bringing in our Friend's< name & Anias—here Shcherbatov promised Massalov that he wld. try to stop them, but as it comes fr. Moscou [sic], he did not know how. But it must be forbidden; & Samarin will go on for sure—such a hideous shame, & only so as to drag me in too.—Be severe. And what about [the Elder Count] Yussupov—he does not intend returning & gave in this demission [request for retirement] tho' one never does during war. Is there no capable general who might replace him?—only he must be energetic indeed. All men seem to wear peticoats [sic] now!— Mme Zizi< lunched as its her namesday—& then we talked & I explained a lot, at wh. she was most grateful, as it opened her eyes upon many unclear things. You know ramoli[e]< Fredericks told Orlov (who repeated it to Zizi) that I felt he disliked me—so he went only disculpiating himself & proving his innocence. Countess [Maria] Benkendorff told A. she was delighted he leaves & ought to have long ago, as the things he allowed himself to say were awful.—It was the kind couple Benkendorff that hinted last night to A. that I shld. go & see the refugees, so I at once did it, as I know meant well & may help people taking more interest in those poor creatures.—The fabrics [factories in Petrograd] began working again—not so in Moscou I fear.—[c, d]

Kussov< wrote (he gets none of Ania's letters & feels very sad we shld. have forgotten him). Is full of the news about You [assuming command] & he explained it all to his men. He longs to say heaps, & thinks you for sure don't know & wh. are not right, but he cannot risk writing frankly.—Zizi asked me who the General Borissov? is with Alekseev as she heard, he was not a good man in the Japanese war!—I was half an hour in Church this morning & then at the hospital (without working)—there were 8 of yr. 3d Rifles [Regiment] fr. here wounded on the 30th—one of them, the first I have ever heard, said one longs for peace;—they chattered a lot!—Now my Sunshine, dearly beloved Angel, I kiss & bless you & long for you. Ever yr. very own old Wify. [e]

I told Mitia Den, that you thought of sending the Suite to as many fabricks [factories] & workshops as possible, & he found it a brilliant idea & just the thing, as then all will feel your eye is every where.—Do begin sending them off & make them come with reports to you.—It will make an excellent impression & encourage them working & spur them on.—Get a list of your free Suite (without German names), Dm. Sheremetev as he is free. Komarov (as he spoke to you), Vyazemsky, Zhilinsky, Silaev, those who are less "able men" send to quieter & surer places; Mitia Den<, Nik.[olai] Mikhailovich (as he is in a good frame of mind), Kirill<—Baranov. But do it now Deary.—Am I boring you, then forgive me, but I must be yr. note-book. [f]

Now Miechen< writes about the same man as Max< & Mavra<. Fritzie vouches for him [Ploto] not being a spy & a real Gentleman.—The papers concerning him I think lie in town at the general-staff; it was Nikolasha< ordered him to be shut up. He is since beginning of the war in a real cell with a wee window, like a culprit—only let him be kept decently like any officer we have, if one wont exchange him for Kostia's< a.d.c. He writes to Adini [Alexandrina, queen of Denmark] that he was auf einer Studienreise durch den Kaukasus begriffen [on a scientific mission] up in the [Caucasus] mountains [when] he heard rumours of impending war, & so he flew off on the shortest road. He reached Kovel July 20 & at the station heard of the declaration of war. The train did not continue. He announced himself as officer & begged to be permitted to pass over [to] Sweden or Odessa; instead one took him prisoner in a cell at Kiev, where he is still now, regarding him as spy. He gives his word of honour to Adini that he "was only traveling without any ugly sidedeeds, & that he kept himself far from anything like spying". He suffers away fr. wife & children & not being able to do his duty.—He begs to be exchanged, or at least a better position. Poor Ploto, if one has wrongly shut him up in a cell, the quicker one takes him out & treats him as a German officer taken as being in Russia when war was declared, that would only be decent. When Miechen enquired, one said they had nothing against him. Sazonov only said that he had given out he was unmarried or on his honeymoon, in any case not correct, but that means nothing (perhaps there was a croocked novel [i.e., crooked intrigue?]) & when they begged again, I think Nikol.[asha] or Yanushkevitch one answered that one did not remember why he was shut, but probably they had a reason & therefore he must remain there—that's "weak" as the children would say. [g]

Ah, here Miechen sends me a letter of his [Ploto's] wife to Adini. They wanted to travel & he wanted to show her Petrograd & Moscou & take a rest, after hard work & freshen up his Russian. They left beginning of July 1914 [from] Stettin. For safety sake her husband took a diplomatic Pass (?). The last moment friends in Kurland told them not to visit them, so they spent 8 days in Petrograd & 8 in Moscou & did sightseeing. There they separated because of her bad health wh. prevented her accomp. him to friends in the Caucasus. She daily got news fr. him, & fr. Tiflis & near there he went to a H.[err N. F.] v.[on] Kutschenbach, who during the war was murdered with his wife. Through the german Consul at Tiflis he got a ticket to Berlin over Kalish—but only reached Kovel.—The only red cross German sister [i.e., nurse], von Passow [Erica von Passov] is his sister in law—she is now here to see the prisoners. Do have him well placed, please he can have his health for ever ruined—& Fritzy vouches for him. If you cant have him exchanged, then at least lodged & with light & good air. Excuse my writing all this, but its good you should know what Adini heard, & one cant be cruel, its not noble & after the war one must speak well of our treatment, we must show that we stand higher than they with their "kultur". [h]

How I bother you, am so sorry, but its hard for others & you don't persecute as N.< & Yanushk.[evich] did mercilessly in the B.[altic] provinces either, & that does not harm the war nor mean peace.—Goremykin comes to me to-morrow at 3—tiresome hour, but is only free then.—Tell N.P.< that we thank him very much for his letters of thanks &—messages.—God bless you, once more thousand warm, warm tender kisses Sweetheart.—Cold & raining. My love & goodwishes to Dmitri<.—My yesterday's letter I marked wrongly, it must be 344, please correct it.— [i]

No. 436/ Telegram 31. Stavka> Tsarskoe Selo. 5 Sept 1915. 9.46> 10.29 p.m. To her majesty. Many thanks for yours and Marie's letter. Too bad about Ortipo.[142] Just got your telegram. Be quite sure about my firmness with Shch[erbatov]. [I] wrote today. Cold, rainy. Fondest kisses. Niki

142. Ortipo, the family's pet female bulldog, had just died.

No. 437/ Telegram 50. Tsarskoe Selo> Stavka. 6 Sept 1915. 4.15> 7.00 p.m. To his majesty. Tenderly thank you for dear letter. In heart and soul am with you, pray to and believe in God's mercy. Cold, rain. [We] are going for tea to Pavlovsk. All tenderly kiss [you]. She [Anna Vyrubova] heartily thanks you. Alix

No. 438/ Telegram 35. Stavka> Tsarskoe Selo. 6 Sept 1915. 4.58> 5.55 p.m. To her majesty. Thank you from all my heart for letter and flowers wh[ich] arrived fresh. Cold, rainy, stormy. Vilna has been left this night. Hope in a few days news will be better up there. Fondest kiss to all. Niki

No. 439/ Telegram 55. Tsarskoe Selo> Stavka. 6 Sept 1915. 8.30> 9.26 p.m. To his majesty. Received your telegram, my dear, in spirit and heart [am] sharing everything with you. All your aspirations are in hands of the Lord God Who must hear our prayers and lighten these dark days with a ray of sunshine to the joy of all. Difficult to be far from you. [I] tenderly kiss [you]. May God bless you. Alix

No. 440/ Her No. 346.   Tsarskoe Selo. Sept. 6th 1915.
Beloved Nicky dear,
    Every morning & evening I bless & then kiss your cushion & one of your Images [icons]. I always bless you whilst you sleep & I get up to draw open the curtains. Wify sleeps all alone down here, & the wind is howling melancholy to-night. How lonely you must feel, wee One. Are your rooms at least not too hideous? Cannot N.P.< or Drenteln photo them? All day impatiently I await your dear telegram wh. either comes during dinner or towards 11.— So many yellow & copper leaves, & alas also many are beginning to fall—sad autumn has already set in—the wounded feel melancholy as they cannot sit out but rarely & their limbs ache when its damp—they almost all have become barometers. We send them off as quickly as possible to the Crimea. Taube left yesterday with several others to Yalta as a surgeon must watch his wound & my little Ivanov's too.—A.[nia]< dined with us yesterday upstairs. To-day is Isa's< birthday, so I have invited her with Ania to luncheon.—Oh beloved One—2 weeks you left,—me loves you so intensely & I long to hold you in my arms & cover your

sweet face with gentle kisses & gaze into your big beautiful eyes—now you cant prevent me from writing it, you bad boy. [a, b]

When will some of our dear troops have that joy? Wont it be a recompense to see you! [Teimur Bek] Navruzov wrote, he at last tried to return to his regiment after 9 months, but only got as far as Kars, his wound reopened again a fistula & he needs dressings, so once more his hopes are frustrated—but he begged Yagmin for work & he has sent him to Armavir with the young soldiers to train them & look after the youngest officers. It is so nice to feel ones dear wounded remember one & write. Madame Zizi< also often hears from those that lay in the big palace<.—Have you news from Misha?< I have no idea where he is. Do get him to stop a bit with you—get him quite to yourself.—N.P.< writes so contented & spirits up—anything better than town<. It seems Aunt Olga< before coming to me had flown half wild to Paul< saying the revolution has begun, there will be bloodshed, we shall all be got rid of, Paul must fly to Gorem.< & so on—poor soul! To me she came already quieter & left quite calm—she & Mavra< probably got a fright, the atmosphere spread there too from Petrograd.—[c, d]

Grey & only 5 degrees.—The big girls< have gone to Church at 9 & I go with the others at 10½.—Isa has cought [sic] cold & 38 this morning, so has to keep in bed. The news is good again in the south, but they [the Germans] are quite close to Vilna wh. is despairing—but their forces are so colossal.—You wired you had written so I am eagerly awaiting your letter, Lovy—its sad only with telegrams in wh. one cannot give any news, but I know you have no time for writing, & when working hard to have still to sit down to a letter, that dull & wearisome work; & you have every moment taken too, Sweetheart. I had Markozov from 6¼ to 8 so have to write whilst eating—most interesting all he told & can be of use to abolish misunderstandings, cant write about anything of that to-night.—Old man [Goremykin] came to me—so hard for him, ministers so rotten to him. I think they want to ask for their leave & the best thing too.—Sazonov is the worst, cries, excites all (when it has nothing to do with him), does not come to the conseil des Ministers, wh. is an unheard of thing—Fred.< ought to tell him fr. you that you have heard of it & are very displeased, I find. I call it a strike of the ministers. Then they go & speak of everything wh. is spoken of & discussed in the Council & they have no right to, makes him so angry. You ought to wire to the old man that you forbid one talking outside what is spoken of at the Council of Ministers & wh. concerns nobody. There are things that can & wh. are known later, but not everything.—[e, f]

If in any way you feel he [Goremykin] hinders, is an obstacle for you, then you better let him go (he says all this) but if you keep him he will do all you order & try on his best—but begs you to think this over for when you return to seriously decide, also Shcherbatov's successor & Sazonov.—He told Shcherbatov he finds absolutely a person chosen by Shcherbatov ought to be present at Moscou [sic] at all these meetings & forbid any touching of questions wh. dont concern them—he has the right as Minister of the Interior; Shcherbatov agreed at first, but after having seen people fr. Moscou he changed his mind & no more agreed—he was to tell you all this, Goremykin told him to—did he? Do answer.— Then he begs D. Mrazovsky should quickly go to Moscou, as his presence may be needed any day.—I don't admire Yu.[supov] leaving (its her [his wife's] fault) but he was not worth much [as governor of Moscow].[105]—And now we have left Vilna—what pain, but God will help—its not our fault with these terrible losses. Soon is the Sweet Virgin's feast 8-th (my day, do you remember Mr. Philippe)—she will help us. [g]

Our Friend wires, probably after her letter His wife brought, telling about all the interior difficulties. [The following quote is in Russian.] "Do not fear our present embarassments [sic], the protection of the Holy Mother is over you—go to the hospitals though the enemies are menacing—have faith." Well I have no fright, that you know.—In Germany one hates me now too.— Mark.< said & I understand it—its but natural.—How I understand, how disagreeable to change your place—but of course you need being further from the big [battle] line. But God will not forsake our troops, they are so brave.—I must end now, Lovebird.—Alright about Boris, only is it the moment? Then make him remain at the war & not return here, he must lead a better life than at Warshaw & understand the great honour for one so young.—Its a pitty [sic], true, that not Misha. The German nurses left for Russia & M. [Maria Fedorovna, the tsar's mother] had no time to see them, me they did not ask to see, probably hate me.—Oh Treasure, how I long to be with you, hate not being near, not to be able to hold you tight in my arms & cover you with kisses—alone in yr. pain over the war news—yearn over you. God bless help, strengthen, comfort, guard & guide.—Ever yr. very own Wify. [h, i]

No. 441/ Telegram 59. Tsarskoe Selo> Stavka. 7 Sept 1915. 10.38> 11.28 a.m. To his majesty. Cold, windy, intense day. Going for operation. Suslik[143] arrived, his supervisor [Samarin] still spreads awful rumors about our Friend<, and orders Suslik to admit that he told you a lie. [I] telegraphed the old man [Goremykin] and asked [him] to receive the bishop [Varnava]. [I] bless and kiss [you]. In thoughts together. God will help. Alix

143. A suslik is a squirrel-like rodent with a thick body and a bushy tale. "Suslik" was Alexandra's nickname for Varnava, bishop of Tobol'sk and Siberia and an ally of Rasputin. (See Footnote 111.) In June 1915 Varnava petitioned the Holy Synod to canonize John Maximovich, a local holy man buried in the cathedral at Tobol'sk. The Synod investigated and rejected the proposal. Incited by Rasputin and with the secret support of Nicholas II, Varnava proclaimed John's beatification in a spectacular ceremony in the Tobol'sk cathedral on August 27/ September 9, 1915. (Beatification is the first stage in canonization.) The Synod summoned Varnava to the capital to account for his actions. Samarin met Varnava at his hotel the day before his "trial," hoping to persuade him to turn against Rasputin. Varnava stood firm. At his hearing on September 8/21, 1915, Varnava produced the tsar's telegram authorizing the beatification. Nicholas was defying, ridiculing—and undermining—the leaders of his church. This scandal confirmed the conviction many held that Alexandra and Rasputin manipulated the tsar and were the real power in Russia. This was an important milestone in the collapse of Nicholas's government. See Fuhrmann, *Rasputin*, pp. 77, 128, 134-139.

No. 442/ Telegram 53. Stavka> Tsarskoe Selo. 7 Sept 1915. 7.48> 8.55 p.m. To her majesty. So many thanks for your's and [daughter] Olga's letter. Also for news. That man's [Samarin's] behavior begins to enrage me. Cold but finer. Tender kisses to all. Niki

---

No. 443/ Her No. 347.   Tsarskoe Selo. Sept. 7th 1915.

Beloved Huzy dear,

Cold, windy & rainy—may it spoil the roads [and hinder the advance of the German armies]. I have read through the papers —nothing written that we left Vilno—again very mixed, success, bad luck & it cannot be otherwise, & one rejoices over the smallest success. It does not seem to me that the Germans will venture much more further, it would be great folly to enter deeper into the country—as later our turn will come.—Is the amunition [sic], shells & rifles coming in well? You will send people to have a look [at our factories]—your Suite?—Your poor dear head must be awfully tired with all this work & especially the interior questions? Then, to recapitulate what the old man [Goremykin] said: to think of a new minister of the interior, (I told him you had not yet fixed upon [A. B.] Neidhardt; perhaps, when you return, you can think once more about [A. N.] Khvostov); a successor to Sazonov, whom he finds quite impossible, has lost his head, cries & agitates against Goremykin, & then the question, whether you intend keeping the latter or not. But certainly not a minister who answers before the Duma, as they want,—we are not ripe for it & it would be Russia's ruin—we are not a Constitutional country & dare not be it, our people are not educated for it & thank God our Emperor is an Autocrat & must stick to this, as you do—only you must show more power & decision. I should have cleared out quickly still Samarin & Krivoshein, the latter displeases the old man greatly, [he lurches] right & left & [gets] excited beyond words. [a]

Goremykin hopes you won't receive Rodzianko. (Could one but get another instead of him, an energetic, good man in his place wld. keep the Duma in Order.)—Poor old man [Goremykin] came to me, as a "soutien" [someone needing support] & because he says I am "l'énergie". To my mind, much better clear out ministers who strike & not change the President [of the council of ministers, Goremykin] who with decent, energetic, well-intentioned cooperates [i.e., colleagues] can serve still perfectly well. He only lives & serves you & yr. country & knows his days are counted & fears not death of age, or by knife or shot—but God will protect him & the holy Virgin. Our Friend< wanted to wire to him an encouraging telegram.—Markozov—no I must finish about Goremykin, he beggs [sic] you to think of somebody for [governor of] Moscou [sic] & besides get Mrozovsky to come quicker, as these sessions may become too noisy in Moscou[144] & therefore an eye & voice of the Minister of Interior ought to be there, & one has the right to, as Moscou [sic] is on a military footing and is under the minister of Interior—true? Neratov he finds no good for replace Sazonov (I only like that mentioned his name), he knows him since he was a boy & says he never served out of Russia, & that is not convenient at such a place. But where to get the man. We had enough of Isvolsky & he is not a very sure man—Girs is not worth much, Benk.[145]—the [German] name already against him. Where are men I always say, I simply cannot grasp, how in such a big country does it happen that we never can find suitable people, with exceptions!— [b, c]

My conversation with Markozov was most interesting (a little too sure of himself) & he can tell one many necessary things & clear up misunderstandings. Polivanov knows him well & already he has cleared up one thing. It seems there was an order to take off of the prisoner officers their epaulets, wh. created an awful fury in Germany & wh. I understand—why humiliate a prisoner & that is one of those wrong orders of 1914 fr. the Headquarters—thank God one has now changed it.—He also understands that we must always try to be in the right, as they at once otherwise repay us equally—till for that[tit for tat?]—& when this hideous war is over & the hatred abated, I long that one should say, that we were noble. The horror of being a prisoner is already enough for an officer & one wont forget humiliations or cruelties—let them carry home remembrances of christianity & honour. Luxury, nobody asks for. They are really improving the lot of our prisoners, I saw a photo, Max< did of our wounded at Saalem (A.[unt] Maroussia's[139] place) in the garden, near a Russian toy hut, Max used to play in & they look well fed & contented. Their greatest hatred has passed, & ours is artificially kept up by the rotten "Novoye Vremya"<.—I must fly & dress, as we have got an operation & before that I want to place my candles & pray for you as usual; my treasure, my Angel, my Sunshine, my poor much-suffering Job.[146] I cover you with kisses & mourn over your loneliness.—The operation went off alright—in the afternoon we went to the big Palace< hospital. Kulomzin came to me to present himself & bring lists, to show me what the Romanovsky committee has done;—most interesting talk about all sorts of questions.— [d, e]

Well, Dear, here are a list of names, very little indeed, who might replace Samarin. A.[nia]< got them through Andron.< who had been talking with the Metropolitan [Makary of Moscow?] as he was in despair Samarin got that nomination [as director of the Holy Synod], saying that he understood nothing about the Church affairs. Probably he [Samarin] saw Hermogen at Moscou, in any case he sent for Varnava, abused our Friend, & said that Hermogen had been the only honest man, because he was not afraid to tell you all against Greg.[ory] & therefore he was shut up, & that he, Samarin wishes Varnava to go & tell you all against Gregory;< he answered that he could not, only if the other ordered him to, & as coming from him.[147] So I wired to the old man [Goremykin] to receive V.[arnava] who would tell him all, & I hope the old man will speak to S.[amarin] after & wash his head. You see, he [Samarin] does not heed what you told him—he does nothing in the Synod & only persecutes our Friend, i.e. goes straight against us both—unpardonable, & at such a time even criminal. He must leave.—Well here. [A. A.] Khvostov (minister of justice) very religious knowing much about the Church, most devoted to you & much heart. Guriev (Director of the Chancellary [sic] of the Synod) very honest, serves long in the Synod (likes our Friend). He mentioned Makarov ex minister, but he would never do, & a small unknown man. [f]

But he [Prince Andronnikov] goes on singing a praise of [A. N.] Khvostov & tells it to Gregory as he wants to bring him round to see, that this is a man ready to have himself chopped to pieces for you (will stand up for our Friend, never allow one mention him [in the press]); his manqué de tacte [tactlessness[148]] after all [we] don't mind so much now, when one needs an energetic man who knows people in every place, & a Russian name, Kulomzin also hates the "Novoye Vremya"< & finds the Moscov. Ved.< & "Russkoye Slovo"< much better. I am a bit anxious what they are producing in Moscou. The Petrograd strikes, Andron.< says, are thanks to colossal gaffes of Shcherbatov who shut up people who had nothing to do in that respect.—I hope Voeikov listens less to Shch. —he is such a nullity & weak & by that does harm.—What dull letters I write, but me

wants to help you so awfully, Sweetheart, & so many use me as an organ to give
over things to you.—Sonia Den< took tea with us, she leaves for Koreiz, as needs
a better climate, is so happy you are out there [at Stavka] & understands perfectly well that you went now when all is so difficult.— Yesterday we took tea at
Pavlovsk with Mavra—A.[unt] Olga< turned up too—she looks unwell, worked in
Sunday fr. 10-2½ in the hospital—she overtires herself, but wont listen to reason.
I understand her—myself of experience have realised [sic] one must do less, alas,
so I work rarely, to keep my strength for more necessary things. [g, h]

Yesterday evening we were at Ania's, also Shurik<, Yuzik< Marie's friend &
Aleksei Pavlovich [Sablin], who told us about the Headquarters—he leaves for
there again to-morrow.—I enclose a letter from Ania about her brother [S. A.
Taneev], tho' I advised her not to send it as if the name comes to you, of yr. own
accord I know you will do what is right for the boy who worked so hard.—Now I
must dress for Church. Cold, wet and rainy,—may it spoil the roads thoroughly
at least [and hinder the advance of the German armies].—Awfully anxious to get
news—God will help.— Goodbye & God bless you my sweetest of sweets.—I
cover your precious face with tenderest, warmest kisses & long to hold you in
my arms & forget everything for a few moments. Ever yr. very own old
<u>Sunny</u>.   [P.S.] Here is Babysweets< letter too.— [i]

144. Alexandra is referring to the Congress of Zemstvoes and Municipalities that convened in
Moscow on September 6/19, 1915. This independent organization was critical of the government's
conduct of the war. See Oldenburg, *Last Tsar*, III, pp. 49-50.

145. M. N. Giers was Russian ambassador to Constantinople at the outbreak of the war. A. P.
Izvol'sky had been minister of foreign affairs and at this time was Russian ambassador to Paris. A.
C. Benckendorff was the Russian ambassador to London.

146. Nicholas II was born on May 6/18, the day on the Russian church calendar dedicated to Job.
Nicholas found meaning in this date, he was convinced (as he told Stolypin) that "I am destined for
terrible trials" and "shall not receive my reward on *this* earth."

147. See Letter No. 441 and Footnote 133. Note that nomination of candidates to replace Samarin
was in the hands of Andronnikov and the "metropolitan," probably Makary of Moscow. Andronnikov and Makary handed their "list of names, very little indeed" to Vyrubova, who gave it to Alexandra, who forwarded it to her husband. Rasputin's allies also installed A. N. Khvostov as minister of
internal affairs on November 23 (O.S.), 1915. Rasputin was not important in this maneuver, but it
had his blessing; the architects were a "troika" comprised of Andronnikov, A. N. Khvostov and
Stephen Beletsky, who became assistant-minister of internal affairs and police director. The troika
also secured A. N. Volzhin's appointment as director of the Holy Synod, though he quickly turned
against them.

148. Alexandra recalls that Nicholas considered A. N. Khvostov as minister of internal affairs in
1911. Khvostov was then governor of Nizhnyi-Novgorod. Rasputin went to "gaze into Khvostov's
soul" and evaluate his suitability for the office. Rasputin believed even the highest officials should
receive ordinary citizens courteously; he appeared at Khvostov's office, unannounced and unidentified, requesting a reception. Khvostov did not know who Rasputin was—and he failed his test. A. A.
Makarov was made minister of the interior. Rasputin actually had little to do with the decision, but
Khvostov attributed his bad luck to a lack of "tact" in receiving Grigory. When A. N. Khvostov had
another chance to become interior minister in 1915, he was careful to win Rasputin's support. See
Fuhrmann, *Rasputin*, pp. 72-73, 143-147.

No. 444.   Mogilev. Sept. 7 1915.
My sweet beloved Sunny,

Tender thanks for your dear letter in which you wrote about having visited to
the bezhentsy [refugees] in different places in town! What an excellent idea &

how good of you to have gone there & seen it all for yourself! How your dear brain works I can judge from. [sic] the amount of subject ideas & names you speak about in your letters. I shall inquire about Ploto & try to do what is possible! It is good to send the memb[ers] of the suite to these fabrics that work for the army & I will tell it to the old man [Fredericks], who lays himself at your feet! Georgii suddenly turned up yesterday looking brown & well; He saw about 30 army corps, but could not get up to the guards & the northern armies, as hard fighting was going on. He told me lots of interesting things. Today I have sent Kirill< to visit gen. Ivanov & his three splended [sic] armies after their recent successes. He takes over 4200 crosses with him and also officer's decorations. He was delighted to have this work. [a, b]

Yesterday, though a Sunday was a busy day. Church at 10. From 11 till 12.30, work in the staff, a large luncheon, then Shcherbatov's report; I told him all. Half an hour's turn in the garden, fr 6-7.30, Polivanov's report in Alekseev['s] presence & after dinner his private report and then lots of rotten papers to read. Shcherbatov made me this time a much better impression than in Tsarskoe; he was much less frightened & reasoned soundly! Also about Moscow, he said there was no reason to worry about the s"ezd [assembly], because if they made stupid resolutions it would not be allowed to be printed & no harm could come out of it. True! Me also love[s] you & would give much to nestle around you in our comfortable old bed. My camp bed is so hard and stiff! But I must not complain—lots sleep on damp grass or in dirt! God bless you my love & the children. I kiss you all over & over tenderly & passionately times without number. Ever your old huzy   Nicky. [c]

No. 445/ Telegram 56. Stavka> Tsarskoe Selo. 8 Sept 1915. 12.36> 12.55 p.m. To her majesty. Fondest thanks for dear letter. Have written. Thoughts so much on this day especially. Shocking weather, cold, rainy. Have been to church this morning. Tender kisses to all. Niki

No. 446/ Telegram 64. Tsarskoe Selo> Stavka. 8 Sept 1915. 2.40 p.m.> 4.35 p.m. To his majesty. Heartily thank you for telegram. It would be right to drive away quickly whoever troubles you. Give order to old man [Goremykin] this very day. He knows everything concerning abominable position and what horrors Suslik< was forced to hear from his superior [Samarin] for 3 hours. But he told them nothing definite and then relayed to old man everything which troubled him to depths of his being. They nearly laughed at your telegram, disregarded it and forbade [Varnava] to continue the glorification [i.e., beatification of John Maximovich]. Metropolitan Makary was completely for Suslik. Only severe measures can stop this anarchy. Wisdom [Goremykin] says that nothing like this was ever said at such meetings [of the Holy Synod]. Forgive me for disturbing you, but it is necessary to act more quickly. Cold, windy. Attended church. [I] bless and kiss [you]. Alix

No. 447/ Her No. 348.   Tsarskoe Selo. Sept. 8th 1915.
My own beloved One,

Am so anxious what news—its 10½ & the "Novoye Vremya"< has not come &
I don't know what is going on, as never get the telegr. any more as before were
sent me, when you were at the Headquarters. So cold, 3 degr. only in the night,
grey & windy. The eldest [two daughters] went to mass at 9 & the little ones
now, I shall follow, have been reading through an immense fat report fr. Rostovtsev.—There is Prince Ukhtomsky in the 4-th rifles & his wife is terribly worried, as some of the comrades said they had seen him fallen, wounded, whereas
no sanitary has yet brought him. Did Boris< bring the lists? But it may have
happened since. In town< one says all the guard was surrounded, but I wont
believe anything that is not official. I must dress for Church. Service was nice
last night & they sang well. Dear one, it is so difficult when there are things one
must tell you directly—& I dont know whether anybody reads our telegrams.
Again I have had to wire an unpleasant thing to you, but there was no time to
loose [sic]. I have asked her [Anna Vyrubova], as well as she can, to write out
Suslik's conversation in the Synod. Really the little man has behaved with marvellous energy, standing up for us & our Friend<, & gave back slapping answers
to their questions. Tho' the Metropolitan [Makary] is very displeased with
S.[amarin], yet at this interrogation he was feeble & held his tongue, alas.—They
want to clear Varnava out & put Hermogen in his place, have you ever heard
such an impudence! They dare not do it without yr. sanction, as by yr. order he
was punished. [a, b]

Its once more Nikolasha's< doing (egged on by the women[1]) he made him[155a]
come out of his place, without any right, to Vilna to live with Agafangel & of
course this latter, S.[ergei, bishop of Finland] & Nikon [archbishop of Vologda]
(the awful harmbringer to Athos)[149] attacked Varnava about our Friend for 3
hours; Sam.[arin] went to Moscou [sic] for 3 days I think, no doubt to see Hermogen—I sent you the cutting about his having been allowed to spend 2 days in
Moscou at Vost.[okov]'s by Nikolasha's order— since when was he allowed to
mix in such questions, knowing that by yr. order the punishment was inflicted
upon Hermogen! How dare they go against yr. permission of the "salutation"
[i.e., the beatification of John Maximovich]—what have they come to, even there
anarchy reigns & once more Nikolasha's fault, as he (purposely) proposed Samarin, knowing that that man would do all in his power against Greg.[ory] & me,
but here you are dragged in, & that is criminal, & at such a time quite particularly. [c]

Several times the old man [Goremykin] told S.[amarin] not to touch that subject, therefore he is fearfully hurt & said so to V.[arnava] & that he found
S.[amarin] must at once leave, otherwise they will drag it into the public. I find
those 2 bishops [mentioned above, Serge and Nikon] ought at once to be taken
out of the Synod—let Pitirim come & sit there,[174] as our Friend feared
N.[icholasha] would harm him if he heard that P.[itirim] venerates our Friend.
Get other, more worthy Bishops in. Strike of the Synod —at such a time, too unpatriotic, unloyal—what does it concern anybody—may they now pay for it &
learn who is their master. Here is a cutting "again" you will say, but V. J. Gurko
says (I will write it better out instead of sending you the paper). In Moscou
[sic], [G. E.] Lvov allowed him to speak. "We want a strong authority—we mean
an authority armed with extraordinary powers, authority with a horse-whip (now

you show it them in every way, where you can, you are their autocrat master) but not such an authority which is itself under a whip." A slandering pun, directed against you & our Friend [& especially me!],[150] God punish them for this;—its not Christian to write this, then better, God forgive them, but above all make them repent.— [d]

Varnava told Gor.[emykin] all about the Governor [of Siberia?]—how nice he was with Gregory until he came here & got horrid orders fr. Shcherbatov, i.e. Samarin. About me he said to Suslik "a foolish woman" & about A.[nia]< abominable things wh. he cld. not even repeat. Goremykin says he must at once be changed. Look through my letters of about 5 days ago, there I named one, our Friend would have liked to have. Only all this must be done quickly, the effect is all the greater. Samarin knows yr. opinion & wishes & so does Shcherbatov & they don't care, thats the vile part of it. Give orders to the old man [Goremykin], that is then easy for him to fulfil. He told Varnava how hard it was to have all against him, if only you would give him new ministers to work with.—Samarin had ordered Varnava to go to you—now it would have been good, he could have told you all, only it will take up your time & one must hurry with ones decisions. You see he is like S.[ophia] Iv.[anovna Tyutcheva], incorrigible & narrow-minded. He ought to think of his churches, clergy & convents & not of whom we receive. That is his bad conscience now. Once more "who digs a pit for others, falls into it himself", like N.[icholasha].—Quicker also change the ministers, he cannot work with them—if you give him categorical orders, then he can give them over, thats easier—but to talk with them he cant. Excellent to send several flying & keep him, serves them right, please think of it. [e, f]

Despairing not to be with you & talk all over quietly together.—About the war news our Friend writes (add it to yr. list of telegrams) Sept. 8. [The following quote is in Russian.] "Don't fear it will not be worse than it was, faith and the banner will favor us."—I enclose a telegram of E. Witgenstein, born Nabokova [Elizabeth Sayn-Wittgenstein] (Groten's great friend, was in Marie's train). She wants medals, perhaps you would give Fred.< the order—& the telegram too. The Images [icons] I can send her straight.—Here my love is [A. N.] Khvostov's speech in reading you will understand why Paul< disapproved because he openly speaks against Dzhunkovsky. You better keep it, in case one makes remarks about him, you can always fall back upon it; its clever & honest & energetic—a man longing to be of use to you.—Are you having more justice done in the Baltic provinces, one would like that, I must say poor people suffer enough.— [g]

Khvostov's speech I have just read through, very clear & interesting, but I must say our own lazy slave [Slavic?] natures without any initiative have been at fault, we ought to have kept the bank in hand [i.e., Russian ownership] before—earlier nobody paid attention now all eyes hunt for the German influence, but we brought it on ourselves, I assure you by our lazyness [sic]. Pay attention to page 21, 22 about Dzhunkovsky, what right had he to telegraph such a thing, it was only possible in quite particular cases —& that sounds rotten. I think it will interest you as it shows you his ideas about the banks etc. Then Ania's paper I enclose about Varnava & the Synod. Anastasia kisses you & begs pardon for not having written but we went for a little drive (of course the girls froze) &

then to the Invalid-house where it lasted 1½ hour talking to all. We picked up Ania again at Css. Shulenburg's ideal little cottage. Then they went to their hospital & after tea to Ania's to play with some young girls.—One's head is ramolished< fr. conversations—but the spirit is good, Lovy, & ready for anything you need. Varnava comes to me to-morrow. Go on being energetic Sweetheart, use your broom—show them your energetic, sure, firm side wh. they have not seen enough. Now is the fight to show them who you are, & that you have enough—you tried with gentleness & kindness, but that did not take, now you will show the contrary—the Master-will. Kussov< wrote to A.[nia] amongst other things, sad that a man like Miheyev [B. A. Mikheev] came in yr. name as he represents nothing & does not know how to represent—nor to speak. [h, i]

Manny mine, Angel Sweetheart, so sorry to daily bore you with things, but I cant otherwise.—I long to kiss you & gaze into yr. beloved eyes. I bless & kiss you without end in true & deep devotion.   God bless, guard, guide & protect you. Ever yr. very own old   Wify. [P.S.] Are you thinking of sending Dmitri< back to the regiment? Dont let him dawdle about doing nothing, its his ruin, he will be worth nothing, if his caracter [sic] does not get formed at the war—he was not out [at the front] more than one or 2 months. [j]

149. On this see Fuhrmann, *Rasputin*, pp. 78, 136, 146, 156.
150. The first in this double pun suggests the tsar was under two whips, one Rasputin's, the other his wife's. The second pun refers to the khlysty (Flagellants), who supposedly used whips in worship. Rasputin was widely (and falsely) regarded as a khlyst.

No. 448/ Telegram 61. Stavka> Tsarskoe Selo. 8 Sept 1915. 7.34> 8.15 p.m. To her majesty. Thanks [for] telegram. Difficult to send him [Samarin] away without having chosen someone to replace him. Could old man [Goremykin] give you a list for choice and you send it on to me?[151] Saw Mordvinov today who accompanied Georgi<, told me lots of good [news] from the army. Loving kisses. Niki

151. Notice the difference between Nicholas and Alexandra in selecting candidates for appointmen to the rank of minister. The empress relied on such "friends" as Andronikov and Metropolitan Makary. The tsar would ask the chairman of his council of ministers to list suitable candidates. In either case, final selection belonged to the emperor.

No. 449/ Telegram 68. Tsarskoe Selo> Stavka. 9 Sept 1915. 10.30> 11.29 a.m. To his majesty. At last clear, sunny day; am going to hospitals in Petrograd. [I] asked old man [Goremykin] for a list [see No. 447] since everything should be done quickly.[151] Did they[144] really have the arrogance to send this telegram to you from Moscou [sic]? Shcherbatov should have foreseen all this in time. Be firm and show an iron will. There has already been enough of their interference. They have enough of their own work to do, cannot raise this racket. A firm hand is needed from above to put them in their place. [I] am sending flowers from [all of] us. Dear old Savina died. [I] bless and warmly kiss [you]. Alix.

No. 450/ Her No. 349.   Tsarskoe Selo. Sept. 9th 1915.
My very own Sweet One,

At last a sunny morning, & "of course we go to town", as [daughter] Olga says; but I must go to hospitals, there is nothing to be done. Yesterday we went to the Invalid-hospital, I spoke to 120 men 1½ [hours], & the rest en gros as they stood in one room, —why I told you all this yesterday, I am quite foolish. Thank God the news is a bit better, I find, to the north, i. e. Vilna—Dvinsk, You said we left Vilna the other night, but they have not yet entered, have they? Am eagerly awaiting your promised letter to-day, such a joy always.—There! I have got your precious letter & I thank you for it from the depths of my heart, I hold it in my left hand & kiss it, Sweetheart. Wont Mme Plautin be mad with joy to have news that her sons are safe, thanks so much for enquiring. What a lovely telegr. from our Friend<.— [a]

Thats good you use Kirill< now after Georgie<, so that each goes in turn, only don't send Dmitri<, he is too young & it makes him conceited—wish you would send him off!—Only don't say its I who ask this.—Well, you have a lot to do. You had a better impression of Shcherbatov, but he is not good, I fear at all, so weak and wont work properly with the old man [Goremykin]. Well look what they spoke about at Moscou [sic],[144] again those questions, wh. they had come to the conclusion to drop, & asking for an answerable minister[385] wh. is quite impossible, even Kulomzin sees this clearly—did they really have the impertinence of sending you the intended telegram? How they all need to feel an iron will & hand— it has been a reign of gentleness & now must be the one of power & firmness—you are the Lord & Master in Russia & God Almighty placed you there & they shall bow down before your wisdom & firmness, enough of kindness, wh. they were not worthy of & thought they could hoist you round their finger. What they said at Moscou was printed yesterday.— [b]

I saw poor Varnava to-day my dear, its abominable how Samarin behaved to him in the hotel[152] & then in the Synod—such cross-examination as is unheard of & spoke so meanly about Greg.[ory]< using vile words in speaking of Him. He makes the Gov.[ernor of Rasputin's home province, Tobol'sk, in Siberia] watch all their [Rasputin's and Varnava's] telegrams & send them to him—vicious about the salutation [beatification of John Maximovich] that you have no right to allow such a thing—upon wh. Varnava answered him soundly & said that you were the chief protector of the Church, & Samarin impertinently said you were its servant. Colossal insolence & more than ungentlemanlike—lolling back in his chair with crossed legs crossexamining a Bishop about our Friend. When Peter the Great of his own accord also ordered a "salutation", it was at once done, in the place & round about. After the salutation, the funeral services cease (as when we were at Sarov, the salutation & glorification, were done together)—& they have reordered funeral services & said they would not heed what you said. [c]

Lovy, you must be firm & give the strict order to the Synod that you insist upon your order being fulfilled & the Synod that yr. order has to be fulfilled and the salutation is to continue—more than ever one needs those prayers now. They ought to know that you are most displeased with them. And please do not allow V.[arnava] to be sent away, he stood up splendidly for us & Gr. & showed them how they on purpose go against us in all this. Old Goremykin was more than hurt & horrified & beyond words shocked, wenn [sic] he heard that the Gov. (whom Dzhunkovsky had made change his opinion & instigated) said to V. that

I was a crazy woman & Ania< a nasty woman etc.—how can he remain after that? You cannot allow such things. These are the devil's last trials to make a mess everywhere & he shant succeed. S.[amarin] said highest praise of Feofan & Hermogen, & wants to put the latter in V.'s place. You see the rotten game of theirs. Some while ago I begged you to change the Gov. [of Siberia] he spies upon them, every step Varnava took at Pokrovsk[oe, Rasputin's home] & what our Fr.[iend] does & what telegrams are written, thats Dzhunkovsky's work & S.[amarin]'s excited on through Nikolasha< by the black women<.—Agafangel spoke so badly (fr. Yaroslavl)—he ought to be sent away on the retiring list & replaced by Sergei [bishop of] F.[inland] who must leave & get out of the Synod— Nikon ought to be cleaned out of the Council of the Empire [State Council], where he is a member & also out of the Synod, he has besides the sin of Mt. Athos on his soul.[149] This Suslik< rightly all said, so as to give the Synod a good lesson & strong reprimand for their behaviour, therefore quickly change Samarin. Every day he remains, he is dangerous & does mischief, old man [Goremykin] is of the same opinion, it is not woman's stupidity—therefore I cried so awfully when I heard they had forced you to name him at the Head-quarters & I wrote to you in my misery, knowing N.[icholasha] proposed him because he was my enemy & Gr.'s & through that yours.— [d, e]

In conversation Metropolitan Vladimir said (they have made him mad too), when V. said that S.[amarin] was breaking his neck by behaving thus, & that he is not Over-Procurator [director of the Holy Synod] yet. "The Emperor is no boy and ought to know what he is doing" & "that you earnestly begged S.[amarin] to accept" [the position of director] (I told Goremykin then that it was wrong)—well let them see & feel that you are not a boy & who calumniates peo-ple you respect & insults them—insults you, that they dare not call a Bishop to account for knowing Gr.—I cant repeat to you all the names they gave our Friend. Pardon my boring you again with all this, but its to show you, that you must quickly change S.—I shall have to suffer for it if he remains, as I shall get it onto my head, you heard what the Governor said, & here one is not kindly in-tentioned towards me in some sets & its not the time to drag ones Sovereign or his wife down. Only be firm (he begged not to remain long, you remember) & don't put him into the Council of the Empire< as a bonbons after he behaved & spoke openly like that about whom we receive & such a tone about you & yr. wishes—that cannot be borne, you have not the right to overlook it. These are the last fights for yr. internal Victory, show them yr. mastery. [f]

Remember, in 6 days [in office] he [Samarin] kicked out old Damansky (be-cause of Gregory) & gave 60.000 [rubles] for his successor to arrange the ap-partments [sic]—hideous actions. I invented to-day the aid to the new one—Prince Zhivakha you remember him, quite young, knows all about the Church questions, most loyal & religious (Bari-Bielgorod) don't you agree?[153] Clean out all, give Goremykin new ministers to work with & God will bless you & their work. Please Lovebird, act quickly. I wrote to him [Goremykin] to give a list, as you asked [see No. 448] but he begged you to think of Sazonov's suc-cessor & Shcherbatov he is far too weak, tho' you liked him better this time. I am sure Voeikov (his bosom friend) told him how to be—dont listen to

V.[oeikov], he has been wrong all this heavy time & a bad adviser.—it will pass, he is conceited & got a fright for his own skin.—Oh dear, humanity! [g, h]

My Image [icon] of yesterday, of 1911 with the bell[103] has indeed helped me to "feel" the people—at first I did not pay enough attention, did not trust to my opinion, but now I see the Image & our Friend have helped me grasp people quickly. And the bell would ring if they came with bad intentions & wld. keep them fr. approaching me—there, Orlov, Dzhunkovsky, Drentel'n who have that "strange" fright of me are those to have a special eye upon. And you my love, try to heed to what I say, its not my wisdom, but a certain instinct given by God beyond myself so as to be your help.— [i]

Precious one, I send you the paper one of our wounded wrote by my request, as I was afraid of giving our the wish wrongly—it wld. be good if the regiment could get that bit of ground for building a mausoleum for their fallen officers.—Perhaps you would tell Fred.< to give the order from you to Shcherbatov you have not the time for doing all yourself.—The little Image is fr. Ania< she went to the Chapel to-day whilst we were visiting hospitals, both under my protection. The one for 60 officers on the Horse Guards Boulevard, very nice indeed & then to the Vyborg suburb between the prisons (a new hospital for the prisoners) wh. was now at once used for 130 men.—so nice & clean—several Semenovtsi [men of the Semenovsky Guards Regiment] fr. Kholm & rifles etc. & one who had been for a year in Germany. The pavement was atrocious. You see I choose the smart & quite poor places to turn up in—they shall see that I don't care what one says & shall go about as always. Now that am feeling better, I can do it.— [j]

Such sunny weather. From Znamenia< I went in my droshki round the Boulevard to the hospital to get good air in the morning.—Is there a chance of your coming now?—I was thinking about Novgorod (don't tell V.[oeikov]) & Ressin< is making inquiries. By boat, or motor even fr. the broad railway too far, 60 Verst—so one must get into the narrow gauged waggon [sic]. Sleeping here in the train—reaching there in the morning, lunching there etc. back by 10½ in the evening—because must look at the Cathedral. The new soldiers are there & that makes me doubt whether I ought not rather await yr. return. If so, wire to me, "wait about Novgorod" & I shall then.—Our Friend wants me to go about more, but where to? [k]

Did you copy out his telegr. for yourself on the extra sheet? If not, here it is again: "Sept. 7, 1915. [The following quote is in Russian.] Do not fall, when in trouble God will glorify by his appearance."—[Daughter] Olga has a committee this evening.— Aleksei's train (Shulenburg) sticks at Opukliki since 4 days, was stopped there until called to Polotsk; he asked the Comm.[ander] of Polotsk by wire, but received no answer yet—are we cut off from there?—My train returned, said there were lots of sanitaries waiting out there without being able to move, I hope it means that our troops are being brought up there? Then masses of women were brought to work near the lakes, but not told for how long, so that they had no time to take warm clothes, got wages per day for the journey, 30 kopecks & the journey lasted 5 days—are the Governors mad. Never any order here, it drives me to distraction— that lesson we ought to learn fr. the Germans. [l, m]

[Your s]ister Olga's train is bringing many wounded officers & men & 90 refugees. I told them always to pick them up on the way.—Dear me, what a lot one might do—I long to poke my nose into everything (Ella< does it with success)—to wake up people, put order into all & unite all forces. All goes by fits & starts—so irregular—so very little energy (my despair, as have enough, no matter if I feel ill even, wh. thank God I don't just now)—am wise & don't do too much.—Now the endless letter must be finished. Do I write too much? Courage—energy—firmness will be rewarded by success, you remember what He [Rasputin] said, that the glory of yr. reign is coming & we shall fight for it together, as it means the glory of Russia—you & Russia are one.—Beloved one, yes, my bed is much softer than yr. camp-bed—how I wish you were here to share it. Only when you are away I dream. 2 weeks & ½ since you left. I bless you & cover you with kisses, my Angel, & press you to my heart. God be with you. For ever yr. very own old Sunny. [n]

152. Varnava appeared before the Synod on September 8, 1915, to account for his beatification of John Maximovich. The authorities instructed Varnava to return on September 10 to answer nine questions he was given to study. Varnava objected to a second inquest—as we see here —and refused to appear. For reference to the "hotel," see Footnote 143.

153. Peter Damansky (1859-1916) was a Synod official, a Rasputin supporter and a favorite of the empress. Samarin dismissed him after being in office six days. Alexandra is saying whoever Nicholas might choose to replace Samarin, she has just met a young man who would be an excellent assistant-director ("aid"): Prince Nicholas Zhevakov. Zhevakov was a student of religion— and an opportunist. Previous Synod directors refused him even minor positions, but the disorder created by Samarin's ouster plus an alliance with Rasputin brought Zhevakov new opportunities. He is discussed at length in Fuhrmann, *Rasputin*.

No. 451/ Telegram 64. Stavka> Tsarskoe Selo. 9 Sept 1915. 7.04> 7.50 p.m. To her majesty. Tender thanks to you [my] love, [also daughter] Tatiana and Tiny<. Hope not too tired. Misha< asked to come, am very glad to see him soon. News a bit better. God grant in a few days they may be quite comforting. Cold clearer weather. Loving kisses. Niki

No. 452/ Telegram 74. Tsarskoe Selo> Stavka. 9 Sept 1915. 9.30> 10.25 p.m. To his majesty. Heartily thank you for letter which touched me very much and telegram. Lovely, sunny day. Were in town<, in two hospitals. Not very tired. Thanks be to God, news better. [We] embrace and kiss [you]. Sleep well, darling. Alix

No. 453.   Mogilev. Sept. 9th 1915.
My beloved dearest Sunny,
  So many thanks for your sweet long letters wh now come more regularly about 9.30 of the evening. You write quite as you talk. The behaviour of some ministers continues to astonish me! After all I have told them at the famous evening sitting, I thought they might have understood me & that I meant seriously what I said. Well, so much the worse for them! They were afraid of shutting up the Duma—it has been done! I left for here & changed N.< against their advice; the people have taken this step naturally & have understood—as ourselves. The

proof—lots of telegrams I get from different parts and in most touching expressions. All this shows us clearly one thing—that the ministers, living always in town< know extremely little of what goes on in the whole country. Here I can judge rightly of the real nastroenie [mood] among the different classes of people: everything must be done to carry on the war to a victorious end & no doubt is expressed about it. This all the deputations I received the other day told me officially, and so it is everywhere in Russia. The only two exceptions are Petrograd & Moscow—two needle dots on the map of our country! [a]

Dear Shavel'sky came back fr two corps he visited[, the Second] near Dvinsk & the other[, the Third] outside Riga. He told me lots of comforting [things] & sad ones also of course—but the spirits prime over everything. The same I hear from Georgi, Mordvinov and fat Kakhovsky who accompany him. They are still waiting for the first opportunity of going to other troops further north. Misha< has wired to ask if he may come for the end of the week, I am very pleased to see him here. Well, my precious Love-bird, I must end. God bless you and the children. Me loves you so & prays for you fervently daily. I send two telegrams fr. our friend's< [sic]—so his son has been taken![154] Bless you & kiss you tenderly. Ever your own Nicky. [b]

---

154. See Footnote 134 concerning the draft of Rasputin's son, Dmitry. Rasputin wired Vyrubova: "Have suddenly received a telegram that my son is called up. I say in wrath—is it possible that I am Abraham?" Few Russians were as optimistic about the war as the tsar was at this point. "The number of men who reported 'sick' was enormous. Any excuse was good enough to get away from the front. They said there was no good in their fighting, as they were always beaten." (Vulliamy, p. 86, citing Knox, *With the Russian Army*, p. 350.)

No. 454/ Telegram 77. Tsarskoe Selo> Stavka. 10 Sept 1915. 1.40> 2.26 p.m. To his majesty. Glorious, absolutely mild, sunny day. [We] are going to Peterhof hospital, first time this year. Will see our favorite sea and think of you there even more than usual. All embrace and kiss you, darling. Alix

---

No. 455/ Her No. 350.   Ts.[arskoe] S[elo]. Sept. 10th 1915.
My own Sweetheart,

Yes, indeed the news is better—I just looked through the papers. What a blessing if the reinforcements from the south can soon get to their destination; one prays & prays.—The article about Varnava in the papers is untrue, he gave exact answers to all questions & showed yr. telegram about the salutation. Last year the Synod had all the papers about the miracles & Sabler would not have the salutation this summer. Your will & order count, make them feel it. V.[arnava] implores you to hurry with clearing out Samarin as he & [the] Synod are intending to do more horrors & he has to go there again, poor man, to be tortured.[152] Goremykin also finds one must hasten (alas, no list from him yet).[151] One praises the redfaced Prutchenko too—only his brother and wife horrid about our Friend<. Gorem.< wants quickly to see you, & before any others when you return, but if you dont soon—he wants to go to you, he is ready to scream at the bishops, V. said & to send them off. You better send for the old Man [Goremykin].—As one wants a firm Government, instead of the old Man going; clear out the others and get strong ones in. Please, speak seriously about [A. N.] Khvostov as Minister of the Interior to Goremykin am sure he is the man for the moment, as fears nobody & is devoted to you. [a]

Again an ugly thing about N.[icholasha<] I am obliged to tell you. All the Barons sent to the Headquarters B.[aron] Reitern to N. He begged in all their names that these persecutions should cease, because they could not bear them any more. N. answered that he agreed with them, but could do nothing as the orders came from Tsarskoe Selo [i.e., from Alexandra]. Is not this too vile. S. Rebinder of the Artillery told it to Alia<—Reitern was astonished to see Suvorin being received by N. This must be cleared up, such a lie dare not lie upon you; they must be told that you are just to those that are loyal & never persecute the innocent. A man who wrote against N. was shut up for 8 months now, there they know how to stop the press, when it touches N.—When the prayers for you were being read those 3 fasting days, fr. the Synod, in front of the Kazan Cathedral, 1000 of portraits of N. were being devided [sic] out [among] of the crowds. What does that mean? They had intended quite another game, our Friend read their cards in time, & came to save you by entreating you to clear out N. & take over the Command yourself. One hears always more and more of their hideous, treacherous game. [b, c]

M.[ilitsa] & S.[tana]< spread horrors about me in Kiev & that I was going to be shut up in a Convent—the married daughter of one of the Trepovs was so hurt when they spoke, that she begged to leave the room. He wrote this to the Css. Shulenburg. Oh Lovy, Ivanov's army (some) heard these rumours—is not that a mean scandal? I see Dzhunkovsky has gone for an unfixed time to the Caucasus—there: "birds of one feather flock together" what new sin are they preparing? They better take care of their skin there. [d]

We, i.e. [daughter] Olga, Ressin<, A.[nia]< & I went to Peterhof—we left her [Anna Vyrubova] at her Parents [A. S. & Nadezhda Taneev] & drove on to the local hospital—clean this time & no very heavy wounded—then to the tiny red cross station near the English E.[mbassy], where there were a few officers—then to the new Bathhouse near the lake, where were also wounded—nothing very bad. Took a cup of coffee at the Taneyev's & came home. Then Tatiana Andreievna [Gromova] came to say goodbye, after wh. Mere Catherine & the Abbess, & talked without end. She brought a paper about flying machines wh. the inventor showed before at the Headquarters—it was approved & the papers now stick somewhere, so I enclose a paper about it & can you have the thing hurried up. There is a Rubinstein who has given 1000's already, who is willing to give 500.000 [rubles] for this [aircraft] invention being made, if he receives the same [honorary state service rank] as Manus—pretty these beggings at such a time, charity cant go unbought—so ugly.— [e]

Then Marie [Pavlovna] came and now I am writing & quite gaga—the road tired me in motor. The sea, my sea! Felt, oh, so sad, reminded me of happy peaceful times, our house without you—we passed it—pain in my heart & full of remembrances.—I received sweet letters [from Germany] from Ernie<, Onor< & Frl. Textor. He gave them [to] Sister [i.e., nurse] Baroness Uxkull who came [on a visit from Germany to Russia]—he hoped I would see & help her—yr. Mama [Maria Fedorovna] did not receive her & then I was not asked—a great mistake of hers. These Sisters could have told us about our Prisoners. Ernie thinks so much of you too—I enclose his letter.—Frl. Textor lives at W. to give the children German & English lessons. The heather blooms & it is lovely they say—I will show you his letter, when you come—asks for nothing only full of love. Yr. regiment has better luck than the [German] red Dragoons, who have only one officer not wounded. Moritz [Ridezel of Hesse] youngest son is slowly recovering fr. wounds. B.[aron] Ridezel (who was with Sandro< in Bulgaria—a dear) has lost 3 sons already.—Onors nephew has also been killed. [f]

The weather was divine to day. I was in the hospital this morning —another Crimean is coming.—Now must send off my letter, high time.—Every blessing & fondest, tenderest, warmest kisses & endless love fr. yr. own old   Sunny. [P.S.] Am glad you will see Misha<.—Have you a list of the losses in the guard? All are so anxious, the wives anxious about their husbands—cannot somebody copy them out & send them me.—Tell Fredericks that young Mme Baranov (he was just killed) is fearfully poor, you kept him in the regiment by paying him, now she looses [sic] that & Shulgin begged me whether something could be done for her, as he was such a good officer. Mme Lutke [sends] thanks for the flowers I had sent from us both.—Maria Plautin thanks colossaly. [g]

No. 456/ Telegram 69. Stavka> Tsarskoe Selo. 10 Sept 1915. 6.53> 7.35 p.m. To her majesty. Loving thanks for dear letters [from] the girls< and Aleksei<, also [for] telegram. Glad you went to Peterhof. Hope feel none the worse [for the trip]. [Here it is] also fine and warmer. Tender kisses to all. Niki

No. 457/ Telegram 80. Tsarskoe Selo> Stavka. 11 Sept 1915. 11.30 a.m.> 12.08 p.m. To his majesty. Clear but very fresh. Laid down in the morning as I felt tired from automobile trip and visits to three Peterhof hospitals. [We] embrace and tenderly kiss you. If you do not return, they [the ministers] will go to old man [Goremykin, for a conference]. Alix

No. 458/ Telegram 84. Tsarskoe Selo> Stavka. 11 Sept 1915. 5.57> 7.20 p.m. To his majesty. [Daughter] Tatiana and I warmly thank for dear letters—we were very much gladdened by them. Please summon old man [Goremykin] on Sunday. It is extremely necessary for him to see you more quickly. Wonderful sunny weather. [They] are driving. [We] embrace and kiss [you]. Is it possible for me to receive a list of those lost in the guard? Alix

No. 459/ Telegram 72. Stavka> Tsarskoe Selo. 11 Sept 1915. 7.41> 8.25 p.m. To her majesty. Many thanks for dear letter, and [daughter] Tatiana's. Again fine [and] warm. Misha< just arrived, looking well. Saw some troops today. [I] am writing. Tender kisses to [all]. Thank her [Anna Vyrubova] for image [icon]. Niki

No. 460/ Her No. 354.   Tsarskoe Selo. Sept. 11th 1915.
My own beloved Darling,
It was so grey, that I felt quite sad, but now the sun is trying to pierce its way through the clouds. The colouring of the trees is so lovely now, many have

turned yellow, red & copper. Sad to think summer is over & endless winter awaits us soon. It was strange to see the beloved sea, but so dirty—pain filled my heart when I saw the [imperial yacht] Alexandrie from far & remembered with what joy we always saw her, knowing that she was the means for taking us to our beloved "Standart" [a larger imperial yacht] & fiords! Now all but a dream. [a]

What are the Bulgarians up to, why is Sazonov such a pancake [i.e., so wishy-washy]? It seems to me that the people want to side with us & only the Minister & rotten Ferdinand [tsar of Bulgaria] mobilize to join the other countrys [Germany, Austria-Hungary and Turkey] so as to squash Servia & throw themselves greedily upon Greece. Get rid of our Minister at Buccarest [sic] & the Rumaniens [sic] cld. be got to march with us, I am sure.—Is it true that they intend sending [N. I.] Guchkov & some others from Moscou [sic] as a deputation to you? A strong railwayaccident in wh. he alone wld. suffer wld. be a real punishment fr. God & well deserved, they go too far, & that fool Shcherbatov gained nothing by only blotching out parts of what they said—indeed a rotten government—wh. wont work with, but against its leader. [b]

I am remaining in bed till luncheon, the motordrive shook me too much & I am tired from seeing hospitals three days running.—Do so much wonder when you will be able to return & for how many days—how you have arranged with Al.[ekseev], when you leave?— The old man [Goremykin] has asked to see me this evening, & as I know he must see you, I have already wired to you. He finds it absolutely indispensable S.[azonov] should at once leave, he told it to Andr.<—another man they propose is Makarov, but that won't do, as he did not show himself at all well in the story of Hermogen.[155a] Now another is the editor of the "Government Bulletin[,]" Marshal of the Horse, Prince [S. P.] Urussov an other man, very loyal to you, religious (made our Friend's< acquaintance)—that would be best I think & at once. I write all this for you to have it clearly in yr. head—now I suppose he may bring yet candidates. The story of V.[arnava] is going too far—he did not go again to the Synod, because he will not hear yr. orders mocked at[152]—the Metropolitan [Vladimir or Flavian?] calls yr. telegram [a] "foolish telegram"—such impertinence cannot be borne—you must set yr. broom working & clear out the dirts that has accumulated at the Synod.—All this row about V. is only so as to drag our Friend's name into the Duma. When S.[amarin] accepted this place he told his set at M.[oscow] that he takes it only because he intends to get rid of Gr.< & that he will do all in his power to succeed.—One betted in the Duma, that they would prevent you fr. going to the war.—you did go—they said nobody dare close the Duma—you did—now they have betted that you cannot send S. away—& you will. [c, d]

The Bishops too, that sat there & mocked at yr. orders—you have not had time no doubt to read the articles about the accusation against V.[arnava] at the Synod about the worship. You show yourself the master. We cleared S. Iv. [Tyutcheva] out & her friends shall flie too & with this ridiculous, unloyal, mad idea of saving Russia. Lots of grand words. Goremykin must tell him, that you chose him believing him to be a man, who would work for you & the Church & he has turned out a spy upon the doings & telegr.: of V.[arnava] & Gr. & has posed as an accusing advocate & persecutor—& doubter of your wishes & orders. You are the head & protector of the Church & he tries to undermine you in the eyes of the Church. At once my Love, clear him out & Shcherbatov too. This night he [Shcherbatov] sent out a circular to all the papers, that they may print anything they like against the Governement (your governement)—how dare he—only not against you. But they do all in a hidden way, des sousentendu [between the lines]—and he plays fast & loose a very fool indeed.— [e]

Please take [A. N.] Khvostov in his place. Did you look through his book? He wants very much to see me, looks upon me as the one to save the situation whilst you are away (told it Andr.<) & wants to pour out his heart to me & tell me all his ideas.—He is very energetic, fears no one & is colossally devoted to you, wh. is the chief thing now a days.—His gaffes, one can warn him against making them—he knows the Duma people well, will not allow them to attack one, he knows how to speak; please Sweetheart seriously think of him, he is no such a coward & rag as Shch.[erbatov]. The Government must be set to right & the old man [Goremykin] needs good, devoted & energetic men to help him in his old age working; he cannot go on like this. [f]

You must tell him all, ask everything—he is too discreet & generally waits to be asked & then says his impressions or what he knows. Keep him up, show him you need & trust him & will give him new workers—& God will bless the work.—Take a slip of paper & note down what to talk over, last time you forgot about [A. N.] Khvostov, & then let the old man have it as a help to remember all questions.—1) Samarin, 2) Shcherbatov-Synod, 3) Sazonov, 4) Krivoshein who is an underhand enemy & false to the old man the whole time.—5) How to let the Barons know that it was a great untruth N.[icholasha<] told them, that he got the orders from Tsarskoe to persecute the Barons—that must be cleared up cleverly, delicately.—The old man begs always you should hasten & be decisive; when you give him categoric answers or orders to fulfil its far easier for him & they are forced to listen.— [g]

I do bother you, poor wee one, but they come to me & I cant do otherwise for your sake, Baby's< & Russias. Being out there, your mind can see all clearly & calmly—I am too calm & firm, only when changes must be made to save further horrors & filth, as that at the Synod headed by the soi disant [so-called] "gentleman" Samarin—then I get wild & beg you to hasten. He dare not treat your words like dust, none of the Ministers dare behave as they do after the way you spoke to them. I told you S.[amarin] is stupid insolent fellow—remember how impertinently he behaved to me at Peterhof last summer about the evacuation question & his opinion of Petersburg in comparison to Moscou [sic] etc., he had no right to speak to his Empress as he did—had he wished my good, he would have done all in his power for me, to take it as I wished, & he would have guided & helped me & it would have been a big & popular thing—but I felt his antagonism—as S. I. [Tyutcheva]'s friend; & that why he was proposed to you, & not for the Churches good.— [h]

I am inconvenient to such types, because I am energetic & stick to my friends wherever they may be. When the Duma closed, in a private sitting there, they said filth about Gregory[,] Ania< & her poor father [A. S. Taneev]—so loathsome. Is that devotion, I ask you? Show yr. fist, chastisen [sic], be the master & lord, you are the Autocrat & they dare not forget it, when they do, as now, woe into them.—Over & over let me thank you for your very sweet & dear letter, I was overjoyed to receive it & devoured it up. How glad I am you get lots of nice telegrams.—Thats the proof & your recompense, God will bless you for it, you saved Russia & the throne by that action.—I wish you could have a real good talk with Shavelsky about all that has been & about our Friend—get him to tea a 2.—A.[nia] spoke to him once, but he had his ears filled with horrors & I am sure N.< continued thus. [i]

[Daughter] Olga thanks Mordvinov for his letter.—I fear Misha< will ask for his wife to get a title—she cant—she left two husbands already & he is yr. only Brother,[82] Paul< is of no consequence. —Why is Boris< still with you, he ought to be back with his regiment, not so? Gr. wrote despairing wires about his son & begged him to be taken into the United Regiment wh. we said was impossible, A.[nia] begged Voeikov to do something, as he promised to before & he answered he could not. I understand the boy had to be called in, but he might have got him to a train as sanitary or anything—he always had to do with his hous[e] in the country, an only son, its awfully hard of course. One longs to help without harming Father or Son.—What lovely telegrams he wrote again. [j]

I had old Rauchfuss—we have got masses of cribs in these three last months all over Russia for our Society for Mothers & Babies —its a great joy to me to see how all have taken it to so quickly & have realised [sic] the gravity of the question, now especially every Baby must be cared for, as the losses are so heavy at the war. One says the guard has again lost colossally now.—We drove to Pavlovsk, lovely air & so sunny, the beautiful Cossacks with St. George's Crosses follow one.—Now I must end, Sunshine my beloved One. I long for you, kiss you without end, hold you tightly clasped in my arms. God bless you & protect you, give you strength, health, courage, surety of your opinion, wisdom & peace. Ever Nicky mine yr. very own old Wify Alix. [P.S.] The Children's joy over your letters is intense, they are all well, thank God. [k]

155a. See Fuhrmann, *Rasputin*, pp. 81-84, 87, 90-92.

No. 461.   Mogilev. Sept. 11th 1915.
My precious Sunny,

Bless you for your dear letters! I often read over and then it seems to me that you are lying on your sofa & that I am listening to you, in my armchair near the lamp. When will that happy moment come? God will[ing,] if the affairs near Dvinsk improve & the positions of our troops become stronger there[,] perhaps I will find the possibility of flying off to Ts.[arskoe] S[elo]. Because there is work to be done—those changes of ministers, & the strengthening of the old man's [Goremykin's] position. I will make him come here—not to lose time! Old Fred.< understands this perfectly and he urges me to stick up for Gor.<, wh is very good of him. I have explained all this to V.[oeikov] too, during our walks he seems to grasp it rightly at last! This morning V. told me about a ridiculous slukh [rumor] here in town [Mogilev], as if a german cavalry patrol had been seen somewhere near Orsha (90 versts from here). So at once gendarmes were sent into all directions— and a bit of the convoy. Till now of course one has seen [not even] a rat. It is all so stupid and it makes me laugh quite sincerely. [a, b]

When I motored this afternoon, I stopped to see a field battery wh arrived from afar to protect this town from aeroplanes. This I understand. It gave me great pleasure to see the off[icers] & men & horses, who look so well & healthy. 17 men were decorated. As I drove on I met a large body of men marching towards the town. I stopped & got out—& saw them pass. It was the 2nd Battalion of the Vladivostok Garrison Artillery; coming from Brest-Litovsk, marching exactly one month on the High road & going up north to Orsha. The men looked in very fine condition, they had a few sick lying in carts whom they leave in hospitals as they go on. Just now Misha< turned up. He sits in my room & reads papers. He asked to remain a little while on. Two of his regiments made a fine attack yesterday & took 23 officers & over 400 prisoners—all Hungarians. You ask me about going to Novgorod—certainly, go now without me, as probably I wont have time when I am back home. I must not think of leaving here before the 15th-20th. Now, my love bird, I have to end, me love[s] you passionately with an ever lasting love. 1000 thanks for your dear [Letter] No. 350, wh just came. God bless you and the children. I kiss you all very tenderly. Ever, my darling Sunny, your old Nicky. [c, d]

No. 462/ Telegram 89. Tsarskoe Selo> Stavka. 12 Sept 1915. 10.04> 10.46 a.m. To his majesty. Heavy rain. Saw old man [Goremykin]. He cannot arrive [at Stavka] earlier than Tuesday. I wish you were here if only for three days to put everything in order. They [dissident ministers] continue to act in an impossible way, and this must be brought to an end. [I] have not gone out because I feel completely tired out. [I] bless and warmly kiss [you]. Together in thoughts. Hearty greetings to Mistchenko<. Alix

---

No. 463/ Her No. 352.   Tsarskoe Selo. Sept. 12th 1915.
My own beloved One,
   It is pouring and dreary. Slept very badly, head aches rather, am still tired from [my trip to] Peterhof & feel my heart, am awaiting Becker<.—How I wish the time would come for me to write only simple, nice letters, instead of bothersome ones. But things dont at all go as they should, & the old Man [Goremykin] who came to me yesterday evening, was very sad. He longs for you to come quickly, if only for three days, to see all & to make the changes, as he finds it more than difficult working with ministers who make opposition. Things must be put clearly—either he leaves, or he remains & the ministers are changed, wh. of course would be best. He is going to send you a report about the press—they go after orders N.[icholasha]< gave in July, that one may write whatsoever one likes about the government, only not touch you. When Goremykin complains to Shch[erbatov] he throws the blame on Polivanov & vica versa. Shch. lied to you when he said one would not print what is said at Moscou [sic].—They go on writing everything. Am so glad you declined seeing those creatures. They don't dare use the word constitution, but they go sneeking [sic] round it— verily it would be the ruin of Russia & against your coronation oath it seems to me,[155b] as you are a autocrat, thank God.—The changes must be made, cant think why the old Man is against [A. N.] Khvostov [as the new minister of the interior]—his Uncle [A. A. Khvostov] does not much care for him & they say he is a man who

thinks he knows everything.[117] But I explained to the old Man that we need a decided caracter [sic], one who is not afraid, he is in the Duma, so has the advantage of knowing everybody & will understand how to speak to them & how to protect & defend your government. He proposes nobody, au fond, & we need a "man".— [a, b]

He [Goremykin] begged me to let Varnava know that he must not appear at the Synod but say he is ill—wh. is the best thing, tho' the papers are furious that he wont appear.[152] But he has told them all & answered everything—great brutes, I cannot call them otherwise. If you could only come, then at once see the Metropolitan [Vladimir] & tell him you forbid that subject [the canonization of John Maximovich] to be touched & that you insist upon your instructions being fulfilled. He [Varnava] cried of despair when Samarin was appointed & now he is completely in his hands—but he must have a strong word from you. Yr. arrival here will be a punitive expedition & no rest, poor Sweetheart, but its necessary without delay, they go on writing without ceasing. But they cant propose anybody—Makarov—no good—[V. S.] Arseniev fr. M.[oscou] screams against our Fr.[iend]<—Rogozin [Rogovich]— hates our friend.—Prince [Yu. D.] Urussov (don't know him)—knows our friend, one says much good of him. My head aches from hunting for men [to serve as the new director of the Holy Synod], but anybody rather than Samarin, who openly goes against you by his behaviour in the Synod. [c, d]

Can you really not return soon, Lovy, things seem taking a better turn, thank God & will still. Wonder what troops you saw pass. Old man has a sitting of Ministers on Sunday, thats why he cant leave to-day. If you come Thursday, he says he need not go there before, but I find you can see him quieter now & speak over & prepare all for yr. return. He says Sazonov is pitiful to behold, like "une poule mouillee" [a wet hen]—what has happened to him? He tells Goremykin nothing at all & he must know what is going on. The ministers are rotten & Krivoshein goes on working underhand he says—all so ugly & ungentlemanly;—they need your iron will wh. you will show, won't you. You see the effect of yr. having taken over all, well do the same here, i.e. be decided, reprimand them very severely for their behaviour & for not having listened to yr. orders given at that sitting here—I am more than disgusted with those cowards.— [e, f]

Can Aleks.[eev] spare you 3 days, soon? Do answer this if you can. You cannot imagine how despairing it is not being able to wire all one would & needs too & not to get an answer. You have not time to answer my questions of wh. there are 1000, but always the same ones, as they are pressing & my head is weary from thinking & seeing things so badly—& beginning to spread in the country. Those types go talking against the government everywhere, etc. & sow the seed of discontent. Before the Duma meets in a month, a new strong cabinet must be formed & quicker, so as that they have time to work & prepare together beforehand.—He [Goremykin] proposed I should see Samarin but what good? The man will never listen to me, & just do the contrary out of opposition & anger—I know him also but too well by his behaviour now, —wh. did not surprise me, as I know he would be thus.—Goremykin wants you to return & do all this, but waste no time. You are calm out there, & that is right, but still Sweetest, remember you are a bit slow too in deciding & dawdling is never a good thing.

The big girls< have gone to the hospital, the 3 young ones [Maria, Anastasia, Aleksei] are learning, A.[nia]< is going to town to Alia< & her mother [Madame Taneeva] till 3, & I shall lie again till luncheon as heart a little enlarged & feel so tired.—Now Yuzik< must be already at the Headquarters. Is it true that we are only 200 versts from Lemberg again? Are we to hurry on so much & not come round and squash the Germans? What about Bulgaria? To have them in our flank will be more than rotten, but they have surely bought Ferdinand [I, tsar of Bulgaria].—[g, h]

How is Misha's< humour? Kiss the dear boy from me. Have no news yet from Olga [your sister,] somehow her visit was sad—we scarcely got a glimpse of her & she left sad & anxious.—Just received a perfumed letter fr. Olga Palei. [Her husband] Paul< is better—she at last had news fr. their boy, [Prince Paley,] it took him a week to get to the transport of his regiment & now he hopes to find the regiment.—I believe the lancers are not far fr. Baranovichi; a river one speaks of near there, where was heavy fighting—what fighting everywhere! [i]

Mackensen is not the one we knew. There is a Furst Bentheim at Irkutsk (a sort of relation of Marie Erbachs). Ernie< asks in Max< name whether there would be any possibility for him to be exchanged—he seems to be the last of his family—perhaps somebody of ours cld. be returned in exchange. He only asks like that, not knowing whether its possible. I shall let Rost.[ovtsev] know the same thing,—I doubt it being possible unless he gives his word of honour not to fight any more against any of the allies—only under that condition, I find, one can change him. I shall write this to Rost.< & whom it concerns will know what to do, I have no idea whom one can ask for in return, nor whether its al-lowed.—About the gases E.[rnie] is also disgusted, but he says that when he was near Reims beginning of Sept. last year, the English used the gasses there—& German chemical industries being better, they made worse gasses.—A.< was at the Church of "Joy to all grieving" in town & brought this little Image [icon] for you.—[j]

Fancy our surprise—suddenly Kusov< turned up. All his cavalry is being sent down to Dvinsk & during their move he flew off here, arrived in town< this morning, probably goes on to-morrow, meets his wife & off to Dvinsk to meet his regiment. He had heavy losses —is in despair with Yuri Trubetskoi who makes fault upon fault & others dare not say anything, because one says you particularly care for him (wh. K.[usov] doubts). Thanks to him K.'s men got surrounded, because Yury took the three battalions of infantry away wh. guarded them, for himself—but they got through & only many horses were taken, as it was the place where they were standing together—he told his mind rather clearly to Trubetskoi. He came flying off to know how things were going, as letters never reached him & he wanted to hear all. Is already disgusted with town & furious with the "rotten atmosphere". Was sorry you sent Mikheyev [Mikheev], because he is so very unrepresentive [sic] & does not know how to collect all round him & speak & thank in yr. name.—He saw the Kabardintsi passing a little while ago. Asked questions without end & says the "spirit" in the army splendid. It does one good & refreshes one seeing such a man straight from there—one also gets musty fusty [despondent] here, tho' I fully trust & be-lieve all must go well, if God will give us the necessary wisdom & energy. Don't you find Baby's writing is getting very nice & tidy? I remained quietly at home to-day, saw Mme Zizi< too.—Why is Boris< not with his regiment? 3 of our Cav. divisions got the order to break through the Germans wh. they did & are in their rear now, [our daughter] Tatiana's regiment is there too.— Blessings & kisses without end & tenderest love, Sweetheart, lovy mine, fr. yr. very own old Wify. [k]

155b. Richard Pipes notes that Nicholas "convinced himself (or perhaps was convinced by his wife) that on the day of his coronation in 1896 he had sworn to uphold autocracy. In fact, he did nothing of the kind." The ceremony made no reference to Russia's form of government, the word "autocracy" (*samoderzhavie*) did not even appear. "But Nicholas believed otherwise and said on many occasions that giving up the authority to name the cabinet would have violated his oath of office." (Pipes, *Russian Revolution*, p. 227.)

No. 464/ Telegram 79. Stavka> Tsarskoe Selo. 12 Sept 1915. 9.30> 9.40 p.m. To her majesty. My very tenderest thanks for dear letter.Old man [Goremykin] wired will arrive Monday; wrote to him strengthening letter. Impossible for me to come before a week. Lovely summer weather. Thoughts ever together, kisses. Nicky.

No. 465/ Telegram 102. Tsarskoe Selo> Stavka. 13 Sept 1915. 7.57> 9.20 p.m. To his majesty. Drab, dull day. Now going with Aleksei to church. All are healthy. Still feel total weariness. [I] bless and warmly kiss [you]. Sleep peacefully. Greetings from all. Alix.

No. 466/ Her No. 353.   Tsarskoe Selo. Sept. 13th 1915.
My very own Treasure,
    I am glad you have fine weather, here it is real autumn, there was a little sun an hour ago & now there is again a grey haze.—The 4 Girls have gone to early Church—"Engineer Mechanic"< came, so [it] keeps me company. So you cannot come before the end of the week, I feared so, as things are still very serious near Dvinsk—but how brave both sides are—God help & strengthen our dear troops. —The papers continue aggravating me, discussing & groaning that there will be a censure—& that [the press] ought to have been regulised [deregulated?] months ago.—There is a messenger leaving for England this afternoon, so I must quickly profit to write to Victoria—this I will finish later in the day, as usual.— [a]
    Sazonov says it concerns Aleks.[eev] the exchange of prisoners, so I don't know what to do about Furst Bentheim [see Letter No. 363j], I cannot ask for a German (and I believe not wounded or long ago well by now)—whom could one exchange him with?—I am glad you wrote a good letter to the old Man [Goremykin], it will help him in his difficult task.—3 weeks to-day that you arrived at the Headquarters—when is N.[icholasha<] going to Tiflis? To-day it is put in the papers that Dzhunkovsky is going to the Army & not any more under Alekseev's orders for Sanitary questions. Sweet Manny mine—am always in thoughts with you, yearning to see what you look & feel like; I have no doubt much better than when you were here. I told you about Y. Trubetskoi yesterday, so as that one should have an eye upon him, if he really is so very little famous & confuses them all. Am I meddling? I don't mean to, I only repeat what Kussov< said, as I

know he tells me things in the hope I give all over. What news fr. the Black Sea & Baltic? [b, c]

I spent the afternoon on my sopha in the corner of my big room and A.[nia]< read to me, tea we had at 4 & then the 5 Children went to A. for an hour to see some Children. I have crawled into bed, so as to go to church, service to-day is from 6-8, & I shall go at about 7, more I have not the strength for, as cannot take drops & feel tired, but to-day the heart was not enlarged. A dreary day.—In Moscou [sic] Mme Gard. [i.e., Valentina Gordeeva] finds the things better than they expected, Petrograd she finds horrid just now & I think all agree.—I gave Zizi< papers about John Maximovich & how they found his tomb, and she was grateful & emotioned as it showed her all in quite another light, & now I made A. send it to o.[tets, i.e., Father] Alex.[ander Vasil'ev, the royal family's chaplin]—I want others to understand the thing & the wrong behaviour of the Synod. If they choose to find you had not the right to give such an order, nevertheless, all the more they ought to have stood up for it, legalised [sic] it still from their side, instead of purposely going against your orders—& all that simply out of opposition & to harm Varnava & throw again a bad light on our Friend<.— [d]

My letter is dull, I have seen nobody interesting.—A. is going over to [stay at] the big Palace< for a week, so as to have her rooms cleaned, the shaky plafond [ceiling] seen to and windows arranged for winter. Danini is going to see it! She can meanwhile go through a cure of electrifying & strong light wh. we have next door in the hospital and Vl. Nik.< will do it, & her Fedosia Stepanovna works there too & does massage for the wounded officers.—I enclose a letter fr. [daughter] Olga, & am sending you flowers again—the frezia last very long & every bud will open in your vase.—The leaves are turning very yellow & red, I see it from the windows of my big room.—Sweetheart, you never give me an answer about Dmitri<, why you dont send him back to his regiment, as [his father] Paul< had hoped;—he worrys [sic] so about the boy wasting his best years & at such a grave moment, doing nothing. It does not look well, no Granddukes are out, only Boris< from time to time, the poor Constantin[e']s boys always ill.—I do so hope to get your letter before closing this, so I will rest & then finish it up.—Well I must send it off. I kiss & bless you over & over again, my very own beloved Treasure, Sunshine. I cover you with tender kisses—God bless & keep you. A tender kiss fr. yr. very own old Wify. [f]

No. 467/ Telegram 87. Stavka> Tsarskoe Selo. 13-14 Sept 1915. 10.31 p.m.> 12.10 a.m. To her majesty. Loving thanks [for] dear letter and telegram, also to [our children] Anastasia and Aleksei. Divine warm weather. Was twice in church. News better. Cannot find out yet Exactly about losses. Told Boris< to let me know. He is now returning. Good night. Tender kisses. Niki

---

No. 468/ Telegram 105. Tsarskoe Selo> Stavka. 14 Sept 1915. 10.20> 11.35 a.m. To his majesty. Tenderly thank you for dear telegram which I read this morning since it arrived when I was already in bed [last night]. Thanks be to God—news is better. Cold here, only 34 degrees. [We] warmly embrace and kiss

[you]. Always together in thoughts. Still feel total weariness. Paul< greets you.
Alix

No. 469/ Her. No. 354.   Tsarskoe Selo. Sept. 14th 1915.
My own beloved Darling,
   I found your dear telegram this morning upon getting up, I was so grateful as
had been anxious getting no news all day. Being very tired I went to bed at
11.20[−]yr. wire left the Headquarters at 10.31 & reached here 12.10. Thank
God the news is better. But what will you do for the army, so as not to have
Alekseev the only responsible one? Do you get Ivanov to come here [i.e., to
Stavka] & [Gen. D. G.] Shcherbachev to replace him out there? You will be
calmer & Alekseev wont have to carry the responsibility all alone.—So after all
you have to move [Stavka] to Kaluga—what a nuisance, tho' from here I should
say the distance is less than now, only you are so far from the troops. But if
Ivanov helps Alekseev then you could go straight from here to see some troops
at least. [a]
   What has been going on at sea, I know nothing & read this morning of the
losses of the Captain of the 1-st rank, S. S. Vyazemsky (heroic death in battle) &
the officers & men of the ship announce it, & his body is brought from the
Baltik [sic] Station. Then Capt. of the 2-nd rank, Vl. Al. Svinin also fell as a
hero. What does this mean? Peter Vasil'evich< told the Children some days ago
that the Novik had been in battle, but as one keeps the naval news out of the
papers, one feels anxious to know what it means. When you are not here of
course I only get my news in the morning out of the "Novoye Vremya". If there
should be anything good, do wire it, as one hears often false news wh. of course
I tell all not to believe. [b]
   How is Voeikov<, I cannot forget his madness here and horrid behaviour to
A.[nia]<. Do take care that he does not take things too much in hand there &
does not meddle, as poor old Fred.< is old and, alas, becoming rather foolish, the
other with his dominating spirit & being most ambitious & sure of himself, &
try to fulfill functions wh. don't concern him. Don't you need somebody else
still because of the foreigners, or deputations, or orders to be given over, wh.
you have not the time to do yourself—a General aide de camp or something like
that?—Have you got rid of useless people there? I am glad Boris< has gone back
again.—I hope he can get the lists of the losses as the wives are in all states.—One
says Leichtenberg [N. N. Lichtenberg] is wounded, I forget what regiment he
commands but its the Preobr. ladies especially who are nervous.—I wonder what
troops you saw the other day.—Now the old Man [Goremykin] is with you. Its
stupid one prints when he comes to me, thats fr. town<, my people don't know it
even, as people get angry I mix in—but its my duty to help you. Even in that I
am found fault with, sweet Ministers & society, who criticise [sic] all, & themselves are occupied with things not concerning them at all. Such is the unedify-
ing world.—Still I am sure you hear far less gossip at the Headquarters & I thank
God for it.—Church began at 6-8 yesterday, Baby< & I came at 7¼. [c, d]
   Slept badly, am tired & my head rather aches, so keep in bed till luncheon.
Paul's< asked to come for tea. Oh my sweet One, thanks & thanks ever so tenderly for yr. sweet letter of the 11-th, I received it with intensest gratitude & joy.

It has been kissed over and over again & reread any amount of times. Yes indeed, when will that happy moment arrive, when we shall be cosily [sic] seated together in my mauve room![267] We continue drinking tea in the big room, tho' by the time Paul left at 6½, it was already quite dark. [e]

Yes, the changes of ministers. In the train Kussov< went with Shcherbatov< & he called the old man "crazy old man"[−]thats going far; some in the Duma want Shcherbatov in Goremykin's place, & I understand them because they could do whatsoever they like with him. Paul was disgusted with the goings on at Moscou [sic] & the deputation that wished to present themselves to you!− For the old woman's letter, warmest thanks−it pleased me very much & I read it aloud to A.−P.< does not care for Mrozovsky, said he is such a cad, he remembers him fr. his service−I remember he screamed at the Guard's Convoys once, because a man cld. not say the words of the anthem by heart; the poor Grenadier divisions were so very little famous at the war now. Is it true Kuropatkin, got it, or are those gossips? Wonder how he will show himself this time−God grant alright−being in a lower position it may go better. [f]

P. asked why N.< is still in the Country & whether it was true you wrote he was to rest in the Caucasus, at Borjom−I said yes, & that you had allowed him 10 days at Pershino. Lovy order him south quicker, all sorts of bad elements are collecting round him & want to use him as their flag (God wont permit it) but safer he should be quicker in the Caucasus, & you said 10 days and to-morrow its 3 weeks he left the Headquarters.−Be firm in that too, please. I am so glad, that P. has realised [sic] the game N. was to play−he rages about the way N.'s a.d.c. speak.−I am glad you made V.[oeikov] understand things−he is so obstinate & selfsure & a friend of Shcherbatov's.−How happy I am you saw some artillery−what a recompense to them.−Keep Misha< with you still, do.−P. again repeated, that he hopes very earnestly that you will send D.[mitry]< to his regiment, he finds the life he now leads [to] his ruin, as he has absolutely nothing to do & wastes his time, wh. is perfectly true.−If ever you get news of the hussars, do let me know, as Paul is anxious, his boy [Prince Paley] being now in the regiment. Paul is now well, but very weak, pale & thin.−Old Aunt Sasha I. [Naryshkina] has come to town & will take tea with us on Wednesday, Xenia & Sandro lunch that day with us too. The news to-day about our allies is splendid, if true−thank goodness if they are beginning to work now, it was hard time. And to have taken 24 artillery & made thousands of prisoners, but thats quite beautiful!− [g, h]

I do find it so wrong, that the Ministers do not keep to themselves all the discussions, wh. go on in the Council of Ministers. Once questions are decided, its early enough to know about them. But our uneducated, tho' they imagine themselves intellectual public, read up everything, only grasp a quarter & then set to discussing all, & the papers find fault with everything−hang them! Miechen< wrote to ask again about Plotho [Ploto, see Letters Nos. 435g,h and 444a], whether anything can be done.−I do thoroughly bore you.−In sweet Petrograd one said you were here some days−now−that Gr.[egory Rasputin] is at the Headquarters,−they are really becoming always more cretinised<, & I pitty [sic] you when you return. But we shall be wild with joy to have you back again, if ever so short−just to hear your precious voice, see yr. sweet face & hold you long, long in my yearning arms.—My head and eyes ache, so I cant write any more now. Goodbye, Sweetheart, Nicky love. God bless & protect you & keep you fr. all harm. I cover you with kisses. Ever yr. very own old wify Alix. [i, j]

I feel quite sad without our hospital, where I have not been since Thursday.—A. has gone over to the big palace<.—Lovy, are you sending people of your suite to the fabrics [factories]? Please don't forget it.—My "Alexandrovtsi"< are near Dvinsk & have rather heavy losses amongst the men.—The Children all kiss you, Marie is overjoyed with your letter.—Yuzik never went to the Headquarters, the children imagined it.—I like the story about the hunt for the germans near Orsha; our cossacks would have found them fast enough. Are they aiming at Riga again? Lovy sweet, me wants you, oh so, so much, precious Darling. Your letters & telegrams are my life now.—Kiss dear Misha<, Dmitri<. My love to the old Man [Fredericks] & N.P.< Think over about Ivanov sweet one—I think you would feel calm—or if he were with Alekseev at the Headquarters & then you would be free to move about—& when you remain longer at the Headquarters he could go round inspecting all & give you news how things are going & have an eye on all, & his presence would be good everywhere.—Sleep well, I bless & kiss you! [k, l]

No. 470.   Mogilev. Sept. 14th 1915.
My beloved darling Sunny,

Foundest thanks for your dear letters wh are always a source of joy and comfort for me. The old man (Gor.<) has just arrived & I am going to see him at 6 o['clock]. Such a bore you are feeling tired after those busy days—but it had come especially before Mme B.< It is difficult yet to fix the date of my arrival home, because it is in connection with the day the Stavka is to be transferred to Kaluga; wh will take five or six days—so God grant, we may spend about a week together! What happiness! [a]

The story of the German patrols ended, as I thought [it would], in a ludicrous manner. It was our own patrol of 7 Cossacks, who took a wrong direction from one of the cavalry divisions far to the north of Minsk—they were looking for the german cavalry & got so far south as Mogilev. Stupid to have invented such a story! The weather continues to be lovely. I motor with Misha every day< & we spend most of my free time together—like in bygone years. He is so quite & nice—and sends you his best love. On the whole the affairs at the front are not bad. They continue pressing at the top [of our line]—Dvinsk and in the direction from Vilna to the east, also from Baranovichi. Very serious fighting is going on all these days at those places. Now my sweetest One, I must end. God bless you & the dear children. I will write next time to [daughter] Anastasia. With loving kisses to all. Ever your own Nicky. [b, c]

No. 471/ Telegram 97. Stavka> Tsarskoe Selo. 14 Sept 1915. 7.40> 8.54 p.m.
To her majesty. Tender thanks for telegram. Just saw old man [Goremykin]. Have decided to make all ministers come here. He asked for it. Have written. Weather warm. Sorry old Arsenev died. Please order Shcheglov to take back to library all the papers and letters which I allowed him [Arsen'ev] to use. Fondest kisses. Niki

No, 472/ Telegram 112. Tsarskoe Selo> Stavka. 14 Sept 1915. 10.30> 11.10 p.m. To his majesty. Heartily thank you for dear letter and telegram. Gave order concerning papers of Arsenev. All might quieten down and go well after you see them [the ministers]. Am in despair not to be with you. [I] bless and kiss [you]. Sleep peacefully, my dear. [Daughter] Marie heartily thanks [you] for letter. Baby< will now pray with me. He kisses you. Alix

No. 473/ Telegram 117. Tsarskoe Selo> Stavka. 15 Sept 1915. 3.40> 5.10 p.m. To his majesty. Cold, raining. Now session of my committee on matter of prisoners abroad. Feeling better. All my thoughts are with you. [I] bless and kiss [you]; my dear, don't forget to comb your hair with the little comb [from Rasputin, see Nos. 474c, 477]. Greetings to Misha< and Dmitry<. Alix

No. 474/ Her No. 355.   Tsarskoe Selo. Sept. 15th 1915.
My very own precious Darling,
   Grey and raining & quite cold. Am still not feeling famous & head continues aching rather—nevertheless I have a committee for our prisoners in Germany. A private society all over Russia now has begun the same thing, instigated by Suvorin, as he finds Pr. Galitzin [N. D. Golitsyn] does not work enough—I do not like the idea as its only so as to hinder me, instead of asking to become part of our society.—Not feeling well, I have been unable to go to old Arsenev's services but shall go either to-morrow evening to the funeral & service at Znamenia< or to the funeral there Thursday morning. I sent a cross of flowers from us both & wrote to poor little Nadinka [Arseneva] & sent expression of your sympathy to her brothers.—A bit of old history dies with him. I at once gave over yr. order about the papers & letters he had, wh. belonged to yr. library. To-day it was put in the papers about the naval losses & now I understand all. And how good the French & English at last began—& with success, may they continue thus—it is as they had promised in September. But what obstinate fighting on our side, despairing feeling that taking & retaking of places & positions several times running.—Its sad you will have to go to Kaluga, wh. is such a big town & yet further away—but I suppose on account of the railway line?—So strange you should have lived at different places & gone through so much there & that I do not know them & had no share on yr. life there.—Lovy, can one have an eye upon what is going on at Pershino not good rumours come from there.— [a, b]
   How I wish I had something interesting, cheery to tell you, instead of harping always on the same subject.—Remember to keep the Image [icon] in yr. hand again & several times to comb yr. hair with His comb before the sitting of the ministers. [See Nos. 473 and 477.] Oh how I shall think of you & pray for you more than ever then, Beloved One.—A.[nia]< sends you her love.—One says Theo Nirod has left the service so as to follow N.< I find he is taking far too big a suite of a.d.c. yr. g. ad. [adjutant-general] & [Fat] Orloff<—its not good coming with such a court & clique, & I very much dread they will try to continue making messes.—God grant only that nothing shld. succeed in the Caucasus, & the people show their devotion to you & allow no playing of a grand part—I fear Militsa< & her wickedness—but God will protect against evil. Well, the sitting went off allright, 10 people. I took [daughter] Olga to sit near me & then she

will get more accustomed to see people & hear what is going. She is a clever child, but does not use her brains enough. Before that I had Kussov< for an hour, because he would not go away without having seem me once more. Quite disgusted with town< & so pained by everything & that my name is always mentioned, as tho' I had cleared O.[rlov] & Dzh.[unkovsky] away because of our Fr.< etc. He began to have a constant eye upon the going on in the Caucasus, that they should not spoil everything there & to send people to find out fr. time to time to "feel the atmosphere"—he certainly, one sees, has a very bad opinion of them all. [c, d]

Shch.[erbatov] told him [Kusov] in the train that Goremykin is a decrepit old man (not "mad" as A.< said) & that he finds one must make concessions, wh. K.[usov] said to him would be most dangerous, as one gives a finger & the whole arm is cought [sic] hold of. People want Shch.[erbatov] instead of Gore-mykin, I understand them, as he is weak & one can do anything & he is like a weathercock, alas.—[P.C.] Benkendorff< let me know, that he is sending Gebel to Moscou [sic] on account of the demenagement [relocation]—that means yours I suppose. How sad, that you really have to go so far away & be near that rotten Moscou.—A. went to town to her Parents [A. S. and Nadezhda Taneev] till 5—she took Groten to Nat. Br. and back again, he enjoyed the change after the sick room.—Am so anxious, how it will be with the ministers—now you cant change them once they come there & its so essential, only you must get a look at the others first. Please remember [A. N.] Khvostov.—You know my committee will have to ask the government for big sums for our prisoners, we shall never have enough, & the number will be, alas, several millions—its most necessary, otherwise bad elements will profit & say we are not thinking of them, they are forgotten & many bad things can be inculcated into them, as amongst our pris-oners for sure there are rotten red [Bolshevik?] creatures. [e, f]

The organisation [sic] of the Union of Cities are also forming a society for the same thing, that makes 3—we must keep in contact with them. Do take every-thing in hand, so as to say afterwards that the government does nothing, & they everything, the same for the wounded & refugees—they turn up & help every-where—& their deligates [sic] need watching.—Now goodbye my love, I am tired & head & eyes ache.—Goodbye, dear Beloved, my own sweet husband, joy of my heart—I cover you with tender longing kisses.—Ever yr. very own old Wify. [P.S.] Please, give this other letter enclosed to Misha<. My love to old man [Fredericks] & N.P.< How are you contented with Vilna, & Dvinsk, & Barano-vichi,—are things going as you wish? Sleep well & feel my warm presence.—[g]

No. 475/ Telegram 104. Stavka> Tsarskoe Selo. 15 Sept 1915. 7.11> 7.58 p.m. To her majesty. Tender thanks for yours and [daughter] Olga's letters, also for delicious flowers and telegram. News good. Ideal weather. Glad you feel better. In thoughts together. Do not worry about my sitting [of ministers at Stavka] to-morrow. Shall give it them nicely. Loving kisses to all. Niki

---

No. 476/ Telegram 119. Tsarskoe Selo> Stavka. 15 Sept 1915. 8.30> 10.23 p.m. To his majesty. Deeply happy with dear letter, warmly thank you. Committee went well, I even decided to speak. Thick fog. We are dining in play-room. All kiss you. Sleep peacefully. Alix

---

No. 477/ Telegram 124. Tsarskoe Selo> Stavka. 16 Sept 1915. 3.10> 5.20 p.m. To his majesty. In prayers and thoughts with you. Going to place a candle. May God help you. Don't forget the comb [see Nos. 473 and 474c]. Clear, sunny. Xenia< and Sandro< wish that I were with you. [I] warmly kiss you. Alix

---

No. 478/ Her No. 356.   Tsarskoe Selo. Sept. 16th 1915.
My very own beloved Darling,

Ever such tender kisses & thanks for your treasure of a letter. Ah, how I love to hear fr. you, over & over I reread your letters & kiss them. Shall we really soon have you here—it seems to be too good to be true. It will then be four weeks we are separated—a rare thing in our lives, we have been such lucky creatures & therefore one feels the parting all the more. And now when times are so very hard & trying, I long quite particularly to be near you with my love & tenderness, to give you cheer & courage and to keep you up to being decided and energetic.—God help you my beloved One, to find the right issue to all the difficult questions—this is my constant earnest prayer. But I fully believe in our Friend's< words that the glory of your reign is coming, ever since you stuck to your decision, against everybody's wish—& we see the good result. Continue thus, full of energy & wisdom, feeling more sure of yourself & heeding less to the advice of others. Voeikov< did not rise in my opinion this summer, [though it is true] I thought him cleverer & less frightened. He has never been my weakness, but I appreciate his practical brain for simple affairs & orderliness. But he is too selfsure and that has always aggravated me & his mother in law [Madame Gedviga Fredericks]. All this must have been a good lesson to him, lets hope. Only he sticks too much to Shcherbatov<, who is a null—tho' he may be a nice man—but I fear that he & Samarin are one.—Heart & soul I shall be praying for you—may the committee go off well—they made me mad last time, & when I looked through the window I did not like their faces & I blessed you over & over again from far. God give you force, wisdom & power to impress them, & to make them realise [sic] how badly they have fulfilled your orders these three weeks. You are the master—& not Guchkov, Shcherbatov, Krivoshein, Nikolai III (as some dare call N.<) Rodzianko, Suvorin—they are nothing & you are all, anointed by God. [a, b]

I am too happy that Misha< is with you, thats why I had to write to him—your very own brother, its just his place, & the longer he stops with you, away from her bad influence[82] the better it is & you will get him to see things with your eyes. Do speak often about [your sister] Olga, when you are out together, don't let him think badly of her [for opposing his current, scandalous marriage]. As you have much to do, tell him simply to write for you to her to tell her what you are doing—that may break the ice between them. Say it naturally, as tho' you never imagined it could be otherwise. I hope he is at last nice with good Mord-vinov & does not cut that devoted, loving soul who tenderly loves him. [c]

I do so wonder, what the English wrote after you took over the command, I see no Engl. papers, so have no idea. They and the French really seem continuing to push forwards; thank goodness, that they at last could begin & let us hope it will draw some troops away from our side. After all its colossal what the Germans have to do, and one cannot but admire how well & systematically all is organised [sic]—did our "mashene" [war machine] work as well as theirs, wh. is of long training & preparation & had we the same amount of railways, war would for sure already have been over.   Our Generals are not well enough prepared—tho' many were at the Japanese war, & the Germans have had no war since ages. How much there is to learn from them, wh. is good & necessary for our nation and other things one can turn away from with horror. There was little news in the papers, and you wired last night that the news was good, so that means that we are firmly keeping them at bay.—There are 9 degr. this morning, and it is grey & rainy, not inviting weather.—Little Nadinka Arseneva is coming to me this morning—poor girl, she was so touched by my letter & yr. sympathy I expressed them all, that she begged me to see her, as none had written so kindly. Poor, foolish child, what will become of her & her brother with all their old nurses & governesses. Her Father was everything to her in life.—All my thoughts are with you, Sweetheart & those odious Ministers, whose opposition makes me rage—God help you to impress them with yr. firmness & knowledge of the situation & yr. great disapprouval [sic] of their behaviour—wh. at such a moment is nothing else but treacherous.   But personally I think you will be obliged to change Shch.[erbatov], S.[amarin] probably longnosed S.[azonov] & Kr.[ivoshein] too— they wont change & you cannot keep such types to fight against a new Duma. [d, e, f]

How one is tired of all these questions—the war is quite enough & all the misery it has brought & now one must think & work to set all to rights & see that nothing is wanted for the troops, wounded, cripples, families & refugees.—I shall anxiously await a telegram fr. you, tho' you wont be able to put much in it.—I am glad my long letters don't bore you & that you feel cosy [sic] reading them. I cannot not talk with you on paper at least, otherwise it would be too hard, this separation and all the rest wh. worries one.—Gr.< telegraphed that Suslik< shld. return & then made us understand that [A. N.] Khvostov wld. be good [as the new minister of the interior]. You remember, he went once to see him (I think by yr. wish) to N. Novgorod.[148]—I do so long for at last things to go smoother & let you feel you can quite give yourself up to the war & its interests.—How do you think about what I wrote of Ivanov as aid, so as that Al.[ekseev] wont carry all the responsability [sic] when you are off & on away, here or inspecting the troops, wh. I do wish you could soon do—en passant, without preparation [i.e., advance notice to the places inspected] by motor fr. a bigger place—nobody will watch 2 motors or 3 even & you could rejoice yr. heart & theirs.— [g, h]

Xenia< & Sandro< lunch, Aunt Sasha [Naryshkina] comes to tea & then, I think, I must go for the carrying out of the body of Arsenev as that not long & then to-morrow to the funeral at Znamenia<. I am so glad the flowers arrive fresh—they cheer up the room & they come out of my vases with all my love and tenderness.—I wonder, whether you asked Shcherbatov what he meant by telling you that nothing wld. be printed in the papers about the speeches at Moscou [sic], when they wrote whatsoever they wished. Coward that he is!— [i]

I am choosing photos I made, so as to have an album printed for Xmas (like A.[unt] Alex.'s<) for charity, & I think it will sell well, as the small albums with my photos sold at once here this summer —& in the Crimea.—Went for a drive to Pavlovsk with [two daughters] A.[nastasia], M.[arie] & An.[ia]<,—the weather was lovely, the sun shone & all glittered like gold, a real treat such weather. At first I placed candles before the Virgin's Image, & St. Nicolas [sic] at Znamenia and prayed fervently for you. Church was being cleaned up, palms being stood and blue carpets arranged for poor old Arseniev. Aunt Sasha took tea & chattered a lot & abused nobody, I could not keep her long as wanted to go with Olga to the funeral procession—of course because of the old woman we were late & they were just carrying him out, so we followed with Nadinka [Arseneva] till the street & he was put on the funeral car & then we came home, as I go to-morrow to the funeral. [M. P.] Stepanov,—Ella< had—Skariatin, her old brother was there, Balashov<; the 2 sons, Benk.<, Putyatin<, Nebolsin & 2 officers of the Naval corps.—Nadinka had been with me in the morning—talked a lot & did not cry, very caressing & grateful. She begs you whether she might remain on living in the little house with her poor brother, as they lived there so long with the Parents & their graves are at Tsarskoe [Selo].—Perhaps one might for the present at least, don't you think so? Ella wrote and wishes me to give over how much she thinks of you & with what love & constant prayers. I send you a paper of hers wh. read through & find out the truth about it, please—Voeikov< can do that, or still better from your new staff.—I don't need the paper again. [j, k]

How one longs to fly away together & forget all—one gets at times so weary—my spirit is good but so disgusted with all one says. I fear Gadon is playing a bad part at Elagin<, because one says the conversations there against our Friend< are awfull—old Mme Orloff had heard this—she knows ladies who go there. When you see poor Motherdear<, you must rather sharply tell her how pained you are, that she listens to slander & does not stop it, as it makes mischief, & others wld. be delighted, I am sure, to put her against me—people are so mean.—How I wish Misha< could be a help in that.—Precious one we met some of the cossacks riding at P.[avlovsk] & I loved them not only for themselves, but because they had seen & guarded you & been in battle.—Beloved, I must end. God Almighty bless & protect, guard & guide you now & ever. I kiss you with endless tenderless & fathomless love, ever yr. very own   Sunny.   [P.S.] Xenia< looks better, they told nothing interesting. So anxious how all went off [in your meeting with the ministers]. [l, m]

No. 479/ Telegram 115. Stavka> Tsarskoe Selo. 16 Sept 1915. 9.52> 10.22 p.m. To her majesty. Best thanks [for] dear wishes. Sitting went off well. Told them in the face strongly my opinion. Sorry had no time to write. Divine weather. News much better. [I] love you and kiss [you] tenderly. Niki

---

No. 480/ Telegram 132. Tsarskoe Selo> Stavka. 17 Sept 1915. 9.36> 11.35 a.m. To his majesty. Warmly thank you for yesterday's telegram. Lord will help. Thanks be to God, news is better. Bright sun. [We] are going to funeral. Iza< is having lunch—it is her name-day. Sunny [the empress herself] saw the

Tail<. Petia is taking tea with us. In tender thoughts and prayers always together.
All kiss [you]. Alix

No. 481/ Her No. 357.   Tsarskoe Selo. Sept. 17th 1915.
My very own beloved Darling,
    It was with a feeling of intense relief, that I got your dear telegram telling me
that the committee went off alright & that you strongly told them your opinion
into their faces. God recompense you for this my treasure. You cannot imagine
how hard it is not being with you, near you at such times, not knowing what is
being discussed, hearing such horrors here. Deary, [A. N.] Khvostov came to
Ania again & entreated to see me, so I shall to-day. From all he told her one sees
he thoroughly understands the situation & that with skill & cleverness, he thinks,
one can manage to set all to rights. He knows that his Uncle [A. A. Khvostov[117]]
& Goremykin are against him [being appointed minister of the interior], i.e. they
are afraid of him as he is very energetic. But he is above all devoted to you &
therefore offers his services to you, to try him & see whether he cannot help. He
esteems the old man [Goremykin] very much & would not go against him. Once
already now he stopped the question in the Duma about our Friend< in time[152]
—now they intend bringing it up as one of the first questions. S.[amarin] &
Shch.[erbatov] spread so much about Greg.< & Shcherbatov showed your telegrams, our Friends & Varnava's to heaps of people—fancy the hideousness
(about John Max.[imovich]) of such an act—private telegrams—this Khvostov
told—& Varnava too, how did they dare take the telegrams, when the people at
the telegr. office have to take oaths—consequently it came through Dzhunkovsky
before, the governor, Shcherbatov & Samarin (just as V.[arnava] already told
me)—he will put a stop to this, knows all the parties in the Duma & will know
how to talk to them. [a, b]
    He proposes his Uncle (Minister of Justice [A. A. Khvostov]) instead of Sama-
rin [as director of the Holy Synod] being a very religious man & knowing much
about the Church, & in his place Senator Krasheninnikov, whom you have sent
to Moscou [sic] to investigate things & they say everybody praises him highly.
[See Letter No. 486h.] Now that Gr.< advises [A. N.] Khvostov I feel its right &
therefore I will see him. He got an awful shock as in the evening papers one said
[S. E.] Kryzhanovsky] (is that the name) had left for the Headquarters, he is a
very bad man & you very much always disliked him & I told the old Man
so—God forbid him having advised him again. Did you look through [A. N.]
Khvostov['s] book? Only as soon as you can come & quickly make the changes,
they will go on working against our Friend & that is a great evil. He will not
play fast & loose with the press like Shch.[erbatov] but watch it & stop whenever necessary wrong articles. Its madning [sic] not to know what you think,
what you are deciding—its a cross going through this anguish fr. far—& perhaps
you are making no changes until you return & I am uselessly worrying. Only
wire a word to quieten me. If no ministers yet changed—simply wire "no changes
yet", & if you are thinking about Khvostov say "I remember the tail"< & if not
"dont need the tail", but God grant you will think well of him—therefore I receive him as he begs for it quicker—why he believes in my wisdom & help I

don't know, it only shows he wishes to serve you & yr. dynasty against those brigands & screamers.—[c, d]

Oh my Love, how dear you are to me, how infinitely do I long to help you & be of real use—I do so pray to God always to make me be yr. Guardian Angel & helper in everything—some look at me as that now—& others cannot find nasty enough things to say about me. Some are afraid I am meddling in state affairs (the ministers) & others look upon me as the one to help as you are not here (Andron.[nikov], [A. N.] Khvostov, Varnava & some others) that shows who is devoted to you in the real sense of the word—they will seek me out & the others will avoid me—is it not true, Sweetheart? Do read the 36-th Psalm, it is so lovely & strengthening & consoling.—Ah me loves Zoo so, so, so much & so passion-ately. Only 6 degrees, but such a glorious, sunny morning —a real gift of Gods.—Slept midling [sic], got off only after 3, sad thoughts haunted me.—Why was Kaluga chosen [as the new site for Stavka], so far to the south? Do you pass by Pskov coming here, so as to see Ruzsky< & perhaps some troops? How dis-gusting that Guchkov, Ryabushinsky, Weinstein (a real Jew for sure) Laptev, Zhukovsky have been chosen into the Council of the Empire< by all those brutes. Indeed one will have nice work with them. Khvostov hopes that in 2, 3 months one can put all into order with cleverness & decision. Ah, if he [A. N. Khvostov] could but be the one to do it, even if the old man [Goremykin] is against him—from fright. One can be sure he will act carefully, & once he in-tends standing up for our Friend, God will bless his work & his devotion to you.—the others S.[amarin] & Shch.< sell us simply—cowards! I see also Prince Tumanov instead of Frolov will be here—thats surely a good choice. Keep al-ways an eye on Polivanov, please. The painter Makovsky has had a horrible accident, his horse bolted & flew into a tram—he lies in a hospital with concus-sion of the brain & a cut on his head.—Now I must quickly get up & dress for the service of old Arsenev. Mass begins at 10, so we shall go at 11—I take [daugh-ters] O.[lga] & T.[atiana] too.— [e, f, g]

Well, Sweetie, I have talked with "the tail" for an hour & am full of the best impressions. I was honestly, rather anxious, as A.[nia]< is sometimes carried off for a person—but we talked over every possible subject & I came to the conclu-sion, that to work with such a man would be a pleasure. Such a clear head, un-derstanding so perfectly the gravity of the situation, & understanding how one must fight against it. That is much, as here one criticises [sic] & rarely proposes antedotes [sic]. He is also of course horrified that Guchkov & Ryabushinsky have got into the Council of the Empire—it is indeed a scandle—& one knows Guchkov's work is against the dynasty. I wish you could get him for a good talk.—Entre autre he told me, that Shcherbatov shows about all yr. telegr. & our Friends to whomsoever he wishes—many are disgusted & others enchanted. What right has he to potter in his E.[emperor]'s private affairs & have the tele-graphs shown him? How do I know if he wont watch ours to[o], after that you can, alas, never more call him a gentleman or honest. Krivoshein is too well acquainted with Gutchkov being married to a lady fr. Moscou (also of the mer-chant families & that makes one). [h]

I have so much in my head, that I don't know what to begin with nor what to tell.—In any case he finds you must quicker change the ministers, above all

Shch.[erbatov] & S.[amarin] as the old man cannot stand with them opposite to the Duma. Now, having spoken with him—I can honestly advise you to take him without any fear. He talks well & does not hide this fact, wh. is a plus, as one needs people to speak easily & be ready with a word to answer back at once & to the point. He could fight that duel with Guchkov & God would bless him, I think. Of course he had too much tact & was too clever to hint about himself—he only thanked me many times for having allowed him to pour out all that was on his soul, as he puts his hope & trust on me to help for the good cause for you & Baby< & Russia. All is in Moscou & Petrograd wh. is bad—but, the government must look ahead & prepare for after the war & this question he finds one of the most serious. And if he stands in the Duma, he must for his country's sake say all this [i.e., these] things & then unwillingly again he will show up the weakness & not thinking beforehand (what abominable English) of the Government. [i]

When the war is over, all those 1000[s] of men working in fabrics [factories] for the army will sit without work & of course be a discontented lot to do with—therefore already now that must all be thought of, all the places, fabrics written down, the quantity of working hands etc. & settled what one will give them then to do, not to leave them in the street—& that will take long to prepare & think out & is of greatest gravity wh. of course is absolutely true. Then will be so many discontented elements, now they have money, then the troops return, the men to the villages, many ill & maimed, many whose patriotism & spirit now keep them up, will then be lowspirited & dissatisfied & act badly on the workmen, therefore it is of them one must think—& one sees he would do it. Wonderfully clever, does not matter if he is a bit selfsure, its not offensively noticed—only an energetic devoted man, who yearns to help you & his country. Then the preparations beforehand for the elections into the Duma (later)—the bad prepare, & so must the good "canvass",[156] as one says in England.— [j]

He says Mme Stolypin[157] is trying hard for Tatiana's [A. B.] Neidhardt, hoping to play a part again herself—but he finds him quite incapable. You would enjoy working with this man & you would not have to be keeping him up, pushing him on—with you here or there, one feels he wld. work just as honestly. He got safely through in his governments [of Vologda province] during the revolution [of 1905-6] (& shot at). It seems it was he who asked to have the relics of Paul Obnorsky arranged, I had quite forgotten.—He says the old man [Goremykin] is afraid of him because he is old & cannot bend into new ideas (as you yourself told me) & does not realise [sic] that one cannot do without new things & must count with them & cannot ignore them. The Duma exist—there is nothing to be done,[156] & with such a hard worker, the old man would get on alright. [k]

Excellent you did not see Rodzianko, at once their noses went down—you shut the Duma wh. they thought you wld. not dare to—all quite right. Now you don't, thank God, receive the Moscou deputation, all the better—again they intend asking, & don't you give in, else it looks as tho' you acknowledge their existence (whatever you may even say to them). That you went to the war was splendid, & he [A. N. Khvostov] is horrified that people dared be so blind & unpatriotic & frightened as to be against it. Sees the way how to act with the press, & not as Shch. has been playing with it.—Now I must end, Lovy, its 7 o'clock—I have written all this in half an hour so excuse atrocious writing. Really, my Treasure, I think he [A. N. Khvosotov] is the man [who is most suitable as minister of internal affairs] & our Fr. hinted [this] to A.< in his wire;—I am always careful in my choice—but I have not the feeling wh. I had to Shch. when he came to me. And he understands one must watch Polivanov since Guchkov has got into the Coun. of the Em.<, is not oversure of him. He sees & thinks like us—he did nearly all the talking.—Try him now, because Shch.< must leave, a man who openly shows about your telegrams & Greg.'s wh. he has kidnapped & S.[amarin] too—are utterly unworthy ministers & no better than Makarov who showed my letter to our Friend, to others too—& Shch. is a rag & stupid.—If the old man grumbles—does not matter—wait & see how he proves himself to be, worse than Shch. he cannot be, but I think 1000 time[s] better, God grant, that I am not mistaken & I honestly believe I am not. I prayed before seeing him, as was rather frightened of the talk. Looks one straight into the eyes.— [l, m]

I drove with my 5 girls [Alexandra's four daughters plus Anna Vyrubova] to Pavlovsk, glorious weather. Were 1½ hour in Church, Nadinka [Arseneva] held herself well.—Petia< hopes still to see you here, then must go South for his lungs.—Blessings & kisses without end. [A. N.] Khvostov has refreshed me, my spirit was not down, but I yearned to see a "man" at last—& here I saw & heard him. And you together would keep each other going.—I bless you my Angel, God bless you & the holy Virgin. Cover you with longing, loving, tender kisses. Ever, huzy mine, yr. very own old <u>Sunny</u>. [P.S.] Nobody is any the wiser I saw him.—[Daughter] Anastasia intensely proud & happy with yr. letter.—Bow to Fredericks & N.P. Love to Misha< & Dimitri<. [n]

156. Nicholas II minimized the Duma's role by keeping it in recess as much as possible. A. N. Khvostov thought the tsar should cooperate with the Duma, though on his terms. Khvostov argued that rightist supporters of the throne should make a concerted effort to win seats in the elections to the Fifth Duma which would occur in 1917. As we see here, Alexandra was impressed with this strategy—as well as the fact that Khvostov was already thinking about postwar problems: the proper way to demobilize the army, the need to combat leftist agitators in that situation, etc.

157. Olga Borisovna Stolypina was the widow of Peter Stolypin. Born Neidhardt, Madame Stolypina was a relative of A. B. Neidhardt, briefly considered as minister of the interior. The "Tatiana" mentioned here might have been Neidhardt's wife or some relative.

No. 482.   Mogilev. Sept. 17 1915.
My own beloved Sunny,

The messenger leaves at such an hour in the afternoon that I have never time to write quietly. Misha< often sits with me & like that I lose my free time, having to gobble up my papers late in the evening. Thank God our affairs are going well & our splendid troops are advancing between Dvinsk & another place near Sventsian. This gives me the possibility of coming home for about a week—I hope to arrive on Wednesday morning! That will [be] a happy day! Alekseev hopes that now perhaps the Stavka need not change place, which is a good thing, especially from the moral point of view. The sitting yesterday showed one clearly that some of the minist[ers] <u>won't work</u> to work with old Gor.< notwithstanding my strong words to them. Therefore changes must take place when I return. Sorry I have no time to answer all your questions. God bless you, my darling precious Wify. Looking so much forward to our meeting. I kiss you and all the children tenderly & remain ever your own old Nicky. [P.S.] Misha thanks and sends love.

No. 483/ Telegram 140. Tsarskoe Selo> Stavka. 17 Sept 1915. 9.15> 10.45 p.m. To his majesty. [Daughter] Anastasia passionately thanks you for letter. Tail< made beautiful impression on Sunny[, i.e., me]. Fully suitable person. [We] drove, splendid sunny day. [We] attended funeral. Petia< and Marie< had tea. [I] love you forever. In prayers and thoughts with you. Sleep peacefully. Alix

---

No. 484/ Telegram 117. Stavka> Tsarskoe Selo. 17 Sept 1915. 9.56> 11.30 p.m. To her majesty. Tender thanks for your dear letter and [daughters] Marie and Anastasia's Misha< left for home but will come again next time. Wrote to-day. Hope [you are] feeling well. Lovely weather. News continue good. Kiss all lovingly. Niki

---

No. 485/ Her No. 358.   Tsarskoe Selo. Sept. 17th 1915.
My own beloved Angel,
   Only a word before going to sleep. Have been so anxious all evening because I got no telegram from you, at last whilst my hair was being done it came at 5.m[inutes] to 12—think, how slow it went, it left the Headquarters at 9.56 & reached here 11.30, & I fool got nervous & anxious. I sent you 4 wires because of [A. N.] Khvostov & hoped you would mention a wee word. I asked you by letter some days ago about seeing him as he wanted it & you did not answer, & now he begged again before going to the country & therefore I wired it in the morning, & at 8.30 after seeing him.—So thankful, you say news continues good—that means very much, & people's spirits will rise.—Misha< wired, to thank for my letter, from Orsha—thats good you will have him with you after-wards again. Marie< said Dmitri< wrote that he comes here with you, why Dar-ling, Paul< earnestly begs for you to send him to the regiment, he asked again when he took tea with me on Monday.—Marie looks alright, her hair is growing thick—she has worries with her chief Dr. & wants to get rid of him.—The Orloffs are still in town it seems & continue talking—Fredericks must forbid it, its dis-graceful, only the old man [Fredericks] must not use my name again.— [a]
   Fancy, Stana< has sent away her faithful Mlle Peters.[on]—I suppose she sud-denly found the name too German & will choose a Caucasian lady to help her & be popular. Oh, wont she try to charm all there!—Now I must try and sleep. I have blessed & kissed & laid my head upon your empty cushion as usual. It only can receive my kisses, but, alas, cannot respond to them.—Sleep well, Sweet-heart & see wify in your dream & feel her arms caressingly around you. God bless you, holy Angels guard you, good-night my Treasure, my Sunshine, my long-suffering Job.— [b]
   18th.Good-morning wee One—grey & pouring—I found the evening so lovely, moon & stars shining, that I even opened half the window (ventilator always)—& then now, when I drew up the curtains, I was quite disappointed & only 6 de-

grees again.—As am feeling better, went to peep in to A.[nia]< in the big Palace<
(after Znamenia<) on my way to a new young officer who has just come —only
20 years old, with a bad wound in the leg, Vladimir Nikolaevich< thinks it ought
to be taken off, as blood-poisoning is setting in there & in the wound in the
shoulder—he feels well, does not complain, that is always a bad sign—so difficult
to decide when death is so near leave him to die in peace or risk it, I should, as
there always is a flicker of hope when the organism is so young, tho' now very
weak & high temp.—seems 7 days he was without having his wound dressed,
wretched boy,—& so I want to have a look at the child. I have not been into that
room for 6 months —no, I was there once since my poor Grabovoy died.—From
there I will go to our hospital, as have not been there for a week & I miss them
& they even told me. One says one of my lancers, a volunteer Luder (something
like that) has come to us—not wounded but squashed somehow, they could not
explain it properly. With pleasure I continue thinking over [A. N.] Khvostov's
talk & wish you had been there too—a man, no petticoats—& then one who will
not let anything touch us, & will do all in his power to stop the attacks upon our
Friend<, as then he stopped them & now they intend beginning again, &
Shch.[erbatov] & S.[amarin] wont certainly oppose, on the contrary for popularity's sake. I am bothering you with this talk, but I should like to convince you,
having honestly, calmly the opinion that this (very fat young man of much experience) is the one you would approve of & that old woman [i.e., the empress
herself] who writes to you I should say [is correct] too[.]—He knows the Russian
peasant well & closely having been much amongst them—& other types too &
does not fear them. [c, d]

He knows too that fat Priest, now archimandrite. I think, Gregory's & Varnava
friend, as he helped him 4 years when he was governor during the bad years, &
he spoke so well to the peasants & brought them to reason. He finds a good
Priest's influence should always be used & he is right—& they arranged together
for St. Paul Obnorsky & he is now at Tobolsk or Tyumen & therefore S.[amarin]
& C°. told V.[arnava] they do not approve of him & will get rid of him—his body
is colossal A.< says, but the soul high & clear.—I told Khvostov how sad I find
it, that evil intentioned have always far more courage & therefore sooner success—upon wh. he rightly answered, but the others have the spirit & feeling to
guide them & God will be near them, when they have good intentions & guide
them.—[e]

The Zemstvo Union, wh. I too find has spread too far & taken too many things
in hand, so as that later one can say, the Government did not enough look after
the wounded, refugees, our prisoners in Germany etc. & the Zemstvo saved
them, ought to have been held in bounds by Krivoshein, who set the things going—a good idea, only needed watching carefully as there are many bad types
out at the war in their hospitals & feeding stations. Finds Krivoshein too much
in contact with Guchkov.—Khvostov in his paper never attacked german names
of the Barons or devoted servants, when they speak of this German influence but
drew all the attention upon the banks, wh. was right, as nobody had yet—(& the
Ministers saw their faults). He spoke of the food & fuel question—Guchkov,
member of the Petrograd Duma, even forgot that, probably intentionally so as
that one should throw the fault upon the government. And it is its very criminal

fault not having thought—months ago of getting big stocks of wood—we can have disorders on that account & quite comprehensible—so one must wake up & set people working. Its not your business to go into these details—it is Shch.<, who ought to have seen to that with Krivoshein & Rukhlov—but they occupy themselves with politics— & try to eat away the old man [Goremykin].— [f]

Well, I was happy to receive your dear letter from yesterday, & thank you for it from the depths of my heart. I understand how difficult it is for you to find time to write, & I am therefore doubly happy, when I see your dear handwriting & read your loving words. You must miss Misha< now—how nice that you had him staying with you, & I am sure that it must have done him good in every sense.—I am enchanted, if you need not have to change the Headquarters, I was quite sad about it, just on account of the moral side of it, and as God blesses the troops & really things seem to be going better, & we keep firm where we are—then no need for you to move.—But what about Al.[ekseev] remaining alone—you wont get Ivanov to share the work & responsibility with him & there you can be more free in your movements to Pskov or wherever you wish. [g]

Well dear, there is nothing to be done with those Ministers, and the sooner you change them, the better. [A. N.] Khvostov instead of Shch. & instead of Samarin there is another man I can recommend devoted old N. K. Shvedov,—but of course I do not know if you find a military man can occupy the place of Over-Procurator [director] of the Holy Synod.—He has studied church history well, has a known collection of Churchbooks—in being at the head of the Accademy [sic] for Oriental studies, he studied the Church too—is very religious & devoted beyond words (calls our Friend Father Gregory) & spoke well of him when he saw & had occasion to speak to his former scholars in the army, when he went to see Ivanov. He is deeply loyal—now you know him much better than I do & can judge whether its nonsense or not—we only remembered him, because he longs to be of use to me, to make people know me & be a counterbalance to the "ugly party"—but such a man in a high place is good to have, but as I say, you know his caracter [sic] better than I do, otherwise—[A. A.] Khvostov of the justice [ministry] & the other one [reference is to I. S. Krasheninnikov] in his place, whom I mentioned to you the other day, who clears up the stories at Moscow, but whom instead of longnosed Sazonov, if he will be an opponent the whole time![158]— [h]

I received this from Ella< to-day, as she read in the papers that Yussupov [the Elder] is retired from the service.—not said, that according to his petition wh. wld. have sounded prettier & this makes people probably think he did not act well. He wld. gladly (I believe) have returned, had one given him the military power he asked for, but she [his wife, Zinaida?] spoiled all. Well, he is no loss there, tho' I am sorry it was not better worded, & he meant honestly—you might have written a wee word if you had had time but its true, one does not ask ones demission [retirement] in time of war. "Just read old Felix officially suspended, when he wrote asking demission, must be an error, cant one do something as most painful impression, even people sent away one puts "in accordance with request". I have also wired it to you, as don't know what to answer her [Ella]. One must make the difference, I find, between a Dzhunkovsky & a Yussupov, the one utterly false—the other stupid but honestly devoted.— [i]

Paul's< wife [Princess Paley] was alright, but bored with her way of saying how devoted she is etc. Ladung [Leding]'s lovely daughter marries on Sunday, my Godchild, so I blessed her to-day! The afternoon I remained quiet & A.< read to me. In the morning I was with that poor boy [see No. 386c above] & then in our hospital, sat knitting and talking.—Wet, grey day.—Ania had a long conversation with Mme Zizi< about our Friend & [Fat] Orloff & cleared up many things to her. She made her promise not to tell on the story of [Fat] O.[rloff] at the Headquarters & N.P.< telegr.—she was horrified & went green—and said she remembers, all the a.d.c. used daily to write their reports during the war to (she did not understand quite, to Anpapa [Alexander III]).—She will see her again & clear up many more things for the old lady to know, as she is utterly devoted to us & can be of use if she sees the things rightly. I explained lots of other things the other day wh. she was, most grateful to know.—Is it true what Pss Palei!![sic] says that Bark telegraphed he cannot make the loan without the Duma being called together? That is a catch [trap,] I fear. [A. N.] Khvostov entreated that one should not think of calling it together before 1-st of Nov. as was announced. He knows people are working at this, but finds it would be a wrong concession, as one must have time to prepare ones actions clearly before they assemble—& be ready to meet all attacks with answers. Fat Andronnikov telephoned to Ania that Khvostov was very contented with his talk, & other amiabilities wh. I shan't repeat. [j, k]

Have you any place for my letters? I write such volumes—Baby sweet< gently began speaking again, whether you would take him back to the Headquarters & at the same time he feels sad to leave me. But you would be less lonely—for a bit at least, & if you intended to move & see the troops, I could come & fetch him. You have Fedorov<, so he would only need Mr. Gilliard, & you could let still one of the aide de camp[s] accompany him out motoring. He could have his French lessons every morning & drive with you in the afternoon—only he cant take walks—he could remain behind with the motor playing about. Have you a room near you, or he could share yr. bedroom.—But that you must think over quietly.—[l]

Our Friend always wires about Pokrov [Festival of the Protection of the Virgin Mary]—I am sure Oct. 1-st. will bring some particular blessing, & the Virgin help you. To-morrow its four weeks that you left us—shall we really have the intense joy of getting you back by Wednesday? Ania is mad with joy. I carry it in me. And, alas, you will have more disagreeable than pleasant things to do;—but what a joy to hold you again in my arms, caress you kiss & feel your warmth & love I so long for. You don't know how I miss you, my Angel Dear. Now my letter must be sent off.—God bless you. Goodbye my own sweet Nicky dear, my husband, my joy & light, the sunshine & peace of my life. I bless & kiss you over and over again.— Ever yr. very own tenderly loving old wife Alix. [m]

P.S. How are the foreigners? Is the nice young Irishman still there,?— Messages to the old man [Fredericks] & N.P. Nini< is now here again, reasonable & clever & still in despair at her husband's [V. N. Voeikov's] behaviour last month & anxious how is behaving now & hopes he tells you things rightly & honestly. Don't you tell him this Lovy.—All the children kiss you. Baby bakes potatoes &

apples in the garden. The girls went to hospitals. Why Boris< is again here, I do not know.—Frolov was in despair. All abused him for allowing the articles about our Friend, tho' it was Shch.'s fault & was watching now carefully to avoid anything again, & now he has been changed. [A. N.] Khvostov also has ideas about the press. You will think, that I have now got a "tail"[135] growing.—Gadon does great harm to our Friend speaking horrors about him wherever & whenever he can.—1000 thanks for the well written cuting [sic] about the general situation. This morning's papers with the news fr. the Headquarters pleased me, not dry & explaining the situation so well to all readers.— [n]

158. The empress is telling Nicholas that if he does not think N. K. Shvedov would be suitable as director of the Holy Synod, he might make Minister of Justice A. A. Khvostov the director and appoint I. S. Krasheninnikov (1857-1918)—"the other one ... whom I mentioned to you the other day" in Letter No. 482c—to serve as minister of justice. Alexandra thinks Krasheninnikov did a good job of investigating the various accounts ("stories") of the anti-German riots at Moscow. As for S. D. Sazonov, he should be dismissed as minister of foreign affairs "if he will be an opponent the entire time," but she is not sure who would be a suitable replacement. Nicholas did not appoint Shvedov, A. A. Khvostov or Krasheninnikov to these offices, though Sazonov was eventually demoted and sent to represent the tsar's government in London. Nicholas placed Krasheninnikov on the State Council (November 14, 1915). On January 1, 1917, Krasheninnikov became president of the high criminal court.

No. 486/ Telegram 146. Tsarskoe Selo> Stavka. 18 Sept 1915. 3.45> 4.55 p.m. To his majesty. Damp, cold. Were at hospital<. Received Paul's wife [Princess Paley]. Feel better. [We] embrace and tenderly kiss you. In thoughts together. Only just received your precious letter, endless thanks. What lovely telegrams! Alix

No. 487/ Telegram 118. Stavka> Tsarskoe Selo. 18 Sept 1915. 7.22> 8.10 p.m. To her majesty. Warmest thanks for dear telegram. Thank God news from everywhere quite satisfactory. So happy with allies great success. Lovely weather. Tenderest kisses. Niki

No. 488/ Telegram 147. Tsarskoe Selo> Stavka. 18 Sept 1915. 7.43> 8.35 p.m. To his majesty. What am I to say in reply to Ella's< telegram? Only just read that old Felix [Yusupov] was officially dismissed at time he requested retirement. Must be mistake. Impossible to do something of that sort—made very bad impression on me. Even when they dismiss someone they add in agreement with [his] request. What can I say to sister [Ella] and what can be done? Seems to me she is right. Will count days [until you return home] with anticipation. Sleep peacefully. God be with you. We all kiss you. Please [send] reply. Alix

No. 489/ Telegram 124. Stavka> Tsarskoe Selo. 18 Sept 1915. 10.05> 10.25 p.m. To her majesty. Have at once told old man [Fredericks] to find out about old Felix [Yusupov]. Think it is a misunderstanding. French General d'Amade and two officers sent by Joffre are here. They leave for town to-morrow<. Will ask to be received by you; do see them please. Good night. Tender kisses. Niki

No. 490.   Mogilev. Sept. 18th 1915.
My precious, beloved Sunny,

Your dear letters touch me <u>so</u> deeply that I feel in despair not to be able to answer in the same way, perhaps only one tenth part I give back of what you show in your loving lines! The longer the separation lasts, the deeper and firmer become the ties that link one together—I find. A month is much. Strange how accurately our Friend< foresaw the time I would be away. [The following quote is in Russian.] "Thou wilt spend a month there, and then thou wilt return." When I go now, of course, our cossacks (konvoi [the convoy]) will remain here; at Tsarskoe is other half, so [M. N.] Grabbe begged me to ask you to dispose of the barracks—new ones—for your wounded until the end of the war! He came and told me to write this to you, knowing it would give you pleasure. [a]

I just got your last dear letter fr. the 17th, in wh you speak about the good impression which young [A. N.] Khvostov made upon you. I was sure of that knowing knowing [sic] him from former times when he was governor of Vologda and later at Nizhny[-Novgorod]. So as not to lose time I shall see him at once the day I come home at 6 o'clock. Perhaps the elder [i.e., A. A.] Khvost[ov] will do in S.[amarin]'s place [as director of the Holy Synod]. The other day after our sitting he[159] asked to see me & came in shaking with indignation against the rest [i.e., the other ministers]. He wanted to know whether I would keep him longer—so I of course said I would—only now he will be at another post—this I did not tell him [because I] did not know [it myself] then. [b, c]
Sept. 19. It is true the old man [Goremykin] named Kryzhanov.[sky], but I refused him. Krasheninnikov is an excellent, strong minded man & will do as min[ister] of jus[tice]. These are the principal questions I hasten to answer. And now one must end. God bless you my beloved precious Lovebird. I kiss you and the children passionately and tenderly. Thank A.[nia]< for her letter. Ever your own huzy <u>Nicky</u>. I let Dimitri go to his father. [d]

159. Reference here is apparently to A. A. Khvostov, minister of justice, who was being considered for "another post": to replace Samarin. The Synod directorship finally went to Alexander Volzhin. A. A. Khvostov continued as minister of justice until July 7/20, 1916, when he became minister of the interior. See Footnote 158.

No. 491/ Telegram 127. Stavka> Tsarskoe Selo. 19 Sept 1915. 10.05> 10.52 a.m. To her majesty. Thanks for dear letter. I remember the Tail<. Would like to see him Wednesday [at] 6 o'clock. Could you let him know? Ideal, warm weather. Loving kisses. Niki.

No. 492/ Telegram 150. Tsarskoe Selo> Stavka. 19 Sept 1915. 1.28> 2.23 p.m. To his majesty. Heartily thank you for telegram. Am exhausted. [We] were at hospital<. Weather becoming overcast. Bless, kiss [you]. In thoughts always together. Alix

No. 493/ Her No. 359.   Tsarskoe Selo. Sept. 19th 1915.
My own sweet Darling,

To-day its four weeks you left us, it was a Saturday evening—Aug. 22-nd. Thank God we may hope to see you soon back again, in our midst—oh what a joy that will be! Grey & rainy again.—Thanks for having at once answered me about Yussupov [the Elder], I directly telegraphed it on to Ella<, it will quieten her.—I am glad Vorontsov's escorts were so nice. How will it all be there now—that nest [Nicholasha< and his admirers] collecting again together—& Stana< has taken there Krupensky's wife as her lady—her husband did the most harm in the talking set at the old Headquarters—& is not a good man. One must have an eye on their behaviour the whole time, they are a dangerous foe now—& as not being good people, our Friend< ends your telegr. [the following quote is in Russian]: "In the Caucasus there is little sunshine".—It hurts one that he [Nicholasha] should have changed so, but those women [the black princesses<] turn their husbands round their fingers.— [a]

I see Ducky< has been to Minsk to visit hospitals & refugees! Boris< is coming to tea.—I placed my candles at Znamenia< & prayed so earnestly for my Love. Then I went to our hospital< & sat knitting in the different wards—I take my work so as to keep from being in the dressing station, wh. always draws me there. I only did one officer.—In the morning I finished Rost.< papers, wh. I could not get done with before, tho' I read till 2 in the night in bed.—I saw Dr. Pantyukhin fr. Livadia & we spoke about all the hospitals, sanatoriums, wh. he hopes can begin their work in Jan., it will be a great boon when they are ready.—We drove to Pavlovsk, mild, fr. time to time rained.—Boris told me about his new nomination, wh. has overjoyed him I think, as he will have a lot to do—then I had Isa< with papers. At 7 I shall go to Church with Baby<. [M. N.] Grabbe wrote to his wife that the ministers' sitting had been stormy & that they wont do as you bid, but that you had been very energetic, a real Tsar—& I was so proud when A.[nia]< told me this—ah Lovy, do you feel yr. own strength & wisdom now, that you are yr. own master & will be energetic, decisive & not let yourself be imposed upon by others.—I liked the way Boris spoke of you & the great change in the Headquarters, & how one always gets news there now from all sides, & how cheerful you are. [b, c]

God be blessed—our Friend was right.—I had a wire fr. my Veselovsky, that he is ill & had to go from the regiment to look after his health.—Perhaps you are in Church at the same time as we are, that will be a nice feeling.—My supply train No. 1 is at Rovno & fr. there goes out & with a motor column, wh. a Prince Abamelek (fr. Odessa) formed & gave me (he is with it) they take things linnen [sic] etc. along the whole front—& they continued without harm under heavy firing—I am so glad [N. K. von] Mekk wired fr. Vinnitsa where my big store< is.—Varnava has left for Tobolsk, our Friend said we were to send him back. The old man [Goremykin] said he was no more to show himself at the Synod. One announces S.[amarin]'s return fr. th. Headquarters & that he at once began the work about Varnava & that he must be dismissed. Please forbid this if it is true & should reach you.— [d]

I must end now & dress for Church. Every evening fr. 9-9½ [daughter] Marie, Baby, I and either Mr. G.[illard] or Vladimir Nikolaevich play "Tishe Yedesh, Dalshe Budesh." [If You Go Quieter, You Will Go Farther]—Dinner is very cosy [sic] in the middle of the playroom.—Goodnight my beloved One, God bless and protect you guard & guide you & I cover you with kisses. Ever, Nicky, mine yr. very own loving Wify. [P.S.] I see the French people Monday at 4½, as they lunch at Elagin<. Its such scandle—no flower [flour] to be had in town nor here—people stand in long files in the streets before the shops. Abominably organised, Obolensky is an idiot—one must foresee the[se] things— not wait till they happen.— [e]

No. 494/ Telegram 160. Tsarskoe Selo> Stavka. 20 Sept 1915. 12.25> 1.28 p.m. To his majesty. Was at church. Overcast, frosting, nevertheless am going for drive, then to station at Red Cross for Te Deum; we give diplomas to nurses finishing course. In thoughts and prayers always together. All warmly kiss [you]. Alix

No. 495/ Telegram 161. Tsarskoe Selo> Stavka. 20 Sept 1915. 3.10> 4.00 p.m. To his majesty. Terribly happy with your dear letter. Tell [M. N.] Grabbe I am very grateful and enchanted to be getting beautiful new barracks. Very grateful for all that you write. Drove with children. [I] bless and kiss [you]. Alix

No. 496/ Her No. 360.   Tsarskoe Selo. Sept. 20th 1915.
My own beloved Darling,
    I read the papers this morning with much interest—the promised explanation of our position at the war, clearly put & the work of a month that you are there keeping the enemy at bay.—A grey, rainy morning again but not cold.—This afternoon we have a Te Deum in the red cross & then I give the diplomas to the ladies who have finished their courses as nurses & received the red cross. We are always in need of nurses, many get tired, ill, or wish to go out to the front positions to receive medals. The work here is monotonous and continual—out there, there is more excitement, constant change, even danger, uncertainty & not always much work to be done; certainly it is far more tempting. One of our Trepov's daughters worked nearly a year in our Invalid's hospital—but after her Mother's death she always felt restless, so off she went—& has already received the medal on the St. George's ribbon.— [a]
    I send you a letter from Bulatovitch he sent you through Ania & a summary of her talk with Beletsky<—that does indeed seem a man who could be most useful to the minister of the Interior, as he knows everything—Dzhunkovsky eat [i.e., ate] him out; just when one needs to have all the threads in hand. He says everywhere one complains of Shch.[erbatov]'s inactivity & not understanding of his work & duties. Has very bad opinion of fat Orloff< & feels sure that my long lost letter from the Standart in C.[rimea] to A.[nia]< in the country is in Orloff's hands. Says Dzhunkovsky gave over those filthy papers about our Friend to Maklakov's brother, as they intend bringing up that question in the Duma & papers. But God grant, if you find [A. N.] Khvostov suitable, he will put a stop to all. [b]
    Luckily he [A. N. Khvostov] is still here & even went to Goremykin to place all his ideas before the old man. Andr.[onnikov] gave A. his word of honour, that nobody shall know, that Khvostov comes to Ania (she sees him in her

house, not in the palace) or Beletsky, so that her & my name will remain out of this.—Alas Gadon & Sherv.[ashidze] seem to spread very many bad things about Gr.[egory], as Dzhunkovsky's friend of course—& knowing poor Ella's< ideas & wishing to help—thus he does mischief— before others' eyes sets Elagin< against Ts.[arskoe] S.[elo] & that is bad & wrong—& its he who ennervates [sic] Xenia< & Motherdear<, instead of keeping them up bravely & squashing gossip. It was with deepest joy that I received your precious, tender letter—your warm words did my yearning heart good. Yes, my treasure, separation draws one yet closer together— one feels so greatly what one misses—& letters are a great consolation. Indeed he [Rasputin] foretold most accurately the length of time you would remain out there. Still I am sure you long to have more contact with the troops, & I shall be glad for you when you will be able to move a bit. Of course this month was too serious— you had to get into your work & plans with Alekseev & the time has been such an anxious out there—but now thank God, all seems going satisfactorily. [c, d]

Tell [M. N.] Grabbe I am delighted with his proposition —Vil'chkovsky wanted the new barracks badly & wrote I believe to him & Voeikov about it—I said I could say nothing until you came. Long ago I had my eye upon it—but discreetly held my tongue —now I can only say I am enchanted—it is near the station—so big & lofty & clean, brand new & we have an red cross station waiting to be placed. Thank him very much from me.—The old man [Goremykin] has asked to see me at 6 to-morrow, probably to give over things to you, or to tell about Khvostov's talk.—It will be interesting what he will tell about the sitting [of ministers] at Mogilev. What a beautiful telegram from our Friend & what courage it gives you to act firmly.—Certainly, as soon as S.[amarin] goes, one must clear out the members of the Synod and get others in. Our Friend's wife [Praskovaya] came, A. saw her—so sad & says he suffers awfully through calumnies & vile things one writes about him— high time to stop all that—Khvostov & Beletsky are men to do that. Only one must get the 2 Khvostov[s] to work well together—all must unite. [e]

But about Sazonov what do you think, I wonder? I believe, as he is a very good & honest (but obstinate) man, that when he sees a new collection of Ministers who are energetic, he may draw himself up & become once more a man—the atmosphere around him cought [sic] hold of him & cretinised him. There are men who become marvels in time of anxiety & great difficulties—& others show a pittiful [sic] side of their nature. Sazonov needs a good stimulant—& once he sees things "working well" instead of fomenting & at the same time dropping to pieces—he will feel his backbone grow. I cant believe he is as harmful as Shch.< & S.[amarin] or even my friend Krivoshein—what has happened to him? I am bitterly disappointed in him. [f]

Lovy, if you have an occasion in the train, speak to N.P.< & make him understand, that you are glad to make use of me. He wrote to me once very upset that one mentions my name so much & that Goremykin sees me etc. & he does not understand that its my duty, tho' I am a woman, to help you when & where I can, once you are away, all the more so. Don't say I mentioned it, but bring the conversation onto that topic à deux. He has a cousin's husband in the Duma & perhaps he sometimes tries not rightly to tell him things or influence him. He told

Axel Pistol'kors that I give officers Greg.['s]< prayer belts—such rot, one loves those belts with different prayers & I give them to every officer that leaves to the war fr. here—& two whom I never saw begged for them fr. me with a prayer to Father Seraphim.—One told me that those soldiers that wore them in the last war were not killed. [g]

I see N.P. so rarely to talk to longer, & he is so young & I always lead him all these years—& now he suddenly comes into quite a new life—sees what hard times we are going through & trembles for us. He longs to help & of course does not know how to. I fear Petrograd will fill his ears with horrors—please tell him not to heed what one says, because it can make one wild—& nasty ones drag my name about a good deal.—We were in Church this morning, later drove & after the [R]ed Cross called on Silaev.—His wife is so like her son Raftopulo, too amusing—their little Children are sweet. Now our 5 chicks [our four daughters and Anna Vyrubova] are at Ania's in the big palace<, playing with Rita Kh.< & Irina Tolstaya. —What intense joy—on three days, God grant, we shall have you back again—its too beautiful. My love, my joy, I await you with such eagerness. Goodbye, Sweetheart, I bless & kiss you without end with deep & true devotion, better, better, every day. Sleep well, agooweeone.—I shall still write to-morrow, if a man goes to meet you, as may have something to tell after my talk with Goremykin. Ever, precious Nicky mine, yr. own, tenderly loving old wife <u>Alix</u>. [h, i]

No. 497/ Telegram 137. Stavka> Tsarskoe Selo. 20 Sept 1915. 6.46> 7.32 p.m. To her majesty. Fond thanks [for] dear letter and two telegrams. Gave over message to [M. N.] Grabbe. Astonishing, heavenly weather, last three days 16 deg. in the shade. Took a delightful row on the river, with my gentlemen in three boats. Kiss you and children very tenderly. Niki

---

No. 498/ Telegram 161. Tsarskoe Selo> Stavka. 21 Sept 1915. To his majesty. Had 2 operations on badly wounded [soldiers]. [We] are expecting son of old Rattsikh, wounded in head. Cool weather. Am receiving French officers and old man [Goremykin]. God bless you. Warmly kiss you. We see Paul< to congratulate him. Alix

---

No. 499/ Telegram 141. Stavka> Tsarskoe Selo. 21 Sept 1915. 9.41> 10.07 p.m. To her majesty. Many thanks you [for] dear letters, yours and the childrens', also for telegram. News continue good. Made delightful trip down river in a motor boat. Summer weather. Too happy to meet soon. Loving kisses to all. Niki

---

No. 500/ Telegram 185. Tsarskoe Selo> Stavka. 22 Sept 1915. 1.53> 2.43 p.m. To his majesty. .Only four degrees. .Was at two operations. We await wounded, going for a drive. Dmitry< will have tea with us. Very pleased news is good. Impatiently awaiting to-morrow. Have a good trip. We all tenderly embrace and kiss [you]. Alix

No. 501/ Telegram 142. Stavka> Tsarskoe Selo. 22 Sept 1915. 2.15> 3.07 p.m.
To her majesty. Leaving at 4.30, hope to arrive at 10 in the morning. Saw San-
dro< today. News good. Tender thanks for dear letter last evening. Kiss all lovingly. Niki

---

No. 502/ Her No. 361.   Tsarskoe Selo. Sept. 20th 1915.
My own Beloved,
    You will read these lines when the train has already carried you from us. This
time you can part with a quieter heart, things, God blessed, are going better—exteriorly as interiorly our Friend< is here to bless your journey. The holy
feast of Pokrov [Festival of the Protection of the Virgin] may it shed its blessings upon our troops and bring us victories and the holy Virgin spread her man-
tle over your whole country.—Its always the same pain to see you leave & now
Baby< too for the first time in his life [is going with you to Stavka], its not easy,
its awfully hard. But for you I rejoice, at least you wont be quite alone & wont
agoo wee one be proud to travel with you without any of us women near him.
Quite a big boy. I am sure the troops will rejoice, when the news reaches them
that he is with you—our officers in the hospital were enchanted. If you see
troops beyond Pskov, please, take him also in the motor,—awfully much hope
you can see some no matter how few, but it will already create joy & content-
ment. Wire a word from Pskov about your plans, so that I can follow you in
thoughts & prayers. [a]
    Lovy my Soul! Oh how hard it is to let you go each time, tho' now I have got
the hope to see you soon, but it will make you sad as I come to fetch Aleksei—but not before 10 days, I suppose.—Its so lonely without Your caresses wh.
mean everything to me—ah how me loves oo, "better better every day, with unending true devotion, deeper than I can say". But these days have been awfully
tiring for you & the last evening we could not even spend quietly together—its
sad.—See that Tiny< does not tire himself on the stairs, I regret that he does not
sleep near you in the train—but at Moghilew it will be cosy—it is not necessary[160]—even, too touching & sweet. I hope you will like my photo of Baby in
the frame. [b]
    Derevenko[161] has got our presents for Baby—the tipe writing mashene [type-
writing machine] he gets here & a big game when he returns—a bag in train. You
will give him some writing paper & a silver bowl to have near his bed when he
eats fruits in the evening, instead of a china saucer.—Ask him from time to time
whether he says his prayers properly, please Deary.—Sweet One, I love you &
wish I could never be parted from you & share everything with you.—Oh the joy
it was having you here, my Sunshine, I shall feed on the remembrances.—Sleep
well huzy, wify is ever near you, with & in you. When you remember the picture
books think of old wify for ever & ever.—God bless you & protect you, guard &
guide you. Ever Your very own old Sunny. [P.S.] I bless you. I kiss & caress every tenderly beloved place & gaze into your deep, sweet eyes wh. long
ago conquered me completely. Love ever grows.— [c]

---

    160. A note to the Soviet edition of the Nicky-Sunny Correspondence says this was an
"[e]xpression used in the family of Nicholas Romanov." (Sergeev: Nicholas and Alexandra,

Perepiska, III, p. 381) Both Nicholas and Alexandra repeat it in various ways: see, for example, Letters No. 517c and 675c. "It is not necessary" or "don't" is rendered in Russian "ne nado!" As used in the letters, it means, "stop!" or "I'm not going to let myself do that!!" It is an appeal for strength, a summons to oneself to not do something one is prone to do, *e.g.*, to be sentimental or self-indulgent.

161. The sailors Derevenko and Nagorny attended Aleksei. Derevenko turned on the tsarevich after the March Revolution, and, in leaving, cruelly abused him. Derevenko is said to have ended as a Bolshevik commissar. The faithful Nagorny accompanied the royal family to Siberia, and was shot for defending Aleksei from harassment.

No. 503/ Telegram 16. Tsarskoe Selo> Pskov. 1 Oct 1915. 6.48> 7.25 p.m. To his majesty. [I] wish you both goodnight. Terribly dull without Sun Light and Sun Beam<. How totally empty. We drove to Pavlovsk. Placed candles [there]. Just visited poor dying boy who recognized me and spoke several words. God bless you, my dear ones. All of us five tenderly kiss you. Greetings to Marie<. Alix

---

No. 504/ Her No. 362.   Tsarskoe Selo. Oct. 1st 1915.
Sweet precious One,
    It seems a messenger leaves this evening, so I profit to send you a word. Well there we are again separated—but I hope it will be easier for you whilst Sunbeam< is near you—he will bring life into your house & cheer you up. How happy he was to go, with what excitement he has been awaiting this great moment to travel with you alone. I was afraid he might be sad, as when we left for the south to meet you in Dec. he cried at the station, but no, he was happy. [Daughter] Tatiana & I felt very hard to be brave—you dont know what it is to be without you & the wee one<. I just looked at my little book & saw with despair that I shall [illegible] the 10-th [illegible] to travel & inspect hospitals the two first days I really cant, as otherwise shall get again one of my raging headaches—is it not too stupid!—[a]
    We drove this afternoon to Pavlovsk—the air was very autumnal —then we went into Znamenia< & placed candles & I prayed hard for my darlings. Hereafter Ania< read to me. After tea I saw Isa< & then I went to the poor boy[—]he has changed, a good deal since yesterday. I stroked his head a while & then he woke up—I said you & Aleksei sent messages wh.delighted him & he thanked so much—then went to sleep again—that was the first time he had spoken to-day. My consolation when I feel very down & wretched is to go to the very ill & try & bring them a ray of light & love—so much suffering one has to go through in this year, it wears one out. So Kira< went with you, thats good & just—may he only not be stupid & sleep. Do so hope you can manage to see some troops to-morrow. Sweet Huzy mine, I kiss & bless you without end & long for your caresses—the heart is so heavy. God be with you & help you evermore. Very tenderest, fondest kisses, sweet Beloved, fr. yr. very own   Wify. [P.S.] Sleep well, dream of old Sunny.—I hope Paul< will be allright & not fidgety. Did the little Admiral< answer you? [b, c]

No. 505/ Telegram 25. Pskov> Tsarskoe Selo. 1 Oct 1915. 9.55> 10.43 p.m. To her majesty. Tender thanks [for] dear telegram, we miss you very much. Sat with Aleksei, played games, walked at [train] stations. Just dined with Marie<

and generals. Shall see troops to-morrow further on. Good night, sleep well, kisses. Niki

---

No. 506/ Telegram 20. Tsarskoe Selo> Rezhitsa. 2 Oct 1915. 10.20> 11.08 a.m. To his majesty. Warmly thank you for telegram. Terribly glad you will see troops. In thoughts am with you constantly. Am very lonesome without you, my dear ones. God keep you. Going to hospital<. [We] all tenderly kiss [you both]. Greetings to others. Alix

---

No. 507/ Her No. 363.   Tsarskoe Selo. Oct. 2nd 1915.
My own beloved Sweetheart,
   Goodmorning my precious ones, how did you sleep, I wonder! I did not [sleep] very well its always so when you are away, Lovy mine. So strange to read in the papers, that you & Baby< have left for the front. I am sure you felt cosy [sic] sitting & playing with Baby, not this perpetual loneliness; for N.P.< I too am glad, as he feels lonely there often, none are such particular friends, tho' he likes most of them & they get on splendidly but he misses us all— & now Aleksei being there, it will warm him up & he will feel you nearer to him too. Mr. Gill[i]ard will enjoy all & he can speak with the French.—You did have such hard work here, that I am glad it is over now, more or less, & you see the troops to-day! Oh, how pleased I am, the heart of a soldier's daughter & soldier's wife rejoices for you—& I wish I were with you to see the faces of those brave fellows when they see for whom & with whom they go out to fight. I hope you can take Aleksei with you.—The impression will remain for his whole life & theirs. Oh how I miss you both! The hour for his prayer, I must say I broke down, so hurried off into my room & said all his prayers in case he should forget to say them.—Please, ask him whether he remembers them daily.—What it will be to you when I fetch him! You must go off too somewhere, not to remain alone.—It seems to me as tho' you were already gone ages ago, such yearning after you—I miss you, my own Angel, more than I can say.— [a, b]
   I went to A.[nia]< this morning & took her to Znamenia< & the big Palace< fr. whence she left for town<, & I went to the poor boy —he had recognised [sic] nobody & not been able to speak, but me he did at once & even spoke a little. From there I went to our hospital<. Two new officers have come. The one poor fellow has the ball or splinter in his eye—the other deep in his lungs & a fragment probably in the stomach—he has such a strong internal hemorrhage wh. has completely pushed his heart to the right side so that one clearly sees it beat, near his right niple [sic]. Its a very serious case, & probably he must be operated to-morrow—his pulse is 140 & he is awfully weak, the eyeballs so yellow, the stomach blown up—it will be an anguishing operation.—After luncheon we received 4 new Alexandrovtsi< just promoted going off to the war —2 Elisavet-gradtsi< & 4 Vosnesentsi?<—4 wounded & [D. S.] Arsenev's son. Then we drove, [ate] a pear & apple—& went to the cemetry [sic] to have a look at our wee temporary Church for our dead heroes. From there to the big Palace to a Te Deum before the Image [Icon] of the Virgin, wh. I had told them to bring fr. Znamenia it passed through all the wards—it was nice.—After tea I saw Russin<

& gave him letters for Victoria< & Toria<—then Ressin< about our journey—only what date to settle, because of Bekker<, wh. spoils everything.—[c, d]

Got your telegram at 5½ & we all enjoyed it, thank God you saw the troops,
but you do not mention whether Tiny< accompanied you.—Wont you let the
soldiers, wh. stand now at Moghilev, show you some exercises & then they can
see Baby. His having gone to the army will also bring its blessing our Friend<
told Ania; even agoo wee one< helps. He [Rasputin] is furious with the way
people go on in Moscou [sic—see Letter No. 511a].—There, the Pss. of the Palace
[Paley] has already sent her first perfumed letter so I forward it to you. Personally I think she ought not to ask for him—what wld. it look like, both Paul's<
sons [Prince Paley and Dmitry Pavlovich] living lazily, comfortably at the
Headquarters, whilst their comrades shed their blood as heroes. [e]

I shall send you the boy's [Prince Paley's] pretty verses to-morrow. If I were
you, I should tell Paul about this letter, even show it to him, & explain that its
too early to call him back—its bad enough one son not being out at the front & it
would harm the boy in the regiment, I assure you;—after a bit of service he can
be perhaps given a place as courier of one of the Generals, but not yet, I find I
understand her Mother's heart bleeding—but she must not spoil the boy's career—dont speak to Dmitri< about it.—I must now write to Miechen< & Aunt
Olga<, so to speak to invite them to the consecration of our microscopic
Church—officially I cant, as the Church is too small, but if I don't, Miechen is
sure to be offended. The Pavlovsk family (ladies) [of Kostia's< family] I must
[invite] then too, as their soldiers are buried on our ground.—Goodbye my Love,
sweetest One, Beloved—I bless & kiss you without end. Ever yr. very own old
Wify. [P.S.] [A. N.] Khvostov has asked to see me after the 5-th.—[f]

No. 508/ Telegram 118 in Russian. Rezhitsa> Tsarskoe Selo. 2 Oct 1915.
4.28> 4.54 p.m. To her majesty. Thanks for news. Had great joy today of seeing wonderful 21st Corps. Weather is remarkable, sunny. In thoughts am with
you and children. [We] are now going to Mogilev [to Stavka]. Aleksei and I
warmly embrace all. Niki

No. 509/ Telegram 25. Tsarskoe Selo> Stavka. 2-3 Oct 1915. 10.25> 12.00
p.m. To his majesty. Terribly glad you saw troops. Was Tiny< with you? Sleep
well, soundly. [We] kiss [you both]. Alix

No. 510/ Her No. 364.   Tsarskoe Selo. Oct. 3rd 1915.
My own beloved Darling,

A gloriously bright, sunny day—2 degr. of frost in the night. What a pitty [sic],
nothing is written in the papers about your having seen the troops—I hope it will
appear to-morrow. It is necessary to print all such things without mentioning of
course what troops you saw.—Am eagerly awaiting details how it all was. So
silly, in Moscou [sic] they want to give Samarin an address when he returns fr.
the country—it seems that horror Vostokov has sent him a telegram in the name
of his two "flocks", Moscou & Kolomna—so the dear little Makari [Makary]
wrote to the Consistory [an office in the Holy Synod] to insist upon a copy of

Vostokov's telegram to Samarin & to know what gave him the right to forward such a telegr.— how good, if the little Metropolitan [of Moscow, Makary] can get rid of Vostokov, its high time, he does endless harm & its he who leads Samarin.[162] Moscou is in a rotten state, but God grant nothing at all will be—but they need feeling yr. displeasure. Sweetheart, me misses you very, very much, I want your kisses, I want to hear your dear voice & gaze into your eyes.—Thanks ever so much for yr. telegram—well Baby< must have been pleased that he was present at the review. How cosy [sic] yr. beds must be in the same room. And a nice drive too.—I always give over by telephone all you write to Vladimir Nikolaevich<. This morning I went in to the little Boy—he is fast sinking & the quiet end may come this evening.—I spoke with his poor mother & she was so brave & understood all so rightly. [a, b]

Then we worked in the hospital< & Vladimir Nikolaevich made an injection to the new officer—probably to-morrow will be the operation. Pss. Gedroits has [a temperature of] 39 & feels so ill—eresypelis in the head one fears, so she begged [Dr. V. N.] Derevenko to replace her for serious operations. Nastinka< lunched, then I received generals Prince Tumanov, Pavlov, Benkendorff<, Isa<. The inauguration of the Winter-Palace hospital can only be on the 10-th as the red cross has not brought the beds etc. yet—our part is done—so you see I better keep quiet after that ceremony (& Bekker< no doubt) & the 11 & 12—if so, then I would be at Moghilev 15-th morning at 9 if that suits you? Thats a Thursday, just 2 weeks fr. the day you left. You let me know. That means I am the 13-th at Tver, 14-th other places nearing you.— [c]

A lovely bright moon, its 10 minutes past 5 & becoming rather dark, we took tea after a drive to Pavlovsk, so cold—the little ones [daughters Maria and Anastasia] are trying on [surgical assistants' garb?] & the big ones [daughters Olga and Tatyana] have gone to clean the instruments in our hospital. At 6½ we go to the evening service in our new little Church.—In the evening we see our Friend< at Ania's< to bid goodbye. He begs you very much to send a telegram to the King of Servia [Peter I], as he is very anxious that Bulgaria will finish them off—so I enclose the paper again for you to use it for yr. telegram—the sense in yr. words & shorter of course reminding them of their Saints & so on.—Make Baby show you Peter Vassilievitch['s]< envelope, its sweet. I shall also address my letter separatly [sic] to him, he will feel prouder. Derevenko[161] has got our presents for him & can arrange them in the bedroom before your dinner.—Wonder, how you will feast the Convoy. Now I must end my letter, Sweetheart. God bless & protect you & the holy Virgin guard you from all harm. Every goodwish for our sweet Sunbeam's< Namesday. I kiss you without end & hold you tightly clasped to my old heart wh. yearns for you ever, Nicky sweet, yr. very own wify   Alix. [d, e]

---

162. Vladimir Vostokov was a Rasputin foe, the pastor of two parishes—his Moscow church had a large working class congregation; he also edited *Responses to Life*. As Alexandra notes, Vostokov sent Samarin telegrams of support when he was dismissed as director of the Holy Synod. Metropolitan Makary, a Rasputin ally at the Holy Synod, brought charges of heresy against Vostokov which forced him to leave Moscow. Bishop Andrew, another liberal, invited Vostokov to join him at Ufa, 700 miles east of Moscow.

No. 511/ Telegram 3. Stavka> Tsarskoe Selo. 3 Oct 1915. 2.33> 4.00 p.m. To her majesty. Tender thanks [for] dear letter by messenger. Of course Tiny< was present at splendid review yesterday and was so pleased. [We] arrived this night, left our train at 10 this morning and have arranged ourself quite cosily [sic]. Fine but cold. Going out in the woods. Fondest love from both. Niki

No. 512/ Telegram 38. Tsarskoe Selo> Stavka. 4 Oct 1915. 9.07> 10.25 a.m. To his majesty. Wonderful, sunny, cold morning. Am going at 10 for consecration of [my] little church at cemetery. Later operation. Saw our Friend<. He greets you. Please thank Mon. Gilliard for his first letter. Congratulate you on the feast day of [your] dear convoy. Regret we are not together. Think of you tenderly. Embrace and kiss [you]. Alix

No. 513/ Her No. 365.   Tsarskoe Selo. Oct. 4th 1915.
My own beloved Darling,
With all my heart I congratulate you with our sweet Child's namesday [sic]—
—He spends it quite like a little military man. I read the telegram our Friend< sends him, its so pretty. You are in Church this evening, but I was feeling too tired, so went into Znamenia< just now to place candles for my darling instead.—A glorious sunny day, zero in the morning, 3 at night. At 10 we went off to the Consecration of the dear little Church—last nights service was also very pretty—many sisters [i.e., nurses] in their white headdress give such a picturesque aspect. Aunt Olga< & we both were also as sisters, as its for our poor wounded, dead we pray for there. Miechen< & Mavra< & Princess Palei & many others were there. About 200 men of the convalescent companys stood round the church, so they saw the procession with the cross.— [a]
    At 1 went to our hospital & Vladimir Nikolaevich< performed the operation wh. went off well—then we had dressings after wh. I went to see poor Princess Gedroits<. She had 40.5 temp., took Communion in the evening & felt calmer later—spoke about death & gave all her orders. To-day she suffers less, but its very serious still as descending towards the ear—eresypeles. But our Friend promised to pray for her.—Then we fetched A.[nia]< & drove to Pavlovsk, everything looked lovely, & to the cemetry [sic] as I wanted to put flowers on poor Orloff's grave—7 years that he is dead! After tea [we went] fr. Znamenia to the big palace< to the poor boy. He recognised [sic] me, extraordinary, that he is still alive, poor child. A.< & Lili Den< come to dinner. Yesterday we saw Gr.< at Ania's<—nice—Zina< was there too—he spoke so well. He begged me to tell you, that it is not at all clear about the stamp money, the simple people cannot understand, we have enough coins & this may create disagreablinesses [sic] [See Letter No. 525a,d.]—I think me wants [he wants me?] to tell the tail< to speak to Bark about it.—One, of course, did not accept his wire to Baby<, so I send it[163] [to] you to read to the tiny one<, perhaps you will wire to me to thank [him].—How do you find the news? I was so happy to get your telegram, Baby's & Mr. G.[illiard]'s letters to-day—they warmed me up & I cld. picture all to myself.—So strange not to be with him on his namesday [sic].—His letter was sweet—I also write every day—probably with many faults [i.e., mistakes in French] too.—The big girls< go in the evening to clean instruments. Its quite funny to have "for the

time being" no affairs to write about, nor to bore you with.—Your bedroom is cosy [sic]? Did he sleep quietly & the creaking boards not disturb him?—Oh, I miss you both awfully.—Now goodbye my love, God bless you, protect you. I cover you with kisses my own Beloved, & remain yr. fondly loving very own Sunny. [b, c, d]

Sweety, I do not think it right that Zamoisky's wife is going to take appartments[sic] at the Headquarters. It was known her goings on at Varsovie [Warsaw] with Boris<, in the train, at the Headquarters & now in Petrograd—it will throw a bad light on the Headquarters. —Fred.< admires her so wont disapprove, but please, tell Zamoisky its better no ladies come to settle down at the Headquarters. Therefore I do not either. A. kisses yr. hand & congratulates you with Aleksei['s nameday]. [e]

163. Rasputin's telegram was not delivered to the tsar. This might have been due to the army's hostility to Rasputin, it might have been military procedure to block wires from a "private citizen." On December 7, 1916, Nicholas wrote: "Yesterday I was inundated with telegrams, as they were not forbidden: an enormous number arrived! I have not yet finished answering them." (See Letter No. 1611.)

No. 514/ Telegram 7. Stavka> Tsarskoe Selo. 4 Oct 1915. 2.47> 3.45 p.m. To her majesty. Loving thanks [for] dear letter. Had no time to write yet. Thanks also [for] telegram. A small review with moleben [prayer service] for the convoy feast. Lunched with and goes [sic] to church this evening. First night together, very cozy.[164] Tender thoughts and love from both [Aleksei and me]. Niki

164. Nicholas and his son were models of aristocratic simplicity. Nicholas never bothered with advancements beyond colonel, the last promotion he gained from his father, Alexander III; to the end, Nicholas proudly wore the insignia of that rank. For his part, Aleksei was delighted with his private's uniform and an eventual promotion to corporal. Both slept at Stavka in a bare room on ordinary cots. When Nicholas appeared before the troops, he "raised tremendous enthusiasm among the men who saw him." Similarly, "wherever Alexis appeared he became a center of great excitement." (Massie, *Nicholas and Alexandra*, pp. 282-288.) Even as it moved towards collapse, monarchy in Russia enjoyed reserves of love and support.

No. 515/ Telegram 48. Stavka> Tsarskoe Selo. 5 Oct 1915. 7.21> 8.20 a.m. To his majesty. All of us, girls and I, send warm wishes on Sunbeam's< nameday. Very sad not to be together. Passionately pray for health and happiness of the dear [one, Aleksei]. All five of us warmly kiss [you]. She [Anna Vyrubova] heartily congratulates you both. Alix

No. 516/ Her No. 366.   Tsarskoe Selo. Oct. 5th 1915.
My own Sweetheart,

Once more many happy returns of this dear day—God bless our precious Child [Aleksei] in health & happiness. I am so glad that one at last printed that you had seen [the] troop[s] & what you said —otherwise none out at the front would be any the wiser, as before. —And every bit of your movements to the troops, when known, will yet more raise their spirits & all will hope for the same luck.[164] —Glorious, sunny, cold morning. We went to Church at 10, then I changed & we worked at the hospital till 10 m.[inutes] to 2. After luncheon I drove with the girls. Miechen< came to tea, was nice & cosy [sic], is so delighted that Plotho [Ploto] has been set free—now he gets transported to Siberia, but its quite different. [See Letters No. 435g,h, 444a, 469j.]—She [Miechen] goes with her train now, Ducky< returned with a terrible cough—so she wishes to go, as its not far nor long—well, lets hope no bombs will be thrown upon it.— [a]

We have just returned fr. a funeral service in the new Church—the little boy in the big palace died peacefully this night & in M.[aria's] & A.[nastasia']s hospital one died too—so both coffins stood there—I am so glad we have got that little Church there.—I received still several officers & feel now mighty tired, so excuse a short letter.—Lili Den< was very handsome yesterday evening & dear. How sweet that you say prayers with Baby<, he wrote it to me, the treasure—his letters are delightful.—I am so grateful, that you told Grigorovich to send me every evening the papers—I eagerly read & then return them after having sealed them myself.— Sweetheart, beloved Treasure, I wish I had wings so as to fly over to you & see how you both sleep in wee bedybys—& would love to tuck you up & cover you both with kisses—very "not necessary".[160]—Ever, my Treasure, yr. very own, tenderly loving old <u>Wify</u>. [P.S.] God bless & protect you. At night 2 & 3 degr. of frost, nevertheless I sleep with the little window open.—Its so empty—miss you both terribly. How does Paul< get on?—You may like to read Putyatin's letter, so I send it to you.— [b, c]

No. 517/ Telegram 15. Stavka> Tsarskoe Selo. 5 Oct 1915. 2.57> 4.25 p.m. To her majesty. Many thanks for dear wishes. Were in prayers with you and girlies. Last evening gave him [Aleksei] our presents. He was overjoyed, especially with the big knife, which he slept with. He is tremendously gay and up to anything. Better come a few days later, as you wrote. Fondest tender kisses from both. Niki

---

No. 518/ Telegram 65. Tsarskoe Selo> Stavka. 5 Oct 1915. 8.31> 10.40 p.m. To his majesty. Heartily thank you for telegram. Were in church, then at hospital<. After hospital [we] drove. Miechen< had tea, then funeral service in new church where both coffins stood. Boy died peacefully this night. Cold, sunny day. All my thoughts [are] with you both. Sleep peacefully. God bless you both. [We] kiss [you]. Alix

---

No. 519/ Telegram 72. Tsarskoe Selo> Stavka. 6 Oct 1915. 9.55> 11.30 a.m. To his majesty. Cold and foggy. Going to hospital<, then to [Petrograd for the] opening of my new school of people's art [see Letter No. 521a], [then] back after tea at Elagin<. Tenderly kiss you both. God bless you, my dear ones. Alix

---

No. 520/ Her No. 367.   Tsarskoe Selo. Oct. 6th 1915.
My own beloved Treasure,
A cold foggy morning. Have read through the papers, thank God, the news continues being good. I was glad to see, that one already speaks of changing the stamp money, thats good. [See Letter No. 525a,d.]—P-ss Gedroits< is happily

better, the temperature less high.—We have just returned from town<. The school is really charming—4 stories high so I was carried up, the lift not being ready; a part of the necessary things are at Archangelsk.—Really the girls have made wonderful progress. I went through all their workrooms weaving, carpets, embroidery, paintings, where they prepare the dyes & dye the silk threads & stuffs they make out of blackberry.—Our priest [Father A. P. Vasil'ev] officiated [at] the Te Deum. Bark, [A. N.] Khvostov, Volzhin & Krivoshein etc. were there, the later offered us 24,000 Rubles for keeping up the school one year.—Then we took tea at Elagin<,—she [Motherdear<] looks well & thinks of going for a tiny visit to Kiev to see [your sister] Olga whilst Xenia< is away, wh. I find an excellent idea. In the morning, I had much to do in the hospital. [a]

Sweety, why did Dzhunkovsky receive the "Preobrasentsi"< & "Semenovtsi"<—too much honour after his vile behaviour—it spoils the effect of the punishment—he ought to have got [ordinary] army regiments. He has been continuing horrors against our Friend< now amongst the nobility—the tail< brings me the proofs to-morrow—ah no, thats far too kind already to have given him [Dzhunkovsky] such a splendid nomination—can imagine the filth he will spread in those two regiments & all will believe him.—I am sending you a very fat letter from the Cow [Anna Vyrubova!], the lovesick creature could not wait any longer [for your next return home], she must pour out her love otherwise she bursts. [b]

My back aches & I feel very tired & long for my own sweet One. One keeps up alright, but there are moments when it is very difficult.—When sanitary trains pass do you sometimes have a look to them? Have you gone over the house, where all the small people of your staff work, take Baby< with you & that will be a thanks to them for their hard work & serve as an encouragement; have the different officers of yr. staff been invited to lunch on Sundays?—Has the English Admiral arrived yet?—There is so much to do, people to see etc. that I feel mighty tired & fill myself with medicins [sic]. How is your health my Beloved?—Are no troops for you to see near Orsha? or Vitebsk? An afternoon you might give up to that?—You think me a bore but I long for you to see more troops & I am sure young soldiers pass by on their way to fill up regiments—they might march pass you at the station & they will be happy. You know our people often have the false idea of not telling you, as it might prevent your habitual drive as tho' one could not often combine all quite well.— [c]

What does Paul< do of an evening? And what have you settled about Dmitri?<—Oh Deary, how I long for you yearn after you both its horrible how I miss you. But I am sure, all seems different now the little man [our son] is with you. Go & have the regiment drill before you & let Baby see it too it will be a nice remembrance for you both my sunshine< & sunbeam<. The letter must leave.— Good bye my very own Huzy heart of my heart, soul of my life—I clasp you tight in my arms & kiss you with ever such great tenderness, gentleness & devotion. God bless & protect you & keep you from all harm. A thousand kisses fr. yr. own old   Wify. [d]

No. 521/ Telegram 49. Stavka> Tsarskoe Selo. 6 Oct 1915. 7.21> 7.48 p.m. To her majesty. Tender thanks for dear letters also to our Friend< for message.

In thoughts always together. We both were very busy answering and thanking for congratulations [on Aleksei's nameday]. [Weather] is fine, a little milder. News good. Fondest kisses from both. Niki

---

No. 522.   Mogilev. Oct. 6th 1915.
My own precious Lovebird,
   So many tender thanks for your loving letter. I truly am in despair that I have not written once since we left, but truly I am occupied here every moment except from 2.30 till 6. And having Tiny< of course takes a part of the time, wh. I certainly do not regret. His presence brings light & life to us all–the foreigners included! It is awfully cozy sleeping near each other.[164] I pray with him every evening since the [time when we were on the] train, he says the prayers much too quick & it is difficult to stop him. He enjoyed the review enormously[–]he followed me & stood the whole time during the march part, wh. was excellent. That review I shall never forget. The weather was perfect and the whole impression remarquable[sic]. [a]
   The life here is the same as usual. Only the first day Aleksei lunched with Mr. Gilliard in my room, but then he begged very much to lunch with everybody. He sits on my left & behaves well, but is sometimes inclined to be rather gay & noisy, especially while I am talking to others in the saloon. In any case it makes them smile & pleased. We motor out in the afternoon (in the morning he plays in the garden), either in the wood or to [the] river bank, where we make a bonfire & I take my walk round about. I am astonished how much he can & wants to walk & does not complain of being tired on returning home! He sleeps quietly, I too notwithstanding the strong light of his lampadka [icon lamp]. In the morning he wakes early between 7 and 8, sits up in bed & begins a gentle talk with me. I answer him half sleeping & then he lies down & remains quiet till they come in to awake me. Paul< is very nice & modest; we have had a good delightful talk. He knew about his wife's letter & is not pleased with it. God bless you my Sunny, my beloved Wify. I kiss you & the girlies tenderly. A.[nia]< too. Ever your own Nicky. [b, c]

No. 523/ Telegram 90. Tsarskoe Selo> Stavka. 7 Oct 1915. 10.07> 11.50 a.m.
To his majesty. First snow is falling. [I expect an] operation and big reception. Terribly tired but should receive those who must see me. We all tenderly kiss you both. God bless you [both]. Alix

---

No. 524/ Her No. 368.   Tsarskoe Selo. Oct. 7th 1915.
My very Own,
   Sweetest Darling, I try to picture to myself how you sat answering congratulations. I also got [telegrams] from some of Baby's< regiments (I collect his regimental ones [telegrams] for him during the war) & I answered that he was at the Headquarters, as I was sure it would rejoice their hearts to know Father and Son [are] together.–Since yesterday evening it gently snows, but scarcely any remains lying–does seem so early already to have real winter beginning. Lovy Dear, I send you two stamps (money) fr. our Friend<, to show you that already

one of them is false [i.e., a counterfeit]. People are very discontented—such wee papers flie [sic] away, in the darkness they cheat the cabmen & its not a good thing—he entreats you to have it stopped at once.—[a]

That rotten Bulgaria, now we shall have them turning against us from the south, or do you think they will only turn against Servia & then Greece—its vile. Did you wire to old King Peter, our Friend wanted it so much. Oh my love, its 20 m.[inutes] to 8 & I am absolutely cretinised have heaps to say & don't know how to begin.—10-12½ operation, & gips [plaster cast] being put on—12-1 Krivoshein, we only spoke about home manufactures committee how to arrange it, whom to invite etc. Girls came late to lunch, had to choose cloaks for them, received officers—Bark for ½ hour, then to big palace<. Then got yr. precious letter for wh. I thank you without end, you sweet One—I loved to get it & have reread it & kissed it & Tiny's< too.—Our Friend is rather anxious about Riga, are you too?— [b, c]

I spoke to Bark about the stamps—he also found the stamps wrong, wants to get the Japanese to make coins for us—& then to have the papermoney, instead of wee stamps, like the Italian lire, wh. is then really papermoney.—He was very interesting. Then Mme Zizi<, then young Lady Sibyl de Grey, who has come to arrange the English Hospital & Malcolm (whom I knew before, was at Mossy's< Wedding, our Coronation as a fair curly young man in a kilt), both remained 20 minutes each. Then [A. N.] Khvostov till this minute & my head buzzes from everything. As remplacant [replacement] of Dzhunkovsky for the Gendarmes he thought Tatishchev (Zizi's son in law) might do, discrete[sic] & a real gen- tleman—only then he ought to wear a uniform—you gave [A. N.] Obolensky one again & Kurlov & Prince [I. M.] Obolensky general governor of Finland for 12 years—he [A. N.] Khvostov asked me to tell you this beforehand so as that you should think whether it would suit you. He wishes to ask to be received next week by you & he told me the different questions he will touch. To-morrow I'll try & write more, when can calmly shape all into words—I am too idiotical this evening.—Our Friend was very contented with yr. decree about Bulgaria, found it well worded.—I must then end now. Thanks again over & over for yr. sweet- est letter, beloved Angel. I can see you & the wee one in the morning & be talking to you whilst you half sleep. Bad Boy wrote to-day: Papa made smells much and long this morning. Too noughty [sic]! Oh my Angels how I love you—but you will miss him shockingly later. Just got your telegram. What news Deary, I long to have some, it seems very difficult again, does it not? Goodbye my Sun, I cover you with fond kisses. Bless you my Love. Ever yr. very own old <u>Sunny</u>. [d, e]

No. 525/ Telegram 72. Stavka> Tsarskoe Selo. 7 Oct 1915. 7.02> 7.35 p.m. To her majesty. Thanks for news. Also cold, grey weather. Drove out in shut motor, walked in a pretty wood, made fire. We both kiss you and girls very ten- derly. Niki

---

No. 526.   Mogilev. Oct. 7th 1915.
My precious Wify-sweet,

Tenderest thanks for your dear letter. Your two last ones you suddenly began to number 465 & 466, you have given them a whole hundred ahead—the last one before being 364. Agoo! Please thank all the girls< for their letters. Today for the first time we have no sun—it is grey & dull. My doklad [report] ended earlier than usual so I went into the little garden where Aleksei was marching about singing loudly & Derevenko[161] along another path, whistling. I had not been there since our arrival. His left leg hurts a tiny bit having worked yesterday he worked in the sand on the beach of the river bank, but he does not mind it & is very gay. He always rests over half an hour after luncheon & M. Gilliard reads to him while I write to you. At the table he sits on my left: Georgi [Georgy Constantinovich] generally is his neighbourgh [sic]. Aleksei loves teasing him. It is curious how little shy he has become, he always follows me when I say good morning to the gentlemen & stands quietly during our zakuska [hors d'oeuvres]. You must not get overtired now so as to be able to stand the fatigue of your journey here. Please! [a]

The news from the whole of our front are good—except from near Riga, where our troops have left too quickly their front positions. Three Generals will pay for that—I ordered Ruzskii to send them away & have them replaced by better ones. They are my first victims, but for the right cause. The little Admiral< did not answer my letter then, but now he asks for a leave to Kislovodsk for a short cure. Now my Love-bird I must end as the train leaves earlier than usual. God bless you & our girlies! With very tender wish[es] & fondest love ever my precious Darling your own loving old Nicky. [b]

No. 527/ Telegram 94. Tsarskoe Selo> Stavka. 7 Oct 1915. 9.12> 10.02 p.m. To his majesty. Hearty thanks to you both for dear letters. Was terribly gladdened. Was very busy today. All kiss [you]. Sleep well. May God bless you. What news? Alix

---

No. 528/ Telegram 96. Tsarskoe Selo> Stavka. 8 Oct 1915. 11.03 a.m.> 12.37 p.m. To his majesty. What unexpected joy your letters were this morning. Warmly bless and kiss you both. Feel very tired, did so much this morning. After diner going to town< on visit to Countess Hendrikova's hospital. [Daughter] Olga receiving donations at Tatiana's committee. Overcast, cold. May God bless you, my dears. What news? Alix

---

No. 529/ Telegram 75. Tsarskoe Selo> Stavka. 8 Oct 1915. 2.35> 3.00 p.m. To her majesty. Thanks for dear letter. News good. Our attack yesterday near Baranovichi successful, made lots of prisoners. Again no time to write. Grey, cold. We kiss you all very tenderly. Niki

---

No. 530/ Telegram 101. Tsarskoe Selo> Stavka. 8 Oct 1915. 7.46> 8.22 p.m. To his majesty. Returned from town< successfully but [am] tired. Received. Was with Countess Hendrikova and at hospital of oboryanskogo sobranie [military assembly, see Letter No. 532g]. At same time meeting occurred there. 300

wounded. Glad news good. Volzhin[159] made excellent impression on me. We all kiss you both. Sleep well. God bless you. Alix

---

No. 531/ Her No. 369   Tsarskoe Selo. Oct. 8th 1915.
My very own Love,
   A grey and dreary morning. You too have cold weather, I see, its sad, as winter is so endless.—I am glad tiny< behaves well, but I hope his presence does not prevent you from seeing troops or anything like that. Am I a bore, always mentioning that? Only I have such a longing you should go about & see more & be seen. Do not reserve regiments stand at Vitebsk, or are only the horses kept there? Baby< writes such amusing letters & everything that passes through his head.—Does he speak with the foreigners, or has he not the courage?—I am glad his little [icon] lamp does not keep you from sleeping.—[a]
   Well, about the Tail.< I spoke to him concerning flour, sugar, wh. are scarcely [i.e., scarce] & butter, wh. is lacking now in Petrograd when [according to Rasputin] cars full are sticking in Siberia. He says its Rukhlov this all concerns, he has to see & give the order to let the waggons [sic] pass.[165] Instead of all these necessary products, waggons with flowers & fruit pass wh. really is a shame. The dear man is old [Rukhlov was born in 1853]—he ought to have gone himself to inspect all & set things working properly—its really a crying shame, & one feels humiliated before the strangers [foreigners] that such disorder should exist. Could you not choose somebody & send him to revise it all & oblige those to work properly out there at the places where the waggons stand & the things rot. [A. N.] Khvostov mentioned [Vladimir Iosifovich] Gurko as a man to send and inspect as he is very energetic & quick about all—but do you like such a type? Its true he was unjustly treated by Stolypin but some energetic means ought to be taken.—I wrote to you about Tatishchev for the gendarmes[,] only I forgot to tell Khvostov that he is terribly against our Friend,< so he ought to speak to him upon that subject first, I think.—Fancy, how disgusting, the warministery has its own detective work[ers] to look out for spies, and now they spie [sic] upon Khvostov & have found out where he goes & whom he sees & the poor man is very much upset by it. He cannot make a row, as he found it out through a clerk (!), I think, who told him all about it, his Uncle [A. A. Khvostov] also had heard things wh. came from the side of Polivanov—the latter continues being Guchkov's friend & therefore they can harm [A. N.] Khvostov. One must have a firm watch over Polivanov.—Bark also dislikes him & gave him a smacking answer the other day. But perhaps you are satisfied with Polivanov's work, for the war. In any case when you find he needs changing, there is Belyaev his aide, whom everybody praises as such a clever, thorough worker and real gentleman & utterly devoted to you.— [b, c]
   All the papers against our Friend, kept in the ministery [sic] of the Interior, Dzhunkovsky, took copies of (he had no right to) & showed them right & left at Moscou [sic] amongst the nobility— after he was changed.—Once more Paul's< wife [Princess Paley] repeated to A.[nia]< that Dzhunkovsky gave his word that you had given him in winter the order to have Greg.< severely judged—he said it to Paul & his wife & repeated it to Dmitri< & many others in town. I call that dishonesty, unloyalty to the highest extreme & a man who deserves no recom-

penses or high nominations. Such a man will continue unscrupilously [sic] doing harm & speaking against our Friend in the regiments. Gr.< says he can never bring luck in his work, the same as Nikolasha<, as they went against him,—against you. What a delightful surprise, your dear letter was brought me so early—I thank you for it over & over again my Sweetheart. That is right, Dear, that you have at once ordered those 3 generals who were at fault, to be changed; such measures will be lessons to the rest & they will pay more attention to their actions. I wonder who the 3 are.—But God grant Riga wont be taken, they have enough. [d, e]

What an idiot I was to wrongly number your letters [see No. 527a], please correct the fault. Tiny does love digging & working as he is so strong, & forgets that he must be careful—only watch he should now not use it [his left leg which recently suffered swelling and internal bleeding from hemophilia]—wet weather can make it ache more. I am glad he is so little shy, that is a great thing.—I am not going to the hospital< this morning & shall only get up for luncheon, because my back continues aching & I feel very tired, but must still go to town,< its necessary, as people are so very unfriendly & misjudge one—then one must just show oneself, tho' its tiring.—I am astonished the little Admiral< did not answer yr. letter—I think a change of air will do him & his wife good; A.< went to see them, as I begged her to—at first he was stiff—he had not seen her for a year & never enquired after her when she had the accident, but afterwards he got alright, talked a lot about the Headquarters & the good change since you are at the head. [f]

Well, I am tired. In town I received the Baroness Uxcull of the Kaufmans hospital—it is the first time I saw her & we had a charming talk. She is very fond of our Friend.< Then I went with the 2 little ones to Css. Hendrikov, whom I had not seen for a year—it was indeed "fatiguing" with her, poor soul.—Then the big girls< joined us and we went to the Noblemen's Assembly.—By chance I fell upon a day when they were all assembled at a sitting —well, let them, perhaps all the better & will make them amiable. We had tea in the train. Upon our return I found yr. sweet telegram for wh. tenderest thanks—how glad I am that our attack near Baranovichi was successful.—Ella< wired that my Grodno hospital with Mme Kaygorodova has settled down at Moscou [sic], in a nice house.—Then I received Volzhin[159] with whom I talked for three quarters of an hour, he made me a perfect impression, God grant all his good intentions be successful & he have the strength to bring them into life—he indeed seems the right man in the right place, very glad to work with energetic young Khvostov.—In going away he asked me to bless him wh. touched me very much—one sees he is full of the best intentions & understands the needs of our church perfectly well. How awfully difficult it was to find the right man—& you got him I think.—We touched all the most vital questions of our Priesthood[,] refugees[,] Synod etc.—Gunst [Gyunst, a midwife] comes at nine to say goodbye, she is going to Belgorod to join her mother.— [g, h]

Now Lovebird I must send off my letter. God bless & protect you & keep you from all harm. I kiss you my both Treasures over & over again. Ever yr. very own old   Wify.   [P.S.] I send you some of the postcards I ordered to have made, they cost 3 kopecks & are sold for 5, so Massalov [A. A. Mosolov] pro-

poses I should use the money for some charity organisation [sic] & it must be
printed on the back, so I shall think out for what.— [i]

---

165. Here we see an argument between two ministries as to which was responsible for a problem.
Minister of Communications S. V. Rukhlov controlled railroads, which gave him a role in supplying
cities. The ministry of internal affairs included the police—who might be used to see that supplies got
to their destinations. It is not clear if A. N. Khvostov, who was formally appointed minister of the
interior on November 23/ December 4, 1915—wanted to invade Rukhlov's turf or to avoid helping
him. Alexandra here conveys a thought gotten from Rasputin: Siberia (and other rural areas) had
food and fuel in abundance at this time; urban shortages were due to transportation inadequacies, not
a lack of goods.

No. 532/ Telegram 104. Tsarskoe Selo> Stavka. 9 Oct 1915. 2.10> 3.00 p.m.
To his majesty. Warm thanks to Aleksei for his letter. Snowing. Mordvinov
lunched with us. Heaps of things [to do] before departure. [We] tenderly embrace and kiss you both. Hope little one's< arm not worse. Alix

---

No. 533/ Telegram 87. Stavka> Tsarskoe Selo. 9 Oct 1915. 7.54> 8.31 p.m.
To her majesty. Loving thanks for letters and postcards, find them very good.
Hope [you are] not too tired. Admiral Phillimore came and lunched today,
brought me a letter from Georgie [King George V]. Cold, grey. [Our son's] arm
[is] well. Tenderest kisses from both. Niki

No. 534/ Her No. 370.   Tsarskoe Selo. Oct. 9th 1915.
My own precious One,
   It is snowing—the men were cutting the grass this morning & raking it away
under the snow, I wonder why they wait so long.— Well, I have had again a day.
This morning I had Rostovtsev's papers to read until 11, then dressed, went to
Znamenia< called on Ania< & at 12 was at hospital< till 1. Mordvinov lunched
with us, then I had pr. Galitzin [N. D. Golitsyn], Rauchfuss, had to see about
coats—then A.[nia] came & read to me (as I cant talk the whole time), the head is
so tired as so many things to remember— caviar, wine, postcards to the hospital—our prisoners—babies etc. Then A. has heaps to tell after all her conversations & her humour to-day is not famous (as I go away). Then after tea officers,
Duvan fr. Evpatoria, again papers & lots more people to see before leaving & all
must be fitted in. Our friend< is with her [Anna Vyrubova], & we shall probably go there in the evening—he puts her out by saying she will probably never
really walk again, poor child, better not tell her with her caracter [sic].—I am
going to see Zhevakha< to-morrow—to hear all about the image, it will be interesting to hear all—it would be good to draw him to the Synod as [a] worker.[166]—I
wonder how Baby's< arm is—he so easily overtires it, being such a strong child
& wanting to do everything like the others—you know Lovy, I think I must bring
[our daughters] Marie and Anastasia too, it would be too sad to leave them all
alone behind. I shall only tell them on Monday morning, as they love surprises.— Mme Zizi< wants to come as far as Tver as its her old town & she
knows everybody, so she can be of much help to us.— [a, b]
   Lovy, wont you go to Vitebsk with Baby, before we come, so as to see the
army-corps wh. stands there, its interesting to see, Mordvinov says—or let us all

go there together & from there you leave to the south somewhere to [General] Ivanov. Think that over —it would be awfully interesting to see the troops, only 2 versts from Vitebsk by motor—our friend always wanted me also to see the troops, since last year till now he speaks of it—that it would also bring them luck. You speak it over with Voeikov & let us go all together. We arrive 15th morning at 9, I think & then you say for one or 2 days.—What intense joy to meet again, I do miss you both so dreadfully! Yesterday it was a week you left us, our precious sunny ones!— [c]

Beletsky presents himself to-morrow. It seems he spoke very energetically to Polivanov & told him, that he knows his detective work & spy & so do his watch, & that rather upset him. Mordvinov was full of his best impressions of all he had seen—oh what good it does being out there, far from these grey, nasty, gossiping towns.—Forgive my bad writing, but I am as usual in a hurry—Shall see our friend this evening at 9 at her [Anna Vyrubova's] house. Sweetheart, how are things working near Riga, who are the 3 generals you cleared out?—I cannot imagine what N.[icholasha]< does, now he has taken Istomin (who hates Greg.[ory]) who was Samarin's aide, as the chief of his chancellery. Miechen< is off with her train. Igor returned very ill, inflammation [sic] of the lungs & pleurisie [sic]—now he is out of danger, poor boy—he lies in the [hospital at the] Marble palace—what bad health they all of them have, I pitty [sic] poor Mavra[, his mother].< Now my Sunshine I must end. My longing is great for you & I eagerly count the days that remain still. God bless & protect you, guard & guide you now and ever. I cover you with tender kisses, my Treasure, & remain yr. fondly loving very   Own.   [P.S.] I send you some flowers again.—I always kiss & bless your cushion morning & evening. [d, e]

166. The opportunistic young Prince Zhevakov was about to meet the empress, hoping to gain a position at the Holy Synod. (See Letter No. 567c and Footnotes 137, 143, 149.) Zhevakov, "one of the silliest of Christian enthusiasts," told Alexandra of a vision calling upon him to defeat the Germans "by transporting to the front an unwieldy but very holy icon." (de Jonge, *Life and Times of Grigory Rasputin*, p. 145). As we see here, the idea interested Alexandra. After a two-hour conversation with "Zhevaka" the following day (see 539h) she admitted that had she met Zhevakov earlier, he, not Volzhin, would have been named Synod director. Volzhin opposed the idea that Zhevakov be made his first or second assistant-director. Rasputin suggested that a number three position be created for Zhevakov, a "second assistant-director general." The Duma was about to go into session, and Volzhin protested that this would create difficulties for him before he had a grip on his office. Beletsky backed him and Nicholas decided Zhevakov must wait. (Fuhrmann, *Rasputin*, pp. 159-160) Zhevakov finally became assistant-director of the Holy Synod in September 1916, under Nicholas Raev.

No. 535.   Mogilev. Oct. 9th 1915.
My own beloved Sunny,

So many loving thanks for your dear letters wh overjoy me daily! As the trains seem to go better the messenger leaves now fr. here at 2 o['clock] in the afternoon—that is the reason why I have no time to write. Always somebody to receive after luncheon, while Baby< rests. Then out at 2.30 because the afternoons become short. After to-morrow on Sunday we leave for Berdichev where old Ivanov stays. I wanted quickly to visit him & perhaps some troops if there are any near while Sunbeam< is with me and be back on Tuesday —the latest on

Wednesday according to the day you arrive here. I hope you approve of this expedition. [a]

I on purpose did not wire. Paul< leaves for Tsarskoe Selo on Sunday—the reason is this: I am sure you remember my old wish to have our Guards in one group as <u>my personal</u> reserve. It took a month to fish them out of the fighting lines. Bezobrazov will be at the head of this group, wh will be composed of two guard corps[:] the 1st (now existing) & the 2nd composed of our rifles and the Varsovie [Warsaw] guard division. Gen. Olokhov will command the latter & the first I proposed to Paul who accepted with joy and gratitude. That is why he goes back to prepare to go out for a long time! I hope & think that he will do his duty well—he gets on well with Bezobrazov & they will all help him—their former commander! When I told Paul of my intention he cried & nearly throttled me—he wants so much to take part in the war. Well, my Lovebird, my own precious Darling, I must end. May God bless you and your journey! With tender love & passionate kisses. Ever your own old <u>Nicky</u>. [b]

No. 536/ Telegram 107. From Tsarskoe Selo to Stavka. 10 Oct 1915. 10.20 a.m.> 11.20 a.m. To his majesty. Snowing. Only just received Baby's< letter, for which warmly thank [him]. Must receive heaps of people. Then leaving for Winter Palace< for opening of hospital [there]. All tenderly embrace and kiss [you both]. Alix

---

No. 537/ Telegram 109. Tsarskoe Selo> Stavka. 10 Oct 1915. 2.02> 3.14 p.m. To his majesty. Now going to town.< Received heaps of people, completely worn out. Hope Sunbeam< will be near sunshine [i.e., you] everywhere it shines so as to warm all together. Will Thursday be convenient? [We] warmly embrace and kiss [you both]. Will you write me before departure? Alix

---

No 538/ Her No. 371.   Tsarskoe Selo. Oct. 10th 1915.
My own beloved Darling,

Snowing & one degree of frost & grey; but still I slept with an open window.—What a lot of prisoners we have made against, but how is the news near Riga, that point disturbs one.—Our Friend,< whom we saw last night, is otherwise quiet about the war, now another subject worries him very much & he spoke scarcely about anything else for two hours. It is this that you must give an order that waggons [sic] with flour, butter & sugar should be obliged to pass. He saw the whole thing in the night like a vision, all the towns, railway lines etc. its difficult to give over fr. his words, but he says it is very serious & that then [with the cities well supplied] we shall have no strikes. Only for such an organisation [sic] somebody ought to be sent from you. He wishes me to speak to you about all this very earnestly, severely even, & the girls are to help, therefore I already write about it beforehand for you to get accustomed to the idea. He would propose 3 days [when] no other trains should go except these with flour, butter & sugar—its even more necessary than meat or amunition [sic] just now. He counts that with 40 old soldiers one could load in an hour a train, send one after the other, but not all to one place, but to Petrograd—Moscou [sic]—& stop some waggons at different places, by lines and have them by degrees brought on—not all to one place, that also would be bad, but to different stations, different buildings—if passenger trains only very few would be allowed and instead of all 4 classes [each of which occupies at least one separate coach] these days hang on waggons with flour or butter fr. Siberia. The lines are less filled there coming towards the west & the discontentment will be intense, if the things dont move. [a]

People will scream & say its impossible, frighten you, if can be done & "will hark" as he says—but its necessary & tho' a risk, essential. In three days one could bring enough for very many months. It may seem strange how I write it, but if one goes into the thought—one sees the truth of it. After all one can do anything, and one must give the order beforehand about these three days, like for a lottery or collect[ion]—so that all can arrange themselves good—now it must be done & quickly. Only you ought to choose an energetic man to go to Siberia to the big line & he can have some others who will watch at the big stations & embranchments [branches] & see the thing works properly, without unnecessary stoppages. I suppose you will see [A. N.] Khvostov before me, therefore I write all [this to you]. He told me to speak it to Beletsky [Khvostov's assistant] & to-morrow to the old man [Goremykin], so as that they should think about it quicker. Khvostov says its Rukhlov's fault, as he is old & does not go himself to see what is going on, therefore if you send somebody quite else to see to the thing, it would be good.—If one looks at the map one sees the branching off lines & from Vyatka. Also one ought to get sugar from Kiev.—But especially the flower & butter wh. overflows in Yalutersk [Yakutsk?] & other districts—old men, soldiers can be used as there are otherwise not enough men to pack up & load the waggons.—Make it spread like a network & push on them & fill up—there are sufficient waggons.—Well, please, seriously think this over.— [b, c]

Now enough of this topic.—A.[nia]< is very put out [because] He [Rasputin] wont let her go anywhere, Belgorod for instance, whilst we are away—& when I encouraged her to go [anyhow,] she found her house so cosy [sic], that she did not wish to leave it; its always the same thing & it does not improve her mood and spoils ones pleasure when one rejoices to see you Darlings soon.—He finds it necessary to remain on here to watch how things are going, but if she leaves then he will too, as he has nobody otherwise to help him. Yes, He blesses you [in advance] for the arrangement [which he, Rasputin, suggests above] of these waggons, trains.—Again I cannot go to the hospital, as have four people to receive before luncheon; & each will have a lot to talk about. At 2.20 we go to the Winter Palace< for the opening of the hospital.—I take the 4 Girlies —Mother dear< will be there too & heaps of people—if there is time I shall pass through the Store.<[2] At 6 I receive again—its madning [sic].—In the train I must speak with Ressin< about our journey.—I am so tired & M. Becker< will be coming too. [d, e]

Here we are back again from town. The hospital in the Winter Palace is really splendid—a marvel how quick all the works have been done—one does not know where one is with [large] rooms made in[to smaller] rooms[—]quite excellent, & the baths, any amount of them. You must come & see it some day, its certainly worth while seeing. From there we went to the Store right through. —Beletsky told me, that you are leaving to-day or to morrow for Chernigov, Kiev, Berdi-chev, but Voeikov only mentioned yr. name, therefore I wired about Baby,< because he can remain in the train when necessary & appear too sometimes—the more you & he show yourselves together, the better it is & he does love it so, & our Friend is so happy about it; & so is your old Sunny when Sunbeam< accompanies sunshine< through the country. May God bless you, my Angels.—We think of leaving monday evening at 10½—reaching Tver at 9-9[:30] & remaining there till 3 or 5—the next morning, Wednesday at 8½ at Velikia-Luki for several hours —& in the evening 8½ at Orsha where we can see several establishments of Tatiana's committees³—its too late to go on to Moghilev so shall spend the night there and be at 9½ at Moghilev Thursday morning. You will then tell us how long we are to remain. It will be such a joy! [f, g]

Zhevakha is charming & we had a thorough talk about every thing—he knows all Church questions & the clergy & Bishops a fond, so he would be good as a help to Volzhin.[166] The latter spoke well at the Synod it seems.—Beletsky pleased me, another energetic man.—Now I have been talking to the American Mr. Hearte for 1 h. & 20 m. about our prisoners in Germany & Austria & he brought me photos I'll show you. He helps a lot now he goes again to visit the Germans & Austr. here.—Well my Sunshine, Goodbye & God bless you. If you see [your sister] Olga kiss her tenderly from me—my prayers follow you everywhere so tenderly.—Very tender kisses. Sweetheart fr., yr., own deeply endlessly loving old Wify. [P.S.] Its too late to go to church. I am sending you a paper from our Friend, please give it to Alekseev to read. [h]

No. 539/ Telegram 94. Stavka> Tsarskoe Selo. 10 Oct 1915. 7.30> 8.16 p.m. To her majesty. Many thanks for dear letter and news. Thursday suits perfectly. Better not write any more. News continue good.[158] Leaving to-morrow [at] lunch time for a couple of days, details in my last letter. Paul< in bed again[,] his old illness. Has to remain there. Fondest love from both. Niki

No. 540/ Telegram 110. Tsarskoe Selo> Stavka. 11 Oct 1915. 11.20 a.m.> 12.05 p.m. To his majesty. Terribly gladdened by your dear letter. [I] kiss you both. Wish you happiness and success. Finally [a] sunny day, am going to an operation. How is poor Paul?< What disappointment for him. God keep you, my dear ones. Alix

No. 541/ Telegram 121 in Russian. Zhlobin> Tsarskoe Selo. 11 Oct 1915. 4.25> 5.11 p.m. To her majesty. Thank you very much for telegram. Are travelling well. Weather sunny. Aleksei and I warmly kiss [you]. Nikolai

No. 542/ Telegram 184 in Russian. Berdichev> Tsarskoe Selo. 12 Oct 1915. 10.15> 10.46 p.m. To her majesty. Are going for several hours to Rovno with General Ivanov.[167] Wish you a happy journey with all our heart. Warmly embrace [you]. Nicky Aleksei

167. "This was the first visit of the Tsarevitch to the front. Ivanov joined the train at Berditchev, and General Broussilov joined the party at Rovno. After inspecting the troops, the Tsar and his son

paid a surprise visit to a dressing-station after nightfall. It was a little building, faintly lit by torches. The wounded men could hardly believe that the Tsar was among them, and one of them raised his hand and touched his coat as he passed, to assure himself that it was no dream. Alexey was 'profoundly moved' (Gilliard, p. 126)." From Vulliamy, p. 100n.

No. 543/ Telegram 113. Tsarskoe Selo> Shepetovka, S.W. [Front]. 12 Oct 1915. 11.28 p.m.> 12.12 a.m. To his majesty. Rovno. God keep you. Gladdened by telegram. All thoughts, prayers together. Going to operation. We depart this evening after service. Snowing. Greetings to all and General Ivanov also. [We] warmly kiss you both. Alix

No. 544/ Telegram 60. Tver> Berdichev. 13 Oct 1915. To his majesty. Were at church, three hospitals, reservists' orphanage. Snowing. [We] warmly kiss you both. Am a bit tired. Alix

No. 545/ Telegram 1477. Kiev> Velikie Luki. 14 Oct 1915. 9.15> 10.32 a.m. To her majesty. Spent unforgettable day among troops yesterday. Very best impressions. [We] thank you for last letters. Look forward to meeting to-morrow and kiss [you]. Niki

No. 546/ Telegram 130. Velikie Luki, Vind.> Zhlobin. 14 Oct 1915. 12.30> 7.35 p.m. To his majesty. [We] are happy with news. Again saw many hospitals today. Snowing. Look forward to to-morrow. [We] warmly kiss you both. Alix

No. 547/ Her No. 372   Tsarskoe Selo. Oct. 27th 1915.
My very own Sweetheart,
    There off you are again my two treasures—God bless your journey & send His Angels to guard & guide you. May you only have beautiful impressions & everything go off well. What will the sea be like? Dress warmly Lovy, its sure to be bitterly cold— may it only not be rough.—You will take Baby on some ships—but not out to sea & perhaps to the forts, depending how you find his health. I feel so much quieter for you knowing that precious child [is] near you to warm & cheer you up with his bright spirit & by his tender presence. Its more than sad without you both. But we wont speak of that.—See that he dresses warm enough.—I wish the old man [Fredericks] wld. stay at home—I find it a shame he goes with you as you will feel nervous on his account—but insist upon Fedorov< being severe with him.—Give me news whenever you can, as shall anxiously follow your journey; I know you wont risk anything & remember what He [Rasputin] said about Riga.—Sweet Angel, God bless & protect you—ever near & with you my own Sweets, its such pain every time & I am glad its in the evening at least, when one can go straight home to ones room. Yr. warm caresses are my life & I always recall & remember them with infinite tenderness & gratitude.—Sleep well, Lovebird—Holy Angels guard yr. slumber—tiny< is near by to keep you warm & cheer you up. Ever yr. very own, endlessly loving Wify.

No. 548/ Telegram 212. Tsarskoe Selo> Revel. 28 Oct 1915. 10.30> 10.54. To his majesty. Bright sunny day. Very cold. Are lonesome without you, my dears, very much so. [I] hope all is well. In prayers and thoughts invariably together. Are leaving for hospital. We all kiss you both. Paul< slept better, no pain but hiccups continue. Alix

No. 549/ Telegram 1. Revel> Tsarskoe Selo. 28 Oct 1915. 12.40> 1.35 p.m. To her majesty. Arrived well, motored the whole morning along fortifications, saw lots of troops, among which Sherekhovsky's regiment and artillery from Osovets. All look splendid. Bright, cold weather. Tender thanks [for] news and kiss all. Niki

No. 550/ Her No. 373.   Tsarskoe Selo. Oct. 28th 1915.
My own sweet One,
    Such tender thoughts follow you both darlings everywhere. I am glad you saw so many troops, I did not think you would at Reval [i.e., Revel]. How I wonder whether you will go on to Riga & Dvinsk.—So bitterly cold, but bright sunshine. Miss you both quite horribly, but feel much quieter for you as sunbeam< is there to cheer you up & keep company. No need to motor with Fred.< & Voeikov now. Do have the old man [Fredericks] always watched, our Fr.[iend]< is afraid he may do something stupid before the troops. Let somebody follow & have an eye upon him. A.[nia]< gave me this paper for you—she forgot to tell it to me, probably not grasping what it would mean to us about Baby's< health & the great weight lifted at last fr. ones shoulder after 11 years of constant anxiety & fright![168] [a]
    Forgive me bothering you already with a paper, but Rost.[ovtsev] sent it to me—Voeikov can send the answer to Rost.—that would be best. I was not long at the hospital< as had much to read. We had Valia<, Iza<, Mr. Malcolm & Lady Sibyl Grey to lunch—they are such nice people (arranging the hospital in Ella's< house—the operation room will be in the room of Ella's with the 3 lights wh. you used to watch).—Then I received our 3 sisters [i.e., nurses], who go to Austria & Kazbek my lancer. Please remember about [D. M.] Knyazhevich. —Went straight to bed fr. the station, sad & lonely—saw yr. sweet faces before me—my two St. George's treasures.[168]—Goodbye Sweetheart! God bless & protect you now & ever. Cover you with kisses & yearn for yr. embrace. Ever yr. very own old Sunny. [P.S.] I wonder whether this [letter] goes to the Headquarters or Pskov, wh. wld. have been cleverest.—Am so glad I know now where & how you live & the drives, country around & Church—can follow you everywhere. All my love. [b]

168. Aleksei was born on July 30 (O.S.), 1904, so at this time he was ten years old. The St. George Council had bestowed the St. George Cross upon the tsar and the St. George Medal on his son.

No. 551/ Unnumbered Telegram. Venden> Tsarskoe Selo. 29 Oct 1915. 10.00> 11.05. To her majesty. Yesterday afternoon visited our and English submarines. Most interesting ship building yards and naval hospital. Charming young fellows. Then two manufactories and naval hospital. To day much warmer. Shall wire in the evening. Tender love from both of us. Niki

---

No. 552/ Telegram 28 in Russian. Tsarskoe Selo> Riga. 29 Oct 1915. 11.52 a.m.> 12.20 p.m. To his majesty. Am glad you saw so many troops yesterday. All thoughts and prayers surround you. Not going out because very tired and [have] many receptions. [We] warmly kiss you both. Paul< slept well. [His temperature is] 37 [degrees]. Alix

---

No. 553/ Her No. 374.   Tsarskoe Selo. Oct. 29th 1915.
My own beloved,
   I just received yr. wire from Venden, wh. came fr. 10-11.[0]5, so now I suppose you are at Riga. All my thoughts & prayers surround you my darlings. How interesting all you saw at Reval[i.e., Revel]—can imagine how enchanted the English submarines must have been that you inspected them—they know now for whom they are so valiantly fighting. The manufacteries [sic] & ship building yards are sure to work doubly hard & energetically now.   Wonder whether Baby< accompanied you & what you did with the old man [Fredericks].—Here too its a little bit warmer, 5 degree of frost & sunshine. I remain in bed till 12 as heart a little enlarged & aches as does my head (not too bad) since yesterday. Then I have several gentlemen to see with doklady [reports] & that is fatiguing when the head is tired. I shall finish this later, as may have more to tell then. [a]
   Sweety, again I come with a petition, wh. the widow Mme Belyaeva brought me to-day.—Groten came to A.[nia]< to-day, in despair to be without a place—he is well now & will go to the regiment to give it over and then he has to go to Dvinsk with Reserves—but perhaps you will think about getting him a nomination.   His eldest officer got a regiment & now a brigade already.—I am quite ramolished< after all the people I saw. Mlle Schneider was interesting & talked like a fountain—we just arranged with her to keep Krivoshein in the new Home Manufactures committee, as he can be most useful.   Excuse such a beastly dull letter, but am incapable of writing a decent letter. I bless & kiss you over & over again—sad lonely nights & don't sleep very well. God be with you. Ever yr. very own old Wify. [P.S.] Remember about [D. M.] Knyazhevich. [b]

No. 554/ Telegram 1771. Venden> Tsarskoe Selo. 29 Oct 1915. 7.11> 10.07 p.m. To her majesty. Saw beyond Riga three regiments of different Siberian troops and cavalry. Warm, rainy, no snow. Were in one large, beautiful hospital. Heard some shooting far away. Such good impressions. Tender love. Niki

---

No. 555/ Telegram 220. Tsarskoe Selo> Vitebsk. 30 Oct 1915. 11.41 a.m.> 12.58 p.m. To his majesty. Terribly gladdened by yesterday's telegram. Hope your visit will be published. Thawing, raining, overcast. Rested in the morning, then received at Big Palace<. Paul< slept well. Doctor now satisfied [with his progress]. We all kiss you both. Greetings to Dmitry<. God bless you [both]! Alix

No. 556/ Her No. 375.   Tsarskoe Selo. Oct. 30th 1915.
My precious Darling,

It is thawing, raining and terribly dreary and dark this morning. Many thanks for last nights telegram again from Venden. I am happy you managed to go beyond Riga—it will be a consolation to the troops and make the town inhabitants more reassured.—Was Baby< excited to hear the distant shooting? How different your life is now, thank God, with nobody to keep you from traveling about and showing yourself to the soldiers. N.[icholasha]< must now realise [sic] how false his ideas were and how much he personally lost by never having shown himself anywhere. [a]

Old Mme Belyaeva told me yesterday, that she had a letter from her son yesterday from England (all 6 serve in the artillery). He is attached to Kitchener and has to see about our orders being executed there.—Georgie [King George V] received him and spoke about you[;] just that you are with the troops and K.[itchener] wont allow him to go [to visit the British troops] wh. is a sore point. B.[elyaeva] answered him, that here there is a great difference, we are fighting on our own territory wh. he would not be doing. This simple answer seemed to console him and K. was very contented when B. repeated their conversation. I was sure it wld. torment Georgie—but he does visit the troops in France from time to time.— Markosov is off to Sweden to meet Max< etc. & speak over the questions of all the prisoners. M. just returned from Tashkent as he wanted to see how they were cared for there, & found 700 Austrians, officers, but only 15 intelligent people to look after them, to answer their questions etc.—I think he can be of use, as he is very just, wh. people are not inclined to be now. But one sends him without any instructions wh. is foolish, & its the business of the red cross who sends him to do so.—Thank goodness the Epaulets have been restored to the officers.—I hope, Deary, that as soon as you reach the Headquarter one will print in the papers where you have been and what you have seen. [b, c]

How does the old man [Fredericks] get on? I hope Fedorov< keeps an eye upon him & that he wont gaffe before the foreigners. Strange at the Headquarters without us? The noisy girls not there. Eristov wrote to Ania<, that you will be receiving a petition from Molostvo's widow, to receive a yearly substitute [i.e., pension]. It seems he left her scarcely a penny & she is in an awful dilemma. ["]He squandered his small capital sold his estate to his brother & the crumbs which remained will with difficulty cover the debts which were left after his death. Unfortunately the victims of an epidemic have not the same privileges as those who fell in Battle.["] He is delighted that Afrossimov has been advanced as General, and in the suite, an honour to the regiment.—Would Groten have done for [commander of] yr. lancers, how do you think? I had old Shvedov for ½ hour & I told him I shall go one day & see where the young men work. Sazonov is a nuisance—always jalousie de metier [jealousy of the expert], but in my Imperial academy of oriental sciences we have to prepare good consuls who know the languages, religions, customs etc. of the east.— [d, e]

Isa< lunched with us—then I received 3 young officers returning to the war after wh. we went to the big palace<—the hospital exists since a year, so we had lots of groups taken. Later I received Joy Kantakuzen who talked a lot, her husband is delighted to command yr. curassiers. Then Pss Galitzin [Vera Golit-

syna] of Smolna [the Smolnyi Institute], then I read—A.[nia] went to town< &
returns only at 9½ (with Groten) as they dine at Mme Orloff's in town.—I do so
wonder whether you reached the Headquarters to-day or went to Dvinsk. Sweet
Angel, goodbye & God bless & keep you, endless passionate kisses fr. yr. old
<u>Wify</u>.   [P.S.] Massages to the old man [Fredericks] & N.P.< [f]

No. 557/ Telegram 01483 in Russian. Orsha> Tsarskoe Selo. 30 Oct 1915.
7.00> 8.15 p.m. To her majesty. Thank you very much for two letters and telegram. In Vitebsk inspected wonderful fighting Division. Extremely satisfied
with its magnificent appearance. Aleksei accompanied me everywhere during
these days. Today we again spend night in train as we are travelling behind time.
All is well. [We] both warmly embrace [you] all. Niki

No. 558/ Telegram 222. Tsarskoe Selo> Stavka. 31 Oct 1915. 10.10> 11.15
a.m. To his majesty. Terribly glad you saw them in Vitebsk. Was it strange to
be again in our old rooms? Thawing. Am staying home because heart much enlarged. [Daughter] Olga's condition still not famous. [We] warmly embrace and
kiss you both. Alix

No. 559/ Telegram 145. Stavka> Tsarskoe Selo. 31 Oct 1915. 2.42> 3.08 p.m.
To her majesty. Tender thanks [for] news. Came back to our old house in the
morning. Lovely sunny weather, all snow gone. Miss you here very much. Loving kisses. Niki

No. 560/ Her No. 376.   Tsarskoe Selo. Oct. 31st 1915.
Beloved One,
    I am so glad that you saw the splendid troops at Vitebsk[—]you have done a lot
in these days—such joy Baby< can accompany you everywhere.—Its grey, thawing, raining; I remain at home as my heart more enlarged & don't feel very nice
all these days. It had to come sooner or later as I had done so much & still a lot
ahead to be done. [Daughter] Olga only got up for a drive & now after tea she
remains on the sopha & we shall dine upstairs—this is my treatment —she must
lie more, as goes about so pale & wearily—the Arsenic injections will act quicker
like that, you see.—All the snow has melted away. [a]
    I just heard through Rostovtsev that my lancer [Baron] Tiesenhausen [Tizen-
gauzen] <u>suddenly died on his post as a guard</u>— it seems to me very strange—he
had no heart complaint. His young wife died this winter. Our Fr.[iend]< is
happy you saw so much, says you walked all in the clouds. Isa< lunched & bid
us goodbye, she leaves to-morrow early fr. town for Copenhagen, to see her
Father [A. S. Taneev] for 5 days, after 2 years' separation.—Do you look at our
names on the window sometimes? Paul< is better but I think [Dr.] Varavka
speaks of an operation wh. Fedorov dreaded on account of his heart. The wife
[Princess Paley] says he cannot take any food, only a cup of tea.—Alas, no
Church for Olga & me—and I cannot go on Monday to the Supreme Council, it
had to come, I had overtired myself—& I do so miss you my own Treasures.—Well Love, Goodbye & God bless you. I cover you with tenderest kisses

& remain yr. very own old <u>Sunny</u>. [P.S.] What is Greece up to? Does not sound very encouraging—hang those Balkans all. Now that idiotical Roumania, what will she do? [c]

No. 561.   Mogilev. Oct. 31st 1915.
My own precious Sunny,
   Here we are again in our old rooms, which have been nicely cleaned & put in order. The weather luckily is sunny & dry—8° of warmth, so agreeable after the bitterly cold day at Reval [Revel]. Else the day there was most successful & interesting. The whole morning Baby< and I motored about the country, getting out to see the troops near to their positions and fortification, remarquably [sic] hidden in the woods or made quite flat in the open fields. It astonished me how much has been done during the war, but there remains still more work to finish all that is necessary. Though in a shut motor & warmly dressed we all felt cold, and enjoyed returning for lunch to the train. At 2.o['clock] we continued our round & visited the old "Evropa" wh. is now the mother ship of our's & the english submarines. Fancy, little Podgursky commands the whole lot of them. I was so pleased to have been on board and to have spoken to the english officers and men. I thanked them all on deck & decorated some for their last exploits ([on the submarines] Prince Albert & Undine). Ours praise them enormously and they have become great friends, real comrades! [a, b]
   Aleksei climbed all over & through every hole he could find—I even heard him talk deliberately to a lieutenant, asking him about various things! Then we drove to two new naval factories— shipbuilding [yards] & machinery, very interesting! Payed [sic] a short visit to the naval hospital—250 sick and only four wounded sailors. It got dark when we reached our train. After tea till dinner time I had a long doklad [report] of Adm. Kanin in the presence of Grigorovich. All the naval authorities & the four english commanders dined and at 9.o we left Reval after a tiring but instructive day. Travelled in the night in a snowstorm & arrived Thursday morning at Wenden, where general Gorbatovsky met us and got into the train. At 1 o'clock we streamed through Riga & stopped at a little station at the outskirts of the town. [c]
   [G]en. Radko-Dmitriev was waiting there next to a fine guard of honour of the 4th dragoons Ekaterinoslav reg[iment]. Not far off was the place where the review of two mixed regiments of Siberian Rifles took place—among them were Mamma's and Aleksei's regts. They looked very well. We heard our guns booming in the distance, just then our successful attack was going on! On the way back to our train we went into a large hospital full of miserable fellows severely wounded. As we were an hour too late when we left—we passed Pskov at 12.15 of the night & I had to receive Ruzskii for about an hour, so I never got to bed before 2.o. Slept beautifully till 10.30 Friday morning! The weather was warm but it poured in torrents. At 2.o we arrived at Vitebsk & went straight to the review of the 78th inf. division. The rain was falling & the field was covered by lakes of water to Baby's great delight. [d, e]
   This Division distinguished itself in the battles on the Carpathians; when it arrived here a month ago it counted only 980 men—a division! Now it is again war strength—15,000. Over 3000 wounded come back to their regiments—all

with St. George's crosses. They looked splendid, like the guards! Going to the station we went into the cathedral wh[ere] the people made a crush. After dinner we reached Mogilev but spent the night in our cozy train. This morning we came over at 10. Aleksei flew off to the garden & me to the doklad [report] wh. was of course a long one. Today along the whole front it was quiet—only perestrelka [cross-fire]. All our foreign friends met us with amiable faces—Aleksei and his fat Belgian[169] grinned at each other across the table. We took our usual motor drive, walked & made a fire near the high road. Now my beloved darling I must end. Thank you so for your dear letters. I kiss you and the girlies most tenderly. God bless you. Ever your own old huzy Nicky. [f]

169. This was Baron de Ricquel, head of the Belgian mission to Stavka. "He was the special friend of the Tsarevitch, and used to take part in the improvised games of football." (Vulliamy, p. 103n).

No. 562/ Telegram 1. Tsarskoe Selo> Stavka. 1 Nov 1915. 12.02> 12.40 p.m. To his majesty. Overcast weather. [I feel a] bit better. I thank Aleksei for charming letter. What news from Roumania? [I am] very uneasy. All warmly kiss and embrace [you]. In thoughts together. Alix

No. 563/ Telegram 4. Tsarskoe Selo> Stavka. 1 Nov 1915. 2.55> 3.42 p.m. To her majesty. Thanks for dear letter and news. Have heard nothing about Roumania, but Greece becomes very suspicious. [Aleksei's] little arm hurts since yesterday slightly. Nice warm weather. Tender kisses from both. Niki

No. 564/ Her No. 377.   Tsarskoe Selo. Nov. 1st 1915.
My own precious Darling,
    I just got Baby's< letter & enjoyed it thoroughly, he does write amusingly. What a pitty [sic] there was such rain & mud—but then at least the Dvina wont yet freeze. Am so anxious about Roumania, if its true what Vesselkin< wired (Grigor.[ovich]'s papers [i.e., secret accounts of the news]) that at Rustchuk one says Roumania has declared us war [i.e., declared war against us]—I hope it is unfounded & that they only spread such news to please the Bulgarians. It would be horrid, as then Greece I fear will turn against us too. Oh, confound these Balkan countries. Russia has only been as an ever-loving helping mother to them & then they turn treacherously & fight her.—Really you never get out of worry and anxiety.— [a]
    I read the whole description of your journey in the papers—what a lot you did; & then Mr. G.[illard] explains all nicely.—last night we dined upstairs in the corner room—horribly sad & empty without Sunbeam<—I prayed in his room afterwards—no little bed! & then I remembered that where he is now he has another beloved Being lying near him. What a blessing that you can share all together, its so good for him to be your little companion it developes [sic] him quicker;—he is not too wild before guests, I hope. He writes so happy to be again at the Headquarters.—To-day I bid goodbye to my Crimean, Gubariov, Vatchnadze [Vachnadze] & Botkin's son, who all return to the front. The Crimeans all are anxious to reach the regiment as they are sent to the new front. [b]

Grey, rainy weather.—The heart is better this morning, but does not feel nice,
so I wont go out, nor to church, I must put myself to right again.—I send you a
touching telegram from Aleksei's Georgians;< I answered them & said I should
forward it to him—so perhaps you would thank them in his name again. How
did you find poor Kanin, not too bad I trust. [Your s]ister Olga wrote she is so
happy in her work—Motherdear< runs about all day in hospitals & finds Olgas
especially cosy & nice.—[c]

Beloved, I have popped [sic] into bed after seeing [A. N.] Khvostov who
begged urgently to be received. Well, our good old Fred.< had gaffed quite colossaly again, wh. shows that one must no more tell him anything serious or wh.
is not to be repeated. Khvostov got a letter fr. (his former brother in law) Drentel'n—he will bring it to you, for you to see in what terms it is written. He tells
him that Fredericks sent for him and told him that he wishes to know why
Khvostov judges Dzhunkovsky so unjustily etc. Drentel'n furious, sees in it the
result of that black force (one understands [this to refer to] our Friend<) & that
he pities you & russia if Khvostov perverts all <u>orders</u> in that way.—Khvostov
told Fred. that one must beware of Dzhunkovsky because of his different actions, police etc. Moscou meeting of the nobility, making himself out as a martyr because of Gr.[egory]< & so on, & finding that in the society & clubs one
ought to pay attention to his talks—and not let him receive a nomination [i.e.,
appointment to a post] in the Caucasus. [d]

Oh, that awful gaffeur—now that runs the round of the Preobrazhensky reg. &
the Governors excomerades [sic] & hinders Khvostov terribly. He begs you not
to tell anything to Fredericks, who will make it yet worse, nor Drentel'n, who
will be furious that I saw the letter. Such an unfortunate affair & binds Khvostov's hands. The regiment is not, alas, famous [i.e., good] & hates our Friend, so
he hopes you will soon promote Drentel'n—give him an army brigade, so as that
he should not yet more influence the regiment. Drentel'n writes that [V. N.]
Orloff sent for Dzhunkovsky (soit disant [one says] his brother being very
ill)—N.[icholasha]< proposed him to become hetman of the Tersk troops but
Dzhunkovsky refused. According to "spied upon" correspondance [sic] N. intends proposing him to be his aide. For God's sake don't agree, otherwise we
shall have the whole lot of evil doers brooding harm & mischief there. Give him
any command in front rather, he is a dangerous man pretending to be a martyr. I
said in future Khvostov is to address himself to Voeikov instead of the old
ramoli< gaffeur—no its too, too bad. Tell it V.[oeikov] if he promises to hold his
tongue until he has seen Khvostov. He begs you to receive him one of these
days for affairs. He will send me his answer to Drentel'n.—I begged him to well
think it over, as many will read it, & he must still explain reasons wh. can be
told.—[e, f]

Then as not enough waggons [sic] move, thought it wld. be good if you could
at once send a senator (Dm. Neidhardt) who has often been [on such mis-
sions]—does not matter he has Miechen's< committee and its not for long to
make a revision about the coal in the chief place.[170] Masses are heeped [sic] &
must be moved on to the big towns & if you send him directly it wont be an of-
fense to the new minister.[171] He does not know [A. F.] Trepov, many are against
him as being a very weak & not energetic man. Our Friend is very grieved at his

nomination as He knows he is very against him, his daughter told it to Gr.< & he is sad you did not ask his advice. I too regret the nomination, I think I told you so he is not a sympathetic man—I know him rather well. His daughters were crazy & tried to poison themselves some years ago. The Kiev brother [F. F. Trepov] is far better. Well, one must oblige this one to work hard. [g]

400 waggons ought to come a day with flour, but only 200 do— one must set about things quicker & more energetically—the idea of the revision I think excellent, Senatorial Revision for the coal—if we get that people wont freeze & keep quiet—to send him out to the chief coal places fr. where one forwards it here.[170]—I am sorry to bother you with so many things. I enclose a petition fr. my Galkin for his son. He made A.[nia]< write to several Generals & all say it concerns General (cant spell his name) the little one, Konazarovsky [Kondzerovsky]. Perhaps you would tell Kira< to give it him fr. me. He is a good officer was in the artillery academy, I believe, and Costia< knew about him—so funny for Galkin's son.—Leo< is better, I am glad to say—Volkov is now doing duty [here as my valet in Leo's place]—I am ashamed I took him away fr. the Headquarters. [h]

I do hope the dear little arm [of our son, Aleksei] will be better by the time you get this letter & that it wont spoil the nights rest.— Poor Serbia is being finished off—but it was her lot, had we let Austria do it, our now all the rest—nothing to be done, probably a punishment for the country having murdered their King & Queen. Will Montenegro now be eaten up too, or will Italy help?— Oh & Greece? What shameful game is going on there & in Roumania—I wish one could see clearly. My personal opinion is that our diplomates [sic] ought to be hung—Savinsky has always been the greatest friend of longnosed Ferdinand [I, tsar of Bulgaria] (the same tastes one says) that he always said before he ever went there. Then P. Kozel has neither performed his duty & Elim I think a fool too. Could they not have worked harder?[172a] Look how the Germans dont leave a thing untried so as to succeed. Our Friend was always against this war, saying the Balkans were not worth the world to fight about & that Serbia would be as ungrateful as Bulgaria proved itself.— [i]

Hate yr. having all these worries & I not with you. I find Sazonov might have inquired fr. the Greek Government, why they do not stick to their treaty with Servia[sic]—beastly false Greeks.— How did all the foreigners like being out at the front?—Must quickly end. I miss & long for you quite terribly & kiss & hug you with all the tenderness I am capable off[sic] & yearn for your arms to be around me & rest & forget all that torments one.—Endless fr. yr. old   Wify. [P.S.] On Tuesday [daughter] Olga will be 20. [j]

170. In paragraphs "g" and "h," Alexandra expresses concern for the coal shortage developing in Petrograd and other cities. She urges her husband to dispatch such senators as Dmitry Neidhardt on inspections that could clear bottlenecks. The empress thinks a "revision" must be made in the "chief place[s]" where coal is mined so that an additional 200 train cars ("waggons") will bring fuel "to the big towns" and "here," to Petrograd. See also Letter No. 596a.

171. S. V. Rukhlov was dismissed as minister of communications on October 27, 1915; Alexander Fedorovich Trepov, the "new minister," was appointed to the post on October 30, 1915. Many imagined Alexandra and Rasputin controlled such appointments, but note the empress complains they were not even consulted on this matter. Trepov was openly hostile to Rasputin; despite what Alexandra says, he was anything but "very weak and not energetic."

172a. A. A. Savinsky was Russian envoy to Sofia, 1913-1915. Stanislav Alfonsovich Poklev-sky-Kozell was Russian envoy to Bucharest, 1914-1917. Elim Pavlovich Demidov (Prince San-Donato) was Russian envoy to Athens in Aug. 1912. See Biographical Index entries for additional information on all three.

No. 565/ Telegram 4. Tsarskoe Selo> Stavka. 2 Nov 1915. 12.30> 2.45 p.m. To his majesty. Unspeakably happy with [your] dear letter. Heartily thank you. How is arm [of our son, Aleksei]? [I am] remaining quiet because of [my] heart. Rain mixed with snow. We all tenderly kiss you both. God bless you, dear ones. Alix

---

No. 566/ Her No. 378.   Tsarskoe Selo. Nov. 2nd 1915.
My own Sweetheart,

I send you my very tenderest congratulations for our darling Olga's 20th birthday. How the time does fly! I remember every detail of that memorable day so well, that it seems as tho'—it had all taken place only yesterday.—It is grey & raining, most dreary weather. I wonder how Baby sweet's< arm is, I hope no worse & does not give him too much pain, poor Agooweeone<. How anxiously one waits for news—in Athens an Austrogerman deputation was received, they work hard to attain their aim, & we always trust & are constantly deceived;—one must always be at them energetically & show our power & insistance [sic]. I foresee terrible complications when the war is over and the question of the Balkan territories will have to be settled—then I dread England's selfish politics coming in rude contact with ours—only to well prepare all beforehand, not to have nasty surprises. Now whilst they have great difficulties one must take them in hand.— [a, b]

Yesterday Andron.[nikov] told A.[nia] that Volzhin sent for Zhivakhov [Zhevakhov]< and told that you & I wished him to be appointed, so he gave him the list of all the officials of the Synod, telling him whom wld. he wish to have sent away & replace, one with 8 children, or 6 & so on—of course Zhivakhov declined & the minister of the Interior [A. N. Khvostov] will take him, not to loose [sic] such a perfect gentleman who knows everything about our Church a fond [in depth]. Its downright cowardice & hideous. Why not take him as one of his aides?[166] He [Volzhin] told someone he feared us, but yet more the Duma. Worse than Sabler, how can one do anything with such a poltroon [coward]. If you have papers of his do write that you wish to know "whether you have already appointed Zh.[evakhov]". To you it may seem a mere nothing, but no Deary, he knows all the ins & outs & can be of immense help & he is decided & could support & counsel V.[olzhin] tho' he is a younger man. Why send a poor [i.e., less competent] man because of him, why not as aide, only because we begged for him. Your first wish almost, & he does not fulfil it & no doubt will throw the fault upon Zh. Oh, humanity, so dispisable [sic] only think of themselves, lots of beautiful words & when it comes to deeds—cowardice. [c]

I enclose a charming telr. from the "Erivantsi"<. I find [our daughter] Olga looks better since she lies more—less green and weary. Now its snowing & raining together, such a mess.—O Lovebird, thank you over & over again for yr. sweet letter. I was intensely happy to receive it, it means so much to me a word from you, my Angel. How interesting all you write. I am only rather anxious at Baby's< arm, so asked our Friend< to think about it.—He told me to let [A. N.] Khvostov know, not to answer Drenteln's letter, as it would only be worse, give rise to more talking, be shown about & so forth. He is not obliged, as it was an impertinence & insult writing thus to yr. minister. A.< gave it him over by telephone. She gave me a letter of Kellers for you to read through when you have a free moment; & then as usual a petition. —I am going to give Olga her [birthday] presents in her bedroom as we dine upstairs.—Groten leaves in 2 days to his regiment to give it over & then will remain at Dvinsk, as he has been put en reserve (wh. makes him sad). He looks flourishing & young, can ride again.—To-morrow my Vesselovsky< comes, Vikrestov [Vykrestov] & several petty officers who ran away. I must end now Deary, as I have heaps of papers to read through before dinner.— Goodbye my Beloved, God bless & protect you. I kiss you endlessly, lovingly & longingly.—Ever yr. very own old   Sunny. [d, e]

No. 567/ Telegram 11. Stavka> Tsarskoe Selo. 2 Nov 1915. 7.15> 7.50 p.m. To her majesty. Loving thanks from both [for] dear letters. Arm [of Aleksei] allright[,] so sorry you dont feel well. Fine warm weather. We kiss you all tenderly. Niki

---

No. 568.   Mogilev. Nov. 9th 1915.
My sweet Love-bird,

Many, many thanks for dear letters. So tiresome you again feel worse & that the [heart][172b] is enlarged. Take care of yourself and rest well. But I know that this is a vain wish because one cannot live near the capital without receiving people. Coming here the last evening in the train Baby< was making nonsense & pretended to fall off his chair & he knocked his left arm (under the myshky [armpit]). He felt no pain later on but it became swollen. So the first night here he slept rather restlessly & continually sat up in bed, groaned, called for you & talked to me. A few minutes later he fell asleep again—this went every hour until 4.o['clock]. Except that the house was overheated & the temp. of our rooms was unbearable.[172c] Yesterday he remained in bed. I explained to all that he had simply badly slept & I too, which was true. Thank God today it is over— only he is very pale & had a little more bleeding. Else he is quite himself & we walked in the tiny garden together. At 4.o this afternoon we went to the theatre where they showed us cinema pictures[,] among them your visit south. [a, b]

On the 5th Thursday night, we leave for our visit south. It will last a week, after which we come back here. It will be bad I am afraid for me to give you detailed news by wire—perhaps though I may find time to write to you as the distances between those towns and little places are small—so we shall be standing quietly at some stations probably. Just got your last letter of Nov. 1 in wh you write about Khvost. conversation. Never imagined Drentel'n had been his brother in law. Cannot make out what disturbs him Khv. [sic] in this story of the letter. I wish you paid less attention to such details! I told you a few days ago that I had proposed to Drent the command of the Preobrazh.[ensky Guards Regiment] & I cannot take that back. Please receive General Murray before he leaves for England. Now me must end as I have lots to read. Baby is gone to sleep. God bless you and the girlies. Good-bye my own sweet Sunny-dear I kiss you ever so tenderly & miss you quite awfully. Your own huzy Nicky [c, d]

172b. Instead of writing "heart," Nicholas drew a picture of one at this point in his text. The sketch is quite good!

172c. Is this strange statement a code communication? Sergeev omits the line in his translation: see *Perepiska*, III, p. 426. Sergeev's translation of this important letter is often inaccurate , which is strange considering his normally high scholarly standards.

No. 569/ Telegram 14. Tsarskoe Selo> Stavka. 3 Nov 1915. 9.35> 10.35 a.m. To his majesty. Heartily congratulate [you] on the birthday of our older daughter [Olga]. Sad you are not here. [We] will celebrate Te Deum in my large hospital<. Foggy. Thanks to Baby< for dear letter. We all tenderly kiss you both. What news? Alix

---

No. 570/ Telegram 17. Stavka> Tsarskoe Selo. 3 Nov 1915. 2.45> 3.30 p.m. To her majesty. Loving thanks and good wishes for Olga's 20th birthday. Sad not to be together. Had Te Deum. Warm, grey. Along our front all is quite. Tender kisses Niki

---

No. 571/ Her No. 379.   Tsarskoe Selo. Nov. 3rd 1915.
My very own beloved One,

Many happy returns of our big Olga's 20-th birthday. We are having a Te Deum at 12½ in my big room with the ladies—as it is less tiring for her & me. Such a foggy morning, [our daughter] Tatiana has gone off to the hospital. Rita Khitrovo was yesterday with Olga & touched me by saying, that the wounded are very sad I am not there to do their dressings, as the Dr. hurts them. I always take the worst. So stupid not to be able to work again, but I must keep quiet—one day the heart is more enlarged, the next less & I don't feel nice, so have not even smoked for days; receptions & doklady [reports] are quite enough.—Saw poor Martinov< on crutches, the leg is 4 inches (!) shorter—its now soon a year & by May one hopes he may be able to serve again. Its a marvel that he is alive—how wonderfully he every time escaped, 2 horses killed under him being already wounded & crushed & both bones shot through, broken.—I spoke with Count [N. E.] Nirod about Easter-presents for the army—we did not use up the 3 million roubles you had given fr. the appanage & wh. have to be replaced by the cabinet. A little over 1 m. remains & with that we want to get & order things for Easter. Only each man will get much less, as everything is far more expensive & in such quantities as we need, not even to be had. [a, b]

Then Mr. Malcolm came again with a proposition of a society of the suffragists, who have been working splendidly in France, to look after our refugees, especially the women who are expecting Babys—one can set them to work here under Tatiana's committee[3]—Buchanan must still speak to Sazonov about it. I told Malcolm to see [your sister] Olga, he is off to Kiev to-night & then Odessa—it would have interested you to have seen him, such a nice man & ready to help everywhere. He wrote home to Engl.[and] begging one to collect for our prisoners—most kind, general [Hanbury-]Williams knows him. They have asked me to be the patroness of the hospital in Ella's< house, it will be called after Aunt Alix< I think.—Then I saw my rifles I enclose their names—4 splendid men—one ran away before & was cought [sic] again—50 have already returned—through Belgium & Holland—there they left one now at the Consuls to act as interprator [sic]—they were kindly cared for, fed & clothed, they went at night by the compass. They were made prisoners [N]ov. 11 of last year—Vikrestov's [Vykrestov's] brother is there too, but under another name & as a soldier, so as easier to run away. The one man, the flag-bearer says, that the bits of the flag wh. were not burned by the old Sergeant, different men kept—& the top too.—Then I saw Olga's commander too. And Alia< came with her 2 children for ¾ of an hour, wh. made me very tired. [c, d]

When you see N.P.< alone, tell him to be careful about Dzhunkovsky's book, on account of Drentel'n, who may make a nasty story of it—only that [people] should never guess it came through A.[nia].— The tail< & Bel.[etsky] dine at Ania's—a pitty [sic] I find, as tho' she wanted to play a political part.[58] O she is so proud & sure of herself, not prudent enough, but they begged her to receive them—probably something to give over again & they don't know how to do it otherwise & our Friend< always wishes her to live only for us & such things. Sweetest Treasure I must end now. God bless & protect you & give you wisdom & help. What news about Roumania & Greece? I wish our "fliers" could do something in Bulgaria on the railway lines where so much is being [delivered] in time & succeed. It would be a great thing. Endless kisses of deepest devotion & great yearning. Ever yr. very own old Sunny. [e, f]

No. 572/ Her No. 390.   Tsarskoe Selo. Nov. 3rd 1915.
My own Beloved,

I begin my letter this evening, so as not to forget what Khvostov begged A.[nia] to tell me.

I. It seems the old Man [Goremykin] did not propose the ministery [of agriculture] in a nice way to Naumov, so that he found himself obliged to refuse. [A. N.] Khvostov has seen Naumov since, & is sure that he would accept, or be happy if you simply named him. He is a very right man, we both like him, I fancy Beletsky worked with him before. Being very rich, (his wife is the daughter of Foros Ushkov) so not a man to take bribes—& the one, whom Goremykin proposes, is not worth much—have forgotten his name. [a]

II. Then about Rodzianko of the Duma—Khvostov finds he ought to receive a decoration now, that wld. flatter him & he wld. sink in the eyes of the left party, for having accepted a reward from you. Our Friend< says also that it would be a good thing to do. Certainly it [is a] most unsympathetic [tactic], but, alas, times are such just now, that one is obliged out of wisdom sake to do many a thing one wld. rather not have.— [b]

III. Then he [A. N. Khvostov] begs the police master of Moscou [sic] not to be changed just now, as he has many threads in hand, having belonged to the detective force before. Our Spiridovich won't do there, as it seems he has just remarried a former doubtful singer of gipsy songs—so that one proposes him a post far away of governor I believe.— [c]

IV. Begs you not to have Ksyuin banished to Siberia, as 2 Generals gave him the false news about our disembarkment in Bulgaria (he will bring the names to you)—& the man writes well in the papers & a repremand [sic] might be enough.—[d]

V. Did you get a telegram fr. a woman saying, that you must place Ella< & me in a convent, as he heard something about it, &, if true, wants to have her watched & see what type she is.—[e]

Thats all I think—he dreads meeting Drentel'n, after such a letter finds he cannot give him his hand (ask him to show it you)—if you invite him he must—& if you dont people wld. be unkind & speak. Am so sorry for the poor man.—He brought yr. secret marcheroute (fr. Voeikov) to me & I won't say a word about it except to our Friend to guard you everywhere.[84] If only Kiril< could succeed!— One thing our Friend said, that if people offer great sums (so as to get a decoration), now one must accept, as money is needed & one helps them doing good by giving in to their weaknesses, & 1000 profit by it—it true, but again against all moral feelings. But in time of war all becomes different.—Speak to Khvostov about Zhivakha< (do I still spell it wrongly?) Andr.[onnikov] did not quite give it over as it happened. [f]

Nov. 4-th. Thick snow fell over night, everything white, but zero.—You will receive this letter a few hours before you leave on your journey—God take you into His holy keeping & may your guardian Angels, St. Nicolas [sic] & the sweet Virgin watch over you and Baby sweet<. Shall be near you all the time with heart & soul. How interesting it will be. If you have the chance, give over a greeting & blessing to my Crimeans< & the Nizhegorod.< officers too, if you have the chance, through Yagmin. How I wish we were with you—so emotioning. I read a short description in the "Novoye Vremya" of an eye witness at Riga, & could not read it without tears, so what must be the feelings of those 1000, that see you & Baby together—so simple, so near to them. Can imagine how deeply you feel all this, beloved One, oh the endless blessing, that you command & are yr. own master. Here I send you some flowers to accompany you upon your journey—they stood the day in my room and breathed the same air as your old Sunny, fresias last long in a glass.—[g, h]

If you see our beloved sailors & my giants, think of us & bow to them from us if there should be an occasion.—I hope it will be nice & warm & that will do you all no end of good. For sure Olga Evgenevna< will watch you from somewhere, as she lives at Odessa.—If you do get any sure news about Roumania or Greece, be an Angel & let me know. Elena< fears for her Father [King Peter I of Serbia], because if the worst should happen, he said, he would die with his army—or he may commit suicide. Igor< told us this at luncheon—he says one cant touch the subject of Greece with poor Aunt Olga<. Miss you both this time more than ever, such an endless yearning craving for you, to hear your sweet voice, gaze into your precious eyes & feel your beloved being near me. Thank God, you have Baby to warm you up & that he is of an age to be able to accompany you. Carry this infinite longing alone in my weary soul & aching heart—one cannot get accustomed to these separations, especially when one remains behind. But its good you are away—here the "atmosphere" is so heavy & depressing, I regret yr. Mama [Maria Fedorovna] has returned to town<, fear one will fill her poor ears with unkind gossip. Oh dear, how weary one is of this life this year & the constant anguish & anxiety—one would wish to sleep for a time & forget everything & the daily nightmare. But God will help. When one feels unwell, everything depresses one more—others dont see it tho'.—Our Friend finds Khvostov ought not to shake hands with Dr.[entel'n] after such an insulting letter—but I think Dr. will of his own accord avoid him—am so sorry for the poor fat man [A. N. Khvostov[117]].—Gr.[egory]< has asked to see me to-morrow in the little house [of Anna Vyrubova] to speak about the old man [Goremykin], whom I have not yet seen.—I must end. God bless yr. journey—sleep well, feel my presence near by in any compartment, I cover you with such soft & tender kisses, every little bit of you & lay my weary head upon yr. breast, yr. own old <u>Wify</u>. [i, j, k]

Very fondest thanks my own Sweetheart for your very dear letter, I was more than overjoyed to receive. If you cannot wire details, I can still understand. If you say you saw "ours"—that will mean Marine of the Guard< if "yours"—"Crimeans"< if Edigarov< —"Nizhegorodtsy"<, can always understand more or less—& then what weather—I have the towns & dates, you see, fr. Khvostov to go by & keep it to myself.—I did not mean you should now take the Pr.[eobrazhentsi command] away fr. Dr. but later on.—Read this before you receive Khvostov,—he wants me to prepare you to [cover] several questions. [l]

No. 573/ Telegram 8. Tsarskoe Selo> Stavka. 4 Nov 1915. 11.55 a.m.> 12.45 p.m. To his majesty. Snowed heavily all night. All is white again. Motherdear< arrives at town< this morning. We all kiss and embrace you both without end. Alix

---

No. 574/ Telegram 20. Stavka> Tsarskoe Selo. 4 Nov 1915. 3.30> 4.32 p.m. To her majesty. Loving thanks from both for dear letters. Also snowed over night, but now clear. All came off. Thoughts always together. Tender kisses from both. Niki

---

No. 575.   Mogilev. Nov. 4th 1915.
My own beloved Sunny,
    Many thanks for your dear letters wh arrive here again in the evening. I do hope your poor heart will get alright [sic] soon. I hate to be separated at such moments—understanding so well that it is natural to feel depressed at times when something aches inside. We had a molebin [Te Deum] yesterday for dear Olga[, my sister]—the church was full of generals, officers & men living here[—]most kind, as I ordered this te deum for Baby< & myself. Now many more people are invited to table (thanks to N.P.'s< suggestion); in this way they all pass before one's eyes. [a]
    Several foreigners have left for the front, others for Petrogr[ad]. The tall Montenegrin is returning home, as the King [Nicholas I] needs him. To-morrow we leave for a week. I am glad to go south & especially to see the beloved troops wh I have not seen since the [beginning of the] war. In Odessa we will see the Gvar. Ekip. [Ship's Equipage<] wh. will join all of the guards who are also going to be sent there—in Bessarabia—in about three weeks. Later on I will

explain to you the measures that are to be taken in case Roumania does not allow our army to go through their country. All is quiet along our front. Ask gen Murray's opinion about our state of affairs—it will interest you because he has seen and heard much of [everything] during his visit to our front. Lovy-mine me loves you so very tenderly, me wants you! [b]

Nov 5. Alekseev, Sazonov & I held a council yesterday about Roum & Greece—we came to the conclusion that for the present it is wiser to leave the former quiet & not to send Kyrill<. France & England seem at last to have realised [sic] that greece must be forced to behave decently towards them & the poor Serbians! It is time for me to end. God bless you my Treasure & the girlies & keep you well! I cover your sweet face with endless love & remain ever your own old huzy Nicky. [c]

No. 576/ Telegram 62. Tsarskoe Selo> Stavka. 4 Nov 1915. 10.40> 11.15 p.m. To his majesty. With all my heart I thank you and Baby sweet< for dear letters. What joy to receive them! Sleep well. We all tenderly kiss [you both]. God keep you [both]. Alix

---

No. 577/ Telegram 64. Tsarskoe Selo> Stavka. 5 Nov 1915. 9.50> 10.55 a.m. To his majesty. How charming Baby's< photos are! Very grateful, dear. Will have them copied and those they took of him standing will be made into postcards for sale. [I] thank Aleksei for [his] dear letter. Received him [A. N. Khvostov] at 9, 8 hours earlier than yesterday. Read my letter before [you] receive [him]. [We] all warmly kiss [you]. Alix

---

No. 578/ Telegram 567. Stavka> Tsarskoe Selo. 5 Nov 1915. 6.05> 6.46 p.m. To her majesty. Thanks for news. Afraid letter may arrive after I have seen him [A. N. Khvostov]. Leave at midnight. Rainy, windy. Tenderest love from both. Niki

---

No. 579/ Her No. 381.   Tsarskoe Selo. Nov. 5th 1915.
My own Angel,
   How charming Aleksei's photos are, the one standing ought to be sold as postcard,—both might be really.—Please, be done [i.e., be photographed] with Baby<, also for the public & then we can send them to the soldiers.—If in the south, then with cross & medal without coats & in caps & if at the Headquarter[s] or on the way there, near a wood,—[with] overcoat & fur cap.—Fredericks asked my opinion, whether to permit that cinema of Baby & Joy [his dog] can be allowed to be shown in public; not having seen it, I can not judge, so leave it to you to decide. Baby told Mr. G.[illard], that it was silly to see him "faisant [making] des pirouettes" & that the dog looked cleverer than he—I like that.—We had Mme Zizi< to lunch, she had a whole doklad [report] about all sorts of petitions & ladies, who want to see me.—Rostchakovsky was interesting I told him to write me a Memorandum for you. It concerns the railway line to Archangelsk, wh. he says might work 7 times more than he [i.e., it] does. Ugriumov sent him for affairs concerning P.[utilov iron] works especially, but he profitted [sic] to ask

to see me to tell me how difficult it is for Ugriumov to do anything, as he has no official power given to him all these months. [a, b]

Now one says it will be under Military law, so as to give him help but thats unnecessary, as they are quiet there, no stories or disorders whatsoever. Then he asked for some formal nomination as to see to the railways, the minister of war put it on to Rukhlov etc., if he had a special nomination, then he could give severer orders as he is energetic, the engineers wld. be obliged to listen to him, those who dont work he cld. change, those that are good reward. He could force more goods trains leaving, could hurry on the work of the broad gage & so on. He does not ask, but Rostchakovsky, for the good of the work spoke to me to say a word to you. [The position of] General Gov. is—especially now—during the war—such a very essential place now & much depends upon all being regulated & sent off well and hurried up.— [c]

Do I bore you very much with all these things, poor sweet?—Then of course I add a petition.—General Murray has not yet arrived, but when he comes I shall certainly receive him with pleasure.—Now I had P-ce Galitzin< with his doklad [report] about our prisoners. 4 times a week we send off several waggon [sic] loads of things. How stingy the Synod is, I asked Volzhin should send more Priests & Churches to [our prisoners of war in] Germany & Austria—he wished us to pay, but as it was too much, he made the money be given out of the military fund—really a shame in time of war. Their convents, especially the Moscou [sic] ones are so rich & don't dream of helping. He wrote to St. Serg.[eev Monastery] for them to give us little Images [icons] & Crosses & if they wont gratis we shall pay—and they dont even answer; I shall try now through Ella;<—we have sent 10,000, but what is that wee number.— [d]

I wonder, where this letter will find you! Isa< arrived at Copenhagen & had a good passage.—Maslov sent a Trumpeter with a letter telling the details, of poor Tiesenhausen [Tizengauzen's] death—influenza & heartfailure;—so I told one to give him food & then called him upstairs—he talked nicely. 21 years in the regiment, was on the dear [imperial yacht] Standart with us. I gave him an Image & the envelope of the military-post letter with my name to bring back to the Commander. Now sweetest One, my beloved, my Soul & Sunshine, brightness of my life I must end my letter. I miss you more than words can say & yearn for you my huzy love. I cover you with kisses caresses & undying love. God bless you my A[ngel?]. Ever yr. very own old Wify. [P.S.] Paul< continues being very ill, lost in weight very much—the Drs. wish an operation & to take out the Gall Bladder, [but our] Friend< says he will die then & I remember Fedorov saying he feared an operation because of the heart being weak, with wh. I agree. She [his wife, Princess Paley] says Paul won't hear of an operation; it looks bad their wishing to take it out, is there a bad growth? I should not operate him in the state he is now.— [e, f]

No. 580/ Telegram 68. Tsarskoe Selo> Stavka. 5 Nov 1915. 9.40> 10.30 p.m. To his majesty. [We] sincerely wish you a happy trip, dear ones. God bless and keep you. [We] tenderly kiss [you both]. I will think much of you today. Sleep well. Alix

No. 581/ Telegram 70 in Russian. Tsarskoe Selo> Stavka. 6 Nov 1915. 10.37 a.m.> 1.58 p.m. To his majesty. Terribly gladdened by your dear letters. Warmly thank you both. Hope it is warmer and all is well. [I] feel better but still very tired. The Lord keep you. [We] tenderly kiss you. [I] congratulate you and Voeikov on the regiment's feast day. Alix

---

No. 582/ Her No. 382.   Tsarskoe Selo. Nov. 6th 1915.
My Own,
    Warmest congratulations for yr. dear regiment's feast.—It was an intense joy when your dear letter was brought me this morning & I covered it with kisses—thanks ever so much for having written. So comforting to hear from you when the heart is sad & lonely & yearns for its mate. I am sending you Rost-chakovsky's paper—its quite private, I begged him to write all out so as to have it clearer for you, & I am sure, that you will agree with the chief points. The man is very energetic & full of best intentions & sees that things might work far better with a little help & a few changes—so please read it through.—That is a good plan you intend sending the guards later to Bessarabia after they are reformed & rested—they will be perfection then. Well, may God help those miserable Serbi-ans.—I fear, they are done for & we cannot reach them in time.—Those beastly Greeks, so unfair leaving them in the lurch.[173] [a, b]
    Our Friend<, whom we saw yesterday evening, when he sent you the telegram, was afraid that, if we had not a big army to pass through Roumania, we might be cought [sic] in a trap from behind.—Alekseev is worth 100 longnosed Sazonov's, who seems somewhat feeble, to say the least of it.—Well Lovy, He [Rasputin] thinks I better now see the old Gentlemen [Goremykin] & gently tell it him, as if the Duma hisses him, what can one do, one cannot send it away for such a rea-son[, so you are forced to dismiss Goremykin as chairman of the council of ministers]. You thought out something with [A. S.] Taneev for him, did you not? I feel sure he will understand it. If you get a wire from me—all is arranged or: its done—that means I have spoken & then you can write or, when you return, send for him. He [Goremykin] loves you so deeply that he wont be hurt & I shall say it as warmly as I can—He [Rasputin] is so sorry as venerates the old Man.—But he [Goremykin] can always be yr. help & counsellor as old Mishch. [V. P. Meshchersky] was—& better he goes by yr. wish than forced by a scandle [sic], wh. wld. hurt you & him far more. He [Rasputin] spoke well & it did me good to have seen him. Coughs very much & worries about Greece. Your pres-ence in the Army with Baby< brings new life to all & to Russia, he was always repeating it.—He finds you ought to tell Volzhin you wish Zhivakhov [Zhevak-hov] to be named his aide[166]—he is well over 40, older than Istomin, whom Sa-marin took, knows the Church far better than Volzhin & can be of the very greatest help. Now old Flavian has died, ours [Vladimir] ought to go there [to Kiev] as highest place & Pitirim here, a real worshipper.[174]— [c, d]
    I saw Senator Krivtsov this morning—he gave me his book—I cried reading of the horrors the Germans did to our wounded & prisoners—cannot forget the atrocities, to think that civilised [sic] people could be so cruel—during battle, when one is mad, that [is] another thing. I know they say cossacks did horrors at Memel—a few cases of course there may have been out of revenge. Better to

forget it, as I firmly believe they are better now—but when once we begin to advance & their needs become greater, then I fear our poor men may fare worse.—Mother Elena sat with me for some time, she is intensely grateful that you allowed her with her 400 nuns & 200 children to live at Neskutchnoye where its so peaceful & quiet. They have only got the dining room on the midle [sic] floor as our furniture fr. Belovezh & Varsovie [Warsaw] are kept in the other rooms.—All my tender thoughts dont leave you, Angel dear & agooweeone< on your journey, oh I do hope the weather will be sunny & bright—do Baby good, dampness acts on him & makes him pale always.—Precious One, I kiss you with deep tenderness & loving caresses, passionately love. God Almighty bless and protect you my huzy darling, my bright sunshine.—Ever yr. very own old wify <u>Alix</u>. [P.S.] When you are away, I always dream—shows what it is not to have Sweetheart near me.—Bow to the old man [Fredericks], I do hope he wont hinder yr. movements. Give the little Admiral< & N.P.< also my love. Wonder, whether Dmitri< is with you or not. [e, f, g]

173. Serbia fought back the Austrian attack of 1914, but Bulgaria's entry into the war (September 1915) put Serbia at a new disadvantage. In October 300,000 German, Austrian and Bulgarian troops attacked 200,000 Serbians. The kingdom was completely occupied within ten weeks, though half of the Serbian army escaped. Alexandra's anger at the Greeks was based on their unwillingness to help Serbia. Bulgaria defeated a small Anglo-French expeditionary force. It fled to Thessaloniki with the agreement of Prime Minister Venizelos, who favored entering the war as a member of the Entente. But Constantine I, brother-in-law of Wilhelm II, was pro-German; he was determined to keep Greece neutral and to block aid to the Entente. Constantine dismissed Venizelos in October 1915. In 1916 Venizelos organized a government at Thessaloniki that declared war on Germany and Bulgaria. In 1917 the Allies pressured Constantine to abdicate in favor of his younger son, Alexander, who, with Venizelos as prime minister, finally brought Greece fully into the war.

174. The four most important prelates were, in order of prestige, the metropolitans of Petrograd, Moscow and Kiev, and the Exarch of Georgia. They were also permanent members of the governing council of the Holy Synod. At the outbreak of the war, these posts were occupied by Vladimir, Makary, Flavian and Pitirim. Vladimir and Flavian were hostile to Rasputin; Makary and Pitirim were Rasputin allies. Flavian died in November 1915. In this letter, Alexandra proposes that her husband demote Vladimir to Kiev and promote Pitirim to Petrograd. Nicholas did this. Such "leap-frogging" created a scandal, and was taken as another indication of Rasputin's power in the Church and state. Alexandra's crack—"ours [Vladimir] ought to go there [to Kiev] as highest place [he deserves]"—was sarcastic, though it is true that Pitirim, "a real <u>worshipper</u>," was an old favorite of the royal family and Rasputin. See also Footnote 175.

No. 583/ Telegram 6 in Russian. Novomirgorod> Tsarskoe Selo. 6 Nov 1915. 9.00> 11.25 p.m. To her majesty. [We] thank [you] warmly for letters and news. Weather good, clear. Passing many military trains. Travelling marvellously. [We] warmly kiss all. Nicky

No. 584/ Telegram 75. Tsarskoe Selo> Odessa. 7 Nov 1915. 12.15> 1.25 p.m. To his majesty. My tender thoughts go with you [both]. Thank you for telegram last evening. Same weather, no sun. Yesterday evening went to our hospital< at midnight because one of our officers was very ill. We all warmly kiss you both. Alix

No. 585/ Her No. 383.   Tsarskoe Selo. Nov. 7th 1915.

My own beloved Nicky dear,

Precious one, my thoughts dont leave you. So grateful for yr. telegram yester-day evening fr. Novomirgorod—comforting to see so many military trains pass—God bless the brave souls! I have nothing of interest to tell. Yesterday evening we dined at 7½ because the 3 youngest girls went at 8 to the panikhida [funeral service] of the young officer, who died in the big palace<. From 9-9½ I went to our hospital to see one who is very dangerously ill & I could not bear the idea of not going to him for a little bit—& then I passed through all the wards to bid goodnight. I had not been for a week & was glad to find all the others looking and feeling much better. I had Vil'chkovsky with a long doklad [report], an account of the year, money questions etc. & then Ania got me to sledge for ½ an hour the interior Babol.-park, where you walked near my little carriage—3 degrees of frost, we went much at a footpace, as then it was easier for me to breathe. Mme B.< has come just now!!—Longing for a wire from Odessa, all thoughts were with you.—I feel my letter is mighty dull, but I have absolutely nothing interesting to tell.—Sweet Angel, long to ask heaps about yr. plans con-cerning R.[oumania], our Friend< is so anxious to know. [a, b]

Bezobrazov is inspecting the young soldiers at Novgorod to-day. What now about poor Paul?< I doubt his ever being able to take up his service, to my mind its a finished man, that does not mean that he may not continue living with care, but not at the war, & I pitty [sic] him deeply. Wont you give Dmitri< over to Bezobrazov to use then? Huzy mine, I long for you & love you "with unending true devotion deeper more than I can say, better better every day"—you remem-ber that old song of 21 years ago? God's blessing be upon you my Sweetheart, sunshine. I cover you with kisses. Ever yr. very   Own. [P.S.] Its cosy to get back into the train after a tiring day? Is there still a chance of yr returning the 14th or only later? [c, d]

No. 586/ Telegram 1. Odessa Sup.[reme Command]> Tsarskoe Selo. 7 Nov 1915. 5.20> 7.20 p.m. To her majesty. Fondest thanks [for] news. Had a very good day. Looked through some transport ships and hospital ship. After lunch splendid review of our beauties [probably the Guards Equipage<] and others. Cold, windy, sunny weather. Perfect order in town. Tender kisses from both. Niki

---

No. 587/ Unnumbered telegram in Russian. Tiraspol Railroad Station> Tsar-skoe Selo. 8 Nov 1915. 3.30> 5.20 p.m. To her majesty. We thank [you] very much for letters. Appearance and condition of the troops above praise. Great joy to see them. Weather cold. To-morrow we go to visit Veselkin. We warmly kiss all. Niki

---

No. 588/ Telegram 83. Tsarskoe Selo> Razdel'naya. 8 Nov 1915. 10.00> 11.35 a.m. To his majesty. Poor Echappar< injured [his] head terribly in automobile accident in Minsk last night. Professor Mirotvorets thinks [he suffered] fracture at base of skull. In the night he performed a skull trepanation on him which went off well. Condition remains serious. Has not regained consciousness. Pulse and breathing satisfactory. Yesterday I went sledging for a half hour. Happy with yesterday evening's telegram. We warmly embrace you [both]. God keep [you]. Alix

---

No. 589/ Telegram 96. Tsarskoe Selo> Skinosy. 8 Nov 1915. 6.15> 7.20 p.m. To his majesty. Am happy all was well. To-morrow in thoughts will be even more with you [both]. Greetings to Veselkin<. Poor Echappar< died this morning. Great loss for Georgi< and for my train.[19] [We] warmly kiss [you]. How is count [Frederick]'s health? Sleep well. Alix

---

No. 590/ Her No. 384.   Tsarskoe Selo. Nov. 8th 1915.
My sweetest Huzy dear,
     I am so glad that all went off so well at Odessa & that you saw so many interesting things & our dear sailors too, but what a pitty [sic] that the weather was not warmer. Here it continues, about 3 degrees & no sun.—I wired to you about poor Echappar's< accident & operation, as I got the news this morning. I do hope he will pull through, tho' its a terribly dangerous place—oh those motors, how careful one must be.—And Fredericks keeps on alright? It costs [i.e., worries] our Friend< a lot, & he finds one really must not take him [on a trip] another time, anything may happen—besides he might suddenly take you for somebody else ([Kaiser] William for instance) & make a scandle [sic]—I don't know why he [Rasputin] says this.—Something has got wrong with my pen and my writing is queer.—Alas, again wont go to Church, but wiser not on account of B.<—How glad I am, that you were so contented with all you saw at Tiraspol what good it must do them seeing you, & how refreshing & emotioning for you. I am sending you a telegram. He dictated to me the other day I saw Him, walking about, praying & crossing himself—about Roumania & Greece & our troops passing through, & as you will be at Reni to-morrow, he wishes you to get it before. He wanders about & wonders what you settled at the Headquarters, finds you need lots of troops there so as not be cut off from behind.—In the papers Grigorovich< sends (so grateful you let me get them as most interesting generally) one sees how many guns & troops they send to Bulgaria. Hang those submarines, who hinder ones fleet & any disembarcation & they have time to collect so much.— [a, b]
     When one day our troops will march into Const.[antinople] he [Rasputin] wants one of my regiments to be the first, don't know why.—I said, I hoped it wld. be our beloved sailors, tho' they are not mine, at heart they are nearest to us all.—I long for news about the Guard etc.—Ania's brother [S. A. Taneev] has arrived & its her mothers [Nadezhda Taneeva] & Alia's< birthday, so shall only see her this evening. Do send me a message once for her, she is sad to have none. I am much grieved about Echappar's< death. Georgi< will be awfully sad and all who knew him except Minny [Maria Georgievna]. And for my train[19] a great loss & I was just thinking about arranging for his train to go south, but perhaps I can let Riman's, wh. goes from Kharkov, go to Odessa, as one will need a good train there. [See also Letter No. 1677d.]—So tiresome that cannot go about again because of my health, had wanted to do a lot during your ab-

sence.—We had Nini< & Emma< to tea & we talked long about their Father [V. B. Fredericks] & how to keep him back next time [you travel]. [c, d]

I am going this evening at 8½ for half an hour to our hospital< to see the one who is so bad, as they say he is better since he saw me, & perhaps it may help again. I think its natural, why those who are so very ill feel calmer & better when I am there, as I always think of our Friend & pray whilst sitting quietly near them or stroking them—the soul must prepare itself when with the ill if one wishes to help—one must try & put oneself into the same plan & help oneself to rise through them, or help them to rise through being a follower of our Friends.—Now Lovebird, I must end. God bless & protect you & keep you from all harm. Oh how one longs to be together at such serious times to share all. Endless blessings, fondest, tenderest kisses Nicky sweet, fr. yr. deeply & passionately loving old Wify   Sunny. [e]

No. 591/ Telegram 102. Tsarskoe Selo> Kul'mskaya. 9 Nov 1915. 1.07> 1.57 p.m. To his majesty. Grey weather. [We] go to Echappar's< funeral in church of court hospital. Am receiving General Murray today. Health so-so. My tender thoughts and prayers are with you. We warmly kiss you. Alix

---

No. 592/ Telegram 6 in Russian. Reni> Tsarskoe Selo. 9 Nov 1915. 2.27> 3.20 p.m. To her majesty. Thanks for telegram. After inspection of our troops we visited a church, all institutions and Veselkin's< flagship. [He] has done astonishing amount here, and well. Cold weather. [We] warmly kiss [you]. Niki

---

No. 593/ No. 385.   Tsarskoe Selo. Nov. 9th 1915.
My own beloved Sweetheart,

Grey, thawing & very dark. Well, I went yesterday evening to our hospital, sat some time near the bed of Smirnov[—]temp. still high but breath quieter—said goodevening to the others—3 were lying on their backs playing on guitars & quite cheery.—Xenia< telegraphed, that [your sister] Olga is going to her for a few days, I am glad as it will do her no end of good, as her nerves seem to me rather down, ever since she came to Petrograd & one filled her ears with horrors, & Kiev, wh. Militsa< & Stana< had spoiled by wicked talks.—[a]

In one of the copies of a German newspaper they write, that whilst the allies are wasting time discussing about Roumania, we & the Bulgarians are not wasting time making our preparations—yes, they never dawdle & our diplomates [sic] do most piteously [sic]. I wonder whether energetic Kitchener will manage anything with Tino<.[173] —Could one but get hold of the German submarines in the black sea, they are sending out more of them & they will paralise [sic] our fleet completely. Interesting all Veselkin< will have to tell you, I hope they are all well fortifying etc. all along the Roumanian-Bulgarian frontier—always better to calculate for the worst, as the Germans seem to be collecting all their forces down there now. It sounds absurd my writing all this, when you know a 1000 times better than me what to do;—I have nobody to speak with on such subjects;—but what a lot of men they send down there, wish we could hurry up a bit.—How glad I am that you are satisfied with all you saw at Reni & that Veselkin works well, how proud he must have been to show you his church —may it only not suffer on [account of] have [having] to be taken away.— [b]

I received Altfater, Porgrebnyakov, Rumella & Semenov of the 1-st artillery brigade of the Body-Guards as its their feast, & the touching people gave me 1000 [rubles for use in my charities]— [our daughters] Olga 150, & Tatiana 150.—I went with Tatiana to the panikhida [funeral service] for Echappar<—Baranov. was there, Kotsebu grown quite grey, Yakovlev, Shulenburg, Kaulbars & [D. M.] Knyazhevich & all the ladies. As my train[19] stands without work at Dvinsk have told it to bring his body.—General Murray is enchanted with all he saw, Anias brother [S. A. Taneev] took him about a lot.—Excuse a dull letter, but am tired & achy as slept very badly these last 3 nights.—Very tenderest blessings, fondest, warmest kisses, Precious One, fr. yr. very own old Wify. [c]

No. 594/ Telegram 107. Tsarskoe Selo> Balta Podol'skaya. 10 Nov 1915. 10.06> 11.15 a.m. To his majesty. Terribly gladdened by unexpected letter from Aleksei, tenderly thank him. Warm, dark, everything thawing. All [our] thoughts [are] together. [We] warmly kiss you. God keep [you]. Thank Zhilik< for letter. Alix

---

No. 595/ Telegram 3 in Russian. Balta> Tsarskoe Selo. 10 Nov 1915. 3.17> 5.58 p.m. To her majesty. Many thanks for letters. Only just held review of Nizhegorodtsy<, Severtsy and Khopertsy. All appeared in ideal condition. 4 deg. of frost. Fog. Was glad to see many acquaintances to whom I conveyed your greetings. [We are] now moving on. [We] tenderly kiss [you]. Niki

---

No. 596/ Her No. 386.   Tsarskoe Selo. Nov. 10th 1915.
My own beloved One,

It seems to be darker every morning—nearly all the snow gone & three degrees of warmth.—Now the letters have to leave much earlier, the trains have changed it seems.—By the by did you settle anything about a senator to inspect the railways & coaldepots & see to set all moving, because really it is a shame[170]—in Moscou [sic] one has no butter & here still many things are scarce & prices very high, so that for rich people even it is hard living—& this is all known & rejoiced at in Germany as our bad organisation [sic], wh. is absolutely true.—Such a nice surprise Baby dears< letter from Odessa & Mr. Gillards [Gilliard's]—of course you cant write, I can imagine how even in the train you are bothered with papers.— Perhaps, if you do send me a word, you will give a message of thanks to A.[nia]< for her letters, because when I said you wired thanks for letters, she said it meant ours.—I suppose this letter will find you at the Headquarter[s]. Nini< understood you were probably arriving here on the 14-th, to me it does not seem very likely, as after such a journey you will for sure have lots to speak to Alekseev about.—Stupid heart is enlarged again & the old pain in the legs was very strong—nevertheless have many people to receive to-day,—ex lancer [D. M.] Knyazhevich too, don't know what shall have to tell him.— [a, b]

Our Friend< told me to wait about the old man [Goremykin] until he has seen uncle [A. A.] Khvostov on Thursday, what impression he will have of him [see Letter No. 598f]—he is miserable about the dear old man, says he is such a righteous man, but he dreads the Duma hissing him & then you will be in an awful position.—Is the Zemstvo reform which Nikolasha< wants to bring into the Caucasus a good thing? The people and many different nationalities, can they grasp this—or do you find [it to be a] a good reform? My personal weak brain does not find it yet time [to do this]—you will see "Novoye Vremya" page 7 below of Nov. 10th.—What hideously dull letters I write! Forgive me sweetest. The Austrian sisters [i.e., nurses] have arrived, one is a good acquaintance of Marie Bariatinskys from Italy. Mme Zizi< will beg Motherdear< to see them & the Germans when they return, then I can too; & one must do such things, its for humanity's sake[—]then they will be more willing to help our prisoners too;—& if she sees them one cannot find fault with me.— [c, d]

Volzhin will need a good deal of "picking up" from you, he is weak & frightened—when all is going to be well arranged about Varnava, he suddenly writes to him privately that he should ask for his dismission [i.e., resignation as bishop of Tobol'sk]—young [A. N.] Khvostov told him it was very wrong—but he is a coward & frightened of public opinion, so when you see him, make him understand that he serves you first of all & the Church—& that it does not concern society nor Duma.—Princess Palei says Paul< eats a lot now but looses [sic] daily in weight—he weighs less than Anastasia now, at night sometimes screams from pain & then again feels better. The gall bladder is becoming atrophied & therefore the gall spreads everywhere, tho' he has not become yellow. They want him to be operated at once upon yr. return, in some hospital station—they say its the only thing to save him, & our Friend says he will certainly then die, the heart not being strong enough. To-day Chigaev is to see him. His colour frightened me, the same as [your] Uncle Wladimir [Vladimir Alexandrovich] had the last months, & [your] Uncle Aleksei [Alexandrovich] before he left abroad then, & looking so like Anpapa [Alexander III], hollow under the eyes. He receives nobody, not wishing them to see him; am so awfully sorry for him—at last all his wishes achieved—& nothing of any avail.—Now goodbye Lovebird, God bless—& protect you. Ever such tender, passionately, loving kisses, Nicky sweet, beloved huzy, fr. yr. very own old wife Sunny. [P.S.] How is the little Admiral?< What have you settled about Dmitri?< Love to the boy[, son Aleksei]. [e, f]

No. 597/ Telegram 112. Tsarskoe Selo> Nikolaev. 11 Nov 1915. 11.47 a.m.> 12.57 p.m. To his majesty. Cold, snowing. Received touching telegram from Yagmin, [he] is seeing you.—wonderful impressions but probably quite tiring. In thoughts always together. [I] warmly embrace and kiss [you]. Receptions every day but [I] do not go out because of [my enlarged] heart. Children also tenderly kiss you both. [Our daughters] Tatiana and Marie having tea at Anichkov< after committee [meeting there]. Alix

---

No. 598/ Her No. 387.   Tsarskoe Selo. Nov. 11th 1915.
My own beloved Sweetheart,

I am so glad you saw the Caucasian cavalry—I got a charming telegram afterwards from Yagmin.—Can imagine their enchantment at last to have seen you; &
the Tvertsi [soldiers from Tver saw] Baby< for the first time.—Dark, windy,
snowing, 1 degree of frost—the shortest days, so dreary.—Yesterday afternoon
dear Lili Den< came to us for tea, on her way from Helsingfors to the country.
She saw her husband [Karl Dehn], & he told her many interesting episodes of
their fighting, firing from sea on shore.—Oh, my dear, I received Olga Orlov, on
purpose I had [our daughters] Olga & Anastasia in the room & all went well, but
when I got up she begged to speak to me alone & then went off about her husband [V. N. Orlov] & what I had against him & that she hoped I did not believe
all the calumnies spread against him etc. I was sorry for the woman, but it was
horribly painful, as I could not offend nor hurt her—I got through somehow, but I
dont think she went away any the wiser—I was kind & calm, did not fib—well I
wont bother you with the talk & thank God its over—one has so to pick out ones
words, that they should not be turned against one afterwards.—[a, b]

The Russian motor sanitary detachment of Verol[y]as wh. is under my protection, worked splendidly in France, a while ago I got the telegrams from him &
Mme Isvolsky [Izvolskaya] & to-day I read a description in the "Novoye Vremya"—the one motor got holes.—Then I saw Prince Gelovani to speak about Eupatoria wh. he looked after for me. Now he goes for 10 days to his family to the
Caucasus & then straight to the regiment. He is delighted the Css. Worontzov
[Elizabeth Vorontsova-Dashkova] has been taken away as the harm she did was
very great. About the Zemstvo he is very contented & says its obligatory to be
arranged as they must see to the state of the roads & railways & so on;—he is
such a nice, cosy [sic] man, with his amusing Russian. Poor Petrovsky sat for
nearly an hour with me & we talked over the question of his divorce without
end[,] all so complicated.—A week to-day that you left us—but it seems much
longer & I have such a yearning for you my two Darlings.—Wont you have a lot
to tell us! I continue receiving daily, my heart is still enlarged so do not go out &
miss my hospital, but I want to get decent for your return. [Our daughter] Olga
looks better and less tired, I find.—[c, d]

Well Deary, I saw [D. M.] Knyazhevich & found him looking very well, fresh,
good look in the eyes & nothing about him like last year. Feels well, so of
course I could not say anything. He leaves at the the [sic] same time as this letter for the Headquarters, Alekseev told him to be there on the 14[-th], well he
will be already [on] the 13-th. He has good complexion—his wife [Lidiya
Knyazhevicha] finds him also quite alright—a momentary weakness—I should
not personally listen to Erdeli, as he is not famous & a jealous nature—Georgi<
heard such strange things too—but you will see he is just now looking flourishing
& bright too.—He thinks, that perhaps [E. C.] Arsenev may receive our brigade,
that would be lovely.—Goodbye, Beloved, God bless & protect you. I cover your
sweet face with kisses and tender caresses.—Ever, Huzy love, yr. very own wify
Alix. [P.S.] How is the old man Fred.< In town< one grumbles again so awfully against dear old Goremykin so despairing. To-morrow Gr.[egory]< sees
old [A. A.] Khvostov & then I see him in the evening—He wants to tell his impression, if [he would be] a worthy successor [as prime minister] to Goremy-

kin,—old Khvostov receives him like a[n ordinary] petitioner in the ministry [of justice]. [e, f]

No. 599/ Telegram 119 in Russian. Novopoltavka> Tsarskoe Selo. 11 Nov 1915. 7.30> 11.40 p.m. To her majesty. Heartily thank you for telegram. To-day it was warm at last. Magnificent review of a division at Kherson in morning, and during day of another [division] at Nikolaevo. Very brightest impressions. To-morrow evening [we] return to Stavka. Warmly embrace all. Niki

---

No. 600/ Telegram 16 in Russian. Tsarskoe Selo> St. Uza. 12 Nov 1915. 12.18> 1.50 p.m. To his majesty. [I] thank you for yesterday's telegram. Is it still necessary [for me] to write a long letter? Health still not famous, heart enlarged. Receptions every day. [We] warmly embrace you both. God keep [you]. Alexandra

---

No. 601/ Her No. 388.   Tsarskoe Selo. 12 Nov 1915.
My own beloved Nicky dear,
    Is this the last letter to you, I wonder. One says the Erivantsi< are preparing for the 17-th when you go to see them—the guard awaits you too—you arrive only this evening at the Headquarters so, that it seems to me impossible you should leave the 13-th— besides Bark awaits you at Moghilev, & for sure heaps of work. In case therefore if we do not see each other the 14-th [the day of their wedding anniversary], I send you my very, very tenderest loving thoughts & wishes & endless thanks for the intense happiness & love you have given me these 21 years —oh, Darling, it is difficult to be happier than we have been, & it has given one strength to bear much sorrow. May our children be as richly blessed—with anguish I think of their future—so unknown! Well, all must be placed into God's hands with trust & faith.—Life is a riddle, the future hidden behind a curtain, & when I look at our big Olga, my heart fills with emotions & wondering as to what is in store for her—what will her lot be. Now about affairs again. Groten suddenly turned up, he bid his regiment goodbye & was touched to tears by their kindness & the regimental farewell. He went to the Headquarters presented himself to General Konazarovsky [Kondzerovsky], who did not receive him over amiably & said he could not tell him anything as you were away. He [Groten], the stupid [boy], left again for the country instead of patiently awaiting yr. return. He is perfectly well & can serve—wonder what brigade he will get? As regiment I believe the Horse grenadiers are free, my fat Toll, I fancy, receives the Pavlogradtsi (not a beauty, but one says thorough).— Does Dobriazin [Drobryazin] get a brigade? Kusov waits for a regiment. The Severtsi are free too, I believe. Heaps of questions, you see— But get work for Groten, he is young & strong & its no good his sitting in the country in the reserves. [a, b]
    I sleep abominably, get off only after 3, and this night after 5—so dull. Heart still enlarged.—A.[nia]< walked on her crutches guided by Zhuk< from Fed.[orov] hospital through our garden to Znamenia<, of course far to much, already twice, & now feels very tired. —I received again yesterday, to-day I have

Rostovtsev< & I read already a fat doklad [report] of his this morning. At midnight I got yr. telegram yesterday about Kherso and Nikolaev—it took 4 hours coming & I was beginning to get anxious without any news. [c]

It will seem strange to live in a house again, I am sure, after your long roaming about.—Fancy, Olga Orlova telephoned to her friend Emma< (she has broken with Nini< for her finding Voeikov at fault in everything), that she had seen me & not spoken a word about her affairs—such a lie! And when she gave her word of honour to me she had never said anything against me, the old Css. [Emma Fredericks] says she did speak against me, & he [her husband, V. N. Orlov] said nasty insinuations at Livadia against me to his friend Emma & she, Olga O.[rlova,] says he never did, nor wld. try to harm a woman's reputation— one nest of lies—they don't touch me, because I know both be liars, only I hate words of honour, when one does not know how to answer.—Now my sweetest love, I must end my scrawl. Let me know about when to expect you. God bless and protect, guard & guide you.—I kiss you with deepest tenderness and boundless love & devotion, & long to rest my weary head upon yr. breast.—Ever, Huzy mine, yr. very own old Sunny. [d]

P.S. Darling, I forgot to speak about Pitrim, the exarch of Georgia —all the papers are full of his departure fr. the Caucasus & how greatly he was beloved there—I send you one of the cuttings to give you an idea of the love & gratitude one bears him there. Shows that he is a worthy man, and a great Worshipper, as our Friend< says[174]—He [Rasputin] foresees Volzhin's fright & that he will try to dissuade you, but begs you to be firm, as he is the only suitable man. To replace him [as exarch] he [Rasputin] has nobody to recommend, unless the one who was at Belovezh, I suppose thats the Grodno one? A good man he says—only not S.F. or A.V. or Hermogen,[175] they would spoil all with their spirit there. [e]

Old Vladimir already speaks with sorrow, that he is sure to be named to Kiev—so it would be good you did it as soon as you come, to prevent talks & beggings fr. Ella<[175] etc.—Then Zhivakhov [Zhevakov] he begs you straight to nominate as help [i.e., assistant] to Volzhin,[166] he is older than Istomin so age means nothing & knows the Church affairs to perfection—its your will & you are master.—There, that was a long post scriptom.— W[ify]. [f]

175. Discussion concerns the "bishops' leapfrog" explained in Footnote 174. Alexandra foresees it would be opposed by Volzhin and her own sister, Elizabeth ("Ella"), mother-superior and a church leader in her own right. Rasputin warns against appointing Sergei, archbishop of Finland ("S.F."), Antony, bishop of Volhynia ("A.V.") or Hermogen to the soon-to-be vacant exarchate of Georgia. Thanks to Rasputin, Aleksei, the unsavory and disgraced bishop of Pskov, followed Pitirim in Georgia. Fuhrmann, *Rasputin*, pp. 155, 246-247, discusses the thirteen of the some 70 bishops of the Russian Orthodox Church who were more or less members of Rasputin's "party" at this time.

No. 602/ Telegram 001425. Mogilev> Tsarskoe Selo. 12 Nov 1915. 10.40 p.m.> 12.43 a.m. To her majesty. Just arrived. [Will] spend night in train. Lovely impressions of whole journey. Tender thanks [for] many dear letters received on the way back. Better write still. Give her [Anna<] my love. Weather mild, snowing hard. Hope you will soon feel better. Kiss you and the girlies lovingly. Niki

No. 603.   Mogilev. The Train.   Nov. 12 1915.
My own beloved Darling,

Here we are back again having been away fr. the Stavka exactly a week to the
hour. One feels nearer to you <u>somehow</u> as the letters arrive on the next day, but
during our trip we received them only on the third. I cannot say yet when we
will return home, but I think it might happen in about six days. That will be a
happy moment—& there will be so much to tell you. [a]

Well, thank God, our journey passed off & ended splendidly! A whole rainbow of impressions! Only, alas! the weather was not friendly—we hoped for a
little warmth, but the south received us quite coldly with sharp wind. Only in
Odessa did we have a single sunny day. We were met there by Kyrill<, Boris<
& Shcherbachev. The streets were packed with young soldiers, cadets, military
school students & ordinary people—it was quite like my visit there last spring.
But this time I had our Treasure [Aleksei] with me. He sat with a serious face,
saluting all the time. Through the noisy crowd and the shouts of "hurrah" I could
hear women's voices calling out: "The heir, the angel, the beautiful boy!" So
touching! He heard them too, & smiled at them. After visiting the cathedral we
drove to the port & got on board a large French ship converted into a floating
hospital; [we also boarded] the new cruiser "Pruth"—formerly "Medzhidie"—a
fine ship almost entirely rebuilt; then [we boarded] the korabl'-priyut [home
ship] for boys whose fathers are serving in the war, under Aleksei['s patronage]
(pretty Mme. Sosnovskaya heads it); & at the end one of seventy transports under command of Admiral Khomenko. A large inspection took place before evening. What a magnificent appearance the Ekip.< presented! I offered Polushkin
& Rodionov a few words while motoring past, but have not said good bye since
I hope to see them when the guards are assembled. [b]

There were many troops, inspection lasted a long time, and it was quite dark
when we returned to the station. I spoke long with Shcherbachev, whom I promoted adj.[utant]-gen.[eral]. The following morning, Nov. 8th, I inspected an
entire army corps, very close to the train, near a village called Eremeievka. The
troops were magnificent, well trained, equipped, and so on. I lunched in the
train on the way to Tiraspol, where we were on the day we journeyed to Kishi-
nev. Here we saw another corps, this stationed at Odessa—[it appeared] even
better. We travelled through the night to Reni, reaching it on morning of 9th, at 9
o.c[lock]. The regular railway is old & terribly bumpy here, the train rocks as a
ship on the sea. The Danube is a powerful, wide river between beautiful forested
banks, they reminded one of eng.[lish] lakes. Our fat friend Veselkin met us in
early morning, he explained everything in advance. What we saw was <u>so</u> interesting. I must own he has a gift of good organisation [sic], he knows to make
people of different sorts work well in full agreement. Describing all this in a
letter would take too long! [c]

Here I inspected the 3rd Turkestan rif.[le] brig.[ade]—they were like our best
guard reg.[iments]. We also had a look at several of the recently equipped
heavy batteries which cover the river Pruth as it flows into the Danube. They
are very well situated. Again we travelled all night, arriving at Balta on Nov.
10th, just after breakfast. 4 deg.[rees] frost, fog. That was a pity because the
country is charming. After a ¼ hour motor drive we arrived at the locale of the

inspection of the Cauc.[asian] cav.[alry] div.[ision]. All four regs. were splendidly beautiful! I was so sorry you could not admire them! [d]

I gave your greetings to the officers of the three dragoon regs. On the way to
Kherson we met many trains filled with young soldiers we inspected at stations
where we stopped. Insp.[ection] of the 2nd Finnish rif.[le] div.[ision] took place
in this town, & after noon the 4th Finnish rif.[le] div.[ision] at Nikolaevo. It finally became warmer, & my fingers stopped aching when I rode. Aleksei took
the strain of the week amazingly well, tho' occasionally he suffered fr. a slight
nose bleed. He was cheery the whole while. All is well with the old man
[Fredericks]. He is at times rather pale at table, but has no fatigue fr. our activity
& walking.[e]

Nov. 13th. We returned home at 10 o.c[lock] in the morning. Found the rooms
breezy, cool & freshened. Alekseev's doklad [report] lasted long—each [of us]
had much to tell the other. To-morrow I will give him the newspapers you sent
me. I woke up with a strong cold in the left nostril, I think of spraying it yet
with cocaine. Aside fr. that I feel strong—much energy! The schedule for the
trains has been changed. They arrive at 11 in the morning & leave at 6, which is
more convenient—at least for me. I do so hope yr. poor heart will get better &
not cause you further pain. I always feel for you, my Wify-darling, when I hear
your health is not good & you suffer. Every one here learned with sorrow of
Echappar's< death. Such a capable, energetic man! Such a loss! Well, my
treasure, I must end. God bless you & the girlies! With countless kisses, ever
your old huzy Nicky. [f]

No. 604/ Telegram 120. Tsarskoe Selo> Stavka. 13 Nov 1915. 10.44> 11.50
a.m. To his majesty. Glad that you got back successfully. Dull weather. Heart
still not at all famous. Very happy you have wonderful impressions, such a comfort in this difficult time. [We] tenderly kiss [you] both. May the Lord bless you
[both]. Alix

No. 605/ Her No. 389.   Tsarskoe Selo. Nov. 13th 1915.
My own beloved Husband,

21 years that we are 1, sweet Angel, I thank you once more for all you gave
me these long years, wh. have passed like a dream— much joy and sorrow we
have shared together, & love ever increased in depth and longing. Last year, I
think, we were neither together; on that day you had left for the Headquarters &
Caucasus? Or no, you were with us at Anichkov?< All is so mudled [sic] up in
my brain.—Congratulate you with Motherdear's< birthday—our Olga's Christening day.—I shall choose a present & the children can take it to-morrow.— [a]

I was to have gone to Paul< to-day, but my heart being more enlarged it would
have been unwise. I have asked Botkin to find out the exact truth fr. Varavka—I
always fear cancer, & the [F]rench Drs. some years ago thought, that he had the
beginning of cancer. By telephone one told me that Chigaev is of the same
opinion as Varavka & that to-morrow he is to be looked at through Rontgen
rays—now that shows, that they think there is something wh. might appear, because to be fed every 2 hours & decrease in weight shows that things are bad.
Our Friend< entreats there should be no operation, as he says Pauls organism is

like that of a wee childs—& Fedorov then told me, that he would not like an operation, fearing for Paul's heart. Now if it is cancer in the liver, then one never, I believe, operates—in any case I fear he is a doomed man, so why shorten his days & he does not often suffer. I only think they ought to let little Marie [his daughter, Maria Pavlovna, the younger] know how bad he is, as the Child is devoted to him & might have cheered him up. The Prss. [Palei] continues her long walks twice daily to become thin, & I do not think realises [sic] how seriously ill poor Paul is.—I see Bezobrazov to-day. What are you going to do now, you will have to think of another man now instead of Paul, as were he to recover, in any case there would be no question, alas, of his serving at the war. —Remember to nominate Groten somewhere.—Well, I saw our Friend from 5½-7 yesterday at Anias. He cannot bear the idea of the old man [Goremykin] being sent away, has been worrying & thinking over that question without end. Says he is so <u>very wise</u> & when others make a row & say he sits ramoli< with his head down —it is because he understands that to-day the crowd howls, to-morrow rejoices, that one need not be crushed by the changing waves. He thinks better to wait [to dismiss Goremykin], according to God one ought not to send him away. [b, c, d]

Of course if you could have turned up for a few words, quite unexpected at the Duma (as you had thought to) that might change everything & be a splendid deed & it wld. later be easier for the old man—otherwise better he should be ill a few days before so as not to personally open the Duma not to be hissed, but he thinks better to wait until you return, and when I said I should [agree], it was a weight lifted fr. his mind—& I know you think so too.[176] He [Rasputin] saw the old tail [A. A. Khvostov], very dry & hard, but honest, but not to be compared with Goremykin—one good thing that he is devoted to the old man—but is obstinate.— Emma< saw Him [Rasputin] afterwards & like a child poured her whole heart out to Him.—He thinks Greece wont move & Roumania neither, then the war will last shorter—He hopes not more than to spring.— Would to God it were true! [e, f]

Do you know a Count [V. S.] Tatishchev from Moscou [sic] (banks)?—I think [he is] a son (or nephew) of the old General a.d.c., a most devoted man to you, says you know him. Likes Gr.[egory]< much, disapproves of the Moscou nobility to wh. he belongs—is an older man already. Came to A.[nia]< to talk, sees very clearly the faults Bark made, about the loan I believe & the fatal results it may have. Our Friend says Tatishchev is a man to be trusted, very rich & knows the bank world very well—would be good, if you could have seen him & heard his opinion—says he is most sympathetic. I can make his acquaintance, only my brain I am sure would never grasp money affairs—I do dislike them so. But he might put things clearly to you, & help you advise [i.e., with advice]. Just this moment got Mr. Gill[i]ard's letter of the 8-th describing the day at Odessa—that was nice that you rode & Baby< drove with the old man [Fredericks]—he wired home enchanted too.—I shall have a mass to-morrow in the house at 12½ for Olga & me, the others will go for 11 oclock to Anichkov. Now I must end. Goodbye & God bless you, my Treasure. Live through these days 21 years ago with tender, grateful love, I kiss you without end in deepest love & devotion caressing you gently. I bless you & commend you to our Lord's care & the Holy

Virgin's love. Ever yr. very own old   Wify. [P.S.] Will Bezobrazov take Dmitri?< If my Commander General Veselovsky< receives a brigade, please, let his
successor be Sergeev<, he is the eldest in the reg.[iment] & commanded when
Veselovsky was wounded. [g, h]

176. Alexandra refers to the possibility that Nicholas could prevent the Duma from abusing
Goremykin by accompanying him to its next session. Apparently the tsar had entertained this idea
("as you had thought to"), but decided against it; Rasputin and Alexandra were now urging such a
visit. It would mollify critics by suggesting that Nicholas was now willing to work with his legislature. But Goremykin continued to be fearful, he begged Nicholas to not convene the Duma until
early 1916. Nicholas agreed. He also dismissed Goremykin as chairman of the council of ministers
and appointed Boris Sturmer in his place on January 20, 1916. Nicholas and Sturmer made the
"surprise appearance" before the Duma in February 1916. Perhaps Alexandra's desire to appease the
Duma flowed from Rasputin's new flexibility on the subject.

No. 606/ Telegram 35. Stavka> Tsarskoe Selo. 13 Nov 1915. 7.47> 8.36 p.m.
To her majesty. Tender thanks from both for dear letters. Sad not to be together
to-morrow, our wedding day, for which my most loving wishes. Fondest kisses
from both. Niki

No. 607/ Telegram 123. Tsarskoe Selo> Stavka. 13 Nov 1915. 9.35> 10.53
p.m. To his majesty. Warmly thank you for dear telegram. Also sad not to be
together on our wedding day. Send you tender good wishes, dear. God keep you
both, my dear ones. Sleep well. Alix

No. 608/ Telegram 129. Tsarskoe Selo> St. Uza. 14 Nov 1915. 9.16> 10.25
a.m. To his majesty. Heartily congratulate you on Motherdear's< birthday.
Hard not to be together on this day. May the Lord send you a special thought. [I]
tenderly kiss you both [i.e., Nicholas and their son Aleksei]. Clear. 10 degrees of
frost. Will be a Te Deum in my room before lunch. Alix

No. 609/ Her No. 390.   Tsarskoe Selo. Nov. 14th 1915.
My own sweet Treasure,
   Every loving thoughts & prayer are with you, all my love & caresses. So sad
to spend this day apart, but what is to be done, we can only thank God for the
past & that up to now we spent that day always together. Foolish old wify cried
a lot this night.—A bright morning, the sun rose beautifully behind the kitchen,
10 degrees of frost—a pitty [sic] the snow has all melted.—Once more, Huzy
mine, thank you for all during these 21 years! What a lot you have to do for sure
now after your journey —wonder how you spend this day! Is Baby-kins< not too
tired from all the walking? Mr. Gill[i]ard's letters are so interesting, as he relates
about all you saw —& what splendid French, it makes me quite jealous. [a]
   I am sending off the 3 youngest girls with Mme Zizi< to Church & lunch to
Anichkov< & Nastinka< also meets them there. The rest of us will have a Te
Deum in my big room at 12½. I have not been to mass since you left & it makes
me so sad.—I am so glad, that you have named Naumov definitely [minister of
agriculture in place of Krivoshein] and am full of hopes, that he will be the right
man—he always pleased me, I like his frank eyes & he always spoke enthusiasti-

cally & eager[ly] about his [experience in provincial] governments and all the work to be done & went into all the details, so it is knowledge he has gained personally by work. [b]

Bezobrazov came to me yesterday & we had a nice talk—you saved him as he says.—Then the Dr. of my train, who brought poor Eshapar's body, presented himself to give me all the details, & then a wounded officer returning to his Siberian regiment No. 18, wh. you must have seen near Riga.—Slept badly, again heart still enlarged & head rather aches, still shall have to go to Pauls<, as he begged to see me. I asked A.[nia]< to invite Rita [Khitrovo?] & Shah Bagov [Shakh-Bagov] & Kikinadze [Kiknadze] & Danelkov [Demenkov] for the Children at 4½, to spend a cosy afternoon, as they dont go to the hospital to-day and would have missed their friends.—I wonder how Shvedov [Shurik<] is, he fell ill again at the Headquarters—A. wired to Zborovsky on his namesday [sic], asking about Shurik, but got no answer—perhaps private telegrams are not let through.[163] Its quite strange to see the sun again after these dark days, such a consolation.—My letter is dull & must now come to an end. God bless & protect you, my very own Darling, my Beloved, my One & All. I cover you with tender kisses and hold you tightly in my yearning arms. Ever yr. very own old   Wify. [Next to her signature Alexandra wrote a large Roman numeral "XXI" with a large exclamation mark; under it she drew two glowing hearts penetrated by an arrow.] [c, d]

No. 610/ Telegram 41. Stavka> Tsarskoe Selo. 14 Nov 1915. 3.32> 4.40 p.m. To her majesty. So touched by tiny frame and best wishes for this day. Hearty thanks for letter. Leave on Tuesday. Were in church to day. Snowing, 5 degr. frost. Tender kisses. Niki

---

No. 611/ Telegram 139. Tsarskoe Selo> Stavka. 14 Nov 1915. 7.05> 8.17 p.m. To his majesty. Deeply happy and grateful for precious, interesting letter. Also thank Baby<. Feel in poor health. Even so had to visit Paul<. Found he has gotten quite thin. Voice stronger, quite talkative. Tenderly kiss and embrace [you]. Alix

---

No. 612/ Telegram 146. Tsarskoe Selo> Stavka. 15 Nov 1915. 1.55> 2.44 p.m. To his majesty. Wonderful sunny day. Children strolling. Good old man Rauchfuss died yesterday. Please read my letter [No. 613] to-morrow before report [from Trepov]. [We] all tenderly kiss you both. God keep you. Alix

---

No. 613/ Her No. 391.   Tsarskoe Selo. Nov. 15th 1915.
My own Beloved,

Heart & soul were overjoyed to receive your dear letter, & I thank you for it ever so tenderly. Everything you wrote was most interesting & did one good to see how contented & well pleased you are with the state of the troops you inspected. Can imagine the wild joy of your Nizhegorodtsi and all the rest scampering after you—their dream fulfilled, to see you during the war!—And perhaps you will be home on Wednesday, oh wont that be too lovely, after 3 long weeks.

I have never been separated so long from Agoowee one<—now it seems already such ages.—Now, before I forget, I must give you over a message from our Friend<, prompted by what He saw in the night. He begs you to order that one should advance near Riga, says it is necessary, otherwise the Germans will settle down so firmly through all the winter, that it will cost endless bloodshed & trouble to make them move—now it will take them so aback, that we shall succeed in making them retrace their steps—he says this is just now the most essential thing & begs you seriously to order ours to advance, he says we can & we must, and I was to write it to you at once.—[a, b]

Then from [A. N.] Khvostov. He says Trepov is very much against the revision you ordered [D. B.] Neidhardt to do, & does not wish him to mix in his affairs, but Khvostov begs you to stick to yr. order & insists upon it, because the well-thinkers and in the Duma too are delighted, as they see that will save the situation & clear much up. Khvostov read [in a] delighted [mood your] telegr. about it & that will touch different commissions, entre autre Guchkov< will be shown up, and its absurd Trepov being against it. I have a paper (copy) of Shakhovskoy's begging Khvostov to take energetic measures otherwise he cannot guarantee for the result—Trepov ought to be glad—no fault touches him as he is new [as minister of transportation] & is also trying his best. Khvostov thinks it wld. be very advisable if you had the pay of the railroad men augmented, as with the post, the result was glorious gratitude towards you, boundless, a stop to strikes—given by you personally before they had time to ask for it. He came on purpose to dine with A.[nia]< & Bel.[etsky], to-night, so as that I should write this for you to read before Trepov's doklad [report] on Monday.—[c]

Lovy, you wrote me that the railway line to Reni is old & rotten, please order it categorically to be at once improved to avoid accidents, as our sanitary trains, amunitions [sic], provisions & troops will need it. Cannot you quickly have small lines branching off laid, to facilitate the communication, as we sorely need more lines there, otherwise our communication will stick, and that can be awful during winter battles. This I write of my own accord, because I feel sure it could be done and you know, alas, how very little initiative our people have—they never look a head until the catastrophe comes suddenly right upon us & we are taken unaware. Several short branches towards the Roumanian frontier & Austria, have sleepers for broad gages prepared beforehand, you remember what trouble it was to reach Lemberg. I was at Paul's<, he lay in their bedroom, is allowed to move about in the room & sit a bit on the armchair—terribly thin, but not those dark spots on his cheeks I disliked, voice stronger, talkative, interested in everything. I begged him to put off having Roentgen photo taken till Fedorov returns, as Dmitri< wired Fedorov< begged it—she [Paul's wife, Princess Paley] hurrys things too much. He puts all his trust in Fedorov< & leaves it to him to decide about the operation, he of course hates the idea, but if Fedorov insists, of course he will do it; I should not risk it. [d, e]

I felt rotten all day with my heart. Received my Toll< (lancer), who gets a regiment, one says yr. Pavlograd Hussars—but he does not know for sure. Samoilov is also a candidate for a regiment & [E. C.] Arsenev for our brigade.—Paul imagines he will be well enough to go, she says—I told her I doubted it, I did not speak reassuringly when we were alone, as she was so cool about it

& eyes so hard. You know its strange, the eve before he fell ill, he had a discussion with Georgi at the Headquarters about our Friend. G.[eorgi] said the family call him a follower of Rasputin, where upon Paul got furious & said very strong things—and fell ill that night. Her niece heard this from her [his wife]—told it to Gr.[egory], who said, that no doubt God sent it him because he ought to have stood up for a man you respect & his soul ought to have remembered that he received everything fr. you & brought a letter fr. his wife she had asked Gr. to write to me begging for them.—Our Friend was struck by this.—It was a sad day without you—Sonia< & Trina< lunched, Olga fed Sonia and I lay as usual on the sopha. Your letters were then brought to me & I have reread them more than once since & kissed them tenderly—your sweet hands rested on the paper & Baby's< too.—Good old Rauchfuss died yesterday morning, a great loss for my society "Mothers' and Infants" as his head was marvelously fresh for his great age.—Botkin is not well, so can't come this morning.—A[nia].< manages to walk half an hour on crutches through our garden—how strong she is, tho' complains at being a cripple— nearly daily shaken by motor [trips] to town<, climbs up to the 3rd story to see our Friend —her back aches especially in the evening. But I feel its the hope of meeting you in the mornings that gives her the strength to walk. —Zhuk< accompanies her now again, as it wld. be dangerous her going alone, she might fall & then, the Drs said, she wld. be sure to rebrake [sic] her leg. Her brother [S. A. Taneev] returned for 6 days. [f, g]

Mavra< is going to the country as she feels her nerves so shaken & cant sleep a bit, poor thing. Tatiana [Constantinovna] has gone to the Caucasus for the 6 months of her husband's death & then returns again from Mskhed.—The old man [Goremykin] is coming to me to-day, but I don't know why.—Such glorious sunshine! Remember about Riga! And now goodbye & God bless you my sweetest husband, love of my soul. Endless kisses fr. yr. own wife.   <u>Alix</u>.   [P.S.] Went to sleep after 4.— [h]

No. 614/ Telegram 43. Stavka> Tsarskoe Selo. 15 Nov 1915. 7.31> 7.58 p.m. To her majesty. Best thanks [for] sweet letter and news. Also sunny day. 10 deg. frost, lots of snow. Thoughts always near you. We both kiss you all very tenderly. Niki

---

No. 615/ Her No. 392.   Tsarskoe Selo. Nov. 15th 1915.
My own beloved Darling,

I began my letter already to-day, but I saw old Goremykin just now & am so afraid of forgetting what I am to give over, by to-morrow.—He was to have a sitting of all the ministers this evening, but had to put it off as you sent for Trepov—he will have them Wednesday evening & begs to see you on Thursday. He is perfectly calm for the interior quiet, says nothing will be [i.e., occur]. The young ministers, [A. N.] Khvostov & Shakhovskoy he finds get a bit excited before anything is the matter, to wh. I answered better foresee things than sleep, as one generally does here.—Well, its the question about calling the Duma together now— he [Goremykin] is against it.[176] They have no work to do, the budget of the minister of Finances [Bark] has been presented 5 to 6 days late & they have not begun the preliminary works, wh. are needed before giving it over to the whole Duma. If they sit idle, they will begin talks about Varnava & our Friend< & mix into governmental questions, to wh. they have not the right. (now Khvostov & Bel.[etsky] told A.[nia], that the man who intended speaking against Gr.[egory]< has taken back his paper & they say that subject won't be touched)—well, this is the old man's council after long consideration & yester-days talk with a member of the Duma, whose name he begged not to mention. He would advise you writing two rescripts, one to Kulomzin (I find you might change him) & the other to Rodzianko, giving as reason that the budget has not been worked through by the commissions & therefore too early to assemble the Duma, that Rodzianko is to make his doklad [report] to you when they are ready with their preliminary work. I am going to ask A.< to quite privately speak of this to our Friend, who sees & hears & "knows much", to ask what He would bless—as He thought otherwise the other day. Goremykin wants me to write all this to you before seeing you, so as to prepare you to his conversation. Always calm, only very wretched about his wife who suffers now from asthma beside all the rest & therefore can scarcely take her breath. [a, b, c]

From Khvostov he heard that all your orders to Polivanov or his papers to you are all shown to Guchkov<—now that cannot be stood, simply playing into yr. enemy's hands. He told me you had mentioned Ivanov to him—the same thing also our Fr., I believe, & Khvostov said—especially our Friend—then all would be perfect in the Duma & everything one needs, pass through. Belyaev is a good worker & the old man's [i.e., Goremykin's] prestige would do the rest. And he is tired at the war—& if you have a man to replace him, perhaps it would be good now.—Then he touched other questions of less interest to you.—But our Friend said last time, that only if we have a victory, then the Duma should not be called in, otherwise yes, that nothing will be said so bad—that the old man must be ill a few days so as not to appear there—& that you should turn up unawares & say a few words.[176]—Well, when we meet I'll tell you what he now says. Lovy mine, is this really the last letter, & are you coming on Wednesday?—How lovely.—A. had a charming letter fr. N.P.< telling all about the journey & his im-pressions—full of the beauty of the troops, as tho' they were fresh & never been to the war yet.—All this gives you strength for your work & a clear mind.—[d, e]

16-th. Goodmorning Lovy. Cold & windy. Feel very tired after again a badish night & everything aches rather—so have been lying with shut eyes this morn-ing—I have a doklad with Senator Pr.[ince] Galitsin [N. D. Golitsyn] about our prisoners & then see Kolenkin & hereafter the 3 Austrian Sisters [i.e., nurses].—I hope your cold has passed & that the cocain[e] helped well. Pitty [sic] no long walks for you, with the roads covered in deep snow.—I suppose you come for barely a week if you must be back again for the St. George's feast—how will that be, I wonder. Oh what joy, God grant, if I shall have you home again in two days—to-morrow 3 weeks that you left! Such a longing for you, my Treas-ure.—Well, goodbye my Love, I bless & kiss you over & over again with deepest love & tenderness. Ever Nicky mine, yr. very own old <u>Sunny</u>. [f]

P.S. I reopened my letter—she [Anna Vyrubova] spoke to our Friend who was very sad & said, it was quite wrong, what the old man said. One must call the Duma together even for quite short, especially if you, unknown to others, turn up there it will be splendid, as you had thought before of doing—that there wont be any scandals, one wont make a row about him [Rasputin], B.[eletsky] & Khvostov are seeing to that & that, if you do not call them together, it will create unneccessary [sic] displeasure & stories—I was sure He wld. answer so, & it seems to me quite right. Probably one frightened the old man that he would be whistled at, its people who were sorry personally for him—because I understand having sent them away when they did not expect it, one cannot again uselessly offend them—of course he loathes their existence (as do I for Russia). Well, one must see to their [convocation] at once & quickly sitting to work over the Budget. I feel sure you also will agree to Gr. sooner than to the old man, who this time is wrong & been frightened about Gr. & Varnava.[176] [g]

No. 616/ Telegram 148. Tsarskoe Selo> Stavka. 16 Nov 1915. 9.19> 9.47 p.m. To his majesty. Heartily thank you for telegram. We also await your arrival with impatience. So distracted this morning [I] forgot to telegraph. Cold day. We all tenderly kiss you. May God keep you [both]. Sleep well. Alix

No. 617/ Telegram 53. Stavka> Tsarskoe Selo. 16 Nov 1915. 7.50> 8.07 p.m. To her majesty. Tender thanks for dear letter. Lovely sunny weather. Counting the hours of our meeting. We both send you all our love. Niki

No. 618/ Telegram 152. Tsarskoe Selo> Stavka. 17 Nov 1915. 1.05> 1.43 p.m. To his majesty. We all wish you a good trip. Mild weather, snowing, 4 degrees. May God keep you [both]. [We] warmly kiss [you]. If [I] feel well, hope to meet you, dear ones. Alix

No. 619/ Telegram 57. Stavka> Tsarskoe Selo. 17 Nov 1915. 2.43> 3.30 p.m. To her majesty. Fondest thanks [for] dear letters and telegram. Fine cold weather. So eager to see you soon. Your flowers are quite fresh. Sleep well. Tender kisses. Niki

No. 620.   [No place indicated.] Nov. 24th 1915. My own beloved One,
    It's hard parting again, having spent a mere 6 days together. Duty!—there is the reason. Please take care of yourself, do not over tire your poor heart. I love you so! In thoughts & prayers I am constantly with you, above all in the evening when we are accustomed to be together. I hope time is not behind the mountains [i.e., I hope good times such as those we have had will come again] & nothing will distress you. God bless you & the dear girlies! I kiss you tenderly & love you infinitely. Always, my dear Sunny, your own old huzy Nicky.

No. 621/ Her No. 393.   Tsarskoe Selo. Nov. 25th 1915. My own precious One,
    Off you will be storming when you read this note. My tenderest prayers & thoughts will as ever follow you everywhere. Thank God, I had you 7 days—but they flew by, & again the heartache begins. Take care of Baby<, don't let him run about in the train, so as not to knock his arms—I trust he will be able to bend

his right arm alright [sic] by Thursday.—The idea of having to let him leave you alone afterwards, makes me sad. Before you decide speak with Mr. Gill[i]ard, he is such a sensible man & knows all so well about Aleksei.—You will be glad to get away from here with all your receptions, worries & doklady [reports],—here life is no rest for you, on the contrary.—Your tender caresses warmed up my old heart—you don't know how hard it is being without you both Angels.—I am glad, that I shall go straight to Church from the station at 9½ in the darkness & pray for you—the home coming is always so particularly painful. Sleep well and long, my Treasure, my one & all, the light of my life! I bless you & confide you unto God's holy care—tightly I hold you in my arms & press tender kisses upon yr. sweet face, lovely eyes & all dear places. Goodnight, rest well. Ever yr. very own old   Wify.

No. 622/ Telegram 199 in Russian. Tsarskoe Selo> Vitebsk. 25 Nov 1915. 11.10> 11.32 a.m. To his majesty. Terribly gladdened by your dear note. Slept as usual. Very sad. Going for a while to hospital<. Many receptions to-day. How are [Aleksei's] arms? [We] miss [you]. 10 degrees. God keep you. Alix

No. 623/ Her No. 394.   Tsarskoe Selo. Nov. 25th 1915.
My very own beloved One,
   Your sweet note, you left me, is a great consolation, I read it over and over again & kiss it & think I hear you talk. Oh I hate those goodbyes! We went straight to [the hospital] church, upstairs, so I remained in my verkhnyaya tserkov [upstairs chapel]—the moleben [prayer service] had already begun, so lasted quite short. What pain in the soul! Came home & went to bed very soon, could not want to see A.[nia]< I prefer being alone when the heart is so sore. 10 degrees this morning. Wonder how Baby's< arms are—am a bit anxious until he will be quite right again—only careful in his movements.—Alek< is arranging something in the narodnyi dom [People's House] for to-morrow [in honor of] St. George's heroes. Now I can congratulate you too, my Angel, & do so with heart & soul. You deserved the cross for all yr. hard labour & for the pod'em dukha [uplift in spirits] you bring the troops. Regret not being with you & our little St. George's cavalier, Baby sweet, to bless & kiss you that day.[168]—I went to Znamenia< & placed a candle for you—service was going on and they just brought out the chaska [chalice]. Then went to the hospital & spoke to all. We are lunching & this letter must be sent at once. Goodbye my own precious Darling, I cover you with tender kisses. God Almighty bless & keep you—Sunny. [P.S.] The Children kiss you. Had you an answer from Georgie? [King George V]

No. 624/ Telegram 73. Stavka> Tsarskoe Selo. 25 Nov 1915. 5.25> 6.05 p.m. To her majesty. Best thanks [for] dear telegram. Arrived well. Since morning thawing. Strange and empty to be here. We both kiss you fondly. Niki

No. 625/ Telegram 202. Tsarskoe Selo> Stavka. 25 Nov 1915. 8.20> 9.35 p.m. To his majesty. Heartily thank you for telegram. Only just returned alone from church. Remember, in gold chest with chains you have relics of St. George in case you wish to take him to Te Deum. Good night to you both. [We] tenderly embrace and kiss [you]. Congratulate you both and Fath.[er] Georgy Shavel'sky on to-morrow's festival. Alix

---

No. 626/ Telegram 205. Tsarskoe Selo> Stavka. 26 Nov 1915. 9.52> 10.48 a.m. To his majesty. Are proud to be able to congratulate you both on this great festival. May St. George bring special blessings to our soldiers. She [Anna Vyrubova] sends you both her very warmest congratulations and greetings. 5 degrees, very warm. [We] miss you terribly. All heartily kiss you both. Alix

---

No. 627/ Her No. 395.   Tsarskoe Selo. Nov. 26th 1915.
My own beloved Darling,
    I wonder how all is going off at the Headquarters to-day, great excitement, I am sure. Hope Baby dear's< arms are much better.— Am going later to Church with [daughter] Olga, last night I went alone, upstairs in my prayer-house Church [see Letter No. 623a] [which] is my consolation. Stupid heart rather bothers me.—Saw M-me Pogulyaev, M-me Manskovskaya [Manikovskaya],— fancy, her sister is young [A. N.] Khvostov's mother—he asked to see me to-day, I don't know why. Our Friend< dined with him yesterday & was very contented. —5 degrees & so dark.—A.[nia]< just got a wire fr. N.P.< about his nomination & that he is off to Odessa. I am awfully sorry he wont be any more with you, was so quiet for you both—we shall miss him awfully—but its a splendid nomination —but you will be so lonely!—Our Friend is in all states that [N.P.] leaves, as one "of his" & ought to be near you, as have few such true, honest friends as He says only Ania & N.P.—wished me to telegraph to you, but I declined & begged Him neither to—I know what this means to him & his comerades [sic], tho' he will horribly suffer leaving us, who are his nearest & dearest as he always says! [a, b]
    What news from Georgie [King George V]? How delighted [V. N.] Orlov & Drentel'n will be that N.P.< leaves—their jealous hearts will be contented.—And 3 of yr. players at once gone, whom can you get? Silaev is quiet & nice & utterly devoted.—Came to half of mass & Te Deum. Had a long telegr. fr. [V. V.] Mekk about all my flying [i.e., mobile] stores<—M-me Hartwigs< is at Rovno—have put our pokhodnaya tserkov [field church] & twice daily there are also at Rovno. Our flying detachment of the store is 40 versts north, on the new line near the front. Then our Bacteriological disinfection unit works for all the army, another supply train at Podvolochisk, another at Tarnopol, but he moves it to Kamenets-Podolsk where the Bacteriological Section will have more work. I only tell you this in case you pass any.—Goodbye my Lovebird, the man leaves earlier.—Blessings & kisses without end & great yearning. God bless you. Ever yr. very own old   Wify. [c]

No. 628/ Telegram 79. Stavka> Tsarskoe Selo. 26 Nov 1915. 5.20> 6.21 p.m. To her majesty. Loving thanks [for] dear letter and congratulations for this day. The review and celebration went off perfectly, though quite otherwise than usually. Spring weather, but rainy. We both send you all, and her [Anna Vyrubova], our thanks and best love. Niki

No. 629.   Ts.[arist] Stavka. Nov. 26th 1915.
My own beloved Wify,
   The journey was dull & quiet; we [Aleksei and I] felt so sad without you & the
girlies. We were met by Alekseev, several generals fr. the staff and old Pilz
[Pil'ts], & drove to our house. Then I was bothered with questions about today's
festivities. Baby< slept well, his legs & arms did not hurt. It was warm &
damp. Fedorov was worried about the review and the wet ground [posing a
danger to our son]. Thanks be to God, everything came off well, & movingly.
At 10 in the morning we appeared. All the officers fr. the army stood left of the
porch, & opposite them a splendid company[177] of non-commissioned officers &
ensigns holding St. George crosses 2nd, 3rd & 4th [class], & with all the medals
on their breasts. Then, with backs to the street, a large assembly of the wounded
sent to serve at the Stavka, & on down soldiers & cossacks etc. [a, b]
   After a thanksgiving moleben they all marched past, with the generals & officers at their head. I addressed a few words to them, & then went to the doklad
[report]. At 12 we came to the dinner wh. was arranged for everyone, & I drank
to their health with kvass. After this Aleksei went home, & I with the others to
the gorod. duma.[178] We lunched in two large halls—170 in all. When we rose, I
spoke with each officer, wh. took an hour & a half—but I did not mind as it was
interesting to hear their answers. At the end, I promoted all to their next rank.
The scene was marvellous ! Amongst the officers I saw & spoke with [Teimur
Bek] Navruzov & Kratt and bowed to them fr. you & the girls. Nik. Pav.
[Sablin] leaves for Odessa to-morrow to take command of the Ekip.< fr. Polushkin. God bless you, my darling Wify! I kiss you & the dear children tenderly.
Ever yr. own old huzy Nicky. [P.S.] Please give my letter over to Malcolm. [c]

   177. This was the St. George Battalion, consisting of men who had been decorated with the Cross
of St. George, an award for conspicuous bravery in the field. (Vulliamy, p. 113n)
   178. "Gorodskaia duma" refers to the town duma, an elected council that, together with the mayor,
governed the town which elected them. Nicholas refers here to the building (the "People's House,"
narodnyi_dom) where the Mogilev duma met.

No. 630/ Her No. 396.   Tsarskoe Selo. Nov. 27th 1915.
My very own Huzy,
   I am glad everything went off so well yesterday—Georgi< telegraphed that it
had been one of the finest sights he had ever seen in his life. How emotioning.
One says it was splendid at the People's House—greatest order—18,000 men—sat
together according to the wars [in which they served]—got heaps of food & were
allowed to take their plates & mugs home. In each hall there was a Te
Deum—Valia< was there. I spent yesterday afternoon reading, the Children<
were out & Ania< only returned from town at 4.20 —but I liked the calm, only
the air in my big room was stiffling [sic] they let on the hot air—& out of doors
the glass on 1 [degree] of warmth. So after tea & having seen officers, I sledged
for half an hour with [daughter] Olga—it was mild & snowing. This morning
there are 10 degrees—those ups & downs are so bad for the ill. A.< dined with
us—all worked, even she at last, then they sang churchsongs & Olga played.
Khvostov did not come yester-day as he felt unwell. [a, b]

My letters are dull, I have nothing interesting to tell you, & the thoughts are not gay—its lonely without Sweetheart< & agoowee-one<.—I feel my heart enlarged, but still I want to go to our lower Church, as little Metropolitan Makari[179] is going to serve, simple, without pomp—its the feast of Znamenia<. So in the afternoon I hope to go in & place a candle for you & I believe our Friend< wants to see me at 4.— Just back from Church, little Metropolitan served beautifully, so quietly—looked a picture, all gold, glittering, & the golden Church round the Altar & his silver hair. I went away before the Te Deum, Olga to the hospital, & I to finish my letters, receive Isa< & then Valia< before luncheon.—Goodbye my Angel sweet, my Treasure, my Lovebird. God bless & protect you —1000 of kisses, Nicky love, fr. yr. old wife   Alix. [P.S.] Any idea about your plans? I sent for Joy [Aleksei's dog] & he lies at my feet—a melancholy picture, as he misses his little master. [c, d]

179. Moscow Metropolitan Makary was in the capital because he was ex officio a member of the thirteen-man governing council of the Holy Synod. See also Footnotes 174 and 175.

No. 631/ Telegram 215. Tsarskoe Selo> Stavka. 27 Nov 1915. 2.20> 3.12 p.m. To his majesty. Wonderful service in lower church. Little metropolitan [Makary of Moscow] presided.[179] Snowing. 10 degrees frost. We all tenderly kiss you both. Alix

---

No. 632/ Telegram 216. Tsarskoe Selo> Stavka. 27 Nov 1915. 6.24> 7.40 p.m. To his majesty. Terribly gladdened by your letters, yours and Aleksei's. Heartily thank you. God keep you. [We] tenderly kiss [you]. Sleep well. Alix

---

No. 633/ Telegram 100. Stavka> Tsarskoe Selo. 27 Nov 1915. 7.56> 8.43 p.m. To her majesty. Fondest thanks for letters and news.To day feast of my Nizhegorodtsy<. [Teimur Bek] Navruzov and Chavchavadze lunched. They want to see you soon. N.P.< took leave, am glad for him. Light frost. Tender kisses. Niki

---

No. 634/ Her No. 397.   Tsarskoe Selo. Nov. 28th 1915.
Darling Sweetheart,
    Ever such very tender thanks for yr. dear letter, wh. I never expected. I am delighted that the St. George's feast was so splendid—I just read the description & all yr. lovely words in the papers. Fancy [Teimur Bek] Navruzov, my Hooligan as I always call him, & Krat[t]. having been there, that is nice. Well, yr. 2 Nizhegorodtsy< must tell us about it—we shall eagerly await them. I saw our Friend< for ¾ of an hour—asked much after you, goes to-day to see the old man [Goremykin]. Spoke about N.P.<, regrets terribly he wont be near you, but that God will protect him & that after the war (wh. he always thinks will be over in a few months) he must come back to you again.—Please dear dont let Spiridovich< be named as Chief of police in Petrograd—I know he & Voeikov< (whom Spiridovich, sorry to say, holds in hands) want to place him there. It wld. never do, he is not enough gentleman, has now made a useless marriage & then on account of Stolypin's story at Kiev, it would not be good.[180] One proposed him to be governor at Astrakhan (yes?) & he refused,—& one thing more, why I do not

know, but Spiridovich puts Voeikov up against Khvostov, with whom everything went so well at first. Now one must get Trepov to work in harmony with
Khvostov—its the only way of setting things to rights & making work go
smoothely [sic]. [a, b]

The dear little Metropolitan Makari [Makary] came to me after luncheon &
was sweet.—Loman had feasted him & all the clergy—Ania & Mme Loman were
there too.—Then I saw two German sisters [i.e., nurses]; Countess Uxkull had
been to Wolfsgarten before coming, but she is still going to visit more
places;—the other is from Mecklenburg—she asked me whether one could not let
home to Germany old men & children fr. Siberia, whom ours transported there
fr. East Prussia, when our troops were there. Does it [this question] concern
[Assistant-Minister of War] Belyaev or [Minister of the Interior A. N.] Khvostov? I should say, the latter.—Can you tell me as then I can ask about it—of
course only the quite old men & tiny children [should be permitted to return to
Germany?]—she saw them in Siberia, Samara.—I went to Znamenia< and placed
a candle for you. Then I got Loman so as to speak about a wee pokhodnaya
tserkov [field church], I want to send to the Gvard. Ekipazh< as our priest [Fa-
ther A. P. Vasil'ev] is with them. I am remaining quiet this morning, as don't
feel very famous.—One of our wounded officers died last night—yesterday he
was operated—he was several times at death's door—I used to go to him in the
evenings when he was so bad—but I think he never could have recovered—his
soldier[-servant] is an Angel.—This evening Shavel'sky officiates in our Church.
In the evening Nik. Dm. Dem.[enkov] & Vict. Erast.< come to Ania's< at 9, to
say goodbye to the latter; so sad we shant see Shvedov before he leaves. All
ones dear friends go off at the same time to the war! [c, d]

11 degrees of frost & thick snow. I am sending you a paper of Rostovtsev, I
think it concerns Alekseev & can be quicker done through you, if you agree—I
saw the wretched officer & yr. Mama [Maria Fedorovna] too.—Ortipo [a dog] is
lying on my bed & sleeping fast.—I have sent your letter to Malcolm to give over
to Georgie [King George V]—he leaves to-morrow.—Now my sweetest One, my
sorely missed & deeply yearned for Huzy, Goodbye & God bless—and protect
you. Endless tender kisses do I press upon yr. sweet lips & beloved eyes. Ever
yr. very own old   Sunny. [e]

180. Gen. Spiridovich was faulted for lax security in the assassination of Stolypin at Kiev in 1911.

No. 635/ Telegram 105. Stavka> Tsarskoe Selo. 28 Nov 1915. 6.38> 7.21 p.m.
To her majesty. Fondest thanks [for] dear letters. All is well. Baby's< health
too. Mild weather. Silaev arrived. Have written about plans. [See Letter 634c.]
Tender kisses to all. Niki

No. 636.   Ts.[arist] Stavka. Nov. 28th 1915.
My own darling Sunny,

My warmest thanks for yr. two dear letters. I have again been busy all morning & after dinner & could scarcely snatch ¼ hour to write a few words. [M. N.]
Grabbe begs you send 70 images [icons] for our 4th Kuban sotnia [Cossack
squadron] here who soon go to the front. Just this moment Voeikov brought me

a paper with the time table for our trip. We start on Dec. 3rd for Zhmerinka and will spend 4th, 5th & 6th with the guard div[ision]s. I am glad that it has turned out this way, & I will spend my namesday [sic] with them. Pardon this hasty writing, I have but a few minutes left. Silaev just looked in—he looks well. He gave me greetings fr. the girlies<, for wh. I thank them very much. I send you Georgie's [King George V] reply—keep it. I hope yr. poor heart will soon be better; I am so sorry for you! God bless you, my dear little bird, my treasure, my dear Wify! I tenderly kiss you & the dear children. Ever yr. own old huzy Nicky.

No. 637/ Her No. 398.   Tsarskoe Selo. Nov. 29th 1915.
My own beloved Sweetheart,
    Only the 5 th day since you left, & it seems already such ages. Dark, snowing 11 degr.; last night 16.—yesterday evening Shavel'sky served, it was so nice & I like his voice. He is kindly going to take two antiminsi [communion cloths] with him, as I am sending the Gvard. Ekipazh< & 4 rifles [regiments] pokhod-nye tserkvi [field churches] for the 6 th.—Marie P.< came to tea— looked really pretty when she took off her kosynka [scarf], her short hair had been curled. She has greatly improved & becoming so different to what she was before. To-day she returns again to Pskov, but does not know when Dmitri< leaves.—In the evening we went to Anias< & there were besides us, Demenk.[ov] & Zborovsky. It seems Al.[eksei] Konst.[antinovitch Shvedov] has also come, so shall see him before his departure for the war. This morning Gulyga comes to bid us good bye:—Pss. Lolo D. [Olga Dolgorukaya] lunches with us & after [that] I see Sandra Shuvalova with her doklad [report].—Every day somebody to receive & affairs & nothing interesting to tell you. My jaw has jumped out and I eat with difficulty. I enclose a letter fr. A.[nia], perhaps you will in your wire say I am to thank her and for the present.—Beloved one, I do wish yr. letter had come, now the man is always late.—I bless you over & over again my one & all and kiss you with all the fervour of my love—Ever, Nicky mine, yr. very own old Wify.

No. 638/ Telegram 223. Tsarskoe Selo> Stavka. 29 Nov 1915. 3.18> 4.49 p.m.
To his majesty. Tenderly thank you both for dear letters. Thank you for news. Had just intended to send some little images [icons] and soon will do so. Cold, snow. Saw Sandra Shuvalova. She leaves for Crimea since her father had stroke. [We] all kiss and embrace [you]. Alix

No. 639/ Telegram 106. Stavka> Tsarskoe Selo. 29 Nov 1915. 6.45> 7.08 p.m.
To her majesty. Loving thanks for letters. Delightful, sunny day. Thoughts al-ways together. Sorry about old [I. Iv.] Vorontsov[-Dashkov]. Tenderest love to all. Niki

No. 640/ Her No. 399.   Tsarskoe Selo. Nov. 29th 1915.
Sweet Beloved,

I begin my letter already to-day, so as to thank you ever so fondly for yours, wh. I just received. That is nice, that you will spend your namesday [sic] with the troops, tho' sad we cannot be together, am glad you will spend that big feast-day in yr. army & may St. Nicolas send special blessings to all & help.—I don't like Georgie's [King George V's] answer, to my mind its quite wrong. [a]

How interesting you saw K. Krutchkov [Kryuchkov]; its snowing so hard, A.[nia]'s< train left an hour late from here & took a whole hour to town, she fears sticking on her way back. Ira [Irina Sheremeteva], Larka< & Sandra< leave to-night for Alupka as the old Count< had a stroke. She has four St. George's medals. It looks so strange on a smart dress. Mme Orjewsky [Orzhev-skaya] is going to propose to your Mama [Maria Fedorovna] that one should send her to see the prisoners here, wh. I find perfect, as there are things one must see into. Our government gives enough money for food but it seems its not given as ought to be, I fear, dishonest people keep it back & that wont do; I am glad she & I had the same idea—I have no right to mix in, & she can advise. Thank God, Baby< is better so I hope he will get through the journey al-right.—Does Drentel'n take over the regiment now, or how is he arranging? I have got a fly buzzing round my lamp, reminds one of summer; but the wind is howling down the chimney. Oh sweet Love, I long for you so terribly—thank God you have Sunbeam< to keep your heart warm.—What do you do in the eve-nings, have you anyone for domino? [Teimur Bek] Navruzov & Chavtchavadze [Chavchavadze] took tea cosily [sic] with us—it was awfully nice seeing them again after so many months & to get news of you both. You see us 5 taking tea with 2 officers, but with them it seems somehow so natural. They also are en-chanted that [old Count] Vorontsov< left the Caucasus.—I am sending [M. N.] Grabbe on Tuesday 170 Images [icons], 170 little books, 200 ordinary store post-cards, 170 packets for officers—to Zborovsky & Shvedov I shall give the things myself. And then a small Image of St. Nicolas for the company, you can bless them with it, Deary. [b, c]

Well, our Friend was with the old man [Goremykin] who listened to him very attentively, but was most obstinate. He intends asking you not at all to call the Duma together (he loathes it)—& Gr.[egory]< told him it was not right to ask such a thing of you, as now all are willing to try & work & as soon as their pre-liminary work is ready it would be wrong not to call them together—one must show them a little confidence.—Nov. 30 th. I am lunching & writing. At 10 I went to the zaupokoinaya liturgiya [memorial liturgy] for our officer, the chil-dren came for the otpevanie [requiem]. Then sat in the hospital, [Teimur Bek] Navruzov turned up, he leaves to-night again for Armavir. Ravtopolo turned up, looks flourishing! Its 2 [degrees] of warmth & pouring [rain?].—The guard offi-cers heard, that the promotion did not count for them.—Do you return straight to the Headquarters or over Minsk? The Erivantsi were asking. Melik[-]Adamov turned up fr. Eupatoria.—Have to receive & so must end & swallow my food.—I bless & kiss you over & over again with unending deep devotion. Ever, Sweet-heart, yr. very own old   Sunny. [d, e]

No. 641/ Telegram 229. Tsarskoe Selo> Stavka. 30 Nov 1915. 2.06> 2.35 p.m. To his majesty. Warm, snowing. Were at hospital< and obednya [Mass] there.

Kiss Baby< for his dear letter. We all send tenderest kisses and [we] embrace
[you]. Alix

No. 642.   Ts.[arist]. Stavka. Nov. 30th 1915.
My own Wify-dear,
   My warmest thanks for your letters. I always look forward to them with a
beating heart. After opening the envelope, I put my nose into it and breathe
your scent! Thinking it will be more convenient for the guards and ourselves,
we set out on Thursday Dec. 3rd & return here either on Dec. 7th or 8th. The
troops are now moving forward & we shall see them closer to the frontier than
originally expected. Drenteln takes leave here the day of our departure, he goes
directly to Petrograd on family business. Nik. Pav. [Sablin] returns fr. Odessa
for ten days. I may not see the Ekip.< again as they remain as long as possible
in that town. Such a pity! [a]
   The french gentleman (Paul Doumer) I received my last day at home arrived
here this morning. He lunched, then I spoke with him. I just received your dear
letter No. 398, for wh. many thanks, my treasure! In a previous letter you mentioned Spiridovich. I believe I told you before my departure that the Tail<
talked to me about this and asked he not be appointed to Obolensky's post, with
wh. I quite agree. [A. N.] Khvostov then gave his opinion that our Veselkin
would be a suitable man. But there is no rush as Obolensky remains for the present. As concerns the old men & children fr. East Prussia who are now in Siberia, I have arranged to have them sent to Germany. The doklad [report] this
morning was short, so before lunch I finally took a walk with Tiny<. He
marched about with his rifle, singing loudly. God bless you my Sunny, my darling. I love you & kiss you tenderly. Ever yr. own old huzy   Nicky. [b]

No. 643/ Telegram 109. Stavka> Tsarskoe Selo. 30 Nov 1915. 7.06> 7.35
p.m. To her majesty. We thank you for dear letters. Also quite warm, pouring.
Saw very good cinema this afternoon. Loving kisses. Nicky

No. 644/ Her No. 400.   Tsarskoe Selo. Dec. 1st 1915.
My own Beloved,
   Dark, cold, 11 degree of frost. Sonia< has fallen ill, very weak, a noise in the
lungs & dozing state, scarcely speaks & when does, scarce to be understood. I
had Vl. Nik.< to come & he will bring his brother too. V.N.< put ban'ki [cup-
pings] on whilst I was there —she took no notice & hung like a lump in the 2
maids' arms— pittyful [sic] sight this paralised [sic] body. In the night she was
worse so they got a sister [i.e., nurse] fr. the big palace< to make camphor injections & then the heart got a bit better. I know she likes to take holy Communion
when so ill, so shall try & get the priest [A. P. Vasil'ev ?]. She only said [talked]
yesterday "like Mama", she always thinks of her mother's death when feels ill.
Mitia Den< & Isa< sat long next door—I shall go up soon this morning—still
when ill, she is accustomed to have me near her always. [a]
   Only since yesterday morning everything [which I described above happened],
& at once [she is] so weak & broken & yesterday only 37.3 & pulse 140—to-day

38.7 & pulse 82-104.—I had Pss. Gedroits< for a doklad [report] 1½ hour yesterday about Evpatoria, where I sent her to clear up things wh. were going on.— Shurik<, Victor Er.< & Ravtopolo were in the evening at Anias<,—Nast.< eyes glittered fr. joy.—I hear Erdeli let the staff know you have said my [V. M.] Andronnikov is to be aid to Vil'chkovsky<. Well, then we must add a place as second aid, as have already one.—Tchitchagov[181] was at A.[nia's] & told her that he leads Varnava's story[171] to-day & that to-day the Synod issues the glorificate [glorification] decree of St. John M.[aximovitch]—Tchitchagov found a paper at the Synod, wh. the metrop. & all had forgotten (scandal!), in wh. the Synod asked you to permit his glorification (a year ago or a little more) & you wrote "agree" on the top—so they are at fault in everything.—Shall finish this during luncheon, must go up to Sonia, when dressed. Sweetheart, me wants you.— [b, c]

Are lunching in the play-room to be nearer to poor Sonia. Lovy, she is very bad. Inflamation of the lungs, but whats worse the paral.[ysis] is creeping round the muscles of her heart wh. is very weak—there is little hope & she looks so bad. At 3 she will take holy Communion. Does not speak to-day, hears when I tell her to drink & cough. Eyes always shut—bad complexion—They say her left zrachok [eyeball] does not react. Her Aunt [Elizabeth] Ivanova & a sister [i.e., nurse] fr. the Alex.[ander hospital] Station (fr. the convoy) have come to look after her.—For yr. beloved letter, endless thanks, always an intense joy, Sweetheart. Excuse short letter, but am worried about Sonia. Our Friend< says better for her she shld. go & we all feel it—I am very calm, seeing so many going off, dying, makes one realise [sic] the grandeur of it & that He knows best. Sun shines. Endless blessings & kisses fr. own Wify. [d, e]

181. Reference is probably to Seraphim, archbishop of Tver'. Seraphim was presumably a member of Rasputin's "party" in the Church. At any rate, he intended to present Varnava's "story" (argument) that Varnava acted properly in the glorification of John Maximovich which occurred when Samarin was director of the Holy Synod.

No. 645/ Telegram 3. Tsarskoe Selo> Stavka. 1 Dec 1915. 2.16> 2.45 p.m. To his majesty. Tenderly thank you for precious letter and chestnuts. Sonia< has pneumonia, heart muscles grow more paralyzed, very serious situation. [I] insisted [we] eat in nursery to be closer [to her]. Clear, cold. We all warmly kiss you. God bless you. Alix

No. 646/ Telegram 1. Stavka> Tsarskoe Selo. 1 Dec 1915. 7.11> 7.30 p.m. To her majesty. Loving thanks for letters. Sorry about Sonia. Again frosty weather. Thank her [Anna Vyrubova] very much for letter and present. Tender kisses. Niki

No. 647/ Telegram 6. Tsarskoe Selo> Stavka. 1 Dec 1915. 6.50> 7.45 p.m. To his majesty. Dear little Sonia< died quietly. This is so painful because she lived a long time with me, but I am glad for her. God keep you [both], my beloved darlings. [We] tenderly kiss [you]. Alix

No. 648/ Telegram 2. Stavka> Tsarskoe Selo. 1 Dec 1915. 8.35> 10.38 p.m.
To her majesty. Awfully upset by Sonia's< sudden death. Feel so for you, but
for her its real delivery. Entreat you not to get tired. Blessing [and] fondest
kisses from both. Niki

No. 649/ Telegram 12. Tsarskoe Selo> Stavka. 2 Dec 1915. 10.50> 11.38 a.m.
To his majesty. Tenderly thank you for dear telegram. Spent the night badly.
Not moving about because heart enlarged. Hope to go in evening to carrying out
of [Sonia's<] body from the church. Very much want to receive communion to-
morrow morning, if I feel better. Clear, cold day. All tenderly embrace and kiss
[you]. Alix

No. 650/ Her No. 401.   Tsarskoe Selo. Dec. 2nd 1915.
My very own sweet One,
    One more true heart gone to the unknown land! For her I am glad that all is
over, as in the future life might have been a yet worse phisical [sic] trial to her.
Went so quickly that one cannot yet realise [sic] it—she lies there like a wax ball,
I cannot call it otherwise, so unlike the Sonia< full of bright life & roy [gay?]
colours we knew. God took her mercifully without any suffering. I wrote to you
during luncheon yesterday, then just began doklad [report] with Vil'chkovsky &
I was called to her, heart very weak, [she had a temperature of] 39.7 & was
taken Holy Communion (2½), she could not open her eyes—the only thing she
said, was to me, & [it was] "forgive"—that was all & then no more heeded [?]
[—]when one told her to swallow, the end began. I asked the priest [A. P. Vasil'ev] to read the prayers & give her the last unction—it brings peace into the
room [with] prayers & I always think helps the parting soul. She changed rapidly. At 4¼ her Aunt [Elizabeth Ivanova] begged me to go & rest—so I lay in
Isa's< room & there we took tea—at 5.10 they called me—the priest read the
prayers for the dying & she quite peacefully went to sleep. God let her soul rest
in peace & bless her for all her great love to me through these long years. [a]
    Never did the child complain of her health—even paralised [sic], she enjoyed
life to the end.—It was the heart wh. failed, they gave her camphor & other
strong injections, nothing acted upon the heart. What a great mystery life is—all
waiting round for the birth of a human being—again all awaiting the departure of
a soul. Something so grand in it all & one feels how small we mortals are &
how great our heavenly Father. Its difficult to express ones thoughts & feelings
on paper—I felt as tho' were giving her over to God's care alone now, wanting to
help her soul to be happy—a great awe & holiness of the moment overtakes
one—such a secret, only to be fathomed yonder. The girls & I went at 9 to the
panikhida [funeral service]. Now they are going to place her into her coffin in
her sittingroom, but I shall spare my forces [until] the evening, to accompany
her out of our house to Znamenia<. I scarcely slept—too many impressions! I
am quiet—calm—numbed feeling you know fr. crushing all in. Botkin for the first
time turned up this morning—begged me to keep quiet because of the enlarged
heart. I want to go to holy Communion to-morrow morning— Christmas Fast &
now it will be a help.—A.[nia]< will go to Peshcherny Chapel< at 9. So Sweetheart, I tenderly, lovingly beg your forgiveness for everything— word &

deed—bless me Lovy.[129] It will be a comfort, as you leave on your journey to-morrow, to pray for you there. God grant all will go well. Sad you won't see the Gvardeisky Ekipazh<. After your letter yesterday, we arranged to send Popof [Popov] to Odessa with my [field-]church & Andreev with the one for the 4-th reg. to Zhmerinka or wherever they are. It will be interesting [for you to see it as] you go on further.—[b, c]

I send you a small present to-day (the letterbox awaits your return) & you open it the 5-th evening. Its a photo taken out of a group last year & enlarged.—I send it to-day, in case it might not reach you on the 6-th & in any case also my very tenderest blessings goodwishes & kisses for your precious Namesday [sic]. Heart & soul ever with you my beloved Angel, also a few flowers —the others must have faded, as yesterday it was a week that you left us. God grant you a good journey in every respect.—A. kisses you.—Yr. Mama [Maria Fedorovna] is coming to the panikhida [funeral service], so I must go to it, because Olga & Tatiana are obliged to go to town<, they cannot put off a big committee & receipt of donations. God bless & protect you my Love, 1000 fond kisses fr. yr. own old   Wify. [d]

No. 651/ Telegram 23. Stavka> Tsarskoe Selo. 2 Dec 1915. 7.15> 8.26 p.m. To her majesty. Tender thanks [for] dear letter. Thoughts so much with you. Do not overtire yourself. Leave to-morrow, [will have] lunch in train. Frosty, clear weather. Loving kisses. Niki

---

No. 652/ Telegram 20. Tsarskoe Selo> Stavka. 2 Dec 1915. 9.40> 10.23 p.m. To his majesty. Now going to her [Sonia<] to take her with me to Znamenia<, then to confession. [I] ask forgiveness for everything.[129] Motherdear< left for funeral service. 15 degs. frost. Brother of poor Trina< just died. How many woes surround [us]. Sleep peacefully. [I] warmly embrace and kiss you. Alix

---

No. 653/ Telegram 22. Tsarskoe Selo> Stavka. 3 Dec 1915. 8.54> 9.40 a.m. To his majesty. Now going to church and my heart is full of you. She [Anna Vyrubova] also asks forgiveness of you.[129] May God bless you, my darlings, and your journey. Will await your telegrams impatiently. Clear, cold. We all kiss you very, very warmly. Alix

---

No. 654/ Her No. 402.   Tsarskoe Selo. Dec. 3rd 1915.
Sweet precious One,

It was a great consolation to go to Holy Communion this morning & I carried you in my heart. So peaceful & lovely & our singers sang beautifully—nobody was in Church—only [daughter] Olga dear came. Ania< went with me—but everywhere one misses & thinks of Sonia<—how I used to wheel her up to the Czar Gates. —We took a cup of tea, then Ania went to town & Olga & I a moment to place candles at Znamenia<. A nun was reading,—she was covered right over and only her faithful servant stood there—so lonely. As nobody thought, of 40 days mass, I had it ordered.—Yesterday the officers of the United Regiment carried her in the house down the stairs & in[to the] Church, in the street the ser-

vants, [daughters] T.[atiana] & M.[aria] followed on foot [while] I drove behind
with O.[lga] & A.[nastasia]—snow—so quiet & quick all. But one cannot grasp
that being [once] so full of life [she] is lying there so still—yes, the soul is gone
indeed.—[a]

Ania had confession in our bedroom too, it was simpler for the priest [A. P.
Vasil'ev]. I had wanted to go this lent & now it came as a great consolation—one
is a bit tired from more than a years suffering & that gives one new strength &
help.—To-day its the anniversery [sic] of Botkin's son's death. Sonia died the
same day as my Mother 34 years ago;—she was much pittied [sic] & loved &
heaps of people came. During the panikhida [funeral service] in the house, I kept
near the bedroom door so saw nobody, wh. was easier. Kind little Mother dear<
came, as she wanted to see her in her own room still, and than she told me she
wants all those pictures of [the court painter M. A.] Zichy's taken out of the
frames again and put in a map [case] & sent to her, as they are remembrances of
the journey & she says were before at Gatchina. I shall get Shcheglov.< to do it,
only after one has taken Sonia's things away & put order. [b]

It's cold & snowing—I wonder how you are getting along on your journey, my
sweetest sweets. Such an intense longing for you, but I am glad you are not here
these sad days. Petia< comes to tea.—I had Mme Zizi<, as there was a lot to talk
about an on account of the funeral too.—Its snowing away the whole time.
Lovebird, treasure, how I think of & lovy [i.e., love] you & my Sunbeam<. God
bless you & your journey & bring you safely back again I cover you with very
tenderest kisses, & remain, Huzy Love, yr. very own old Sunny. [c]

No. 655/ Telegram 34. Stavka> Tsarskoe Selo. 3 Dec 1915. 12.27> 12.47 p.m.
To her majesty. God bless you. Heart and soul with you since yesterday. Aleksei has rather strong cold. So tiresome if he has to remain in the train and not see
the troops. Give Trina< over my sympathy. Leaving directly. Tender love from
both. Niki

No. 656/ Telegram 10 in Russian. Stavka> Tsarskoe Selo. 3/4 Dec 1915.. 10.10
p.m.> 12.05 a.m. To her majesty. Because of his cold Aleksei has had bleeding
at the nose at intervals the whole day. Have decided, on Fedorov's advice, to
return to Stavka.[182] Shall be very glad if you come to spend 6th December together. [I] warmly kiss [you]. Nikolai.

182. The tsarevich was a hemophiliac, and bleeding of any kind posed danger to him. Nicholas
and Aleksei were travelling to inspect the guard regiments when the boy's condition became alarm-
ing. At 3 a.m. Dr. Fedorov woke the Tsar to advise him to return immediately to Stavka. "They got
back to Mogilev on the same day, but Alexey grew rapidly worse, and it was decided to take him to
Tsarskoe Selo (Gilliard)." (Vulliamy, pp. 116-117n)

No. 657/ Telegram 25. Tsarskoe Selo> Stavka. 4 Dec 1915. 10.35> 11.12 a.m.
To his majesty. Most distressed that all [your] wonderful plans have been ruined. This is also a disappointment for all of you. Really, should you not now
cauterize his nose, as [Dr. F. P.] Polyakov advises in such cases? Do not worry,
[our] Friend< says all this comes from weariness and will now pass. Am dis-

turbed not to be with you. Am taking [daughter] Olga with me, will telegraph as soon as it will be known when we will arrive, in all probability not earlier than to-morrow. Will bring Vl. Nik.< Then you will not be tied down by our movements. [I] embrace and kiss you. [I] know there is no danger and am not worried by anything. Alix

---

No. 658/ Telegram 7. Stavka> Tsarskoe Selo. 4 Dec 1915. 12.41> 1.15 p.m. To her majesty. [We] arrived well, remain in train. As his temp. has risen to 39, have decided to return home [to Tsarskoe Selo] at once. Leave to day at 3; hope to arrive to morrow [at] 11 [in] morning. He slept rather well, is gay. Bleeding much less, coughs rarely. Tender thanks for letter. Kisses from both. Niki

---

No. 659/ Telegram 8. Stavka> Tsarskoe Selo. 4 Dec 1915. 2.10> 3.00 p.m. To her majesty. Thank God he feels better now. Temp. 37.5. Bleeding stopped though can easily begin from his moving about or coughing. To day no headache. Eats on the whole well. Shall wire in the evening. Fondest thanks [for] second dear letter. So happy to meet you soon at home. Niki

---

No. 660/ Telegram 29. Tsarskoe Selo> Stavka. 4 Dec 1915. 2.57> 3.30 p.m. To his majesty. Tenderly thank you. Very worried about [my] dear one. Glad you are arriving together. [Dr.] Polyakov says it is necessary to cauterize nose with that medicine again quickly. Derevenko should have a vile of it. [I] hope [his] throat is not worse. God bless your trip. [I] warmly kiss [you] both. Alix

---

No. 661/ Telegram 9. Vitebsk> Tsarskoe Selo. 4 Dec 1915. 8.50> 10.23 p.m. To her majesty. Spent second half day well. At 8 o'clock [his] temp. 38.1. [He is] in excellent spirits and rather astonished why we are going home. Please [let there be] nobody to-morrow at station.[183] Tenderest kisses from both. Niki

---

183. "According to Gilliard, the journey was 'agonising.' The train had to be stopped several times in order that the dressings might be carefully renewed. The boy had two attacks of syncope during the night, but towards the morning there was a slight improvement. He was taken to the palace with infinite precautions, and the wound was cauterised. It was on this occasion that the Tsaritsa attributed her son's escape from death to the timely presence of Rasputin (Paléologue, II, p. 138.)." (Vulliamy, p. 117n)

No. 662/ Her No. 403.   Tsarskoe Selo. Dec. 12th 1915.
My very own,
    Sweetheart, beloved Darling, its with an aching heart I let you go—no Baby sweet< to accompany you—quite alone. Tho' I suffered without my Child, it was a great consolation to give him to you & to feel his sweet presence would be ever near to brighten up your life. And no N.P.< anymore to accompany you—I was quiet when I knew him with you[—]"He is ours" as our Friend< says so rightly & his life is so knitted to ours since all these years, he has shared our joys & sorrows and is quite our very own and we are his nearest & dearest—he too dreads the long absence now from us all, I do hope you will see him with the battalions, it would be a blessing for his new work.—Thank God, your heart can

be quiet about Aleksei & I hope, that by the time you return, you will find him as round & rosy as before.—He will be very sad to remain behind, he loved being with you alone like a big fellow already.   Altogether separations are horrid things & one cannot get accustomed to them.   Nobody to caress & kiss you for long now— in thoughts I will be always doing it, my Angel.   Your cushion gets the morning & evening kisses & many a tear.   Ones love always grows and the yearning increases.   God grant you may have fine & warmer weather there to the south.   Its a pitty [sic] all has to be crowded into one day—one cannot so thoroughly enjoy all one sees, nor have enough time to talk, as one would wish.—May your precious presence bring them great blessings & success. [a, b]

I wonder, whether you will return for Xmas or not, but you will let me know as soon as it is settled, now of course you cannot tell.—My own, my own, I hold you tightly clasped to my heart & cover you with kisses—feel me with & near you, holding you warm & tenderly.   The first hour will be horrid in the train without Baby< —so silent & you will miss the prayers too.   Sweethearty mine, oh me loves so deeply, deeply "with unending true devotion deeper far than I can say".—When you are away, there is a feeling of the chief thing in my life missing—everything has a sad note, & now I keep Agoowee one, its worse for you by far.   Sleep peacefully my Love, God send you strengthning [sic] sleep & rest.— [c]

I have given the Image [icon] for the Chasseurs regiment, the bag is lined with their ribbon they gave and our Friend blessed on their Feastday 1906 at Peterhof. The rest of it I have kept; but He [Rasputin] said it would be in a war & they would do great things.   Now He cannot exactly remember, but said that one must always do what he says—it has a deep meaning.   Perhaps you wont wish to give it personally, not to hurt the other reg. (as this one has nothing to do with Baby or me)—then have it given them fr. me when you leave,—Remember Georgi's< good idea of having all yr. a.d.c. to do service 10 days—then you will hear fresh news & they will get a rest.—Goodbye my own Huzy, my Own, own, very Own, my Life, my Sunshine, God bless & protect you, St. Nicolos [sic] hear our prayers. Kisses without end. Ever yr. very   Own. [d]

No. 663/ Telegram 3 in Russian. Semrino> Tsarskoe Selo. 12 Dec 1915. 6.15> 7.07 p.m. To her majesty. Made inquiries about frost-bitten Cossacks. Turned out to be absolute lie from some doctor. In thoughts am with you [all]. Very sad alone. Warmly kiss all. Niki

---

No. 664/ Telegram 112 in Russian. Tsarskoe Selo> Dno. 12 Dec 1915. 8.30> 9.58 p.m. To his majesty. Very sad. [We] are lunching together. Difficult that you are alone. Sleep well. [We] warmly kiss [you]. Thank you for telegram. God keep you. Alix

---

No. 665/ Telegram 114. Tsarskoe Selo> Stavka. 13 Dec 1915. 10.42> 11.50 a.m. To his majesty. Snowing. 12 degrees. Slept poorly. Terribly sad, feel awfully alone. Clear. [I] am going to church briefly. Received telegram from N.P.<

from Podvolochisk: they arrived safely. God bless your trip. [We] all warmly kiss [you]. Little one< slept well, [his temperature is] 37. Alix

---

No. 666/ Her No. 404.   Tsarskoe Selo. Dec. 13th 1915.
My own Beloved,
   It was a lonely night & I miss you awfully—but for you its far worse & I feel so much for you my Sweetheart. Was so hard parting! God bless & protect you now & for ever.—I slept midling [sic]—its snowing since the evening, 12-15 degrees only, such luck and I hope you will find it much warmer on your journey.—Just got a wire fr. Zhukov, very touching, before their departure & one from N.P.< from Podvolotchisk, that they arrived there safely yesterday—so I hope he will still see you there.—Dined upstairs & then a letter from Paul< was brought me & one to him from Marie< all about Ruzsky<, despair etc.; after a talk of hers with B.[onch]-Br.[uevich], who complained of course that one protects the Barons here—that when he sent away the 2 of the red cross, Beletski got them back—that Ruzsky is against this plan of Alekseev to the south & abuse of Alekseev—so, as Paul left it to me to choose, whether to send his & Maries< letters to you—I returned them to him with a few explanations—as I disagree with all she writes. As tho' one simply sent Ruzsky off, after his letter to Polivanov, wh. soi disant [one says] the latter never showed you—lots of rot.— [a]
   Tiny< slept well, [he had a temperature of] 37, but left arm rather stiff, no pain.—As heart a little better, & not so cold, am going at 11 to mass—Pitirim serves and I will feel grateful to pray in Church, tho' miss you there quite awfully.—God bless you Lovy, I must get up, & dress. I feel still your goodbye kiss on my lips & hunger for more. Goodbye my Angel, my Sunshine. I cover you with tender fond kisses.—Ever yr. very own old <u>Wify</u>. [P.S.] Thoughts don't leave you, nor my prayers with endless yearning. [b]

No. 667/ Telegram 9. Stavka> Tsarskoe Selo. 13 Dec 1915. 1.01> 1.31 p.m.
To her majesty. Thanks for telegram. Arrived well. 3 degr[ees] of frost, windy. Leave at midnight. Less lonely in the train as always occupied. Tender kisses to all. Niki

---

No. 668/ Telegram 117. Tsarskoe Selo> Stavka. 13 Dec 1915. 9.00> 9.30 p.m.
To his majesty. [We are] lunching upstairs. All kiss you and wish [you] a good night. Voronov and wife had tea with us. Little one< healthy. My tender thoughts [are] constantly with you. [We] tenderly embrace [you]. Alix

---

No. 669/ Her No. 405.   Tsarskoe Selo. Dec. 13th 1915.
My own Sweetheart,
   I begin my letter this evening, as shall not have much time for writing to-morrow morning, as the dentist [Dr. S. S. Kostritsky] awaits me & Ella< arrived. Excuse another ink, but the other pen is empty. Baby< has been quite alright [sic]—we lunched, took tea & dined with him & after seeing [P. C.] Benkendorff & Sonia's Aunt Sister Ivanova, I remained with him. The Metropolitan Pitirim served beautifully, & at the end said a few warm words & prayer

for you, Lovy dear. Loman gave him a big clerical luncheon at wh. Ania also assisted. It was comforting praying in Church with our dear soldiers.—Ania<, Voronov & wife took tea, Baby was delighted to see them. He leaves on Thursday to join the crew with his 160 sailors, over Moscou [sic], as that way to Kiev seems quicker. [a]

He says poor Melnovets has grown terribly thin & his lungs are in a seriously bad state.—To-morrow is already the anniversary of Butakov's death—how the time flies!—Then I had a Pr. Obolensky, brother of M-me [Olga] Prutchenko, tho' she hates Ania on account of our Friend<, he came to me through A.[nia] to bring me photos of the frescos in the Feropontievsky monastery, wh. he is helping to restore—they need still 38.000 rub.[les], so I told him he must wait to the end of the war, now all sums are needed elsewhere. Then Pr. Galitzin [N. D. Golitsyn] came with his doklad [report] of my committee for our prisoners.—Then I rested an hour. Ania dines too, as I shall see her less these days, tho' Ella leaves again Wednesday evening & will spend half her days in town & I with the dentist. Alas, I cannot go to the consecration of the little Church—its too tiring & I am not fit yet; in ten days Xmas & so much to be done before that.—It was warmer, so the children drove to Pavlovsk,—met the Countess Palei, son & little girls on snowshoes. Now I must try & sleep. [b, c]

Dec. 14-th. 17° of frost. Good morning, Sweetheart! Babykins< slept well, I not famously.—I wonder whether my letters catch you up on the way back or whether you will only find them upon yr. return to the Headquarters; well, as they are numbered, you wont make any confusions.—The pink sky behind the kitchen & the thickly covered in snow trees look quite fairylike—one longs to be an artist to paint all.—I told [P. C.] Benkendorff about the gospels to be sent to you through Rostovtsev. Ella comes at ¼ to 12 -3 ½ & then goes to town for Akafist [a series of doxological prayers] & evening service before to-morrow's consecration & dines at Anichkov<. And I have the dentist before 11 in consequence.—His arm is alright again & [he has a temperature of] 36.6 & gay. All my thoughts follow you the whole time and ernest prayers—miss you greatly, my Sweetheart & long for your tender caresses to warm me up.—There, Ortipo jumped upon my bed, Tatiana has gone off to the hospital, Anastasia was at the dentists.—Leo< is still alive—ups & downs, poor man.—I kissed one of our little pink flowers & enclose it in this letter.—Now I must get up—such a nuisance—& end my letter. Goodbye my Beloved, I bless you & kiss you without end. Ever Husy sweet yr. very   Own. [d]

No. 670/ Telegram 119. Tsarskoe Selo> Kiev. 14 Dec 1915. 1.13> 1.30 p.m. To his majesty. Kiev. Sunny. 17 degrees early in morning. Ella's< trip running four hours late, as result of which she probably is still in city. Sunbeam< healthy. [We] are now going to lunch together. In thoughts and in prayers with you. All warmly kiss [you]. [We] miss [you] terribly. Alix

---

No. 671/ Telegram 2. Kiev> Tsarskoe Selo. 14 Dec 1915. 6.42> 7.55 p.m. To her majesty. Arrived well. One degree of warmth. Thanks for news. Xenia<, Sandro< [and my sister] Olga after tea are sitting with me talking cosily [sic]. Leave at 7. Tenderest kisses to all. Niki

No. 672/ Telegram 126 in Russian. Tsarskoe Selo> Volochisk. 15 Dec 1915. 10.55> 11.20 a.m. To his majesty. Tenderest thoughts and prayers surround you. [I] hope all is well. Probably splendid impressions. Little one< better. Ella< healthy. [We] all warmly kiss [you]. Heart enlarged. 20 [degrees of] frost. Alix

No. 673/ Her No. 406.   Tsarskoe Selo. Dec. 15th 1915.

My very own sweet Darling,

All my thoughts are with you, wondering how all is going on.—We have again 20° of frost, & glorious sunshine.—Such a fidgeting from early morning on, hundreds of questions about Xmas presents for the wounded & personal of the hospitals—the number always increases.—The 900 gospels, images [icons] & postcard-groups have been sent to Kyra<.—I only saw Ella< a second at 9 before she flew off to church—it is 1, & she has not yet left town< again. Sat with the dentist [Dr. S. S. Kostritsky] for an hour.—Heart more enlarged this morning.—Baby< slept till 11, alright, but still has a cold.—Had Sophie Fersen [Ferzen] for nearly 2 hours yesterday and we had such a nice talk—such a pleasant, good woman.— [a]

I send you a petition of Prince Yurevsky's sister-in-law, a not good person, you will do as you like with it.—Css. Rebinder, Kharkov, wrote to Ania, that her brother Kutaysov [Kutaisov] got the news of his nomination there: "At first he would not believe in his good fortune, & now he is aflame with the desire to prove his worth to bear the insignia of his beloved Monarch & ready to sacrifice for him all his powers, all his life." She says he has become quite another man since—God bless you for what you have done to him, Sweetheart. How glad I am you saw Xenia< too.— Ania sends you her tender kisses, she has left for town at 1, over night.—Must send this off now.—Blessing & ever such warm, tender, fond kisses, Lovebird fr. yr. very own little Sunny. [b]

No. 674/ Telegram 3 in Russian. Podvolochisk> Tsarskoe Selo. 15 Dec 1915. 9.36> 11.12 p.m. To her majesty. All three reviews passed off very successfully. Appearance of troops magnificent. Weather warm—2 deg. Leaving now, remembered Aleksei in these places. Warmly kiss all. Niki

No. 675/ Her No. 407.   Tsarskoe Selo. Dec. 16th 1915.

My very own Darling,

I was so happy to receive your dear telegram last night from Podvolotchisk & to know, that all had been so beautiful. Our Friend< prayed & blessed again from afar.—N.P.< wired after 4 already, that you had promoted him after the review & that he was awfully happy—I am glad you saw him before the battalion.—We made Baby< tell Ella< all about Volotchisk & your inspections there & the Pss. Volkonskaya—he told it very well and with lots of details.—Ella had been there a year ago in autumn. Her humour and looks are excellent, quiet & natural—of course has to rush every morning to town & receives besides here still. She leaves again to-morrow evening—to-day I am going to look at the china & drawings from the fabric with her & Strukov. 26° of frost again, so that & my enlarged heart keep me quietly home. Ania was yesterday at the Metropolitans [Pitirim], our Friend too—they spoke very well, & then he gave them luncheon—always the first place to Gr.[egory]< & the whole time wonderfully respectful to him & deeply impressed by all he said. You have only left us 5 days, & it seems to me such ages already. Oh Lovy, Baby & I are already thinking of your loneliness at the Headquarter[s] & it fills us with great sorrow. "You really mustn't"[160] I find, precious Angel mine. Now I must dress & go to the dentist [Dr. S. S. Kostritsky], after wh. I shall finish my letter.—[a, b, c]

Here I am upstairs & he [Dr. Kostritsky] is arranging my (false) tooth—we spoke about the big military Sanatorium, wh. is being finished with yr. sums & now he hears the Yalta medical society (wh. the "Union of Cities" helps) wants you to give it over to them —he finds it principally quite wrong (belongs himself to the society), therefore I warn you not to agree if you get such a petition —speak it over with me when you return, please—one needs it for those tubercular patients, who must be kept separately & have no place at Yalta—& it must be yours [i.e., a state facility].—Now I am sitting next to Aleksei's bed & he is writing to you. P.V.P.< watches how he spells. "Joy" lies sleeping in the floor. The sun shines brightly—I am giving an Image [Icon] of St. Nicolas [sic] for Ella to bring Prince Chir.-Chakhmatov [A. A. Shirinsky-Shikhmatov] from you, as thanks for his work,—he was ill & could not be at the consecration of the Church.—I fear my letter is very dull, but I have nothing of interest to tell you. Now it is time to go down to luncheon.—Goodbye, my very own beloved Sweetheart. The empty house at the Headquarters will make you sad, poor Lovy mine & you will miss our Sunbeam. God help you, Deary. I cover you with tenderest, fondest kisses, blessings. Ever yr. very own old Wify. [d]

No. 676/ Telegram 11 in Russian. Bakhmach> Tsarskoe Selo. 16 Dec 1915. 2.30> 4.08 p.m. To her majesty. Still under splendid impressions of all I saw yesterday. Thank you very much for letter. Am glad [your] health is better. Here 4 deg frost. Warmly kiss all. Niki

---

No. 677/ Telegram 132. Tsarskoe Selo> Uza, Libavo-Romen r.[ail] r.[oad]. 16 Dec 1915. 3.15> 6.10 p.m. To his majesty. Am glad everything was so good yesterday. In thoughts [we are] together entire time. Tiny< better. 26 degrees. Ella< leaves to-morrow. Health so-so. [We] warmly kiss you. [Your sister] Olga coming for tea. God keep you. Alix

---

No. 678/ Telegram 13. Stavka> Tsarskoe Selo. 17 Dec 1915. 10.32> 11.30 a.m. To her majesty. Arrived well. Feel very lonely here in the house, rooms are so empty. Tender thanks for two letters. Shall try and write. Fondest kisses. Real winter, lots of snow, 10 deg. Niki

---

No. 679/ Telegram 135. Tsarskoe Selo> Stavka. 17 Dec 1915. 11.51 a.m.> 12.20 p.m. To his majesty. Think of you with tenderness. God bless you. We all warmly kiss you. 22° of frost. Heart bothers me all the time so am staying at home. Little one< hopes to get up to-morrow. Alix

No. 680/ Her No. 408.   Tsarskoe Selo. Dec. 17th 1915.
My own Darling,

Again no time to write even a decent letter. I had to read through any amount of doklady [reports], must get up at 10½ to go to the dentist [Dr. S. S. Kostritsky]—then Vil'chkovsky with a doklad [report], in the evening [A. N.] Khvostov I don't know why, & my heart more enlarged & hurts & I ought to keep quiet.—22° of frost. —I send you a paper Ella< brought from Kursk—she thought you would perhaps send someone with medals. The other is to remind you whom to telegraph for Xmas—it's no good my sending them, as we are not together.—Baby< hopes to be up & dressed to-morrow if his temp. keeps normal to-day; the cold had thrown itself unto his tommy, so that he has to keep to a diat [diet].—Ella< leaves this evening, as has much to do—her visit was cosy, calm & homely &, I think, will have done her good. [a, b]

I got a telegram fr. N.P.< that he comes on the 20-th fr. Kiev, no, not true, thinks of leaving the 20-th, but the wire comes fr. Kiev & he writes "not well," perhaps cought [sic] cold—rather unclear.— Ones thoughts are "out there" wondering how all are moving along.—Your lonely homecoming to the empty house makes me sad—God help you. Blessings & very tenderest kisses without end fr. yr. very own old <u>Wify</u>.   [P.S.] Excuse short letter, but really have no time—when Ella leaves & dentist finished, shall be free'r— but all is worse before Xmas wh. is in a week.—How was & is the old Man [Fredericks]? [c]

No. 681.   Ts.[arist] Stavka. Dec. 17th 1915.
My own darling Sunny,

Here I am again and filled with the best impressions. First, tenderest thanks for yr. four dear letters: two I received on the way & two after arriving here. [My sisters] Xenia< & Olga kiss you; we spent two nice hours in the train, Sandro< too. It became quite warm that evening, I opened the window in your couch & its doors into mine, so I slept well. The 15th I rose early because the first inspection of the 1st G.[uards] cav.[alry] div.[ision] was to begin at 8.30. The weather was delicious, just as it was in April, in the spring, only the fields & roads were quite muddy. I was so happy to see the dear regiments wh. I had not visited since the war began! Two cossack reg.[iment]s were there & three batteries of horse artil.[lery], and all passed very well. I invited all the commanding officers into the train & fed them on the way to Volochisk. Among them were Dmitry< & [A. N.] Linevich, who feels much better he said. [a]

At Voloch.[isk], quite near the train, the second inspection of the 5th Guards div.[ision] (Warsaw) occurred. Our rifles, now formed in a whole division, the splendid Ekip.< bat.[talion], the sappers & their artillery. The appearance of the troops was marvellous. The deep thick mud prevented their marching past, they wld. have lost their boots under my very eyes. The gen.[eral]s, Kyrill< & N.P.< lunched in my train—after which I promoted him [N. P. Sablin, to commander of a naval battalion of the Life Guards Ship's Co.]. Later we passed on to austrian territory. The last inspection, wh. began at 3.30, took place within three versts of the Podvolochisk station, as I had been detained at the earlier inspections. The 1st & 2nd Guar.[ds] inf.[antry] div.[ision]s with their artillery were there. It was already getting dark, so I again rode twice along the ranks from front to

rear, after wh. Shavel'sky held a Te Deum in the centre of a large square in total
darkness. After sitting in the motor, I shouted "good-bye" to the troops, & fr.
the invisible field there arose an enormous roar wh. accompanied me to the
train. Here the last party came to dinner. On that day I inspected 84,000 soldiers—Guards alone—& fed 105 commanding officers! Now I must end God
bless you & the dear children! Tell Tiny< I miss him terribly. Tender kisses fr.
your own old   Nicky. [b]

No. 682/ Her No. 682.   Tsarskoe Selo. Dec. 18th 1915.
My own beloved Sweetheart,
   Glorious bright sunshine, 8° of frost in the morning—the dentist [Dr. S. S.
Kostritsky] finished with me for this time & the teeth ache still. Yr. loneliness
makes us sad—fancy yr. dreary walks in the garden, call Mordv.[inov] or
Sil.[aev] to come with you, they have always something to tell. And the empty
bedroom! Come back quicker & we shall warm you up & caress you, Lovebird
tenderly I longed for.—The amount I have to do these days makes me wild, so as
that I have not even time to write to you quietly. I am smoking because my
teeth ache so more the nerves of the face. [a]
   Alas, I must bother you with papers, a thing you dont like. I enclose
Miechen's< letter, its simpler than writing out all the story about Dellingshausen,
when you have read her explanation, you will see whether anything can be done
for him—she is very careful whom she asks about, but also wants us to help set
right things if one can, & if an injustice has been committed through people
having hastily judged people.—Manus never died, it was simply a game of the
bourse wh. made the papers rise & fall—an ugly trick.[184]—My conversation with
the Tail< I shall write to-morrow, to-day I have no time & my brain is too
tired.—Things to settle for Xmas are always tiring & so complicated.—Baby< has
got up & will lunch in my room, looks sweet, thin with big eyes.—The girls alright. Tell me to thank her [Anna Vyrubova] for letter & goodies & send a message.—Must end. Blessings without end & 1,000 of very, very fond kisses. Ever,
Huzy mine yr. very own old Alix. [b]

   184. Ignaty Porfir'evich Manus was a prominent Jewish capitalist (see Biographical Index for
details); the "bourse" was the Petrograd stock exchange. The "ugly trick" must have been a false
rumor of Manus's death, as a consequence of which the "papers" (stocks and bonds) rose and fell—no
doubt to the profit of the people behind the ruse.

No. 683/ Telegram 140. Tsarskoe Selo> Stavka. 18 Dec 1915. 2.45> 3.22 p.m.
To his majesty. In thoughts together. 10° frost. Clear, sunny day. Aleksei
lunched with us upstairs. Feel wonderful. Ella< left yesterday evening. [We]
warmly embrace and kiss [you]. Alix

No. 684/ Telegram 33. Stavka> Tsarskoe Selo. 18 Dec 1915. 4.36> 5.16 p.m.
To her majesty. Many thanks for dear letter and list of New Year's greetings. In
the day occupied but very lonely in the evenings and nights. Thank her [Anna
Vyrubova] for [her] letter. Tenderest love, kisses. Niki

No. 685/ Telegram 143. Tsarskoe Selo> Stavka. 18 Dec 1915. 8.31> 8.55 p.m.
To his majesty. Tenderly thank you for dear letter. Terribly happy to receive it.
Fully understand your terrible loneliness. May God help you and bless you. Lit-
tle one< and I miss you very much. Alix

No. 686.   Ts.[arist] Stavka. Dec. 18th 1915.
My own beloved Sunny-dear,
    Warmest thanks for your dear letter & list of New Year's telegrams. Thank
Tiny< & the girlies< for their letters. Beletsky, among others, dined here today;
he told how Masha V.< behaved before & after leaving Town<, & how she was
received on her sister's estate.[81]   I have some hope of returning home for the
Christmas holidays. My plan is as follows: I leave to-morrow night, the 19th, for
the western front (Evert [is the commander]) & arrive by way of Minsk, at the
little station of Zamire, near Baranovichi. I will stay there for two days, & expect to inspect many troops.   Tuesday morning I will hold an inspection at
Molodechno, & another Friday at Vileiki, whence I shall return— through Minsk
& Orsha—home, arriving Thursday at 5.30 in time for the evening service. That
would be splendid! [a]
    There is very little news from the south as thick fog hinders our artillery fire;
nevertheless, some of our infantry regiments went up, or crawled up, to the wire
of the austr.[ian] positions, and even took the front lines in some places. But
you must not speak of this to anyone—please do me that favour. I have no more
time to write, so I must end.   The old man's [Fredericks's] health is excellent; the
other day he persuaded me to allow him to lead his squadron of chass.[eurs] de
le g.[uarde, i.e., cavalry guards] on horseback, tho' at a walking pace.   He was
tremendously happy after it. God bless you my darling-Sunny, my Little Lovebird. I shower you with kisses, also the dear children.   With tender love I am
ever your own old huzy   Nicky. [b]

No. 687/ Telegram 146. Tsarskoe Selo> Stavka.   19 Dec 1915. 12.49> 1.34
p.m. To his majesty. Only 4 degrees. Very dark. Tired out from pile of reports.
Little one< healthy. Sad to be far away. Embrace and kiss [you] without end.
Alix

No. 688/ Her No. 410.   Tsarskoe Selo. Dec. 19th 1915.
My own Sweetheart,
    You cannot imagine what a joy & consolation your precious letter was. I miss
you quite terribly, & all the more knowing how intensely lonely you must feel,
& no soft kiss to warm you up, no little voice to cheer you. Its more than hard
knowing you [are] all alone & not even N.P.< near you. How I wonder what
news you have from the front, is the move going satisfactorily—black crows<
croak with whys & wherefores, in winter such an undertaking—but I find we
have no right to judge, you & Alekseev have your calculations & plans & we
only need [to be] praying with heart & soul for success—& it will come to him
who knows how to wait. Its bitterly trying & hard, but without great patience,
faith and trust nothing can be achieved. God always tries one & when least we

expect it sends His recompense & relief. And how different all will be interiorly [i.e., domestically] when once our arms are crowned with success.— [a]

We talked a lot about the supply question with [A. N.] Khvostov, he says the ministers really try working together (putting Bark & Polivanov beside), but its the Duma's fault wh. hung comissions [sic] with 70 members onto them & the Minister of Interior's powers consequently are greatly diminished & he can take no particular measures, without it having passed through the comission. Certainly with one's hands tied like that, little can be achieved—he told it at the Duma the other day & they held their tongues. He therefore asked me to remind you of his conversation with you when he begged you to give an order—to the Council of ministers (I think) for the people to know, that you are thinking of their needs & wont forget them—it wont be much of a help, but as a moral link, to show them, that tho' you are at the war, you remember their needs. I fear, I explain things badly, but my head aches—I had such masses to read through—yesterday was dead tired 2 hours looking through Sonia's< things with her brother [D. I. Dzhambakurian-Orbeliani] & choosing Xmas presents & receiving. To-day I shall only have V. Kotchubey [Kochubei] about the Easter-gifts fund he is thinking we might found [i.e., establish]. [b]

One person, whom not only the tail<, but many good intentioned people are against & find not at the hight [height] of his place is Bark. He certainly does not help Khvostov—ever so long one has asked for money for him to buy the "Novoye Vremya" partly (the ministers, alas, told Bark to do it instead of Khvostov who wld. certainly have succeeded, whereas B. dawdles for his own reasons) —& the result is Guchkov with Jews, Rubinsteins etc. buy up the paper, put in their own mendacious articles. He [Bark] himself does not feel his sitting [i.e., position with you] very firm since he signed that letter with the other ministers, who partly left since[119] & so tries to get on with the party of Guchkov more or less. They say a clever Minister of Finance cld. easily catch Guchkov [in] a trap & make him harmless, once he wld. have no money from the Jews. Now this Pr. Tatishchev whom I saw (was in the Cavalry school, no, Cadet-corps, I think, which command.[er][185] is a great friend of his) is a very competent man, knows & venerates our Friend< deeply & gets on to perfection with Khvostov; a sort of relationship besides between them—a most loyal man & only wanting yr. & Russia's good. His name [Tatishchev's] is in many mouths, as a man capable of saving the financial situation & the gaffes Bark made. He is a man with an opinion of his own & seeks nothing personal, is rich, a prince, & an enemy of the Tjutchev[a]<-Samarin set—"he is one of our own men, ours, and will not betray us", as Khvostov says, & loving our Friend is certainly a blessing & gain. Do think about him & when you see Khvostov speak about him, as he of course has not the right to meddle in the affairs not concerning him—but they wld. work harmoniously together! He hates Guchkov & those Moscow types[101]—made a really good impression upon me. It was Andronnikov who spoke without any reason, nastly [sic] about T.[atishchev] to Voeikov<, & he confessed this afterwards—fancy, Pss. Palei knows even this (A.[nia]< pretended utter innocence & no knowledge of anything) —& said what good one says of Pr.[ince]Tatishchev.—I enclose a paper about him, I asked Khvostov to write [it] down for me. [c, d]

In his Luzhskoe estate he [Tatishchev] has just found a sulphour (?) spring &
coal, this I only tell you for a point of interest.—Do see him when you come &
have a quiet talk.—Certainly if the Cabinet becomes always more united, everey
[sic] thing will work better & they will besides stick up for our Friend from love
for you & veneration for Him. Baby< has written you a French letter, you send
him a telegr. it will rejoice the child. Now I must end. Goodbye my own precious Husband, heart of my heart, longsuffering Darling. I cannot think of you
quietly, the heart draws itself together from pain. I long to see you at last relieved from worries & anxieties—seeing people honestly fulfilling yr. orders,
serving you for your own precious self. You have so much to carry.—God indeed has laid a heavy burden upon yr. shoulders—but He will not fail you, will
give you the wisdom & strength you need & recompense your unfailing patience
& humility. I only wish I could be of more use to you—all is so difficult, complicated & hard now—and we cannot be together, that is the worst of it. Do you
think there is a chance of yr. coming soon?—God bless and protect you, comfort
you in yr. loneliness & hearken unto yr. prayers. I cover you with tenderest
warmest kisses, press you tightly to my heart & long to rest upon yr. breast &
keep quietly so, forgetting everything that tears the heart to pieces. Ever,
Sweetheart yr. very own Sunny. [e]

185. A. A. Sergeev thinks this person was "perhaps" Grand Prince Constantine Constantinovich
Tatishchev, inspector-general of Russian military schools. (See *Perepiska*, III, p. 501n)

No. 689/ Telegram 45. Stavka> Tsarskoe Selo. 19 Dec 1915. 5.27> 6.22 p.m.
To her majesty. Fondest thanks [for] dear letter. Tiny [is] up. Fancy, Georgie
[King George V] Has named me Field-Marshal of the British Army.[186] Am
leaving at 10 this evening. You will find explanation in my second letter. Tender
kisses to all. Niki

186. Hanbury-Williams notes that the Tsar's appointment as a Field-Marshal of the British Army,
which he heard on New Year's Day, caused him "real satisfaction and pleasure." (Vulliamy, p.
121n)

No. 690/ Telegram 149. Tsarskoe Selo> Stavka. 19 Dec 1915. 6.25> 6.45 p.m.
To his majesty. Heartily thank you for precious letter and news. We all tenderly
kiss [you] and wish [you] a safe trip. Not going to church because am too tired.
Will be happy if we see you in coming week. Greetings to all. Alix

No. 691/ Her No. 411.   Tsarskoe Selo. Dec. 20th 1915.
My own Sweetheart,
    Well, that was a surprise receiving yr. second dear letter, & I thank you for it
with all my heart. I am glad you are off & away again, you will have less time to
feel lonely & then those troops have been so long waiting to see you. It is also
less cold now, wh. is a good thing for inspections. Fancy the old Sinner [Freder-
icks, see Letter No. 686b] having ridden past at the head of his Squadron,—thank
God it went off well;—but I hope he otherwise does not bother you in your active
movements.—What joy you can be here on the 24-th, then you drink tea in the

train & we can light the Children's tree when you come—we shall have finished
the servants & ladies trees by then too. Ones head goes round from all there is
to do and I feel rotten—still I want to go for a bit to Church as Lili Den's Boy
["Titi"] becomes orthodox this morning in the lowerchurch—& upstairs will
stand during mass & go to Holy Communion for the first time in his life—my
Godchild. As Drentel'n lunches at Isa's< we have asked him to come down after,
to bid him goodbye, as probably he won't think of doing it himself. [a]

   Fancy yr. being English Fieldmarshall! That's nice. Now I am going to order
a nice Image of the English, Scotch & Irish Patron Saints, St. George, St. Michel
[sic], St. Andrew for you to bless the English Army with—St. Patrick is the Irish
au fond.—I saw in the papers to-day what you wrote about our advance to the
south till the wire-lines & so forth. God bless the troops with success. I wonder
what B.[eletsky] told you about Masha.[81] 10 degrees—of frost this morning &
the trees as thickly covered in snow as when you were here. Sunbeam< is at last
going out & I hope he will quickly regain his pink cheeks again.—To-day it's 20
days that Sonia died! One has no idea of time now—it seems like yesterday &
then again as tho' it happened ages ago—one day like a year at these serious
times of suffering and anguish.—Lovebird, I must be getting up to dress for
Church. Goodbye my very own beloved, my joy, my life, my one & all. I bless
& kiss you tenderly as it is only possible & cuddle close to you.—Ever, Sweetheart, yr. very own old wify   Alix.   [P.S.] How nice if you see the Erivantsi<,
Georgians< & the other Caucasians now—perhaps my Siberians?< I got a very
pretty telegram from the Chasseurs of the Guard thanking for the Image [icon]
& ribbon. [b]

No. 692/ Telegram 151 in Russian. Tsarskoe Selo> Train of the Supreme
Command, west.[ern] front. 20 Dec 1915. 1.35> 3.00 p.m. To his majesty.
Thoughts and prayers together. Little one< strolled about. 10 degrees. [We] were
at church. [We] wish you well. [We] warmly kiss [you]. Alix.

No. 693/ Telegram unnumbered in Russian. Tsarskoe Selo. 20 Dec 1915. [ar-
rived] 8.15 p.m. To her majesty. Thank you for news. In morning held grand
review. Very pleased with brave, healthy appearance of troops. Weather not
cold. Roads good. Warmly kiss all. Niki

No. 694/ Her No. 412.   Tsarskoe Selo. Dec. 21st 1915.
My own Sweetheart,

   How glad I am that you were satisfied with all you saw yesterday, & that the
weather was not too cold. To-day we have only 3 degrees—& Baby< enjoys his
outing twice daily in the garden.—I went to mass yesterday—the latter half, because I wished to be present when Lili Den's boy ["Titi"] took holy Communion
for the first time—he is my Godchild. She became [O]rthodox yesterday morning. The discription [sic] of her journey with Groten last time from here to the
country—is delightful—please, they slept in one compartment, he over her head
as there was no other place—good it was not Ania<.—Erdeli comes to me to-day,

I don't know why, perhaps after the false order he gave in your name & wh. he wants to clear himself probably, but I don't see how he can.— [a]

Yesterday Drentel'n took leave of us—eyes full of tears—he leaves the 26-th evening & hopes to have a chance of bidding you before goodbye. Won't yr. days here be madning [sic], 3 days Xmastrees in the manege [riding school] there are such masses! Then I had Mitia [Dzhambakurian-]Orbeliani to look through little Sonia's< jewels & devide [sic] them according to her wish—painful work seeing all her little things she was so fond of.—Tudels< is such a bore, never remembers anything, asks hundred times the same things, & that does not make my writing better. Head & heart bother me & I am awfully tired. For the other's sakes I went to A.[nia']s house yesterday as there were 2 of the Childrens wounded friends & [daughter] Marie's fat fellow—so I had to keep A. company. —Beloved Darling, I must say goodbye now. Keep well, heart & soul never leave you. Blessings & kisses without end, Huzy mine, fr. yr. own old <u>Wify</u>. [b]

No. 695/ Telegram 154 in Russian. Tsarskoe Selo> Zamir'e. 21 Dec 1915. 3.56> 4.50 p.m. To his majesty. Warmly thank you for yesterday's telegram. Today warmer. Snowing. Everything as usual. In thoughts together. [We] tenderly kiss [you]. Alix

---

No. 696/ Telegram 4 in Russian. Army in the Field> Tsarskoe Selo. 21 Dec 1915. 6.03> 7.15 p.m. To her majesty. Heartily thank you for dear letter. Today drove around the fighting fronts of two corps in a place familiar to me. [Received] most pleasant impressions from troops I saw. Full thaw. Warmly kiss [you]. Niki

---

No. 697/ Her No. 413.   Tsarskoe Selo. Dec. 22nd 1915.
My own Lovebird,

I congratulate you with our little Anastasia's namesday [sic]. It was sad giving her the presents without you. We have a mass in my room at 12½ & perhaps after I shall go for a little airing, as there are 2 degrees of warmth & no wind, from time to time a little snow. The first day that snow has fallen from the trees & they are quite uncovered.—Our Friend< is always praying & thinking of the war—He says we are to tell him at once if there is anything particular—so she [Anna Vyrubova?] did about the fogg, & He scolded [her] for not having said it at once—says no more foggs will disturb. [a]

Aleksei & Shot [the dog] have just gone off into the garden, it does him such good these walks.—Veselovsky< telegraphed, that you saw my Company on the 20-th—I am so glad for them, our wounded Kunov may also have been there or the other wounded Maleev. I saw Erdeli—well! the story is most unclear to my mind, as he protests [denies] ever having spoken to you personally about [V. M.] Andronnikov & that he never wrote such a telegr., he thinks at the telegraph they did it, to wh. I firmly protested, as they never would invent or use your name & for what reason besides. Then says it [is] Maslov's fault, may be the idea was a mistake of his—but I told him to find out in the staff in town who wrote & who got the order fr. Erdeli & "by your order"—I honestly believe Erdeli did it, because he told me other words & tho' my name were mentioned—bosh,—you know I don't like him nor his shifty eyes & manners. Then he told me good things about Groten (looks upon him as my protege & Ania's no doubt, as Erdeli was awfully rude the last years, during his great friendship with Stana<, towards Ania). [b]

My lancer Gurev sat an hour with me (also spoke well of Groten & Maslov) & was nice, interesting, excellent <u>spirit</u>—the thing for a young officer.—How strange it must have seemed to you to see our troops in the places you knew from the old Headquarters. Do we at all advance there, or have we stuck fast since the retreat?—To the south we seem to be making lots of prisoners and slowly but firmly advance.—I have been making up things for N.P.<—we sewed him a silk shirt, I knitted stockings, then got india rubber basin & jug like those I gave last Xmas to Rodionov etc.—Seeing the troops must be refreshing. I suppose you go by motor & walk—not possible to get your horses there—Sweetheart, I must now end, I bless, & kiss you without end, caress & love you beyond words.— Ever yr. very   <u>Own</u>.   [P.S.] [A. N.] Khvostov told A. that he, Naumov & Trepov have made a plan for the food distribution for 2 months—thank God, after 15 months, these have at last worked out a plan.—M-me Antonova returned from Livadia—I enclose a violet, snowdrop & other smelling buds from there.— [c]

No. 698/ Telegram 160. Tsarskoe Selo> Usha. 22 Dec 1915. 1.34> 4.50 p.m. To his majesty. [We] congratulate you on name day of [our daughter] Anastasia. So glad you saw my company. Thaw [is occurring]. Hope, finally, to take drive for a bit. [We] all warmly kiss [you]. Alix

---

No. 699/ Telegram unnumbered in Russian. Army in the Field> Tsarskoe Selo. 22 Dec 1915. - [Arrived,] 4.40 p.m. [I] thank you with all my soul for letter. Congratulate you on Anastasia's names-day [sic]. In morning review troops of army here, saw our Caucasian friends. All sections look remarkably well. Warmly kiss [you]. Niki

---

No. 700/ Telegram 9 in Russian. Army in the Field> Tsarskoe Selo. 23 Dec 1915. 1.55> 2.45 p.m. To her majesty. This morning held final review of army on Western Front. Troops look wonderful. Weather is warm. Am now leaving. Warmly kiss [you]. Niki

---

No. 701/ Telegram 183 in Russian. Tsarskoe Selo> Minsk. 23 Dec 1915. 2.58> 3.22 p.m. To his majesty. We all warmly kiss [you]. Dark, warm days. Are happy over your arrival soon. How good that you saw a lot! Aleksei was terribly happy over your telegram. God keep you. Alexandra

---

No. 702/ Her No. 414.   Tsarskoe Selo. Dec. 30th 1915.
My very own beloved One,

Off you go again alone & its with a very heavy heart I part from you. No more kisses & tender caresses for ever so long—I want to bury myself into you, hold you tight in my arms, make you feel the intense love of mine. You are my very life Sweetheart, & every separation gives such endless heartache—a tearing away from one, what is dearest & holiest to one. God grant it's not for long—others would no doubt find me foolish & sentimental—but I feel too deeply & intently & my love is fathomlessly deep, Lovebird!—And knowing all your heart carries, anxieties, worries,—so much that is serious, such heavy responsibilities wh. I long to share with you & take the weight upon my shoulders. One prays [again] & again with hope & trust & patience the good will come in due time & you & our country be recompensed for all the heartache & bloodshed. All that have been taken[, Rasputin once said,] "& burn as candles before God's throne" are praying for victory & success—& where the right cause is, will final victory be! One longs just a bit quicker for some very good news to quieten the restless minds here, to put their small faith to shame.— [a]

We have not seen each other quietly this time, alone only ¾ of an hour on Xmas Eve, & yesterday ½ an hour—in bed one cannot speak, too awfully late always, & in the morning no time—so that this visit has flown by, & then the Xmastrees took you away daily —but I am grateful that you came, not counting our joy, your sweet presence delighted several thousands who saw you here. The new year does not count—but still not to begin it together for the first time since 21 years is still a bit sad.—This letter I fear sounds grumbly, but indeed its not meant to be so, only the heart is very heavy & your loneliness is a source of trouble to me. Others, who are less accustomed to family life, feel such separations far less. Tho' the heart is engaged, I'll still come to see you off & then go into Church & seek strength there, & pray for your journey & victory.—Goodbye my Angel, Husband of my heart[,] I envy my flowers that will accompany you. I press you tightly to my breast, kiss every sweet place with gentle tender love, I, your own little woman, to whom you are All in this world. God bless & protect you, guard you from all harm, guide you safely & firmly into the new year. May it bring glory & sure peace, & the reward for all this war has cost you. I gently press my lips to yours & try to forget everything, gazing into your lovely eyes—I lay on your precious breast, rested my tired head upon it still. This morning I tried to gain calm & strength for the separation. Goodbye wee one, Lovebird, Sunshine, Huzy mine, Own! Ever your unto death wife & friend. Sunny. [P.S.] A big kiss imprinted here. [A large circle is drawn after these words on the original letter.] This little calendar may still be [a remembrance?] of me to you. [b]

No. 703/ Telegram 46 in Russian. Peredol'skaya> Tsarskoe Selo. 30 Dec 1915. 6.00> 7.43 p.m. To her majesty. Lonely and empty alone. In thoughts am with you all. Warmly kiss [you]. Good night. Niki

---

No. 704/ Telegram 242 in Russian. Tsarskoe Selo> Novosokolniki. 30 Dec 1915. 7.16 p.m.> 12.15 a.m. To his majesty. All [our] thoughts surround you. Sad, empty. [We] warmly kiss you. [We] wish you a good night. [We] will lunch in play room. God keep you. Alix

No. 705/ Telegram 50. Stavka> Tsarskoe Selo. 31 Dec 1915. 10.10> 10.40 a.m.
To her majesty. Arrived well, could not sleep. Weather the same. Loving thanks
[for] dear letter. Thoughts always together. Tenderest kisses. Niki

---

No. 706/ Her No. 415.   Tsarskoe Selo. Dec. 31st 1915.
My own Sweetheart,
   This is the last time that I write to you in the year 1915. From the depths of
my heart & soul I pray God Almighty to bless 1916 quite particularly for you &
our beloved country. May He crown all your undertakings with success, recompense the troops for all their bravery, send victory to us—show our enemies of
what we are capable. 5 m.[inutes] the sun shone before you left, & so has even
Shah Bagov [Shakh-Bagov] also noticed it each time you left for the army &
to-day it shines brightly, 18 [degrees] of frost. And as our Friend< says always
to pay attention to the weather, I trust that forsooth it is a good augury. [a]
   And for interior calm—to crush those effervescing elements, wh. try to ruin the
country & give you endless worry.—I prayed last night till I thought my soul
wld. burst, & cried my eyes out. I cannot bear to think of all you have to carry,
& all alone away from us—oh, my Treasure, my Sunshine, my Love. We went
straight to Znamenia< from the station, Baby dear< also placed his candles. I
don't know how we shall meet the new Year—I like being in Church—it bores the
Children—my heart is worse, so I cannot make up my mind yet,—in any case, its
very sad not to be together & I miss you quite horribly.—And yr. empty rooms
without our Sunbeam<, poor Angel; such endless pitty [sic] fills my heart for
you & such a craving to hold you tightly in my arms, & to cover you with
kisses. Baby< has just gone off into the garden.—Now I must end—Once more
every blessing & goodwish for the coming Year. God bless you, Lovy sweet,
beloved Angel! I kiss you without end, & remain yr. deeply, deeply loving,
loving very own old Wify Alix. [P.S.] A.[nia]< sends every blessings, goodwish, love & kisses for the New Year.—Just got yr. wire, so sorry you did not
sleep, for sure too hot, overtired & worried & sad. My humour too is of the sad-
dest. [b]

No. 707/ Telegram 247. Tsarskoe Selo> Stavka. 31 Dec 1915. 11.35 a.m.>
12.12 p.m. To his majesty. Thank you for telegrams. Terribly sad without you.
What a pity you cannot sleep. Here bright, sunny day. 18 degrees frost. We all
warmly kiss you. May God bless, strengthen and help you. Baby< strolling in
garden. Alix

No. 708.   Ts.[arist] Stavka. Dec. 31st 1915.
My beloved.
   Fond thanks for the dear letter wh. you gave to Teter.< & wh. surprised me as
I was going to bed! Warmest thanks for all the love and kindness you showed
during our six days together. If you only knew how it supports & rewards me
for my work, responsibilities & cares etc. I do not know how I wld. have en-
dured the burden had God had not give you to me as wife & friend! I speak in

earnest. It is difficult to say such truths, it is easier for me to write it out on paper—due to foolish shyness. [a]

Yesterday after parting fr. you, I received Fat [A. N.] Khvostov—for 1 ½ hour. We had a good, serious talk. After tea I took up "The Millionaire Girl" [by A. W. Marchmont] & read much of it. Very interesting, & calming to the brain; it has been several years since I read English novels. I slept badly, or better to say little—my feet were so cold I could not get to sleep; I finally put my head under the sheets, this warmed the side of the bed & the situation improved. Arriving here this morning, I found the weather as cold as at home—10 deg. Now the cold is less severe, no wind, lots of snow. After a lengthy doklad [report], the usual lunch with all the foreigners. I gave Aleksei's greeting over to them, & they asked much about him, they were sorry not to see him now. Our prayers will meet to-night—the Te Deum takes place in the church at 11.45. God bless you my darling Wify & the dear children! Ever my dearest Sunny, yr. own old huzy Nicky. [b]

No. 709/ Telegram 2. Tsarskoe Selo> Stavka. 1 Jan 1916. 12.36> 1.10 a.m. To his majesty. [They] just now celebrated Te Deum. Prayed for you with my soul and heart, my angel. May God bless you and our beloved country, may he give strength and courage to our heroes to victorious end! We all tenderly kiss [you] and are terribly lonesome without you. Sleep well, dear. Alix

---

No. 710/ Telegram 12. Tsarskoe Selo> Stavka. 1 Jan 1916. 2.35> 3.47 p.m. To his majesty. Just now received [your] dear letter for which [I] tenderly thank you—[It was the] best present for me on a day when I lie in bed thanks to my old heart. 22 deg. frost, clear, sunny. We all tenderly kiss [you] and send you best wishes. Hope you slept well, I did not. Alix

---

No. 711/ Her No. 416.   Tsarskoe Selo. Jan. 1st 1916.
My own beloved Angel,

The new year has begun & to you I send the first words my pen traces. Blessings & boundless love I send you. We had a mass in the other side of the house at 10 ½ & then I answered telegrams & got to my prayers before 12—I heard the Churchbells ring lying on my knees, crying & praying with heart & soul. Sweet Lovebird, what are you doing? Have you been to Church? Alone in yr. empty rooms, a sad sensation! One happy man I saw this evening, that was Volkov, as I have named him my 3-st [i.e., 3rd] page, the others beeing [sic] old & so often at death's door—he cried when thanking me—we remembered how he brought us in a present at Coburg, when we were engaged & I remember him yet before at Darmstadt.—I can't write any more to-night, my eyes are too sore. Sleep well, my precious One, my Sunshine. [a]

Goodmorning Huzy, my own! 22° of frost, bright weather. Slept badly, head ached—this morning more enlarged so have to spend the day in bed—sorry for the children—if better, shall get over onto the sopha in the evening to have this room aired. Got a telegram from Sandro< from town<, glad [his wife] poor little Xenia not alone, as she feels so very unwell. Longing for news from you, as only had a wire upon your arrival 24 hours ago & my thoughts dont leave you,—As Baby< has a wee bit scratchy throat, he remains at home.—The others have gone to Church.—Darling treasure, I trust this bright sunshine will bring many blessings to our brave troops & dear country and shine into your life with bright hope, strength & courage.—Have any amount of telegram[s] to answer.—Yesterday I received Mme Khvostov (wife of Minister of Justice) & pretty daughter, who marries next week, before the young Artillery officer returns to the war—he had 17 wounds. Then received 4 wounded officers, Vil'chkovsky< & a Kalmyk & Priest of theirs, who ask me to send wounded earlier in this year to their hospitals for mare's milk—they want to arrange also a sanatorium, wh. wld. be splendid.—Well, in bed one wont get at me & that will be perhaps better & help getting my heart sooner into order.—[b, c]

A.[nia]< spent the night in town, she went after 5 already—& after her telephone, by our Friend's< order. She told me what to tell you at once about [what is worrying Rasputin:] the trams. I know, Alek< once tried to stop it & at once there were rows—what general gave the order now?[187a] It is perfectly absurd, as they have often to go great distances, & a tram takes them there in no time. It seems an officer, because of the order, kicked a man out of the tram & the soldier tried to beat him—its bitterly cold too—& really, gives rise to nasty stories—our officers are not all gentlemen, so that their ways of explaining things to the soldiers are probably often "with the fist".—Why do people always invent new reasons for discontent & scandal, when all goes smothely [sic].—Beletsky got hold of a gang & brochures, wh. were being printed for the 9-th, to make filth again[—]knowing our Friend, God will help them serve you. [d]

The children are lunching next door & making wonderful noises. Inzhmekh< has arrived unexpectedly & so prevents [me from taking] med.[icine] wh. is a bore.—This instant, quite unexpectedly your sweetest letter was brought—oh thank you Lovy mine, thank you tenderly for yr. sweet words wh. warmed up my aching heart— the best gift for the beginning of the new year. Oh, Lovy mine, what good it does a tender word like that! you don't know, how much it means to me, nor how terribly I miss you—I yearn for your kisses, for your arms, shy Childy only gives them me in the dark & wify lives by them; I hate begging for them like A., but when I get them, they are my life, & when you are away, I recall all your sweet looks & every word and caress.—Baby received a charming telegram fr. all the foreigners at the Headquarters in remembrance of the little room in wh. they used to sit & chat during Zakuska [hors d'oeuvres]. A. brought a flower from our Friend for you with His blessing, love and many good wishes.—Goodbye my Angel Dear, I bless & kiss you over & over again yr. own Wify. [e]

No. 712/ Telegram 3. Stavka> Tsarskoe Selo. 1 Jan 1916. 3.32> 4.42 p.m. To her majesty. Loving thanks [for] dear letters and wishes. Have at once ordered forbidding about the trams to be taken back.[187a] Have always found it unjust. Hope [you are] not too tired. Tenderest kisses. Niki

---

187a. Enlisted men were not allowed on Russia's overcrowded streetcars during the war. Even before 1914, they were subjected to such "indignities as having to walk on the shady side of the street or to ride on streetcar platforms." The decree Nicholas issued at this time did not resolve the problem, and the "resentments which these discriminatory rules bred were a major cause of the mutiny of the Petrograd garrison in February 1917." Pipes, *Russian Revolution*, p. 83.

No. 713/ Telegram 49. Tsarskoe Selo> Stavka. 2 Jan 1916. 11.08> 11.52 a.m. To his majesty. Lay on couch for 2 hours last evening, headache continues to-day, hence am lying down again. 20 deg. frost. A year to-day since that tragic incident with Ania.[59] [She] has gone to take communion. We all tenderly kiss our dear, lonesome soul. God bless you. Alix

---

No. 714/ Her No. 417.   Tsarskoe Selo. Jan. 2nd 1916.
My own beloved Darling,
   Nice bright sunshine, 20 of frost. Did not sleep well as head continues aching, so excuse short letter. Was on the sopha yesterday fr. 9-11, but the head began aching thouroughly [sic] then—therefore I remain again in bed to-day, as head & heart ache more when I move. [Daughters] M.[arie] & A.[nastasia] went for an hour to church, because of Ania<, who takes Holy Communion[. T]he others were in the hospital & now they are lunching next door. No news from the front—shows the weather has not yet changed for the better.—I made a mistake, Sandro< is not here it's the other one ["Sandro L."] who telegraphed to me. Sergei< too is in town again. Nikolasha< wired from his family.[a]
   My Beloved, my lonely Sweetheart, my old heart aches for you, I so well understand that feeling of emptiness, tho' there are many people around—no one to give you caresses. When A. speeks [speaks] of her loneliness, it makes me angry, she has Nini< near whom she tenderly loves, twice a day comes to us—every evening with us four hours & you are her life & she gets daily caresses fr. us both & blessings; you have nothing now—only all in thoughts and fr. far. Oh, to have wings & fly over every evening to cheer you up with my love. Long to hold you in my arms, to cover you with kisses & feel that you are my very Own, whoever dares call you "my own",—you nevertheless are mine, my own treasure, my life, my Sun, my Heart! 32 years ago my childs heart already went out to you in deep love.—Of course you are your country's first of all & that you show in all your deeds, precious One.—I just read what you write to the army & the navy as New year's greeting.— have you let know about W[ilhelm II]'s birthday, that they [German pows in Russia] may feast it in the same way as yours was [by Russian pows in Germany—see Letters Nos. 737h and 738a]? Baby began writing his first diary yesterday,—[Daughter] Marie helped him, his spelling is of course queer.—Cannot write any more to-day.—Every thought is with you. I bless you fervently & sent warm "soft" kisses. Ever Huzzy mine, very own tenderly loving, deeply devoted little <u>Wify</u>. [P.S.] I reread your letter & love it. [b]

No. 715/ Telegram 27. Stavka> Tsarskoe Selo. 2 Jan 1916.[187b] 2.28> 3.27 p.m. To her majesty. Fondest thanks [for] letters. So tiresome to know you are not well. Do keep quiet for some time. Only 3, deg. frost. Nothing of interest going on. Tenderest kisses to all. Niki

187b. This and two of Nicholas's other telegrams—No. 720 sent on January 3 and No. 753 sent on January 10—are dated 1915, but that is a mistake which should be corrected to 1916.

No. 716.   Ts.[arist] Stavka. Jan. 2nd 1916.
My own beloved darling Sunny!
    Heartfelt thanks for both dear letters. I am distressed to hear you are ill, & live in anxiety when I am separated fr. you. My loneliness is nothing compared to this. My dear, be careful & take care of yourself. These telegrams are for you to read, tear them up when you are through. You ask how I greeted the New Year. We also had a Te Deum in the church at midnight. O.[tets, i.e., Father] Shavel'sky spoke well & directly.—My head ached so I laid down as soon as he was through.—I felt quite well again on New Year's Day. At 10 o.c[lock] I received several pleasant people from the town, then I went to church. A few papers came along with several telegrams, mostly family and foreign ones, which are always more difficult to answer. Of the regiments, only the Erivantsy< telegraphed. [a]
    I confess the book I am reading [see Letter 708b] is totally fascinating. When I finish I will send it to you. You will probably guess the parts wh. interested me most. The foreign officers begged my permission to telegraph Aleksei, they were impressed with his well written reply. Tell him they still take zakuska [hors d'oeuvres] in the little room & remember him. I also think of him, especially in the garden & during the evenings, & miss my cup of chocolate. The weather is fine, mild, 3° with much snow, but there has been no sunshine since I returned.—The days have become much longer. I must end now. God bless you my darling Wify-dear I kiss you & the children tenderly. Ever your own old Nicky. [b]

No. 717/ Telegram 64. Tsarskoe Selo> Stavka. 3 Jan 1916. 1.20> 2.55 p.m.
To his majesty. Today only 5 deg. Headache not so bad but heart still enlarged so that [I] am not getting up from bed. We all tenderly kiss and embrace our lonely and dear [one]. Alix

No. 718/ Her No. 418.   Tsarskoe Selo. Jan. 3rd 1916.
My very own Sweetheart,
    This morning only 5 degrees—such a great change. Scarcely slept this night— after 4-5½—after 7-9—head better, heart more enlarged, so remain in bed again. Yesterday was up from 9-11 again on sopha.—Am sorry one takes Masha's Chiffre off,[81] but once that [is] done, there are gentlemen who allow themselves to say things, whose golden coats & aiguillettes can now in future well be taken from them. Give Maximovich[188] the order to pay attention in the club—[A. N.] Khvost.[ov] begged Fred.[ericks] to help him, but the latter could not or did not understand the necessity.—Alas, Bor. Vasil'ch.[ikov] has changed much for the worse & many another [as well]—oh, they need to feel yr. power—one must be severe now.— [a]
    A.[nia]< was awfully happy with yr. telegram & says she wrote a rotten answer with the Parents, tho' she did not add half the official things the old man [her father, S. A. Taneev] wanted her to write.— I send you a whole collection of

letters. Excuse bad writing, I don't know why I cannot write evenly with this selffilling pen, because its so hard probably. I enclose a postcard made of Baby's< photo by Hahn at the Headquarters when we were there—it's such a good one.—It's snowing.—How dull I write. But I am squashed & humour not bright, so cannot write nicely. The Children are eating next door, chattering & firing away with their toy pistols.—Oh, my Angel sweet—my Own, very own—do so long for your loving arms to be around me, to hold me tight. The consolation of yr. loving letter! I continue rereading it & thanking God that really I can be something for you—I long to—I do love you so intently with every fibre of my heart. God bless you my sunshine, my one & all—I kiss and kiss you without end, pray without ceasing, that God may hearken unto our prayers send consolation, strength, success, victory, peace, peace in every sense—one is so dead tired and weary fr. all the misery.—Ever Huzy mine, life of my life, the blessing of it, the gratitude for every second of love you have given me. Yr. little woman, Yr. Wify. [b]

188. Gen. C. K. Maximovich, was known to be an informant of the empress, and was widely disliked for that reason. (See Letters No. 413f, 414b,d,e and 738b.) He was attached to the tsar at Stavka. In this letter Alexandra asks her husband to order Maximovich to note what was being said in the officer's club about Maria Vasil'chikova being deprived of court rank. (See Footnote 81.) A. N. Khvostov apparently asked B. V. Fredericks to inform him of gossip on this matter at Stavka, but the honorable old count was unwilling to do that.

No. 719.   Ts.[arist] Stavka. Jan. 3rd 1916.
My own dearest One,
   So far I have not received one letter fr. you. The train is six hours late owing to an enormous snowstorm. A storm has also raged here since yesterday, & last night the wind moaned in the chimney like that terrible tremolo in the "Ahnfrau."[189] I am quite grateful for yr. dear telegram. I am glad your headache is nearly gone, but the heart insists on being troublesome! Today I can write to you & the children, as no papers have come. I telegraphed Ania< yesterday, and received a nice reply.—No one remembered this anniversary, so I reminded Fred.< & Voeikov about it. Valia< is in bed with a high temperature, I just visited him. He feels better, but his face is swollen & red fr. the cold. [a]
   A great deal of snow fell during the night. I was glad to find a wooden shovel in the garden and have cleared one of the paths.— That is a very useful & pleasant occupation for me, as for now I am not exercising. And thanks to this I do not miss Tiny< so much. The morning doklady [reports] are short now because everything is quiet, but our troops have begun an offensive on the Caucasus, & fairly successfully. The Turks did not expect it during the winter. In Persia we are also dealing strong blows to those cursed gendarmes under the leadership of german, austrian & Swedish officers. By the way, I received a very cordial telegram fr. Harding, the Viceroy of India, in the name of the gov.[ernment], the princes & the people. Who would have expected this ten years ago?[190] I was touched by the flower our Friend< sent. Good bye until our next meeting, my darling Sunny. God bless you. I kiss you tenderly & love you without end. Ever your own old Nicky. [b]

189. In the last act of this drama by Franz Grillparzer, the family ghost (*die Ahufrau*) rises from the grave to receive a dying member of the household. The wind howls, and, " when the play is given with incidental music, the orchestra reinforces the effect with an appropriate tremolo. This drama was popular with Russian audiences." (Vulliamy, p. 126n)

190. Nicholas refers to traditional British anxiety that Russia had designs on India. "[T]en years ago," 1906, was when France drew her separate allies, Great Britain and Russia, into the Triple Entente.

No. 720/ Telegram 37. Stavka> Tsarskoe Selo. 3 Jan 1916.[187b] 6.40> 7.15 p.m. To her majesty. Loving thanks [for] dear letter. Got it only now as train was late owing to snowstorm. Warm weather. Again freezing. Hope you will feel soon strong. Loving kisses. Niki

---

No. 721/ Telegram 65. Tsarskoe Selo> Stavka. 3 Jan 1916. 8.20> 8.45 p.m. To his majesty. Warmly thank you for dear letter and telegram. Snowing here too. 5 deg. In thoughts always together. All 6 [of us] kiss and embrace [you]. Sleep well. Alix

---

No. 722/ Telegram 67. Tsarskoe Selo> Stavka. 4 Jan 1916. 2.42> 3.00 p.m. To his majesty. 15 deg., cold, windy. Health same, continue to lie down. Three of the children have colds, nothing serious. They are lunching in next room and shoot with their pistols. We all kiss and embrace you. Alix

---

No. 723/ Her No. 419   Tsarskoe Selo. Jan. 4th 1916.
My own Sweetheart,

It was such an unexpected joy to receive your sweet letter yesterday afternoon, & I thank you for it with all my deeply loving heart. My day passed as usual, A.[nia]< read to me a little in the day. Got on to my sopha from 9-12, N.P.< came to tea from 10-12—had not seen him since last Monday, missed you, Lovy, as never had him to tea without you, but he leaves probably the 8-th, according to the day he has to meet Kirill< at Kiev. To-night he leaves for 1 day to bid his sisters goodbye. He told us how touchingly kind Motherdear< was to him; kept him half an hour, talked about the Ekipazh<, politics, the old man [Goremykin] whom she finds honest, but a fool because he offended Buligin[191]— said how deeply she regretted N.P. was leaving her son [the tsar], such a true & honest friend, fished an image [icon] out of her pocket & blessed him—he was awfully touched by her kindness. [a]

It seems Sablin 3 (whom other[s] believe, alas, to be his brother)[192] spread the story about his being sent out there, away fr. you for having spoken against our Friend<, such a beastly shame & it has made him again less willing to go to Gr.[egory]<, as tho' now it would look as if he went to beg for himself; & he ought to see him before going to the war, his blessings can save him fr. harm, I shall see him again & then beg him to go—its a subject one has to handle gently—Manus did all the harm then.—Ebikin [A. N. Chebykin] saw him several times & will do all about getting the men, I think they look at them together before he leaves. K.[irill]< begged Grigorovich to ask Kanin to send officers from the "Oleg". They have sent for Kozhevnikov to prepare the men for his Company—that goes together with 3 weeks leave,—then Rod.[ionov] & so on they got no leave till now, since [E]aster, as had to be always ready at S.[evastopol'] & Odessa.—[b]

Guchkov is very ill—wish he would go to yonder world for you & Russians blessing, so its not a sinful wish.—The Children went to the Silaievs yesterday, O.[lga] & T.[atiana] & enjoyed them.—I slept so badly, heart enlarged & head aches rather, so remain in bed.—A. "rushes" about arranging her refugee-home, as wants to take some men in on the 6-th [see Letter No. 728g]—I scrape up things for her too & order other [thing]s she needs. They say the house looks so cosy [sic], T.[atiana] went to look at it!—15 degrees of frost to-day. Bichette [Maria Radziwell] wrote in despair to Mme Zizi< to crave your forgiveness, that her son was not at Nieswicz [Nesvizhe] when you went there. Since 17 months he had not left, & only then went for 2 days to see his mother & Grandmother, who was feeling ill. Had they known you were coming, she too would have flown to meet you.—Baby< seriously writes his diary, only is so funny about it,—as little time in the evening, he writes in the afternoon about dinner.—Yesterday as a treat he remained long with me, drew, wrote & played on my bed— & I longed for you to be with us—oh, how I want you, beloved One, but its good you are not here, as I am in bed & I should never see you, as they have the meals next door.—Very windy & cold, Baby remains in, because of his cold, & [Dr. F. P.] Polyakov says he must never go out above 15 degr. for some years still, tho' I sent him out before to 20. Olga & Anastasia also have colds, but go to [the] hospitals [where they work as volunteer nurses] & drove yesterday—sledged in a sleigh driven by three horses. [c, d]

Papa-Fedorov & O.E.< have come to town< & hope to see her.— How is the little Admiral<, & do they get on with Mordvinov at domino? What news has [A. N.] Grabbe from our dear Convoys. The Children are eating & firing away with their rotten pistols. Xenia< feels still very weak fr. her influenza—Felix [Yusupov the Younger] has got the mumps.—Sweety, are you seriously now thinking about Shtyurmer, I do believe its worth risking the German name, as one knows what a right man he is[193] (I believe yr. old correspondent lady spoke of him?) & will work well with the new energetic ministers. I see they have all gone off in different directions to try & see things with their own eyes—a good thing —also that communication will soon be stopped between Moscou & Petrograd. I am glad you enjoy the book [see Letters No. 708b and 716b], am not sure; but fancy you gave it me once to read, did not Sandro< give it you?—Now my Sunshine, my joy, my Husband beloved, Goodbye. God bless you & protect you & help you in everything. I cover you with tenderest gentlest & yet passionately loving kisses, Lovebird. Ever yr. own unto & beyond death   Wify. [e]

---

191. A. G. Bulygin was prominent during the Revolution of 1905 as minister of the interior. At this time he was the head of Maria Fedorovna's own chancellery.

192. "Sablin 3" was Nicholas Vasil'evich Sablin, naval capt. 2nd grade of the Life Guards Ship's Co.

193. Reference is to Boris Vladimirovich Sturmer, soon to follow I. I. Goremykin as chairman of the council of ministers. Sturmer's elevation to this office marked a new stage in the disintegration of Nicholas II's government. See Fuhrmann, *Rasputin*, pp. 171-173, for a discussion of this bumbling mediocrity.

No. 724.   Ts.[arist] Stavka. Jan. 4th 1916.
My own darling Sunny,

Warm thanks for yr. dear letter wh. arrived yesterday evening after mine was already sent. The train was late again to day, but the wind is quieter & it is snowing. I sincerely hope yr. headache is gone & yr. poor heart is better.—I gladly read yr. long New Year's telegram to old Gorem.[ykin]. It is very well written. All is quiet on our front. Our offensive is proceeding well but slowly in the caucasus due to deep snow. Our troops fight courageously & have taken many prisoners, equipment, stores etc.—So far as I can judge fr. what Alekseev told me this morning, Nikolasha< is confident & pleased. [a]

My dear, I long for you, yr. kisses & caresses! Here, away fr. ministers & visitors, we would have time to talk quietly over various questions & spend a few cosy [sic] hours together! But what can we do? You put it quite well in one of yr. last letters, our separation is our own personal sacrifice wh. we make for our country in this terrible time. And this thought makes it easier for me to endure. Kind old gen.[eral] Pau is a delightful neighbour at table. I like his simple, sound views & straightforward talk. I still get masses of postcards fr. various English regiments. Sir [John Hanbury-]Williams gave me a large number of them for Aleksei; I will gradually forward them to you—tell him to keep them in order. Farewell until our next meeting, my darling Wify! I kiss you passionately & them [our children] tenderly. Your own old huzy   Nicky. [b]

No. 725/ Telegram 40. Stavka> Tsarskoe Selo. 4 Jan 1916. 6.40> 7.08 p.m. To her majesty. Thanks for news. Train again very late. Will arrive about 9 o'clock. Rather cold. Have written. Hope [you] will feel better. Tender kisses. Niki

---

No. 726/ Telegram 71. Tsarskoe Selo> Stavka. 5 Jan 1916. 10.13> 10.40 a.m. To his majesty.   [We] received [your] dear letters. Warm thanks from six< thankful, loving hearts which feel at one with their dear soul. 15 deg. this morning, sunny, very cold wind. Heart better but everything still hurts. [I] tenderly embrace and kiss [you]. Today is birthday of her [Anna Vyrubova's] father [A. S. Taneev]. Alix

---

No. 727/ Telegram 42. Stavka> Tsarskoe Selo. 5 Jan 1916. 11.54 a.m.> 12.13 p.m. To her majesty. Only this morning got your dear letter for which tender thanks[,] also for telegram. 15 deg. of cold. Bright, sunny weather. Feel well. Loving kisses. Niki

---

No. 728/ Her No. 420.   Tsarskoe Selo. Jan. 5th 1916.
My own Sweetheart,

What joy, I received your sweet letter from the 3-rd this morning—nice snow-storms must have retained the trains. We all 6< are intensely happy over our letters & thank you for them as tenderly as we only can. A bright, sunny morning, 15 degrees & a very cold wind. Thats good you found a spade to work, get Mordvinov to come & help you, otherwise this solitude must be distracting, & I can feel how you miss sweet Sunbeam< everywhere. I slept a little better this night & my heart too is better, tho' aches a good deal & I feel rotten, so keep to my bed. Have not yet been able to begin my medicines.—Hope poor spineless[194] Valia< will soon be better—give him over compliments. [Daughter] Anastasia has a cold, 37.5 & Bekker<, & did not get to sleep till very late, [Daughter] Olga has a slight one too & Baby< a tiny bit.— [a]

How good the things go well in the Caucasus—what Grigorovich['s confidential military] papers say fr. German & Austrian sources of course is always different—& as tho' on the Roumanian frontier they had good luck & we terrible losses—but the latter you knew still [the last time you were] here, yes? And not too terrible, therefore you stopped.—Guchkov< is better!! [See Letter No. 723c.]—How nice that Harding wired from all [the colonial government in India as well as the Indian princes & people]—yes, how things do change in this world.[190]—The 3 eldest [girls] are off to church—[I] long to go, get consolation & strength there.—Oh my Lovebird, "me love oo" quite terribly!— Here I send you card from Louise<. Your sweet letters are such a joy to me & I reread & kiss them incessantly. Dearly beloved One, sunshine of my aching soul, I wish I were with you, far from all these worries & sorrows, quite by ourselves & the wee ones, to rest a while & forget all—one gets, oh, so tired! [b, c]

Mita Benk. [D. A. Benckendorff] told at Paul's<, that Masha< had brought letters from Ernie<, Ania said she knew nothing, & Paul said it was true—who told him? They all found it right the chiffre[188] was taken from her (I personally find, that S. Jv. T[yutcheva]. & Lili [Obolenskaya], who behaved so badly & were my own personal ladies ought far sooner to have suffered, & other men too)—it seems a letter fr. a Pss. Galitzin [Golitsyna], to her [Masha] was printed, a horrid one, accusing her of being a spy etc. (wh. I continue not to believe, tho' she has acted very wrongly fr. stupidity & I fear, greed of money). But it's a nuissance [sic] that my name & Ernie's name are mentioned again.—Paul is still offended about Rauch—whenever I see him, I shall certainly explain things to him wh. are as clear as day.—I saw in the papers that nice Tkatchenko died at Khar'kov—am so sorry—many a remembrance of the peaceful, happy bygone are linked with his name! An old friend of the [imperial yacht] Standart.—Kilhen [Kil'khen] (I thought it was written with a "G") has died—such a shame they cleared him out from Bessarabia because of his German name—I never heard that name before. There are german names here wh. do not, I believe, exist elsewhere.— [d, e]

I read an endless letter fr. Max< to Vicky<, wh. he wished me to read—he tries to be just, but it was more than painful, as many things alas, were true about here & the [German] prisoners—I can only repeat that I find one must send a higher placed official with Mme Orjewsky [Orzhevskaya] to inspect our prisons, especially in Siberia. It is so far away, & certainly people, alas, in our Country, do but rarely fulfil their duties well, when out of sight. The letter hurt me, much truth was in it & also things that were wrong, & he says ours wont believe things said against the treatment [of German prisoners] here (— neither do they vice versa)—I saw what the sisters [i.e., German nurses who had just visited Russia] had told him, also about the cossacks [sic]. But all that is too painful, only I find in [this point] that he is right, when he says they [the Germans] have not enough food to feed their prisoners much, as all [the Anglo-French blockade] cut off their food from outside (now [food from] fr. Turkey I think its great gain for them)—& we can give more food [to the prisoners Russia is holding]—& more grease they need, & in Siberia the trains go alright—& warmer barracks & more cleanliness. Out of humanity['s] sake & that one dare not [have others] speak badly of our treatment to the prisoners one longs to give severe orders, & that those who don't fulfil them will be punished—& I [say this even though some say I] have not the right to mix in [the matter] as a "German"—one, some brutes, persist on calling me so, probably so as to hinder my interference [in the pow question]. [f]

Our cold is too intense, with more food one can save their lives, 1000[s ?] have died—our climate is so terribly trying. —I hope Georgi< & [I. L.] Tatishchev will inspect [the prison camps] on their way back & thoroughly—especially the small towns[;] & poke their noses well into everything, as one does not notice all at first sight.—Fredericks might have wired a cypher [sic] to G.[eorgi]< with yr. order, only yr. Mama [Maria Fedorovna] & I begged him to go & look.—He must not say it [i.e., announce to the camp authorities that he is coming for an inspection] before hand, otherwise they will prepare things on purpose—Tatishchev can be a help as he speaks German well & will know how to be with the German officers & found [find] out the real truth about their treatment & whether they have really been beaten, as that [is] disgusting if true & may have happened out there—as [it will be] better for us, they too will [be forced to] do things more humanely, as Max< intends helping in his mother's memory—so if Georgi does, it wld. be excellent; & send someone else also here about, & Mme O.[rzhevskaya] to Siberia to meet G.[eorgi]<,—these are wify's ideas.— [g]

Why dont you, now that you are, free'er, prepare all for the old man's change [i.e., replacement of Goremykin as chairman of the council of ministers]—I am sure he feels he has not acted wisely latterly [i.e., lately, in refusing to appear before a hostile Duma], because he long has not tried to see me—he realises [sic] he is, alas, not in the right.—Precious One—I have sent Baby to church for the blessing of the water[195]—he had masters [lessons] before. Such sunshine!—I am so glad Ania< has that work to do about her "home" [see Letter No. 723c],—several times a day she goes there to see to all, to order things, & what a lot one needs for 50 invalids, sanitarys, sisters [i.e., nurses], doctors etc. Vil'chkovsky< & Loman & Reshetnikov< (fr. Moscou) help her—I think she has 27,000 [rubles]—all been given to her, not a penny yet of her own. Its so good at last she has something like that to do, not time to have "the blue devils" [depression] & God will bless her for this work. She has lost a pound this week in consequence, wh. delights Zhuk<. To-morrow she takes in her first soldiers.— [h]

So you, Sweetheart, also only got my letter this morning—is it possible so much snow or our railways once more a fault—when will there at last be order, wh. in every sense our poor country needs & wh. is not in the Slave [Slavic] nature! I read one has evacuated Cetinje [Tsetine] & their troops are surrounded—well, now the King [of Montenegro, Nicholas I] & sons & black daughters< here, who wished so madly this war, are paying for all their sins towards you & God, as they went against our Friend< [who opposed the war in

August 1914] knowing who He is! God avenges Himself. Only I am sorry for the people, such heroes all— & the Italians are selfish brutes to have left them in the lurch— cowards!—Baby will write to-morrow, he slept long to-day.—I bless you & kiss you without end, with fervent love. yr. very own little   Wify. [P.S.] The Priest [Father A. P. Vasil'ev] I hear is coming to bless the rooms, so I must put on a teagown & crawl back to bed —its nice he remembered to come, tho' Church is not in the house to-day. [i]

194. This seems to be a slip. Alexandra liked "Valia" (Vasily Dolgorukov), she did not regard him as "spineless." See Letter No. 719a for the illness he had at this time.
195. Russians celebrate the "great blessing of the waters" at Epiphany on January 6. This ceremony is "often performed out of doors, beside a river or on the sea shore." Timothy Ware, *The Orthodox Church* (Baltimore, Penguin Books, 1964), pp. 282, 307.

No. 729/ Telegram 72. Tsarskoe Selo> Stavka. 5 Jan 1916. 5.25> 6.05 p.m. To his majesty. Received second dear letter and English [newspaper] cuttings, both today, though yesterday there was not a single [word from you]. Father [Vasil'ev] sprinkled all the rooms [with holy water], I am very glad. [Daughter] Anastasia lying down, she has a mild cold and a cold passes away more quickly in bed. God bless you. All kiss [you]. [We] miss [you] terribly. Alix

No. 730.   Ts.[arist] Stavka. Jan. 5th 1916.
My own beloved Sunny-Dear,
    There were no letters yesterday, but to day as compensation I received two—one in the morning & the other soon after in the afternoon. I thank you tenderly for both of them. Tell Aleksei I am glad he has begun to write a diary. It teaches one to express his thoughts clearly & concisely. How sad you do not feel better, & the d—ned headache persists!—I am glad to hear Mama [Maria Fedorovna] was kind to N.P.<—Perhaps we will be able to see the others—Kozhev.[nikov], Rod.[ionov] etc. when they arrive for a brief leave. Today the weather is clear but cold—15 deg. & windy. I hope it will be warmer to-morrow; it will be more pleasant attending the blessing of the waters on the river near the big bridge.[195]—This morning, after the service O.[tets, i.e., Father] Shavel'sky went thru the house, sprinkling with holy water, beginning with my blue room, where he read several prayers!—The foreigners will have to eat fish & mushrooms to-day, but they assure us they like it. [a, b]
    I continue to think about a successor for the old man [Goremykin as chairman of the council of ministers]. In the train I asked Fat Khv.[ostov] his opinion of Shtyurmer. He praised him, but thinks he is too old & his head is not as clear as once. Incidentally, this old Sht.[yurmer] sent me a petition to change his surname & adopt the name of [his wife's family,] Panin.—Through Mamant.[ov] I told him I could not grant such permission without the agreement of the surviving Panins. The little Admiral< is well but angry with [the Jewish capitalist] Manus, who desires to receive the [non-Jewish] name of Nilov. [See Letter No. 737a.] So what do you think of that? I must end now, my precious Wify. God bless you & the children! I kiss you & them tenderly and remain yr. faithful huzy   Nicky. [c]

No. 731/ Telegram 75. Tsarskoe Selo> Stavka. 6 Jan 1916. 11.54 a.m.> 12.50 p.m. To his majesty. [Daughter] Anastasia slept very poorly. Painful [for her] to swallow, 38 [degrees temperature] —bronchitis and bad cold. Others healthy. [My] heart still quite enlarged. Only 5 deg. Will lie a bit on balcony. We all tenderly kiss and embrace [you]. Alix

No. 732.   Ts.[arist] Stavka. Jan. 6th 1916.
My own dearest One,
    Warm thanks for yr. dear letter No. 420, & for the marvellous idea of dispatching Georgi< & [I. L.] Tatishchev to look over how the prisoners of war are being kept in Siberia. I will do it. The blessing of the waters went well today.[195] When I got up there were 15 degs. of frost; as the time for the blessing of the waters approached, the temp. reached 7, now it is 5—strange fluctuations. The sun already begins to warm things up—quite like spring.   Good bishop Constantine [of Mogilev] celebrated in our church, then the krestnyi khod [Procession of the Cross] proceeded down to the river.   All the troops in the town were lined up on both sides, the battery saluted 101 times & 2 aeroplanes passed over our heads. Masses of people & perfect order! Returning I left the procession near the house where the staff is quartered as I had to go to the doklad [report]. The crowd cheered me. The old man [Fredericks] insisted on attending me during the ceremony, as he was feeling well. The Little Admiral< was more cautious & stayed at home because of a cough. Both bow low to you! [a]
    Friday I will have a cinema for all the school-boys, & I will enjoy it too! I just received yr. telegram saying that Anastasia is suffering fr. bronchitis; how tiresome! I hope it will soon pass. I finished my book and will read it to you & the children when I return home—so interesting & quite proper. [See Letter No. 708b.]   Now I must end this letter, my own precious Wify. May God bless you & the children! I press you passionately to my heart—& lower (forgive me) & remain ever yr. own faithful   Nicky. [b]

No. 733/ Her No. 421.   Tsarskoe Selo Jan. 6th 1916.
My very own Treasure,
    It was such a joy having two letters to reread ever so often yesterday & to cover with kisses. I was in bed at 2 ½ & only got to sleep after 3 ½ (as usual now) & reread them again & hovered over every tender word. The heart is again enlarged, tho' I twice took my adonis yesterday—I told Botkin, I need a moments fresh air—so he said I might go unto the balkony [sic], there being only 5 degrees & no wind. Poor [daughter] Anastasia has [a temperature of] 38 this morning & slept very badly. At first I feared it might be the beginning of measels [sic], but they say that no—so I suppose only influenza—[daughter] Marie will sleep this night with the big sisters<, its better. They went to Church at 9 & now are in the hospital, Tiny< is going there too.—I miss my hospital so much— but whats to be done.— [a]
    Ah yes! I often think how lovely it would be in your free hours to sit cosily [sic] by yr. side & chatter away calmly, with no ministers etc. to bore us—it seems as tho' all difficulties & sad things come together for you.—Our Friend< is

sad about the people of Montenegro & that the ennemy [sic] takes everything & is so pained that such luck accompanies them—but always says the final victory will be ours but that with great difficulty as the enemy is so strong. He regrets one [i.e., you, the tsar] began that movements I think without asking him—he wld. have said waited—he is always praying & thinking when the good moment will come to advance, so as not to uselessly loose [sic] men.—Please, thank General [Hanbury-]Williams in Baby's name for the pretty cards—it is interesting for him to have the collection.—Anastasia has bronchitis, head is heavy & hurts her swallowing, coughed in the night, she writes about Ostrog.[orsky]. "Although he said that I look a little better than yesterday, but I am pale & my appearance is foolish in my view" just like the "Shvibzik"< to say such things;— such a bore I cant sit with my Beloved Darling, I think of you so endlessly lovingly & suffer over your loneliness—Nobody young & bright near you, a thing one needs so much to keep one going when worried & hard-worked.—Just collected 10 simple Images [icons] for Ania's< Invalid-house, she takes in her first men to-day. [b, c]

Well, I lay for ¼ an hour on the balkony [sic]—nice air, heard the bells ringing—but was glad to get into bed again—still not feeling famous. I send you a petition from our Friend, its a military thing, He only sent it without any word of comment[—]& then again a letter from A.[nia]. A week to-day that you left us—to me it seems very much longer, wify misses her own, her Sunshine<, her one & all in Life & longs to caress & cheer him up in his loneliness, Sweetest of Sweets. I have nothing of interest to tell you, as I see nobody. Had a wire from Miassoyedov Ivanov [S. V. Myasoedov-Ivanov] yesterday thanking for pretty Reg.[imental] book I send them—they have moved on to Belozorka wherever that may be. [d]

Malama wrote a card to A. saying that they leave "for business & go on that account West. The place is not especially pleasant, to rest in a hole is also not well, but not for long. Yesterday went to the dance arranged by the detachement [sic], the whole village 'monde' [the *mir*, the peasant village collective], was there I enjoyed myself much & am arranging similar affair to-night". Now my Beloved, my Angel, my one & all I hold you tightly in my arms, gaze long & tenderly into your sweet lovely eyes, kiss them, & every bit of you—& "me" alone has the full right to this—true? God bless & protect you & keep you from all harm. Ever yr. very own old <u>Sunny</u>. [P.S.] Lovy, you burn her [Ania's] letters so as that they should never fall into anybody's hands? [See Letter 742a.] [e]

No. 734/ Telegram 76. Tsarskoe Selo> Stavka. 6 Jan 1916. 6.35> 6.52 p.m. To his majesty. Warm thanks for precious letter. [Daughter] Anastasia has [a temperature of] 37.6. Spent 20 minutes on balcony because weather mild. We all tenderly kiss you. God bless you. Sleep well. In thoughts always with you. Alix

No. 735/ Telegram 44. Stavka> Tsarskoe Selo. 6 Jan 1916. 7.00> 8.18 p.m. To her majesty. Hearty thanks [for] letter and news. Tiresome [daughter] Anastasia's strong cold. Ceremony to day went off perfectly on the river.[195] Fine sunny calm day. Fondest kisses. Nicky

No. 736/ Telegram 78. Tsarskoe Selo> Stavka. 7 Jan 1916. 1.22> 2.00 p.m.
To his majesty. [Daughter] Anastasia has [temperature of] 36.5, feels better.
Little one< has a cold, staying home. I am laying on balcony, 2 deg. warmth.
Slept badly again. Very gladdened by your dear letter, [I] heartily thank you. [I]
kiss and embrace you. Moved over to couch for lunch. Alix

No. 737/ Her No. 422.   Tsarskoe Selo. Jan. 7th 1916.
My very own beloved Darling,
   I received your sweet letter after having sent off mine—thanks for it with all
my heart. It is lovely that you can write to me every day & I devour your letters
with such endless love.—N.P.< dined with A.[nia]< & then spent the evening
with us. He was disgusted with Moscou [sic] & all the filth one says there & it
took him lots of trouble to clear up many horrors his sisters had heard & false
opinions they had. Here he avoids the clubs, but friends tell him lots of things.
The train fr. Sebastopol was late, so he stuck at Moscou station from 11-4 in the
night, & reached Petr.[ograd] at 5 instead of 2.—He says about Manus its not true
about his wishing to change his name [see Letter No. 730c], enemies of his
spread things about him, because they are jealous he got that rank & he had a
row with with [sic] Milyukov, who wrote lies about him & now people want to
set the little Admiral< against him out of spite. N.P. went in the train with old
Dubensky, who spoke very frankly to him about the old Headquarters & all the
stories & "nice" things about fat Orloff< & plans he & others had, coinciding
with what our Friend< said, I'll tell you when we meet. [a]
   Have you any plans in view or any journeys, as you have less to do now & it
must be so dull at the Headquarters. Lovy, I don't know, but I should still think
of Shtyurmer, his head is plenty fresh enough—you see [A. N.] Kh.[vostov] a
tiny bit hopes to get that place—but he is too young[201]—Shtyurmer would do for a
bit, & then later on if you ever want to find another you can change him, only
don't let him change his name "it would do him more harm than if he kept his
old & venerated ones" as you remember, Gr.[egory]< said[201]—& He very much
values Gr. wh. is a great thing. You know Volzhin is an obstinate nuisance &
wont help Pitirim[,] wont give into things unless he gets yr. special order—frightened of public opinion. Pitirim wishes Nicon (the brute) to be sent [to
head a diocese] to Siberia, you remember & V.[olzhin] wishes him to go to Tula
& the Metropolitan [Pitirim] finds it not good he should be in the centre of Russia, but further away, where he can do less harm.[196] Then he [Pitirim] has other
good plans about paying the clergy & V. wont agree & so on. Shall I ask P. to
write me a list of the things he finds neccessary [sic] & then I can give them you
to order V. to fulfill. Pit. is so clever & largeminded & the other just not, fr.
fright. [b, c]
   [Daughter] Anastasia's temp. in the evening was 37, she spoke with me by
telephone. Aleksei came to our dinner already in dressing gown at 8.20 & wrote
his diary wh. he is sweet about. Your message came in time, as he was already
beginning to get a bit bored about it, not knowing when to have time to
write.—Such a craving for your caresses, yearning to hold you in my arms and
rest my head upon your shoulder, as in bed & to cud[d]le up close & lie quite
still upon yr. heart & feel peaceful & at rest. So much sorrow & pain, worries &

trials—one gets so tired & one must keep up & be strong to face everything. I should have liked to see our Friend, only never ask Him [Rasputin] to the house when you are not there, as people are so nasty. Now they pretend he has received a nomination at the F.[edorovsky] Cathedral wh. obliges him also to light all the <u>lamps</u> in the palace in all the rooms! One knows what that means[197]—but that is so idiotic that any sensible person can but laugh at it;—as do I.— [d]

You don't mind my seeing N.P. often now? But as he leaves in a few days (his friends left), the whole days he is occupied & in the evenings quite alone & downhearted. After all these talks here & in Moscou that he has been sent away because of our Friend—its not easy for him leaving you & us all, & for us too its horrid to have to say goodbye—one has so few real friends & he is our very nearest. He will go to our Friend, thank God. Ania spoke lots to him & then I did all about the great change this summer—he did not know that it was He [Rasputin] who kept you & us up to the absolute necessity for you, our & Russia's sake. I had not spoken to him alone for months & was afraid to speak about Gregory, as I knew he was doubting him—it has not yet quite passed I fear[200]—but if he sees Him he will feel calmer—he believes so in Manus (I don't) & I believe he set him against our Fr. & now he calls him Rasput.[in], wh. I don't like & I will try & get him out of this habit.[198] [e]

So much milder, 1 degree in the evening only—those changes are bad for the health.—What do you say about Montenegro? I don't trust that old King [Nicholas I] & fear he may be up to mischief as he is most untrustworthy & above all ungrateful. What have the poor Servian troops done wh. had gone there? Italy is disgusting to my mind & so cowardly, she easily might have saved Montenegro.—bow to nice old Po [Pau] from me & to General [Hanbury-]Williams & Baby's< dear Belgian [Baron de Ricquel].— I am sure the blessing of the waters must have been very fine[195]— such a pretty place down by the river, the steep street & mild weather. Anastasia is better, [her temperature is] 36,5, feels clearer in the head & the cough already less—it seems only the tops of the bronchi were touched. I slept most rottenly & feel idiotic, so will go out on the balkony [sic]—1 degree of warmth—& Isa< will keep me company. [f]

Am sorry to bother you with petitions, but Bezrodny is a good Dr. (he knows our friend already long) & only you can help, so write a word on his <u>memorandum</u> (there was no petition) to say one is to give him the divorce & sent it to Volzhin or Mamantov. Then there is a paper from a Georgian, Gregory & Pitirim know [him] & ask for [it]—well you can send it to Kotchubei [Kochubei], tho' I doubt he can do anything for this Prince David Bagration- Davidov—or do you know him?—Then a paper from Mamantov (Gr.[egory]< knows him [i.e., whichever petitioner is the subject of this "paper"] many years)—it seems an injustice was done, can you just look it through & do according to what you think right with it. Sorry to bother you, but they are for you—simpler ones I send straight to our Mamantov without any commentary. Baby's throat is a bit red, so he wont go out—it's the real weather for catching cold—these great changes.— [g]

Did you repeat the order about [Kaiser] William's birthday being allowed to be feasted [among German pows in Russia] the same as yr. namesday [sic] was [among Russian pows in Germany—see Letters No. 714a and 738a.]?—Did you think over again, that people of the Duma, such as Guchkov<, shld. no more be allowed to go to the front & speak to the troops? He is recovering, honestly I must say, alas! One ordered molebny [services] for him at the cathedral & now he becomes yet more of a heroe [sic] in the eyes of those that admire him. Here is a letter from Aleksei. Sweetheart, me thought so quite particularly of you this sleepless night & with such tender longing & compassion!—How is you?[199] Now Goodbye, my Sunshine, my long-loved Huzy, God Almighty bless and protect you & help you in all yr. decisions & give you great firmness of caracter [sic]. Kisses, tender & passionate without end, fr. yr. very own fondly loving Wify. [P.S.] Bow to Mordvinov & Silaev. Where is Misha<, no living sign fr. him since he left in Dec. [h, i]

196. Although Volzhin flattered Alexandra and Rasputin to become director of the Holy Synod, in office, he turned on the "Rasputin gang" and worked to curb its influence. Disappointed with this setback, the empress and Grigory pursued their plan to bring Pitirim to the capital as metropolitan of Petrograd. Another battle developed over Nikon, the anti-Rasputin archbishop of Vologda and a member of the Synod's governing council. As we see, Alexandra wanted Nikon transferred to a diocese in Siberia, whereas Volzhin would have promoted him to the ancient and prestigious city of Tula, 120 miles south of Moscow. Working through the tsar, Alexandra prevailed. After the March Revolution, Nikon retired to the Troitse-Sergieva Monastery north of Moscow; he died in 1918 and was buried at Zagorsk.

197. Alexandra is laughing at those who complained that Rasputin held a sinecure as "lampidary," tender of holy candles in the Fedorovsky Church at Tsarskoe Selo. There was no such office! In fact, Rasputin held no salaried post. Yet the "lampidary" rumor abounded and even made its way into print.

198. Alexandra called Rasputin "our Friend" or "Grigory." She and other admirers avoided "Rasputin," because enemies charged the name was derived from the verb *rasputnichat'*, "to lead a dissolute life," "to be drunken and dissipated." Even scholarly literature has perpetuated this myth. Two recent biographies correct the record: de Jonge, *Life and Times of Grigorii Rasputin*, pp. 31-32, and Fuhrmann, *Rasputin*, pp. 227-228, n. 14. See also Footnote 262.

199. A. A. Sergeev thinks this was an "intimate expression." See *Perepiska*, IV, p. 32.

No. 738.   Ts.[arist] Stavka. Jan. 7th 1916.
My own precious Treasure,

Again the train is late, so I have received neither letters nor newspapers. I receive Trepov & Naumov, who arrived fr. Kiev, & later gen.[eral] Belyaev from the War Ministry—I do not know on what matter. I shall tell the last about the german prisoners, Wilhelm's birthday, etc. [See Letters No. 714b and 737h.] I intend sending Georgi< a ciphered telegram telling him what to look out for when visiting the prisoners of war, besides other matters I want him to investigate. [a]

To-day I asked Fredericks to write very sternly to Maximovich about the clubs, & to [tell him to] watch all that goes on in them. He must cut short any gossip & criticism which he hears personally, and warn those who wear the gold uniform or aiguillettes they will be taken away if they continue behaving in this way. I forgot to thank you for dear Baby's< photograph, which I find charming. It stands on my writing table. Somebody took the shovel from the garden—actually there is nothing more to be cleaned up there. I prefer to walk there alone, as is my custom, as it gives a chance to think quietly, & good ideas often come to me on my walks. [b]

I keep racking my brain over a successor to the old man [Goremykin as chairman of the council of ministers] if Shtyurmer should prove not young enough or sufficiently up to date. Our troops attack very successfully in the caucasus, & are not far from Erzerum,[214] the only Turkish fortress there. I think the black sisters< must be very depressed over the fate of their unhappy country[, Montenegro]. May God bless you & the dear children! I kiss you all tenderly, my dear ones. I kiss you passionately & tenderly, my beloved Sunny. Ever your own old huzy   Nicky. [c]

No. 739/ Telegram 46. Stavka> Tsarskoe Selo. 7 Jan 1916. 7.38> 8.50 p.m. To her majesty. At last your dear letter arrived. Thanks. Weather grey, thawing. Received two ministers who came from Kiev[−]Trepov and Naumov. Very useful visit. Kiss all fondly. Niki

---

No. 740/ Telegram 80. Tsarskoe Selo> Stavka. 8 Jan 1916. 10.43> 11.20 a.m. To his majesty. Baby woke up only twice−[he has a temperature of] 37.6. Does not feel too bad. [Daughter] Anastasia has 36.8. Ania< had a temperature of 38 last night. [She] slept badly, strong cough, headache. All about here people have colds. Rainy weather, 2 deg. warmth. Slept not famously, as is my habit. We "all" tenderly kiss and embrace [you]. Alix

---

No. 741/ Her No. 423.   Tsarskoe Selo. Jan. 8th 1916.
My own Darling,
   Very tenderly do I thank you for yesterday's precious letter.−The end was so sweet & full of tender meaning−lady thanks for the caress wh. she returns with great love!−Well Babykins< went up after luncheon with a heavy head, rather red throat, ached swallowing, so I told him to lie down & get a compress on. Later he had [a temperature of] 38.4 but the head got better. I no more saw him, we only spoke to him & [daughter] Anastasia by telephone, she felt better, 37.2.−Ania< coughed 2 days & was feeling feverish when she came in the afternoon, so I made her measure her temperature, 37.9. so I sent her home instead of to her wounded, Akelina [Akilina Laptinskaya] remains the night with her, the Dr. gave her medicine, she drank hot red wine blessed by our Friend<−I hope she will be better by to-morrow. She wrote in a very sad mood−& begged to say she kisses you.−I remained on the sopha after the balkony [sic] till 6−& then up for dinner again−feel weak all day & not very nice. [a]
   N.P.< came after 9 & kept us company & the children tried all sorts of music for the gramaphones I want for our, & Ania's hospital. He says one sends Rodionov now instead of Kozhevnikov, & as soon as he arrives, Saturday or Sunday, he supposes Kirill< & he leave. If you are at the Headquarters, Kirill wanted to pass there for 2 days, then N.P. thought better to join him at Kiev so as not to look pushy at Moghilev, but if you are away, as Dubensky hinted to him you might be, then he & Kirill will go straight fr. here together. He bought masses of shoes for their horses & nails etc. & things without end [needed for his new assignment]. He is bringing six cadets: one is baron Geiden (I suppose, the son of ours [A. F. Geiden]), Koni, & the other names he had forgotten. It

freshens one up to see him—its lovely—to-day a week that I am so to speak in bed & one does not feel bright nor over gay—& neither does my own Love-bird.—Its been raining & "dirty" weather.— [b]

Am so glad Trepov's & Naumov's journeys were useful & I hope they woke up everybody thoroughly—one must go about oneself & poke ones nose into everything, then people work harder & feel that one is watching them & can turn up [unannounced for an inspection at] any moment. How good you have a cinema for all the children & then they can see you nicely too. Anastasia slept well, 36.8, Aleksei only woke up twice in the night, 37.6, is in the playroom, in bed & very gay. I hope to go upstairs this afternoon to see them both. In the morning I am to lie on the balkony [sic] again. 2 degr. of warmth, rainy, windy, dark, dull weather shall get Isa< there again to speak over affairs. Did not sleep again very well & had nasty dreams, head aches rather, heart too, tho' just now got enlarged. Ania slept very badly, to wh. she is unaccustomed, coughed much, head aches & 38. [Daughter] Olga has gone there for a little & [daughter] Marie will at 12—stupid I cant. Perhaps you will tell me to give her your love to cheer her up—All about people have influenza, rotten thing.— [c]

Could you not have got Shtyurmer to quietly come to the Headquarters, you see so many people, to have a quiet talk together before you settle anything.—Look here, when you see Dubensky cleverly draw the question to speak about fat Orloff< & make him tell you things about him—if he has the courage to show up the man's vileness wh. drags in others too high placed of the old Head-quarters—Fed.[orov]<, I think, knows it too. Me, he always spoke of as "she"—& that he was sure I wld. not let you come soon to the Headquarters again after they had forced "their" ministers upon you,[99]—ask about Drentel'n too, who had the convent in view for me ultimately.—Dzh.[unkovsky], [Fat] Orloff ougt [sic] straight off to have been sent to Siberia—after the war is over you ought to have a punishment made—why should they go, free with good places [appointments], when they had prepared all to have you changed & me shut up, & also Samarin who did all, to be nasty to yr. wife—& they wander about & other people think they were unjustly cleared out [from earlier appointments], as they went scott-free. Its vile to think of the falseness of humanity—tho' I long knew & told you my feeling about them—thank God, Drent. has also gone—now these are clean people round you, & I only wish N.P. were of their number.[200] We [the empress and N.P.?] spoke long about Dmitri<—he says that he is a boy without any caracter [sic] and can be lead by anybody. 3 months he was under the influence of N.P. and held himself well at the Headquarters & when in town< with him, kept himself like the other [N.P.?] & did not go to ladies companies—but out of sight—gets into other hands. He finds the regiment perverts the boy, as their coarse conversations, jokes are horrid & before ladies too & they draw him down. Now he is used as aide de camp.— [d]

Shvibzik< just wrote one of her funny notes—to-day she has to keep still in bed.—I spent my time writing notes to all the invalids. A.[nia] had a letter from dear Otar Purtseladze—tell it to Silaev. He [N.P.] sends lots of good wishes, feelings, love to the family;— & is happy we have seen his wife & boy. Learns French & English—gets up & goes to bed early—does not say how kept or fed nor any details—only in despair to be there instead of serving at such a time.

Now Sweetheart, Beloved, my Own, My very Own, I bless you —, kiss you, press you tightly in my arms, with infinite love & gratitude for 21 years [of] perfect happiness for wh. morn & night I thank God. Oh, how I long for you & yr. tender caresses—I send you all, all, all, the s-a-m-e as you did. Ever yr. own old   Sunny.   [P.S.] Does the paper smell good!!! [e]

200. N. P. Sablin had been a friend of Rasputin. In Letter No. 737e, Sablin seems to be turning against Rasputin, and—as was often the case with newly disillusioned supporters of the "holy man"—sought to enlighten Alexandra about the "real Rasputin." Sablin, like the others, would almost certainly have paid for such a change with the loss of Alexandra's friendship. This letter suggests Sablin backed away from further attacks against "Our Friend," and so his good relations with the empress continued.

No. 742.   Ts.[arist] Stavka. Jan. 8th 1916.
My darling, beloved wify,
   I thank you warmly for yr. dear letter, wh. I received after lunch. Then I had to read through my papers, walked for about a ½ hour, and now I have sat down to write a few lines to you. The cinema for the schoolboys begins at 4.o['clock]. I am glad for every time you see N.P., especially now when he leaves for God knows how long! You ask where Misha< is? I am certain he has returned to Gatchina< after spending two weeks in the country. Why not see him at once? True, you have not been feeling well enough to receive. I always tear A.[nia]'s letters into small pieces after reading them, so you need not worry. None of her letters will be saved for posterity. [See Letter No. 733e.] My dear, I have nothing of interest to tell you—I only repeat the old story wh. you have known for 22 years—that I love you, I am devoted & faithful to you to the end! I love you passionately & tenderly, my own darling Sunny! May God bless you & the children! I kiss you all tenderly. Ever your old   Nicky. [P.S.] Greetings to A[nia].

No. 743/ Telegram 82 in Russian. Tsarskoe Selo> Stavka. 8 Jan 1916. 6.26> 7.05 p.m. To his majesty. [I] thank you very tenderly for dear letter. Was on balcony. [Daughter] Anastasia has [temperature of] 37.2, Baby< 37.1, she [Anna Vyrubova] 38.6. [She] asks priest [A. P. Vasil'ev] to pray [for her]. Warm weather. [We] drank tea in playroom [with Aleksei, who was in bed at that time]. Sleep well. [I] kiss and embrace [you]. Alix

No. 744/ Telegram 83. Tsarskoe Selo> Stavka. 8 Jan 1916. 8.20> 8.46 p.m. To his majesty. Glad you liked cinematograph. Can imagine joy of children. Hope you received letter. He [Rasputin] hopes you did not decide to permit [Shtyurmer] to change [his] name and [that you] will appoint the one of whom you and I spoke, he [Shtyurmer] is suited best of all for the present time.[201] [I] tenderly kiss [you]. [I] always deeply long for you. Alix

201. Rasputin formed an alliance in the fall of 1915 with Andronnikov, A. N. Khvostov and Beletsky to install Khvostov as minister of the interior with Beletsky as asst.-minister and police director. The troika was unraveling, however, due to friction with Andronnikov and because Rasputin opposed Khvostov's next ambition, which was to become chairman of the council of ministers as well as minister of the interior. Rasputin insisted that Khvostov at 43 was "too young" for the

higher office; Alexandra concurred. (See Letters No. 737b and 746a.) Sturmer was a terrible choice for any office, but see Fuhrmann, *Rasputin*, pp. 171-172, for the factors that made Nicholas favor him, and for the agreement between Sturmer and Rasputin that won Grigory's support. Khvostov was deciding at this point to have Rasputin murdered, hoping this would clear the way for the promotion he coveted.

No. 745/ Telegram 85. Tsarskoe Selo> Stavka. 9 Jan 1916. 12.31> 1.30 p.m. To his majesty. Tenderly thank you for dear letter. Baby< has—[a temperature of] 36.4, [daughter] Anastasia has—36.3, she [Ania<] has—35.8—very weak. Thawing, raining and snow, dark. [I] still feel entirely not famous and am not going out. [We] all warmly kiss and embrace [you]. Alix

---

No. 746/ Her No. 424.   Tsarskoe Selo. Jan. 9th 1916.
My own Sweetheart,
   Mild, snowing, raining & dark. The 2 little ones [daughter Anastasia & son Aleksei] slept well, have [temperatures of] 36.3 & 36.4. I shall go again up to them in the afternoon.—Have been reading doklady [reports] & Isa< came to help about a few questions & yesterday evening too.—The Children went in several times yesterday to see Ania<—& [daughter] Tatiana late, still after cleaning instruments in the hospital. She [Anna Vyrubova] had people all day, her Father [A. S. Taneev], then our Friend< & nice Zina<, then her Mother [Nadezhda Taneeva], then Axel P.< who has come for 3 days, & Zhuk<. The Metropolitan [Pitirim] hearing she is ill, wants to see her too—awfully kind & she does not know what to do. Her maid last night [had a temperature of] 40.2, [and is suffering from an] Angina, so the Dr. took her off to the hospital & her old Zina came in to help Akelina [Akilina Laptinskaya]. She did not sleep the night because of her cough—now she is better no doubt, as has not let me know about her temp.—She said to kiss you & beg for yr. prayers, therefore I had to wire & also [tell you] what our Fr.< said about Shtyurmer not to change his name & to take him for a time at least,[201] as he is such a decided loyal man & will hold others in hand,—let one scream if one wishes, they always will at any nomination. [a]
   N.P.< spoke by telephone: Kirill< sends him off to-night to Helsingfors to see Kanin & the staff—because Grigorovich< told Kirill they make difficulties about fulfilling your orders to K.—so the quickest & best was to send N.P. to explain matters & that K. got the order from you,—its not Kanin but others in the staff & he fears Timirev may be disagreable [sic] as he is offended with the Gv. Ek.<, wh. he left.— [b]
   Ania slept from 8-11 & has 35.8—so feels very weak. Sergei< goes to the Headquarters soon, I hear—better not, keep him there long, as he is always a gossip, alas, & such a sharp, criticising [sic] tongue & his manners before strangers are not edifying—& then there are very unclear, unclean stories about her[202] & bribes etc. wh. all speak about, & the artillery is mixed up into it.—Just got your letter, 12 o'clock nice and early, such an endless joy to have news fr. you, you cannot think what your sweet letters are to me & how I kiss & reread them ever so often. Such a treat to get them now daily, they warm me up, as I miss my treasure quite terribly & kissing your cushion & letter is still not quite satisfying to a hungry wify. Ah, My Angel, [G]od bless you for your marvellous love & devotion wh. I am not near worthy enough of.—Bless you for it,

sweet One. You too, Huzy mine, know what you are to me & what depths of love my old heart is capable of—these separations kindle the fire yet more & make the great love yet more intense.— [c]

Will you be moving about to the other corps as you have less work now? Its good you let the ministers come out there to you. Oh, how I wish you could get rid of Polivanov, wh. means Guchkov<—[I would prefer] old Ivanov in his [Polivanov's] stead [as minister of war], if honest Belyaev< too weak—all hearts in the Duma would go out to "grandfather" [Ivanov, who was born in 1851], am sure, but perhaps you have no one ready in his place.—To-day 40 days little Sonia< died.—In a few days its Tatiana's namesday [sic]; to-day the famous 9-th.—How much we have lived through together & what hard times & yet god never forsook one & kept us up—& so he will now, tho' we need great patience, faith, trust in His mercy. And your work resignation & humility must be recompensed & God I feel will do so, tho' when, we cannot guess.—Yesterday evening I laid patiences, read, saw Isa< & played with [daughter] Marie.—Took tea with the little ones upstairs—the three then stood still & their beds were in the middle of the room—Anastasia looks green with shades under her eyes, but he [Aleksei]—not bad. My Love, I send you just one paper to do what you like with.— [d]

You must get the old man [Goremykin] out & calmly tell him yr. decision [to replace him as chairman of the council of ministers]—now its easier as you dont agree quite & he did not have that circular printed (showing he is a bit old & tired & cant grasp, alas, everything, dear old man)—you have time to speak, & its better the other [Shtyurmer] shld. have time before the Duma is called in to have sittings with the ministers & prepare himself—& Shtyurmer being an older man, won't offend Gorem.: & then you give him the title of old Solsky, not of course Count (wh. is rotten [i.e., insufficiently prestigious]), but the other thing[203][—]I should calmly do it now at the Headquarters & not put it off any longer, believe me Deary. [e]

Well, now goodbye, Sweety mine, Husband of my heart & soul, light of my life—I hold you in my arms & clasp you tightly to me, kissing yr. sweet face, eyes, lips, neck & hands with burning tender kisses,—"I love you, I love you 'tis all that I can say" you remember that song at Windsor 1894? on these evenings!! God bless you Treasure. Ever yr. very own unto death   Wify.   [P.S.] Hope my flowers will arrive fresh & smelling good. Here is a big kiss.[204] [f]

---

202. Reference is to the famed ballerina Mathilde Kschessinska. She and Nicholas II had been lovers before his engagement to Alexandra. According to A. A. Sergeev, at this time Kschessinska was seeing Serge Michaelovich, also referred to in this passage. (*Perepiska*, IV, p. 41n)

203. Alexandra is saying that one measure which would sooth Goremykin's hurt at being dismissed would be to receive the title which had been granted Dmitry Sol'sky: *deistvitel'nyi tainyi sovetnik First Class*. The only higher rank in state service was *kantsler* (chancellor). Rasputin tried but failed to have the higher title conferred on Goremykin; the old man retired as a d.t.s. First Class. Rasputin hated to see Goremykin step down, but he felt Nicholas needed a new chairman who would work with the Duma.

204. Alexandra drew a square, followed by this explanation.

No. 747/ Telegram 50. Stavka> Tsarskoe Selo. 9 Jan 1916. 5.10> 7.08 p.m. To her majesty. Best thanks [for] dear letter. Glad all are better. Give her [Ania<] my love. Here same weather as with you. Tenderest kisses. Nicky

No. 748.   Ts.[arist] Stavka. Jan. 9th 1916.
My own beloved Darling!

I warmly thank you fr. dear letter No. 423. How tiresome & boring that the little ones are not entirely healthy, & that you, poor dear, are not sufficiently well to go upstairs to see them! I sincerely hope this situation will end. The weather is annoying; it snows, rains, & a strong wind is blowing—exactly as it was with you. I am beginning to plan short trips—of course, to review troops. Several cavalry & cossack divisions along the line of Orsha, Vitebsk & further towards Dvinsk are resting & being reformed. I will let you know as soon as I finally decide upon anything. As to [your suggestion of] Sht.[yurmer] coming here, I think that unsuitable. I receive here only people who have some connection with the war. His arrival, therefore, would simply provoke various rumours & speculations.—I want his appointment, if it takes place, to come like a clap of thunder. For this reason, I will receive him as soon as I return.—Believe me, it is better so. [a]

Ella< has written, asking me to give the next award to Bazilevsky. He already had one conferred upon him last year, at New Year's. But I intend to reply to her that January 1st has already passed, & it would be better to wait till Easter, which will be here in three months! He is, of course, an excellent man & good worker, & is, according to what she says, very useful to her committee. I have heard or read nothing about Samarin, which is rather strange![205] You alone mentioned him in your last letter. I must end now. God bless you & our chicks! I kiss you tenderly & passionately, & remain, my precious Wify, your loving old hubby Nicky. [b]

205. Apparently Nicholas expected Samarin to make difficulties as revenge for being dismissed as director of the Holy Synod. Samarin's behavior was entirely to the contrary. Monarchy exercised power in Russia even as it was declining—and to the end, Nicholas enjoyed loyalty among people he injured in various ways: Samarin, Kokovtsov, Hermogen, Rodzyanko.

No. 749/ Telegram 87. Tsarskoe Selo> Stavka. 9 Jan 1916. 7.53> 8.17 p.m. To his majesty. Children have normal temperatures, they are merry, [I] had tea with them. Heart enlarged. Metropolitan [Pitirim] will ask you to receive him since you are less busy now and he could quietly talk over many important questions with you. Dull weather. [We] all kiss and embrace [you]. Alix

No. 750/ Telegram 90. Tsarskoe Selo> Stavka. 9 Jan 1916. 11.20 a.m.> 12.22 p.m. To his majesty. All the invalids [now] have normal temperature. They send their greetings. I the same. [It is our] Friend's< namesday [sic]. Thawing, sometimes snowing. God bless you. [I] bow to all. Alix

No. 751/ Her No. 425.   Tsarskoe Selo. Jan. 10th 1916.
My very Own,

Warm & snowing again. Our Friend's< Namesday [sic].—I am so glad, that thanks to measures having been taken, all passed quietly in Moscow & Petrograd & the strikers behaved themselves. Thank goodness, one sees the difference of Beletsky< & Dzhunkovsky or Obolensky[, who preceded him as police director]. I hope you dont mind I wired about Pitirim, but he wld. so much like to see you quietly (here you never have time) and tell you all his ideas & improvements he wld. like to make. He sat near Ania's< bed yesterday, kind man. She slept only for about 4 hours this night, (so did I) coughed much, [her temperature is] 36.8, & Becker<, & tired, & Gr.[egory]< wanted her to come to-day, but she really has not the strength to go & it would be utter folly fr. the human point of view.—[Daughter] Anastasia slept well, 36.3. Aleksei still sleeps. The big ones< are off to Church.—I lay in their room yesterday fr. 4½- 6½—Baby< was playing bezigue with Mr. Gibbs, who spent the day with him. [a]

Evg. Serg. [Botkin] turned up, his foot was better & found my heart enlarged this morning too, but I knew that—so must take more Adonis & other drops to quieten the heartbeating.—I have absolutely nothing of interest to tell you, am so sorry—but I see nobody & hear nothing. Xenia [Sandro's< wife?] feels still very weak and is only half dressed, & up half.—How well our cossacks "worked" near [the Turkish fortresses of] Erzerum![214]—Anastasia may get up in her rooms only on Tuesday, its a bore, but wiser & she does look still green.—Baby slept very well till after 10, woke only once, [his temperature was] 36.2. Why, there is the sun out for our Friend, that is lovely indeed, had to be so for Him!—Ania thanks for yr. love & sends a letter, asks me whether you will be angry, I answered she must know better than me whether you allowed her to write often.—Isa< lunched with us—shall spend afternoon again quietly & alone till go up to the pets [i.e., our children].—Just got precious letter for wh. endless thanks, Sweetheart. You are right about Shtyurmer & a "thunderbolt". Glad you will manage to see troops. Kiss & bless you without end, press you to my big, aching heart, yearn for yr. tender kisses & caresses wh. mean so much to yr. very own little Woman yr. wife, yr. <u>Sunny</u>, who lives by you & whose Sun and light you are, purest & best One. [b]

No. 752.   Ts.[arist] Stavka. Jan. 10th 1916.
My own dearest One,

I tenderly thank you for yr. sweet letter No. 424.—I am glad to hear our invalids have a normal temperature, as you wired me.— Fedorov told me various childrens' illnesses are prevalent here, so it seems fortunate that Sunbeam< is not here. The walks in the garden bore me no end; I am never there more than 50 minutes, otherwise I could not read & write & finish everything by 5.o['clock] as the train leaves at 6.o. Later, when the weather becomes better, I will change my schedule as it is extremely necessary for me to get enough fresh air! Tomorrow I hope to tell you my plans. Possibly towards the end of the week I might come home!! My sincerest thanks also for the sweet flowers, wh. reached me quite fresh. Give A.[nia]< my greetings, tell her I often think of her! I write in a terrible hurry, because there is much for me to look through, so forgive this short & uninteresting letter. May God bless you & the dear children!—In thoughts I will be with you on Tatiana's namesday [sic]! I kiss you tenderly, my beloved Sunny-dear. Your Nicky

No. 753/ Telegram 52. Stavka> Tsarskoe Selo. 10 Jan 1916.[187b] 6.39> 7.05 p.m. To her majesty. Loving thanks [for] letters and news. Glad all are better. English Gen. Callwell arrived for some affairs. Very warm, slippery. Tenderest kisses. Niki

No. 754/ Telegram 96. Tsarskoe Selo> Stavka. 11 Jan 1916. 2.47> 3.39 p.m. To his majesty. Heartily thank you for dear letter. What joy if we soon see each other. All are much better. Possible that she [Ania<] might even come to me this evening. Still do not feel at all famous. Lay on balcony. Clear, 2 deg. frost. We all tenderly kiss and embrace [you]. Tatiana thanks [you] very much. Alix

No. 755/ Her No. 426.   Tsarskoe Selo. Jan. 11th 1916.
My own Sweetheart,
   A brighter day at last & 2 degrees of frost & the dear sun shining—its a pitty [sic] you have such "dirty weather".—Is the English General [Callwell] nice? I suppose he was sent to you from the army to welcome you as fieldmarshal?—But there is nothing you can give Georgie [King George V] in exchange, as he does not command, & one cannot play with such nominations.—I don't quite understand what has been going on in Montenegro—it says the King [Nicholas I] & Pietro [Prince Peter] left over Brindisi for Lyon, where he is to meet his wife & 2 youngest daughters & that [Peter's brother, Prince] Mirko remained to try & unite with the Montenegran, Servian & Albanian troops. Only now Italy has landed 70,000 men in Albania—an ugly game theirs. But if the King surrendered, how about his troops? Where are Jutta & Danilo? Why does one allow him to go to France—all most uncomprehensible [sic] to me.—Ania< was up an hour on the sopha in the evening & spoke with quite a strong voice—she is already dreaming of coming here—what a strong health after all, to pick up in a second, after she thought she was so fearfully ill & miserable!—Now don't think me mad for my wee bottle, but our Friend< sent her [Anna Vyrubova] one from his namesday [sic] feast, & we each took a sip & I poured this out for you—I believe its Madeira, I swallowed for his sake (like medecine [sic]), you do it too, please, tho' you dislike it—pour it into a glass & drink it all up for His health as we did—the lily of the valley & wee crust[206] also are from Him for you, my Angel Sweet. One says heaps of people came to Him & He was beautiful. I wired congratulations <u>from all of us</u> & got this answer. "Inexpressibly overjoyed—God's light shines on you, we will fear nothing." [a, b]
   He [Rasputin] likes [it] when one is not afraid to wire to Him direct, I know He was very displeased she [Anna Vyrubova] did not go, & it worries her, but I think He goes to her to-day. The little ex Xmas-tree smells so deliciously strong this morning! All [Ania and the entire family] have good temperatures this morning. —I am sorry my letters are so dull, but I hear nothing & see nobody.—Vassilievsky [Ya. T. Veselovsky] telegraphed so happy to have received the brigade in wh. my regiment is, & Sergeev enchanted to have taken the 21[st E. Siberian] reg. fr. him as he has served there so long.—I had to take another pen, as there was no more ink in the other one.—Slept better, so far heart not enlarged this morning. I shall go & lie for a bit on the balkony [sic] as had no air since two days.—Thoughts & prayers never leave you, Sweetheart & I think

of you with intense love, tenderness & longing. God bless you, 1000 kisses fr. yr. very   Own. Ania just writes that N.P.< returned fr. Helsingfors & that she would like to come with him to dinner, that her Dr. has allowed her to go out in a shut carriage in the evening—I find Drs[.] queer, or she is wonderfully strong & when she wants to do a thing she always does it & somehow succeeds—Youth & strength.—Very tenderest thanks for sweetest letter—what joy if you come end of the week home again!!

206. Rasputin had rusk made from black bread; this became famous in Petrograd as "Rasputin rusks."

No. 756.   Ts.[arist] Stavka. Jan. 11th 1916.
My beloved darling Wify,
   I thank you tenderly for yr. dear letter. It is always such a joy to get them. I breathe in their scent and re-read every page with delight. I do so hope you are better, & that you will feel stronger when I return. Try to lie on the balcony every day or drive in the park. In any event, you must know that fresh air along with rest are undoubtedly the best cure for you. That is true—true!! The weather is very changeable—frost at night but everything thaws in the sun. The streets & paths in the garden are quite slippery. [a]
   At 4 o'clock I must go to the cinema wh. is being arranged for the other half of the schoolboys. I will sit in the centre box with old Fred.<, who is totally deaf.—We cannot converse as I do not want to answer all of his questions with a roar amidst the deadly silence of the theatre! This very second Tet—e [Teteryatnikov] brought me your dear letter No. 425, as well as Tatiana's & A.[leksei]'s letters. I kiss you fondly for all that you write, beloved one. Pitirim comes tomorrow. Beletsky has told Voeikov about it. Gen.[eral] Callwell is a quiet & extremely clever man. He brought me a letter from Georgie [King George V]. There is a whole eng.[lish] colony here now. It is strange listening to the eng.[lish] conversation at the table. Good bye till our next meeting, my tenderly beloved Sunny. May God bless you & the children! I kiss you & them fondly & remain your faithful huzy Nicky [b]

No. 757/ Telegram 55. Stavka> Tsarskoe Selo. 11 Jan 1916. 6.47> 7.03 p.m. To her majesty. Much thanks [for] dear letter, also Tatiana and Aleksei. This afternoon was the second cynematogr. [See 756b.] Also successful. Sunny, warm. Tender kisses to all. Niki

---

No. 758/ Telegram 101. Tsarskoe Selo> Stavka. 12 Jan 1916. 11.05> 11.31 a.m. To his majesty. We all tenderly kiss and congratulate you on Tatiana's nameday. [We] regret you are not here on this day. She heartily thanks you for all [your] presents. 2° frost. Te Deum will be in my room. May God keep you. Alix

---

No. 759/ Her No. 427.   Tsarskoe Selo. Jan. 12th 1916.
My very own Treasure,

Tenderest good-wishes for our [daughter] Tatiana's Namesday [sic]. She & Olga have flown off to the hospital & at 12½ we have a moleben [prayer service] in my room—sad you are not with us, sweetheart.—I can so well realise [sic] the utter boredom of your daily walks in that tiny garden, better cross the bridge in a motor & at the end of the town walk—or near the train on the big road; you indeed need air & exercise, but soon I suppose the snow will quite melt in yr. parts.—What joy if you can really come end of the week, sweet Angel mine!—the time seems long & weary when you are not here.—[a]

Well, Ania< & N.P.< came to dinner, she remained only little over an hour, looks stout, rosy, tho' shades under her eyes. I had not seen either since last Thursday. He had lots of difficulties at Helsingfors, they dont wish to give the quantity of officers needed, so now Kirill< must work on at it. Rod.[ionov] arrived, & they both will come at 9, so as give Tatiana pleasure too on her Namesday.—[Daughter and son] Anastasia & Aleksei are allowed to be dressed & up, but not to come down yet to-day—Baby< slept till nearly 10—[he has a temperature of] 36.2. Its much better he was up, as felt well & did such awful nonsense [sic] in his bed & could not be kept quiet.—The Germans are evacuating Pinsk? I wish one cld. "pinch" them before they have time to.—At last 2 nights that I have slept quite nicely & the heart has not been enlarged in the morning.—Such a surprise, both the little Ones< turned up & may lunch with us—& really its much better. Both look rather thin & green still.—Now Goodbye Sweetheart, Beloved. God bless you, kiss you ever so tenderly & fondly, & remain, Nicky mine, yr. very own old   Wify. P.S. Just received yr. sweet letter, thanks 1000 times my very, very own Beloved, cover you with burning kisses. Oh how dull [for you] to sit with the old man [Fredericks]!!! Wish it were me, wld. not Boysy< like lady? She [I] wanted him [you] frantically. [b, c]

No. 760/ Telegram 57. Stavka> Tsarskoe Selo. 12 Jan 1916. 3.16> 4.16 p.m. To her majesty. Tender thanks [for] letters and little bottle. My very best wishes for Tatiana. Sorry we not to be together. Just had most friendly talk with our Metropolitan [Pitirim]. Wet and warm. Fondest kisses. Niki

---

No. 761.   Ts.[arist] Stavka. Jan. 12th 1916.
My own darling One,

I warmly thank you for your dear letter, & for the little bottle & flowers from our Friend.—I drank the wine directly fr. the bottle to His health & happiness; I drank it all, to the last drop. This was after lunch—young Ravtopulo also lunched with us. He has been sent here from his reg.[iment] to obtain boots & various sorts of warm things. I was very glad to see him & talk to him. He congratulated me on Tatiana's namesday [sic], & requested me to give his greetings to you & the girls. I congratulate you also! In the afternoon I received Pitirim. He spoke of the Synod, the clergy & especially of [summoning] the Gos.[udarstvennaya—i.e., State] Duma. This surprised me, & I should like to know who influenced him in this matter.[207] He was very glad to be received & to be able to speak freely. Now I must end as I have no more time. God bless you, my beloved darling. I warmly kiss you & the dear children. Give her

[Anna Vyrubova] my greetings & thank her for her letter. Ever yr. own old Nicky.

207. Apparently Nicholas II did not think his clergy should meddle in this political issue. Pitirim was one of those newly "enlightened" monarchists—their number now included Alexandra and Rasputin—who believed the tsar should work with the Duma. This rejected the policy personified by Goremykin, though in truth, he had merely reflected Nicholas's views. Pitirim backed Sturmer as a replacement for Goremykin, hoping Sturmer would be more flexible with the Duma. Pitirim's visit was probably calculated to advance Sturmer's candidacy.

No. 762/ Telegram 212. Tsarskoe Selo> Stavka. 13 Jan 1916. 2.10> 2.55 p.m. To his majesty. [I] tenderly thank you for dear letter. Warm, windy, overcast. [We] are going with [daughter] Marie for bit of a sledge drive in park, then to Znamenia< to place candles. We all warmly kiss [you]. Alix

No. 763/ Her No. 428.   Tsarskoe Selo. Jan. 13th 1916.
My own Sweetheart,
Grey, dull weather, 2° of warmth again & very windy.—Lay out on the balkony [sic] yesterday for half an hour. The little ones are so happy to be able to come down again, but look pale.—To-day the two eldest lunch at Anichkov,< have committees, receipt of donations & tea at Xenias<. It seems Motherdear< was not quite well, & so was lonely & could only go to Xenia once.—It was cosy having N.P.< & V.N.[208] yesterday from 9¼-11.50—they talked much about there. N.P. lets him live in his appartments [sic] as nearer to the escort. He & Kirill< leave Saturday evening, I believe. There is still masses to be done—people are so obstinate & wont do things—he goes to Grigorovich< this morning. [a]
How dull, poor Angel, to sit near the old man [Fredericks] at the cinema—why, its to run up the walls. I am glad the new English general [Callwell] is nice.—What are the stories going on about the Montenegrians? As tho' he [King Nicholas I?—see Letter No. 755a] had sold his country to the Austrians, therefore one wld. not receive him in Rome nor in Paris—or is this all gossip—he is capable of anything for money's sake & his personal profit, tho' he loved his country I thought—in any case I understand nothing.—I want to go in the little sledge in the garden, tho' strong wind, with [daughter] Marie, & enter into Znam.[enia]< for the first time in 1916, & place candles there & pray for my own sweet Lovebird.— Nice Zina<, who likes our Friend,< sat for an hour with me yesterday. Now goodbye my Sunshine, my one & all. I bless you & cover yr. beloved face with ever such tender kisses. Yr, very own little Wify. [P.S.] Fancy Raftopolo being at Moghilev, he wrote to Ania he was sent there from the regiment. [b]

208. Context suggests "V.N." was one of N. P. Sablin's sons.

No. 764.   Ts.[arist] Stavka. Jan. 13th 1916.
My precious Wify,
My plans are now fixed. To-morrow, Thursday, I board the train & Friday morning will inspect the Zabaikal'skaya kazachaya [Trans-Baikal Cossack] div.[ision] in Bobruisk.[210]—I return here the same day & will spend the night in

the train. Saturday morning there will be my usual doklad [report], then I shall leave right away for Orsha.—Three Cossack divisions are in the neighbourhood —the 1^{aya} & 2^{aya} Kuban and Ural—after which I continue my journey home, arriving at Ts.[arskoe] S.[elo] Sunday at 12 o'clock.—Alas, I will miss the church service! Perhaps I shall spend 8-9 days at home—that would be splendid! My dear little Sunny, I burn with impatience to see you as soon as possible, to hear your voice, to look into your eyes & to feel myself in your arms! I think separation actually makes love stronger & mutual attraction greater. I hope you will feel well & strong by then. [a]

[Our daughter] Tatiana's namesday [sic] was celebrated in town with great fanfare. There was a concert & presentations in the theatre. It seems it was crowded & quite successful, it lasted from 9 till 1.30.—The governor [of Mogilev, A. I. Pil'ts] was unable to tell me how much had been collected during the whole evening.— Tatiana's portrait with autograph was sold along with the programme. Fedorov has slight pains in the left side of the abdomen & slight temperature the last two days, so I asked him to lie down. He looks cheerful, as he always does. At this moment— 2.30—your dear letter No. 427 was brought to me. I kiss you tenderly & thank you for all you write.—May God bless you & the dear children! Your deeply loving old huzy   Nicky. [b]

No. 765/ Telegram 60. Stavka> Tsarskoe Selo. 13 Jan 1916. 5.15> 5.45 p.m. To her majesty. Loving thanks to you and [daughter] Marie [for] dear letters. Warm, windy, dark. Glad you went out. Tender kisses to all. Niki

---

No. 766/ Her No. 429.   Tsarskoe Selo. Jan. 14th 1916.
My very own Lovebird,
Very windy, mild, sun shone a little. Feel rotten as had such pains in my tommy in the night & such faintness, even rang for Madeleine< to fill up my hotwaterbottle & give me opium. Probably it comes from Adonis. But I feel so weak to-day.—Olga Evgenjevna< lunches & then I receive Yagmin, who came to hurry his wife, at last.—How nice that Raftopolo [Ravtopulo] lunched with you—Silaev< will have been delighted—it was the boy's sisters namesday too on the 12-th. To-day is [Kaiser] Williams birthday! There now its snowing.—I wonder whether this is my last letter & you return on Saturday or not?— [a]

The Children found Motherdear< rather thin, they lunched with her upstairs—then after their committees they took tea at Xenias,< who neither looks flouroushing [sic].—Yr. friend Plevitskaya brought [daughter] Olga money fr. the concerts she had given.— She had sung to [your sister] Olga at Kiev where by chance Mahalov [Mochalov] ("Rodotchka") was, & he accompanied her & Rodionov came with her here.—Ania< read some stories out of yr. book to us, about Children, whilst we were laying patiences—she has brought a new book for you for yr. return.—Cannot write any more, feel too idiotic.—Goodbye my Sweetheart, God bless & protect you now & ever & help you in all the difficult moments of your life.—I cover you with tenderly caressing, yearning kisses, & remain, precious One, yr. very own fondly loving old wife   Sunny. [b]
No. 767/ Telegram 225. Tsarskoe Selo> Stavka. 14 Jan 1916. 5.10> 6.30 p.m. To his majesty. Tenderly thank you for dear letter. In thoughts together. Wish

you all the best. Children healthy though little ones< still not walking. Olga
Evg.< lunched with us, sends greetings. [We] warmly kiss [you]. May God keep
you. Alix

No. 768.   Ts.[arist] Stavka. Jan. 14th 1916.
My own precious One,
     This will be my last letter. Yesterday many generals & high people arrived for
the commission under Alekseev's presidency to discuss questions of
prod.[ovol'stvie, production], coal & other things. Pr. [N. P.] Urusov, who
works in the R.[ed] Cross as well as with the bezhentsy [refugees] has arrived,
along with gen. Ivanov. Then to my great amazement, came the mayor of Moscow, Chelnokov, the president of the soyuz gorod.[ov],[209] & other important
persons from other ministries. I invited them to dinner.— I received Chelnokov
privately a few minutes before dinner—he presented me with a warm address fr.
Moscow in wh. he thanks the troops for the good reception accorded the delegation sent to distribute presents to the soldiers.—He breathed heavily, & jumped
every second from his chair while he was spoke. I asked him if he felt well, he
said he did but added he was accustomed to present himself to Nikolasha< &
had not at all expected to see me here. This reply & his overall manner pleased
me this time! [a]
     Poor Alekseev sat with them yesterday evening from 9 to 12. And again to
day. After Fedorov, Voeikov has now taken ill with influenza: foolish man, two
days ago he had shivering & when he took his temperature it was 39 deg. With
difficulty I persuaded him to remain in bed this morning, but now he is up again.
Our [Dr. S. P.] Polyakov placed 17 cuppings on his chest & back, wh. helped
considerably, otherwise he might have gotten inflammation of the lungs! I
thank you & kiss you warmly for your dear letter No. 428, wh. only just arrived.
Well, goodbye. God bless you, my beloved Sunny, my precious darling! I kiss
you & the dear children tenderly. In 2 days, God willing, we will be together
again. Your Nicky. [b]

209. The *soyuz godorov* (union of towns) was a voluntary organization that strove to harness
popular forces for victory. Independent of the government, it supported the Duma and was often
critical of the tsar and his bureaucracy. The Union of Zemstvos and the Central War Industry Committee, which coordinated the work of War Industry Committees in every province, were other important "voluntary organizations." "M. V. Chelnokov ... was a Liberal, and his audience with the
Tsar had for its object the representation of public opinion. That, no doubt, accounted for his nervous
demeanour." (Vulliamy, p. 138n)

No. 769/ Telegram 62. Stavka> Tsarskoe Selo. 14 Jan 1916. 6.56> 7.23 p.m.
To her majesty. Many thanks [for] dear letter. This evening [we] get into the
train, leaving in the night for Bobruisk. Warm, grey weather. Tender love to all.
Niki

No. 770/ Her No. 430.   Tsarskoe Selo. Jan. 15th 1916.
Sweetheart,
     Only a few lines as feel very rotten. Slept well, but head aches still, difficult
to keep eyes open, feel so weak, fievrish [sic], nasty, [I have a temperature of]

37.1, but will probably rise, heart enlarged—as tho' I were going to have influenza, so B.[otkin] said I was to remain all day in bed. Yesterday also felt nasty & cretinised. Olga Evgenjevna the same as always, begged to send her compliments. Yagmin has news the regiment is well into Persia now. Ania< & N.P.< dined—I felt too rotten to fully enjoy them— Sunny day, 6° of warmth in the sun.— Such happiness you come Sunday, but want to be well by then. Hope good weather— all will go off well, see dear Cossacks.—How was it a beastly Zeppelin came as far as Rezhitsa? Children well, tho' Olga was sick in the night without any reason. Beloved, I cant write any more, eyes ache & are so heavy. Poor Css. Worontzov—she will miss her dear old husband—but for him it must be a relief. [See Letter No. 773.] —How is Fedorov?< Blessings & kisses without end & great longing to have you back again, Lovebird, sweetest of Sweets— Press you tenderly to my heart—Ever yr. own old wify Alix. [P.S.] You will get this no doubt at Orsha.

No. 771/ Telegram unnumbered. Bobruisk> Tsarskoe Selo. 15 Jan 1916. [Arrived,] 1.46 p.m. To her majesty. Just held inspection of Zabaikaltsy.[210] Very pleased. [I] thank you for yesterday's telegram. Weather sunny, windy. Warmly embrace all. Niki

210. "Za Baikal" means "beyond Lake Baikal," these men were from the far eastern region of Siberia. See Letter No. 764a.

No. 772/ Telegram 289. Tsarskoe Selo> Orsha. 15 Jan 1916. 1.57> 2.58 p.m. To his majesty. Thank you for telegram. Splendid sun. Lay on balcony, today better. [We] all warmly embrace [you]. May God keep you. Alix

No. 773/ Telegram 280. Tsarskoe Selo> Stavka. 15 Jan 1916. 5.52> 7.30 p.m. To his majesty. Tenderly thank you for dear letter and telegram. Glad all is going successfully. Sunny, quiet weather. Spend day in bed because did not feel well, now better. Will move over to sofa for dinner. Sad that dear old [Count I. Iv.] Vorontsov[-Dashkov] died. Warmly embrace and kiss [you]. Alix

No. 774/ Telegram 64. Stavka> Tsarskoe Selo. 15 Jan 1916. 9.48> 10.48 p.m. To her majesty. Loving thanks [for] letter and telegram. Just came back. Freezing beastly wind. [You] must get well for Sunday. Tender kisses. Niki

No. 775/ Telegram 65. Stavka> Tsarskoe Selo. 16 Jan 1916. 12.18> 12.56 p.m. To her majesty. Leaving directly. Cold fine day. Hope [you] are feeling better. Tender kisses. Niki

No. 776/ Her No. 431.   Tsarskoe Selo. Jan. 16th 1916.
My Own,
    I hear that a messenger leaves even to-day still to worry you—so I write a few lines. Bright sunshine, calm & 2° of frost. Went to sleep after 3, feel a bit better to-day, but still a strange feeling in my inside & I keep a hotwater bottle on my tommy—but heart by chance this morning not enlarged.—I got up for dinner yes-

terday & lay on the sopha till 11—laying patiences as usual, as less tiring than working.—Sandra [Shuvalova] is with her mother, Ira [Sheremeteva] & Maia [Musina-Pushkina] here in town<.—Such consolation you return to-morrow, lovebird. Yr. dear letter made me so happy.—But how strange Chelnokov having been with you— can imagine that he felt small & not sure of himself—he ought to have stood all the time, doublefaced man![209]—Fancy Voeikov< also having fallen ill—you have had to wander from one to the other. What a dull letter! Excuse my not coming to the station, but have not the strength to stand about there.—Kiss & bless you my own Love & am more than happy to clasp you soon to my breast again. Ever yr. very own old Wify.

No. 777/ Telegram 0761 in Russian. Orsha> Tsarskoe Selo. 16 Jan 1916. 4.35> 5.58 p.m. To her majesty. Heartily thank you for letter. Returned very pleased with review. Weather favored [us]. My invalids V.[oeikov] and F.[edorov] better. Tenderly embrace [you]. Niki

---

No. 778.   Ts.[arist] Stavka. Jan. 28th 1916.
My own darling One,

   Again I must leave you & the children—my home, my little nest—& I feel so sad & downcast, tho I don't want to show it. God grant that we will not be separated for long—I hope to return on Febr. 8th. Do not be sad, do not worry! Knowing you as I do, I fear you will brood over what Miechen< told us to day, & this question will torment you in my absence.[211] Please leave it alone! Joy of my life, my Sunny, my adorable little Wify, I love you & long for you terribly! Only when I see the soldiers & sailors am I able to forget you for a few moments—if possible! With regard to the other questions, I go away this time with greater peace of mind because I have unlimited confidence in Shtyurm[er]. God bless you. I kiss you all tenderly. Ever your Nicky.

No. 779/ Her No. 432.   Tsarskoe Selo. Jan. 28th 1916.
My very own beloved Sweetheart,

   Once more the train is carrying my Treasure away, but I hope not for long—I know I ought not to say this, & for an old married woman it may seem ridiculous—but I cannot help it.—With the years love increases & the time without your sweet presence is hard to bear. When I could be about & nurse the wounded it was more bearable. For you its worse, my Own. I am glad you see troops already to-morrow, that will be refreshing & to all a joy, I hope you will have the same sunshine as there is here to-day.—It was so nice you read to us & I hear your dear voice now always! And your tender caresses, oh how deeply I thank you for them— they warmed me up & were such a consolation; when the heart is heavy with care & anxieties, every tenderness gives one force and intense happiness. Oh, could but our children be equally blessed in their married lives—the idea of Boris< is too unsympathetic & the child [your sister Olga] would, I feel convinced, never agree to marry him & I should perfectly well understand her. Only never let Miechen< guess other thoughts have filled the child's head & heart—those are a young girls holy secrets wh. other[s] must not know of, it would terribly hurt Olga, who is so susceptible.[211] That conversation has made me feel far from cheery, & as it is I feel very low at yr. going & my old heart cramps itself in pain—cannot get accustomed to our separations. Here, Baby's note will amuse you. The lilies of the valley are to brighten up yr. writing table. [a]

You will talk seriously to Kedrov, wont you—because the joy & honour of this journey comes almost like a recompense & so as to cover the reprimand he so rightly deserved. Why you saved him being judged again [I cannot understand] &, tho' a nice man, needs to be held in hand, the Admiral [C. D. Nilov] ought never to be so familiar with him—he is terribly ambitious. But you take him for short [time], I suppose.—What rejoicings there will be, when you get rid of Br.-B. (can't spell his name) [M. D. Bonch-Bruevich]—but he ought to be made to understand first the wrong he has done & wh. falls upon you—you are too kind, my Sunny Angel, be firmer & when you punish, don't forgive at once & give good places— one does not fear you enough—show yr. power, one profits of yr. marvellous kindness & gentleness. Sad I cannot take you to the station, but I am not up to it, the heart being enlarged—& the eng.-mech.< came. My Own, my light, my love, sleep well & peacefully, feel my tender arms encircling you, & your dear sweet head rest it in thoughts upon my breast, (not upon the high cushion you dislike).—Goodbye, my Treasure, my Husband, Sunshine beloved, God bless & keep you, holy Angels guard you & the force of my intense love. Oh my Boy, how I love you! Words cannot express it, but you can read it in my eyes. Ever yr. very own old   Wify.   [P.S.] Oh, the lonely night! [b]

---

211. At this time, Nicholas II's younger sister Olga was estranged from her husband, Peter Alexandrovich ("Petia"). Maria Pavlovna the Elder ("Miechen") apparently hoped to see her son, Boris Vladimirovich, marry Olga. See Footnote 212.

No. 780/ Telegram 320 in Russian. Tsarskoe Selo> St. Vyshki. 29 Jan 1916. 1.20> 2.20 p.m. [We] all warmly kiss you. Feel not famous, slept little. Comforted by [your] dear letter. Am lonely. Hope all is well. Snowing. Have written. May God keep you. Alix

---

No. 781/ Her No. 433.   Tsarskoe Selo. Jan. 29th 1916.
My own Treasure love,

I thank you very, very fondly for yr. sweetest letter you left me as a consolation—over & over again I have reread it, & in the night when I could not sleep & my eyes ached fr. crying.—We went to bed at 10½—bad night & head aches this morning. Have just finished heaps of papers from Rostovtsev<. It is gently snowing—2 degrees of frost. Ania< peeped in a second on her way to town< & she begged me yet again to thank you fr. the depths of her heart for the money. She telephoned it to our Friend<, & He said it would bring you blessings—& that she is to put it aside in the bank to be a fund she must collect for building the home for the cripples.—I shall see whether we cannot give her a bit of ground—it would be good if it were not far from the Invalid House, as then they could profit of our bathhouse & shops<. [a]

I wonder whether you will begin the French book, you will see how exciting it is.—How did my Lovebird sleep? How I miss my Sunshine!! Do think about Ivanov, it would indeed be a splendid change—& clean beginning for 1916—Polivanov needs no place to bother you about, Shcherb.[achev]< can replace Ivanov & then somebody energetic in his place. What a bore old Ruzsky< is not yet well enough.—How glad I am that you have got Sht.[yurmer] now to rest upon; one who you know will try & hold all the ministers together. Now I must be getting up for luncheon. Later Benkendorff< wishes to see me & Mme Volzhaninova from the Crimea. The Children want to see Rodionov to-morrow evening, as he wishes to go to our Church for service.—Sweetest of Sweets, then now goodbye & God bless and protect you. I cover your beloved face with very tenderest kisses, & remain Ever yr. own wify Alix. [P.S.] Fedorov slept well, coughs less, [has a temperature of] 37. Mme Zizi< feels better, 36.4, tell this to Kira<, who does not think enough about his mother. Have a quiet talk with Mordvinov about Misha's< story & then about [your sister] Olga & ask what sort of a man her N.A. is.[212] [b, c]

212. Discussion here is of a possible second marriage to N. A. Kulikovsky. "N.A." and Olga were soon married. See Footnote 211.

No. 782/ Telegram 499 in Russian. Vyshki r.r.> Tsarskoe Selo. 29 Jan 1916. 3.50> 5.10 p.m. To her majesty. [I] thank you very much for letter yesterday evening. Very pleased with review. Saw many troops. My company of Kabardintsy was in Guard of Honour. Not cold, snowing. Warmly embrace all. Niki

---

No. 783/ Her No. 434.   Tsarskoe Selo. Jan. 30th 1916.
My own Sweetheart,
   We were so happy to get yr. telegram during tea, & to know that all went off so well—how nice that you had a guard of honour of your Cabardintsy at the station.—There must have been heavy fighting as Baby's< train brings 15 wounded officers & over 300 men from Kalkuny—Drissa, that is where Tatiana's regiment is & where you will be, it seems to me.—All looks so white to-day, a good deal of snow fell yesterday—3 degrees. of frost—Had a bad, restless night, went early to bed—head ached & continues to, heart the same. I saw Mme Volzhaninova fr. the Crimea—(wine-makers) you remember her I am sure, she met me on the pier with flowers, lunched at Livadia & sold at the bazaars. You made acquaintance with her old mother (over 70) at the opening of a children's sanatorium beyond Massandra—Mme Zheltukhin born Ilovaiskaya, daughter of the hero of Borodino. Her property near Bielovezh was completely destroyed & she had no time to save anything & she possessed many historical things. You are the 5th Emperor she has seen. [a, b]
   Our Friend< is very happy that you see the troops now again, he is quiet about everything, only anxious Ivanov should be named [minister of war], as his presence in the Duma can be of much help.—I have again several officers waiting to be received—that continues the whole time—& I do feel so tired. Wish I could at last get to Church again—not once in the month of Jan:—& I long to go to Znam.[enia]< and place my candles there.—Old Professor Pavlov died—he got

poisoning of the blood, after an operation he had performed, I think.—Lovy sweet, I miss you awfully. The evenings are dull—Ania< is aggravated we all play patiences, but it rests the eyes after much working & to sit with folded hands is awful. She likes reading aloud, but grabbles [i.e., chatters] awfully —but one cannot sit & talk all day, & I have nothing to speak of—I am weary. Dear Sweetheart, I am not boasting, but nobody loves you so intensely as old [S]unny—you are her life, her Own! God bless you Precious one, I cover you with tender, passionate kisses & long to have you back into my arms again. Ever, Nicky mine yr. very own old girly   Wify. [c]

No. 784/ Telegram 1 in Russian. Army in the Field> Tsarskoe Selo. 30 Jan 1916. 1.55> 2.45 p.m. To his majesty. Just finished big review. Saw [daughter] Tatiana's regiment. Found all in splendid condition and order. Weather warm. Warmly embrace all. Niki

No. 785/ Telegram 321 in Russian. Tsarskoe Selo> Borkovichi. 30 Jan 1916. 3.40> 8.00 p.m. To his majesty. Warmly thank you for news. [Daughter] Tatiana terribly happy for [her] regiment. Here all are the same. Lonely. [We] tenderly kiss you. May God keep you. Alix

No. 786/ Her No. 435.   Tsarskoe Selo. Jan. 31st 1916.
My own sweet Treasure,
   [Our daughter] Tatiana was delighted that you saw her regiment & found it in good order. I had always hoped to go about more, in sanitary trains too, & to have the chance of seeing at least one of my regiments.—Rodionov was in Church yesterday evening, dined with A.[nia]< & then came to us. He leaves to-morrow. Again they stand in a new village, he said, only 8 versts fr. Volo-chisk & all the officers together in a landlord's estate—they have changed already four or five times. He showed us some groups he had made & of some of them on horseback—Massoyedov's [S. V. Myasoedov-Ivanov's] horse looks quite an-tidiluvian.—[a]
   A grey morning, 5 degrees. Got to sleep late, but then slept alright, head scarcely aches, but heart & eyes do, & I am writing in specks, so as to tire them less.—I saw one of my Crimeans yesterday—now they all deeply regret that Dro-byazgin leaves them —all stories had finished, & now they appreciated him & much regret the change.—We receive military cadets to-day who will be pro-moted to-morrow I believe, and then leave. Then Varnava, Arch.[bishop] Sera-phim,—Kuptsov (Eriv.[anets]<) who was here on leave & wants to see me before returning to the regiment, then Alek!!< what can he want? probably to talk about Gagri, but then I shall have to tell him about Skalon. [b]
   At 6 comes Captain of the 1-st rank Schults (such a purely German name, alas), who leaves for England—suppose its the one with the long beard who commanded the "Africa", if I don't invent, occupies himself with hypnotism, & his sister was nurse in my hospital during the Japanese war and died later at Kronstadt. One of the wounded I received yesterday, gave me a charming col-lection of photos, he had taken at [the Crimean town of] Eupatoria—some lie out

taking sunbaths, others covered in mud, others in baths, having douches, being electrified—quite amusing.— Yesterday was the silver Wedding [day] of the Putiatins [M. S. Putyatin and wife]. I am trying to give you all the news I can, tho' its not interesting. alas.—Sweetheart, I wonder whether you get my letters on the way, probably they will await you at some big station —I wish I were in their place & could feel your sweet lips upon mine & could gaze into your beloved eyes. Sorely do I miss my own Sweetheart & his tender kisses, wh. mean so much to me.— Well, Lovy, I will end now. Goodbye & God bless you now & evermore. Endless kisses fr. yr. very own old   Sunny. [c, d]

No. 787/ Telegram 11 in Russian. Army in the Field> Tsarskoe Selo. 31 Jan 1916. 1.30> 2.56 p.m. To her majesty. Splendid review today of two cavalry divisions. Thank you very much for yesterday's letter, and for the second, just received. 3° frost. [I] warmly embrace all. Niki

---

No. 788/ Telegram 326. Tsarskoe Selo> Orsha [R.R.] St[ation]. [No date]. 4.50> 7.45 p.m. To his majesty. From my soul thank you for dear telegram. Received many [people], very tired. Alek< comes to you on Tuesday. 5 [degrees of] frost. We all tenderly kiss [you]. Alix

---

No. 789/ Her No. 436.   Tsarskoe Selo. Feb. 1st 1916.
My very Own,
   Colder this morning, 7 degrees & snowing. Scarcely slept this night & heart aches more this morning, head alright. I send you a little snowdrop from Livadia. Miechen< wrote again yesterday begging for Baron Dellingshausen to be let free. He is kept in the prison Kresti at Petrogr.[ad], Viborg side. His son, the dragoon may visit him. But its such a hideous shame that can only be helped by having him quickly let out by telegraph. One wont know how to look him in the face later on.— [a]
   Alek< did not say anything particular to me—only it seems is not contented with the wounded officers—then those that have to be sent to the south (fr. Moscou [sic] by the commission), stick there for 2 months without leaving—disorder wh. he is going to try and set to rights;—then he spoke about the prisoners he visited—indeed one must think of having some moved as they die from illnesses, the climate being unbearable for them.—Many people find it wld. be good if you had, for a time only, given over the food supply question to Alek, as really it is scandalous in town< & the prices are impossible; he would poke his nose into everything, fly at the merchants who cheat & ask impossible prices & would help getting rid of Obolensky< who is really no good whatsoever and does not help one bit. Our Friend< is anxious if it continues still for 2 months that we may have disagreeable rows and stories in town—& I understand it, as its shameful making the poor people suffer so—& the humiliation before our allies!! We have got everything in quantities, only they wont bring it, & when they do, the prices for all become unattainable. Why not ask him [Alek] for 2 months to take all in hand, or one month even, & he wont allow cheating to go on. He is excellent in any place to set order, shake up people—but not for long. I write this

to you, as you will be seeing him I believe on Tuesday.—Schultz was charming, we talked for half an hour upon every sort of subject—he is the brother of the black one [i.e., the one] who still commands the "Africa" & all the divers. To-day I have Shvedov with a doklad [report], & M-lle Schneider & that will be endless as we have much to talk over about the artschool, & reorganisation [sic] of my patriotic schools—& the Home Manufactures Committee wh. it seems to me Krivosh.[ein] has forgotten all about.—Then the Commander [E. E. Vyshinsky] of the Erivantsi< asked to see us, he was here on leave & returns to the regiment.— [b, c]

How you miss Baby sweet< again at the Headquarters,—your lonely life begins once more again, poor precious Angel mine!— The Children enjoyed themselves at Anias yesterday & the soldiers too—I suppose Tatiana< will have discribed [sic] all. Anias names-day [sic] is on the 3-st [sic] in case you care to send her a telegram. —Tatiana is bidding Rodionov goodbye by telephone & I shall too. How awfully difficult the fighting in such terrible cold in the Caucasus, Alek says less men have frozen feet, 1 per cent, & officers—8 [per cent],—to[o] lightly dressed, going south they no doubt thought it would be warmer.—Now Sweetheart I must end my letter. God bless & protect you, precious One & keep you from all harm. I cover you with tender kisses & clasp you to my breast.— Ever yr. very own loving old   Wify. [d]

Has "everything" passed with you & do you no longer need the things I gave you? I do wish you could take more exercise, it would be the best thing for you. Tell boysy< that lady sends him her tenderest love & gentlest kisses & often thinks of him in lonely, sleepless nights.—Loman drinks again heaps & is most crazy, A.[nia] simply dreads him—he ought absolutely to be sent to Finland to a sanatorium for 2 months complete rest—otherwise I assure you he will shoot himself or others. The Drs[.] also find he needs a change & rest, he had a nervous stroke already.—This green ink smells abominably, hope the scent will take the odour away. [e]

No. 790/ Telegram 2. Tsarskoe Selo> Stavka. 1 Feb 1916. 11.56 a.m.> 12.12 p.m. To his majesty. Snowing, 7 deg. frost. Hope you can read my letter tomorrow before Alek's< departure. Nearly did not sleep, heart aching, tired after long doklady [reports]. Children feel wonderful. [I] imagine your loneliness in [your] empty rooms. All tenderly kiss and embrace [you]. Alix

---

No. 791/ Telegram 1. Stavka> Tsarskoe Selo. 1 Feb 1916. 2.48> 3.03 p.m. To her majesty. Tender thanks [for] dear letter also [daughter] Olga. Came over from the train in the morning. Not cold, 3 deg. Slight snow. Till now under excellent impression of reviews. Kiss all very fondly. Niki

---

No. 792.   Ts.[arist] Stavka. Feb. 1st 1916.
My own beloved Sunny!

At last I find a free evening to talk quietly to you. I long for you terribly. First, I thank you for yr. three dear letters. They came quite irregularly, of course, because the train jerked back & forth on the rails as near Dvinsk, where bad birds [i.e., enemy aircraft] fly. Much snow fell the last three days, which makes it useless for them! The review of 1ᵃʸᵃ Army was held near the little rr. station of Vyshki. To my great satisfaction, a company of the Kabardinsky reg.[iment] was stationed there, but it had only one officer I knew, as well as several men who were at Livadia! Among the cavalry regiments were two regs. of Mama & Xenia[213a] (I could not find Gordinsky). But your Alexandrovtsy< & my Pavlovtsy< were not there. Such a pity! They had just been sent to relieve the infantry in the trenches. My God!—your poor Plehve looks terrible. Green as a corpse, blinder & more stooped than ever, hardly able to move his legs. Seated on his horse, he threw himself back so far that I thought he was fainting. He assured me he rides often, but I doubt it. [a, b]

The troops were in fine condition, also the horses. After lunch I spoke with Plehve. He reasons quite soundly & normally, his head is fresh & thoughts clear, & seated he seems alright [sic], but when he stands up he offers a terrible sight. I spoke to him severely about [his chief of staff] Bonch-Bruevich—that he must be rid of him etc. I then had a good walk along the highroad. [We returned to the train and a]t 6.o['clock] passed through Dvinsk. The streets are lighted as usual. I saw only one searchlight illuminating the dark horizon! We passed the night near Polotsk, and on the morning of Jan. 30th returned to Drissa. There I was met by Evert & gen. Litvinov of the 1aya Army & three cavalry div.[ision]s—the 8ᵗʰ, 14ᵗʰ & [one of] the Siberian cossacks. Tatiana's lancers looked to be fine fellows, [as did all the] other troops. So neat clean & well dressed & armed, such as I have seldom seen even in peace time! Truly excellent! They all have such a good appearance in their grey papakhi [Caucasian fur caps], though at the same time they look so much alike it is difficult to determine their regiments. [c, d]

Yesterday Jan. 31ˢᵗ the last review was held. The 6ᵗʰ & 13ᵗʰ cavalry divisions were there—the same fine fellows as before. The weather is not at all cold—3-4 degs. frost & it is again snowing. The old man [Fredericks] rode on horseback again of course, & was very proud of it—he speaks to all about it, wh. drives Nilov wild! After lunch, the train left Borkovichi station at 3.o['clock]; we proceeded through Vitebsk & Orsha, & arrived here at 11 in the evening. The air was so lovely that Voeikov, [A. N.] Grabbe, Kedrov & I took a refreshing walk before retiring. Today at 10 in the morning I moved into my quarters & spent 2½ hrs. with Alekseev. I found Sergei< in Mogilev, he has already settled there, but not the foreigners as they have all gone to Odessa for a while, except for [Hanbury-]Williams. I walked in the garden during the afternoon, there was no time to motor about. I settled down to my papers, & only finished them before dinner. Now it is late, I am very tired, so I must wish you good night, my darling Wify, my only & all! Why can you not sleep, my poor dear one? [e, f]

2 February. I just finished lunch with the foreigners; they arrived yesterday evening. I went to church this morning & then had a long talk with Alekseev about retiring Plehve & Bonch-Bruevich. It seems the latter is (apparently) hated by everyone in the army, starting with the highest generals! To-morrow I must find a successor to him (Plehve). I received yr. dear letter No. 436 & telegram. I thank you tenderly. How tiresome you have pains in yr. face, it is even swollen! My dear, I am so sorry for you! The water in Mogilev has again af-

fected my stomach badly, in other respects I feel fine. I thank you also for the charming flower. Now I must end, my beloved. God bless you & the children! I embrace you tightly & kiss you tenderly. Ever yr. own old huzy   Nicky. [g]

213a. Maria was Nicholas's mother, Xenia his older sister.

No. 793/ Telegram 4. Tsarskoe Selo> Stavka. 2 Feb 1916. 10.40> 11.15 a.m. To his majesty. Did not sleep all night. Strong pain in face, swelling. Sent for Crimean friend. 4 deg. frost. [We] all tenderly kiss [you]. May God keep you. Alix

No. 794/ Her No. 437.   Tsarskoe Selo. Feb. 2nd 1916.
Sweet Angel,
    Excuse a short letter to-day, but I am cretinised<, did not sleep all night from pain in my cheek wh. is swollen & looks hideous. Vl. Nik.< thinks its from the tooth & has wired to our dentist [Dr. S. S. Kostritsky] to come. I had a compress on all night, changed it too—sat smoking in the sitting room, wandered about. Good you were not there for me to disturb. It is not as bad as those madning [sic] pains I used to have, but hurts quite enough & incessantly. I made all dark from 11-1 but without any result & the head begins to ache & the heart is more enlarged. I have begun my medicines again to-day.—4 degrees of frost, tiny bit snowing. Gorodinsky of [your sister] Xenia's reg. said you saw the reg.[,] thanked them & they were awfully happy. In to-day's papers there is a description of yr. inspections, but am not up to reading it, so shall keep that number. Yesterday I had Shvedov's doklad [report] for ¾ of an hour & Mlle Schneider 1½ hour till I was quite done for. Beloved Sweetheart, I think & long for you & cover you with very tenderest kisses. God bless & keep you. Ever yr. very own old   Wify.   [P.S.] The Children kiss you; they were in church & hospital.— Shall keep in bed till teatime & see then how I feel.—Beloved One, think incessantly of you.

No. 795/ Telegram 3. Stavka> Tsarskoe Selo. 2 Feb 1916. 6.30> 7.10 p.m. To her majesty. Fondest thanks [for] dear letter. Feel so much for you [because of] that pain [in your] face[—]horrible nuissance [sic]. Took a longer walk on highroad. Snowstorm beginning. Tender love [and] kisses. Niki

No. 796/ Telegram 8. Tsarskoe Selo> Stavka. 2 Feb 1916. 8.13> 8.27 p.m. To his majesty. Tenderly thank you for telegram. Face aches much less though quite swollen. Drank tea on sopha and and [sic] returned there after dinner. What did you do with petition Shulenburg wrote me? All warmly kiss [you]. May God bless you. Sleep well. Alix

No. 797/ Telegram 12 in Russian. Tsarskoe Selo> Stavka. 3 Feb 1916. 11.03> 11.29 a.m. To his majesty. Slept better, almost not aching, swelling less. Snowing, 5 deg. frost. [We] all tenderly kiss [you]. May God keep you. Alix

No. 798/ Her No. 438.   Tsarskoe Selo. Feb. 3rd 1916.
My own Sweetheart,

I got to sleep after 4—the cheek is less swollen—yesterday evening I looked too ridiculous one had to laugh at this croocked [sic] face. [Daughter] Olga & A.[nia]< read to us Avertchenko stories about children & I laid patiences, tho' head ached & felt cretinised<.—Baby< was sweet, when I told him yesterday that there wld. be blinis for him for luncheon as he loves them—"how, when you have got pain you order me blinis, I wont eat them on purpose—it is not necessary"[160] but I said it would just please me and it seems he ate a lot.—We played douratscki [durachki] before he went to bed.—5 degrees of frost & snowing.— [a]

Our Standart officers & the priest wired her their good wishes [to Anna Vyrubova on her name day], so touching, & Rodionov from the way too.—N.P.< writes[213b]: "I am happy that I have enough work even for 24 hours a day; I don't know whether it is good or bad, but I push myself everywhere, yesterday I even picked horses for every carriage [Sablin was in a transport unit]—this I was taught to do by the senior officers, & indeed I thus learned everything. My brother visited me, spent with me a whole day—it is unimaginably easy in his regiment, he has been a month here & he has been given another leave—this is because in his regiment instead of 29 officers there are almost 89—cannot understand it—in my opinion what is happening in our army regarding officers is not right—this is my deep conviction." [b]

Your three Sharpshooters dined with us.[213c] They had music & singing & my "giant" Petrov is the zapevala [choir-leader][14] & splendid.

"We arrived at another village, this is 8 versty [1 versta = 3500 ft.] to the southwest—it is more convenient for us here because we are stationed alone[, i.e., apart from the other units in this area] and are all together, and there are 2 companies there and machine guns are placed every 3 and 6 versty. Here with us is posted a Red Cross station named for Rodzyanko[;] and his wife, a beautiful English woman (the successor of Tamara), is the director of the station. We accommodated ourselves wonderfully in the priest's ward-room—a big, good living room—it even has a large portrait of the sovereign. I live with the landowner in the house, they are a very nice newly married couple, she is pleasant and he is too—a former officer, a dragoon,—his father was a member of the Pavlovtsy guards and was wounded in 1877—now he died not long ago. They look after me marvellously, from 6½ in the morning tea is always ready for me, and during the day as well—and moreover she also very much likes my adjutant (Kern). They go to sleep at 10 o'clock at night—such rascals! There is thick fog all the time. Kir. Vlad. [Cyril Vladimirovich] is arriving—and so we'll get some news. His arrival here goaded everyone into action, and in Rodz.[ianko's] station everyone took me for him and reported to me as if to him. I am the garrison commander here, and all the peasants call me a general, no less—is it possible I am already that old—I do not want that! Everything is quite serious—now I see that myself, I hear from people who are knowledgeable about military affairs—[generally speaking, they maintain that] there is little energy [in the Russian army], they[, i.e., these unworthy people] deceive each other." [c]

(He [N. P. Sablin] would eat me if he knew that I copied this for you, but all the same I think that his impressions will be interesting to you.)[213c]

"It is necessary to strengthen those places where we are stationed—yet all here say that only on paper everything is right—there are no roads at all and all say that everything has been written down and reported and the responsibility has been shifted to [General] Ivanov's sector of the front. It is painful for me to hear all this, all say that they often report to the sover.[eign] untruthfully, that they absolutely do not know the truth at Stavka. This is all the talk here among the guard—it would be good if his maj.[esty] would see the commanders of the regiments when he is in Petrogr.[ad] and they happen to be there on leave. They want Kir. Vl. to say this, but what can he do if he himself does not understand much? Usov is coming, [he is the] commander of the 3-rd rif.[le] regiment, which has gotten[, i.e., which has been assigned] our brigade now—he is a person who spent the entire war with the regiment and at the Gen.[eral] Staff itself, but only as an officer serving in line; he also says a lot of interesting things, he also observes [matters] seriously—he says we must win, but to accomplish that all must work harmoniously and carry out their tasks and not lie and just write reports." [d]

"Forgive me for writing all this to you,[213d] but know that everything I tell you is always everything that lies on my soul and heart with joy and seriously. Have to go soon. Here is my horse, my 'Miko', already waiting for me—first I am going to the office, then I will watch the exercise of the horses used in transport and [then I] will go to the field used for training all the regiments. We are all living quite harmoniously and well." [e]

There, my letter became quite long, as personally I have nothing interesting to tell you, only that [I] love you intensely & long for your tender, soothing caresses. How was Alek?< What answer about Shulenb.[urg]'s paper? Can the young man be sent to the army [see Letters No. 799 and 803b]? What about Dellingshausen? Ivanov? God bless & protect you. I cover you with tenderest kisses. Ever yr. very own old   Wify. [P.S.] You wld. laugh at my face!—Glad you took a longer walk. How good we have taken so many of the forts around Erzerum.[214]—Are you reading the French book? Will you be here by next Monday? Oh that will be too beautiful my own sweetest Treasure, my shining One! Just received yr. precious letter wh. endless thanks Sweetheart—such a joyful surprise.   And all you saw—so good.   Yes, get quickly rid of Br.-Br. [Bonch-Bruevich] only dont give him a division if he is so hated. And what about Ivanov? Try & take a glass of quite cold water after yr. breakfast it may help yr. tommy [tummy] working. [f, g]

213b. The following quote from N. P. Sablin's letter is in Russian; see *Perepiska*, IV, pp. 77-79, for the original text. The 1923 Berlin "Slovo" edition of the empress's letters, and its London reprint of that year, omit Sablin's account after the words: "Petrov is the choirleader and splendid ..." Some of Sablin's passages make but slight sense and suggest he was a man of limited intelligence.

213c. The words in these paragraphs are those of the empress, she writes in English.

213d. Sablin and the empress were friends, but he addresses her by the formal "you" (*vy*) rather than the informal *ty*.

214. "The capture of Erzerum, with 13,000 prisoners and 323 guns, was an important military success." (Vulliamy, p. 143n) See also Footnote 251.

No. 799/ Telegram 10. Stavka> Tsarskoe Selo. 3 Feb 1916. 2.55> 3.40 p.m.
To her majesty. Just received news that Erzerum has been stormed and taken.[214]
Thank God. Have sent petition to War Minister [Polivanov] with order to dispatch man to the front. [See Letters No. 798f and 803b.] Saw Alek< [who]
showed experiments with antigaz [sic] masks. Tenderest kisses. Niki

No. 800/ Telegram 15. Tsarskoe Selo> Stavka. 3 Feb 1916. 6.45> 6.58 p.m.
To his majesty. Heartily thank you for unexpected dear letter. In rapture at news
of taking of Erzerum.[214] Congratulate you with all my soul. She [Anna Vy-
rubova] thanks [you], terribly gladdened by telegram received just now at her
return from church. Older girls< in town<. Kiss [you]. Sleep well. Alix

No. 801/ Telegram 12. Stavka> Tsarskoe Selo. 3 Feb 1916. 6.55> 7.50 p.m.
To her majesty. Fondest thanks [for] dear letter and Marie's. Hope [you] feel
better. Good night. Sleep well. Bless and kiss you all. Niki

No. 802/ Telegram 20. Tsarskoe Selo> Stavka. 4 Feb 1916. 1.35> 1.58 p.m.
To his majesty. Gently snowing. Slept better, swelling on cheek less but do not
feel famous. [We] all tenderly kiss [you]. In thoughts always together. Alix

No. 803/ Her No. 439.   Tsarskoe Selo. Feb. 4th 1916.
Beloved One,
    With all my heart I congratulate you that Erzerum has fallen. Splendid fighting
it must have been, & how quick it went. Such a comfort—& to the others[, i.e.,
the enemy] a good moral crush. May it only remain in our hands now.[214]— Now
a perfectly private question of my own—as one reads always that the [G]ermans
continue sending [supplies?] & artillery & troops to Bulgaria, if, when we advance at last, they come from behind through Roumania—who covers the back of
our army? Or does the guard get sent down to the left of Keller & to protect
towards Odessa? These are my own thoughts, because the enemy always finds
our weak points—they prepare everywhere & for all emergencies always & we
very superficially as a rule, therefore lost in the Carpathians etc. as had not suf-
ficiantly [sic] fortified our positions. Now, if they force their way through Roumania upon our left flank—what has remained to protect our frontier. Excuse my
bothering you—but involuntarily all such thoughts come.— [a]
    What are our plans now that Erzerum has been taken, how far off from us are
the English troops?   Wonder whether Aleks< antigas [mask] is of any
good.—Thanks deeply for having saved that poor fellow's life—out at the front he
can prove his thanks—poor civilian tho' he is. [See Letters Nos. 798f and
799.]—4 "Plastuni" officers[75] have been brought to our hospital & some to the
big palace<. I have not been to our wounded since Dec. 23 & [for] ages [have]
not [been] to the big palace. I miss them all so much, & the work I love.
Baby's< right arm is swollen, but does not hurt, so its difficult for him to
write.—Got to sleep late, but then the night was alright—face less swollen, but
not yet normal & feels still stiff.—Fedorov is getting on well, tho' temp. not quite
normal—in a few days he hopes to leave the house. Mme Zizi< feels still

weak.—Here is a fat letter of love for you fr. the cow!!< 2 degrees of frost, gently snowing. To-day its a week we parted, my Sunshine, & to me it seems such ages already. My life has been very monotonous & dreary this week—& still the days flew & the nights dragged. [b, c]

O, Love, I do so terribly miss you—the light seems gone out of everything when you are not here. Oh, my Own, my one & all, I long to clasp you to my heart, I am sad and weary & want yr. caresses. Goodbye Lovebird, my own & not hers, as she [Anna Vyrubova] dares to call you, God bless you little One and keep you from all harm, guide you to success & ultimate glorious, yearned for peace. Girly covers you with kisses, Huzy Sweet. Ever yr. very own old Wify. [P.S.] Whom have you named instead of Pleve [Plehve]? What is long-nosed Ferdinand [I, tsar of Bulgaria,] doing in Vienna? Now I must dress for luncheon, have invited Ania< as she found she scarcely saw me yesterday, as had masses of people.—Sleep peacefully, my Sun Beam, joy of my life! Feel how my loving arms embrace you with tender longing and deep love. Your Wify. You will find on your desk a few flowers—I kissed them with love. [d, e]

No. 804.   Ts.[arist] Stavka. Feb. 4th 1916.
My own darling Sunny,

My warmest thanks for yr. dear letter. I read with interest the excerpt you sent fr. N.P.'s< letter. I am very happy about our great success in the caucasus—I never supposed Erzerum would be taken so soon. It seems that our troops had to stop after attacking the forts, but their sweep was so intense that they reached the rear of the Turks & so took the town.—This information came to me from Tiflis from N.< in 7 minutes, just as we were rising from the table.[214] Alek< was quiet & not excited. He made a long doklad [report], & then offered to show me experiments with asphyxiating gases.—Three officers & two chemists in various masks went into a carriage & stayed there over 30 minutes. I watched them through the windows as they stood and walked about in those terrible yellow fumes. Even in open air the terrible stench could be detected. Strange people! They carry out these experiments joyfully—as if it is a sport! [a, b]

Now about my plans.—I want to return to be present at the opening of the G. duma & the g. soviet.[215] Please do not speak of this as yet. I leave Saturday to review the splendid 1st siberian corps & arrive at Tsarskoe [Selo] on Monday, the 8th.—I will stay two days & quickly return here, because I have ordered our military conference for Thursday 11th, all the commanders-in-chief taking part.[218] I intended this from the outset, but it could not be arranged somehow. I will be so happy to see you & the children—if only for 2 days, it is better than nothing. Now, my darling, my dear, swollen-cheeked Wify, I must end. God bless you all! I kiss you & the children tenderly & remain your faithful & ever-devoted Nicky. [c]

---

215. Nicholas is referring to a scheduled joint meeting of the "G.[osudarstvennaya, i.e., State] Duma" and the "G.[osudarstvennyi] Soviet," the State Council. See Footnote 96.

No. 805/ Telegram 19. Stavka> Tsarskoe Selo. 4 Feb 1916. 6.39> 7.10 p.m.
To her majesty. Best thanks for dear letters [and] telegram. Have written.
Warm, thawing. Tender love. Niki

No. 806/ Telegram 22. Tsarskoe Selo> Stavka. 5 Feb 1916. 1.48> 2.07 p.m.
To his majesty. Terribly gladdened by contents of dear letter, heartily thank
you. [Aleksei's] ruchka [little arm] better but [he is] in bed so as to keep quiet,
[he is] quite merry. Am going upstairs a bit later. I do not feel especially well.
Thawing, windy, snowing. [We] all tenderly kiss [you]. Alix

No. 807/ Her No. 440.   Tsarskoe Selo. Feb. 5th 1916.
My own Sweetheart,
    Zero this morning, windy,—snowing hard. Thank God Baby's< night was on
the whole good—woke up several times, but not for long & did not complain.
His both arms are bandaged & the right ached rather yesterday—but our Friend<
says it will pass in two days. The last nights his sleep was restless, tho' painless
& he did not complain about his arm, tho' could not bend it. Probably hurt himself holding on to the cord of the sledge when several are tied together. But
Derevenko[207] says he is quite cheery, so don't worry, Lovebird. We dined upstairs, so as that he should be in bed & move less. The quieter he keeps, the
better.—[Daughters] Olga & Tatania go to town< for T's committee.— [a]
    I got to sleep after 4—scarcely swollen, but felt it still & the head whole time
strange & jaw too—more like a chill in the head, without a cold & difficult to
open the mouth again in the jaw.— Heart aches all these days & don't feel
nice—do hope that Aleksei & I shall be decent for your return.—It may interest
you to know, that the sums my store< & chancelry [sic] received since June 21,
1914:

To Jan. 31, 1916 collected — 6,675,136 r.[ubles] 80 k.[opecks]
Given out   — 5,862,151 r.[ubles] 46 k.[opecks]
Remains   —   812,985 r.[ubles] 34 k.[opecks]

Immense sums of it goes [sic] to my Moscow, Kharkov, Vinnitsa, Tiflis
stores,[2] to my 6 supply trains, sanitary trains etc.,[19] regiments etc. But the big
stores collect sums & things too. Supreme Council[216] gave me big sums—then
yours all along you get & from English flag days[, i.e., days on which English
flags are sold].— [b]
    Why have our troops again evacuated Galicia? It seems to me so from Re-
binder's account as so many officers of the reg., wh. have gone back fr. Galicia,
come to Kharkov to my store and ask for linnen [sic] & "individual parcels". I
cannot understand, what happened down there or they are being more concentrated together & these are the troops ready to defend one['s] rear to the south?
Ania makes her excuses for bad writing yesterday, but was in an awful hurry—&
she forgot to tell you that she had a dear card of congratulations fr. [your sister]
Olga.—She lunched with us yesterday & stayed till 5—read aloud & even played
cards with me. Shall go up to Baby in the afternoon—remain lying till luncheon,

as feel still rotten.—Eagerly awaiting yr. letter yr. telegram announced. Do hope
you are really coming & wont put off this joy of a few days happiness. [c, d]

Are you quite content with Alekseev, energetic enough? How is Ruzsky?
Some here say that he is quite well again, but I dont know whether its true or
not, wish it were, as Germans fear him.— Fancy only, I saw Miss Eady yesterday, Dona< & Loos[217] nurse.— She had to leave D.[armstadt] to E.[rnie]'s< &
Onor's< deep sorrow, last Nov., the ministers found it necessary she shld. leave—
they all were wretched. Poor woman cld. get no situation in England, as she had
been at D.—even in England they are quite unnormal[, i.e., prone to anti-German
hysteria]—so she came over here, as must earn her living, keep up her old mother
(4 brothers & many nephews at the war). She is at the Osten-Sackens (Vo-
loshev) here & the change fr. D. is very great. I told her to come often to
Madelaine< & us, so as to feel less lonely.—She told M.[adelaine] how sad many
were, Ludwig[217] had to leave & that they greatly venerate him and go after his
plans. The first ideas of his at the outset of the war, they did not follow, & now
have seen how wrong they were & deeply regret it. It was so nice seeing her
—reminded me of old home & all & of Friedberg & Livadia especially. She
hears from them sometimes. But in Engl. one got angry with her [Miss Eady]
because she wld. not speak against the Germans but she had only received greatest kindness in Germany. This war seems to have acted on all the brains.— [e]

Just read in the "Nov. Vrem."< the heroic deed of the sr. und.-offic. [senior
under-officer] of Baby's Siberian reg., his portrait is there too—yes, we have
many a hero in the army & were but our Generals as perfect, we might do marvels!—I see Misha< has not yet left, do get him to the army, I assure you its better he should be in his place there, than here with her[82] bad set.—Sweetest of
Sweets, just this minute, 1 o'clock 20 minutes, your precious letter was brought
to me & I thank you for it with all my tenderly loving heart. Oh Lovy, what joy
to have you even for two days.— God bless all yr. undertakings, yr. appearance
will do wonders I feel sure, & God will inspire you, with the right words—& to
see you—is already immense—you yourself do not half realise [sic] the power of
yr. personality wh. touches every heart, the worst even. I am glad you will have
the council of war, to thoroughly go into all questions—you wld. not have sent
for Ruzsky for that day, as he commanded nearly the whole time & is such a
capable man, & tho' often disagrees with Alekseev, it wld. just be advisable to
have one who perhaps sees things differently & then you can choose the right
way easier—& as God grant you can have R.[uzsky] back when he is well again,
he ought to know and share all the plans, I shld. say.— [f, g]

How splendid what you write about Erzerum;—marvellous troops indeed![214]—
Yes, I too admire those men who go on working at these vile gases & risking
their lives. Oh, to think that humanity should have stopped [stooped] so low.
They find it splendid technics—but the "Soul" where is it in all this? One can cry
aloud at the misery & inhumanity this ghastly war has provoked.—You will get
this letter somewhere on the way. I wonder at what hour you arrive on the 8-th?
This letter, no doubt, is then the before last. Goodbye, my Own—I bless & kiss
you with unending love & tenderness, & remain, sweet Nicky yr. very own old
wife Alix. [h]

216. *Verkhovnyi sovet po prizrennuyu semei lits, prizvannykh ha voinu*, the "Supreme Council for the Relief of the Families of Those called to Service in the War."

217. "Derevenko" might have been Doctor V. N. Derevenko, but A. A. Sergeev thinks in this case it was the sailor of that name who was assigned to help care for the tsarevich. Sergeev identifies "Loo" as "probably Louis-Hermann, Hessen prince, relative of A.[lexandra] F.[edorovna]," while "Ludwig" was "the Prince of Battenburg, husband of Victoria of Hesse, a sister of A.F." See *Perepiska*, IV, p. 86n.

No. 808/ Telegram 31. Stavka> Tsarskoe Selo. 5 Feb 1916. 7.05> 7.22 p.m. To her majesty. Fondest thanks for dear letter, also [daughter] Olga and her [Anna Vyrubova]. Also for news. Drove out and took a good walk. Tenderest kisses. Niki

---

No. 809/ Telegram 25. Tsarskoe Selo> Stavka. 6 Feb 1916. 10.18> 10.40 a.m. To his majesty. Tiny< spent night well though woke up several times; [I] think he is able to get up to-day. Have a good trip. Thousands of kisses from all. 2° frost. Alix

---

No. 810/ Her No. 441.   Tsarskoe Selo. Feb. 6th 1916.
My Treasure,
    The men are cleaning the roof, making a great noise as they clear the snow away—2 degrees of frost.—Baby< woke up several times, but did not have pain, so I hope will be quite alright [sic] for yr. return. Oh how lovely it will be to see you again, my Sweetheart, I do miss you so terribly! They will be tiring, those 2 days here. Xenia writes that [her husband] Sandro arrives on Wednesday for a few days—I am so glad for her. She walks a tiny bit in her garden & Mother-dear< goes to her daily.—What did you do about poor Dellingshausen?—I read yr. telegram & answer to the Moscou [sic] nobility & to the widow of the former governor of Erzerum— strange feelings for her, who saw the last fall of the fortress 38 years ago [during the Russo-Turkish War of 1878].— [a]
    Have nothing interesting to tell you, my Sunshine.—I am glad you took a good walk at last, it is sure to have done you good—as going round & round in the little garden must have been distracting.—Karangozov wrote to Ania< that in Odessa the weather was lovely, 12 [degrees] in shade, the ladies walk in light dresses—from there he went to Kiev—into snow. His regiment got only leave to the south, not to Tsarskoe Selo so his mother & sister arranged to meet him at Odessa.—I wonder when & where you see the first Siberian corps.—Goodbye Lovebird, God bless yr. journey & bring you safely to us. I cover you with tender kisses & remain yr. fondly loving old <u>Wify</u>. [P.S.] All the children kiss you warmly. [b]

No. 811.   Ts.[arist] Stavka. Feb. 6th 1916.
My own beloved Wify,
    I warmly thank you for yr. last two letters. I cannot understand what was wrong with you—I speak of the pains in yr. face. I hope they will be gone by the time I return, & that Aleksei's arms will be both better. Kiss him tenderly for me. After a lengthy & involved discussion with Alekseev, I have decided to put Kuropatkin in Plehve's place.—I know this will produce much rumour & criti-

cism,[218] but what can one do if there are so few good men? So I sent for him & told him about it yesterday. You ask about Ruzsky. He wrote a little while back, complaining of his health & saying that since October he has been unable to get rid of the polzuchii plevrit [creeping pleurisy]. I believe with God's help, Kuropatkin will be a good commander-in-chief. He will be directly under Stavka, & so will not have on his shoulders the same responsibility as in Manchuria. You can be quite sure the armies under his command will welcome the appointment. He spoke very well & judiciously of his new position, & will return here for the military conference. [a, b]

The sums received & spent by yr. [Red Cross] depot are enormous—I would have never expected them to reach such a size.[219] I look forward impatiently to to-morrow's review, at wh. I hope to see the first eight siberian regiments, with mine at the head. It snows to day & a strong wind is blowing.—If it would only stop for Sunday! May God bless you & the children. And so, in a day I will be able to press you to my heart, my dear child, my Sunny. I kiss all tenderly. Ever yr. own old   Nicky. [c]

218. Aleksei Kuropatkin (1848-1925) was Russian commander in the Far East during the Russo-Japanese War. He proved incompetent and resigned after Russia's defeat at Mukden. Alexandra doubted the wisdom of Kuropatkin's return to active service in 1914. (See Letter No. 469f.) It was incredible for Nicholas to make Kuropatkin commander of the n. Front. Kuropatkin was inactive during the Brusilov offensive, spring 1916. (Russia lacked a centralized command, so each commander was responsible for his own strategy and tactics.) Kuropatkin was replaced by Gen. Dragomirov in July 1916. Other commanders during the Brusilov offensive were P. A. Plehve (n.w. front), A. A. Brusilov (s.w. front) and A. E. Evert (w. front).

219. To give but one example of Alexandra's ability as an administrator, by late 1914, 85 hospitals operated under her patronage in the Petrograd area alone. Her work as a nurse, by contrast, was less valuable: if some of the wounded appreciated Alexandra's attentions, others were uncomfortable at being tended by the *empress*. (Massie, *Nicholas and Alexandra*, p. 308)

No. 812/ Telegram 35. Stavka> Tsarskoe Selo. 6 Feb 1916. 5.23> 6.10 p.m. To her majesty. Tender thanks [for] dear letter and Tatiana. Have written. Hope to return by 10 in the morning. Blowing, snowing, leave tonight. Fondest love [and] kisses. Niki

No. 813/ Telegram 29. Tsarskoe Selo> Seslavino. 7 Feb 1916. 2.09> 3.15 p.m. To his majesty. Heartily thank you for dear letter. [We] all warmly kiss [you]. [We] await to-morrow impatiently. Snowing. May God keep you. Alix

No. 814/ Telegram 59 in Russian. Polotsk> Tsarskoe Selo. 7 Feb 1916. 8.54> 9.25 p.m. To her majesty. Thank you for news. Am delighted with review of Siberian rifles. Road was difficult. Lots of snow, therefore am two and a half hours late. Warmly embrace [you]. Nikolai

No. 815/ Her No. 442.   Tsarskoe Selo. Feb. 10th 1916.
My own precious Sweetheart,

It has been such a gift this flying visit of yours, beloved one—& tho' we saw little of each other—yet I felt you were here. And your tender caresses have warmed me up again.—I can imagine the deep impression your presence at the

Duma & Council of the Empire[215] must have made on everybody—God grant that it will be a stimulant & make all work hard & in unity for the blessing & grandeur of our beloved country.—To see you, means so much!— You just found the right words.—We, Ania< & I, had gone through very trying days because of this story against our Friend<—& no man near to advise—but she was brave & good about it all—even stood a hideously rude talk with Voeikov on Monday. I really feel rather anxious about her now—as she saw through an ugly story one was trying to drag in Khvostov with—the jews—& just to make a mess before the Duma, so tendencious [sic] all.[220]—Seeing you— has given one again courage & strength as humanity is so low especially around us & the "rear" minds are ill still.—All my prayers & thoughts will surround you to-morrow—a great thing you are doing & such a wise one—& all the chiefs can speak out their thoughts honestly & give you a clear picture of everything [See Letter No. 804c above.] —God bless their work under yr. guidance. Sleep well, my Treasure—I shall miss you again most awfully—you brought such sunshine to me & I shall live in re-memberance of yr. sweet presence.   Soon again, lets hope, I shall have you home again.—God bless & protect you, my own Lovy dear, my husband, my Own—a thousand tender kisses fr. yr. very own little   Wify.

220. Details were now breaking of A. N. Khvostov's plot to kill Rasputin. Beletsky and other police officials had pretended to support the scheme, while avoiding actual involvement. Frustrated, Khvostov turned to an embezzler, a Red Cross official by the name of Boris Rzhevsky, who agreed to carry out Khvostov's plan and travelled to Norway to enlist the support of Rasputin's old enemy, Iliodor. Seeing an opportunity to expose Khvostov, Beletsky had Rzhevsky arrested when he re-turned to Russia on February 7/20, 1916. Khvostov and Beletsky were now open enemies; their charges and counter charges rocked the ministry of internal affairs. On March 2/15, 1916, Alexan-dra apologized to Nicholas for thrusting Khvostov upon him (Letter No. 838a)—though neither she nor her husband used the experience to reevaluate their method of appointing people to office. Nicholas dismissed A. N. Khvostov on March 3/16, 1916. The episode discredited Nicholas's re-gime. Before this, the tsar's ministers had been remote figures who reflected a bit of their master's grandeur. Khvostov now stood revealed as a common criminal. Nicholas's "mystique began to erode at this time," the "Khvostov scandal lowered the tsar's prestige in circles where he had not been criticized before." (Fuhrmann, *Rasputin*, pp. 175-176)

No. 816/ Her No. 443.   Tsarskoe Selo. Feb. 11th 1916.
My very own precious One,
   Bright & sunny, 12 degrees of frost. All my tenderest thoughts are with you, beloved Sweetheart, & I hope, the great military council will go off well & ac-cording to yr. wishes. [See Letter No. 804c.]—I can imagine how refreshed you will feel to be amongst military people, as these days here have not been of the pleasantest & you must have been delighted to get away again. You generally have some painful impressions here—Tuesday brought splendid good—& then that wretched story about our Friend<.[220] She [Anna Vyrubova] will try her best with him [i.e., Rasputin]—tho' in his present humour he screams at her & is so awfully nervous. But its sunny wheater [weather] & so, I hope, he will have changed again into what he always was. He is frightened to leave, says one will kill him—well, we shall see how God turns all! [a]
   All this gave you pain & worry & you could not get any joy out of yr. visit, beloved Sunshine—but you warmed up old Sunny & she feels your last kiss still

upon her lips! Yr. visit was like a dream—so empty now again!—I have nothing to tell you yet to-day. Yesterday evening we worked, laid patiences & [daughters] T.[atiana] or A.[nastasia] read aloud "Ours Ab.[road]"[221]—but my thoughts were with you & not in the book.—Precious Sweetheart, I must get up now as Prince Golitzin [N. D. Golitsyn] comes at 12½ with his doklad [report] about our prisoners, & after luncheon Vil'chkovsky<. Goodbye & God bless you my own Love. I cover you with kisses & remain, Ever yr. very own <u>Wify</u>. [b]

221. Reference is to "Nashi za granitsei" (Ours Abroad), a humorous tale by Nicholas Alexandrovich Leikin.

No. 817/ Telegram 57. Tsarskoe Selo> Stavka. 11 Feb 1916. 1.50> 3.00 p.m. To his majesty. Sun, 12 deg. frost.[I] miss [you] very much. In thoughts together. Hope all goes well. Bow to all. [We] all kiss and embrace you. Alix

---

No. 818/ Telegram 44. Stavka> Tsarskoe Selo. 11 Feb 1916. 4.52> 5.17 p.m. To her majesty. Arrived at 4. Was met by all commanding generals. Council begins at 6 o'clock. Fine, cold, sunny weather. Thanks so much for dear letter last evening. Tender kisses. Niki

---

No. 819/ No. 444.   Tsarskoe Selo. Feb. 12th 1916.
My own Sweetheart,
   A bright, sunny morning, 7 degrees of frost, last night 12. I wonder how the generals all spoke—nice they met you. So refreshing such talks, however serious & difficult they may be. But I hope that they are contented on the whole with the amunition [sic], or is there still a great scarcity of rifles? [a]
   I had a nice long letter from Victoria<, she is now in London—Ludwig[, prince of Battenburg] & Louise are going north to see Georgie[, prince of Battenburg] & she will go later. They have been having great gales & very cold weather & when the "New Zealand" was out cruising last month, the sea washed right over her & one wave came into Georgie'[s] turret through the gun openings & washed one of his men down a liftshaft & Georgie had to crawl in after him & found him wedged in at the bottom halfdrowned & with his legs broken. Some of the sailors have been allowed to go & see the fighting in France & a ship's corporal of the N. Z., who was of the lot, was in a trench, when a German mine exploded under it & killed the men of the machinegun— whereupon the bluejackets promptly manned it under their corporal & did such good work, that he has been decorated & the ship is very proud of him.—Dickie [Ludwig-Frantsisk] & the cadets of his term are not to go straight to sea after easter, but to the engineering college at Kegham (Plymouth) first. The best 26 or 30 of them will go to sea in June, & as his place in the term [i.e., team] is about 15-th always, he hopes to be one of the lot. Of course he is disappointed at the delay, but I feel selfishly grateful for it. [b]
   Alice writes that the english are liked at Salonica, the officers are courteous, the men well behaved; with the french, I am sorry to say, she says it is the other way round, & in one small town they have behaved as horribly to the women, as the Germans in Belgium, whilst the officers at Salonica, from the general

downwards, are insolent & rude even to Andrea [Prince Andrew of Greece].—Louise is enjoying her holiday at home, she will probably go back to Nevers at the end of this month.—Sandro is at the Headquarters? Little Marie< lunches with us to-day & before & after I have [to] receive. Precious Treasure, Goodbye & God bless you, many a tender, longing kiss fr. yr. deeply loving old wife Alix. [c]

No. 820.   Ts.[arist] Stavka. Feb. 12th 1916.
My own dearest One,
   Warm thanks for your dear letter—the first I received here. I am returning the french book; I read the new english one greedily when there is time. The journey was absolutely quiet. I insisted our train not exceed 40 versts per hour [26.5 mph]. Four commanders met me at the platform.[218] I saw Alekseev a minute, then at 6 went to staff quarters, where the conference dragged on till 8 & continued right after dinner until nearly 12.30. Poor Plehve seemed like a dead man, he was so pale. Today he is lying in his sleeping car and is unable to move—probably over-fatigued! In general, I am well pleased with the results of our long meeting. They[218] argued a lot with each other. I asked them all to speak out, as truth is of utmost significance in such important matters. I prefer not to write on this, but will tell you all about it when we meet. It is very cold & windy. I must end. God bless you, my dear! I kiss you & the dear children tenderly. Ever yr. own old Nicky.

No. 821/ Telegram 62. Tsarskoe Selo> Stavka. 12 Feb 1916. 4.50> 5.15 p.m.
To his majesty. Sunny morning. Marie< lunched with us. Received. In thoughts always together. We all warmly kiss and embrace [you]. This evening will see Lili Den< and her husband. Alix

No. 822/ Telegram 48. Stavka> Tsarskoe Selo. 12 Feb 1916. 6.58> 7.42 p.m.
To her majesty. Best thanks for letter and wire. Council was over after midnight. Pleased with result. Cold, windy. Tenderest kisses. Niki

No. 823/ Her No. 445.   Ts.[arskoe] Selo. Feb. 13th 1916.
My own Sweetheart,
   2 degrees of frost & gently snowing. I happily sleep well now, wh. is a rare treat—also cough a little like Baby<.—Saw Neklyudov yesterday—he speaks alright, only from time to time becomes an affected diplomate, wh. is distractingly aggravating. Then I saw Dr. Brunner who gave me an account of how the German & Austrian [prisoners] are kept in Siberia—satisfactorily! Then a Psse Francoise Woroniecka [Voronetskaya] (born Krassinsky) who organised [sic] many hospitals at Varsovie [Warsaw] & got the medal there. Now her hospitals are doing well and she travels and inspects them. Her husband & 2 sons remained at Varsovie & she rarely has any news of them. She seems most energetic, tho' looks rosy, plump & comfortable in highest narrowest heals & funny little cap to her sister's dress.—To-day I have Pss. Gedroits<— probably to grumble.—Lili D.[ehn] & husband came for an hour & evening tea—she is a real dear

& so amusing always—but his foolish laugh [is] rather trying.—Is he going to receive [command of] the "Variag" [cruiser <u>Varangian</u>]? I am so glad that you are contented with the result of the military council—it is a beautiful thing that you called them all & gave them the chance to speak together in your presence.—Little Marie< lunched with us, looks quite well, only covered in pimples—she says Dmitri< arrives to-morrow—pitty [sic], as he will get into a bad set again & ways. How I wish somebody wld. speak to him seriously—I know N.P.< did many a time & kept him several times fr. evening escapades—the boy behaves according to the person whom he for the moment cares for. [a, b]

The oftener I think about Boris<, the more I realise [sic] what an awful set his wife wld. be dragged into. His & Miechen's< friends, rich french people, russian bankers, "the society", Olga Orlov & the Bielos. & all such types—intrigues without end—fast manners & conversations & Ducky< not a suitable sister in-law at all—& then Boris'[s] mad past. Miechen gave into U.[ncle] Wladimir's ways so as to share all together, but she found pleasure in that life—with her nature that was easy.—Well, why do I write about this, when you know it as well as I do. So give over a well used half worn out, blase young man, to a pure, fresh young girl 18 years his junior & to live in a house in wh. many a woman has "shared" his life. Only a "woman" who knows the world & can judge & choose with eyes open, ought to be his wife & she wld. know how to hold him & make a good husband of him. But an inexperienced young girl would suffer terribly, to have her husband 4, 5-th hand or more—a woman could put up with this of course easier if she loved.—Therefore Dmitri ought to be held tight in hand by you too & explained what married life means. Now I must end.—Goodbye my Angel, my Lovebird. Holy Angels guard you—God bless you. Endlessly tender, yearning kisses fr. yr. very loving old <u>Wify</u>.   [P.S.] In the Duma one makes horrid speeches—but they fall flat, nobody picks them up. Purishkevich made an awful one—why to be so mad always. But you brought great good there, as the speeches have <u>no</u> effect. [c]

No. 824.   Ts.[arist] Stavka. Feb. 13th 1916.
My own beloved Sunny-dear,

The messenger has not yet arrived. I finished my papers, & therefore have more time for a letter. Today is the feast day of my lancers—they are resting some place in southern galicia. In honour of the day, I promoted Zamoisky aide-de-camp. I inherited him from Nikolasha<, he was attached to him as orderly. There has been much bother these recent days, especially for me. First, the conference, wh. lasted 6 hrs. At the same time, I had to speak seriously with several of the generals, to receive Sandro< with a long doklad [report], Boris< after his inspection, Polivanov & ad.[miral] Phillimore, who has returned fr. Arkhangelsk. Yesterday Dmitry< appeared unexpectedly, passing through on a 10-day leave. I will see him for a little while this afternoon. [a]

Sandro is in fine form. He goes home for five days—I will try to see him. [My sister] Olga writes she is leaving Kiev for a few days to visit her regiment, as she does not have much to do at this time. When free, I enjoy reading "The Room of Secrets" [by William le Queux]. It often reminds me of a book we read together. For the last two days, the weather has not been favourable for long walks—a strong wind blows with frost & snow, so I was forced to walk in the tiny garden!!! Poor little me!!! They just brought me yr. dear scented letter & [daughter] Olga's.—I thank you warmly for them & for the interesting news from Victoria's< letter. The scent excites me & brings wonderful memories; it quite drew me to you! I must end now. I hope you feel better. God bless you & the children! I kiss you tenderly. Your old Nicky. [P.S.] Give her [Anna Vyrubova] my greetings. [b]

No. 825/ Telegram 63. Tsarskoe Selo> Stavka. 13 Feb 1916. 6.50> 7.14 p.m. To his majesty. Tender thanks for letter. How gratifying to receive news. We all warmly kiss [you]. May God keep you. Sleep peacefully. Mild weather. Alix

---

No. 826/ Telegram 51. Stavka> Tsarskoe Selo. 13 Feb 1916. 7.23> 7.40 p.m. To her majesty. Tender thanks for letter. Just came back from church. Dmitry< took tea before leaving for home. Loving kisses to all. Niki

---

No. 827/ Her No. 446.   Ts.[arskoe] S[elo]. Feb. 14th 1916.
My very Own,
    Your sweet letter made me intensely happy & I read it over many a time & tenderly kissed each page wh. yr. dear hand had touched. I am a foolish old woman, yes? But a deeply loving one who sorely misses her Sweetheart. Poor Pleve, fancy his having become such a wretched little being—before the war he was already pityful [sic] to behold. I am glad that they all spoke themselves well out & even squabbled—its the very best thing & clears up all misunderstandings & pictures the caracters [sic] far better. [See Letters No. 820a,b, 822, 824a.] The big girls< go to a concert in our hospital<, & the 3 youngest [children] to Ania's< refuge [home] this afternoon for a concert & old Davidov wanted to come too, so as to see Baby<. Her Parents [A. S. Taneev and his wife Nadezhda] will also be there, so as to cheer them up, after a vile letter her mother got fr. Mme Rodzianko full of vilest abuse of Ania. And Nik. Dm. D.[emenkov] & Irina Tolstoy, Vl. Nik.< & Mr. Zhilik<. I cannot go, am not famous, cough rather & [have a temperature of] 37.3 this morning—to catch things without going out is really too bad.—Greyish morning calm, 3½ degrees of frost.— I receive then people. [a, b]
    Poor Isa< is very depressed as one wrote nasty things about her Father in the papers—my ex Stern [E. K. Shtein, formerly an officer in Alexandra's Crimean Cavalry Regiment], they also accuse of being a spy—& altogether I find people somewhat unbalanced, to say it gently.—Mme Zizi< is still not yet fit to come out here.—I got the [F]rench book alright—when you finish the English one, I can send another. Such innocent lecture [i.e., literature] is a rest to the tired brain & gives one other thoughts.—I hope you will get some good walks again. Have you arranged about yr. aide-de-camp doing two weeks service at the Headquarters? Now whilst things are calmer you could get commanders of regiments even, tho' there are scarcely any more. But it would be a great gain to you, they could tell you many truths wh. the generals even don't know, & I am sure be of help to you. And all will try their best & work harder, if they know that one of

their officers will be at the Headquarters & have to answer frankly to all yr. questions. They notice more things than others do—& then it is a constant living link with the army.—Aleksei got a wire fr. Eristov fr. yr. lancers.—Now, my Sweetheart, I must end my letter. God Almighty bless & protect you. I cover my Huzy love with fond kisses. Ever yr. old   Sunny.   [P.S.] The Children kiss you very tenderly. [c, d]

No. 828/ Telegram 66. Tsarskoe Selo> Stavka. 14 Feb 1916. 2.30> 2.53 p.m. To his majesty. Just received your precious letter. Tenderly thank you for it. We all kiss you. [We] are lunching, then they will go to concert. Weather grey. [My] health not famous. May God bless you. Alix

---

No. 829/ Telegram 53. Stavka> Tsarskoe Selo. 14 Feb 1916. 6.20> 7.10 p.m. To her majesty. Loving thanks [for] dear letters. Had no time to write to day Sossy.[222] Took a good walk out of town. Cold, bright, sun. Kiss all tenderly. Niki

222. "Sossy" may be Queen Sophia of Greece or perhaps the tsar intended to write "Sunny," one of his nicknames for his wife.

No. 830/ Her No. 447.   Tsarskoe Selo. Feb. 15th 1916.
My very own Beloved!
    Ever such tender thanks for yr. sweet letter, I received yesterday. You have indeed had busy days & I am glad you at last got a good walk yesterday to freshen you up.—Fancy only, Esi[223] lunches with us to-day! I have not seen him since he left for the war, & he asked to present himself as G.[eneral-]a.d.c., so I thought better to invite him to luncheon. It will be rather stiff work making him talk, & without you to help me.— [a]
    A glorious sunny morning, 8 degrees of frost. A.[nia]< begs me to go out every day, but I know it wld. be folly with my cough. Did not sleep very well as it disturbed me. Sometimes don't cough for long & then it goes off again, just like Baby<. [Daughter] Marie has a cold.—To-day they all go to the big palace< to see small theatricals for the wounded—"Krivoye Zerkalo" [The Distorting Mirror]. Old Goremykin was with me yesterday. I gave him all the news I have of you, & [he] was happy to hear of yr. military Council [See Letters No. 820a,b, 822, 824a.] His wife had just been taking leave of her "hospital" when she got an access at the heart [heart attack] from emotion, & they had to leave her the night there—poor old people, I am so sorry for them. He looks alright, but the first days he had suddenly no work to do, he was in a constant half sleep—after the great strain of these heavy months. When he says goodbye, it always seems to me that he thinks it may be the last time that he sees one—at least the kind old eyes have that look. [b]
    The French are having a hard time round Verdun, God grant them luck, how one longs for them & the English at last to advance.—What was Fillimore's [Phillimore's] impression of Arkhangelsk? Does he now realise [sic] our diffi- cult position there & does he find one is working hard? A foreign critical eye can always be of use.—Zuev comes to-day, as he leaves on Wednesday for

England-France.—Emma Fr.< was at Sashka's< marriage, says the bride's profile is pretty, en face the nose too aquashed [flattened], fine eyes, very black hair—not tall & plump.—Irina (Drina)< came to me in despair that O. Lamkert has been told to leave after all these years.[224] The money affairs he put into splendid order, after having received his place wh. was deeply indebted. Sturmer comes with his own candidate (Gurlin I think or Gurland), who has already much work to do, so wont be able even personally to lead this.[224] If I see Shakhovskoy (?) whom I expect to ask to be received because of the supreme Counc.[il], I shall ask him about it.—I am glad you like my nicely scented letters—I want them to remind you of your old girly who longs for you so much, so much!—In thoughts I tenderly press you to my heart, hold you tightly in my embrace & cover your sweet face with loving kisses & caresses.—Now goodbye my Lovebird. Ever so many blessings & kisses fr. yr. own old Alix.   [P.S.]   Been reading through some of my letters to Sonia< & tearing them up—quite like diaries & bring back the past so vividly. To-morrow would have been her birthday. [d]

223. Reference is to Michael Georgievich, duke of Mecklenburg-Streletsk, adj.-gen., lt.-gen., former commander of the First Artillery Brigade; before and at the beginning of the war assigned to ministry of war, then promoted to inspector of the Artillery Corps.

224. O. I. Lamkert was a member of the Supreme Council for Press Affairs. I. Ya. Gurland was important in the ministry of internal affairs under Stolypin, editing the semi-official newspaper *Russia* from 1907. His importance declined after Stolypin's murder in 1911. As governor of Yaroslavl, Sturmer knew and respected Gurland; when Sturmer became chairman of the council of ministers, Gurland returned to importance, becoming a member of the council of the ministry of internal affairs. Gurland emigrated after the March Revolution.

No. 831.   Ts.[arist] Stavka. Feb. 15th 1916.
My own darling One,

I thank you warmly for yr. dear letters—my old heart beats faster every time I open & read them. All is totally quiet here now. All plans for the coming[225] are ready & now being placed into execution—so Alekseev has suggested I go home.—I leave Wednesday afternoon & hope to return [home] on Thursday at 11.o['clock] in the morning.—will stay a week & half. Will that not be splendid, darling? Just now, after lunch, I found yr. letter No. 446 on my table, & thank you most warmly for it. How tiresome that you have a cough & a temperature of 37.3! Why? [a]

This morning, after I got up, I allowed Botkin to sound & examine me.—He asked to do it here, as there is more time here—he had not examined me like this since the Crimea. He found everything in order, the heart even better than last time! Strange! Georgi< has arrived, but I have not yet seen him since his train was late.   Sir Arthur Paget comes to-morrow, & will present me the Field-Marshal's baton. [See Letters No. 689 and 691b.] I have asked all the eng.[lish] officers staying here to be present at this little ceremony. I received Georgie's [King George V's] letter before—it was brought by Gen. [John Hanbury-]Williams, who saw Paget in Petrograd. Now, my dear Wify, I must end this, my last letter. God bless you all! [I] warmly embrace & kiss [you]. Yr. old Nicky. [b]

225. Nicholas might have written a word such as "attack" or "offensive" here, but he did not do so. The tsar was referring to what would prove to be the greatest Russian effort of the war, the Brusilov offensive in the spring of 1916.

No. 832/ Telegram 73. Tsarskoe Selo> Stavka. 15 Feb 1915. 2.55> 3.07 p.m. To his majesty. Very sunny day, 8° frost in morning. Iza [apparently this should read "Esi," see Letter No. 830a] lunched with us. [We] all tenderly kiss you. May the Lord keep you. Alix

---

No. 833/ Telegram 57. Stavka> Tsarskoe Selo. 15 Feb 1916. 6.28> 6.59 p.m. To her majesty. Fondest thanks [for] dear letters and wire. To-morrow [you] will get my letter which may give you pleasure I hope. Lovely, sunny, frosty. Took a long walk. Tender kisses. Niki

---

No. 834/ Her No. 448.   Tsarskoe Selo. Feb. 16th 1916.
My own Sweetheart,
   A bright, sunny morning again, there were 6 degrees of frost. I dont venture on to the balkony [sic] yet, because of my cough.—At 12½ I have Witte with his doklad [report], then after luncheon still people & at 6—Sturmer. To-day would have been Sonia's< birthday —so sad, I have not once been to her grave.—Yesteday evening we had A. P. Sablin, he was not in the least bit shy & quite natural. He returns to-morrow again to the terrible mud of Proskurovo—he talked away cheerily.—[Daughter] Olga made nonsence [sic], sitting on a tiny table, until she happily smashed it. Its so funny, he has some of his brother's [N. P. Sablin's] movements; a refreshing change to see him, as one dries up in sorrows & worries.— [a]
   I am eagerly awaiting yr. letter, wh. you wired about—does it bring news of your return, that would indeed be lovely; me wants Sweetheart badly.—Mme Zizi< is still not famous [i.e., does not feel well], went out in town< in a close carriage, & felt worse after. I must stop a little, my eyes ache, as I have written a long letter to Victoria< for Zuev to take to-morrow.—Excuse my dull letters, Lovy, but life is very monotonous & I myself am not of the gayest—& what I hear is nothing to cheer one up.—It will be interesting to hear fr. you, your opinion upon the Generals & what was spoken of & settled. I long to hear about military things, of wh. I of course cannot [hear], except from you.—Just got yr. sweetest letter, a big kiss for it. So this is my last. Oh what joy! Thursday home again, this is indeed splendid news—to-morrow just a week you left us. How good to have you back, & the children are free the last 3 days so will be wild of joy you are home & I hope Baby< can go out by then again. Wish you heartily a good journey. God bless & protect you. Cover you with kisses. Ever yr. own old <u>Wify</u>. [b]

No. 835/ Telegram 74. Tsarskoe Selo> Stavka. 16 Feb 1916. 1.15> 1.37 p.m. To his majesty. Just now received your dear letter with joyful news. No words to express how happy I am. Clear, cold weather. [We] all warmly kiss and embrace [you]. Alix

No. 836/ Telegram 60. Stavka> Tsarskoe Selo. 16 Feb 1916. 7.48> 8.35 p.m.
To her majesty. Fondest thanks [for] dear letters. Just received Sir A. Paget with
the baton. Had cinema in the theater [spelled according to U.S. usage] for girls.
[It] was nice. Tender love to all. Niki

No. 837/ Telegram 77. Tsarskoe Selo> Stavka. 17 Feb 1916. 12.45> 1.25 p.m.
To his majesty. Tenderly embrace and wish [you] a good trip. Clear, sunny.
Marie< and Dmitri< will have lunch with us. [We] warmly kiss [you]. With joy-
ful impatience we await to-morrow. Alix

No. 838/ Telegram 63. Stavka> Tsarskoe Selo. 17 Feb 1916. 2.35> 3.06 p.m.
To her majesty. Tender thanks [for] dear letters. Leaving at 4 o'clock. Bright
cold weather. Over happy to meet [you] soon. Loving kisses. Niki

No. 839/ Her No. 449.   Ts.[arskoe] S[elo]. March 2nd 1916.
My own Sweetheart,
   I cannot tell you what joy it has been to have you here, tho' to you it brought
again worry without end & was tiring. Its hard you cant come home to feel
quiet, but on the contrary—therefore I have even to be glad for you when you
leave. Such a blessing we could go to Holy Communion together.—These last
days my horrid pains cretinised me, so that I was good for nothing—& many a
question before parting I should have liked to touch, & could not remember
them.—[a]
   Am so wretched that we, through Gregory recommended [A. N.] Khvostov to
you—it leaves me not peace—you were against it & I let myself be imposed upon
by them, tho' fr. the very first told A.[nia]< that I like his great energy but that
too selflove & something not pleasing to me; & the devil got hold of him, one
cannot call it otherwise. I wld. not write to you about it last time not to bother
you—but we passed through trying times, & therefore wld. have been calmer if,
now that you go, something could be settled. As long as Khvostov is in power
and has money & police in hands—I honestly am not quiet for Gregory &
Ania.[201] Dear me, how weary one is! Your beloved presence & tender caresses
soothe me & I dread your departure. Do remember to keep our Friend's< Image
[i.e., the icon Rasputin gave you] near you as a blessing for the coming "move
forwards"[225]—oh how I wish we were always together, to share all, see all! Such
an anxious time is ahead! And when we shall meet again—is a vague thing. All
my prayers will incessantly follow you, sweetest love. God bless you & yr.
work & every undertaking & crown it with success. The good will come & [i.e.,
if] you are patient & [you] will be blessed, I feel so sure, only much to be gone
through still. When I know what the "losses" of lives mean to yr. heart—I can
imagine Ernie's< suffering now. Oh this hideously bloody war!—Excuse bad
writing, but head & eyes ache & heart feels weak after all this pain. [b, c]
   Oh Lovy mine, beloved, precious Sunshine—its so depressing when you
go—you are yet far more lonely, so I ought not to complain—but to feel yr. sweet
being near me is such a consolation & calm.—Goodbye Sweetheart, love of my
soul—God Almighty bless & protect you & keep you fr. all harm, guard & guide

you on all yr. ways & bless all yr. undertakings. May He help you find a good successor to Kh.[vostov] too [as minister of the interior], so that you should have one worry less.—Farewell Sunshine. I hold you tightly clasped in my arms & cover you with tender kisses. Beloved, & remain yr. very own girly, Wify. [P.S.] Am glad S. Petr. [Fedorov] is with you—prefer him to all the rest who accompany you & good Mord.[vinov] too. N.P.< also became good friends with Fed.[orov]< just because he is so devoted to you—Voeikov is selfsure & gets blown about by the wind sometimes, [if it] is better for him personally [i.e., if he has a personal, greedy interest in the matter]. Thank you over & over again for all yr. love, wh. is my life. [d]

No. 840/ Telegram 4 in Russian. Tsarskoe Selo> Rzhev, Tversk. 2 Mar 1916. 7.30> 9.20 p.m. To his majesty. Very sad in the soul, empty. All warmly embrace you, sleep well. Do not feel very famous, on sopha during day. May God keep you. Bow to S. Nik.[226] Alix

226. Alexandra meant to write "S. Pet." since she is referring to Sergei Petrovich Fedorov, M.D. See Letter No. 840d.

No. 841/ Telegram 18 in Russian. Likhoslavl> Tsarskoe Selo. 2 Mar 1916. 9.20> 9.55 p.m. To the sovereign empress. In thoughts am with you all. Heartily thank you for letter. Read a lot. Good night. Warmly embrace [you]. Niki

---

No. 842/ Telegram 7. Tsarskoe Selo> Stavka. 3 Mar 1916. 12.52> 1.10 p.m. To his majesty. Fairly mild weather. Slept well. Pain not so bad but still feel abominable. Very lonesome, miss you terribly. Children healthy. [We] warmly embrace and kiss [you]. Alix

---

No. 843/ Her No. 450.   Ts.[arskoe] S[elo]. March 3rd 1916.
My very own Sweetheart,

Oh its lonely without you & I miss you awfully. So sad to wake up & find an empty place beside me. Thanks tenderly for yr. evenings telegram. How melancholy without you, every moment you expect you to drop in!—I slept well, the effect of the medicine still acts,—& I feel my heart not nice in consequence. Vl. Nik.< continues electrifying the face. The pains only come from time to time, but I feel rather gid[d]y & nasty & have to eat carefully, not to bring on the pains in my jaw. [Daughters] O.[lga] & A.[nastasia] have Becker<.—A.[nia]< coughs worse, so remains home & will only come in the afternoon, wh. is much wiser. Here is a petition fr. the Athos monks living at Moscou [sic]. I send it [to] you, hoping you will forward it to Volzhin with a strong resolution upon it, that you insist (once more) that all are to be allowed to take Holy Communion & that the priest may personally serve. Volzhin is somewhat a coward, so you personally write your order, not a wish, upon the petition. Its shameful to get on as one does with them. You remember Metr.[opolitan] Makari allowed it them & you too,—& the Synod of course protested.[227] [a, b]

N.P.< just telephoned to A.< that he arrived this morning & leaves again this evening,—so will come to us this afternoon; is in despair you have left, as came for affairs with the 6 officers for the "Variag" [cruiser <u>Varangian</u>]. Seems in a wretched state, that had to give up good officers & 400 men, things all must better be finished off, that cannot continue [to] command the battalion with again less officers & men. He goes to talk to Kiryll<. I shall have a good talk with him, as I think all can be managed, tho' I understand its more than depressing when you have well organised [sic] a thing, to have to break it up again. I personally find they ought to talk to Grigorovich< & both go straight off to you & explain matters & ask yr. wishes. I shall do my best to quieten him. I felt it wld. be so, when you told me of it a few weeks ago. Already then they lacked officers & how they have to give up their best,—but as they are in the reserve they wld. have time to get & prepare men fr. here, only where to get the officers from. A sort of bad luck & preventing them going with the guard.—[c]

I shall tell you all to-morrow after have seen him.—The Children are alright [sic]. Sturmer has asked to see me on Saturday,—he asked through A. & told her that all is now in his hands,—nothing is of course as yet in the papers [about Sturmer replacing Goremykin as chairman of the council of ministers].—How are you getting on with the book, is it not exciting,—it was so sad & dull without your reading yesterday.—I see your beloved, sad eyes still before me, when you left,—its an awful wrench each time. O Lovy, thanks again & again for all yr. tender caresses wh. warmed me up & were such a consolation. The heart is so heavy & sad & when phisically [sic] run down, one gets yet more depressed. I try not to show it to others.—Very mild to-day again. Sweetheart, I must say Goodbye now & God bless you. I cover you with tender kisses & remain your fondly loving, endlessly devoted, own old   <u>Sunny</u>. [P.S.] A. is sad she never had an occasion to see you alone,— personally I think she gets calmer & more normal, less aggressive when she has less chance [to see you],—because the more one has, the more one wants,—if you need talks, then of course its another thing. But she gets over those things much better now,—you have trained her & in consequence her temper is calmer & we have no stories. She was killing [i.e., talked amusingly] about telephones & visits & stories about our Friend<, flinging her stick about the room & laughing—Oh now I long for you!!! [d]

227. Curtiss, *Church and State*, pp. 356-357, discusses this controversy among the Russian monks at Mt. Athos, the international center of Eastern Orthodox monasticism. These monks developed heretical notions about the meaning of God's name. Rasputin supported them and apparently influenced the empress in their favor.

No. 844/ Telegram 1. Stavka> Tsarskoe Selo. 3 Mar 1916. 3.40> 4.10 p.m. To her majesty. Arrived and travelled well. Rather cold in the night. Here quite mild. Finished book to day. Feel lonely, but well. Tenderest, fondest kisses and thanks for wire. Niki

---

No. 845.   Ts.[arist] Stavka. March 3rd 1916.
My own precious darling,
    Yr. telegram, in wh. you said you slept well & yr. face had not ached much, consoled me greatly, as I was worried at leaving you in such a condition! The trip was good, but I felt so tired in the train yesterday that I remained lying down

in my compartment till tea, & after dinner I read this interesting book.—After sleeping for 10 hours yesterday, I feel well again today. This morning, passing thru Orsha, I inspected an echelon of the guard of the Litovsky reg.[iment] wh. goes north; they jumped fr. the carriages, & I walked around them twice. Such fine fellows! I arrived here at 2.45, & was met by the usual public, including the new governor—Yavlensky—who made a good impression on me! From 3.15 till 5.15 I was busy with Alekseev, who thanks you very much. He showed me that nearly everything is ready for our offensive.[225] I talked for a long time with gen. Palitsyn, whom Nikolasha< has sent here. He understands quite well that we cannot spare troops for the caucasus. Now, my dear, I wish you good night and pleasant dreams. [a]

4 March. Only three of the foreigners appeared at dinner; old Pau is laid up with rheumatism, the others have gone away. Georgi< arrived here a few hours before me. Sergei< is not here. There was 1 deg. of frost last night; it thawed during the day. The weather is the same as at home, & everything is covered with a light mist. Last night I played dominoes for an hour; the Admiral [Nilov] was very charming & modest this time! Only this moment, returning fr. lunch, I received your dear letter with the pretty postcard & a letter from [daughter] Marie. Now I am going for a drive in the motor along the high road. It is thawing & dull. Be well. God bless you, my beloved Sunny! I kiss you & the dear children tenderly. Give A.[nia]< my greetings. Ever yr. own old hubby   Nicky. [b]

No. 846/ Her No. 471.   Ts.[arskoe] S[elo]. March 4th 1916.
My very own Sweetheart,

I can imagine how lonely you must feel again at Moghilev, poor Sweetums,—wify too misses you terribly.—I am glad you also found mild weather there. Is the book not palpitatingly interesting; when you return again you must finish reading it aloud.—Well, N.P.< came in the evening. They [Sablin and Kirill<] had a long & serious talk & now go to you to ask for the decision. Over 400 men have been taken—the lists sent fr. here, so that the best men who are accustomed to the Machineguns are taken,—to form new ones takes a long time. But with the men things could be arranged, if it were not, that in a month one will again take 400 away for the "Svetlana", then the work is bitterly hard—to form all well & then have it picked all to pieces. You gave the order 6 officers were to be given to the battalion—they never were, & 6 have instead now been taken, so that now Babys< midshipmen command the companies—they know nothing & the sailors of many years service know better than them & can find fault & judge all their actions. Voronov is to replace Popov here—Koshevn. [Kozhevnikov], senior officer [on the] "Variag" [cruiser Varangian]—[and junior officers] Kublitsky, Taube, Lukin. I forget the other two. Like that the battalion cannot remain, as it will not be what it was, & not what you could expect it to be. So you will have to decide (don't ask the ramoli< Admiral's [Nilov's] advice as he councils badly)—better now give away the men already for the "Svetlana" & then have two small battalions, wh. anybody can command & wh. won't have much significance. Its a sad thing after puting [sic] one's soul into a work to have it picked to pieces. N.P. of course brought the officers, & men all as ordered. The men of course are enchanted to go, a comfortable ship, no marching & much better pay. For them its harder serving now in the army with smaller rations after what they were accustomed to for years—in the army most men are new & young. Therefore they need also older officers to keep them in hand & explain things.—I only tell you this as I see how terribly it has worried N.P. He is quiet & sad & awaits yr. decision when they come & what will become of him too. [a, b]

I asked about Lyalin. Kirill< is also in despair the Admiral [Nilov] recommended him. When Miass.-Ivanov [S. V. Myasoedov-Ivanov] wrote & asked L.[yalin] to join the battalion, as they needed him, he declined as got more pay & prefered [sic] the ship in the black sea or living without work in town. They were horrified with him. And he, who was in no far before, now did nothing, received such a splendid nomination. N.P. you remember one said was too young to receive [command of] the [royal yacht] Standart, tho' had been in the war & had commanded the "Oleg" during some time & was yr. aide-de-camp—Saltanov or Den< were far more worthy of it. Now she [the *Standard*] does not go to sea. Kirill & all hoped Shir.[insky]-Shakhmatov wld. be named as such an excellent man, but the Admiral [Nilov] hates him. Alas, more than ever one feels the admiral takes no interest in the crew how much he could have helped,—& he does the contrary & presents the things to you as he chooses. I wish you had another in his place; and he dislikes Grigorovich< as much as Kedrov hates him [Nilov] too. Very interesting all N.P. told about where they stand—they followed the "Preobr"<—he left Wednesday evening & arrived Thursday morning here.—I felt all this would come when you told me about the "Variag". He returns this evening to Rezhitsa & probably fr. there to you & meets K.[irill] Tuesday. Css. Kleinmichel who married the Dr. came to A.[nia]< looking young & handsome. I am really anxious about A.; once a man[220] was capable to try & buy others to kill our Fr.< he is capable of revenging himself upon her. She had an awful row by telephone with Greg.[ory]< for not having gone [to visit Him] to-day,—but I entreated her not to—besides she has a terrible cough & Mme B.< Then the woman[228a] came & made a scene to her for not going to town< & He [Rasputin] sort of predicts something is going to happen to her wh. certainly makes her yet more nervous. [c, d]

This war has made everything topsy turvy & turned all minds.—I saw by the papers you have said Sukhom.[linov] is to be judged [i.e. tried],—thats right,—have his aiguillettes been taken fr. him. One says there will come out bad things against him,—that he took bribes,—thats her [his wife] for sure,—its so sad. Dear me, what bad luck one has, no "gentlemen", thats what it is—no decent bringing up & inner development & princip[al]s wh. one can rely upon.—One gets so bitterly disappointed in Russian people,—they are so far behind[;] still we know such masses & yet when one has to choose a minister,—none is capable to hold such a post.— Remember about [dismissing Minister of War] Polivanov. [e]

Have you talked with Fed.[orov], wld. be interesting for you—he is so devoted & he has nothing to gain, has received all & can have no higher position to aim after.—A mild day again.—Have been reading through heap of papers from Rostovtsev< & feel cretinised. My head & eyes became weaker since these pains, the jaw is so heavy & pains still continue, tho' at times almost pass,—but it makes me feel good for nothing. How does Po [Pau] look upon the state of affairs in France? Oh, my precious One, all my thoughts are with you & tenderest prayers. Lonely without sweet Huzy dear's caresses.—I hope you can take good walks. [f]

N.P. enjoyed riding a good deal. They stand in the different villages all about, he is lodged in a splendid house of a millionaire—friend of M. Ivanov—beautiful rooms, hothouse, garden, stables, carriages—watched fishing with the nets under the ice.—I said goodbye to a young wounded officer who returns to his regiment. Now I have no more news to give you. I wrote out our conversation for you to have an idea in yr. head when they [Sablin and Kirill] come to you next week for yr. decision—one thing well done better than many bits unsatisfactorily—well, they will tell you all their ideas & you will know what is best.—Goodbye my Sweet One, God bless & protect & help you in all your decisions & undertakings. Fondest, tenderest kisses fr. yr. very own old Wify.   [P.S.] Bow to Fedorov & Mordvinov if you have an occasion. Mr. Dodd's book is an example of how history is made? [g]

228a. One of Rasputin's lady followers, probably Akilina Laptinskaya.

No. 847/ Telegram 9. Tsarskoe Selo> Stavka. 4 Mar 1916. 2.40> 3.03 p.m. To his majesty. Mild weather. [My] face not yet quite normal. Am writing daily. My thoughts follow you with tenderness. Remember A.[unt] Olga< tomorrow —day of death of U.[ncle] Willi<. All are healthy. [We] all warmly kiss and embrace [you]. Alix

No. 848/ Telegram 3. Stavka> Tsarskoe Selo. 4 Mar 1916. 6.33> 6.55 p.m. To her majesty. Tender thanks [for] dearest letter, also for [daughter] Marie's long one. Have written. Had a good walk. Weather mild, grey. Loving kisses to all. Niki

No. 849/ Her No. 452.   Ts.[arskoe] S[elo]. March 5th 1916.
My Sweetheart,

Very tenderly do I press you to my loving old heart wh. is ever full of deepest love and yearning. Thats good you took a nice walk, it will make you feel much fresher, and the time will pass quicker. Are you reading now the french book "La Dame au parfum"? I had a collection of English ones brought me to-day, but I fear there is nothing very interesting amongst them. No great authors already since a long time & in no other country either, nor celebrated artist, or composer—a strange lack. One lives too quickly, impressions follow in rapid succession—machinery & money rule the world & crush all art; & those who think themselves gifted, have ill minds.—I do wonder what will be after this great war is over! Will there be a reawakening & new birth in all—shall once more ideals exist, will people become more pure & poetic, or will they continue being dry materialists? So many things one longs to know. But such terrible misery as the whole world has suffered must clean hearts & minds & purify the stagnant brain & sleeping souls;—oh, only to guide all wisely into the right & fruitful channel. [a, b]

Our Friend< came to A.[nia]< yesterday, he finds it a good thing that the Putilov Plant has been taken by the warministry & doubts that there will be any more troubles—others set the workmen on to strike. He thinks you will return here still before our attacks begin, as there is still such deep snow. When N.P.< left [at the] beginning of Jan. he said that he would be back in less than three months, & so it turned out too.—Lovy, have an eye on Nilov<. Nini< finds his influence upon her husband [V. N. Voeikov] not good—says they are inseparable & that he sets V.[oeikov]< up against A.< I know the little Admiral< gets himself under bad influences.—I had a vile anon.[ymous] letter yesterday— happily only read the 4 first lines & at once tore it up. Fancy Andron.[nikov] & [A. N.] Khvost.[ov] used to occupy themselves writing anon. letters sometimes:—our Friend got one a month ago & is convinced Andron.[nikov] wrote it. What a vile thing it is!—A. continues getting them & with black crosses on them & telling her what dates she must fear,—so cowardly! [c]

Its again mild & grey. I receive [V. V.] Mekk & Apraxin as they are off to inspect my supply trains. G. M. Gurko of the 5-th Army wired fr. Dvinsk thanking me for my supply train, wh. stands there & is such a help to the regiments,—its a comfort to know that small organisation [sic] of Mekks works so well.—I had to name Apraxin now my ch.[ief] manager for the 5 trains,—over Mekk as people were so unkind & jealous of the young man (in Moscou [sic]). I tell you all this in case you hear of him travelling about.—Eagerly I am awaiting your promised letter to-day—beloved Huzy mine, sweet Treasure! Already a week to-day that we went to Holy Communion—how the time flies.—Molostvov comes to present himself—he has one of my waggons [sic] (Mme Sukhomlinov's), wh. takes linen & presents to the front & brings back wounded or sick. [d]

Such a bore I have nothing interesting or amusing to tell you,— "me want oo." Are you going to find some work for Igor< to do, as [his mother] Mavra< hoped you would use him so that he should not dawdle about,—& to keep him from drinking—he got into a rather too wild life, it seems, when he lived in town. Its sad she has so many worries with her children,—one sees the father ["Kostia"<] never occupied himself with them & Mitia[228b] was not the man to bring them up & Mavra was not permitted to say a word,—hard lines on [i.e., fate for] a mother.—Sweetheart, your precious letter has just been brought to me, & I thank you for it with all my heart. Such happiness to hear from you. That was nice you saw some of the Lithuanians passing. So nearly all is ready for to advance, must just get the snow to melt a bit first.[225] I daily have my face electrified for ¼ of an hour—the pains are rare, only such a stiff feeling in the jaw—am sure its gouty. Now Beloved, I must end. Many a fond kiss & blessing fr. yr. very own old wife   Alix.   [P.S.] How is Fedorov< feeling? [e]

228b.   Nicholas II's second cousin Constantine Constantinovich ("Kostia") and Elizabeth Mavrikievna ("Mavra") had four sons, Georgy, Igor, Ioann and Oleg. Kostia died in 1915; Alexandra suggests Kostia's younger brother Dmitry ("Mitia") had some interest in his nephews, but was "not the man to bring them up. See the Biographical Index entries on these people, and Massie, *Nicholas and Alexandra*, pp. 497-498, for their fate at Bolshevik hands.

No. 850/ Telegram 14. Tsarskoe Selo> Stavka. 5 Mar 1916. 2.50> 3.20 p.m.
To his majesty. Much gladdened by [your] dear letter. Tenderly thank [you].
Mild weather. Am still not entirely healthy. Warmly kiss and embrace [you].
Alix

No. 851.   Ts.[arist] Stavka. 5 March 1916.
My very own One,
    Warm thanks for yr. long letter with details of yr. conversation with N.P.<, as
well as letters fr. [daughter] Olga & [son] Aleksei. They arrived quite punctually today. I am very grateful to you for writing all this beforehand, thus preparing me for a talk with him [N. P. Sablin] & Kirill<.—Why are you still anxious about A.[nia]<, now that everything is in Sht.[yurmer]'s hands? I hope his
appointment will be made announced on Monday. [A. N.] Khv.[ostov] wrote
me a long letter; he speaks of his devotion etc., does not understand the reason
[for his dismissal as minister of the interior],[220] & asks to be received. I forwarded this to Sht. with a note that I never doubted his loyalty & shall receive
him in time if his good behaviour & tact shows he deserves it. The whole story
is d—-mnable! [a]
    The weather is mild & foggy,—I walked only in the little garden as there was
no time [for more]—church is at 6.o['clock]. Sergei< returned to day. Poor old
Pau is in bed with rheumatism in the knee, Fedorov visits him from time to time.
So far as I know, he is much at ease regarding the battle at Verdun. The french
have lost 42,000 men, but german losses must be at least four times as great!
The messenger leaves in a quarter of an hour. I have finished the book regret-
fully & shall re-read it aloud with pleasure.—May God bless you, my beloved
Sunny! I kiss & embrace you & the children tenderly. Ever your own old
Nicky. [b]

No. 852/ Telegram 7. Stavka> Tsarskoe Selo. 5 Mar 1916. 7.49> 8.10 p.m. To
her majesty. Fondly thank you, [daughter] Olga and [son] Aleksei for letters.
Mild, foggy, damp. Just back from church. Tender kisses. Niki

No. 853/ Her No. 453.   Ts.[arskoe] S[elo]. March 6th 1916.
My own Sweetheart,
    I reread your precious letter with such happiness & feel warmed up by it.—You
say you felt so tired in the train—I am sure it was the result of 3 hours daily
standing in Church[229] the first week, & moral worries wh. pulled you down.
Now being amongst military people, it will set you up again.—Dull, grey weather
continues—2 degrees of frost this morning, Baby< has just gone out before
Church. He & some of his sisters go for an hour to A.[nia]'s< hospital to see a
conjurer in the afternoon. The face continues improving.—The heart still a little
enlarged, saw [Dr.] Sirotinin as he came to Ts.[arskoe] S.[elo] for Ania. [a]
    Well Sturmer sat with me nigh upon an hour. We talked about the strikes—he
finds the fabrics [factories] ought to be militarised [sic] during the war, & that
paper [authorizing this act] is a long time at the Duma, but does not get looked
through as they are against it. He is rather adverse to Pr.[ince] Tumanov's wish

of very strong measures & would prefer Kuropatkin naming some cleverer man in his place.—Of course that f.[ood] comm.[ittee] makes him despair & they had a strong talk about sending representatives fr. the committee to London, as Russin< brought the invitation. Judging by the example of the behaviour of those delegates in America, its clear one cannot permit them to go as they act against the Government.[230] Polivanov & Grigorovich< & Ignatiev< (the liberal!) are for it—but Grig. only because Russin brought the invitation. [b]

Poliv.[anov] is his despair—and [Sturmer] longs you would change him, but understands you cannot do so without having a good successor. He says his one aid[e] is such a bad man & does such harm—have forgotten his name, a very firm man but not good. Pol. simply treacherous, the way he repeats at once all that is spoken over in secret at the Council of Ministers—its too hideous!—Spoke of the <u>responsible</u> government wh. all scream for, even good ones who do not realise [sic] we [Russians] are not at all fit for it.[385] (As our Friend< says it wld. be the utter ruin of everything.)— [c]

Then, how weak [A. N.] Obolensky is. (Fancy, his wife, born Princess Mingrelskaya went to Greg.[ory]< to beg her husband shld. not be changed—think of that, Lili's< sister-in-law!) Volkonsky he [Sturmer] finds no good in his place, also disapproves of his running about behind the scenes at the Duma. Well we went through all the ministers, & his aids. God help him in his great task to serve you & his country well—makes him also sad that such a capable man as [A. N.] Kh.[vostov] should have gone so utterly wrong.[220]— It seems there was a horrible article in the "Retch" [the liberal (Kadet) newspaper <u>Rech'</u>] against A.[nia]<—how vile people are to drag a young woman in like that!—I am glad you find the new governor [of Mogilev, D. G. Yavlensky] a nice man—where was he before? [He was governor of Pskov.]—Oh you dear one to have written to me again, thanks ever so tenderly & with many a kiss. I saw the nomination & changes [whereby Sturmer replaced Goremykin as chairman of the council of ministers] came out this morning in the papers— yesterday at 6 Sturmer did not know yet when he would get yr. paper [authorizing the change?] back. [d, e]

Yes, [A. N.] Kh.[vostov] told Sturmer he did not understand why he left [i.e., was dismissed as minister of the interior], if on account of that story[220]—the other did not answer anything particular. In any case he [Khvostov] did not come up to what you expected of him, did not work properly,—was most promising at the beginning & then all changed![220] Now he does certainly not behave as a gentleman. He showed about A.'s< letter to members of the Duma, in wh. she asks [Khvostov] to see that one shld. make no <u>search</u> in Greg.[ory]'s rooms a certain night "if its not again a chantage [blackmail] story", she wrote. No harm in the letter, but ugly to give others to read—he was to return the letter to Sturmer, as the parents [A. S. Taneev and Nadezhda] heard of it—but Kh. did not,—now a friend of his [Prince Andronnikov?] said it was untrue, he was shocked one sh. say such a thing & that he had <u>just now</u> found the torn fragments in his basket!! (he got it more than a week ago) & that he wld. glue them together & return them [to] her to-morrow. Can only be a big lie this answer of the basket—hang that dirty story & I am glad you are put of it.—The Children have gone to the big palace< to see the wounded. Now I must end. God bless you, Sweetheart. Many a tender kiss, precious One, fr. yr. deeply loving old wify   <u>Alix</u>. [f]

229. Able-bodied people stand in the Russian Orthodox Church and, as we see from this passage, the Liturgies are lengthy.
230. Note that the empress did not consider the Duma to be part of the "Government."

No. 854/ Telegram 15. Tsarskoe Selo> Stavka. 6 Mar 1916. 4.45> 5.01 p.m. To his majesty. Tenderly thank you for nice letter. Weather mild, overcast. We all warmly kiss and embrace [you]. Alix

---

No. 855/ Telegram 8. Stavka> Tsarskoe Selo. 6 Mar 1916. 10.23> 10.54 p.m. To her majesty. Fond thanks [for] dear letters. Had no time to write as very occupied. Tenderest love. Niki

---

No. 856/ Her No. 454.   Ts.[arskoe] S[elo]. March 7th 1916.
My own Love,
   Its gently snowing, grey, 2° of frost. Feel my heart still & face— not pain, but heavy, stiff.—I am going to see Grigorovich< to-day with photos. of the naval Sanatorium at Massandra—I asked that he should bring them, as have not seen him for more than a year. Then I see Mme Ridiger (widow of a Georgian Reg.[iment's] officer), who will look after my Sanatorium at Massandragates, below the naval one. Its a very big building & we can send wounded there in a week, I am so glad. We collected the money for it with bazars [sic], then as there was not enough, you allowed the udelam [the tsar's local estates] to finish building, as we had not enough money (later I hope we can by degrees pay it back). It was to be for [the] usual sick who come to Yalta & have no place to live, below richer ones & at the top [i.e., primarily for the] poor, tired out school-mistresses, dressmakers who can't pay much. Now of course it goes only for the military & I gave it over to the "Zdravnitsa" [sanitorium] to keep up.—Nikolai Dmitrovitch Dem.[enkov] comes to say goodbye. Then Yakovlev about [daughter] Marie's train; one of our wounded returning to the army & Kaulbars.—Always people to see.— [a]
   You have much to do & so could not write yesterday, poor Darling, but I hope you are contented with the way things are going & the preparations, wh. are being made for the great advance.[225] Had a letter fr. Irene<, (in german) asking about some prisoner officers. Bobbie will be promoted officer in summer (he is Tatianas age, Toddie was yesterday 27, Louise will be the same already in July)—she says the boy has seen already many trying things—was he out on a ship, I do not know. She sends love to all. —Then Daisy[231] kindly wrote & asks for prayerbooks for our Priests in Germany for lent & easter services & she will forward them, so as that it [delivery] should go quicker.—I read a most exciting english book yesterday, wh. we must read aloud with you later on. I end in haste. Every blessing & kiss, Treasure, fr. yr. very own old   Sunny. [b]

---

231. Irina ("Irene") was Alexandra's older sister and the wife of Prince Henry of Prussia. Sigismund-Wilhelm ("Bobbie") and Waldemar-Wilhelm ("Toddie") were Prussian princes and relatives of the empress. Louise, princess of Battenburg, was Alexandra's niece. "Daisy" probably refers to Margarita, a Swedish princess who was born a British princess.

No. 857/ Telegram 19. Tsarskoe Selo> Stavka. 7 Mar 1916. 2.13> 2.52 p.m.
To his majesty. Overcast, dull weather. We all kiss you. Many people to see
today. Warmly kiss [you]. Alix

No. 858.   Ts.[arist] Stavka. March 7ᵗʰ 1916.

My own precious Sunny,

I warmly thank you for yr. dear letters. I was greatly annoyed not to be able to
write you yesterday, but I was indeed quite occupied. I received all day & was
left in peace only at 10.15 in the evening. Gen. Callwell arrived fr. england
along with another very interesting man–Major Sykes, he has travelled all his
life in Asia Min.[or] & Mesopotamia, knows the Turks & Arabs well. He told
me much wh. is strange & remarkable. He already set out for Tiflis to give
N.[icholasha]< the information he needs. Callwell goes there soon, as Georgie
[King George V] commissioned him to present the highest engl.[ish] Order to
[Gen.] Yudenich. Yesterday dear old Pil'ts went to Petrograd, to his new appointment.[232] He was feasted here, & all saw him off in a remarkably warm &
touching way. Bidding me farewell in my room, he wept & begged me to be
careful in the story about our Friend<–his intentions were the best, of course, &
for our own good.[233] [a]

The weather is gradually getting warmer, but it is unfortunate that we never
see the sun! I am glad you saw old Shtyurmer, and now know his opinion of
some ministers & things in general. I cannot understand why you think the
adm.[iral Nilov] has a bad influence on V[oeikov]. They meet only at table &
say very rude things to each other. The adm. is much attached to Fedorov; I had
a long, thorough talk with the latter. I must end this letter. God bless you my
darling, & the children. I kiss you all tenderly (her [Anna Vyrubova] as well).
Ever yr. own old   Nicky. [b]

---

232. "Brigadier-General Sir Percy M. Sykes['s] travels in Persia and Baluchistan are well known.
In 1916 he raised the South Persian Rifles, and was G.O.C. in Southern Persia till the end of 1918."
(Vulliamy, pp. 153-154n) Yudenich was chief of staff in the Caucasus before the war; he was now
serving there with Nicholasha<. Yudenich commanded a White army in the Baltic region during the
civil war and died in France in 1933. A. I. Pil'ts, the governor of Mogilev, replaced Beletsky as
asst.-minister of the interior and police director on Feb. 14, 1916. (See Fn. 233.) Beletsky was to be
sent to Irkutsk as governor, but on March 15, 1916, this plan was cancelled. It was Pil'ts who became governor of Irkutsk! Beletsky was made a senator with a yearly stipend of 18,000 rubles.
Hoping Sturmer would prove to be a "new Stolypin," Nicholas II appointed him both chairman of
the council of ministers and minister of the interior. Neither Sturmer nor Alexandra knew it, but at
this point Nicholas was considering a military dictatorship. Under this scheme, the Duma would be
dismissed, and Nicholas would command the army while Sturmer would direct civilian affairs with
an "iron hand." The plan collapsed as the tsar realized Sturmer was not suited for such a role.
(Fuhrmann, *Rasputin*, pp. 166, 173-175.)

233. Although Nicholas II was approachable on most subjects, he was touchy about his private
life. The tsar considered Rasputin a "private" matter. Nicholas liked Pil'ts; he realized that Pil'ts
mentioned Rasputin with the "best intentions," "for our own good." Nicholas chose to overlook the
intrusion. He was not always so indulgent.

No. 859/ Telegram 9. Stavka> Tsarskoe Selo. 7 Mar 1916. 6.50> 7.00 p.m. To
her majesty. Tender thanks for dear letters [and] Anastasia's photos. Tame, dull
weather. Motor out daily. Fondest love. Niki

No. 860/ Her No. 455.   Ts.[arskoe] S[elo]. March 8th 1916.

My Beloved,

Quite cold, 10° of frost, but in consequence lighter. I had the woman for the first time to mass[ag]e round my heart,—gently stroking to make the muscles stronger (did not like it) & then she did my face because of the continual aching, & the back of my nape of the neck & shoulders wh. was agreable [sic]—felt tired after it all.—Sweet Lovy mine, I do <u>so</u> miss you, no sun without you, tho' I have a Sunbeam< in the house & bright girlies<, but my Own, my one & all is ever missing & I yearn for yr. consoling, tender caresses!—Yesterday evening, after they had dined at Anias<, Lili Den< & husband [Karl]—Kozhevnikov & [G. N.] Taube spent from 9-11 with us. Sad saying goodbye to them,—so far away, endless voyage they & we without news. Awful to be away from home at such a time. All our Friends spread away, all over the place. [Karl] Den has managed to get 20 officers & is enchanted. He & Lili & the most of the officers leave to-day—the kitchen follows a few days later with the men. For Lili it will be awfully hard—she has already grown thinner & the eyes all the time swim in tears.—Oh this hideous war!!—[a, b]

I had the American Harte [Hearte] for 2 hours yesterday—he is off to Germany now. He told several things wh. decidedly can be done here [on behalf of pows] & I begged him to speak again with G. Rudiger [Ridiger]. To-day I have Vil'chkovsky< with a long doklad [report] & other people. My Lovebird, to-morrow its a week you left us! How lonely you must feel. I am glad you will see N.P.< to-morrow, it will remind you of the time when he lived with you at the Headquarters. Wonder what you will settle?— A.[nia] just brought me in a big letter for you, so have to use a large envelope to stick it in. She is quite well & the cough has passed & [she has] walked even—strong health, recovers so quickly. Georgi< at Pavlovsk has got the mumps, poor boy!— Yakovlev with [daughter] Marie's train was ordered to Riga yesterday. Look here, do a clever thing & tell Kirill< you <u>strongly</u> disapprove of Boris< having that beast Plen [I. M. Plehn]. His reputation—vile,—kicked out of the navy, sent away by Kirill, received into Baby's< "Atamantsi" [a Cossack regiment]—honour far too great to wear that uniform & covered with war decorations & high rank—for no military bravery & service—but some private dirty service. Speak to Kirill & N.P. about him, all are horrified, & Petrograd talks enough about it,—(also Miechen's< ambition to get him nearest to the throne is well known.) Much dirt everywhere.— So sad the lowness of humanity—Sodom & Gomorrah verily,— many must still personally suffer through the war & only then will they be loitered [i.e., cleansed] & change[d]. Its all very painful & one can have so little veneration or respect of anyone.— [c, d]

Has Kuropatkin at last cleared out Br.-Bruievitch [Bonch-Bruevich]?—if not, do have it done quiker [sic]. Be firmer & more authoritative, Sweetheart, show yr. fist when necessary—as old Goremykin said still the last time he came to me: "the Emp.[eror] must be firmer[—]one <u>needs</u> to feel his power"[—]& its true. Your angelic kindness, forgiveness & patience are known & one profits [i.e., takes advantage] of it—<u>show you alone</u> are the master & have a strong will.—Oh, my Angel love, I long to be near you, to hear yr. beloved voice & gaze into yr. lovely, deep eyes! God's holy Angels guard & protect you & bless your life &

works & send success. Thousand tender kisses do I press upon yr. lips & press you fondly to my heart.—Ever yr. very   Own. [P.S.] Just got yr. sweetest letter [No. 858] for wh. fondest thanks. How good you saw those Engl.[ishmen] & nice Yudenich gets a decoration from Georgi [King George V]. Wonder for what occasion Alekseev will be made General a.d.c.?—So one has probably talked to Pil'ts already against our Friend<, pity.—Glad you had a conversation with Fedor.[ov]<. She [Anna Vyrubova] will be happy with yr. kiss.—God bless you. Endless tender kisses.— [e]

No. 861/ Telegram 24. Tsarskoe Selo> Stavka. 8 Mar 1916. 1.00> 1.32 p.m. To his majesty. Endlessly thankful for precious letter. 10 deg. frost. [We] all warmly kiss and embrace [you]. Alix

---

No. 862/ Telegram 11. Stavka> Tsarskoe Selo. 8 Mar 1916. 7.40> 7.50 p.m. To her majesty. Thank you and [daughter] Olga fondly [for] dear letters. Did not write. Saw now good cinematograph. Tender kisses. Niki

---

No. 863/ Her No. 456.   Ts.[arskoe] S[elo]. March 9th 1916. My Love,

    15 degrees in the night, now 12 degrees, snowing finely & one sees too, sun wishes to appear.   Once again winter seems to have set in, but not for long.—How strange it is what one reads in the Naval Minister's paper [i.e., confidential bulletin prepared by Grigorovich] fr. foreign news [of the Central Powers], that every little success we have, they call theirs, really it would be interesting to print the announcements next to each other, to see the difference. I am sorry I did not heed the story of the "Moewe" & so missed what they did.[234]—I slept alright [sic], only had rather strong pains in my face till I smeared it with a new mixture & wrapped my whole head in a thick shawl.—Lili Den's< boy comes to A.[nia]< for two days & 2 nights, I am so glad for the lovely child, & I shall get him to come to me too & the children can take him into the garden. The big ones go to town< for a committee, donations & tea at Anichkov<. Xenia< again is feverish & does not go out—a wretched winter for her—she & Motherdear< ought to go to Kiev for 2 weeks to get a change & have their rooms, wh. are full of microbes, thoroughly aired.— [a, b]

    I have people to see again & doklady [reports]. Shtyurmer again too, don't know why.—He had a long talk with Vil'chkovsky—one sent our "station" at Luga, two hospitals fr. Rezhitsa & yet another comes, military ones, as of course the greater mass will come straight to us. There is much to do to prepare things before hand.—What a wind & snow! Now you will be having yr. talk with Kirill< & N.P.<,—always I try to live my life with you[, though we are separated,] & wonder how you are getting on. I send you again fresh flowers, as yours have for sure already faded—a week that you left—I lie in the corner of my big room in the afternoon, as its lighter & we took tea there too.—Sweetest of Treasure, heart of my heart, Goodbye & God bless & protect you. Endless tender kisses my Own, fr. yr. deeply loving old wife   Sunny. [P.S.] In case N.P. is still at the Headquarters when you get this, give him our love.— [c]

234. The *Moewe*, Germany's most successful commerce raider, began life as a 4,800-ton banana boat. Her first military mission lasted two months: she sank 15 ships and returned home in March 1916. Her second mission began in November 1916 and lasted four months. She then destroyed 27 vessels and disrupted Allied shipping over a large area. The *Moewe* was an auxiliary minelayer for the rest of the war.

No. 864/ Telegram 28. Tsarskoe Selo> Stavka. 9 Mar 1916. 2.10> 2.35 p.m. To his majesty. Strong wind, snowing, 12 deg. frost. Big girls< go to town<. With great tenderness my thoughts surround you. We all warmly kiss and embrace [you]. Alix

---

No. 865.   Ts.[arist] Stavka. March 9th 1916.
My own beloved Sunny-dear,
I thank you warmly for yr. dear letters & the love wh. enriches every line. I delight in them, drinking in each word of a letter, breathing its perfume & pressing the paper yr. hands have touched to my lips. How strange yr. weather has changed suddenly & severe frosts have started! Here it is thawing rapidly—that is the chief reason our offensive will begin in a few days.[225] If we wait another week [the spring thaw will begin], the trenches in many places on our front will flood with water & the troops would have to be moved back. In that event, they lose the chance to move forward for a month or 1½ month, till the roads dry. Then the germans would surely attack us with an great quantity of heavy artillery, as they did last summer. It has, therefore been decided to seize the initiative, taking advantage of the onslaught at Verdun. May God keep & bless our valiant troops! I beg you not to tell <u>anyone</u> of this.[235] [a]
Yesterday I saw a cinematograph wh. was particularly interesting, because we saw many photographs of Erzerum immediately after its fall.[214] The high mountains are remarkably beautiful, covered by deep snow, glistening in the sunlight. After this, we saw 2 funny pictures with [the renowned French comedian] Max Linder in the chief role—this would probably have appealed to the children. I am glad you found a new book for us to read aloud [when our family is together again]. Have those two books from Marshton [Marston] come yet from england? So far I have no time to read for my own pleasure, although I play dominoes in the evening every other day. Well, I think it is time to end my letter. God bless you my darling Wify, & the children. I kiss & embrace you all tenderly. Yr. own old huzy   Nicky. [b]

235. Nicholas was probably concerned that the talkative Rasputin be kept ignorant of Russian battle plans. "In connection with this offensive (preceding the great offensive of Broussilov) the following passage from Ludendorff is worth quoting: 'From the 18th to the 21st of March [March 5-9, O.S.] the situation of the 10th [Germany] Army was critical and the numerical superiority of the Russians overwhelming. On the 21st they won a success on the narrow lake sector which affected us gravely, and even the attack west of Postovy was only stemmed with difficulty' (p. 211). By the end of April, however, the 10th Army had regained the ground which it had lost between Lake Narotch and Lake Vishniev." (Vulliamy, p. 155n).

No. 866/ Telegram 14. Stavka> Tsarskoe Selo. 9 Mar 1916. 6.45> 7.17 p.m. To her majesty. Tender thanks [for] dear letters, [daughter] Tatiana and [son]

Aleksei also. Snow fell in the night, now melted. Storm blowing. Fondest loving kisses. Niki

---

No. 867/ Her No. 457.   Tsarskoe Selo. March 10th 1916.

My own Sweetheart,

Snowing, blowing, 8° of frost. Little Titi< came to me yesterday afternoon for an hour—we looked at books together, [he] took tea with us & played with Aleksei. Now he has begun speaking English quite nicely, a tall, clever boy for 7½; writes alone to his mother in Russian. He spent the night at Anias< & we hope he will come again on Saturday. Had doklady [reports] & received. Shtyurmer came to speak about that story [concerning Rasputin[220]] as things must be seriously cleared up & I had to give him over letters fr. Iliodor relating everything & he will have investigations made still as to the truth of what he wrote,—alas, it seems truthful!—Then he told me to warn you that N.[icholasha]< wants to have Uncle [the reference is sarcastic] Krivoshein as a help [i.e., aide]. During [Old Count] Vorontsov's< time there was a Nikolsky. He has to represent N's. interests when necessary in the Duma & Council of the Emp.[ire]< & it wld. be impossible Krivoshein filling such a place. It would be the ruin of the Caucasus, he [Krivoshein] cleverer than anybody & unscrupulous now—friend to N. & fat O.[rlov]< & Yanushkevich—would be awful. As it must come to you for yr. approval, I warn you.— [a]

Its madness of N. to take a man you sent away [Nicholas dismissed Krivoshein as minister of agriculture on October 26, 1915] & who did all the harm then.—Shtyurmer was much less shy & quite open this time—one sees what a real love & veneration he has for you.—Is worried about the Convention in Moscow wh. will be soon, is sending for the General fr. there to speak over matters, personaly [sic] I fear that neurasthenic Shebeko [the new governor-general of Moscow] will be a useless rag there, if there should be any stories [i.e., difficulties]. Of course he [Shtyurmer] also finds a General Governor must be there, without having any man in view. —He wishes I could show myself often in town< & go about & to Kazan Church—but my stupid heart & now face prevent & [i.e., although] I know it would be good. Motherdear< neither can [appear] & Miechen< is playing a popular part in town & going about a lot & to musical evenings & acting her part as charmeuse [charmer]. The Benkendorffs< are also in despair about this, the Css. told A.[nia]<. They came back quite sick after a few days spent in town. [b]

Everyone horrified by Khvostov.[220]—She [Countess Benckendorff?] took tea at Pauls< (after ages again)—[he was in] good humour. The boy [Paul's younger son, Prince Paley?] goes about quite green as returns to the regiment to-day. The terrible, forced drinking in the Hussars made him ill & acted on his heart. They & the Garde à cheval continue drinking colossaly at the war, its loathsome & degrading before the soldiers who know that you prohibited it.[236]—If you have an occasion, tell Bezobrasov [Bezobrazov] to have an eye on the regiments & make them understand how hideously unmoral it is at such a time. The Css. B.[enckendorff] is shocked with Dmitris goings on in town during the war & finds one ought to insist upon him returning to the regiment—I fully agree, town & women are <u>poison</u> for him. Just read in the papers about our advancing—thank

God its going quietly, steadily well[235]–God grant this may change the rotten minds of the "rear".–To-day Css. Carlov< comes to me, as she leaves for Tiflis for 3 months as her daughter is expecting–then Mme Nikitina (ex Odessa) & a lady of my store.–Tatiana is at an operation of one of our officers this morning.–Poor old Zaltsa died yesterday–a remembrance of our young married days here. Dear me, how much we have seen & lived through in these 21½ years of married life– but all is so distinct & clear in my memory!–oh how lovely the times were! Sweetheart, Sunny's love ever increases, fuller, richer & deeper & she dreams of our youthful happy love in the bygone, how mad we were!–Precious one, I bless & kiss you without end & yearn for yr. tender, consoling caresses more than ever. [c, d]

One just brought me you[r] beloved letter for wh. very tenderest thanks. So, my Angel also kisses my letters as I always do yours, every page & more than once. To-day it smells of cigarets.–I see now why we advance, it being again winter here, I did not think it wld. be thawing yet there. [See Letter No. 865a.] In the papers to-day the news is so good about our advance, 17 officers & 1000 men taken etc. oh, God bless our troops,[235] I am sure he [God] will & its good we waste no time, before they profit attacking us. All are so happy & full of it here. I am glad the cinema was amusing as well as interesting. Did Kiryll< & N.P.< not turn up yesterday as I thought they intended to? No, those English books have not yet come. Motherdear finished the 2-nd, so I sent her the French book you read. Now I must end & get up, as the oculist [Dr. L. G. Bellyarminov] comes to see to my aching eyes.–Sweetheart, goodbye & God bless you over & over again & all yr. undertakings & our beloved troops. Ah how full the heart is & our prayers must be redoubled. I cover you with kisses, my Huzy, & remain yr. very own   Wify. [e]

Belarminov says I need stronger specks to read with, eyes overtired & the aching comes also from gout–the same as my face nerve pains too–but he is contented with the eyes themselves & says they are very good, only I overtask [sic] them. I am glad to have seen him, as the pain is often very strong & that acts on my head, & I see worse for reading. (I personally know they get bad fr. much crying) & fr. many unshed tears too, wh. fill the eyes & that must drink themselves up again–this all I did not tell him.) Then he gives me an ointment to rub in exteriorly if they ache much. [f]

---

236. Nicholas II decreed prohibition of alcoholic beverages until the war ended. In part, this was to save grain. The measure had also been long demanded to improve the nation's health and morals. Prohibition was not only ineffective, it deprived the state of tax revenues from its monopoly on the sale of alcohol.

No. 868/ Telegram 30. Tsarskoe Selo> Stavka. 10 Mar 1916. 2.00> 2.23 p.m. To his majesty. Warmly thank you for dear letter. News in papers today[235] filled all hearts with joy. Each of our successes brings consolation. May God bless our brave troops! 8 deg. frost, snowing, strong wind. [We] all kiss and bless [you]. Alix

---

No. 869.   Ts.[arist] Stavka. March 10th 1916.

My own beloved One,

I thank you warmly for yr. dear letters—they are recompense for my loneliness here. The days seem to fly; I have heaps of work, see crowds of every sort of people, & yet do not feel tired. Alas, I have no time for reading! Yr. lovely lilies of the valley smell deliciously—many thanks for them! I was very glad to see N.P.< Kirill< & he dined with me yesterday & lunched today—now they have gone. I talked with them a long time last night, & agreed to leave the battalion [of the Guards Equipage<] at its present strength—4 full companies; it ought not to be reduced by one man until the end of the war. [a]

Today Kirill spoke to me about the "P. Zvezda" [the imperial yacht *Polyarnaya Zvezda*, "Polar Star"]. I told him Mama [Maria Fedorovna] & I agreed to appoint Lyalin, but he should ask her again if he wished, although I very much doubted whether she would change her decision. Shir.[insky]-Shikh.[matov] is an excellent man, but he has not been on a ship for many years. At last I found a successor for Polivanov [as minister of war]— Shuvaev, whom I can trust absolutely. I have not spoken with him yet. I also intend to attach old [Gen. N. I.] Ivanov to myself, & to appoint Brusilov or Shcherbachev to his post—probably the former. After P.'s removal I shall sleep in peace, and all the Ministers will feel relieved as well.[237] [b]

11 March. The morning work with Alekseev takes all my time till lunch, but now it has come to be of absorbing interest. Cold weather has set in here as well—at Riga the frost reaches 10 deg.[rees] at night—it is terrible for the poor wounded & for the troops who are positioned in the snow on many sections of the front, right opposite the enemy's [barbed-]wire barriers. God bless you & the children, my dear! I kiss you all tenderly. I thank A.[nia]< for her dear letter. Ever yr. own old huzy Nicky. [c]

237. Polivanov was an able minister of war; Hindenburg thought he saved the Russian army in 1915. But Polivanov's continuing ties to Guchkov made him increasingly unacceptable to Nicholas II, who also remembered that Polivanov was among the ministers who urged him not to dismiss Nicholasha<, and who then attempted to resign when the decision stood. Shuvaev, by contrast, was totally "devoted" to the royal family. Alexandra's first choice to replace Polivanov was Gen. N. I. Ivanov, her second choice was Gen. M. A. Belyaev. (See Letter No. 874c; Rasputin also favored Ivanov: see Letters No. 783c and 880a.) Nicholas probably selected Shuvaev because, as Oldenburg notes, he had run the "[war] ministry's quartermaster and supply department effectively" since 1909. Shuvaev was passionate over footwear, a contemporary claimed every question he discussed "invariably turned to that of boots." (Pipes, *Russian Revolution*, pp. 241-242; Oldenburg, *Last Tsar*, IV, pp. 80, 117, 194; Vulliamy, p. 156n) Shuvaev was not a wise choice as minister of war; the fact that Nicholas chose him shows how badly the tsar's judgment was slipping. Shuvaev's selection in the face of Alexandra's opposition (see Letters No. 874e and 877b) also shows how little influence she—much less Rasputin—had in military matters. Belyaev replaced Shuvaev in January 1917 and was the last tsarist minister of war.

No. 870/ Telegram 16. Stavka> Tsarskoe Selo. 10 Mar 1916. 6.57> 7.30 p.m. To her majesty. Loving thanks to you and [daughter] Marie. Saw Kirill< and N.P.<. That question [see Letter No. 869a] now settled once for all. 3 [degrees] of frost. Strong wind. Tenderest love. Niki

No. 871/ Her No. 458.   Ts.[arskoe] S[elo]. March 11th 1916.
My very own Sweetheart,

At last glorious, bright sunshine—what a difference it makes. I have ordered service in the house as its Friday & I have such a longing to go to church. All ones thoughts & prayers are with our troops & one flies to read the news every morning. Should there ever be anything quite particularly good, perhaps you wld. send me a short wire? one feels so anxious—but God will bless the troops & send success, if we only all pray enough! All our sanitary trains have been called out & heaps of otryady [units] & 15 hospitals have gone to Dvinsk. I got yr. wire that you settled that question once for all with Kirill< & N.P.< & am anxiously awaiting what conclusion you came to [concerning a shortage of officers and men in various units; See Letters No. 869a and No. 874b].—Have again ladies to receive. Excuse my having wired about M-me Nikitina's husband, but she entreated me to,—of course you will do as you think right. She thought he was the oldest general with the St. George's cross who could fill that vacancy!— [a]

The children say the tower [snow-tower, see Letter No. 877b] in the garden has become quite magnificent—I long to go & look at it—hope to soon, if can risk with my face.—Beloved One precious Darling, you feel wify holding you tightly in her arms, caressing you tenderly & gently? Oh, hard not to be together at such times.— There are rumours that some guard reg.[iments] have already had great losses,—but have they already been used? Oh, the beautiful sunshine! Beloved, I must end. Heart & soul with you. God bless & protect you & help you, give strength & energy & success. More than ever I pray for you. I want to see you blessed, happy, successful, I want to see the recompense for all your endless heartache, sorrow, anxiety, work, & that the prayers of all those who fell for their Sovereign & Country shd. be heard. My Own, endless kisses from your own old   Sunny. [b]

No. 872/ Telegram 34. Tsarskoe Selo> Stavka. 11 Mar 1916. 8.12> 8.34 p.m. To his majesty. Sunny day. Received. N.P.< coming now, hope [he] will have much to say. He leaves this evening. Finally face does not hurt any more. Embrace and kiss [you]. Alix

---

No. 873/ Telegram 22. Stavka> Tsarskoe Selo. 11 Mar 1916. 8.13> 8.48 p.m. To her majesty. Fondest thanks to you, [daughter] Olga, [son] Aleksei. Cold, snow, wind. Just come home from English cinema that [we] saw together. Love to all. Niki

---

No. 874/ Her No. 459.   Ts.[arskoe] S[elo]. March 12th 1916.
My own Lovebird,

I scarcely slept this night from pains in my face again. It began in the evening, just after I had told Vl. Nik.< that I thought I was quite rid of it & might go this evening to Church,—the krestopoklonnaya subb.[ota],[238] so disappointing. Had massage again this morning, smeared the face with all sorts of things. It is a little better now, but aches & the eye is half shut. Have again sent for the poor dentist [Dr. S. S. Kostritsky]—have seen so many other Drs. now, that I think he better come & have a look & perhaps change a filling[;] there may be a new cavity. Of course feel cretinised & have to receive Mrozovsky & our three Sisters [i.e., nurses] who returned from Austria & have a lot to tell.—Two of our sanitary trains are returning with heavy wounded. Is it true our loses are very heavy? Of course attacking, it cannot be otherwise— still we made many prisoners & took a lot (whilst the Germans said they did not let us advance one step, that we have immense losses & that they took 17 officers & 800 men prisoners).[235] [a]

Sweety, remember you have that special telegrapho-telephon, or however you call it & if anything particular let Voeikov< speak to Ressin< or you to me. One feels so anxious & longs for more news than waiting 24 hours for the papers.—N.P.< came yesterday fr. 7½-9 (such a pleasant surprise). A joy to get direct news. He was sad for you [with] that very dull atmosphere around you, no young, fresh a.d.c. & you seemed so lonely. Its that wh. worries me too. He told me about all yr. decisions, & hurried off last night back to Rezhitsa.—It is provoking that lack of officers.—He says the Admiral [Nilov] spoke again very much against Grigorovich<, wh. always hurtes [sic] him, as he [N. P. Sablin] venerates him very much & sees [i.e., understands that] N.[icholasha]< wants to fight him out [i.e., see Grigorovich dismissed as minister of naval affairs]. [b]

He [N. P. Sablin] said he had a good talk with Fedorov< & about Polivanov too. Maklakov was at A.[nia]'s< & entreats to see me also[—]beseeching that I shld. implore you quickly to get rid of Polivanov, that he is simply a revolutionist under the wing of Guchkov<—Shtyurmer begged the same. They say that in that odious War-ind.[ustries] comm.[ittee] they are intending to say horrid things, they come together in a few days, & [N. A.] Maklakov says therefore quickly clear out Polivanov, any honest man better than him. If you cant [appoint Gen. N. I.] Ivanov, why not honest, devoted Belyaev[237] & give him a good help[er, i.e., assistant-minister of war]. Shtyurmer much dislikes the other help of Polivanov, says such a very bad man, I did not catch the name. Lovy mine, dont dawdle, make up yr. mind, its far too serious, & changing him at once, you cut the wings of that revolutionary party; only be quicker about it—you know, you yourself long ago wanted to change him [Polivanov]—hurry up Sweetheart, you need Wify to be behind pushing you! You above all need an honestly devoted man, and that Belyaev is, if Ivanov is too obstinate. Please, do the change at once, then propaganda & all can at once be stopped energetically. Maklakov adores you & spoke to her [Anna Vyrubova] with tears in his eyes about you & so I shall see him soon. Promise me you will at once change the M.[inister] of War, for your sake, your Sons & Russias,—& it is high time— otherwise I shld. not have written again so soon about this question! You told me you wld. be soon doing it & who knows if God won't sooner bless our troops if this "choice of the old Headquarters" is at once cleared out. Rodz.[yanko] & Guchk.[ov] knew well why they & Janushk.< made Nik.[olasha]< propose him to you & fat Orloff< [stood] behind [it] all. Maklakov loathes Orlov says he is a man to stoop before nothing, the same as [A. N.] Khvostov.— [c, d]

Saw Shebeko yesterday & had a good talk; & my ex lancer Vinberg.—Our Friend< leaves to-morrow, cld. not get any [railway?] tickets for last Wednesday.—I wish my face did not ache so, long to write a lot more & can't, & want to ask heaps about the troops.—Heart & soul with you longing to be together!—There, your sweet letter [No. 869b] has just come, thanks ever so tenderly, Sweetheart.—So you think Shuvaev the right man (tho' less of a gentleman than Belyaev) & is he really the right type? I only once spoke to him when found him most obstinate, so cannot judge. But who to succeed him? In any case—hurry up, Lovebird. [e]

Excellent that you intend attaching Ivanov to yr. person, as all down there complain of the dear man being so tired & "getting old".—Cannot understand why Keller & Brussilov always have hated each other & when he can Brussilov is not just [to Keller]—& the other in return abuses him (privately). Wont the ministers be happy when Polivanov leaves? Oh, the relief. Alas, Ignat.[ev] is neither a man in his place [i.e., is not competent as minister of education], tries to play the popular man & is left, alas, as too Boris Vas.[ilchikov], his brother-in-law,—the smart set. Can imagine how palpitatingly interesting the work now is, & long I were near you to follow all together on the map & share anxiety & joy with you. From far we all do, heart & soul.—Yes, that frost is despairing for the troops. [This Russian passage may be a message from Rasputin:] "There is nothing to be done,—God will help." God bless & protect you my Angel, my Own, my Love, my Huzy Sweet—guard & guide you. Endless tender, passionately loving kisses fr. yr. own old   Sunny. [f]

---

238. Alexandra refers to the "Exaltation and Adoration of the Cross"; *subbota* is the Russian word for Saturday, the day the service was observed that year in the Russian Orthodox Church.

No. 875/ Telegram 39. Tsarskoe Selo> Stavka. 12 Mar 1916. 2.16> 2.35 p.m. To his majesty. Very thankful, gladdened by your precious letter. Overcast weather but not so cold. In thoughts with you. God keep [you]. We all kiss you. Alix

No. 876/ Telegram 23. Stavka> Tsarskoe Selo. 12 Mar 1916. 9.31> 10.07 p.m. To her majesty. Warm thanks [for] dear letters and Shvybzik< too. Very busy day. On the whole events are good. Much warmer. Tenderest kisses. Niki

No. 877/ Her No. 460.   Ts.[arskoe] S[elo]. March 13th 1916.
My very Own,

Warm & lovely sunshine, so God grant our troops have the same weather. Our train is just being emptied out & [daughter] Maries comes later in the day with very heavy wounded. Despairing not to be able to go and meet them and work in the hospital—every hand is needed at such a time. Slept alright, but the strong pain in my eye continues, the cheek gets better when V.N.< electrifies it, so I do it now twice a day. Baby< went out already early before Church. A.[nia]< goes for the whole day to town<, as Greg.[ory]< leaves, then she sees her parents [A. S. Taneev and his wife Nadezhda] & dines at the Css. Fredericks.—My poor Rostoftzev's< twin-sister has just died from cancer & one says he is quite wretched—is ill himself the whole time but goes on working.— Little Titi< played on the snowtower with the children yesterday & enjoyed it, to-day he returns again to town<.—I am thinking so much about Shuvaev & do greatly wonder whether he can fill such a place, know[s] how to speak in the Duma, as one time one abused him & the ordnance department—but is that alright now? My eye aches so writing—I could not use it all day yesterday, & whilst I was receiving it was distracting—as if one stuck [a] pencil into the centre & then the whole eye aches too, so better stop now & finish later on.—[a, b]

So anxious for news. The children were all in Church & are now going out, hot sun, wind, frost in the shade, last night rain.—You cannot imagine how terribly I miss you—such utter loneliness—the children with all their love still have quite other ideas & rarely understand my way of looking at things[,] the smallest[,] even—they are always right & when I say how I was brought up & how one must be, they cant understand, find it dull.—Only when [I] quietly speak with T.[atiana] she grasps it. Olga is always most unamiable about every proposition, tho' may end by doing what I wish. And when I am severe—sulks me. Am so weary & yearn for you.—There are also many thing wh. A.[nia], with her bringing up & being out of another set, does not understand & many a worry I would never share with her—I used to with N.P.< because he, as a man with inborn tact, understood me.—We all have our ways & thoughts & I feel so horribly old at times & low spirited—pain pulls one down & perpetual anxiety & worry since the war goes on. Your precious calming presence gives me strength & consolation—I take things too deeply to heart—try to master it—but, I suppose, God gave me such a heart wh. fills up my whole being. Forgive my writing all this & pay no attention to it, I am only a bit down. Oh, I must be off to Vl. N.< to electrify myself.—I bless you, kiss you over & over again & press you to my yearning heart, Sweet Angel, Treasure, Beloved! Ever yr. very own weary old Sunny. [c]

No. 878/ Telegram 45. Tsarskoe Selo> Stavka. 13 Mar 1916. 1.22> 1.45 p.m. To his majesty. Glorious warm sun, strong wind. 5 deg. frost in shade. Rained last night. In thoughts and prayers with you. What news? Warmly kiss [you]. Pain continues, especially in eye. Alix

---

No. 879/ Telegram 25. Stavka> Tsarskoe Selo. 13 Mar 1916. 7.15> 7.45 p.m. To her majesty. Anxious about your pains always continuing. Thanks tenderly [for] dear letter, also Tatiana. Again had no time to write, so sorry. Lovely sunny day. Long to be out more. No particular news. Fondest kisses. Niki

---

No. 880/ Her No. 461.   Tsarskoe Selo. March 14th 1916.
My own sweet Treasure,

I send you an apple & flower from our Friend<—we all had fruit as a goodbye gift. He left this evening—quietly, saying better times are coming & that he leaves spring-time with us.—He told her [Anna Vyrubova] He finds Ivanov wld. be good as Minister of War on account of his great popularity not only in the army, but all over the country.—In that He is certainly right—but you will do what you think best. I only asked He should pray for success in yr. choice, & He gave this answer.—[a]

I spent the whole long afternoon from 1-4 alone, reading with an aching eye. It seems [A. B.] Neidhardt is ill with the same pains & high fever. The dentist [Dr. S. S. Kostritsky] has left the Crimea yesterday evening.—The girls went to see Marie's sanitary train whilst half full still—it left to the front in the evening

again. Three trains came. Forgive my having seemed to grumble in my last letter, its a shame—only I was feeling so low & wrongly forgot to hide it. Such
constant pains pull one down a bit. Oh yes, yet another thing He [Rasputin] said
to tell you that the Metropolitan [Pitirim] told him, the Synod wants to present
you a wish of theirs that seven metropolitans should be in Russia. Vladimir very
much for it—but our Friend begs you not to agree as its certainly not the moment
& we cant even find scarcely 3 decent ones fit to occupy such a place.[174] How
utterly absurd of them. Nikon is still here, [in Petrograd, at the Holy Synod,] too
bad. [b]

One says Uncle [A. A.] Kh.[vostov], hopes to whitewash his nephew [A. N.
Khvostov], tho' all are against him & wants to drag Beletsky< in, who really
seems quite innocent concerning the zagovor [conspiracy] & wishes him no
longer to be Senator,[220, 232] but then you must be just & have [A. N.] Kh.'s
courtrank taken away—I deeply regret it was left him—as in the Duma they
say—if he wished to get rid of Greg.< because he did not suit him, he can do the
same with any of us who may displease him. I don't like Beletsky but it wld. be
very unfair if he suffered more than [A. N.] Kh. He has forfeited Irkutsk
through his imprudence, but thats enough. The other tried to instigate a murder.—Enough of this story.[232] Excuse this ink, but my other pen is empty &
needs refilling. [c]

What a pitty [sic] you cannot get out more! I know how wildly you long for
the sun & air towards spring—so was I in the bygone, could not live without air
& then through being ill everything changed & I learned to be weeks without air
& never any walks.—And you do so need it with all the work you have to do.
How vile that they [the Germans] shoot again with explosive bullets. But God
will punish them.—Sweetheart, if you only knew how yr. little wify longs for
you & now we shall for sure long not meet again! There is nothing to be done
but you are so <u>lonely</u>, Lovebird & I long to caress you & feel yr. sweet tenderness. Precious one, you feel wify's love enveloping you with fathomless tenderness? You feel my arms round you & my lips pressed to your warm ones with
such utter love? God keep you, my one & all, my own Sunshine.—Got to sleep
late, because of the aching—its not any longer madning [sic] pain, but aches &
these last day's especially my right eye. 4° of warmth this morning—the sun did
not shine long.—Its the feast of the Fedor.[ovskaya] H.[oly] Mother & consequently of our Church. Igor comes to present himself as yr. a.d.c. & lunches
with us. I also receive the commander of my Crimeans<—I wonder what he is
like. Alia< has asked to see me she drives here to-day, so will come to tea. All
that with these pains is not gay, but difficult to refuse. Now Lovebird, Goodbye
& God bless you. I cover you, sweet Nicky, with very tenderest kisses. Ever yr.
very <u>Own</u>. [d, e]

The Children are alright—Tatiana busy at the hospital—Olga has gone there on
foot with Shura, Anastasia after her lesson is off for a run with Trina< as the
priest [Father A. P. Vasil'ev] officiates in Church this morning. Marie is writing
to you. Baby< is out. I must get up for my electricity.—It does not concern me,
but whilst I could not sleep, I was thinking over what you said about Kedrov;—
wld. not M. P. Sablin be better instead of Planson,—such a serious, quiet man &
not an ambitious "Sterber" [careerist]. Tho' Kedrov is clever & talented, yet he

is somewhat an insolent fellow, judging by his letters to the Admiral [Nilov?]—
& the other so discreet & an older man [is better fitted] for such a place. This is
my very own opinion, not prompted by any talk with N.P.< as you might think.
We never mentioned his brother last time, there was no time even.— [f]

Poguliaiev [Pogulyaev] such a young admiral & in yr. suite— colossal honour,
the couple wild of joy & he is going to fly off to the old Father to present himself—he is also ambition itself & insolent & therefore has luck & both these men
turn the Admiral [Nilov] round their little finger. Eberhardt< needs a serious
help [assistant] and I find a man fr. the Black sea [fleet] is the one just to occupy
such a place. Pardon my interference, Sweety, but in the long, lonely night I
thought of this & felt I must write it honestly to you,—tell me whether you don't
agree.—Paul< told A.[nia]< he takes over the command [of the Guards Corps] in
April, can it be true? I personally strongly doubt his succeeding & honestly find
it not right his insisting, as after all he is quite out of everything since ever so
long & one cannot be sure of his health.—Now I really must get up. Farewell my
Angel.—A bow to Fed.[orov]< & Gen. Alekseev. [g]

No. 881/ Telegram 47. Tsarskoe Selo> Stavka. 14 Mar 1916. 2.40> 3.12 p.m.
To his majesty. Warm. thawing. Igor lunched with us. Face a bit better but
everything still hurts. May God bless you. We all tenderly kiss [you]. Alix

---

No. 882.   Ts.[arist] Stavka. March 14th 1916.
My own beloved Wify-dear,
For the last 3 days there has been no time whatsoever to write you; I was quite
busy with military operations & the repositioning [of the troops]. I had to write
Pol.[ivanov] & explain why I was dissatisfied.[239] I am certain that dear old Shuvaev is exactly the right man for the post of minister of War. He is honest, absolutely loyal, not at all afraid of the Duma & knows all the faults &
short-comings of these committees! Then I had to receive [people] & read my
beastly papers—all in a rush! The ministers are beginning to arrive now, one after another—first was Naumov, then Shakhovskoi etc. Today I had a conversation with gen.[eral] Manikovsky, nachal'nik Glavn. Art. Upr. [director of the
main artillery dept]. He told me he wished to resign, as Pol.'s behaviour towards
him was quite impossible. When he heard that P. is dismissed and Shuv. named,
he crossed himself three times.[239] Old Ivanov will be replaced by Brusilov.
You see, yr. huzy has been working these days—many changes have already
been made & more will occur—including Ronzhin. [a, b]

How sad you have pains in yr. face & eye! Is it due to nerves? I am so sorry,
my dear, that I cannot be with you & console you when you are suffering.
Things move quite slowly at the front; in some places we have sustained heavy
losses, & many generals are making serious blunders. The worst is we have so
few good generals. It seems to me that during the long winter rest they lost all
the experience they acquired last year! Lord! I am beginning to complain, but it
is ne nado [not necessary[160]]! I feel firm, & believe totally in our final success.
God bless you my own, my all, my treasure, my darling! I kiss you & the children tenderly. Greetings to A[nia]<. Ever yr. own old hubby Nicky. [c]

239. In faulting Polivanov for not exerting sufficient control over the War/Military Industry Committees, Nicholas was "expressing displeasure with Polivanov's closeness to Guchkov, the chairman of these committees, and through him to the business community." (Pipes, *Russian Revolution*, p. 241; see also Footnote 237.) This letter shows how marginal men attempted to manipulate Nicholas by playing upon what they perceived to be his likes and dislikes. A. A. Manikovsky, the tsar's interlocutor in this instance, was finally dismissed and tried for treason.

No. 883/ Telegram 29. Stavka> Tsarskoe Selo. 14 Mar 1916. 7.33> 8.07 p.m.
To her majesty. Awfully thankful [for] dear letter also Olga's. Cooler today. At last wrote to you. Hope [you are] feeling better, no pains. Tenderest love. Niki

No. 884/ Her No. 462.   Ts.[arskoe] S[elo]. March 15th 1916.
My own Sweetheart,
    There, glorious sunshine with 10° of warmth, but windy—& yesterday afternoon & evening it snowed hard. My head & eyes go on aching, the woman has been masseing [massaging] my face & head, neck & shoulders & soon I go up to my electricity. I dare not risk going out until have seen the dentist [Dr. S. S. Kostritsky] & to be sure my cheek wont swell up.—Lovy, I send you here a letter I got from Rostchakovsky[242][;] when read through & if you agree, wire to me "all right" & I shall have it wired on to him. He is a strange chap, not like others—but certainly devoted & energetic & as he so funnily writes, must be used.—I wish you could shut up that rotten [war] ind.[ustries] commit.[tee] as they prepare simply antidynastic questions for their meeting.—I have V. P. Schneider with a long doklad [report]—I like her as she is so energetic & understands half words already [i.e., she understands me from only half of what I say]—only my head is not fresh at all. Later Emelianov comes to bid goodbye before returning to my regiment. —Last night Baby's< train came. It seems of the 20-th Sib. reg. only 5 officers have remained—fearful losses. But are you on the whole contented? Of course in attacking heavy losses are inevitable. [a, b]
    Mme Zizi< has at last returned here & I shall see her this afternoon.—So tiresome I cant take medicines now, something came on 8 days too early. Am eagerly awaiting yr. promised letter. Excuse bad writing.—One says Dmitri< is still scandalling about in town< such a pitty [sic]! He wont become a better husband for that.—Did you see the Sultan [Muhammed V] received the fieldmarshal's staff from [Kaiser] William, such mockery!—Missy [Maria, queen of Roumania] has sent another pretty fairytale book of hers to [our daughter] Olga.—Beloved One, I kiss you, oh so tenderly & wish I could share yr. loneliness; you have not a soul to talk to, to feel near you, who understands you & with whom you can talk about anything wh. comes into yr. head;—sad N.P.< is no longer with you—he had shared our life so much & knew & understood so many little things, wh. the other a.d.c.[s] dont. Wont you have them [i.e., those] on duty change about [i.e., rotate assignments] with you? Would be good for them and interesting for you. [c]
    Thanks tenderly, my beloved One, for yr. sweetest letter, am glad you have settled all about P.[olivanov]. God grant Shuvaev may be the right man in the right place, in any case a <u>blessing</u> you are rid of him [Polivanov]. I shall read through Greg.[ory]'s telegr. with Ania when she returns from town & then explain it to you.—Hang those Generals, why are they so weak & good for nothing,

be severe to them. You have indeed been busy, Sweetheart. But I must end now. God bless & protect you. Warmest, tenderest kisses, Huzy mine fr. yr. very own old Wify. [d]

No. 885/ Telegram 54. Tsarskoe Selo> Stavka. 15 Mar 1916. 2.16> 2.48 p.m. To his majesty. Warmly thank you for dear letter, glad all is decided. 10° warmth in the sun, snowed all day yesterday and in evening. Entire face still hurts, especially eyes and head. Now awaiting news with impatience. We all kiss you. May the Lord God keep you. Alix

---

No. 886.   Ts.[arist] Stavka. March 15th 1916.
My own Precious One,
    Tender thanks for yr. dear letters. I cannot tell you how I feel for you when you are bothered by those awful pains in yr. face, & how I long to be with you to comfort you! It is absolutely impossible to determine when I will be able to return [home] for a few days— perhaps not for some time & perhaps in a week! What I feared has happened. Such a strong thaw has set in that our troops' forward positions are flooded with water knee-deep, so one cannot sit or lie down in the trenches. The roads are deteriorating rapidly; the artillery & transport are scarcely moving. Even the bravest troops cannot fight under conditions when it is impossible even to entrench oneself. As a result, our offensive had to be stopped & another plan must be worked out. To discuss this, I am thinking of summoning the three commanders-in-chief to the Stavka, wh. will give me an opportunity to see Brusilov before his new activity [i.e., the next phase of the grand offensive].[235] [a, b]
    You write there is much talk in town< of losses among some of the guards regiments. That is a fantasy, they are 50 versts [33 miles] fr. the battle line & I still hold them in reserve in the deep rear. They have moved a bit forward towards Dvinsk—that is all. I agree with your thoughts about M. P. Sablin. It would be splendid if Eberhardt took him as chief of staff, but I never insist upon such appointments as the ch. of s. must give absolute satisfaction to his commander. A while back adm.[iral] Eberhardt went to Batum & had a lengthy discussion with Nik.[olasha]< concerning the planned combined military [and naval] operations against Trapezund [Trebizond]. Our dear plastuni[75] will play a large role in them. As far as I know, all loyal & right-thinking people applaud Shuvaev's appointment. Now, my darling, I must end. God bless you & the children. I kiss & embrace you tenderly & sincerely hope yr. pains will disappear soon & completely. Ever yr. own old huzy Nicky. [c]

No. 887/ Telegram 31. Stavka> Tsarskoe Selo. 15 Mar 1916. 7.45> 8.28 p.m. To her majesty. Loving thanks [for] precious letter, also [our children] Marie [and] Aleksei. Thick fog, rather warm. Thoughts ever together. Tenderest kisses. Niki

---

No. 888/ Her No. 463.   Ts.[arskoe] S[elo]. March 15th 1916.
My own Lovebird,

I begin my letter to you this evening. It was such happiness hearing from you & I can imagine how comforted you feel to have at last settled the question of the minister of war. God bless your choice with success, & may he [Gen. Shuvaev] prove himself worthy of your trust! Is it true that things are going very bad with Sukhomlinov?—Igor had heard as tho' he wld. have to be shot—but I don't know where he got the news from. Certainly he had his great faults—but his successor [Polivanov] is yet a greater traitor to my mind. I return Gr.[egory]'s telegram to you. He means Beletsky<, because he does not find just that he, who has scarcely been to blame, should so severely suffer & the other [A. N. Khvostov] got off better, who committed the greatest sin.[220, 232]—My eye has been hurting me madly all day (& head too)—its from the triplex nerve in the face. One branch to the eye, the one took the upper row of teeth, the other the lower, & the knot before the ear. I have heard of more people suffering now fr. these pains —[A. B.] Neidhardt had it so bad, that Drs. send him to the south for a rest. Its fr. a chill in the facial nerves, the cheek & teeth are much better, the left jaw goes popping in & out this evening, but the eyes ache very much—therefore I wont write anymore now.— Here is a letter fr. Poguliaiev [Pogulyaev] for you to read through, & copy of a telegr. fr. the "Tvertsy"< Baby< got to-day.—"On March 7-th the 3-d squadron of the Tver Regiment named after your Imperial Majesty [the tsarevich] penetrated into the ranks of a Kurdish cavalry body [of the Ottoman army] more than three times as large as ours and sabered many, thereby extricating our infantry from a dangerous situation—I am happy to felicitate with this our Worshipped August Chief[, the tsarevich]. Colonel von Harten. (Field Telegraph branch 116.)[240] [a, b, c]

One says [A. N.] Kh.[vostov] is at Moscou [sic] talking away & saying he was sent off because wished to get rid of the German spies near our Fr.<—so low. Ah, indeed he ought to be judged or his embroidered coat[241] be taken fr. him. He [Rasputin?] said you ought to punish those that talk in the clubs.—A.[nia]< continues getting anon.[ymous] letters, her Father [S. A. Taneev] & poor Zhuk< too, telling him not to go with her [on walks], otherwise he will die a violent death with A.< She spoke to Spiridov.[ich] & he will have her guarded, knows one is after her. Begs her only to walk in our garden, not go on foot to Church nor in the street, to get quicker into her carriage—certainly this makes her nervous. Sht.[yurmer] told the Father [S. A. Taneev] he has her safely guarded in town<.—I wish one cld. stop Ignatev's popular (left) speeches in the Duma about universities wh. one needs all over Russia etc.—he will break his own neck seeking for popularity. [d]

March 16-th. Again splendid sunshine, 13° in the sun & thawing hard—strange you had such a thick fogg [sic]. Slept alright, but the pains gently continue tiring me. I have the dentist [Dr. S. S. Kostritsky] after luncheon. Titi< will walk with the children & before tea I shall have his hair cut—Lili< could never make up her mind because his standing out ears were hidden by his long hair— so she let me do it, it wld. be less painful to her & I am sure he will look much nicer, being such a big boy. To-morrow he leaves for Reval to live with her relations.—I am sorry, as he is a nice boy for Aleksei to play with. The big girls< go to town as Olga has a committee & then they take tea at Anichkov<. Sweetest Love, its two weeks to-day, that you left us and I miss you quite terribly. Its good you have much to do, so that you cannot feel the loneliness so much. Only the evenings must indeed be sad & dull, poor Sweetheart. I send you again some lilies of the valley & the little sweet-smelling blue flowers you like—I have kissed them & they bring you my love, wh. is deep and tender.— [e]

I don't read at all now, so as to rest my eyes wh. ache so & in the evening lay patiences with Marie, in the daytime A. reads sometimes aloud to me. I shall send Motherdear< an exciting book again. My "Buyan" has come back again to the big palace< & this time wounded.—I got telegrams fr. Yalta, my Sanatorium is quite ready—such luck as it gives us from 50-60 officers' places, than we can turn "Kutchuk Lambat [Kuchuk-Lembad]" into a hospital only for soldiers, as the officers bored themselves to distraction there & always tried to go off to Yalta & there was no place for their wives to live, as its only a fishermens' village.—I do so wonder how Shuvaev will manage, is he energetic? What a blessing if he is the right man.—Yes, alas, our generals have never been very famous—what can it be? Clear them out then & bring forward young energetic men, as for instance [E. C.] Arsenev—during a war one chooses the capable men & does not go by the age & rank, I find,—its for the whole armie's [sic] sake & one cannot suffer men's lives to be shed in vain by blustering generals.—I wonder what Admiral Filimore [Phillimore] will tell you about the north?— [f, g]

I had a letter fr. Malcolm expressing the wild enthusiasm all over England, about Erzerum[214]—in the streets & clubs it was the reigning talk.—Unfortunately he did not succeed with the English red cross to get them to send their 3 sisters [i.e., nurses] over to Germany as we did, & he is muchly disappointed. Then Daisy< arranged him a meeting with Max< in Switzerland—when he got there, Max had fallen ill & cld. not meet him. He went over our organisation [sic] at Bern for the help of our prisoners & found it excellent. I shall finish this after luncheon, as now must be getting up. I cover you with kisses, every sweet place & hold you tightly clasped to my heart—Treasure, sweetest of Huzys!—We had Nastinka< to luncheon & before that Maklakov sat with me for ¾ of an hour talking hard. True, devoted soul. Intensely relieved you have changed Poliv.[anov] but he wld. have cleared out some others too. When we meet again I can talk over many things he said & I shall speak with Sht.[yurmer] when see him, as some things are really true & need thinking over.—He entreats you not to agree with all the Moscou [sic] vostrebovaniya [demands]. Of course one cannot sanction the soyuz gorodov [Union of Cities] etc. becoming legalized & stable institutions. Their money is governemental [sic] & they can use as many millions as they like & the "people" don't even know its crown money—that must be made known officially. [h, i]

Should they exist on later they wld. inevitably be the nest of propaganda & the workers of the Duma in the country. He was minister [of internal affairs] when you allowed it, as they came straight to you before Maklakov cld. make his doklad [report] & then he begged you after [you allowed the formation of these voluntary, semi-private organizations] only to sanction it during the war. Please, Lovy, remember this. You have now sent them a wire thanking for their work—but that must not mean they they [sic] should continue [after the war]. If ever such sort of organisations [sic] are needed, it must be in the hands of Governors.—He is over disgusted with [A. N.] Khvostov's behaviour. He spoke like an honest, well-meaning, deeply loving & devoted loyal friend & servant of yours.—Now for to-day I must end, the man leaves. Goodbye & God bless & keep you, my Angel. Tenderest kisses fr. all. Ever yr. very, very Own. [j]

240. The "Nicky-Sunny Correspondence" contains a copy of this telegram in pencil on a separate sheet. It is not placed in correct order in the Soviet edition: rather than appearing (as it does) at the bottom of *Perepiska*, IV, page 151, it should begin on line 14 of page 154.

241. Men and women in Russian state and court service displayed embroidered monograms indicating their rank. Although dismissed as minister of the interior, A. N. Khvostov continued to hold the high rank of *deistvitel'ny statsky sovetnik* (d.s.s.).

No. 889/ Telegram 57. Tsarskoe Selo> Stavka. 16 Mar 1916. 2.32> 3.00 p.m. To his majesty. Warm, glorious sun, now cloudy. Big girls< in town<, little ones< strolling. Entire face still hurts, though less. In thoughts always together. Await good news with impatience. God bless you. Warmly embrace [you]. Alix

No. 890/ Telegram 32. Stavka> Tsarskoe Selo. 16 Mar 1916. 7.35> 7.45 p.m. To her majesty. Fond thanks [for] dear letter and Anastasia. Horrid fog continues. The ice has broken up, water in river very high. Also got letter from energetic naval man[242] in the far north. Tender love. Niki

242. This was M. S. Roshchakovsky, "a retired naval officer, who had become an intimate friend of the Court circle during the Japanese War. During the Great War he appears to have been a supervisor of various undertakings on the Murman Coast." (Vulliamy, p. 160n)

No. 891/ Telegram 60. Tsarskoe Selo> Stavka. 16 Mar 1916. 8.50> 9.53 p.m. To his majesty. Thank you for telegram, sorry you have rotten weather, here [it is] good. How am I to answer energetic R?[242] Asked about that in my letter. Sleep well, dear one. God bless you. [Our] children found Motherdear< getting better, coughs less, but still has not come downstairs. Xenia< has been in bed for a week now with a cold. We all kiss you. Alix

No. 892/ Her No. 464.   Tsarskoe Selo. March 17th 1916.
My Beloved,
    A grey morning, 3° of warmth. How annoying that the fogg [sic] continues at Moghilev & such mud, swamps, inundated rivers all along the front. Really its bitterly hard all the difficulties our poor troops have to fight with; but God wont forsake them. Only Lovy, punish those that make faults [mistakes], you cannot be severe enough—some firm examples will frighten all the rest.—Thats good yr. clearing away Ronzhin—he is the despair of all—& red Danilov?[243] Css. Carlov [Natalya Karlova] is furious her friend Polivanov has been changed [i.e., dismissed as minister of war] & has at once offered him to live in her house—that pictures to you the state of many in society now. Formerly they would never have dreamed of doing such a thing—she with aplomb shows the opposition—her son in law is at Tiflis, N.[icholasha]< chose P.[olivanov], thats all one [group] & [explains] her unamiability when she came to me. She is Volzhin's great friend & therefore sits upon the week [sic] man and crushes him. I know this all fr. A.[nia]'s< Mother [Nadezhda Taneeva] as the Css. & Sisters are her Father's [A.

S. Taneev's] relations & they have changed in their behaviour towards them [Anna Vyrubova's parents] too.— [a, b]

Cannot one be more careful as to who gets put into the Council of the Empire?< Makl.[akov] says it makes all the good ones say, that many one does not approve of, find a home there, as for instance Dumitrashko whom Trepov wishes to get rid of & therefore begs him to be put there. One needs good men & not any body (else it becomes like the retired officers). It must be the loyal right.—I never knew that nice Pokrovsky is a known left[ist] (their nicest luckily), a follower of Kokovtzev [Kokovtsov] & of the "[Progressive] Block".[244] Wish you could think of a good successor to Sazonov,—need not be a diplomat! So as now already to get into the work & to see we are not sat upon later by England & that when the questions of ultimate peace comes we should be firm. Old Goremykin & Shtyurmer always disapproved of him [Sazonov] as he is such a coward towards Europe & a parlamentarist—& that wld. be Russia's ruin. [c]

For Baby's< sake we must be firm as otherwise his inheritance will be awful, as with his [mild?] c[h]aracter [we must see that] he wont bow down to others but be his own master, as one must in Russia whilst people are still so uneducated—Mr. Philippe & Gr.[egory] said so too.—And another thing Lovy, forgive my bothering you, but its for yr. sweet sake they speak to me. Wont you give Sht.[yurmer] the order he is to send for Rodz.[yanko] (the rotten) & very firmly tell him you insist upon the [Duma] budget being finished before Easter; as then you need not call them together till, God grant, when everything is better—autumn—after war. They want to dawdle on so as to come back in summer with all their horrible liberal propositions. Many say the same thing & beg of you to insist they shld. finish now. And you cannot make concessions, an answerable ministery[244] etc.: & all the rest they wish. It must be your war & your peace & your & our Country's honour & as no means the Duma's they have not to say a word in those questions.— [d]

Ah, how I wish we were together, I cant write all, I should like to, tho' my pen flies like mad over the paper & the thoughts tear through my head—its difficult to put all plainly on paper—& besides I have to get up & be off to the dentist.—He [Dr. S. S. Kostritsky] is killing a nerve in my last tooth to the right, thinks that may calm the other nerves, because the tooth does not require the nerve being killed at all. He is quite put out about my pains. Head & eye go on aching to-day, but I slept well.—My little Malama came for an hour yesterday evening, after dinner at Anias. We had not seen him for 1½ years. Looks flourishing more of a man now, an adorable boy still. I must say, a perfect son in law he wld. have been—why are foreign Pces. [princes] not as nice!—Ortipo [the dog] had to be shown to his "Father" of course.—Quite nice what they wrote about Shuvaev. Must make A.[nia] read what Men.[shikov] says about P.[olivanov]—am so relieved he has gone—the "socie" [society of his supporters & our critics] of course will grieve, it interests me what Paul< will say at tea to-day.—I must be off, shall finish after luncheon.— [e, f]

Oh thank you so, so much my beloved Sweetheart for your precious letter wh. was joy to receive & every loving word warmed me up.—Yes, thats Albert Grancy's son who told that—at least one told that—at least one who honestly said that the Germans began. —Its most despairing[, a] thaw having set in at the front & that one cant advance & are deep in water. Such bad luck, but perhaps will pass quickly. Good, you have sent for the 3 chiefs[218] to speak over with them.—[Your] Sister Olga arrives on Sunday, to everybody's great surprise. I fear she comes to speak about her wishes for the future—what am I to say about yr. thoughts on that subject [of her marriage to N. A. Kulikovsky]. The moment when all minds are so unpatriotic & against the family its hard she should think of such things & his part is unpardonable, and personally I fear Sandro< has been egging her on—I may be wrong—but that story worries me very much & I don't find she ought to have brought up this theme now. Perhaps she wants to follow him to the Caucasus as one says his regiment goes off there—that would be more than unwise & give occasion for much talk & ugly talk.[235] I am so glad to hear that people are contented at Shuvaev's nomination—God grant him success.—Now my Darling I must close my letter. All the children fondly kiss you & I cover you with tender, gentle kisses & deep love, sweet Huzy mine. Ever yr. old Wify. [g]

243. A. A. Sergeev thinks "red" indicates Gen. N. A. Danilov had red hair. (*Perepiska*, IV, p. 158) It may also be significant that Gen. G. N. Danilov was known as the "black one"; perhaps a humorous connection developed whereby people referred to N. A. Danilov as "red" to distinguish him from the "other" Danilov.
244. Alexandra refers to the demand of the "progressive block" in the Duma for a "ministry of public confidence." According to this proposition, ministers would no longer be solely responsible to the tsar. Some claimed that if the ministers were responsible to the Duma—at least to some extent—they would begin to enjoy the *confidence* of the public.

No. 893/ Telegram 65. Tsarskoe Selo> Stavka. 17 Mar 1916. 2.20> 2.55 p.m. To his majesty. [Daughter] Olga and I heartily thank [you] for dear letters. Plunged into despair that you have such poor weather there, thawing here as well. In thoughts together. Think of you with love and yearning. We all 6 kiss and embrace you. Alix

No. 894. Ts.[arist] Stavka. March 17th 1916.
My own beloved Sunny,
Shuvaev will hand you this letter—so I hope you will receive him soon. I also return R.'s[242] letter, wh. is similar to the one sent a few days ago through admir.[al] Phillimore. I will show it to you when I return home. For three days solid we have been sitting in a thick fog, & truly that has a depressing effect. The spring quickly approaches; the Dnepr broke up yesterday and has risen considerably. But to date there are no floods in this area. [a]
Yesterday I motored, & took one of my favourite walks fr. last autumn towards the bank, to the spot wh. Baby< liked so much. The scene was truly magnificent—the entire river was covered with blocks of ice; they moved quickly & quietly, but sometimes one could hear the sharp sound of two huge ice-blocks clashing. We all stood a long time, admiring the scene. Just fancy, for the first time in my life I saw such a nature scene—not counting, of course the Neva in town<, wh. is, of course a very different affair. It may soon be possible to go out in boats!! [b]

Just fancy, the little adm.[iral]< asked [N. A.] Grabbe the other day to provide a gentle cossack horse for him to ride. He [Admiral Nilov] is delighted, enjoys his rides, feels well & sleeps better. But he always leaves & returns in such a way as for us to not see him—strange fellow! Now I must go to the doklad [report]. Fancy, Alekseev told me I could return [home] for a week! The commanders-in-chief [218] all come here about the 30th or 31st, as I have perhaps already written. I am most pleased with this unexpected luck. God bless you my Sunny, my beloved Wify-dear, my girlie. I kiss you & the children tenderly. Ever your own old huzy   Nicky. [c]

No. 895/ Telegram 33. Stavka> Tsarskoe Selo. 17 Mar 1916. 5.36> 6.00 p.m. To her majesty. Answer R.[242] Am very pleased with his work. Loving thanks [for] dear letters. Can leave to-morrow, arriving home Saturday evening. Please receive Shuvaev in the afternoon. He leaves to day with a letter from me. Overjoyed to meet. Tender love. Niki

No. 896/ Telegram 69. Tsarskoe Selo> Stavka. 17 Mar 1916. 7.18> 8.17 p.m. To his majesty. Terribly glad over unexpected joy on Saturday. Of course will receive him [Gen. Shuvaev, the newly appointed minister of war] to-morrow. Embrace and kiss you. Sleep well. Necessary to take a small break [in the Brusilov offensive] and then all will go well. He [Rasputin] said so. Alix

No. 897/ Telegram 34. Stavka> Tsarskoe Selo. 18 Mar 1916. 4.38> 5.15 p.m. To her majesty. Fondest thanks [for] dear letter, also Olga. Rainy, cold weather. Happy to return. Enjoy sweet flowers. Tender kisses to all. Niki

No. 898/ Telegram 70. Tsarskoe Selo> Stavka. 18 Mar 1916. 10.15> 10.45 p.m. To his majesty. Glorious sun. Wish you a happy trip. [We] await to-morrow with impatience. Face better, eye still hurts a lot. All tenderly kiss [you]. Alix

No. 899/ Her No. 465.   Ts.[arskoe] S[elo]. March 26th 1916.
My very own precious Love,
   Once more the train will be carrying you off from us, when you read my letter. This week has flown; it was an unexpected joy you came & you can tell Alekseev, with kind messages, that I think of him with a grateful heart. I am glad Dmitri< accompanies you now, it will make the journey brighter & less lonely. The idea of you going off all alone again, is great pain. If I feel this terrible loneliness everytime, tho' have the dear children, what must yr. sensations be all alone at the Headquarters! And Passion-week & Easter approaching, those lovely services, you will be sad standing all by yourself in Church.[229] God help you, my own Lovebird.—You never can come here without there being some story to pain you or make you anxious & give worry, now [your] poor [sister] Olga's intentions & plans for the future have assailed us & I cannot tell you the bitter pain it causes me for you. Your own sweet sister doing such a thing![245] I understand all & don't & cant grudge her longing first for liberty & then happiness, but she forces you to go against the family laws, when it touches ones own

nearest, its far worse. She, an Emperor's daughter & sister! Before the country, at such a time when the dynasty is going through heavy trials & many counter-currants are at work,—is sad. The society's morals are falling to pieces & our family, Paul, Misha & Olga show the example, not speaking of the yet worse behaviour of Boris, Andrei & Sergei.[245] How shall we ever stop the rest from similar marriages? Its wrong she puts you into this false position & it hurts me its through her this new sorrow has been inflicted upon you! What would yr. Father [Alexander III] have said to all this? We have been far to[o] weak & kind to the family & ought many a time to have thundered at the young ones. [a, b]

Do, if only possible, find an occasion of speaking to Dmitri about his goings on in town<, & at such a time.—I, wickedly perhaps, did hope Petia< would not give the divorce. It may seem cruel & I don't mean to be so, because I tenderly love Olga, but I think of you first & that she makes you act wrongly. Nice sun-shine, I hope it will shine upon yr. way too. Please give many messages to Count Keller fr. me, ask after his boy (second marriage)[—]he had him with him a time, I know.—I hope to go to Church to-night when you have left, it will be a comfort to pray for you with all the rest. I hate goodbyes & the awful separa-tions. You have warmed me up again with your tender, loving caresses, they soothe the constant aching heart. All my deepest, warmest, unceasing love sur-rounds you, all fervent, burning prayers, heart & soul undying together through all eternity. My Own, my Life, my Treasure! God bless & protect you & give you success in all undertakings, guide & guard you fr. all harm! Passionately I press you to my heart & kiss you with infinite tenderness, eyes, lips, forehead, chest, hands, every tenderly loved place wh. belongs to me. Goodbye, Sunshine, my happiness, God grant the separation may not be too long. The chief thing is missing when you are not here & the evenings are sad & we try to get early to bed. Ever, Nicky mine, yr. own true wify Your Own.— Alix. [c, d]

245. By law, members of the imperial family could marry only with permission of the tsar. Al-though the Orthodox Church permits divorce, Romanovs were to avoid divorce as well as marriage to divorced people and commoners. The sovereign could grant exceptions to these rules. Olga wanted a divorce from her husband "Petia"< to marry N. A. Kulikovsky. Nicholas granted the di-vorce in the fall of 1916; Olga and Kulikovsky then married. The emperor's Uncle Paul had a mor-ganatic marriage with Countess Hohenfelsen; Nicholas gave her the title "Princess Paley." The tsar's brother Michael ("Misha") provided the severest test to the dynasty's good name. (See Letters No. 213 and 227a.) Boris and Andrew ("Andrei") Vladimirovich were brothers. Boris, a notorious roue, proposed to Olga, the tsar's eldest daughter. See Letter No. 823c for the furious anger with which the empress reacted to this idea. Andrew's mistress was Mathilde Kschessinska, the famed ballerina who had an affair with Nicholas II before his engagement to Alexandra.

No. 900/ Her No. 466.   Ts.[arskoe] S[elo]. March 27th 1916.
My very own Lovebird,

Glorious warm sunshine, do hope you have the same weather. Such a sad feeling when I awoke this morning & turned to kiss you & found the dear place empty "Me don't like dat" at all. And the evening was melancholy, laid pa-tiences & talked. Went to evening service & prayed hard for my lonely One whom I had just parted with in great pain. The priest [Father A. P. Vasil'ev] preached about Maria of Egypt. Baby< wrote his diary with grumbling. They all go to Ania's< hospital this afternoon to hear singing & see conjurers, she wants me to go, but do not feel up to it. After Church must finish this, then must look at some of Streblov's pictures [i.e., paintings], change & go to the big pal-ace< hospital, where I have not been since about 4 months, & then for a drive, as they say the roads are better.—Isa< lunches with us. Now I must quickly get up.—Always in a hurry, so my letter will be short. Have you got on with the book? Oh, my Sweetheart, how I miss you & long for you. I cover you with tender kisses. God bless & protect you. The Children kiss you over & over again. Ever, my Angel love, yr. very own old   Wify.

No. 901/ Telegram 111. Tsarskoe Selo> Kursk. 27 Mar 1916. 1.40> 3.23 p.m. To his majesty. Glorious warm sun. [We] were at church, now going to big pal-ace< hospital and for a drive. In thoughts and prayers always with you. [I] miss [you] terribly. We all kiss you and Dmitry<. Alix

No. 902/ Telegram 1600 in Russian. Orel> Tsarskoe Selo. 27 Mar 1916. 2.30> 3.15 p.m. To her majesty. Warmly thank you for dear letter. Sunny weather, cold. Hope all are well. Warmly embrace [you]. Niki

No. 903/ Telegram 113. Tsarskoe Selo> Proskurovo. 28 Mar 1916. 9.55 a.m.> 2.05 p.m. To his majesty. Glorious weather. Drove yesterday at Pavlovsk. Am going to hospital<. Most thankful for yesterday's telegram. [We] miss you. [In] thoughts together. God keep you. [We] all warmly kiss [you]. Alix

No. 904/ Her No. 467.   Tsarskoe Selo. March 28th 1916.
My own Sweetheart,
   Another glorious morning with splendid sunshine, I am glad, then the snow will sooner melt & the roads become better. We drove yesterday at Pavlovsk. I am so disaccustomed to the movement in a big carriage & driving quickly, that it makes my back ache & gives me a not very pleasant sensation (the movable heart & kidneys), but after a while that is sure to pass. I so very rarely drive these last years.—At Ania's< hospital it was quite nice, fancy my having gone for an hour, I watched everything with a sort of interest, heart & soul being far away from all that. 2 tiny children played remarcably [sic] well on the gicelyra, that wooden instrument with wooden hammers. Then Mme Beling sang, very pretty voice indeed. The soldiers were enchanted. Nini< sat next to me and was a goose. I saw Kotchubei [Kochubei] about presents for the "Plastuni" [Cossack infantry] from Baby<, he will give money & then our store< can make the things for the 6-th of May, as they cannot possibly be got ready for Easter. To-day I see the Priest of the [imperial yacht] Standart. He came here for the men's devotions on board & now goes back to Rezhitsa. Then Shagubatov presents himself.—I found 4 "Alexandrovtsi"< & 2 Crimeans< in the big palace< [hospital] yester-day, also one of yr. 1-st Siberian regiment, I had seen him wounded after the last war; he said the losses a week or 2 ago were terrible[—]in yr. regiment nearly all the officers again killed or wounded,—such a cauchemar [nightmare]. [a, b]
   In the afternoon we went into Znamenia< & placing candles & praying there reminded me of the last day we knelt there side by side, as one. Oh, my Lovy

sweet, if you knew the solitude without your precious presence! Such a yearning besides in my arms to close them around you & press you to my heart & feel peaceful & calm in yr. great unfailing love! I must stop now because of the masseuse & then I go to our hospital<.−A.[nia] spends the day in town< till 5, so I shall be free to visit another hospital & take Isa< for a turn [walk] perhaps. Three new officers arrived fr. Tarnopol & I made their dressings, One old one had served many years in baby's "Lithuanians" & remembered seeing me when I arrived 22 years ago at Simferopol. We are going to the Matf. lazaret [Maternity] Hospital after luncheon. One brought me quite charming Images [icons] painted by wounded soldiers, who had never drawn before, & the setting made by them too. I am writing during luncheon, as have to receive after. Just got yr. wire from Zhmerinka, glad you have spring weather, hope you can take a little walk upon yr. arrival this evening. Now goodbye my Nicky sweet, my own Huzy. Endless kisses & blessings. Ever yr. very own old <u>Sunny</u>. [c]

No. 905/ Telegram 1 in Russian. Zhmerinka> Tsarskoe Selo. 28 Mar 1916. 12.30> 1.05 p.m. To her majesty. Thank you for telegram. Absolutely spring-like here. Dmitry< is touched [that you remembered him in No. 901 above] and with me embraces all [of you]. Niki

---

No. 906/ Telegram 21 in Russian. Kamenets-Podol'sk> Tsarskoe Selo. 29 Mar 1916. 9.44> 10.15 a.m. To her majesty. Thank you for news. Arrived yesterday with rain. Better today though cool. Going to review now. Warmly embrace all. Niki

---

No. 907/ Telegram 118. Tsarskoe Selo> Pol. tel. otd. lit. E. [Emperor's field telegraph unit]. 29 Mar 1916. 2.25> 3.21 p.m. To his majesty. Grey weather, was at hospital<, now going to lancer hospital. [We] all warmly kiss you. [We] kiss [you]. May the Lord bless you. Alix

---

No. 908/ Her No. 468.   Tsarskoe Selo. March 29th 1916.
My Beloved,
   I have no idea when and where you will receive my letters. Just now one brought me yr. wire from Kamenets-Podolsk, wh. came in half an hour only. Here too its grey this morning & dull. Do so wonder whether you will see my Crimeans< anywhere, they are at 20 versts about from where you spent the night.−Poor little Nikita[, your nephew,] had an operation done yesterday, but I don't know the details,−the ear,−anyhow the Drs. seem satisfied.−The Children worked in the ice & I sat in the sun for ¾ of an hour looking on.−Dr. Zuev has returned & I hope to see him, he went to Victoria to Darmouth to bring her my letter. Dicky [Ludwig-Frantsisk] walks on crutches, he broke his leg some time ago toboggaining [sic]. He spends [E]aster with his parents at Kent House. Easter falls [i.e., finds them] together this year. Louise is in France in the hospital again.−A.[nia]< read to us yesterday evening, poor girl, she does not read well & makes endless faults [mistakes] in English.− [a]

Lovy, do have that question stopped about the lot of new metropolitans, it is again being discussed in the Synod believe me, its not right, we have not the men & it will only do harm to the Church. First our Bishops must be better men before we can think of making them metropolitans, its too early & will do much mischief & bring yet more frictions in the Church. [See Letter No. 880b.]—Have been to A.'s hospital & dressed the wounds of three of the worst. Now I am going to my lancer hospital, & before that, must receive.—Tatiana Andreevna [Gromova] comes to tea; alas, [your sister] Olga says she cannot come to us, so sad, as I had hoped to have a talk with her. [See Letters No. 892g and 899a,b,c.]—Goodbye, my Angel, God bless & protect you. I cover you, my own sweet One, with very tender kisses & such craving. Ever yr. very own old Wify. [b]

No. 909/ Telegram 36 in Russian. Kamenets-Podol'sk> Tsarskoe Selo. 29 Mar 1916. 7.24> 8.07 p.m. To her majesty. Returned from review near Khotin. Troops showed themselves in excellent condition. Saw our Kuban [Cossack] company. Wind, rain, hail. Visited two hospitals. Warmly embrace all. Niki

No. 910/ Her No. 469.   Ts.[arskoe] S[elo]. March 30th 1916.
My own Sweetheart,
    I am writing, to you during luncheon, as had no time in the morning. Read through my prayers, had the masseuse, went to our Peshcherny Church< for service (thought so much of you) & then to our hospital<, where I made 10 dressings,—now am tired. Have to receive. At 4 go to the red cross & I give the graduates of the courses their papers & they get the cross. Then A.[unt] Olga<, Mavra< & Helene< dine with us, as I have not yet seen them this year.—A grey day, wanted to snow but not [sufficiently] cold, so shall dine with the girls to freshen up my brain. A.[nia]< has gone for the day to town<, saw her in Church. — I was awfully grateful to get 2 telegr. from you yesterday, Lovebird. We are enchanted that you saw our [Kuban Cossack] Company.—3 people of "Pate" [the film company Pathe] come to bring Aleksei an apparatus [film projector?] & some films.—Baby< improves playing on the balalaika, [daughter] Tatiana also had a lesson yesterday,—I want them all to learn to play together, it wld. be charming. Sweetheart, I must end now. God bless & protect you & keep you fr. all harm. I cover you with fond, longing kisses.—Ever, Huzy love,   Wify.

No. 911/ Telegram 52 in Russian. Kamenets-Podol'sk> Tsarskoe Selo. 30 Mar 1916. 2.30> 3.09 p.m. To her majesty. Finally, good, warm day. Held fine inspection of [Third] Trans-Amur division. Visited two hospitals. Am leaving now. Tenderly embrace you [all]. Niki

No. 912/ Telegram 122 in Russian. Tsarskoe Selo> Grechanyi, Pod.[ol'skaya] gubernaya. 30 Mar 1916. 3.27> 4.52 p.m. To his majesty. Attended mass at hospital this morning. Now have taken a drive. [We] all warmly kiss [you]. God keep [you]. Alix

No. 913/ Telegram 2. Zhmerinka> Tsarskoe Selo. 30 Mar 1916. 10.40> 11.30 p.m. To her majesty. Heartily thank you for dear letter, received in Proskurov. Good night. Niki

---

No. 914/ Her No. 470.   Ts.[arskoe] S[elo]. March 31st 1916.
My own sweet One,
   I hope you will find this letter upon yr. arrival to-morrow. How glad I am that all went off so successfully & that the weather got warmer.—Mavra< & Helene< dined, A.[unt] Olgas< chill prevented her coming,—Christophor [Christo<] ar-rives to-day. Helene read to us a most interesting letter she received fr. Vera[, Queen of Montenegro], all about the last terrible days they went through in Montenegro & their marvellous [sic] escape. She writes so cleverly & full of life,—a regular nightmare, poor thing.—Mavra wanted you to send for Igor< so as to get him away from a bad, fast set here,[—]Ella Benkendorff, etc: she will speak again to [Dr.] Varavka about the boy's health.—A lonely homecoming to the Headquarters again, poor agoo wee one, I long to hold you tightly in my arms & to cover you with kisses,—and you?— [a]
   Now I know Vl. Nik.< & Danini[, the imperial architect] are working out plans for this institute of Fedorov & the plans will be sent to him & Voeikov< to choose,—but please, tell Fed. that I must see them as may have ideas to pro-pose,—& I beg of you to insist upon Ania< being permitted to buy that bit of ground she chose ([priced at] 10 to 12,000 [rubles]) & wh. Voeikov knows about. Only he wont stand up for Ania, he is not a real friend of hers when it does not suit him. You give him & Fed. your & my order that she is to be al-lowed to buy that bit of ground now they need not have it, only have ample place [i.e., land] next to it. Its opposite the photographers, where the Baron [a dog] fell into the water, a little higher up & she could have some green there. Voeikov arranged the buying & selling of those grounds with a man & is obsti-nate & very angry that A.[nia] & Putyatin spoke about it & looked at the ground & arranged with the man that they would like to buy it for her invalid hospital house. Before she has the money for building, she can already plant vegetables, wh. will be a profit to her refuge[e home]. I dont want Vl. Nik. Der.< & Fed. to be greedy. So you give that order—Fed. will remember it. Both things are under my protection,—so Voeikov can give Kharlamov (I think thats the man's name) the order to sell the bit Ania chose already before we had thoughts of that ground for the medical Institute (and there is ample place still), so as that she can buy it now & he can write to her, we both wish her to have that ground to buy (or we can give for Easter it to her, 10[,000] to 12,000 [rubles], as you think)—only please have it done at once, & don't let them cheet [sic] her.— [b, c]
   Excuse my bothering you, but I know she is in all states about this ground & its good she has that work to think about & the plans and the planting etc.—We leave the house before 10, as at 10½ is the consecration in town< of the little church in my school [of] Pop.[ular] Artcraft. Then 12½ lunch at Anichkov<. At 2 [daughter] Olga has a committee & receives offerings. I shall probably go to the store^{2} with [daughter] Tatiana or [to the] hospital in the palace, or to [visit] Nikita. He is getting on alright [sic—see Letter No. 908a.]—A bright morning,—I wish had not to go to town, its always so tiring such an expedition.—You will

feel dull when Dmitri< leaves again. Css. Palei [Paley] wrote me a long letter, begging you to keep him away fr. the regiment, because his health is so bad & he so sad to go. If one could find him work of some sort to do, or send him to a sanatorium for 2 months complete rest in good air,—only not town, or dawdling about.— Now must get up & dress, Goodbye, my very own Treasure, my joy & sunshine, my very own Precious One. God bless & keep you. I kiss you with unending true devotion & remain, yr. own old Sunny. [d]

No. 915/ Telegram 1 in Russian. Mena> Tsarskoe Selo. 31 Mar 1916. 11.50 a.m.> 1.20 p.m. To her majesty. Warmly thank you for two dear letters. Hope to be in Mogilev this evening. Weather is excellent. Warmly embrace [you]. Niki

No. 916/ Telegram unnumbered. Tsarskoe Selo> Zhlobin. 31 Mar 1916. 5.10> 5.40 p.m. To his majesty. Tenderly thank you for telegram. Were in town< since morning for dedication of church, lunched at Anichkov<. Were at Kazan cathedral for skoroposlushnitsa[247], [then visited] Xenia's< store. Good weather. [We] warmly kiss you. God keep [you]. Alix

No. 917/ Telegram 42. Stavka> Tsarskoe Selo. 31 Mar 1916. 11.15> 11.50 p.m. To her majesty. Arrived safely. Fondest thanks [for] dear letter of yesterday. Mild weather. Good night, sleep well. Niki

No. 918.   Ts.[arist] Stavka. March 31st 1916.
My own beloved Sunny,
    At last I have taken a minute to sit down & write you after a silence of five days—a letter is a substitute for conversation, unlike telegrams! I tenderly thank you for yr. dear letters—it seems the first came so long ago! What a joy it is to get several in a single day, on the way returning home! During the journey I read fr. morning until night—first I finished "The Man who was Dead," then a french book & to day the marvellous [sic] tale about little Boy Blue![246] I like it, as does Dmitry<. I had to use my handkerchief several times. I enjoy re-reading some of the parts separately, though I know them almost by heart. I find them so true & beautiful! I dont know why, but it reminded me of Coburg & Walton[-on-Thames, where as tsarevich Nicholas stayed with Prince Ludwig of Battenberg in 1894]! I am pleased with my trip. Thank God, all came off well. You can fancy how I was pleasantly surprised when, riding round the troops at a big inspection, I saw our dear cossacks who grinned & smiled broadly, beginning with Zhukov & down to the last soldier—among them Shvedov & Zborovsky. I gave them greetings fr. you & the girlies! They had just returned fr. the trenches. The weather was beastly— strong wind with sun, hail & rain. Unfortunately I did not see your Crimeans!< [a, b]
    The staff of the 9th army prepared a simple lunch for me in the little village of Khotin, where I also visited 2 hospitals. We spent 9 hours in the open air that day. The generals dined with me in the train at Kamenets-Podol'sk. I spoke much with Keller, & gave him your regards. He has not changed a bit. The following day, that is yesterday, I inspected the newly formed division—the 3rd

Trans-Amur infantry div. It made an excellent impression —splendid, tall fellows, real guardsmen. During the review we heard our guns firing at austrian aeroplanes wh. were dropping bombs on both of our bridges over the Dnestr. Then I visited 2 more hospitals and [saw] Lechitsky; he is starting to recover, but still lies down. I left Kamen.-Pod. after lunch; by then the weather was warm & clear, & I arrived here to-night at 9.30. I went to bed rather late, as I had to prepare myself for the military council. [c]

April 1st. A warm, grey morning after rain last night—just the right weather for a long conference. It began at 10.o['clock] & lasted till lunch-time, & will be resumed immediately. Dmitry< leaves this evening; he will spend three days at home & then return to his regiment. I asked him to see you. I forgot to tell you I saw Misha< twice at Kam.-Pod. He left before me for his division, which is stationed not far from Kam.-Pod. Now, my angel, my sweet darling, I must end. God bless you & the children! I kiss you & them tenderly. Ever yr. own old huzy   Nicky. [d]

---

246. "The Man who was Dead" was a story by A. W. Marchmont. "Little Boy Blue" was the hero of *Through the Postern Gate*, a popular novel by Florence L. Barclay. "This book seems to have appealed profoundly to the Tsar and the Tsaritsa, and there are several pathetic and playful allusions to it in their correspondence. [For example, see Letters No. 923a and 948.] The choice of such a book and the impression which it made are facts of some significance, and help us to realise vividly the tastes and proclivities of the royal couple." (Vulliamy, p. 164n) I read the Barclay novels referred to in the Nicky-Sunny Correspondence, asking myself if a liking for these tales indicated a lack of taste and discretion on the part of the royal couple. Barclay was a competent writer who offered light, romantic literature. Interestingly enough, in captivity Nicholas turned to the classics of Russian literature, a much "heavier" fare, indeed.

No. 919/ Telegram 2. Tsarskoe Selo> Stavka. 1 Ap 1916. 1.03> 1.15 p.m. To his majesty. [I] think of you with tenderness, of your lonely return [to Stavka]. Glorious, warm sunny morning. Window open. Now becoming overcast. Feel completely tired and sick after yesterday. [We] all warmly kiss [you]. God keep you. Alix

---

No. 920/ Her No. 471.   Tsarskoe Selo. April 1st 1916.
My own sweet One,
    Now you are back again at the Headquarter[s] & I fear, will feel awfully lonely. And to stand all alone during those lovely Church services will be sad,[229]—have you at least got Georgi< with you?—I have the window a little open & hear a little birdie chirruping away, at Gatchino the first little blue flowers are out; its beautiful this sunshine & so calm to-day. [Daughter] Olga wrote to you all about our doings in town<,—I must only add where [daughter] Tatiana & I were, whilst Olga was in the Winter Palace. We drove to the new little Bari Church of the "Skoroposlushnitsa" & saw the lovely Image [icon] there,—such an ideally sweet face & one has such a nice feeling when praying before it,—I placed a candle for you there[247] & at the Kaz.[an] Virgin too, where we went. I send you a tiny Image I brought back from there,—you have already many, but when you read the inscription behind, it may help you in your heavy tasks.—Then to the store,[2] went right through it,—alas, not very many peo-

ple.—Sat then at Xenias<,—for years I had not been to her & so found changes in her room. Nikita is getting on alright. [See Letter No. 908a.] [a]

Have not slept very well, that happens when I am overtired & everything aches, therefore shall remain lying this morning.—Had news from N.P.,< says its spring there, lots of birds, 25 storks even arrived. Kirill< spent a week with them & seemed sorry to leave. In the mornings they rode to the different Companies, wh. are several versts away,—watched the shooting. They have not yet been excerising [sic] as the roads are impossible & everything [is] under water. After luncheon they walked in the garden & then went off again,—& in the evening bridge. The Companies make their devotions by turn,—my little Church is in a barn & so quite cosy & not cold & can stand[229] without caps. The priest is happy to have more services, as Polushkin did not much care about it,—& on board ours are accustomed to it. I am going to get a small plashchanitsa[247] for them & my lancers to send out.—He [N. P. Sablin] is awfully happy that old Ivanov will be with you.—I remember him always hinting to me how good it would be.—If all is quiet, hopes to come about the 16-th for 5 days.—Groten turned up for a few days here & Kussov< too it seems.—Passed Linevich in town,—Dobriazgin [S. A. Drobyazgin] in a vile, small papakha [fur-cap]. [b]

Oh Lovy, how sad the "willows" all alone![247] I hate to think of you without any of us,—those at the war have all their men & comrades around them,—you carry all the weight & have such dull people with you. I yearn after you, miss you more than I can say, my One & all, my Life, my Sunshine,—my Own, very, very Own.— Shall sit in the garden this afternoon whilst the children work & before that go in to Znamenia<,—feel quieter when [I] have carried my prayers there to her [the Virgin], for you, my Angel. Lovy, why dont you get a.d.c. from different regiments to come & do their duty with you for 2-3 weeks, it would be an honour to them, times are still quiet & they could tell you interesting things during your walks,—gayer than Valia<, Kira< & even blissful Mordvinov & selfsure Voeikov<,—please squash the latter sometimes, he needs it, is too awfully contented with himself, it puts me out every time I talk to him. Dont let him again speak against our Metropolitan [Pitirim], & pay less attention to what he says,—there, I meddle again, but he is a man I always found needs holding in hand, & being watched. He is not amiable enough to others & thinks of his personal safety, position I mean, first. Goodbye my Manny dear, my Boysy sweet, Huzy love. Feel my loving warm presence & prayers near you when you kneel with your candle & "willows"[247] in yr. hand. I cannot imagine our not spending these great days together. May yr. life & reign also turn from anguish and misery to glorious sunshine & joy & holy Easter bring its fathomless blessings.—Farewell, Sweetheart. We shall make our devotions as usual,—but it will be awfully sad without you. I gather you to my breast & hold you in tender embrace kissing every loved place, with fondest, most complete devotion. God bless you! yr. Own. [c, d]

247. Alexandra refers to the "Icon of the Virgin of Swift Aid." Prayers before this image were said to be answered with dispatch, hence the name "skoroposlushnitsa," "swift aid." Russians receive willows rather than palms on "Palm Sunday." A "holy winding sheet" (*plashchanitsa*) representing the shroud in which Christ was buried is carried in Good Friday processions in the Orthodox Church.

No. 921/ Telegram 3. Stavka> Tsarskoe Selo. 1 Ap 1916. 21.30> 22.18.[248] To
her majesty. Tender thanks [for] dear letters. From 10 of the morning till late
afternoon was at [military] sitting. Quite exhausted. Delightful spring day.
Fondest love. Niki

---

248. Beginning with No. 921, the telegrams Nicholas and Alexandra exchanged generally abandon
the a.m./p.m. notation and shift to the 24-hour clock familiar in military usage.

No. 922/ Telegram 4. Tsarskoe Selo> Stavka. 2 Ap 1916. 1.21> 1.50. To his
majesty. Terribly gladdened by dear, unexpected letter, tenderly thank you.
Good weather. All still feel weariness from town<. Will think of you this evening in church. [We] all warmly embrace and kiss [you]. Alix

---

No. 923/ Her No. 472.   Tsarskoe Selo. April 2nd 1916.
My own beloved Sweetheart,
    Oh, what an unexpected joy it was when Madelaine< brought me yr. precious
letter, I never thought you would find time to write.— How deadtired you must
have been yesterday after that endless war-council. I hope you were contented
with all the plans.—As you liked that sweet English book, I am sending you another by the same author[, Florence L. Barclay], wh. we also like. It is also
charming & interesting; tho' not as sweet as the Boy. Yes Lovy, it reminds one
of 22 years ago, & I would give much to be alone with you in such a garden, its
so true; every woman has in her the feeling of a mother too towards the man she
loves, its her nature, when its real deep love!—I love those pretty words & how
he sits at her feet under the tree & he has such a lovely, sunny soul, "my little
boy blue". We all of us read the story with wet eyes.[246]— [a]
    Paul< comes to us to tea to-day, I suppose Dmitri< will turn up to-morrow, if
it does not bore him. I lay out on the balkony [sic] yesterday & A.[nia] read to
me,—to-day I'll sit near the children whilst they work. [Daughter] Marie is in a
grumpy mood & grumbles all the time & bellows at one, she & [daughter] Olga
have B.<—Olga has become better humoured I find, it shows she is feeling
stronger.—I feel still awfully tired after town & ache all over. Must be back at 4
for a doklad [report] with Lili Ob.[olenskaya]; amongst others, I saw Baron
Kussov< for 10 m.[inutes] yesterday, full of questions, looking brown &
well.—Shall read over your letter lots more still. Through Groten am sending
to-day 3 small plashchanitsy[247] for his regiment fr. Baby<, for the lancers & Gv.
Ekip.<fr. me.—Shall think of you quite particularly this evening when we get our
"Willows",[247] oh sweet One, God bless & protect you, all my tenderest, passionate love fondly surrounds you & I long to hold you tightly in my arms & let your
head rest upon my breast like in bed & feel your sweet loving presence, & to
cover you with kisses. Ever Huzy mine, yr. very own old Wify. [b]

No. 924/ Telegram 5. Tsarskoe Selo> Stavka. 2 Ap 1916. 8.38> 9.33. To his
majesty. Just now returned from church, [we] are lunching and miss you terribly. Sleep well, [we] tenderly kiss [you]. May the Lord God keep you. Crimean,
Atamanets, Elizabeth Guardsman, Voznesenets, Kazanets, Kaspisets.[249]

249. Each title indicates a guards regiment whose titular commander was a member of the royal family. Alexandra was honorary colonel and commander of a Crimean cavalry regiment, Aleksei was ataman ("chief") of a Cossack regiment. The girls are in order of birth: Olga (commanded the Elizabeth Reg.), Tatiana (Voznesentsky Reg.), Maria (Kazan Reg.) and Anastasia (Caspian Reg.).

No. 925/ Telegram 6. Stavka> Tsarskoe Selo. 2 Ap 1916. 10.20> 22.48. To her majesty. Thank all tenderly for evening message, also for dear letters and image [icon]. Heavenly weather. Fondest love. Good night. Niki

---

No. 926/ Telegram 7. Tsarskoe Selo> Stavka. 3 Ap 1916. 2.17> 2.54. To his majesty. Aunt Olga< and Christo< were with us in church and had lunch. Wonderful weather, [we] are going for a drive. Tenderly embrace and bless [you]. Miss [you] terribly. Alix

---

No. 927/ Telegram 9. Stavka> Tsarskoe Selo. 3 Ap 1916. 2.53> 15.35.   To her majesty. Awfully thankful for dear letters, flowers and book. [See Letter No. 929.] Delicious warm weather. Hope [you] feel better. Saw Vyshinsky, who will see you before leaving. Tenderest love.   Niki

---

No. 928/ Her No. 473.   Tsarskoe Selo. April 3rd 1916.
My own Sweetheart,
Several times I have again reread & kissed your dear letter, I received yesterday, yes,—its like talking & a whole week without a word in your own handwriting was sad (tho' most comprehensible).—How one would sometimes like to relive happy, peaceful moments as those when we were alone, together with our beautiful love, wh. every day brought new revelations. These constant partings wear out the heart, because one suffers so, but the sweet words in letters, wh. you, silly old Boy, are shy to use except in the dark, fill my heart with silent bliss & make me feel younger & the few nights we spend together now are so quiet & full of loving tenderness. Always being inseperable [sic] for years, one loose [loses] the habit of showing ones tenderness & feelings, whereas now one cannot keep them back they bring such untold consolation & joy.— [a]
[Daughter] Marie wrote to you all about the nonsense on the ice. I went into Znamenia< & placed candles & brought some flowers to the Virgine [sic].—Paul< took tea with us, to-day Dmitri< & we have A.[unt] Olga< & Christo< for Church & luncheon. D.[mitry]< came with that rotten Marianna [Mariana Ericovna von Derfel'den, his step-sister] & A.[nia?]< in the train, [— he is] in despair [over having] to go back to the regiment & all the more before the holidays, finds it no use being in the regiment, no work & constant drinking. Longs to go to the Caucasus, to be sent down there to see something else in a warm climate & with some order to fulfil. And disappointed not to have been left at the Headquarters with you. Oh these young men of the family with bad health & love of pleasure instead of duty! Felt so sad without you in church, I was not [with you] last year either [at this time]. The boys will only be out of quarantine for Easter[,] I fear,—such a bore. But the men sang very well, masses of soldiers & people were in church, when we left there were still heaps waiting to approach the Image [icon] & receive their "willows".[247] [b]

How was Brussilov?< Did he speak out his opinions & did they seem good? I do wonder whether he is capable to fill such a responsible place, God grant it!—How grateful we must be, that those aeroplanes were got to move off, you were in a precarious place,—hang them, they prevent you going further to the front & trenches.—The papers say [Kaiser] William was wounded at Verdun by shell-fragments, is it true, I of course dont know.—Here I send you a petition (through Paul) fr. Mme Speier,[250] perhaps one can help her a little? Paul begs you to remember General Novos.[iltsev]—He longs for a place, hoped for Tougaku's place,[250] but that is to[o] great a one for him, I think, but as ex Garde à cheval, Paul asks for him some place. [c]

You will be in despair when you see this big envelope, but its the otchet [inventory] of Ella's< obshchezhitie dlya yunykh dobrovol'tsev [home for young volunteers] & she asks whether you would allow Aleksei to be the pokrovitel' [sponsor]. Therefore I send you the paper, only just to look through it, let Mordvinov read it & tell you if he finds all correct & then let me know, whether Baby< may be named the pokrovitel' & I shall send a wire to Ella for Easter announcing yr. sanction. The paper kindly return. Aunt Olga< was very sweet, Christo< looks the same as ever, a big fat Boy. Came over London, Paris, Switzerland, Berlin, Sassnitz.— Says untrue all one said about Sophie, [250] she kept herself very quietly & did not scream out her feelings, never left the country. Tino's< wound has never healed up & every day the Drs. have to clean it & change the trubochka [tube]. A.[unt] Alix< he found as well as ever, Minny very busy with her hospitals at Harrogate.— They were delighted with our Churches, showed them also the little one. Glorious, warm sunshine, so we shall go for a drive. Dmitri< comes to tea. Sweetest Love, precious Darling, Goodbye & God bless & protect you. Will you be going to Church twice daily? Do you make yr. devotions, or is it difficult at the Headquarters? All my thoughts surround you in endless love, Treasure. Fondest kisses fr. yr. ever deeply loving & devoted old Sunny. [d]

---

250. Anna Shpeier was widow of Senator A. N. Shpeier, who died March 19, 1916. "Tougaku" was N. L. Gondatti, governor-general of the Amur region. "Sophie" was Sophia, wife of King Constantine I ("Tino") of Greece and a sister of the kaiser. "Aunt Alix" was Alexandra, widow of King Edward VII. "Minny" was Maria Georgievna, Greek princess married to g.p. Georgy Michaelovich.

No. 929.   Ts.[arist] Stavka. April 3rd 1916.
My own beloved One,

Fondest thanks for your dear letters; now [that] I don't see any troops they are my only comfort. Thanks also for the little image [icon]—I have put it on my chain! Now I will wear something from you! Here are three flowers I found yesterday during the walk. Again no time to write[—]always people who want to see me & make endless doklady [reports]. I hope that during Passion week they will leave me quiet. Thank you so for the new book you sent me. [See Letters No. 918a, 923a and 927.] Lovy-mine, me loves you so, really more than ever & miss you so these days especially. I must finish already. God bless you and the children. I kiss you and them tenderly. Ever my beloved Wify, your own old huzy Nicky. [P.S.] The mandation [petition] is splendid. [See Letter 928c.]

No. 930/ Telegram 9. Tsarskoe Selo> Stavka. 4 Ap 1916. 12.56> 13.30. To his majesty. Very happy with dear letter and flowers, received them after mass. Missed you terribly at my corner [of the church]. Today cold and overcast. All tenderly kiss [you]. Alix

---

No. 931/ Her No. 474.   Tsarskoe Selo. April 4th 1916.
My own Beloved,
   I was so glad to get news of you through Dmitri<, only we saw him quite short; he came at 10 minutes past 5 & left at 10 m.[inutes] to 8. Hartmann is in town & he hopes he will allow him to remain on for the holidays. He wont ask, but he will make him understand his wish. Sad, how he dislikes going to the regiment & does not like the commander & the officers I think neither—all his comrades were killed. He looks better than when you left, & was in good humour.—We drove through Tyarlevo, the road already perfect—very little snow in the woods & one feels spring in the air —but there was rather a sharp wind. I fetched A.[nia]< at her house, slipped on her balkony [sic] & came down with a great bang. Jumped up at once, but am bruised & achy—my hands were in my muff—to[o] idiotic—& some wounding [i.e., wounded soldiers] were standing opposite & saw the sight. But my hat, a very big one, did not move luckily—so absurd.—Mme Zizi< sat with me for an hour. She does not feel famous, such flow of blood to her head, wh. make the back of her head ache, the whole left side of her face & arm, & she fears a stroke like A.[unt] Eugenie[53]—it does begin so. So one gives her strong purgatives & she eats no meat—poor dear, it makes her so nervous & every worry makes her feel worse.—A.< read to us in the evening whilst we laid patiences. D.[mitry] said that the people on the railway said you would be coming [home] for 3 days—if true it wld. be too beautiful for words. I know Voeikov< told Ania he could not understand why you wld. not do it. Well, all lies in yr. hands & how you think right, & I will not meddle in any way. [a]
   Its grey this morning, & only 1° of warmth—I shall remain at home or lie on the balkony, don't want to be shaken about, as feel a bit achy fr. my fall, (a bump besides on the knee, wh. is most uncomfortable when I kneel) & the left arm feels heavy & uncomfy.—I am glad I have not ...[391]—there, I was disturbed, had to choose [Easter] eggs & don't know what I wanted to write.—Old Kundiger's [Kyundiger's] brother, Heinrich died.—We have Church at 11 & 6½ as usual—the girls go before to the hospital.—Will you make Alekseev G. A. d. c. [General Aide de Camp] for Easter? —How is old Fredericks, not too gaga [i.e., senile]? How I wish we had somebody in view for his place.—[b]
   Do get yr. a.d.c.'s to do duty with you, now they have nothing to do, later it will be more difficult for the commanders of regiments to get free. I hate your loneliness at the Headquarters & yr. dull people.—I cannot say how intensely happy I was to receive yr. precious letter, upon our return from Church. The sweet little blue flowers I put into my gospel. I do so love to get little flowers fr. you, they are a token of such sweet love. Not every husband wld. think of sending his old wife flowers. The first blue ones this year. I hope you get good walks & that one wont bore you too much this week.—Can imagine how lonely you feel with none of your own near you—if N.P.< were near you I shld. feel

quieter, as he is a man you are so accustomed to, can bang [speak with frankly?] when you want, understands any joke—have lived so much together all these years—& your [other Stavka] people are really such bores. —Am so happy & awfully touched that you wear my image [icon], may it bring you blessings & helps & consolation & let you feel my presence always quite close to you.—Ah, I too have such a deep great love filling my heart for you & such a yearning to be together. Baby< was in my molel'nya [chapel] with me, the girls< in Church. Ania outside at the door. Goodbye Lovebird, Sunshine —me is so sad & feel your absence intensely, & hate your loneliness. God Almighty bless & protect you. Endless kisses, Darling, fr. yr. very own old   Wify. [c, d]

No. 932.   Ts.[arist] Stavka. April 4th 1916.
My beloved Wify,
    Fond thanks for your letter and for everything you write there, the sweetest words of love which are so comforting & soothing in my lonelyness [sic] Of course I go to church morning and evening; o.[tets, Father] Shavel'sky officiates so well, exactly an hour. Alekseev & many of the staff are going to take Holy Communion on Thursday. I am sorry not to do it with them, but one must not change one's confessor! I forgot to choose & bring with me Easter cards & neither small eggs to send to you & the children! Porcelain eggs for the rest I have & a pretty good number too. It rained this morning & as I had much to read & to sign before Easter, I had no expedition by motor, but walked a bit in the garden & am now writing to you. The view from there is really a fine one—the river has become an enormous lake, with any amount of houses in the middle of it. The current is very strong. The adm. [Nilov] ordered the two sailors yesterday to try & pull about [i.e., row] in one of the boats, & they could row up the river! A pity as I had hoped to have a try, but I intend to nevertheless.— [a, b]
    Now there is a lull in SEAT of war, but in the Caucasus, along the coast of the Black Sea, our troops are pushing the turks on, & I hope that Trebizond [Trapezund] will soon be ours—the fleet helps very much the land operations.[252] I forgot to mention about my talk with Misha< at Kamenets-p[odol'sk] the other day. He begged to be recalled in June & taken to the Stavka. So I preeched [sic] to him about our Father [Alexander III], the feeling of duty, the example to others & so on. When I finished & we said good-bye he once more cooly asked [me] not to forget his request—as if I had not spoken at all. I was disgusted. But now I must end. God bless you & the ch[ildren]. I kiss you all so tenderly & remain ever your own huzy. Nicky   [P.S.] My darling, I love you so deeply and fervently! [c]

No. 933/ Telegram 12. Tsarskoe Selo> Stavka. 4 Ap 1916. 20.04> 20.20. To his majesty. All my prayers were about you, was terribly difficult in church without you, especially during [the singing of] two beautiful canticles. [We] are having lunch. [We] all warmly kiss [you] and wish [you] a good night. Alix

No. 934/ Telegram 12. Stavka> Tsarskoe Selo. 4 Ap 1916. 21.50> 22.35. To her majesty. Many thanks [for] dear letters and two wires. Fine weather, a bit cooler. Thoughts incessantly together. Am doing small puzzle, as [I] read much. Blessings. Kisses. Nicky

---

No. 935/ Telegram 15. Tsarskoe Selo> Stavka. 5 Ap 1916. 12.58> 13.20. To his majesty. Just now received [your] dear letter, heartily thank you. Petia< is lunching with us. Overcast weather, beginning to snow lightly. As an exception one might change his confessor [See Letter No. 932a] when in a different place, and this will be a big comfort to you and will give you new strength. We all warmly kiss [you]. Alix

---

No. 936/ Her No. 475.   Ts.[arskoe] S[elo]. April 5th 1916.
My own sweet Treasure,
   To think of you sitting all alone over a small puzzle,—its quite "not neces-sary".[160] Ah my poor wee One, it shows your loneliness. I understand after this heaps of work & reading you have to get through & people to see,—such a harmless occupation is a rest. We don't either lay patiences now, & to-day I began drawing on wooden [Easter] eggs,—with specks on. Cannot knit or hold my work comfortably because the left hand shakes & arm aches. Myself I smeared it for the night with white iodine & then put a hot compress on & ban-daged it beautifully & tidily with my right hand,—I was quite proud of it. [a]
   All through the service I had to think of you, all the prayers & yr. favourite lovely passion-week singing,—I cant understand your not being near me,—& somehow I have the feeling that I carry you in my soul & bring you to God with all my love.—How Christ must suffer now, seeing all that misery and bloodshed around! He gave up His life for us, was tortured and calumniated, bore all & shed His precious blood for the remittance of our sins. And how do we all pay it Him back, how do we prove our love & gratitude? The wickedness of the world ever increases. During the evening Bible [reading] I thought so much of our Friend<, how the bookworms & pharisees persecute Christ, pretending to be such perfections, (& how far they are from it now!) Yes, indeed, a prophet is never acknowledged in his own country. And how much we have to be grateful for, how many prayers of His [Rasputin's] were heard. And where there is such a Servant of Gods,—the evil crops up around Him to try & do harm & drag him away. If they but knew the harm they do!—why He lives for His Sovereign & Russia & bears all slanders for our sakes. How glad I am that we went all with Him to Holy Communion the first week in lent.—You don't want a book so as to follow the service in? I can send you mine if you would care to have it, as I use the one wh. belongs to the molel'nya [chapel] now.—I have had the foot-stool placed again next to my chair for Aleksei to sit upon,—but on my right side the corner is, oh, so empty! [b]
   Our Friend writes so sadly, that as He was driven away fr. P.[etrograd] there will be many hungry ones there this Easter. He gives such a lot to the poor, every penny he receives goes to them & it brings blessings too to those who brought Him the money.[251] A grey morning & slightly snowing. I send you a petition fr. the wife of a colonel Svechin, who asks her son to be placed as can-didate for the pages corps. The boy's grandfather was promoted to general after he had left the service as a reward; the father commands the 6-th Fin.[nish]

Rif.[le] Regiment. Your chancelry [sic] answered her it cld. not be done, so through A.[nia]< she sent this, as a last trial to see whether you wld. not allow it. Her husband has the gold sword & [Order of] Vladimir 3-rd class. Am sorry to bother you with these petitions, but perhaps you could write a word on them & send them to yr. chancelry. The other is fr. a widow asking for help. [c]

Here Lovy, I send you 8 Eastercards for the Children, [your sister] Olga & A.;< perhaps you would send them on Friday already. I have sent still to Uralsky [a store in Petrograd which sold fine stone from the Urals] for [stone Easter] eggs & shall make a small choice for you to-morrow, as it will give more pleasure if you send the eggs, and they will know they come fr. & were chosen by you. For yr. precious letter my very tenderest kisses and thanks. Lovy mine, you can go to another Confessor when [you] are in another place & Father Al.[exander Vasil'ev] wld. perfectly well understand it—if you do, wire it directly to me, & I shall tell it [to] the Priest at Confession & yr. scruples, & I feel convinced he will only rejoice with you, as he knows how much you need that strength & blessing now,—& to go with Alekseev & yr. people would be a special blessing to them & yr. work. [See Letters No. 932a and 935.] If Shav.[el'sky] speaks about our Friend or the Metropolitan [Pitirim], be firm & show that you appreciate them, & that when he hears stories against our Friend, he is to stand up with energy against all & forbid their talks & they dare not say he has anything to do with the Germans— & he is generous & kind to all, as christ was, no matter what religion, as a real Christian should be. And once you find His prayers help one bear one trials, & we have had enough examples—they dare not speak against him, you be firm & stand up for our Friend. [d]

Do go to Holy Communion, we shall feel quite together then. —Thank God, things are going so well in the Caucasus.[252] What you tell about Misha< is strange [See Letter No. 932c.]—I know Dmitri< & he had some conversation & correspondence & they probably settled this together. One suffers in one's relations & their lack of feeling of duty—as poor Olga[, your sister,] too. Petia< lunched with us & talked after & cried, poor Boy. He begs me to tell you, that he goes to-morrow straight to Ai-Todor[, the Crimean estate of his father, "Sandro," Alexander Mikhailovich], as wld. be to[o] painful at Ramon[, estate of the Ol'denburg family in Voronezh gubernaya]. Must end. Blessings & kisses without end. Tenderly do I beg yr. pardon for word or deed, wh. may have displeased or caused you pain & believe it was not done willingly.[129] Ever Sweetheart, Treasure, yr. own old   Wify. [e]

251. Rasputin must have been speaking figuratively when he referred to being "driven away fr. P.[etrograd]" in 1916. The tale Rasputin offers here about his charity was probably calculated to head off displeasure on Alexandra's part were she to hear he was taking bribes. In fact, Rasputin *was* concerned about the poor. He often told an obviously wealthy petitioner waiting to be received that the price of his favor was to give everything in his wallet to another petitioner who was needy and had come to ask for financial aid. Even so, Rasputin died a rich man. (Fuhrmann, *Rasputin*, pp. 32-33, 61, 121-124, 145, 163-165, 195)

252. Nicholasha< now commanded Russian armies in the Caucasus. His subordinate, General N. N. Yudenich—one of the most capable Russian commanders—began a drive against the Turks on December 29 (O.S.), 1915. The Turkish Third Army fell back to Erzerum with a loss of 25,000 men. Russian armies took Erzerum on February 3/16, 1916. (See Letter No. 804.) As indicated here, the Russian armies (with naval support) captured Trebizond on April 5/18, 1916. The Turkish Third

Army's counterattack was a disaster: Yudenich's brilliant counterstroke split the Turkish force, inflicted 34,000 casualties and routed the enemy. In August 1916, Yudenich turned on the Turkish Second Army, defeated it and regained ground seized by its impressive commander, Kemal Ataturk. Both sides then took up early winter positions. (Dupuy and Dupuy, *Encyclopedia*, p. 964)

No. 937.   Ts.[arist] Stavka. April 5th 1916.
My own darling Sunny,
    Thank God our gallant troops with our Black Sea fleet have occupied Trebizond [Trapezund].[252] I got the news from N.[icholasha]< already sitting in the motor for going out. Such a success & this week too. After that I drove to the pier & went up the river in a fine big motor-boat with neat cabins. The current is beastly strong, but yet advanced well & reached a place where Aleksei used to play last autumn. One can hardly recognise [sic] the country because everything is deep under water. The morning was lovely but of course while I was on the river a thunderstorm came up & it poured like a deluge & became colder after. But I felt happy to have been on the river & to have seen the two fine sailors fr. the "Razvedchik" & the "Dozorny" at the pier with our sweet <u>dvoika</u> [dinghy]. The messenger must leave & I hasten to finish this scribble. To-morrow you go to confession −please Lovy-mine[,] forgive me if I have hurt you in any way.[129] I shall think of <u>you</u> especially & on Thursday morning, I always do, but those moments still more. May God bless you & the children. Tenderly do I kiss you & them & miss you awfully. Ever your own huzy <u>Nicky</u>.   [P.S.] Give A.[nna Vyrubova] my love.

No. 938/ Telegram 13. Stavka> Tsarskoe Selo. 5 Ap 1916. 21.17> 21.41. To her majesty. Loving thanks [for] sweet letter. So happy about Trapezund.[252] Hope you are none the worse after your fall. How very imprudent. Dear me! Tenderest kisses. Nicky

No. 939/ Telegram 17. Tsarskoe Selo> Stavka. 5 Ap 1916. 22.35> 23. To his majesty. Tenderly thank you for dear telegram. In rapture over good news from Trapezund.[252] Only [my] left arm still hurts. Letter [sent]. God bless you. Sleep well. We all kiss you. Alix

No. 940/ Telegram 19. Tsarskoe Selo> Stavka. 6 Ap 1916. 13.04> 14.04. To his majesty. Tenderly thank you for dear letter. Glad you are rowing on river. Drab day. Tiny's< arm hurt terribly to-night, now he is asleep. In all probability he injured it with a heavy dirk on the ice. Because pain is very strong it is possible that it will quickly pass. We all warmly kiss you. Alix

No. 941/ Her No. 476.   Ts.[arskoe] S[elo]. April 6th 1916.
My own sweet Darling,
    I send you a book & collection of eggs wh. I think would please the children & Ania< [for you to send as Easter presents to them in your name].−Several times I have reread your dear letter & kissed it over & over again. Yes, it must be a fine sight, the inundated country before you & the immense river now.−How splendid Trebizond has been taken by our splendid troops[252]−I congratulate you

with all my loving heart! It makes me sad that all the luck is down there—but the
good will come here too in time.—My arm is better, but aches still a bit—but its
really nothing at all, and nobody notices it. Kneeling on the bruise has made it
every colour of the rainbow. Baby< was awfully cheery & gay all day & till he
went to bed—in the night he woke up from pain in his left arm and from 2 on
scarcely got a moments sleep, the girls< sat with him a good while. Its too despairing for words & he is already worrying about Easter—standing with candles
to-morrow in Church, & holy Communion, poor little man. It seems he worked
with a <u>dirk</u> & <u>must have done too much</u>—he is so strong, that its difficult, for
him always to remember & think that he must not do strong movements. But as
the pain came with such force in the night & the arm wont bend, I think it will
pass quicker—generally 3 nights pain, but perhaps God will mercyfully [sic]
make it pass quicker—its too hard about Baby [suffering this before] Holy
Communion.   I hope he will sleep now—she [Anna Vyrubova] wires to
Gr.[egory]<.—I shall finish my letter after luncheon, by then can say more about
him. Perhaps one can bring him Holy Communion upstairs. Ania probably cant
go [to church] before Saturday as B.< came. N.P.< telegraphed to her that they
go to-morrow too; Rodionov is coming to town.— [a, b]
    Grey morning.—The big ones [daughters Olga and Tatiana] are in the hospital
& the little ones [Maria and Anastasia] have gone to the big Palace< hosp. so as
to have the afternoon free to sit with Baby & we can paint [in his bedroom] up
there our [Easter] eggs. Oh such thanks, Lovebird, for yr. sweet letter, tender
words. Yes, indeed I shall think of you quite especially during confession &
Holy Communion. Its more than sad we shall not be together this great moment
but our souls will be. Once more Darling, forgive me for everything, everything.[129] —Feel awfully sad & lowspirited to-day and cried like a Baby in
Church. Cannot bear when the sweet Child suffers and know what it costs you.
But Mr. G. said it [the blow] came as sudden[ly] & terribly strong as on
board—& then it passes quicker.[253]—He [Aleksei] is sleeping. [c]
    We had a bit of the Metrop.[olitan Pitirim's] choir in Church (The Priest [A. P.
Vasil'ev's] & A[nia]'s doing, I did not want [it], as knew they wld. sing differently, & so they did). But our boys are ill all the time—really they might separate ours for Ts.[arskoe] S.[elo] fr. the others, when there are such a lot of
them.—How nice going up the river must have been—always nice being on the
water—I hope [A. N.] Grabbe photographed. I have not been out these days, so
as to keep quieter on account of Church.—Now my own beloved Treasure,
Goodbye & God bless you, I kiss you without end—& shall feel you so, so near
me. Oh how I love you, long for you, beloved One.—Think of Coburg[254] & all
we went through these days. Ever yr. very own old <u>Sunny</u>. [d]
    I send you the petition of one of Aunt Olga's< wounded men. He is a Jew, has
lived since 10 years in America. He was wounded & lost his left arm on the
Carpathians. The wound had healed well, but he suffers fearfully morally as in
August he must leave, & looses [sic] the right of living in either of the capitals
[Petrograd and Moscow] or other big towns. He is living in town< only on the
strength of a <u>special</u> permit, wh. a previous minister of the Interior[255] gave him
for one year. And he could find work in a big town. His English is wonderfully
good, I read a letter of his to little Vera [Constantinovna]'s English governess &

Aunt Olga says he is a man with good education, so to speak. 10 years ago he left for the United States to find the opportunity to become a useful member of human society to the fullest extent of his capabilities, as here [it] is difficult for a Jew who is always hampered by legislative restrictions. Tho' in America, he never forgot Russia & suffered much from homesickness & the moment war broke out he flew here to enlist as soldier to defend his country. [e]

Now that he lost his arm serving in our army, got the St. George's medal, he longs to remain here & have the right to live wherever he pleases in Russia, a right the Jews don't possess. As soon as discharged fr. the army, as a cripple, he finds things have remained the same as before [with regard to restrictions on Jews], & his headlong rush home to fight, & loss of his arm has brought him no gain. One sees the bitterness, & I fully grasp it—surely such a man ought to be treated the same as any other soldier who received such a wound. He was not obliged to fly over here at once. Tho' he is a Jew, one would like him to be justly treated & not different to the others with similar losses of a limb. With his knowledge of English & learning he could easier gain his bread in a big town of course; & one ought not to let him become more bitter & feel the cruelty of his old country. To me it seems one ought always to choose between the good & bad jews & not be equally hard upon all—its so cruel to my mind. The bad ones can be severely punished.—Can you tell me what decision you write on the petition; as Aunt Olga wanted to know.— [f]

4 big eggs are for:

1. Father Shav.[el'sky]	3. G.[en.] Alekseev
2. G.[en.] Ivanov	4. G.[en., i.e., Admiral] Nilov

(Fred.[ericks] already has one.)

12 small eggs:

1. Voeikov<	6. Mordv.[inov]
2. [A. N.] Grabbe	7. Kira<
3. Dol.[gorukov]	8. Fed.[orov]<
4. D. Sherem.[etev]	9. Zamoi.[sky]
5. Silaev	10. Pustov.[oitenko] as he works with you always.

Our Friend wired to me [the following quote is in Russian:] "Christ has risen, [this day] is a holiday & a day of joy,[—]in trials joy is brighter,[—]I am convinced the church is invincible & we, its children, are joyous with the resurrection of Christ." [g]

253. The text here and twice in Letter No. 945a reads "Mr. G." Ordinarily, "G" denotes Gilliard, and Nabokov thinks such is the case in these three places. (*Pis'ma imperatritsy*, II, p. 72) Charles Sydney Gibbs, however, is identified in Letter No. 945b. I agree with A. A. Sergeev (*Perepiska*, IV, p. 195) that in these three cases, "Mr. G." probably refers to Gibbs. Whether the man in question was Gibbs or Gilliard, he apparently compared this hemophiliac episode with a similar attack he

observed when the royal family was on a ship ("as on board"), noting that in such cases it seemed to him that Aleksei's pain "passes quicker."

254. On April 7, 1916, Nicholas and Alexandra celebrated the twenty-second anniversary of their engagement at Coburg in 1894.

255. Alexandra discusses restrictions that confined most Jews in the Russian Empire to the "Pale." Judging from the text, the empress now hated to refer to A. N. Khvostov—once a favorite—by name: he is called "a previous minister of the Interior!" Khvostov built his career upon an anti-Semitism extreme even for Russia, but this Jew touched a sense of justice: Khvostov gave the veteran permission to live in Petrograd for a year. Alexandra was prejudiced against Jews. This statement—written during one of Aleksei's most severe bouts with hemophilia—suggests her views were changing to some extent and in some ways.

No. 942.   Ts.[arist] Stavka.   April 6th 1916.
My precious Sunny,

Thank you so much for your letter [No. 931] in which you write about Dmitry's< visit. I don't understand people talking or still less Voeik[ov] telling A.[nia]< that I was coming home for 3 days? Now during Passion week, or later? I have yet no plans & have therefore not said a word to any one. Yes, I think to name Aleks.[eev] g.a.d.c [general aide de camp] for Easter. Old Freder.< is quite fresh—only at times he forgets in conversations what people have told him before, at least I hear with one ear what's going on accross [sic] the table—sometimes most funny confussions [sic]! He rode alright at both reviews.— [a]

You always seem to want me to have some of my a.d.c.'s on duty —I quite agree, but you know there are not many left. Several are promoted—others are difficult to get at. I have always the whole list before my eyes to remind me. Do you know who is going to get the Erivantsy? Silaev! Vyshinsky gave me that good idea—he finds he is just the man now. These are not pretty stories in the regiment wh. V found out—intriques of the senior officers (natives [i.e., Armenians]), especially against S.—but now that is finished & they will be cleared out! For the first time I questioned S. upon this subject yesterday & he confirmed every word of the ex commander. So I told him about the coming nomination wh. made him awfully happy.—[256] [b]

I don't feel so lonely now as I have much to do & when free a nice book to freshen me up. This moment your dear letter No. 475[257] was brought, thank you so much for it & also for Easter cards.—I do not feel inclined to confess with Shav.[el'sky] because instead of bringing peace & calm to my soul it might have just the contrary effect! And morally I feel alright. Shall think so of you to-morrow morning. How tiresome poor A.[leksei]'s arm hurts. I hope it wont last long. Kiss him fondly. God bless you my beloved Sunny, my One & All. I kiss you & the girls tenderly & may the Holy Communion bring you peace & happiness. Ever my darling your own   Nicky. [c]

---

256. According to Vulliamy (p. 169n), Silaev " refused the command of the regiment, on the grounds of ill health."

257. The tsar seems to be referring to the letter Alexandra numbered as No. 476, which is published here as No. 941.

No. 943/ Telegram 14. Stavka> Tsarskoe Selo. 6 Ap 1916. 19.54> 20.55. To her majesty. Many thanks [for] letter [and] post cards. Hope your and his arms better. Delicous [sic] weather. Had a capital row up the river[,] fought violently against the current. Thoughts together. Tenderest love and blessings. Niki

---

No. 944/ Telegram 22. Tsarskoe Selo> Stavka. 6 Ap 1916. 22.08> 22.40. To his majesty. Heartily thank you for telegram. Glad you sailed up river well. The three little children [Maria, Anastasia and Aleksei] went to confession to-day, we three [the empress, Olga and Tatiana] are going to confession at 10 o'clock. With you in thoughts and prayers. Tiny's< arm hurt almost all day. [He] slept very little, was more peaceful when [they] read to him aloud. Hope to take a stroll now. God bless you. Sleep well. I wish you were with us. [We] all kiss [you] warmly. Alix

---

No. 945/ Her No. 477.   Ts.[arskoe] S[elo]. April 6th 1916.
My own beloved One,
    I begin my letter still to-night, after once more having reread your sweet letter. The afternoon I spent in Baby's< room painting [Easter eggs], whilst Mr. G.[253] read to him or held Foen[, a heating apparatus]. He suffered almost the whole time, then would half doze for a few minutes & then again strong pains. Eat[s] next to nothing. Reading is the best thing, as for a time it distracts the thoughts when the suffering is less great. I hope he will have a pretty calm night. He confessed with the two youngest & the priest [A. P. Vasil'ev] will bring him Holy Communion like last year. A.[nia]< dined with us & remained till ten—she had been all day in town & motored back.—Sat with Tiny< after dinner, poor wee one. The swelling is not much & less than in the night, so I hope it will soon pass. Seeing him suffer makes me utterly wretched.—Mr. G.[253] is so gentle & kind with him & knows exactly how to be with him.—We had confession at 10—sad without my Angel & I miss you quite horribly—do wish you had gone to Holy Communion & the priest agreed.—After, I read through the doklady [reports] & arranged some Easterpackets. There was a colossally thick fogg [sic] this evening.—Now its very late, so I better bid you goodnight. I know yr. prayers will be with us & I carry you with me. God bless and protect you. I cover you with tender, yearning kisses—in thought clasp you tenderly to my loving old heart, stroke and caress you & whisper of deep love.— [a]
    April 7-th. Ever so many fond thanks, my own sweetest Darling, for your beloved letter and telegram. Missed you awfully in Church this morning. Service was lovely & such a blessing & I prayed & longed for you quite unspeakably. The sun was shining splendidly & drove the fogg away.—The priest brought Baby the Holy Communion. Thank God, he slept much better, woke up only once, or twice for a short time. He would not touch anything even no water before Communion, wh. he partake only towards 11½. He is far brighter to-day—we took tea with him [i.e., in his bedroom] & are going to lunch there too. I lay upstairs painting, whilst Mr. Gibbs read to him & then came down to finish my letter & change. After lunch shall go for a short drive as the air is so divine & go into Znamenia< to place candles for you, sweetheart, & our Sunbeam<. [b]
    Fancy, Silaev receiving the Erivantsy!< Yesterday I asked Vyshinsky & he said he did not know who his successor would be.—They had hoped for a

guard[s] officer, as for one fr. there its difficult generally, as they either side with the Russian[s] or Georgians. [This was actually an Armenian regiment.] But I am glad for S. & as his health is now better on the whole; at least if he can have the honour to command for a time.—Precious One, more than ever shall I think of you to-morrow, the 22-nd anniversary of our engagement[254]—dear me, how the time flies & yet how vividly one remembers every detail! Unforgetta- ble days & the love you gave me then & ever since! Its sad not to spend that day together & feel your warm kisses & live through all again. God bless my One & all & thank you over & over again for yr. endless, tender love wh. is my life.—Goodbye now Lovy, Huzy mine, the letter must go. I cover you with kisses & remain yr. very, very own <u>Bridy</u>. [P.S.] All the children kiss you aw- fully tenderly. [c]

No. 946/ Telegram 17. Stavka> Tsarskoe Selo. 7 Ap 1916. 11.08> 11.50. To her majesty. In thoughts and prayers united together. Send all my fondest blessings. Nicky

---

No. 947/ Telegram 24. Tsarskoe Selo> Stavka. 7 Ap 1916. 12.05> 13.00. To his majesty. We all six received communion, it [was a] great consolation but sad that you were not with us. [We] will drink tea upstairs [in Aleksei's bed- room]. [He] spent the night better, arm much better. Glorious sun. [We] warmly and tenderly kiss [you]. Alix

---

No. 948.   Ts.[arist] Stavka. April 7th 1916.
My own Lovebird,
    Only a few lines because me again has no time, the ministers having sent me hills of papers—probably [so that I might deal with them] before Easter. I wrote on that petition of the wounded jew from America—[the following passage is in Russian] ["]to be granted universal domicile in Russia["] & sent it to Shtyurmer. [See Letter No. 941e,f.] Tenderest thanks for y[r] dear letter & for the little [painted Easter] eggs. I do hope Baby's< arm will not hurt for long. I thought so much of you in our little church this morning—it was very nice & peaceful here, lots of officers in the Staff & their families took the Commun[ion]. The mornings, when I can't get out it is always sunny, and when I drive out or row it becomes cloudy—so me cannot get brown. To-morrow is the 8th[254]—my prayers and thoughts will surround you, my girli, my own Sunny. I did fight for you then & against yourself too!! Like little Boy Blue, but more tenacious.[258] God bless you & the children. I kiss you over & over & them too. Ever your own <u>Nicky</u>. [P.S.] The album I sent Alexei [sic] is fr. an english war photographer.

---

258. Vulliamy thinks the "time I fought for you,' refers to the time of the Tsar's courtship, when he persuaded his future wife (then Princess Alexandra of Hesse-Darmstadt) to become a member of the Orthodox Church." (p. 170n) "Little Boy Blue" was a heroic figure in the novel *Through the Pos- tern Gate* by Florence L. Barclay. Nicholas and Alexandra had recently read that book. On several occasions, Nicholas compared himself to Little Boy Blue. (See Letters No. 918a [Footnote 236] and 923a.)

No. 949/ Telegram 26. Tsarskoe Selo> Stavka. 7 Ap 1916. 21.50> 22.20. To his majesty. [We] had lunch and dinner upstairs [in Aleksei's sickroom], [it was] quite gay. Wonderful warm weather, window [is] wide open. Church services were so sad without you. What answer to Ella's< paper? [See Letter No. 956b.] Sleep well. God keep you. We all warmly kiss you. Alix

No. 950/ Telegram 24. Stavka> Tsarskoe Selo. 7 Ap 1916. 22.14> 22.32. To her majesty. Tenderest thanks for beloved letter also Tatiana. Awfully pleased with the [Easter] eggs. Misha the ass wired to announce engagement of his second daughter with Georgi Bat.[259] Shall answer from both of us. Good night. Loving kisses. Niki

259. As explained in Footnote 245, members of the imperial family were held to certain marital standards. Nicholas's cousin Michael Michaelovich ("Misha") violated the law by marrying a commoner. Nicholas indicates his feelings for this cousin by such nicknames as "ass" and "fool!" Young George ("Georgi Bat."), prince of Battenburg, was the son of Alexandra's sister Victoria. George at this time was a lieutenant on the cruiser *New Zealand*; later he was the Marquis of Milford Haven. George's fiancé and subsequent wife was Michael Mikhaelovich's second daughter, Nadezhda Mikhailovna.

No. 951/ Telegram 27. Tsarskoe Selo> Stavka. 8 Ap 1916. 7.50> 9.00. To his majesty. Good morning and may the Lord bless you, my love. Today is day of our dear anniversary.[254] Thoughts fly to the past, am suffering from fact that we are not together. Tenderly kiss and love [you]. Is it possible that Georgi[, son of] Victoria, is getting engaged? Seems quite improbable. He is all of 23 and has been at sea all the time. What answer to Ella?< [See Letter No. 956b.] Alix

No. 952.   8 April 1916.
Christ has risen![260]   [This is a post card]
I send you, my darling, my precious Sunny, my sincerest, loving Easter greetings. It is even harder [than usual] to be separated during these days! May God bless you in all your undertakings! I love you tenderly and cover your dear face and hands with passionate kisses. Always your Nicky.

260. The Russian Easter greeting is "Khristos voskres!" ("Christ has risen!"), the reply to which is "vo istinu, voskres!" ("Truly, He has risen!"). This document is no longer in the State Archive of the Russian Federation (GARF). The text here is translated from A. A. Sergeev: Nicholas and Alexandra, *Perepiska*, IV, p. 203. Vulliamy notes the tsar sent the greeting on Good Friday to be sure it arrived in time for Easter. (Pp. 170-171n.)

No. 953/ Telegram 31. Tsarskoe Selo> Stavka. 8 Ap 1916. 13.43> 14.20. To his majesty. Tenderly thank you for dear letter and wonderful flowers, they arrived absolutely fresh. Gave some to all. He [our son Aleksei] generally slept fairly well, will get up later. His head spins a bit from medicine. Drab weather. We all warmly kiss you. Alix

No. 954/ Telegram 27. Stavka> Tsarskoe Selo. 8 Ap 1916. 14.34> 15.07. To her majesty. Tender loving thanks [for] telegram and letter. Inseparable in thoughts. Warm, rainy. Off to church now. Tell Ella< I find the work done very well. [See Letter No. 956b.] Fondest kisses. Niki

---

No. 955/ Her No. 478.   Ts.[arskoe] S[elo]. April 8th 1916.
Christ has risen!   My own sweet Nicky love,

On this our engagement day all my tenderest thoughts are with you, filling my heart with boundless gratitude for the intense love & happiness you have given me ever since that memorable day, 22 years ago.[254] May God help me to repay you hundredfold for all your sweetness! Yes, verily, I doubt there being such happy wives as I am—such love, trust & devotion as you have shown me these long years with happiness & sorrow. All the anguish, suffering & indecision have been well worth what I received from you, my precious bridegroom & husband. Now-a-days one rarely sees such marriages. Your wonderful patience & forgiveness are untold—I can only ask God Almighty on my knees to bless & repay you for everything—He alone can. Thank you, Sweetheart & feel my longing to be held in your arms tightly clasped & to relive our beautiful bridal days, wh. daily brought new tokens of love & sweetness. That dear brooch will be worn to-day. I feel still your grey suit, the smell of it by the window in the Coburg Schloss. How vivid[ly] I remember everything; those sweet kisses wh. I had dreamed of & yearned after so many years & wh. I thought, I should never get. You see, as even then, faith & religion play such a strong part in my life. I cannot take this simply—& when make up for sure mind, then its already for always—the same in my love & affections. A far too big heart wh. eats me up. And the love for Christ too—& it has always been so closely linked with our lives these 22 years! First the question of taking the orthodox faith & then our two Friends [Philippe and Rasputin] sent to us by God. Last night['s] gospels made one think so vividly of Gr.[egory]< & His persecution for Christ & our sakes—everything had a double meaning & I was so sad not to have you standing by me. [a]

Last year I was in the afternoon near Ania's bed in her house (our Friend too), listening to the 12 Gospels—a part of them. To-day at 2 the vynos plashch. [carrying out of the winding-sheet][247] & at 6 the pogreb [burial]. Loman begged [for this to be done] upstairs instead of [during] the night, as then none of the soldiers can go. And you alone at the Headquarters—ah Sweet One, I cry over yr. solitude! Baby< slept well, woke up only 3 times &, I hope, will be up to-day, as he badly wishes to come to the zautr. [morning Mass] but without you I cannot imagine that great and holy feast. Think its Wify kissing you 3 times in Church,[266] I shall feel yr. kisses too & blessings.—My head goes round, & during my writing one interrupts me & I have to choose [Easter] eggs & write cards, so as to send off most things to-day—after all lots have to get things—& now must get up for luncheon at 12½, & after that shall finish my letter.—I send you my little Eastergifts—the bookmarker for the novels you read.—We lunched near Baby's bed in the big room, he feels rather giddy fr. his medicines—but will get up later.—The Image [icon] I thought you would perhaps all kiss in Church & then it will be a double remembrance. The egg is kustarnoe [handmade], can hang with yr. war Images in Church if you don't know where to put it. Its grey & now raining.—Your sweet blue flowers are too nice, thanks awfully for them, the Children & I love them & I gave some bunches to the ladies, who were quite delighted.—Baby fears he cant go to-morrow night & that worries him. [b, c]

1000 thanks, Lovebird, for yr. sweet letter—I shall at once let Aunt Olga know about the Jew. [See Letters No. 941e,f, and 948.] Shtyurmer comes to me this evening.—Yes, me loves oo, my little Boy Blue[258] & already 31 years [we have known each other] & [I] belong to you 22.—Now I must end. 3 Easter-kisses, blessings without end, my own lonely Angel, whom I love so endlessly—oh, your sad Easternight—shall miss you more than words.—Ever yr. very own old Wify. [P.S.] I send you a "Sketch" of Baby< for you to keep at the Headquarters—later can have it a wee bit arranged [framed?]—& I send you Stredlov's [Streblov's] photos he made, lovy. I shall tell Ella< you find the work very well done, only please, wire to me at once, may Baby be Protector [see Letter No. 928d and Footnote 261], then shall telegraph it to her to-morrow, or will you,—please.—Must be off. These flowers bring all my love.— [d]

No. 956.   Ts.[arist] Stavka. April 8th 1916.
My own precious Love,

I must begin my letter on this date in remembrance of what happened 22 years ago![254] I think there was a concert that evening at Coburg and a Bavarian band played; poor n. [Uncle] Alfred [Duke Alfred of Coburg] was rather tired fr. his dinner & kept dropping his stick with a crashing noise! Do you remember? Last year too we were asunder this day—it was just before the journey to Galicia!! It is really trying to be far away from each other during Passion Week & Easter. Of course I did not miss our service. To-day both times Alekseev, Nilov, Ivanov & I carried the plashchanitsa.[247] All our cossacks & lots of soldiers were standing outside the church along the way of the procession [of the cross]. It rained the whole day so I was hardly out[—]also on account of Church being at 2.30. This evening Roshchakovsky[242] suddenly appeared at dinner, I will receive him to-morrow in the evening. He has become old & reminded me somehow of Pimenov & of Bezkrovny together. He has become much calmer. I told him that you would be glad to see him on his way back. [a]

In your telegrams you asked me several times what you were to answer Ella?< I simply looked through her paper at the drawings & had not the least idea what I was supposed to say, so I wrote that I thought the work very well done! But what work I meant I do not know. Ha! Ha![261] My sweet Love, I want you so! Please do not have M.[me] B.< when I come home! Now me must go to bed. Good-night my beloved Darling, sleep well & dream gently—not about catholic priests!— [b]

9 April. Ending this letter after lunch. Just got your dear one [letter] with the tiny eggs, as book marker, for wh. I thank you so fondly. The image [icon] & egg I will place in church opposite to where I stand. Today there were lots of people & children who took Holy Communion, the latter would stare at me & bow many times after stumbling against each other! Now me must end. God bless you, my precious Treasure & send you a happy and peaceful Easter. Many tender kisses to you & the dear children from your ever loving & truly devoted huzy Nicky. [c]

261. Elizabeth ("Ella"), Alexandra's sister, was building a home for young volunteers crippled in
the war. Ella's "paper" was a request that Nicholas permit his son, the tsarevich, to be the home's
"protector" (or patron). See Letters No. 928d, 949a, 951, 954, 955e.

No. 957/ Her No. 479.   Ts.[arskoe] S[elo]. April 9th 1916.
Christ has Risen!   Sweetest Darling,
    Three very tender Easter-kisses[266] & blessings. I do so wonder how you will
spend these feast-days—all alone amongst heaps of people. All my thoughts
incessantly surround you, & I do wish we were together to meet this great holiday, but the joy of your precious letters must be my consolation. I send you a
matchbox fr. Mme. [Lyubov] Khitrovo. The big egg is from the Stroganov
school—they sent me an ideal one too—perhaps Fred.[ericks] might wire Globa
thanks from us both. The picture Ella< ordered a little painter to do for you &
she hopes you will have it always with you when you travel.—The verses on the
card I send you are written again by Mme Gordeeva. [a]
    My brain goes spinning round fr. all there has been to do again—sorting out
things, the services, tho' I sat or knelt were also very tiring, tho' lovely—& I have
a slight cold.—The sun peeps in and out to-day—I want it to remain out & let
Baby< get some air. I fear this night will be too tiring for him & yet he longs to
go. —Rodionov came for four days & leaves to-morrow—so we asked him to-day
to tea. N.P.< lets them all off for a few days now. Tchistiakov [Chistyakov] sent
a postcard fr. where they live—& his staff, in a lovely property wh. originally
belonged to Kublitsky's wife's family; now very rich people have it. Big lake,
terraces & steps down to it.—Now they have put my little Church on the terrace
& there they took holy Communion on Thursday whilst aeroplanes were flying
over their heads & our artillery & the Ekipazh< machine-guns were firing at
them, but the shells burst far away. Every day they fly & they threw bombs onto
the town, not far from the bridge. During service masses of storks promenade
about close by & [make] merry before all eyes—the priest [A. P. Vasil'ev] forbids the sailors looking about during service (wh. is most tempting there), so
they tease him, that he at least looks through a chink of the little Church.— [b]
    They say its so warm & N.P. says you wld. enjoy ideal walks in the woods &
along the roads & rowing on the lake. They heard & my lancers too that you are
going to inspect the guard now.—Does Silaev's nomination come out
to-morrow?—Babykins< is going out & then intends colouring [Easter] eggs,
[he] is very cheery—hope, the little sketch will have pleased you. For the 6-th I
intend another picture being made [by Streblov], & you must choose fr. the
photos more or less wh. pose pleased you best—tell me the No. only. Of course
one must never do completely en face, as no face is completely regular & one
eye is bigger than the other.—Ania goes to holy Communion this morning.
Shtyurmer [will be] in town< too.—I must end now as shall be having to get up
for Church—I shall go half an hour later, as service is very long to-day.—Excuse
dull letter, but am cretinised. I bless & kiss you without end, my own sweet
Sunshine, my Joy & Life, dearest of husbands.—Ever yr. very own old   Wify.
[P.S.] General-M[aj]. Fok who died from wounds, was he not the hero at
Port-Arthur on the railway engine? When was he wounded? The relief & joy
was great yesterday, when I read that our dear troops had arrived safely at Mar-

seilles & just for Easter.[262] God bless them & may they do great deeds & have immense success on French soil.—Do wire to our Friend for Easter, Novy,[263] Pokrovskoye, the government of Tobolsk. 1000 tender, touched thanks for yr. awfully sweet words on the card—I shall wear it in my dress against my heart in Church to-night to feel your love, blessing & kisses with me.—[c]

262. Reference is to a Russian expeditionary force sent to help her allies on the western front.

263. As explained in Footnote 198, the name "Rasputin" has amusing connotations to Russians, being related to "drunkenness," "dissoluteness," etc. *Rasputin* is actually a common Siberian surname, Gregory's family held it for generations. (Fuhrmann, *Rasputin*, pp. 227-228 note 14.) Even so, its negative connotations bothered the healer-mystic, and in 1907, he officially changed it to *Novyi*, "New." This is the name Alexandra uses in stating "Our Friend's" address: first the name ("Novy"), then the town ("Pokrovskoe"), finally the gubernaya (Alexandra calls it "government") of Pokrovskoe in Siberia.

No. 958/ Telegram 35. Tsarskoe Selo> Stavka. 9 Ap 1916. 14.40> 15.28. To his majesty. We all heartily thank you for dear [Easter] eggs [and] post card. Will take it with me to church this evening. Baby< taking a drive with pleasure. We lunched in my room after Mass. Rodionov comes for tea. Warmly kiss [you]. Alix

No. 959/ Telegram 29. Stavka> Tsarskoe Selo. 9 Ap 1916. 19.18> 20.30. To her majesty. So awfully thankful for dear letters and Easter presents. Enjoying them. Lovely weather. Thoughts together. Tenderest love. Niki

No. 960/ Telegram 47. Tsarskoe Selo> Stavka. 9 Ap 1916. 21.59> 22.45. To his majesty. Christ has risen![260] We all tenderly kiss you. Faberge [the jeweler] just now brought your charming egg, for which [I] thank you 1000 times. Miniature group is splendid and all the portraits are superb. In thoughts and prayers [I am] with you in your heavy loneliness. No words to express how utterly sad and empty [I am] without you on this great festival day. All [five] children going to church with me. Heartily congratulate all. Alix

No. 961/ Telegram 36 in Russian. Stavka> Tsarskoe Selo. 10 Ap 1916. 8.43> 9.55. To her majesty. Truly, He has risen![260] In thoughts I greet all of you on Easter Day. Thank you again for my Easter presents. Very fine midnight service ended at quarter to two, after which all senior ranks broke their fast with me.[264] Tenderly kiss [you]. Niki

264. "Breaking the fast (Rasgovliatsia) concluded the seven weeks' fast of Lent by the eating of food which had been blessed in the church." (Vulliamy, p. 172n)

No. 962/ Telegram 76. Tsarskoe Selo> Stavka. 10 Ap 1916. 12.56> 13.18. To his majesty. Heartily thank you for telegram, dear letter and dear little blue flowers. Some 700 people were at reception. Later today [go to] hospital<. Drab weather. How do you like Baby's< portrait [by Streblov]? Embrace and kiss [you]. Alix

No. 963/ Her No. 480.   Tsarskoe Selo. April 10th 1916.

My own sweet One,

A blessed Easter to you, peace in heart & soul—strength for all your work & success & rich blessings! I kissed your photo three times last night & this morning—the big Image [icon], on wh. you are three times.—Your card lay on my breast during the whole service—cannot tell you how unutterably sad I felt the whole night, such pain in the heart & with difficulty kept back my tears—your loneliness is too hard—God bless & richly recompense you for all your sacrifices! Just got yr. beloved letter & dear flowers.—Fancy that sinner Roshchakovsky[242] having turned up—yes, I also found him calmer & much older—his wife is an angel of goodness & patience, A.[unt] Olga< says—as his character is trying.— [a]

You sweet ramoli<, you forgot what I wrote out to you on an extra paper, that Ella< asks whether Baby< can take over the protectorship of that school of little hero boys of the war.[261]—How did you like the picture of Aleksei, the sketch of Stredlov [Ivan Bogdanovich Streblov]? How nice that you 4 carried the plash-chanitsa.[237]—Oh Pussy[-cat], M[me] .B.< is sure to come to-morrow! [See Letter No. 956b.]—The 5 Children walked round [in the church procession] last night & I sat on the top of the stairs (in a chair, not on the Churchsteps)—a lovely sight, only I dont like fireworks & crackers whilst the Priest is singing & saying prayers before the entry. Baby< had lovely pink cheeks as he had slept before. He went home after the Easter service & broke fast with Der.[evenko] & Nag.[265]—we did [so] with A.[nia]< after mass, 10 m.[inutes] to 2.—One had to wake him at 10½ he was sleeping so fast this morning. The Easter congratulations was fr. 11-12. Now [daughters] M.[arie] & A.[nastasia] go to their hospital, & then I go with the 4 girls to our hospital<—[Daughter] Olga is the whole time grumpy, sleepy, angry to put on a tidy dress & not nurses [attire] for the hospital & to go there officially—she makes everything more difficult by her humour. [Daughter] Tatiana helped me with the eggs & yr. men—so unnatural all without you!—Can you kindly give over the eggs I sent you [to those specified, see Letter No. 942g]. A.< wore yr. egg & was enchanted with it & yr. card.—Must end. Goodbye & God bless you. 1000 tender kisses fr. yr. very tired old   Wify. [b, c]

265. Derevenko and Nagorny were sailors assigned to care for the tsarevich. Dr. Derevenko (no known relation to the sailor) was another important figure in guarding Aleksei's health, so the reference might be to him, but the pairing of the names suggests "Derevenko" was the sailor.

No. 964.   Ts.[arist] Stavka. 10 April 1916.

My dear Sunny,

I thank you once more for all the pretty things which you sent me for Easter—they made my two rooms look more animated & cozy. Fancy, I may leave on Tuesday and be at home on Wednesday. That will be a joy & great bliss for me. To-day the weather is perfect, not a cloud & the birds are singing gaily & the bells are ringing the whole time. At 10.30 this morning I had the khristosovanie [Easter greetings][266] with all my people, men [the escort], staff and priests. It went off smoothly, but I had to give the eggs myself—for the first

time in my life,! To-morrow afternoon it is the turn of the Cossacks and the soldiers & it will be out of doors near the barracks out of town.–On my way back I
will inspect the guards properly. Yes, Silaev is being [promoted] now, though it
[this type of change] always comes out late–I mean the nomination. The foreigners alas came for the congratulations & received an egg each. I must say I
prefer these eggs with one's chiffre [initial letters] to the old ones [with flowers]
& besides they are much easier to make.–I have just had a good pull [row] on
the river & feel oily [supple] in all my limbs. This time [I rowed] in our [impe-
rial yacht, the] Standart['s] dvoika [dinghy]. It is 5 o'clock & I must be off to the
vechernya [vespers]. God bless my angel, my darling Girlie & Wify. I kiss you
all so fondly. Ever your own huzy Nicky.

266. Easter ceremonies are joyful occasions in Russia. "'Khristosovat'sya,' or Easter greetings ...
included three kisses–one on each cheek and one on the lips. Eggs were presented to friends and
relatives, and these were specially prized if they had been taken to church and blessed before the
presentation. The eggs given and received by persons of high rank or of wealth were often of immense value, made of gold encrusted with jewels, and containing elaborate trifles worth many thousands of pounds." (Vulliamy, p 173n)

No. 965/ Telegram 49. Stavka> Tsarskoe Selo. 10 Ap 1916. 19.30> 21.20. To
her majesty. Fond thanks [for] dear letter and his [our son Aleksei's] picture [by
the artist Ivan Streblov], wh I like very much. Divine weather. Hope [you are]
not tired. Had a good pull [row] on river. Loving kisses. Niki

No. 966/ No. 481.   Ts.[arskoe] S[elo]. April 11th 1916.
My very Own,
    Sweetheart mine, I wonder it is true that you are arriving on Wednesday at 3?
Voeikov's officer [Col. D. I.] Rost.[ovtsev] told it privately to Nini< that her
husband is returning then. Nini told me the guard had been warned you were
going to inspect them one of these days, so Sophie F.[erzen]'s boy was recalled
to the regiment yesterday evening. These are all the "rumors" wh. buzz around,
but fr. the chief person, you Lovebird, I know yet nothing, so [I will] wait quite
patiently & send this letter.– Of course, M-me. B.< had to arrive this evening
because you did not want to see her, but maybe I will be successful in getting rid
of her early so that she will not bother you. Three days I am fighting with a
cold–beastly nuisance, as it may make my face ache again. [a]
    Again grey weather, the second day already. Am tired & head rather aches, so
have not gone to Church–this afternoon at 2 khristosovanie[266] in the big pal-
ace<, over 500 people & then below in the hospital.–It went off alright in our
hospital yesterday, we remained there an hour. To-morrow I must go to the red
cross & Matf. lazaret [Matthew Hospital], but if you return on Wednesday, then
I will go earlier to the Kokor.[sky] hospital.–So tiring when not well & cannot
keep the heart up with medicines. Sweet Angel, fancy what joy if you really do
come now, the best treat of all [for] my heart, my Sunshine, my radiant Love!
Easternight Baby< khristosovalsya [kissed[266]] all the clergy in Church–& will
[also kiss] his 101 officers (I hope) to-day.–I am dreading saying goodmorning
& congratulating the men to-day. Probably in a smaller hall, as I said.– [b]

The blue flowers look charming in a big flat bowl.—You remember the prim-
roses we picked these days at Rosenau? Oh, yes I remember U.[ncle] Alfred
dropping granny's stick & being rather "tired".—I live in the past & the poetry of
it all—& long for the hero of those days to return, to clasp him tightly to my
bosom & cover him with kisses. Olga Evg.< wrote & begged me to give you
over her best Easter-wishes.—Thats good you get your rows on the river, good
exercise at least.—Georgi< met Easter with my lancers—such a nice idea! Taube
& Shesterikov said, that your 1-st rifles were full of hopes that you would see
them on their feast day. Everybody wants to see my Treasure, & I understand
them & share that wish.—Morning & evening & when I rest in the afternoon I
kiss the words on yr. Easter-card—your hand lay on it & you wrote all those dear
words to your little woman & they must warm me up. Cant' bear your being
alone, such pain!—There is that lovely little French song I have, wh. Emma F.<
gave me. "Partir, c'est mourir un peu, c'est mourir à tout ce qu'on aime" [To part
is to die a little, It is to die to all that one loves] etc.—so true—one feels an inner
death when bidding goodbye!—Baby slept splendidly again— woke only at 9 &
continued till 10.—He has grown paler fr. the pain & no sun, feels very sad without you!—Now sweetest of Husbands, my very own Treasure, Lovebird
mine—my bridegroom that was—goodbye & God bless you. Ever yr. very own
wife   Alix. [c, d]

1000 burning kisses.—Yr. card & telegram rejoiced her [Ania's<] heart colossally [sic] & she loves the [Easter] egg—I enclose her thanks.—Endless thanks for
yr. sweet letter & heavenly news that you are really coming, oh what bliss indeed, joy untold!—Excuse vile writing, I am eating, they are making an unearthly
row & teazing [sic] the wolf [a pet dog?] atrociously.—Fancy, a "dvoika" [din-
ghy] of our beloved [yacht] Standart's being there. Yes, for the soldiers the
monogram eggs are best—tho' they love the flowers too.—Hope you can without
hurrying see the guard in different places, more interesting & less stiff. Goodbye my Manny—my Angel love, I kiss you without end, every tenderly beloved
sweet place & the beautiful big eyes—write it I may, you cant stop me. [e]

No. 967/ Telegram 112. Tsarskoe Selo> Stavka. 11 Ap 1916. 13.16> 13.46.
To his majesty. Much gladdened by news you conveyed, very good. Thank you
for dear letter. Again overcast day. Am going to Big palace< and hospital<.
What a shame engineer-mechanic< came. [We] all kiss [you]. Alix

---

No. 968/ Telegram 65. Stavka> Tsarskoe Selo. 11 Ap 1916. 19.22> 19.40. To
her majesty. Fondest thanks [for] dear letters. Today kissed thrice[266] over 900
soldiers. Beautiful warm weather. Shall try and bring it with me. Georgi M.<
arrived from the front. Tenderest kisses. Niki

No. 969/ Telegram 130. Tsarskoe Selo> Orsha train station. 12 Ap 1916.
12.14> 13.27. To his majesty. Wish you a good trip. Finally, again a splendid,
warm sunny day. Every day I have exchange of Easter greetings.[266] Await
to-morrow with impatience. May the Lord bless you. [We] all warmly kiss
[you]. Alix

No. 970/ Telegram 67. Stavka> Tsarskoe Selo. 12 Ap 1916. 12.21> 12.50. To her majesty. Leaving now. Hope to arrive to-morrow afternoon at 3.30. Much colder weather. Wordless joy to meet you. Will find your letters probably in train. Tenderest love. Niki

No. 971/ Telegram 587 in Russian. Smolensk> Tsarskoe Selo. 12 Ap 1916. 6.15> 18.37. To her majesty. Thank you very much for dear letter. Travelling well. Clear weather. Warmly embrace [you]. Niki

No. 972/ Her No. 482.   Tsarskoe Selo. April 24th 1916.
My very own Beloved,
   Sweetheart, I cannot tell you what your dear presence has been to me, the light & calm you brought to my heart, as without you everything is harder to bear & I miss you <u>always</u> beyond words! Your tender caresses & kisses are such balm & such a treat—I always yearn for them—we women long for tenderness (tho' I do not ask for it nor show it often)—but now that we are so often separated I cannot help showing it. I live afterwards upon the sweet remembrances.—God grant we shall soon be together again—you tell it privately to Voeikov. Please, see the guard before as they are so impatient to present themselves—& then to go to-gether to the south would be splendid. Now you will get a certain sort of rest, as these days here are really a torment to you—people fr. morn. to night with you, fidgeting & bothering. I am so glad our Friend< came to bless you before leav-ing. I think He will return home as soon as A.[nia]< has left.—What weather! O my Love, my Own, my Soul, my Life, my One & all—fare well. I hold you tightly clasped to my heart & cover you with kisses. God bless & keep you & guard you fr. all harm. Ever yr. very own <u>Wify</u>.

No. 973/ Telegram 59 in Russian. Malaya Vishera> Tsarskoe Selo. 24 Ap 1916. 18.35> 19.05. To her majesty. Lonely and hot in carriage. In thoughts with you. Am reading.[269] Warmly embrace all. Niki

No. 974/ Telegram 341. Tsarskoe Selo> Likhoslavl. 24 Ap 1916. 21.35> 22.50. To his imperial majesty. Tenderly thank you for telegram. [We] dined on bal-cony. Just now went for drive. Lonely, empty. Sleep well. [We] warmly kiss [you]. God keep [you]. Alix

No. 975/ Telegram 1194. Smolensk> Tsarskoe Selo. 25 Ap 1916. 12.10> 13.00. To her majesty. Tender thanks for dear letter. Much cooler, rainy wea-ther, agreeable for journey. Thoughts incessantly together. Fondest kisses. Niki

No. 976/ Telegram 343. Tsarskoe Selo> Orsha, train station. 25 Ap 1916. 13.55> 15.15. To his majesty. Happy with [your] dear telegram. Very hot, wounded lying on balcony. Warmly kiss [you]. [Our] thoughts are together en-tire time. God keep [you]. Alix

No. 977/ Her No. 483.   Ts.[arskoe] S[elo]. April 25th 1916.

My own Boy Blue,[258]

How do you like that, my sweet One? Yes, I love the book[258] & shall bring it with me & read the tender passages when sad & heartsick.—I do miss you so, so much, Lovy mine—yr. lonely journey is yet worse.—Marvellous weather again[—]they are putting up the marguin [window awning] outside—it will be darker in the rooms, but the sun spoils the furniture.—We went all over Baby's< train, you had seen it already & there is a little commemorative plate on the wall. Schmidt was there & persisted in speaking French, [A. F.] Trepov too—we had to wait till 3 as the train had been sent to the Aleks.[ander] station to wait. Very clean—a sweet little Church with bells too—299 wounded soldiers & 6 officers—I gave medals to the worst.—Then I lay on the balkony [sic] till 6.— A.[nia]< came for an hour—her humour is rather aggressive, aggravated to see me little these days, [the reason being] that [she] has [so] much to do, people to see, that [she] did scarcely see you; so that in some respects it will be a relief when she goes.—[a]

We dined out & then I motored with the Children to Pavlovsk—heard the first nightingale. She [Anna Vyrubova] came back from town< in the evening.—I am writing with another pen, as [I] am in my mauveroom.[267] Was ever so happy to get yr. dear wire fr. Smolensk.—Our Friend< told Ania about one having shut up Sukhomlinov that "it is a bit not well [i.e., just]".[268]—Such marvellous weather, our wounded all lay & sat out on the balkony [sic] & in the garden, even the worst, the sun being the best cure, & then morally it does them good.—Sweety, you won't forget to speak to Voeikov about Bressler (A.< gave you her private letter fr. him about his brother).—We are going to the hospital of the Aleks. Obshch.[estvo, Alexandrovsky Society] in the barracks of the convoy & I shall give medals to the worst. Visiting hospitals in the heat is somewhat fatiguing & the heart beats hard.—Must end, my Sunshine, my joy.—We all kiss & bless you. I cover you with kisses & miss you horribly, my Angel—you did take the fortress, you sweet Boy Blue[258] & she was like yr. very own   Wify. [b]

267. Massie calls the "Empress's mauve boudoir," the "most famous room in the palace—for a time the most famous room in Russia." See its description in *Nicholas and Alexandra*, pp. 117-118.
268. Gen. Sukhomlinov, former Minister of War, was arrested on April 20, 1916 and imprisoned in the Peter and Paul Fortress. He faced trial, and, if convicted, could have been sentenced to death.

No. 978/ Telegram 78. Stavka> Tsarskoe Selo. 25 Ap 1916. 18.08> 18.21. To her majesty. Arrived well. Everything beautifully green, smells so good. Finished [that] nice book[269] with moist eyes. Miss you greatly. Tender kisses. Niki

269. Nicholas refers to *The Rosary*, by Florence Barclay, "a 'best seller' of an ultra-sentimental type." (Vulliamy, p. 175n) In Letter No. 982b, we find Alexandra sending her husband the "continuation" of *The Rosary*; she promises "you will find the same people again in this book." See Footnote 276 and Letters No. 1023 and 1073.

No. 979/ Telegram 346. Tsarskoe Selo> Stavka. 25 Ap. 21.08> 21.55. To his majesty. Are dining on balcony with N.P.< and Rodionov. Glorious breeze. Miss [you] terribly. Glad you enjoyed [that] touching book.[269] Sleep well. May [the] Lord keep you. Thank you for telegram. Alix

No. 980. Ts.[arskoe] S[elo]. April 25th 1916.

My beloved,

It was horrid saying good-bye & leaving you and the children behind. I ran away into my compartment because a lump was rising up my throat! Your dear letter soothed me & I re-read it many times over. I looked out as we passed the Aleksandr.[ovsky] station & saw the sanitary train full of poor wounded, doctors & sisters [nurses]. The heat in our cars was awful in the beginning–23°, toward the evening it became tolerable and today it was perfect, as it rained the whole morning & was much cooler. [a]

I read away at that charming book, "The Rosary" and enjoyed it thoroughly[269]; sorry to have finished it already. But I have some Russian ones left. I told Voeik.[ov] to work out the plans for our combined journey south. Shall speak about it to Aleks[eev] also. He looks well & sunburnt–I am pleased to say. They are putting up the tent in the garden. Trees & bushes are quite green, the chestnuts will be out in a day or two & everything looks bright & smells so good! The river has gone down to its normal height–I hope to row to-morrow. Igor behaves well & seems to get on alright [sic] with the rest. Just got your second wire–so glad you had N.P. and Rodion.[ov] for dinner–it is refreshing to see them–especially now! Now me must go to beddy-bye, so good night my precious Wify–sleep well & dream gently. [P.S.] April 26. A divine morning, got up early & walked for half an hour in the garden, then breakfasted & went to Aleks[eev]. As usual the first report was very long. I must finish as it is time to go out on the river. God bless you & the children my own darling Sunny. I kiss you & them so fondly. Ever your own huzy Nicky. [b]

No. 981/ Telegram 350. Tsarskoe Selo> Stavka. 26 Ap 1916. 14.20> 14.59. To his majesty. Again wonderful weather. Had an operation in our hospital–appendicitis. Am now lying on balcony. Tenderly kiss and embrace [you], miss [you] very much. Alix

---

No. 982/ Her No. 484. Ts.[arskoe] S[elo]. April 26th 1916.

My very Own,

Another splendid day, such a blessing; but the night was cooler & there is a breeze this morning.–We had N.P.< & N. N. [Rodionov] to dinner & sat out on the balkony [sic] till 10½–at 11 they left to catch their train at the Aleks.[ander] station. Missed you so much, reminded one of the bygone.–In conversation N.P. told me of an idea one had proposed (probably [some] banker, but to my mind excellent)–that one should a little later on make a loan in the country for a milliard to build railways of wh. we are in sore need. It would be covered almost at once, as the bankers & merchants, who are colossaly rich now, would give big sums–as they understand the gain. Then by this one [could] find work for our reserves when they return fr. the war, so as not to let them at once return to their villages, where discontent would soon begin–& all must try to avoid histories [i.e., tales] & disturbances by thinking out means of occupying them beforehand & for money they will be glad to work. The prisoners can begin all.–And thus one can find heaps of places for wounded officers along the line, at the stations etc. Don't you agree with the idea—you & I once had it, do you remember? [a]

May I speak of it to Shtyurmer when next I see him, so as to work out a plan how it might be done & he can speak to Bark about it?—We had an operation—appendicitis to-day.—This afternoon I shall remain, on the balcony, as my heart is tired.—As you finished the Rosary, I send you the continuation, you will find the same people again in this book.[269]—When do you go to the guard? Have you thought about our journey? Is it not beastly the Breslau[53] shot at Evpatoria—our wounded must have got a good fright.—Sweetheart, I must end now. I miss you more than words can say & yearn for your kisses. God bless you. Ever yr. very Own. [b]

No. 983/ Telegram 352. Tsarskoe Selo, the palace> Stavka. 26 Ap 1916. 17.40> 18.30. To his majesty. Wife of General Sakharov wants to know if her son was killed or only wounded, he is a lieutenant in 8th Lubensky Hussar Regiment. She was upset, came to me and asked me to investigate. [I] ask you to learn about this. [See No. 988.] [We] are drinking tea on balcony. [We] warmly kiss [you]. Alix

---

No. 984/ Telegram 81. Stavka> Tsarskoe Selo. 26 Ap 1916. 18.40> 19.25. To her majesty. Very loving thanks [for] letter and wire. Wonderful weather. Took a delightful row. Boy Blue[258] loves and wants you. Tenderest kisses. Niki

---

No. 985.   Ts.[arist] Stavka. April 26th 1916.
My own precious Sunny,

Ever so many loving thanks for your dear letter. If you knew the great joy they bring me and the excitedness I am in when I see them lying on my table! And today the one I got begins with the words "Boy Blue."[258]—I was so touched by it. That will be good if you bring it[269] with you! The weather today is delightful & I enjoyed our trip down the river. We went in three dvoiki [dinghies]. The weather is beautiful to-day, and I enjoyed my trip down the river. We went in three dinghies, Igor<, Fedorov and Dm. Sher.< followed in the big motor launch. The former cannot row, he says that after a few strokes he begins to cough & spit blood! Cannot walk quick for the same reason—poor chap considering he is only 22. [a]

We rowed half way back too in the blazing sun & after a while got into the motor. Then for fun Fedorov tried our pulses—after pulling hard against the current—Valia's< was 82, mine 92, Voeik.[ov]'s 114 and Kira's< 128. So we chaffed him about his abstention from eating meat & told him he had not seemed to profit much—at least not his heart! Ten minutes later Fed. tried us again; Valia and I had normal pulses, but the other two continued very excitedly to throb. If you arrive here on a fine afternoon you must come with all the children on a trip like this—you will enjoy the fresh breeze after the hot train! [b]

Georgi arrived from Moscow, he saw Ella, who sent me a very pretty image [icon] of the Vladimir Virgin—where she had just been to.[270a]—Try and see Motherdear[.]< I think she leaves on Saturday & give her my love. Oh! This morning while I was drying my face & hands by the open window I saw two little dogs pursuing each other along the trees in front; a moment later the one was riding on the other & a minute later they were stuck & turned around with their 6.> [sic] touching & they squeeled & for a long time could not get asunder—poor beasts. But that was a real spring picture & I had to mention it to you. I saw that the sentries were also enjoying the sight! [P.S.] 27th April It is much cooler & it rained hard in the morning. Here are programs[270b] for you to choose—I of course prefer the one that brings you quicker or earlier here. God bless you my own Love. Many tender kisses fr. your old   Nicky. [c]

270a. This famous icon of the Virgin was originally from the ancient city of Vladimir-in-Suzdal', just east of Moscow. Until this time it had been in the Uspensky Cathedral of the Moscow Kremlin. It was one of several images that "were believed to possess miraculous powers, and their presence gave confidence and courage both to the leaders and to the troops." (Vulliamy, p. 188n) On May 22 (O.S.), 1916, Nicholas had the icon brought to Stavka just before he unleashed the full force of the Brusilov offensive. (See Letters No. 992e, 1045a, and 1062b.)

270b. The sheet that presumably contained this information does not seem to be in the State Archive of the Russian Federation (GARF).

No. 986/ Telegram 355.   Tsarskoe Selo> Stavka. 27 Ap 1916. 13.59> 14.48. To his majesty. Happy at [your] dear letter, tenderly thank you. Thunderstorm came, fortunately, since heat was terrible. She [Anna Vyrubova] and our wounded soon leaving. [We] all warmly kiss and embrace [you]. Alix

No. 987/ Her No. 485.   Ts.[arskoe] S[elo]. April 27th 1916.
My own beloved Sweetheart,
   My heart leaped with joy when Tudels< gave me your precious letter upon my return from the hospital. The air was terribly heavy, my heart ached & [this] made me cough so, & left arm ached; felt the thunderstorm wh., thank God, came, and passed by, heard it twice in the distance & it poured, all has become much greener. It will lay the dust for A.[nia]'s< journey & all our wounded,— when the train leaves is still not yet settled, they change every minute on account of the movement of the other trains— probably at 7.—Great excitement in the hospital & Ania full of fidgets.—Placed my candle for you at Znamenia<. Petrovsky came to the hospital to say goodbye.—Yester-day Tolia B. [Anatoly Baryatinsky] came & did not know what to do, whether he would find you at Moghilev or not. So glad, you can row again on the river—that one arranges a tent in the garden.—When do you go to the guard? Heart & soul long for you. You cannot imagine how wildly my face ached again yesterday, whole afternoon & evening ever,—since the motor drives it has been preparing.[270c] To-day its better. Goodbye, Sweetheart, I bless you & cover you with passionate kisses. What joy to meet soon, I hope! Blessings & thousands of kisses, Huzy mine. Ever yr. very, very Own.

270c. Sergeev understands the empress to be saying that the "[pain in my face begins] as soon as I am seated in the automobile," (Perepiska, IV, p. 226). Nabokov renders the passage "it [the pain] appeared from the time of my trips in the car." (Pis'ma imperatritsy, II, p. 83)

No. 988/ Telegram 87 in Russian. Stavka> Tsarskoe Selo. 27 Ap 1916. 14.52>
15.10. To her majesty. Cornet [Sakharov] of 8th Lubensky Hussar Regiment is
alive and well, and is present here in person. [See No. 983.] Colder today and
drizzling with rain. Warmly embrace [you]. Niki

No. 989/ Telegram 89. Stavka> Tsarskoe Selo. 27 Ap 1916. 19.37> 20.04. To
her majesty. Best thanks [for] dearest letters. Weather again fine but cooler. So
pleased with new book.[269] Endless love and kisses. Niki

No. 990.   Ts.[arist] Stavka. April 27th 1916.
My beloved wify,
    Tenderest thanks for your dear letter together with the one from Olga & fr.
Aleksei. Tiny< begins his like this [the quote is in Russian]–"I count the
days–why, you know yourself!" Rather sweet! It rained till noon & became
suddenly cold–only 10°–after the heat on the previous days. The french ministers arrived[271] with several officers–they had long conferences with Alekseev,
Belyaev, Sergei etc. and dined, both being my neighbours; in this way I escaped
the necessity of a talk extra. [a]
    The idea of making a new large loan in the country, wh. you write about, I
think a very good one–so please talk about it to Shtyurmer & even to Bark. I
am sure it would [be that] the latter would be awfully honoured & touched & in
the same time he might at once tell you the manner how to do it & wherein
might be difficulties if there are any? Before leaving I told the ministers to work
out a large plan for years to come for a new railway building scheme–so this
new idea about the money–would just help the other to be brought into execution. Just now I got the following telegram: "La centenaire met aux pieds des
Vos. Maj. sa profonde reconnaissance, sa fidélite à un passé toujours
présent.–Leonille Wittgenstein."[272] Very prettily expressed, I think. I enclose a
letter from [my sister] Olga wh. please send me back. Poor girl! it is only natural that she worries; so long she has kept her feelings back–that she had to let
them out & craves for a real personal happiness, which she has never had. [b]
28th April Luckily a fine warm day! Last night it got very cold, only 4 degrees,
so I even had to shut the window! Tender thanks for your sweet letter, with
Tatiana's. I do hope your face won't hurt you much. God bless you my own
Wify darling. I kiss you & the children tenderly & thank them all for their letters! Ever your own huzy Nicky. [P.S.] Could not settle yet when to leave for
the guard for several reasons wh. shall explain. [c]

271. The ministers were Viviani and Albert Thomas. French ambassador Maurice Paléologue had
presented them to Nicholas II "about a week previously at Tsarskoe Selo." (Vulliamy, p. 178n)
272. "A century-old woman places her deep gratitude at the feet of Your Maj., being true to a past
which always remains present." This statement of loyalty was signed by Princess Leonille Ivanovna
Sayn-Wittgenstein, born Princess Baryatinskaya in 1816.

No. 991/ Telegram 359. Tsarskoe Selo> Stavka. 28 Ap 1916. 9.59> 10.28. To
his majesty. She [Anna Vyrubova] left yesterday evening. Everything covered

by white blanket, snowing heavily. Going to town< to English hospital, tea at Anichkov<. Warmly kiss and embrace [you]. Alix

No. 992/ Her No. 486.   Tsarskoe Selo. April 28th 1916.

My own precious Darling,

There we are into winter again—everything white & snowing hard, I am so sorry for trees & bushes, wh. after yesterday's rain had become so green!—It will be less tiring for going to town<, that is true. I take the four girls with me to see the English hospital in Ella's< house—in the evening their <u>unit</u> leaves for the guard.—Then we take tea at Anichkov<. I cant take Baby< as his left leg is bent all these days & one must carry him—he has no pain at all & its getting better and he is careful on account of the journey.—I wonder, why you have not left yet for seeing the guard, they are all so impatient—& now the weather has suddenly changed.— [a]

I send you the report about the little Dr. Matushkin of my 21st Siberian regiment—last winter he was in our hospital. Cannot he present the papers again to [receive] the St. George Cross, as it seems to me most unjust he did not get the cross—tho' he is a doctor, he did the work of an officer.—Well, that was a <u>trial</u> for A.[nia]< yesterday—never could one settle when my sanitary train wld. get to Ts.[arskoe] S.[elo] from town to pick her up—after endless changes, we at last took her off there after 6 [o'clock] & went all over the train, found lots of our & big palace hosp.< officers, and from town, Gebel's son too—& soldiers—5 of Ania's poor wretches too & 5 sisters [i.e., nurses] going to Livadia to rest, & some wives accompanying their husbands.—Vilchk.< went too so as to look at all the sanatoriums of the Crimea belonging to our Ts.[arskoe] S.[elo] station & Duvan went. A. had a whole court to accompany her—Zhuk<, Fed.[os'ya] Stepan.[ovna—both doctors' assistants], [Dr. S. A.] Korenev, Loman takes the train. She is placed in his charming compartiment [sic] with her maid in the sisters [i.e., nurses] waggon [sic]—her wounded are right at the other end. At 7½ at last they left (she was utterly wretched)—& when going to bed I got a letter from her fr. town, saving that they would stick [be delayed] there till 10½—God knows when they will reach Evpatoria. She sends you many loving kisses, but had no time to write these last days of fidgeting. [b]

Oh, what a snow!—I did not sleep well, something went wrong with my "minister of the interior." [Digestive problem?!]—We spent our evening working, & Olga & I read aloud change about [i.e., taking turns reading aloud] an English story we had begun long ago & forgotten all about it. What do you say to Nikolasha< having presided [at] the opening committee "on the question of Zemstvos in Trans-Caucasia?" I see by the papers that Grevenitz [V. E. Grevenits] has died—what will become of Dolly, [his wife,] I wonder.—Just got your beloved letter, my Treasure, & I thank you for it with all my heart. Yes, Lovy certainly we shall take the marcheroute reaching Moghilev at 2, otherwise we should have no quiet time before Church. What joy to meet in a week! That is good Fed.[orov]< watches your pulses, as all hearts are not equally strong & too much rowing against the current may harm them— they need gentle training.—You say, Motherdear< probably leaves Saturday—here nothing is known, so for safety [security's] sake Ressin< sends the soldiers & cossacks off to-day—Zina [Mengden] neither knows & all are in trances, as its difficult to arrange [i.e., travel] quickly, especially now.—Poor Igor< is distressed with me [i.e., is embarrassed] that he is still so weak—the health of all these boys[228] is not at all famous [i.e., good]. [c, d]

Ah my Boy Blue,[258] me's coming soon to gather him to my breast and to cover his sweet face, eyes & lips with tender kisses!!!—Oh, those 2 poor dogs! [See Letter No. 985c.] Do you remember [our dogs] Iman & Shilka at Peterhof, when we saved them? Its after 12 & still snowing & blowing, the sun tries to break through, but has not yet succeeded.—How is it you dont go to see the guards yet? Will one arrange to stop at Vinnitsa on the way south, so as that I can see my store[2] there? If I know the date beforehand, I can let Apraxin< & [V. V.] Mekk know to be there then.—If you have any rough plan, let me know please, as we must calculate for our linen & clothes; and then can we go to Evpatoria by train, not all the waggons fr. Simferopol, one wld. be less tiring & we could lunch in the train, see the Sanatorium & Ania. Have you thought about giving the order that the [icon of the] Vlad.[imir] Virgin fr. the Usp. Cath.[270a] should be brought to the Headquarters? Now I must get up & dress.—Goodbye & God bless you Sweetheart, little wify misses you terribly. I cover you with burning kisses & rest yr. head upon my breast. Ever yr. very own old Sunny. [e]

No. 993/ Telegram 93. Stavka> Tsarskoe Selo. 28 Ap 1916. 19.34> 19.56. To her majesty. Tender thanks letters. Hope not over tired from town<. What a pity show [i.e., snow]—with you. Here very fine. Love to all. Niki

---

No. 994/ Telegram 366. Tsarskoe Selo> Stavka. 28 Ap 1916. 21.02> 22.05. To his majesty. Warmly thank you for letter and telegram. Am tired from town<. Motherdear< healthy, kisses you, leaves on Sunday. Was clear during day, now snowing again. Received news from my sanitary train travelling south. Embrace and kiss [you], sleep well. Alix

---

No. 995/ Her No. 487.   Ts.[arskoe] S[elo]. April 29th 1916.
My own Boy Blue![258]

Warmest thanks my treasure for yr. dear letter just received & for poor little Olga's[, your sister's]. I fully understand & deeply feel for her—but had to put all before her, for your sake. Of course one can only long for her happiness at last—but will she gain it thus. May I ask our Friend<, of my accord, whether he would think it better for all reasons it should be now or after the war? [See Footnotes 201, 202 and 235.] I shall see him to bid goodbye a second in Ania's< house, as he wants to bless me before the journey; & then you can answer her. I saw Xenia< at tea yester-day,—she also leaves south on Saturday & wont probably see me before the talk. Vol.[odia] Volk.[onsky] told her now & to Petia< he said better after the war—he is such a man, tries to please all parties, the same as he does in the corridors of the Tauride [Palace where the Duma met]. [a]

Been snowing hard all morning & very damp indeed, the wounded & my cheek feel it. I went to our hospital< this morning, now must receive. Then shall go to Ania's hospital & then doklady [reports]—always busy. Baby's< arm is also swollen (does not hurt) fr. the damp & the leg is not yet quite right. Pitty [sic] about the guards, but you have your reasons no doubt.—Excuse short letter but must receive.—Precious Boy Blue,[258] me loves oo, oh, so much & so endlessly.—God bless & protect you. I cover you with very, very tenderest kisses. Ever yr. very Own. [P.S.] Motherdear< looks well, but thin & longs to get off, as perpetual receptions tire & bother her. She leaves on Sunday—so we all now disperse [i.e., travel in various directions].—[b]

No. 996/ Telegram 369. Tsarskoe Selo> Stavka. 29 Ap 1916. 14.17> 14.58. To his majesty. Tenderly thank you for dear letter. Snowing a lot, such a pity. Was at hospital<. Kiss and embrace [you]. Alix

---

No. 997/ Telegram 94. Stavka> Tsarskoe Selo. 29 Ap 1916. 19.47> 20.35. To her majesty. Fond thanks [for] dear letters and wire. Got one from her [Vyrubova?]. Fine weather. Tenderest kisses to all. Niki

---

No. 998.   Ts.[arist] Stavka. April 29th 1916.
My very Own,
    Yesterday I had more to do & could not begin my letter as usual before going to bed. I wrote a scolding one [letter] to Boris< on account of the treatment he gives to the chief of his staff—gen. Bogaevsky. In the afternoon I looked on at some experiments made with burning spirits of wine & kerosine [sic] being thrown at a certain distance![273] After that I took a splendid row with the others in our three dvoiki [dinghies] up the river. In mornings here are fine, also the evenings, but at noon the sky becomes cloudy wh. makes me angry as I want to become sun burnt & not look like all or most of the staff officers look! [a]
    Your dearest letter No. 486 has arrived—tender thanks. I am glad you have chosen 2 o'clock for coming here. I will order Voeik[ov] to work out the plan for our journey. In broad lines it is this. we leave Mogilev on the 7th & stop at Vinnitsa for several hours on the 9th. Then we go to Kishinev where is quartered one new division & back to Odessa, wh.[ere I] shall see the servian troops—probably the 11th. From there to Sevastopol for as many days as you like! We can go together till Kursk and separate there on our own way back—arriving at the same time—you at Ts.[arskoe] Selo & me here! Probably the 17th or 18th of May! There, my darling Sunny, now I must end. God bless you & the children. I kiss you & them very tenderly and miss you wildly. Ever your own huzy Nicky. [P.S.] Many thanks for the dear blue flowers! [b]

273. The Germans introduced the flamethrower in 1914, but its usefulness was limited by a short range of 25-40 yards and low destructive power. The ghastly weapon did not become effective and widely used until the Second World War.

No. 999/ Telegram 376. Tsarskoe Selo> Stavka. 30 Ap 1916. 13.56> 14.17. To his majesty. Warmly thank you for dear letter. Plan is good. Weather, fortunately, is better, sometimes sun shows through. Was at hospital<. Reception

[next]. Am going to Big palace<. Christo< comes for tea, leaving to-morrow. Embrace and kiss [you]. Alix

---

No. 1000/ Her No. 488.   Ts.[arskoe] S[elo]. April 30th 1916.
My own precious One,
   Very tenderest thanks for dear letter & the progr. of our journey, it seems quite good, shall I only have time to see any hospitals & [my] store< at Odessa? What a nice journey together—hang Becker< for wishing to accompany me then! You better find out whether that rotten Plen [I. M. Plehn] has nothing to do with Boris'< behaviour—do get that man away.—To-day at last finer, warmer, the sun peeps in & out.—Baby< looks thin & pale, left arm also wont bend well, but no pains & as soon as its warmer, its sure to pass.—Sat in the hospital<, worked & continued teaching my little Crimean English & [G. N.] Taube talked like a waterfall.— Christo comes to tea & Tatiana's Children,[274] as I have not seen them since last summer. [a]
   The children are eating & talking bosh & laughing.—Went all over Ania's< hospital from top to cellar, kitchen & stables. In the evening we work & read.—Nikolai [Michaelovich] has asked to see me—alone.—Cant imagine why, so shall see him to-morrow & Shtyurmer too. We go to the big palace<—(so dull). Sweetest Treasure, beloved Darling, I do so long for you & your tender caresses.—Awfully busy, tho' heart tired—strange enough, don't miss her [Anna Vyrubova] a bit, can't understand how that is.—Pss. Odoevsky comes to me now & two wounded officers who return to the front. What real news from the front? Goodbye my Treasure— sorry dull letter.—Metropolitan [Pitirim] was very nice yesterday, shall tell you our conversation, nothing particular.—Fondest kisses, Huzy mine. Ever yr. very, very own old woman   Alix [b]

---

   274. "Christo" was Prince Christopher, son of King George I of Greece. "Tatiana" was a Russian princess (knyaginya), the older daughter of Constantine Constantinovich and the wife of Prince C. A. Bagration-Mukhransky, a junior officer in the 13th Erivan Grenadier Reg. who was killed a few days later on May 19, 1916.

No. 1001/ Telegram 100. Stavka> Tsarskoe Selo. 30 Ap 1916. 19.43> 20.14.
To her majesty. Best thanks [for] dear letter and wire. Hope [your] sweet face [is] better. Cold, windy. Tenderest kisses. Niki

---

No. 1002.   Ts.[arist] Stavka. April 30th 1916.
My beloved wify,
   So many loving thanks for your dear letter. I am again much occupied & have to receive people one after the other. These receptions take away lots of one's free time, wh. is generally used for reading the daily papers & writing letters. I no more look through the newspapers or illustrations. [N]either do I play domino in the evening any more. It is true we are only three of those who used to play. I am bitterly disappointed at not having gone to see the guard, but it was impossible for me to have left, as there was a constant correspondence going on between Alekseev and Evert concerning the future plans, in which the guard is

also concerned. So [V. M.] Bezobrazoff has been sent for. I shall explain [to you] the reason when you come. [a]

The shutting up of poor S.[ukhomlinov] puts me out very much.[268] Khvostov ([Minister of] justice) warned me that would probably happen, by the order of the senator who has got the affair in his hands. I told him [in] my opinion it was unjust & unnecessary; he said it was done to prevent S. from escaping out of the country & that one has already spread that news to excite people's minds! Disgusting at all events! Now my own beloved Sweetheart I must end. God bless you & the children! I kiss you with passionate kisses & them with [a] fatherly one and remain Ever your own huzy Boy Blue[258] Nicky. [b]

No. 1003/ Telegram 3. Tsarskoe Selo> Stavka. 1 May 1916. 13.47> 14.12. To his majesty. Heartily thank you for dear letter. Left cheek hurts a bit. Wind, snow, rain, sun—[they continually] change about,—so dreary. We all tenderly kiss [you]. Lonely without you in church. [I] bless [you]. Alix

---

No. 1004/ Her No. 489.   Ts.[arskoe] S[elo]. May 1st 1916.
My beloved precious One,

From all my loving heart do I send you these lines again. Yesterday, no, to-day a week that you left us—it seems ever so much longer & I am counting the days when we shall meet—4 have remained. I again did not sleep famously & my left "ternary" nerve of the face began aching, an awful nuisance—now its better.—Were in church yesterday evening, its so empty without you, but I feel our prayers are together & all our thoughts. Fresh, windy, sun & rain change about—for Baby< sunny weather is so essential, he is quite pale again—you both need the sunny south.—Excuse my bothering you with petitions, but our Friend< sent them [to] me.— A.[nia]< arrived last night at her destination.—I have nothing interesting to tell you, perhaps [I will] after Nikolai M.[ichaelovich] has been [to visit]—he asked to see me alone, cannot simply imagine why.—Then I have —Ioanchik [Ioann Constantinovich] & Putyatin with the plans for the Church. [a]

The last days there is always so much to do & see to & finish off before leaving. "Do you love his mouth, his eyes, his hair". Yes, my little Boy Blue, I do, & I long to press my kisses tenderly & passionately upon them.—Sweet Boy Blue, with that deep true love![258]—Tenderest thanks Sweetheart, for yr. precious letter. What a nuisance you have so much to do, my Treasure, & I too am disappointed for you, the guard & N.P.< who were longing for you to come. Snow, rain, hail & sunshine, strong wind, nuisance & my face aches.—Find it a shame about Soukhoml.[268] as if he wld. dream of running away.—Thanks for sweet forgetmenot.— [b]

Well I had Nikolai [Michaelovich] for an hour—very interesting about the letters he wrote you etc. & he wants me to talk all over with you. I am very tired after it, but he meant & spoke well (tho' I don't like him). Now I must send this. Its snowing hard & we are going to [daughters] M.[arie] & A.[nastasia]'s hospital. Goodbye, Sweetheart, Boy Blue—ah, could I but help you more & be an adviser & of real, real use to you. I bless & kiss you without end, my one & all. Ever yr. very own old Wify. [c]

No. 1005/ Telegram 2. Stavka> Tsarskoe Selo. 1 May 1916. 19.47> 20.05. To
her majesty. Loving thanks [for] dear letter, also [daughters] Olga and Tatiana
for photo. Finer but still cold. Hope cheek [pain] will pass soon. Tender kisses to
all. Niki

No. 1006.   May 1. 1916.[275]
My very Own!
    Tenderest thanks for your dear letter. Yesterday was much occupied & to day
Sunday also. So cannot write a letter. The weather is slowly improving but still
very cold. A few bits of snow fell this morning. I am counting the days for our
meeting! God bless you & the children. Tender wishes to all fr. your very own
loving Nicky

---

275. Nicholas did not note where he wrote this post card, but it was probably at Stavka at Mogilev.

No. 1007.   Ts.[arist] Stavka. May 1st 1916.
My dear darling,
    Many loving thanks for your dear letter N° 488. We are now in the middle of
May & the nearer the date of your arrival approaches the more impatient I grow!
I only wish that the weather may get warmer & be fine when you are here. As
much as I remember last year you did not a stay at Mogilev. That as usual makes
all the difference! At Odessa we remain 24 hours—so I think you will have ample time to see what you want.—From Boris< came at once a very amiable answer by wire, so it did him good to be shaken up! [See Letter No. 1000a.] Very
possible that Plen [I. M. Plehn] had to do something [i.e., had something to do]
in [with] the story. Veselkin turned up today looking thin & sad. He told me
there is a set of men who were try to break his neck by spreading calumnies
about him. I have heard some stories & was glad to hear that they were all pure
inventions; he left me very relieved.—I mean he was relieved by telling me everything so. His work down there goes on well & smoothly. Please tell Paul<, if
you see him, that his nomination will come out a little later than the 6th of May.
Bezobrazoff is coming here to-morrow—I will talk it over once more with him.
Now, Lovy-mine, I must go to bed as it is late. Night-night. [a]
May 2[d]. The weather is decidedly better & warmer. Have just come back from
the doklad [report]. I forgot to say that yesterday [G. M.] Romanovsky dined,
he is now on his way to France whereto he is being sent with two others for
some time. He looks thin but well—so this letter is my last one! God bless you
& the children! I wish you a safe & pleasant journey! God grant in three days
we may be together. With many tender kisses ever, my beloved Wify, your own
old huzy Nicky. [b]

No. 1008/ Her No. 490.   Ts.[arskoe] S[elo]. May 2nd 1916.
My own beloved Treasure,
    Grey and windy, despairing weather as my cheek continues aching—the left
one now, and I slept badly notwithstanding a compress & it is a little swollen.
In my sisters [i.e., nurse's] kosynika [triangular scarf] it hides it.—Last evening
we were for two hours in our hospital to cheer them up, as our departure grieves

them.—Well, Shtyurmer found the idea about the loan for railways ingenious &
just the right moment, as all grumble now about the railways & will sooner give
money. He will send me Bark at 5.—Then I spoke of Sukh.[omlinov][268]—he said
Frederiks got a letter (like mine probably) fr. the wife, but he said it did not concern him to speak to you of it & gave it to Sh.[tyurmer], who showed it to the
Minister of Justice[, A. A. Khvostov]. The latter wrote a whole answer why it
had to be, & S. thought of bringing it to you now but I said you wld. have no
time to receive him these days & he will ask for an audience after yr. return, he
has never been at the Headquarters. He did not wish to grieve you about Sukh.
as he knows you liked him. So I asked him to speak again to Khvostov [who]
comes to me at 4½. Look at me with all the ministers suddenly!— [a]

Sh.[tyurmer] has nothing in particular—only [wanted to say that] if you receive
Rodzianko (one says [i.e., it is rumored] he goes to you) do tell him you wish
[to] insist the Duma to finish her work in a month & that its the place for him &
all the rest to be in the country & see to their fields [i.e., estates].—He does not
approve of the question of zemstvo for the Caucasus as is sure they will always
fight—the different nationalities—I thought you did not agree, but according to
yr. answering telegram to Nikolasha<, you wish them luck.—Paul< took tea with
us yesterday,—is waiting for news, so I said you have sent for Bezobr.[azov] to
talk over things concerning the guard.—A.[nia]< writes she lies on the beach in
the sun, that its like a dream, like paradise, people bathing all round. Am going
to our hospital—hang the cheek!—1000 thanks for lovely card, sweet words—so
you too have cold weather, disappointing. I am bringing Vlad. Nik.< till the 7-th
(except Mr. Gill[i]ard of course)—for safety sake as we travel for 27 hours its
safer, tho' his [Aleksei's] right arm is again alright [sic], the left leg also much
better.—Fondest blessings & warmest, tenderest kisses, Lovebird. Ever yr. very
Own. [P.S.] Soon, soon together. [b]

No. 1009/ Telegram 13. Tsarskoe Selo> Stavka. 2 May 1916. 14.04> 14.42.
To his majesty. Warmly thank you for dear post card. Cold, overcast. Cheek
hurts, a bit swollen, slept badly. Was at hospital<. Big reception. Kiss and
warmly embrace [you]. God keep [you]. Alix

No. 1010/ Telegram 8. Stavka> Tsarskoe Selo. 2 May 1916. 19.38> 20.11. To
her majesty. Tender thanks [for] sweet letter. Wrote my last one. Fine weather,
strong wind. Rowed on river, was tossed about from waves, great fun. Thought
of Tiny<. Kisses to all. Niki

No. 1011/ Telegram No 38. Tsarskoe Selo> Stavka. 3 May 1916. 17.14> 18.20.
To his majesty. Warmly thank you for dear letter. Forgive me for not writing
today, there was no time. Reception, [then] our hospital<, Zizi< and Trina< to
lunch, cemetery, Ania's< hospital. Over-cast, rain. Await to-morrow impatiently.
Embrace and kiss [you]. Alix

No. 1012/ Telegram 14. Stavka> Tsarskoe Selo. 3 May 1916. 22.45> 23.45.
To her majesty. Many thanks [for] dear letter and Marie's. Very busy day. After

heat strong rain and thunder. Understand perfectly could not write to day. Loving kisses and blessings. Niki

---

No. 1013/ Telegram 45. Tsarskoe Selo> Stavka. 4 May 1916. ___ .37> 1.10. To his majesty. Thank you for telegram. Forgot to say that in my opinion it would be excellent to send Georgy< to Nizhnyi[-Novgorod], as I consider that at such a national festival, especially in war time, a representative of our family ought to be there, and Georgy< is the most suitable. Warm, raining almost entire day. Sleep well. [I] embrace and kiss [you]. Alix

---

No. 1014/ Telegram 47. Tsarskoe Selo> Stavka. 4 May 1916. 10.15> 10.55. To his majesty. Are leaving in an hour. Awaiting to-morrow with impatience. Rain, windy. [I] kiss and embrace you. Alix

---

No. 1015/ Telegram 15. Stavka> Tsarskoe Selo. 4 May 1916. 10.19> 10.25. To her majesty. Thanks [for] dear wire. Quite agree. [See No. 1013.] God bless your journey. Fondest kisses. Niki

---

No. 1016/ Telegram 41 in Russian. Likhoslavl> Stavka. 4 May 1916. 20.50> 22.26. To his majesty. Are travelling quite well. Glorious weather in the day. Await to-morrow with impatience. Sleep well, [we] warmly embrace [you]. Alix

---

No. 1017/ Telegram 2 in Russian. Krasnoe> Stavka. 5 May 1916. 10.28> 12.32. To his majesty. [I] slept well. Pity, seems weather still not famous. [We] all warmly kiss you. Strong wind, brief rain. What do you propose [we] do during the day so that [we] will know how to dress? Alix

---

No. 1018/ Her No. 491.   In the train. May 17th 1916.
My own Beloved,
   In a few hours we shall part—our lovely journey together at an end! Oh, I hate saying goodbye to you my both treasures, sunshine< & sunbeam< & feel already a heavy, sore heart! But its a comfort to know that you are together & so you will feel less lonely & Baby< will bring life into yr. so dull life [at Stavka].—The lovely south[ern trip, see Letter No. 998b] did him good—you get him to play in the sand without making too strong movements. Wonder, when we shall meet again? Sweetest One, it has been a dream these 10 days & so cosy being next to each other—& such sweet remembrances of all your love & tender caresses wh. shall sorely miss at Tsarskoe [Selo].—Our hospital< will be my consolation; if only the weather is nice.—Goodbye, my Angel, my own Sweetest of sweets, little Boy Blue[258] with his great big heart. God bless & protect you & Babykins<—kiss him very tenderly & think of me when you say prayers together. I hold you tightly & yearningly in my arms & cover you with kisses. Ever yr. very, very own little Sunny. [P.S.] A kiss [I am placing here].

No. 1019/ Telegram 53 in Russian. Glushkovo M.K.V.> Moscow. 17 May 1916. 17.10> 22.—. To her majesty, Moscow. Very empty and sad without you. Have finished the book.[276] Heartily thank you for letter. Aleksei and I warmly embrace all. Niki

---

276. Nicholas II finished Florence L. Barclay's novel, *The Rosary*, on April 25, 1916. (See Letter No. 978.) He praised it so highly to his wife that on the following day she sent him "the continuation," assuring her husband "you will find the same people again in this book." This may have been the title he reports finishing at this time. See Letters No. 982b, 985a, 989 and especially 1023 and 1073.

No. 1020/ Telegram 31. Nakhomovo> Zhlobin. 17/18 May 1916. 10.52> 4.05. To his imperial majesty. The following. Are travelling well. The two of us had supper together. Am sewing and am quite lonely without you, my dears. Sleep well. [We] tenderly kiss you [both]. Quite sad. God keep [you]. Alix

---

No. 1021/ Telegram 262 in Russian. Bologoe> Stavka. 18 May 1916. 9.52> 11.05. To his majesty. [I] slept well. Only 6 degrees. Am terribly lonely without you both. Warmly kiss and embrace [you]. Heartily thank you for dear telegram. Alexandra

---

No. 1022.   Ts.[arist] Stavka. May 18th 1916.
My own Darling,   [This is a post card]
    Tender thanks for your sweet letter, I did not expect it! Oh, how I miss you! Our trip together and the time spent on the Black Sea have passed like a dream. It is a consolation for me that Sunbeam< remains with me. I love you with an eternal love which grows continually. May God bless you, my darling! I kiss you and them tenderly. Your Nicky.

No. 1023/ Her No. 492.   In the train. May 18th 1916.
My very own Sweetheart,
    All my heart's thoughts are with you my both treasures; miss you sorely—had my lonely luncheon wh. was very quiet & sad without Sunbeam's< lively prattle.—Its nice the book, is it not? I am glad you know so many of them now, they [novels by Florence L. Barclay] do one really good, so healthy, simple & warm up the lonely heart.—When I got up yr. dear telegram was brought me. It was horrid saying goodbye!!—Spent the whole afternoon & evening till 10¼ with Ella<, who then went to try & get some sleep till Moscou [sic]—[We should arrive there at] 2.15.—I took tea with all, so as to be able to speak with her people. At Kursk I received the handsome new governor.—I have finished my third piece of embroidery since this 2 weeks' journey & feel quite proud.—The 2 youngest [daughters] & Olga are grumbling over the weather, only 4° & they said one saw one's breath out of doors,—so they play ball to get warm or play on the piano—[Daughter] Tatiana sows [sic] quietly. But the sun shines at least brightly.— [a]
    Yesterday, whilst still warm & Tudels< was arranging my compartment, we sat in the saloon—the girls sprawling on the floor with the sun shining full upon them so as to get brown. From whom have they got that craze? Now you like the heat, but not when you were their age; & I run away fr. the sun—tho' the air

in the south did me good I think, as there was always a breeze.—Our last stop-page now & Valuev has come—the platform [was] close & the exact hight [sic] for all to look in, so I quickly had to draw the curtain. I am not yet dressed & quite [want to stay] in bed till 2, so as to thoroughly rest.—Babykins< I am sure keeps you all gay & now 2 sweet campbeds stand cosily together.[164]— [b]

I shall give this to the Feldjager who goes on to town, then it will reach the other in good time.—I slept well, thank God & got through this journey much better than I ever expected.—To-morrow [daughter] Tatiana & I have our regi-mental feasts.—Lovy, tell Shtyurmer to come now, speak about the railway loan; & let him know to bring Sukhoml.[inov]'s journal & letters to his wife, wh. are compromising, better you should see for yourself & judge rightly & not only go by their words—they can have [been] read in another sense than you will.—Then, remember please, [to see] both the Metropolitans [probably Pitirim and Vladi-mir—see Letter No. 1055] with Volzhin, upon yr. return here. Tatiana's birthday [is] May 29, Anast.[asia's] June 5, Marie['s] 14-th—now Heart of my heart, my Own, my Sunshine sweet, whose caresses I yearn for— Goodbye & God bless & keep you. 1000 of endless, tender kisses. Ever yr. very, very Own. [P.S.] The 4 girls kiss you very much. [c]

No. 1024/ Telegram 103. Stavka> Tsarskoe Selo. 18 May 1916. 14.36> 15.25. To her majesty. Tender thanks [for] telegram. Hope [you] arrived well. Here fine warm weather. Since yesterday going out to play on the sand. Both [Aleksei and I are] quite well. Miss you terribly. Fondest kisses to all. Niki

---

No. 1025/ Telegram 72. Tsarskoe Selo> Stavka. 18 May 1916. 16.30> 18.45. To his majesty. [We] just now arrived. Clear sun. Only 4°—cold. Empty, sad rooms seem vast after 2-week trip in train. Children returned home with sadness. [We] kiss [you] and are terribly lonely without you both. [I] wish you [both] all the best. Am going to hospital for vsenoshchnaya [vespers], this will be unex-pected for them. Heartily thank you for dear telegram. Glad you are playing on the sand. Alix

---

No. 1026/ Telegram 79. Tsarskoe Selo> Stavka. 19 May 1916. 13.40> 14.17. To his majesty. Very gladdened by dear post card and letter of Baby<, tenderly thank you. 1° frost during night, clear sunny day, cold. This morning was at church at hospital<. Yedigarov< will have dinner with us. Am terribly lonely without you both. We all embrace and kiss [you]. Thank Zhilik< for letter. Am going to moleben [Te Deum] at my lancers' hospital. Alix

---

No. 1027/ Telegram 107. Stavka> Tsarskoe Selo. 19 May 1916. 14.53> 15.16. To her majesty. So touched by dear letter. My best wishes for your lancers and Tatiana's. [Weather here is] also cold and bright. Thoughts always together. Tenderest love from both. Niki

---

No. 1028/ Her No. 493.   Ts.[arskoe] S[elo]. May 19th 1916.
My own Beloved

Ever such tender thanks for yr. dear sweet words on the card. Bless you, my Treasure. I miss you 2 quite awfully, therefore am glad to be in our hospital< instead of at home. Well, yesterday vsenoshchnaya [vespers] in the hospital< itself ½ an hours [sic], & then sat & talked with all. Spent the evening quietly working. This morning 9½ to the hospital Church & then to our wounded. Karangozov turned up, Anushevitch [Anyshevich], Yedigarov<— last moment, so have invited him to dinner—leaves to-morrow & came only so as to see us, such a dear—we were all shy & silent, meeting after 15 months,—here it will be better.—After luncheon went to moleben [Te Deum] & cup of chocolate to my lancers' hospital. All the ladies were there, Baranov, Trubnikof & one or 2 old ones, but not one active one, all are in the regiment. Then to Lyanosov's hospital to see Silaev; have told him <u>by your order</u> to go to Sebastopol for a cure at the Rom.[anov] Inst.[itute], 2-3 weeks; he wanted to return to the regiment, wh. I told him, was absolute folly—so by yr. order he will go in a few days. Its quite essential I find.—1° of frost in the night—sunny & cold—small oakleaves, lilacs not thinking of coming out. Must quickly send this off, else the man wont catch the train. Blessings & tenderest kisses, sweet Angel, fr. yr. very own little <u>Wify.</u> [P.S.] Tenderly I clasp you to my breast with endless love. —

No. 1029.										19 May 1916.[275]
My own Darling,								[This is a post card.]
   Tender thanks for your dear letter wh. was such a lovely surprise! Thank God you don't feel tired after our journey! To-day the weather has suddenly become cold with a bright sun. We both [our son Aleksei and I] slept very well near each other. Played nicely yesterday on the sand. God bless you & the girls. I kiss you my own Sunny very fondly & them too. Ever your own Nicky.

No. 1030/ Telegram 86. Tsarskoe Selo> Stavka. 20 May 1916. 13.59> 14.39. To his majesty. Tenderly, tenderly thank you both, my dears, for dear letters. Warmer. [We] were at hospital. Now I have doklady [reports]. [We] embrace and warmly kiss [you]. Miss [you] quite badly. Alix

No. 1031/ Her No. 494.						Tsarskoe Selo. May 20th 1916.
My own Beloved,
   Ever such tender thanks for yr. dear card I received upon my return from the hospital. I do wish it wld. get really warm at the Headquarters—to-day its better. I have a long doklad [report] with Rostovtsev< & then Shvedov, so fear I shall again not have time to go out. I placed a candle for you my Sweetheart at Znamenia<,Yedigarov< was very dear, kept him for 2 hours & he told us a lot of interesting things. Dear me, how difficult & hard it is for them in that terrible heat, & the wretched horses suffer awfully & never any rest. We bid him goodbye this morning at the hospital, Raftopolo [Ravtopulo] & Shah Bagov [Shakh-Bagov] also were there;—I photographed them all.—I send you 3 photos. I took [them] in April when you were here. Its so nice being with them all & I feel the loneliness less than here in my rooms.—Botkin was an hour with me & has still not yet finished all about Livadia & Yalta hospitals, to-morrow morning

he will continue his doklad. Trina< lunched with us.—How do you spend your evenings? Always reading, poor wee One? But Tiny< must be a consolation & bring life into your solitude, I am sure. Happily I keep alright [sic], so can get about more, this fresh weather keeps me up.—Sweetest of Sweets, dearly beloved One, I cover you with tender, burning kisses. God bless & protect you & help you in all your undertakings. Ever yr. very   Own. [P.S.] The girlies all kiss you very fondly;—they have gone out driving with Trina. Bow to Igor< fr. me;—speak to him about his sister Tatiana [Constantinovna]. —

No. 1032/ Telegram 111. Stavka> Tsarskoe Selo. 20 May 1916. 20.20> 21.32. To her majesty. Tenderest thanks [for] receiving beloved letter and wire. Fine, warm weather. Receiving continually. [We] both kiss you all. Niki

---

No 1033.   Ts.[arist] Stavka. May 20th 1916.
My tenderly beloved Wify,

Thank you for your dearest letter [written] before you reached Tsarskoe [Selo] & which I did not at all expect to receive so soon. It was horrid seeing you leave with the girlies—Baby< & I at once got into our train; it left Kursk 10 min.[utes] later. I took him to your cabin & made him sniff at your cushion & at the curtain of the window on the right—he was quite astonished to smell y^r scent thereon & shyly remarked that he was frightfully sad without you. So I kissed him & told him to go & play the "nain jaune"[277] & promised to walk with him at the next station. I was of course occupied with my rotten papers. Only in the evening after he had said his prayers, could I begin the new book.[269] It was very cold in the night but luckily for our arrival here the weather was fine & quite warm. He motored in the afternoon & found a good place with soft sand, where he enjoyed playing on! Yesterday the weather suddenly changed & became cold—4° in the night, but the sun warmed up the air & the temp. rose to 10 in the shade. For our second drive we followed a small road along the banks of the river & halted about three versts lower of [i.e., below] the new big bridge. There the sand was as white & as soft as that of a sea beach. Baby rushed about on it shouting—sovsem kak v Evpatoria [just like at Evpatoria] because it was so warm! Fedorov allowed him to run about bare-foot & he was delighted of course! I walked along the river up to the bridge & back again & thought the whole time of you & of our drive on the first day of your arrival here. It really does seem like a dream now! [a]

My evenings now are rather busy, as ministers & other people want to see me. We dine at 8.o to have more time after tea. The tent as yet is not inviting to eat in—the evenings are too cool. Aleksei behaves much better at table & sits quietly by my side. He brings so much life & light in one's existence here, but nevertheless I crave & yearn for your sweet love & caresses! These separations teach one great lessons! Being so often away one learns to treasure that, which passes unnoticed or not so strongly felt when at home in quiet times! Now my Love I must end. God bless you & the dear girlies! I kiss you all very tenderly & want you fearfully. Ever your own Nicky. [b]

---

277. "Nain Jaune" was a card game also known as "Pope Joan."

No. 1034/ Telegram 95. Tsarskoe Selo> Stavka. 21 May 1916. 14.05> 14.47.
To his majesty. Heartily thank you for precious letters [from] you and Baby<.
Warm today. What news about the English naval engagement?[279] [We] were at
hospital. [We] kiss and embrace [you]. Alix

No. 1035/ Her No. 495.   Ts.[arskoe] S[elo]. May 21st 1916.
Sweetheart beloved,
   I cover you with kisses & thank endlessly for <u>precious</u> letter. Yes, Lovy, its
true what you say—when apart one doubly realises [sic] that one has not sufficiently appreciated the many marks of love, wh. one has taken as natural &
usual. Now every caress is a double treat & terribly longed for when not to be
had.—I send you & Baby< each a pansy. Dear, can you give the enclosed paper
over to Frederiksy [Count Fredericks]—poor M-lle Petersen[278] has really nothing
to live upon—her old Aunt left her 50.000—that means 2000 a year for lodging,
food & clothes—if she could have got 2000 yearly fr. you, Katia Ozerov [Cath-
erine Ozerova] says it would be a Godsend. Can you have it done as an exception— they[278] did behave too badly sending her off with a penny & no-where to
live—life so expensive now.—What is the news about the English naval battle—awfully anxious to know whether Georgi [George, prince of Battenburg]
was out too on the [cruiser] New Zealand & wh. English ships were
sunk.[279]—[Daughter] Maries & Babys< trains have been sent for to Pskov.
[Daughter] Olga says she has much work now, many wounded again. Sorry,
you have again such a lot to do.—Were in hospital—operation. Zizi< lunched,
now [V. V.] Mekk comes with doklad [report];—so must end.— Blessings & very
tenderest kisses, sweet Angel, fr. yr. very, very. <u>Own.</u>

278. Judging from this letter, Anastasia, Nicholasha's< wife, had just dismissed her fraulein, Anna
Karlovna Peterson, leaving her in a difficult situation.

No. 1036/ Telegram 118. Stavka> Tsarskoe Selo. 21 May 1916. 15.00> 15.17.
To her majesty. Found thanks [for] dear letters. Today Georgie's [King George
V's] birthday. Again very warm. [We] both kiss you and girlies tenderly. Niki

No. 1037.   Ts.[arist] Stavka. May 21 1916.
My own beloved One,
   Tenderly do I thank you for your dear letter. Now they arrive before 12
o'clock. To-day the weather is quite warm, the glass is falling, we may have a
thunderstorm. I am so glad it has also improved with [sic]. How nice you saw
Iedigarov & the others! I received [A. F.] Trepov who just returned from the
caucasus. He was at the front & at Trebizond [also Trapezund] & also saw
Nikolasha<. His impressions of him are very good—as well as about the whole
country. People of there [sic] told Tr[epov] that the feeling of loyalty among all
the tribes are much stronger than they were & <u>they give</u> credit for that to the tall
cousin[, i.e., my cousin, Nicholasha]. So much the better if it is so. This morning I will receive Shtyurmer. I have written down all the difficult questions.
Yesterday I saw Naumov who has been travelling about in the cast & the south.
Laguiche is leaving for town [i.e., to the French embassy in Petrograd], as he has

been replaced, or rather he & old Pau, by the new general[,] Janin—who is Jof-fre's favourite. Old Pau must go off for a cure before he leaves for France. We all want him to go to Sevastobol, but he is afraid of going away so far. Then there remains only Staraia Russa[, a town near Novgorod noted for its clinical mud baths,] for him. Now we [sic] must finish. God bless you and the girls! My darling, my One & All, my tenderly loved Wify, I kiss you passionately & softly & with non resisting lips. Ever your very own Nicky.

No. 1038/ Telegram 100. Tsarskoe Selo> Stavka. 22 May 1916. 13.00> 13.49. To his majesty. Warmly thank you for dear letter, Aleksei also. They are my comfort. Warm, overcast. [We] were in church, krestnyi khod [procession of the cross will be] at 2 o'clock. [I] kiss and embrace [you]. All [are] healthy. Alix

No. 1039/ Her No. 496.   Ts.[arskoe] S[elo]. May 22nd 1916.
My own Sweetheart,
    From all my loving heart I send you thanks for yr. beloved letter —how I love all your write! Me too longs for Huzy's fond caresses & soft, warm kisses!—Its warm, grey & trying to rain. We were in Church, then Isa< & Nastinka< lunched. After my letter we go to the big palace< & at 2 to the Cross Procession i.e. to the Te Deum; one has brought the miraculous Image [icon] of St. Nicolas [sic] fr. Kolpino.—Yesterday we spent the evening cosily in the hospital. The big girls cleaned instruments with the help of Shah B. [Shakh-Bagov] & Rafto-polo [Ravtopulo], the little ones chattered till 10.—I sat working & later made puzzles—alltogether [sic] forgot the time & sat till 12, the Pss. G.[edroits] also busy with puzzle!—Its more cosy than at home now.—I am sorry to bother you again with a letter fr. Mme Sukhomlinova.—The other paper is fr. one of the wounded who returns to the war, but is anxious to know about his decora-tion.—Silaev leaves to-day. We took chocolate with them yesterday—his brother and wife (hideous) too, Shah Bag.[ov] & Raftopolo too.—Shuvaev comes af-ter—Betsy Sh.<—Always heaps to do.—Heart bleeds to think of all the losses at sea—all those lives done for—oh such a tragedy![279]—Now must end. Goodbye, my one & all. Blessing & kisses without end, Nicky mine fr. yr. very, very own Sunny. [P.S.] One says Kitchener comes the 28-th here or to the Headquarters.

No. 1040/ Telegram 120. Stavka> Tsarskoe Selo. 22 May 1916. 19.37> 19.55. To her majesty. Loving thanks for dear letters. Divine weather. [We] have be-gun eating in the tent. Had a delightful trip down the river from the new bridge. Fondest kisses. Niki

No. 1041.   Ts.[arist] Stavka. May 22^{d} 1916.
My own beloved Sunny,
    Ever so many tender thanks for your dearest letter & for the two pansies—I gave Baby< one. Now the weather has at last become fine & warm. Last even-ing when Aleksei was already in bed a thunderstorm came on, there was a very large crash somewhere near town [Mogilev], it poured hard & after that the air became delicious & cooler. So we slept with an open window which he ap-

proved of very much. Thank God he looks brown & healthy. I am sure you got details of the naval battle from Grigorovich, if not ask him to send you what one knows. The english have acknowledged the loss of the "Queen Mary", the "Invincible" & the "Warspite" and of six destroyers. The germans must have lost at least the same quantity—certainly more than they have announced up to the present! Of course it is sad; but remember what we lost at Tsushima 11 years ago!! Almost the entire fleet! This night we have begun the bombardment of some austrian positions a little to the north of Rovno. God bless our troops, who are so eager to get on![279] The naval expedition in the Black Sea has ended beautifully in the landing of another division to the west of Trebizond [also Trapezund]! Good-bye my Love, my Sunshine, soul of my soul. God bless you and the girls. With tenderest loving kisses ever your own <u>Nicky.</u>

279. "The naval battle" was Jutland (May 31 and June 1, 1916.) The British lost three battle-cruisers, three cruisers and eight smaller ships; the Germans lost one battleship, one battle-cruiser, four cruisers and five smaller vessels. The "Russian fleet was annihilated [at Tsushima Straits] on the 27th May, 1905—the anniversary of the Tsar's coronation, ... when hundreds of people were crushed to death. Of the thirty-six [Russian] ships ..., twenty-two were sunk, six were captured and six interned. Thus the Japanese fleet, led by Admiral Togo, won the most complete naval victory of modern times." Brusilov's "offensive began on the following day, and led to a series of brilliant victories on the Carpathian front." (Vulliamy, p. 187n)

No. 1042/ Telegram 103. Tsarskoe Selo> Stavka. 23 May 1916. 13.55> 15.12. To his majesty. [I] tenderly kiss you both. Thank you for dear letters. [We] are lunching on balcony. [We] miss you very much. [We] were at hospital<. Beautiful weather. May the Lord bless you. Alix

No. 1043/ Her No. 497.   Ts.[arskoe] S[elo]. May 23rd 1916.
My sweetest Treasure,
   Over & over I thank you for yr. precious letter. I always get them when I return fr. the hospital< & read them at once, & then still later on several times & kiss them with fond love. We at last lunched on the balkony [sic]—ideal weather—everything now quite green at last.—I drove with the big girls< to Pavlovsk yesterday & the smell of the birches was divine—now I am going again with 3 of them, whilst [daughter] Tatiana rides (I envy her this joy).—I just saw Misha Grabbe.—Yesterday Betsy< sat with me for an hour. One says you wished her to be one of the sisters [i.e., nurses] to go to Germany & this disturbs her as she cannot speak German & is tired & does not find herself capable for such an undertaking. I told her I was convinced you never chose her, but that one proposed her & you said yes, and that you wld. perfectly well understand her not going—and that I wld. write you all this. She was much consoled.—Our Friend< begs very much that you should not name Makarov as minister of Interior—a party wants it, & you remember how he behaved during the stories of Iliodor & Germogen & never stood up for me—it would indeed be a great mistake to name him.[280]—I spent yesterday evening in the hospital<.—Have Mlle [Barbara] Schnider with a doklad [report]. Must end now, Lovy dear. God bless you, my One & all—I cover you with kisses. Ever yr. own old <u>Sunny.</u>   [P.S.] To-morrow I shall be 44!!!

280. When they were friends, Rasputin gave Iliodor letters written to him by Alexandra and her daughters. Some could be read to suggest a sexual relationship between their authors and Rasputin! Rasputin and Iliodor later became enemies, and in 1912 hectographed copies of the letters appeared in St. Petersburg in an effort to discredit Rasputin and force him from the capital. Minister of the Interior A. A. Makarov, a Rasputin foe, retrieved the originals and returned them—but in such a way as to offended both Nicholas and Alexandra. Makarov was dismissed in December 1912. Despite the opposition of Alexandra and Rasputin, Makarov returned as minister of the interior from July 7 to December 20, 1916.

No. 1044/ Telegram 125. Stavka> Tsarskoe Selo. 23 May 1916. 20.20> 21.05. To her majesty. Warmest thanks [for] dear letters. Splendid dry weather. Happy about our first success in the south west.[279] Tender kisses. Niki

No. 1045.   Ts.[arist] Stavka. May 23[d] 1916.
My own precious Wify,
    Loving thanks for your sweet letter. I gave Fred.< the paper about Mlle. Pe-terson[278]—she will get the 2000 r[ubles]. He inquired why she was sent away—it seems she has two brothers serving in the german army & used to correspond with them through german prisoners and notwithstanding a warning she received fr. Nikolasha to stop she continued—that is the reason! Last night in the garden I told Shavelsky to write & have the image of the Vladimirskoi Bozh'ei Materi [Icon of the Mother of God of Vladimir] sent here. I hope she will arrive soon just for the serious times now approaching.[270] This morning I learnt very good news about the beginning of our attack in the southwest. Up to now during [i.e., and as of?] yesterday we took several guns and over 12,000 prisoners, mostly hungarians. God grant it may continue so! [a]
    From this you can see that now I cannot move from here & unluckily cannot go to see the guard. Very tiresome, especially that it may happen that [they] will be employed without my inspecting them since the month of December last. You will get this letter before your dear birthday. I am in despair to have nothing to give you, my beloved One. Please pardon me for this. I can only offer you my boundless love & faithfulness and regret terribly to be separated from you on that day. But the one consolation lies in the fact that duty towards one's country needs this sacrifice! God bless you & the girlies! I kiss you and them very ten-derly. Ever my darling Sunny, my own little Wify, your very own Nicky. [b]

No. 1046/ Telegram 111. Tsarskoe Selo> Stavka. 24 May 1916. 14.25> 15.05. To his majesty. Tenderly thank you both, my dears, for dear letters. Operation went off well. Very hot, are having lunch on balcony, then reports. Warmly em-brace, kiss and love [you]. Alix

No. 1047/ Her No. 498.   Tsarskoe Selo. May 24th 1916.
My own precious Huzy,
    Tender thanks for your sweet letter.—I think Fred.< is mistaken about Mlle Peterson.[278] Her sister is married to a Bavarian (Monjelas, I believe) & this is her son who is our prisoner here, to whom she therefore sent presents (very natural) & no brother at all. They[278] behaved very badly to her, thanks, Darling, for saving her.—Very hot indeed, I am roasting on the balcony [sic] &

ramoli<—had 2 reports fr. 1¾-3½ & am cretinised. The operation was rather long but went off well, I gave the instruments. Thats nice Sweety, that you told Shavel'sky about the Image [icon] to be brought now,[270]—thank God the news was good—such a comfort! Wonder, whether my Crimeans have been fighting??— [a]

Touching [P. D.] Shipov sent me a soldier with flowers he picked on the 14-th under fire, had blessed them & sent for my birthday.— Of course you cannot move now, I felt sure it would be so—well, we had our treat together and my old birthday does not matter—its really to-day. Very sad I am, you wont probably see the guard, why did they keep you fr. seeing them before they were moved off!—What about Paul< I wonder? He comes to tea.—Beloved, I need no present yr. love is <u>more</u> to me than anything you might have given me—yr. letters are such a joy to me.—Yesterday afternoon we drove to Pavlovsk, to-day I prefer keeping quiet.— Now I must end, heart & soul are with you in endless love & prayers. God bless & protect you, give you strength & success. Ever, my One & all, yr. very own old   <u>Wify</u>. [P.S.] I cover you with burning kisses.— [b]

No. 1048/ Telegram 133. Stavka> Tsarskoe Selo. 24 May 1916. 20.15> 20.30. To her majesty. Best thanks for dear letter. We both send you our most tender good wishes and blessings. Divine weather. Loving kisses. Niki

---

No. 1049.   Ts.[arist] Stavka. May 24th 1916.
My own Sweetheart,

Loving thanks for your beloved letter. I enclose a letter from [my sister] Olga which Sandro< brought fr. Kiev. To-day is your old birthday—my prayers and thoughts surround you more fervently than ever! God bless you & may He send you all that which my old heart begs Him for daily. I cannot tell you how deeply I regret not to spend these two days near you & not to lie beside you clasped in your loving soft arms!! [a]

Thank God the news continue to be good—our troops have made on the whole 30,000 prisoners and many guns & pulemety [machine guns]. Our dear Crimean rifles have behaved as real heroes & took in one rush several austrian positions! If our success goes on, lots of our cavalry will be able to get through & inundate the rear of the enemy.—I got a very good answer from Georgie [King George V, to] whom I sent a wire after the naval battle.[279] It seems that only their cruiser squadrons engaged the whole german fleet, but when the great english fleet came up, the former quickly retired to their ports.— Please let Betsy Sh.< know that she certainly need not go to Germany, I had only thought of her, as she is such a capable & good woman.—Certainly Mak. does not do as M. of Int.[280] I wonder where that news came from. Now my Love, my Wify darling, I must end. God bless you once more. I kiss you and the children very tenderly & clasp you tightly in my arms. Ever your very own   <u>Nicky</u>. [b]

No. 1050/ Telegram 125. Tsarskoe Selo> Stavka. 25 May 1916. 1.20> 1.50. To his majesty. Tenderly thank you both for good wishes. Am very lonesome without you both, my loved ones. What a terrible catastrophe with English

cruiser on which Kitchener was.[281a] Terrible loss for Georgie [King George V].
Sleep well. [I] spent evening at hospital<. Kiss and embrace [you]. Alix

281a. Lord Horatio Herbert Kitchener was British secretary of state for war. He trip to Russia at
this time was to bolster Russian morale and improve coordination of military efforts between the two
allies. Kitchener was killed when his ship, the cruiser *Hampshire*, hit a German mine and sank on
June 5 (N.S.), 1916.

No. 1051/ Telegram 138. Tsarskoe Selo> Stavka. 25 May 1916. 13.15> 14.05.
To his majesty. Tenderly kiss you and Baby< for dear letters. Sad lunching
without you on balcony. Very hot. What terrible fate for Kitchener.[281a] May the
Lord bless and protect all of you. Kiss [you] both. Alix

No. 1052/ Her No. 499.   Tsarskoe Selo. May 25th 1916.
My own beloved Angel,
    Quite grey, colossal downpour—will refresh the air. Lunched on the balkony
[sic]. Ever such tender thanks for your dearest letter, Sweetheart. All your loving words warm me up, I miss you sorely —such lonely nights!—How awful
about Kitchener![281a] A real cauchemar [nightmare], & what a loss for the English. Were in Church—to tea come Miechen< & Mavra<. Paul< took tea yesterday, is full of hopes to get his nomination. Going to Church met Misha<,
stopped, talked a minute & than he went back to Gatchina,—not a hair on his
head, completely shaved off.—Excuse dull letter, am cretinised.—Mary [Maria
Pavlovna the Younger] congratulates you many times. Children are driving, I
must answer telegrams. At 7 see our Friend< in little house [of Anna Vyrubova,
who at that time was actually visiting the Crimea]. Believe Kolenkin has new
nomination; all hope very much, that the Horse-Grenadier (of course have forgotten his name), who has been a year in the regiment, will receive it—you know
him.—Ania< has sent you photos. Let me know if you got them safely, as she
was anxious about them.—Must end now—blessings without end. So happy
[over] good news—God grant will continue. Kiss you fervently with ever increasing love, my boy Blue,[258] yr. very   Own.

No. 1053/ Telegram 137. Stavka> Tsarskoe Selo. 25 May 1916. 19.51> 20.40.
To her majesty. Thank you lovingly for letter. Once more we both send you our
innermost tender wishes. Miss you horribly. Lord Kitchener's[281a] loss is indeed
great for Georgie [King George V]. Fondest soft kisses. Niki

No. 1054/ Telegram 226. Tsarskoe Selo> Stavka. 26 May 1916. 14.12> 14.32.
To his majesty. Warmly thank you for letters. Inexpressibly happy with good
news. May the Lord bless our valiant troops. Am praying for them and for you,
my dear. [P. C.] Benckendorff, Derevenko, leaving, am giving them a peek.
Embrace and kiss you. Alix

No. 1055/ Her No. 500.   Ts.[arskoe] S[elo]. May 26th 1916.
My very own Sweetheart,

I send you my tenderest thanks for yr. dearest letter. We saw our Friend< yesterday [see Letter No. 1052] & he is so happy over the good news. Was delighted that we had fine weather & several showers yesterday, says its a particular blessing of Gods on ones birthday—repeated it several times. He had just returned fr. Moscou [sic]—saw Shebeko & had a good impression of him, thinks he will be good in his place.—Begs very much if you receive Volzh.[in] & Vlad.[imir], also to send for Pit.[irim] with them. Says the peasants, cannot choose a suitable priest, that one cannot allow.[281b]—Says for A.[nia]< wld. have been good to have remained on still a bit at E.[vpatoria] only if she continues fretting, it will do her more harm, than good. I fear she returns in a week! Its noughty [sic] to say so, but its been a holiday without her as I cld. do what I liked without having to combine & arrange things & hours to suit her. She dislikes our hospital< & disapproves that I go often so how I shall do when she returns & will want her afternoons & evenings above all with me—I don't know. The Children make grimmaces [sic] already.—Miechen< was in a vile humour[—]she left last night for Minsk with her train & then to inspect her organisations in other towns.—for ever jealous with Ellas< organisations [sic], & tries to do the same things wh. don't concern her & make too many alike.—Fine days but clouds. Going to big palace< & for a drive. Blessings & endless, longing kisses fr. old <u>Wify</u>. [P.S.] Sending you flowers & for the table & [Sir John Hanbury-]Williams.

281b. V. N. Shebeko succeeded Yusupov as *gradonachal'nik* (governor) of Moscow. Judging from this text, Shebeko cultivated Rasputin, who, as in other instances, visited an official being considered for promotion to "peer into his soul." Choosing "a suitable priest" refers to one of many reform issues then under debate in the Russian Orthodox Church: should parishes elect priests or should they still be appointed by bishops? Synod Director Volzhin favored the innovation, as did his anti-Rasputin ally, Metropolitan Vladimir of Kiev. Rasputin and such friends as Pitirim opposed the change, rightly seeing in it a threat to their power.

No. 1056/ Telegram 140. Stavka> Tsarskoe Selo. 26 May 1916. 20.20> 21.10. To her majesty. So many thanks [for dear] dear letters. Today much over fifty thousand prisoners [have been taken] from beginning [of the current offensive]. Ideal weather. Got her [Ania's<] photo. Shall I send them [to] you? Fondest kisses. Niki

No. 1057.   Ts.[arist] Stavka. May 26th 1916.
My treasure,
Fondly do I thank & kiss you for your dear letter. I found this lilac-luck[282] on a bush in the garden on your birthday & send it to you in remembrance! My feelings yesterday were rather mixed as a cause of our successes & on account of the sad news about Kitchener.[281a] But such is life & especially in war time. Of course you know from the papers in what proportions grow the numbers of prisoners & other material taken by our troops. I told the italian general[282] that I thought their losses were well counterbalanced & avenged by the russian army! He gladly gave in & said that the italians would never forget our great help. He is a fool & the rest of our foreign officers don't care for him. At last old Pau has

consented to go on a cure to Essentuki, before he quite returns to France. Gen. Janin seems to be a good military man & behaves modestly & keeps silent. [a]

Georgi< has returned from the Crimea; all the three brothers[283] were together for two days. Today Sandro< left for Kiev. This morning I received with Baby< a deputation of Emp.[eror] Alexander II's 1st Life [Guard] Grenadier Ekaterinoslav Regiment as this is the anniversary that I became [their] chef at the grand review at Moscow after the Coronation–20 years ago. Only two lieut.-colonels have remained since then! The old man [Fredericks] leaves now for 10 day[s] & I have asked [P. C.] Benckendorff[, chief marshal of the court,] to come for that interval. Now my beloved I must end. God bless you and the girls. I shower upon you many passionate kisses, my own darling Wify & remain ever your own   Nicky. [b]

282. A. A. Sergeev translates "lilac-luck" as "eto 'schast'e' na kuste sirenii," and Vulliamy, following this Russian text as the basis of his English version, renders it as a "lucky bit." Vulliamy adds the following explanation: "A 'lucky bit' is a lilac bloom with five or more petals instead of the usual four. It is particularly efficacious if the finder eats it." "The Italian general" referred to here was actually Colonel Marsengo, military attaché to Stavka. (Vulliamy, p. 191n). Italian "losses" probably refers to the Battle of Asiago, fought from May 15 to June 25 (N.S.), 1916. On that occasion, in an effort to take Italy out of the war, fifteen Austrian divisions struck in the Trentino over a 40-mile front. The Italians retreated, but their excellent railway network permitted them to reinforce their army and check the Austrian advance. The Brusilov offensive, however, forced the Austrians to transfer forces from this army to the Russian front and to return to defensive positions against the Italians. Italy lost 147,000 men (including 40,000 prisoners), 300 guns and a large quantity of supplies; the Austrians lost 81,000 men, 26,000 of whom were prisoners. (Bruce, *Illustrated Companion*, pp. 35-36; Dupuy and Dupuy, *Encyclopedia*, pp. 961-962)

283. These were the sons of g.p. Michael Nicholaevich: Georgy and Alexander ("Sandro"), both mentioned here. The third brother was Nicholas Michaelovich. See also Footnote 415.

No. 1058/ Telegram 235. Tsarskoje Selo> Stavka. 27 May 1916. 1.–> 14.39. To his majesty. [We] are lunching on balcony, glorious weather. Please kiss Baby< for post card. In thoughts together. Are going for drive. May the Lord bless you both, my dears! Tenderly kiss [you].   Alix

No. 1059/ Her No. 501.   Ts.[arskoe] S[elo]. May 27th 1916.
My own Beloved,

The good news makes my heart rejoice for you quite especially, such a comfort & recompense for all yr. hard work & patience. To me its like a second war we are beginning again & may God bless it & all act with wisdom & forethought.–In the hospital< one says after they have read the papers they scream hurrah with joy–they only all long quickly to get back to the war to help their comrades. –Yesterday afternoon went to the big palace< & then for a drive. At 6 I went for ½ hour to Ania's< hospital to see them all and give them news. Keep the photos till we meet, they were for your album, Deary.–Mine succeeded too & I have ordered duplicates.– Dined in as cooler & damp and I was afraid for my cheek. Spent the evening in the hospital<.–Fancy yr. having made Baby< corporal on the 25-th, its too sweet!–Botkin left for Livadia via Evpatoria [to] fetch his daughter for his son's marriage at Abaza's estate.–Why do all your people fly off at once? [a]

[P. C.] Benkendorf is delighted to have been called to the Headquarters & to be nearer the news—one longs for more details wh. of course cannot be given. I am glad Baby lives through these days with you—such great moments for his whole life.—I am, oh, so happy for you, Angel beloved. Endless love & tenderness surrounds you & in thoughts I cover you with kisses & press you to my heart wh. burns for love of you!— A grey morning, the weather cannot make up its mind to rain or to let the sun break through the clouds. With greed one throws oneself every morning upon the papers & with heartbeating—too much at times for the human—the joy & anxiety.—It is true new regiments are being formed to send to France? [See Letters No. 957d, 1075b, 1150b, 1313, 1587b.]—How does Baby like P.V.P's< letters, does he quite understand them? Yr. enemy, the crows, are making a vile noise opposite to my window. I must be getting up and dressing for the hospital—shall place my daily candle at Znamenia< with tenderest love for you my one & all, my joy of joys, my Huzy dear! The weather became quite divine. Sat in the hospital garden working whilst some played croquet. Now Tatiana rides, Maria & Anastasia are going to dig out weeds in the little garden, as they are spoiling the lilies of the valley;—Olga & I are going to a hospital & then to drive.—Endless, tender kisses & fervent blessings Sweetheart, fr. yr. own old <u>Sunny</u>.   [P.S.] Shtyurmer comes at 6. [b, c]

No. 1060/ Telegram 147. Stavka> Tsarskoe Selo. 27 May 1916. 19.27> 19.37. To her majesty. Loving thanks [for] dear letters [and] lovely flowers. Did you find my letter from yesterday in large envelope? Thoughts always near you. News very good. Tender kisses. Niki

---

No. 1061/ Telegram 236. Tsarskoe Selo> Stavka. 27 May 1916. 19.39> 20.19. To his majesty. Just now opened large envelope from you with precious letter, tenderly thank you for it. Beautiful weather. Terribly glad news continues to be very good. May the Lord bless our valiant troops and both of you. Warmly kiss [you]. Alix

---

No. 1062.   Ts.[arist] S[tavka]. May 27th 1916.
My own Sweetheart,
    Tender thanks for your dear letter. [P. C.] Benckendorf has just arrived & gave me the latest verbal news about you. A great pity it was not you yourself, my beloved One! Thank god, the news continue very good. The staff estimates the total german & austrian prisoners up to 70000 men and a thousand officers! And in the official announcement made the word "victory" was used for the first time. N.[icholasha]< sent me a very warm telegram fr. himself personally. I quite understand what you say about A.[nia]<. Please, Sweety, be first of all <u>your own mistress</u> & arrange your time according with your duty & your wishes. Quite enough if you give her either your afternoons or your evenings[,] but not both. I really mean good for her, but of course I think you should do with a quiet conscience what you find best & according to your own habits! [a]
    Just now Aleksei & I received a deputation of peasants fr. the gov. of Kherson (Odessa). Fancy those touching people brought me 600,000 r.[ubles] from the

whole population for the needs of the war! Do think where we could use this enormous sum or whether you want me to send it [to] you? I have no idea yet how to use it. The weather is beautiful & awfully warm, a light heat, but perspiration runs down my face—we shall go on the river. The image fr. Moscow[270] arrives to-morrow—it will be received with pomp & ceremony. Now I must end. God bless you my sweet Sunny! I kiss you and the girls very tenderly & remain ever your very own Nicky. [b]

No. 1063/ Her No. 502.   Ts.[arskoe] S[elo]. May 28th 1916.
My own Beloved,
   I don't know how it happened, that I did not discover yr. letter till the afternoon when I opened all the big envelopes with doklady [reports]. My joy was all the greater when I read yr. sweet words.—No time for much to-day. For an hour have been reading doklady & writing & now must be getting up & go to the hospital<—have two heavy perevyazki [dressings] to do.—Fred.< & wife lunch, then must go to opening of a hospital for refugees children—& then look over the Drozhdin lying in [maternity] hospital etc. to settle what hospital to build.—Ella< wired [from Moscow to say that] the Krestn. khod. s Vlad. b. m. [procession of the cross with the icon of the Mother of God of Vladimir] was most touching, great crowds.[270]— [a]
   What good news again, ones heart rejoices & to-day interesting fine facts are mentioned, wh. is a good thing. Glorious weather. Yr. group at the Khadzhib. Liman [a concert hall in Odessa] succeeded very well, M-me Sosnovsky sent it me.—Drove yesterday afternoon with [daughter] Olga—whilst picking daisys [sic], Pss. Palei turned up—she has a birthday present just come for me fr. Worth (dressmaker in Paris) & wants to bring it me—what next? Wish she wld. leave me in peace.—Now beloved I congratulate you with Tatiana who will be 19 to-morrow! How the time flies!—I kiss & hug you, press you to my yearning heart & whisper words of deepest love & devotion, Treasure Dear. God bless you & yr. undertakings. Yr. own old Wify. [P.S.] Tenderest thanks for beloved letter.— [b]

No. 1064/ Telegram 243. Tsarskoe Selo> Stavka. 28 May 1916. 16.52> 17.27. [To his majesty.] Endless thanks to you both, my dears. Terribly hot, awfully tired. Was at opening of sanitorium for children of refugees at Tsarskoe Selo. N.P.< arrived in town for one day, is coming to tea, [we] will be glad to see him again. Embrace and kiss [you]. Alix

---

No. 1065.   Ts.[arist] Stavka. May 28th 1916.
My own darling Sunny,   [This is a post card.]
   I have no time to write much. Everything goes well with us. Today they bring the S[t] image Vlad. B. M. [Holy icon of the Mother of God of Vladimir] to our church.[270] I feel sure Her blessing will help us much. I love you so & miss you exceedingly. Gen. [Hanbury-]Williams thanks [you] very much for flowers. God bless you my beloved One. Thousands of soft kisses fr. your own Nicky.

No. 1066/ Telegram 149. Stavka> Tsarskoe Selo. 28 May 1916. 22.44> 23.16. To her majesty. Loving thanks [for] letter and wire. The image[270] was brought to day and placed in our church. Masses of people followed. Also colossal heat. Fondest kisses from both. Bless you! Niki

No. 1067/ Telegram 249. Tsarskoe Selo> Stavka. 29 May 1916. 9.22> 10.40. To his majesty. Heartily congratulate you over our sweet, dear girlie. [This day was Tatiana's 19th birthday.] Again terribly hot. Birds chirping merrily. Fredericks couple had lunch yesterday. Warmly embrace and kiss you. Very happy the h.[oly] image[270] is with you, may it bring happiness and success to us and give protection from every evil! Alix

No. 1068/ Her No. 503.   Ts.[arskoe] S[elo]. May 29th 1916.
My own dearly Beloved,
    I congratulate you with our sweet Tatiana's 19th birthday—how the time flies! Well do I remember this day at the farm.—The heat is quite tremendous—the rooms are far cooler, but I am lying on the balkony [sic]. My heart feels the heat & protests.   Church-bells are ringing—service lasts so long to-day.—Many thanks, Lovebird, for your dear card. Thank God, all continues well—where on earth are we to put these masses of prisoners—in Siberia there is ample place, only give orders that all should be quickly & decently, hygienically arranged for them, so as to be safe from epidimies [epidemics].— [a]
    Such a surprise when N.P.< telephoned that he had come for the day for affairs—so we got him to tea for a short hour, looks well & much thinner. They are standing in front of [i.e., superior to?] all the rest, [he] told lots of interesting things, asked much after you;—wont return [here] probably for very long now—was here 5 weeks ago with Rodionov who will also be coming soon for a few days. Says Kirill< intends going out to see them soon.—Zizi< comes to tea as she leaves to-morrow for the country.—I feel quite cretinised—have, alas, to go & look at a "home" & future hospital to give my orders.[219]—Spent the evening in the hospital<, but I lay back in a comfortable chair in one of the wards as was very tired.—Excuse the unutterably dull letter. I bless & kiss you without end, my Own, my very Own. God be with you.—Ever yr. old Sunny. [P.S.] Have you been able to bathe in the river?—Do you know how great our losses are?—My darling, I yearn for your kisses and tender caresses. My tommy [tummy] becomes impossible in this heat as every summer & gives me no peace.— [b]

No 1069/ Telegram 159. Stavka> Tsarskoe Selo. 29 May 1916. 15.26> 15.40. To her majesty. Loving thanks [for] dear letter. We both congratulate you and dearest Tatiana. Enormous heat. Excellent news. Fondest kisses. Niki

No. 1070/ Telegram 278. Tsarskoe Selo> Stavka. 29 May 1916. 18.40> 19.20. To his majesty. Warmly thank you both for post card and telegram. Thanks be to God that news is again good. Terrible heat. [We] all kiss and embrace [you]. Alix

No. 1071.   Ts.[arist] Stavka. May 29th 1916.
My beloved wify,
   Tenderest thanks for your dear letter. All my thoughts go back to what happened 19 years ago at the Farm at Peterhof. God bless dear Tatiana & may she
always remain the good, loving & patient girl she is now & a consolation in our
old days! Again no time to write. The heat is stupendous, my hands sweat
abominably. Yesterday the image was carried through the streets by soldiers;[270]
it reminded me of Borodino.[65] To-morrow she will go to the front to those
troops, wh. will soon begin to attack the german positions! Then she will be
brought here. Thank God the news are very good, our armies advance and push
the enemy away. The number of prisoners exceeds 100.000 men—one general—I
don't know his name yet. Now Sweetheart mine, I must close. God bless you.
Tenderly do I kiss you. Ever your own Nicky.

No. 1072/ Telegram 405. Tsarskoe Selo> Stavka. 30 May 1916. 13.29> 14.07.
To his majesty. Tenderly thank you both for dear letters. Thanks be to God for
good news. Beautiful weather, and heat not so strong—after evening rain. Lilac
[is] in full bloom. [We] all warmly kiss and embrace [you]. Alix

---

No. 1073/ Her No. 504.   Ts.[arskoe] S[elo]. May 30th 1916.
My own Sweetheart,
   Very tenderest thanks for yr. precious letter. Really the good news fill ones
heart with endless gratitude. How good you send the Image [icon] out to the
front, may the holy Virgin give strength & wisdom to all to bless the final successes.[270] What are our losses? Two of my Crimeans< are wounded & they told
a lot.—The heat yesterday was quite unbearable, so I took a refreshing bath at 6½
before resting. Early this morning there was rain, so that to-day it is quite ideal.
We went to service in the hospital Church; as early [i.e., because the service
there was early] & [so then we] could do our perevyazki [dressings] afterwards.
—Shall go for a drive with the big girls< now. A.[nia] leaves Simf.[eropol'] this
evening at 8 o'clock—am sure she will miss the lovely sea, peaceful calm & all
[of the mayor of Evpatoria] Duvan's kindnesses[—]but she is mad to get home.
Her Father [A. S. Taneev] leaves with the grandchildren to-day to the country.
—Mme Zizi< took tea with us yesterday & has now gone off to her country-place
for the whole summer.—Just now Nikolaev[42] (former Crimean<) bid me goodbye, he is off to his 4-th Ulans again (near Segewoldt). He was so happy to have
seen you at Evpatoria.—I suppose you have not yet begun the "Wall of partition"[284]—I don't read a bit now, only work.—Beloved Angel, heart & soul never
leaves you. God bless & protect you & give you success—I cover you with tenderest caresses & warmest kisses.—Ever Huzy mine, sweet Boy Blue,[258] yr. very
own old Wify.

   284. This was yet another novel by Florence L. Barclay, a British author and one of the royal
family's favorite writers.

No. 1074/ Telegram 181. Stavka> Tsarskoe Selo. 30 May 1916. 20.07> 20.57.
To her majesty. After very rayny [sic] morning now fine and cool. Many thanks

[for] dear letters. Just home from cinematograph. News continue good. Warm kisses. Niki

---

No. 1075.   Ts.[arist] Stavka. May 30ᵗʰ 1916.
My own beloved One,
   Tenderest thanks for your sweet letter. We also had a tremendous heat these last days but yesterday after much rain & a real storm, the temp[erature] fell luckily to 13° & now I can again breathe easily. It seems strange that even I felt this heat; and our rooms were stifling—19° degrees in the bedroom!—I slept rather badly on account of that. This morning it poured in torrents & in such rain we had a large te deum in front of our house, with all the troops & people. Then every one approached & kissed the image.[270] It leaves for the front this afternoon & comes back in about a fortnight. Our heads & necks were jolly wet, to Baby's< infinite delight. After kissing the image I went in for my doklad [report], but he stood a long time at our porch watching the crowd! It was over at 12.30—having begun at 10.30—that the people & soldiers came up. [a]
   The last night's storm did much damage to the telegraph wires & therefore there is a lack of news fr the southwestern front, but what we got is good. By now we are far over 1600 officers and 106.000 soldiers prisoners. Our losses are not great on the whole, of course they vary in different armies. I am glad you saw N.P.<, [I] have a great wish to visit them [the guards regiments?] myself, but now it is utterly impossible! New regiments are being formed for sending to France & to Salonika. My sweet Lovebird, me wants to nestle near you oh! so tightly! God bless you & the girlies. I kiss you gently and softly many a time & remain ever your very own   Nicky. [b]

No. 1076/ Telegram 418. Tsarskoe Selo> Stavka. 31 May 1916. 13.54> 14.25.
To his majesty. Tenderly thank you both for precious letters. Much fresher, very pleasant after the heat. She [Anna Vyrubova] arrives to-morrow. Very happy about image.[270] We all lunched on balcony. [We] warmly kiss [you]. May the Lord bless you. Alix

---

No. 1077/ Her No. 505.   Ts.[arskoe] S[elo]. May 31ˢᵗ 1916.
My own Beloved,
   From all my heart I thank for sweetest letter & tender words. I too have such a yearning after yr. caresses & love!—Really the news is beautiful! Idiotical Petr.[ograd] does not nearly enough appreciate it. God bless you & our heroes—so glad the Image[270] has gone [from Stavka to the front] to bless them all. The mass must have been very touching before the house—she[270] brings them yr. love & prayers too & they will feel how near you are to them. A glorious day & cooler, wh. is a great boon after the colossal heat.— Placed my candles, worked in the hospital<, now am going to drive with 3 girls whilst Tatiana rides [her horse].—Was Purishkevich's train alright [sic], please, tell me which Number, 1 or 2, as my Crimean< Sedov has a sister in Number 2, & it interests him so much to know wh. you visited.—I have nothing of interest to tell you.—When about will the guard be advancing? —Beloved Treasure, prayers & thoughts ever

surround you. I miss you, oh, so much. To-day its 2 weeks we parted at Kursk! How horrid it was.—God bless & protect you. I cover you with tender kisses, Huzy my Love, & remain yr. very   Own.

No. 1078/ Telegram 196. Stavka> Tsarskoe Selo. 31 May 1916. 22.47> 23.14. To her majesty. [We] both thank [you] warmly for [your] dear letters. Lovely weather. Was much occupied. Good night. Endless love. Niki

No. 1079.   Ts.[arist] Stavka. May 31st 1916.
My darling wify,
    Many fond thanks for your dear letter. Now it is lovely after yesterdays [sic] downpour. The rooms became quite cool again. I took a long walk through woods & fields with Valia D.<, while Baby< played near the highroad. After that we went to the cinematograph which was entertaining. Today we will have an expedition on the river after seeing some passing troops at our plat-form-station. On the whole our actions continue alright [sic] except in one place, just in the centre of both of our attacking wings. The austrian troops & some of the german divisions are making desperate efforts to break through at that place, but without result. The necessary measures to relieve our corps are being taken & reserves are brought up. Of course here our losses are heavy, what is to be done! But these have gallantly done their duty valiantly—they were to attract the enemy's attention & thus help their neighbours.— [a]
    I have not heard anything about your Crimeans!< I hope Keller will produce something with his cavalry; perhaps he will be able to occupy Chernovitsy. Then our Cossacks will advance & our 1st Kuban [Division] also towards that town.—Sweet-love me wants oo very much! Since our arrival I have not touched the new book,[284] wh I want to read, but have no time.—God bless you, my be-loved Wify! I kiss you passionately & the girlies tenderly. Ever your own old Nicky. [b]

No. 1080/ Telegram 4. Tsarskoe Selo> Stavka. 1 June 1916. 14.27> 15.30. To his majesty. Warmly thank you both for dear letters. Big girls< are going to town<. Cooler. Celebrated funeral service on Sonia's< grave. Today 6 months [since she died]. [We] were at hospital<. Tenderly kiss and embrace [you]. Alix

No. 1081/ Her No. 506.   Ts.[arskoe] S[elo]. June 1st 1916.
My own beloved Treasure,
    Ever such fond thanks for yr. sweet letter. Its a comfort to know our losses have not been so very great in comparison with what we have gained in every sense. That we have the weak point in the centre is comprehensible, but with care & reinforcements it will, with God's help be alright.—All think of you in the joy of victory, first thought of all the wounded is,—how happy you must be. Such a recompense for your intense suffering, patient endurance & hard work! Its much cooler to-day, rained a bit. The big girls< have gone to town, as Olga receives podnosheniya [offerings], & then they go to Tatiana [Constantinovna].

The little ones< are in their hospital & as soon as I have finished writing I shall fetch them for a drive. Ania< comes to tea, she arrived to town< alright [sic]. [a]

We worked in the hospital< & then I went with [daughter] Marie to the ceme-try [sic] as there was a panikhida [funeral service] for little Sonia—already six months since her death. The birds were singing so gaily, the sun lit up her grave covered with forgetmenots—it made a cheery impression & not sad.—Pss. Palei came yesterday & brought me a very pretty chiffon thing to wear. [See Letter No. 1063b.] She says Paul< is full of excitement & quite well & the Drs. are perfectly quiet about his health.—I too have had no time for reading, as were so much in the hospital, then received, drove, work & wrote.—I congratulate you with [your dear] sister Olga['s birthday on June 1/13]. Two weeks that we re-turned & five that Ania left fr. here—the time simply flies.— To-morrow shall have to be going for service to town, anniversary of Costia's< death!—Think of my Huzy with great longing & intensest love. I cover you with tender kisses & press you to my heart. God bless you my Angel. Keep well—am always near you. Ever yr. very own old   Sunny. [b]`

No. 1082/ Telegram 8. Stavka> Tsarskoe Selo. 1 June 1916. 18.40> 19.05. To her majesty. Fond thanks [for] dear letters [and] wire. Dull, rainy weather. Good news.[285] Many kisses. Niki

285. "During the fighting at Lokachi and Kolki in the Lutsk sector 31,000 prisoners were claimed." (Vulliamy, p. 196n)

No. 1083.   Ts.[arist] Stavka. June 1st 1916.
My own darling Sunny,

Many loving thanks for your dear letter. This second [P. C.] Benckendorff came in & brought me a letter from Miechen< who sits at Minsk & sent Etter with it & the polozheniya [regulations] of the whole organisation [sic] of hers. I have sent him to Alekseev, because the thing is much too serious to confirm at a stroke of the pen! Thank goodness she has not turned up in person. I forgot in the hurry I was in the other day about our visit to Purishkevich's train. That was not a sanitary [i.e., hospital] one—it contained three cars with a library for offi-cers & men and a polevaya apteka [field pharmacy] very neatly arranged & enough to help three army corps. He dined with us and told [us] lots of most interesting details! Wonderful energy! and excellent organizer! There were no sisters [i.e., nurses] in that train, only men. The visit took place at our platform where I also saw troops passing to the south. [a]

If the guard moves—it will probably be a little nearer [to] the lines. The whole cavalry is already moving to the west to take the place of the 7th cavalry corps wh has advanced. The weather changes the whole time—to day it is rainy and cooler.—My sweetest girlie, I miss you so—already over a fortnight that we sepa-rated. God bless you & the girlies. I kiss you and them very tenderly, nestle to your breast & feel cozy there on! Ever my beloved one your own   Nicky. [b]

No. 1084/ Telegram 13. Tsarskoe Selo> Stavka. 2 June 1916. 14.32> 15.20. To his majesty. Heartily thank you for dear letters. [We] have returned from fort.[286] Colder, clear. [We] lunched on balcony. Ania< arrived safely, looks healthy, in good mood. We all kiss and embrace you both. [We] are now going for drive. Alix

286. Deceased Romanovs were buried at the Peter and Paul Fortress, located on Zayachii Island in St. Petersburg.

No. 1085/ Her No. 507.   Ts.[arskoe] S[elo]. June 2nd 1916.
My own precious One,
   A very tender kiss & thanks for yr sweet letter; how I love hearing fr. you, it warms me up to read yr loving words & I try to imagine I hear you saying all those dear words to lonely wify.—Little sun to-day, but it was better for [a trip to] town<. In the morning went for ½ hour to bid all good morning in the hospital<. Like Babies they all stared at us in "dresses & hats" & looked at our rings & bracelets (the ladies too) & we felt shy & "guests".—Then with [daughters] O.[lga] & T.[atiana] to the fortress to mass. Oh, how cold that family vault is,[286] difficult to pray too, one does not feel its a church at all.—Now are going for a drive with A.[nia]< too.— [a]
   Yesterday afternoon [daughters] M.[arie], A.[nastasia] & I got into a colossal downpour, so were out quite a little. In the evening I went to A.< for ¾ of an hour & then joined the Children [i.e., the wounded] in the hospital. They were wild of joy as did not expect us at all. The good news is such a boon & helps one to live.— Really Miechen!< She can drive one wild—I have to see [G. G. von] Witte to-day to speak over all, on her account [see Letter No. 1089b], as she really is very pretencious [sic]—only one does not wish needlessly to offend her, as she means well, only spoils all by her jealous ambition.—Don't let her come bothering you & above all give her no promises.—Sweetest Angel, I clasp you to my breast & hold you long & calmly there, whispering tender words of deepest love.—God bless & protect you. Holy Angels guard & guide you. Ever, Nicky mine yr. very, very own old girlie   Alix.   [P.S.] Saw Leo< the other day—looks very thin, but not so bad— wanted to begin [i.e., return to] his service [as valet], but I told him to wait still & pick up more strength. Kondratieff serves again, also very thin—I don't let him help at table so as that he should walk about less.—your Own. [P.P.S.] Ania was very happy over telegrams. [c]

No. 1086/ Telegram 16. Stavka> Tsarskoe Selo. 2 June 1916. 19.15> 19.40.
To her majesty. Loving thanks [for] dear letters. Very warm, some passing showers. Give her [Anna Vyrubova] our love. Tenderest kisses from both. Niki

No. 1087.   Ts.[arist] Stavka. June 2nd 1916.
My own Lovebird,
   Ever so many thanks for your dear letter No. 506 (fancy what a big N°). Every evening before praying with our Sunbeam< I tell him what you have wired to me & then read to him all his letters [i.e., the letters addressed to Aleksei]. He listens, lying in bed and kisses your signature. He becomes talkative & asks many questions, because we are alone. Sometimes if it is late I have to hurry him to say his prayers. He sleeps very well & quietly & loves having the win-

dow open. The noise of the street does not disturb him. I send you some of the last photos.—the first represent the arrival of the image[270] & the last the te deum under pouring rain. Choose whichever you like! [a]

Yesterday I saw Bark; he is working out that loan for the railways wh interests you. He leaves in a week for England & France. To-morrow I receive Mamantov & then I hope there will be a lull in the stream of people who come here to bore me. Since spring I have less time for reading because we remain much longer out of doors—generally fr. 3.0 till 6.0; when we come home we take tea & Baby< dines at the same time.—Now my Sweetheart I must end. God bless you and the girlies. I kiss you all over your beloved face & [me] loves oo [i.e., you] so tenderly. Ever, Wify-mine, your own   Nicky. [b]

No. 1088/ Telegram 16. Tsarskoe Selo> Stavka. 3 June 1916. 14.19> 14.52. To his majesty. Tenderly thank you both. Photographs delightful. [We] are lunching on balcony. Now raining but warm. All tenderly kiss [you]. Are sending you photographs we took. [We] warmly embrace you. Alix

---

No. 1089/ Her No. 508.   Ts.[arskoe] S[elo]. June 3rd 1916.
My Sweetheart,

Please, change the N°. in my yesterday's letter, I made a mistake, it ought to have been 507 only.—Fine & sunny & then suddenly clouds.—Spent the evening quietly. A.[nia]< sat with me, showed photos, talked endlessly of the Kakham, it seems he is also very devoted [to us;[287] Anna] read to me, the children were in the hospital<. She proposed to me to go, but I said I was tired from town< & wld. remain quietly with her.—Had a long letter fr. Irene<, Gretchen [Margarita Fabritse], Anna Rantzau [Countess Anna Ranttsau]. My poor Friend Toni's< boy has been killed at the war (only 19, my godchild, went in 1914 already as freiwilliger)—was an excellent officer it seems already & received the iron cross—too sad for words, she adored the boy.—Aunt Beatrice[44] also wrote & sends you her love—she imagines I am at Livadia, resting.—Now I must get up & dress for the hospital. I send you & Baby< my photos, I took. The water is fr. the black sea, Ania had it filled for you & Baby< & sends it with much love—the goodies are also for you from her.—[a]

Please if you settle any thing about Miechen<, have it written to Senator Witte or Shtyurmer, as it concerns the supreme Council[298] & I feel she intends making a mess in going to you behind my back—a revenge wh. is ugly.—I had just Professor Rein [Rhein] & a long talk—I have told him to ask Shtyurmer to receive him, to explain all, because really his work ought to be begun as you said, & Alek< said you said all was to be put off.—Would you let him come to you some day, as when you are here you have yet less time.—Pouring cats & dogs.—Such warm thanks for sweetest letter. How charming the photos are, I have kept one. Goodbye, my Angel Love, God bless you. I love & kiss you without end. Yr. very, very   Own. [b]

---

287. Reference is to S. M. Shapshal, spiritual leader (*gakham*) of the Karaites. "The Jews of the Karaite sect differ entirely from the orthodox Jews both in worship and in mode of life. They, too, are inclined to trade, but they also carry on agriculture successfully. Those inhabiting the Crimea

[i.e., Shapshal's group] speak Tatar, and the few who are settled in W. Russia speak Polish. They
[both] are on good terms with the Russians." *Encyclopaedia Britannica*, XXIII (11th ed., 1911), p.
885. The Karaites were a strict Jewish sect that rejected Talmudic interpretation in favor of literal
reading of scripture. In 1904, 10,000 of the world's 12,000 Karaites lived in Russia. (*Ibid.*, XXII., p.
705) Karaite communities still existed in the Crimea and Israel as of 1998.

No. 1090/ Telegram 27. Stavka> Tsarskoe Selo. 3 June 1916. 17.40> 18.07.
To her majesty. Best thanks [for] precious letters. Also showers and has become
cooler. Just now came home from drive and good walk. Tenderest kisses. Niki

---

No. 1091.   Ts.[arist] Stavka. June 3^d 1916.
My own sweetest Darling,
   Ever so many tender thanks for your dear No. 508. What a joy it is to come
back fr. the doklad [report] & to catch the sight of an envelope with your beloved handwriting on my table! Then I run up after lunch in the garden & quietly enjoy your letter by myself. Today the band played in the public gardens
near ours. It was such a treat to everybody to hear music during lunch—it plays
still & lots of people are listening. I told the colonel of the regiment here to pass
through the town [of Mogilev] with the band—it lifts one up. So he did several
times already. [a]
   I have not heard anything about Zborovsky being wounded, I only know that
their division has not moved anywhere. I will astonish by what I am going to tell
you: these last weeks our railways here at the front have begun to work much
better. The last movements of troops fr the north to the south were accomplished
much quicker & more accurately than before. It used to take a fortnight to carry
over one army corps; now each corps was transferred in a week or six days! So
yesterday for the first time, I told a few kind words to Ronzhin and his people!
One must be just. My beloved Angel! How I miss you & how I want to see you
& talk to you & kiss you. I feel that soon I will write & ask you to come here
for a couple of days to visit —to refresh us all with your sweet presence.—God
bless you & the girlies! I press you gently & long to my loving heart & cover
you with endless kisses, dearest old Wify. Ever your own Nicky. [b]

No. 1092/ Telegram 22. Tsarskoe Selo> Stavka. 4 June 1916. 15.25> 15.58.
To his majesty. Warmly thank you both, my dears. Strong rain fell all day, now
bit better. [I] am going for drive. Fredericks, Emma< and Ania< lunched with
us. Saw [A. N.] Grabbe. Bekker< arrived. Warmly kiss and embrace [you]. Alix

---

No. 1093/ Her No. 509.   Ts.[arskoe] S[elo]. June 4th 1916.
My own Lovebird,
   From all my heart I send you tender thanks for yr. precious letter. A.[nia]<
forgot to tell you, that our Friend< sends his blessing to the whole orthodox
army. He begs we should not yet strongly advance in the <u>north</u> because he says,
if our successes continue being good in the south, they will themselves retreat
from the north, or advance & then their losses will be very great—if we begin
there, our losses will be very heavy—He says this is an advise [advice].—Becker<
has just come. I too throw myself upon yr. letters & devower [sic] them up &

the children stand by, waiting for me to read aloud what is for them of inter-est—& then later I reread & kiss the dear pages. Thats good the music passes through the streets it brightens up the spirits.—Am trying to get hold of Zborov-sky (wounded through the chest, not too bad), Shvedov typhoid, Skvortsov wounded—with my sanitary train, Yuzik< will help through Kiev, I told all to [A. N.] Grabbe.— [a]

How glad I am at what you write about the trains at last moving quicker with the troops!—I assure you "where there's a will there's a way"—only not too many cooks to spoil the broth.—Just had long wire fr. Apraxin<—my little trains are working hard at Lutsk, Rovno, Rezhitsa, Tarnopol, Trembol., a branch of the Vinnitsa store at Shchertkov all grateful, the military say they could not get on without us, thank god for helping us succeed.—Yes, Angel, we can fly to you some day to cheer you up with joy.— Pouring.— Emma<, her Father [Count Fredericks] & Ania< lunched.—Spent evening in hospital, to-day at home. End-less kisses, burning love. God bless you! Yr. very Own. [b]

No. 1094/ Telegram 32. Stavka> Tsarskoe Selo. 4 June 1916. 19.50> 20.24. To her majesty. Many thanks for sweet letters and delightful photos. Awful weather, cold, rainy. News good. Fondest kisses from both. Niki

---

No. 1095.   Ts.[arist] Stavka. June 4th 1916.
My own beloved Sunny,

So many loving thanks for your dear letter & charming photos. Please thank also [daughters] Tatiana, Marie and Ania< for theirs. —I was delighted to receive such a lot & enjoy looking at them. Only have nothing to glew them with. No fear about Miechen< & her wishes. Alekseev gave a very cold reception to Etter & kept back the papers I got from her. [See Letter No. 1083a.] I enclose her letter which you can tear up. She sent me this polozhenie [Regulation] of all her organization[s].—If you think it concerns the Verkh. Sov.,[298] I can return them to you. Alekseev finds that it concerns also the Red Cross but still more different questions having to do with the military [i.e., the Regulation concerns the mili-tary authorities to a still greater degree]! [a]

You ask whether I would see prof. Rein; it is no use, I know beforehand what he is going to tell me. But Alek< begged me to put it off to the end of the war & I consented.[288] I cannot change my mind every two months—it is quite sicken-ing! Yesterday col. Kireev of the escort told me that Vict. Er. [Zborovsky] was seriously wounded in the leg, a young one slightly wounded & Shvedov has got the typhus. So no officer [is] left for the moment in the sotnya [company]! I cannot make out whether they were with Keller or by themselves? Now [I] must end. God bless you my own sweet Wify. Every best wish for [daughter] Anastasia's birthday. With tender kisses, ever your own Nicky. [b]

---

288. Professor Georgy Rhein, M.D., was a member of the State Council and Honorary Surgeon to the Court. Presumably he wanted to confer with the tsar on health policy. Although Nicholas re-jected Rhein's proposals at this time, in July 1916 he did come to support them against the continu-ing objections of Alexander Petrovich ("Alek"). (See Letters No. 1280, 1281, 1284.) On Sept. 22 (O.S.), 1916, Rhein was made director of the Public Health Department.

No. 1096/ Telegram 24. Tsarskoe Selo> Stavka. 4 June 1916. 21.21> 22.30.
To his majesty. Just now read papers, congratulate you on your successes, my
dear. Thanks be to God, Pochaevskaya lavra [monastery] is again in our hands.
[I] love and pray for you [both] endlessly. Sleep peacefully, loved ones. God
keep you [both]. Alix

No. 1097/ Telegram 28. Tsarskoe Selo> Stavka. 5 June 1916. 10.00> 10.55.
To his majesty. With all my heart [I] congratulate you on the birthday of our
merry little girl [Anastasia]. Only 8 degrees, rainy. Strong rain fell yesterday all
day. Tell [A. N.] Grabbe that Loman telegraphed from Kiev that he is going to
Novoselitsy to get Zborovsky and Skvortsov. Warmly kiss and bless you both.
Alix

No. 1098/ Her No. 510.   Ts.[arskoe] S[elo]. June 5th 1916.
Darling beloved One,
I congratulate you with our little girlie's [Anastasia's] birthday—fancy her being
already 15, its quite sad—no babys [sic] any more.—Such cold, rainy weather
only 7.8 degrees—we drove in thick coats & [daughter] Olga is freezing.—From
all my heart I thank you for your sweet letter. Shall send you still more photos,
as soon as get them.—Really one cannot let Miechen< mix up in things wh. do
not concern her—she has become so grasping— military things are not her business.—Am sorry about Rein[288]—he is right & Alek< quite wrong, I see it
clearly.—Ania< has just left for Terioki to see her family & will be back by
Tuesday afternoon. She forgot to tell you, that our Friend< says its good for us
that Kitchener died[281a]—as later on he might have done Russia harm & that no
harm papers were lost with him. You see he always fears about England at the
end of the war when the peace-negociations [sic] begin.—He said that Tumanov
is excellent in this place & has no wish to leave & is better than Engalichev—I
did not know he was to be changed.[289]— [a]
    I asked the priest [A. P. Vasil'ev] to have thanksgiving prayers, wh. he did
after a short good sermon about our successes & the Pochaev monastery being
again ours, & how God harkened unto all prayers & so forth.—Yesterday evening A.[nia]< read to me, whilst they were in the hospital. Anna Alekseevna Korovtchuk [Korobchuk] had a daughter 3 days ago, and I am going to christen it
to-morrow.—Must send this off now. All thoughts, longing love, kisses, blessings, great yearning, Sweetheart. Ever yr. very own Wify.   [P.S.] Sweet Boy
Blue![258] Just got enclosed wire fr. my 21 Siberians [i.e., the 21st E. Siberian
Infantry Regiment]—poor X [i.e., Vykrestov—see No. 1100—was killed in battle
—] am awfully sorry—such a nice man, had St. G.[eorge]'s [Cross]. [b]

289. Prince N. E. Tumanov, an engineer-general, was *nachal'nik* of the Petrograd military region.
In June 1916 he was promoted to chief-director of communications of all Russian armies on the
western front. For whatever reason, as we see, Rasputin approved of him. Prince P. N. Engalychev
had been governor-general of Warsaw, now occupied by the Germans.

No. 1099/ Telegram 40.   Stavka> Tsarskoe Selo.   5 June 1916. 15.22> 16.06.
To her majesty.   Fondest wishes for today[, 15th birthday of our daughter
Anastasia] and best thanks for dear letters and wire. Chernovets was taken. Our
troops pursue down there the enemy. So happy. Loving kisses. Niki

No. 1100/ Telegram 51.   Tsarskoe Selo> Stavka.   5 June 1916. 17.05> 17.40.
To his majesty.   Tenderly thank you both.   Thanksgiving Te Deum [was cele-
brated] in church. [We] drove. Terribly cold. Glorious Vykrestov of my Siberians [see Letter No. 1098] killed in battle. Am sending you the telegram. We all
warmly kiss you. May the Lord keep you [both]. Alix

No. 1101.   Ts.[arist] Stavka. June 5[h] 1916.
My own Sweetheart,
    Tenderest thanks for your dear letter. I saw [A. N.] Grabbe & he told all your
messages.   So little time unluckily to write.   A few days ago Alekseev & I decided not to attack fr. the north, but to concentrate all our efforts lower
down.[290]—But please don't mention this to any body, not even our Friend<. Nobody must know this. Even the armies in the north believe that they are soon
going to attack & that keeps their spirits up. Demonstrations & strong ones will
continue up here on purpose. Strong reinforcements are being sent down to the
south. Brusilov is firm & calm. Yesterday, to my utter astonishment, I discovered two white acasias [sic] blooming in the little garden & I send you a few
flowers. The weather is a little better & warmer. Yes, I quite forgot to send you
my best wishes for Anastasia's birthday. God bless you my Angel & the girlies!
I cover your sweet face with burning kisses. Ever your own   Nicky.

290. "The following quotation from Ludendorff is of special interest: 'Russia's amazing victories
over the Austro-Hungarian troops induced her to abandon her proposed offensive against the [Ger-
man] front of the Commander-in-Chief in the East, except for the move in the direction of Baranovitchi, and concentrate all her efforts against Austria-Hungary. The more the German front proved
itself inviolable, the more eagerly did the Russians turn from it to hurl themselves against their
weaker foe.'" (Vulliamy, p. 201n)

No. 1102/ Her No. 511.   Ts.[arskoe] S[elo]. June 6th 1916.
My own Sweetheart,
    I congratulate you with all my heart for our successes & the taking of Czerno-
vitzy—thanks be to God almighty.   Only that we don't rush too wildly forward—are we laying small railway lines to bring provisions & amunitions [sic]
nearer to the front? I made Tatiana at once telephone the news to the hospital—the joy was immense. We spent the evening there. The little ones play
games, the big ones with Raftopolo [Ravtopulo] & Shah-Bagov [Shakh-Bagov]
prepare material for the dressing-station, I sometimes play a little & wander fr.
ward to ward, sitting with those that lie—then rest in a comfortable armchair in
little Sedov['s] ("Crimean"<) room & work & talk, and then V.[arvara]
Viltchkovskaja [Vil'chkovskaya] brings a stool & sits at my feet & its very cosy
[sic] a 3. Now another youngster who suffers awfully, lies next door & wants
me also to bring my work and sit there, so that I shall be torn to pieces now [by
his suffering].—[a]

Have little Mme Kotzebu [Kotsebu] ([wife of my] ex-lancer) after lunch, then
the christening [of] Korovtchuk [Korobchuk] & to see Olga's (Caucasian nobility) train.—Shall give medals to the worst & go through the whole train. Prince
Tseretelli (ex nizhe-gorodets) is at the head of it.—Such loving thanks, Lovebird,
for your very sweet letter & the delicious white acacia. I am glad my rifles also
wired to you, brave fellows!—Oh what weather! cold, grey, rainy— autumn simply. Excuse short letter but must receive. All my thoughts are with you & love
of the deepest, deepest, Sweetheart. God bless & protect you. Cover you with
tenderest kisses. Ever, Nicky mine, yr. very own Sunny. [b]

No. 1103/ Telegram 70. Tsarskoe Selo> Stavka. 6 June 1916. 17.54> 18.45.
To his majesty. Cold weather. Heartily thank you for dear letters. [We] were at
hospital< and at christening. [I] visited [daughter] Olga's sanitary train. [We]
drove a bit. Acacia smelled so strongly, very grateful. [We] all kiss and embrace
[you]. Alix

No. 1104.   Ts.[arist] Stavka. June 6th 1916.
My own dearly Beloved,
   I thank you heartily for your dear letter. Today the weather is better, but the
air feels more like autumn than June. We drove along a new road & crossed the
river over a splendid new bridge at a place called Dashkovka, 15 versts [10
miles] lower down fr. Mogilev. I walked some distance & of course we got wet
through from a downpour. Baby< climbed into one of the motors & remained
dry. He always takes with him his little gun & walks up & down by the hour on
a chosen path. This I write in the morning [—]now after lunch it has become
warmer. Your Siberians & the whole 6th sib.[erian] rifle division behaved like
heroes & kept all their positions against strong German attacks. In two days
they will be reinforced & I hope a new advance shall be made towards Kovel[291].
If you look at the map you will understand why it is important for us to reach
[that point] & why the germans are helping the austrians to resist our movement
forward? Today Voeikov returned fr. his country place very pleased with what
he saw & heard in Moscow—of course on account of our victory. Darling
mine—me loves oo [i.e., you] & wants oo tremendously. I have seldom missed
you so strongly as now, probably after our last trip together notwithstanding
Sunbeam's presence. God bless you my Love & the girlies. Thank A.[nia]< for
her good photo. Thousands of tender kisses from your ever loving old Nicky.

   291. "Kovel is an important junction on the line midway between Brest-Litovsk and Rovno."
(Vulliamy, p.202n)

No. 1105/ Telegram 60. Stavka> Tsarskoe Selo. 6 June 1916. 19.45> 20.07.
To her majesty. Warmest thanks [for] dear letters and A.[nia]< for photos.
Weather much better, warmer, went down river. Tenderest kisses. Niki

---

No. 1106/ Telegram 76. Tsarskoe Selo> Stavka. 7 June 1916. 15.07> 15.47.
To his majesty. Warmly thank you both. Finally, clear. Lunched on balcony,
there were Mavra<, Vera [and her brother] Georgy [Constantinovich] since they

are leaving. At cinematograph will show [the Russian capture of] Trapezond [also Trebizond] and Erzerum, which you have seen. We all kiss you [both], are very lonesome without you both. God keep you. Alix

No. 1107/ Her No. 512.   Ts.[arskoe] S[elo]. June 7th 1916.
My own sweet Angel,
     Very fondest thanks for yr. dear letter. I think so, oh so much of you, my Pet, in yr. loneliness, tho' Sunbeam< is with you. I miss you both more than you can guess & live over all your sweet tenderness.—The good news keep one up. Thank god the dear Siberians have been so brave again.—At last sunshine & warmer so we could lunch on the balkony [sic]. Mavra<, Vera & Georgi too as they leave for Ostashevo. [See No. 1106 above.] She asked whether Igor was going to be sent out somewhere to the war in the warmer parts as you had once thought.—Worked in the hospital. The Commander of the Tekintzi [S. P.] Zykov my Alexandr.[ovets] is with us. He was wounded in the foot during their splendid cavalry attack. He always wears their tiny cap. Interesting all he tells, he is very deaf fr. contusion & the heart enlarged.—To-day at 4 we have the cinema you saw of Sarokomishch & Trapezund [also Trebizond] in the manege [riding school] for all the wounded.—A.[nia]< returns at 5 fr. Terioki. Sweetheart, I press you to my heart & cover you with very tender kisses, God bless you—I love you beyond words. Ever yr. very own little   <u>Sunny</u>.   [P.S.] Zelenetzky [Zelenetsky] brought me 96 r.[ubles] from our sailors again, too touching. —

No. 1108.   Ts.[arist] Stavka. June 7th 1916.
My own Sunny,
     Loving thanks for your dearest letter & for the glew. Like in old days on board when it rained we all used to glew our photos in albums, so shall I do now when the weather is bad. After a glorious day yesterday it began to pour early in the morning & goes without stopping. Too tiresome! I told Alekseev how interested you were in military questions & about those details you asked me in your last letter No. 511. He smiled and listened silently.[292] Certainly those things [you mention] were & are taken into account; our pursuit will stop at a river called Suchava (in russian) & all the large & narrow gauge railway lines are at once improved & new ones [are] being laid down to follow our troops close up.[293] You must not be astonished if there is a lull in the operations for a few days. Our troops down there won't move until reinforcements come up & until another diversion is made near Pinsk. Please, this is only for <u>you</u>, not another soul must hear about it! [a]
     Judging by all this, I come to the conclusion I will remain here for an unlimited time and have therefore told Voeikov to send my train home for the necessary repairs of which it is sorely in need. Yesterday the Vlad. Bozh'e mater' image returned fr. the front.[270] The old priest of Moscow [who brought it here] is quite in rapture with the troops he saw & their spirit. God bless you [&] the girlies. [I] fondly clasp you in my arms & cover your sweet face with burning kisses, my precious little Wify. Ever your very own <u>Nicky</u>. [b]

292. Even if Alekseev dismissed rumors that the empress was a German spy, he disliked her interest in military affairs. The general's "attitude towards the Tsaritsa, always irreproachably courteous,
but firm and reserved, may be gathered from a statement which he made to General Denikin: 'When
the Empress's papers were examined [in the spring of 1917] she was found to be in possession of a
map indicating in detail the dispositions of the troops along the entire front. Only two copies were
prepared of this map, one for the Emperor and one for myself. I was very painfully impressed. God
knows who may have made use of this map' (Denikin, p. 20). Alekseev is said to have opposed the
Tsaritsa's suggestion that Rasputin should visit the Stavka, and even to have threatened resignation if
such a visit took place." (Vulliamy, p. 203n)
293. "For strategical reasons the Russians had retained the broad gauge. But although this prevented the invader from making immediate use of the Russian railways, it also prevented the Russians themselves from making use of captured rolling-stock and from sending their own trains into
the enemy's territory." (Vulliamy, p. 203n)

No. 1109/ Telegram 67.   Stavka> Tsarskoe Selo.   7 June 1916. 20.10> 20.29.
To her majesty. Tender thanks [for] dear letters. Have also been to cinema.
Morning rain storm, now fine sunny weather. News good. Fondest kisses. Niki

---

No. 1110/ Telegram 85.   Tsarskoe Selo> Stavka.   8 June 1916. 14.02> 14.25.
Tenderly thank you both. Weather average. Lunched in our rooms with Sashka<.
Warmly embrace and kiss [you]. [unsigned]

No. 1111/ Her No. 513.   Ts.[arskoe] S[elo]. June 8th 1916.
My own Beloved,
    Many a tender kiss & warmest thanks for your sweet letter. I understand per-
fectly well that you wont be coming now for some time, your presence is too
much needed. Thanks for the news about the plans, of course I wont repeat
them. [See Letter No. 1108a.]—Sashka< lunched with us—he has 3 week's leave
& lives at Ts.[arskoe] S.[elo] with wife & mother—he has remained the same &
teased [daughter] Olga as usual.—Were in the hospital, now are going for a little
drive. Yesterday evening I spent at home & Ania read aloud to me whilst I
worked. The weather is so changeable, & my cheek in consequence is rather
swollen. In my sister's [i.e., nurse's] dress its not seen & I can drive with a black
shawl over my headdress—but to-morrow at the sup.[reme] Council[298] I wont be
very pretty.—The roses I send you come from dear Peterhof, the sweetpees fr.
here, they smell so deliciously that I must send you some.—I think of you so
much, my joy & happiness[,] & cover you with passionate, tender kisses.—The
cinema of Erzerum & Trapezund [also Trebizond] was interesting, some pictures very pretty, others so dark that one scarcely saw anything;—must have an
amusing one once for all, so as that the men can laugh;—heaps looked on.—Now
my Huzy dear, my Own, Goodbye & God bless you. Excuse my dull letters,
but, alas, have nothing interesting to tell you.—I send you all that is tender &
fond—clasp you in thoughts to my breast & let you rest yr. sweet head upon my
heart. Ever yr. very   Own.

No. 1112.   Ts.[arist] Stavka. June 8th 1916.
My tender darling,   [This is a post card.]
    [P. C.] Benckendorff leaves today. He very much wants to take a letter to you,
so I sending you this post-card and a sprig of acacia. Today is the anniversary of

my arrival at Walton-on-T.[294] in 1894. It all seems so distant now! With tender, passionate love, always your Nicky.

294. Reference is to Walton-on-Thames. "The Tsar (then Tsarevitch) arrived at Gravesend on 20th June, 1894, and left the same day by special train for Walton, where he was the guest of Prince Louis of Battenberg. He came by sea in the 'Polar Star' from Kronstadt, and, to ensure his safety, a new department of the Civil Service was created by his father, Alexander III. Princess Alix or Alexandra of Hesse, then betrothed to Nicholas, came from Harrogate to stay with her sister, Princess Louise of Battenberg, at Walton. On the 24th the betrothed couple arrived at Windsor Castle as the guests of Queen Victoria. The Tsarevitch left England on 24th July." (Vulliamy, p. 204n)

No. 1113/ Telegram 76. Stavka> Tsarskoe Selo. 8 June 1916. 18.42> 19.13. To her majesty. Loving thanks. Weather improved but uncertain. Many people to receive. Old Man [Fredericks] arrived well. Fondest kisses. Niki

No. 1114/ Telegram 21. Tsarskoe Selo> Stavka. 9 June 1916. 1.20> 2.00. To his majesty. Please, quickly telegraph Silaev in Sevastopol categorical order to continue treatment, doctors insist on this. He is in no condition to return now and his reg. is likewise worried about that. Would be better if you personally ordered him to stay, otherwise he leaves on 12th. Tenderly embrace [you]. Alix

No. 1115/ Telegram 94. Tsarskoe Selo> Stavka. 9 June 1916. 14.58> 15.30. To his majesty. Saw Count [P. C. Benckendorff]. Tenderly thank you both for dear post-card. Weather changeable. Now going to town< to Supreme Council.[298] We all warmly kiss [you]. May the Lord bless you [both]. Alix

No. 1116/ Her No. 514.   Ts.[arskoe] S[elo]. June 9th 1916.
My own Lovebird,
     Tender thanks for yr. dear card Benkendorf [P. C. Benckendorff] just now brought me; I am glad he found you both looking so well, tho' the weather [is] also bad [here] & even out [i.e., there] at the war.—We are off to town< directly to the Supreme Council[298] & back to tea, as Paul< comes to bid us goodbye, he leaves to-morrow.—Were in the hospital<, yesterday evening too, so I sat an hour with her [Anna Vyrubova] before as she seemed rather hurt I went—tho' understood it,—this evening she will spend with me.—I see by the papers Motherdear< goes about, has been to the old [Countess] Branitzkaia at Be-laya-Tserkov,[295] I think.—[a]
     To-morrow our prayers will meet at Tobolsk.[296] Lovy, I told Zaionch-k.[ovsky] to tell Volzhin to go [there for the ceremony], they got no answer fr. you (he wrote too, I find) & I said I was sure you wld. wish it, as it is customary for the Over-Proc[u]rator to go & not the assistant—I hope it was right I said so;—he ought to have known that, but as its far [to Tobol'sk], he [Volzhin] thought you might need him [to stay here in the capital,] etc. Ella<, alas, has not gone, I was sure she would not.—Lunched on the balkony [sic], but rather cold—weather not inviting. Such a strange summer. Yes, dear Walton![294] What lovely, sweet, tender & passionate remembrances—ah, dear, how intensely deeply I love you, more far than I can ever say—you are my life, my sunshine,

my one & all.— God bless & protect you. I cover you with tenderest kisses, ever
Huzy mine, yr. very own old girly   <u>Alix</u>. [b]

295. Alexandra is referring to Maria Branitskaya, wife of Count Michael Branitsky. After the
Germans occupied Warsaw, the family continued to live on their estate at Belaya Tserkov' (White
Church). Note by A. A. Sergeev: Nicholas and Alexandra, *Perepiska*, IV, p. 298n.
296. Alexandra refers to *proslavlenie* ("glorification"), one of the stages of canonization. Nicholas's support for an earlier stage of this process (the *velichanie*, "laudation") in the fall of 1915 shook
the Church because it suggested the tsar was a tool of Bishop Varnava and his ally, Rasputin. (See
Letters No. 413c and 644c, and Footnote 181.) The director of the Holy Synod would ordinarily
attend such an event. But this canonization was irregular—which is why Volzhin was sending in his
stead his assistant-director, N. Ch. Zaionchkovsky. Note that Alexandra's own sister Ella< would
have nothing to do with "Saint" John Maximovich. The ceremony occurred in the cathedral church at
Tobol'sk on June 10, 1916. See Footnote 301.

No. 1117.   Ts.[arist] Stavka. June 9th 1916.
My own Treasure,
    Yesterday I had so much to do that [I] could not write you a real letter. Today
also shall be busy as [I] have to see old Kulomzin, Markov—minister for Finland
& gen Stakhovich. That will take all my time till dinner, and in the evening I
shall have to race on as usual with my papers & go late to bed. Last night I lay
down at 2.o'clock. I have wired to Silaev to remain & continue his treatment, as
he has got time for that. [a]
    As I expected, the germans are bringing more and more troops over towards
Kovel[291] & now there are very bloody battles, raging in that region. All available troops are being sent to Brusilov to reinforce him as much as possible. And
that cursed question of heavy artillery ammunition is beginning to be felt. All
the stores from Evert & Kuropatkin have to be sent down there; this together
with great transportations of troops—makes the work very hard for the railways
& staff. But God is merciful & I hope in a few days or in about a week this
critical moment will have passed! The weather is not to be understood; regularly one day it is fine & the next it pours.—The train was late, so I got your letter
[only] this instant. Fondly do I thank you my darling Wify, my own Pet. God
bless you & the girlies. With many tender kisses ever your very own   <u>Nicky</u>. [b]

No. 1118/ Telegram 86. Stavka> Tsarskoe Selo. 9 June 1916. 18.40> 19.07.
To her majesty. Very fond thanks [for] letters and photos. Sun occasional,
squals [sic], rain. News good. Tender kisses. Niki

No. 1119/ Her No. 515.   Tsarskoe Selo. June 9th 1916.
Beloved sweet Angel,
    Before going to sleep I begin my letter to you. I have told Ania< to write to
you, as she was told [by Rasputin] to give over 5 [of his] questions to you, & its
easier for her to write them, who must remember. Do you wish me to send for
Shtyurmer & speak to him about these subjects to prepare them, if so wire at
once to me: "agree to yr. question", then shall see him on Sunday, speak over all
& tell him to ask when you can receive him. Our Friend< hoped you could have
come [back to Tsarskoe Selo] now for 2 days to settle these different questions,
wh. he finds most essential should be thought of quicker, especially about 1.—the

Duma—I remember I told you Sht. begged you should say, that they were to finish quickly & go to the country & watch the fieldworks [i.e., tend to agriculture on their estates].—Only send for Sh.[tyurmer] soon, as things do dawdle so. You can show him Miechen's paper [see Letters No. 1083, 1085b, 1089b, 1095a, 1098a] just to look through.— [a]

2. Obolensky to be changed—why not name him governor somewhere—only who is the right man to replace him [at Petrograd]? He has never gone against Gregory so he [Rasputin] is sorry to ask for him to be changed, only he says he really does nothing—& one must seriously begin the collecting of provisions quicker—people file along again in the streets before the shops.— [b]

3. That wld. it not be wiser to give over all that question about food & fuel to the minister of Interior, whom it concerns more than the minister of Agriculture. The Minister of Interior has his people everywhere, can give orders & direct instructions to all the Governors—all are under him after all & Krivosh.[ein], [a former minister of agriculture] took it [jurisdiction in this matter] out of greed into his hands &—I don't want to insinuate worse things. I remember young [A. N.] Khvostov also thought it wld. have been better in the Ministry of the Interior. This is one of the most serious questions, otherwise fuel will be too awfully expensive. [c]

4. About the Soyuz gorodov [Union of Cities], that you should not thank them any more personally. That means should be found for now publishing all about what they do and saying especially that you, the Government, give all the money & that they spend it largely—its yours & not theirs. The public must know this. I spoke it over several times with Sh.[tyurmer] how it cld. be made known —by an order of yours to Sh. or a paper fr. him to you—shall talk it over with him as they try to play too great a part & it becomes a political danger, wh. now must already be taken into account, otherwise too many things will come at a time to settle.[297] [d]

No. 5—she [Anna Vyrubova] could not remember what He [Rasputin] told her.—The Supreme Council[298] lasted fr. 3-4½ —Rodzianko & Chelnokov talked a good deal, & Miechen's< [D. M.] Neidhardt aggravated me—Stichinsky [Stishinsky] spoke well, not famously Boris Wassiltchikov [Vasil'chikov]. [A. F.] Trepov gave me over yr. messages, thanks Lovebird. Am sorry had no time to see Mitja Den< before he left—heard of it too late.—Dear old Goremykin was too at S.[upreme] C.[ouncil] so tiny, very thin with big eyes—said the heat at Gagry had disagreed with him, whilst his wife, on the contrary, has greatly improved & her eyes are better. [e]

Paul< & Marie< came to tea (she covered with pimples again)—he leaves to-morrow. Seems Dmitri< is here several weeks & up & down to Moscou [sic]—has not shown himself once— cannot understand the way he serves!—As they say, he is attached to Skoropadsky. Olga & I drove in my droshki & as service was going on at Tiarlevo we got out & went there till we kissed the Bible & then returned home. A nice, cosy [sic] Church. The other 3 [of our daughters] & Isa< went for a walk. The evening A.[nia]< spent with me.—Yr. first acacia lies in my gospel, this one will go into another prayerbook. Now I must put out my lamp, shall finish to-morrow. [f]

We have Church at 9 ([it is] St. John Maximovitch['s day] now) & then go to
the hospital< for an operation. Saturday shall see our Fr.< in her [Anna Vyrubova's] house to say goodbye—he leaves next week home.—Sleep well my
Treasure, I always, morn. & evening bless & kiss your cushion—its all I have!
Why on earth this ultimatum to Greece, for sure England & France are at the
bottom of it—to my simple mind, it seems unjust & hard—cannot imagine how
Tino< will get out of it & it may harm his popularity. One more thing I was to
tell you, that Gen. Selivanov is the judge of Sukhomlinov & one says he cannot
be unbiased as he had formerly been discharged by Sukhomlinov from Siberia
and that it would be better to appoint the member of the Council of the Empire,
General Shumilov.[299] I only tell you this as He wished me too, but I told Ania I
doubt yr. mixing in this affair. [g]
    10-th. Warmest thanks [for] sweetest letter, so happy to receive it, my Angel.
It has begun to rain several times. Were in Church, then an operation, 7 new
officers were brought to us, Ingermanlandian Hus.[sars], Belomorsky and Be-
loozersky regiments etc. Now saw Malevsky-Malevitch—[he is] glad to be back
fr. Japan as has both sons serving in the Preobrazhentsy<. He longs to be presented to you, but knows you have no time.—Thanks for wiring to Silaev. Endless, burning kisses & many blessings fr. yr. old   Wify.   [P.S.] St. John
Max.[imovich:] may He send you both & our Country His blessings.—[h]

    297. Alexandra refers to a fear she and her husband shared: if liberal "popular" volunteer organi-
zations such as the Union of Towns and Union of Zemstvos played a key role in securing victory,
this would strengthen the Duma's position after the war—and further weaken the power of the tsar.
    298. Alexandra refers to the "Supreme Council to Aid the Families of those Serving in the War"
(*Verkhovnyi sovet po prizrenniiu semei lits prizvannykh na voinu*).
    299. This seems to be a slip of the pen: judging from context, the empress meant to indicate
Nicholas Pavlovich *Shatilov*, infantry general and a member of the State Council.

No. 1120/ Telegram 99. Tsarskoe Selo> Stavka. 10 June 1916. 14.37> 15.09.
To his majesty. Warmly thank you both, my dears. [We] were at church, then
hospital<, operation,—very tired. Newly wounded just now arrived. Dmitry<
comes for tea. We all embrace and warmly kiss you both. Alix

No. 1121.   Ts.[arist] Stavka. June 10th 1916.
My sweet Lovebird,   [This is a post card.]
    So many loving thanks for your letter. Again had no time to write longer.
Received old Persian Prince, Zilli Sultan who goes back to his country. He is a
brother of the former Schah [Shah], whom we saw at Peterhof.—Aleksei sat near
his son & talked the whole time in french.—God bless you my own beloved
Sunny. I kiss & love you dearly & tenderly. Ever your own   Nicky.

No. 1122/ Telegram 90. Stavka> Tsarskoe Selo. 10 June 1916. 19.35> 20.00.
To her majesty. Loving thanks. Received to day old Persian Prince [Zilli Sul-
tan] with his son. Took tea at Georgi['s]< little country house[300] along highroad.
Fine weather and showers have ceased. Tender kisses. Niki

300. Nicholas wrote "little country house," but the Russian term is *dacha*: a "lightly constructed summer residence. Those who were unable to maintain a dacha of their own used to hire one for the summer months. These houses ranged from mere huts or bungalows to handsome wooden buildings." (Vulliamy, p. 206n)

No. 1123/ Her No. 516.   Ts.[arskoe] S[elo]. June 11th 1916.
My own beloved Angel,
   Tenderest thanks for yr. dear card.—Its pouring as usual. Were at the hospital<, then panikhida [funeral service] for poor Zhukov— what can have induced him to commit suicide?—Then I saw my column of ambulances wh. are going off to the army of Shcherbachev—where he needs them! Now saw von Harten[,] Com.[mander] of the Tvertsy & he begs to be allowed to be presented to Aleksei, so I told him to go to the Headquarters & ask Voeikov<.—Had a wire fr. my Siberian rifles—again many losses amongst the officers, heaps [are] heavily wounded—one of ours [i.e., an officer who already recovered in our hospital is here] again, now 2 wounds in the head. [The following quote is in Russian.] "Killed as a result of extraordinary heroism the senior under-officer of the unit of reconnoitring [sic] infantry, B. P. Akimov, formerly a naval lieutenant". Zborovsky has already arrived (my train hunts for him) & comes to the Children hospital— they have gone off there in great excitement. I sent Vil'chk.< the names of the cossacks we must get here. To-morrow I think my train arrives, it has been picking up in different towns.—Has Georgi< arranged himself cosily? [sic]—Despairing this perpetual damp—for Baby< too. The dentist [S. S. Kostritsky] has arrived & will soon be worrying me.—We see our Friend< a moment this evening in her [Anna Vyrubova's] house to say goodbye, as he leaves [on a visit home to Pokrovskoe, in Siberia]. Suslik's< telegram is really killing.[301]—Beloved of beloveds, I bless & kiss you without end & yearn for you. Ever yr. very Own. [P.S.] Where has the Ekipazh< gone off to again? Dmitri< [is] in good spirits & funny as usual.

301. Alexandra received a congratulatory telegram from Metropolitan Makary of Moscow and Bishop Varnava ("Suslik") of Tobol'sk on June 10, 1916, day of the glorification (*proslavlenie*) of the new saint, John Maximovich, along with a new Siberian prayer book featuring a salutation to the royal family. A few days later, Synod Director Volzhin presented Varnava with the Order of St. Vladimir Second Class. (Nabokov: Alexandra, *Pis'ma imperatritsy*, II, p. 116n)

No. 1124/ Telegram 107. Tsarskoe Selo> Stavka. 11 June 1916. 17.46> 18.24.
To his majesty. Warmly thank you for dear post card. Strong rain fell almost all day long. Were at hospital and at panikhida [funeral service] for poor Zhukov. Viktor Erastovich< arrived, they placed him in children's hospital, wounded in chest, quite thin, just as ever. Tenderly kiss and embrace [you]. Alix

No. 1125/ Telegram 96. Stavka> Tsarskoe Selo. 11 June 1916. 18.54> 19.10.
To her majesty. Warmest thanks. Speak to Sh.[tyurmer] about those questions. Showers continue. Thank [daughter] Olga for photos. Tender kisses. Niki

No. 1126.   Ts.[arist] Stavka. June 11th 1916.
My own darling wify,

Fondest thanks for your dear letter, wh. was full of tiresome questions, most of which I have often touched on in conversations with Sht[yurmer]. He is an excellent honest man, but cannot decide himself to do what is necessary—seems to me. The great thing needed most is fuel & metals—iron & copper for ammunition —as not having enough metal, the fabrics [factories] cannot work enough cartridges & shells. The same with the railways, [A. F.] Trepov insists that they work better than last year & has got proofs, but everybody else complains that they do not transport all they could! Confound these affairs, from thinking about them so much my brain does not grasp any more where is the true solution? But something very energetic must be done, a very firm step to resolve it once for all. As soon as the Duma is gone away I will send for the ministers & work & settle it here! They continue coming nearly every day & that takes all my time up; I go to bed after 1.30 a.m. normally, having to make haste on writing, reading & receiving!!! Simply desperate! [a]

It is warmer to day, though it rained twice. I received yesterday two Persian princes [Zilli Sultan and his son—see Letters No. 1121 and 1122]. Baby< amazed all by conversing in French during lunch with the younger! God bless you!—I kiss you passionately and tenderly, my treasure, the girlies the same. Give her [Anna Vyrubova] my love. Ever your own old Nicky. [b]

No. 1127/ Telegram 110. Tsarskoe Selo> Stavka. 12 June 1916. 14.25> 14.53. To his majesty. Warmer but overcast. Tenderly thank you both. Now going [to visit] Victor Erastovich<. [We] were at church, then drove. [Am going] to hospital< in evening. Embrace and tenderly kiss [you]. Alix

---

No. 1128/ Her No. 517.   Ts.[arskoe] S[elo]. June 12th 1916.
My own dearly Beloved,

For yr. sweet letter my very tenderest thanks. How tired & weary you must be of all those people bothering you, & I with my tiresome letter the other day too!—Yesterday I had the joy of seeing our Friend< in the evening in the little house [of Anna Vyrubova] before going to the hospital<. He was in excellent spirits & so affectionate & kind—happy over the good news, asked much after you. It did me good to see him and I was glad to go to our wounded straight from him. The poor old Colonel is so bad, but I hope, with God's help that we can pull him through. He took Holy Communion this morning as I proposed it to him.—I always put all my hope into that blessing.—The hospital is very full, we have 23 officers.—[Daughters] Olga & Tatiana are working & abusing each other [so much] that they "skull",[302] absurd girls. [a]

We came back from a drive after having been at the little ones hospital. Victor Erastovitch looks brown & alright, pretends he has no pains, but one sees his face twitch. He is wounded through the chest, but feels the arm.—A.[nia]< has gone for the night to Finland. Our exhibition opens to-day at the big palace<, like last year—the works of all our wounded of here—& our own things we do.—Were in Church.—Have Sht.[yurmer] & then Rost.< with a long doklad [report], as he leaves for 6 weeks rest to Finland. The weather is finer, warmer, but scarcely any sun. Beloved Angel, I long to press you to my heart and to whisper words of endless love and tenderness, Sweethearty mine! I cover yr. dear face and eyes and lips with burning kisses. God bless & keep you. Ever yr. very, very Own. [P.S.] Thanks, my Pet, for the [cotton wool] wadding!!!—Excuse such a dull letter.— [b]

302. The empress is rendering in English the root of the Russian verb *skulit'*, "to whine" or "to whimper," as dogs do.

No. 1129/ Telegram 104. Stavka> Tsarskoe Selo. 12 June 1916. 19.55> 20.58. To her majesty. Fondest thanks. Weather decidedly better. Thoughts always together. Tender kisses to all. Niki

No. 1130/ Telegram 112. Tsarskoe Selo> Stavka. 12 June 1916. 21.05> 21.46. To his majesty. Fairly cold, but we are having lunch on balcony so as not to forget that it is now summer. Greatly touched by cornflowers and blue bells. Anastasia is fighting with Wolf [a pet dog?]. Sleep well. May the Lord bless you. Warmly kiss [you]. Alix

No. 1131.   Ts.[arist] Stavka. June 12th 1916.
My beloved,
  Many loving thanks for your dear No. 516. Yes, it is very sad about poor Zhukov. [A. N.] Grabbe does not yet know the reason, but thinks it must [have been] the gryzha [hernia] wh. prevented him from riding just [at] the moment when our cavalry began pursuing of the austrians. He probably found it humiliating to have to remain behind in the hospital & shot himself—leaving a note in which he says he commits suicide! Alekseev told me he had a letter fr one of the commandering [sic] generals saying that the soldiers are in need of writing paper & postcards. Could you be an Angel & order as much of them as you can? And later send them in batches to the komanduyushchim armiyami [commanding officers of armies] with your little trains. [a]
  The splendid 6th Siberian division has lost much but it has inflicted colossal losses to the newly arrived german troops, from Verdun. Wherever the enemy uses dum-dum bullets—our men don't take any prisoners! It was officially announced the other day because it is good the world should know it. Ask your wounded about this. Our brave Keller has driven the austrians downwards out of the Bucovina & managed to take 60 officers & over 2000 men prisoners. Lechitsky cannot stop him. K.[irill<] just wired to Grabbe that with regret he lets our 1st Kub.[an] sotnya [company] —it will be now replaced by the 4th Terskaya; please find out when it leaves & bid them good-bye! God bless you & the girls. Tenderly I hug you in my arms & kiss you softly all over! My treasure, my sweet Wify! Ever your own Nicky. [b]

No. 1132/ Telegram 116. Tsarskoe Selo> Stavka. 13 June 1916. 14.27> 15.02. To his majesty. Warmly thank you both, my dears. Wonderful weather. [We] are having lunch on balcony. Will find out about the cossacks. [See Letter No. 1132b.] Tenderly embrace and kiss [you]. Alix

No. 1133/ Her No. 518.   Ts.[arskoe] S[elo]. June 13th 1916.

My own sweet Angel,

Such a lovely day, & the birds are singing away so merrily enjoying the sun—but there is a strange light, a sort of haze in the sky—can it not be from all the shooting? Beloved, I thank you very very fondly for your sweet letter. Thank God the news is good & that Keller behaves so splendidly.—More wounded are being brought. We had to operate [on] the old Colonel—it was serious, thank God his heart so far bore it alright, but its still very grave. I feel tired, it lasted 50 m.[inutes] & I stood all the time so as to give the instruments quickly and be ready for anything. Css. Vorontsova [Elizabeth Vorontsova-Dashkova] sat a long time with me—begs to be remembered to you. Lives here, has grown very old indeed, friendly & kind. Now the dentist [S. S. Kostritsky] is going to worry me (just when its fine!) then a long doklad [report] with V. P. Shneider [Varvara Schneider]. The evening remain at home, Ania< returns fr. Terioki. Gardinsky [Gordinsky] turned up for 2 days—[Ania] always feels still the results of the railway accident.[59] [a]

Lovy, excuse my bothering you, but can you ask Alekseev, is it absolutely necessary to give up Baby's< splendid hospital of mine (ex Sukhoml.[inov]'s) at the Military Academy—its such a splendid one, you remember, & beautifully arranged, one of the very best in town. [See Letter No. 1171b.] Al.[ekseev] says he wishes to renew his studies, as needs more off.[icers] for the Gener.[al] Staff.—Are they so much needed now, don't the line officers do yet better & understand all more during the war. They even ask us to have 50 beds for these officers who are to learn there. Its more than a pitty [sic] as I doubt our ever finding an equally suitable big house anywhere. Be an angel and ask Al. quite sure again, must we clear out—can he not have us there? Kindly answer me as all are very anxious about it. [b]

Thank Zhilik< for his letter, he finds Baby not quite so well & therefore the lessons are not quite so good—I think it is owing to the weather being so damp & unsettled.—Must end & fly off now. Saw Sh.[tyurmer and] told him all, he wrote down the questions all, will prepare everything for when you send for him. Hopes the Duma will finish [on the] 20-th.—I bless you, kiss you without end in yearning love & adoration.—Ever, Huzy mine, yr. very own old   Wify.
[P.S.] As the Pss. [Gedroits] has left with a [train] wagon to the front to fetch wounded, I feel responsable [sic] for the hospital< and they turn to me as their head.— [c]

No. 1134.   Ts.[arist] Stavka. June 13th 1916.
My beloved Sunny,   [This is a post card.]
Fondest thanks for [your] dear letter. My best wishes for [daughter] Marie's birthday. Sad to be separated. Today at last it is fine and warm so we lunched in the tent, wh. we have not done for the last 10 days.—The news are good. [A. N.] Grabbe goes back for a short time & wants to see you. Tenderly I clasp you in my arms & whisper words of love into y[r] ears! God bless you, my Darling! Ever y[r] own   Nicky.

No. 1135/ Telegram 113. Stavka> Tsarskoe Selo. 13 June 1916. 22.15> 22.48.
To his majesty. Loving thank [for] letters and best wishes for dear [daughter]

Marie's birthday. Was occupied whole evening. Weather atlast [sic] fine, no rain. May God bless you. Tender love. Niki

No. 1136/ Telegram 120. Tsarskoe Selo> Stavka. 14 June 1916. 10.17> 11.43. To his majesty. Congratulate you with all my heart on birthday of our dear girlie [Marie]. Glorious weather— such a treat. [We] are going to hospital<. Te Deum at 2 o'clock in new childrens' hospital, to which their [i.e., Marie's and Anastasia's] wounded were sent this morning. Kiss you both, my dears. Alix

No. 1137/ Her No. 519.   Ts.[arskoe] S[elo]. June 14th 1916.
My own beloved Darling,
    Warmest, tenderest thanks for yr. sweet card. Such lovely weather, a real treat. All our wounded lie out on the balkony [sic] & enjoy the beautiful air. Taube lay in the sun under a parasole [sic], so as to have a sunbath for his poor stump.—Now we are directly off to [daughters] M.[arie]'s & A.[nastasia]'s new hospital, next to their old one, & there will be a Te Deum. I warmly congratulate you with our big Marie['s birthday]—she is overjoyed with yr. dear letter.—Our Friend< hopes there will be a good victory (perhaps Kovel[291]) & if so, He begs on that account you should have "vzyat' na poruki" ["release on bail"] Sukhomlinov. Give the order privately, without much ado, to [A. A.] Khvostov, or the Senator who looks after him [i.e., his case]—and let him live at home under the trust of 2 others. He is old—of course the judgement remains, but it will make the heavy load easier for the old man to bear—He begs you to do it, if we have a big victory.— [a]
    The cigarets [sic] came to an end, so [daughter] Tatiana fished out a little box as you had told her to.—I am glad you can lunch out again, we also with gratitude take our meals on the balkony. Titeriat [Teteryatnikov] will bring you flowers again.—A.[nia]< came to the hospital in her little pony-carriage to see all our wounded—such a sunny friendly smile must cheer them up.—After my perevyazki [dressings] were over, I embroidered (always for our exhibition-bazar [sic]—& the things sell splendidly) & Gardinsky [Gordinsky] & Sedov helped me sowing [sic].—I fear the Colonel is dying, so sad!—To-day 4 weeks we parted—ah, my Love, I love you so intensely, my own my very own Boy Blue[258] & cover you with kisses. God bless & protect you now and ever! Yr. very Own.
[b]

No. 1138.   Ts.[arist] Stavka. June 14th 1916.
My sweet, darling Wify,
    Fondest and loving thanks for your dear letter. I congratulate you for [daughter] Marie's 17th birthday. How the time flies!—I shall ask Alekseev about the house of the academy. I am almost sure the building must be cleared as the need of officers of the Gen. st.[aff] is very serious. Lots of vacancies are filled by those who have finished only one year in the Academy & yet there were not enough. Think—our army has been doubled & there have been losses among the Gen. H.[eadquarters] officers—therefore the need increases daily.—I think it a mistake to send so many wounded to the capital, it is better for them to lie and

recover in the interior of the country. Again no time to write.—Yesterday I received Ignatev, today will have to see Naumov & to-morrow Shuvaev. God bless you my beloved treasure! Many tender & burning kisses from your ever own old Nicky.

No. 1139/ Telegram 116. Stavka> Tsarskoe Selo. 14 June 1916. 15.08> 15.45. To her majesty. Congratulate and thank [you] tenderly for letters. Also divine weather [here]. Going on a trip down river. Warm kisses from both. Niki

No. 1140/ Telegram 124. Tsarskoe Selo> Stavka. 14 June 1916. 18.46> 19.40. To his majesty. Warmly thank [you] both for postcards. Marie in raptures over letters. Childrens' hospital charmingly cosy. Bless and tenderly love my dear ones. Alix

No. 1141/ Telegram 152. Tsarskoe Selo> Stavka. 15 June 1916. 15.27> 16.28. To his majesty. Tenderly thank you for dear letters. Glorious weather. Big girls< gone to town<. [I] will stroll with little ones<. Received [A. N.] Grabbe and [P. C.] Benckendorff. Poor old colonel died this evening, [we] attended panikhida [funeral]. Warmly kiss and embrace you. Alix

No. 1142/ Her No. 520.   Ts.[arskoe] S[elo]. June 15th 1916.
My own Beloved,
   Ever such grateful thanks for yr. sweet letter.—I send you a paper fr. Duvan wh. A.[nia]< told me to give you with her love, & a petition fr. Ania's future sister-in-laws Mother, Princess Dzhordzhadze. [Daughters] O.[lga] & T.[atiana] have gone to town<, as Tatiana has a committee—I shall drive with the little ones<. Every day the dentist [S. S. Kostritsky] worries me & my cheek aches in consequence rather.—Our poor old Colonel died peacefully this night—we shall bury him on our fraternal cemetry [sic], the wife agrees to this; she & the daughter seem to feel it less than his touching soldier [i.e., orderly] who never left him.—What a downpour! Will refresh the air.—A. has gone for the night to Finland to see her brother [S. A. Taneev], (after 8 months) who has come for 3 days.—Miechen< lives now here!! Thanks dear for the paper about the ex Naval officer.—Heart & Soul ever near you with burning love & yearning. How the Ministers must bore you, my Angel. I kiss you as only wify knows how to, true? God bless you. Endless kisses fr. yr. own Sunny.

No. 1143.   Ts.[arist] Stavka. June 15th 1916.
My own precious Sunny,
   I thank you ever so fondly for your dear letter. Yesterday busy day yesterday: [daughter] Marie's birthday, church, a long doklad [report], lunch, writing a letter in all haste, an expedition down the river in a quick new motor boat, at 6.o cinematograph & after dinner also a long doklad with Naumov. After that I had to read lots of papers till 11.30 & then tea à trois with Den and Vlad. Nik.< Today I receive old Shuvaev. As soon as the Gosud. Soviet [State Council] & the Duma leave—I will collect all the ministers here—about the 24th. After that per-

haps you might come, if our military affairs don't go against [it]. Not once have I looked into that dear story of the Boy Blue![284] [a]

My precious darling, I also yearn for you & for your sweet caresses! It is sad not to kiss [anyone] except Babykins<—once in the morning & in the evening; but that is not enough for me! The weather is really ideal—a delicious & dry [day?]. One would like to be out on the river or in the wood the whole day! Kirill< came yesterday fr Poltava on his way to the Gv. Ek. [Guards Equipage<]—they are somewhere not far fr Molodechno.[303] God bless you & the girlies. I kiss you and them very tenderly. Ever my darling Wify your own Nicky. [b]

303. "Molodechno, a small town on ... the eastern border of Lithuania." (Vulliamy, p. 210n)

No. 1144/ Telegram 125. Stavka> Tsarskoe Selo. 15 June 1916. 20.20> 20.36. To her majesty. Fondest thanks. Ideal weather. Sorry about old colonel. We both kiss all tenderly. Niki

No. 1145/ Telegram 162. Tsarskoe Selo> Stavka. 16 June 1916. 14.00> 14.45. To his majesty. Tenderly thank you both, my dears, for letters and Baby< for flowers. Wonderful weather, but my heart feels approach of thunderstorm. Warmly kiss and embrace [you]. Today am receiving our sisters [i.e., nurses] who are going to Germany and Austria. Alix

No. 1146/ Her No. 521.   Ts.[arskoe] S[elo]. June 16th 1916.
My own beloved Sweetheart,
    Warmly do I thank & kiss you for your sweet letter. Excuse my bad writing, but I have a compress & bandage on my first finger. When we operated [on] the poor colonel, I pricked my finger & now have a gathering [infection].—Its splendid weather, but I think a thunderstorm is in the air, my heart felt so bad in the hospital.—I receive to-day our sisters [i.e., nurses] who are leaving to-morrow for Germany & Austria—Mme Orjevsky [Natalya Orzhevskaya] does not seem to be of the number.—Then Sister Kartzeva [Anastasia Kartseva, a nurse] (Mme Hartwig's sister) I send to Eupatoria as popechitel'nitsa [inspectress] & starshaya sestra [senior nurse], so as to put all in order there and to better look after everything. [Daughter] Olga is working here on the balkony [sic]—the 3 others have gone riding.— [a]
    A.[nia]< returns fr. Terioki where she spent the night with her whole family[, the Taneevs].—I forgot to tell you that our Friend< begs you should give the order that one should not augment [i.e., increase] the prices of going in town in trains—instead of 5 kop.[ecks] now one must pay 10 kop.[ecks] & thats not fair upon the poor people—let the rich be taxed but not the others who daily have often more than once, to go by train.—Write it on one of yr. papers to Shtyurmer to tell [A. N.] Obolensky, who I suppose gave this foolish order.— [b]
    It will be nice to go & see you afterwards! If we do, Gr.[egory] begged me to take A.<—I said its not convenient as there are always guests & foreigners—then he said she need not come to the meals and remain in the train, but he said it would be kinder to give her that joy;—I should bring Nastinka< this time & then

the 4 Girlies[, our daughters].—Beloved Angel, I must stop now. My heart is full of very deep, great love for my Angel love & I cover you with kisses.—God bless & protect you, Nicky mine. Ever yr. very own old   Sunny. [P.S.] I use Baby's envelope again, it will amuse him to see it.—[c]

No. 1147.   Ts.[arist] Stavka. June 16th 1916.
My own darling Wify,
    Today the messenger is a little late, probably on account of new movements of troops fr north to south. I send you a telegram which Aleksei got fr his regiment. Again good news thank God fr Lechitsky![304] Yesterday his army made 221 officers & 10,200 men prisoners! So many new hands for working in our fields & manufact.[ories]. Miechen< wrote me a cold letter asking me why I have not approved the polozhenie [Regulation]?[304] I sent it through Alekseev to the Verkh. Soviet.[298] Perhaps you will let Ilin[, president of the Russian Red Cross,] know that they are to look at it through [sic] & send me their opinion. She is really insufferable—if I have time, I shall answer her sharply.—We have finished lunch & on coming up to my room I found your dear letter No. 520. [P. C.] Benckendorff also arrived, as old Fred.< intends going back for affairs. [a]
    Please thank A.[nia]< for the papers fr. Duvan. How I miss your sweet kisses! Yes, beloved One, you know how to give them! Oh, how naughtily! B...y hops from remembrances. It is very hot & now a few drops of rain fell out of an isolated cloud. I hope to bathe in the river higher up while Aleksei runs about with naked legs. Did he describe to you how the small peasant boys play all sorts of games before us? Now, my precious Darling, I must end. God bless you & the girlies. With many fond kisses ever your own Nicky. [b]

    304. P. A. Lechitsky, commander of the Ninth Army, "played a dashing part" in the Brusilov offensive which was "entirely successful." "More than 144,000 prisoners were claimed at this time, 4031 officers and 219 guns." (Vulliamy, p. 211n) See Letters No. 1083, 1085b, 1089b, 1095a, 1098a, 1119a,e, and 1142 for a discussion of the "Regulations" Maria Pavlovna the Elder ("Miechen") was trying to get approved for her charitable institutions.

No. 1148/ Telegram 128. Stavka> Tsarskoe Selo. 16 June 1916. 19.30> 20.00.
To her majesty. Warmest thanks also for flowers. Splendid weather. Bathed in the river, very enjoyable. Good news. Tender kisses. Niki

No. 1149/ Telegram 166. Tsarskoe Selo> Stavka. 17 June 1916. 10.09> 12.03.
To his majesty. Heartily thank you, again good news. Just now received telegram from Keller. Wounded by bullet in other leg, bone not perebita [broken] but rasshcheplena [splintered]. He hopes to soon return to the front. Telegram from Kimpolung. Warmly embrace and kiss you both. Husband of Sasha Kozen has died. Alix

No. 1150/ Her No. 522.   Ts.[arskoe] S[elo]. June 17th 1916.
My own beloved One,
    Still a bad writing, because the finger disturbs me. From all my heart I congratulate you with the good news again, over 10,000 prisoners.—This morning I

got a telegr. fr. Keller fr. Kimpolung. [The following quote is in Russian.] "Fulfilled the given task, cleared southern Bukovina of the enemy. Was wounded to-day in the other leg by a bullet the bone has not been shattered but splintered. With the help of God I hope soon to return into the ranks for further service to Your Imperial Majesty."—Ania's< brother [Sergei Taneev] told her much about him, how the soldiers adore him & when he goes to the wounded, how each tries to sit up to see him better. He rides, followed by an immense banner with the image [icon] of the Saviour, & 40 cossacks, of wh. each has 4 St. George's crosses, otherwise they dont guard him—they say its an imposing & emotioning picture. How glad I am for him—he always yearned for this great chance to prove to you his intense love, loyalty & gratitude. So prettily he told Sergei Tan.[eev] that he (Keller) & Ania serve us alike, each in our place & therefore he is so fond of her.—So I told Ania to ask our Fr.< to pray for him, I told her last night to give it over to-day (he leaves for Tobolsk and home)—and this morning I already had a wire he [Keller] is wounded—but thank God seems not serious. [a]

Splendid weather. Spent the evening with Ania, sent for the dentist (S. S. Kostritsky) in the evening (3-rd time in one day) to take out the filling, because of the pain, you see the inflammation of the periosteam makes the treatment so difficult. I must get up now so shall finish this after luncheon. We have a French cinema at 4 in the manege [riding-school], a count shows it—our troops arrival in France—Verdun, fabrics [factories] where they make cartridges & amusing pictures.—Sweetest Angel, my thoughts forever suround [sic] you with yearning love.—Yes, One begs you should not allow the districts (Metropolitan) wh. Volzh.[in] wishes to bring in now with Vladim.[ir] its not the time & Gr.< says would have fatal results. She [Anna Vyrubova] goes to see him of this morning.—Forgive my bothering you with the enclosed paper, but He [Rasputin] wished you to know it.—I hold you tightly in my arms & whisper words of infinite tenderness & love.—Heartfelt thanks my treasure for yr. dear letter; none came fr. Baby< or Zhilik< thanks for Aleksei's telegram, shall show it to Rita< & then return it for Der.[evenko, the sailor attending the tsarevich] to keep.— Hang Miechen< on 60 apple trees! So uncomfy writing with this bandaged finger. I cut the thing open with an operations-knife.—Ah my big wee one, I kiss you endlessly—the balkony is so empty without you and Tiny<.—God bless and protect you my Own, my Sunshine, my life's joy. Ever yr. very own <u>Wify</u>. [b, c]

No. 1151/ Telegram 135. Stavka> Tsarskoe Selo. 17 June 1916. 15.05> 15.20. To her majesty. Best thanks [for] letters and wire. Strong downpour in the night, now fine. Tiresome about Keller['s wound]. Fondest kisses. Niki

No. 1152.   Ts.[arist] Stavka. June 17th 1916.
My own Sweetheart,
    Ever so many thanks for your dear letter No. 521. How tiresome your poor finger has a gathering & you wear a bandage. Take care & look after it well.—There, again poor Keller got wounded. I heard of it this morning & then directly I got your wire. I do hope it will not last long. Brave man, he has payed[305a] three times during the war with his own self! Next Tuesday begins our

our [sic] second attack down there & higher up along the whole line nearly. If only we had enough ammunition for our <u>heavy</u> guns.—I would be quite easy then. Because till now we have always to stop after a week or so—to refill our stores, wh. are already much too slowly [replenished?] on account of lack of fuel! Thus we are hampered in our military operations—simply because the armies do not receive the necessary quantity of heavy shells. It is really to run up the walls from despair! For the first time I bathed yesterday in the river higher up [from] the town—the water was refreshing & rather clean, the current very strong. My sweet Lovebird, I love oo [you] & me yearns for your caress! God bless you & the girlies! I kiss you & them very tenderly & remain ever your own <u>Nicky</u>.

305a. After writing "paid," Nicholas neatly crossed out the word and wrote "payed."

No. 1153/ Telegram 169. Tsarskoe Selo> Stavka. 17 June 1916. 19.05> 20.10. To his majesty. Tenderly thank you both, my dears, for letter and post card. It was interesting at cinematograph, only I felt drowsy since it was quite stuffy in the manege [riding school]. Glorious weather. Warmly kiss and embrace [you]. Please, summon Shakhovskoi, [the acting minister of trade and industry,] he would like to tell you many things. Alix

No. 1154/ Her No. 523.   Ts.[arskoe] S[elo]. June 18th 1916.
My ever beloved One,
    Ever such tender thanks for your precious letter, my Treasure. Such heavy air, in the distance a thunderstorm happily. Finger is a little better, & I nevertheless work, but my writing is ugly.—Again good news, they say such a necessary place has been taken for the railways.—I wired to you about Shakhovskoy, because Gr.[egory]< begs you to see him, they have been thinking over things together, & he has got propositions to make, where to get things one needs, wh. you wrote about.—When you see all the ministers He [Rasputin] begs you to be very firm with them. Sht.[yurmer] is honest & excellent, [A. F.] Trepov seems rather against him.— Petrovsky is awfully happy you have sent for him—I saw him to-day. Get Sashka< another time too.— [a]
    The dentist [S. S. Kostritsky] bothers me daily, it goes so slowly on account of the inflamation [sic] of the periosteam.—Drove with A.[nia]< yesterday evening to Pavlovsk,—no, what ugly ladies one sees, its [sic] extraordinary— dresses!—Miechen< asked to take tea, I said I could not ([since first I must] have Kostritsky & later Church).—Gr.< says Keller will soon be well again.—I feel my letter is beastly dull, so sorry, my Angel.—Thats nice you bathe, so refreshing.—Am quite ramolie<.—Valia< waits to see me & another officer.—The cinema was interesting, only too long.—Have said [i.e., told] Witte ([a member of the] Supreme Council [to Aid Russian POW Families]) [that he] is to tell Iljin [Il'in] to look through Miechen's paper.[304]—Beloved, I long for you & yr. caresses. Keep well & of good cheer. I kiss you with endless, tender love. Holy Angels guard and God bless you. Ever yr. very, very   <u>Own</u>. [b]

No. 1155/ Telegram 170. Tsarskoe Selo> Stavka. 18 June 1916. 13.55> 14.35. To his majesty. Warmly thank you both. Congratulate [you] on good news. Glorious weather. There was a thunderstorm in the distance and, fortunately, it freshened the air. We all kiss and warmly embrace [you]. Alix

No. 1156. Ts.[arist] Stavka. June 18th 1916.
My own darling,
    I kiss you & thank [you] tenderly for [your] dearest letter. Again no time for writing, as old Ivanov talked like a water fall after luncheon. I am sending him on inspection to Finland. He leaves today with old Fred.[ericks], whom I said to deposit a kiss on your forehead with your permission. He seemed very pleased with this commission but was not sure how he will carry it out. It is fine & cooler thank goodness—I hope to bathe. Of course everybody here regrets that Keller has been wounded just at the time when his cavalry corps is so useful. I do hope his wound won't take long to heal. How is your poor finger getting on? Me misses you awfully, my sweet Wify. We have never been so long away fr. each other as now! Let us hope that such separation is not useless & counts somewhere! Now I must end. God bless you & the dear girlies! I kiss you fondly & passionately. Ever, beloved One, your own Nicky.

No. 1157/ Telegram 138. Stavka> Tsarskoe Selo. 18 June 1916. 19.15> 19.30. To her majesty. Fondest thanks. So happy about good news. Bathed with delight. Tender kisses from both. Niki

No. 1158/ Telegram 177. Tsarskoe Selo> Stavka. 19 June 1916. 13.00> 14.00. To his majesty. Are having lunch on balcony. Tenderly, tenderly thank you both. [I] warmly kiss [you]. May the Lord bless you [both]! Finger better. Alix

No. 1159/ Her No. 524. Ts.[arskoe] S[elo]. June 19th 1916.
My own beloved One,
    Such fond thanks for yr. sweetest letter I found after church. Shall think of you when Fr.[edericks] will give me over yr. kiss, that will make it bearable. [See Letter No. 1156.] Ah, Sweetheart,—how long this separation is! Both of you far away—but we are doing it for our country & when the news is good, one stands it better. All my very most fervent prayers will be with our beloved troops on Tuesday[, when the Brusilov offensive resumes].—God Almighty help & send them strength, courage & wisdom to have success!—We are on the balkony [sic], working, Ania< & [daughter] Anastasia [are] glueing [sic] photos—one thunderstorm after the other, but not heavy air! [a]
    Were in Church.—I wired to Konzarovsky [Kondzerovsky], to ask about freight trains [V. V.] Mekk needs. You see, my tiny supply trains fetch the wounded far in front & take them to Novoseltsy etc., w[h]ere real sanitary trains await them—our motors are not enough—& we shall arrange barracks to bind up their wounds before sending them on. Brussilov agrees, as he needs our help. In 1 day we can 4 times transport the wounded, thats good is it not?—Brinken wired my ambulance column (of my train Loman's) arrived alright, he needed

it—the first year we helped the guards & now Shcherbatchov< wanted us.—Such a comfort to know that thanks to Mekk I can help our troops so much. How its pouring!— A.[nia]< goes for the night to Finland [to visit her family.]—Now, beloved Huzy, Goodbye & God bless you. I cover you with yearning kisses and love you beyond words. Ever yr. very, very own   Sunny. [b]

No. 1160.   Ts.[arist] Stavka. June 19th 1916.
My own darling Sunny,
    I thank you heartily for your dear No. 523. I know how difficult it is to write a letter when the weather is hot. Since this morning, after strong rain, the air became much cooler, which is very agreeable. As the weather is grey and not invigorating, I will go with Aleksei at 4.o['clock] to the cinematograph, wh is really meant for soldiers—Thursday afternoons. Of course his excitement is great! Shakh.[ovskoi] asked me to see him, so I will receive him on Thursday. I wired to old Sasha K.[ozen], & received a very warm answer. The troops fight splendidly & so many gallant deeds are performed during a battle by lots [by individual soldiers?] & even companies that it is difficult to remember [them all].—Our Odessa rifles fight like heroes—but, alas! only one quarter of them remain!—Your Crimeans are preparing to pursue the austrians deep in their rear. Your Siberians are drawn back to have a well gained rest & to be refilled. In two days, with God's help & with many fresh troops the attack will be resumed! Now my Love, I must end. God bless you & the girlies! I kiss you and press you to my longing heart. Ever, my precious One, your own   Nicky.

No. 1161/ Telegram 142. Stavka> Tsarskoe Selo. 19 June 1916. 19.10> 19.48. To her majesty. Loving thanks. Rainy, cooler. Have again meals in doors. Very good cinema today. Fondest kisses. Niki

No. 1162/ Telegram 181. Tsarskoe Selo> Stavka. 20 June 1916. 17.54> 18.30. To his majesty. Tenderly thank you both, my dears. Thunderstorm, raining. Fredericks had lunch with us. Miechen< comes for tea, no longer so pleasant [to receive her]. Warmly kiss and embrace you [both]. In thoughts together, am praying especially for you in these days. Alix

No. 1163/ Her No. 525.   Ts.[arskoe] S[elo]. June 20th 1916.
My own sweet Angel dear,
    Warmest thanks for your precious letter. Again a thunderstorm & raining, the air was so heavy this morning. Frederiks< lunched & gave "the kiss" on my "grain de beaute" ["beauty spot," see Letter No. 1156]. He begs to be remembered to you. Found him fresh & looking well; will live here & go every day to town< for doklady [reports]. Rita< just heard that her brother has now been wounded and already operated [on] at Voronezh—she and her Father leave at once this evening, anxious as don't know what operation has been, I have wired to the Governor.— [a]
    I saw Sht.[yurmer], who begs to come a little later, as the Duma finishes to-day, the Conseil de l'Empire [State Council]< closes the 22-nd & then he has

to see lots of people—but wld. like to see you before all the Ministers as has several questions & things to say beforehand.[305b] Says now he will be energetic, that it was difficult until he had quite got into the work & the Duma only hampered him in everything—he has got answers to all those questions I put to him & told you about.—One thing I this time forgot to remind him about, was what Nikolai [Mikhailovich] mentioned [see Letter No. 1004c] & wh. is most essential—now already to choose people to study and work out ideas for the future congress, when the war will be ended—they must already now thoroughly prepare and think over all—speak over that please, its so urgent.—[b]

I am glad my poor Siberians can rest now.—The regiment has just sent for Korovtchuk [Korobchuk] to come, probably after their heavy losses, so he comes to say Goodbye. Have the amusement of Miechen< to tea!—& twice the dentist [S. S. Kostritsky]—such a nuisance.—Congratulate you for to-morrow feast of yr. yellow Curassiers.—Beloved, I must end now. God bless & protect you. I cover you with burning kisses. Ever yr. very, very Own. [P.S.] Do speak with Vl. Nik.< as he fidgets so much about mud for Baby<,[318] cld. one not have arranged the mud compresses at the Headquarters, because it seems cruel to take him fr. you now. [c]

305b. Sturmer arrived at Stavka on June 26, 1916, the remaining ministers the following day, June 27. Footnote in Nabokov: Alexandra, *Pis'ma imperatritsy*, II, p. 124.

No. 1164.   Ts.[arist] Stavka. June 20th 1916.
My own Lovebird,

Many fondest thanks for your dear No. 524. I am glad your finger gives you no trouble. Yesterday the weather suddenly changed, it was very windy, poured & became cool. To-day it is again fine, curious these constant changes. We went to a very interesting performance (cinema) for the soldiers, with lots of laughing. I am sending Georgi< to Archangel to look at the works [work?] there and also to wish a safe journey to our other brigade wh is going to sail around to Salonika. They leave one of these days. To-morrow I expect to see our 1st Kub.[an] sotnya [company] on its way to Tsarskoe [Selo]. That will be a joy! When they arrive home, the 4th Tver [company] will leave for the front. Last night our troops began an attack in the direction of Baranovichi, the first line of trenches has been taken. The french and english have also begun with some success! Now my beloved Treasure I must stop. God bless you & the girlies. Thank them for their letters & A[nia]< too. Tell her [Anna Vyrubova] I will write her soon. Fondly & fondly I kiss you, my beloved Wify. Ever your own old Nicky.

No. 1165/ Telegram 149. Stavka> Tsarskoe Selo. 20 June 1916. 19.49> 20.29. To her majesty. Warmest thanks [for] dear lines. Today again fine [weather]. Motored on river. Bathed. Thoughts always together. Loving kisses. Niki

---

No. 1166/ Telegram 187. Petrograd> Stavka. 21 June 1916. 14.50> 3.10. To his majesty. Tenderly thank [you] both for dear letters. Tell little lance-corporal [our son, Aleksei,] that I am sending him an allowance. [See Letter No. 1167b.] Strange weather. In thoughts and in prayers am at front. Lady Sybil Grey[306] badly wounded in face, but not dangerously so. They brought her to town;< she was in trenches, how carelessly stupid. May the Lord bless you. Warmly kiss you both. Congratulate you on festival day of your curassiers. Alix

---

306. A British nurse who served in the English hospital in Petrograd. She was wounded by a hand-grenade while at the front.

No. 1167/ Her No. 526.   Ts.[arskoe] S[elo]. June 21ˢᵗ 1916.
My own Sweetheart
   We just received [N. M.] Lavrinovsky, who came to congratulate in the name of yr. curassiers—he reminds one very much of the poor brother who died[, N. N. Lavrinovsky], only that he is fair.— All my thoughts are out at the war—God help them. The news fr. near Baranovichi was good yesterday. If there is anything particular, do let it be given over to me by the straight telegraph-telephone, [over] wh.[ich news] comes in 5 m.[inutes]—Two of my Alex.< officers are wounded at Novoseltsy,—shows, [I think, that] they have been sent down there now. [See Letter No. 1172a.] Does the guard take part yet, or not? Forgive these questions, but I am interested for my lancers & the Equipage<. [a]
   Strange sky, looks as tho' there wld. be a thunderstorm again.—Ania< had a slight heartattack yesterday, wh. frightened her & she of course thought the end was coming. I spent the evening near her bed. She will lie out in the garden & we shall take tea with her, Vict. Erast.< & Yuzik.—Fancy, poor little Lady Sybil³⁰⁶ being wounded in the face—it does seem horrid.— Miechen< was most amiable & did not say a word.³⁰⁴—Remember to wire to Toria< on Thursday for her birthday.—Baby< writes sweetly [in Russian]. "I have no more money, beg you to send an allowance"—I entreat (its me)." His notes are often too dear, precious Child.—Zhilik< finds he develops very well and that the life with many people does him much good—I too am sure of it—yet miss you both, sorely.—I suppose we better come a little later, as you wont be seeing the ministers so soon? Pss. Gedroits has not yet returned [to our hospital, from her trip]. Blessings & very tenderest kisses, my longed for Angel, fr. yr. very own old   Wify.
[P.S.]   Thats good you send Georgi< about again.— [b]

No. 1168.   Ts.[arist] Stavka. June 21ʰ 1916.
My own beloved One,
   Thanks so much for your dear letter No. 525, & for your congratulations for my cuirassiers feast. I am glad to have Petrovsky here, he at once came into our life here & is such a good & cheery boy. I like Mitia Den< too, such a quiet reasonable man & a perfect gentleman. I will speak with Vld. Nik.< about mud compresses for Baby<³¹⁸—it seems to me not difficult to arrange here. I wonder what Miechen< spoke to you about:—was it about her affairs & that paper she sent me or another subject?³⁰⁴ [a]
   Gen. [Hanbury-]Williams told me about a stupid conversation Boris has had with an English officer in the rifle's club at Tsarskoe [Selo] the other day. It seems B. had said he was sure we would fight with the english after this war & that Baghdad was not taken because they would not allow us to do it. All this is a lie. B. pretends having heard this at the Stavka, but would not name the per-

son; Buchanan and Sir [Edward] Grey have heard about this jabbering & certainly it is most unpleasant![307a] The news on the whole are good. God bless you & the dear girlies, my darling little girlie of old days. I kiss you so tenderly & so fondly & remain ever your own Nicky. [b]

307a. "The 'stupid conversation,' between Grand Duke Boris and the English Intelligence Officer, Thornhill, is circumstantially described, with the sequel, by Sir Alfred Knox (p. 429). The matter was reported to the British Foreign Office, and caused great indignation in diplomatic and military circles, though it must have been clear that it had no significance whatever. Sir Alfred Knox and Thornhill visited the Grand Duke and forced him to withdraw his allegations." (Vulliamy, p. 215n)

No. 1169/ Telegram 160. Stavka> Tsarskoe Selo. 21 June 1916. 20.14> 21.12. To her majesty. Tender thanks. Sorry for Lady Sibyl Grey.[306] Divine weather. News good. Fondest kisses. Niki

No. 1170/ Telegram 189. Tsarskoe Selo> Stavka. 22 June 1916. 13.57> 15.12. To his majesty. Tenderly thank you both. Very hot. Very glad news is better. Enchanted over lovely photographs by Derevenko. [We] embrace and warmly kiss [you]. Alix

No. 1171/ Her No. 527.								Ts.[arskoe] S[elo]. June 22nd 1916.
My own beloved One,
   Such tender thanks for yr. dear letter. I am glad Petrovsky is with you, a nice cheery young fellow wh. must brighten up yr. walks.—Get Eristov & others too [to] change about [i.e., take turns walking with you].—I find you ought to send for Boris & wash his head—how dare he say such things—can think what he likes, but to have the impertinence of speaking to an Englishman before others, is rather strong—you must have him reprimanded, he dare not behave so, the insolent fellow.[307a]—I just saw the Mufti of Orenburg[307b] & he said all sort of nice things, prayers & wishes for you.—Such heavy air to-day, rained a tiny bit too.—My little trains & transports are working hard at Vinnitsa, only the distances are great, they brought in 6 days 839 wounded 90 versts awful roads, so the horses are in a sad state & the changing of carts acted on the horses, 4 fell ill, one died, thats why I asked for light freight wagons & Konozar. [Kondzerovsky] promised them.— [a]
   Shuvaev comes to-day to speak about the Academy. [See Letters No. 1133b and 1138.] I want him to try & get us a decent big house for our hospital.—Derevenko's photos of Baby< were sweet, please ask him to send me 12 of each still, with his gun, running, learning in the tent, & you in the boat, as I have to glue albums for our exhibition & have mostly old photos.—He might send me some other nice ones he did before of Aleksei & you, please.—I shall give her [Anna Vyrubova] yr. letter, she will be wild of joy. Am just going to drive with her & [daughter] Olga,—[daughter] Tatiana is riding and the others are in their hospital. Lady Sibyl[306] feels alright one says.—Most uncomfortable writing with such a swollen, stiff finger.—So anxious for news.—Goodbye my Sunshine, my joy, my life. God bless & protect you. 1000 of tender kisses fr. yr. own old Sunny. [b]

307b. Orenburg was the third largest of the eleven Cossack hosts in the Russian Empire. Their realm stretched north from the Caspian Sea along the Ural River, then east along the Ui, an affluent of the Tobol'. (*Modern Encyclopedia of Russian and Soviet History*, XXVI, pp. 84-85) The Cossacks were Orthodox. "Mufti" were Moslem authorities on religious and legal matters. This otherwise unidentified person was probably a leader of Moslems in the Orenburg region; he was apparently devoted to the Royal Family. Writing her husband in Letter No. 1673c, Alexandra refers to the man again, this time as "your Mufti."

No. 1172.   Ts.[arist] Stavka. June 22nd 1916.
My own precious Angel,
    Ever so many thanks for your dear letter N[o.] 526. I cannot understand why two of your Alexan.< were wounded near Novoselitsy—when I know that they are along the Dvina, a little to the north of Dvinsk! [See Letters No. 1167a and 1175.] Perhaps they may have been attached for a time to another regiment—those two officers! At Baranovichi the attack develops slowly—for the same old reason that many of our commanding generals are foolish idiots, who even after two years of war cannot learn the first & simplest lessons in warfare! I cannot tell you how angry I feel with them, but I shall get to the end & know the truth. About the guard I am unable to say anything, because it is not yet quite clear where they ought to be sent. I am inclined to think it will be somewhere to the southwest; but this is only my supposition. I will let you know in time. Yesterday I received Grigorovich. Today I will see gen. Baranov about the affair of Kurlov in the Baltic provinces.[308] The ministers come here on Tuesday, after which I will be more free. God bless you & the girlies. I kiss you very tenderly, my Love, my Sunny-dear. Ever your own Nicky.

308. Gen. P. G. Kurlov was asst.-minister of the interior and police director under Stolypin; he "retired" in disgrace when his chief was assassinated in 1911. When the war broke out, the unsavory Kurlov reentered service as governor (*gradonachal'nik*) of civil administration—as opposed to military affairs—of the Baltic provinces. Kurlov was dismissed from this post on June 29 (O.S), 1916. At this point, Kurlov was an ally of Dr. Badmaev, the famous Buryat "healer," businessman and influence peddler; they worked with Rasputin, using his influence to secure war contracts. In September 1916, this "troika" secured the appointment of Protopopov as minister of the interior, with Kurlov returning to the post of asst.-min. Kurlov's reputation was so bad that Nicholas did not publish the decree appointing him. This was contrary to law; and on December 3, 1916, Kurlov was again dismissed. His memoirs are valuable but, as one would expect, must be used critically.

No. 1173/ Telegram 165. Stavka> Tsarskoe Selo. 22 June 1916. 20.28> 21.05. To her majesty. Fondest thanks. Just saw our 1aya Kubanskaya sotnia [First Kuban Company]. So interesting all they did. Lovely weather. Kiss all tenderly. Niki

No. 1174/ Telegram 195. Tsarskoe Selo> Stavka. 23 June 1916. 13.54> 14.20. To his majesty. Warmly thank you both, my dears. In thoughts always together. Weather is glorious. Must receive many, and also [the dentist, Dr.] Kostritsky. We all kiss you. May the Lord bless you. Alix

No. 1175/ Her No. 528.   Ts.[arskoe] S[elo]. June 23rd 1916.
My own Sweetheart,

Ever such tender thanks for yr. precious letter. I understand that our Generals make you wild when they act stupidly & make faults. —It was a mistake of [V. V.] Mekk's [see Letters No. 1167a and 1172a]—its 2 "Crimeans"< & not "Alexandrovtsy"<, who were wounded.—Nastinka< lunched with us as its her birthday, then I receive Belosselsky—[and then Dr. Kostritsky,] the dentist for an hour, perhaps A.[nia]< brings her brother [S. A. Taneev] & sister [Alia<] to me.—At 5½ Shtyurmer & the dentist again for 1½ hour. —There is a rumor that Sergei M.< is to be at the head of the question for provisions in the country—such rot.[314]— Sht.[yurmer] has a good idea about all that if you [i.e., you should] give it [the responsibility of supplying the cities] over to his ministery [the interior] where it has been for hundreds of years & only [a few months ago] sly Krivoshein [the former minister of agriculture] took it to himself. In the Ministery of Interior its all easier as he [Sturmer, who was both chairman of the council of ministers and minister of the interior] has all the necessary people and influence & can put a good, energetic man at the head of a special commission.[309] Now I hear as tho' Naumov keeps it, that wld. be a real pitty [sic], as he is not energetic enough & thinks too much of the Duma's opinion & the Zemstvo Union.[209] Shtyurmer thought of a Pr. [N. L.] Obolensky (Gov. of Kharkov), who could head the commission & travel about and see all & go energetically into all the details. I don't know, why he [Sturmer] comes to-day—he begged so much you should send for him before the other Ministers so as to talk over quietly with you all the questions you allowed me to tell him.[305]—Very warm again. Must end now Deary. I long for you & cover you with burning kisses. God bless & keep you.—Ever yr. very, very   Own.   [P.S.] I cover yr. letters with kisses & try to think, I hear you talk, ah, me misses you madly!

309. In late July 1916, Prince N. L. Obolensky was made president of the commission to combat high prices.

No. 1176/ Telegram 171. Stavka> Tsarskoe Selo. 23 June 1916. 20.20> 20.36. To her majesty. Fond thanks. After great heat just passed a mighty thunderstorm. News good. Very loving kisses from both. Niki

No. 1177.   Ts.[arist] Stavka. June 23rd 1916.
My own Sunny-dear,
    Warmest thanks for your sweet letter No. 527. I thought your poor finger was healed by now, but you say it [is] disturbed still! Yesterday between 6 & 7 of the evening Baby< & I went to the station & saw our dear cossacks of the 1st Kuban Sotnia [Company]. Nearly every man has been decorated. They behaved splendidly of course & a very high tribute was given them by Keller & by the commander of the 2nd Kizlyaro-Grebensky, wh. they were attached to. So many palpitating things I heard from many of them. I invited Rashpil and Skvortsov for dinner—they looked quite black amid the other guests. Probably they arrive at Ts.[arskoe] Selo on the 25th[—]it would be awfully kind if you saw them before or after the tedeum [sic] in the Fedorovsky sobor [cathedral]. From Brusilov the news are good—I hope in a day or two our armies down there, being reinforced, will be able to attack & drive the enemy further away. Our losses

from the beginning—from May 22^d are appalling—285,000 men! But the success is also great! I have spoken to V. N.< about the mud-compresses[318] & everything will be arranged easily he said.   God bless you my own beloved One.   With many thender [sic] kisses & much love to the girlies ever your own   Nicky.

No. 1178/ Her No. 529.   Ts.[arskoe] S[elo]. June 23rd 1916.
My own beloved Angel,
     It is 12½ already & I am just in bed, but I want to begin my letter whilst I still remember my conversation with Shtyurmer. The poor man was much disturbed by rumors, wh. had been brought him fr. people who had been at Moghilev, but as Rodzianko pounced upon him, he began to get quite surprised.[310]   As tho' there was to be a military dictatorship with Sergei M.[ikhailovich] at the head, that the Ministers wld. be changed etc. & Rodz. the fool came flying to ask him his opinion on the subject etc. etc. He answered that he knew nothing whatso-ever & therefore could not form any opinion. I consoled him, saying that you had written nothing to me upon this subject & that I was convinced, that you wld. never put a Grand Duke at such a place & least of all S. M., who has enough to do to try & put his business in order. We discussed it being possible that Generals think it advisable a military man being at the head of such a com-mission (food) so as to unite everything for the army and to be able to take military measures for punishments—tho' certainly the Ministers wld. be placed in an awkward position.[314]— [a]
     Then we spoke of Naumov, who again said to him, that he was tired of his work & did not feel well & wld. like to leave. (He does not agree with the Gov-ernment, looks at things quite fr. another point of view. Tho' being a loyal & charming man, he is obstinate and sticks to the ideas of Duma's, Zemstvo etc. & trusts their work better than the Governments; this is not famous [i.e., good] for a minister & makes work with him very difficult.)[311] He wished Sht.[yurmer] to tell you he wants to ask to be dismissed, but Shtyurmer protested & said he must ask himself, tho' he finds he has no right to ask for his dismission during the war—but for Sht. it would be easier without him. [b]
     Yesterday was the last sitting of the Conseil de l'Empire [State Council], Golubev presided. Nearly all the right were missing, had left some time ago as had enough of it—Kokovtsev lead [sic] the other party & is altogether an abomi-nable element.—This party intended pour la bonne bouche [as the final touch] to draw [A. F.] Trepov, Shakhovskoy & Naumov to account for things not being as they ought to [be] & to insist upon their answering to all questions. Tr. & Shakh. said they were ready with all documents, but agreed with Sht. that ques-tions might be touched [upon], wh. they were not yet ready to answer—Naumov delighted said he would with joy answer everything and that there wld. not be one question he wld. not find his explanation to—it was very unpleasant but Sht. insisted upon Golub. not allowing these questions to be touched at all—so when all came together it ended decently.— [c]
     Then another thing, S. M. twice already asked Sht. that all the fabrics [facto-ries] should be militarised [sic]—but Sht. said during the Duma it cld. not be done—& now he has found a much better way out of the thing. One fabric (of course have forgotten in wh. town) is just an example, there were strikes, so one

ordered at once all the people & workmen to be called in, & instead of sending them out to the war, make them work in the fabric as before, only being now soldiers, if they dare do anything wrong, they are judged by military judgement. This can be done smoother & with less noise than all the fabrics together—its the best example and all will tremble that their turn may come.—He [Sturmer] is becoming far more energetic now & feels a heavy load off his shoulders now that the Duma has left.—What will that odious Rodz. have spoken about—there is much chance he wont be reelected [president of the Fourth Duma], because his [Octobrist] party is furious he did the thing clumsily & asked you should shut up the Duma as they were tired—and Sht. said no, that they of their own accord must go.—I beg your pardon for bothering you with all these questions, but I wanted to warn you beforehand about Naumov['s defiance of the Duma] & what was worrying the good old man [Sturmer].—I saw dear Lili Den at A.[nia]'s this evening—just back—& our ships gone off—God guard them. She spent 2 weeks in Japan as her husband [Karl Akimovich Dehn] was sent there. At Kioto she lived in the house & very room you did. She is full of Japan & managed to see a great deal. She created much surprise in the streets & little japanese women took a fancy to her & hung on either side of this giantess. She brought me an ivory elephant and each of the girls & Baby< too, wh. I send him. Elephants are for luck & especially the number 7, so our elephants make 7, as Baby has two.—Seriozha Taneyev told lots about the war & Keller.—I had awfully much to do to-day & heaps of doklady [reports] to read. [d, e]

I had a wire fr. the Commander of my 21 S. R. [21st Siberian Rifle Regiment] about the losses of the 13-th [of June 1916]—really terrible the mass of the old officers killed & lots severely wounded. Pss. Gedroits saw them now.—Then I got at last a map & report fr. my Crimeans< of 3 weeks ago. And this evening's paper mentioned my dear regiment in the announcement fr. yr. staff—am so proud—my 2 wounded are in despair not to be there now when work is going on hard.—Now its 1 o'clock, I must put out the lights & get to sleep & rest my weary old head. I would give much to have another precious & dearly beloved one lying next to me & to feel Sunshine's caresses.— [f]

June 24-th. Sashka V.< lunches with us & says goodbye, as he returns to the front. His wife is expecting it seems. Then I have Naumov, Pr. Golitzin [N. D. Golitsyn] & Shvedov. Just finished [A. S.] Taneyev's papers and must be getting up & dress for the hospital. Sashka< lunched with us, he leaves on Sunday.—Thank you very tenderly, my Lovebird, for yr. sweetest letter. Certainly with joy shall see our dear Cossacks, was just thinking how to do it (rather shy work without my own Huzy & Baby). [g]

I am glad that the Kust.[arnyi] Komitet[312] has now understood what they must do, Naumov talked just now long with me—Witte helps him much—that man is a real pearl & is my right hand in everything, & V. P. Shneider [Barbara Schneider] gives useful advice & they want to unite it [the Kustarnyi Komitet] with the Supreme Council.[298] Excuse my finishing in pencil, no more ink in the pen & I must quickly finish (and am on the balkony [sic].) We shall interest the governors & spread it [these Kustarnie Komitety] all over the country & for the wounded and then have art & taste in it like in my School of Popular Artcraft.[312] Oh Sweety, what a lot one can do, & we women can help so much, at last all have woken up and are ready to help and work—like that we shall get to know the country, peasants, governments always better & be in <u>real union</u> with all. May God help me in that way to be of some use to you, Sweetheart! And they are glad to work with me, you helped & set all going through giving me the supreme Council & the "Infants' and Mothers Home", all goes together, all for the "people" wh. are our strength & the devoted souls of Russia.—Must end now. Cover you with yearning, endless kisses & blessings. Ever, Nicky mine, yr. very own old   <u>Wify</u>. [h]

310. As president of the Duma, Rodzyanko reported directly to the tsar. He travelled to Stavka on June 23 (O.S.), 1916, to brief Nicholas on the Duma session that had just been concluded. Sturmer arrived there three days later, on June 26. (Cf. Footnote 305.) Alexandra, *Pis'ma*, II, pp. 124n, 127n.
311. In recommending appointments to office, Alexandra is conventionally depicted as stressing devotion to her husband and Rasputin over ability, experience, etc. The empress's determination to see A. N. Naumov on the council of ministers was a striking exception to this supposed "rule." Naumov was a friend of Alexander Samarin, former director of the Holy Synod. Alexandra hated Samarin, she must have known of his ties to Naumov, but she was apparently willing to overlook them. Even here, as Naumov was about to resign, the tsarina—now all too aware of what she would call his "faults"—is judicious in assessing the man. Nicholas II relieved Naumov of office on July 21 (O.S.), 1916, and appointed him to the State Council. Note how resolutely Naumov defended his tsar's position against the Duma in the episode recounted in this letter.
312. Alexandra refers to the "Home Manufactures Committee," which encouraged home handicrafts. The empress had long sponsored "popular art," i.e., handicrafts; as we see here, she now saw them as a way to employ disabled veterans. Russia had various "Supreme Councils," each of which dealt with a particular problem caused by the war. The "Council" referred to in this letter was probably the Supreme Council to Aid the Families of Those Serving in the War.

No. 1179/ Telegram 201. Tsarskoe Selo> Stavka. 24 June 1916. 13.56> 14.47. To his majesty. Tenderly kiss you both for letters. Sashka< will have lunch with us, leaves after several days. Terribly hot. [We] warmly embrace [you]. God keep [you]. Alix

No. 1180.   Ts.[arist] Stavka. June 24th 1916.
My own beloved Sunny,
    Thank you ever so fondly for your dear letter 528. Sht.[yurmer] wrote to me about those questions & yesterday I saw Shakh.[ovskoi] & spoke longly with him. During our conversation a thunderstorm came on; it became quite dark & strong lightning fell near the town. All the electric wires began to shine, as if on fire—it was rather unheimlich [weird]! After dinner it went away & the night was quiet—only it poured vehemently. Today it is grey & uncertain, luckily cooler. Olga's Martynov[313] appeared looking well; he hopes to continue his active service—a real molodets [fine fellow]! [a]
    What nonsense one says about Sergei<, he is just right in his place now! How can one put a Grand Duke at the head of the provision question?[314] The news are good; the difficult place near Galusia, Novoselki, Kolki are being cleared by our troops wh. drive the enemy away from there, through a boggy & woody country. Thus our front become much shorter, whereas it made a long curve until now. Shcherbachev's troops [of the Seventh Army] have had a good success near their flank with Lechitsky's [Ninth Army]. Now I must say the outlook is decidedly better than it was these last 12 days. I am looking forward to

our meeting, perhaps in the beginning of July; only that you sh-ld not suffer of
the heat [by] remaining in the train! God bless you my own Sweetheart! I kiss
you & the girlies very fondly & remain ever your very own Nicky. [b]

313. Maj.-Gen. A. I. Martynov was the former commander of the Third Elizabeth Guards Regiment, the titular head of which was the tsar's oldest daughter, Olga. At this time, Martynov commanded the Second Brigade of the Fourth Cavalry Division.

No. 1181/ Telegram 180. Stavka> Tsarskoe Selo. 24 June 1916. 18.55> 19.22.
To her majesty. Many thanks from both [of us, our son and I]. Very good news.
Much cooler now. Tender kisses. Niki

No. 1182/ Telegram 207. Tsarskoe Selo> Stavka. 25 June 1916. 13.35> 14.10.
To his majesty. Thank you both very much for dear letters. Thanks be to God,
news good. Terrible heat. Old man [Fredericks] will lunch with us, then Te
Deum for the sotnya. [See No. 1173] Kiss and embrace [you]. Alix

No. 1183/ Her No. 530.   Ts.[arskoe] S[elo]. June 25th 1916.
My own beloved One,
    Thank you ever so tenderly for yr. precious letter. What colossal thunderstorm
you must have had, Zhilik< also wrote about it.— How glad I am Martinov
[Martynov] will be able to continue his military service. I enclose a wire I had
yesterday fr. Count Keller. —Thank God the news is good & you are contented.
All that lie here are craving to get back. In the "Novoye Vremya"< of June
24-th there is an article "Armor-clad" wh. describes the heroes [sic] who lies in
our hospital—only he did not like how it was written, found one spoke too much
of him & little of his officers & men who were splendid. Siro-Boyarsky<,—he
has got all the decorations one can have & one asked for him to get the 2 cross
now for entering Lutsk first and how he continued firing, fallen under the
bridge, lying on his dead comrade etc.—but they say its against the rules, he being too young (I don't understand there being rules for heroes.)— [a]
    Were at the Te Deum & then saw the splendid [First Kuban Cossack?] Sot-
nia—said good morning, congratulated them for their safe return & gave all my
hand and spoke to some with 3 crosses.— Colossal heat. Just had a long doklad
[report] with Witte, my head quite goes round. Fred.< lunched & I send you the
enclosed paper, about a feast Miechen's< committee[317] arranges. Why so colossally official—& before whom do our troops pass, before the German trophies or
Miechen? Please, say what you wish, am I to assist or not, perhaps I must, else
Miechen will play too great a part, only she has the medal. Tell me what you
wish, as soon as possible please wire, because they await an answer and I don't
know what to say, having no idea how you look upon the whole question. All
the St. George knights will be invited one says.[320]—And then later on, off into
my Angel sweet's loving arms. Ever blessing & endless kisses, my Nicky sweet,
fr. yr. very Own. [b]

No. 1184.   Ts.[arist] Stavka. June 25th 1916.
My own beloved Sunny,

So many fondest thanks for your interesting long letter. Having heard also those questions you write to me—I admire the clear way you put them on paper & give your opinion wh. is quite right to my mind. I will see old Sht.[yurmer] on Monday & calm him in that sense,[314] while spurring him in other affairs. Rodzyanko of course talked much rot, but his tone is different, it has become more beseeching—than it was last year! Among the rot he told me the greatest was about changing Sht.[yurmer] & putting Grigorovich (during the war) in his place & also changing [A. F.] Trepov & Shakhov[skoi]. Instead of the former he proposed an engineer Voskresensky (don't know him) & in the latter place, his tovarishch[,] Protopopov.[315] I think our Friend once mentioned [him]. I smiled & thanked him for the advice. [a]

The other subjects concerned the Duma & the committee where he sits that works for the supplies of the army. He looked sad & resigned; that was Alekseev's impression too. Petia< has just arrived, he wants to have a talk; he only mentioned that his father knows everything fr. himself personally.[316] This is a flower fr. our garden, a small token of huzy's love & yearning for Wify. God bless you, my precious Darling & the girlies! I kiss you all very tenderly. Ever your own Nicky. [b]

---

314. Nicholas II is referring to the rumor that Serge Michaelovich was to be appointed director of supplies. (See Letters 1175, 1178a, 1180b.)

315. This is the first reference in the "Nicky-Sunny Correspondence" to the ill-fated A. D. Protopopov (1866-1918). "Tovarishch" in Russian means *comrade* or *associate*; here it indicates Protopopov was vice-president of the Fourth Duma, Rodzyanko being the president. Both were members of the Octobrist Party. Protopopov was a wealthy landowner in Simbirsk province; he had been local marshal of the nobility and was one of Russia's prominent capitalists. As a young officer, Protopopov contracted syphilis which was now manifesting itself as insanity. The charming Protopopov led a Duma delegation that visited Russia's allies in the spring of 1916. Protopopov impressed those he met, especially King George V, who (with others) was soon urging Nicholas II to make serious use of the man's talents. (An unfortunate aspect of the trip—and one that would haunt Protopopov later—was a clandestine meeting on the way home with a German diplomat in Stockholm, the purpose of which was to discuss a separate peace.) As for "our Friend mention[ing] him on some occasion," Rasputin befriended Protopopov at the clinic of the Buryat folkhealer, Dr. Badmaev, where Protopopov underwent secret, lengthy "root and herb" treatments for syphilis. Protopopov was a member of the Duma's "progressive block"; Rodzyanko hoped that as a minister, his vice-president would bridge the gap between tsar and Duma. But as minister of the interior, Protopopov infuriated Nicholas's critics by identifying with the autocracy and its determination to rebuff those who would bring Russia closer to a parliamentary regime.

316. Peter Alexandrovich ("Petia"), prince of Ol'denburg and the husband of the tsar's sister, Olga," evidently wished to discuss his divorce. Petia's father was Alexander Petrovich ("Alek").

No. 1185/ Telegram 188. Stavka> Tsarskoe Selo. 25 June 1916. 19.46> 20.16.
To her majesty. Many thanks. Splendid weather. I hope seeing off the cossacks went well. Both [of us] tenderly embrace [you]. Niki

---

No. 1186/ Her No. 531.   Ts.[arskoe] S[elo]. June 25th 1916.
My own sweet One,

I want to begin my letter this evening. Its still uncomfortable holding the pen —the skin of my finger is all pealing [sic] fr. the spirit-compresses I wore & there are blisters, so I cant well bend my finger.—Lovy, I forgot to tell you, that I saw the Metropolitan [of Petrograd Pitirim] yesterday & we spoke over the question of Hermogen, who is in town since some days & receives reporters etc. He has no right to be here, as you never gave the permission, he received it fr. Volzhin & Metropolitan Vlad.[imir] in whose Kiev house he is living. Several papers speak about him, the "Novoye Vremja"< writes that the <u>disgraced</u> bishop will probably soon be named to Astrakhan and in the same place they say the Synod allowed him to come. Sht.[yurmer] also by chance heard of it and was displeased, so I asked the Metr. to go to Shtyurmer fr. me & beg him in his own name to tell Volzh., that he cannot trouble you upon this subject, but that he finds it not at all proper, nor the moment for Hermog. to be here as one cannot forget, why you had him sent away[155a] & that stories may arise again; especially now all such things must be avoided—they chose the moment Gr.[egory]< is away. That he lived already some days here & it was kept a secret even fr. Sht., to whom the police ought to have told it at once—is strange. I only write all this, in case you hear about it—he must be sent back to his place [of exile at the Nikolo-Ugreshsky Monastery near Moscow] & I hope Sht. told Volzh.,—you ask Sht. [a]

As long as Volzh. remains, things wont ever work, he is quite unfit for this place, [the Holy Synod, he] is a handsome man of the world & works exclusively with Vlad.[imir, the anti-Rasputin metropolitan of Kiev]. On Monday I receive Raiev (brother of the Dr., son of old Metr. Pal[l]adi)—[Raiev is] a professor I believe—an excellent man, knowing the Church by heart since his childhood. Write down to ask Sht. about him, he [Pitirim?] found him very good indeed (his looks certainly not like Volzhin and wears a wig)—you probably know him—has the kursissky [girls' school] under him, & when there were rows in all the schools & universities [during the Revolution of 1905], his girls behaved beautifully. It interests me to see him as he is so well versed in everything concerning our Church. Please, remember to speak about him to Shtyurmer. [See Letter No. 1192.]— [b]

26-th. No, what a heat! Thank you my Angel over & over again for yr. sweet letter. I am so glad my long letter did not bore you & that you agree with all.—Sandro L.< lunched—he leaves to-morrow to take over his regiment near Riga.—He has much improved, become so quiet & eyes too less nervous.—Poor O.[lga] & T.[atiana, our daughters,] have gone off to town<, A.[nia]< off to Terioki with Becker< probably on the way. The little ones[, daughters Marie and Anastasia,] are in the hospital and I shall meet them & take them for a drive.—Well Lovy, if we go on the 3-rd to town, wh. I think wld. be right as its such a big military thing—who takes the review—who says good-morning, who thanks—without you I cannot imagine how things are done.— [c]

Paul has wired for his wife [Princess Paley] not to come to him for his names day, wh. means the guard will probably move then.—Had the dentist [Dr. S. S. Kostritsky] fr. 5-7 & to-day again, odious in the heat.—Must end now—what joy if we soon meet—tell me about A[nna Vyrubova]. Can I bring her extra with me, as our Friend< wanted it so much, she too wld. bring blessing for the troops as, He says, Wify does when [she] goes there.—God bless & protect you. Kisses without end fr. yr. own old roasting   <u>Sunny</u>. [P.S.] Thanks, my Angel, for the sweet pansy. [d]

No. 1187/ Telegram 209. Tsarskoe Selo> Stavka. 26 June 1916. 7.50> 8.10.
To his majesty. All went well with [inspection of the 1st Kuban Cossack] sotnya [Company]. She [Anna Vyrubova] is going to take communion, asks forgiveness of you[129] and blessings, during the day leaves for Finland. Divine
weather. Warmly kiss you. Alix

No. 1188/ Telegram 211. Tsarskoe Selo> Stavka. 26 June 1916. 14.07> 15.05.
To his majesty. Thank you both with all my soul. Terribly hot. Sandro L.< will
have lunch with us. After service big girls< are going to town for consecration
of hospital for refugees. [We] all kiss and embrace [you]. Alix

No. 1189.   Ts.[arist] Stavka. June 26th 1916.
My sweet angel,
    Loving thanks for dear letter. I find it quite unnecessary that you or the girls
should be at the opening of the trophies exhibition.[320] Don't understand why they
make such a fuss about it. Have no time to write more, but love you deeply &
fervently. God bless you, my beloved One! Many tender kisses fr. your own
Nicky

No. 1190/ Telegram 193. Stavka> Tsarskoe Selo. 26 June 1916. 19.05> 19.41.
To her majesty. Many loving thanks. Enjoyable weather. Thoughts surround
you. Fondest kisses. Niki

No. 1191/ Telegram 216. Tsarskoe Selo> Stavka. 27 June 1916. 16.31> 17.20.
To his majesty. Warmly thank you both for dear letters. Apraxin< had lunch,
[he] just now returned from front. [We] are now going to hospital< for concert
of artillery balalaechniki [balalaika players]. Terrible heat. Kiss you both very
tenderly. May the Lord bless you. Alix

No. 1192/ Her No. 532.   Ts.[arskoe] S[elo]. June 27th 1916.
My own sweet Angel,
    I thank you very tenderly for yr. precious letter—such an intense joy to hear
from you, its my recompense after working in the hospital. Pss. Gedr.< returned
with her wounded. She worked three days in a front unit, where there was no
surgeon (just left)—made 30 operations, lots of trepanning; [she] saw my poor
dear Siberians.—Apraxin< lunched with us, told many interesting things, been
with my supply trains, was at Lutsk, Czernowitzy, returns there soon again.
Then saw Senator Krivtsov—oh, what a rottenly affected man he is with sweet
phrases—makes me sick every time. Raev made me an excellent impression.
[See Letter No. 1186b.]—Then Col. Domashevsky, my ex page, happy to have
seen you. Now my brain is utterly gaga. Going to hear the artillery balalaiki
(guitars) in our hospital—they leave Wednesday for Lutsk—then dentist[, Dr. S.
S. Kostritsky]. No brains for writing—& so awfully hot—quite ramolie<.—Once
more I ask about this tiresome trophy exhibition ceremony—why is it so official—ask Fred.< & Minister of war [Shuvaev] about it. If we dont go, does it
matter that Miechen< does all? Only wire—don't go—or—better go to it, so as to

be quite sure, please answer at once.[320]—Shall think of you much to-morrow [when you will hold a meeting of the ministers at Stavka]. Be energetic, lovy mine.—Cannot write any more. Kisses without end. Ever, Sunshine mine, yr. very own old   Girly.   [P.S.] God bless & protect you.—Hope, Baby's arm not too bad.[318]

No. 1193.   Ts.[arist] Stavka. June 27th 1916.
My darling,

So many thanks for your dear letter. You can certainly bring A.[nia]< with you, though it would have been quieter if we were alone those few days! I send you back Keller's wire—I told Alekseev to let him know his corps will remain vacant until he returns! How insupportable that Herm.[ogen] has again appeared on the horizon![155a] I will speak to Sht.[yurmer] today. To-morrow in the afternoon my sitting with the ministers [takes place]. I intend to be very disagreeable to them—& make them feel how I value Sht., & that he is their first chief. I cannot make out why & how that opening of the trophys [sic] celebration has grown into such an enormous ceremony & I continue to find it quite unnecessary you [sic] or even the girls were present. It seems to me that the Georgievsky committee of Misha's<[317] are doing it all for their own glorification. I got a wire from their vice-pred. sen. [vice-president of the Senate] Dobrovolsky (Misha's friend) letting me know about the date of the opening. How good it would be if you came [here] between the 3[d] and 11th July! That [the 11th] is [daughter] Olga's namesday[sic]. To-morrow Baby< begins mud comp[ress treatments]. Mr. Gilliard hopes to get a month's leave, the poor man is really tired.[318] God bless you and the girlies. With many tender kisses, my own sweet Sunny. Ever your own   Nicky.

317. The Knights of Saint George was a rightest, "patriotic" organization. "Misha" here refers to "Miechen," Maria Pavlovna.

318. Gilliard felt the tsarevich's presence at Stavka was dangerous. The tutor's protests were in vain, so he travelled to Petrograd—pleading the need for a "leave"—to confront Alexandra directly. The empress understood Gilliard's concerns, but she thought her son should remain at headquarters where contact with people would help him overcome the shyness Nicholas II suffered. (see Footnote in Nabokov: Alexandra, *Pis'ma imperatritsy*, II, p. 134.) The "mud packs" (Letter No. 1192 indicates they were applied to his arm) suggest the dangers Aleksei faced as a hemophiliac.

No. 1194/ Telegram 197. Stavka> Tsarskoe Selo. 27 June 1916. 20.20> 20.41. To her majesty. Loving thanks. Splendid weather. Just received Shtyurmer. News good. Tender kisses. Niki

---

No. 1195/ Telegram 281. Tsarskoe Selo> Stavka. 28 June 1916. 14.56> 15.32. To his majesty. Tenderly thank [you] for dear letters. Thought much about you to-day. Hope you are not very tired. Terrible heat, rather small thunderstorm in distance. [We] all kiss and embrace you. Tell Zhilik that he may, of course, take a leave which he fully deserves.[318] Alix

---

No. 1196/ Her No. 533.   Ts.[arskoe] S[elo]. June 28th 1916.
My own beloved Angel,

Such tender thanks for yr. very dear letter. Poor one, so sad you have to see all those Ministers in this great heat.—In the distance there is a thunderstorm. We had awfully much to do in the hospital, I did the 11 new ones, who are very heavily wounded. The dentist[, Dr. S. S. Kostritsky,] every day is madning [sic]—I hope to finish to-morrow. Lili< & Titi< came to tea and then they leave for the country. A.[nia]< sends you both radishes, wh. her wounded planted. Hermog.[en] has left [Petrograd].—Certainly Zhilik<[318] must have a rest—does he think Mr. Gibbs ought to go in his stead not for lessons, but to read more to Baby< & to give him the chance of speaking more English. Please, ask him, & if he thinks it good, he can tell, write it to Peter Vas.<, [one of Aleksei's other tutors,] or should Peter Vas. come [to Stavka] for a time, please, speak it over with Zhilik. It will be lovely to come there—Becker< will be about the 3-rd, so as to be the 11-th with you. I must end now. Goodbye my love, my Sweetheart, whom I yearn after. God bless & protect you. Endless kisses and passionately loving ones fr. yr. very   Own.

No. 1197.   Ts.[arist] Stavka. June 28th 1916.
My own dear Sunny,
   Thanks very fondly for your letter. Yesterday began & today continues a great fidget for me.—I saw Sht.[yurmer] we talked about everything.—Well! Then Grigorovich with Rusin till 11.o in the evening. Today arrived the others—my sitting [with the ministers] begins at 6.o till dinner. Then several want to be received—shall have to put them off till to-morrow! Have alas! no more time! God bless you my Angel, my own beloved girly. I kiss and love you endlessly. Ever your Own.

No. 1198/ Telegram 199. Stavka> Tsarskoe Selo. 28 June 1916. 20.20> 20.49. To her majesty. Tender thanks for letter. Just got up from sitting, [it went off] alright [sic]. Lovely weather. Fondest kisses. Niki

No. 1199/ Her No. 534.   Ts.[arskoe] S[elo]. June 29th 1916.
My own Sweetheart,
   Warmest thanks for yr. dear letter. Glad, all went off well at the sitting, judging by yr. wire—it was dear of you still having written. We went to the hospital< Church for service & then did our work. Isa< lunched—now a Colonel comes to her about this odious holiday [i.e., display of German trophies][320]—we take tea at Miechens< & she is sure to speak about it too—I wont answer till yr. wired answer comes. I have told I.[sa]< to ask details—because, if Miechen intends playing a part, its better we 5 go—because of the St. George knights[317] who will all be there. Think it over again with Fred.< Will you? Its only because of Miechen. Am as usual in a beastly hurry, as people are waiting to be received. [a]
   I send you a paper about Zhuk; Ania< & Loman very much beg for him & he deserves this—write a resolution on it, & I can send it then to be done quicker. Excuse bothering, but they wanted Ania to ask for him.—Becker< came to [daughter] Tatiana & me to-day, so kind before time, will be all the better for

journey.—A.[nia] will remain more in the train, not appear at meals—so we shall have time to be more to ourselves—she for nothing wishes to disturb, and never asked—our Fr.'s< wanted [i.e., requested it].—Lovely weather. Must end. I hold you tightly in my loving arms & cover you with kisses. God bless & protect you yr. very own old Sunny. [b]

No. 1200/ Telegram 232. Tsarskoe Selo> Stavka. 29 June 1916. 18.56> 19.20. To his majesty.   Tenderly, tenderly thank you both, my dears. Wonderful weather, after evening rain fresher. Had tea at Miechen's<. In morning were at hospital< church. Warmly kiss and embrace [you]. Alix

No. 1201/ Telegram 210. Stavka> Tsarskoe Selo. 29 June 1916. 18.57> 19.42. To her majesty. Fondest thanks. Had to receive three ministers to day and could not write therefore. Delicious weather. All well. Tenderest kisses from both. Niki

No. 1202/ Telegram 235. Tsarskoe Selo> Stavka. 30 June 1916. 14.52> 15.20. To his majesty. Georgi< had lunch with us, [he] will be with you on Saturday. Thank Aleksei for letter. Understand that you are not able to write. How will this silly holiday come off? I only fear that [people] may think I do not want to be there because of the trophies, and she [Miechen<, sponsor of the event] will play an important role. Ask you, telegraph what I am to do, darling.[320] We all kiss you and embrace [you]. Alix

No. 1203/ Her No. 535.   Ts.[arskoe] S[elo]. June 30th 1916.
My own Angel dear,
    We had Georgi< to lunch—he will be with you on Saturday. Aunt Olga< goes for 10 days to Kiev,—Motherdear< invited her—soon Nicky & Andrea[319] arrive.—Had much work this morning, operated upon poor Taube's leg again.—Said goodbye to our 5 Cossack officers.   Shall be to-morrow at 4 at the Te Deum before the Fed.[orovsky] Sob.[or, i.e., Cathedral]—the men on horseback, as they go straight fr. there to the train.—Excuse my always bothering you about that. beastly feast on Sunday, but I fear one may think I don't want to come because of German trophies [which will be on display].—Miechen you see goes[320]—& one has gathered over 1000 St. George's cavaliers[317] to be present.—Nice weather.—I finish with the dentist[, Dr. S. S. Kostritsky,] at last this evening.—Took tea at Miechens yesterday—most amiable, & touched absolutely no [difficult] subjects.—God grant soon, next week we shall be together—too lovely—not leave here before the 5-th—for how many days can we remain. I cover you with yearning kisses & boundless love. Beg yr. pardon for the smudges, the wind blew the page too—God bless & protect you—yr. very own old Wify.

319. Olga Constantinovna ("Aunt Olga") was the daughter of g.p. Constantine Nicholaevich and the widow of King George I of Greece. Her sons were Nicholas ("Nicky") and Andrew ("Andrea").
320. Alexandra was aware, as we see here, that many thought she was a German sympathizer. This was untrue, of course, but in this instance popular opinion was more important than the truth. The situation was complicated for the empress by the fact that g.p. Maria Pavlovna the Elder

("Miechen") organized and expected to dominate the event discussed here. Alexandra stews over the matter in Letters No. 1183b, 1189, 1192, 1193, 1199a and 1202. She *did* pester her husband with the matter, and his irritation shows in Letters No. 1189 and 1193. Nicholas resolved the issue by canceling the parade, an act for which his wife was grateful: see Letters No. 1205 and 1206.

No. 1204.   Ts.[arist] Stavka. June 30th 1916.
My own precious One,
   Tenderest thanks for your two dearest letters. I could not possibly write to you as [I] was walking on [the top of] my head on account of all those ministers, who each wanted to see me after the sitting. Now at least I have done with them! [A. N.] Grabbe beggs [sic] you to order Zborovsky to be sent now to the Crimea to restore his health.[321] If it were possible for him to live in the escort's barracks of Livadia—he might take his old mother & sisters with him!—My head is still boiling with difficult questions I have thought about or heard of when the ministers were here & it is rather difficult to put my ideas to rights. Your soon coming here makes everything better for me. Babykins< constantly asks me the day of your arrival & also whether you will come for his birthday [July 30 O.S.]? He stands the mud compr[esses][318] very well & is just as cheery as usual. Vl. Nik.< proposed me to take iodine, wh. I do & neither feel its disagreeable results. The weather is good, not hot & the nights deliciously cool happily. I bathe every day. Igor< leaves for a month for Ostashevo. Petrovsky's turn [for a leave] has also come too; instead of them will arrive Daragan & Genritsi (dragoon). God bless you & the girlies. I kiss you and them tenderly. Give A.[nia]< my love & thank her for her radishes [which were grown by the patients at her hospital]. Ever, my beloved Sunny, your very own Nicky.

   321. V. E. Zborovsky ("Vikt. Erast.") was a Cossack lieutenant in Her Majesty's Own Convoy, and as such was subject to her orders.

No. 1205/ Telegram 217. Stavka> Tsarskoe Selo. 30 June 1916. 20.12> 20.35. To her majesty. Thanks for letter and [daughter] Olga for photo. Today interesting French cinematograph. Fine weather, cooler. [You] need not go, have ordered no troops to be present.[320] Both kiss [you] tenderly. Niki

No. 1206/ Telegram 237. Tsarskoe Selo> Stavka. 30 June 1916. 21.10> 21.50. To his majesty. Thank you for telegram. Am glad [I] do not have to go and that you cancelled parade.[320] Strong rain fell, now colder. Sleep peacefully. Tenderly kiss [you]. Alix

No. 1207/ Telegram 1. Tsarskoe Selo> Stavka. 1 July 1916. 16.03>16.30. To his majesty. Warmly thank [you] both. Zhilik<[318] will have lunch with us. Now going to Te Deum for [First Kuban Cossack] sotnya [Company] in front of the Big Palace< since they are on horses. Sad and difficult without you. Tenderly kiss you [both], my dears. Alix

No. 1208/ Her No. 536.   Ts.[arskoe] S[elo]. July 1st 1916.
My own Darling,

Such endless thanks for yr. dear letter. Zhilik<[318] will dine with us & then shall get news of you all.—Can well imagine how tired yr. poor head must be fr. all the hard work—so difficult to remember always everything. I have told [daughter] Marie to speak with Zborovsky & then we can arrange all—he had wanted to go to the Caucasus, I know.[321]—I am glad you take iodine again, its so good for you from time to time.—Are going to bid our Company goodbye—there is the Te Deum before the big palace (so frightening all that without you). Am glad that need not go on Sunday, & that you have ordered off the military part of the feast.[320]—Now we have a little boy of 8 in the hospital<, a nephew of Jediga-rov<, he lies with the officers, as they begged to have him with them & one big young hero was laying puzzles with him—"You needn't!!" [which is the name of the puzzle game.]—Taube is getting on nicely, tho' the leg hurts very much.—Weather changeable to-day.—Ania< sends you both radishes again.—Am sure Baby must feel sad without Zhilik,—that man is a pearl.— How nice I shall see then Daragan.—I also had a wire fr. Gr[egory]<. Had letters fr. Victoria< & Louise<.—The red cross forbids the Germ. & Austr. sisters [i.e., nurses] fr. in-specting the prisoners on account of the loss of the second red cross ship—I find it foolish and wont help a bit.—Sweetheart, goodbye now. I cover you with endless, burning kisses. God bless & protect you. Ever yr. own old Sunny. [P.S.] Old Lolo D.< will lunch with us to-morrow.

No. 1209.   Ts.[arist] S[tavka]. July 1st 1916.
My own Sweetheart,
    Thank you so much for your dear No. 535. How nice you go to the molebin [Te Deum] & say good-bye to our cossacks. Today my uryadnik [orderly] Muravetsky has left me and a new one with four crosses has taken his place. He is called Svetlichny. The first one was such an excellent fellow. Baby< liked him—he used to play funny tricks in the water while bathing, with Nagorny[265] and spoke little russian [i.e., Ukrainian] to Igor. I send you lots of photos [Dr.] Derevenko made, he begs you to take whichever you like. The cinema we saw yesterday was interesting, it represented Verdun. I said the families of the mili-tary could come & so all the side boxes were filled with ladies & children, the chairs were occupied by the husbands & all the top by the soldiers as usual. The air was not as good as when the ladies were absent.—I wonder why? Now I must end. Daragan has arrived for 10 days. God bless you my precious Sunny-dear. I kiss you & the girlies very tenderly. Ever your very own Nicky.

No. 1210/ Telegram 3. Stavka> Tsarskoe Selo. 1 July 1916. 19.35> 20.18. To her majesty. Fondest thanks. Am sure it went off well, your saying goodbye. Shall see them [First Kuban Cossack Company] here. Atlast [sic] am free. Kisses from both. Niki

No. 1211/ Telegram 7. Tsarskoe Selo> Stavka. 2 July 1916. 14.57> 15.20. To his majesty. Tenderly thank you both. Terrible thunderstorm. Lolo< and Valia< had lunch with us. Now cinematograph for wounded. Please permit me to issue in your name permission for young cavalry guardsman Bezobrazov to continue leave for 2 months to regain his health. He has still not yet entirely recovered but his leave has ended and he must return to [his] regiment; your permission will save him. He is here, so telegraph me your decision. Kiss and embrace [you]. Alix

No. 1212.   Ts.[arist] Stavka. July 2ᵈ 1916.
My precious wify,
    Many fondest thanks for your dear No. 536. As usual I am writing after lunch & have come up fr. the garden with wet sleeves & boots, as Aleksei made us wet at the fountain. That is his favourite little game together with Solovoi [Solo-vovo], the french gen. Janin, Petrovsky, gen. [Hanbury-]Williams & the japa-nese. Frightful excitement & laughter prevails—sometimes other guests also take part—I look after the order & see that things do not go too far!! I hope you will see this game when you come! Now it is so warm one dries in an instant. Solovoi is such a gay kind fellow & Baby< is very fond of him. Georgii< has arrived, thanks for messages through him. He is interesting about Arkhangel'sk & goes so well into everything. [a]
    Old Sht.[yurmer] has already asked to see me, so will receive him to-morrow Sunday, probably he brings me the scheme worked out of the principal question of our sitting the other day. Now there is a lull in the battle wh. will be resumed I think about the 7th & the guards are also taking part, because it is time to tear the enemy's lines through & take Kovel.[322] Then you being here—I shall be still happier! God bless you and the girlies! I kiss you passionately. Ever, my sweet Love, your own Nicky. [b]

322. "Ludendorff wrote: 'On 16th July the Russians, in enormous force, poured out from the Riga bridge-head ... and gained ground at once. We went through a terrible time until the crisis here was overcome. ... These battles were not yet over at the end of July, when there were some indications that the attacks at Baranovichi and along the whole course of the Stockod would be resumed. We awaited these with a sinking heart[,] ... our nerves were strung to the highest pitch' (pp. 226-7)." (Vulliamy, p. 226n)

No. 1213/ Telegram 5. Stavka> Tsarskoe Selo. 2 July 1916. 19.06> 19.43. To her majesty. Very fondest thanks. Of course young Bezobrazov may look after his health for two months more. Also thunderstorm but weak. Tender kisses from both. Niki

No. 1214/ Her No. 537.   Ts.[arskoe] S[elo]. July 2ⁿᵈ 1916.
My own Lovebird,
    I am writing in my room by lamplight, as there is a colossal thunderstorm & rain—terrible loud claps as tho' it had struck near by. Pss. Lolo< & Valia< lunched—he will bring you this letter.— Very tenderest thanks to you, Angel dear, for your beloved letter. The photos [Dr.] Derev.[enko] did are perfectly delight-ful, especially of you both my sweet Darlings. How big Alexei [sic] has grown, no more babies! Ah, how I miss you both!! The hospital< is my real saving & consolation. We have many heavy wounded, daily operations and much work we want to get through before leaving. The "Kakham"[287] has come & spent the evening at Ania's yesterday—to-day she has asked me to spend the evening with

her & him and to hear him tell pretty stories.—There, its clearing up.—One begged me to ask for Bezobrazov (chevalier garde) as the boy is still ill, but his term is up & he wld. have to leave the regiment unless I get yr. order that he may remain still 2 months, then they keep him in the regiment.—Now my Sunshine, Goodbye & God bless & protect you.—I cover you with very tenderest & warmest kisses. Ever, Nicky mine, yr. very <u>Own</u>.

No. 1215/ Telegram 10. Tsarskoe Selo> Stavka. 3 July 1916. 15.00> 15.28. To his majesty. Heartily thank you both, my dears. Beautiful weather. ... [The ellipsis is in Sergeev's text.] Hope to be with you on Thursday during the afternoon, what joy! [We] attended Mass at hospital< church. Tenderly kiss and embrace [you]. Alix

---

No. 1216/ Her No. 538.   Ts.[arskoe] S[elo]. July 3rd 1916.
My own beloved Angel,

Ever such tender thanks for yr. sweetest letter.—God grant we shall be together by Thursday after luncheon. Wont that be too lovely, at last again together after 7 long, long, weeks?—We bring P. V. Petr.[ov, one of Aleksei's tutors] with us.—So the guard moves! N.P.< wrote that they were just going off, probably to Lutsk. So we shall be with you those great days [when the Brusilov offensive will resume]—God almighty help our troops. Gr.[egory]< said if I went to you, God wld. again send His blessing to the army—may it be so.—St.[aff]-Cap.[tain] Liubimov [Lyubimov], com.[mander] of Baby's< Company of the [89th] Belom.[orsky] Regiment soon leaves our hospital<, has never seen Alexei [sic], so we told him to pass by the Headquarters [and] ask to see Baby through Valia<—he is such a nice little man. [a]

There is another I wish you could see—our hero, I wrote to you already once about him of the <u>armoured machine-gun cars</u>—he has never seen you—thats why came to our hospital to see us at least—wld. be nice if he cld. also have passed the Headquarters (26 years old st.[aff]-cap.[tain], father [Col. V. A. Syroboyarsky] was in the Jap. war; commanded at Poltava the artillery & died there just before this war began)[.]—[The young man I am referring to here, A. V.] Siro-Boyarsky<, [has the] St. George's sword, [also the St. George's] cross [and] all [the decorations] one can have, three times already wounded. May they pass like that, can I tell him anything (they never asked)—he leaves now for a week to his mother at Poltava & then returns to SPB [St. Petersburg] for business;—if they come to M[ogilev], whom must he ask, so as to be presented? One wants to give pleasure to such brave fellows, and you will listen with interest to all his [i.e., he] tells.— [b]

Glorious weather. Ania< has gone to Finland for the night. Miechen< is in town< feasting with [i.e., showing] her medal.—I spent yesterday evening at Ania's with the "Hakham"!! [See Letter No. 1214 and Footnote 287.] Very clever, pleasant man—she [Anna Vyrubova] has quite melted.—Now must go to the big palace< (such a bore)!—S. P. Feod.[orov]< will be at the Headquarters about July 15. Every blessing & 1000 kisses fr. yr. own old <u>Wify</u>. [P.S.] Shall come to you & leave Becker< behind! [c]

No. 1217.   Ts.[arist] Stavka. July 3^d 1916.
My own beloved Sunny,
   Ever so many thanks for your dear letter. V. Dolg.[oruky] arrived & with the
same train passed A.[unt] Olga< on her way to Kiev. I could not see her as I
was occupied at the staff. Again no time! Good news from the Caucasus.—Oh!
how happy I am, Baby< too, that soon we will meet. God bless you my darling
Wify! Many burning & loving kisses from your own ever devoted old   Nicky

---

No. 1218/ Telegram 16. Stavka> Tsarskoe Selo. 3 July 1916. 20.17> 20.35.
To her majesty. Tender thanks. What joy on Thursday! Divine weather. Loving
kisses from both. Niki

No. 1219/ Telegram 18. Tsarskoe Selo> Stavka. 4 July 1916. 15.36> 16.23.
To his majesty. Warmly thank you both. Petia< had lunch with us. Was thunderstorm, now overcast, and breeze fresher. Tenderly kiss and embrace [you].
Am going to hospital<. Am bringing Silaev along since it is better that he personally report to you on doctors' conclusion concerning his health. Alix

---

No. 1220/ Her No. 539.   Ts.[arskoe] S[elo]. July 4th 1916
My own Sweetheart,
   Fondest thanks for yr. precious letter. Petia lunched & send[s] his very tenderest love & good wishes for success.—There was a thunderstorm.—Now we are
bringing Silaev with us—you will think me crazy, but I thought it best he should
present himself to you & tell you all the details about the Dr's opinion, as it
needs a long treatment still & he does not know what to do about the regiment,
poor man. Writing up and down takes so long, & like this it is simplest you talk
it over together & give him yr. orders.—The operation[,] gryzha [hernial rupture]
of Yedigarov's< 8 year old nephew[,] went off well—now I am going to the hos-
pital< to see the men, as many of my 21-st [Siberian Rifle] reg. have been
brought.—Ania's< Raduta (refugee, nurse) marries her sanitary & they have a
feast in the hospital.—There is nothing you wish me to bring you? Shurik< &
Vict. Er.< take tea with us.—Now must end. Cover you with tender kisses &
blessings. Ever yr. very, very Own. [P.S.] To you & Baby< each a cornflower!
Saw Vera Volkova who came for a few weeks and now returns to England.

No. 1221.   Ts.[arist] Stavka. July 4th 1916.
My own tenderly beloved One,
   Many thanks for your dear long letter. Today Nikolai Mikh. [ailovich] arrived
to talk over questions concerning the Imper.[ial] Historical Soc.[iety] & also
about his last trip on the northern rivers. Shall certainly receive any brave officer you may intend sending to me. They must ask through the staff. I continually see officers, colonels & generals who come from the front & invite them to
lunch or dinner. Many of those who are put out of their places come here with
complaints & their affairs are looked through. Mogilev is like an enormous hotel where people pass through & one always sees any amount of different sorts
of types. The weather is delicious[—]one would like to sit in the water the whole

day. While Aleksei paddles—I bathe near him, also Kira<, Petrovsky, my cossack[s] & the sailors. This morning the 4$^{\text{aya[th]}}$ sotnia [company] arrived & passed the house. I look leave of them, though they start really to-morrow morning. Such a lot of good acquaintances!—God bless you & your journey! This is my last letter. I kiss you & the girlies very tenderly & wait for you with yearning love. Ever, Sunny-mine, your own Nicky.

No. 1222/ Telegram 22. Tsarskoe Selo> Stavka. 5 July 1916. 14.14> 14.40. To his majesty. Warmly thank you both. Terrible heat. We all tenderly kiss you [both]. May the Lord bless you. Alix

No. 1223/ Telegram 20. Stavka> Tsarskoe Selo. 5 July 1916. 14.45> 15.13. To her majesty. Fond thanks [for] dear letters [and] cornflowers. Very hot. Both excited before your arrival. Loving kisses to all. Niki

No. 1224/ Her No. 540.   Ts.[arskoe] S[elo]. July 5th 1916.
My very Own,
    Such loving thanks for yr. last dear letter. To-day 7 weeks that we separated—it was a Tuesday. The heat is tremendous, I am perspiring & broiling.—Thanks so much about the officers, they will be wild with joy, all the more so, because they did not dare ask;—they will come whilst we are there so as to feel less shy.—Groups were taken in the hospital to-day.—Nastinka< has fallen ill, so we bring Isa<, who is overjoyed.—Shtyurmer comes to-day, & [there are] still others [for me] to receive.—What joy to feel I shall soon have you in my loving old arms again.—Excuse rotten letter, but am ramolie< & in a haste.—God bless & protect you. I cover you with kisses. Ever yr. very own old   Sunny.   [P.S.] Dediulin [A. N. Dedyulin] came to say goodbye, the regiment has sent for him.
No. 1225/ Telegram 30. Tosno> Stavka. 6 July 1916. 12.45> 13.45. To his majesty. Are travelling well. Terribly hot. As we are arriving earlier, would you not like for us to have lunch with Aleksei? [We] warmly kiss you both. Alix

No. 1226/ Telegram 26 in Russian. Stavka> Bologoe. 6 July 1916. 14.49> 15.08. To her majesty. Thank you. [We are] very glad to have lunch with you. [We] await your arrival impatiently. [We] warmly embrace [you] all. Niki

No. 1227/ Her No. 541[A].   Moghilev. 12 July 1916.
Lovy my Angel,
    I have asked Ania to drop these papers for you to give Alekseev to read and then to return me the doklad [Report], the telegram I dont need as have another. What rain! Do hope my Baby< is alright [sic], they let know he woke up and went to sleep again, hope the night was good—do say they are to let me know as soon as he wakes up, the temp.[erature,] etc.[—]then I can came up earlier to sit with him. I hope its nothing and a good sleep will set the sweet child to rights again.—I cover you both with kisses yr. own old   Wify.

Note.- This seems to have been a message the empress left her husband after he and their son had retired to their bedroom. Her next letter duplicates the number "541"; I distinguish the two as "[A]" and "[B]." Letter No. 1233 suggests that 541[B] was a farewell note the empress left for Nicholas to read after she had left Mogilev.

No. 1228/ Her No. 541[B].   Ts.[arist] Stavka. July 12th 1916.
My own Beloved,
    Again goodbye, but thank God not for long—but nevertheless I hate leaving
you & Sunbeam<. Its so lonely without you & knowing yr. hard work & dreary
life, makes it very sad. Thanks my Angel, for having let me be with you, for
having sent for us, it was a joy and gives strength again to continue. We have
enjoyed our holiday and go now back to our work. Thursday morning straight
to perevyazki [dressings] & then to receive the German & Austrian Sisters [i.e.,
nurses] (I don't look forward to that).—She [Anna Vyrubova] has wired to Our
Friend< about the weather & I hope God will bless the front with Sunshine.
Please, wire this evening how Tiny's< temp.[erature] is & to-morrow morning.
We reach Ts.[arskoe] S.[elo] to-morrow evening at 8.—Farewell, my Sunshine,
my Love. I fear our visit was too fidgeting for you, so much running about &
still yr. work to be done. I shall remember every caress with yearned longing.
God bless & protect you, give you strength, courage, success. I cover you with
endless, burning kisses. Ever yr. very, very   Own.

No. 1229/ Telegram 157 in Russian. Stavka> Smolensk Al. 12 July 1916.
20.19> 21.25. To her majesty. Am touched, grateful for the letter. General condition [of our son[318] is] better, temp. 36.6. [Here it is] very sad and empty. Have
a good trip. [We] both warmly embrace [you]. Niki

No. 1230/ Telegram 0565. Orsha train station> Stavka. 12 July 1916. 20.30>
21.10. To his majesty. Hope [Aleksei's] temperature is normal. [We] kiss you
both warmly. [I] remember cosy days [we just enjoyed]. Sleep well, the Lord be
with you. Alix

No. 1231/ Telegram 159 in Russian. Stavka> Likhoslavl. 13 July 1916. 10.27>
11.05. To her majesty. [Aleksei] slept wonderfully. Completely healthy. Temp.
36.1. Rain has stopped, warmer. [We] remember and embrace [you]. Niki

No. 1232/ Telegram 87. Likhoslavl> Stavka. 13 July 1916. 11.23> 12.25. To
his majesty. Are travelling well, weather marvellous [sic], not hot. [I] remember
everything about you [both]. [We are] all embroidering shirts. [We] warmly kiss
you both. Greetings to all. Alix

No. 1233.   Ts.[arist] Stavka. July 13th 1916.
My own beloved,
    Tenderest thanks for your two dear letters—the morning note fr. the train wh. I
only read in the afternoon & the goodbye letter that Baby< gave me during
Sht.[yurmer]'s doklad [report]. Thank God he is quite well, slept very soundly
near his old father & is full of life & energy as usual. It is for me to thank you,
my Darling, for coming here all that way with our girlies & bringing here life &
sunshine notwithstanding the rainy weather. I am afraid that you felt tired from

the constant running up & down & to & fro. Of course, as usual, I did not tell you half the things I had intended to say, because when we meet after a long separation, somehow I get stupidly shy & sit & gaze at you—wh. already is a joy for me! I am looking so much forward to our meeting before A.[nia]'s< birthday! When we drove back fr. the station Baby was thinking aloud & suddenly said "opyat' odin" ["alone again"]! Very short & clear! Now we will steam up the river to his favourite beach with a comparatively small company. The weather is calm & half cloudy—very mild. God bless you my beloved Sunny & the girlies! Ever so many tender kisses from your old loving devoted & adoring old huzy Nicky

No. 1234/ Telegram 160. Stavka> Tsarskoe Selo. 13 July 1916. 19.45> 20.20. To her majesty. Hope [you] arrived well. We both miss you awfully. God bless you. Sleep well. Niki

No. 1235/ Telegram 40. Tsarskoe Selo> Stavka. 13 July 1916. 20.45> 21.25. To his majesty. [We] arrived successfully. Was very hot, now marvellous [sic] breeze. I will rest on balcony. In thoughts with you, my dears. [I] miss [you] terribly. [I] warmly kiss you. Sleep well. Alix

No. 1236./ Telegram 41. Tsarskoe Selo> Stavka. 14 July 1916. 13.37> 15.08. To his majesty. Tenderly thank you for both dear letters. What joy to receive them as [I am] very lonely without you [both]. Worked a lot at hospital<. Wonderful weather. Pleasant little breeze. We all warmly kiss you [both]. God keep you. What news? Alix

No. 1237/ Her No. 542.   Ts.[arskoe] S[elo].   July 14th 1916.
My own beloved, precious One,
    Such endless joy to receive yr. dear letter & I thank you for it with all my fondly loving old heart. Sweetums, every tender word of yours is my greatest, deepest joy & I carry it deep in my heart and live by it. Seems a dream, our journey. Had to relate heaps in the hospital<, all full of interest & wanting to know everything.—The weather is very warm & a divine breeze, so that we are going for a drive.   Just receive[d] 6 German & 5 Austrian sisters [i.e., nurses]—real ladies, nothing like our bad selection, wh. was sent.—They brought me letters fr. home & Irene[,] & all send you their love. You must excuse a stupid letter, but am slightly cretinised.—Went early to bed & enjoyed a bath.—Lovy, do say about Sukhomlinov being let home, the Drs. fear he will go mad if kept shut up any longer—do this act of kindness of your own sweet self.—My Siberians< were so happy over Sergeev's telegr. that they had succeeded again.—I am so glad you took us everywhere, now we know how & where you spend your afternoons.—Beloved Angel, now Goodbye & God bless & keep you.—I cover you with endless burning kisses & live in the past. Ever yr. very, very   Own.

No. 1238.   Ts.[arist] Stavka. July 14th 1916.

My own darling Love,

Today the train with Nicky is over three hours late, something happened to the engine. So I will see him before dinner. The weather is fine & warm. I intend sending Baby< down the river & going myself round by motor & walking the last bit of the road across both long bridges, getting into the boat near that white villa you saw & joining Baby at his place. Next time you are here I hope to take you there, as it is a new drive!—In the Caucasus the operations are very successful. To-morrow begins our second attack along Brusiloff's whole front;[323a] the guard pushing toward Kovel![291] God bless them & help our brave troops! I can't help feeling nervous[323b] before the moment has come; after the beginning a sort of calm arrives & a great impatience to have news as quick as possible.—Brusilov is an interesting man & talks about everything cleverly & rightly. His ideas about the war are also very sound. Our walks & teas are the most convenient times for these conversations.—Beloved One, please tell [daughter] Tatiana to send me a blue box with my writing paper of this sheet's shape. Now I must end! God bless you & the girlies! Many tender kisses to you, my own Sunny, & to them & A[nia]<. Ever your own Nicky.

323a. "Our second offensive" refers to the brilliant advance of the Russian 11th Army under Gen. Sakharov. (Vulliamy, p. 229n)

323b. Nicholas injects humor into his letter at this point. His penmanship becomes odd, the letters are oversized and awkwardly drawn, as if he were *n e r v o u s* in writing this one, single word.

No. 1239/ Telegram 163. Stavka> Tsarskoe Selo. 14 July 1916. 19.12> 19.49. To her majesty. Loving thanks [for] wire. Also glorious weather. Both [of us are] well. Tender kisses. Niki

No. 1240/ Telegram 56. Tsarskoe Selo> Stavka. 15 July 1916. 13.50> 14.30. To his majesty. [We] warmly kiss you both. Tenderly thank you for dear letters. Beautiful weather. In thoughts and prayers am with you especially in these days and with our dear troops. Alix

No. 1241/ Her No. 543.   Ts.[arskoe] S[elo]. July 15th 1916.

My own beloved Darling,

Very fondest thanks for yr. dear letter.—All my thoughts & prayers are with you and our dear troops—God help & send success—it will be very hard for them I fear, [so I ask:] if you get news—let me know, feel so anxious.—Weather fine, not too hot & now even grey, in the evening there were only 9 degrees.—To-morrow is Ania's< birthday, please wire to her, if in the evening then to Terioki, Estate of Mikhailov. She leaves for there at 4 to-morrow & spends the night with her parents[, A. S. and Nadezhda Taneev]. I saw Maximovich< this morning—I am glad the old man [Fredericks] goes on leave again, it will freshen him up, as I found him pale, thin & not looking well.—How is Grigoriev's health? [Dr.] Derevenko sends you photos, he took on the river.—The bedroom is so empty & big after the train!!—Sweet Angel, soon we shall be back again with you & I long for your caresses & kisses.—I have got to receive three officers now, who are returning to the front. Have nothing interesting to tell you.— Goodbye Sweetheart, God Almighty bless and protect you; I cover you with fond kisses & remain, yr. very own old   <u>Wify</u>.   [P.S.] My compliments to Alekseev. All were wonderfully kind & amiable to Ania. —

No. 1242.   Ts.[arist] Stavka. July 15 1916.
My own beloved One,
   Most tender thanks for your dearest letter, such a happiness to see & read the dear handwriting. Yesterday I had a long & interesting conversation with Nicky<. He left this morning for Kiev to visit Mama[, Maria Fedorovna] & then goes back to Pavlovsk & will certainly see you. I found him looking old & very nervous[,] therefore I let him speak out & explain Tino's< messages. I must own that the diplomats of the allies have blundered [with regard to Greece] very often, as usual; in upholding that Veniselos[173] we can come to grief. Tino thinks that perservering [sic] in this way the allies may force the dynastical question to rise & that might be playing with fire—for no reason. Everything Nicky told me is based on official documents, copies of wh. he brought with him. He intends speaking to [i.e., on] a little on the subject[,] that is why I wanted you to know the substance before he comes.—The old man [Fredericks] leaves today.—Now I must end. God bless you my One & All, my girly, Sunny! Many tender kisses from your own old   Nicky

---

No. 1243/ Telegram 169. Stavka> Tsarskoe Selo. 15 July 1916. 20.12> 20.55.
To her majesty. Fondest thanks to you and [daughter] Olga. Good news. Lovely day also with breeze. [We] both kiss [you] tenderly. Niki

---

No. 1244/ Telegram 61. Tsarskoe Selo> Stavka. 15 July 1916. 21.10> 22.27.
To his majesty. Fairly cool breeze. To-morrow is her [Anna Vyrubova's] birthday. Kiss you both. Sleep well. God keep [you]. Hope news is good. Alix

---

No. 1245/ Telegram 64. Tsarskoe Selo> Stavka. 16 July 1916. 13.50> 14.40. To his majesty. Happy over joyful news of taking Brody. May the Lord bless our brave troops with success. Tenderly thank you both my dears, for dear letters. We all tenderly kiss and embrace [you]. Rain fell just now, rather freshened the heavy air before it. Alix

---

No. 1246/ Her No. 544.   Ts.[arskoe] S[elo]. July 16th 1916.
My very own Treasure,
   Warmest thanks for yr. sweet letter. Let me congratulate you with all my heart for the good news—what a surprise it was when Rita announced it to us this morning in the hospital—I had not had time to read the papers. Brodi taken—how lucky—the straight line for Lemberg & the <u>breakthrough</u> begun—the good is coming, as our Friend< had said. I am so <u>happy</u> for you—a great consolation & recompense after all yr. anxiety & hard preparatory work! And how are the losses? Heart & soul are with you out there!—Thats right you let Nicky< speak himself out, it will have quietened him & I really think the other powers do not act fairly towards Greece, tho' its a rotten country.— [a]

Heavy air, the rain did good, a tiny shower—good luck for Ania<—she is 32 to-day. She begs yr. excuse for blotching her letter—now she is off to Finland till to-morrow evening.—I have Witte's doklad [report] at 5½ & to-morrow Shtyurmer, whom I must speak seriously to about the new ministers[324]—alas, that Makarov has been chosen (again a man against yr. poor old wify & that bring no luck) & I must have our Friend< guaranteed against them & Pitirim too. Volzhin does act so wrongly—Pitirim chooses the man to be at the head of his Church [in Petrograd] & Volzh.[in] forbids it—he has no right to do so.—Goodbye my One & All, my Huzy Love, my precious Sunshine. I bless & kiss you without end in fond & deep devotion. Yr. very   Own. [b]

324. While Alexandra was at Stavka (July 6-12, 1916), Sturmer replaced Sazonov as minister of foreign affairs, A. A. Khvostov followed Sturmer as minister of the interior, A. A. Makarov replaced Khvostov as minister of justice. This was the beginning of what came to be known as "ministerial leapfrog." Although the empress was widely blamed for these changes, she actually had little to do with them. As Sturmer was anxious to escape hard work at interior, he asked to be transferred to foreign affairs, which he thought would be less demanding. Khvostov was a logical choice to follow Sturmer. Alexandra was unhappy to see Makarov return to power. She wanted Rasputin and Pitirim "guaranteed against" Khvostov and Makarov because she knew they could cause trouble at interior and justice. Sazonov's ouster troubled Russia's allies. French ambassador Paléologue learned of Sazonov's dismissal on July 7/20, 1916. Paléologue and his British colleague Buchanan informed Minister of the Court Fredericks of their concern; they requested that Sazonov be retained. (Alexandra: *Pis'ma imperatritsy*, II, p. 140n) Nicholas made Sazonov ambassador to Great Britain. As we see in Letter No. 1250b, the tsar's critics made much of this shakeup of the ministers.

No. 1247.   Stavka. July 16 1916.
My beloved Sunny,   [This is a post card.]
    Fondest thanks for your dear letter. Again no time to write, as old Kulomzin came with a doklad [report]. The guard made their attack yesterday & advance well, thank God. They and Sakharov's army[325] have taken over 400 officers, 20,000 men & 55 guns. God bless you and the girlies! I kiss you tenderly my darling Wify. Ever yʳ own   Nicky

325. "General V. V. Sakharov, commanding the 11th Army, had been one of the most efficient staff officers in the Japanese War. On the previous day [July 15] he had entered Brody—Boehm-Ermolli's headquarters—and in twelve days he took 40,000 prisoners and many guns." (Vulliamy, p. 230n) This action was near the Roumanian front.

No. 1248/ Telegram 177. Stavka> Tsarskoe Selo. 16 July 1916. 19.35> 20.39. To her majesty. Fondest thanks [to] you and [daughter] Tatiana. News continue good. Delicious weather. Think of you, kiss tenderly. Niki

No. 1249/ Telegram 68. Tsarskoe Selo> Stavka. 17 July 1916. 13.52> 14.34. To his majesty. Heartily thank you both. Raining. This morning attended hospital< church, now going to christening of Loman's grandson. Embrace and kiss [you]. Alix

No. 1250/ Her No. 545.[326a]   Ts.[arskoe] S[elo]. July 17th 1916.
My very own Lovebird,

A kiss for yr. dear card I received to-day. So the guard has already taken part—Taube was very much interested to know about it. The amount of prisoners taken again is indeed splendid.—Darling, can you please let me know where my Siberians< are just now, as one of my officers returns to them in a few days & does not know where to go & one looses [sic] so much time looking for one's regiment & I thought you might know—can you?—We have just christened Loman's grandson, a splendid baby—old Sirotinin & I were the godparents.—Its pouring cats & dogs, so we shall be good & go to some hospital< [i.e., go some to the hospital?]. In the morning we went to the lower hospital Church & then worked. Yesterday to the Fedor.[ovsky] Cathedral & evening in the hospital. [a]

I wonder how the weather is along the front. The glass [i.e., barometer] has fallen a good bit.—Had a long letter fr. [your sister] Olga, says Motherdear< is well, in good spirits & enjoys herself at Kiev & does not speak about leaving; she sees her but rarely & works very hard since 3 months. In 3 or 4 days her friend goes back to the front & she thinks of it already with despair.[326b] He came for her Namesday [sic]—he was somewhere with the horses the last 2 months.—How the papers are down upon Sazonov,[324] it must be very unpleasant for him, after imagining he was worth so much, poor long nose.—Now, my Sunshine, goodbye & God bless & protect you & keep you from all harm. Ever yr. very own old   Sunny. [b]

326a. In Letter No. 1427 (dated September 19 [O.S.], 1916), Nicholas says the following: "Last night I looked through all your letters, and noticed that in June you suddenly jumped from No. 545 to No. 555. So that now all your letters are numbered wrong." I have retained the empress's numberings whether they are "correct" or not. We see how much Alexandra's letters meant to her husband; he would reread what she had written months earlier.

326b. This is probably a reference to V. A. Kulikovsky, the man Olga married after she divorced Petia< in September 1916.

No. 1251.   Ts.[arist] Stavka. July 17th 1916.
My beloved Sunny,

Fondest thanks for your dear letter. Thank God, our splendid troops, though with heavy losses, tear through the lines of the enemy & advance. The number of prisoners taken & heavy guns augments every day. Of the artillery mostly german—among the prisoners one third are germans. In the open field they cannot withstand our rush. The guard are also advancing & doing beautifully of course. I am so glad for Paul< [as the new commander of the Guards Corps]. That is good you receive Sht.[yurmer]. He likes to hear your instructions. When we go out on the river we take that tiny cadet Makarov with us. He is a good little man & plays quietly with Baby<. The vaccination took with both of us, so alas! we [Aleksei and I] cannot bathe these days. Now I must end. God bless you my Angel! I kiss you and the girlies very tenderly. Ever your own   Nicky

No. 1252/ Telegram 183. Stavka> Tsarskoe Selo. 17 July 1916. 20.00> 20.35. To her majesty. Warmest thanks [to] you and [daughter] Marie. Lovely weather. Enjoyed to days [sic] trip up river. News good. Fondest kisses. Niki

No. 1253/ Telegram 73. Tsarskoe Selo> Stavka. 18 July 1916. 14.25> 15.15. To his majesty. Hearty thanks, my dears. Rain, fresh. Send you telegrams received by Kirill< from N.P.< They [Guards Equipage<] handled themselves marvellously; fortunately, only 16 [of our] soldiers were killed. Kiss and embrace [you]. Alix

No. 1254/ Her No. 555.[326a]   Ts.[arskoe] S[elo]. July 18th 1916.
My own Angel dear,
   Every tender thanks for yr. sweet letter. To-morrow already 2 years of the war—terrible to think. As it's St. Seraphim's day too, we shall have service in the little Church below.—Yesterday evening Kirill< came with the 2 telegr. I copied out for you— because N.P.< told him I always wished to know all about them.— We read them with great emotion.—Wonder, who the 16 men are who were killed—thank God no great losses.—Generally kindly let me know whenever you get lists of deaths & wounded—because the families all telephone for news fr. me. Several of our trains are down there—lots of 4-th rifle officers are wounded. One waits with such anxiety!—Just had Apraxin<—I told him he might pass by the Headquarters soon, to see the different Generals with whom he, [V. V.] Mekk & I have to do!—Many showers to-day. Sorry cant write any more. We went to A.[unt] Olga< yesterday, she was very dear—asked after you.—God bless & protect you. Ever such fondest kisses, my own Sunshine—yr. very   Own.

No. 1255.   Ts.[arist] Stavka. July 18th 1916.
My own precious One,   [This is a post card.]
   Again no time to write longer. Our Wielopolsky[326c] came & I had a long talk with him. He would so much like to see you & explain in a few words the whole polish question. You know it & therefore it won't last long. Fedorov arrived and V.N.< leaves today. Fine but windy. I love you so! God bless you my own Sunny & the girlies! With tender kisses ever your own   Nicky

326c. The issue probably concerned Polish autonomy, noted in Letter No. 1257a. See also Letters No. 1380c (Fn. 345), 1515a (Fn. 379), 1520 (Fn. 381), 1527a, and 1434b. Count Sigismund Iosifovich Velepol'sky (Wielopolsky), mentioned here, was a *shtalmeister* in state service and master of the imperial preserves in Poland. He was a large landholder— see Letter No. 233; his fellow Polish landowners elected him to the State Council in 1909, 1912 and 1916. Letter No. 1270a suggests Velepol'sky advocated Polish autonomy within the Russian Empire.

No. 1256/ Telegram 191. Stavka> Tsarskoe Selo. 18 July 1916. 20.10> 21.00. To her majesty. Fond thanks to you [and daughter] Anastasia. Your Sib.[erians]< are war [i.e., attacking?] Brody and doing wonders. Fine dry day. [We] both kiss [you] tenderly. Niki

No. 1257/ Her No. 556.   Ts.[arskoe] S[elo]. July 19th 1916.
My own Beloved,
   All my thoughts and very tenderest prayers were with you this morning in our Peshcherny chapel. We ordered a service below for ourselves & afterwards there was in the big Church a krestnyi khod [Cross Procession] & feasting & lunch in the Childrens' hospital. We had fewer perevyazki [dressings] to-day.

Your messenger came late—fondest thanks for yr. dear card, my Sweetheart. Again quite cold, only 8 degrees & showers from time to time.—Shtyurmer spoke with me about the Polish question—one must indeed be very prudent[345]—you know, I like Zamoisky, but know he is intriguer [sic], so one must well weigh over this serious question.— [a]

I deeply regret one made you rename Metrop. Wladimir [Vladimir, metropolitan of Kiev] for the summer session of the Synod—it ought to have been Pitirim. Wladimir belongs to Kiev & has only been a week there in all these months [since he was demoted as metropolitan of Petrograd so that Pitirim could follow him at the capital]. He harms ours in everything,—not one thing can P.[itirim] do in his own town [Petrograd], for everything Wlad. must be asked, so that the clergy don't know who is the master, & its very unfair towards him. The other metrop. [Flavian] had the tact of remaining at Kiev more—one ought to do something for this poor one.—Now I must end. Heart & soul with you.—2 years this awful war! God bless & help you. 1000 fond kisses fr. yr. own old Wify. [b]

No. 1258.   Ts.[arist] Stavka. July 19th 1916.
My darling Wify,

Many loving thanks for your letter & for N.P.'s< telegrams, which I return. I never heard they [the Guards Equipage<] had already taken such a serious part in the battle. God bless the dear fellows; only that they should not rush headlong madly forwards! That is my usual anxiety! The names of officers killed or wounded are sent to Petrograd to Glavnaya Shtaba [Main Staff]. Here we get those of colonels—commanders of regiments only. [This is a reply to a request in Letter No. 1254.] There is again a lull down there, more reinforcements are being sent. Probably about the 23[d] the attack will be renewed. The whole time one must refill the regiments and that takes several days. Yes, to day it is two years since this awful war was declared—Heaven knows how long it is still to last! Yesterday I received our Wielopolsky & a Count [D. A.] Usoufieff of the Cons.[iel] of Emp.[ire, i.e., the State Council] who has been in England, France & Italy. He has quite lost his head about stupid Misha's daughter![259] Too funny! He saw [our daughters] Olga and Tatiana at Isa's< and told them the same I think. Now, my sweet Angel, I must end. God bless you & the girlies. Many loving & tender kisses from your own old huzy Nicky.

No. 1259/ Telegram 199. Stavka> Tsarskoe Selo. 19 July 1916. 19.32> 20.10. To her majesty. To you and [daughter] Olga loving thanks. Cooler, two showers. Read with interest copies of both wires. [We] both kiss [you] fondly. Niki

No. 1260/ Telegram 82. Tsarskoe Selo> Stavka. 19 July 1916. 20.27> 21.45. To his majesty. Tenderly thank you both. Cold, overcast, [we] will all have lunch and dinner outside. We all tenderly kiss [you]. In thoughts and prayers are with you on this day. May the Lord bless you. Alix

No. 1261/ Telegram 86. Tsarskoe Selo> Stavka. 20 July 1916. 14.25> 14.49.
To his majesty. Tenderly kiss you both. Colder, grey weather. Big girls< going
to town<. [I] warmly kiss [you]. God keep [you]. Alix

No. 1262/ Her No. 557.   Ts.[arskoe] S[elo]. July 20th 1916.
Sweetheart mine,
    Fondest thanks for yr. dear letter. I saw Vl. Nik.< yesterday & was glad to get
news of you all. He thinks of quietly remaining here, as there is much work in
the hospitals & we are daily expecting new trains. Cold & grey weather, tho' the
glass [i.e., barometer] is rising—reminds me of autumn, we dine in coats— because its dull indoors.—[Daughters] O.[lga] & T.[atiana] have gone to town< for
donations. Nicky< has asked to see me, so shall probably to-morrow, if he is not
with Shtyurmer—Saw Voeikov who stank of cigars & is full of his millions &
constructions & selfsure as always—absolutely positive the war will be over by
Nov. & in Aug. now the begin of the end—he aggravates me & I told him God
alone knows when the end will be & many have said it wld. be Nov. but I doubt
it—in any case its unwise to be always so cocksure as he is. Nekliudov of Stockholm's son has fallen (Preobrajenetz)³²⁷ & the son of Uncle Mekk<—too
sad!—Excuse a dull letter, but my head rather aches. Remember to wire to
Miechen< on the 22nd. Goodbye, my Angel sweet, my Sunshine & joy. God
bless & protect you. I cover you with tender kisses. Ever yr. very own old
<u>Sunny</u>.

---

327. The empress is saying that the son of A. V. Neklyudov, the Russian ambassador to Stockholm, was killed; the young man was a member of the Preobrazhensky Guards Regiment.

No. 1263.   Ts.[arist] Stavka. July 20th 1916.
My own darling Wify,
    So many loving thanks for your dear letter. I send you this little paper I got in
[my sister] Olga's letter—please tell me what I am to answer her to her first
question.³²⁸ You see I am writing with a new pen, you have just sent me &
Chemodurov brought me. Today Teteryat.[in] leaves after five weeks. Today
also is the anniversary of the molebin [Te Deum] & sortie in the Winter Palace!!
You remember the squash on the quay when we left. How long ago it seems &
how much has happened. Yesterday I saw a man who who [sic] pleased me
very much, Protopopov— tovarishch predsedatel' gos. Dumy [Vice-President of
the State Duma]. He went abroad with the other members & told me lots of
interesting things. He is an ex-officer of the konno-grenadery [Cavalry Grena-
diers Regiment], and Maximovich knows him well.³¹⁵ It seems that now atlast
[sic] the roumanians seem ready to participate in the war! The Turks have been
ordered to send some of their troops fr. Constant.[inople] to Galicia to help the
austro-german army. Curious indication but up until now they have not appeared. Now my beloved Sunny I must end. God bless you & the girlies! With
tender & passionate kisses from your own old huzy <u>Nicky</u>.

---

328. The empress refers to plans of Nicholas's sister Olga to divorce Petia< and marry V. A. Kulikovsky. Olga would then be in a degree of disgrace, she "wont wish to appear at official occasions"

and usually "will no longer be in need of a lady in waiting." If she did make such appearances, Olga could borrow a lady-in-waiting from her mother, the Dowager Empress Maria Fedorovna.

No. 1264/ Telegram 200. Stavka> Tsarskoe Selo. 20 July 1916. 20.12> 21.02. To her majesty. Thank you and [daughter] Tatiana. Also grey and cool. Fondest kisses from both. Niki

---

No. 1265/ Telegram 1265. Tsarskoe Selo> Stavka. 21 July 1916. 14.03> 14.48. To his majesty. Warmly thank you both. Rain, colder. In thoughts together. Very busy. [I] warmly kiss [you]. Alix

---

No. 1266/ Her No. 558.   Ts.[arskoe] S[elo]. July 21st 1916.
My own Treasure,
   Again grey & cool & the glass [i.e., barometer] is falling—really, where is summer flown to, we have seen so little of it.—Last night at 10 [daughter] Anastasia's train arrived & I went all over it with her. Heaps of very heavy wounded—they had been endlessly long on the way. There were several of her "Caspian" officers.— Khrapov's grandson—the cousin of one we had 2 months before. Soldiers fr. Finland regiments etc. "Belomortsy" a few with many crosses—all fr. the Austrian front. I gave medals to the worst of wh. many were going to Pavlovsk to Aunt Olga's< hospital.—We want to enlarge our little hospital, so as to be able to always have 35 officers—now 6 of them lie in the room we had for the men (where Ania< lay). We want to build out a wing with a room for 20 men, add a bathroom for them & rooms for sanitaries—they can do it quickly—last autumn we added on the large sittingroom.—The men love coming down to us, & its a pitty [sic] not to look after them. Formerly we worked also in the big house—& this is more comfy. Vil'chk.[ovsky] & Danini come this morning with the plans & all are already deeply interested in it; it has become such a home to all & all the more so, since we spend the evenings with them. I shall finish this after luncheon, now must be off to Znamenje< & our work. Thank God, that He has given me the strength to be of use again;—such consolation in one's work.— [a]
   Ever such tender thanks for yr. sweet letter. Our Friend's< wire is comforting, as this constant rain & cold are sad for July & will make the movement again impossible.—Nevertheless I am going for a drive as my head is heavy. I think you better answer Olga's first question, that she ought to write a nice kind letter to the Pss. as she is so fond of her, & it will hurt less coming straight fr. her, thanking her for all these year's service, but that now she will no longer be in need of a lady in waiting & therefore must part with her. Tho' she remains a grand Duchess, she may at times need a lady—she wont wish to appear at official occasions, but still there may be moments after the war, & when our Children marry & so forth—then Motherdear< must lend her one—I suppose [it is also desirable for Olga] to ask her [Maria Fedorovna's] advice.[328] [b]
   Nicky< will come to-morrow to tea, as he is now with Shtyurmer. We had news of Yedigarov<, poor boy—fancy, the commander did not wish him to come to Russia even to find an occupation, but now he is coming. He wld. not give him yr. squadron, & this has been the great blow, as he ought by right to have

got it. What can I propose him to do? Go over to my Crimeans< or what on earth. What can you council?—Now must end. Congratulate you with Mother-dear & our big [daughter] Marie. Remember Minny [Maria Georgievna] and little Marie P.< God bless you. 1000 burning kisses fr. yr. own, very Own. [c]

No. 1267.   Ts.[arist] Stavka. July 21ᵗ 1916.
My own precious One,
   So many thanks for your dear letter. I just now saw Voeikov who brought me your greeting. Yes, he is pleased to be relieved of that Kuvaka business.[329] [See Letter No. 1262.] I also tell him not to be so self-sure, especially upon such serious subjects as the question of the end of the war! I like old Maximovich<, he is such a gentleman, honest & quiet[,] so agreeable to have to do with. Please insist that the "old man" [Fredericks] does not come here before the 6ᵗʰ of Aug. He was to go for a cure to the Romanov Inst.[itute] at Sevastopol and Voeikov says he wishes now to come back here very soon! I think this quite silly. As you are the only one he obeys—please let him know that he is to rest three weeks at Siverskaya. God grant in six days I will be once more in your arms & feel your solf [i.e., soft] lips—something hops within me at the mere thought! You must not smile when you read these words! Eristov and Kozlyaninov left—the former to Kiev & his regiment, so I gave [him] a letter for Mama [Maria Fe-dorovna]. Mordvinov and Raevsky have come. The second has become fat & quite wild fr. the war presumably. It is raining. Now I must end. God bless you, my darling Sunny & the girlies! I kiss you tenderly & lovingly. Ever your own old Nicky.

   329. Voeikov had just sold a factory in Penza province that bottled a popular brand of mineral water known as "Kuvaka."

No. 1268/ Telegram 204. Stavka> Tsarskoe Selo. 21 July 1916. 18.30> 19.30. To her majesty. Thank you and [daughter] Marie. Variable, warm weather. Thoughts together. Fondest love. Niki

No. 1269/ Telegram 138. Tsarskoe Selo> Stavka. 22 July 1916. 13.50> 14.50. To his majesty. With all our hearts we all congratulate [you] on nameday of Motherdear< and our [daughter] Marie. Heartily thank you both. Saw [A. N.] Grabbe in church. [We] all kiss you both. Alix

No. 1270/ Her No. 559.   Ts.[arskoe] S[elo]. July 22ⁿᵈ 1916.
My own precious One,
   There, a downpour again. Such tender thanks, Lovy mine, for your sweet let-ter I was so happy to receive.—We had service in the Fedor.[ovsky] Cathedral, Css. Voronts.[ova-Dashkova], Css. [Maria] Benk.[endorff], Princess Dol-gor.[ukaya], Mme Nilova, Dediulina & our ladies were there.—Now I have Velep.[326c]—I rather dread it, because I feel sure I shan't quite agree with him—& think wiser one shld. wait a bit, but in any case not give too great liberties, oth-erwise when Baby's< turn comes [to reign as tsar] he will have very hard times to go through.—Then to [daughters] M.[arie's] & A.[nastasia's] hospital for a

concert—a visit to Miechen<—Nicky< to tea, then Shtyurmer—between that Ania<—& the Hospital< begging me to come in the evening & I shld. like to—its the only thing wh. helps me now you are away. Yet I know, A.[nia] is sad [not to accompany us on this trip to Stavka]—tho' she has Alia< lying not well in her house & might naturally sit more with her, I find. Forgive therefore a short letter, as am in a great hurry & fidgeted (wh. I don't like).—I cover you with kisses & count the moments till we shall be together. God bless & protect you & keep you fr. all harm. Always miss & yearn for you—Ever yr. very, very   Own. [P.S.] Shall do my very, very best about the old man [Fredericks]. [See Letter No. 1269] —

No. 1271/ Telegram 219. Stavka> Tsarskoe Selo. 22 July 1916. 15.16> 15.46. To her majesty. We both[, Aleksei and I,] send our best wishes for Marie and thank you [and] Anastasia. Bad, rainy weather. Tender kisses. Niki

---

No. 1272.   Ts.[arist] Stavka. July 22nd 1916.
My own Lovebird,

Loving thanks for your dear long letter. I am glad you want to add a wing to your hospital so as to have place also for the men. That is right & just. Basically I do not know what to advise Yedigarov<. If he wants to continue military service (and that one must during war) then the best for him would be to go to the Caucasian division; not to your krymtsy [Crimeans]< because they have over 100 officers! Or perhaps into one of the three Zaamurskie konnye polki [Trans-Amur Cavalry regiments] which are splendid regiments. I am very sorry for the poor fellow, but I cannot mix into interior home affairs of the nizhegorodtsy<. I forgot to congratulate you for our [daughter] Marie's namesday [sic]. The weather is atrocious[—]it is cool & it pours every half hour, but we shall go out in our motors, as it does not do to remain in doors. Besides we have a cynema [sic] this evening. Grigorovich came—I saw him yesterday. He leaves for Arkhangel'sk. Baby< & I are already eagerly awaiting your arrival. Your sweet presence is worth the running about or "sueta" ["bustle"] as you call it. Now my Angel I must end. God bless you & the girlies! With many tender burning kisses from your own old   Nicky.

No. 1273/ Telegram 308. Tsarskoe Selo> Stavka. 23 July 1916. 14.12> 14.53. To his majesty. Warmly thank you both. Grey, cold, windy, all are having lunch on balcony. Tenderly embrace and kiss [you]. Alix

---

No. 1274/ Her No. 560.   Ts.[arskoe] S[elo]. July 23rd 1916.
My own Lovebird,

From all my heart I thank you for yr. dear letter—yes, I too am eagerly looking forward to our meeting on Wednesday. What a nice wire from Tino!<—I also wrote to him, Nicky< begged me to. He was very contented with his talk with Sht.[yurmer]. It was a tiring day yesterday. Church, Velep.,[326c] to the Childrens' hospital, visit to Miechen<, [then had] Nicky, Shtyurmer—till 7½— A.[nia]< dined & remained with me till 10—then to our hospital<.—Cold, grey &

windy.—We have to go to the big palace< for a concert & before want to drive a
bit. Are awaiting trains [bearing more wounded].—We used to work in the big
house & have heaps of men—& this will be much better near us.—Frederiksy<
cld. not come to lunch, not being well. Benkendorf [P. C. Benckendorff] is also
still not well.—I am glad you like old, nice Maximovich<. —Now, sweetest Angel, wify's lovebird, I cover you with burning kisses & remain yr. own old
Sunny.   [P.S.] Ania's goodies will only be ready to-morrow, she begs pardon.

No. 1275. Telegram 233. Stavka> Tsarskoe Selo. 23 July 1916. 16.20> 18.08.
To her majesty. To you and [daughter] Olga fondest thanks. [Aleksei's] left el-
bow a little stiff, no pain. Excellent spirits. Rainy, warmer. [We] both kiss all.
Niki

No. 1276.   Ts.[arist] Stavka. July 23[d] 1916.
My beloved Sunny,
   Many thanks for your dear letter. The weather continues to be strange & disagreeable! Every quarter of an hour—the sun shines or it rains like cats and
dogs. This morning while we were both in ours beds—Aleksei explained to me
that his left elbow is stiff, then he measured his temp. & coolly [sic] announced
to me he had better remain in bed the whole day. The temp. was 36.5. As the
weather is damp I found it right he should remain quiet. Now he is playing
"nain jaune"[277] with Voeik.[ov] and P.V.< in our bedroom. Just before lunch
one of our pages died suddenly while shaving! So sad! He served years ago in
the Semenovsky p[olk. i.e., regiment] in the Svodnaya rota [mixed company] in
Gatchina. And after lunch I heard that the inspector of the river communications
here, who always goes with us on our expeditions, had his leg broken by a motor
in the street.— Yesterday we saw an interesting cynema [sic] wh. all enjoyed.
Baby< is making a great row playing & is very cheerful—no pain. Certainly the
cause is this tiresome damp weather! My Love, how impatiently do I await your
arrival! Baby too of course.—God bless you & the girlies! I kiss you all very
tenderly. Ever, Sunny-mine, your own Nicky.

No. 1277/ Telegram 330. Tsarskoe Selo> Stavka. 24 July 1916. 14.13> 14.55.
To his majesty. Tenderly thank you both. Weather remains wonderful. Just now
visited one of my trains, filled with guards officers and soldiers. [I] warmly embrace and kiss [you]. Alix

---

No. 1278/ Her No. 561.   Tsarskoe Selo. July 24th 1916.
My own beloved Sweetheart,
   From all my tender heart I thank you for your sweetest letter.— The train (I am
ramolie<) bringing mostly guard officers & men arrived to-day & we went over
it—2 sailors were there too—some remained here, others went on to town. The
poor couple Verevkin (ex. gov. of Kiev—"Preobrajenetz"<) came to meet their
son's body. We had service in the hospital< & then did perevyazki [dress-
ings]—without any doctors, as they were all occupied at an operation of a lady
upstairs.—At last! divine weather—our Friend< has brought it, He arrived to

town< this morning, & I am eagerly looking forward to see[ing] Him before we leave.—A.[nia]<, I think, is more than grieved I don't take her [to visit you at Stavka] this time, tho' she does not say it in words—but He [Rasputin] has come & Alia< is ill in her house & its unnecessary this time. I think my going so often to the hospital in the evening puts her out, but really her sister [Alia<] is there [in her house] & ill to sit by—& there I forget the solitude & misery & they warm us all up.—[A. N.] Grabbe is coming with us, I am delighted, as Nastinka< & Ressin [Resin] are dull.—Sweet Angel, goodbye & God bless & protect you. Ever yr. very own endlessly loving old   Wify. [P.S.] Thousands of kisses. Am awaiting Becker< for the journey —hideous nuisance! —

No. 1279.   Ts.[arist] Stavka. July 24th 1916.

My precious,
    Tender thanks for your dear letter. I can well imagine how occupied & tormented you are by those people you receive or go to see. Poor Sunny! Here perhaps you will have a little rest, if I don't come with my fidgeting about driving or motoring here & there!! Sandro< is here for two days. He told me lots about Mama [Maria Fedorovna], Xenia<, who is there for a fortnight & about [my other sister] Olga. Baby< is, thank God, alright [sic]. He slept well and is getting up now [at] 2.30. Fedorov won't let him to go out, not to romp too much; but his two little comrades are coming & they will play quietly in the rooms. The weather has improved & bright sun [shines] again. Darling, this will be my last letter as you arrive in three days. God bless you & your journey. All my prayers & thoughts will surround you quite especially. Ever, my beloved Wify, your own old   Nicky

No. 1280/ Telegram 334. Tsarskoe Selo> Stavka. 24 July 1916. 17.45> 18.40. To his majesty. Rhein asked Alek< to receive him, but has not gotten a reply. Now he comes to you and it would be very undesirable if one refused him a second time as he works on something which has already waited 8 years and which has just been sanctioned by you. Hope you will be firm as this is a really necessary and marvellous project.[288] Tenderly kiss [you], hope [Aleksei's] elbow [is] better. God keep [you]. Alix

No. 1281/ Telegram 238. Stavka> Tsarskoe Selo. 24 July 1916. 19.50> 20.48. To her majesty. Fond thanks [for] letter [and] wires. Shall be firm and insist upon my will being executed [regarding Dr. Rhein's proposal].[288] [Aleksei's] elbow better, got up in the day but not out of doors. Warmer, only one shower. Tender kisses from both. Niki

No. 1282/ Telegram 337. Tsarskoe Selo> Stavka. 25 July 1916. 15.13> 15.37. To his majesty. Warmly kiss [you], thank you both for letters. Await Wednesday with impatience. Am bringing Botkin with me since [my] heart is hurting. Tired, staying home all day. Sunny and rain. May the Lord keep you both. Alix

No. 1283/ Her No. 562.   Ts.[arskoe] S[elo]. July 25th 1916.

My own beloved Huzy dear,

Changeable weather—at moments lovely sunshine & then such dark clouds again. I am in bed this morning as my heart is a good deal enlarged, I felt it all these days—I overtired myself—so remain quiet to-day & only go to A.[nia]< this evening to see our Friend<. —He finds better one shld. not advance to [sic] obstinately as the losses will be too great—one can be patient without forcing things, as ultimately it [victory] will be ours; one can go on madly & finish the war in 2 months, but then thousands of lives will be sacrificed—& by patience the end will also be gained & one will spare much blood. [a]

I bring Botkin, as he was anxious to let me go now alone—before B.[ecker]< its often worse—& then I worried rather much latterly over the nomination of Makarov[280,324] & the Polish story [i.e., situation][345]—etc.—Endless thanks for yr. precious letter—this too is my last to you.—Ania wanders about with a long face & is aggressive—the hospital< aggravates her because I so often spend the evenings there ([but the work there is] my rest fr. talks & one needs other faces when the heart is heavy with anxiety & loneliness—very, very sad without you both & she, poor soul, does not brighten me up always.)—I prefer not speaking of the [people who are] absent & remembering the past & cry[ing] over what cant be— our interests are different generally—when her sweetheart the Caraim[, S. M. Shapshal, leader of the Karaites[287]] was here and caressed her [the statement is ironic]—she was splendid. But we get on calmly; & now I don't take her [on this trip to Stavka] of course she is, I see, very hurt—forgets her sister [Alia<] is ill in her house & Gr.[egory]< [has returned from his last visit home, to Siberia, and] is here.—Now its raining. God grant in 2 days we shall be together!! 1000 kisses & blessings fr. yr. longing old <u>Wify</u>.   [P.S.] We shall lunch in the train? & if heart bad I can dine home too, yes?— [b]

No. 1284/ Telegram 252. Stavka> Tsarskoe Selo. 25 July 1916. 18.50> 19.20. To her majesty. Loving thanks. Saw Alek< this morning. Talked about several questions but never mentioned a word concerning R[hein]. [Aleksei's] elbow alright [sic]. We went up the river. Now again raining. Tenderest kisses. Niki

---

No. 1285/ Telegram 48. Malaya Vishera> Stavka. 26 July 1916. 14.18> 14.58. To his majesty. [We] are travelling well. Warm, good weather. [We] await to-morrow with impatience. Heart so-so, [I] am very tired. [We] warmly kiss you both. Alix

---

No. 1286/ Telegram 256 in Russian. Stavka> Bologoe. 26 July 1916. 14.40> 14.55. To her majesty. Letters today are running late[, so we do not yet have any word from you]. [We] wish you a good trip. Raining entire time. [We] warmly embrace [you]. Niki, Aleksei

---

No. 1287/ Telegram 259 in Russian. Stavka> Rzhev, Tver gub.[ernaya]. 26 July 1916. 14.40> 14.55. To her majesty. Heartily thank you for letters. Will be glad to see you to-morrow. Waiting to have lunch [when you arrive]. Good night. Embrace [you]. Niki, Aleksei

No. 1288.   Ts.[arist] Stavka. The Train. 3 August 1916.
My very own beloved Angel,
   Alas, the day of departure has arrived again, but I thank God for this happy,
restful week.   Now I can return with new strength to my work and live upon
sweet remembrances of your tender love.   Its very hard leaving you alone to yr.
heavy responsability [sic] & masses of tireing [sic] work—wish I cld. be of more
use to you! I long to guard you fr. all useless worries & vexations, but often [I]
have myself to come [to you] with tiresome papers—but nothing is to be
done.—Beloved One, God Almighty give you wisdom & success—patience for
the others not to hurry obstinately forward & spoil all by useless losses [see
Letter No. 1283a]—steadily forward, every step firm & no dashes with retracing
again one's steps backwards—thats far worse.—[a]
   If only Alekseev has taken our Friend's< Image [icon] in the right spirit, then
God is sure to bless his work with you.   Don't fear to mention Gr.[egory]'s<
name to him—[it is] thanks to Him that you remained firm & took over the
commandment a year ago, when all were against you, tell him [Alekseev] that &
he will understand the wisdom then—& many wonderful escapes to those he
prays for at the war who know Him—not to speak of Baby< & Ania<.—Sweetest
One, heart & soul remain with you & all my passionate love.   God bless you &
precious Baby hundertfold— shall miss you both horribly—& you will feel yr.
loneliness, alas, again.   I cover you with burning, tender kisses, Sunshine of my
life —& remain yr. very own old   Wify. [P.S.] Sleep well, hold you both tightly
in my arms.— [b]

No. 1289/ Telegram 0140. Orsha, train station> Stavka. 3 Aug 1916. 19.55>
21.20. To his majesty. [We] warmly kiss you both. Sleep well. Sad, melancholy in the soul. God keep [you]. Alix

No. 1290/ Telegram 49 in Russian. Stavka> Tsarskoe Selo. 3 Aug 1916.
20.04> 21.21. To her majesty. Vitebsk, Al. r. r., the following. Once more [I
wish you a] good trip. Thank you for dear letter. We are both lonely. Goodnight,
[we] embrace [you]. Niki

No. 1291.   Ts.[arist] Stavka. August 3^d 1916.
My own beloved Angel,
   How I do hate when you leave & to see the train taking you & the girlies
away! I have such calm in the soul when you are near me, I want to send all
worries & nuisances far away & enjoy your presence without speaking—of
course when we are alone. Thank you oh! so tenderly for having come & given
me this treat & rest of the heart's yearning & craving for you. Now I will be
strong & calm till your next visit. Loving thanks also for your dearest letter
which soothed a bit the pain of separation! Baby< went to drive with his two
tiny friends & I received C^t [Count A. A.] Bobrinsky who did not remain long &
made a good impression upon me. We dined in the tent—it was rather cold &
damp inside—I would prefer the balcony another time. After playing with Baby
I managed to finish all my papers, which gives me always some satisfaction!

And took a delightful drive along the highroad & round by the long bridge by a beautiful moonlight. The air was very cool; so good before going to bed. Sleep well my precious Sunny! [a]

August 4th. A glorious day & very warm. I hope you slept well & are travelling comfortably! Baby & I will feel lonely at lunch & during our expedition—in fact all day till night. God bless you, my beloved Wify, my Treasure. I cover you with burning tender kisses. Much love to the girlies. Ever your very own Nicky [b]

No. 1292/ Telegram 25. Likhoslavl> Stavka. 4 Aug 1916. 11.25> 12.03. To his majesty. Heartily thank you for yesterday's telegram. Miss [you] very much, [I] remember the wonderful days [during our visit], again divine weather, 17° in shade. Slept so-so. [We] warmly kiss you both. God keep [you]. Alix

---

No. 1293/ Telegram 54. Stavka> Tsarskoe Selo. 4 Aug 1916. 18.54> 20.29. To her majesty. Best thanks for dear wire. Hope [you] arrived well. Lovely weather. Miss you quite madly. Tenderest love. Niki

---

No. 1294/ Telegram 4. Tsarskoe Selo> Stavka. 4 Aug 1916. 20.45> 21.16. To his majesty. Arrived safely, travelled well. Ideal weather. [I] miss my dears terribly. We tenderly kiss you both. Sleep peacefully. Alix

---

No. 1295/ Her No. 564.   Tsarskoe Selo. August 4th 1916.
My own sweet Angel[,]

It is already 10 o'clock, but I want nevertheless to begin my letter to you [as] to-morrow I shall be so busy.—We travelled alright [sic] & my heart behaved itself; I only took tea with the others, lunch & dinner I had in my compart-ment—lay the whole time & embroidered, whilst my thoughts were with you both treasures & I lived over that happy, peaceful week. Alone in my big empty bedroom, only your cushion to bless & kiss! Lovely moon & so quiet—the weather splendid to-day & not too hot.—A.[nia]< spent the evening with us—grown thinner this week, looks tired & one sees has cried much. Scarcely spoke—only after the children went to bed. She leaves on Monday with our Fr.< & dear Lili for Tobolsk to pray before the relics of the new Saint [John Maxi-movich].[330] [Anna Vyrubova is] In despair to leave without yr. blessing for so far [a trip], & just when I returned, but He wishes her to go now, finds it the best moment. [a]

He [Rasputin] asks whether its true what the papers write that the Slavic war prisoners will be set free,[331] hopes not true, as wld. be a great fault [mistake] (do answer this question).—Is grieved one says Guchkov< & Rodzianko< have gone to give the order to collect copper—if true, says one ought to take the initiative from them, its not their business. Begs you to be very severe with the generals, that are at fault. You see, from all sides terrible cries against Bezobrazov arise, that he let the guard be slaughtered—that Lesh 5 days running gave B.[ezobrazov] the order to advance & he always put it off & then lost all through his obstinacy. The wounded rifles & others don't hide their anger. [b]

Ania got a most interesting, but sad letter fr. N.P.<—writes about what they did too—but with despair about the Generals— Bez.[obrazov] —now they know nothing, ordered the guard to advance where the bogs were <u>known</u> to be impregnable—& told to avoid other bogs where one cld. quite well pass—says, the worst impression—[it] grieves [N.P.] to make me sad, but begs her [Ania<] to tell me this.—All here hope you will change Bez.—I hoped it fr. the beginning, surely not difficult to find a successor & at least [to find] one who is not as obstinate as a mule. The guard will never forgive him & wont be pleased you stick up for him, & that he profits [i.e., takes advantage of you] as an old comrade.[332]—Forgive me, but the more I quietly thought all over in the train what Paul< wrote, Dmitri< & others said, I honestly find [I agree with N.P. that] he ought to leave, & it will be a glorious example of your wisdom. Its yr. special guard he has thrown sinfully away—& he will again disagree with Lesh & Brussilov—you kindly saved him after the story last year & gave him a glorious chance wh. he shamefully misused—one cannot act thus unpunished. Let him suffer & others be saved by this example. Regret, I did not speak more vehemently at the Headquarters & not to Alekseev—yr. prestige will be saved—one will say you are weak & don't stand up for yr. guard wh. you always loved—& one can't risk another calamity. [c]

The generals know we have men in Russia still, & don't care about the lives—but these were so beautifully prepared & all—for nothing. I know how it has made you suffer—but be reasonable, Lovebird—listen to old wify who only thinks of yr. good & knows this step is the right one.—Let Aleks.[eev] think otherwise—only better quite put him [Bezobrazov] away, as you said a strong reprimand wld. make him nervous—do it for yr. brave guard's sake & all will thank you for it, they are too deeply hurt by his rashness in letting all their men be killed. [d]

Ania told our Friend< what I said about Sandro's< despair & He [Rasputin] was very much put out about it. He had a long talk with Sekretev on the subject & he says that he has heaps of things one cld. perfectly well use for the machenery [sic] of the aeroplanes. Don't you want to send for him & have a talk on the subject, or send him to Sandro[333] to talk the question over—it wld. be in deed lucky if they cld. find a way of making the machenery here. —Forgive me, if my first letter [since returning home from our trip] is already about [serious] affairs—but all concerning the army is so vital to us all & we live for it.— [e]

By the [wrist-]watch I live through all you are doing all day, my own Lovebird. Only yesterday we were still together & it seems already much longer ago. Did you remember about putting off the calling in of the young soldiers till Sept. 15 if possible, so that they can finish their fieldworks [i.e., agricultural work] everywhere.[93]— Isa< came to [meet us at] the station but still looks ailing—Trina< keeps to her room yet with a cold. Mme Zizi< was there & asked where we came from!!! The Pss. Palei< was there too—without a veil, but I did not kiss her.—I congratulate you with the Preobrajensky< feast, my one & all. [f]

5-th. Ever such loving thanks for yr. precious letter [No. 1291], Sweetheart. Yes, the joy of being together is inconceivable & I live on remembrances now. For you its yet worse, poor Angel dear!—Again lovely weather—got to sleep after 3. Worked in the hospital<, lots of new faces. Pss. Gedr.<, Taube & Emelianov

[Emelyanov] send touched thanks for messages.—I enclose a paper about good Lapukhin [Lopukhin],—Botkin begs for him again & Makarov acts not fairly.—A.[nia]< got a wire fr. N.P.<,—he will be at the Headquarters about the 12-th. Sweety, I want to go to holy Communion this lent, so think Monday morning, as this evening is Church, to-morrow morning & evening, Sunday morning & then I'll order twice [i.e., two services] more—it will be a great consolation. Ania leaves Monday for [Tobol'sk][330]—she does not know how long the journey will be. Wont you send her a card with wishes & blessing for the journey, only then write in time.— Lovely weather, are lunching on the balkony [sic].— [g]

I receive a lady now & then [V. V.] Mekk & Apraxin< who goes to the front at 4 o'clock.—Lovy, you wont forget about the decorations for the wounded by bombs fr. aeroplanes. A. thanks for the teaglass.—Goodbye now, my Sunshine, my joy. In thoughts press you tenderly to my heart, cover you with burning kisses. God bless & protect you & help you in all yr. undertakings.—Think about Bezobrazov. Ever, Angel mine, yr. very own   Sunny. [h]

330. "Mme. Vyrubova and Mme. Lily Dehn, accompanied by Rasputin, were starting for Tobolsk, to pray before the relics of a new saint, recently canonised through the influence of Rasputin. This journey was undertaken by the wish of the Tsaritsa, who had vowed either to visit Tobolsk herself or to send thither her chosen representatives. The party, in a special saloon, followed the same route which was taken, a year later, by the Imperial Family on their way to exile and death." (Vulliamy, pp. 239-240n)

331. Perhaps the plan was for "Slavic war prisoners" taken from the Austro-Hungarian army to "be set free" to fight their former masters, knowing that if Dual Monarchy collapsed, its Slavic lands would become independent states. The "Czech Legion" was one result of this idea. While moving eastward through Siberia to join the Allied armies in France in 1918, it clashed with local communist forces and ignited the Red-White Civil War of 1918-1921.

332. Bezobrazov was a comrade-in-arms with Nicholas II from the time both were young men enrolled in the Hussar Life Guards Regiment.

333. Alexander Michaelovich ("Sandro") was in charge of Russian military aircraft during the war. Maj.-Gen. P. I. Sekretev directed automobile repairs on the western front. Note his ties with Rasputin.

No. 1296.   Ts.[arist] Stavka. August 5th 1916.
My own beloved one,

Our normal grey life has begun. The bright "Sunny" days have flown away & I live by sweet remembrances of the past! My Darling, how I love you & deeply I have grown accustomed to your continual presence! Every separation is so hard to bear & one longs more and more to be always together! But duty comes before everything, so we must submit & try not to grumble though it is not easy. After the most divine weather we had yesterday, this night several showers have come down & it is rather uncertain to day whether to get fine or to go on raining! The air is very warm & we intend to motor out to the place which we call "skerries." Every day I receive one minister & that with my papers—prevented me from seeing Botkin's naval brother & old [retired Gen.] Dudel Adlerberg. Now my sweet Love I must end. God bless you & the girlies! With many burning kisses ever your own old Nicky.

No. 1297/ Telegram 6. Tsarskoe Selo> Stavka. 5 Aug 1916. 18.43> 19.30. To his majesty. Tenderly thank you both, my loved ones, for dear letters. [We] are going to church. Beautiful weather. [I] worked in hospital<, many newly wounded, motored. Please, read my letter to-morrow, before you receive Makarov. Warmly kiss you both. Miss [you] very much. Alix

No. 1298/ Telegram 58. Stavka> Tsarskoe Selo. 5 Aug 1916. 20.02> 20.37. To her majesty. Hope you are well and found all your wounded alright. Miss [you] greatly. Very warm. Tender kisses from both. Niki

No. 1299/ Telegram 8. Tsarskoe Selo> Stavka. 6 Aug 1916. 13.41>14.46. To his majesty. Heartily congratulate you on Preobrazhentsy< festival day. Beautiful weather. Were at church, then hospital<. Heartily thank you both for dear letters. [We] all tenderly kiss [you]. Greek Nicky< leaves this evening. Alix

No. 1300/ Her No. 565.   Ts.[arskoe] S[elo]. August 6th 1916.
My very own Sweetheart,
    Fondest thanks my Angel for yr. precious letter. Yes, the blessing to be together is intense, & one feels the longing & missing quite awfully. Ah, your tender caresses, big sad eyes when we parted haunt me always. It is good to have a nice time to look forward to again, poor A.[nia]< hopes to be back by then, or the girl can catch us up at the Headquarters, it will refresh her & then N.P.< will be there & we all once more together. Remember to give him [command of] the yacht [*Standard*], that makes a good reason for his not being out there & he ought to have it.—Lovely weather again, so shall remain the afternoon on the balkony [sic]. Have 4 officers. Mr. Gibbs & Pr. Golitzin [N. D. Golitsyn] with a doklad [report] & then Nicky< to see—there cld. not finish, they come one after the other & now the Feldjager must leave. Nicky< begs to thank you again ever so much for everything.— [a]
    Beloved, we had evening service in the F.[edorovsky] S.[boor]< & to-night again, this morning in our Peshch.[ernaya] ts.[erkov', i.e., Church] & to-morrow morning in the lower hospital Church. Hope to go on Monday morning to Holy Communion—heart & soul I beg yr. pardon my one & all for word or deed by wh. I may have unwillingly hurt you;[129]—I am so glad to go [to Holy Communion], long for this moral strength—one goes through so much & has to give out such a lot. Confession Sunday evening at 10—perhaps A.[nia]< may come too—otherwise I shall be alone, the girls don't care about going now.—Goodbye, Angel Sweet. I see our Friend< in her [Ania's] house to-day, you speak about Him [Rasputin] to Mr. Gibbs.—I cover you with fondest kisses & bless you over & over again. Ever yr. very own, deeply loving & longing old   Wify.   [P.S.] As [I found it] interesting, I told Ania to write out [the enclosed episode] about her Brother [S. A. Taneev] for you.— [b]

No. 1301.   Ts.[arist] Stavka. August 6th 1916.
My own precious Sunny,

Ever so many loving thanks for your dear letter. Again I have no time to write properly & answer your questions. Always ministers or other people to receive! It seems Yury Trubetskoi has arrived—shall see him before dinner. It is very hot. I have got piles wh. are very uncomfortable. Could you send me my box with those candles [i.e., suppositories]—it is in my dressing-room to the left of the door on a small shelf. Please give A.[nia]< my very best love & wishes for her journey[330]! I simply could not find a minute to write to her. God bless you, my beloved Wify! 1000 tender kisses to you & the girlies. Ever your own old Nicky

---

No. 1302/ Telegram 69. Stavka> Tsarskoe Selo. 6 Aug 1916. 19.55> 20.13. To her majesty. [We] both thank you fondly for dear letters. Divine weather. Thanks also for [congratulations on the Preobrazhensky] regiments feast day. Loving kisses. Niki

---

No. 1303/ Telegram 10. Tsarskoe Selo> Stavka. 7 Aug 1916. 13.50> 14.39. To his majesty. Tenderly thank you both. Grey, small shower. Were at church and hospital<. [We] warmly kiss [you], may the Lord bless you, my dears. Alix

---

No. 1304/ Her No. 566.   Ts.[arskoe] S[elo]. August 7th 1916.
My own beloved Angel,
    I thank you fr. all my heart for yr. sweet letter—understand its difficult for you to write when you have so much to do.—A grey day—rained a little. Saw our Friend< yesterday evening in the little house [of Anna Vyrubova]—[He] sends you these flowers and much love. They leave Tuesday evening. A.[nia]< and I go to confession at 10 and to-morrow morning service at 9 in our Peshch.[erny] Khram [Chapel]<—quite particularly shall pray for you, my one and all and carry you in my soul. I cover you with tenderest kisses and send you endless love.—What news fr. the war? Pretty quiet? Excuse a dull, short letter, but have no time for more.—I send you the "candles"—what a nuisance you suffer again fr. them. [See Letter No. 1301.]—Goodbye, my bright Sunshine. God bless and protect you. Ever yr. very own tenderly loving old Sunny.

No. 1305.   Ts.[arist] Stavka. August 7th 1916.
My beloved darling,
    So many thanks for your dear letter. Thank A.[nia]< for the copy she sends me.[334] Again no time to write as Alek< suddenly appeared this morning; I saw him just now after lunch. Luckily he was quiet, spoke about Rein's affair[288] & others, but did not grumble. This morning I receive Mamantov & only to-morrow Monday Makarov. I will tell him to stop that story [i.e., affair] about Lopukhin. It is very hot—I am afraid a thunderstorm is preparing. Now good-bye! God bless you my sweet Wify-dear! I kiss you & the girlies very tenderly. Ever your own old Nicky

---

    334. Nicholas refers to a " copy of a letter from N. P. Sablin, making serious allegations against General Bezobrazov, then commanding the special Guard Corps. [See Letter No. 1295c.] It was by such letters and messages that the Tsar was swayed in making appointments and in ordering dismissals." (Vulliamy, p. 240n)

No. 1306/ Telegram 11. Tsarskoe Selo> Stavka. 7 Aug 1916. 19.18> 21.11. To his majesty. Now going to church. Confession at 10 [o'clock]. Again ask you with all my heart to forgive me.[129] Kiss you both, my precious ones. She [Anna Vyrubova] also going to confession. Please, telegraph her— congratulate her and wish her a happy trip.[330] She will be madly happy. [We] went for drive. Heavy rain. Sleep well. May the Lord bless you! Alix

No. 1307/ Telegram 73. Stavka> Tsarskoe Selo. 7 Aug 1916. 20.03> 21.10. To her majesty. Fondest thanks for dear letters. Will think especially of you, darling, this evening. Lovely day. Tender kisses. God bless you. Niki

No. 1308/ Telegram 79. Stavka> Tsarskoe Selo. 8 Aug 1916. 10.56> 11.20. To her majesty. [May God] bless you. Heart and soul together. Tender love. Niki

No. 1309/ Telegram 12. Tsarskoe Selo> Stavka. 8 Aug 1916. 13.21> 14.06. To his majesty. Tenderly thank you for precious telegram and letters. This is such comfort for me. This morning after church [we] went directly to hospital< to work. Colossal heat, heavy air. We all warmly kiss you. May the Lord bless you, dear ones. Alix

No. 1310/ Her No. 567.   Ts.[arskoe] S[elo]. August 8th 1916.
My own Beloved,
    Warmest thanks, my Angel, for your dear letter. What a nuisance you have to see so many people.—Colossally [sic] hot to-day and such heavy air—also a wee breeze—shant drive, prefer remaining quiet.—It was a great consolation and so calming to go to Holy Communion—carried you both with me in my innermost soul. Can pray so much better in our wee Church below. From there went straight to the hospital where they gave me a glass of tea; and then I did my per-evyazki [dressings]. The foundation work of our new wing is getting on nicely—hope it will be ready by the end of October. On Wednesday 10-th, will be the second anniversary of our hospital and all want it awfully to be called His Majesty's own Hospital No. 3—as there are for ever confusions between Palace Hospital and Hos.[pital] of the [Bolshoi] Palace. Wonder, what you are doing about the guard,—will they keep quiet now for some time.—Our Friend< hopes we wont climb over the Carpathans [sic] and try to take them, as he repeats the losses will be too great again.—Tchebikin [Chebykin] comes to me to arrange about a hospital in the new barracks of the 3-rd rifle regiment.— Must end now. Goodbye my beloved Treasure, my one and all, my sunshine dear; cover you with burning kisses. God bless you. Ever yr. very own old Wify.

No. 1311.   Ts.[arist] Stavka. August 8th 1916.
My own beloved One,
    So many thanks for your dear short letter. My thoughts surround you particu-larly last evening & this morning, when you went to Holy Communion in our cozy underground church. It must be a year ago that we took it together during

those hard days before my coming here! I remember so well that which [sic] I was standing opposite our Saviour's big picture upstairs in the big church [when] an interior voice seemed to tell me to make up my mind & write about my decision [to assume personal command of my armies on the Western front] at once to Nik.[olasha]<—apart from what our Friend< told me. Please thank him [Rasputin] for the two flowers he sent me. Mr. Gibbs has arrived, but much later than we had expected. Baby< seems pleased to see him. [a]

There is a lull for the moment at the front—till the 15th—though in some places fighting continues at Bucovina.[335] At the Caucasian front a strong attack of ours is progressing more or less in our centre. I quite agree that N.P.< must be named captain of the Standart [see Letter No. 1300a]; but I have to find a place for Zelen.[etsky, the present captain,] first of all. One cannot kick a good man off his place to give it to a better one & leave him in the lurch. I am sure you did not mean that! It is raining to day but very warm. God bless you my sweet Wify & the girlies! Tell [daughter] Tatiana to send me now a silver cigarcase of mine! With fondest & tenderest kisses ever your own old Nicky. [b]

335. "According to the Russian official figures, 350,845 men and 7757 officers had been taken by Brusilov's armies. Falkenhayn admits Austrian losses of 'far more than 200,000 men in three days' (p. 249)." (Vulliamy, p. 242n)

No. 1312/ Telegram 15. Tsarskoe Selo> Stavka. 9 Aug 1916. 13.48> 14.25. To his majesty. Heartily thank you both. Very warm, again clear. Were at hospital<. She is leaving for Tobolsk.[330] [We] all embrace and kiss [you]. Alix

---

No. 1313/ Her No. 568.   Ts.[arskoe] S[elo]. August 9th 1916.
My own beloved One,

Ever such fond thanks for yr. sweet letter. Shall ask our Friend< to pray quite particularly on the 14-th.-15-th. to bless the beginning. They leave fr. town< at 7.[330]—Pouring and sun shining, very damp and hot.—She [Anna Vyrubova] is sorry she answered yr. wire so officially, but her mother [Nadezhda Taneeva] was there.—Kaufmann is coming to me, as I want them to send an unit [Red Cross unit] out with our troops to France and Alekseev agreed to the idea.—Lovy, I have forgotten what Zelenetsky's place is as aid to Kirill<, you speak with him and think the question over together.—Tchebikin [Chebykin] was very nice yesterday and most willing to help—and so I get another wing still for Aleksei's hospital (ex Academy).—Our Friend< had a good, long and nice talk with Shtyurmer—he told him to come to me every week.[336]—Now I must end, Zikov [Zykov] is waiting to see me—always somebody and have to write in a hurry. Goodbye, my Treasure Sweet—I cover you with tender, passionate kisses and remain yr. fondly loving old   Wify. [P.S.] God bless you.

336. Sturmer used Alexandra, Rasputin, and Pitirim to become chairman of the council of ministers. Rasputin was the first to realize that Sturmer, in office, planned to sever his ties with these "friends" and to be independent. In part this was because Sturmer really did hope to improve relations with the Duma. Grigory's insistence that Sturmer be in close contact with the empress—recorded here—was calculated to keep him "in line" as much as possible. (See Fuhrmann, *Rasputin*, pp. 171-175)

No. 1314.   Ts.[arist] Stavka. August 9th 1916.
Sweet Lovebird,   [This is a post card.]
   No time to write long. Thousand loving thanks for your dear letter. Am so glad
you took Holy Com.[munion]. For the moment all is quiet, only Sakharov[,
commander of 2nd Army,] continues his attacks. Today the weather is fine &
cooler. Mr. Gibbs arrived & begins to grow accust.[omed] to the life here. God
bless you my precious darling. Many tender kisses fr. your own old   Nicky

No. 1315/ Telegram 85. Stavka> Tsarskoe Selo. 9 Aug 1916. 20.01> 20.25.
To her majesty. Fondest thanks [for] dear letters. Again fine [weather]. [We]
came back from cinema. Tender kisses from both. Niki

No. 1316/ Telegram 12. Tsarskoe Selo> Stavka. 10 Aug 1916. 14.45> 15.16.
To his majesty. Warmly thank you both. Today two years since our hospital<
existed, hence we are treating today as a holiday. [We] all kiss and embrace
[you]. Alix

No. 1317/ Her No. 569.   Ts.[arskoe] S[elo]. August 10th 1916.
My own sweet Angel,
   Ever such tender thanks for your dear card. Grey and rather fresh. Go again
to the hospital< at 2½ for the Mass and feasting the 2 year's anniversary of our
hospital. It will be shy work [i.e., it will be a busy day] and we do not look forward to it.—Got a wire fr. Vologda, they[330] are traveling alright [sic]—before
leaving, she begged me to send you her blessing and kisses.— You will think
about sending for Raev, won't you, to have a good talk with him.— Shvedov and
then [A. A.] Bobrinsky come—every day have people to see.—Just had a wire
from Sergeev with the names of my wounded Siberian officers, Aug. 1 and
8-th,—losses of men he does not give. Now have to receive a Dr., who has to do
with my "Infants' and Mother's Home" [reference is to the "Society to Protect
Mothers and Children formed under the Patronage of Alexandra Fedorovna"] he
went on an inspection—its spreading well over all Russia.—Am glad Mr. Gibbs
gets on nicely, he was awfully happy to go [to Stavka].—Don't you think it
would be good if I stopped a few hours at Smolensk to look at some hospitals—and then reach you probably for dinner on the 23-rd? Yes, dear?—Now I
must be off.—God bless you, my Angel, long for you and yr. caresses. I cover
you with tender kisses. Ever yr. very own old   Girly.

No. 1318.   Ts.[arist] Stavka. August 10th 1916.
My own precious wify,
   Thank you many many times for your dear letter. I just [received] Kirill<
yesterday evening on his way from the guard, where he stayed 6 six [sic] days.
He saw many commanders & officers—they all told him the same thing about
old Bezobrazoff, as you know. So today I spoke upon this question to Alekseev
& told him I want to change B. He of course agreed it was better to relieve him
& name a good general. We are both thinking who could replace him—perhaps
one of the brothers Dragomirov!—such a pity I forgot to ask Kir.[ill]< about

Zelenetsky. [See Letter No. 1311b.] But as he returns in a week I can do it
then[,] I think. N.P.< arrives here on the 12th. Shall be awfully glad to see him
again. Dmitry< is so on [i.e., soon] passing through, I want to keep him here a
few weeks, because I heard from Georgi< that the boy has again that idea in his
head—that he is going to be killed. I am already counting the days before your
arrival! Sweet love, I must end. God bless you and the girlies. I cover your
beloved face with burning kisses. Ever your own old <u>Nicky</u>.
    P. S. I am worried how to explain to old Fredericks about [my sister] Olga's
divorce?[326] It is difficult writing [about] such an affair.

No. 1319/ Telegram 96. Stavka> Tsarskoe Selo. 10 Aug 1916. 20.05> 20.40.
To her majesty. Fondest thanks. Congratulate [you] with two years [of] hard
work in your hospital<. Fine, warm. [We] both kiss [you] tenderly. Niki

---

No. 1320/ Telegram 25. Tsarskoe Selo> Stavka. 11 Aug 1916. 14.20> 15.03.
To his majesty. Heartily thank you both. Very happy with your wise decision
[to remove Bezobrazov]. Weather fresher. [We] kiss, embrace [you]. Alix

---

No. 1321/ Her No. 570.   Ts.[arskoe] S[elo]. 11 August 1916.
My own Sweetheart,
    Heartiest thanks for yr. dear letter. I am grateful you are changing
B.[ezobrazov],—it wld. have hurt the guard sorely had he remained, as all knew
it was his fault the losses were so great and useless, alas! One speaks good of
the one brother [A. M.] Dragomirov—God grant he may be fit for that place and
work in harmony with the other Generals! Only they must have a better <u>intelli-
gence service</u> than he had, he knew next to nothing. Have not seen Dmitri<, yes,
I suppose his nerves are again, alas, good for nothing, its indeed a great pitty
[sic]. Don't let him go to that lady so often—such society is his ruin—nothing but
flattery and he likes it and then of course service becomes dull. You must keep
him firmer and don't let him be too free with his tongue either.—If Fred.< is not
well enough, I can send for C.[ount N. E.] Nierod [Nirod] and tell him to go to
Siverskaya and explain all to the old man [Fredericks, minister of the imperial
court] and find out what must be done [to process your sister Olga's divorce].
Only have I to say any date for it to come out, please, answer by wire. Operation went off well and yesterday's feast too. Now [daughters] O.[lga] and
T.[atiana] count as serving in the hospital.— Weather cooler. The girls have been
photographed whole afternoon by Funk, as they needed new ones for giving
away to their committees etc.—Tender blessings and 1000 kisses fr. yr. old
<u>Own</u>.

No. 1322.   Ts.[arist] Stavka. August 11th 1916.
My own beloved Girly,
    Ever so many tender thanks for your dear letter. Certainly if you stopped for a
few hours at Smolensk—it would be excellent & will give such pleasure to the
wounded & the people. Excuse the blotch I made on this envelope, but your pen
is very capricious & wont write for some time & then suddenly it shoots out a

blue fountain. Everything here is calm here [sic] along the front; in the Caucasus we have taken two Turkish regiments prisoners. I am expecting N.P.< to-day. I send you this paper of Maximovich—I think it is better to have them each pair for a fortnight! Don't you think? [See Letter No. 1325a.] Please send it me back [sic]. The japanese Prince Kan-in< arrives here in September, so [I. L.] Tatishchev & Bezak are going to meet him at Vladivostok & bring him here & Georgi< will look after him here. Now my Lovebird I must finish end. God bless you & the girlies! I kiss you so fondly & tenderly & remain ever your own old huzy Nicky.

No. 1323/ Telegram 1323. Stavka> Tsarskoe Selo. 11 Aug 1916. 22.08> 22.15. To her majesty. Tender thanks. N.P.< arrived, looks very well. Delicious warm weather. Good night. Fondest love. Niki

---

No. 1324/ Telegram 29. Tsarskoe Selo> Stavka. 12 Aug 1916. 14.10> 15.02. To his majesty. Tenderly thank you both. Today glorious, sunny. Very busy. Spent entire morning in hospital<. Tenderly kiss and embrace [you]. Very happy that N.P.< is with you, give him our heartfelt greetings. Alix

---

No. 1325/ Her No. 571.   Ts.[arskoe] S[elo]. 12 August 1916.
My own Sweetheart,
   Ever such loving thanks for yr. dear letter. I am glad things go well in the Caucasus.—Yes, its quite good if you have 2 a.d.c. doing duty a fortnight & then change them—but keep N.P.< for a bit longer so as to have a naval one with you & he has nowhere to go for sure;—& for you I am much quieter, when he is there—one of ours; & his influence upon Dmitri< is good. Got news fr. A.[nia]<, she sends you a kiss; to-morrow they arrive at Tobolsk[330] to-day they are on the river.—Weather finer.—Sorry have nothing of interest to tell you;—have much to do in the hospital< as such heavy cases, & daily operations.—Irina [Yusupova]'s Baby[, "Little Irina,"] is much worse again, lives here with the Grandparents[, Prince Felix the Elder and his wife Zinaida]—Irina [is] at Krasnoye with an "an-gina"—always ill, poor girl.—Am sure N.P. must have many interesting things to tell you about the battles. [a]
   Are remaining on the balkony [sic] so as to be near in case poor Rei-shakh[-Rit] has suddenly to be operated.—Am sorry my pen produces such an-tics—they are always capricious at the beginning. —Got a long & interesting doklad [report] fr. my Crimeans<. It will be a joy to be together again, tho' just now we are much needed in the hospital<.—Goodbye, my Sunshine. God bless & protect you & help you in all yr. difficulties. Had an interesting talk with [A. A.] Bobrinsky.—Cover you with fond & tender, longing kisses—Ever yr. very own old Sunny. [b]

No. 1326.   Ts.[arist] Stavka. August 12th 1916.
My beloved One,
   So many tender thanks for your dear letter. Yesterday I was rejoiced to see N.P.< who looks health itself. He is awfully interesting to listen to—after even-

ing tea we sat up & till 12.30 in the night & he was speaking about their life & their experiences. He praises so much our officers & men—Kirill< told me he had heard from all the generals & officers of the guard the same highest admiration for the battalion. Of course we expected it but it is good to hear it spoken out so eloquently.—Do make C^{nt} [N. E.] Nirod come to you & explain all for the old man [Fredericks]. —There is no date [for the announcement of my sister Olga's divorce] fixed.[326] Olga only wished it to come out after Aug. 15th. One thing she begged [is] that her upravlyayushchii kontory [estate steward] Rodzevich should be asked & spoken with about their affairs—in order that there should be less difficulty. Today I saw colonel Tatarinov—our mil.[itary] att.[ache] in Roumania. He brought the famous paper signed by them. The 15th the [offensive] will at last begin & attack the Austrian forces across their frontier. Now good-bye my beloved precious Sunny. God bless you & the girlies! I kiss you all tenderly & remain ever your own old   Nicky.

No. 1327/ Telegram 108. Stavka> Tsarskoe Selo. 12 Aug 1916. 19.32> 19.50. To her majesty. Warmest thanks. No date fixed, but it [the public announcement of my sister Olga's divorce] must be prepared very soon. This is an answer to your question. Tenderest love. Niki

---

No. 1328/ Telegram 34. Tsarskoe Selo> Stavka. 13 Aug 1916. 14.21> 15.10. To his majesty. Warmly thank you both, my dears. Rained just now, dull weather. Had operation, much work. Told [P. C.] Benckendorff to tell everything to old man [Fredericks] through [N. E.] Nirod. Warmly kiss and embrace [you]. Alix

---

No. 1329/ Her No. 572.   Ts.[arskoe] S[elo]. 13 August 1916.
My very own Angel,
    Ever such fond thanks for yr. dear letter. I told all about Olga's affair [i.e., divorce] to Benkendorf [P. C. Benckendorff], who was going to give it over to Nierod [Nirod], who after collecting necessary papers will tell all to the old man [Fredericks].—Can imagine how interesting all is that N.P.< has to tell you!—The weather is not very nice & it rained too, so I remain on the balkony [sic] & then go to the big palace<. Dmitri< has at last asked to come to tea.—Shtyurmer[336] begged to see me to-morrow.—Had an operation of one of my young Siberians, & heavy perevyazki [dressings], so lunched only at 1½.—Thank goodness the Roumanians will at last move—& what are our movements for the 15-th?—Benkendorf finds I must give a luncheon for Prince Kanin in September—a bore during the war, but I suppose necessary. —Well, are you thinking about Belyaev [the asst.-minister of war] as Minister of War—I think it wld. be after all a wise choice.—[A. A.] Bobrinksy finds things cant work well, whilst Sht.[yurmer] has so much to do, he cannot give himself over to one thing properly & entirely as he ought to & our Friend< found the same thing too.— Now Sweetheart, beloved One, I must end. God bless & protect you. I kiss you with unending true devotion & love you more than ever. Yr. very, very Own.

No. 1330.   Ts.[arist] Stavka. August 13th 1916.
My own beloved Sunny,
   Tenderest thanks for your dear letter. I have not either any interesting news to
give you. Old gen. Pau arrived fr. the Caucasus looking well, thin & [with] a
neat white beard. He leaves today and hopes to have a chance of taking your
leave! Instead of Dragomirov I have chosen gen. Gurko,[337] who commands the
5th army & is acquainted with the work of a large staff,—I mean to name him
instead of Besobrazov [i.e., Bezobrazov]. No more time, my angel. God bless
you & the girlies. I kiss you passionately & fondly, my precious little girly.
Ever your own old   Nicky.

337. General Vasily Gurko was an able "and at times a very brilliant commander. He was
fifty-three. As a young soldier he had seen active service in the Pamirs. In 1899-1900 he was military attaché to the Boers, and was captured by the English. He served with distinction in the Japanese War, and became military adviser to the Octobrist party. At the beginning of the war he commanded the 1st Cavalry Division, and he succeeded in retiring with small losses after the disaster of
Tannenberg. He was then promoted to the command of the 6th Corps, and in 1916 to the 5th Army.
His book, in spite of certain prejudices, is remarkably fair and reasonable, and in many respects a
valuable document on the war." (Vulliamy, p. 246n)

No. 1331/ Telegram 113. Stavka> Tsarskoe Selo. 13 Aug 1916. 19.37> 20.45.
To her majesty. Loving thanks. Warm, misty weather. So grateful [to you] for
telling Benk.[endorff] to give over commission. Tender kisses from both. Niki

No. 1332/ Telegram 88. Tsarskoe Selo> Stavka. 14 Aug 1916. 14.23> 15.04.
To his majesty. Tenderly thank you both. Foggy, grey, colder, hence [we] are
having lunch in our rooms. In thoughts together. Were at our Peshchernyi khram
[Chapel]<. [We] all warmly kiss [you]. Alix

No. 1333/ Her No. 573.   Ts.[arskoe] S[elo]. August 14th 1916.
My own Beloved,
   Warmest thanks for yr. sweet letter. Well, one hears much good of Gurko.
God grant him success & bless his commandment. More than ever my thoughts
are & will be with you these days [when the Brusilov offensive resumes], & I
have asked our Friend< to remember & pray much.—I send you my Image [icon]
back again, I have had a little border & safe ring[338a] made to it.—Also foggy,
grey & rather cold, a September day.—Dmitri< took tea with us yesterday—his
heart is not in a good state, [it] moves like mine also therefore of course has at
times pains, feels weak & gets out of breath. He ought to make a cure, as it is
only beginning & then he can be quite cured.—We went to our Peshcherny
Chapel< this morning. Afterwards we go to the store in the big palace< for me
to give jetons [medals] to all the workers.—Irina & Felix [Yusupov the Younger,
her husband] take tea.—Shirinsky-S[h]akhmatov has died—probably he had cancer —am sorry for his wife.—Dear Sweetheart, I long for caresses & to show you
all my deep, unending love & devotion—its hard, always being seperated [sic]!
Goodbye & God bless you sweet Sunshine. I cover you with kisses & remain
yr. deeply loving old   Wify.

338a. Sergeev translates these two words as "zapor na kolechke" (lock on the ring)(*Perepiska*, IV, p. 417); Nabokov renders them as "prochnoe kol'tso" ("solid ring")(*Pis'ma imperatritsy*, II, p. 161). What the empress is saying is not clear; she probably had a glass cover with a lock affixed to the front of this icon.

No. 1334.   Ts.[arist] Stavka. August 14th 1916.
My own precious Darling,
    Many loving thanks for your beloved letter. It is so good of you to have told [P. C.] Benckendorff [about] Olga's case,[326] because it would be so disagreeable for me to write it all out for the old man [Fredericks]. What [A. A.] Bobrinsky told you.[338b] I was affraid [sic] of the whole time. But it is really awfully diffi-cult to find such a man to be at the head of the munition departm[ent]. Sht.[yurmer] being the president of the council [of ministers] holds the rest of the ministers under him, but as soon as one of them should get the upper hand the rest will not bow down, or if they even do—there might begin intrigues & things would not go smoothly. There is of course one way out, Krivoshein's idea, to make the Min.[ister] of War—master of the whole situation. I doubt though Shuv.[aev] or even Belyaev succeeding in such a place. The second is a very weak man—he always gives way & is a slow worker. He & Sh.[tyurmer] have had difficulties & therefore they have to separate. B.[elyaev] is being named to the voen. sovet [Council of War]. Now I must end. God bless you my sweet Wify, my own Girly! I kiss you and the dear daughters very tenderly & remain ever your own old   Nicky.

338b. "Bobrinsky (the Minister of Agriculture) had said that Sturmer had too much to do, and that it was difficult to work with him. Sturmer's insufficiency and arrogance were weakening his posi-tion on all sides." (Vulliamy, p. 247n)

No. 1335/ Telegram 119. Stavka> Tsarskoe Selo. 14 Aug 1916. 19.00> 19.35. To her majesty. Best thanks. Also uncertain weather, cooler after tremendous downpour by night. [In] thoughts together. Tenderest love. Niki

No. 1336/ Her No. 574.   Ts.[arskoe] S[elo]. August 14th 1916.
My beloved One,
    I have remained at home this evening as am very tired and want to go to bed at 10 and drink something hot, as am fighting a cold down. The weather is quite sad, raining and cold and so dark all day.—Went to Alia< this afternoon and sat a while with her and her husband [A. E. von Pistol'kors], she looks and feels very unwell, has lost 15 pounds since spring. Then I went to Ania's< hospital, found all in good order. Afterwards—to give jetons [medals] to 70 people in the big palace<. Irina and Felix [Yusupov the Younger, her husband,] took tea—they were quite nice and natural, she very brown and he looking very thin, short hair and as page looks much better and holds himself properly.—Then to rest had Shtyurmer (therefore this big sheet of paper). If only I can write clearly and properly with a stupid, tired head. [a]
    Well, to begin with, it was a great blow to him [Sturmer] that Belyaev has been dismissed [as asst.-minister of war], as he [Sturmer] had given him the question over about the prisoners whom one must have for coalmines, etc.: all

over the country, and wished him to speak with the Commanders of armies to arrange with them how many they can spare etc:—he [Sturmer] gave him over this necessary and urgent commission for the <u>food</u> questions. Now he [Belyaev] is no longer in the ministery, [Sturmer is] not liked by Shuvaev, will no longer be able to help him, and he [Belyaev] <u>really</u> is a capable man and works far more than Shuvaev, who never appears at the Council of Ministers but sends his representants [representatives]. I so much hoped you wld. name him [Belyaev] minister of war [in place of Shuvaev]—[Belyaev] is a real gentleman and knows all questions, and a really able man, tho' Shuvaev cld. not appreciate him.—We [Sturmer and I] spoke long about the food question and wondered, whether it wld. not be more advisable to choose a military man (for example Shuvaev himself, who cld. manage for sure that question well as it resembles all he did so well for the Quartermasters Department—instead of being minister). [b]

Alekseev does not care for Shtyurmer, has clearly let other ministers feel this, perhaps because he is a civilian, and a military man wld. be more welcome. He [whoever would grapple with the supply problem, even if a military man,] wld. have to have the rights of Minister, wld. remain what you named him, at the head of it all, wld. see that all work together, help the ministers—and you wld. not have to change anything. He is not tired of the work nor affraid [sic] of it, only we thought perhaps you might prefer a military man to do it.[338b] So I said I shld. find out, and in case you wish to speak it over with Sht. and please send for him—he does not wish to bother you and wld. wish the initiative to come fr. you. Then about Volzhin he will give him the paper [granting his wish to be replaced as director of the Holy Synod] now—and wont you see Raev to have a good talk with him and see whether he suits you [as Volzhin's successor].— I believe that he, with Zhevakhov as aid[e] wld. really be [a] Godsend for the Church.[339] If you wish to see him, wire the date to me, without mentioning the name and Sht. will let him know. The other candidates I find quite unfit and knowing next to nothing about the church. [c, d]

When I spoke with [A. A.] Bobrinsky, he also found a special man ought to be at the head of the <u>food supplies</u> and who wld. have no other thoughts in his head and only live and think of this.—The old [A. A.] Khvostov comes to present himself to-morrow. So sorry to bother you with such a letter, but the old man [Sturmer] always feels relieved, when he can pour out his heart to one and is glad, when I go to the Headquarters. I daily pray God to help me be of use to you and come with right advice, our Friend< encourages Sht. to speak with me always,[336] as you are not here for him to talk over things with. I am touched the old man has confidence in yr. old woman. [e]

Why was Belyaev cleared out? [See Letter No. 1334.] Does it make it now easier for you to name him Minister [of War]?—I got 2 wires fr. Ania with lovely impressions fr. Tobolsk, where she has prayed for us all.[330] To-night they already leave again, to-morrow are on the river and 16-th reach Pokrovskoye[, Rasputin's home town in Siberia]. I shall finish this letter to-morrow. Sleep well Sweetheart, beloved Angel, my one and all, my dear patient sufferer.—My prayers and thoughts are at the front—for sure they [the renewed attacks of the Brusilov offensive] begin at 4 in the morning as usual—God help them and the holy Virgin, whose great feast it is—may she bless our troops.— [f]

15-th. Good morning my own Treasure. Fondest thanks for yr. dear letter I found upon my return from the hospital<. I am sorry you have not such a very high opinion of Belyaev, he seems always so exceedingly willing and does try his best, but I think it has been more than hard for him working under these 2 last Ministers of war [Polivanov and Shuvaev]—and he was going to help Sht. now so much and he [Sturmer] intensely regrets he wont have his [Belyaev's] help now—Perhaps independant [sic., i.e., as the minister of war] he [Belyaev] might be alright?—I had a letter fr. Olga Evg.<—you know she is always so grieved her husband no longer has his "eagles" [indicating the rank of colonel]. Now she read the Commanders of Military ports (rear or vice-admirals) are being called up to active duty in conformity with order [dated] 26/ 5. 1916[,] and of course her hopes and apetite [sic] arose, she begs me only to know this—but I mention it to you feeling, I must say sure, you cant do anything and Nilov I know is against him and [will] laugh at the idea of her wanting Papa F. [G. N. Papafedorov, the husband of "Olga Evg." referred to above] to get the "eagles" back again.— [g]

Not nice weather, raining and grey, the sun tried twice to break through the clouds, but without any success.—We were in our Peshch.[erny] Chapel< and then in the hospital—little work by chance, so had more time to sit and embroider and then fed some of those who cld. not eat alone.—Tho' I went early to bed, 10, only got to sleep after 2½ and woke up for good again at 7½.— Remaining on my sopha, so as to rest more.—Now sweet Angel, Goodbye and God bless you. Endless tender kisses fr. yr. very loving old Sunny. [P.S.] Poor Pr. [S. A.] Shirinsky-Shakhmatov died. [h]

---

339. In the fall of 1915, Alexandra hoped to see the post of "second assistant-director of the Holy Synod" created for her new favorite, N. D. Zhevakov. Director Volzhin, his assistant (Zaionchkovsky) and the Duma were hostile to doing favors for this notorious Rasputinite, so Nicholas withdrew the proposal. Despite Volzhin's opposition, Zhevakov received another Synod appointment. After a year of conflict, Volzhin wanted to resign. The emperor dismissed Volzhin (the "paper" Alexandra mentions making this official was dated August 7, 1916) and appointed him to the State Council. Nicholas Raev—who had ties to Pitirim and Rasputin—became the new director; Zhevakov was to be "second asst.-director." This stirred renewed opposition, and the scheme was dropped a second time. Zaionchkovsky was "promoted" to the Senate on October 13, 1916, and Zhevakov took the now-vacant position of "first" asst.-director. Note the difficulty Nicholas was having at this point finding men to serve as ministers. People were concluding the tsarist regime would soon collapse, talented men were waiting to join their fortunes to whatever would follow it.

No. 1337.   Ts.[arist] Stavka. August 15th 1916.
My own Lovebird,

Many thanks for your dear letter. Today is my Shirvantsy's holiday. If I am not mistaken they are going to be sent south to stand behind Sakharov and Shcherbachev. On the 18th Brusilov has decided to begin his attack with all his armies. Now you know that Roumania has declared war against Austria. That will certainly help our troops in Bucovina. Yesterday, as was decided, Zaionchkovsky's troops have crossed the Danube & are marching through Dobruzha & a bit of our Black Sea fleet came into Constantsa to help the roumanians, in case they were attacked by German submarines. It is pouring, it is blowing & sometimes appears sunshine—such a funny weather. Now I must end.

God bless you my darling little Wify! I kiss & the dear girlies tenderly. Ever
your Nicky.

No. 1338/ Telegram 96. Tsarskoe Selo> Stavka. 15 Aug 1916. 18.35> 19.00.
To his majesty. Warmly kiss and thank you both. Heavy rain. Miechen< had tea
with us. Seems that Nicky< is still at Pavlovsk, 2 times tried to leave but Tino<
ordered him to stay. May the Lord keep you! What news? Alix

No. 1339/ Telegram 124. Stavka> Tsarskoe Selo. 15 Aug 1916. 19.10> 19.25.
To her majesty. Warmest thanks [for] letter [and] image [icon]. Cooler and
finer. In thoughts together. Fondest kisses. Niki

No. 1340/ Telegram 101. Tsarskoe Selo> Stavka. 16 Aug 1916. 14.07> 14.40.
To his majesty. Tenderly thank you both, my dears. Rain continues. [I] worked
at hospital.< Pictures will be taken at Big palace<, very dull. [I] warmly kiss and
embrace [you]. Alix

No. 1341/ Her No. 575.   Ts.[arskoe] S[elo]. August 16th 1916.
My own truly Beloved,
   A big kiss for yr. dear letter. Benkendorf [P. C. Benckendorff] will bring you
the papers about [your sister] Olga['s divorce] in a few days. It continues pouring, wh. is really depressing.—Had an operation & many heavy perevyazki
[dressings] with tears & moanings!—Saw Maltsev a moment, he says their guns
help immensely & the aeroplanes keep away. They are at Lutsk & helped at
Rezhitsa—he has come for a few days.—I am sending [daughter] Marie's train off
& have asked the Headquarters to say where it is to go, quite to the left or to the
guards.—Siroboyarsky< has been sent south, passed the 8-th to the 11-th Army-
corps for whatever place needed. My Crimeans are not very far fr. Halicz, Sedov reached them alright [sic]. [a]
   I hear Sandro L.< intends marrying an awful woman, Ignatiev, born Coralli,
former cocote [sic] with a dreadful reputation—her sister is ruining old Pistolkors
for 3 years.[340a] I do hope it can be prevented—will only bring the foolish boy
great misery.—A.[nia]< & Lili Den reached Pokrovskoe this night.[330]—Miechen<
took tea & was alright, enjoyed her visit to Belaja Ts.[erkov'] & to Antoinette
(Josef) Pototzky. Real summer weather, everybody bathing & in summer
dresses.—Have to go now to the big palace< to be photoed with the
wounded—dull.—Spent the evening in the hospital,< lay there also on a sopha so
as to rest more. Goodbye my Treasure Sweet. God bless & protect you. Very
tenderest kisses fr. yr. own old   Girly.   [P.S.]   How nice the photos of Aleksei with the boys.—So Germany has declared war to Roumania, I thought as
much. Endless kisses lovy. [b]

340a. The "awful woman" was Nadezhda Nicholaevna Ignat'eva, the former wife of V. A. Ignat'ev. I have not been able to identify her sister; "old Pistolkors" was Lt.-Gen. Erik Augustinovich
von Pistol'kors, who had been married to Olga Valerianovna Gogenfel'zen. His son, Alexander
Erikovich von Pistol'kors ("Aksel'"), and his wife ("Alia"<) often appear in the Nicky-Sunny correspondence. The young man was an official in the state chancellery; he was interested in religious
questions and was a devotee of Rasputin.

No. 1342.   Ts.[arist] Stavka. August 16th 1916.
My own Lovebird,
    Thank you so much for your dear long letter, wh. gave me great pleasure. I
send these photos back to [daughter] Tatiana. Sometimes my head feels like
wanting to crack when I turn over those questions about naming this or that
name & trying to guess how it will go. The one cardinal question for us—is the
prodovol'st.[vennyi, i.e., supply] one. If the right man were found—all would go
well & the fabrics [factories] would work full speed. Perhaps Shuv.[aev] will do
these [things]; may be also Bel.[yaev] as min.[ister] of war will also be at his
place! I will speak it over with Alekseev.—I sent my order to poor Bezobrazov—as Gurko is gone already to take his place.[334] It will not be a pleasant
meeting for us both!—I will send for Sht.[yurmer] and let you know about Raev.
You know fr. the papers that Germany has declared war on Roumania & Italy to
[i.e., on] Germany. Now remains the question whether Bulgaria will follow suit.
Now my own darling Sunny I must end. God bless you and the dear girlies!
With many tender kisses I remain ever your own old <u>Nicky</u>.

No. 1343/ Telegram 136. Stavka> Tsarskoe Selo. 16 Aug 1916. 18.19> 19.03.
To her majesty. Tender thanks. Weather fine. Going directly to cynema. Fondest kisses from both. Niki

---

No. 1344/ Telegram 105. Tsarskoe Selo> Stavka. 17 Aug 1916. 14.20> 15.00.
To his majesty. Heartily thank you both. Rain continues, such a bother. [I] kiss,
embrace [you]. Am receiving La Guiche. Alix

No. 1345/ Her No. 576.   Ts.[arskoe] S[elo]. August 17th 1916.
My own Sweetheart,
    Warmest thanks for yr. dear letter—can imagine how awfully tired & weary yr.
poor head must be. Sunny will come & freshen her Treasure up with caresses.
God grant we shall be together Monday at 5½ for tea in the train, yes? Am
yearning for my 2 Beloved ones. Rain continues, still hope to get out at last if
clears up a bit.—Now La Guiche comes to me.—Am sending Yedigarov< off
with Yakovlev in [daughter] Marie's train to-morrow to see if he can manage. If
he went to another regiment he wld. sit on the head of others.—Lady Muriel Paget[, a British nurse working at the English Hospital in Petrograd and at the
front,] takes tea with us this afternoon. Always daily people to see & many
doklady [reports]. [a]
    Of course its sad for you about Bezobrazov,[334] but you saved him once, gave
him this beautiful chance—& he was not fit for it—whats to be done—one cannot
keep one & loose [sic] thousands because of his obstinacy.—Yes, send for
Sht.[yurmer] & speak to him about Raev.—Really I think Belyaev wld. be a good
choice & Shuv.[aev] more capable for the food question, as he managed the
Quartermasters Department well—& Shtyurmer remains at the head still, so will
watch that the Ministers do what the other asks.—Must end now. Cover yr. beloved face with tender kisses & remain yr. deeply loving old   <u>Wify</u>.   [P.S.]

God bless & protect you & help our troops & send success—all prayers & thoughts with them. [b]

No. 1346.   Ts.[arist] Stavka. August 17ᵗʰ 1916.
My own Treasure,
   Tender thanks for your sweet letter. I send you [Dr.] Derev.[enko]'s photos to choose, make a sign on those you wish to have & send them back. Dmitry< came today, we spoke long about difficult questions. He begged to be allowed to go for five days to town< & bring his things here for a longer stay. He is delighted at the thought of seeing you again. O.[tets, i.e., Father] Shavel'sky returned from an inspection of his from Shcherba.[chev]'s army full of splendid impressions. I was pleased to hear excellent accounts about Misha's< behaviour with his 2ᵈ cavalry corps. He asked, I mean Misha[,] to come & see me for a couple of days. Yesterday I saw Gurko & had a thorough talk with him & then together à trois with Alekseev. Thank God I think it [sic] is the man I wanted. He understands so well how the guards must be kept etc. Bezobrazov has not yet arrived.³³⁴ The weather is good on the whole, but in the afternoon it generally becomes cloudy. To-morrow Baby's< little comrade also leaves—he will miss him greatly! Good-bye and God bless you, my beloved own girlie. I kiss you and the dear little daughters very tenderly & remain ever your own old Nicky.

No. 1347/ Telegram 142. Stavka> Tsarskoe Selo. 17 Aug 1916. 19.15> 19.39. To her majesty. Fondest thanks. Sad you have such weather, here fine. Count the days before [your] arrival. Many kisses from both. Niki

No. 1348/ Her No. 577.   Ts.[arskoe] S[elo]. August 18ᵗʰ 1916.
Sweetest Lovebird,
   Very tenderest thanks for yr. dear letter.—Grey weather, but warmer. Do you manage still to lunch out, do hope so.—Lady Muriel Paget [see Letter No. 1345a] goes out to the guard again, she was there during the battles & had much to tell—envy her.— Also got a wire fr. [Rasputin, from] Tyumen to-day. [The following quote is in Russian.] "A bad tree will fall whatever be the axe which cuts it. St. Nikolai is with you—by his miraculous appearance he always does wonders." So glad you are contented with Gurko—is it the one who lay at us [i.e., was in our hospital] & whom Pss. Gedroits< saved at the Japanese war? Worked hard this morning, now must go to the blessing of [daughter] Olga's [train] wagon, arranged by Thekla Orlova Davidova [Fekla Georgievna Orlova-Davydova]. Fancy, poor Petrovsky wrote to Ania that Sandra had a son in July—not his certainly & he has no idea who is the father (may be several) & it counts him³⁴⁰ᵇ so to speak as they are not divorced—poor boy, am so sorry for him, he had no idea that she was expecting—she has been for months in the country.—Must end now. In four days, God grant!! Of course Becker< will catch me up at the Headquarters, am furious.— Goodbye my Sunshine, God bless & keep you! Endless tender kisses fr. yr. very   Own.

340b. The empress is saying that N. A. Petrovsky (see Biographical Index) expects this illegitimate child to be "counted" as one of his.

No. 1349.   Ts.[arist] Stavka. August 18th 1916.
My very own Lovebird,
    Tenderest thanks for your loving letter. Today at last the weather is lovely &
warm like in summer. Well! I saw Bezobrazov yester-day, had a long talk with
him & am pleased with his behavior—wh. proved me once more what a gentleman & honest man he is!³³⁴ I gave him a two month's leave, he intends to go
through a cure at the caucasian waters & begs to get any commandment in the
army. So I promised him, if his health allowed & if one of the guard corps were
vacant to name him there! At the head of a guard corps he was very good, why
not give a man after a higher place—a lower one wh.[ere] he can be of use according to his capacities? Gurko, with whom I spoke the other day upon the
same subject, told me it would be a wise system to name generals who had not
behaved badly of course, back to their last posts—like Scheidemann or Mishchenko etc. I quite agree to [i.e., with] this point of view. Dmitry< goes back
today. I am waiting for you terribly impatiently! and intend keeping you as long
as possible. God bless you my Love, my Sunny-darling. Many tender kisses
from your own old   Nicky.

No. 1350/ Telegram 116. Tsarskoe Selo> Stavka. 18 Aug 1916. 18.40> 19.20.
To his majesty. Tenderly thank you both, my dears. Sorry that Aleksei's friends
left. Forgot to send letter of our [daughter] Tatiana, will do it to-morrow. Mild
weather, we had a light rain. Went driving. Received (seven) Japanese[, including Prince Kanin<]. [I] warmly kiss and embrace [you] both. What news? Alix

No. 1351/ Telegram 146. Stavka> Tsarskoe Selo. 18 Aug 1916. 19.45> 20.28.
To her majesty. Loving thanks. Real summer day, now thunder storm beginning. Thoughts together. Fondest kisses from both. Niki

No. 1352/ Her No. 578.   Ts.[arskoe] S[elo]. August 19th 1916.
My own Treasure,
    Always in a hurry. Fondest thanks for yr. dear letter. Glad you are over yr.
conversation with Bezobrazov.—Just had a good talk with Zhilik< about Baby's<
lessons & ideas I have & he is writing them to P.V.P.< We bring Ania< with
us.—Then I had Sekretev—a long & interesting talk—so grateful to you for having
saved him in Polivanov's time, a young general of 38, so energetic—we spoke
about the aviation question—that I'll all tell you when we meet.— Frederiksy<
asked himself to come to-day to tea. Now I must fly to the red cross—then Pr.
Golitzin [Princess Vera Golitsyna, director of the Smolnyi Institute].—Great
grief for many over Belyaev's demission—for me & Vil'chkovsky[,] B.[elyaev]
did everything so quickly and through Rostov.[tsev] too & never made difficulties.—To-morrow Sht.[yurmer] asked to see me.—I thought you wld. send for
him. Must end. Excuse untidy flying writing. God bless you—endless kisses fr.
yr. own old   Sunny.   [P.S.] In 3 days [I will meet you at Smolensk]!!!

No. 1353.   Ts.[arist] Stavka. August 19th 1916.
My own Treasure,

Warmest loving thanks for your dear letter. Yes, till now we have always managed to lunch & dine out in the tent when it is fine & on the balcony when it rains. You ask which Gurko got the nomination? It is the little general who commanded the 1st cavalry division fr. Moscow. Groten liked him as his chief. Till now he commanded the 5th army at Dvinsk, & Dragomirov gets his place there. Thank God the news are good[341]—the first day of our attack [we] took 300 officers & over 15,000 austrians & germans prisoner. It seems the Roumanians have also good success for the beginning—they took three towns not far from their frontier. What you write about Petrovsky's wife is too bad! Poor boy! The weather is delicious[,] real summer, I hope it will keep so when you come! I & b-y [Baby<] are terribly impatient to see [you]— Mme. B.[ecker]< would be met with great animosity! Good-bye my love. God bless you & them very tenderly. Ever your own old   Nicky.   P.S. Tell [daughter] Tatiana to bring also 8 boxes of servian tobacco. Kisses.

341. "The military situation in the East was now regarded as so threatening by the German Supreme Command that they decided, in spite of Allied pressure on the Somme, to transfer four divisions from the Western Front. But the great Russian offensive was already losing impetus, and it was not long before the turn of the tide. Broussilov's advance was certainly one of the most notable military achievements of the war. Nearly a million of the enemy were put out of action, and the Russians captured an enormous amount of material. ... An extremely interesting passage in this correspondence (21st to 24th September) shows how the influence of Rasputin was really the decisive factor [in ending the offensive]." (Vulliamy, pp. 247-248n) Actually, the Nicky-Sunny correspondence shows no such thing. True, Rasputin (and Alexandra, as well) opposed continuation of the offensive, so costly in Russian life. So, too, at this point, did Russian military experts. I doubt Nicholas's decision to terminate the engagement was much affected by the opinions of his wife or "Friend." Nothing in the tsar's letters and telegrams suggests such influence.

No. 1354/ Telegram 152. Stavka> Tsarskoe Selo. 19 Aug 1916. 22.40> 23.40. To her majesty. Fond thanks. Very good news. Summer heat, occasional showers. Good night. Loving kisses. Niki

No. 1355/ Her No. 579.   Ts.[arskoe] S[elo]. August 20th 1916.
My own Beloved,

This is my last letter & again written in flying haste—the confusion of the last day. Fondest thanks for yr. dear letter! What joy if we are going to enjoy sunshine & warmth—we only have rain, its pouring since the morning & the leaves are turning yellow. Had a lot to do in the hospital, then Mme Zizi< lunched & Dmitri< has asked to come to tea. Bezobrazov came & talked much[334]—I shall repeat all to you.—Poor Masha Stenbok[-Fermor] has died, I regret it for the poor lovely Orlov boys—she managed well for them and I fear for Aleksei without her to keep him fr. a foolish marriage. Now Sht.[yurmer] comes—then must put my things together & arrange some paper[s], say goodbye to Alia< to whom I go every second day & who also looks upon me as a second mother. My "Children" [i.e., the wounded] augment and so many like to pour out their hearts to old me!—Thanks God for the good news, oh how lovely it is & now the 23-rd comes! Am bringing Botkin as S.P. [Fedorov] goes away.—Of course beastly

Becker< is coming—awful nuisance spoils everything. Feel rather rotten to-day & look forward to my "rest" with you, Sweetheart.—Endless kisses & blessings. Ever yr. very, very Own. [P.S.] Poor Liza Rebinder ([nee] Kutaissov) died. —

No. 1356.   Ts.[arist] Stavka. August 20. 1916.
My beloved Sweetheart,
    Ever so many thanks for your dear letter. I am also in a hurry as I had many people to talk to after lunch. Mad with happiness of seeing you soon! I send you this little paper [A. N.] Grabbe gave me. I don't know in what fight those poor fellows were killed & wounded! It was quite near the roumanian frontier—Dorna-Vatra. Our troops got the orders to advance down there. Atlast [sic] we have got warm weather! [P. C.] Benckendorff arrived & brought me a paper from Fred.< concerning [my sister] Olga's divorce. It must be sent to the Synod & all is done. Now my precious One, I must end. God bless you and the girlies! This is my last long letter. Many kisses from your own old loving & expecting huzy   Nicky.

No. 1357/ Telegram 126. Tsarskoe Selo> Stavka. 20 Aug 1916. 16.05> 16.45. To his majesty. Rain continues, [I] dream of your sun. Very busy, as always in the last days (before trip). Dmitry< will have tea with us. Zizi< had lunch. Warmly embrace and kiss [you]. Alix

No. 1358/ Telegram 156. Stavka> Tsarskoe Selo. 20 Aug 1916. 18.59> 19.55. To her majesty. Tender thanks. Feel for you, how tiresome to receive so much. When do you leave? Loving kisses from both. Niki

No. 1359/ Telegram 131. Tsarskoe Selo> Stavka. 20 Aug 1916. 20.53> 21.38. To his majesty. [We] are arriving to-morrow at 12.30, after Mass and hospital.< Heavy rain. Glad to see my dears. [I] warmly kiss you. Sleep well. May the Lord bless you! Dmitry< had tea with us. Alix

No. 1360/ Telegram 133. Tsarskoe Selo> Stavka. 21 Aug 1916. 9.50> 10.47. To his majesty. Bit of sun trying to break through, only 8 degrees. Now going to our lower church, then to hospital< for final perevyazki [dressings]. Am terribly happy over to-morrow. She [Anna Vyrubova] from afar sends kisses to you both and N.P.< May the Lord bless you, my dears! We all tenderly kiss [you]. Alix

No. 1361/ Telegram 161 in Russian. Stavka> Bologoe. 21 Aug 1916. 15.00> 15.25. To her majesty. Heartily thank you for letters, [we] are quite joyful over [your] arrival. Today colder, no sun. [We] warmly embrace [you]. Niki

No. 1362/ Telegram 31. Malaya Vishera> Stavka. 21 Aug 1916. 16.45> 16.54. To his majesty. Tenderly thank you both for dear letters. Terribly sorry about poor Zolotarev. [We] are travelling, freezing. In thoughts together. [We] all warmly kiss [you]. God keep you. Alix

No. 1363/ Telegram 91 in Russian.   Krasnoe, Al.> Stavka.   22 Aug 1916.
14.10> 16.12.   To his majesty.   Were at cathedral, four hospitals. Am tired,
weather was good, now getting worse again. Only 5 degrees during night. [We]
await seeing you soon with impatience. [We] warmly kiss [you]. Alix

---

No. 1364/ Her No. 580.   Ts.[arist] Stavka. September 4th 1916.
My own beloved Sweetheart,
   Its horribly hard leaving you my both treasures again, tho' we were 2 weeks
together, its never enough for loving hearts. And above all at such time when
you have such a terrible load to carry upon your poor, dear shoulders. Could I
but help you more—I pray so hard for God to give me wisdom & understanding
so as to be a real help for you in every way; & to advise you always rightly. Oh,
my Angel—God will send better days, luck & success to our brave troops—may
He enlighten the Chiefs that they should leed [sic] them right & wisely.—You
will be having the ministers now & speak on energetically to them—they do try,
are only so slow & heavy to move.—Only my Sunshine—please, I entreat you—do
not <u>hurry</u> with the Polish affair³⁴⁵—dont let others push you to do it until we get
over the frontier—I fully trust in our Friends< wisdom endowed by God, to
council what is right for you & our country— He sees far ahead & therefore His
judgement can be relied upon.— Your loneliness will be great—& so dull—no real
friend near you—shall be quieter when N.P.< returns again—he is one of ours,
blessed by our Friend to be of use to you—& now he has learned & seen much in
these months.—What shall I do without yr. caresses & beautiful love! I thank
you over & over again for all & for this holiday—shall live upon sweet remembrances. Keep well. God bless you. Cover you with endless, burning kisses &
hold you tightly in my arms. Ever Sweetheart, yr. very own old   <u>Wify</u>.

No. 1365/ Telegram 21 in Russian. Stavka> Smolensk, Al. 4 Sept 1916. 19.55>
20.55. To her majesty. Orsha, Aleks.[androvskaya gubernaya], the following.
Hearty thanks for dear letter. Melancholy and lonely. Good night. Have a good
trip. We both tenderly embrace all. Niki

No. 1366/ Telegram 0182. Orsha, train station> Stavka. 4 Sept 1916. 20.12>
23.15. To his majesty. Very empty, sad without you both, [we] warmly kiss
you, wish you a good night. Am melancholy. Alix

No. 1367.   Ts.[arist] Stavka. September 4th 1916.
My own beloved Wify,
   Ever so many loving thanks for your dear letter & also for those few lines you
wrote on a sheet of paper & left in my note book.^{342a} It is for me to thank you
for coming here to see us two & living after all not so comfortably in the train
with all that row [i.e., noise] & whistling of engines going on the whole night!
We are better off here in this house—so it is certainly for Aleksei & me to be
grateful to you. Coming back from the station was very sad— we both felt
lonely. I pounced upon my papers & he went to his dinner. He is fast asleep
after having said hastily his prayers. It is cold & dreary out of doors & I intend

going to bed early. At dinner Sergei< and Kirill< were my neighbours; the second has just come from an inspection of our naval flotilla on the river Pripyat, & told me some interesting things. The rest made a great row [racket] at table as I had foreseen today at lunch. [a]

My girly, how I miss you & our talks in the evening. Though the others sometimes disturbed us (Dmitry< and Igor,< etc.)—still it was a joy we saw each other. This time luckily there was no bustle whatever & that was a great luck. I was so happy too you came to spend the anniversary here. I am sure your stay gives very great pleasure to the people of the whole staff, especially the smaller ones. Dmitry is sorry the girls are gone—their presence always puts him in a gay humour. I suppose Igor also regrets they left, but I am not going to find that out from him! [b]

September 5th. Good-morning, my own Darling! The sun is so bright & warm, but in the shade it is cold. And you, poor things, are rattling away towards the north, where it is real autumn & the leaves are yellow & falling. Your beloved letter is a real comfort for me & I have often reread it & kissed the dear lines. Today is the feast of the Chevaliergardes [Cavalry Guards]. We have just finished our lunch & intend motoring out in the woods, as it has again become grey.—Along the front [we see] artillery fire & strong counter attacks in the 7th Army where our troops repulsed them with heavy losses for the enemy.   In Roumania near the Danube their troops have behaved better,[342b] & the general outlook is good. At Salonica the Servians are moving forward & have pushed the Bulgars away. My Lovy-mine I must end. God bless you & the girlies! I kiss you most tenderly and remain your own old Nicky. [c]

342a. This extra "sheet of paper" seems to be lost; I did not find it with the letter in question (published here as No. 1364/ Her No. 340) in the State Archive of the Russian Federation (GARF).
342b. On August 19/ September 1, 1916, "Russian troops were advancing in Volhynia, and at the same time the Roumanians were moving forward and had occupied Hermannstadt." By September 4/ 17, 1916, " heavy fighting was in progress at Merisor in Transylvania. The Russian and Roumanian forces were compelled to retire, and [to fall] back to the Rasova-Tuzla line." (Vulliamy, pp. 251n, 253n)

No. 1368/ Telegram 12. Likhoslavl> Stavka. 5 Sept 1916. 11.15> 12.11. To his majesty. [We] are travelling well, slept so-so. [I] miss [you] very much. Tenderly thank you for last evening's telegram. Clear day. [We] all warmly kiss you. Alix

No. 1369/ Telegram 25. Stavka> Tsarskoe Selo. 5 Sept 1916. 19.35> —-. To her majesty. Thanks for two wires. Hope [you] arrived well. Thoughts continually together. Tender love [and] blessings. Niki

No. 1370/ Telegram 14. Tsarskoe Selo> Stavka. 5 Sept 1916. 21.15> 22.16. To his majesty. [We] arrived safely. Very cold. Just now received poor widow of count Reishakh[-Rit]. Ania< arrives today. In tender thoughts am with you. [I] embrace and warmly kiss you. Thank you for telegram. Sleep well. Alix

No. 1371.   Ts.[arist] Stavka. Sept. 5th 1916.

My own beloved one,

I begin this letter before going to bed, because I feel a great wish to talk silently to you. All my papers are sealed & I have just finished tea with a few of my suite. Happy to know you [are] safe at home. A pity the weather is so cold. Here also it is fresh. Babykins< & I both felt cold in our rooms, so I had the stoves just slightly heated only to take away the dampness. With open windows in the day the air like that is good. My pen is hard & writes abominably; when I have finished & shut it up it squirts the ink like a bubble! Today we went along a very pretty new road— the beginning of which we have often passed—it looks like the roads at Spala. Very nice country & fine trees along the whole road. After tea I received Shakhovskoi & had a long talk with him. He is truly a good honest man. He told me rather interesting things about N.[icholasha]< & others in the Caucasus, where he has been lately & seen them all! Now good-night, my own Sweetheart; it is time to go to bed.   [P.S.] Sept. 6th. It is fine & warm again. My morning was busy so have no time to write long. God bless you my own Lovebird & the girlies. I kiss you & them very tenderly, her [Ania<] also & our Friend<. Ever your very own Nicky.

No. 1372/ Telegram 20. Tsarskoe Selo> Stavka. 6 Sept 1916. 14.00> 14.30. To his majesty. Warmly thank you both for priceless letters. Clear sunny day. Today Paul< comes for tea. [I] miss [you] terribly, so empty here. Am going for a drive. [We] all warmly kiss and embrace [you]. Alix

---

No. 1373/ Her No. 581.   Ts.[arskoe] S[elo]. September 6th 1916.
My own beloved Angel dear,

I was intensely happy to receive your dear long letter & kiss & thank you for it over & over again. Oh, my Love, how I miss you, so empty here—but notwithstanding I slept like dead beat & did not wake up once in the night, wh. for me is a more than rare thing. A bright, sunny day—the leaves are so yellow & red—quite autumn—a great difference in these 2 weeks. Found our wounded all much better. Placed our candles at Znamenje< & then did our work. Taube & Pss. Gedroitz< thank very much for yr. messages.—Paul< has already asked to come to tea. Colonel Maltsev is coming now as wants to see me before returning to Lutsk. Saw Yedigarov<, who went with [daughter] Marie's train for a trial. He wants to get service now in Persia where is being formed a cavalry unit—against the Turkish gendarms [sic] or something like that—& I shall try & help arranging it for him.—Long talk with Vil'chk.<—affairs—& Isa< to lunch as [it was] her birthday & now feel quite stupid in my head already. [a]

Poor Countess Reishakht Rit came yesterday—holds herself very bravely, & then A[nia]<. She showed me our Friend's< wire to you. He says from to-day on the news will be better. The Image (ikon) in the Monastery to wh. I several times went (He knows it, years ago prayed there when He walked all over Russia); says its a very miraculous one & will save Russia.—Do go to it once, its so close to the house—& the Virgin has such a sweet face.—He [Rasputin] spoke with Raev over an hour,—says he is a real God's send, & spoke so well about all Church questions & in such a spiritual way.—Is sad that heaps of people write nasty letters against Him (Gr.<) to Alekseev.—We traveled well, it was so cosy having N.P.< with us & reminded one of the Headquarters so much.—Had good long talks about all the serious questions. He is so grateful to you for all yr. great kindness to him.— [b]

Lovy dear, please dont let them present Mme Soldatenko[va] to you—you remember I told you I had the conviction [A. N.] Grabbe wants to do it. And fancy that nasty man had the idiocy of telling Nini< his friend, that he hoped I wld. not be going now to the Headquarters so as to get you acquainted with her & that she might become yr. mistress. What a vile, low thing to say—she was furious & gave it him nicely. (Thats, no doubt, why he [Grabbe] gives you these exciting books to read.) Don't repeat this to him, but keep her away—she tried to get Isa to come to her, but she thanked & refused. Her reputation is very bad—N.P. knows with whom she "lived" before—this is her second husband—& he said he wld. not set his foot in her house. She tries to catch [seduce] the grd. [grand] Dukes & suite—to play a part [i.e., be important]—I saw how she looked up at their box & found it strange she stood below when we passed—I told you then I felt sure they want to get her presented.—Its a dirty, mean thing of Grabbe, when we are so kind to him.—I should not have allowed her to remain living there—its a bad tone at the Headquarters & will give rise to talks. To-day at the cynema [sic] she is sure to turn up again.—Excuse my writing all this but I want you to take care of Grabbe. [c]

Another thing he said to Ressin< (know all this fr. A.<) that Voeikov< will be leaving & that one will propose it to him—this astonished Grabbe greatly.—Must hold him in hand—he plays the fool & is amusing with the Children, not clever but sly & not "clean minded".—Forgive change of pen, but the other needs refilling—I have 2 such pens, only this one is thicker.—It was good having some cosy, calm talks in my compartment—only too little, on account of the boys. I live on the remembrances & thank God He lets us meet—4 months is a very long time to be away.—Me too kisses oo sweet letters & reread them with a yearning heart.—Its cosy living in the train [when I visit you at Stavka], I like it. But with joy I took my bath last night.— [d]

You know Pustov.[oitenko] is one of the men of yr. staff I like best—such kind, honest straightforward eyes.—Thank God, news better. Our Friend wld. have liked if we had taken the Roumanian troops in hand to be surer of them.—We are going to drive. Sad, already autumn before we scarcely had any summer here.—Must end. I send you some photos I did.—Love to Dmitri< & Igor<.—I bless & kiss you without end, long to feel yr. tender arms around me & kiss yr. sweet lips. God be with you, Nicky mine. Ever yr. very own old   <u>Sunny</u>. [e]

No. 1374/ Telegram 26. Stavka> Tsarskoe Selo. 6 Sept 1916. 20.17> 21.12. To her majesty. Tender thanks for dear wire. Your last letter is No. 580. Weather finer. Just saw interesting cinema. Loving kisses from both. Niki

---

No. 1375/ Telegram 23. Tsarskoe Selo> Stavka. 7 Sept 1916. 0.33> 1.41. To his majesty. Heartily thank you for telegram. [We] drove during day, will sit home peacefully in evening since heart is still not entirely right. Daisy< answered that older son of poor Mossy [Princess Margarita of Hesse] is killed, now she has lost both. Is simply terrible. Sleep well. [I] kiss [you] warmly. Alix

No. 1376/ Telegram 26. Tsarskoe Selo> Stavka. 7 Sept 1916. 15.43> 17.12.
To his majesty. Warmly thank you for both dear letters. Were at funeral of little
Zolotarev, very emotioning. Silaev had lunch with us, he comes to you Friday.
[I] warmly embrace and kiss [you]. What news? Alix

No. 1377/ Her No. 582.   Ts.[arskoe] S[elo]. September 7th 1916.
My own sweet Angel,
    Thank you from the depths of my heart for yr. beloved letter. I cover you with
kisses for it, Lovy.—Here one is always in a hurry. From the hospital to the otpevanie [funeral] of poor little Zolotarev.—His sisters remind one of him. His
horse followed in the procession—& the men of his squad stood watching on
crutches —so pathetic.—Then Silaev & Raftopulo to lunch. The Prof. is very
much against his returning to the front & spoiling his health completely—he
agrees its unwise—but he wants to try & put order in the regiment & clear away
bad elements. If you wld. let him try that & then say you will keep him in the
suite, that wld. be best of course. His heart is in a bad state & he is so weak &
unfit. He leaves to-morrow for the Headquarters. To my mind he wont stand it
above a few days at the front. He can be of use to you always & such a perfect
pure man, as one rarely finds—but no health, alas, any more; & so worried.— [a]
    Then I received officers—Kazakevich too, who needs still treatment & hopes
later to get service in the south.—A. has just come & sends much
love.—Shtyurmer comes at 5½ & I see our Fr.< in the evening.—[Daughter]
Tatiana worked for me & I sat & looked on, as must take care of my
heart.—N.P.< was with our Friend & He [Rasputin] was contented with him &
[thought] that through suffering [N. P. Sablin] had quite come back to Him &
God.—Baby< wrote a sweet French letter all alone, too nice;—I send him his
money [i.e., allowance].—I send you a petition of the widow of Sauvage—he died
at the war—she is a nice woman, very poor, has two big daughters & asks for a
bigger pension.—The other 2 petitions are fr. a poor official who asks his son to
be put into a cadetcorps. [b]
    Your dear letters are my joy—miss you oh, so, much Sweetheart!—Now must
end, beloved Angel.—Ah yes, I had Paul< for tea & a long talk. Well, I think he
will really be of use & has quite sound ideas.—Seems again losses amongst our
sailors, & a young officer (we dont know) wounded through the mouth. Do
wish they wld. take them back, they are much to [sic] good to be wasted like
that.—[Daughter] Olga has a committee this evening.— God bless & protect you.
Remember wify to-morrow, Sept. 8-th— my day. If not too tired shall try & go
to Church this evening. Very, very fondest endless kisses & boundless love, my
Own, fr. yr. little   Sunny. [P.S.] My love to Dmitri & Igor.— [c]

No. 1378.   Ts.[arist] Stavka. Sept. 7th 1916.
My own Lovebird,
    Your letter has not arrived as the train is late on account of a slight accident
that happened with another train. Mamantov was to come with it. Luckily the
weather is again much warmer—today it is grey & windy. The cinema yesterday
was really most interesting & exciting! We all spoke about it in the evening!
Grigorovich came with Rusin & explained that things were not going so well in

the higher commandment of the Baltic fleet. Kanin became tired from not seeing well & let the reins loose. Therefore it is absolutely necessary to replace
him. The best man in his place is a young admiral Nepenin, the Chief of the
Liaison Service of the Balt.[ic] Fleet. I consented & signed the nominations.
Already today the new admiral left for the sea. He is a friend of Kolchak of the
Black sea, being two years older & has the same strong will and great capacities! God grant he may show himself worthy of his distinction. I think so much
of you, my darling; I am glad our Friend< has arrived [in Petrograd]. God bless
you my own beloved Wify and the girlies! With many tender kisses ever your
own old Nicky.

No. 1379/ Telegram 28. Stavka> Tsarskoje Selo. 7 Sept 1916. 19.42> 20.25.
To her majesty. Fondest thanks for dear letters and photo, also for two wires.
No news. Everything quiet these days. [I] kiss you all tenderly. Niki

---

No. 1380/ Her No. 583.   Ts.[arskoe] S[elo]. September 7th 1916.
My own Sweetheart,
   Tho' I am very tired I must begin my letter this evening, so as not to forget
what our Friend< told me. I gave yr. message & He sends His love & says not to
worry, all will be right.—I told Him my conversation with Shtyurmer, who says
Klimovich must absolutely be sent away (he becomes senator [i.e., he should be
appointed to the Senate]) & then old [A. A.] Khvostov will go, as he cannot get
along without him. Khvost. is nervous & feels ill (I know he dislikes Sht, & so
does Klimovich, who is a bad man, hates our Friend & yet comes to him pretending & cringing before him).[343]   Now Sht. wants to propose this Pr. [N. L.]
Obolensky fr. Kursk-Kharkov (before that at the old Headquarters with Niko-
lasha<!!), now works at the food-question, to become minister of the Interior,
but Gregory begs you earnestly to name Protopopov there. You know him & had
such a good impression of him— happens to be of the Duma (is not left) & so
will know how to be with them.[315] Those rotten people came together & want
Rodzianko to go to you and ask you to change all the ministers & take their candidates—impertinent brutes![344] [a]
   I think you could not do better than name him [Protopopov]. Poor [A. A.]
Orlov was a great friend of his—I think Maximovich knows him well. He likes
our Friend since at least 4 years [Rasputin and Protopopov actually met in 1913]
& that says much for a man—& this Obolensky is sure to be again of the other
clan.—I don't know him, but I believe in our Friend's wisdom & guidance. He is
sad you never come here—yr. presence is also needed here, even if only for 2
days, unexpectedly, they will all feel the Master has come to have a look. It
would have been lovely, & not difficult for a flying visit & make people
happy.—I told Him [Rasputin] that Sht.[yurmer] spoke to me about announcing
officially about Constantin[ople]:[73]—you know what you said to Georgi [King
George V]. [b]
   He also thinks it wld. be good as it [the secret agreement giving the city to
Russia] binds France & England before the whole of Russia & then they must
keep their word after.—About Poland He [Rasputin] begs you to wait,[345] Shtyurmer too; only not before we cross the frontier—do listen to Him who only want

yr. good & whom God has given more insight, wisdom & enlightenment than all the military put together. His love for you & Russia is so intense & God has sent Him to be yr. help & guide & prays so hard for you.—I told Sht. again about having the paper [decree] about the money given to the Union [of Zemstvos and the Union of Towns] to be printed—you told it him long ago—he said the ministers were looking it through—you remind him again. So as not to forget write out—or no, here I shall write out for you to remember, when you have him on Saturday.— [c]

Our Friend finds it excellent to send our units with priests or monks fr. all the different monasteries—to be in the front hospitals & go out & bury our poor dead, where the regimental priests have no time—I shall speak to Raev to-morrow.—I must go to sleep now, its after 12 & I am very tired. Rested fr. 6-7 & then went to Church.—Goodnight & sleep well, my Pet—think of you so constantly—so empty & quiet here. 4 months we have not slept together—even more.—Bless you, Lovebird, God give me strength to be yr. help & find the right words to give over everything rightly & to persuade you as our Friend & God would wish. [d]

8-th My day.—Thank you my Huzy sweet for your precious letter. Such joy to hear fr. you.—That new Admiral [Nepenin], is he not the one Fillimore [Phillimore] appreciates so much? God grant him success—one does need energetic ones & poor Kanin's ill health no doubt made him less capable latterly.—Just saw Benkendorf [P. C. Benckendorff] about the Japanese.—The girls have gone driving with Irina [Tolstaya?] & I take the others & Ania<.—Now must end. God bless you my Life & joy.—I cover you with kisses & remain yr. own old Wify. [e]

343. At his request, A. A. Khvostov was relieved of the post of minister of the interior (September 16/29, 1916). E. C. Klimovich, the assistant-minister and *ex officio* police director, was dismissed on September 15/28, 1916, and "promoted" to the Senate.

344. A meeting occurred in Rodzyanko's office on September 6, 1916. Those present requested, among other things, a speedy reconvocation of the Duma, which according to the tsar's plan was not scheduled to go back into session until November 1916. (Nabokov: Alexandra, *Pis'ma imperatritsy*, II, p. 172n)

345. Hoping to gain the support of Poles against Russia, Germany and Austria announced that after the war they would unite Poland and grant it independence. Sazonov responded with a plan for Polish autonomy, and the tsar reacted favorably to it on June 30/July 13, 1916. Alexandra, Rasputin and all but three of the ministers opposed Polish autonomy. Although Sazonov was dismissed as minister of foreign affairs on July 7/23, 1916, this was not due to the Polish question. (Pares, *Fall*, pp. 339-341) The reference in this letter to Poland was caused by the fact that rumors were appearing in the press that the anticipated edict granting Polish autonomy was to be revised. (Nabokov: Alexandra, *Pis'ma imperatritsy*, II, p. 173n)

No. 1381/ Telegram 34. Tsarskoe Selo> Stavka. 8 Sept 1916. 14.04> 14.33. To his majesty. Tenderly thank you both for dear letters. Was at our church and hospital<. Sunny, am going for drive. Embrace and kiss [you] many times. She [Anna Vyrubova] sends greetings. Alix

---

No. 1382.   Ts.[arist] Stavka. Sept. 8th 1916.
My own beloved Sunny,

Your dear long letter with several petitions gave me an enormous pleasure & I thank you heartily for it. What you wrote yesterday about [A. N.] Grabbe & what he told Nini< astonished me greatly. [See Letter No. 1373c.] I remember that in the summer Igor< was speaking about the lawn tennis arranged here & the hope that I might go there & watch the games. I answered that he was to mind his own business. The same evening at tea I was alone with Grabbe & he told me how right I was in declining to go to that place, where Mme. Soldat.[enkova] & other ladies usually went, as that would certainly lead to stupid stories etc. So I do not know how to put those two facts together—I mean what Gr.[abbe] said to N.[ini]< & then to me. Lovy-mine, you can be quite sure I will not make her acquaintance, whoever may want it. But also don't allow A.[nia]< to fill your ears with stupid gossip—it does no one good—nor yourself nor those included! Yes, the losses of the poor Guards[346] have again been heavy—I dont know the details yet! Good-bye & God bless you, my own darling Wify. With many tender kisses ever your own old Nicky.

346. Letters No. 1403 and 1413c below suggest these losses were occurring in the naval guards battalion, the Guards Equipage<. This unit was soon transferred to the Black Sea for rest and rehabilitation. The idea of using them for an assault against Constantinople was discussed at this time, but it never materialized.

No. 1383/ Telegram 30. Stavka> Tsarskoe Selo. 8 Sept 1916. 20.08> 21.05. To her majesty. We both thank you heartily for letters and photos. Rainy morning, now fine. Fondest kisses, bow to all. Niki

No. 1384/ Telegram 43. Tsarskoe Selo> Stavka. 9 Sept 1916. 14.37> 16.39. To his majesty. Tenderly kiss, thank [you] both for dear letters. Just now returned from town<. Saw poor Countess Hendrikov, [she] is utterly unconscious, dying. Placed candles at Kazan cathedral. Clear, sunny. Warmly embrace [you]. N.P.< had tea with us yesterday. Please read today's letter with attention. Alix

No. 1385/ Her No. 584.   Ts.[arskoe] S[elo]. 9 September 1916.
My very Own,
    Warmest thanks my own Sweetheart for your so sweet letter.—Went to Znamenje< for half an hour to the hospital< & then to town< with Isa< & (Ania<) to see poor Css. Hendrikov, who is quite dying—utterly unconscious, but I remembered she had asked me to come when she wld. die. Inotchka[, Alexandra Balasheva, a daughter,] also just arrived fr. the country looking awfully ill; [Hendrikova's other daughter,] Nastinka< very brave only cried when I went away. Then I placed candles in the Kaz.[an] Cathedral & prayed for you, my Angel. Back at 1¾. Lovely, sunny day. Too tired to go out. Despairing that the losses of the guard again are so great[346]—but have they advanced at least.—Paul< has not a good impression of Kaledin, says he never seems sure of success—& that is not a good thing, as then he is less wise & energetic—wish they wld. spare the guard more.—Dear Sweetheart, all my tender, tender love & thoughts surround you with great longing & love—hate yr. loneliness. [a]

You know deary, I shld. not have Dmitri< & Igor< on duty at the same time, am sure Igor feels he is at a disadvantage then—& notices the difference of ones treatment with Dmitri & then he comes more silly & his amour propre suffers. We had N.P.< for tea yesterday—he left for 2 days to Moscou [sic] to see (only) his 2 sisters who had just come there—the widow with her boys & the youngest sister.—Miechen< has gone off for 10 days to Odessa etc.! Since Aug. 10th my Siberians have 43 men killed, 281 wounded, 2 lieutenants killed, 2 wounded & 2 contusioned.—Had Raev for nearly an hour—interesting & understanding so well all the necessary questions. Zhilik's< letters about the "hand" are most interest-ing—can imagine how excited Babykins< was.[424]—A triumphal arch for the Japanese is being erected in town near the station—seems strange in war-time.—[b]

Ania has begun reading an interesting English novel to me. I spend the eve-nings at home, too tired to go to the hospital<. —Greek Nicky< seems still to be at Pavlovsk. Now sweetest of Loves, whom I miss so greatly & long to clasp to my burning old heart—goodbye. God bless & protect you & help you in all. A tender kiss fr. yr. old   Sunny.   [P.S.] Please, take Protopopov as minister of the Interior, as he is one of the Duma, it will make a great effect amongst them & shut their mouths.[315]— [c]

No. 1386.   Ts.[arist] Stavka. Sept. 9th 1916.
My very own Lovebird,
Tenderest thanks for your dear long letter in which you give over some mes-sages from our Friend<. That Protopopov, is I think, good a [sic] man, but he is much in affairs with fabrics [factories] etc.[315] Rodzianko proposed him long ago as minister of commun.[ications] instead of Shakhovskoi. I must think that question over as it takes me quite unexpectedly. Our Friend's idca's [sic] about men are sometimes queer, as you know—so one must be careful especially in nominations of high people. That Klimovich I do not know personally. Is it good to send away both at the same time—I mean the Min. of Int. & the man at the head of the police?[343] That must all be thought out carefully! And whom to be-gin by? All these changes exhaust the head. I find they happen much too often. It is certainly not at all good for the interior of the country because every new man brings changes also into the administration. I am sorry my little letter has become so tiresome, but I had to answer your questions. God bless you [&] the girlies. I kiss you all tenderly. Ever, my sweet Sunny, your own old Nicky.[347]

347. Rasputin was urging Nicholas to make Protopopov minister of the interior and also to replace Klimovich who, as assistant minister, headed the police. The appointment was made the following month, "but the Tsar's hesitation is noteworthy. ... The Tsaritsa desired [Klimovich's] dismissal because he 'hated our Friend'—a reason which was generally sufficient." (Vulliamy, p. 257n) Actu-ally, Shakhovskoi was acting minister of trade and industry since February 1915. S. V. Rukhlov was minister of communications from 1909 until October 27, 1915, when he was replaced by A. F. Tre-pov.

No. 1387/ Telegram No 31.   Stavka> Tsarskoe Selo.   9 Sept 1916.   20.22> 20.33. To her majesty. Fondest thanks for dear letters. Bright, colder. Silaev arrived. Tenderest kisses. Niki

No. 1388/ Telegram 46. Tsarskoe Selo> Stavka. 10 Sept 1916. 10.04> 12.02. To his majesty. Countess [Hendrikova] died this night. Will you not telegraph [your regrets] to Nastinka?< Clear day. Tenderly kiss you both. What news? Please, do not forget my letter since the one the old man[348a] wants to suggest is again among those who are against you and what we love. Keep him in his place. Alix

348a. Alexandra is saying that the "old man" (Sturmer) wanted N. L. Obolensky (see Letter No. 1390a) to become minister of the interior. Obolensky had been governor of Kharkov. From August 1, 1916, he headed the special commission to combat high prices; later he was governor of Yaroslavl. Obolensky disliked Rasputin and, in turn, Alexandra and Rasputin opposed Obolensky.

No. 1389/ Telegram 49. Tsarskoe Selo> Stavka. 10 Sept 1916. 14.35> 15.07. To his majesty. Tenderly thank you both, my loved ones, for dear letters. Clear, sunny day. Very busy, tired, am going this evening to [Countess Hendrikova's] funeral service in town<. [I] embrace, kiss you. Greetings to the boys. Alix

No. 1390/ Her No. 585.   Ts.[arskoe] S[elo]. Sept. 10th 1916.
My own beloved One,
    Warmest thanks for yr. dear letter. So sorry I had to bother you about all those questions, only I wanted to prepare you. Shakhovskoy too good to be changed, & as [A. A.] Khvost.[ov] wants to leave & Protop.[opov] is a suitable man, Gr.< says—had to tell you[348b]—& that Pr. [N. L.] Obolensky[348a] would be again of the opposite clan & not a "friend".—Such a busy day & feel so tired.—Two of my Crimeans came en passant, & told me about the regiment.—See old Ivanov—then an (American) [Red Cross?] unit under [daughter] Tatiana's protection presents itself—then Gussiev (the younger one) who returns to the regiment.—Then go to a Refuge[e fund-raising event] for Children ([under daughter] Olga's [sponsorship]) in the hussar barracks or manege [riding-school]. Then Pr. Golitzin [N. D. Golitsyn]—& at 8.20 off to town to a panikhida [funeral service] for Css. Hendrikov, who died this night at 4.—I enclose a touching wire from old Frederiks<—tear it [up] when read. Thanks for the English papers—don't you and Mr. Gibbs read them? [a]
    Baby wrote me his first English letter to-day.—Glorious, sunny day, orange & yellow leaves glitter beautifully, 15° in the sun, but I think, there was frost this night.—Sweet Angel mine, always in thoughts with you & so tenderly.—Cant understand why the guards loose [sic] so many & have such little luck[346]—always worries for you.—A.[nia]< has gone for the night to Terioki.—Must receive now.—Goodbye & God bless you, my very precious Treasure, Sun of my life & love. Cover you with fond, burning kisses.—Ever yr. very, very Own. [b]

348b. Alexandra is saying that Protopopov should not replace Shakhovskoi as acting-minister of trade and industry since the latter is "too good to be changed." A. A. Khvostov, on the other hand, was asking to be relieved as minister of the interior, and Protopopov "is a suitable man" for that post. These were the opinions of Rasputin ("Gr."), so "[I] had to tell you [that]." These passages from the Nicky-Sunny correspondence document the fact that Protopopov was appointed minister of the interior thanks to the influence of Rasputin on Alexandra who, in turn, influenced her husband. The fact that Nicholas initially opposed the appointment makes the point even clearer.

No. 1391.   Ts.[arist] Stavka. Sept. 10th 1916.

My own beloved One,

Tenderest thanks for your dear letter. Please thank the girls for their letters, which I have no time to answer. The photos Demenkov sent them are interesting. For to-morrow's reception of the japanese prince[Kotohito Kan-in,] Shtyurm[er] & C.[ount] Nirod have come. I will receive each today before dinner. So poor C.^{ss} Hendrickoff has atlast [sic] died, as I see fr. your wire. It is a great relief to herself & even to the children. You want me to come [home] even for two days, but for the moment it is alas! quite impossible, as there is so much preparatory work for the coming operations and I cannot be away from my staff now. I am afraid it is the atmosphere of Petrograd which is worrying you & wh. you do not feel here. Certainly I would come home with joy, first of all to sleep with you & secondly to bathe in my big bath. God grant later in the autumn that may happen as like last year. Baby< probably wrote you that we are making excavations near the little chapel. Now I must end. God bless you [&] the girls. With many tender kisses to you my darling Sunny & them, ever your own old Nicky.

No. 1392/ Telegram 29. Stavka> Tsarskoe Selo. 10 Sept 1916. 20.16> 20.45.

To her majesty. Heartfelt thanks [for] dear letters. It will be done.[349] Please tell Nastenka< how sad her mother's death made me. Fine, cold weather. Burning kisses from both. Niki

349. Nicholas is agreeing to make A. D. Protopopov head of the ministry of internal affairs. As a sign of his continuing reservations, however, the tsar appointed Protopopov *acting* minister (*upravlyayushchii ministr*). See Footnote 353.

No. 1393/ Telegram 35. Stavka> Tsarskoe Selo. 11 Sept 1916. 12.13> 12.46.

To her majesty. Better to send your seventh train to Caucasus. Leaving directly from the station to meet the prince [Kotohito Kan-in]. Beautiful, sunny weather. Love Niki

No. 1394/ Telegram 55. Tsarskoe Selo> Stavka. 11 Sept 1916. 14.10> 15.02.

To his majesty. Tenderly thank you both. Had to tell poor batyushka [see Letter No. 1395a] that his older son—[from the] Pavl[ovsky] Reg.[iment]—is killed, and his body has not been found; was very difficult. Rain, dark. [I] embrace, warmly kiss [you]. Thank you for telegram. Alix

No. 1395/ Her No. 586.   Ts.[arskoe] S[elo]. Sept. 11th 1916.

My own beloved Angel,

Raining & grey.—Very tender thanks for your precious letter, Lovebird & wire. Shall arrange then for my 7-th supply train to be sent to the Caucasus as soon as ready.—[Your] Sister Olga's sanitary train (off our section) has been much bombarded, the officers' wagon quite spoiled & the Apothecary Compartment much damaged, but nobody, thank God, hurt.—Did not go to Church as too tired. Then Loman begged me to tell poor batyushka [the priest A. P. Vasil'ev] that his eldest son (the favourite) had been killed & one had been obliged to leave his body.

I had never had such a task before—he took it as a brave Christian with big tears rolling down his face!—Then I went to the hospital, made 4 perevyazki [dressings] & sat knitting & talking long to Taube.— [a]

Now have 5 officers to receive, then Mme Zizi<, Senator Witte. Were yesterday evening at the poor Countess [Hendrikova's] funeral service—she lies there with such a peaceful face—at last her long martyrdom has ceased.—No, lovy, its my heart I feel & the whole body aches, so, so tired—it always comes fr. time to when I have been tiring myself.—Oh, I do so long for yor, my boysy sweet—so lonely without you! One hears nothing about the war, only sees by the death announcements the losses in the guard.[346]—Shall see Apraxin< about my little stores—his wife is expecting her 5-th baby.—Goodbye now, my one & all, my Treasure dear. I bless you, God be with you. A thousand tender kisses fr. yr. very own old Girly. [P.S.] To-day a week we parted, seems much longer!— [b]

No. 1396.   Ts.[arist] Stavka. Sept. 11 1916.
My beloved,   [This is a post card.]

Tender thanks for dear letter. Just finished lunch with prince [Kotohito] Kan-in. He is a nice man & speaks good French. He came to us in 1900. Luckily the weather is fine & warm. He brought Baby< & me pretty japanese presents. No more time to write. With fondest love to you my own darling & the girlies<. Ever your very own Nicky.

No. 1397/ Telegram 68. Tsarskoe Selo> Stavka. 12 Sept 1916. 13.33> 14.15. To his majesty. Glorious weather, got to hospital< only at 11 as was so tired. Tenderly thank you both for post cards. [We] all warmly kiss [you]. Alix

---

No. 1398/ Her No. 587.   Ts.[arskoe] S[elo]. Sept. 12th 1916.
My own Sweetheart,

Warmest thanks for yr. card. Nice, sunny weather, so after a week am at last going for a drive. [Daughters] T.[atiana] & A.[nastasia] have gone riding.—Went late to the hospital< as felt too tired. —Just saw Maslov, begs to thank you ever so much for having made him general & kept him in the Suite—it came then so unexpectedly & he had no occasion to thank [you].—To-morrow is the funeral of the Countess [Hendrikova]—I think I must get out of it, too tiring—& yet its unkind not being near [her daughter,] poor little Nastinka<.—My Crimeans, son of Emanuel arrived—slight wound, gained at that last attack of theirs.—I thought of giving the Japanese [Prince Kotohito Kan-in] my photo in a very big fine frame of Fabergé's for his wife—shall I add some Vases of the fabric [factory] too? I think Kirill< brought him to lunch to the farm in 1900?—Benk. [P. C. Benckendorff] tells me Frederiks< let him know that Miechen< arrives at Livadia 15-th for 3 days!! (what confounded cheek) & we are to send linen, 2 servants & silver—I strongly protested & said first to find out whether she asked you—we have no Hotel there—beastly impertinence, needs sitting upon [i.e., to be disciplined]—[she] can live at Yalta. Long for you my Sweet Sunshine—cover you with longing, tender kisses. God bless & protect you. Ever yr. very own old Wify. [P.S.] Perhaps you will send the batushka [the priest A. P. Vasil'ev] a

wire to Elagin<.—Nastinka< sends touched thanks. Enclose a letter fr. A.[nia]<
—What news fr. the front? So anxious to know.—Goodbye agoo wee one.

No. 1399.   Ts.[arist] Stavka. Sept. 12th 1916.
My very own Lovebird,
   Many fond thanks for your dear letter & all the kind things you wrote in it.
Yesterday the japanese visit went off perfectly. We received him grandly & the
weather was perfect. In the afternoon Georgii< drove out with the prince [Koto-
hito Kan-in] & we met them at the place where we dig near the future chapel.
He brought Aleksei & me pretty presents from the Emperor [Taisho] & himself.
I am going to send them to Tsarskoe [Selo]—please have the cases opened &
have a look at those things. The finest among them is a cloisonne picture of a
peacock—a tremendous weight to carry, but a splendid work. Alexei [sic] was
glad to see the former japanese general who he played with last year here—he
came now in the prince's suite. Georgii superintended them in a very good
way[—]towering over them like a governor over children. Today Mama [Maria
Fedorovna] receives them at Kiev. You see them the 15th.—Me also wants to
pay you a little visit, my beloved little girly. I wonder when it will be possible?
Now I must end. God bless you & keep you in good health. With tenderest love
to you & the girlies & her [Anna Vyrubova<] also ever my own Sweet heart
your very own   Nicky.

No. 1400/ Telegram 38. Stavka> Tsarskoe Selo. 12 Sept 1916. 19.02> 19.48.
To her majesty. Tender thanks. Yesterday's visit [with Prince Kotohito Kan-in]
went off successfully. Splendid weather. [We] both kiss [you] fondly. Niki

No. 1401/ Telegram 71. Tsarskoe Selo> Stavka. 13 Sept 1916. 13.26> 14.10.
To his majesty. Heartily thank you both, my dears. Beautiful weather. Was late
at hospital<. Embrace and warmly kiss [you]. Alix

No. 1402/ Her No. 588.   Ts.[arskoe] S[elo]. Sept. 13th 1916.
My own sweetheart,
   A lovely sunny morning—am only going to the hospital again at 11 as too
tired—[Daughter] Tatiana will dress the wounds for me.—We had N.P.< to dinner
yesterday—so strange without you— he met all the Japs in Moscow by
chance.—So it seems you gave the permission to Miechen<—hope she asked you
personally— nevertheless, most incorrect she did not wire to me too—so impertinent.—Such beautiful weather, that shall go for a little drive with the big girls<.
Sht.[yurmer] has asked to see me to-day & Schulenburg & then I had wounded.
Saw Benkend. [P. C. Benckendorff] & then I told him better to invite the relations who are here [to the luncheon for Kotohito Kan-in and the other Japanese
visitors?], as they be offended if I dont.—Paul< & his boy [Prince Paley] come to
bring me his poetry, wh. [has] now been printed.—Sent for Botk.[in] & made
him give me pills, wh. generally did me good, as feel so rotten;—therefore the
girls wld. not let me go to the Css. [Hendrikova's] funeral.— [a]

Went to the hospital at 11.—Very, very fondest thanks for yr. precious letter, Sweetheart.—Glad, all went off well with the Japanese. You know Misha's< wife [the Countess Brasova][82] was at Mogilev!! Georgi< told Paul he sat near her at the cynema [sic]. Find out where she lived (perhaps [in a train] wagon) & how long, & forbid strictly it happening again.—Paul is sad about the guard's losses[346]—one places them in such impossible places. Beloved Sweetheart, must end & send this off.—God bless you—very tenderest kisses fr. yr. old   Wify. [P.S.] Love to Dmitri<.— [b]

No. 1403.   Ts.[arist] Stavka. Sept. 13th 1916.
My beloved wify,
    Tenderly do I thank you for your dear letter. This time I must excuse Miechen —she passed here the other day, asking if she could stop in one of the court's houses at Livadia, adding it would not do for her to live in a hotel in Yalta. So I wired my consent. What was there to do otherwise! I send you some pictures of [i.e., from] a newspaper & a letter from Mavra< with a cutting I have not read. Today it is quite warm[,] 11° in the shade & the air is delicious, so we will go as usual up the river, wh.[ich] we have not done for about a week. Yesterday we made excavations at another place, but found nothing. Funny how Aleksei likes digging. From the front the news are very scarce, as we are preparing a new attack. Kira got a long letter from Drentel'n, he is going to bring the copy, then I can send it you on [sic]. To save our sailors [of the Guards Equipage< from such heavy losses in the current offensive] I think the only way is to take them away now & send them to the Black Sea—there they will rest & prepare for the final expedition, if God allows, for Constantinople, as was intended last year in [the] spring.[346] Now good-bye & God bless you & the dear girlies. I kiss you, my own Darling & them very fondly[;] ever your own   Nicky.

No. 1404/ Telegram 41.   Stavka> Tsarskoe Selo.   13 Sept 1916.   21.59> 23.36. To her majesty.   Loving thanks.   Was in church and much occupied. Lovely summer day. Thank [daughter] Marie for photos. Good night. Kisses. Niki

---

No. 1405/ Her No. 589.   Ts.[arskoe] S[elo].   Sept. 14th 1916.
My own beloved Angel,
    A lovely sunny, fresh morning. I have not gone to Church, as too tired—was [there] last night for ¾ of an hour. Alia< lunches & then I receive officers as usual [and] in the evening I see our Friend< in the little house [of Anna Vyrubova]. Yesterday had Sht.[yurmer] & spoke alright—I begged him quickly to change [A. N.] Obolensky,[350] otherwise we may have great disorders in the streets (on account of food) & he will at once loose [sic] his head & all are against him. God bless yr. new choice of Protopopov—our Friend says you have done a very wise act in naming him.—Paul< told me of the paper he has sent to the Headquarters after their decision where to get young officers, lieutenants, from. His boy [Prince Paley] is taller than he, goodlooking, reminds one very much of the Princess [Paley].

The Children have gone to Church—I shall join them at 11 in the hospital<—we have little work, so I leave it to [daughter] Tatiana, except the 2 heaviest [wounded] who feel quieter if I do it.—I shall finish this later, after getting your letter.—Beloved Angel, fond thanks for yr. dear letter. Thank goodness, Miechen< asked you still, tho' its very rude not to ask the lady of the house too, in my opinion. Shall read through Mavra's< paper & then tell you what is in it—Emelianov [Emel'yanov] suddenly turned up again.—He brought me reports fr. the commander, with the map & read them to me. The sky is clouding over, alas, so we shall quickly go for a little drive.—Precious One, goodbye & God bless you. Very tenderest kisses fr. yr. own old <u>Sunny</u>. [P.S.] I got this wire fr. Daisy<, what am I to do with it? To give it, or speak of it to Sht.?

350. Rasputin worried about food shortages. The people of Petrograd often stood in lines ("tails") for hours, only to learn that supplies were exhausted and there was nothing left to buy. Rasputin wanted Governor A. N. Obolensky replaced and the shops reorganized: food should be weighed and priced in advance and multiple lines would insure that sales moved quickly. Officials professed to find merit in Rasputin's ideas. (Letter No. 1430c) But goods were scarce because at this point peasants were hoarding grain and the civilian supply system was breaking down. Contrary to what one often reads about Nicholas, he was aware of the situation—but its solution baffled him. (Letter No. 1431) Letter No. 1434f also indicates that officials lied to the tsar. Trade Minister Shakhovskoi, for example, had not solved Petrograd's fuel problem, as he claimed.

No. 1406/ Telegram 77. Tsarskoe Selo> Stavka. 14 Sept 1916. 15.24> 16.10. To his majesty. Heartily thank you for dear letters. Warmly kiss [you] both. Remember about matushka[, your mother, Maria Fedorovna]. Just think, it has already been 50 years since she arrived here. [See Letter No. 1411.] Morning was delightful, now cloudy. May the Lord bless [you]. Alix

No. 1407. Ts.[arist] Stavka. Sept. 14th 1916.
My own Lovebird,
Fondest thanks for your dear letter. So tiresome you feel weak, do take care, if not for your sake, at least for mine & the wounded. I send you Drent.[el'n]'s letter to Freder[icks]. I was quite sure of the fact that the guard would be left to itself from the moment Bezobrazov was taken away—I think I told you about this! No doubt Gurko would have done better at their head than gen. Kaledin—though he is a good general & had great success in the beginning of our attack in May! I had no time to take the guard into my own reserve because they were marched off at once into their new positions. The enemy had of course the possibility of fortifying their lines & bring[ing] up an enormous amount of heavy artillery & troops. God only knows how this new advance will end! The last days the weather was delicious[,] warm & fine; today it is much cooler! God bless you my own darling Wify. I kiss you & the girlies tenderly. Ever your very own Nicky.

No. 1408/ Telegram 42. Stavka> Tsarskoe Selo. 14 Sept 1916. 20.16> 21.14. To her majesty. Warmest thanks. Fine but cold. Just back from cinema. Fondest love from both Niki

No. 1409/ Telegram 53. Tsarskoe Selo> Stavka. 14 Sept 1916. 15.02> 16.12.
To his majesty. Just now received Japanese Prince [Kotohito Kan-in]. Very
pleasant and talkative. Rested after lunch as was quite tired—lay down until time
he arrived. Warmly thank you both for dear letters. Embrace, kiss [you]. Alix

No. 1410/ Her No. 590.   Ts.[arskoe] S[elo]. Sept. 15th 1916.
My own beloved Darling,
    Cold, sunny morning—am going to lie in bed till I receive the Japanese, as the
heart is a little enlarged & I feel so tired.—I have chosen [as gifts for our Japanese visitors] a lovely big pair of China Vases, wood[s] in winter & summer & 2
high crystal ones with eagles—so a pair for each of them.— Saw our dear Fr.<
yesterday evening in the little house [of Anna Vyrubova]. So happy that you
named Pokr. [the empress meant to write "Prot." for Protopopov]— [Rasputin]
thinks it a most wise nomination, of course some may be discontented,—but for
the next (not this) Duma he can influence for the elections.—He told me to speak
to Raev about the poor monks fr. St. Athon [Mt. Athos?—see Letter No. 843b]
who may not yet officiate [i.e., celebrate the liturgy] & die without receiving
Holy Communion.—[a]
    I read the cutting Mavra< sent—vile—the hell for Germ. & Austr. prisoners,
who have to work to death with us—sensationally written & I fell full of lies. I
shall tell Igor< to-day, that you thank Mavra for her letter, then you need not
bother to write.—He sends you much love. Begs quickly to change [Prince A.
N.] Obolensky & when the new man is named to tell him to give the order that
in the breadshops they should already have everything weighed out beforehand,
so that as soon as one asks, that piece already is ready according to price &
weight & then the work will go quicker & those long tails [i.e., lines] in the
street be sooner appeased—one must trust to the honesty of the men [the bread
merchants] not to cheat the poor people & see that the police has an eye upon
those shops & the chief of police must himself begin by looking himself to see
all is honestly & quickly done.[350] [b]
    Resting after the Japanese—headache, very tired—suppose B.< soon coming
too. He [Prince Kotohito Kan-in] was talkative & nice, so no trouble. Was delighted to see Baby's< 2 friends & talk to them. He gave me fr. the [Taisho]
E.[mperor] of J.[apan] two marvellous gobelins—such exquisite work & beauty
of colouring. He was so touched by yr. reception & kindness, & Motherdears<,
& the crowd all along the streets to the Winter Palace.—Css. Benkendorf [Maria
Benckendorff] was awful—much too badly died red lips—ghastly sight.—Ducky<
[was wearing a] too short velvet dress & badly coiffed, such a pitty [sic].—[c]
    Very fondest thanks for yr. sweet letter. Drent.[el'n]—I shall return to-morrow.
One must save & spare the guard.[346]—We spoke with Kirill< who was my
neighbour at table, about the [Guards Equipage<] battalion—also finds it a good
idea what you write. I told him to be more energetic with Admirals & Ministers
to get the officers he needs as yr. order must be obeyed.—Grigorovich told me
you gave him the order through Kirill about N.P. to be made Commander of the
beloved [imperial yacht] "st." [Standard] & [Admiral] Zelen.[etsky]—[should be
transferred from command of the Standard to serve as] Commander of the port
(which suits the latter very well he says)—does the little Admiral< not rage? But

I am glad its done—how happy dear Johnny[351] wld. be that his son, as he always called N.P. shld. receive the yacht.—Head aches—can't write any more to-day.—Goodbye & God bless you.—A fond, fond kiss fr. yr. very own deeply loving old   <u>Sunny</u>. [d]

---

351. Alexandra refers to Ivan Ivanovich Chagin ("Johnny"), rear-admiral in His Majesty's Suite, and commander of the *Standard*; he shot and killed himself in the autumn of 1912.

No. 1411.   Ts.[arist] Stavka. Sept. 15th 1916.
My own Sweetheart,
   Many many thanks for your beloved letter. I think it better you should ask Sht.[yurmer] about Daisy's< telegram, as it concern[s] two ministries—the War & For.[eign] Affairs. [See Letter No. 1405b.] I send you also a letter I got yesterday from Dolly [Darya Grevenits—see Letter No. 1413c], Eugene's [Eugene Maximilianovich, the duke of Leuchtenberg's] daughter. She brought it herself & wanted absolutely to see me. Through all sorts of lies at the station she got into Fedorov's room & told him a long story about an otryad [detachment] of her's & that she wants to get down to the south away fr. Dvinsk etc. Nilov, who is now instead of Voeik.[ov],[352] was furious & only got her out of the house only by promising to hand over her letter. Too bad. What she asks for is to get the title of D[ss] [Duchess] of Leuchtenberg—after that you may be sure she will ask for money from the udely [districts], wh. of course she has no right to. I saw Silaev a few days ago, he is gone to the regiment, but does not know how long he may be able to remain with it. Such a pity! My love! I am already looking forward to our next meeting! Though [I have] much to do I am always in thoughts with you! Yes, fancy Mother dear< being 50 years in Russia. [G]od bless you. With many loving kisses to you, my beloved One, & the girlies, ever your very own   Nicky.

---

352. Admiral Nilov became Nicholas II's aide at Stavka, replacing Maj.-Gen. Voeikov. Rumors held that Alexandra was behind these changes; in fact, the empress had long turned against both men, once among her favorites, and her opinion had no bearing on their recent assignments.

No. 1412/ Telegram 44. Stavka> Tsarskoe Selo. 15 Sept 1916. 20.01> 20.43. To her majesty. Tender thanks. Glad visit [of Prince Kotohito] went off well. Sandro< came from Kiev for a day. Fine, cold weather. Burning kisses. Niki

---

No. 1413/ Her No. 591.   Ts.[arskoe] S[elo]. Sept. 16th 1916.
My own sweetheart,
   Grey, windy, rainy morning. The Children have gone off to see [daughter] Olga's sanitary train—then to the hospital & at 12| to a funeral service for the batushka's son [see Letter No. 1395a]—he begged us to come. I remain in bed till luncheon as heart enlarged & dont feel well. Had hideous headache yesterday, but passed. N.P.< dined with us & then we read Drentel'n's letter together; & one he had from Rodionov—full of despair. 3 times in one day they were all obliged to attack (I think Sept. 4) & the place impregnable, the Germans were completely hidden & their maximguns [Maxim machine guns] fired without

ceasing. A prisoner told them [i.e., the Russians] they have dug themselves down 10 meters, & somehow push the guns up & down as needed, so our artillery did them no harm—they (Germans) all know our guard[346] is against them—they feel one [i.e., the Russian high command] sacrifices them for nothing.—[a]

I begged our Friend< to particularly pray for the success of your new plans, & he does so & hopes God will bless them.—All say the comm. of the "Pavlovtzy" (Schevitch [D. D. Shevich]) is a real pancake [i.e., is wishy-washy] & that regiment has no success & rarely advances. It seems to me our Generals are fearfully weak. Ah yes, He [Rasputin] said I was to tell you, not to worry when you send a General away, if he has been innocent. You can always forgive him afterwards & recall him to service & him it will never do harm, to have suffered, as it makes him realise the fear of God. —Ania< goes for 2 days to Finland as [it is] her Mama's [Nadezhda Taneeva's] namesday [sic].—Do hope we shall have nice sunny weather when we meet again!— [b]

Thats a good idea about the battalion[346]—told N.P.< you thought about it—only hopes they will not be in Odessa or S.[evastopol'] but in some smaller place, to keep them better in hand & less temptations, than in a big town & to keep them up to work all the while.—Just got yr. sweet letter, for wh. very tenderest thanks.— Tell Nilov to answer Dolly< that she cannot receive the name (without any [appropriate] reason). [See Letter No. 1411.] What does she mean, that her marriage with Grevenitz did not count? She is cracked, I believe. The less one has to do with her the better—& Nilov can answer best—as she was a relation of his wifes & as Frederiks< is not there.— [c]

"Me" too is looking forward to our meeting with great longing—hope to feel better by then, now am really rotten.—Fancy, Greek Nicky< is still at Pavlovsk in an awful state of nerves they say. Cannot imagine why they dont let him home at last he cant help here, or perhaps its to show their good feelings towards us.—I send you a paper about a general Oganovsky [Oranovsky?], read it through & do what you like with it.—Now must end. Its cleared up, sun shining. Becker< has come.—Feel rotten, blessings & kisses without end. Ever yr. very own   Wify. [d]

No. 1414/ Telegram 88. Tsarskoe Selo> Stavka. 16 Sept 1916. 15.00> 15.45. To his majesty. Heartily thank you both, dears. Heavy rain in morning, now sunny. Am resting as heart enlarged, feel not well. Tenderly kiss and warmly embrace you both, my loved ones. Alix

---

No. 1415.   Ts.[arist] Stavka. Sept. 16th 1916.
My own Sweetheart,
Loving thanks for your dear letter. I am glad the japanese visit & lunch went well off [sic], but am sad you felt tired. Do take care of yourself & don't over tire your poor dear heart! I wrote this morning to Motherdear [Maria Fedorovna] with Sandro<. It seems that idiot of Rodzianko wrote a very impertinent official letter to him, to which Sandro is going to answer sharply. He read to me bits of each—his answer is well written. [a]

There is a slight misunderstanding about the [imperial yacht] "Standart" according to what Kirill told you. I never ordered Grigorovich anything, but simply enquired about that place for Zelenetsky[, the current commander,] in the future[,] and explaining my wish that N.P.< is to receive the yacht after Z. I spoke about it to the Admiral [Nilov] too who took it quite cooly, but only asked if it would be done at the end of the war, when the boilers & other repair works in the yacht will be finished. Except this Z. really does everything in the [Guards] Equipage< for Kirill, who is often away. And lastly, as I want N.P. during the war near me, he could not stay away fr. that work if he were now captain. Understood—yes? Now, my beloved little girly, I must end. [G]od bless you & the dear daughters. With many tender kisses ever your own old <u>Nicky</u>. [b]

No. 1416/ Telegram 48. Stavka> Tsarskoe Selo. 16 Sept 1916. 19.26> 20.05. To her majesty. Fondest thanks. Hope you will feel better. Today warmer. Went as usual up river. Kisses from both. Niki

---

No. 1417/ Telegram 98. Tsarskoe Selo> Stavka. 17 Sept 1916. 16.25> 17.01. To his majesty. Tenderly thank you both. Very cold, had frost during night. Am resting. Warmly kiss you both, my dears. [I] wish [you] all the best. Alix

---

No. 1418/ Her No. 592.   Ts.[arskoe] S[elo]. Sept. 17<u>th</u> 1916.
My own dear Sweetheart,
    Fancy, only 1° of warmth & yesterday evening 2° of frost—no sunshine.—I enclose a paper fr. our Friend< for you, as I asked Him to think particularly of you to bless your new combinations.—Lovy, do tell somebody to go & <u>see</u> to the <u>4</u> heavy <u>batteries</u>, wh. stand since some time quite ready here at Ts.[arskoe] S.[elo] (one tells me) & nobody thinks of sending them off. They have munition (if not sufficient, can be sent after [they leave for the front]). If old Ivanov is still at Petrogr.[ad], give him the order to go & see & look at all in detail (officers told this to Botkin as they have seen them quite close). It wld. be good to get them off, because the men are not quite famous [admirable]—several weeks ago there were stories & [some] rifles [infantrymen] were sent to catch them in a wood where they were occupied with propaganda papers.—These 40 guns stand <u>without guard</u> on the place—a young lieutenant has written paper after paper begging for men to watch them as every morning he finds some screw or little thing taken off, missing & nobody takes heed to this.[353a] I think a general <u>unexpectedly</u> being sent here by you to make an inspection wld. be best & quickest —we so sorely need them out at the war, but dont warn Sergei—let all be done unexpectedly—& <u>then</u> he will also see that ones eyes must be <u>everywhere</u>. He [Sergei] ought to move about more—& why does Andre stick here—is there no nomination for him anywhere out at the war—active, not as all these 2 years?[353b]—need not be in the guard as there are no vacancies—Misha< also served elsewhere.—Make the family move about more.— [a]
    In the battalion Rod.[ionov] wrote there have been 50 cases & more of dissentry—autumn—here Css. Nierod's child & one of our wounded too.—Lying till luncheon. Saw [A. A.] Bobrinsky yesterday—touched me. Asks to see you next

week.—Now the sun is coming out brightly—but I shall remain on the sopha, must get decent again.—Fondest thanks, Beloved, for yr. dear letter just given to me. Lovy, it was Grigorov.[ich] [who] told me, not Kirill< about Z. & N.P.< [See Letter No. 1415b.] How I wish one cld. hang Rodz.[yanko], awful man, & such a insolent fellow. Kiknadze has again been wounded & lies in our hospital—told [daughter] Tatiana lots about our sailors. We have 4 new wounded besides him—have not been to the hospital since Wednesday, alas.—Goodbye my Treasure, & God bless you. A big & tender kiss fr. yr. very own old Wify. [P.S.] Did you let Petia know he is free?[316] What does Sandro say about [your sister] Olga's intentions?[326] [b]

353a. This episode is interesting as a warning sign of the coming March Revolution. (See also Letters No. 1426c, 1427, 1430d.)
353b. The empress asks why Andrew Vladimirovich ("Andre") has been hanging around "here" (Petrograd)? is there no place for him in the "active" army "anywhere out at the war?" has this not been going on "all these two years?" By contrast, she praises the tsar's brother Misha< for serving in the field, while warning her husband not to let Andre wheedle a prestigious assignment with a guards unit, "as there are no [legitimate] vacancies" in those regiments.

No. 1419.   Ts.[arist] Stavka. Sept. 17th 1916.
My tenderly beloved One,
   Many thanks for your dear letter. I am so sorry that you are feeling rotten & B.< has also come! You must not have headaches & be sick. After a few fine days this night the weather suddenly changed—& now it is raining incessantly, very dark & warm. In one sense it does not matter, as we would not have gone out in any case, as Baby's< left foot or rather his instep is a little swollen, he cannot put on his boot, but luckily it does not hurt him. He is dressed & spends his whole day in the bow-window room! Of course I will take a turn in the garden. On board [our yacht] or in Livadia it would have been a good occasion to glew [sic] photos in the album. [a]
   I told Alekseev about the battalion of our sailors[346] & they will be sent back directly after this battle.   [S]even corps are going to attack these [enemy lines]—if only God blessed them with a fine success! Since weeks I worry over this! If only we had more heavy artillery—there would not be the slightest doubt as to the results. Like with the french & english armies—they crush every resistance only with their enormous heavy fire. So we did in the beginning of our March forward. God bless you & the girlies! I kiss you passionately, my own Sunny, my One & All! Them too. Ever your own Nicky. [b]

No. 1420/ Telegram 52. Stavka> Tsarskoe Selo. 17 Sept 1916. 19.36> 20.10. To her majesty. Loving thanks. Pouring [rain] without stopping. [We] both kiss [you] all tenderly. Niki

No. 1421/ Telegram 101. Tsarskoe Selo> Stavka. 18 Sept 1916. 14.02> 14.27. To his majesty. Tenderly thank you both, my dears. Hope [Aleksei's] leg is better. Cold, grey, snowing, sun occasionally pokes through. On the whole feel so-so. We warmly kiss you both. May the Lord bless you. Alix

No. 1422/ Her No. 593.   Ts.[arskoe] S[elo]. Sept. 18th 1916.
My very own Treasure,

Fondest thanks for yr. sweetest letter. As I lie in bed in the mornings I get yr. letters much earlier to read, wh. is a very great joy.—Sun, clouds, snow change about—real autumn. This change may take Tiny< feels less well;—but that weakness in the foot by a false movement or over exertion can easily swell up—thank God, that no pain.—We can help glueing yr. photos in the evenings, if you like.—Put all my trust in God's mercy, only tell me when the attack is to begin, so as that He [Rasputin] can particularly pray then;—it means too much & He realises [sic] your suffering. [a]

Lovy, I hear Pahlen's court rank has been taken fr. him because one read a private letter of his to his wife, where he calls the ambassadors scoundrels[353c] & I understand him saying so. But that surely is a mistake, one has hooked onto a German name again [i.e., he is being punished because of his German surname] —& he really is so devoted to you.—Much sooner & with right one ought at once in winter to have taken off Khvost.[ov's] uniform [see Letter No. 1430]—he behaved vilely & everybody knows it, only Voeikov< & Andronn.[ikov] (whom I again warned Shtyurmer against) stuck up for Kh.[vostov].—Now a correspondance [sic] between Alekseev & that brute Guchkov< is going on & he [Guchkov] fills him [Alekseev] with vile things—warn him, he is such a clever brute & Al. will certainly, alas, listen to things against our Friend< too—& that wont bring him luck.—Now my Sunshine & Joy—Goodbye & God bless & keep you. Very tenderest kisses fr. yr. very, very Own. [P.S.] Must quickly get up & dress for luncheon. Think of you incessantly with longing love & earnest prayers—soul & heart with you, Lovebird. [b]

No. 1423.   Ts.[arist] Stavka. Sept. 18th 1916.
My own Sweetheart,

The doklad [report] having been finished earlier than usual I profit by beginning my letter before luncheon. There will come many people as it is Sunday—Alex< has also arrived from his trip to Reni and Rumania. The weather is fine & cold, such a difference from what it was yesterday. Baby's< swollen foot is better—he is very gay. We played "Nain jaune"[277] together in the afternoon till tea-time. I went to the evening service after which o.[tets, i.e., Father] Shavel'sky presented me an old priest of here [sic]—who is 95 years old, but looks as if he were 70 not more.— Just finished lunch & talking & Alex too. Fondest thanks for your dear letter. No, I did not let Petia< know he is free [i.e., divorced from my sister Olga]—it will soon be published! Sandro< finds Olga ought to wait [to marry N. A. Kulikovsky], but she does not want to heed.—I am going to speak to Sergei about those 40 guns at Ts.[arskoe] S[elo—see Letters 1418a, 1426c, 1427 and 1430d]. He told me some time ago that heavy artillery was being formed there. Why go behind his back?[353a] Who sent me the last photos? Am I to choose fr. them or are they all for me or Aleksei? Old [Gen. N. Yu.] Ivanov arrived here a few days ago from Finland, he can't bear that country! Now my Love-bird I must end. God bless you & the girlies! I kiss you all tenderly & her [Anna Vyrubova] too. With fondest love ever my own Treasure your old   Nicky

No. 1424/ Telegram 53. Stavka> Tsarskoe Selo. 18 Sept 1916. 19.01> 19.11.
To her majesty. [We] both thank [you] heartily. Again fine, cool. [Aleksei's]
foot better but [he] remained in doors. Loving kisses. Niki

No. 1425/ Telegram 106. Tsarskoe Selo> Stavka. 19 Sept 1916. 14.14> 15.02.
To his majesty. Thank you both with all my soul, my dears. The Holy Virgin is
with you, do not fear, He [Rasputin] says. Cold, overcast getting ready to snow a
bit. [I] embrace, kiss [you]. Health so-so. Am lying down a lot during hours free
of receptions. Alix

No. 1426/ Her No. 594.   Ts.[arskoe] S[elo]. Sept. 19th 1916.
My very own beloved One,
    A cold morning, snow on some leaves & patches on the grass—its very early
this year.—N.P.< dined with us yesterday—he leaves to-day—had a blooming cold
& cough. Was twice at our Friend's, I am pleased to say. Perhaps you will be
able to find him some work to do for you?—One of the men just came from the
battalion—says they are used very much. In the morning they are sent back & in
the evening out again—I find it horribly anguishing they will take part in the big
battles now—each man is in himself a perfection—the only bit of the whole army
who has got men of so many years service—God spare them for work hereafter
& in the "South".[346]—Have got two doklady [reports], Silaev & Shtyurmer
to-day, Trina< and Isa< for affairs.—To-morrow Raev etc. & so it goes
on.—Heart still enlarged & tired, but lying much is resting me, the back & legs
ache less. I do so want to get quicker well again, have more work to do & all lies
upon [daughter] Tatiana's shoulders. [a]
    Now it seems a most interesting young American Dr. with 3 sisters [i.e.,
nurses] has been sent here by the rich Guld—we want to use them & put them up
in the big palace<. He will operate there & in any other hospital. To-morrow he
does [so] in our soldiers' ward. He cuts out & fits in bones with electric machine
like a fine puzzle—one can never be so exact with the hand. I looked through a
most interesting book with drawings & explanations. One Dr. went with such
an apparatus to England, 2 to France (the inventor himself) & this one here. The
red Cross did not need him & we accept him with delight—always good to learn
& see new methods. Have forgotten his name. Worked in Servia a year during
the war & so can speak a little Servian. For sure, Pss. Shakhovskoy will fall in
love with him. We have by chance a French Dr. as patient in the big palace<,
but as not very ill, also helps Vl. Nik.< [b]
    How is the air now in the diningroom—I told it Valia< a good while ago &
repeated it to Benkendorf [P. C. Benckendorff]—but they dawdled over it, & its
not so complicated to have the upper windows made to open upwards.—But
when we come, cant we keep to the cosy habit of dining in the train—its so much
less tiring & for you I think more refreshing too & comfortable.—You must be
feeling dull now, I am sure, as the walks are less inviting & soon I fear too cold
on the river—we came in Oct. for the first time last year, & I remember it was
very cold already, we went in closed motors & then you got out and walked—what joy to meet again! Ever such tender thanks, my own Darling for yr.
very sweet letter.—Those photos were fr. me for yr. album, lovy dear.—I think

still you ought to let Petia< know. Sandro can write him [a] letter or you a short wire.—Yes, find out about those guns, do. [See Letters No. 1418a, 1423, 1427 and 1430d.] Horrid weather. Paul's< birthday is on Wednesday—they have asked us to chocolate—doubt I shall be up & about by then. Now goodbye my one & all. Fondest, burning kisses & blessings without end yr. very, very   Own. [c]

No. 1427.   Ts.[arist] Stavka. Sept. 19ᵗʰ 1916.

My very own Sweetheart,

Very tenderest thanks for your sweet loving letter. Yesterday evening I looked through them all & found that in June you suddenly jumped fr. No. 545 to No. 555! [See Letters No. 1250 and 1254 and Footnote 326a.] So now the letters are all wrongly numbered! How do you know that Guchkov is in correspondence with Aleks.[eev]? [See Letter No. 1422b.] I never never [sic] heard about it before. Is it not a curious coincidence that the colonel at the head of the new heavy artillery being formed up at Ts.[arskoe] S.[elo] came here for affairs & lunched with me just now. So I asked him several questions & he told me that there is a sentry for each battery, that twice thefts were committed in the night, because it is dark, in one case by the sentry himself; & that a certain metal wh. is very dear, is generally stolen out of the big engl.[ish] guns on their way from Arkhangel'sk to Ts. S. Sergei knew all this & measures will be taken. [See Letters No. 1418b, 1423, 1426c and 1430d.] Before Fred.< left he sent me a whole lot of letters written by Cᵗ Pahlen to his wife, in wh. he wrote violent expressions against the milit.[ary] censure & the rear, and so forth.³⁵³ᶜ The old man [Fredericks] begged me to take away his [i.e., Pahlen's] court rank & I gave in, but own [admit] that the punishment is too severe. Mama [Maria Fedorovna] also wrote to me about it. Now my own Wify I must end. God bless you! I kiss you my Lovebird-darling & the girlies. Ever your own   Nicky.

353c. "The examination of private correspondence in the "Black Box" department of the Post Office was a matter of routine; but it is probable that the statement concerning this correspondence came from Mme. Vyroubova. Count Pahlen's letters, referred to below, were doubtless intercepted by the postal authorities in the course of their duty. ... Count C. C. Pahlen was a Marshal of the Court, a Senator and a Privy Councillor." (Vulliamy, pp. 265-266n)

No. 1428/ Telegram 56. Stavka> Tsarskoe Selo. 19 Sept 1916. 18.55> 19.29. To her majesty. Tenderest thanks for letter and message. Also cold and grey. Hope [you] will feel better. Loving kisses. Niki

---

No. 1429/ Telegram 111. Tsarskoe Selo> Stavka. 20 Sept 1916. 13.55> 14.34. To his majesty. Heartily thank you for dear letters. Marie< had lunch with us. Cold, dull weather. [We] warmly embrace and kiss [you]. What news? Alix

---

No. 1430/ Her No. 595.   Ts.[arskoe] S[elo]. Sept. 20ᵗʰ 1916.

My own sweet Angel,

Grey, cold, trying to snow. Little Marie< has arrived & comes to us to luncheon. Ingeborg's girls sent [daughter] Tatiana an adorable postcard of little Lennard [Lennart, son of Kaiser Wilhelm II]—such a sturdy, splendid, goodlooking

boy with big, sad eyes—nothing of their family. How can she live so calmly
without him all these years is to me quite uncomprehensible & most unnormal.—Had doklady [reports] from 5-7 yesterday. Sht.[yurmer] has not yet found
a Chief of police for town<—those he proposed wld. never do—have told him to
hurry up & think again.[350]—Guchkov< is trying to get round Alekseev,— complains to him against all the ministers (egged on by Polivanov)—Sht., [A. F.]
Trepov, Shakhovskoi—& that makes things clear, why Aleks.[eev] is so against
the ministers, who are really working better & more together & things are getting better & we fear no real crisis if they continue thus.[354]— [a]

Please, Darling, don't let kind Aleks. begin to play a part with Guchkov as one
did at the old Headquarters. Rodz.[ianko] & he [Guchkov] make now one & are
trying to get round Al., pretending nobody can work but they. He must only
occupy himself with the war—the others answer for what goes on behind.—Protopopov comes to me to-morrow & I have heaps to ask him & some
ideas wh. propped up in my own old mind to make a counter propaganda against
the Union of Cities out in the army—to have them watched & those that one
catches at [unacceptable behavior?] cleared out; the Minister of the Interior must
get nice, honest people to be "his eyes" out there & with the military help, see
what they can do—we have no right allowing them to continue filling their ears
(the soldiers) with bad ideas—their Drs. (Jews) & sisters [i.e., nurses] are awful—Shavel'sky can tell you about them.—I told Sht. to tell this to Prot. & he will
think it over till to-morrow & see whether anything practical can be done. I dont
see why the bad shld. always fight for their cause, & the good complain, but sit
calmly with folded hands & wait for events.— [b]

You dont mind my coming with ideas, do you deary, but I assure you, tho' ill
& with bad heart, I have more energy than the whole lot put together & I cant sit
calmly by. [A. A.] Bobrinsky was glad to see me so & says I am therefore disliked, because one feels (the left set) I stand up for yr. cause, Baby's< & Russia's. Yes, I am more Russian than many another, & I wont keep quiet. I begged
them to arrange (what Gr.[egory] said) that good[s], flower [flour], butter, bread,
sugar shld. all be weighed out beforehand in the shops & then each buyer can
get his parcel much quicker & there won't be such endless tails [lines]—all
agreed its an excellent idea—now why did not they think of it before.[350]— [c]

Shakhovskoi comes to-day, as I want to hear how about the watertraffic—I
think he is quite calm about the wood, there will be enough—but I want to ask
whether, before the rivers freeze, whether one cannot bring other provisions wh.
are not of his ministery, down by water—as they must all help each other—& he
adores you.[350] He was with Ania< yesterday. Then I see Bishop Antony Guir-
sky from the Caucasus.—You see, all day people—at least have time to write
[during] the morning in bed. But I long to get back to the hospital work—love it
so.—Just brought me yr. sweet letter for wh. fondest, fondest thanks, I am glad
you had an occasion to speak about the artillery ready here. [See Letters No.
1418b, 1423, 1426c and 1427.]—About Guchk.[ov] & Al.[ekseev] I'll tell you
to-morrow, Sht. told me & Shakhovskoi has seen the copies of the letters—I'll
tell you to-morrow after having personally spoken to Shakhovskoi. [See Letters
No. 1422b, 1427.]— [d]

Certainly if one heeds privately[-written] letters between husband & wife—far more reason to watch others. [See Letter No. 1427.] Forgive me, but Fred.< acted very wrongly—one dare not judge a man so severely because of private letters (opened) to his wife—thats mean, I find. I should have made Fred. understand this utterly wrong thing. [A. A.] Khvostov[, who as minister of the interior is in charge of these surveillances,] ought to have had his dress [i.e., uniform indicating rank] at once taken off—enough proofs & scandalous, dirty affair—& here quite private. I wish one cld. set it to rights for Baby's< namesday [sic]. [Count Pahlen] is still happily Senator—& the punishment has lasted enough— spying at times goes too far—& I am utterly convinced that far more write like that & openly speak so—Kokovtsev, Krivoshein & many others got through scot-free—& they went in action, against Sovereign & country & the Pahlens quite privately—an awful gaffe of Fred. & certainly because the man has a German name. You have not got the head for all such things, you are far too much occupied—& others are responsable [sic] for "putting you in" & that vexes me as they oblige you being unjust.— [e]

You say I have numbered yr. letters wrongly, so sorry, cant you change them & add a No: [sic] to the letter I left you unnumbered last time? Heart is better to-day the rest is doing me good.—But the weather is sad indeed.—Fancy yr. having played old Nain Jaune[277] again!—How I wish we could have gone off all together for a few days again to Sebastopol in October, how lovely it wld. have been. An awful thing, sticking at the Headquarters, in town [of Mogilev] for so many months running; and now the long winter is setting in early.—Silaev told me all, poor man.—Now he will go to Sebastopol & ask the Professor what he is to do & where to go & take his family if possible with him—the climate does not agree with them, they need sunshine for a few months & warmth.—Now my very own Sunshine, life of my life, sweetest of dears, goodbye & God bless you. I hold you clasped tightly in my arms & cover you with burning kisses. Ever yr. own old   Sunny.   [P.S.] Does Mr. Gibbs read the English papers first? [f]

354. Note that the empress—cheered by Protopopov's rise and the recent ouster of several officials she disliked—is more positive about the council of ministers than in previous letters.

No. 1431.   Ts.[arist] Stavka. Sept. 20th 1916.
My own sweet Sunny,

Ever so many tender thanks for your dear letter. Maximovich, [A. N.] Grabbe & N.P.< arrived today—till now we were quite a small party among ourselves. Baby's< foot is well again & he walks alright [sic]. What preoccupies me most of all now, except the military affairs, is the old question about the prodovol'stvie [supplies]. Today Alekseev gave me a letter he received from a very good pr. [Prince A. N.] Obolensky who is the president of the committee po prodovol' [supplies]. He openly admits confesses that they cannot do anything to help the situation, that they work, so to speak[,] in the air, the zemledelie [ministry of agriculture under Bobrinsky] does not take heed of what they decide—and prices go up & the people are beginning to starve. It is clear what this state of affairs can bring the country! Old Sht.[yurmer] cannot overcome this difficulty. I don't see another way out of it—than by giving it over to the military authorities, but that also has its inconveniences! The most d–d question I ever came accross [sic]. I have never been a merchant & simply do not understand those questions about provisions & stores! Now, my Lovebird, I must end. God bless you and the girlies! With many loving kisses ever your own old Nicky.

No. 1432/ Telegram 58. Stavka> Tsarskoe Selo. 20 Sept 1916. 20.11> 21.05. To her majesty. Heartily thank you. [We] also [have] overcast, rainy weather. [I] have returned from cinematograph. News not very good. Warmly embrace [you]. Nicky.

No. 1433/ Telegram 114. Tsarskoe Selo> Stavka. 21 Sept 1916. 14.51> 15.27. To his majesty. Warmly thank you for dear letters. Was sunny morning, now overcast. Big girls< went to town<. In thoughts and prayers always together. Warmly kiss [you]. Alix

---

No. 1434/ Her No. 596.   Ts.[arskoe] S[elo]. Sept. 21st 1916.
My own Sweetheart,
   Goodmorning, my treasure! At last again sunshine—such a joy; but in the evening there were at my window already 3 degrees of frost. The leaves are falling, alas, so fast, I can well see the big palace [Bolshoi dvorets] Church fr. my windows. We still take our meals in my big sitting-room.—Am sending Paul< vases and a note [for his birthday], as I cannot go to him, the heart being enlarged. A week I have not left the house to-day. I cannot yet take medicins [sic], wh. is the bore.—Again received for 2 hours yesterday & before that [for] ¾ of an [hour] Apraxin< & Uncle Mekk< about the Caucasus.—Raev (good talk) —Shakhovskoi (long conversation). It seems Polivanov & Guchkov< are working hand in hand again. I read the copy of 2 of Guchkov's letters to Aleks.[eev] have asked for one to be written out cleanly to send you, to see the brute he is! Now I understand why A.[lekseev] rages against all the ministers— after every letter (there have been many one sees) he upsets poor Al. & then his facts are often quite intentionally falsely put to A.—The ministers all feel his antagonism at the Headquarters & now they see why. [a]
   When I send you the letter, then have a serious talk with Al.< as that brute [Guchkov] undermines the whole government in A.'s eyes—really vile, & 10,000,000 times worse than anything Pahlen can have written to his Wife [see Letters No. 1427 and 1430e]—one must pull away Al. fr. Guch. fr. that bad, sly influence. Then I saw Bishop Antony Guriysky—charming impression, cosy Georgian intonation in his voice—knows our Friend< longer than we do—was rector years ago at Kazan [Seminary]. He buried Bagration[355] —have asked him to help me collect things, linen etc. in the Caucasus & to help Apraxin< when I send him there next month. Speaks strongly against Nik.[olasha]< & them all (to Ania)—he [Nicholasha] is too harsh & rude against the Georgians.—Now I have found out who the Exarch is—you remember Platon fr. America [i.e., he was the former archbishop of the Aleutian Islands and America]—whom we saw at Livadia, & who spoke Russian with an American accent, was unsympathetic & terribly sure of himself, perfect for the Americans but not for the Caucasus

—& now I grasp why N. wants him, to become Metropolitain [sic]!!! why the man was always ambitious & sly & clever & has already got round N.—one may have to send him away, if he continues being disliked so. Pitirim they [Bishop Antony Guriysky and other Georgians?] till now simply worship.—He [Bishop Antony Guriysky] came for the ordination of their priest as bishop Melchizedek (our Friend says he will be a marvellous Metropolitan in the future). But of course one must not have a Metropolitan now at Tiflis—they [Nicholasha, etc.] only want a court round them & everything grand, will soon ask for special ministers too. N. says [all this will be necessary] because of the country [i.e., Turkish lands then being conquered] we have vanquished— nonsense—Poland had none either.— [b]

Fancy, the Synod wants to present me with a Testimonial & Image [icon] (because of my work for the wounded, I think)—you see poor me receiving them all? Since Catherine no Empress has personally received them alone, Gr. is delighted (I less so)—but strange, is it not, I, whom they feared & disapproved of always.[370] Well enough about business talks.—Yet more officers have been brought us—the Varsh. Gv. [Warsaw Guard] etc.—despairing [sic] not to be able to work & see them.—The 3 big girls went to [your] sister Olga's train & gave medals & saw lots.—To-day O. & T. [Olga and Tatiana] go to town< for Tatiana's Committee.—Our Fr. wishes to see me this evening in the little house [of Anna Vyrubova] (with his wife [Praskovaya Rasputina] too), says I won't be any the worse for it. Says not to worry too much, God will help out at the war.— To-day I see Protopopov & Ilyin [Il'in]—every day people & ones head has to work so hard, so many questions to ask & get clear into ones head.— [c, d]

I also regret [that your sister] Olga wants to marry now—& how about her hospital then? And generally I cannot help deeply regretting this marriage, tho' want her to be happy at last.—Little Marie< lunched with us—looks well—has little to do, i.e. she does not nurse the wounded, but looks after the economical managment [sic], wh. gives her not much work—& then she has taken over Ella's< committee at Pskov. The summer she lived in a wee house near a monastery [i.e., convent] where a recluse lives she likes.— She made me a good, quiet opinion. [Her brother] Dmitri< mocks at her & that grieves her & the rest too, that she is so hideous as [a] sister [i.e.., nurse], much better in her town dresses etc.—thats all so foolish—instead of being grateful, that the Child has found an occupation wh. satisfies her—what will be [i.e., what she will do] after the war, she cannot imagine.—I enclose a letter Ania received fr. Bresler, do tell me what one is to answer him—can he present himself or send you a petition through me?— [e]

Madelaine< just brought me yr. sweet letter—thanks fondly, my treasure.—I understand how worried you are [see Letter No. 1431], shall talk with Protop. to-day & to our Friend. Shakh.[ovskoi] told me that they have brought ample fuel by the rivers for the whole winter—wood & coal—of course prices high—alas. He has received much money ahead, so as to already prepare the wood for 17-18 autumn [i.e., for the autumn of the coming year, 1917] too.—I asked about the bread. Says the peasants always sold their [grain] quickly, in time of peace, for fear the prices wld. fall—now they know that by waiting the prices rise, & they have no hurry for money as are well off. I said to my mind one ought to send people of the different interested ministeries [sic] to the most essential places for flour & bread & make them speak to the peasants & explain clearly to them. When bad people wish to succeed they always speak & are listened to, now if the good give themselves the same trouble, of course the peasants will listen to them.[350] The Governor, vicegovernor & all their people must take part, shall speak to Protop. & see what he finds to say.—The reason we have not enough sugar—you know.—Now butter gets sent in such colossal quantities to the army (need much fat as [they have] less meat) that one has not enough here.—Fish there is enough, not so meat.—It interests me speaking to a new man & we'll see what his ideas are. Oh, Krivoshein[, a previous minister of agriculture,] he has everything on his rotten conscience. But still, its not as awful as all that, <u>we shall find</u> a way out; & these brutes Rodz.[ianko], Guchk., Poliv. & Co. are at the bottom of far more <u>than one sees</u> (I feel it) so as to force things out of the hands of the ministers.[354] But you will see all soon & speak it over, & I'll ask our Fr.'s advice.—So often He has sound ideas others go by—God inspires Him—& to-morrow I'll write what He said. His being here makes me quieter, says things will go better—people less persecute Him, whenever they are more after Him everything goes worse.— [f]

I hope such an endless letter does not make you wild, Sun of my heart? Wish I were with & near you the whole, whole time to help carrying all together.—I send some bits of cardboard back as am sure you need still lots.—Talked for an hour with Protop.[opov],— really good impression, I have told him to send you a wire he & Bobr.[inksy] sent to all the governors.[356] Must end, 1000 kisses, fond blessings, old   <u>Wify.</u>   [P.S.] Verily think, God has sent you the <u>right</u> man in Protopopov & he <u>will</u> work & has already begun. I think now can have food supply in Governments hands, not need military. [g]

355. Prince C. A. Bagration-Mukhraisky, a lt. and son-in-law of g.p. Constantine Constantinovich, was killed on May 19, 1915.

356. During wartime emergencies, tsarist officials often confiscated goods to supply the armed forces and cities. Protopopov and Bobrinsky, by contrast, urged provincial governors to avoid such tactics. Protopopov believed draconian measures were economically counterproductive: they caused peasants to horde, so fewer goods entered the market, and prices remained high. As a "free trader," Protopopov also favored an end to price fixing. He argued rising prices would stimulate production which, in turn, would lower prices. (Nabokov: Alexandra, *Pis'ma imperatritsy*, II, p. 192n) This philosophy exposed the wealthy Protopopov to the charge (echoed by communist historians) of favoring exploitation of the masses in defense of interests of the ruling class. See Letter No. 1439b.

No. 1435.   Ts.[arist] Stavka. Sept. 21st 1916.
My own beloved One,
   Today the train is very late & your letter has not come. It is again fine & not too cold. Please thank [daughter] Tatiana for her photos & tell her to send me more of my writing paper (one of the blue boxes). The sad feeling I had yesterday has passed. I told Alexeev [sic] to order Brusilov to stop our hopeless attacks, so as to later pull the guards & some other troops out of the front lines & give them time to rest & be refilled [i.e., reinforced]. We must push on near Halich & lower down at Dorna-Vatra to help the rumanians & to cross the Carpathians before the winter sets in. The necessary reinforcements for this will be sent.—N.P.< told me he was pleased with your looks. Do try, Lovy-mine, to

regain your strength when you come here in a fortnight! To day is Paul's<
birthday & Dmitry's< & Dm. Sherem.['s]< namesday [sic]—so we had a little
glass of champagne to give them pleasure at luncheon! The sun shines gloriously & there are lots of green leaves among the yellow ones. Sweet Love, now
me must end! Me loves oo [you] so so much & miss you awfully. God bless you
& the girlies; I kiss you all very tenderly & her [Anna Vyrubova] too. With
fondest & tenderest love—Ever my own Girly your old   Nicky.

No. 1436/ Telegram 62. Stavka> Tsarskoe Selo. 21 Sept 1916. 20.03> 21.37.
To her majesty. Loving thanks [for] long dear letter. Received Ct. [Count] Bobrinsky. [He made] good impression. Splendid sunny day. [We] both kiss [you]
tenderly. Niki

No. 1437/ Telegram 123. Tsarskoe Selo> Stavka. 21/22 Sept 1916. 23.46>
0.55. To his majesty. Many thanks for telegram. Received new minister [Pro-
topopov], made wonderful impression. [We] talked of many things, please advance him more quickly.[349] [I] believe everything will be put in order well and
quickly along with the person you saw today [Bobrinsky], and there will be no
need for further changes [on council of ministers].[354] [We] talked much about
everything this evening. He [Protopopov] asks you to not worry, all will be well.
Sleep peacefully. [I] tenderly kiss [you]. Alex

No. 1438/ Telegram 126. Tsarskoe Selo> Stavka. 22 Sept 1916. 14.05> 14.45.
To his majesty. Tenderly thank [you] both. Weather changeable. [We] all
warmly kiss you [both]. God keep [you]. [My] health not famous [good]. Alix

---

No. 1439/ Her No. 597.   Tsarskoe Selo. Sept. 22[n] 1916.
My own beloved precious Darling,
   I have a lot I want to speak about, but as I scarcely slept at all this night, saw
every hour, ½ hour, except 5 o'clock, on the watch, (don't know why, as had
spent a lovely, soothing evening). I don't know whether I shall find words
enough.—Its not easy giving over conversations, one always is affraid [sic] of
using wrong words & thus making the sense different. To begin with I send you
the copy of one [of] Guchkov's letters to Alekseev—read it through, please &
then you will understand [how] the poor general gets beside himself—&
Guchkov< is untruthful, egged on by Polivanov, with whom they are inseparable. Warn the old man [Alekseev] seriously against this correspondance [sic], it
is made to enervate him—& they [the issues raised in the letters] don't concern
him, i.e. because for the army everything will be done & nothing missing.—Our
Friend< begs you not to too much worry over this question of food supply, thats
why I wired last night again—says things will arrange themselves & the new
Minister [Protopopov] has already set to work at once. [A. A.] Bobrinsky will
have told you about their united telegram to the governors which was a clever
thing.[356] One must make them [the ministers] realise their power & that they
should make more use of it.— [a]

I told Protopopov to write this to you—he said its against etiquette as he has not yet presented himself & did not wish to bother you.—I said that was quite the same, that you & I stick to etiquette for official things, but elsewise prefer knowing always everything.—Another fault [i.e., problem] is, Protopopov said[,] & which I fully agree to, that from one government [gubernaya, province] to the other things may not be exported—this is absurd— in one there is scarcely any cattle, in the other more than they need —of course one must let them get it & so on.—The landlords are to have all their woods confiscated, ([my] other [fountain]pen is being refilled) not fair, as some only live by their woods & life has become very hard for them—so must use one's brain & confiscate little in some properties—& others—more, who have other means beside wood for keeping up their properties—he told this to Shakhovskoy.[356]— [b]

We spoke for 1½ hour[.]—[Protopopov and I had] never [spoken] before, & I did not even remember his face—[He has] Brussilov's sly face, when he puckers up one eye. Very clever, coaxing, beautiful manners, speaks also very good French & English, one sees [he is] accustomed to speak—wont sleep [at his post], he promised me (but needs being kept in hand our Friend says, so as that pride should not spoil all[357])—I spoke very frankly to him, how yr. orders are constantly not fulfilled, put aside, how difficult to believe people, promises made & not kept;—I am no longer the slightest bit shy or affraid [sic] of the ministers & speak like a waterfall in Russia[n]!!! And they kindly don't laugh at my faults [i.e., mistakes]. They see I am energetic & tell all to you I hear & see & that I am yr. wall in the rear wh. is a very firm one & with God's mercy I hope I may be of some wee use to you. Shakhovskoi has begged to come whenever he has important questions, Bobrinsky too & this one [Protopopov] will also, & Shtyurmer, comes every week, so perhaps I can get them to stick together. I am obstinate & over & over repeat the same things & our Friend help with advice (may they continue listening to Him).—Things will & shall go, Lovy. [c]

Prot. is looking for a successor to [A. N.] Obol.[ensky] as its more than necessary—he thought of Spiridovich, I said no, that you & I had spoken that over before, & find him better suited for Yalta then the capital. He has told Ob. to come every morning to him, has given him orders about the quebles [queues or lines] in town<, to have the food measured out beforehand—to put the people under shelter, in courtyards, not out in the streets[350]—till now he has done nothing—utterly unfit for his place—too grand to accept the place of governor. [d]

Well, I wont repeat any more, its dull for you. But its [i.e., Protopopov is] a man who will work, has promised to be truthful, may he prove it (pen made me quite filthy).—But don't give it over into military hands—I fully believe P. can cope with this question & will do all in his power to succeed. Bobr.[inksy] is very devoted, but rather old—together they will manage, Shakh.[ovskoi] (goose, hoped to become min.[ister] of Int.[erior], our Friend told me & therefore is a bit against Prot., tho' an old friend of his) I shall keep him up to [i.e., I will watch to be certain that he does] work with the others, [— Protopopov] begged me to do it (I had already [spoken with Protopopov] on Tuesday). [e]

Lovy, all thats in my power I shall do to help you—sometimes a woman can, when men a wee bit look up to her—these know they have me to comit [i.e., contend] with as yr. guard, eye & ear in the rear.—Its better the food supply remains in the hand of the governm. civil—& the military all [i.e., be responsible solely] for the active army. All has been taken out of the Minister of Interior's hands & Bobr. has it now, therefore they will do things together, beginning by that telegram.[356] Their aids were most displeased but the order was given to despatch [sic] the wire. One must not provoke—& unwillingly military measures might be too hard in the wrong place—& they could not give orders to Gov.[ernors,] vicegov.[ernors,] etc.—No, I believe you can be quiet now on that subject, & our dear Friend says so too.— [f]

Had a lovely evening yesterday & we were very, very sad you were not with us, wld. have rested you, so uplifting! There was besides a bishop, an old man, a friend of his & "very high" therefore persecuted ([from] Viatka) & accused that he kissed women etc. He, like our Friend & all people in the bygone, kissed everybody alike. Read the Apostles—they kiss all as welcome. Well, now Pitirim sent for him & he cleared him completely.[358] He is much higher than the Metropolitan [Pitirim in spiritual strength] & with Gr.[egory]< one continues what the other begins, & still the Bishop looks up to Gr. There was such peace in the atmosphere & I longed so for your sweet presence—such a rest after all yr. endless worries & work—such beautiful talks!—They spoke of the Virgin—that she never wrote anything tho' so very clever—her very existence & being was enough of a miracle in itself—& [she] needed no more, she wld. never speak of herself; (and her life is known to our spirit).— [g]

Just got yr. precious letter—so, oh, so glad you feel less sad. I hate not being with you, you carry [everything] all alone, not a soul to share yr. worries—speak to N.P.<, let him be of use to you, knowing our Friend [as N. P. Sablin does] makes him understand things easier—& he has much developed these last months with that grave responsability [sic] upon his shoulders.—Well, I suppose you are right to stop the attack [see Letter No. 1435] & go at work fr. the south, we must push on over the Carpathians before winter[,] now its already very cold up there.—The Commander of my Siberians is wounded & amongst others, a charming officer, who left us only two months ago—hope he will be brought here.—If we advance to the south then they will be obliged to take their forces down there—& we shall be free'r up here. God will help—just patience, but the enemy is a still [a] very powerful one. [h]

I enclose some photos for you—Nastinka< or Isa< did [them].— Nast. comes to me this afternoon.—A doklad [report] of Rost.[ovtsev]—yesterday had still Ilyin [Il'in] & I spoke about the shocking behaviour of many sisters [i.e., nurses] (not real community ones) etc. We spoke with Prot. about the methodists being called in (10.000 they are on the whole I believe)—we both found it unwise as against their religious convictions (& their number small)—so I proposed he shld. ask the Minister of war to give them as sanitaries & then take all sanitaries (whom they always are trying to take away) to the war; that wld. be good & they wld. be serving.—Or, our Friend says, use them for making trenches & picking up wounded & dead as sanitaries at the war.[359]—Our Friend finds you ought to call in the Tartars now—such masses in Siberia everywhere—but explain it properly to them & not repeat that wicked mistake as in Turkestan[, where an anti-Russian uprising occurred in the summer of 1916].— [i]

Then our Friend said [the quotes that follow are in Russian]: "General Sukhomlinov should be set free, so that he should not die in jail, otherwise things will not be smooth, one should never fear to release prisoners, to restore sinners to a life of righteousness—prisoners until they reach jail become through their sufferings in the eyes of God—nobler than we"—more or less His words. "Every [person], even vilest sinner, has moments where the soul rises & is purified through their fearful suffering—then the hand must be reached out to save them before they are relost by bitterness & despair."—I have a petition fr. Mme Sukh.[omlinova] for you—do you wish me to send it to you? 6 months he is imprisoned, enough punishment—(as [he was] no spy) for all the wrong he did—is old, brokendown & wont live long, wld. be awful if died in prison. Order him to be taken & kept closely watched in his own house, without much fuss—please, Lovebird.—A day is an age now—there is need of wise administrators—the chief of police [Klimovich] should be quickly removed as [he] does endless harm—one is looking for a successor.—Beautifully they spoke of God, reminded me deeply of the Persian book I love—Bogoutshita [Bogouchitsa, "Teachings of God"]. "One must see God every where, in all things, in everything about us—then shall we be saved." "Be as holy as I am", be like God in virtue.—Its difficult to give over what He says [all these were "wise words" from Rasputin]—words are weak—it needs the accompanying spirit to enlighten them.— [j]

Grey, rainy day & so dark, lie in bed with a lamp writing.—These mornings lying—do me good, look rather rottener than when N.P. last saw me—doing everything I can to get stronger, hope by to-morrow to begin my medicins [sic] again. Except when receiving—lie all day.—Want badly to be decent by the time we meet. Sweet one, I miss you both quite awfully. Thoughts always with you. Cover you with tender, tenderest kisses. God bless & protect you now & evermore! Ever, Nicky my Own, yr. deeply loving old <u>Sunny</u>. [P.S.] What on earth is going on in Greece—looks like a revolution impending, God forbid—the allies fault then, alas! [k]

357. Rasputin supported Protopopov for high office, but we see here that even Grigory had reservations about the man.

358. The bishop of Vyatka was apparently charged with scandalous behavior ("accused that he kissed women"). These comments suggest the bishop was an ally of Pitirim and Rasputin. Pitirim helped clear the bishop of the charges before the Holy Synod.

359. Rasputin opposed war, but when it broke out he insisted Russia must fight to victory. Grigory also respected pacifism. Even so, his support for these Russian Methodists was probably secured with a bribe. On an earlier occasion, his fee for rescuing 300 Baptist pacifists from prison was 1,000 rubles per man. Unfortunately, the Baptists could not pay their bill, and Rasputin had to content himself with a mere 5,000 rubles. (Fuhrmann, *Rasputin*, pp. 123, 241 n. 23) By royal decree of October 19, 1916, the Methodists mentioned here were freed from combat duty to serve as medics ("sanitaries"). (Nabokov: Alexandra, *Pis'ma imperatritsy*, II, p. 195n)

No. 1440.   Ts.[arist] Stavka. Sept. 22$^{\underline{d}}$ 1916.
My beloved Sunny,

Many, many thanks for your two dear letters & especially for the last long one! I saw Bobrinsky & had a good talk with him. He knows Protop.[opov] since many years, likes him & is sure that they both shall work hand-in-hand. He also told about a telegram they both wrote![356] I am pleased with this. Al.[ekseev] has never mentioned to me Guchk.[ov]'s name—I only know that he hates Rodzianko & mocks at that man for always pretending he knows much better than others. No, what distresses him since months, is the quantity of letters he gets from officers, their families, soldiers etc. & also anonymous ones—all begging him to draw my attention to the difficulties of life in the towns & small places on account of the high prices of food & stuffs. I send you a few photos—duplicates as am putting my album in order before glewing them in.—Brusilov begged to continue the attack as Gurk[o] will help him on his right wing—so I allowed it.[360] The pen is very stupid. Good-bye & God bless you my own darling Lovebird & the girlies. With tenderest love & kisses ever your own old Nicky.

360. "After reading this letter on the following day the Tsaritsa telegraphed: 'He [Rasputin] approved of your original plan to stop [the offensive] and begin in another place. Now you write otherwise. May God help us.' [See Letter No. 1442.] The 'original plan' to which she refers (to stop the main offensive and to attack near Galitch and at Dorna-Vatra) will be found in the Tsar's letter of the 21st [see Letter No. 1435.]. The [present] telegram appears to have been delayed, and the Tsar did not receive it till the 24th." (Vulliamy, pp. 268-269n)

No. 1441/ Telegram 65. Stavka> Tsarskoe Selo. 22 Sept 1916. 19.55> 21.04. To her majesty. Many loving thanks. Warm, windy. Hope [you] feel better. Grateful for long wire last night. Tenderest kisses. Niki

No. 1442/ Telegram 138. Tsarskoe Selo> Stavka. 23 Sept 1916. 12.59> 14.21. To his majesty. Warmly thank you both for dear letters. He [Rasputin] approved of your original plan to halt [attack] and begin [it] at another place. Now you write otherwise, God help us.[360] Wonderful sun. [I] kiss, embrace [you]. [Greek] Nicky< comes for tea, leaves on Sunday. Alix

No. 1443/ Her No. 598. Ts.[arskoe] S[elo]. Sept. 23rd 1916.
My own beloved Angel,
   A glorious, sunny morning—shall lie out a little in the sun. Sat out yesterday for ¼ of an hour—as could not get any air, even kept the ventilator open all night.—Gr.[eek] Nicky< comes to tea—leaves on Sunday at last, poor boy.—[Daughter] Marie has gone out riding I am glad to say.—Our Friend< says about the new orders you gave to Brussilov etc.: "Very satisfied with father's orders, all will be well." [Cf. Letters No. 1435 and 1442.] He won't mention it to a soul, but I had to ask His blessing for yr. decision.—Very tenderest thanks for yr. dear letter, just received. Do hope Brussilov is sure & doing no folly & wont again sacrifice the guard in an impregnable place.—Am glad you liked yr. talk with [A. A.] Bobrinsky.—Baby< wrote me such a nice letter, sweet Child.— Have great, great longing for you, my one & all—am trying to get better—the air may help & now medicins [sic].—Excuse a short letter. Fondest kisses & blessings fr. yr. very own old   Wify.

No. 1444. Ts.[arist] Stavka. Sept. 23. 1916.
My own beloved One,

Tenderly do I thank you for your dear long letter, explaining so well your conversation with Prot[opopov]. God grant he may be the man we want just now! Fancy, Shakh.[ovskoi] who wanted to have to be in that place! Yes, verily, you ought to be my eye and ear there—near the capital while I have to stick here. That is just the part for you to keep the ministers going hand in hand & like this you are rendering me & our country enormous use. Oh, you precious Sunny, I am so happy you have at last found the right work for yourself. Now I will certainly feel quiet & no more worried, at least for the interior. [a]

I sent Bressler's letter to A.[nia]< back, that is [a] hopeless affair as his brother would not clear himself of all accusations. Perhaps better he were to write one a petition. Thanks also for the photos you sent me. The weather is warm but grey, this morning there was thick fog! Today a year ago I came back to Ts. S. for the first time after spending here a month! And today also it is five months I left home on your namesday [sic].—Oh, how Mogilev boxes me! And at [the] same time I have very much to do— scarcely any time to begin arranging the photos in my album. Well now I must end. God bless you my angel, my Heart, Brain & Soul. Fondly do I kiss you & the girlies. Ever your own   Nicky. [b]

No. 1445/ Telegram 66. Stavka> Tsarskoe Selo. 23 Sept 1916. 19.46> 20.34. To her majesty. Fondest thanks [for] letter and great help. So grateful and touched. Warm, fog, rain. [We] both [are] alright [sic]. Tender love to all. Niki

---

No. 1446/ Telegram 140. Tsarskoe Selo> Stavka. 24 Sept 1916. 10.55> 12.04. To his majesty. Cold, foggy, rain. He [Rasputin] very pleased that you did not follow your plan—you totally correctly foresaw all, and [A. A.] B.[obrinsky] there should hear and carry out your commands [so that] now again [there will not be] useless sacrifices. Your thoughts [are] inspired from on high. May God keep you, dear ones, [I] warmly kiss [you both]. Alix

---

No. 1447/ Her No. 599.   Tsarskoe Selo. Sept. 24th 1916.
Sweet beloved One,

A grey, foggy, pouring morning—slept & feel midling [sic]. Shevich [D. D. Shevich's] daughter (ex rifles) comes to be blessed by Paul< & me—she marries Dellingshausen of the 4-th reg. to-morrow. Then I see poor Kutaissov whose sister (Rebinder) died so suddenly.—Lovy, our Friend< is much put out that Brussilov has not listened to yr. order to stop the advance—says you were inspired from above to give that order & the crossing of the Carpathians before winter & God wld. bless it.—Now he says again useless losses.—Hopes you will still insist, as now all is not right.—One of my wounded wrote to me in a way for me to understand, that its utterly in vain just now, the chiefs themselves not too sure & useless losses. So you see, something is not rightly managed; more than one tells the same story. It coincides with what Paul said about Kaledin not being sure at all of success;—why obstinately go against a wall, break yr. heart for nothing—& throw away lives like flies.— [a]

There is your letter! how beautifully early[—]10½. Thanks over & over again, Lovebird. So touched by all you write that will let me be a help to you—tried before, but the ministers I felt did not like me.—Wish—I were only quicker a bit stronger again—as then the hospital< does one good in between for the soul & rests the head.—Had Mme Orjewsky [Orzhevskaya] 1½ hour yesterday & then Greek N.[icky]<. He leaves to-morrow—hopes you got his last letter, as you never wired. Will write again to-day—I must say our diplomates [sic] behave shamefully & if Tino< is kicked out, it will be our fault—horrid & unjust—how dare we mix into a country's private politics & force one government to be sent flying & intrigue to get a revolutionist back to his post. I believe if you cld. get the French Government to recall Seraille [Sarrail] (this is my private opinion) things wld. at once calm down there. Its an awful intrigue of freemasons, of wh. the Fr. General & Venizelos are members—& many Egyptians, rich Greeks etc. who have collected money, & have even payed [sic] the "Novoye Vremya"< & other papers to write bad & forbid good articles concerning Tino & Greece. Vile shame!—[b]

(Cant write any more to-day.—Red cross [workers] all say Miechen's< papers, [expressing] wishes of a special department— quite wrong, cannot be apart fr. red cross.) Godbless you. Very tender kissis [sic] fr. yr. very own old Wify. [P.S.] This a strictly private letter of [the] Pahlens to Taneyev [A. S. Taneev] & as such I must still forward it to you—one has made you do an unjust thing. I honestly should give him back his rank, he undeservedly lost—Guchkov does far worse things & is in no way touched or reprimended [sic]—& Pahlen has suffered innocently. Give it him back now, before I come, so as to show its you alone who have done it—or if you seek an occasion, then Oct. 5 [Aleksei's name-day]—but please, do it, Tell Maxim.[ovich] to write all to Fred.[ericks] & have it quickly done—so pleasant to set an injustice to rights—else Taneyev wld. never have sent me this private letter. He does not know I even send it [to] you.— [c]

No. 1448.   Ts.[arist] Stavka. Sept. 24. 1916.
My own Precious Darling,

Again the train is late & your letter has not reached me yet. Read this wire fr. Miechen< & tear it up.—Once more I thank you, Lovy-mine, for your dear long letter. Verily, you will help me enormously in speaking with & looking after the ministers. Just got your wire where you say our Friend< is put out that my plan is not followed out.[361] When I gave this order I did not know that Gurko decided to draw nearly all his available forces & prepare an attack together with the guards & neighbour troops. That combination makes our troops doubly stronger at this point & gives one faith in the possiblity [sic] of success. That is why when Al.[ekseev] read the explanation telegrams from Brus.[ilov] & Gurko begging to continue the operation, wh. was in full development—the next morning I gave my consent.—Today Br. asked to send gen. Kaledin down to Lechitsky & make Gurko the chief of all these troops[,] the guards included, which is perfectly right & correct fr. the milit.[ary] point of view & pleases me highly! Now I shall be quiet [i.e., calm] & sure that G. will act energetically but wisely! These details are only for you—please Lovy! Tell Him [Rasputin] only: "Papa prikazal prinyat' razumnie meri"! [Papa has ordered sensible measures taken!] Thank you fondly, my Sweet One, for your dear letter that just arrived [at] 2.15 instead of 11.30. The weather is very warm but dampish with occasional show-

ers. Now I must end. God bless you my One & All, my beloved Sunny. I kiss
you & the girlies & yearn frightfully for you. Ever your own old Nicky.

---

361. Vulliamy claims these " passages are of great historical interest, for they exhibit Rasputin's
influence on the course of military operations —with the result shown in the Tsar's letter of the 27th,
three days later [Letter No. 1462]. In reply to the present letter, the Tsaritsa begs her husband to 'stop
this useless massacre,' and on this day she telegraphed: 'He is very disturbed that your plan was not
carried out. You foresaw everything quite correctly, and B.[rusilov] ought to obey and fulfill your
orders. Now there are again useless sacrifices.'" (Pp. 270-271n) But a more careful reading of this
letter indicates it was *Alekseev* who favored a continuation of the Brusilov offensive, and Nicholas
accepted his recommendation. See also Letter No. 1462 and Footnotes 338 and 372.

No. 1449/ Telegram 143. Tsarskoe Selo> Stavka. 24 Sept 1916. 18.22> 19.26.
To his majesty. Very happy with dear letters. Paul< and Marie< had tea with us.
Grey, thick fog, rain. Poor Komarov had stroke, feels bad, left side paralyzed.
Kiss [you] both and tenderly embrace [you]. Alix

No. 1450/ Telegram 68. Stavka> Tsarskoe Selo. 24 Sept 1916. 20.15> 20.40.
To her majesty. Thank [you] lovingly also [for] two wires. Fog, rain, warm.
Sorry about Komarov. With love from both. Niki

No. 1451/ Telegram 150. Tsarskoe Selo> Stavka. 25 Sept 1916. 11.50> 13.04.
To his majesty. Heartily thank you for both dear letters. Drab, rainy, dull
weather. Today receive Synod with image [icon], am embarrassed.[370] Embrace
and kiss you [both], my loved ones. Alix

No. 1452/ Her No. 600.   Tsarskoe Selo. Sept. 25th 1916.
My own beloved Darling,
    Grey, dull weather—yet more leaves have fallen, so dreary.— Sweetheart, I saw
Kutaisov yesterday & we had a long talk—then Paul< told me about interesting
letters fr. Rauch & Rilsky [C. I. Rylsky];—& fr. others I have heard—& all say
the same thing, that its a second Verdun, we are sacrificing 1000[s] of lives for
nothing, pure obstinacy. Oh, give your order again to Brussilov—stop this useless sloughter [sic]—the younger ones feel their chiefs have neither any faith of
success there—why repeat the madness of the Germans at Verdun. Yr: plane
[i.e., plan was] so wise, approved by our Friend<—[strike at] Galitsch, Carpathians, Dona-Vatra [Dorna-Vatra], [to help the] Roumanians. Stick to it, you are
head master & all will thank you on their knees—& our glorious guard!— Those
boggs [sic], impregnable—open spaces, impossible to hide, few woods, soon
leaves will fall & no saving shelter for advance. One has to send the men far
round the boggs, the smell is so awful—the unburied comrades!! Our generals
don't count the "lives" any—hardened to losses—& that is sin—when you are convinced of success, its another thing. God blesses yr. idea—have it executed—spare those lives—Sweety, I know nothing—but is Kaledin the right man
in the right place, when things are difficult?— [a]
    Now other things.—Am hunting for a man in [A. N.] Obolensky's place (by the
by, [he, Obolensky?] has asked to see me—very unpleasant, does not concern me
to speak about with him)—would Andrianov [Adrianov] not do? Is he still in the

Suite? Was completely aquitted [sic]—does it matter he was under judgement? But he came out clean. If you have nothing against this idea—wire at once that you agree [with proposal] No. 1; then shall propose him to Sht.[yurmer], who can talk to the M.[inister] of Int.[erior Protopopov]—not your order, but that you would have nothing against him.   He was very good in Moscou [sic], Dz[h]unkovsky tried to break his neck & Jussupov's [Yusupov the Elder]—of all, Andr. was the least at fault. But you can judge best.[362]—Then to finish Obolensky, how wld. it be to give him Komarov's place—long, I doubt his [Komarov's] living—even if life spared, will be an invalid. A splendid place, Preobrazh. [i.e., as a former member of the Preobrazhensky Guards Regiment, Obolensky deserves a good appointment] & I think [he is] quite fit for such a place. If you agree to this—wire No. 2 yes. I have it written out on a paper you see, I shall probably see him [Obolensky] on Tuesday, then if he makes a fuss, I cld. tell him that you think of him in future for the W.[inter] P.[alace, i.e., director of the imperial court at Petrograd]—he is in the Suite—& Zeime[, the current director,] is not & he [Obolensky] is more suited.— [b]

The Children have all gone to Church—I am still unable to go— such a nuisance.—Paul will be with you on Thursday, has a big doklad [report] & wld. like to go to the guard (very good thing) & return to the Headquarter[s], if time, for the 5-th.—What have you done about Guchkov's< letter? [See Letters No. 1439a and 1440.] At last our Botkin has fully understand what a man he is—they are relations—but only now he has fully understood the great evil in him—he & Polivanov tried to harm his naval [officer] brother.— You saved him now, by wiring to Russky [Ruzsky], who did not wish to obey yr. order about Botkin before—but he was received like "a dog there".— [c]

Paul & I blessed the little Shevich [daughter of D. D. Shevich— see Letter No. 1447a]—pretty girl—to-day is her wedding—the mother, old, fat, with no teeth scarcely—& she is my age!—had a baby 3 years ago, happy woman!—Sorry, nothing interesting to tell you, dull letter.—Fondest thanks precious letter come so nice & early, can't imagine why mine are so often late.—Well, I am glad that Br.[usilov] has sent Kal.[edin] south & given over all to Gurko, thats far the wisest thing to do—may he be reasonable & not obstinate, make him understand that clearly. [d]

Oh, I too yearn for you fearfully—soon, soon God grant again some happy days together. Babykins<, you keep him in hand, see he does not play at table or put his arms & elbows on the table, please—& dont let him shy [throw] breadballs. 5 months from here—ah when shall you be able to get away fr. that old place & see something else again!—Goodbye, sweet One, sun of my life. Kiss you ever so tenderly. God bless & protect you—yr. very own old   Wify. [The following P.S. is written in pencil, not ink.]   Please pay attention to what A.[nia]< has written about rising [sic] the wages to all poor officials all over the country. It must come straight from you[371]—there is always money had fr. some capitals—a check to all revolutionary ideas.—Our Friend says if you agree to Adrianov,[362] then as temporary prefect (hold. office)—then nobody will have anything to say against him.[363]— [e]

362. Maj.-Gen. A. A. Adrianov was governor of Moscow (*gradonachal'nik*) when an anti-German riot broke out there in the spring of 1915. The Senate investigated Adrianov for behavior that some thought brought on the pogrom; Alexandra notes he was acquitted. Although Adrianov was considered as A. N. Obolensky's successor as *gradonachal'nik* of Petrograd, the appointment did not materialize.

363. Rasputin is saying that if Nicholas feared appointing Adrianov *gradonachal'nik* of Petrograd would cause an uproar, he could make him *acting* governor: *upravlyayushchii gradonachal'nik*, "one carrying out the duties of the governor." Such an appointment was considered temporary, pending location of someone who would receive the title without qualification. Protopopov, for example, was "upravlyayushchii" minister of the interior; Alexandra thought he should be made full minister, and Nicholas did this on December 16 (O.S.), 1916. See Letters No. 1647c and 1652b.

No. 1453.   Ts.[arist] Stavka. Sept. 25th 1916.
My own precious Lovebird,
    Many thanks for your dear letter. I send you Pahlen's letter back. Yesterday I wrote old l. [sic] Nirod that injustice to be corrected & that he is to get back his rank on Octob. 5th. [See Letter No. 1447c.] I send you my photo at Evpatoria as I have one already. Today is a lovely summer weather—12° in the shade—such joy! Two new rumanian officers have arrived—the one is old Rozetti's son (mother born Giers) quite like his father, only does not cry every instant.[364] The other a young boy, who pleased Aleksei —; he may become his friend.—You must come for the Oct. 4—our Cossack feast, better of course on the 3^{d}. My love, my Treasure, how happy that idea makes me to think that in about a week I may be able to see you, to hear your dear voice & clasp you in my arms! Excuse this pen but it is very old & needs changing. Just got your wire. I can you see [sic] receiving the Synod[370]—only one disagreeable member—Serg.[ei, archbishop of] Finland[—]to look at.—Now me must end. God bless you my beloved Darling & the girlies. Many tender kisses from your own old Nicky.

364. Nicholas II refers to Fedor Georgievich Rosseti-Solesko, former attaché of the Roumanian embassy in Berlin; his father, G. K. Rosseti-Solesko, was the former Roumanian envoy to Russia. (Sergeev: Nicholas and Alexandra, *Perepiska,*V, p. 68n)

No. 1454/ Telegram 69. Stavka> Tsarskoe Selo. 25 Sept 1916. 18.49> 19.30.
To her majesty. Fondest thanks. Lovely summer day. Now down pour. Thoughts always together. Tender kisses. Niki

---

No. 1455/ Telegram 155. Tsarskoe Selo> Stavka. 26 Sept 1916. 10.30> 11.20.
To his majesty. Clear, marvellous, sunny day. Cold. Shall lie on balcony. Heart not famous [i.e., good], perhaps air will help. Synod gave me a marvellous ancient image [icon]. Khogandokov is being recommended for place I wrote about in my letter [see No. 1456a] as the best [to replace A. N. Obolensky as governor of Petrograd]. [I] warmly kiss [you]. Alix

---

No. 1456/ Her No. 601.   Tsarskoe Selo. Sept. 26th 1916.
My very own Treasure,
    There—you will say—a big sheet, means she is going to chatter a lot again!—Well, Prot.[opopov] dined with A.[nia]<—she knows him already a year or two—& he proposed my friend Konst. Nik. Hagandokov [Constantine

Nicholaevich Khogandokov] instead of [A. N.] Obolensky, i.e. V. Volkonsky proposes him. I have the whole account about him—tho' we know him—& that looks really so good. Now he is Military Governor and Ataman [Hetman] of the Amur cossacks; has been through Chinese campagne [campaign], Jap.[anese War of 1904] & this war; participated in the repression of the sedition in Manchuria 1900—probably my age or younger—in service (officer) [since] 10 aug. 1890 has all military war decorations for his rank. Our Fr.< says if the [i.e., he] likes us—why not take him—I was much taken aback, never wld. have dreamed of him.[365] Rank major-general. Perhaps this all is better than Andr.,[362] who of course has enemies.—I think Hagan. told me he left because of his kidneys—& this service is not tiring, needs an energetic man—& his white cross will already make effect.— [a]

Things were not very nice in Moscou [sic] yesterday, so Prot. sent off Volkonsky at once & made Bobr.[insky] sent [send] off his aid there too to see into the affairs.[366] He does not waste time—I am glad to say—& they & the military will let's hope at once quieten down all. But its sure to begin here, & Obol. will be absolutely no good[350]—we say what he was in the reg., where he might have stopped that story [i.e., episode].[367]—I send you the petition of a medical field surgeon, who killed a man—just read it through—he begs to be a field surgeon out at the war—only you can change the judgement by mercifully letting him go—our Fr. gave it to me[365] & Rost.[ovtsov] says only you can help. My chancellry [sic] made the red marks.—Then I send you photos I did—also 1 for Alekseev, 1 for Maximovich, 1 for Mordv.[inov], 1 for [A. N.] Grabbe & 2 for cossacks [sic]—give Baby< to give them over if you cant, dear. [b]

Protopop. has asked to see you—wont you tell him to let Sukhoml.[inov] out, he says it can of course at once be done, he will tell M.[inister] of Justice [A. A. Makarov], write this down to remember when you see him & also speak to him about Rubinstein to have him quietly sent to Siberia, not left here to aggravate the Jews—Prot. quite agrees with the way our Fr. looks upon this question. Prot. thinks it was Guchkov, who must have egged on the military to catch the man, hoping to find evidences against our Friend<. Certainly he [Rubinstein] had ugly money affairs—but not he alone.[368]—Let the man [Protopopov] speak out frankly to you, I said you always wish it, the same as I do.— [c]

He [Protopopov] quite cleverly thinks of using Kurlov[308] in some things of foodsupplies, wh. is right—not to waste the man.—He got the thing at once to be printed about the millions the Union got & wh. the others were dawdling over—only its not what I wanted—I did not want bare facts—they are bad enough—but it was to be cleverly written—this is too naked for my taste.[369] One can cry to think of half a milliard [billion] has been thrown to the Union— when existing organisations [sic] could have done marvels with a quarter of the sum.—I enclose it for you to read.—Very, very tenderest thanks for your dear letter just received. So happy you have given that order about Pahlen, thank you for yr. justice.—How nice you had such warmth. This morning 1 degree of frost, but sunshine thats everything, so shall lie out on the balkony [sic] before luncheon—my heart is more enlarged again & its difficult breathing. Fear, I shant be good at much this time, I am sorry to say, for much motoring. And I do so want to get to the hospital<—& cant—great nuisance.—Fancy, Rosetti's son being with you [see Letter No. 1453]—what a type! [d]

How lovely it will be to be with you again soon, sunshine< & Sunbeam< & old mother sunny! Miss you both horribly. These break downs come regularly 3 or 4 times a year—I fill myself with medicins [sic].—Now my Angel, goodbye & God bless & protect you. Kisses without end on every dearly beloved, very own place —yr. Own. [P.S.] The Synod gave me a lovely old Image (icon) & Pitirim read a nice paper—I mumbled an answer. Was rejoiced to see dear Shavel'sky.[370] Our Fr.< worries that one did not listen to you (Brussilov) as your first thought was the right one & a pity you gave in, yr. spirit was right wishing the change. He took up the Virgin's Image & blessed you fr. far & said "May the Sun rise there". A.[nia]< just brought these messages fr. town< & kisses you.—[A. N.] Obolensky's wife whole time bothers our Fr. in tears that husband leaves, begs for a good place [i.e., assignment]. [e]

365. These are almost certainly examples of bribes winning Rasputin's support for the favor or appointment in question.

366. Reference here is probably to some public disorder connected with a shortage of food, supplies, etc. Note Alexandra's conviction that the problem would spread to the capital unless more forceful leadership was found.

367. This refers to a well-known uprising in the Preobrazhensky Regiment during the Revolution of 1905. (Nabokov: Alexandra, *Pis'ma imperatritsy*, II, p. 202n)

368. Dmitry Rubinstein was a promimant Jewish capitalist. Alexandra used him to forward money to relatives in Germany during the war, which may be behind her statement, "[c]ertainly he had ugly money affairs—but not he alone." Rubinstein was reputedly pro-German; his ties to Rasputin and the empress fed the notion they were likewise disloyal. General N. S. Batyushin's commission arrested Rubinstein after a press campaign that accused him of "illicit financial speculation." Alexandra apparently feared a public trial would stir Jewish resentments ("aggravate the Jews"), hence she suggested having Rubinstein "quietly sent to Siberia." Rubinstein was released from custody in early December 1916. He was born in 1876 and died in emigration. (Katkov, *Russia 1917*, pp. 68-69; Fuhrmann, *Rasputin*, pp. 123-125, 169, 241-242)

369. On September 25, 1916, the semi-official newspaper *Novoe Vremya* (New Times) published figures of monies the various Unions had received from the government.

370. This event celebrated the power of the "Rasputin gang" in the Holy Synod. It occurred at the Alexander Palace on September 26 (O.S.), 1916. The Synod delegation was headed by Pitirim, metropolitan of Petrograd, and Director Raev. Chief Chaplain of the Armed Forces G. I. Shavel'sky attended; he claimed Raev was so obsequious it "made the eyes hurt." The group gave Alexandra an ancient icon and a commendation for her work with the wounded and other activities. A mishap occurred at the end. Bishop Michael understood that one should take leave of the empress without turning his back to her. Doing his best with this difficult maneuver, he knocked over a pedestal and smashed a costly vase. "This accident," according to Shavel'sky, "left the superstitious empress in a depressed mood." (Fuhrmann, *Rasputin*, p. 161)

No. 1457.   Ts.[arist] Stavka. Sept. 26th 1916.
My own Lovebird,

Tender thanks for your dear letter. You put so many questions in it wh. I must think about before answering them. Wednesday I receive Prot.[opopov] & will speak about the petrogr. gradon.[achal'nik, i.e., the governor of Petrograd]. I think it would not be wise to place there Adrian.[ov] who is an honest man but awfully weak, a real pancake, an ex-milit.[ary] judge. He would not do there during the present difficult times.[362] As for [A. N.] Obolensky, if you have nothing against him, one might promise him the Wint.[er] Pal.[ace, see Letter

No. 1452b] after poor Komarov. Your friend Khogandokov is nakazhym ata-manom Amursk. kaz. voiska [i.e., hetman of the Amur Cossack army]—named there a few months ago! I really do not know how he would be as grad.[o-nachal'nik, governor]? I send you [Greek] Nicky's< letter and a paper of Sht.[yurmer] about the question that interested you. Now I must end! God bless you my sweet Sunny & the girlies. With fondest kisses ever your own Nicky.

No. 1458/ Telegram 73. Stavka> Tsarskoe Selo. 26 Sept 1916. 19.36> 8.10. To her majesty. Fondest thanks. After rainy morning [weather] now better. Shall think over what you wrote. Kisses from both. Niki

No. 1459/ Telegram 161. Tsarskoe Selo> Stavka. 26 Sept 1916. 20.37> 21.05. To his majesty. Heartily thank you for dear letters, was very happy to receive them. Am lying on balcony, very clear. Sleep well. Embrace and kiss you both. Any interesting news? Alix

No. 1460/ Telegram 166. Tsarskoe Selo> Stavka. 27 Sept 1916. 10.44> 12.20. To his majesty. Yesterday evening was 5 deg. frost, this morning 1, grey. Be-lieve A.[nia]< will not appear [with me to visit you] because it was suggested to her [that she stay home]. Am sending you her explanations. Heart still quite en-larged. Will try to not receive anyone to-morrow, instead lie in bed all day so as to get well more quickly. Warmly kiss and embrace [you] both. Alix

No. 1461/ Her No. 602.   Ts.[arskoe] S[elo]. Sept. 27$\underline{th}$ 1916.
My own Angel,
    When I went to bed there [was] already 5° of frost, this morning still 1° and grey.—As heart still enlarged, shall arrange to see nobody to-morrow & remain all day in bed—perhaps that will help more—so few days have remained [until we meet]—leave already in 5!—Sweetheart, you are receiving the new M. o. t. Int. [Minister of the Interior Protopopov] to-morrow—he is emotioned.—let him re-alise yr. power of will & decisiveness that will help & stimulate his energy. Let him talk with Aleks.[eev] so as that the latter may feel he has to do with a clever man who wastes no time—it will be an antedote [sic] to Guchkov's< let-ters.—Speak to him about Sukhomlinov he will find means of doing it—the old man will die else in prison & we shall <u>never</u> be at peace about it. Au fond, to save Kshess. & S. M. [reference is to Mathilde Kschessinska,[202] and Serge Michaelovich] he also sits there, & one dare not bring up that subject before law on account of those 2—even Andr.[ew] Vlad.[imirovich] said as much to the Rudiger-Belyaev [reference is to A. F. Rediger and M. A. Belyaev] tho' he [An-drew Vladimirovich] is Kschess. love[r]. Then speak about Rubinstein,[368] he [Protopopov] will know what to do.—Am so happy about Count Pahlen.—You are right about Adrianov[362] I suppose, just had a paper fr. Prot. showing he wont do—I only mentioned him like that as he came into my head.—If Hagandokov [Khogandokov] can be spared—may be good, at least all his military decorations let one hope it—still you may find another. Sht. proposed a Meyer [Maj.-Gen. P. P. Meier, recently made *gradonachal'nik* of Rostov] who was years at Varshaw

[Warsaw], but the name is to[o] appallingly German for the wild anim.[al] ears nowadays.— [a]

10½[—]yr. sweet letter has just been given to me—endless thanks & kisses for it, Treasure sweet.—Shall bring A.[nia]< too, our Fr.< begged it, as the girl is good & so honestly helps when & how she can, & several of "us" together will bring more peace & strength. She can lunch in the train, as shy work [i.e., she is shy] in the room with many people—[Anna Vyrubova] will enjoy the rest, nice air, drives, tea etc.—& we shall still be to ourselves—she does not fidget now.—I bless & kiss you without end in passionate love. Ever Huzy mine, yr. very own old wify   <u>Alix</u>. [b]

I return [Greek] Nicky's< letter to you—exactly as he spoke to me—please talk to Sht. severely about it—we are driving them [the Greeks] into a republic [by undermining their king], we, [their fellow] orthodox—its really shameful.—Why cant you beg Pointcare [Poincaré] (president [of France]) to recall Seraille [Sarrail] & make Fr.[ance] & Engl.[and] insist too (thats my idea)—& make them stand up for Tino<, the King & not side with Venesuelos [Venizelos] the revolutionist & free mason. Call out Sht. as its difficult to write—give him severe instructions, we are behaving most unfairly & understand poor Tino going half wild. [c]

Keep my little list before you—our Friend< begged for you to speak of all these things to Protopopov & its very good if you mention our Friend that he should listen to him & trust to his advice;—let him feel you dont shun his name. I very calmly spoke of him—he came to him when he was very ill, some years ago.—Badmaev called him.[315]—Tell him to be warned against Andronnikov coming to him (Prot.) & keep him away. Forgive my bothering you, Deary—but am always affraid [sic] as you are so terribly hard worked—that you may forget something—& so [I] act as your living notebook.— <u>Sunny</u>.

Speak to Pr.[otopopov] about:

1. Sukh.[omlinov], order to find a way to get him out of prison].

2. Rubinstein to send away [from Petrograd][368]

3. Prefect [i.e., a new *gradonachal'nik* of Petrograd to replace A. N. Obolensky].

4. Augment wages of the officials as your kindness to them, not fr. the ministers.[371a]

5. About food supplies tell him strictly, severely that all must be done to set it to rights—you order it.[350]

6. Tell him to listen to our Friend's councils, it will bring him blessings & help his work & Yours—please say this, let him see yr. trust in him—he knows him several years already.

Keep this paper[371b] before you. [d]

371a. Three days later, on September 30 (O.S.), 1916, Russian newspapers reported this was done. (Nabokov: Alexandra, *Pis'ma imperatritsy*, II, p. 201n)

371b. After signing her letter "Sunny," Alexandra wrote this "check list" on both sides of a much smaller sheet of paper.

No. 1462   Ts.[arist] Stavka. Sept. 27 1916.
My own beloved Sunny,
    Ever so many thanks for your dear letter & photos. Am in despair you don't
feel well & that your poor heart is again enlarged! Certainly you have over
worked yourself & overtired the heart. Do look after your health. The weather is
once more warm & fine at intervals between rain. These days nothing was going
on in [i.e., at the] front, because preparations are being pushed forward and a
great concentration is taking place at furthest left [flank]—Dorna-Vatra to help
the rumanians. Darling—Brusilov at once gave the necessary orders upon receiving mine to stop, but asked whether the troops wh. were marching west were
to be sent back or would be allowed to continue their movement.[372] Then he
proposed Gurko instead of Kaledin. [See Letter No. 1448.] After that he sent a
paper with Gurk[o's] ideas about a new combined attack wh. he thoroughly
shared, as also Alekseev & Pustov[oitenko]. To this new plan I gave in. That is
the whole story in short.—I managed to write to [our daughter] Olga last evening—please give her my letter. At the end of every walk we eat potatoes &
chestnuts. Baby< enjoys these meals out of doors—others too. Now my sweet
heart & love I must end. God bless you & restore you quickly to health! I kiss
you, the girlies & her [Anna Vyrubova] & thank her for her letter. With fondest
love ever, my own Treasure, your own old Nicky.

372. "Broussilov's offensive was now definitely brought to an end. That the ending was ... largely
caused by the influence of Rasputin, is now made clear. This influence was ... indicated by the following passage in Gourko's book: 'The weariness of the troops had its effect ... but there can be no
question that the stoppage of the advance was premature, and founded on orders from Headquarters,
under a pretext which could not be openly spoken about, whereas, amongst our Allies, if not in the
Press, such reasons were publicly mentioned or whispered.' It is true, however, that the Russian
losses had been considerable." (Vulliamy, p. 273) The fact that Alexandra and Rasputin criticized
the offensive is no proof they were responsible for its termination. Such military advisors as Alekseev were more influential in shaping Nicholas's *military* decisions than were the empress or Rasputin. The Russian army was exhausted: each side lost a million men, half of whom were prisoners
of war. Austria-Hungary never recovered from the ordeal. In truth, the Brussilov offensive was
almost as hard on the Russian army, particularly the junior officer corps.

No. 1463/ Telegram 75. Stavka> Tsarskoe Selo. 27 Sept 1916. 22.12> 22.35.
To her majesty. Fondest thanks. Received Rumanian minister and officers with
letters from there. Warm, dry. Thoughts together. Loving kisses. Niki

No. 1464/ Telegram 170. Tsarskoe Selo> Stavka. 28 Sept 1916. 11.23> 13.38.
To his majesty. Heartily thank you both. Warmer, overcast. Know Lili's brother[373a] has other hopes, about which [I] shall write you. Read my letter before
reception [of Protopopov]. [I] warmly kiss and embrace [you]. Old man [Stur-
mer] asked me to receive him at 6 before which time shall remain in bed. Alix

373a. "The Lily referred to here is Princess Elizavieta Nicolaievna Obolenskaia, a lady-in- waiting." (Vulliamy, p. 275n)

No. 1465/ Her No. 603.   Ts.[arskoe] S[elo]. Sept. 28th 1916.
My own Beloved,

Now, I said I wld. lie all day in bed & Apraxin<, who was disgusted with my looks, also begged me to. Of course Sht.[yurmer] has just telephoned, begs absolutely to see me—so must of course at 6. Schwedov [Shvedov] & [A. N.] Obolensky ask again—well I put them off to the next days—its always so, probably they have got wind that we are leaving [to visit you at Stavka] & then each time all come flying.—To-day warmer, poured, was a moment's sun. [a]

Sweety, fancy only, Obolensky asked to see our Friend< & sent a splendid motor for him (knows Mia, Obolensky's wife several years). Received him very nervously at first & then spoke more & more till at the end of the hour began to cry—then Gr.[igory]< went away as He saw it was the moment the Soul was completely touched.—Spoke about all, openly, how had tried his best tho' it had not succeeded, that he heard as tho' one wanted him to paint the roofs of the palaces (probably somebody also imagined the same as we)—but that such a place he wld. not like—he wants work to wh. he is accustomed—& his great dream is to be General Governor of Finland—that he will always ask our Friend's advice about everything. Spoke all out against Ania<, & was astonished when our Fr. said she was from God—& that she suffered so.—Then showed all the 20 letters our Friend had these years sent with petitions all tidily tied up—& said he had fulfilled when he could—when Gr. asked him about bribes—he said no, but his aid had taken much.—I old. [could] not get over the idea that he, that proud man, had come round, because in his misery he felt only with Him wld. he find strength. The wife must have worked hard at him—& he to have cried!—Then our Friend says things wont go until yr. plan [to halt the Brusilov offensive] is obeyed. [b]

Just got yr. precious letter—kiss & thank over & over again for it. A.[nia] was just here, thanks & kisses [you] tenderly.—Am glad nothing has being going on at the front—was so anxious; that left move is the cleverest—near Brody even [though] its so colossaly [sic] fortified & such heavy artillery to go against—a real wall. Thanks, dear, for explaining about Brussilov<—had not quite grasped before.—In any case our Friend says to go by your ideas, your first [thoughts] are always the most correct.—Those meals outside are excellent for Baby<—am bringing two camp chairs & pliable table for him too to take out with him—& I can profit to sit out then too.—There is a wonderful young, just ordained Bishop Melchizedek—whom Pitirim brought fr. the Caucasus—Bishop now of Cronstadt etc. Churches full w[h]ere he serves—very high—(will in the future be a metropolitain [sic])—fancy, he was several years superior of the Bratsky monastery at Moghilef & adores & intensely venerates the miraculous Image [icon] there of the Virgin to wh. we always go—please Love, go there with me & Baby—am bringing a lamp too to place before the Image, I promised it to the superior some time ago.— [c]

I am to make Melch.'[s] acquaintance on Friday at her [Vyrubova's] house, with our Friend—they say his conversation is marvellous;—it does one no end of good, lovely talks & helps the soul to rise up over the worldly worries for a time—but I want you here too always to profit with me.—We think of leaving Sunday at 3—reaching M.[ogilev] for tea 5 on Monday—alright? After yr. walk & then I can lie longer.—What a joy to meet soon—in 5 days!! Seems incredible.—Cover you with tenderest kisses. God bless & protect you & keep you fr.

all harm! Ever yr. very own little <u>Wify</u>. [P.S.] Our Fr. says its very much in the <u>spiritual sense</u> that a man, soul like [Melchizedek] shld. have quite come to him. [d]

No. 1466.   Ts.[arist] Stavka. Sept. 28th 1916.
My own beloved One,

Tender thanks for your sweet letter & tidy instructions for my talk with Protop[opov]. Yesterday evening I was rather occupied. They showed a bit of a most interesting english film of the war. Then I received the rumanian minister Diamandi & Nando's [Roumanian King Ferdinand's] a.d.c.[,] Angelesco, who brought me letters from both. It seems they are going through a stage of panic at Bucarest, fright of an enormous invading german army (imaginary) & a general disbelief in their own troops! who bolt when the germ.[an] art.[illery] opens fire. Alekseev foresaw this & told me several times it would have been more useful for us had the rumanians remained neutral. Now, in any case, we must help them & therefore our long front becomes far longer still, as their frontier is open to the enemy whom they cannot resist. We are bringing down every corps we can, but the transportation of troops takes such a blessed long time. To-morrow Paul< arrives, Makarov also & a servian deputation from the king [Peter I] with military décorations. The weather continues warm but grey & dull. I have sent for a few of our eastern carpets & they do very well in both rooms. Now good-bye & God bless you, my precious own Sunny. I kiss you & the girlies very tenderly & remain ever your own old   Nicky.

No. 1467/ Telegram 77. Stavka> Tsarskoe Selo. 28 Sept 1916. 21.57> 22.25.
To her majesty. Loving thanks. Received new minister [Protopopov], had a two hours talk. Good impression. Hope [you are] not tired. Warm, stormy. Fondest kisses. Niki

No. 1468/ Telegram 183. Tsarskoe Selo> Stavka. 29 Sept 1916. 12.34> 13.49.
To his majesty. Tenderly thank [you] both. Windy, cloudy weather. [My] health so-so. [We] warmly embrace and kiss you both, [also] Paul< and Dmitry<. Alix

No. 1469/ Her No. 604.   Ts.[arskoe] S[elo]. Sept. 29th 1916.
My own beloved One,

Grey & stormy, barometer very low since two days—& all of us who have bad hearts feel it more. Lay on bed till 6 yesterday.— Sht.[yurmer] sat 3/4 of an hour—nothing very particular—spoke over many questions—told him strongly about my opinion of Greece—Sukhomlinov—ministers—dearth [of food for Petrograd]— prisoners—Guchkov<—all & the Duma people know he corresponds with Aleks.[eev] & it throws amongst good people a deep shade upon Al.—one sees the spider G.[uchkov] & Poliv.[anov] spreading a net round Al. & one longs to open his eyes & pull him out—you can save him—hope very sincerely, that you spoke to him about the letters.[373b]— [a]

Have nothing interesting to tell you—have my lamp burning, yesterday too, so fearfully dark dreary;—pouring.—Such fond thanks, dear One, for yr. nice letters.

Yes, Alex.< told me the same thing about the Roumanians. As what does Bel-
yaev< go there? With a letter or as counsillor [sic]? Hang them, why be such
cowards!—And now of course our line is much longer again—quite despairing
[sic] I find. Did you remember about mobilising [sic] the Tartars in Russia &
Siberia? How tired you must have been after yr. 2 hours doklad [report]—but he
[Protopopov] does talk like a waterfall. Glad, [you] had good impression—hope
he spoke with Aleks[eev]—begged he should. Sandro< spoke by telephone to
the Children, only few days here, some [of his] children not well, says cant
come to me (he never does) & will see us on the 5-th as he brings [his son] Andryusha[, Andrew Alexandrovich,] then as officer to you.—Heart not enlarged,
but aches. Send you my very tenderest, softest kisses, Lovebird! God bless &
protect you. 1000 of caresses fr. yr. own old Alix. [b]

373b. Alexandra refers to letters she believed Guchkov was writing to Alekseev to draw the general into an anti-Rasputin cabal. (See her Letters No. 1422b, 1430a,b,d, 1434a,b, 1439a.) Nicholas
seems to have thought this was all an invention of his wife's imagination. See his Letters No. 1427
and 1440.

No. 1470.   Ts.[arist] Stavka. Sept. 29th 1916.
My own precious Lovebird,
    Only at 2 o.['clock] arrived your dear letter No. 603 and at the same time your
wire—the storm probably delayed the train! Warmest thanks for all you write. It
is truly curious Obolen.[sky] should have come round to our Friend in this
way—Lily's brother![373a] Well, yesterday from 6.15 to 8.15 in the evening I sat &
talked with protop[opov]. I do hope he may prove useful & will fulfill our
hopes—he seemed to be animated by the best desires & knows much about the
interior questions. I had your little lists of questions, but only did not touch the
one about Rub.[368]—it was getting so late & the guests in hall were making a great
row [i.e., racket]! What joy to meet soon! That is perfect if you arrive on Monday at 5 for tea! Baby< & I both find it is time we should meet Mother & wife
[&] sisters & daughters again. The weather is warm but very windy, there is a
gale blowing on the Baltic Sea. At 6 o'clock we go to the cinema to see the
other english war film. The first one was remarkably interesting & impressive.
Shall see Paul< in the afternoon—this will probably be his first doklad [i.e., report as the current guards commander]! Now, my Sweetheart, I must finish.
God bless you & our girlies! With fondest kisses to you tenderly, my beloved
Darling, & them—ever your own Nicky.

No. 1471/ Telegram 79. Stavka> Tsarskoe Selo. 29 Sept 1916. 19.53> 20.20.
To her majesty. Tender thanks. Paul< arrived looking well. Bright evening. Saw
interesting English film. Much love from both. Niki

No. 1472/ Telegram 193. Tsarskoe Selo> Stavka. 30 Sept 1916. 11.30> 12.40.
To his majesty. Tenderly thank [you] both. Had terrible downpour. Now sunny.
In thoughts together. [I] warmly kiss and embrace [you]. [My heart is] not en-
larged, but aches. Shall think much of you this evening. Alix

No. 1473/ Her No. 605.   Ts.[arskoe] S[elo]. Sept. 30th 1916.

My own Lovebird,

Warmest thanks for yr. dear letter just received. What about Obolenksy & Finland? So glad your talk with Protop.[opov] pleased you—may he be worthy of the place you have confided him & work well for our poor, tormented country. You can write still on Saturday, because we leave on Sunday only at 3.—What a joy to meet soon again, my two dearest Treasures!! Am trying hard to get better. Heart not enlarged, filled with drops—but hurts very much. Still this evening go out to see our dear Friend< & get His blessings for the journey.—Such a storm blowing, last leaves being shed—in between there were 5 m.[inutes] rays of sun—not spoiled by sun this year—hope to find it at Moghilev—in every sense of the word.— [a]

Made Varavka see A.[nia]<—not at all contented with her heart (our Fr.< neither), [— Rasputin] is glad she goes with us & hopes it will be a rest—here she runs about fr. morn. to night & has such deep shades under her eyes & breathes badly & feels giddy.—We all come to you to freshen ourselves up morally (after great yearning) & phisically [sic]—good air & no work. Sad, we cant get off for a few days to the south.—Emma Fr.'s [sic] writes that her Father [V. B. Fredericks] slowly gets better—when lies [down]—no angoisse [anguish]—but when up—begins again. Voeikov has asked us to bring him to the Stavka. Now Treasure, Sweetheart, goodbye & God bless & keep you! Endless kisses & love fr. yr. very own old   Wify. [b]

Of course an affair again—its about yr. Erivantsi<, read it through seriously. Lovy, forgive me meddling in what does not concern me—but its the cry of an Erivanski heart (on purpose don't write names) wh. has reached us.—They have heard "admitted col. Georgian reg. Magabeli [E. I. Machabeli]"^{373c} & they with anguish await, whether he is really to receive the reg. Mag. was promised to receive the first free regiment of the division, in every way a perfection dear men, respected, beloved by all these 37 years (but not in this case suitable). Several times he [was] temp.[orary] Commander [of] different of the reg.[iments] when the Commanders were ill, as for instance commanded a long time the Mingrelian regiment, whilst the Comm. was ill. Now that Comm. has been promoted General major—already 5 months & continues commanding the reg. wh. I believe is not correct in an army regiment; now give him a nomination & put Mag. there, as he knows the Mingr. regiment now so well—& all will be perfect. Alas, the Eriv. r.[egiment] became free now first. [c]

"Just now the regiment wants a real master—a commander, who could bring everything back to old conditions and who would be able to understand all personally, by himself, and put everything right, justly and sanely, as it ought to be by the law and it was formerly in the regiment. The commander must be quite unknown to the regiment, independent, from quite another milieu— everything will be quite clear to him, as a fresh man, and only then, only with that condition the regiment will again be like it was formerly—before Mdivani. God knows, what menaces our regiment, what dissensions [sic], if just now the regiment will not have real glory. Col. Magabeli is an excellent soul, soft, easy, a general favourite of the whole division, modest and so on,—he was unceasingly with the regiment, makes part of it; but everybody, except himself will command the regiment. Besides he is more a friend, by his name, his family, his origin of 'those' [the following ellipsis is in the original text, the quoted section of which is in Russian] ... The Eriv. reg. ought just now to receive a command.[er] who would tear up with the roots all contrast between 'us' and 'them' and would command our ancient regiment for its real glory and not for a definitive cleft."—Tell nobody about this letter—but it coincides with what Silaev< begged for an outsider now (of the guard perhaps), who cld. put a stop to the ruin of yr. beautiful, dear to our heart regiment—Mag. is an angel, but too gentle & a Grus. [a Gruzinets, a Georgian] wh. just now is not the thing for the reg. wh. has parties [i.e., factions]. [d]

373c. Vulliamy says that Machabeli "was an ardent separatist, and was supposed to have been in touch with the directors of the German espionage during the war." (p. 278n)

No. 1474.   Ts.[arist] Stavka. Sept. 30th 1916.
My own precious Wify,
   Thank you so much for your dear letter. Belyaev has just left my room. He is being sent to Rumania as a councillor & head of military mission, the same as the french have done. I saw their general yesterday on his way to Bucarest.—Paul< looks much better & rested. He found a cosy house here & has established himself completely. He asked to come only for tea, as he prefers having meals at home. After the 5th he will visit the guard. This evening I receive the servian officers who bring me & you all, it seems, military medals! I don't quite understand what sort of decorations. The weather is warm but very squally with short showers & sun. We will go out on the river nevertheless. Since summer I have had only three free evenings after dinner. I played domino twice & arranged the mass of photos in the album, so as to glew them in at once.—I am rejoicing feverishly to meet you soon! Nothing of interest to add. God bless you my own beloved Sunny! Tenderly do I kiss you & the girlies; her [Anna Vyrubova] too. I do hope the journey will not tire you. With fondest love ever, my own Treasure, your own old   Nicky.

No. 1475/ Telegram 83. Stavka> Tsarskoe Selo. 30 Sept 1916. 18.57> 19.35. To her majesty. Loving thanks. Warm, fine, gale blowing. Thoughts together. Tenderest love. Niki

No. 1476/ Telegram 209. Tsarskoe Selo> Stavka. 30 Sept 1916. 21.05> 22.27. To his majesty. Please permit Metropolitan [Pitirim] and Raev to come to you on Monday with holy image [icon] from Synod.[374] ... Telegraph reply. [We] are all sitting together in little house [of Anna Vyrubova] and thinking of you. Sleep well. [I] kiss [you]. Alix

374. The ellipsis is in A. A. Sergeev's translation of this telegram (*Perepiska*,V, p., 85). Since the original document has been lost, I cannot say if the ellipsis is present there, but wherever it is possible to check Sergeev's work on this type of question, he proves reliable.

No. 1477/ Telegram 84.   Stavka> Tsarskoe Selo. 30 Sept 1916. 23.15> 23.40.
To her majesty. Agree. Good night, blessings. Niki

No. 1478/ Telegram 4. Tsarskoe Selo> Stavka. 1 Oct 1916. 12.45> 13.32. To
his majesty. Tenderly thank [you] both. Windy, overcast. Am writing last letter
[before we arrive]. Health so-so. [We] all kiss and embrace [you]. Alix

No. 1479/ Her No. 606.   Ts.[arskoe] S[elo]. Oct. 1st 1916.
[No salutation:]
   Yr. letters are late.   Such a storm blowing.–Thanks for receiving the Metrop.[olitan Pitirim] & Raev–they begged [you to do so] quickly, before Metr.
Wladimir returns[375]–only to bring the holy Image [icon] fr. the Synod, nothing
else.–You must be tired, by the papers I see the ministers have been one after
the other going to the Headquarters. I had Obol. [Prince A. N. Obolensky] for
1¼ of an hour–till I was dead beat–he talks like a wound up machene
[sic]–only about the food supplies of Petrograd[350]–touched nothing else, no
time, as Vil'chk.< was waiting with a doklad [report].–Feel still rotten–hope
change of air will set me to rights again.–Spent a quiet, peaceful evening
8½-10¼ with our Friend<, Bishop Issidor [Isidor]–Bish. Melchizedek–talked so
well & calmly–such a peaceful, harmonious atmosphere. From there I wired to
you about Pit. & Raev;–I wanted you to feel we were thinking of you.– [a]
   Poor Sirobojarski [Syroboyarsky] is again wounded–3-rd time– shoulder, but
bad or little, don't know, he wired to Vil'chk. fr. Tarnopol. Never received his
Capit. [captain's rank,] only yr. thanks (as in time of peace)–strange, how things
are dishonestly done–real great deeds receive no big recompense–small things
in the rear big ones–how many suffer fr. injustices!–Such darkness.–Sweet
Angel, this is my last letter to you–leave to-morrow at 3 o'clock. Going this
evening to the hospital–shy after 2½ weeks & many new ones, but cld. not leave
without seeing all.–Warmest thanks & kisses for sweet letter. Glad Belyaev [is]
at least used there[, on a mission to Roumania].–My last letter.–Goodbye &
God bless you, my Angel, intensely rejoicing to meet & feel yr. warm
kisses.–Ever yr. own very   Own. [b]

375. Metropolitan Vladimir of Kiev opposed the Rasputin-Pitirim bloc. A cleric of his rank would
have to be included in any Synod delegation to the tsar–hence the need his opponents felt to make
the visit "quickly," while Vladimir was not in the capital. Alexandra stresses the purpose was religious, perhaps recalling Nicholas's dissatisfaction with a previous appearance when Metropolitan
Pitirim raised political questions. (Cf. Letter No. 761)

No. 1480.   Ts.[arist] Stavka. Oct. 1 1916.
My own precious Sunny,
   Loving thanks for your dear letter & the note concerning the Erevan.[sky] reg.
Since my talk with Silaev, last time I saw [him], I am preoccupied with this affair & looking out for his successor. Through Kondr. [P. K. Kondzerovsky] I
inquired who was the first candidate–the answer came–first Machabeli[373c] then
kn. [Prince] Shervashidze & lastly Gelovin [K. L. Gelovani]<. It sounds like a
mockery in this case–doesn't it? I will find out through Paul< who knows the

guard [and who would be a suitable] cand[idate for this position]. It have lost alas! touch with them since a year.—So in two days—God grant—we shall meet again. [a]

Your wire last night put me rather out—I mean the image [icon] fr. the Synod. Why such a frightful hurry? I have already people fixed on Monday, just the day of your arrival & now on the top of them the Metrop.[olitan Pitirim] & Raev![376] Yesterday a general & two officers arrived with their minister from the servian Crown Prince with military decorations for Baby< & me—an order & pretty crosses (krest miloserdiya [the cross of mercy]) for you & all the girlies. What a difference—those men who have lost their country—look confident & re-signed—& the rumanians who have been only thrashed—have completely lost their heads & nerves!! God bless you & your journey, my beloved Wify. I kiss you & the girlies very tenderly & remain your ever loving & awaiting old Nicky. [b]

376. Despite these objections, Raev and Pitirim arrived at Stavka during Alexandra's visit of October 3-12 (O.S.), 1916. The object, apparently, was to demonstrate their access to the tsar. On behalf of the Synod, Raev and Pitirim presented Nicholas with a testimonial and icon—as if duplicating their visit to the empress on September 26 (O.S.), 1916. (See Letter No. 1456e.) Varnava was promoted to archbishop during Alexandra's visit, Pahlen's rank of *gofmeister* was officially restored (see Letters No. 1453, 1456d, 1461a), and Stepanov was dismissed as asst.-min. of the interior. On October 11, 1916, Rasputin wired Nicholas that he had spoken "very briefly and affectionately" with Protopopov, who implored the tsar to make certain "that no one interfere with him, also the counter-espionage [for which he is responsible], let him carry out his business." Protopopov "spoke affectionately of the prisoner," D. L. Rubinstein. (Nabokov: Alexandra, *Pis'ma imperatritsy*, II, p. 211n)

No. 1481/ Telegram 1. Stavka> Tsarskoe Selo. 1 Oct 1916. 20.11> 21.18. To her majesty. Best thanks for dear letters from both. [We] sent our last [letter to you]. Fin[e], cold. Tender love. Niki

No. 1482/ Telegram 5. Stavka> Tsarskoe Selo. 2 Oct 1916. 10.20> 1.15. To her majesty. Wish you happy journey. Awaiting [your] arrival with intense im-patience. Calm, cool. Fondest kisses. Niki

No. 1483/ Telegram 11. Tsarskoe Selo> Stavka. 2 Oct 1916. 12.49> 13.15. To his majesty. Warmly thank you for dear letters and dear telegram. Overcast and cold. Are leaving at 3. Am terribly glad about to-morrow. Embrace, kiss [you]. Alix

No. 1484/ Telegram 5. Malaya Vishera> Stavka. 2 Oct 1916. 19.25> 19.50. To his majesty. Travelling well. [We] await to-morrow with impatience. [We] wish you a good night, warmly kiss you both. God bless [you]. Alix

No. 1485/ Telegram 87. Smolensk, Aleks. r.r.> Stavka. 2 Oct 1916. 11.30> 13.04. To his majesty. Slept not famously [i.e., well], heart still more enlarged. Much warmer than yesterday. Am happy about joyful meeting. Tenderly kiss [you] both. Alix

No. 1486/ Telegram 10. Stavka> Orsha station. 3 Oct 1916. 14.22> 15.05. To
her majesty. Thanks [for] wire. Baby had stomach derangement, therefore will
not meet you. Loving kisses. Niki

No. 1487/ Her No. 607.   Mogilev. Oct. 12th 1916.
My very own Sweetheart,
  Its with a very heavy heart I leave you again—how I hate these goodbies [sic],
they tear one to pieces. Thank God, Baby's< nose is alright, so that is one consolation. Lovy mine, I do love you so beyond all words; 22 years have steadily
increased this feeling & its simply pain to go away. You are so lonely amongst
this crowd—so little warmth around. How I wish you cld. have come for 2 days
only, just to have got our Friend's< blessing, it would have given you new
strength—I know you a brave & patient—but human—& a touch of His [hand?] on
your chest would have soothed much pain & given you new wisdom & energy
from Above—these are no idle words—but <u>my firmest conviction</u>.— Aleks.[eev]
can do without you for a few days. Oh Manny man— stop that useless bloodshed—why do they go against a wall, one must wait for the good moment & not
go on & on blindly.^{360} Forgive my saying so, but all feel it. [a]
  You need not receive anybody else, except Protop.[opov]^{376} wh. wld. be a
good thing, or send for him again, let him oftener speak to you, ask yr. council,
tell you his intentions, it will help the man immensely.—Its for yr. good & our
dear countries I say all this, not from greed to see you (that wish you know will
ever exist) but I too well <u>know</u> & believe in the peace our Friend can give & you
are <u>tired</u>, morally, you cant deceive old wify!—And at home its good they shld.
feel you are sometimes near to all the interior work too—at this present moment
you can be spared here a few days—you have the telephonogram for any question in 5 min.— [b]
  For all yr. endless Love I thank & bless you, I carry it all in my burning soul,
wh. lives for you. Goodbye, my Sunshine, my joy & blessing. God Almighty
watch, guard, guide & bless you. I cover you passionately with tender kisses &
hold you tightly in my arms. —I know there are people who don't like my presence at M.[ogilev, the site of Stavka,] & fear my influence—& others who are
only quiet when I am near you—such is the world. Goodbye wee one, Father of
my Children.—I hope to go to holy Communion on the 21-st—how nice if you
cld. have been with me in Church then, too good & lovely it wld. have been!!
Ever yr. very, very <u>Own</u>. [c]

No. 1488.   Ts.[arist] Stavka. Oct. 12th 1916.
My own precious beloved One,
  Again you leave us two to return to your work & tiresome worries! I thank
you lovingly & deeply for having come here & for all your love & caresses!
How I will miss them!! God grant in two week[s] & a half we may meet again.
For the nearest future I don't see any possibility of my leaving this place[,] alas!
I had hoped so we might have been allowed to go to the south & spend a few
days together in our train. Perhaps it may still happen.—I shall miss you espe-
cially in the evenings, wh. were ours. God bless your journey and your coming
home! <u>Do</u> take care of yourself & don't over tire yourself. I kiss your sweet

face lovingly & tenderly, my own Sunny, my Wify, my little girly of bygone days. Clasping you once more in my loving arms—ever my precious Darling, your very own huzy   Nicky.

No. 1489/ Telegram 147 in Russian. Stavka> Orsha train station. 12 Oct 1916. 19.25> 19.31. To her majesty. Orsha. [We] are very sad. [We] thank you for dear letters. It is lonely in the house. Good night. [We] embrace all tenderly. Niki Aleksei

---

No. 1490/ Telegram 0592. Orsha> Stavka. 12 Oct 1916. 19.55> 20.32. To his majesty. [We] warmly kiss you both, thank you for dear letters. Sleep well. [It is] sad, empty. [I] will dine alone. God keep you [all], Alix

---

No. 1491/ Telegram 26. Likhoslavl> Stavka. 13 Oct 1916. 11.15> 12.20. To his majesty. [I] slept fairly well. Wonderful sunny weather, hope it is same for you. [I] miss [you]. Greetings to all. [I] warmly kiss you both. God keep you! Alix

---

No. 1492   Ts.[arist] Stavka. Oct. 13th 1916.
My own tenderly beloved Sunny-dear,
    Fondest thanks for your dear letter. I have to announce to you a very good news—I will try & come home for 2 or 3 days. I hope to leave on the 18th & spend those three days with you my own beloved one. Alas! I have no more time to write today, but I have told you the principle [sic] thing! God bless you & the girlies! Ever your own old Nicky.

No. 1493/ Telegram 149. Stavka> Tsarskoe Selo. 13 Oct 1916. 20.06> 20.38. To her majesty. Thanks [for] wire. Hope [you] arrived well. No sun. Touched by their letter. Sleep calmly. Tender kisses. Niki

---

No. 1494/ Telegram 59. Tsarskoe Selo> Stavka. 13 Oct 1916. 21.15> 22.11. To his majesty. [We] arrived safely. Foggy, messy. Bekker< met [daughter] Olga and me. Huge, empty rooms. Am terribly lonesome without you both. [We] all kiss and embrace [you]. Alix

---

No. 1495/ Telegram 63. Tsarskoe Selo> Stavka. 14 Oct 1916. 14.56> 15.23. To his majesty. Terribly gladdened by news in your dear letter. [I] tenderly thank you both. Was at hospital<, but am not tired. Wonderful sunny weather. [I] warmly kiss [you]. Now there is something wonderful ahead[, your visit here], I will rely on it. Will lie on balcony. Alix

---

No. 1496/ Her No. 608.   Ts.[arskoe] S[elo]. Oct. 14th 1916.
My beloved Angel,
    Thank you, thank you for yr. sweet little letter [No. 1492] with lovely news—cannot tell you what joy it is & what life & sunshine it brought to my sad heart!—Excuse also quite short letter—had Protop.[opov] for ½ hour, now Benk.

[P. C. Benckendorff] waits, then Nastinka<. This morning hospital<. Only made 3 dressings & then sat with different ones—were at Znam.< placed candles for you, Lovy. Glorious, bright, sunny weather.—Head stupid— Becker< besides.— Prot. saw Sukh.[omlinov]—so happy!—Very interesting talk[, Protopopov] was at the Duma this morning for 48 m.[inutes]—Traveled alright [sic], lay all day—this night slept badly—heart alright, especially since yr. letter.—Endless blessings & kisses fr. us all.—Ever yr. very Own.   [P.S.] Tell Prot. you are glad he goes & speaks with Gr.[igory]< & hope he will continue.

No. 1497.   Ts.[arist] Stavka. Oct. 14th 1916.
My own Treasure,
    Yesterday the whole day Baby< was looking pale & sad—I thought he felt lonely. But in the afternoon he played gaily his usual game in the same little wood of the old Stavka. Only during his dinner he complained about his head so he was put to bed wh. he did willingly. The temp.[erature] rose rapidly & he was sick. Before 9.o['clock] he went to sleep & slept well, only awaking twice to have to run [to the bathroom?]! This morning the temp. is normal & he is quite cheery—but we have kept him in bed. Vl. Nik.< thinks it must be still the consequences of his first chill or having eaten something not digestible. In any case I hope it is the end now. [a]
    Oh! how happy I am at the thought of coming home for a few days & seeing you & the girlies! I asked Al.[ekseev] & he told me it was perfectly easy; he remembered I went home last year for the 20th! Later he found it possible for me to go to the south ... [ellipsis in the original] Reni etc. to see the troops.— What a joy that feeling of not being tied for ever to a certain place. Paul< brought his son [Prince Paley] yesterday, who gave me the book with his poems. Today they have both left for an inspection of the guard. I told P. to speak to Brus.[ilov] & Gurko. Now my beloved Sunny, I must end. God bless you all! Many tender kisses fr. your own   Nicky. [b]

No. 1498/ Telegram 152. Stavka> Tsarskoe Selo. 14 Oct 1916. 20.05> 20.50. To her majesty. Thanks for news. Also glorious day. Kept Tiny< in bed. [Has a] chill of stomach. Very gay. Fondest love from both. Niki

No. 1499/ Her No. 609.   Ts.[arskoe] S[elo]. Oct. 15th 1916.
My own sweetheart,
    Such fond thanks for yr. dearest letter. Hope Babykins< is alright [sic] again—dont let them give him oisters [sic] wh. are not fresh.—I feel quite different since I know you are coming for a few days—such a lovely prospect—after 6 months to see you here again! Then we can again all go to Holy Communion, if you feel inclined —& gain strength together & blessings. You don't need long preparations.—Then I suppose you wld. be going later to Reni etc. in Nov.—It will be good for you to get about again, & for the troops to see you.—I am glad you told P. to speak to G. & B. [see Letter No. 1497b.] —This evening I go to see our Friend<.—He says the "Maria" was no punishment but an "error".377—I shall keep Ella's< letter to think about when you came [i.e.,

come here to visit].— Grey, hoarfrost covers everything, were 5° of frost. Shall go for tiny turn [i.e., walk] with A.[nia]<—Am prudent—did only one perevyazok [dressing] & then sat knitting & had Vil'chkovsky's< doklad [report]. Vesselov-sky has come, shall see him to morrow, has been 3 times contused—nerves shaken, Son in law died (or killed) & he wants to go for a rest to the Crimea.—Beloved One, I bless & cover you with endlessly tender kisses & remain yr. fondly loving old   Sunny.

377. Alexandra is referring to the sinking of the *Empress Maria*, a dreadnought in the Black Sea Fleet named in honor of the tsar's mother, the Dowager Empress Maria Fedorovna. Incredible rumors circulated in connection with the disaster: some held the ship was sabotaged by German spies who were members of Nicholas's circle! At the root of this notion, probably, was the growing public conviction that the empress was a German agent.

No. 1500/ Telegram 64. Tsarskoe Selo> Stavka. 15 Oct 1916. 16.55> 17.54. To his majesty. Tenderly thank you both, my dears. 4 deg. frost. Strolled a bit, now [going to] hospital<. Did Mordvinov sneeze when he received Anastasia's letter? [See Letter No. 1509.] Warmly kiss and embrace [you]. Alix

No. 1501.   Ts.[arist] Stavka. Oct. 15th 1916.
My own beloved One,
    Thank you fondly for your dear first letter fr. Ts.[arskoe] S[elo]. I am so so happy to be able to come [home] for some days. Thank God Aleksei is feeling alright [sic]—he got up today, but as he coughs fr. time to time, it is wiser to keep him in doors. The weather is delicious, such pure air & lovely sun. There was a tiny frost in the night. I am happy you feeling well notwithstanding the tiresome B.'s< arrival. Today Mitia D.< & Dm. Sheremetev< came to change Kira< and Igor<. [a]
    I have got ministers every day, perhaps they will leave me quiet those days I am home! I telegraphed to Tino< after you left & since then I hear fr. Athens that things seem to take a better turn in Greece. God grant it may be so! Except that Shtyurmer wrote for me an official frank & friendly wire, of course cyphered [sic], fr. me to Tino—wh. I hope will smooth matters & help him to declare to the powers that he is going to take on his own initiative those measures, wh. the powers wanted him to accept by brutal force. Now my Sunny-dear, I must end. God bless you & the girlies! I hope to leave Tuesday at 12.30—arriving at Ts. S. at 3.30—before tea. I kiss you all very fondly. Ever your very own   Nicky. [b]

No. 1502/ Telegram 153. Stavka> Tsarskoe Selo. 15 Oct 1916. 20.21> 20.45. To her majesty. Fondest thanks [for] letters [and] wire. Fine, cold, sunny. Tiny< cheery. Tender kisses. Niki

No. 1503/ Telegram 70. Tsarskoe Selo> Stavka. 16 Oct 1916. 10.10> 10.40. To his majesty. Am going to church, then to hospital<. Hope he is entirely well. Could Lili's< brother be one of Kalinin's< assistants, as I am unable to think of another place for him and he has now become much better? With tenderness [I] thought of you last evening. Embrace and kiss [you] both. Alix

---

No. 1504/ Her No. 610. Ts.[arskoe] S[elo]. Oct. 16th 1916.
My own sweet Angel,

Very tender thanks for yr. sweet letter. Shall eagerly await you Wednesday afternoon; hope Babykins< will be quite alright [sic] by that time.—Had a nice evening at A.[nia]'s< yesterday—our Friend<, his son [Dmitry Rasputin] & the Bish.[op] Issidor [Isidor were present]. As Obol. [Prince A. N. Obolensky] behaves well now & listens to him [Rasputin], he thinks it wld. be only good if Prot.[opopov] had taken him as one of his aids—there he wld. have worked alright & so as not to kick him out of service.—Our Friend neither cares for Kurlov, but he is Badmaev's bosom friend, & Prot. was cured by Badm.[aev] & so is grateful to him.[315]— Gr.[igory]< thinks it wld. be better to call in[to military service] the younger men instead of those over 40, who are needed at home to keep all work going & to look after the houses!— [a]

Warmer to-day but grey. Were in our lower Church for half the service & then went to the hospital. Saw Vesselovsky—sad many things he tells & [also what] other young ones [say]—what goes on at the war—dear me, I understand their nerves give way, no union, no confidence in the officers, orders, counterorders, disbelief in what they hear—very sad indeed. Ah this want of education is a misery—each for himself—never together.—Merica< & her Mother [Natalya Karlova] come directly—she leaves in a week to be married.—Little Ivan Orlov is engaged to a Pss. Volkonsky—both such Children.—Kiss you without end & bless you. He [Rasputin] is so happy you are coming.—Ever yr. very, very Own. [b]

No. 1505. Ts.[arist] Stavka. Oct. 16th 1916.
My own Treasure,

Many loving thanks for your sweet letter—also for Tatiana's. This will be my last one as we leave Mogilev in 48 hours.—Yes, my Love, I certainly want to go to the Holy Communion with you, as I have not taken it since the first week of Lent. I will try & receive as little as possible those days. Thank God Baby< is well again & may go out, but has to go through a severe diet. It is strange to hear him complaining of being hungry & not getting enough to eat. After two perfect sunny days the weather is more grey & very cold—0 degr[ees]. The river continues to rise—in some places the meadows are water on account of heavy rains near Smolensk, Kaluga. [a]

Yesterday arrived all the intendants of the armies for a sobranie [conference] under their chief here; they dined & told me lots of interesting things. Every day the whole army needs 2676 railway cars of food & forage for the horses! That alone make 400 trains daily. Now my beloved Sunny, I must let the messenger leave. God bless you & the girlies. Many tender kisses to you & them & to A[nia]< from your very own Nicky. Such joy to meet soon!! [b]

No. 1506/ Telegram 157. Stavka> Ts. S. 16 Oct 1916. 18.27> 18.54. To her majesty. Loving thanks. Cold, grey, nasty wind. Thoughts always together. Both [of us are] well. Tenderest kisses. Niki

No. 1506/ Telegram 157. Stavka> Ts. S. 16 Oct 1916. 18.27> 18.54. To her majesty. Loving thanks. Cold, grey, nasty wind. Thoughts always together. Both [of us are] well. Tenderest kisses. Niki

---

No. 1507/ Telegram 72. Tsarskoe Selo> Stavka. 17 Oct 1916. 14.55> 15.25. To his majesty. Warmly thank you both for dear letters. Sunny, clear day. [We] were at hospital<, then finished Te Deum [commemorating] Borki.[378] May the Lord bless you! [We] all tenderly kiss you both. Please, answer quickly, what you wish: Mass celebrated at 11 at fortress or funeral service at 2. Alix

378. Alexandra refers to the terrorist bombing of Alexander III's train at Borki on October 17, 1888. A requiem (*zaupokoinoe bogosluzhenie*) was celebrated in Alexander's honor at the Peter and Paul Fortress on October 20, 1916. (Sergeev's note to *Perepiska*, V, p. 99) See No. 1510 for Nicholas's reply.

No. 1508/ Her No. 611.   Ts.[arskoe] S[elo]. Oct. 17th 1916.
My Beloved,
    Very heartiest thanks to you, my Angel, for your dear letter.—Worked in the hospital< & then had a Te Deum in the corridor there for this day[388]—was so simple & nice.—5 degrees of frost, bright & sunny, am going with Ania< to see her bit of land & where one is going to begin to build. Yesterday I spent the evening at the hospital, calm & cosy.—To-day receive the Motonos[379] who leave for Japan; [A. N.] Obolensky again—seems our Fr.< is most contented, the man has so much changed for the better, & therefore he thinks it wld. be nice if Prot.[opopov] took him as an aid.— [a]
    How lovely it will be to take Holy Communion all together, cannot say how greatly am looking forward to this blessing & joy;—& to have you once more home again!! Do say that none of the family are to be on service these days[, this will give us all an excuse to be home together during your visit]. Am so glad you wired to Tino<, [see Letters No. 1447b, 1461c, 1501b] will help & give him courage.—You will be glad even to get into the train again cosily after such a long time. One pen has to be refilled & this one—too much ink,—& my fingers are filthy.—How are the Roumanians getting on? At Orsha you will see heaps of sisters [i.e., nurses] at the station. They always came running to see one pass.—Now, my Sunshine, goodbye & God bless you. Soon, soon I shall have you tightly clasped to my breast again,—wont it be lovely! I cover you with tender kisses, & remain yr. very, very   Own. [b]

379. Viscount Motono was Japanese ambassador to Russia from 1908 to autumn 1916, when he became minister of foreign affairs.

No. 1509.   Ts.[arist] Stavka. Oct. 17th 1916.
My own precious Sunny,
    I made a mistake yesterday thinking it was my last letter to you. It has become such a habit that you come here & I remain at this place, that is why I thought I could not write more. In 24 hours we move off. I feel quite excited at the idea of travelling at last & going to see all my dear ones at home. Protopopov was long with me yesterday evening[,] nearly two hours—I do hope so [much that]

God will send his blessing on his new serious work! The man is calmly resolved to carry it through whatever may be the difficulties. And I am afraid they will be great[,] especially the first two months! [a]

Fabritsky appeared for dinner—I was glad to see him—enormous, healthy, sunburnt & energetic. His naval brigade is being formed into a division at Nikolaev where I hope to see them later on. Just now your dear letter № 610 came, tenderest thanks for it. Mordvinov did not sneeze after reading Anast.[asia']s letter [see Letter No. 1500], but coughed very much when I told him what she had done. He cannot invent any punishment for her since two years. Now I must end this my very last letter! Ever, my beloved Wify, with many kisses, your very own Nicky. [b]

No. 1510/ Telegram 160. Stavka> Tsarskoe Selo. 17 Oct 1916. 16.11> 16.28. To her majesty. I prefer service at 11 at fortress. [See No. 1507.] Niki

---

No. 1511/ Telegram 161. Stavka> Tsarskoe Selo. 17 Oct 1916. 20.18> 20.56. To her majesty. Loving thanks [for] dear letters. [Aleksei and I] are completely well. Cold, grey, overcast. Went to cinema [today] instead of to-morrow. Tender kisses. Niki

---

No. 1512/ Telegram 77. Tsarskoe Selo> Stavka. 18 Oct 1916. 9.55> 10.10. To his majesty. May the Lord bless your trip. [I] tenderly kiss you both. Terribly glad about to-morrow. [We] all warmly kiss [you]. Drab day. Alix

---

No. 1513/ Telegram 164. Stavka> Tsarskoe Selo. 18 Oct 1916. 12.16> 13.06. To her majesty. Thanks [for] wire. [We are] leaving directly. Lovely sunny weather. Excited to go. Tenderest kisses. Niki

---

No. 1514/ Telegram 101 in Russian. Stavka> Tsarskoe Selo. 18 Oct 1916. 15.50> 16.42. To her majesty. [We] heartily thank you for letters. Are traveling well. Weather clear. Are happy over to-morrow's meeting. [We] warmly kiss [you]. Niki

---

No. 1515/ Her No. 612.   Ts.[arskoe] S[elo]. Oct. 25th 1916.
My very own Angel,

Once more we part again! I cannot tell you the joy & comfort it was to have you once more home again after 6 long months. Like old times it was—thanks for that calm joy, dear One!—I hate letting you go away to all your worries, anxieties & sorrows—here we at least share them together.—Every caress was a gift & I shall long hunger again. For you, alas, no rest, so much hard work! And now this story about Poland,[380] but God sends things for the best, so I will believe it will be for the best in some way or other. Their troops wont fight against us, there will be a mutiny, revolution, anything you like—thats my private opinion—shall find out what our Friend< has to say.— [a]

Sweetheart, goodbye & God help you.—I don't like Nikol.[asha]< going to the H.Q.—may he brood no evil with his people. Don't allow him to go anywhere now, but streight [sic] back to the Caucasus—the revol.[utionary] party else will hail him again[381]—& one was beginning to forget him; him & Sazonov we have to thank for the Polish question[345]—forbid him to speak about it—get Zamoisky away when he comes.—God bless yr. journey! My heart is very heavy. I cover you with endless, passionate kisses. Cannot bear yr. having perpetual sorrows & anxieties & being far away— but heart & soul are ever near you, burning with love.—Ever, Sweetheart, Sunshine mine yr. very own old   Wify. [b]

380. Prussia, Austria and Russia had divided Poland during the eighteenth century. At this point, German-Austrian armies were occupying all of Poland. Seeking Polish support, Germany and Austria pledged to restore Poland after the war. Implementing this policy, the German governor in Warsaw (Bezeler) and the Austrian governor in Lyublin (Kuch) published a joint statement on October 23 (O.S.), 1916, promising an independent Poland with a hereditary monarch. This put pressure on Russia to make similar concessions. Alexandra and Rasputin opposed Polish autonomy, even—much less independence. (See Footnote 335.) The Bezeler-Kuch decree also announced that a Polish army would be raised. Alexandra is predicting that the Poles ("[t]heir troops") " wont fight against us, there will be a mutiny, revolution, anything you like."

381. Alexandra feared Nicholasha< would take advantage of this trip to Stavka to confer with the Dowager Empress Maria Fedorovna at Kiev. In fact, he did have such a conference on November 14/27, 1916. (Nabokov: Alexandra, *Pis'ma imperatritsy*, II, p. 216n) Alexandra considered Nicholasha and Maria Fedorovna to be members of "the revol.[utionary] party"! For their part, the members of Nicholasha's circle feared it was Nicholas II who was unwittingly provoking a revolution. They were typical of those aristocrats who still felt loyalty to Nicholas but despaired of his weak leadership and the apparent influence of Alexandra and Rasputin. (Rumor held the German-born empress and Rasputin were spies, lovers—and the real rulers of Russia.) Talk abounded of an imminent "coup from the right" which would replace Nicholas with his brother Michael or cousin Nicholasha. For all the speculation, nothing happened and Russia moved towards the March Revolution.

No. 1516/ Telegram 131. Tsarskoe Selo> Likhoslavl. 25 Oct 1916. 19.25> 21.30. To his majesty. [We] miss [you] very much. Visited Ania's< asylum, received and now am going to church. [We] warmly kiss you 2. Sleep well. God keep [you]. Alix

No. 1517/ Telegram 959. Smolensk, Aleks. r.r.> Tsarskoe Selo. 26 Oct 1916. 11.35> 13.00. To her majesty. [We] both slept well, colds much better. Grey, warm weather. Miss you horribly. Tender thanks for dear letter. Loving kisses. Niki

No. 1518/ Telegram 138. Tsarskoe Selo> Stavka. 26 Oct 1916. 13.57> 16.50. To his majesty. Warmly thank you for telegram. Were at hospital<, now going to wedding [see Letter No. 1520]. Greyish weather, empty [here, and] sad. [We] warmly kiss you [both]. Alix

No. 1519/ Telegram 65. Stavka> Tsarskoe Selo. 26 Oct 1916. 17.52> 18.20. To her majesty. Arrived well. Miss you so much and girlies, especially at the platform. Kiss fondly. Niki

No. 1520/ Her No. 613.   Ts.[arskoe] S[elo]. Oct. 26th 1916.
My own Sweetheart,

All my tenderest thoughts surround you—very empty, grey & lonely without sunshine< & sunbeam<. Long, lonely night—joy to get yr. two wires.—Yesterday evening saw our Fr.< with his 2 daughters in the little house [of Anna Vyrubova], spoke so beautifully—was so happy to have seen you. Begs you to answer all who speak or worry you about Poland.[345, 380] [The following quote is in Russian:] "I do all for my son, will be pure before my son"[382] & that will at once shut their mouths—strange, I said the very same to Listopad then too, only let none worry you to stop them talking—you are the master.—The Wedding in our hospital went off well—a handsome couple, I was his "Mother" & Botkin the "Father" of the bridegroom. Then the 4 girls & I motored half an hour to fresh one up, as I receive now Isa<, Kussov< (com.[mander of the] Psk.[ov] reg.[iment]) Hagandokov [Khogandokov], [M. D.] Bonch-Bruevich, [A. T.] Vasilev (police [director]) & three officers. Shall spend the evening cosily in the hosp. whilst A.[nia]< is in town<—she lunched with us.—Grey weather, lit up by the remembrance of yr. sweet presence.—Kiss all at Kiev. God bless your journey. Endless tenderest kisses fr. yr. ever loving old   Sunny. [P.S.] Tell Paul< to be back when Nikolasha< comes—better.—Did you say about Obolensky? [See Letter No. 1508a.]

---

382. In other words, Nicholas II should reject demands for Polish independence or autonomy; the entire Russian Empire must be passed on to his son and successor, Aleksei.

No. 1521.   Mogilev. October 26th 1916.
My own precious and beloved Darling,
   I thank you from the depth of my old heart for your dear letter, you left on my table, in saying good-bye. We both felt so lonely & sad, when the train moved off & we saw you standing in front of the door. And directly after we caught a glimpse of your motor taking you all back to the house. Then Babykins< went to his cabin to play & I received old Trepoff all the time until we stopped at Tosno! After playing with Aleksei—I had a little game of domino with Dmitry<, [A. N.] grabbe & N.P.< All went to bed early & slept soundly! We got up late—Babykins even after 10.o'clock. Stopped at Smolensk where we walked & where I saw Rausch. The whole day I read a very interesting engl.[ish] book "the Man who dined with the Kaiser"[383] newly appeared. When I have finished it I will send it to you. [a]
   Al.[eksei] played at his favourite [card game,] "Nain Jaune."[277] Before arriving his nose bled, so Isanyants was sent for & burnt it—now it is alright [sic]. The same people met us & after a few words I dismissed them. I walked up & down the platform & thought so much of you & of the girls. The silence about the place is rather astonishing—I expected to hear with shrieks of [daughters] Anast.[asia] or Marie tormenting Mordvinov. Instead Al.'s cat[383] ran away & hid under the big logs of timber; we put on our coats & went out to look for it. Nagorny[265] at once discovered the cat with the aid of an electric lamp, but it took us a long time to make the brute come out—it would not listen to Al. At last he caught it by the hind legs & pulled it out through the narrow space. [b]
   Now everything is quiet in the train. I said good-night to Aleksei & many of the suite have gone to the cinema of course! I feel rather lonely, but am happy

to be able to write to you; I imagine I am speaking very slowly. Last evening I got the following telegram from Motherdear: "Is it true we will meet soon? Would very much like to know when and for how long, because M. P. [Miechen<] will come [on the] 29[th of October]. Will I have time to put her off?"[383] I laughed when I read this & immediately wired to her the necessary details. When you get this epistle we will be in Kiev. I'm sorry you won't get any letters from me these days, because I doubt my having any time to write. Anyhow this [long] one may count for two. Ah, my Treasure, my Love! How I miss you! It was such real happiness to be six days together at home. And the nights too! God bless you & the girlies. I kiss you ever so tenderly & nestle closely to you. I hug the children—A[nia]< too. Ever, Sunny-mine, your very own old <u>Nicky</u>. [c]

383. The exact title is "My Secret Service, by the Man Who Dined with the Kaiser," published in March 1916. The cat was Zubrovka, "... a kitten from Mogilev, the favourite pet of the Tsarevitch." In this letter, Nicholas cited Maria Fedorovna's telegram in Russian except for the words "put her off," which are in English. (Vulliamy, p. 285n) This sheet (folded) is larger than the stationary Nicholas ordinarily used in writing his wife. In the top left corner, in red, is printed "novyi Imperatorskii poezd" (new Imperial train), one Russian word on each line.

No. 1522/ Telegram 166. Stavka> Tsarskoe Selo. 27 Oct 1916. 14.32> 14.55. To her majesty. Tender thanks [for] dear letter. Finished lunch now [and will] go back to train. Leave at 6 [o'clock]. Grey, warm. Dining saloon looks gay, bright. Fondest kisses. Niki

No. 1523/ Telegram 139. Tsarskoe Selo> Stavka. 27 Oct 1916. 14.56> 16.50. To his majesty. Wish you happy trip. In thoughts together. [I] miss [you] very much. Greyish, warm weather. [I] worked at hospital<. Sonia Den< lunched, she goes to Crimea to-day. Tenderly kiss you both. May the Lord bless you! Alix

No. 1524/ Her No. 614.   Ts.[arskoe] S[elo]. Oct. 27<u>th</u> 1916.
My own Sweetheart,
A grey windy, warm day.—It must indeed seem strange to you at the platform without the girlies & Mordvinov. Wonder if you have sunny weather at least.— Sonia Den lunched with us, looks awfully ill, green & thin, leaves to-day for Crimea—am glad for poor Xenia< who seems to be sad & poorly.—Rein [Rhein] comes later, wonder what he will have to say, shall beg him to get on better & more delicately with Alek<, as you told me.—Hagandokov [Khogandokov] looked more like in old days, thinner & with a sly face—made me feel shy as left the talking to me. I only spoke about Siberia.—Its so dark in my room, I scarcely see to write on my sopha.—The Children have gone to the big palace<. Wonder, how all will be at Kiev—a bore Miechen< will be there & you not alone! [See Letter No. 1521c.]—Was nice in the hospital yesterday evening, sat in all the wards—at home its so sad & lonely without you, Sweetheart. Have your colds quite passed? Good-bye, my Love, & God bless & keep you. Many a tender kisses fr. yr. old <u>Sunny</u>.

No. 1525/ Telegram [unnumbered]. Tsarskoe Selo> Kiev. 28 Oct 1916. [No times listed] [To his majesty.] Terribly gladdened by precious long letter and Tiny's<

letter. Tenderly kiss you both. Hope you spent this day happily. Overcast, rainy. Now [we] all are going to town<. Big girls< to committee, little girls< going with me to hospital at Winter Palace<. [I] embrace and kiss [you]. Alix

No. 1526/ Telegram 121. Kiev> Tsarskoe Selo. 28 Oct 1916. 12.40> 13.20. To her majesty. Arrived well. Touching reception. Motherdear< met us. Foggy, calm weather. Lunch à trois cosily. Fondest love from us. Niki

No. 1527/ Her No. 615   Ts.[arskoe] S[elo]. Oct. 29th 1916.
My beloved Treasure,
   All my tender thoughts are with you.—I have been reading what the German papers say about the Polish question, & how displeased they are William did it[380] without asking the country's advice & feeling it will be for ever a question of animosity between our 2 countries—etc. [O]thers look at it [endorsement of an independent Poland] as not at all serious & most vague—& I think W. has made a formidable gaffe & will greatly suffer for it. The Poles will not bow down to a German prince & regime of iron under pretended freedom.—How many reasonable Russians, entre autre Shakhovskoi[,] bless you for not having listened to those who begged you to give Poland freedom, when she no longer belonged to us, as it would have been absolutely ridiculous—& they are perfectly right.—[a]
   I saw Rein [Rhein] to-day & told him what you said & he will act accordingly. You know, the man is not sympathetic to me—something mocking in his way—but a clever, very ambitious man & must be held in hand.—You know [M. D.] Bonch-Bruevich made a good impression on the whole upon me, & I was not favourably disposed to him after all one had said [about him]—& I told it him quite frankly. We had an interesting talk for nearly an hour. Now I shall mention some of the things & you profit of them & try & get things improved & changed, only don't say to Aleks.[eev] you heard it from me—he did enough harm telling that lie to Ivanov—& I feel the man does not like me.—We spoke about black Danilov[243]—he says he is a man only of chancelry [sic] work—not live work, always papers & not a good element, old Ruzsky, being rather delicate (bad habit of cocain in the nose) & lazy, needs a strong energetic right hand [assistant] to make things work—good people have been sent away—& others have left as they wld. not continue under Danilov. [b]
   He [Bonch-Bruevich] told me why R.[hein] insisted upon Dan.[ilov] being with him—protection, relation to his wife or something like that (have already forgotten what he said), but it was not because of his brains he took him.—Under Kurop.[atkin] the enemy reconnoitring [sic] (deeply) was almost quite abolished & very weak—they used to know all that went on in Finland, Sweden, Baltic Provinces—now know scarcely anything. Hardly any counter-reconnoitring, only correspondence—papers, papers, looking for laws in everything—no life.—Those 3 people, of the counter-reconnoitring in Petrogr. were formerly under Bn.-Br. with lots more & very good when guided & looked after, but when he was taken away that all ceased & these three are placed by Aleks. & act as his personal staff counter-r. & according to his orders take people shut up etc. & then make their doklady [reports] to Moghilev [i.e., to GHQ at Stavka]— thats not nice, & now I understand many things that happen not rightly.—Fancy, Ruzsk[y] & his staff have

no active operative plans. I asked why they dont advance, as you had given Kurop.[atkin] and R. the order to do so—he says perfectly possible, we have far more troops than the Germans. They train their young soldiers near the trenches to make ours imagine lots are there. R. is contented in his place, his ambitious wife wont let him lose it for anything in the world, & so he prefers sitting calmly—works only 2 hours a day—a good, honest man, but needs a strong right man [assistant] to make him work. They completely neglect the question of food supplies, say the Civil ministery must give it them—quite wrong. In complete neglect the question of civil administration in the front area. [c, d]

Can you make head or tail of what I write?—its so difficult to give over conversations. The points he [Bonch-Bruevich] wrote down for me as I was affraid [sic] to forget them. I can only say I am glad I made his acquaintance & heartily wish you could see him, he wld. tell you much I can't repeat, too complicated & long. He asks & wants nothing, only for your sake & the good he asked to see me to speak all out. Very clever & one can speak easily with him—but he said many sad things as one hears elsewhere.—Such dishonesty everywhere!—But he says its most weak & disorganised [sic] all in that army, but he believes if the old man [Gen. Ruzsky] got a strong help, much could be changed for the good. And keeping the troops for months without moving when they cld. with success—says its demoralising [sic]. Always contrasts—extremes.—[e]

Now enough about affairs. Grey, dull weather. Are off to town, O. & T. [daughters Olga and Tatiana] have a committee, & I shall go with M. & A. [daughters Marie and Anastasia] to the hospital< in the W.[inter] Palace<—358 men just now.—If I did sleep at all this night, it was not more than half an hour—insupportable & without reason—nothing worried or hurt me; no dear "Animal warmth" any more to help me.—Now goodbye & God bless you, my Sweet, I cover you with kisses tender & longing ones. Ever yr. old, very own Wify. [P.S.] Fond thanks [for your] precious long letter. [f]

No. 1528.   Kiev. Railway Station. October 28. 1916.
My own beloved Darling,

We arrived at 10.30 this morning & fancy! were met by Motherdear [Maria Fedorovna], Paul< and Sandro<. Except them there came three generals, the governor & the mayor [of Kiev]. As we— Babykins< & I had to visit the Sofiisky sobor [Cathedral of St. Sophia], Mama drove off straight to the palace & we came a little later. All the military schools, other schools & troops lined the streets. The order was perfect. But the weather was not amiable [—] such a pity—it was foggy & dark, not cold. With intermingled feels [sic] I went through our old rooms —they reminded me so of bygone days & of poor Stolypin's death [in 1911]. We sat till lunch in my room looking at Mama's interesting albums; she likes that room because it is light in the morning. Then we three lunched & Babykins< for once ate with good appetite.—This instant they tell me the messenger must leave directly. God bless you my Love & the girlies! With tender kisses ever your own Nicky.

No. 1529/ Telegram 143. Tsarskoe Selo> Kiev. 29 Oct 1916. 10.22> 10.35. To his majesty. Warm, foggy, rainy. Everything went well in town< yesterday. Glad

that yesterday you were able to spend whole time cosily together. We all tenderly
kiss you all. May the Lord bless you [both]. Alix

No. 1530/ Her No. 616.						Tsarskoe Selo. Oct. 29th 1916.
My very own Sweetheart,
    It was an intense joy receiving yr. dear long letter yesterday—thank you for it with
all my heart. How glad I am to see by yr. telegram that you could cosily lunch a
3—wonder how you got rid of Miechen<. And did you see [your sister] Olga, or
was she still ill?— Warm, grey & raining & a fogg—real "dirty weather" as the
sailors say.—Slept ½ an hour the night before last & this one after 5½ till after
7—insupportably tiresome. Shall go an hour later to the hospital< to rest my legs &
back still wh. ache after the Winter Palace hospital. It took us an hour—back they
wheeled me through the empty halls.—I received Protopopov in town. Then we
went to Skoroposlushnitza^{247} & placed candles—you wear that image [icon] I
brought you once from there. Lunched & took tea in the train—at home received
poor Rebinder whose wife died not long ago. And then Mme Zizi< fr.
8½-9.—To-day I receive Volkov, Fedorov, Shtyurmer, Shebeko fr. Moscou [sic];
ones head gets so tired—during the conversations I am fresh & energetic—but later
on become somewhat cretinised.—Now I must read still through heaps of doklady
[reports]—shall finish my letter after luncheon.—Am going for a little drive to
freshen up my tired brain, as have four doklady this afternoon.—I kiss you, my
Angel, as tenderly & fondly as only possible. God bless & protect you, Lovebird.
Every yr. very, very   Own.

No. 1531/ Telegram 3890. Kiev> Tsarskoe Selo. 29 Oct 1916. 18.52> 21.30. To
her majesty. Tender thanks [for] dear letter. Grey but warmer. [Aleksei and I are]
both well. Went this morning to four military schools. Our gentlemen lunched with
Motherdear<. Drove à trois round the town. Saw [my sister] Olga who is better.
Leave very pleased with all this going [on]. Fondest kisses. Niki

No. 1532/ Telegram 146. Tsarskoe Selo> Bykhov. 30 Oct 1916. 10.12> 12.55.
To his majesty. Many thanks for news. Glad that you saw a lot and are pleased.
Overcast, foggy. Going now to church<, then to hospital<. Tenderly kiss you both.
May the Lord bless you. Alix

No. 1533/ Her No. 617.						Ts.[arskoe] S[elo]. October 30. 1916.
My own beloved Sweetheart,
    Forgive me for what I have done—but I had to—our Friend< said it was absolutely
necessary. Protopopov is in despair he gave you that paper the other day, thought
he was acting rightly until Gr.[igory]< told him it was quite wrong. So I spoke to
Shtyurmer yesterday & they both completely believe in our Friend's wonderful,
God sent wisdom. Sht. sends you by this messenger a new paper to sign giving
over the whole food supply now at once to the minister of Interior. Sht. begs you to
sign it & at once return it with the train 4½, then it will come in time before the
Duma assembles on Tuesday. I had to take this step upon myself as Gr. says
Protopop. will have all in his hands & finish up all the Unions & by that will save

Russia,—that is why it must be in his hands; though it is very difficult, it must be done. In Bobr.'s[384] hands it wld. not work. Trusting our Fr. He will help Protop. & Sht. quite agrees. [a]

Forgive me, but I had to take this responsability [sic] upon myself for your sweet sake. The Duma wld. insist upon it being in one hand & not 3 hands,[384] so better you give it straight beforehand to Protopopov. God will bless this choice.—Sht. is very anxious about the Duma, & their paper is rotten, revolutionary—they (ministers) hope to influence so that the number will change—some of the things they intend saying. For instance that they cant work with such ministers—the colossal impudence of it.[385] It will be a rotten Duma— but one must not fear—if too vile, one closes it. Its war with them & we must be firm.—Tell me, you are not angry—but those men listen to me & when guided by our Friend—it [i.e., the measures they undertake] must be right—they, Pr. & Sht. bow before His Wisdom. My head aches & I feel stupid, so write unclearly, I fear.—Just get yr. precious letter fr. Kiev[—]1.000.000 fond thanks.—So glad, all went off well. Kiss you without end with deepest, boundless devotion. God bless & help you. Yr. own old   Wify. [b]

384. The supply of Russian cities at this point was in the hands of three ministers: interior (Protopopov), agriculture (Bobrinsky) and communications (Trepov). The three were to work together. But the civilian supply problem was actually worsening, in part because the army enjoyed top priority in receiving food and fuel, in part because Russian railways were deteriorating. Some suggested civilian supply be centralized in one ministry. Protopopov was anxious for the honor, though he had but the faintest idea of what to do and failed when he received the assignment he sought.

385. The "paper" was an anticipated declaration from the Progressive Bloc in the Duma demanding a "ministry of public confidence," i.e., ministers responsible to the Duma and capable of working with it.

No. 1534/ Telegram 147. Tsarskoe Selo> Stavka. 30 Oct 1916. 17.05> 17.35. To his majesty. Much gladdened by unexpected dear letter. Heartily thank you. Rainy, overcast. [We] were at concert at Big palace<. Please read my letter to-morrow as soon as it is received, and also papers from old man [Sturmer]. We all warmly kiss you both. God keep you. Alix

No. 1535/ Telegram 168. Stavka> Tsarskoe Selo. 30 Oct 1916. 17.55> 18.20. To her majesty. [We] arrived well. Rain, windy. Both [Aleksei and I are] well, no colds. Thoughts always together. Thanks for two letters. Fondest love. Niki

No. 1536.   Mogilev—train station. Oct. 30. 1916.
My own beloved One,

Just this instant we arrived here in horrid rain & wind. I am writing in the train not to lose time & let the messenger off at the necessary moment. I have brought best of impressions from Kiev. Motherdear [Maria Fedorovna] was so kind & sweet. We had good long talks in the evenings over a puzzle. Olga [my sister] we saw twice, she [was] already up yesterday, looking thin but very well, such a nice quiet expression. She wrote to ask if she could marry on Saturday Nov 5th. She of course asked Mama too & I stood up for her, saying in my opinion it is better to end this state of affairs. Once it is to happen, better it should happen now! She wants to go for two weeks leave & then resume her work. Motherdear intends remaining still at Kiev, wh. she is so fond of. To-morrow I will describe the details of our stay. Now I must end. God bless you, my Love. Tenderest thanks for 2 letters & kisses to all. Ever your own Nicky.

No. 1537.   Ts.[arist] Stavka. Oct. 30th 1916.

My own sweet Treasure,

Many many fond thanks for your dear letter, that I found on arriving here, on my table. It was a great comfort to get the two letters today because I felt rather low coming to this place. Kiev seems like a nice dream, everything went so well there & all the people were so warm! Now I must tell you the events in good order as they followed. On my hasty letter fr. the train in Kiev I stopped at the lunch à trois. At 2.30 one of the shkoly praporshchikov [naval ensigns' academy] came into the courtyard & were promoted. Motherdear [Maria Fedorovna] looked out of the window and was very pleased with the sight, especially by the way Babykins< held himself behind me! Then we drove to [my sister] Olga's hospital & spent nearly an hour with her. She was lying on a straw sopha, a favorite one uses in the garden. I saw several sisters [i.e., nurses] of hers I knew previously & two doctors. [a]

From Olga Motherdear took us back to tea & after that I went to the train. He [Aleksei] had his dinner & I wrote & read. At 8.o['clock] I dined with Mama & spent a cosy evening. The next day 29th from 9.30 till 12.o I visited the four military schools—of which three are quite new and I began by inspecting them. First the Nikolaevskoe voennoe uch. i Nikolaevskoe artiller. uchil. [the Nicholaevsky Military Ac.(ademy) and the Nicholaevsky Artillery Acad.]—both completely outside the town, near each other. Enormous splendid new buildings, not quite finished in some parts.   Then I had to drive right through the town to the Alekseevskoe inzhenernoe uch. [the Alekseev Engineering Ac.,] also a colossal house very well situated & with a grand view down on the Dnepr. Coming back to the palace I played a flying visit to the old milit.[ary] school now called after [i.e., named in memory of] Costia<. Luckily I arrived in time for luncheon at 12.30. Mama invited all my gentlemen & hers and Ignatev (gov.[ernor]) with his wife (Jules Urusov['s] daughter). Babykins had walked the whole morning in the garden & had pink cheeks & astonished those at table with his appetite. He talked well with Zina Mengden & behaved alright [sic]. [b]

In the afternoon Mama took us for a charming drive on the other side of the river. The view from down there onto the town was lovely—only alas! without any sun. We came back accross [sic] another bridge & passed by Olga's hospital, got out there, were glad to see her up. But she felt rather gesanische [weak]. Then to Mama for tea with Paul< and M.P.[, his wife, Miechen<]. She gave Motherdear a very pretty image [icon] fr. the whole family, with all the names written behind. Only our's & the children's of course are not on it. She was lukewarm with me & did not say a word about Livadia! Which Mama found strange. Paul was in an excellent mood, he had just seen all of the guard & was delighted.³⁸⁶ I left Kiev after dinner with Mama, in pouring rain. [c]

Oct 31[!]. I got your dear letter [No. 1533a] & thank you fr. all my heart for your good advice. Thinking about the prodovol'stv[ie, i.e., supply] question I also found it preferable to settle the affair at once, only I had to wait for that paper to reach me. Now it is done: God help us! I feel it is right. The weather is warm. It rained heavily yesterday. Now I must end. God bless you my angel & the girlies! Ever so many loving kisses from your own Nicky. Love to A[nna Vyrubova]. [d]

386. "How false this impression must have been is made evident by an entry in Sir Alfred Knox's diary, dated 28th October, 1916 (p. 488): 'I hear whispers that the Russian infantry has lost heart and that anti-war propaganda is rife in the ranks. It is little wonder that they are downhearted after being driven to the slaughter over the same ground seven times in about a month, and every time taking trenches where their guns could not keep them.'" (Vulliamy, p. 288n)

No. 1538/ Her No. 618.   Ts.[arskoe] S[elo]. Oct. 31st 1916.
My beloved Sweetheart,

Grey & rainy, depressing weather, scarcely slept again—one needs sunshine at last.—All thoughts surround you. Concert nice yesterday —Kuznetzova's voice lovely & danced perfectly Spanish dances. Lersky I heard for the first time—& thought of you.—Protopopov has asked to be received for very important business, after that shall finish my letter. Then have several ladies—later Shakhovskoi & V. P. Schneider—every moment again taken up.—Lovy dear, our Friend< begs you absolutely to have Sukhomlinov's story [i.e., forthcoming trial] stopped, otherwise Guchkov< & others have< prepared nasty things to say—so do it once, wire to Sht.[yurmer], I think it concerns him first? telegraph this: "Having got acquainted with the data of the preliminary investigation in the case of the former Minister of War, General Sukhomlinov, I find that there are absolutely no grounds at all for the charges, and therefore the case should be discontinued." These things need being done before the Duma comes together to-morrow afternoon. [a]

I feel cruel worrying you, my sweet, patient Angel—but all my trust lies in our Friend, who only thinks of you, Baby< & Russia.—And guided by Him we shall get through this heavy time. It will be hard fighting, but a Man of God's is near to guard yr. boat safely through the reefs—& little Sunny is standing as a rock behind you, firm & unwavering with decision, faith & love to fight for her darlings & our country. Shall quickly motor for half an hour to clear up my brain for Protop.[opov].—God will help yr.—precious sake.—I send you a paper about Aleks.[eev]'s secret service—because these people mix in things wh. do not concern them & it ought to be changed—I forgot to send it you before.—Then about Rubinstein, the man is dying. Wire, or give Aleks. the order at once to wire to Ruzsky to give over Rub. from Pskov to the Ministry of the Interior (best you wire yourself) then he will do all at once.[387]—No time to write about our conversation, letter must go [now by courier]. They have managed to stop the Duma fr. giving their rotten declaration.[388] Endless kisses & thanks [for] unexpected sweet letter. Blessings & kisses without end. Yr. own old Wify. [b, c]

387. The case was transferred to the ministry of justice, and on December 6 (O.S.), 1916, Rubinstein was freed of the charges against him. (Nabokov: Alexandra, *Pis'ma imperatritsy*, II, p. 223n)
388. The declaration was issued on November 1/14, 1916. (*Ibid.*, p. 223n)

No. 1539/ Telegram 153. Tsarskoe Selo> Stavka. 31 Oct 1916. 16.15> 16.47. To his majesty. Warmly thank you for dear letter. Glad that you were able to see a lot. Went out a little for breath of fresh air. Terribly busy today. [I] embrace and kiss [you]. Alix

No. 1540/ Telegram 175. Stavka> Tsarskoe Selo. 31 Oct 1916. 18.31> 19.00. To her majesty. Tender thanks. All is donne [sic]. Have wired to old man [Sturmer]. Dont overtire yourself. Warm, a little sun. Fondest kisses. Niki

---

No. 1541/ Telegram 1. Tsarskoe Selo> Stavka. 1 Nov 1916. 13.48> 14.08. To his majesty. Tenderly kiss you both for dear letters. Very glad that everything was so nice there. Today 4 deg. frost, became fresher in evening. [We] all kiss and embrace [you]. Alix

---

No. 1542/ Her No. 619. Tsarskoe Selo. Nov. 1st. 1916.

My own beloved Treasure,

Such very tender thanks for yr. dear long letter with details of your stay in Kiev. I am glad you had cosy evenings with Motherdear< & that you managed to do so much. Miechen's< coolness is too bad—I hope you were stiff too, tho' I doubt that you succeeded to be anything but sweet & polite.—So [your sister] Olga will marry on Saturday—& where will that be & to what country place does she intend going?—Its much better Motherdear stays on at Kiev where the climate is milder & she can live more as she wishes & hears less gossip.— [a]

I am so sorry I had to send you that wire, ciphered by Protopopov— but the Minister all got so nervous on account of the Duma & feared that if it came out to-day, his nomination [as the minister who would deal with civilian supplies], that they wld. make a terrible row at the Duma, not accept him—& then Sht.[yurmer would] be forced to close the Duma. Whereas if put off a bit, then less harm closing the Duma. I disagreed with the paper & knew our Friend< wld., so I sent Protopopov straight to him to speak it over together. Our Friend says its the Ministers' faults because they did not work all these days. Fancy, [A. A.] Bobr.[inksy] never changed his aid, when it was written on that paper Prot.[opopov] showed you—that he should do so. Now I asked Sht. in his name to order him to do so. They are bad, Bobrinsky's men[,] & [they] side with the left parties.—I felt quite crazy yesterday receiving so many people.— Shakhovskoi, I did not agree with, he is against Protopopov (jalousie de métier [professional jealousy]). Then still V. P. Schneider and [in the course of] 1½ hour[s I received] 3 ladies.— [b]

Again got to sleep only after 5½ & not for long.—A.[nia]< comes at 3, so shant close my letter before—she may have something to give over. My 3 cosy Evenings in the hospital< are at an end. What news have you about what happened at Baltic port? Shakhovskoi told me, that in the council of Ministers Trepov was most awfully rude to Grigorovich about that misfortune[, an explosion] at Archangelsk & used very strong, ungentlemanly language. Really, they need smacking & being set to rights.— [c]

I had a nice letter fr. Victoria<—Georgi[e, prince of Battenburg,] comes there to-day, to-morrow is the wedding & then they leave at once for the little house they have taken in the north & he goes to his ship. No leave now, but he hopes every day to see Nada for a few hours in their house. A difficult beginning for such young creatures.[389] Victoria went to France to fetch Louise for a longish holiday—she has been working hard at the hospital & needs a rest.— To-day I receive old Schvedov [N. C. Shvedov] & Mrozosky, fr. Moscou [sic].—Continually people to be seen.—On [T]hursday our [daughter] Olga will be 21! Quite a venerable age!—I always wonder whom our girlies will marry & cannot imagine what their lot will be—could they but find the intense love & happiness you, my Angel, have given me these 22 years. Its such a rare thing now a days, alas!—[d]

How are things going on in Roumania? One hears so little now.— Am already busy about Xmas-presents for my "[hospital] station"— its immense what masses of people—& so difficult to find anything suitable & not to[o] abnormally expensive.—Such darkness, never any sunshine—I hoped the colder weather would bring bright weather.—Miss you so much, my dear precious One, & long for your tender beloved caresses of love. Our Friend is dreadfully angry with Protopop., who out of cowardice wld. not have it announced that the food supply question shld. be in his hands now—on account of the Duma & our Friend had told him he could explain he had taken it & hoped in about a week to have arranged all satisfactorily. Prot. wants to take it in 2 weeks only—wh. is foolish. Gr.[egory] is not so much disturbed about the Duma, as they always scream at anything. I agree to this.—A.[nia]< sends tender kisses & was very pleased to have been in the country & to all the Saints in Moscou—Skopin Shuysky too, quite specially.—She went to the Metropolite [i.e., Metropolitan Makary], who begs to have no bishop as help, and our Friend finds it also.—We all kiss you ever so tenderly. God bless protect & help you.—Ever yr. very own   Wify.   [P.S.] Hope, you wired about dying Rubinstein.—[See Letter No. 1538c.] [e]

389. Nadezhda, daughter of g.p. Michael Michaelovich, married Prince George ("Georgi") of Battenberg. See Footnote 259.

No. 1543.   Ts.[arist] Stavka. Nov. 1ˢᵗ 1916.
My own precious One,

I reread your dear letter many a time—I mean the one in which you write about your talks with Sht.[yurmer] & Prot[opopov]. I have nothing to forgive but to thank you deeply for the mighty push you gave this serious affair[,] helping me immensely! Now I understand the meaning of Gr.[igory]'s telegram I got at Kiev & which I sent you yesterday. But I could not write the necessary words without having the minister's paper under my eyes. Now it is done & I feel quiet, though I am quite aware of the difficulties & great ones wh. are in store the two first months. Well! let us be firm & wait. [a]

The military outlook in Rumania has improved since my last stay here & our army is concentrating itself better than I thought owing to the difficulties of traffic. Coming back from Kiev we met four military trains going down there from Riga; heard songs & saw lots of gay young faces through the windows.—Yesterday we drove to the monument,[390] I walked & later we eat [sic] roasted potatoes. It was quite warm. Dmitry< left to have his cheek (inside) operated! He hopes to see you. Igor< must be coming soon—the joy! The fat belgian [the Baron de Ricquel], [Hanbury-]Williams & Janin arrived from Bucovina enchanted with all they saw & presented thems[elves] to Mama [Maria Fedorovna]. God bless you my one & all! I kiss you lovingly & the girlies. Ever your own old Nicky. [b]

390. This was probably the monument honoring Alexander II and the emancipation of 1861. This statue was unveiled at Kiev in 1911, on the fiftieth anniversary of the event; Nicholas and Stolypin travelled to Kiev for the occasion, Stolypin was assassinated there.

No. 1544/ Telegram 2. Tsarskoe Selo> Stavka. 1 Nov 1916. 21.07> 21.40. To his majesty. Will you not telegram Georgi[e] Battenberg—Kensington House—they are marrying to-morrow, and also Misha[, his prospective father-in-law,],[389] from us both? Sleep well. [I] tenderly kiss [you]. Alix

No. 1545/ Telegram 168. Stavka> Tsarskoe Selo. 1-2 Nov 1916. 23.08> 0.33. To her majesty. Tender thank for dear letter. Were in cinema. Was much occupied. Saw Veselkin. Loving kisses. Niki

No. 1546/ Telegram 4. Tsarskoe Selo> Stavka. 2 Nov 1916. 13.55> 14.47. To his majesty. Thank you with all my soul for dear letters. At last, clear, sunny. 7 deg. frost. [I] warmly kiss and embrace [you]. Alix

No. 1547/ Her No. 690.   Ts.[arskoe] S[elo]. Nov. 2nd 1916.
Beloved Treasure,
Heartfelt thanks for your sweet letter. This morning I got yr. last night's wire—I was feeling anxious & sad, as I knew I must have upset you by my Russian one. I hate worrying you & begging you to change things you have settled, all the more so when I do not agree to what the ministers say.—At last splendid sunshine—such a treat after long, dark weeks—our wounded feel all much brighter & several are going out driving—we too, tho' there were 7 degr. of frost this morning. I again only slept two hours—such a nuisance, perhaps with the change of weather I may manage better. Everything all in order at the hospital<, tho' even there I receive architect [S. A. Danini], [also] generals to speak about sugar & butter etc. . . . [391] [a]
One Officer suddenly had a small artery, wh. burst, so we had at once to perform an operation & sow [i.e., sew] it up—but it went off alright, [daughter] Tatiana gave the chloroform for the first time.— Sad, you both wont be here for [daughter] Olga's 21st birthday. We shall have a mass in my room at 1½.—I am glad things are going better in Roumania—Vesselkin will have told you interesting things;—lucky we have such an energetic man there. Now, Lovebird, joy of my heart—farewell. God bless & protect you. Ever such tender kisses fr. yr. own old   Wify.   [P.S.] Such longing for you! [Your sister] Olga wrote she marries at 4 o'clock on the 4-th at the little Church on the Dneper situated on the place, where the idol perun once stood. God bless the dear & may N. A.[392] really be worth of her love & sacrifice.—[b]

391. Nabokov thinks that dots such as these in Alexandra's letters indicate thoughts that were not finished because "the subject was very disturbing to the person writing [i.e., the empress]." (Alexandra, Pis'ma imperatritsy, II, p. 227n) On occasion, this may be true, but evidently not in this instance. In this case (and those through the remainder of the correspondence), extra dots seem to be used as punctuation. At any rate, the dots are in the original texts. Concerning the problem of supplying Petrograd, see Footnote 350.
392. Perun was the pagan Rus' god of thunder and lightning. When Prince Vladimir of Kiev converted to Christianity in 988/989, Perun was cast into the river. "N. A." was Nicholas Alexandrovich Kulikovsky, the man Olga was marrying now that she had divorced Peter Alexandrovich ("Petia") Oldenburg.

No. 1548.   Ts.[arist] Stavka. Nov. 2nd 1916.
My own precious One,
   Thank you deeply for your dear letter & [I] send you my own loving wishes for
our [daughter] Olga's birthday. Yes! 21 years ago passed—it is almost a generation
back. I remember I lived then in that green old dressing-room of bygone days!
Yesterday it poured & in the night it snowed heavily & now there are 3° of frost.
The view is completely white here. It is even difficult for motors to move about in
the streets. This morning our 4th sotnia [company] presented itself—the officers &
men look in fine condition & very brown. They will go to Tsarskoe S.[elo] in bits,
to get their things & new clothes & boots. Nikolai Mikh.< came here for one
day—we had a long talk last evening wh.[ich] I will write to you about in my next
letter— to-day I have no time. God bless you my beloved Sunny-dear & the
children. With tender love to all[,] ever your old Nicky.

No. 1549/ Telegram 8. Stavka> Tsarskoe Selo. 2 Nov 1916. 19.09> 20.00. To
her majesty. Tenderest thanks. Were you glad to hear your son's voice? Lots of
snow. 5 deg. frost. Thoughts always together. Warm kisses. Niki

---

No. 1550/ Telegram 6. Tsarskoe Selo> Stavka. 2 Nov 1916. 20.16> 20.36. To his
majesty. What joy to hear Baby's< voice, though so distant and unclear. Hope we
will be able sometime to speak with you too. Congratulate you on Olga['s 21st
birthday]. We are now giving her her [sic] presents. [I] will think of you this
evening at the little house [of Anna Vyrubova]. Kiss you both. Sleep peacefully.
Alix

No. 1551/ Telegram 21. Tsarskoe Selo> Stavka. 3 Nov 1916. 16.45> 17.15. To his
majesty. Only now received dear letters. Heartily thank you. Congratulate you on
birthday of our older daughter [Olga]. [We] went for drive. Clear, cold. Kiss you
without end. Alix

No. 1552/ Her No. 621.   Ts.[arskoe] S[elo]. Nov. 3rd 1916.
Sweetheart, beloved One,
   Tenderly congratulate you with our big child. We had a Te Deum in the hospital
& now in my big room. Your letters have not yet come. It was a joy to hear
Babykins< sweet voice—but one hears very badly, in a few days it will be better & I
hope you will also once speak a tiny moment, just to hear the longed for sweet
voice. Victoria wired the wedding was lovely yesterday—Nada wore our
necklace.[389]— [a]
   Spent a lovely evening with our Friend & [Bishop] Isidor: [Rasputin says,] "Calm
Papa, write everything will be all right (that Protopopov will get it into his hands
quite—the food supply) that all is in the future". They dawdled too long, & therefore cld. not name him so late—all their fault & it wld. have gone well. You are not
to worry, yr. decision was right & it will be done a little later. He is very sad
Nikolasha[393] will be at the Headquarters. Spoke beautifully, calmly & very heigh
[sic]—you wld. have loved it.—6½° of frost & bright sunshine—going for a short

drive—difficult breathing in such cold.—Dmitri< is coming to tea.—All thoughts & prayers with you. [b]

Lovy, wld you not send somebody to Oranienbaum to the off. school[—]old General Filatov is at the head—about 300 officers learning for Machine-Guners [sic] & its very badly organised [sic], great disorder, badly tought [sic], so that many leave it. I heard this fr. officers where [i.e., who] have been sent there by their regiments & they say its in a real bad state—unpractical & they are kept there ages & badly organised [sic] (Karangozov etc. spoke seriously to me about it & said it wld. be a blessing if it were changed & real order put). Filatov is an old professor & keeps to his oldfashioned ideas. I thought you wld. have it seen in to seriously by a competent general. Far too few machine-guns for them to practice on, 300 officers—as each must know all the work & go into every detail. Out of their worktime they privately study it, otherwise wld. know nothing. They have to listen to lectures about submarines etc. wh. dont concern them.—Lovy, have you had Rubinstein given over to the Min. of Interior— otherwise he will die still at Pskov—please dear.[387]—Back fr. our drive, found your precious letter, for wh. warmest thanks. Glad N.P.< only remained one day.—Now Lovebird, I must end, the man must go. Blessings & kisses without end fr. yr. very, very   Own.   [P.S.] A.[nia]< sits near & kisses you.— [c]

393. Nicholas II joyfully received his cousin Nicholas Nicholaevich ("Nicholasha") when he appeared at Stavka on November 7/20, 1916. See Letters No. 1570 and 1574 and Footnote 403.

No. 1553.   Ts.[arist] Stavka. Nov. 3[d] 1916.
My own beloved Treasure,

Such fond thanks for your dear letter. Tiny< strained a sinew in the upper part of his right-leg, it is a bit swollen, but not hurt really, only he often awoke this night & moaned in his sleep. Fedorov told him to remain quietly in bed. He is very gay & is and surrounded by all the three masters [i.e., tutors][394] so there is a pretty roar going on in the next room. Vl. Nik.< can give you details about his leg, as it began while he was here. [a]

[A. N.] Obolensky appeared yesterday beaming & happy to have been delivered of his post [as governor of Petrograd]. He will get a nomination in the 3[d] Caucasian corps wh. he chose himself. Gen. Alekseev is not well & has to be kept in bed with high fever. Fedorov says his kidneys are out of order; he has asked Sirotinin to come.[395] This complicates matters for me. I hoped soon to go somewhere to the front, but now I must remain these days. Pustovoitenko knows everything & all details & he is an excellent help. For the moment I do not intend taking an outsider. Perhaps in a week you might come here? I send you Nikolai [Mikhailovich]'s letters, wh. he never sent me but brought with him—they explain the subject of his conversation. God bless you, my own Sunny & our girlies! Tenderest kisses from your own old   Nicky. [b]

394. These tutors were presumably Pierre Gilliard, Charles Sidney Gibbs and Peter Vasil'evich Petrov.
395. "Alexeiev's illness, at this stage, was extremely unfortunate. A week after this letter was written he was sent to the Crimea for a rest, and was succeeded temporarily by General Gourko. Although Gourko was an able and conscientious man, the change of the Chief of Staff at such a moment could only

be regarded as a dangerous necessity. Alexeiev returned to his post shortly before the Tsar's abdication."
(Vulliamy, p. 291n). V. N. Sirotinin, M.D., was physician-in-ordinary to the imperial court.

No. 1554/ Telegram 12. Stavka> Tsarskoe Selo. 3 Nov 1916. 17.19> 17.52. To
her majesty. Congratulate you fondly for [daughter] Olga's birthday. Sorry not to be
together. Cold, grey. Tender kisses from both. Niki

No. 1555/ Telegram 66. Tsarskoe Selo> Stavka. 4 Nov 1916. 14.26> 15.05. To
his majesty. Heartily thank you for both dear letters. Find letter of N.[ikolai
Mikhailovich] disgraceful.[396] He ought to be exiled. How can he speak to you
against Sunny [i.e., me]? It is foul, mean. Overcast, cold. [I] tenderly kiss [you].
Alix

No. 1556/ Her No. 622.   Ts.[arskoe] S[elo]. Nov. 4th 1916.
My own sweet Angel,
    Warmest thanks for yr. dear letter just received. I read Nikolai [Mikhailovich]'s[396]
& am utterly disgusted. Had you stopped him in the midle [sic] of his talk & told
him that, if he only once more touched that subject or me, you will send him to
Siberia—as it becomes next to high treason. He has always hated & spoken badly of
me since 22 years & in the club too (this same conversation I had with him this
year).—but during war & at such a time to crawl behind yr. Mama [Maria Fedorov-
na] & Sisters [Xenia< and Olga] & not stick up bravely (agreeing or not) for his
Emperor's Wife—is loathsome & treachery. He feels people count with me, begin
to understand me & care for my opinion & that he cant bear. He is the incarnation
of all that's evil, all devoted people loathe him, even those who do not much like us
are disgusted with him & his talks.— And Fred.[ericks is] old & no good & cant
shut him up & wash his head [—] & you my Love, far too good & kind & soft—such
a man needs to be held in awe of you— [a]
    He [Nikolai Mikhailovich] & Nikolasha< are my greatest enemies in the family,
not counting the black women<—& Sergei<.—He [Nikolai Mikhailovich] simply
cld. not bear Ania< & me—not so much the cold rooms, I assure you. I don't care
personal nastiness, but as yr. chosen wife—they dare not Sweety mine, you must
back me up, for your & Baby's< sake. Had we not got Him [Rasputin]—all wld.
long have been finished, of that I am utterly convinced.—I am seeing Him a
moment before Shtyurmer. Poor old man [Sturmer] may die fr. the vile way his
[i.e., he is] spoken to & of at the Duma—Milyukov's speech yesterday when he
quotes Buchanan's words that Sht.[yurmer] is a traitor & Buch. to whom he turned
in the box—held his tongue—vile behaviour![397] We are living through hardest times,
but God will help us through, I have no fear. Let they [them] scream—we must
show we have no fear & are firm. Wify is your staunch One & stands as a rock
behind you. I'll ask our Friend<, whether He thinks it advisable I go in a week's
time, or, as you cant move—whether I shld. remain here to help the "weak"
minister.[398] They have again chosen Rodzianko [as president of the Duma] & his
speeches are quite bad & what he says to the ministers. [b]
    I hope Sweetheart's< leg will soon be better. And Alekseev ill—all worries at one
time[395]—but God will not forsake you & our beloved Country through the prayers &
help of our Friend.—Am glad you arranged a place for [A. N.] Obolensky.—Grey

weather again, 4½° of frost—only two days sun.—Weary & sad: you are fighting so hard for the <u>right</u>, and for that reason of course "evil-wishers" try to ruin everything.—I felt that Nikolai [Mikhailovich] was not going to the Hdq. for good, he is a bad person, grandson of a Jew! [c]

Took a drive with her [Anna Vyrubova] and now are waiting for Him [Rasputin] (then have Rost.[ovtsev] and Sht.). Goodbye, joy of my life, my one and my everything. Blessings & kisses without end fr. yr. very, very   <u>Own</u>.   [P.S.] She [Anna Vyrubova] writes me that it is easier for her to write [you] in Russian. Reading Nikolai [Mikhailovich]'s letter, He [Rasputin] said: [the following four quotes are in Russian] "God's goodness never appeared in a single line of his letter, only evil." "As a brother of Milyukov, he [Nikolai Mikhailovich] is like all the brothers of evil." "He's [i.e., Nikolai Mikhailovich is] a ruined man, there is none of God's goodness in whatever goodness he does, no one heeds or is convinced by him." "The Lord shows Mama [i.e., the empress] in a dream that all this [conflict] is worthless." I saw in a dream they were operating on me, cutting off my hand, but I did not feel any pain, and after that [I] received N.[ikolai Mikhailovich]'s letter from you. [d]

396. Nicholas Michaelovich gave the tsar two letters warning of the coming revolution and Alexandra's role in provoking it. These were the letters Nicholas forwarded to his wife. (See Nos. 1558, 1559 and 1561a, also Fn. 399.) They were published after the March 1917 Revolution. (Nabokov: Alexandra, *Pis'ma imperatritsy*, II, p. 227n)

397. The empress refers to Milyukov's famous Duma speech of November 14/27, 1916, attacking the government's conduct of the war. Cataloging abuses that worried so many Russians, Milyukov reiterated the question, "is this folly or is it treason?" The speech was carefully planned and staged, foreigners were present, including, as Alexandra notes, the British ambassador George Buchanan.

398. Probably an ironic reference to Protopopov. Critics of the newly appointed minister called him "weak"; for all her doubts, Alexandra hoped and expected Protopopov would prove to be strong.

No. 1557.   Ts.[arist] Stavka. Nov. 4th 1916.
My own darling Sunny,

So many thanks for your sweet letter. Babykin's< leg hurts from time to time & the first parts of the night he cannot sleep. When I come to bed he tries to stop moaning & gets to sleep quicker. Fedorov says the rassasyvanie [resorption] is progressing. As his temp.[erature] is slightly higher than the normal, I hope in a few days he may be up again! I have little time to write today, as I have received old Pr.[ince S. I.] Vassiltchikoff, Trotsky[36] and Dashkov, who have returned fr. Moscow. They stayed there exactly a month visiting hospitals & saw 76.000 wounded—of whom they decorated 16.000 men. They found everything in great order. I am sending off Georgi< in a few days to the south western front to thank the troops & decorate the heroes. Alekseev is a little better this morning. Fed.[orov] insists he must remain lying for atleast [sic] a week, because except [i.e., besides] his illness he is overtired by his work & did not have enough sleep. He looks fresher! Kirill< came for two days, now he is off to Abo. God keep you my treasure, my beloved Wify & the girlies. Many tender kisses fr. your own old <u>Nicky</u>.

No. 1558/ Telegram 21. From Stavka to Tsarskoe Selo. 4 Nov 1916. 18.21>
18.50. To her majesty. Loving thanks. Sorry I sent you those two letters without
having read them myself.[399] Grey, soft [i.e., mild] weather. Tenderest kisses. Niki

399. One almost wonders if Nicholas were telling the truth. Busy as he was, would the tsar have sent
his wife letters written by someone he knew to be at at odds with Alexandra without reading them?
Nikolai Mikhailovich's *verbal* criticisms must have given the tsar a strong clue to the letters' contents. Is
it possible the emperor wanted Alexandra to see the sort of criticism people were leveling at her, and to
understand the problems this was causing him?

No. 1559/ Telegram 78. Tsarskoe Selo> Stavka. 5 Nov 1916. 10.00> 11.05. To
his majesty. [We] are going to hospital<, then to laying foundation-stone of her
[Anna Vyrubova's] church.[400] 2 deg. frost. How is [Aleksei's] leg? Better to have
torn up the 2 letters which I have returned to you without reading them. Embrace
and kiss [you] both. In thoughts always together. Alix

400. Six weeks later, Rasputin was buried in this uncompleted church at Tsarskoe Selo. During the
March 1917 Revolution, the body was disinterred, desecrated and cremated.

No. 1560/ Her No. 623.   Ts.[arskoe] S[elo]. 5 November 1916.
My own Darling,
    Such fond thanks for yr. dear letter. What a nuisance for Babykins< having to lie,
but of course its the best thing for him to do—only that he should have no
pain!—Thats good you send Georgi< off, the more you make them move about, the
better it is—no good sticking long in one place without any work.—Alekseev ought
to go off for 2 months rest & you get somebody to help you—Golovin for instance,
who all praise very highly—only none of the Commanders of the armies—leave
them quietly in their places where they are alright.   Too much work for
Pustov.[oitenko] & you alone & then you can't move & perhaps a fresh head might
be very good with new ideas. A man who is so terribly against our Friend< as poor
Alekseev is—cannot have blessed work.—his nerves, one says, are run down, & its
compehensible—the continual strain for a man of papers & not much soul to help
him, alas.—[a]
    The laying of the foundation stone [of] Ania's< Church [at Tsarskoe Selo] was
nice,[400] our Fr.< was there, & nice Bishop Isidor—Bishop Melchisedek [Melchiz-
edek] & our priest [A. P. Vasil'ev] etc. were there—shall see Gregory< a moment
to-day.—Shtyurmer is very sad & unhappy they worry you so & that because of him
too. I cheered him up & got calmer & full of good intentions. He finds Rodzianko's
Court dress [i.e., rank, which was indicated by a particular uniform] ought to be
taken fr. him for not having those bad men stopped when they said such strong
things at the Duma & bad insinuations—he told Fred.[ericks] to give him a
reprimand, but the old man misunderstood & wrote to Rodzianko that in the future
he must allow no such things to happen. Won't you say he should have his Court-
rank taken fr. him, or for the next thing he lets pass through wh. touches you
again—horrid man!—What did "Misha the fool" mean, that he & Georgi< got
decorations fr. Georgie [i.e., King George V of Great Britain] "for my invention,
which overjoyed me?"[401]—Our Fr. is so angry, [your sister] Olga married—as she
did wrong towards you & that can bring her no luck. Ah, dear me—I too more than

regret this act of hers tho' understand her human craving for happiness at last.— [b, c]

Lovy, you will be careful not to be cought [sic] by Nikolasha< into any promises or anything—remember Gr.[igory]< saved you from him & his evel [sic] people. Don't let him go to the country, but straight back to the Caucasus where he must be[381, 393]—Be cool, only not too kind to him & Orlov & Yanushkevich—remember for Russia's sake what they wanted to do—to clear you out its not gossip, Orl.[ov] had all the papers ready—& me to a Convent—you won't touch the subjects—as they are over—only make them feel you have not forgotten & that they must fear you. They need to tremble before their Sovereign,—be more selfsure—God has placed you there, its not pride & you are an anointed one & they dare not forget this. One must feel your power, its time for the saving of your Country & your Child's throne. Beloved, goodbye & God bless you. I cover you with unending tender kisses. Ever your old Sunny. [P.S.] I am ramolie<. Just seen our Friend—[he sends the following message to you:] "convoy to him, with kindness, a greeting."—He was very gay after the dinner in the ve[s]try—but not tipsy—[Rasputin has] no time to write—says all will be well. Kisses and blessings without end.—[d]

---

401. G.p. Michael Michaelovich ("Misha the fool") designed anti-aircraft shells that (he claimed) were of interest to the British War Ministry. (Sergeev: Nicholas and Alexandra, *Perepiska*, V, p. 133n)

No. 1561.   Ts.[arist] Stavka. Nov. 5th 1916.
My own precious Darling,

Tender thanks for your dear letter. I am really sorry to have disturbed you & made you angry with N.'s two letters[396], but in my continual hurry I did not read them, as he spoke so long & fully. But he omitted to speak out about you, dwelling only on the stories about spies, fabrics [i.e., factories], workmen, disorders, ministers & the outlook inside the country! Had he said any thing about you, do you doubt huzy would not have upstood [sic] for you? And I must add—he did not want to hand me his letters—I took them from him & he gave them rather unwillingly. Certainly I do not defend him, but explain facts as they were. [a]

Babykin's< leg is a little better, he slept very well & it hurt him for about ¼ of an hour in the evening.—Yesterday I received that good general Manikovsky, the head of the artillery departm.[ent] & he told me many things concerning the workmen & the frightful propaganda among them with the heaps of money being distributed among them to make strikes & that on the other side no resistance is offered against this, the police does nothing & nobody seems to care what will happen! The ministers are as weak as usual—and that is the result. Now my Lovebird I must end. God bless you and the girlies! With fondest kisses ever your own old Nicky. [b]

No. 1562/ Telegram 80. Tsarskoe Selo> Stavka. 5 Nov 1916. 18.35> 19.50. To his majesty. Heartily thank you for dear letters. [We] all warmly kiss you [both]. May God keep you! [We] are going to church, we drove, not very cold, little bit of snow. Alix

No. 1563/ Telegram 22. Stavka> Tsarskoe Selo. 5 Nov 1916. 18.36> 19.50. To her majesty. Deeply grateful [for] dear letter. [Aleksei's] leg is much better. Cold, fine, 7 deg. Got nice answer from Georgie B.[389] Fondest kisses. Niki

---

No. 1564/ Telegram 82. Tsarskoe Selo> Stavka. 6 Nov 1916. 13.38> 14.10. To his majesty. Heartily thank you both for dear letters. Were at church, at hospital<, now going to another [hospital] with medals. Sun is showing through. Congratulate [you] on festival day of your hussars. Alix

---

No. 1565/ Her No. 624.   Ts.[arskoe] S[elo]. Nov. 6th 1916.
Sweetheart dear,
   Very tenderest thanks for yr. dear letter. Thank God the little leg is better. To-day the sun is kindly trying to shine again. Were in our lower church, then worked at the hospital, now go to a soldiers hospital & to the very worst I shall give medals from you.—Later comes ["Uncle"] Mekk< & then Protopopov, shall tell him one must take severe measures against the propaganda you wrote about—I shall make them work Lovy, & I shall tell Kalinin< not to be so fidgety, & be firmer.—Stupid head aches—no doubt Becker< is coming. [a]
   I am glad N. M.[396] did not speak as he wrote,—tho' it wld. have given you reason to wash his head & tell him to mind his own business once in a way.—I shall be anxious whilst N.[icholasha]< is at the Headquarters[—]hope all will go well & you will show you are the master. Cannot help deeply regretting he will be with you[—] remember to be cool to the bad set—hope N. will have the decency not to bring fat Orlov<. Fancy Poguliayev [Pogulyaev] wrote to me he is going to divorce—if she gives it him, he will marry a flame of his youth. She wrote quite miserable to Ania—wld. understand if he married a young person, but not one who is only two years younger than herself, & who would not have him before, he was not good enough—now he is Admiral, it suits her—I don't know her name, neither mentioned it.—Why did he ever marry an older woman—he needed a young one & children as he loves them. Now must end. Thoughts always with you & earnest prayers, kisses & blessings without end, Sweet one. Ever yr. own old   Sunny. [b]

No. 1566.[402]   Ts.[arist] Stavka. Nov. 6th 1916.
My own precious One,
   Ever so many thanks for your beloved letter. Today is the Hussar's feast & also of the naval corps [the Gvardeisky Equipage<], so there were several hussars and naval officers—I spoke long after lunch & that is why I have no time to write longer. The day is bright & so gay—atlast [sic] sun after three weeks of darkness. Babykins< is also feeling much better, but last night had strong pains for about an hour. Please send me back Georgie's [prince of Battenburg] telegram. Now I must end. God bless you my own beloved Sunny & the girlies! With tender love ever your own old   Nicky.

   402. I could not find this letter in the State Archive of the Russian Federation (GARF). The text that appears here is translated from Sergeev: Nicholas and Alexandra, *Perepiska*, V, pp. 136-137

No. 1567/ Telegram 26. Stavka> Tsarskoe Selo. 6 Nov 1916. 18.40> 19.31. To her majesty. Many thanks. Little leg [of Aleksei] much better, no pain. Beautiful weather, so bright. Tenderest kisses from both. Niki

---

No. 1568/ Telegram 84. Tsarskoe Selo> Stavka. 7 Nov 1916. 13.44> 14.12. To his majesty. Heartily thank you both, my dears. In thoughts and prayers always with you, in particular today. Cold weather. Warmly kiss and embrace you both. Alix

---

No. 1569/ Her No. 625.   Ts.[arskoe] S[elo]. Nov. 7th 1916.
My own beloved Nicky dear,
   From all my heart I thank you for yr. dearest letter. Of course its difficult writing, when you have such a lot to do!−Again affairs: I saw Protopopov a long time in the evening, short [time I saw] our Friend<, & both find for the quiet of the Duma−Sht.[yurmer] ought to say he is ill & go for a rest of 3 weeks. Its true (have just spluttered ink all over my sleeve)−he is really quite unwell & broken by those vile assaults−& being the red flag for that madhause [sic], its better he should disappear a bitt [sic] & then in Dec. when they will have been cleared out [i.e., recessed, Sturmer could] return again.[404] Trepov (who I cant help not liking) for the moment is the one who by law replaces him at the Council of ministers [as the presiding minister] & will keep things going. Its only for a time. The Duma comes together again on Friday. If you wire to me you agree, I can do it for you; & kindly without hurting the old man [Sturmer]−for his sake & the quiet, as I know it would be unpleasant for you writing & I want to spare my Sweetheart all I can. He can then ask you for leave for his health.−They will at once cool down & many know he is really now well. So happy, Baby< is better.− Would it suit you if we came the 13-th & what hour, 5, 4 or 4 ½?−Hope, shall find sleep there wh. I cant here. Receive awfully much & have still too these days.−All thoughts with you. Blessings endless kisses fr. yr. own old Wify.

No. 1570.   Ts.[arist] Stavka. Nov. 7th 1916.
My own beloved Sunny,
   Fondest thanks for your dear letter.   N.[icholasha]<[403] arrived today with Petiusha< & decent people of his [i.e., the people in his suite who enjoy my favor]. Fat Orloff< & Yanushk.[evich] remained there! He has not changed & looks alright [sic] in his cherkeska [Circassian coat]. I saw Sirotinin yesterday & he told me what he finds necessary to be done with Alekseev. He must go away to the Crimea for a rest from 6 to 8 weeks. They hope this will be enough to restore his health & put him to rights. I spoke this morning about it all to Alekseev & of course he bows down to their regulations.[395] As the man to take his place for the moment, he recommends strongly Gurko. I also thought of him among others and have therefore agreed to this choice. I saw the man not long ago, every body has got a good opinion of him & at this time of the year he can leave his army for a couple of months. How stupid of Pogul.[yaev] to divorce! Now Babykin's< leg is quite well, I hope he will get up to-morrow. He tried to make a few steps yesterday & it went off alright. He slept without waking once. God bless you my own

darling & the girlies! I am incessantly in thoughts near you. With endless love ever your own old Nicky.

403. Nicholasha's< "visit is referred to by Sir J. Hanbury-Williams (p. 130), who makes it clear that the Tsar did not share the Tsaritsa's hatred of the Grand Duke. The Tsar, he says, was very pleased, and "spoke so cordially about him that it is hard to believe all these stories about jealousy, etc." (Vulliamy, p. 295n)

No. 1571/ Telegram 31. Stavka> Tsarskoe Selo. 7 Nov 1916. 18.30> 18.48. To her majesty. Warmest thanks [for] dear letters, everything here alright. Grey, not cold. Hope [you are] not tired. Tender kisses. Niki

---

No. 1572/ Telegram 87. Tsarskoe Selo> Stavka. 8 Nov 1916. 13.38> 14.17. To his majesty. Tenderly thank you both, my dears, for dear letters. In thoughts together. Happy [Aleksei's] little leg is better. Embrace, kiss [you]. Alix

---

No. 1573/ Her No. 626.   Ts.[arskoe] S[elo]. Nov. 8th 1916.
Lovy, my Angel sweet,
   Such warm thanks for yr. precious letter. Thank goodness N.[ikolasha]< brought decent people.—Thats quite right one sends Al.[ekseev] away for a good rest to the Crimea, its absolutely necessary for him—calm, air & real rest!—I hope Gurko may be the right man—personally I am no judge as don't remember ever speaking to him—the brain he has—God give him the soul. Glad to see him now, I hope, when we come.—Ressin< is in quarantine, Apraxin< in the country, [P. C.] Benk.[endorff] ill—whom am I to bring?—I take A.[nia]< & Nastinka<, no Botkin, if necessary—Vl. Nik.<, but thank God the little leg [of our son Aleksei] seems much better.—Sht.[yurmer] has let me know he is going to the Headquarters & wants to see me before—so I shall gently tell him what I wrote to you (our Fr.< begs me to) & if possible have it known before Friday that he is going on leave for his health,[404] as that day the Duma comes together & they are preparing a row for him that day—& his going on leave will quieten their boiling spirits...[391] [a]
   I find Grigorovich & Shuvaev did not find the right note in their speech, but Shuvaev did the worst thing—he shook hands with Miliukov who only just launched forth things against us.[397] How I wish we had Belyaev (real gentleman) in his [Shuvaev's] place [as minister of war].—Guchkov< has left his place, because he wants to get in with Polivanov, please don't agree to this paper wh. will come to you fr. the Cons. de l'Empire [State Council]—Polivanov who aims at rebecoming Minister of War & promises freedom to the Jews, etc. he is dangerous & ought to have no place in any committee & Guchkov needs to be on a high tree.—Andronnikov will be also one of these days sent off to Siberia. Now I must end. Last evening we spent at Ania's with Yuzik<, V. Erastov [G. N. Eristov], Gromatin & Rita<; to-night go to the hospital.—Blessings & kisses without end— intensely rejoicing for Sunday. Ever yr. very, very Own. [P.S.] What a bore N.P.< wont be at the Headquarters—shall we have that odious Svetchin [V. V. Svechin], or nice Kutaissov at least. Oh lovy mine how I live with you all the time—soul burns—head tired—weary—but spirits up & fight for you & Baby<.—[b]

404. Sturmer did not realize how precarious his position was by this time. He refused to take a "sick leave," as suggested in Letter No. 1569. Nicholas considered forcing him to do this (see Letter No. 1574), but finally resorted to a more thorough measure: he dismissed Sturmer, Bobrinsky and Protopopov—though Alexandra succeeded in saving the latter, her great favorite at this time. (See Letters No. 1576, 1578, etc.)

No. 1574.   Ts.[arist] Stavka. Nov. 8th 1916.
My own beloved Wify-dear,
    Thank you so much for your letter. All these days I have been thinking about old Sht.[yurmer] who is, as you rightly say, the red flag but not only to the Duma, nearly that of the whole country—alas! I hear of that from all sides; people don't believe him & become angry one sticks to him. Much worse than last year with old Goremyk[in]. What I reproach him of is his great prudency [sic] & incapability of taking responsibility upon himself & making the rest work as they ought to. Trepov or Grigorovich would be better in that place [as chairman of the council of ministers]. He comes already to-morrow here (Sht.) & I will let him go on leave now. About the future we will see & can talk about it when you are here.[405b] I am afraid that with him things will not go smoothly & now during war they ought to more than ever! I can't understand [why]—but no one seems to have faith in him! It will be splendid if you came on the 13th. What a funny letter Babykins< wrote to you! He is quite well & I hope will get up to-morrow. N.[icholasha]< and P.[etiusha]< lunch and dine with me, till now the talks were alright [sic]; they leave this evening. God bless you my own precious One and the girlies. Thank her [Anna<] for the image [icon]. With tenderest love ever your very own   Nicky.

No. 1575/ Telegram 31. Stavka> Tsarskoe Selo. 8 Nov 1916. 19.46> 20.58. To her majesty. Tender thanks. Weather warmer. Tiny< quite well, cheery. Kiss ever so fondly. Niki

No. 1576/ Telegram 91. Tsarskoe Selo> Stavka. 9 Nov 1916. 10.09> 10.19. To his majesty. We [Sturmer and I] discussed what I wrote about in letter you received yesterday. He [Sturmer] does not want to understand that there is now an urgent need for his "quick" leave or his transfer to lesser responsibility. Forgive me for disturbing you and please understand that I must convey all of this to you for your welfare. Tenderly kiss [you]. Alix

No. 1577/ Her No. 627   Ts.[arskoe] S[elo]. 9 November 1916.
My own Lovebird,
    Warmest thanks for sweet letter.—Our Friend< says Sht.[yurmer] can remain still some time as President of Council of Minister[s], as that one does not reproach him so much, but all the row began since he became Minister of Foreign Affairs, which Gregory realised [sic] in summer & told him then already that this will be your end. That is why He implores either he should go on leave for a month or at once to name another man in his place as Minister of Foreign Affairs[,] for instance [I. G.] Shcheglovitov, as very clever (tho' hard) & a Russian name, or Giers ([who from 1912 to 1915 was our ambassador to] Constantinople), in that ministery, he [Sturmer] is the red flag & at once all will be quieter if he is changed. But leave

him as President of Council of Minister[s] (if he goes on leave, Trepov by law replaces him)—All want that place, & they are not fit for it. Grigorovich perfect where he is,—others & Ignatev< egg him on to take that place, for which he is unsuited. Ignat. made him & Shuvaev take the wrong note in their speach [sic], wh. had been prepared alright [sic] by the ministers. [a]

Now one calls Mme. Sukhomlinov before judgement on Friday & therefore I wired asking you to have the Sukhomlinov case at once stopped through Senator Kuzmin.—Its vengeance because one let the poor old man out of prison. So horribly unfair!—Just returned fr. mass at my lancers' hospital (1-st rifle regiments mass)—2 years existence. Old Beckmann [V. A. Bekman] was there. 26 lancers, who had been ill or wounded & now return to the regiment.—So glad no conversations with N.[icholasha]<. Baby's< letter too amusing. —yr. letters came 3 hours late.— Weather, 3° of frost, grey.—What are you thinking about the St. George's feast, will you have it here, so as to lift up the spirits by yr. presence in this rotten part of the world.—Now must end, Manny dear. Gr.[igory]< hopes you will soon come here; yr. presence is much needed to keep them all in order.— Sandro L.< said Nik.[olai] Mikh.[ailovich] speaks awfully, all are furious what he says in the club, & he sees Rodz.[yanko] & company continually. Excuse only disagreable [sic] letters, but head weary from affair.—Should I bring Mordv.[inov] or Kutaissov for the journey, as have no gentleman?—1000 tender kisses & blessings Ever yr. very, very, very Own. [b]

No. 1578.   Ts.[arist] Stavka. Nov. 9th 1916.
My own beloved Darling,

Thank you ever so fondly for your letter & for trying to help me about arranging different affairs. I will see Sht.[yurmer] in [an] hour & insist he is to go on leave. Alas! I find he will have to leave completely—no body has any confidence in him. I remember even Buchanan told me last time I received him, he got reports from english consuls in Russia, saying that there would be serious troubles in the country if he remained. And longer every day I hear more and more upon the same subject. One has to reckon with this. Babykins< is up and quite well, though a little pale & thinner. There are such a lot of things I would like to speak about but have no time to do it in writing. So happy we shall meet soon. [G]od keep you my One & All & the girlies. Many tender kisses & much love from your very own old Nicky.

No. 1579/ Telegram 93. Tsarskoe Selo> Stavka. 9 Nov 1916. 20:20> 20:50. To his majesty. Heartily thank you both for dear letters. They were 3 hours late. Was at my lancer's hospital. Received. Sleep well. Tenderly embrace and kiss [you]. Alix

No. 1580/ Telegram 43. Stavka> Tsarskoe Selo. 9 Nov 1916. 22:01> 23:22. To her majesty. Loving thanks. Talked over with old man [Sturmer] who returns to-morrow. [He] will explain to you my decision.[405b] Tenderest kisses from both. Niki

No. 1581/ Telegram 44. Stavka> Tsarskoe Selo. 10 Nov 1916. 0:51> 1:29. To her majesty. Have done it [i.e., dismissed Sturmer]. Good night. Niki

No. 1582/ Telegram 46. Stavka> Tsarskoe Selo. 10 Nov 1916. 12:46> 13:35. To her majesty. As you have, no one to go with[, I] am sending today Voeikov. Tenderest kisses. Niki

---

No. 1583/ Her No. 628.   Ts.[arskoe] S[elo]. Nov. 10th 1916.
My own sweet Angel,
   The kitten is climbing all over my writing table, luckily though scarcely anything [has been knocked] down—she climbs on the palme [palm plant] & whatever she can get hold of.—Been driving—it snowed & was wet.—I received old Sht.[yurmer] & he told me yr. decisions—God grant, all is for the good, tho' it gave me a painful shock you also take him away fr. the Council of Ministers.[405b] I had a big lump in my throat—such a devoted, honest, sure man. Yr. kindness & trust touched him so much & the beautiful nomination. I regret, because he likes our Friend< & was so right in that way— Trepov, I personally do not like & can never have the same feeling for him as to old Gorem.[ykin] & Sht.[yurmer]—they were of the good old sort. The other, I trust, will be firm (I fear at heart a hard man)—but far more difficult to talk to—those two loved me & came for every question that worried them, so as not to disturb you—this one I, alas, doubt caring for me & if he does not trust me or our Friend, things will be difficult. I told Sht. to tell him how to behave about Gr.[igory]< & to safeguard him always. Oh, may it be for the good & [may] you have an honest man, in him to help you. You, Lovy, will tell him [Trepov, the new chairman of the council of ministers] to come to me too sometimes—I know him so little & would like to "understand" him.— [a]
   Thanks, dear, for sending us Voeikov.—Saw Gr. yesterday & then he wired to you, when I told him about the old [Austrian] Emperor's death—(Francis Joseph) he thinks it certainly for our good in every way (I too) & hopes the war may then sooner end, as there may be stories [disagreements] between Germany & Austria. Thanks for Sukhoml.[inov],[405a]—here is a letter fr. S.[ukhomlinov ?] to you. What joy to meet soon—lots to talk over. Please, make Nik. Mikh. go away—he is a dangerous element in town<.[406]—Must end. 10,000,000 kisses & blessings fr. yr. Own. [b]

405a. Nicholas II freed the former minister of war from prison; the charges against the old man were, in effect, dismissed. Sukhomlinov was re-arrested by the Provisional Government, tried, convicted and sentenced to hard labor for life. He was freed by the Bolsheviks, escaped to Finland and died in Germany in 1926.

No. 1584.   Ts.[arist] Stavka. Nov. 10th 1916.
My own precious Sunny,
   Many thanks for your dear letter. When you get this one you will have heard fr. Sht.[yurmer] about the changes wh. are absolutely necessary now.[405b] I am sorry about Prot.[opopov], a good honest man, but he jumped fr. one idea to another & could not stick to his opinion. I remembered that fr. the very beginning. People said he was not normal some years ago fr. a certain illness (when he went to Badmaev[315]). It is risky leaving the min.[istry] of Int.[ernal Affairs] in such hands at such times! Old [A. A.] Bobrinksy needs also replacing. If one can get a strong

& energetic man in his place [minister of agriculture,] then I hope the prodovol['stvie, i.e., supply] question will be rightly settled without breaking the existing system.[384]   While these changes go on the Duma will be shut [i.e., recessed] for 8 days, else they would say one does it [these changes] under their pressure. In any case, Trepoff[, the new chairman of the Council of Ministers,] will try & do his best. He comes back, on Sunday I think, with a list of names, wh. we have spoken about with Sht. & him. Only please don't mix in our Friend<! It is I who carry the responsibility [and] I want to be free to choose accordingly. The poor old man [Sturmer] was calm and touching. God bless you my beloved Darling. Oh! how happy I will be to rest in your dear arms. With tender kisses to you all ever your very own Nicky.

405b. Nicholas II was often accused of lacking the courage to dismiss officials face-to-face. This was certainly not the case with Sturmer. Nicholas told Sturmer that Protopopov, now universally despised, would also be discharged. This was the tsar's last chance, however slight, to regain some control over events. As we shall see, however, Alexandra saved Protopopov—and Russia moved towards revolution.

No. 1585/ Telegram 47. Stavka> Tsarskoe Selo. 10 Nov 1916. 19:35> 20:09. To her majesty. Thanks lovingly [for] dear letter. Bad weather, thawing. [Aleksei and I have] just been at cinema together. Fondest kisses. Niki

No. 1586/ Telegram 100. Tsarskoe Selo> Stavka. 10 Nov 1916. 21:17> 22:00. To his majesty. Warmly thank [you] for dear letters and telegrams. Snow fell, [I] went for a drive, overcast. Saw old man [Sturmer]. Sleep peacefully. [I] warmly embrace and kiss [you] both. Alix

No. 1587/ Her No. 629.   Ts.[arskoe] S[elo]. Nov. 10th 1916.
Beloved Sweetheart,
    Its one in the night & yet I begin my letter to you, as to-morrow have people all day long. Even in the hospital I shall receive a French Dr. as [he] wants to speak about wonderful tables he & other French Doctors take to Rumania. An electric battery & Rontgen apparatus [are] under the table, so that during the operation one can the whole time see where the ball is & that colossally [sic] facilitates of course the extraction of bullets or bits of shells. Then an English consul from Riga I believe will bring me there 10,000 p[ounds].[128] Then at 2 we go to my train to a Mass officiated by the Metropolitan [Pitirim?], as they have newly arranged the church. Then receive somebody in A.[nia]'s< house. Then Frederiks to an early tea. Then N.P.< to real tea. Hereafter (no more ink in that pen) Meliuhin [P. N. Milyutin], Nikolosha's< aid. Then Protopopov, Trepov & our Friend< for an hour in the evening to say goodbye. He is very sad, Sht.[yurmer] did not understand he ought to have gone for a rest.[404] Not knowing Trepov of course he [Rasputin] is anxious for you. But he thinks you ought to have another minister of roads & communication, finds it not good a man has two things to do, as then can never so well fulfil each place—& besides at the present time he must travel about & personally see to all,—would not Valuyev have [been a good choice to follow Trepov as minister of communications]—utterly devoted, good man (so found our

Friend since a good time already).—Lets choose the Minister of foreign affairs together. [a]

I saw Princess Julie Branicka [Branitskaya] to-day, still so handsome, tho' full of [w]rinckles—we saw her last at Kiev. Her husband died before the war. She is a niece of the old lady at Belaya Tserkov[295] & [she] saw Motherdear< there.—Spent a cosy evening at the hospital knitting & chattering. Elena< lunched with us—enjoyed the Crimea. She says [Prince] Peter of Montenegro is fighting with our troops in France.—My head goes round from all the people I have to see—& all must fit in & [I must find] enough time for each. Am greatly intensely looking forward to Sunday 5 o'clock!!! Now at last (thanks to our Fr.<) since 3 nights sleep nearly perfectly well,[406] such a comfort, as the head is then fresher.—Goodnight & sleep well—I have written this in 12 minutes. [b]

Nov. 11-th. Such fond thanks for Your letter, deary. Old man [Sturmer] was wrong in not telling me about your other intention—they have put me awfully out.[407] Forgive me, deary, believe me—I entreat you dont go and change Protopopov, now, he will be alright, give him the chance to get the <u>food supply matter</u> into his hands & I assure you, all will go [well]. Sht.[yurmer] finds him fidgety, because Shtyurmer dawdled & did not answer quick enough & keep them all enough in hand. Bobr.[insky] all the same if you change him, I find, only not Protopopov, now it is not good. Of course I more than regret Ignat.[ev] sits there (very left[ist in his politics!]) & that Trepov is at the head—but choose a new minister of Railroads & Communications—he can't do 2 things at a time, now when everything is so serious.—tho' of course he will say he can.—Makarov cld. be beautifully changed, he is not for us, but Protopop. is honestly <u>for us</u>. [c]

Oh, Lovy, you can trust me. I may not be clever enough—but I have a strong feeling & that helps more than the brain often. Dont change anybody until we meet, I entreat you, lets speak it over quietly together [when I arrive at Stavka]. Let Trep. come a day later [to Stavka] or keep the papers & names back, Lovy dear—for Wify's sake. You dont know how hard it is now—so much to live through & such hatred of the "rotten upper sets". The food supply must be in Prot.'s hands.—Others are intriguing against him, he heard the news from the Headquarters some days ago.—Times are serious—don't break up all at once—Shtyurmer was a big act—now choose—Trepov's successor as minister [of communications] & a younger one [as minister of agriculture] instead of Bobr.—but leave Prot., don't be angry with me, its for you I say all this I know it wld. not be good. Heart & soul are weary fr. suffering, but I must tell you the truth. [d]

Goodbye, my Angel. Once more, remember that for your reign, Baby< & us you <u>need</u> the strenght [i.e., strength, the] prayers & advice of our Friend. Remember, how last year <u>all</u> were against you & for N.[icholasha]< & our Friend gave you the help & strength you took over all & saved Russia—we no longer went back. He told Shtyurmer that he ought not to have accepted being Minister of Foreign affairs, that it would be his ruin—German name & one wld. say—all my doing.—Protop. venerates our Friend & will be blessed—Sht. got frightened & for months did not see him—so wrong & he lost his footing. Ah, Lovy, I pray so hard to God to make you feel & realise, that He [Rasputin] is our caring, were He not here, I dont know what might not have happened. He saves us by His prayers & wise counsils [sic] & is our rock of faith & help.— [e]

M-me Taneyev [Nadezhda Taneeva, Anna Vyrubova's mother] said aloud that Ignat.[ev], Krivoshein and Sazonov[408] & c.[etera] intend breaking Prot.'s neck & will do everything to succeed. Dont let them. He is not mad, the wife[, Madame Olga Pavlovna Protopopova,] sees Bekhterev[, a psychiatrist,] for his [her?] nerves only. For me dont make any changes till I have come, tell Trepov you wish to think it over a day or two & tell him you do not intend sending Protop. & please, give him the food supply question as settled,— believe me, he will manage—in the country one feels it already (only vile Petr.[ograd] & M.[oscow] speak against him).—Quieten me, promise, forgive, but its for you & Baby I fight.—Kisses yr. Wify. [f]

406. Rasputin was crucial in safeguarding the tsarevich's health, but he does not seem to have been called upon to "heal" Alexandra of her ills, real and imagined. In this instance, however, Grigory did help the empress sleep.

407. Although Stürmer told Alexandra her husband had just dismissed him, he withheld the fact that Nicholas was likewise dropping Protopopov and Bobrinsky. This silence was probably at the tsar's request. The empress received Nicholas's letter (No. 1584, dated November 10, 1916) disclosing Protopopov's fate between the time she began this letter and added its post-script. Nicholas usually cushioned a high official's dismissal with an appointment to another post, often to the State Council or Senate. Significantly, the emperor did not do this for Stürmer. (Nabokov: Alexandra, Pis'ma imperatritsy, II, p. 235n) State Controller N. N. Pokrovsky followed Stürmer as minister of foreign affairs; A. A. Rittich replaced Bobrinsky as minister of agriculture; E. B. Voinovsky-Kriger became the new minister of communications. Nicholas disliked Trepov; he planned to use him as a hatchetman to dismiss the Duma; the tsar would then find a new chairman. (See Letter No. 1644a.) Trepov lasted 47 days in his new post; he was succeeded by Prince N. D. Golitsyn, the last chairman of the tsarist council of ministers.

408. The last name is not clear.

No. 1588/ Telegram 102. Tsarskoe Selo> Stavka. 11 Nov 1916. 14:06> 14:42. To his majesty. Many thanks for dear letters. Implore [you] to leave Kalinin<. Sunny asks for this. Wait until our meeting, don't decide anything! Embrace and kiss [you]. Alix

---

No. 1589/ Telegram 49. Stavka> Tsarskoe Selo. 11 Nov 1916. 16:37> 17:05. To her majesty. Best thanks [for] dear letter. Shall wait till [we] meet about settling [these changes on the council of ministers]. Gurko came yesterday, [we] began our work together. Have not written to you, no time today. Tenderest kisses. Niki

---

No. 1590/ Telegram 105. Tsarskoe Selo> Stavka. 11 Nov 1916. 21:40> 22:37. To his majesty. Please, do not undertake appointment again until you have spoken with your Sunny. Tenderly kiss [you]. Sleep well. Alix

---

No. 1591/ Her No. 630.   Ts.[arskoe] S[elo]. Nov. 12[th] 1916. My own beloved One,
    I am writing to you in our hospital in one of the wards—was too dead tired last night to think of anything & had to put my things together & arrange yr. letters. My head goes round in a ring so excuse if I write unclearly—so dark too & d[r]eary. You probably have a paper about Vil'chkovsky< being promoted general, please deary, do it, it will help him for [i.e., in] all his relations with other generals & commissioners, who are a nuisance.— [a]

Lovy, my Angel—now about the chief thing—don't change Protopopov. I had a long talk with him yesterday—the man is as sane as only can [be], of course Trep.[ov] (as I was sure) said the same thing to me—its <u>utterly false</u>,—he is quiet & calm & utterly devoted which one can, alas, say of but few & he will succeed—already things are going better, & it would be folly at such a serious moment to change him. I will tell you details & intrigues when I come & you will see all clearly. Therefore I begged you to put of[f] Trep. till we have met. Its the same story as last year—again [people are] against wify—they know he is completely devoted to me & comes to me as does Shakhovskoi ([our group of enemies] wants to change him too). Change nobody now, otherwise the Duma will think its their doing & that they have succeeded in clearing everybody out. And its bad to begin by sending all flying—others wont have the time to set to work in new places whilst the Duma sits. You know, I have no very good opinion of Trep. & I see by his wishing to clear out people devoted to me—the game. They will then be ministers as the last Headquarters chose, were all against me.[409] They feel I am your wall & it aggravates them—ah, lovy, dont let them do this, its more serious than you think. It took you long then to realise that last year—& now its the bad party, who have got behind Trep.—Voeikov also plays an ugly part with Andronnikov in this affair—he clings to this bad man. [b]

Its difficult writing & asking for oneself, I assure you, but its for yr. & Baby's< sake, believe me. I don't care what bad one says of me, only when one tries to tear devoted, honest people, who care for me— away—its <u>horribly unfair</u>. I am but a woman fighting for her Master & Child, her two dearest ones on earth—& God will help me being your guardian angel, only dont pull the sticks away upon wh. I have found it possible to rest.[410] Trepov will recommend him in Shakhovskoi's place—not if he says he is unnormal.[411] Stick firm & send for Protopop. at once & have a good talk with him, if you like I'll be with you. Only when you tell Trep. you won't change Prot. nor Shakhovskoi, <u>don't</u> for goodness [sake] <u>mention</u> my name—it must be your <u>wise</u> wish. If he says he cant work with them, then tell him you will keep him for the moment & then take another. Be the master—Trep. has a disagreeable character. I never care about people who use lots of words to explain their devotion, I like to see it in their acts—Prot. proves it the whole time (another idiotic wounded [soldier] stands & stares whole time & drives me wild—others make much noise in the corridor, wh. does not make it easier for writing). [c]

I want you to read this before we meet—it will give you time in case Tr. comes [to Stavka] before me. I am very hurt Sht.[yurmer] did not warn me before.[407] Lovy, its no joke, more serious, as its a hunt against wify. Categorically answer you have quietly thought it over & do not for the present intend changing any of your ministers. Leave old Bobr.[insky as minister of agriculture] even. Please, pay attention to all I write (now 3 more [wounded] have come to [where I am writing to stare and] make me wild). Its a lie when Trep. says Prot. understands nothing about the ministery [sic]—he knows well, in the country one feels his firm hand— provisions are coming & its going slowly but rightly for the good. 10 days his papers were not read through by the [other] ministers, such a shame. What joy to rest to-morrow in your arms to kiss & bless you. <u>Wify</u>. [d]

Darling, remember that it does not lie in the man Protopop. or x.y.z., but its the question of <u>monarchy</u> & <u>yr</u>. prestige now, which must not be shattered in the time of the Duma. Dont think they will stop at him, but they will make all others leave who are devoted to you one by one—& then ourselves. Remember, last year Yr. leaving to the Army—when also you were alone with us two [Rasputin and me?] against everybody, who promised revolution if you went. You stood up against all & God blessed your decision. I repeat again—it does not lie in the name of Prot. but in your remaining firm & not giving in—"The Czar rules and not the Duma".—Forgive my again writing, but I am fighting for your reign & Baby's future. God will help, be firm don't listen to men, who are not from God but cowards. Yr. Wify, to whom you are ALL in ALL. True unto death. [e]

---

409. The empress refers to the first "ministerial shakeup" which occurred in June-September 1915, when Nicholas dropped Sukhomlinov (minister of war), Shcheglovitov (justice), Maklakov (internal affairs), Sabler (director Holy Synod) and Rukhlov (communications) in favor of Polivanov, A. A. Khvostov, Shcherbatov, Samarin and A. F. Trepov. The empress was fond of some of the men ousted; she despise their replacements, except for A. A. Khvostov. Since Nicholas was at Stavka when he made these changes, it seemed to his wife "the last Headquarters chose" the new ministers, and "[they] were all against me."

410. Intelligent as she was, the empress was a poor judge of people. Even so, one wonders why Alexandra was so passionately committed to Protopopov. This sentence provides a clue: she was comfortable with Protopopov, he reassured her, he was one of the "sticks ... upon wh. I have found it possible to rest." Letter No. 1600d indicates she held similar feelings for V. N. Shakhovskoi.

411. The sense of this sentence is: Trepov may suggest a compromise whereby Protopopov will give up internal affairs and replace Shakhovskoi as minister of trade and industry—the position Nicholas originally had in mind for Protopopov, a successful businessman. But, the reasoning continues, if Protopopov is able to occupy one position, why not the other?

No. 1592/ Telegram 106. Tsarskoe Selo> Stavka. 12 Nov 1916. 14.55> 15.25. To his majesty. Are now leaving. In prayers and thoughts together. Terribly glad over to-morrow. Read my letter on Sunday as soon as you receive it, deary. We warmly kiss you both. In heart and soul am with you. Alix

---

No. 1593/ Telegram 55 in Russian. Stavka> Bologoe. 12 Nov 1916. 17.47> 18.48. To her majesty. Warmly thank you for letter. Clear, thawing. Have a good trip. [Aleksei and I] are happy at our meeting. [We] warmly embrace [you]. Niki

---

No. 1594/ Telegram 60 in Russian. Yartsevo, Al. r. r.> Stavka. 13 Nov 1916. 9.50> 10.25. To his majesty. Are travelling well. Did not sleep well. All thoughts together. [We] are glad to see you soon. [We] warmly kiss you. Alix

---

No. 1595/ Her No. 631.   Tsarskoe Selo. Dec. 4. 1916.[412]
My very precious One,
    Goodbye, sweet Lovy! Its great pain to let you go—worse than ever after the hard times we have been living & fighting through! But God who is all love & mercy has let the things take a change for the better,—just a little more patience & deepest faith in the prayers & help of our Friend<—then all will go well! I am fully convinced that great & beautiful times are coming for yr. reign & Russia. Only keep up your spirits, let no talks or letters pull you down—let them pass by as something unclean & quickly to be forgotten. Show to all, that you are the Master & your will shall be obeyed—the time of great indulgence & gentleness is

over—now comes your reign of will & power, & they shall be made to bow down before you & listen your orders & to work how & with whom you wish—obedience they must be taught, they do not know the meaning of that word, you have spoilt them by yr. kindness & all forgivingness. [a]

Why do people hate me? Because they know I have a strong will & when am convinced of a thing being right (when besides blessed by Gr.[igory]<), do not change my mind & that they can't bear. But its the bad ones. Remember Mr. Philipp[e']s words when he gave me the image [icon] with the bell. As you were so kind, trusting & gentle, I was to be yr. bell, those that came with wrong intentions wld. not be able to approach me & I wld. warn you.[103] Those who are affraid [sic] of me, dont look me in the eyes or are up to some wrong, never like me.—Look at the black ones<—then [Fat] Orlov< & Drentel'n—[the late ex-Chairman of the Council of Ministers] Witte— Kokovtsov—Trepov, I feel it too—Makarov[280] —Kaufmann—Sofia Ivanovna [Tyutcheva]—Mary [Maria Vasil'chikova]—Sandra Obolensky[, the wife of I. M. Obolensky,] etc., but those who are good & devoted to you honestly & purely—love me,—look at the simple people & military. The good & bad clergy its all so clear & therefore no more hurts me as when I was younger. Only when one allows oneself to write you or me nasty impertinent letters—you must punish. Ania told me about Balaschov[413] (the man I always disliked). [b]

I understood why you came so awfully late to bed & why I had such pain & anxiety waiting. Please, Lovy, tell Frederiks to write him a strong reprimand (he [N. P. Balashov?] & Nik.[olai] Mikh.[ailovich] & Vass. [B. A. Vasil'chikov] make one [i.e., they are aligned together] in the club)—he [N. P. Balashov?] has such a high court-rank & dares to write, unasked. And its not the first time—in bygone days I remember he did so too. Tear up the letter, but have him firmly reprimanded—tell Voeik.[ov] to remind the old man [Fredericks]—such a smack to a conceited member of the Council of the Empire< will be very useful. We cannot now be trampled upon. Firmness above all!—Now you have made Trepov's son A.D.C. you can insist yet more on his working with Protopopov, he must prove his gratitude.—Remember to forbid Gurko speaking & mixing himself into politics—it ruined Nikol.[asha]< & Alekseev,—the latter God sent this illness[395] clearly to save you fr. a man who was lossing [sic] his way & doing harm by listening to bad letters & people, instead of listening to yr. orders about the war & being obstinate. And one has set him against me—proof—what he said to old Ivanov.— [c]

But soon all this [i.e., these] things will blow over, its getting clearer & the weather too, which is a good sign, remember. And our dear Friend is praying so hard for you—a man of God's near one gives the strenght [sic], faith & hope one needs so sorely. And others cannot understand this great calm of yours & therefore think you dont understand[414] & try to ennervate [sic], frighten & prick at you. But they will soon tire of it. Should Motherdear< write, remember the Michels[415] are behind her.—Don't heed & take to heart—thank God, she is not here, but kind people find means of writing & doing harm.—All is turning to the good—our Friends dreams means so much! Sweety, go to the Moghilev Virgin & find peace & strenght [sic] there—look in after tea, before you receive, take Baby< with you, quietly—its so calm there—& you can place yr. candels [sic]. Let the people see you are a christian Sovereign & dont be shy—even such an example will help others. [d]

How will the lonely nights be? I cannot imagine it. The consolation to hold you tightly clasped in my arms—it lulled the pain of soul & heart & I tried to put all my endless love, prayers & faith & strenght [sic] into my caresses! So inexpressibly dear you are to me, husband of my heart! I share your sorrows and joys and am prepared to die for you. God bless you & my Baby treasure—I cover you with kisses; when sad, go to Baby's room & sit a bit quietly there with his nice people. Kiss the beloved child & you will feel warmed & calm. All my love I pour out to you, Sun of my life.—Sleep well, heart & soul with you, my prayers around you— God & the holy Virgin will never forsake you. Ever your very, very   Own. [e]

412. Nabokov notes that Alexandra and her daughters arrived at Stavka on November 13/26, 1916. Protopopov appeared the following day, November 14. Nabokov reproduces the texts of five telegrams Rasputin sent to Stavka in these days, along with five telegrams from Anna Vyrubova. On November 25 (O.S.) the royal family went to Tsarskoe Selo. (Alexandra, *Pis'ma imperatritsy*, II, pp. 240-242n) This explains why Alexandra wrote this parting letter at Tsarskoe Selo. Note that Nicholas and his son returned to Stavka by way of Smolensk.

413. Nicholas Petrovich Balashov (b. 1841) was the wealthiest member of the State Council, sharing 1,409,400 acres with his brother Ivan (b. 1842). The dowry of Balashov's wife, the Countess Catherine Shuvalova, included 459,000 acres. The Balashovs "stood at the very centre of the St. Petersburg aristocracy." For a discussion of this family, see Lieven, *Russia's Rulers*, pp. 19-20, 58, 60, 168.

414. Writing as an historian well after these events had passed, Leon Trotsky noted that during crises—when those around Nicholas II "were depressed, alarmed, shaken—the tsar alone preserved his tranquility [though] thunders rolled over him and lightning flashed." Was this self-restraint or breeding or a conviction that fate rules our lives? Was it inadequate consciousness? Trotsky believed the tsar's "ability to control himself in the most extraordinary circumstances [was more than] mere external training; its essence was an inner indifference, a poverty of spiritual forces, a weakness of impulses of the will." This characterization is memorable, even if not entirely supported by the facts. (Trotsky, *Russian Revolution*, pp. 49-50.)

415. A. A. Sergeev thinks this is probably a reference to the "Mikhailovichi," the sons of g.p. Michael Nicholaevich (1832-1909), the youngest son of Tsar Nicholas I. Michael Nicholaevich and his wife, Olga Fedorovna (1839-1891), had six sons, five of whom were alive at this time: Nicholas (1859-1919), Michael (the tsar often called him "Misha the Fool," 1861-1929), Georgy (1863-1919), Alexander ("Sandro") (1866-1933), Serge (1869-1918) and Aleksei Michaelovich (1875-1895). (*Perepiska*, V, p. 156n)

No. 1596/ Telegram 22 in Russian. Tsarskoe Selo> Bologoe. 4 December 1916. 20.04> 20.40. To his majesty. [We] miss [you] very much. [Our] thoughts are together, prayers—[we] kiss you both. Sleep well. Was at Znamenie<, received; [we] will be at hospital< this evening. The Lord be with you [both]. All is well, tender thanks to Little One< for letter. Alix

No. 1597.   In the train. Dec. 4th 1916.
My own deeply beloved darling Sunny,

I have not read your letter, as I like to do it in bed, before going to sleep. But I thank you before hand for all the love & sweet kindness you have written in it. I will deliver this letter at Tosno & hope it will reach you this evening. Yes, these days we spent together, were indeed hard ones—but tis only thanks to you that I stood them more or less calmly. You were so staunch & induring—I admire you more than I can say! Forgive me if I have been cross or impatient, sometimes one's temper has to get through![416] Of course it would have been bliss if we could have remained together the whole difficult time. But now I firmly believe that the greatest hardship is over—& it won't be as difficult as before. And then I intend becoming sharp & biting. God grant our separation will not be a long one. I am the whole time in thoughts near you, never doubt that. I bless you with all my loving heart & the girlies too. Keep well and strong, my own Lovebird, my One & All! Sleep well & gently! Your very own old huzy Nicky true unto death. Give her [Anna Vyrubova] my love.

416. This refers to the battle over Protopopov. Massie notes this letter contains the only evidence in the entire Nicky-Sunny correspondence of a "serious quarrel." (*Nicholas and Alexandra*, p. 344) Trepov, the new chairman of the council of ministers, was furious to learn Nicholas was retaining Protopopov, and he tried (unsuccessfully) to resign. Trepov actually persuaded Protopopov to step down. (V. S. D'yakin, *Russkaya burzhuaziya*, p. 262) In vain: Protopopov stayed in office until Nicholas's government collapsed.

No. 1598/ Telegram 23 in Russian. Tsarskoe Selo> St. Smolensk.[412] 5 Dec 1916. 9.55> 10.30. To his majesty. Terribly gladdened by dear unexpected letter. Thank you warmly. Slept so-so. 5 degrs. So empty. [We] all warmly embrace you [both]. [We] tenderly embrace [you]. Alex

No. 1599/ Telegram 163 in Russian. Smolensk, Aleks. r.r.[412]> Tsarskoe Selo. 5 Dec 1916. 11.35> 12.06. To her majesty. Both thank [you] for dear letters. [We] are travelling well. Weather clear, 1° of frost. [We] tenderly embrace [you]. Niki

No. 1600/ Her No. 632.   Ts.[arskoe] S[elo]. Dec. 5th 1916.
My own Sweetheart,
   From the depths of my loving heart I send you warmest, heartiest goodwishes & many tender blessings for yr. dear Namesday [sic]. May yr. patronsaint quite particularly be near you & keep you in safe guard. Everything that a devoted, unutterably loving heart can only wish you—Sunny wishes you. Strength, firmness, unwaving [sic] decision, calm, peace, success, brightest sunshine—rest & happiness at last after yr. hard, hard fighting. In thoughts I clasp you tightly to my heart, let your sweet, weary head rest upon my breast. With the candles my prayers rise in burning fervour & brightness for you—to-night shall go to Church, & to-morrow our fogies, court ones, will be there to congratulate after mass.— [a]
   How can I thank you enough for the unexpected, intense joy of yr. precious letter—it was a ray of warming sunshine in my lonely heart. After you both left, I went to Znamenia<. Later received Ilyin [A. A. Il'in], Vsevol.[ozhsky] of my supply trains—Bagrat.[ion]-M.[ukhransky] of the "Savage Division"[417]—[he] will try & see you at the Headquarters—awfully interesting all he tells about the tribes under him—& the Abreki, who behave very well.—After dinner went to the hospital—to forget oneself.—I thank God I could help you a little—you too, Sweet one, become firm & unwavering, show the masterhand & mind. Do not bend down to a man like Trepov (whom you cannot either trust or respect). You have said yr. say & had yr. fight about Protopopov & it shall not be in vain we suffered—stick to him, be firm, don't give in—as then never more any peace, they will begin worrying you in the future yet worse when you don't agree, as they see that by persistent obstinacy they force you to give in—as hard as they, I mean Tr. & Rodz.[yanko] (with the

evil) on one side—I shall stand against them, (with God's holy man [Rasputin]) don't you stick to them, but to us, who live only for you[,] Baby< & Russia. [b]

To follow our Friend's< councils, lovy—I assure is right—He prays so hard day & night for you—& He has kept you where you are—only be as convinced as I am & as I proved it to Ella< & shall for ever—then all will go well. In les "Amis de Dieux" one of the old men of God said, that a country, where a man of God helps the Sovereign, will never be lost & its true—only one must listen trust & ask advice—not think He does not know. God opens everything to Him, that is why people, who do not grasp His soul, so immensely admire His wonderful brain—ready to understand anything; & when He blesses an undertaking—it succeeds & if He advises people—one can be quiet that they are good—if they later on change that is already not His fault—but He will be less mistaken in people than we are—experience in life blessed by God. [c]

He [Rasputin] entreats for Makarov to be quicker changed—& I fully agree. I told Sht.[yurmer] that it was wrong he recomended [sic] him, that I told him that he is far from a devoted man,[280, 324] & now the chief thing is to find really devoted men—in deed & not only in words, & to them we must cling. Don't let Trep. deceive you about people. Prot.[opopov] & Shakhov.[skoi] are only for us, I mean are above all things devoted & love honestly & openly. And Dobrov.[ol'sky] too.—Should Nik. Mikh. [re]turn (wh. God forbid), be hard & give it him for his letter[396] & goings on in town<.—I send you Grigorovich's paper one sent me.— Went at 11 to Znamenia (which I more than ever love) & to the hospital<—sat much—Now receive 4 officers, then we all sledge. Paul< comes to tea then Pogul.[yaev] then Church & in the evening [I will] see our Friend, who will give strength. My spirit is firm & live[s] for you, you & you—my heart & soul.—I wonder, whether you will have a review of the St. George's regiment, wld. be so nice—if not the 6-th, then another day,—Ducky< leaves to-night to see Missy [Maria, queen of Roumania,] & perhaps bring all the Children back, according to circumstances.— [d]

Now I must end. Sleep well & peacefully, beloved Angel. The Holy Virgin guards you & Gr.[igory]< prays for you & we do all so hard. I cover you with tenderest, passionately loving kisses & caresses & long to be of use & help in carrying yr. heavy Cross. God bless & protect you, my Nicky. Ever yr. very own Wify. [P.S.] I hope you will like the book.[419] The cushions are for yr. sopha, wh. is so empty. The ashtrays for the dinnertable or train.—Always near you sharing all—the good is coming, the turn has begun. [e]

---

417. Nicholas II's brother Michael ("Misha") served in the Caucasus as commander of the Second Caucasian Corps and the "Savage Division," also called the *Native Division*. This cavalry division was comprised of Caucasian mountaineers (e.g., the Abreki, mentioned here) who did not speak Russian. It is famous for its role in 1917.

No. 1601/ Telegram 1. Stavka> Tsarskoe Selo. 5 Dec 1916. 17.43> 18.20. To her majesty. We [have] arrived safely [from Smolensk[412]]. Fine, bright evening, two [degrees] of cold. Once more tenderest thanks [for] sweet letter. Hope [you] are feeling well. Fondest kisses from both. Niki

No. 1602/ Telegram 32. Tsarskoe Selo> Stavka. 5 Dec 1916. 20.22> 22.00. To his majesty. Warm thanks for both telegrams. Just now returned from church. All five of us send our most tender and warm wishes, blessings and kisses. Sleep well, dear ones. Alix

No. 1603/ Telegram 38. Tsarskoe Selo> Stavka. 6 Dec 1916. 8.29> 10.10. To his majesty. Good morning, my dear. Hope you will joyfully encounter this great day [(your nameday)] many times yet. [I] tenderly embrace and kiss [you]. [I] thought much about you yesterday evening. Wish you a peaceful, happy mood! [We] feel you with us. [I] warmly kiss you both. Alix

No. 1604/ Telegram 12. Stavka> Tsarskoe Selo. 6 Dec 1916. 9.49> 10.50. To her majesty. Loving thanks for your wishes and presents. Tiny< gave them over from you all last evening. Nice, wintry weather. Thoughts and prayers together. Tender love. Niki

No. 1605/ Telegram 40. Tsarskoe Selo> Stavka. 6 Dec 1916. 10.26> 12.50. To his majesty. Today old Taneev celebrates twentieth anniversary directing your chancellery. Will you not send him telegram? After Mass they will have their luncheon with us. In heart and soul with you. [I] bless and kiss [you] both. Alix

No. 1606/ Her No. 633.   Tsarskoe Selo. Dec. 6th 1916.
My own sweet Angel,
   Many happy returns of the day—tenderest blessings & fondest goodwishes & deepest love! So sad not to be together for your Namesday [sic]—the first time in 22 years! But it was for the good you had to leave, so of course I don't dream of grumbling.—Nice snow covers all & 5° of frost. We sledged yesterday, but it humped [i.e., bumped] still rather. B.< came, hang him.—Paul< took tea & was nice. I wired to you about Papa Taneev being 20 years at the head of yr. chancelry [sic]—she[, his daughter, Anna Vyrubova,] found it out by chance as they give him a big luncheon there.— Yesterday we spent the evening cosily, calmly in the little house [of Anna Vyrubova]. Dear big Lili< came too later & Munia Golovina. He [Rasputin] was in good, cheery spirits—one sees how [he] lives & thinks for you the whole time & that all shld. be well. Is anxious, Trepov come there, fears he will upset you again, bring false things, news I mean & try to come with his candidats [sic].—Take one instead of him for [minister of] the railways—pitty [sic] you don't approve of Valuev for that place—as such a honest & true man. [a]
   Then get quicker rid of Makarov,[324] don't dawdle (forgive me) & I wish you wld. take Dobrovolsky—the story Trepov told you seems untrue (there is another of the same name also Senator)—I send you a paper she copied about a story [i.e., episode] Trepov & good Dobrovolsky had—he thinks it may be a story of revenge.—But Kalinin<—keep—keep him, my Love! I know I bore you, forgive me, but I would never do so, if I did not fear yr. wavering again. Stick to yr. decision—do not give in, how can one hesitate between this simple, honest man who loves us so deeply —& Trepov whom we cannot trust, nor respect or love, on the contrary.—Tell him that question exists no more & you forbid his touching it again & playing with

Rodzianko, who wants Protopopov also to leave. He serves you & not Rodzianko & once you have said you keep Protopopov you do not intend changing & he is to work with him. How dare he go against you—thunder on the table; don't give in (as you said, you wld. at the end)—be the master; listen to your staunch Wify & our Friend<, believe us. Look at Kalinin & Trepov's face—clearly one sees the difference—black & white, let your soul read rightly.—[b]

Its snowing away, but still we want to sledge & get a little air. The couple Benkendorf [P. C. and Madame Benckendorff], Zizi<, Isa<, Nast.[inka]<, Trina<, Ania<, Ressin< and Apraxin< lunched with us & we drank to yr. dear health. Paul was also in Church. The soldiers stood outside afterwards & congratulated.[418] All my thoughts are with you—I fear a very dull day with heaps of people, but I hope you still can get a walk & Baby< his game in the woods. Congratulate you with all the regimental feasts. The eldest Colonel for the 4th rifles [regiment] brought us bouquets. He says he has just received the 4-th rifle reg. & leaves soon.—Agoo wee one, big and small, he [i.e., me] loves you beyond words. [c]

In the evening we shall go to the hospital<.—Our Friend is so contented with our girlies, says they have gone through heavy "courses" for their age & their souls have much developed—they are really great dears & so nice now with A.[nia]<. They have shared all our emotions & it has taught them to see people with open eyes, so that it will be a great help to them later in life. Tiny< feels so much in its little wide awake soul too—& I cannot ever thank God enough for the marvellous blessing He has sent me in you & them—we are one, which is, alas, so, so rare now a days—closely knit together.—[d]

I received 2 lovely telegr. fr. Arkhangelsk from the monarchist party & I answered with our Friend, & He begs you absolutely to allow the telegr. to be printed. Tell Fred.[ericks] to give them the permission—& also their first & mine in the "Novoye Vremya"—it will open people's eyes & be a counteract against the Pss. Vass. [Princess Sophia Nikolaevna Vasil'chikova's] letter (wh. M-me Zizi is quite disgusted & shocked with)[419]—& a smack to old nasty Balashov.[413]—The good is coming, & let "society & Duma" see that Russia loves yr. old Wify & stands up for her against them all.—Zizi admired their touching wire very much; I on purpose answered personally. The snow is such a blessing too, St. Nicolas [sic] blesses my Sweetheart.—Goodbye, my, Sunshine, my adored husband, I love you, love you, yearn over you, kiss & gently caress you, press you to my burning heart. Ever yr. very Own unto death and beyond. [e]

---

418. Nabokov arranges the text that follows as if it were a separate letter, both dated December 6, 1916. (*Pis'ma imperatritsy*, II, pp. 246-249) Sergeev arranges the material as if it were a continuation of the same letter—indeed, the same paragraph. (*Perepiska*, V, p. 164) Stylistically, there seems to be a break, and a new paragraph is certainly indicated. The text which follows was probably a "P.S.," though Alexandra did not so indicate. See No. 1620a,b, and other letters below for similar "Post Scripts."

419. "This was a well-known letter of the wife of Prince B. A. Vasil'chikov imploring the Empress to break with Rasputin." (Nabokov: Alexandra, *Pis'ma imperatritsy*, II, p. 248n)

No. 1607.   Ts.[arist] Stavka. Dec. 6th 1916.
My own beloved One,

Tenderest fondest thanks for your dear kind letter & also for the little presents of yesterday[420] & those that came today with your letter! I drank of every word of love you wrote me! We went to church as usual this morning & coming back I saw all the officers & soldiers, whose holiday it is today, standing along our road & congratulated them. After that I received the people of the Staff & then had the usual doklad [report] wh. was short, as I spoke with Gurko last evening. We have just finished luncheon. It is real fine winter here, lots of snow & such a light dry air. The voyage was very good. We all slept till goodness knows what hour—in the train. Walked with A.[leksei] at every station. I read with delight "The Wall of Partition" & felt rested after such a book.[420] Lots of telegrams as usual. [Our daughter] Olga will be gladly astonished to have been named chef [i.e., colonel-in-chief] of 2nd Kubansk. Plastunsky Battalion.[75] I remembered that two of them had no chefs, so it seemed good to give [her] the 2^d bat. & Boris<, who saw [i.e., inspected] them all down there, the 5th bat. Now good-bye, my own Sweetheart. God bless you & the girlies! Many burning kisses fr. your own old Nicky.

---

420. These presents were to mark the festival day of St. Nicholas on December 6; all Russian men named Nicholas celebrated this as their "nameday"; for many it was more important than their birthdays. *The Wall of Partition* was a novel by Florence Barclay, one of the royal family's favorite writers. The Kuban Cossacks lived on the Black Sea coast between the Dnieper and Bug Rivers.

No. 1608/ Telegram 33. Stavka> Tsarskoe Selo. 6 Dec 1916. 22.17> 23.20. To her majesty. Tenderly do I thank you and [the] children for letters and games.[419] God bless you. Sleep well. Niki

---

No. 1609/ Her No. 634.   Ts.[arskoe] S[elo]. Dec. 7th 1916.
My own Beloved,
    You cannot imagine Olga's joy when she received yr. telegram—she got quite pink & could not read it aloud.—She will write to you herself to-day. Thanks tenderly Darling, for having given her this beautiful surprise—she felt & her sisters as tho' it were her birthday. At once she sent off a wire to the "Plastuni".[75] Did you get news fr. Kirill?< Till now no answer to my telegram I sent the 5-th evening. It seems Irina [Yusupova] is ill again & so Xenia< had to put off going now to Kiev, so disappointing to poor Motherdear<. My Siberians congratulate you & Katia Ozerov. [a]
    5° of frost & looks as tho' it wld. snow more, very grey.—Alas, we heard Baby's< voice very badly by telephone. Mr. Gillard's [sic] is lower & so carries further. Hope you were not too tired & bored yesterday.—Have you begun iodine again, it wld. be good, think.—I go now always at 11 to Znamenia< & hospital<, as not many wounded & then I can finish my papers before.—Lovy, did you have a reprimand written to Balashov?[413] Please, do its the very least you can do.—I cover you with kisses for yr. sweet letter I received, I never thought you would find time for a letter.—I saw Kolenkin in the hospital, had not been on leave for 9 months. They are off & on in their trenches.—Cannot write any more to-day, Lovy my Angel. Only one thing, do put off seeing Trepov, am so affraid [sic] he will worry & make you decide things wh. in a quiet moment you wld. not agree to. Be firm about Kalinin<, for our sake.—Have you said about that nice telegr. to be printed, its a rarely touching one & will do good as Taneev & others also say. [See Letter No. 1606e.]—Blessings & endless kisses fr. yr. very, very own Sunny. [b]

No. 1610/ Telegram 64. Tsarskoe Selo> Stavka. 7 Dec 1916. 14.37> 15.15. To his majesty. From all my heart I thank you both, my dears, for dear letters. Am happy with them. Light snow, mild weather. After hospital< are going sledging. All warmly embrace [you]. Alix

No. 1611.   Ts.[arist] Stavka. Dec. 7th 1916.
My own sweet Sunny,
   Thank you so much for your dear letter. I will tell Fred.[ericks] about those telegrams you got fr. Astrakhan.[421] That man often wires to me—I remember the times when Stolypin lived—he used to send me such well meant telegrams. It is also he who disapproved Shuvaev's and Grigorovich's speeches in the Duma. Yesterday I was overpowered by wires, because they were not forbidden: enormous quantities came, I have not finished answering yet. The cynema [sic] was most interesting last evening; we atlast [sic] know who that "mysterious hand" is? Her cousin & bridegroom would you believe? There was great excitement in the theater on account of this.[424] On Dec. 17th all the glavnokomanduyushchie [commanders-in-chief] are coming here for a military council, as it is time to prepare our plans for the next spring. I hope the day after to be able to leave for home! Be quite sure, my Lovebird, that I shall know how to answer Trep.[ov] when he comes.—In the evenings I hurriedly read some chapters of your engli.[sh] book[420] wh. refreshes to the brain. God bless you my Darling and the girlies. I kiss you all ever so tenderly & remain with fondest love ever your own huzy   Nicky.

---

421. This may be a slip of the pen. Alexandra wrote *Arkhangel'sk* not *Astrakhan* in Letter No. 1606e which provoked this response from the tsar. In Letter No. 1613a, however, the empress follows Nicholas in writing "Astrakhan."

No. 1612/ Telegram 64. Stavka> Tsarskoe Selo. 7 Dec 1916. 18.10> 19.05. To her majesty. Many thanks [for] dearest letter. Much snow. 8 [degrees] of cold. Tenderest kiss from both. Niki

---

No. 1613/ Her No. 635.   Ts.[arskoe] S[elo]. Dec. 8th 1916.
My own beloved Sunshine,
   Fancy, yr. having such cold weather—here are 5 degrees of frost wh. fall to 3 in the day time. We think of going to Novgorod then, as I told you. Get into the train Saturday for the night, leaving very early—reaching then Sunday morning, spending a few hours, looking at Churches & I believe a few hospitals & home again, spending the night in the train & going fr. our wagon Monday morning to the hospital, then we miss no work.—I shall send for Ressin< & tell him all—don't remember who the governor is [he was M. V. Islavin]—shall not keep it a secret this time, so as to see more people. But always so shy without you, my Lovy dear.—My nice old Princess Golitzin ([who is a member of our] committee for our prisoners) found the telegr. fr. Astrakhan[421] lovely & begged they should be printed everywhere. Another Prince Golitzin ([A. D. Golitsyn] from Kharkov) spoke in the Conseil de l' Empire< & not at all well, & one congratulates this one[, his brother N. D. Golitsyn, soon to become chairman of the council of ministers] for the

speech, he was furious—also found that one ought to take off court dresses[422] of such people. [a]

Pity you don't put Shcheglovitov now,[423] he wld. tell you such things at once (if cld. not stop speeches even) & you cld. deprive them of their court rank—one cannot be severe enough now, therefore Balashov[413] needs a strong rebuke—don't be kind & weak—forgive me Lovy.—Such very fond thanks for yr. sweet letter, Lovebird, <u>such</u> joy to hear fr. you.—We also several times thought it might be the bridegroom [who was] the "mysterious hand"—can imagine how excited all were.[424] But to have you back, what joy it will be, my own Sweetheart—only have the Duma cleverly shut—be firm as iron with Trepov & stick to Kalinin the truest friend.—Got dear letters fr. [my sister] Victoria & Georgi, [her son, the prince of Battenburg] who thanks awfully for the present.—Now goodbye, my Angel, sweetest of loves, treasure dear. I bless & kiss you over & over again, yr. own, very own   Wify. [P.S.] Be firm—be the master.— [b]

422. "Court dress" refers to the formal uniform worn by an official, indicating his rank in the service. If an official was discharged, he also lost the right to wear the "dress" of his former rank.

423. I. G. Shcheglovitov was a member of the State Council. As the empress recommended, the tsar appointed him president of the State Council on January 1 (O.S.), 1917. Rasputin had favored him as Sturmer's replacement as minister of foreign affairs, but that appointment went to N. N. Pokrovsky. See Letter No. 1577a.

424. The "Mysterious Hand" was a serial thriller Nicholas and his men were viewing at Stavka. Nicholas saw the conclusion—and it interested him so much that he told his wife the identity of the "mysterious hand" (Letter No. 1611). Alexandra's response to that comment misled V. D. Nabokov, who published Alexandra's letters without enjoying access to the tsar's letters. Nabokov was typical of those who were (and are) everwilling to think the worst of the fallen tsar and his wife. Nabokov concluded that Alexandra's mysterious passage "evidently refers to spiritual seances at Mogilev"! (Alexandra, *Pis'ma imperatritsy*, II, p. 250n) Critics often claimed Nicholas and Alexandra were devotees of the occult. Were that true, evidence of it would appear in the Nicky-Sunny correspondence. It does not—nor anywhere else.

No. 1614/ Telegram 70. Tsarskoe Selo> Stavka. 8 Dec 1916. 16.15> 16.42. To his majesty. With all my soul thank you both for dear letters. [We] went sledging. [I] tenderly kiss and bless [you]. Alex

No. 1615/ Telegram 94. Stavka> Tsarskoe Selo. 8 Dec 1916. 18.57> 19.25. To her majesty. Many thanks [for] beloved letters and photos. Gen. [Hanbury-] Williams' son died from illness. He is going for a week to town<. Bright, cold day. Tenderest kisses. Niki

No. 1616.   Ts.[arist] Stavka. Dec. 8th 1916.
My beloved Sweetheart,

Ever so many thanks for your dear letter. I shall receive Trepoff on Monday Dec 12. Don't worry, my Love. Now I am quiet & <u>firm</u> & will know what to answer. He comes also for serious railway questions to be settled here with Gurko. I gave the telegrams [see Nos. 1606e, 1609b, 1611, 1613a] to Fred.[ericks]. He asked to find out about that man who sent them before printing them, which I find safer, too. The answer will come through Kalinin<, so you can find out from him sooner & decide it there.—Luckily I have not got much papers, but had to receive these days old Dudel (Adlerberg), Solovoi and Ozerov. The book you sent me is very prettily edited, I am glad to possess "Hadzhi Murat".[425] Well can I imagine Olga's wild joy. [A. N.] Grabbe and all our cossacks were also quite excited & he showed me Olga's answer—very good! Every evening I enjoy two chapters of The Wall of Part.[ition],[420] & shall soon finish it. Now we have real fine winter with lots of snow. I must end. God bless you and the girlies! I kiss you my own Sunny with passionate kisses & loves so endlessly. Best love to them & A[nia]<. Please thank her for letter & present. Ever your own old Nicky.

425. Hadzhi Murat (or Murad) was the lieutenant of Shamil, leader of the Moslem tribes which fought the Russians in the Caucasus during the nineteenth century. Russians admired the gallantry and tenacity of these enemies; perhaps the empress sent Leo Tolstoy's story hoping it would have a bracing effect on her husband.

No. 1617/ Telegram 71. Tsarskoe Selo> Stavka. 8 Dec 1916. 22.15> 23.00. To his majesty. Just now learned old count [Fredericks] prevented publication of wonderful telegram. [See Letters No. 1606e, 1609b, 1611, 1613a, 1616, 1619.] This is a disgrace. Consider it essential to do this after this letter. Please take measures. Sleep peacefully. [I] tenderly kiss and bless [you]. Alix

No. 1618/ Telegram 73. Tsarskoe Selo> Stavka. 9 Dec 1916. 13.48> 14.08. To his majesty. Warm thanks to both my dears. In thoughts and prayers always together. Light snow, mild weather. Warmly embrace [you]. Alix

No. 1619/ Telegram 101. Stavka> Tsarskoe Selo. 9 Dec 1916. 18.35> 19.15. To her majesty. Warmest thanks. Told old count [Fredericks] to leave matter about telegram[s] to Kalinin's< care. Fine, 7 deg. [We] both kiss tenderly. Niki

No. 1620/ No. 636.   Ts.[arskoe] S[elo]. Dec. 9th 1916.
My own Angel,
    Ever such warm, burning thanks for your dear letter. I am glad you like that nice English book[420]—its so refreshing amongst the sorrow & worries of this world. We see our Friend< this evening, am very glad. Poor Ania's< leg ached awfully yesterday, sort of Drachenschuss [lumbago] & ischias [sciatica]—screamed from pain—now has B.< so lies to day in bed, dont know whether she can go [with us to Novgorod] to morrow. We take Nastinka<, Ressin< & Apraxin<. The girls rejoice, as they love sleeping in the train—but it will be sad alone.—Sleep so little when you are not there.—Am receiving Rittich, saw Dobrovolsky & spoke much about Misha's< G. obshchina [community station] & the senate.—Poor General [Hanbury-]Williams, am awfully sorry for the poor man. [See Letter No. 1615.]—Please, bow to the Belgian [Baron de Ricquel] fr. me.—How are things going in Roumania? & generally at the war? Lovy my Angel, goodbye & God bless & keep you, cover you with very tenderest kisses. Y. own Wify. [a]
    Got a letter fr. Irene<. Mossy [Margarita, princess of Hesse] lost two sons, & now the eldest couple of twins are out at the war.—A.[nia]< saw Kalinin< yesterday, who said that Trepov has combined with Rodzianko to let go [i.e., recess] the Duma from Dec. 17-Jan. 8.[426] so as that the deputies should have no time to leave

Petrograd for the holidays & to keep them here in hand. Our Friend & Kal.[inin] entreat you to close the Duma not later than the 14-th Feb., [though the] 1-st [of February?] or 15-th [of January?] even [would be still better], otherwise there will be no peace for you & no works got through. In the Duma they only fear this, a longer intermission & Trepov intends to catch you, saying that it will be worse if the people return home & spread their news—but our Friend says, nobody believes these delegates when <u>they are alone</u> in their homestead, [they] only have strenght [sic] when together. Lovy mine, be firm & trust our Friends advice—its only for <u>your good</u> & all who love you think aright. Dont harken, neither to Gurko nor Grigor.[ovich], if they ask for a short intermission they don't understand what they do. I wld. not write all this, were I not so affraid [sic] for you & yr. gentle kindness always read[y] to give in, when not backed up by poor old wify, A.[nia] & our Friend—therefore the untrue & bad hate our influence (which is but for the good). [b]

Trepov was at Kalinin's cousins (Lamsdorf), not knowing they were his relations, & said he was going on the 11-th to you & wld. insist before you (brute he is!) that Protopopov should leave. Lovy, look at their faces—Trepov & Protopopov—can't one clearly see the latter's is cleaner, honester [sic] & more true.—You <u>know</u> you are right, keep up yr. head, order Trepov to work with him—he dare not be against your order—bang on the table. Lovy, do you want me to come for a day to give you courage & firmness? Be the <u>Master</u>. One is against Kalinin for stopping assemblies of "Unions"[427][—]he did quite rightly. Our Friend says [the following quote is in Russian] "that the confusion which was due in Russia during or after the war has arrived and if he (you) had not taken the place of Nik.[olai] Nik.[olaevich], he would now be thrown off the throne". Be of good cheer, the screamers will quieten down—only send off the Duma quicker & for longer—trust me—you know Trepov flirts with Rodzianko—all know it, & to you he slyly fibs its out of politics.—Go to the lovely Image [icon] & get strenght [sic] & power there— <u>remember</u> always our Friends dream, it meens [sic] so, oh so much for you & us all.—[c]

426. Alexandra was offended that Trepov acted independently of the tsar in going to Rodzyanko, president of the Duma, to negotiate a holiday recess. Although one would not think so from what Alexandra writes, Trepov and Rodzyanko were monarchists and personally loyal to Nicholas II. Trepov opposed an expanded role for the Duma in the Russian political system. Alexandra was not impressed, she disliked both Trepov and Rodzyanko. "News of this [that the Duma would be recessed from December 17, 1916, to January 8, 1917] appeared in the papers. In fact, the Duma's work was broken off on the 16th and the papers said that members of the Duma found this to be unexpected." (Nabokov: Alexandra, *Pis'ma imperatritsy*, II, p. 251n) See Footnote 416 for Trepov's relations with Protopopov.

427. The police in Moscow on December 9 (O.S.), 1916, prohibited sessions of the unions of zemstvoes and of towns. (*Ibid.*, p. 252n)

No. 1621.   Ts.[arist] Stavka. Dec. 9. 1916.
My own beloved Sunny,

Tenderest thanks for your dear letter. I am very glad you have decided to visit Novgorod, the oldest town in Russia. You will feel quite different when you come back. I have always remarked that after trips in the country. The governor of Novgorod is an excellent man. I like [him]. His name is Islavin. Please give him my compliments. Hope Mme. B.< will not disturb you or tire you. I have changed the date for receiving Trepoff for [i.e., to] to-morrow Saturday. I intend being firm, cutting & disagreeable. Thank you for the photos–I am afraid I have the same ones already. [a]

Fred.[ericks] got letters at a time [i.e., simultaneously] fr. Wrangel[428] & Larka Vorontsov[-Dashkov], both complaining bitterly about Misha's< wife, [the Countess Brasova,] for not allowing them to speak to him even about his health. According to what they write, the doctors who treated him insisted he should go through a course of treatment & rest in a mild climate. If he would only remain longer in the Crimea, that would help him very much. But he or perhaps she want to return to Gatchina, what [i.e., which] the doctors find bad. And none of them can get to Misha to explain this. So I think I shall wire to him to remain there a month longer.–Now my beloved Darling, I must end. God bless you & your journey. Tenderest fondest kisses fr. your own old huzy <u>Nicky</u>. [b]

---

428. Baron Peter Wrangel was a prominent White general during the civil war of 1918-1920. At this time he was a major-general and a.d.c. to the tsar's brother, Michael Alexandrovich ("Misha").

No. 1622/ Telegram 74. Tsarskoe Selo> Stavka. 10 Dec 1916. 11.52> 13.45. To his majesty. 8 degrees of frost for the first time [this winter]. Tell [our son] Aleksei that I am in despair that he will not receive letter today, but am sure I forgot to write him yesterday because am running late. Today at 2 o'clock opening here of his hospital which has been housed in Military Academy. In prayers and thoughts am with you. Tenderly kiss you. Alix

---

No. 1623/ Telegram 75. Tsarskoe Selo> Stavka. 10 Dec 1916. 14.12> 15.25. To his majesty. Warmly thank [you] both for dear letters. Read mine today as soon as you receive it. Please, dear. Tenderly kiss and embrace [you]. Will be there to-morrow for service in cathedral [at Novgorod]. Will stay until 6, as there are so many hospitals. Will think of you. Alix

---

No. 1624/ Telegram 102. Stavka> Tsarskoe Selo. 10 Dec 1916. 18.17> 19.05. To her majesty. Many thanks [for] letter. Read it with interest. Aleksei understands you could not write. Fondest blessings and love for your journey. Niki

---

No. 1625/ Her No. 637.   Ts.[arskoe] S[elo]. Dec. 10th 1916.
My own beloved One,

Always have to write in a flying hurry, heaps of Rost.[ovtsev]'s papers I had to finish, then Ania's< leg being bad went to her 3 times a day, & received, so that scarcely a free moment. But she hopes to go with us this evening. This morning first time [this winter it was] 7 degrees, its brighter because of the snow, but we have no sun.–I enclose a coin sent for you & an Image on silk;–& then some papers to read through from Kalinin<, in case Voeikov did not give you the duplicates. On Manuilov's paper I <u>beg</u> you to write "<u>discontinue the case</u>" & send it to Minister of Justice [Makarov]. Batiushin [N. S. Batyushin] who had to do with the whole thing, now himself came to A.[nia] to beg one shld. stop it, as he at last understood it was an ugly story, got up by others to harm our Friend<, Pitirim etc. all that fat [A. N.] Khvostov's fault. General Aleks.[eev] knew about it through Batiushin again later. Otherwise in a few days one begins the instruction [trial–see

Footnote 419] & there can be very disagreeable talks all over again, & bring up that horrible scandle [sic] fr. last year.[429] Before others Khvostov said the other day that he regrets that "Tchik"[430] did not succeed to finish off our Friend. And his courtdress was left him alas, alas![422] [a]

Well, please at once without delay send Manuilov's paper to Makarov[430] otherwise too late.—Lovy, wont you quicker change Mak.[arov] & take Dobrovolsky [for his replacement as minister of justice]—Makarov really is an enemy (of me absolutely,[431] therefore of you too), & don't listen to Trepov's protests. He, of course, will speak against Dobrovolsky as has his own candidates—but [Dobrovol'sky] is a devoted man which is much nowadays.—And why won't you have honest Valuev, whom we know so well, honest & devoted as Minister of railways & Communications [in place of Trepov]? I enclose a letter from Sukhomlinov to our Friend, please read it through, as there he explains all clearly about his affair, wh. you must send for & not all to go to the Conseil de l'Empire< as then there will be no saving of poor Sukhomlinov.[405]—He writes so clearly everything—do read it through & act according—why shld. he suffer & not Kokovtzev [Kokovtsov] (who wld. not give the money) nor Sergei< who on account of her[432a] has just as much fault. [b, c]

Just received your letter. From all my heart I thank you for it very tenderly. Now Trepov is with you, & I feel so anxious. I just saw Kalinin—is so glad you got all the papers through Voeikov, so I won't send them again to bother you. He is most anxious you shld. sooner send away the Duma & for longer—in 10 years they have never had a recess like this, so short & then one has no time to do things. The Conseil de l'Empire is mad agreeing with the Duma about freedom of [i.e., from] censorship. My head goes round & I seem to write bosh. —Only be firm, firm.—Thank God one stopped the meetings at Moscou [sic], six times (Kalinin was till 4 in the morning at the telephone), but Lvov succeeded in reading a paper before the police got them in one place.[427] You see—Kalinin works well & firmly & does not flirt with the Duma but only thinks of us.—This letter must go now. Zhevakhov comes directly.—Shall give over your message to Islavin to-morrow—will be a nice change there;—only shall miss you awfully. You will in consequence get this letter on Monday. God bless & protect you! Cover you with kisses & tender caress. Ever yr. very very own old Wify. [d]

---

429. "[T]hat horrible scandle fr. last year" refers to A. N. Khvostov's plot to have Rasputin assassinated. "Tchik" was apparently the empress's code name for the would-be assassin, Boris Michaelovich Rzhevsky. See Fuhrmann, *Rasputin*, pp. 165-166.

430. Ivan Fedorovich Manasevich-Manuilov was an unsavory character with ties to Rasputin and Sturmer. Gen. N. S. Batyushin, chairman of the Commission to Investigate Activities Endangering the Home Front, caught Manasevich-Manuilov in an attempt to extort money from a Petrograd Bank. Manasevich-Manuilov's trial was scheduled to begin on December 15, 1916; it promised to implicate Rasputin (and even the empress) in Manasevich-Manuilov's activities. Although Justice Minister Makarov was loyal to Nicholas, he was willing to let events proceed, even if Alexandra and Rasputin were discredited. Alexandra wanted the trial stopped and Manasevich-Manuilov freed. Nicholas did both, as we see in Letter No. 1647b. The resulting scandal accelerated the decline of Nicholas's regime.

431. Alexandra hated A. A. Makarov because he disliked Rasputin. (Makarov as minister of the interior was also clumsy in retrieving and returning letters the empress wrote to Rasputin which fell into unfriendly hands and appeared in hectograph copies in 1912.) Nicholas dismissed Makarov in late 1912. The increasing shortage of talent available to the tsar led him to restore Makarov to power as minister of justice in July 1915 over objections from Alexandra and Rasputin (see Letters No. 1043, 1246, 1283b,

1297, 1587c, 1595b, 1600d, 1606b). Alexandra pressed Nicholas to correct his "mistake" and dismiss Makarov again. Alexandra favored N. A. Dobrovol'sky, assistant-minister of justice. The tsarina finally had her way. Dobrovol'sky replaced Makarov as minister of justice on December 22 (O.S.), 1916, and held that office until the March Revolution.

432a. "She" refers to Nicholas's former lover, the ballerina Mathilde Kschessinska. See Footnote 115.

No. 1626.   Ts.[arist] Stavka. Dec. 10th 1916.
My own beloved Angel,
    Many thanks for your dear letter. Yesterday driving out to the wood of the old Stavka Aleksei loves so, we went in and prayed a second before the Virgin's image. I feel content having done this, as it was your particular wish. Thank you also for writing those details of Kal.[inin]'s< conversation with A[nia]<. I hope your trip will go off well & Novgorod will please you. I was there once in [the] summer of 1904, just before Babykins< was born. In Rumania things are not famous [i.e., good], for the first reason that our troops cannot get there on account of the railways being blocked by any number of refugees. In Dobrudja our troops have to retreat right till the Danube, as they were in such small numbers that they could not defend their long thin front. By about the 15th Dec. we hope the concentration [of our forces] will be more or less completed & perhaps about Christmas time we might begin the march onward. So you see the situation there is not a gay one. Now, my own Lovebird, I must end. God bless you and our girlies. Give A.< my love and tell her how sorry I am she suffers so fr. her leg. With fondest burning kisses, Sunny-mine, ever your own old Nicky.

No. 1627.[432b]   Ts.[arist] Stavka. Dec. 11 1916.
My own beloved Darling,
    As it is Sunday, I have no time to write a letter—church, doklad [report] & big luncheon. To-morrow I will write about my conversation with Trepoff. I hope your trip to Novgorod will not over tire you. Today it is thawing, very disagreeable. God bless you, my little Lovebird! I kiss you and all tenderly. Your Nicky.

432b. I could not find this postcard in the State Archive of the Russian Federation (GARF). It is translated from Sergeev: Nicholas and Alexandra, *Perepiska,* V, p. 177.

No. 1628/ Telegram 77. Novgorod> Stavka. 11 Dec 1916. 15.10> 17.05. To his majesty. Wonderful trip, 2-hour service in cathedral church, marvellous. Then visited hospitals and ancient church storehouse and residence of the archbishop, very interesting. Am having lunch in my compartment [i.e., train couch]—am tired—and still face looking at a mass of hospitals and churches. Ioanchik< and Andriusha [Andrew Alexandrovich] are here. Tenderly kiss and bless [you]. Governor [Islavin] greets you with deep bow. Alix

No. 1629/ Telegram 103 in Russian. Stavka> Chudovo. 11/XII 1916. 18.40> 21.00. To her majesty. Sincerely thank you for letters and telegram. Am glad you remained pleased with Novgorod. Hope you are not tired; warm, snow, warmly embrace all. Niki

No. 1630/ Telegram 78. Novgorod> Stavka. 11 Dec 1916. 20.49> 23.17. To his majesty. Visited 5 hospitals, Tatiana's shelter [see Letter No. 1633e], churches, monasteries. Spoke with your old Father Nikodim and staritsa [Maria Mikhailovna]. Charming impression. Sleep peacefully. Heartily kiss [you]. Alix

No. 1631/ Telegram 80. Tsarskoe Selo> Stavka. 12 Dec 1916. 9.48> 11.15. To his majesty. Upon my return found both dear letters. Heartily thank you. Spent night on train, very tired, everything hurt, but impression wonderful, cheering. Very happy you were at dear image. [See No. 1626.] We all kiss you [both] warmly. Alix

No. 1632/ Telegram 83. Tsarskoe Selo> Stavka. 12 Dec 1916. 17.40> 18.55. To his majesty. Warmly thank you for dear card. Warm, light snow. Rested during day as was very tired. Will think of you in particular this evening. Sleep well. Blessings and kisses from all. Alix

No. 1633/ Her No. 638.   Ts.[arskoe] S[elo]. Dec. 12th 1916.
Beloved Sweetheart,
     For a precious letter & card my tenderest thanks. I am <u>too</u> happy you went to the dear Image [see Letter No. 1626]—such peace there— one feels away fr. all worries that minute whilst pouring out one's heart & soul in prayer to her [the Virgin Mary], to whom so many come with their sorrows.—Well Lovy, Novgorod was a success—tho' awfully tiring, the soul was uplifted & gave us all strength—I with my heart & A.[nia]< with her aching legs—we got about.—Of course to-day everything aches; but it was worth it. [a]
     I have [daughters] A.[nastasia] & Olga to write to you & Anastasia to Baby<, as each describes differently; & I am a bad one at it. The Governor [Islavin] was perfect, kept us "going" so that we were everywhere in good time & then let the crowd come near too. What a delightful old town, only got too soon dark—lets go together in spring when there are inundations, then they say its yet better & one can go in motor boats to the monasteries. Passing the big monument of the 1000 years of Russia, reminded me of the big picture in the big palace here.—How beautiful the Sofia sobor [cathedral] is, only standing in front one could not see so well. The service lasted 2 hours (instead of 4)—they sang exceedingly well & I was happy to begin all with mass & pray for my sweethearts. Ioanchik< & Andriusha [Andrew Alexandrovich] went everywhere with us.—We knelt to all the saints. A pitty [sic] when one has to do all in a hurry & cannot give oneself enough to prayer before each—nor look at all the details. I give Baby the Image [icon] before which we stood (& sat). Bishop Arseni held an alocution [i.e., speech], when we arrived—very touching, young bishop Aleksei found himself very handsome (a Scholar of the Lyceum) they followed us everywhere, all day long. [b]
     Then after mass 10-12 we went to the hospital next door, [the] diocese [office is] through the bishop's rooms, & to the museum of old church treasures, arranged since 3 years. Lovely old Images wh. had been lying in churches monasteries, hidden away, covered in dust. They have begun to clean them up & lovely fresh colours appear—most interesting & I should have liked to look at all another time in

detail, you wld. love it too.—Back to the train the soldiers had already dispearsed [sic] (luckily).—I lunched on my bed & A.< in her compartment. The children had I.[oanchik] & Andr.[iusha] & Islavin. We were received by his wife & daughter with flowers—bread & salt from the town.—At 2 we went off again to the Zemstvo Hospital small. Everywhere distributed Images.—[c]

Then to the "Dessiatinni" monastery—relicks [sic] of St. Barbara are kept there. Sat a moment at the Abesses [sic] room & then I asked to be taken to the old woman Maria Mikhailovna (Zhevakov told me about her) & we went to her on foot through the wet snow. She lay in bed in a small dark room,[433] so they brought a candle for us to see each other. She is 107, weares [sic] irons (now they lay near her)—generally always works, goes about, sews for the convicts & soldiers without spectacles—never washes. And of course no smell, or feeling of dirt, scraggy grey hair standing out, a sweet fine, oval face with lovely young, shining eyes & sweet smile. She blessed us & kissed us. To you she sends the apple (please eat it)—said the war wld. soon be over [the following quotes are in Russia] —"tell him that we are satisfied". To me she said, "and you the beautiful one—don't fear the heavy cross" (several times)—"for your coming to visit us, two churches will be built in Russia" (said it twice) "don't forget us, come again".—Baby she sent the wafer (too little time & fidgety around, else would have loved to speak to her), gave us all Images. Said not to worry about the children, will marry & could not hear the rest.—Forget, what she said to the girls—I made I.[oanchik] & A.[ndruisha] also go up to her, & sent Ania in;—she will no doubt write about it. I thank God for having let us see her.—It was she who some years ago told people to have that big image of the Virgin of old Russia to be copied & sent to you—one would not, said too big—then the war began & she insisted & they did so & she said we would all be at the church procession & so it was when they brought her last year in July 5 [?] before the Fedor Assembly—you remember? And you had the immense Image kept at the 4 Rifle Regiment[434]—I have a little book about her life an old servant of the Marinsky Palace gave me yesterday (her spiritual son).—She made me a far more peaceful impression than old Pasha of Diveyer. From there to the Yuriev Monastery (5 versts from town), yr. old Nikodim is there, adores & prays for you & sends you love.—[d]

I think [our daughter] Olga writes all these details to you.—Such love & warmth everywhere, feeling of God & your people, unity & purity of feelings—did me no end of good & we are already combining ideas for Tikhvin Monastery with very venerated Virgin (Image)—4 hours from here—& Vyatka & Vologda, Arkhangelsk is going to find out.—Just combine hospitals with holy places, that give strength.—All is so old & historical at Novgorod, one feels removed back to olden times. The old woman meets every one with "be joyous uncrowned bride."—[e]

We went to a little home for boys of Tatiana's committee—they brought little girls there from another one too.—Then we went to Noblemen's Club where the Ladies' Committee gave me 5000 rubles [for charitable work] & saw their hospital—splendid big hall for the men, officers next door. Took tea, quite nice, the Governor's wife & Archbishop sat next to me—few ladies, all hideous—his daughter works there as sister [i.e., nurse].—Then to the Znamenskaya church—I send you an Image I bought of her [the Virgin Mary], as so lovely & do hang her over your bed, her face is so sweet; & the Bride of Christ's (whom they hid fr. us), saw her that same day then, that she wld. help you. Then they brought a miraculous image of St. Nicolas [sic] for us to kiss—how lovely the church is! & vault's (such steep stairs)—no time to look at the "Day of Judgment" on wh. Peter the Great & Menshikov's portraits were painted by Peter's order.—Our motor stuck & the crowd pushed us off. From there to a wee chapel in a garden where on the stove of a holy bread bakery appeared (ages ago) the Virgin—it is intact & only covered in glass & with gems surrounded. Such awfully strong "perfume", the girls & I noticed it. Carried you both everywhere in soul & heart sharing together everything!!— [f]

(Write a little note to A.< as thanks, it will do her good as she shares so warmly everything—govern.[or] so nice to her & Nikodim [was too]).—From there still to Zemstvo hospital, where wounded from surrounding places had been brought—& City Hospital. At the station received an Image & apples from the Merchants. The lancer's march was played by the band of Reserve Regiment of there.—Left before 6—back here 10.20, slept night in train, morning off to hospital—now resting—evening [will see] our Friend<.—So lovely & restful, warming to the soul. Blessings & kisses without end fr. yr.   Sunny.   [P.S.] How odious about Roumania.— [g]

433. At this point in the letter, Alexandra drew a diagram of the room she was describing. A prophetic event occurred during her visit to this place. As the tsarina approached the *staritsa*, the old woman cried out, "behold, the martyred Empress Alexandra Fedorovna!" The empress apparently did not understand the remark to be ominous, but those in her party were shaken and depressed.
434. Alexandra is referring to the Icon of the Virgin of Vladimir. See Letters No. 985c (Fn. 260), 992e, 1045a, 1062b, 1063a, 1065, 1066, 1067, 1071, 1073, 1075a, 1076, 1077, 1087a, 1108b.

No. 1634.[432b]   Ts.[arist] Stavka. Dec. 12. 1916.
My dear Heart,
    Again I have no time to write a long letter. I just received a most interesting civil engineer who returned from Germany after two years there. He was with Dr. Kressen. He told me many things, it was he who kept me so long. His name is Weinberg, grandson of a Jew. I am very glad you were satisfied with what you saw in Novgorod. God bless you my Sunny! With many kisses from your old Nicky.

No. 1635/ Telegram 111. Stavka> Tsarskoe Selo. 12 Dec 1916. 19.47> 20.10. To her majesty. Thanks for two wires, please rest a day or two [so as to] not be overtired. Mild weather. Kisses to all from both [Aleksei and me]. Niki

---

No. 1636/ Telegram 88. Tsarskoe Selo> Stavka. 13 Dec 1916. 11.50> 12.15. To his majesty. Warmly thank you for card. Am very uneasy not knowing details of your conversation [with Trepov—see Letters No. 1627 and No. 1637a]. Remember, read again everything I have written in last week. Rested all morning as am very tired. Clear weather. Warmly kiss and bless [you]. Be firm. Alix

---

No. 1637/ Her No. 639.   Tsarskoe Selo. Dec. 13th 1916.
My own dearest Angel,
    Tenderest thanks for Your dear card. Am so anxious (as you have no time to write) to know about your conversation with that horrible Trepov. I read in the paper that he told Rodzianko now, that the Duma will bee [sic] shut about on the

17-th till first half of Jan. Has he any right to say this, before the official anouncement [sic] through the Senate is made?[426] I find absolutely not & ought to be told so, & Rodzianko get a reprimand for allowing it to be put in the papers. And I did so hard beg for sooner & longer. Thank God, you at last fixed no date in Jan. & can call them together in Feb. or not at all. They do not work & Tr. flirts with Rodz. all know that, 2 [times] a day they meet—that is not decent—why does he make up & try to work with him (who is false) & not with Protopopov (who is true)—that pictures the man. Old [A. A.] Bobrinsky loathes the Trep.[ovs] & knows their faults—& he is so utterly devoted to you & therefore Tr. kicked him out. [a]

My Angel, we dined yesterday at Ania's< with our Friend<. It was so nice, we told all about our journey & He said we ought to have gone straight to you as we would have brought you intense joy & blessing & I fear disturbing you! He entreats you to be firm, to be the Master & not always to give in to Tr.—you know much better than that man (still let him lead you)—& why not our Friend who leads through God? ..[391, 438] Remember why I am disliked—shows it [is] right to be firm & feared & you be the same, you a man,—only believe more in our Friend (instead of Trepov). He [Rasputin] lives for you & Russia. And we must give a strong country to Baby<, & dare not be weak for his sake, else he will have a yet harder reign, setting our faults to right & drawing the reins in tightly which you let loose. You have to suffer for faults in the reigns of your predecessors & God knows what hardships are yours. Let our legacy be a lighter one for Aleksei. He has a strong will & mind of his own, don't let things slip through yr. fingers & make him have to build up all again. Be firm, I, your wall, am behind you & won't give way—I know He leads us right—& you listen gently to a false man as Tr.! Only out of love which you bear for me & Baby—take no big steps without warning me & speaking over all quietly. Would I write thus, did I not know you so very easily waver & change your mind, & what it costs to keep you stick to Your opinion! I know I may hurt you how I write & that is my pain & sorrow—but you, Baby & Russia are far too dear to me. What about Sukhomlinov[405] & Manuilov,[430] I prepared all for you. [b]

And Dobrovolsky—a sure man—& quicker get rid of [Minister of Justice] Makarov, who do at last believe me, is a bad man. God give me the power to convince you—its harder keeping you firm than [enduring] the hate of others wh. leaves me cold. I loathe Tr.'s obstinacy. There were lots of paris [wagers] in the Duma that Pitirim wld. be sent away—now he got the cross,[435] they have become crushed & small (you see, when you show yourself the Master) & more, & more one finds it right Princess W. was sent away.[436]—You never answered me about Balashov,[413] fear, you did nothing & Frederi[c]ks is old, & no good unless I speak firmly to him.—Such a mistake not to have closed the Duma [on the] 14[th of December] & then Kal.[inin]< could get back to his work & you wld. see & talk to him.[437]—Only not a resp.[onsible] cabinet which all are mad about.[385] Its all getting calmer & better, only one wants to feel Your hand—how long, years, people have told me the same—"Russia loves to feel whip"—its their nature—tender love & then the iron hand to punish & guide.—How I wish I could pour my will into your veins! The Virgin is above you, for you, with you, remember the miracle—our Friend's vision. [c]

Soon our troops will have more force in Roumania.—Warm & thick snow.—Forgive this letter, but I could not sleep this night, worrying over you—don't hide things from me—I am strong—but listen to me, wh. means our Friend & trust us through all—& beware of Tr.—you can't love or venerate him. I suffer over you as over a tender, softhearted child—wh. needs giding [sic], but listens to bad advisers whilst a man of God's tells him [better] what to do. Sweetest Angel, come home soon—ah no, you have the Gen...![438] why not before,—I cant grasp; why the same day as the Duma—strange combination again.—And Voeikov, has that also fallen through?—Oh, dear, I must get up. Been writing Xmas-cards all the morning. Heart & soul burning with you—Love boundless, therefore seems harsh all I write—pardon, believe & understand. I love you too too deeply & cry over your faults & rejoice over every right step. God bless & protect, guard & guide you. Kisses without end. Y. truest Wify. [P.S.] Please, read this paper & Anias too. If a lie—have Rodz.'s uniform taken off.[422] [d]

435. On December 6, 1916, Pitirim was awarded a cross for his service to the clergy. Pitirim was indeed active in improving some aspects of clerical life, though he opposed such reforms as restoring the patriarchate, parishes electing their priests, etc. See Fuhrmann, *Rasputin*, p. 150.

436. Princess Maria Alexandrovna ("Masha") Vasil'chikova was an Austrian spy. She was deprived of the court rank of *fraulein* and exiled to her estates (i.e., "sent away") on January 1, 1916.

437. Newspapers reported Protopopov was sick after returning from Stavka on November 23 (O.S.), 1916. If so, it was probably another bout with syphilis. Protopopov's physician, "Doctor" Badmaev, used roots and herbs; his treatments were administered in an elegant clinic that catered to the wealthy inhabitants of Petrograd.

438. Alexandra is referring to the conference the tsar scheduled with General Gurko and other military advisors at Stavka on December 17 (O.S.), 1916. See Letter No. 1644b. The dots are in the original text.

No. 1638.   Ts.[arist] Stavka. Dec. 13th 1916.
My own beloved Sunny,

So many fond thanks for your dear long & interesting letter with lots of details about your trip to Novgorod. You saw more there than I did in 1904. Of course it would be lovely if we could go there together in [the] spring. Thanks also for the image [icon]—I am so glad to have this one particularly. Kirill< passed today with N.P.<, they both lunched and were full of the battalion & Odessa. [See Letters No. 1403, 1426a.] [a]

Well—now about Trepoff. He was low & submissive & did not touch upon the name of Prot.[opopov]. Probably my face was disagreeable & hard, as he sat fidgeting in his chair, speaking about America's note,[439] about the Duma & the near future & of course about the railways. Concerning the Duma he explained his plan—to let it go on Dec. 17th & come back on the 19th of Jan. to show them & the country that, notwithstanding all that was said by them, the gov.[ernment] wished to work together. If in January they begin to make messes & become troublesome—he is going to thunder at them (he told me in short his speech) & shut the Duma completely. That might happen in the second or third day of their New Year's session! After this he asked me what I thought? I did not deny there was logic in his plan & one advantage wh. appeared to my eyes, that, if everything happened as he thinks, we would be relieved of having the Duma by two or three weeks earlier than I had previously thought. (Middle of Jan. instead of beginning of Febr.) [b]

So I approved this idea, but made him solemnly promise he would stick to it & bring it to an end.—I on purpose went to pray before this conversation at the Virgin's image [icon] & felt quiet after. I was glad Paul< arrived yesterday, he came to tea & today he will have a doklad [report]. I just saw Vlad. Nik.<—Serg. Petr. [Fedorov] leaves for Moscow. Yesterday I saw Toll<—the com.[mander] of my Pavlograd Hussars. Looks contented, but is more stupid than ever. Now [I] must end. God bless you my own Darling, my Heart and Soul! Many kisses to you & the girlies & A[nia]< from your own old Nicky. [c]

439. Nicholas is referring to "President Wilson's note, addressed to all the belligerent Governments, asking them to make known their respective views on the conditions under which the war might be terminated." (Vulliamy, p. 306n)

No. 1639/ Telegram 113. Stavka> Tsarskoe Selo. 13 Dec 1916. 19.47> 20.40. To her majesty. Tenderest thanks. Have written today details. Happy to have [your] images [icons]. Mild weather. Fond kisses from both. Niki

No. 1640/ Telegram 94. Tsarskoe Selo> Stavka. 14 Dec 1916. 13.42> 14.30. To his majesty. Tenderly thank you both. Did not go anywhere today as [I] am very tired. Bit of snow. Bless and kiss [you]. In thoughts together. Alix

No. 1641/ Telegram 96. Tsarskoe Selo> Stavka. 14 Dec 1916. 14.20> 17.40. To his majesty. Sent you copies of two telegrams,[442] received in my name. Please, pay particular attention and heed their true words. Have Fredericks thank "warmly" from "us." Necessary to support them. [I] kiss and bless [you]. In spirit [we] are always together. Alix

No. 1642/ Her No. 640.   Tsarskoe Selo. Dec. 14th 1916.
My beloved Sweetheart,
    7° of frost & thick snow. Scarcely slept this night again, remaining till luncheon in bed as all aches still & have a slight chill. Such loving thanks for yr. dear letter. Tr.[epov] was very wrong in putting off the Duma now & wishing to call it beginning of January again, the result being (which he, Rodz.[yanko] & all counted upon), that nobody goes home & all will remain, fomenting boiling in Petrograd. He came to you meekly, as then was sure to succeed with you, had he screamed as usual, you wld. have got angry & not agreed. Lovy, our Friend< begged you to shut it[, the Duma, on the] 14-th [of December]—Ania< and I wrote it to you—& you see, they have time to make trouble now about forbidding the "Unions" to unite[440]—you to Kalinin's< paper through Voeikov[441] yesterday. He also wrote to Trep. begging it shld. be behind closed doors, Tr. never deigned to answer him—so he wrote to Rodz., who did as Kalinin wished, only of course said by Kalinin's wish—coward Trepov wld. not take it upon himself—what ever you like, Trepov behaves now, as a traitor & is false as a cat—do not trust him, he concocts everything with Rodz. together, its only too well known.— [a]
    That paper I sent you yesterday, Rodz. himself wrote—he has no right to print & distribute yr. conversation & I doubt it being literal as he always lies—if not exact then be the Emp.[eror] & at once have his court-dress taken fr. him,[422] [—] don't ask Frederiks' or Tr.'s advice, both are frightened, tho' old man [Fredericks] wld. formerly have understood the necessity, now he is old. Already one spread in town (Duma) that the nobility in Novg.[orod] did not receive me, & when they read that

we even drank tea together they became crushed. About [P. M.] Kaufmann one is very pleased—you see, yr. firmness is appreciated by the good—so easy to continue when once begun—forgive me tormenting you with these letters—but only read the 2 telegr. I wired to you, you will again see what the right [people] say[442]—& they turn to me to beg you. If you hear fr. Kalinin again & he begs to close the Duma—do it, don't stick to the 17-th—time is money, the moment golden, & if dawdled over difficult, impossible to catch up & mend again.—I do hope its not true Nikol.[asha]< comes for the 17-th—formerly it went perfectly without Vorontzov [I. Iv. Vorontsov-Dashkov]—that has nothing to do with the Caucasus, our front here. Keep him away, evil genius. And he will mix into affairs & speak about Wassiltchikov.[419] Be Peter the Great, John the Terrible, Emperor Paul—crush them all under you—now don't you laugh, noughty [sic] one—but I long to see you so with all those men who try to govern you—& it must be the contrary. [b]

Countess Benkendorf [Maria Benckendorff] was so outraged by Princess W.'s letter,[419] that she made a round of visits to the older ladies in town, Princess Lolo<, Countess Vorontzov etc. telling them her opinion & that she finds it a disgrace to what the society has come down to, forgetting all principles & begging them to begin by strongly speaking to their daughters who behave and talk outrageously. It seems to have had its effect, as people speak now of her, so they realise the letter was really an unheard of one, & not such a charming one as some try to pretend. Katoussia W. [Ekaterina Vasil'chikova, personal fraulein of the empress during 1890s] also wrote to me, but after reading I tore it. And here the contrast, telegr. fr. "Union of the Russian People" asking me to give over things [i.e., communicate with, give advice] to you.[442]—One is rotten, weak, immoral society—the other, healthy, rightthinking, devoted subjects—& to these one must listen, their voice is Russia's & not society or the Duma's. One sees the right so clearly & they know the Duma ought to be closed & to them Tr. won't listen. If one does not listen to these, they will take things into their own hands to save you and more harm willingly may be done—than a simple word from you to close the Duma,—but till February, if earlier—they, will all stick here [in Petrograd]. [c]

I cld. hang Tr. for his bad counsels—and now after the papers Kalinin sent Voeikov[441] with those vile, utterly revolutionary representations of Moscou [sic] Nobility[443] & "Unions",[440] wh. have been discussed at the Duma, how can one keep them even one day on still—I hate false Tr. who does all to harm you, backed up by Makarov. Had I but got you here again—all was at once calmer & had you returned as Gr.[igory] in 5 days, you wld. have put order, wld. have rested yr. weary head upon wify's breast & Sunny wld. have given you strength & you wld. have listened to me & not to Trepov. God will help, I know, but you must be firm. Disperse the Duma at once, when you told Trepov 17-th you did not know what they were up to.—I should have quietly & with a clear conscience before the whole of Russia have sent [Prince G. E.] Lvov to Siberia (one did so for far less grave acts), taken Samarin's rank away (he signed that paper fr. Moscou), Meliuk.[ov], Guchk.[ov] & Polivanov also to Siberia. It is <u>war</u> and at such a time <u>interior</u> war is <u>high treason</u>, why don't you look at it like that, I really cannot understand. I am but a woman, but my soul & brain tell me it wld. be the saving of Russia—they sin far worse than anything the Sukhomlinov's ever did.—Forbid Brussilov etc. when they come to touch any political subjects, fool, who wants responsible cabinet,[385] as Georgi writes. Remember even Mr. Philippe said one dare not give constitution, as it would be yr. & Russia's ruin, & all true Russians say the same. [d]

Months ago I told Sturmer about Shvedov to be a member of Gos. Sov. [State Council][444] to have them & good Maklakov in they will stand bravely for us. I know I worry you—ah, wld. I not far, far rather only write letters of love, tenderness & caresses of wh. my heart is so full—but my duty as wife & mother & Russia's mother obliges me to say all to you—blessed by our Friend. Sweetheart, Sunshine of my life, if in battle you had to meet the enemy, you wld. never waver & go forth like a lion—be it now in the battle against the small handful of brutes & republicans—be the Master, & all will bow down to you!—Do you think I shld. fear, ah no—to-day I have had an officer cleared out fr. [daughters] M.[aria]'s & A.[nastasia]'s hospital, because he allowed himself to mock at our journey, pretending Prot.[opopov] bought the people to receive us so well; the Drs. who heared [sic] it raged—you see, Sunny in her small things is energetic & in big one as much as you wish—we have been placed by God on a throne & we must keep it firm & give it over to our Son untouched—if you keep that in mind you will remember to be the Sovereign—& how much easier for an autocratic sovereign than one who has sworn the Constitution!—[e]

Beloved One, listen to me, yes, you know yr. old true Girly. "Do not fear" the old woman [Maria Mikhailovna] said & therefore I write without fear to my agoo wee one.—Now the girlies want their tea, they came frozen back from their drive.—I kiss you & hold you tightly clasped to my breast, caress you, love you, long for you, cant sleep without you—bless you. Ever yr. very Own Wify. [f]

---

440. An inquiry was introduced in the Duma concerning this suppression of the union of zemstvoes and the union of towns. (Nabokov: Alexandra, *Pis'ma imperatritsy*, II, p. 260n)

441. Protopopov forwarded documents to the tsar through Voeikov concerning the recent declarations of the nobility of Moscow referred to here. See Letter No. 1642d, also Footnote 443.

442. These two telegrams were sent by members of the ultra-rightist "Union of the Russian People." They doubtless supported Alexandra's position: refuse concessions to the Duma, hold to the principles of autocracy, etc. On December 14 (O.S.), 1916, Fredericks wired thanks in the name of Nicholas II and Alexandra to those who sent these telegrams: see Letters No. 1645 and 1647c.

443. On December 1 (O.S.), 1916, a congress of the united nobility passed a resolution concerning the current situation in the country. (Nabokov: Alexandra, *Pis'ma imperatritsy*, II, p. 262n)

444. Shvedov was appointed to the State Council for 1917.

No. 1643/ Telegram 114. Stavka> Tsarskoe Selo. 14 Dec 1916. 19.01> 19.20. To her majesty. Many thanks [for] dear letters [and] two wires.[442] Have at once ordered him [Fredericks] to thank those good people from us. Fine, 3 [degrees] of frost. Do not tire yourself. Fondest kisses. Niki

---

No. 1644.   Ts.[arist] Stavka. Dec. 14th 1916.
My own dearest Sweetheart,

Loving thanks for your strong reprimanding letter. I read it with a smile because you speak like to a child.—It is a rotten business to have a man whom one dislikes & distrusts like Trep.[ov]. But first of all one must chose a new successor & then kick him out after he has done dirty business. I mean send him away, when he has shut up the Duma. Let all the responsibility & difficulty fall on his shoulders & not on those of the new comer. I send you two lists of candidates[445] he left me & a letter he sent yesterday where he again comes back to the question of appointing Makarov Pres.[ident] of the Cons.[eil] de l'Empire<. Rukhlov is a very good strong minded and right man—who hates Kokov.[tsov] etc. You know that the Pres. C. de l' Emp is named a new [sic] every year, also all its members. [a]

In Rumania it is not going well. We have sent & are sending more & more troops, but they have to march long distances (three weeks) owing to the atrocious condition of their railway lines. Now it is atlast [sic] been decided to take them over our control.—Dec. 17th was chosen for the generals to come here because Gurko till that date has several sobraniya [conferences]. Now I must end. God bless you my Darling, my Sunny. I kiss you and the girlies ever so tenderly & remain your poor little huzy with no will Nicky. [b]

445. The tsar appointed half of the State Council to one-year terms that expired at the end of the year; he could renew or dismiss "his" members. Apparently, Nicholas sent Alexandra a list of possible appointments for the 1917 term. See Letters No. 1647a and 1651e,g, for an explanation of how Protopopov became involved in the matter. Such favors from the empress made Protopopov increasingly powerful—and despised, even in rightist circles.

No. 1645/ Telegram 115. Stavka> Tsarskoe Selo. 14 Dec 1916. 21.25> 22.12. To her majesty. I did it now.[442] Yesterday I sent the paper[445]. Good night, sleep well. Niki

No. 1646/ Telegram 98. Tsarskoe Selo> Stavka. 15 Dec 1916. 12.07> 12.34. To his majesty. Thank you with all my heart for dear letter, forgive your Sunny.[446] Thank you for yesterday's telegram. Very much liked your wonderful prikaz [order].[443] Kiss and bless [you]. Heavy snow, 6 degrees frost. Still have not gone out at all. Alix

446. See Letters No. 1644a,b and 1647a,b.

No. 1647/ Her No. 641.   Tsarskoe Selo. Dec. 15th 1916.
My own Beloved,

Please, forgive me for my impertinent letters—girly does not mean to hurt her Angel, but writes from deepest love—& sometimes driven to exasperation, knowing one cheets [sic] you & proposes wrong things. How can I feel ever quiet when Trepov comes to you? And still he succeeds in persuading you wrongly— only to find a successor—but many say, that once Mak.[arov is] changed [as minister of justice], he will become better on the whole. You see how he [Trepov?] clings to Makarov (whom I continue saying is false to us) & wants him at head of the Con. de l'Emp. [State Council]<—too bad. Put strong-minded (hard) Stcheglovitov [Shcheglovitov] there, he is the man for such a place & will allow no disorders & bad things to go on.—I shall send you the papers[445] back to-morrow when have studied them through.— [a]

Thanks so much (& fr. Gr.[igory] too) for Manuilov,[430] fancy nice Malama said at 5 yesterday there was no paper fr. you (the Messenger came early in the morning), so I had to wire. One had intended making a whole story, dragging in all sorts of names (out of filth, simply) & lots were going to be present at the trial [of Manasevich-Manuilov]. Thanks again dear one.—Our Fr.< came to her [Anna Vyrubova], I did not go out of the house. He never goes out since ages,[447] except to come here, [to Tsarskoe Selo, usually to Anna Vyrubova's house] but yesterday he walked in the streets with Munia [Golovina], to the Kazan and St. Isaacs (Cathedrals) & not one disagreeable look, people all quiet. Says in 3 or 4 days things will go better in Roumania & all will go better.—How good yr. order is[453]—just read it with deepest emotion.—God help & bless you, Sweetheart. It is not necessary[160] to say poor old huzy with no will [see Letter No. 1644a,b], it kills me—forgive me—you understand me I know & my allconsuming love—yes Lovy mine? Me loves too so terribly, terribly.—Little Kozhevnikov (fr. Murman[sk?]) comes to lunch & N.P.< to tea, to enjoy each separately. Do let N.P. get the yacht for Xmas, please dear.[448]— Our Fr. says Kalinin< must be well now. Why don't you make him M. D. V. not Isp. D. (my idea)[449]—that young Rittich, who only just began, already got his affirmation (to his own surprise).[450]— [b]

Only slept after 4-6 this night, quite lost my sleep again—need you!—The sun is trying to appear very thick snow, 6° of frost. Ania & I want to go to Holy Communion on Sunday, as its Rozhd. post [Christmas Fast]—to get strength & help.—I am glad you liked the Image [icon, see Letters No. 1633f, 1638a and 1639]—is her face not sweet, tho' sad? I am sending 3 little [icon] lamps fr. the Children & me to Nov.[oe] Znam.[ene Church], Vlad. B. M. na pechke & to the old woman [Maria Mikhailovna] with an Image.[451] Did you eat her apple?—So glad you told Frederiks to answer those nice telegr. from us both.[442] Why on earth won't the Generals allow "R.[usskoe] Znamia" (small patriotic paper) to be sent to the army, Dubrovin finds it a shame (I agree) & they can read any proclamations. Our Chiefs are really idiots.[452]—That new Club Trepov has arranged (for officers etc.) not famous—am going to find out about it, Off.[icers] of our United Regiment go there & they all met Rodzianko with manifestations & allocutions [i.e., speeches] there [supporting him]—most tactless.—Lovy, Dubrovin asks to see me—may I or not?[452] [c]

Please, tell Trepov[:] Duma on leave till beginning of Feb. as they must have time to go home (here more mischief if they remain [in Petrograd]—Rodzianko & Trepov arranged it [the recess] together)—believe our Friend's< advice. Even the Children notice how things don't come out well if we do not listen to Him & the contrary—good when listen. [Rasputin says:] "The path is narrow, but one must walk along it straight, in the manner of God and not of man"—one only needs to face all courageously & with more faith.—Now, a miracle (all say) "Variag" [an old cruiser, *The Varangian*, bought from Japan and commanded by Karl von Dehn] arrived before all the others—Storm, 40 knots fr. Gibraltar to Glasgow. The water not simply washes over, but goes in & through, alas, everywhere, machine not famous, must be repared [sic] soon in England. Our Fr. was anxious when they left Vladivostok, but they were blessed & saved because Lili< out of faith went to Verkhoturie & Tobolsk with Gregory & Ania in summer.[330]—Blessings, love, caresses & kisses without end, Huzy my Beloved, fr. yr. very, very Own. [d]

Wish the telephone were not so bad. [See Letters No. 1549, 1550, 1552a, 1609b]—Kozhevnikov was a dear & talked a lot, hope you will see him before he returns, he came with the Adm. they had 3 accidents on the new line. Probably in Feb. the "Variag" will have to go for 5-6 months to England for repairs, as its dangerous leaving her so, she is old & not safe.—The Engl.[ish were] everywhere charming in all the ports helping where & how they could. Poor boy [Lili's husband, Karl von Dehn] had to make speeches in England. Says Den a perfect capt., always calm, never looses [sic] his head. Heat colossal in summer, they went 5 months. They rolled (42 [degrees])—so that the guns sweeped along the sea sideways.—So nice to see him—[he] cld. not get over Anast.[asia, our daughter] being so fat & a big lady.— [e]

447. Popular animosity was now so great that Rasputin went out little, and then under heavy security. On the morning of the following day, December 16/29, 1916, Grigory received a phone call at his apartment threatening his life. (See Fuhrmann, *Rasputin*, pp. 192-195, 201) Rasputin was murdered on the night of December 17/30.

448. Alexandra wanted the family's old friend, Rear-Admiral N. P. Sablin, to replace R. D. Zelenetsky as commander of the imperial yacht *Standard*. The appointment occurred in late 1917.

449. M.V.D. refers to *ministr vnutrennykh del*, "minister of internal affairs" or "minister of the interior." Protopopov did not have that title; he was *ispolnitel'nyi dolgov ministra vnutrennykh del*, literally, "one carrying out the duties of the minister of internal affairs." See Fn. 363 and Letter No. 1652.

450. Alexandra seems to have misunderstood A. A. Rittikh's titles: she speaks as if he were already promoted to full minister of agriculture. Actually, Rittikh was assistant-minister of agriculture from 1912 to 1916. After a brief sojourn in the Senate during 1916, Rittikh returned to the ministry of agriculture as "acting minister" (*upravlyayushchii ministr*— see Fn. 449). He was made full minister on January 12 (O.S.), 1917. Rittikh, too, failed to solve the problem of supplying the cities.

451. The "old woman with an Image" refers to Maria Mikhailovna, the 107-year old *staritsa* ("woman of God") Alexandra recently met at Novgorod. (See Letter No. 1633d.) "Vlad. B. M. na pechke" means the "Church of Vladimir of the Mother of God on the Stove." The following sheds light on the meaning of "on the stove": "[In Novgorod we went] to a wee chapel in a garden where on the stove of a holy bread bakery appeared (ages ago) the Virgin" (See Letter No. 1633f.) The name of this church was presumably the "Church of Vladimir of the Mother of God on the Stove."

452. Dr. A. I. Dubrovin edited *Russkoe znamya* (Russian Banner) and was president of the Union of the Russian People, which published it. It is interesting to note that the tsar's generals, conservatives and monarchists as they were, did not want their soldiers exposed to this "patriotic paper." Nicholas II was sympathetic to the Union, yet even he—for whatever reason—asked his wife not to receive Dubrovin. (See Letter No. 1652.)

No. 1648.   Ts.[arist] Stavka. Dec. 15th 1916.

My own Sweetheart,

Loving thanks for your dear letter. It is so full of questions that I don't know how to answer them all. The most serious one, concerning Voeikov,[441] I shall resolve when I come home. I find it absolutely necessary to bring peace and calm among the whole population of our country. This coupled with the changes in the Cons.[eil] de l'Emp.[ire, the State Council], will do no end of good to freshen up the whole atmosphere. I have just received the Rumanian minister [Diamandy], who brought me a message of thanks fr. Nando [King Ferdinand] in answer to mine, in wh. I tried to encourage him. Diamandi [sic] is a good & honest little man & [one] who views the situation in the right way. I am glad you liked my prikaz [order]. It was written by Gurko—perhaps rather longish, but it was difficult for me to shorten [it], as the sense might lose its clearness![453] On Saturday I have a busy day with my generals & hope to leave Sunday in the afternoon. What joy! To-morrow arrives our Bagration-Mukhran.[sky, who has] been from Stockholm & Copenhagen. Yesterday I saw the other Bagration, who spoke about you & his splendid division with great admiration. Today it is fine & 3 d.[egrees] of frost & I also feel more gay.—Now I must bid you farewell! God bless you, my dearest Wify! I love you and kiss you ever so tenderly, also the girlies. Heart & soul with you. Ever your very own poor little huzy with a tiny will[454] Nicky.

453. This Order of the Day read: "The hour of peace has not yet come.... God will bless your arms: He will cover them with eternal glory and will give us a peace worthy of your glorious deeds, oh, my glorious troops!—such a peace that future generations will bless your holy memory!' [French Ambassador] Paléologue was impressed by this 'noble and courageous language,' but he did not know that it was Gourko's and not the Tsar's." (Vulliamy, p. 309n) See also Nabokov: Alexandra, *Pis'ma imperatritsy*, II p. 268n, and Sergeev: Nicholas and Alexandra, *Perepiska*, V, p. 193n.
454. The reference is ironic: see Nicholas's Letter No. 1644a,b, and Alexandra's apologies in Letters No. 1646 and 1647a,b. See the Biographical Index for an identification of the two "Bagrations."

No. 1649/ Telegram 117. Stavka> Tsarskoe Selo. 15 Dec 1916. 18.41> 19.04. To her majesty. Thanks lovingly [for] dear letter. Thoughts always together. 3 [degrees] frost, calm, fine [weather]. Glad [you are] keeping in. Burning kisses. Niki

No. 1650/ Telegram 106. Tsarskoe Selo> Stavka. 16 Dec 1916. 12.30> 13.25. To his majesty. 10 degrees frost. Still lie down, heart still very enlarged. Please, pay attention to letters of K.[alinin]< and me. Your letters are running late. Bless and kiss [you]. Alix

No. 1651/ Her No. 642.   Tsarskoe Selo. Dec. 16th 1916.
My own beloved Treasure,
    10° of frost this morning & wee pink clouds—everything thickly covered in snow.—Slept five hours this night, quite a treat. Botkin turned up—I have nor seen him for two months at least, because I know by heart what medicines to take when the heart is worse. Well, he gave me stronger drops as its so enlarged & of course said to keep lying, wh. I do. I only have Shvedov to-day, otherwise lie on the sopha. But still I want to go to Holy Communion on Sunday, if only possible & so now beg your forgiveness my Sweetheart for any word, wh. may have hurt you[129]—I fear, I have been rough at times—but out of despair only & endless love & yearning to help you. [See Letters No. 1644a,b and 1647a,b.] Pardon me, Lovy. I want badly to go—am weary—but my spirits are up. Things are going better, & Kalin.[in]< has behaved splendidly. I told him to write openly to you about everything—he was shy to do so—I said to was his duty, once vented in the Duma—Trepov was a coward, Shuvaev worse (wld. that Belyaev were in his place, a gentleman & not one to bow down to the Duma & seek to be popular)—& Rodzia.[nko] listened to Kal.'s letter & became small—bless the man may he continue being as firm & brave as he has up to now. Send him a word of thanks or encouragement, wont you? And affirm him as M. Vn. D.[449] (its wify's idea, & I think the right one).— [a]

People said you would never stand up for him & Pitir.[im] against everybody—& you have! Well done; Huzy mine! Only one thing just torments me,
Gr.[igory]< & Prot.[opopov]—[they insist] the Duma not to be called together
before Febr. so as to give them [the deputies] time to disperse, wh. is <u>more</u> than
necessary, they are in a "group" a poisenous [sic] element in town<, whereas
dispersed over the country nobody pays any heed to them nor respects
them.—[Daughter] Olga had a Committee yesterday evening, but it did not last
long. Volodia Volk.[onsky], who always has a smile or two for her—avoided her
eyes & never once smiled—you see how our girlies have learned to watch people
& their faces—they have developed much interiorly through all this suffering—they know all we go through, its necessary & <u>ripens</u> them. They are happily at times great babies—but have the insight & feelings of the soul of much
wiser beings. As our Fr.< says—they have passed heavy courses. [b]

N.P.< took tea, told heaps about Odessa & the battalion, Olga Evgen.[evna
Byutsova] etc.—Full of Petr.[ograd] horrors & rages that nobody defends me,
that all may say, write, hint at bad things about their Empress & nobody stands
up, repri.[mands], punishes, banishes, fines those types. Only Princess V.[81, 436]
suffered, all others, Meliukov [Milyukov] etc. go free. Yes, people are not to be
admired, cowards! But many shall be struck off future court-lists, they shall
learn to know in time of peace what it was in time of war not to stand up for
ones Sovereign! Why have we got a ramoli< rag as M.[inister] of the Court?
He [Fredericks] ought to have brought all the names & proposed how to punish
them for slandering your wife. Personally I do not care a straw—when I was
young I suffered horribly through those injustices said about me (oh how often)—but now the worldly things don't touch me deeply, I mean nastiness—they
will come round some day, only my Huzy ought really to stick up a bit for me,
as many think you don't care & hide behind me. [c]

You won't answer about Balash.[ov][413]— now why didn't you have him severely written to by Fred[ericks].—I am not going to shake hands with him
whenever we meet, I warn you & I long to fling my fury into his face; Little
snake!—I have disliked him ever since I set eyes on him, & I told you so. He
thinks his high court rank allows him to write vile things—on the contrary, he is
utterly unworthy of it.—Have you said that Prince Golitizin [A. D. Golitsyn] is to
have his court rank taken fr. him.—don't dawdle deary, do all quicker, its the
Danish Bummelzug [i.e., you must be as fast and efficient as this well-known
passenger train]—be quicker in acting strike out people fr. court lists & don't
listen to Fred.[ericks'] protests—he is frightened & does not understand how to
deal at the present moment.— [d]

Now forgive me, if I did wrong, in asking Kalinin's opinion about the list you
sent me.[445] As we trust him (he came for ½ an hour to her [Anna Vyrubova]
yesterday), I asked her to find out what he knows about the people. He promises
to hold his tongue that he saw the names of the candidates.—Only above all begs
Makar.[ov] to quickly leave, without putting him into the Con.[seil de l']
Emp.[ire, the State Council], others neither were put there, & don't need Tr--v's
letter, believe our Fr's advice & now Kal--n's too—he is dangerous & completely
holds Trepov in hand, others, Zhevakhov for instance knows it too.—He spoke a
while ago to Stcheglovitov [Shcheglovitov], who finds Dobrovolsky whom he

knows—excellent in that place [as minister of justice]. I think you would only be right in naming him. I know Dobrov. is much against the reorganisation [sic] of the Senate as projected, (I think agreed to in the Con. Emp. & now presented to the Duma)—says it will be as bad & left as the Duma, & not to be relied upon—he told me that, when I saw him. I only spoke about the Senate & Georgie's committee then.— [e]

Send for Kalinin as soon as you arrive here & then Dobrovolsky to talk to & name Stcheglovit.[ov president of the State Council] quicker—he is the right man in the right place & will stick up for us & permit no rows. Yr. prikaz [order][453] has had a splendid effect upon all—it came at such a good moment and showed so clearly all yr. ideas about continuing the war. Fancy, poor Zizi< was so upset, Meliuk. [Milyukov] in his speech spoke about Lila Narishkin[a] (Lichtenstein), spies etc. & said she was a lady in high sanction at court confounding her with Mme Zizi. Poor old lady heard that it got into small [i.e., local] papers in the country, the Kurakins came all flying & she had to explain to them—her "supervisors" full of horror, a general in the army,—how can we keep such traitors near us (always a bite at me & my people!!)—so she sent for Sazonov (Mel.[i.e., Milyukov]'s bosom friend), & told him to explain all & to insist upon his writing in the papers that he was lead into error. It will appear in the "Retch [*Rech*']," & now she is quite calm again.[455] They touch all near me. Lila N. is at [the Hotel] Astoria, & being watched by the police.— [f]

Poor old Stcheglov [apparently N. G. Shchegol'] died this night— better for him, he was so ill! I am going to get hold of Ressin< one of these days & tell him to pay attention to his officers— Komar.[ov] was always with them, he never, & the tone has become very bad & even left—its the most difficult reg. as so mixed & therefore needs a head to keep them well in hand & guide them, & one does not speak well of them at all. The men don't like him because he is hard—but the officers he does not a bit occupy himself with.—Just had old Shvedov, fancy, when he told Trepov he was to be a member of the Sovet [State Council] by your & my wish, he [Trepov] answered that it did not concern him what orders Shtyurm.[er] got, he did not hear it from you. He brought me the list on one paper of all the members & we can look at it together & strike out & add on new ones.[445] Hates Kaufmann, says he said very bad things, strike him off—now one must come with the brush & sweep away the dust & dirt & get new clean brushes to work. [g]

Warmest thanks precious letter. Poor dear, [you] will be tired to-morrow—God help you—only military & no political questions. [See Letter No. 1644b.] All wild about your prikaz,[445] the Poles of course intensely so.[380]—The kitten has climbed into the fireplace & now sneezes there.—Glad, you saw [D. P.] Bagration—so interesting all about his wild men. "One must not speak"[160]—"with tiny will," but a wee bit weak & not confident in yourself & a bit easily believe bad advices.[456]—Now—I bless, hug, kiss you, my one & all. God bless & protect you. Ever yr. very, very own tiresome   Sunny. [h]

---

455. In his famous "folly or treason?" speech before the Duma, Paul Milyukov apparently confused Elizabeth Alexeevna Naryshkina ("Madame Zizi"), one of Alexandra's friends—"said she was a lady in high sanction at court"—with Elena Constantinovna Naryshkina ("Lila Narishkin"). "Zizi,"

born Princess Kurakina, was the widow of A. D. Naryshkin. "Lila" lived in Florence; married to D. K. Naryshkin, she was also involved with Prince Lichtenstein, a former Austrian envoy to Russia.

456. The empress is saying (paraphrased): "Don't accept the notion that you speak 'with a weak will'—if you are the least bit weak and do not have confidence in yourself, you will accept bad advice from people."

No. 1652.   Ts.[arist] Stavka. Dec. 16th 1916.
My own Sweetheart,

Ever so tenderly do I thank you for your dearest letter. No, me is not angry with the other one [apparently Letter No. 1642 or 1647] you wrote. I understand so well your motive in trying to help me. But change the day the Duma is coming again together (Jan. 12) I cannot, as it is already put in the ukaz [order] wh. appears already to-morrow in the papers. We[, our son Aleksei and I,] eat [i.e., ate] the apple of the staritsa wh. we both found excellent. [See Letter No. 1633d.] I read the description of your visit to Novgorod in the "Russk. Inv.,"[457] the only newspaper I read, & was happy with its subject. I hope to be able to leave on Sunday, if our consiel [i.e., conference] does not last too long. They [i.e., There] are many questions to discuss over! [a]

Today there were lots of foreigners at lunch—two Rumanians, three englishmen & a frenchman. Of course all military. It is astonishing the quantity of foreign officers who arrive to Russia every fortnight. Better not receive Dubrov.[in] now.[452] The other day I told Voeik.[ov] to wire Kal.[inin]< to get well. Yes, I also find it good to affirm him minister.[449] This very minute I looked into his papers & found therein a nice calm letter of his. Now I must end. God bless you my darling Wify & the girlies. Tenderest love & kisses from your poor little huzy with a bit of will Nicky. [b]

457. *Russkii Invalid* (Russian Invalid) was published by the ministry of war. It is astounding to think this was the only paper Nicholas II read, but so he says. In Letter No. 1656b, the tsar claims, "I do not read newspapers here[, at Stavka]."

No. 1653/ Telegram 107. Tsarskoe Selo> Stavka. 16 Dec 1916. 12.30> 13.25.
To his majesty. Warm thanks for dear letters. In thoughts always together. Sleep well. Tenderly kiss and bless [you]. To-morrow will think a lot of you[, during the conference at Stavka]. Alix

---

No. 1654/ Telegram 120. Stavka> Tsarskoe Selo. 16 Dec 1916. 18.53> 19.16.
To her majesty. Fond thanks [for] dear letter. Tiresome you feel the effect of your visit [to Novgorod]. To-morrow at 5 begins my sitting with generals. Colder but clear. Tenderest kisses. Niki

---

No. 1655/ Her No. 643.   Ts.[arskoe] S[elo]. Dec. 17th 1916.
My own beloved Sweetheart,

Again very cold & gently snowing. Slept 5 hours this night, for me quite good—heart not famous & don't feel well. You see my heart for some time was bad again, but I did not keep quiet as ought to have by rights—but I cld. not—I had to be in the hospital< to change my thoughts, had to see many people—the moral strain of these last trying months on a week heart of course had to tell—this lovely journey to Novgorod was phisically [sic] very tiring—& well, the old machine broke down. Hope to be decent for Xmas this year. Since the war I have not been to any [Christmas?] trees in hospital or manege [riding school].—Shall think of you more than ever this afternoon [during the military conference at Stavka]—may all your thoughts & plans be blessed by God! Hope you can go to the Image [icon] before.—I have ordered an all-night mass in the house—(& tho' very foolish) Church to-morrow at 9 in the Peshcherny Chapel<. Ania goes too & we confess at 10. Once more forgive me for every pain & worry, beloved One[129]—shall carry you in my heart & soul to-morrow.—How is the new General instead of Pustov.[oitenko]? The latter must have been sad to leave you—what a nice, honest & devoted man.— [a]

I send you a paper with some ideas of Sukhomlinov about the Duma to read through in the train [as you return to visit us].[458]—I cannot grasp why Voeikov's thing[441,443] was not done 2 weeks ago as intended.—Some gossips: Ania's Mother told her that Krivoshein & Ignatev bless me for having telegraphed to you to leave all the food supply question in Rittich's [Rittikh's] hands—there, & not one single word of truth in the whole thing, ah, how people calmly lie & find it no sin!!—You will finish the nice English novel[420] in the train? Oh the joy, the con-solation of having you home again. At such a time to be separated I assure you is at times absolutely exasperating & distracting—how much easier to have shared all together & spoken over everything, instead of letters wh. have less force, alas, & often must have aggravated you, my poor, patient Angel. But I have to try & be the antedate [sic] to others' poison.— Has Baby's "worm" quite been got rid of? Then he will get fatter & less transparent—the precious Boy![459] [b]

We are sitting together—can imagine our feelings—thoughts—our Friend< has disappeared. Yesterday A.[nia]< saw him & he said Felix [Yusupov the Younger] asked him to come in the night, a motor wld. fetch him to see [his wife,] Irina.—A motor fetched him (military one) with 2 civilians & He went away. This night big scandal at Yussupov's house—big meeting, Dmitri<, Pur-ishkevitch etc. all drunk. Police heard shots, Purishkevitch ran out screaming to the Police that our Friend was killed. Police searching & [agents of the Ministry of] Justice entered now into Yussupov's house—did not dare before as Dmitri there. Chief of police has sent for Dmitri. Felix wished to leave to-night for Crimea, [I] begged Kalinin< to stop him[, and he did]. [c]

Our Friend was in good spirits but nervous these days & for A. too, as Bati-ushin[430] wants to catch things against Ania. Felix pretends He [Rasputin] never came to the house & never asked him. Seems quite a paw [i.e., trap]. I still trust in God's mercy that one has only driven Him off somewhere. Kalinin is doing all he can. Therefore I beg for Voeikov, we women are alone with our weak heads. Shall keep her to live here—as now they [members of this murderous conspiracy] will get at her next. I cannot & won't believe He has been killed. God have mercy. Such utter anguish (am calm & can't believe it).—Thanks dear letter, come quickly—nobody will dare to touch her [Anna Vyrubova] or do anything when you are here. Felix came often to him lately....[391] [Love] & kisses <u>Sunny</u>. [d]

458. Upon Alexandra's urging, Nicholas II freed Sukhomlinov, who, if not a traitor (as charged), was certainly incompetent. This outraged many people. Alexandra now took Sukhomlinov as an advisor on dealing with the Duma!

459. After writing these lines, Alexandra learned Rasputin had disappeared. She wrote the remainder of the letter in pencil.

No. 1656.   Ts.[arist] Stavka. Dec. 17th 1916.
My beloved angel,
   Gurko's doklad [report] was over earlier than normal, so I came home and sat down to write. Everth arrived yesterday & I saw him at dinner, he looks fresh & younger than in April. Today come the others. Belyaev has also appeared fr. Rumania, he remains until our sitting is over, then he goes back to report about the results to Nando [King Ferdinand of Roumania] & Sakharov [commander of the Russian forces in Roumania] & after that he wants to take part in the war & command a division. Just got your dear long letter for which many tender thanks. When I return we will study all those lists & decide all those questions together.[445] About Balash.[ov] I did not tell old Fred.[ericks] neither about that Pz. [Prince A. D.] Gol.[itsyn] not knowing who he is nor what he said. You see I never read [news]papers here.[457]—[a]
   How can you think that generals at a military consiel [sic] are going to discuss political questions? I should like to hear one of them begin that subject before me. I am so intensely happy to come home & perhaps remain a little while on into the New Year. One kiss in the morning & one in the evening to Baby< is not at all sufficient for me—I am hungry for much more! This is my last letter then. I hope you will feel stronger & better; do keep quiet. God bless you, my own Sweetheart, my Sunny beloved. I kiss you and the dear girlies tenderly. Ever your own very own old huzy Nicky.   [P.S.] Shall think of you to-morrow morning!! [b]

No. 1657/ Telegram 110. Tsarskoe Selo> Stavka. 17 Dec 1916. 16.37> 17.07. To his majesty. Warmly thank you for letters. Could you not send Voeikov quickly? His help is needed as our Friend< has disappeared since last night. We are still hoping for God's mercy. Felix [Yusupov the Younger] and Dmitry< are involved. Alix

No. 1658/ Telegram 123. Stavka> Tsarskoe Selo. 17 Dec 1916. 20.05> 20.45. To her majesty. Tender thanks. What an awful thing, no train till to-morrow for Voeikov. Cannot Kalinin< help? Fondest kisses. Niki

No. 1659/ Telegram 111. Tsarskoe Selo> Stavka. 17 Dec 1916. 22.24> 23.10. To his majesty. K.[alinin]< is doing all that he can. So far they have still not found anything. F.[elix] planned to leave for Crimea, is being held. Very much wish you were here. God help us. Sleep well. In prayers and thoughts together. Bless you with unlimited tenderness. Alix

No. 1660/ Telegram 114. Tsarskoe Selo> Stavka. 18 Dec 1916. 11.42> 12.55. To his majesty. Just now took communion in home chapel. They have still not found anything. Searchings [for Rasputin's body] continue. There is danger that these two boys [Dmitry< and Felix Yusupov the Younger] are organizing something still worse.[460] Am not giving up while there is yet hope. Such a clear, sunny day. Hope you are leaving today, I need your presence terribly. Bless and kiss [you]. Alix

460. Rumors abounded that Rasputin's death was the first move in a "coup from the right," which would involve the arrest of Nicholas, Alexandra, Vyrubova, Protopopov, etc. Speculation was rife that Nikolasha< or Aleksei would be proclaimed tsar. In the ltter event, rumors held thatNicholas's brother Michael would be proclaimed regent.

No. 1661/ Telegram 125. Stavka> Tsarskoe Selo. 18 Dec 1916. 14.32> 15.12. To her majesty. Fondest thanks. Leaving [at] 4.30, very busy both days. Also glorious sunshine, fourteen [degrees] of frost. Directly [holding] last sitting. Thoughts with you. Tender love. Niki

No. 1662/ Telegram 116. Tsarskoe Selo> Stavka. 18 Dec 1916. 15.00> 15.45. To his majesty. Ordered Maximovich in your name to forbid D.[mitry] to leave his home until your return. D. wanted to see me today, I refused. He is main one involved. Body [of Rasputin] still not found. When will you be here? Kiss [you] without end. Alix

No. 1663/ Telegram 0770. Orsha train station> Tsarskoe Selo. 18 Dec 1916. 18.38> 19.32. To her majesty. Only now read your letter. Anguished and horrified.[461] Prayers [and] thoughts together. Arrive to-morrow at 5. Great frost. Sitting ended at 4. Blessings [and] kisses. Niki

461. Stavka was hostile to Rasputin; the men there rather openly celebrated the news of his disappearance and presumed death. Observers found Nicholas somber, taciturn—perhaps even relieved at the possibility that Rasputin might be out of his life. These witnesses thought the tsar was "horrified and shaken" only when he arrived home and saw the effect of the murder on his wife. (Fuhrmann, *Rasputin*, pp. 208-214)

No. 1664/ Telegram 119 in Russian. Tsarskoe Selo> Stavka. 19 Dec 1916. 13.50> 14.00. To his majesty. Tenderly thank you for yesterday's telegram and dear letter, received late in day. They found [Rasputin's body] in the water. Thoughts, prayers together. We warmly kiss you [all]. Alix

No. 1665/ Her No. 644.   Tsarskoe Selo. Feb. 22nd 1917.
My very Own precious one,
With anguish & deep pain I let you go—alone, without sweet Baby's< tender, warming, sunny companionship!< And such a hard time as the one we are going through now.—Being apart makes everything so much harder to bear—no possibility of giving you a gentle caress when you look weary, tormented. Verily God has sent you a terrible hard cross to bear & I do so long to help you to carry the burden! You are brave & patient, but my soul feels & suffers with you far more than I can say. I can do nothing but pray & pray & Our dear Friend< does so in yonder world for you—there he is yet nearer to us—Tho' one longs to

hear his voice of comfort and encouragement.—God will help, I feel convinced, & send yet the great recompense for all you go through—but how long to wait still! It seems as tho' things are taking a better turn—only my Love be firm, show the master hand, its that what [the] Russian needs. Love & kindness you have <u>never</u> failed to show—now let them feel yr. fist at times. They ask for it themselves—how many have told me: ["]we want to feel the whip"—Its strange, but such is the Slave [i.e., Slav?] nature, <u>great</u> firmness, hardness even—& warm love. Since they now have begun to "feel" you & Kalinin< they begin to quieten down. They must learn to fear you,—love is not enough. A child that adores its father must still have fear to anger, displease or disobey him—One must play with the reins, let them loose & draw them in, always let the master-hand be felt, then they also far more value kindness—only gentleness they do not understand.— Russian hearts are strange & <u>not</u> tender or susceptible in the higher classes, strange to say. They need decided treatment, especially now. [a]

I am sad we could not be alone [during] our last luncheon, but they are yr. own who also want to see you. Poor little Xenia,< with such boys & her daughter married into that wicked family[, the Yusupovs] & with such a false husband [as Felix Yusupov the Younger][462] I pitty [sic] her deeply. There is so much sorrow & grief all over the world—one great pain in one's heart wh. gnaws at one unceasingly—such a yearning for rest & peace, just to get a <u>wee bit</u> of strength to go on fighting & struggling along this thorny road towards the shining goal. [b]

I hope you will have no difficulties or bothers with Alekseev & that you can come back <u>very</u> soon—its not fr. a pure selfish longing that I speak, but because [I] too well see how "the screaming mass" behave when you are near.—They fear you still & must yet more, so that wherever you are, they should have the same quaver. And for the ministers you are <u>such</u> a strength, & guide—come back soon—you see I don't beg for myself & Baby< even—because that you always know. I understand where duty calls & that is just[, but] now <u>more</u> here than there. So just set things going [at Stavka] & do be home in ten days—til things are really as they should be. — Yr. wall[, yr.] wify remains guarding here in the rear, tho' she can do but little, but the good ones know she is yr. staunch upholder. —My eyes <u>ache</u> fr. crying.—from the station shall go straight to Znamenia,< even if [I] have been there with you before—to get calm & strength & pray for you my Angel—ah, God, <u>how</u> I love you!—Ever increasingly, deep as the sea, fathomless in tenderness. Sleep calmly, dont cough—may the change of air make you quite well again. Holy angels guard you, Christ be near you, & the sweet Virgin never fail you—Our Friend left us to [join] her—I bless you, clasp you tightly in my arms & rest yr. weary head upon my breast. Ah the loneliness of the nights to come—no Sunny< near you—& no Sunshine< either. All our love, burning & warming envelops you, my Huzy, my one & all, the light of my life, the treasure given to me by God Almighty. Feel my arms encircling you, feel my lips tenderly pressed upon yours—always together, never alone. —Farewell Lovy Sweet, come soon back again—to your very own old <u>Sunny</u>. [P.S.] Please, go to the [icon of the] "Virgin" as soon as you can. I have prayed <u>so much</u> for you there. [c]

462. The empress refers to the tsar's older sister, Kseniya. She and her husband Alexander Mikhailovich were the parents of Irina, the wife of Prince Yusupov the Younger, one of Rasputin's assassins.

No. 1666/ Telegram 205 in Russian. Bologoe> Tsarskoe Selo. 22 Feb 1917. 20.55> 21.17. To her majesty. Am travelling well.[463] In thoughts am with all [of you]. [Feel] lonely and sad. Am very grateful for letters. Embrace all. Goodnight. Niki

463. "The Tsar was now on his way to the Stavka for the last time. A fortnight after the dispatch of this telegram he was no longer an Emperor, and was placed under arrest. ... Actually, the first signs of the Revolution had already shown themselves, the army was on the brink of mutiny, and the better part of the population was sick of war, enervated, hungry and desperate. Yet, in his next letter, the Tsar is thinking seriously of 'taking up dominoes in his spare time.' It is this strange blindness, this concern with trifles, which gives the correspondence such a peculiar tragic quality." (Vulliamy, p. 312n)

No. 1667/ Telegram 1. Stavka> Tsarskoe Selo. 23 Feb 1917. 15.40> 16.20. To her majesty. Arrived well. Fine, cold, windy. Am coughing rarely. Feel strong again, but very lonely. Thanks tenderly for wires, Baby< too.[464] Thoughts always together. Miss [you] awfully. Kiss all fondly. Niki

464. The family's telegrams to Nicholas in these days were not published in A. A. Sergeev's edition of the *Perepiska*. Some may be preserved in the State Archive of the Russian Federation (GARF) since Buranov and Khrustalev cite—in Russian—a telegram from Alexandra to the tsar dated March 1: "Thoughts, prayers do not abandon you. The Lord will help. Children's temperature is still high, are coughing hard. [We] all warmly kiss [you]. Aliks." (*Gibel'*, p. 36, the footnote of which to this document reads "TsGAOR SSSR, f. 1779, op. 1, d. 1722, l. 15.")

No. 1668/ Her No. 645.   Ts.[arskoe] S[elo]. Feb. 23rd 1917.
My own angel love,
    Well, now Olga & Aleksei have the measles—[daughter] Olga's face all covered, & Baby< has more in the mouth & he coughs very much & eyes ache. They lie in the dark—we lunched still together in the playroom. P. V. P.[etrov] is reading to him, I hear his voice, I am on Olga's sofa. We are all in summer skirts & white dressing-gowns, & if [I] have to see anybody (who is not afraid), [I will] change into a dress. Our meals we take in the "red room." If the others are to get it, I wish they would fall ill sooner, then gayer for them and wont last so long.
    Now Ania< may get it too, she lies in bed with a cough, had [a temperature of] 38 yesterday & twice after medicines it fell. Only just got yr. wire—that you arrived safely—thank God! Can imagine your awful loneliness without sweet Baby<—he hopped [sic] to wire you, so sad he & Olga cant write to you, as must not use their eyes. All [of] us kiss you very, very tenderly. Oh my love— how sad its [sic] without you—how lonely, how I yearn for yr. love & kisses, precious treasure, [I] think of you without end. Do wear the cross [see Letter No. 1673e] sometimes when [making] difficult decisions, it will help you.—Went to Alex.[androvsk] with [our daughters] T.[atiana], M.[aria] and A.[nastasia] in a shut motor, met lots of sailors & Kublitsky, spoke to him—says Khvotchinsky [Khvoshchinsky] saw you pass. Bright sunny day & not so cold. Shall wire

often how they are if [they are] not so well.[464] Goodbye farewell, my one & all.
God bless & protect you. Cover you with kisses. Ever yr. very Own.

No. 1669/ Telegram 2. Stavka> Tsarskoe Selo. 23 Feb 1917. 18.44> 19.20.
To her majesty. What a bore. Hoped so they [our children Olga and Aleksei]
would be spared of getting measles. Fondest love to all. Sleep gently. Niki

---

No. 1670.   Ts.[arist] Stavka. Feb. 23^d 1917.
My own beloved Sunny,
   Loving thanks for your precious letter—you left in my compartment.—I read it
greedily before going to bed. It did me good, in my solitude, after two months
being together, if not to hear your sweet voice, atleast [sic] to be comforted by
those lines of tender love! I never went out until we arrived here. Today I feel
much better, the voice is not hoarse & the cough is much less strong. It was a
sunny but cold day & I was met by the usual people— Alekseev at their head. He
really looks alright [sic] & the face has an expression of rest & calm which I
have long not seen. We had a good talk for an hour; after that I arranged my
rooms & got your wire[464] about Olga's & Baby's< measles. I could not believe
my eyes—so unexpected was that news, especially after his own telegram[464]
where he says that he is feeling well! Anyhow it is very tiresome & rather troublesome for you, my Lovebird. Perhaps you will put off receiving so many people, as that is a lawful reason not to see so many, on account of their families. In
the 1st & 2^d Cadet corps the number of boys who have got the measles is steadily
rising. I saw all the foreign generals at dinner—they were very sad to hear that
news. [a]
   It is so quiet in this house, no rumbling about, no excited shouts! I imagine he
[Aleksei] is asleep in the bedroom! All his tiny things, photos & toys are kept in
good order in the bedroom & in the bowwindow [sic] room! Ne nado![160] On
the other hand, what a luck that he did not come here with me now only to fall
ill & lie in that small bedroom of our's! God grant the measles may continue
with no complications & better all the children at once have it! I miss my half
an hour's work at the puzzle every evening. If I am free here I think I will turn
to the domino again, because this silence around me is rather depressing—of
course if there is no work for me.—Old Ivanov was amiable & kind at dinner.
My other neighbour was Sir H.[anbury-]Williams, who was delighted to have
seen so many countrymen lately. [b]
   What you write about being firm—the master—is perfectly true. I do not forget
it—be sure of that, but I need not bellow at the people right & left every moment.
A quiet sharp remark or answer is enough very often to put the one or the other
into his place. Now, Lovy-mine dear, it is late. Good-night, God bless your
slumber, sleep well without the animal warmth.
   Feb. 24th. It is a grey windy day with snow falling thick, nothing like spring.
Just got your wire[464] about the children's health. I do hope they will all get it
[the measles] this time. I am sending you & Aleksei each a decoration from the
Queen & the King of Belgians [Albert I]—in commemoration of the war. You
better thank her yourself. Won't he [our son] be pleased to have a new cross!

God bless you my beloved Darling! I kiss you & the dear children ever so tenderly. In thoughts and prayers ever with you all. Your own huzy Nicky. [c]

No. 1671/ Telegram 4. Stavka> Tsarskoe Selo. 24 Feb 1917. 15.22> 16.07. To her majesty. Best thanks [for] two wires.[464] Please do not overwork yourself running between invalids. Train is late because of snowstorm. [My] cough is less. Tenderest kisses to all. Niki

No. 1672/ Telegram 6. Stavka> Tsarskoe Selo. 24 Feb 1917. 21.08> 21.53. To her majesty. Loving thanks for dear letters, also [daughter] Tatiana. Give all the sick my best love. Thoughts incessantly together. Sleep well. God bless you. Niki

No. 1673/ Her No. 646.   Tsarskoe Selo. Feb. 24th 1917.
My own priceless One,
    Milder weather, 4½ dg. Yesterday there were rows [disorders] on the V. ostrov [Vasil'evsky Island] & Nevsky [Avenue] because the poor people stormed the bread shops—they smashed Filipov['s bakery] completely & the cossacks were called out against them. All this I know unofficially. Baby< was cheery yesterday evening & I read "Elena's Babies" [a humorous tale by George Habberton] to him—& P. V. P.[etrov] read to him—[Aleksei's temperature was] 38.1 at 9 [o'clock] —at 6—38.3. Olga both times 37.7. She looks less well & tired. He slept well & has 37.7. At 10 went over to sit with Ania< (she looked like measles—37.7, cough strong, throat ache, may be angina) & then [I visited] with Lili<, N.P.< & Rodionov whom she had for dinner in the corridor whilst she was in bed. [a]
    So, after all the Variag [the Russian cruiser *Varangian*] leaves for England for 6 months [see Letter No. 1647d,e], probably today. She [Lili Dehn, wife of the cruiser's captain] of course is brave, but one sees how sad & disappointed & anxious for the journey [she really is]. How awfully lonely yr. first night must have been— cannot imagine you there without Baby, my poor sweet Angel! I hope one will hang Kedrinsky [A. F. Kerensky?] of the Duma after that horrible speech of his, its the only thing (military law[,] time of war) & [be] an example. One longs & entreats fr. yr. firmness to be seen. I wish you could have found out that story (wh. we know is true & there are artillery officers ready to swear to it) about Andrei [Vladimirovich] & Kutaisov, so as to punish Andr.[ei] for daring to forbid off.[icers] receiving yr. a.d.c. because he fulfilled his duty.—Oh! were but Frederi[c]ks fresher; its his buiseness [sic].—I think Kut.[aisov] will soon be on duty with you, but I hope you can return [to Tsarskoe Selo] before.—Remember to write to Georgie [George V] about Buchanan, don't put it off. [b]
    Well, Ania has the measles, at 3 [o'clock] she had 38.3—Tatiana too & also 38.3. Al.[eksei] & Olga—37.7, 37.9. I wander from one sick room to the other. —have made Marie & Anastasia go back to their rooms. M. Gibbs in a khalyain [dressing-gown] reads to Aleksei, his room has only a few curtains drawn, but O. & T. [have] quite [total darkness], so I write near the lamp (on the sopha).

Received for 1½ hours [a] Belgian, Siamese, Dane, Persian, a Spaniard, 2 Japanese—Korf, Benkendorf [P. C. Benckendorff], my 2 pages, Nastinka< who leaves to-morrow for the Caucasus as her sister is very ill—& Iza< (without touching her [because I carry measles germs]) & Groten fr. Kalinin<—worse disorders at 10 [o'clock], at 1 less, its in Khabalov's[467] hands now. See your Mufti [see Letter No. 1171a] at 6 & a lady too. [c]

Went in a moment to place candles for all of you, my treasures— air seemed lovely. Could not take M. & A. as their throats (& Shura's) have decided signs "suspicious," as the 4 Drs said—so they sat with Ania. I go to her in the morning for an hour & an hour in the evening—such a journey to the other end of the house— but I get wheeled.; she coughs colossally.—So does Tatiana & her head aches. Olga has her face strongly spotted, Baby most on his legs. I saw Bezobrazov yesterday, hopes very much that you wont forget him.—I said certainly not, but he must wait a while so as to get a good place [i.e., assignment]. Excuse dull letter but my days are fidgeti [sic] & lots of talks by phone besides.—The children all kiss you very tenderly. Baby kisses you, & asks how you feel & what is Kulik (the smotritel' [supervisor]) doing. Must end now, my Sunshine. God bless & protect you. Kiss you without end, with tender true devotion, burning love. Yr. own old Wify. [P.S.] Do find out about N.P.'s< cross. [See Letter No. 1668.] He dines today with Maklakov, Kalinin, Rimsky-Kors.[akov] etc. at Burdiukov's. [d]

No. 1674.   Ts.[arist] Stavka. Feb. 24th 1917.
My darling Sunny-dear,

Many hearty thanks for your beloved letter. So there we are with three children & Ania< lying with measles! Do try & let Marie & Anastasia catch it too; it would be so much simpler & better for all of them, and for you also! And this all happened since [I left]— only two days ago. Serg.[ei] Petr.[ovich Fedorov, M.D.] is very interested how the illness will develope [sic]. He finds it absolutely necessary for the children and Aleksei especially, [to have] a change of climate after their complete recovery—soon after Easter. When I asked him what place he was thinking of—he said it was the Crimea. He told me he has a son (never knew it) who got the measles & for a year the boy continued coughing until he was sent to the south which cured him promptly. He had tears in his eyes while he was talking upon this subject. I must say I think his advice an excellent one—& what a rest it would be for you! Besides the rooms at Tsarskoe [Selo] must be disinfected later & you would not care probably going to Peterhof—so where is to live? We will think it over quietly when I come back, which I hope won't take long! My brain feels rested here—no ministers & no fidgety questions to think over—I think it does me good, but only the brain. My heart suffers from being separated & this separation I hate, during such times especially! I won't be long away—only to put all things as much as possible to rights here & then my duty will be done. [a]

Febr. 25th. Just got your morning telegram[464]—thank God no complications as yet. The first days the temp. is always high & decreases slowly towards the end. Poor Ania—I can imagine what she feels & how much worse than the children! Now at 2.30 before driving out for my walk I will peep into the monastery &

pray for you & them to the Virgin! The last snowstorms wh. ended yesterday along all our southwestern railway lines, have placed the armies into a critical situation. If the trains cannot begin moving at once—in 3 or 4 days real famine will break out among the troops. Quite horribly anguishing! Good-bye, my own Love, my beloved little Wify. God bless you & the children! With tender love ever your own huzy Nicky. [b]

No. 1675/ Her No. 647.   Ts.[arskoe] S[elo]. Feb. 25th 1917.
My own priceless, beloved treasure,

8° & gently snowing—so far I sleep very well, but miss you my Love more than words can say.—The rows [disorders] in town< and strikes are more than provoking (I send you Kal.[inin]'s letter to me). The paper is not worth while, & you will get a more detailed one for sure fr. the gradonachal'nik [governor of Petrograd Khabalov]. Its a hooligan movement, young boys & girls running about & screaming that they have no bread, only to excite—& then the workmen preventing others fr. work—if it were very cold they wld. probably stay in doors.[465a] But this will all pass & quieten down—if the Duma wld. only behave itself—one does not print the worst speeches but I find that antidynastic ones ought to be at once very severely punished as its time of war, yet more so. I had the feeling when you go [i.e., left] things wld. not be good.—Do have Batyu-shin[465b] cleared out, remember that Alekseev stands up very firmly for him. Bat. chose as aid now a pol'kovnik [colonel] who was quite poor—his wife brought him 15,000 [rubles—as dowry?] & now he has become very rich. Strange! Batyushin also frightens people into paying him big sums so as not to be sent out (tho' innocent). Get rid of him, my lovy dear—of Bat.—I mean & quicker. [a]

How do you find Alekseev? Will you get good [N. N.] Golovin to come instead of the new man who you do not care for? Have yr. wishes fulfilled first darling.—Hard not to be together.—Ania< sends much love. She is the worst [with the measles], suffers awfully & a terrible cough day & night, the rash is inside [her mouth] & burns so. This morning she has [a temperature of] 38.6 [degrees] too. [Daughters] Olga 37.6, Tat. 37.1—Baby< still sleeps. Give me a message for Ania—it will do her good. Kind Lili< came again, & later when we left A. at 11 [o'clock] she sat with me & took tea til the train left. Nuisance receiving[—]have to [see a] Chinese [man], Portuguese with 2 daughters—the Greek, Argentine with wife. Boisman for Crimea[465b]—hope he will suit. Do go in a moment to the [icon of the] Virgin & pray there quietly for yr. sweet self & to gain strength for our big & little family. Our Knyazhevich's brother[465b] died in Moscou [sic], he was the help [i.e., manager] in my sklad.[2] And old M-me Min[465b] died in town but is being buried here. I thought Anastasia wld get it today, she looked suspicious yesterday—the Drs find her throat doubtful, but temp. so far quite normal. Akilina [Laptinskaya] looks after Ania— all the Drs too.— [b]

I am just reading an account of the Sweedish [sic] Pastor Neander who visited our prisoners in Germany & Austria. Now he has come again, here to continue [the work], shall see him next week. The former Gov.[ernor] of Penza Gen. Goryainov asked him to visit his son's grave in Friedland, & he did so & found it in order under a birch cross made by our soldiers on a German property. Several died there at our arranged hospital in that house [from] 25 Aug. til Sept. 8, 1914.

The [Goryainov] family asked birthday & namesday [sic] [of the Russian dead] so as to put wreaths [on their graves]. Then he went to the town cemetry [sic] & found there many of our graves & one: [with the inscription] Gen.-Maj. Makovsky, Commander of St. P.[etersburg] Regiment, fallen to the glory of Russian arms on the field of battle at Friedl.[and] 2nd June 1807. [c]

Ania sent for me as she felt very bad & could not breathe well, so went over 10½-12. Later I calmed her and she felt quieter, hopes for your "pure prayers"—always gets so frightened. At 1 [o'clock] Baby had 38.5, Olga—38.1, Tat.[iana]—37.4. Sit with all, change about. Am writing by a dark lamp on Olga's sopha. Just placed candles at Znamenia<, tired after receptions, talk with Apraxin< & Boisman.[465b] Of course the latter says one ought to have had a real cavalry reg.[iment] here wh. wld. have put order at once & not the zapasi [reserves] wh. consists of Petersburg people.—Therefore Gurko wld. not have yr. lancers, cld. always have found place[,] Groten said. Boisman proposes Khabalov[465b] shld. take military kitchens [after writing this word the empress crossed it out] ovens & have at once bread baked, as B. also says, there is enough flour. Some bakershops have also striked. One ought at once to have made order, now every day it gets worse. I told B. to go to Kalinin< & tell him to speak the [problem over]with Khabalov about the military ovens because to-morrow Sunday will be yet worse. Cant understand why they dont have the card system [i.e., introduce rationing]—& why not have all the fabrics [factories] military, then there will be not be [sic] disorder, the strikers said not to provoke those, because they wld. be sent to the front or severely punished.—No shooting is required—only [support] order & not let them cross the bridges as they do. That food question is madning [sic]. Excuse dull letter, but so much worry all around. Kiss & bless you. Ever yr. own old   Wify. [P.S.] None feel too bad. Ania suffers & coughs worse. All kiss you 1000 times. [d, e]

465a. This may sound obtuse since Alexandra is dismissing a profound event--the collapse of the tsarist regime—as caused by a minor turn of the weather. But there is some justification for her observation. Steinberg and Khrustalev note that after a long spell of extremely cold weather, the temperature in Petrograd rose above freezing on February 24. The thermometer reached 8 degrees C (46 degrees F) on February 25, and the weather remained warm for several days. (*Fall of the Romanovs*, p. 76)

465b. Nicholas Batyushin had investigated Myasoedov and others suspected of treason. (See Letters No. 1625a, 1655d, also Footnotes 367, 430.) Col. Boisman was appointed governor of Tavrida in place of Maj.-Gen. Nicholas Antonovich Knyazhevich in early 1917, but the tsarist regime collapsed before he assumed this post. The brother of "our" N. A. Knyazhevich was Alexander Antonovich Knyazhevich, also member of the Iversk Society of Nurses. Catherine Sergeevna Min was the widow of the late Maj.-Gen. G. A. Min, a former commander of the Semenovsky Guards Regiment. Lt.-Gen. Sergei Khabalov was military commander of the Petrograd region.

The empress's handwriting in this epistle is strange, the letters are childishly large and poorly drawn; some of what she writes is not entirely coherent. We know the tsarist regime was about to fall, so we might interpret these as signs of the coming collapse. It is also true that Alexandra was exhausted from tending a house full of sick loved-ones.

No. 1676/ Telegram 8. Stavka> Tsarskoe Selo. 25-II 1917. 19.35> 20.20. To her majesty. Tender thanks [for] dear letter. Marie also. Thoughts never leave you. Cold, windy, rather grey weather. Send you and invalids my fondest love. Niki

No. 1677/ Her No. 648.   Ts.[arskoe] S[elo]. Feb. 26th 1917.
Blessed sweet One,

What a joy at 9 [o'clock] this morning I found yr. sweet letter [No. 1670] of
the 23-24th.—Fancy only how long it went! Thanks over & over again for it.—I
covered it with kisses & shall do so yet very often. Its <u>so</u> lonely without
you—<u>nobody</u> to speak to really, as Ania< is very suffering indeed, coughs so
[high temp.—] must have been up to 40 [degrees] I think one time, scarcely slept
a wink this morning[, temp.] already 39.8. Any amount of nurses around her,
Akilina Laptinskaya], Fedosia Stepanovna, sister Tatiana (fr. my train), they
change about 2 at a time & Minny and Zhuk<, the childrens' 4 D^{rs} in the morning, then Evg. Serg.[eevich Botkin] & Vl. Nik.[olaevich Derevenko] 2 to 3 times
a day & her D^r whom she loves & who loves her, even spent this night near her.
The children [visit her] 3 times a day, I twice, Lili< in the evening, sweet creature. You know how difficult & capricious she is as a patient, but she really suffers & now luckily the spots are beginning to cover her whole face and chest. Its
better when they [the measles spots] come out. I went to Znam.[enia]< yesterday
& will to-day again—to go to service all alone, being tired & their needing me—I
think I need not—God sees my progress here. The children are cheery, Anastasia
& Marie call themselves the sick-nurses, sidel'ki—chatter without end & telephone right & left. They are most useful—wonder if they too will break down.
Zhilik< is still very weak & only pays Baby< visits. Mr. Gibbs is with him. All
dark rooms is [i.e., are] depressing, tho' Baby's big room with drawn curtains is
still lighter. [a]

To-day I wont receive anybody, cant continue like that. To-morrow however
must again. Boisman spoke pretty well, only fright[ened] [N. A.] Kniaz-
hevitch^{465b} will be elected mar.[shal] de noblesse, as that will complicate matters. Told me much about the disorders in town< (I think over 200,000 people
[are involved])—finds one does not keep good order. But I wrote all this yesterday, forgive me—I am foolish. But <u>one ought</u> to arrange card system [i.e., ra-
tioning] for bread (as in every country now), as one has it for sugar some time
[ago] & all are quiet & get enough. Our people are idiots. Obolensky wld. not do
it tho' Medem^{466a} wished to, as it succeeded at Pskov. A poor gendarme officer
was killed by the band [i.e., crowd]—a few other[s] too. That beda [misfortune]
does harm, well-dressed people, wounded soldiers & so on—kursistki [female
students] etc. who hit on others. Lili speaks to cab drivers to get news. They said
students came to them & said if they come out in the morning they would be
shot. Such rotten types, of course, cab drivers & tram drivers are on strike, but
they say its not like 95,^{466b} because all adore you & <u>only</u> want bread. Lili talked
for me to Groten as I could not leave Ania. At last I can take my drops again.
Such mild weather—[it's a] bore the little ones can[not ?] even go in a shut motor.—Kind Rodionov sent O., T, A[nia] each a flowerpot with Lilies of the Valley—the [Guards] Equipage< luncheon at the rifles did not take place as the
reg.[iment] were to be ready in case of need. Yr. loneliness must be awful—just
that great stillness around is so depressing, poor beloved one! [See Letter No.
1670b.] [b]

3½. Just got yr. dear letter [No. 1674] of yesterday, fondest thanks Sweetheart.
Yes, certainly a change of air would be good after [this illness,] only Livadia

wld. be too painful & took much fuss now. Well, one can think all over still.—the little ones [Marie and Anastasia] are the whole time with the others & Ania.—they may still catch it. Tatiana coughs awfully—[she has a temperature of] 37.8, O.—39.1, Al.—39.6, <u>Ania</u>—40.1.I just took Marie to Znamenia to place candles, went to our Friend's< grave. Now the church [being built over Rasputin's burial place is] so high that I could kneel & pray there calmly for you all without being seen by the dneval'nyi [orderly]. We went to Aleks<, stopped & talked to M. Ivanov, Khvotchinsky [Khvoshchinsky],[473] to new one [wounded at the hospital?] & with D[r.] Mild, very sunny. I brought you this bit of wood just over his [Rasputin's] grave, where I knelt. [c]

Things were very bad yesterday in town<. One made arrests [of] 120-130 people, chief leaders & Lelyanov drawn to account for speeches in the gor.[odskaya, i.e., the city] Duma. The ministers & some right.[ist] members of the Duma had a council last night (Kalinin< wrote at 4 in the morning) to take severe measures—& they are full of hope that to-morrow it will be calm, they had intended to let up barricades, etc. Monday I read a vile proclamation—but it seems to me it will be alright [sic]. The sun shines <u>so</u> brightly—I felt such peace & calm on this dear place[, Rasputin's grave?]. He died to save us.—Burdukov insists to see me to-day & I did so hope to see nobody. Nastinka< leaves to-night for Kislovodsk—Miechen< reigns there one says. Baby is one rash—covered like a leopard.—Olga has flat spots, Ania too all over, all their eyes and throats ache. Ania had 6 D[rs] & 2 nurses & Zhuk<, Marie and me. Madening—but she likes it, it sooths her nervousness. Bekker< came to her. It does not feel at all like Sunday. I must go back to them in their darkness now. Blessing & kisses without end. God grant the frost may cease in the south. My Riman's train[466a] got off the rails because of the ice near Kiev. God will help—this seems the climax [of our trials]. Faith and trust. So quiet [happy] you went to this dear Image [see Letter No. 1674b]. Ever, sweet Nicky, yr. own old   Wify. [d]

466a. Akilina Laptinskaya was a nun and admirer of Rasputin. Fedosya Stepanovna was a doctor's assistant; "sister Tatiana" and Zhuk— often mentioned in Alexandra's letters—were probably orderlies. Botkin and Derevenko were doctors of the royal family. Maria Georgievna ("Minny") was a Greek princess, the wife of Georgy Michaelovich and a friend of Anna Vyrubova and the empress. Alexander Nicholaevich Obolensky had been recently dismissed as *gradonachal'nik* of Petrograd for his failure to solve the city's supply problem. Nicholas Nicholaevich Medem had been the *gubernator* of Petrograd. Riman was an officer who commanded one of the imperial sanitary trains; see also Letter No. 590d.

466b. Alexandra may be referring to the year *1895*, when some episode (not specified here) made her husband unpopular. Or she may the thinking of the revolutionary year 1905.

No. 1678/ Telegram 10. Stavka> Tsarskoe Selo. 26 Feb 1917. 18.32> 19.15. To her majesty. Loving thanks [for] dear letter, also Anastasia, and [for] news. Glad they dont feel bad. Tenderest love to all. Niki

No. 1679.   Ts.[arist] S[tavka]. Febr. 26th 1917.
My own beloved One,
    The trains are again all wrong; your letter came yesterday after 5.o['clock], but to-day the last one (<u>No. 647</u>) arrived exactly before lunch time. Tender kisses for it. Please do not overtire yourself running accross [sic] among the invalids.

See often Lily Den—a good reasonable friend. I went yesterday to the virgin's image [icon] & prayed hard for you, my Love, for the dear children & our country, also for Ania<. Tell her that I saw her brooch fastened to the image & rubbed it with my nose while kissing [it]! Last evening I was in church; the old mother of the bishop[467]—thanked for the money we gave. This morning during service I felt an excruciating pain in the middle of my chest, wh. lasted for a quarter of an hour. I could hardly stand & my forehead was covered with beads of sweat. I cannot understand what it was, as I had no heart beating, but it came & left me at once, when I knelt before the Virgin's image! If it happens once more I will tell it to Fedorov. I hope Khabalov[467] will know how to stop those street rows [disorders] quickly. Protopopov ought to give him clear & categorical instructions. Only that old Golitsyn does not lose his head! Tell Aleksei that Kulik and Glina[467] are well & think of him. God bless you, my Treasure, our children & her [Anna Vyrubova]! I kiss you all very tenderly. Ever your own <u>Nicky</u>.

---

467. The tsar refers to the mother of Archbishop Constantine of Mogilev and Mstislav. As the military governor of Petrograd, General S. S. Khabalov was responsible for suppressing the disorders that toppled the tsarist regime. Elderly Nicholas Dmitrievich Golitsyn was chairman of the council of ministers. For Kulik, see Letter No. 1673d; Steinberg and Khrustalev identify the two as cadets who were playmates of Aleksei. "Kulik" ("Sandpiper") was Yevgeny Makarov, "Glina" ("Clay") was Vasily Ageev.

No. 1680/ Telegram 11. Stavka> Tsarskoje Selo. 26 Feb 1917. 21.20> 22.08. To her majesty. Loving thanks [for] telegram.[464] Shall leave callidus [code for *day after to-morrow*]. Have settled all necessary questions here. Sleep well. God bless you all. Niki[468]

---

468. "It was on this day that the Tsar received Rodzianko's historic telegram, in which the news of the outbreak of the Revolution and of the peril of the dynasty was conveyed in no uncertain words. He was told that there was anarchy in the capital, that the Government was paralyzed, and that any delay [in announcing a ministry responsible to the Duma] would be fatal." (Vulliamy, p. 317n) Unimpressed, Nicholas put the telegram aside, telling Fredericks, "That fat guy [tolstyak] Rodzianko has again written me all sorts of nonsense, to which I will not even give a reply." (*Padenie*, V, p. 38)

No. 1681.   Ts.[arist] S[tavka]. Febr. 27th 1917.
My own Treasure!
    Tender thanks for your dear letter. This will be my last one.[469] How happy I am at the thought of meeting you in two days. I had much to do & therefore my letter is short. After the news of yester-day from town<—I saw many faces here with frightened expressions. Luckily Alekseev is calm, but finds a very energetic man must be named to make the ministers work for the food question, coal, railways etc. That is right of course. The disorders among the troops come from the rota[469] according to the news I got. I wonder what Paul< is doing? He ought to keep them in hand. God bless you my beloved Sunny! I cover your sweet face with kisses, also the children. Give her [Anna Vyrubova] my love. Ever your own <u>Nicky</u>.

469. This was indeed the last letter Nicholas wrote to his wife, though in the next eight days he sent her nine telegrams that have survived. "After yesterday's news" may refer to Rodzianko's telegram mentioned in Footnote 468; "but it was now generally known that the Revolution had gained the upper hand, and that it was too late to think of concessions." Even so, Nicholas tried that tactic: see Footnote 470 below. The "rota" was made up convalescing soldiers sent to the capital for light duty. (Vulliamy, p. 318n)

No. 1682/ Telegram 12. Stavka> Tsarskoe Selo. 27 Feb 1917. 19.06> 20.02. To her majesty. Many thanks [for] letter. Leave to-morrow 2.30. Guard Cavalry from Nov. [Nizhnyi-Novgorod] ordered at once for town<. God grant vicissm [code for *disorders among*] troops shall soon be stopped. Always near you. Tender love to all. Niki

---

No. 1683/ Telegram 1. Vyazma> Tsarskoe Selo. 28 Feb 1917. 15.00> 16.49. To her majesty. Left this morning at 5. Thoughts always together Glorius [sic] weather Hope [you] are feeling well and [are] quiet. Many troops sent from front [to suppress the disorders in Petrograd] Fondest love. Niki

---

No. 1684/ Telegram 88 in Russian. Likhoslavl> Tsarskoe Selo. 28 Feb 1917. 21.27> 22.10. To her majesty. Thank you for news. Am glad all is well with you [all]. Hope to be home to-morrow morning. Embrace you and the children, God bless you. Niki[470]

470. "The Imperial train was stopped at Vishera, on instructions to the railway staff sent from Petrograd, and was diverted to Pskov. Here the Tsar telegraphed to Rodzianko intimating his readiness to make concessions, and received the grim reply: 'It is too late.' On the evening of 1st March the Tsar sent for General Rouszky (whose headquarters were in Pskov) and handed him a Ukase which made the Cabinet responsible to the Duma. Throughout the night the Commanders-in-Chief were in telegraphic communication with each other, with Alexeiev ... and with Rodzianko, and it was agreed that the only possible course was to demand the abdication of the Tsar (Denikin, p. 50; Gourko, p. 274). On the following day General Rouszky informed the Tsar of this decision. He listened with no visible emotion, and at 3 o'clock he sent Rouszky a signed act of abdication. This act had been prepared at the Stavka and forwarded to Pskov (Denikin, p. 50). He abdicated in favour of his son, but shortly afterwards consulted Professor Feodorov (Gilliard, p. 165): 'Sergey Petrovitch, tell me frankly, is Alexey's malady incurable?' 'Sire, our science teaches us that we have here an incurable disease. Those who are afflicted with it may none the less reach an advanced age. But Alexis Nicolaievitch is at the mercy of an accident.' On hearing this, he changed the abdication in favour of his brother Michael ("Misha"). The same evening, the delegates from the Duma—Schoulgin and the hated Goutchkov—arrived at Pskov and were at once taken to the Imperial train. There, and still with an embarrassing lack of emotion, the Tsar handed them the act. Schoulgin, who was an ardent monarchist, appears to have been the only member of the group who was deeply moved. A coat of varnish was placed over the Tsar's signature, and the delegates returned to Petrograd ·with the document." (Vulliamy, pp. 318-319n) Nicholas wrote in his diary that night, "All around are treason, cowardice, and deception!" (Buranov and Khrustalev, *Gibel'*, p. 39)

No. 1685/ Telegram 23 in Russian. Pskov> Tsarskoe Selo. 2 Mar 1917. 0.15> 12.55. To her majesty. Arrived here at dinnertime. Hope everybody's health is better and that we shall soon see each other. God be with you [all]. Warmly embrace [you]. Niki[471]

471. "This telegram was sent shortly before the ... abdication. It is a strange example of resignation, indifference, concealment or restraint." (Vulliamy, p. 319n)

No. 1686/ Her No. 650.   [No place indicated] March 2nd 1917.
My own beloved, precious angel, light of my life,[472a]

My heart breaks thinking of you all alone, going through all this anguish, anxiety & we know nothing of you & you neither of us. Now am sending off Solovev and Gramotin, each with a letter, hoping one may reach you at least. I wanted to send an aeroplane, but the men have gone. The young men [Solovev and Gramotin] will tell you everything, so that I wont say anything about the situation [here]. Its all so abnormally hideous & the rapidity colossal with wh. events go. But I have the firm belief, wh.—nothing can shake, that all will be well somehow, especially since I got yr. wire this morning—the first ray of sunshine appeared in this swamp. [a]

Not knowing your whereabouts, I finally went through the Stavka. Rodz.[yanko] pretended he did not know why one stopped you. Its clear one does, only not to let you to join with me before you have signed some paper of theirs, constitution or some such horror. And you, who are alone, no army behind you, were cought [sic] like a mouse in a trap, what can you do? Thats the lowest, meanest trick, unheard of in history,—to stop ones sovereign. Now P. [Paul?] cant reach you because of Luga wh. the revolutionaries have taken over. They stopped, seized and disarmed the But. regiment and wrecked the line. Perhaps you will show yourself to troops at Pskov & beyond & get them around you? If you are forced into concessions, you are never bound to keep them because the manner is beyond & below what is legitimate.[472b] [b]

Paul<, after getting a colossal reprimand for doing nothing with the guard [to support your authority], tries to work hard to save us all by means wh. are very grand & foolish. He wrote an idiotical manifesto about a constit.[ution] after the war etc.[472c] Boris [is] off to the Stavka. I saw him in the morning and evening of the day he left, as tho' urgent orders fr. the Stavka,—the purest panick [sic]. Georgi< at Gatchina does not return and gives no news of himself. Kirill<, Xenia<, and Misha< cant get out of town<. Yr. little family misses its Father. By degrees [I] have told the situation to the older [children] & the Cow [Anna Vyrubova]—they were far too ill before—a horribly strong measles, such sickness. Pretending in front of them was trying. Baby< I say [i.e., am telling] the half [of what has happened]. He has [a temperature of] 36.1—quite cheery. Only all wretched you have not come. Lili<, an angel, is inseparable, sleeps in the bedroom; [daughter] Marie with me, we are both in our dressing gowns and with our hair tied up. Whole day seeing people. Groten perfect. Resin< quiet. Old couple Benk.[endorff] sleep at home, Apr.[akin<] gets through here in civil dress. Used Linevich, but now I fear they have kept him too in town. None of our people come [here]. Sisters [i.e., nurses], women, civilians only can teleph.[one] to the W.[inter] Palace. Rataev[473] behaves admirably. We are all up in spirits, uncrushed by circumstances, only anquished [sic] for you & humiliated beyond words for you, patient saint. God almighty help you! [c]

Saw Ivanov last night, 1 til 2½, remains in his train.[473] Here for the moment I thought he could have gone with his train to Dno, but can he get through? He hoped your train would follow his. One burned Fred.[ericks] house, his family lies in the hospital of G. a ch. [the cavalry-guards]. They have taken Grunwald and Stakelburg, shall give a paper for them to bring you we got from N.P.<

through a man we sent to town. He neither can get out—he is registered. Two currents—the Duma and revolutionments [sic]— two snakes which I hope will bite off each others heads—thats [sic] wld. be the reckoning of the situation. I feel that God will do something. Such bright sun today, only to get you here!—The panic that the Ekip: [Guards Equipage<] even left us this night. They understand absolutely nothing, a microbe sits in them. I'll say [send?] that paper for Voeik.[ov] to read—it will hurt you as it did me. Rodz.[yanko] not even once mentions you. But when one hears you are not let on [go?], the troops then safe—stand up against all. They believe the Duma wants to be with & for you. Well let them make order & show themselves fit for something. But they made a too big fire—and how to put it out now? [d]

The children are quite in the dark. Baby lies with them for several hours after lunch & sleeps. I spent my days upstairs, received there too. The lift does not work for 4 days now, a pipe burst. Olga 37.7, T.[atiana] 37.9 & her ear begins to ache, An.[astasia] 37.2 because of med.[icine] they gave her for head ailments[,] pyramidon. Baby still sleeping, Ania< 36.6. Their illness has been very heavy. God for sure sent it, for the good somehow. They are so brave the whole time. I shall go out & say goodmorning to the soldiers now in front of the house. Dont know what to write, too many impressions, too much to say. Heart aches very much, but I don't heed it, my spirits are up & I am like a cock. Only suffer too hideously for you. Must end & write the other letter in case you dont get this one & small for them to hide it in their boots or burn. [This second letter also survived, see No. 1687.] [e]

God bless & protect you, send his angels to guard you and guide you. Never away fr. you. Lili & Ania send tenderest love & prayers. We all kiss & kiss & bless you without end. God will help, will helps [sic] & yr. glory will come. This is at the climax of the bad, the horror befor[e] our allies!! & the enemies joy!! Can advise nothing, be only yr. precious self. If you have to give into things, God will help you to get out of them.[472b] Ah, my suffering saint, I am one with you, inseparably one, old Wify. [P.S.] May this image [icon] I have blessed bring you my fervent blessings, strength, help. Wear his [Rasputin's] cross the whole time even if uncomfortable for my peace's sake. I don't send the image [after all], they can easier crumple up the paper without it.[474] [f]

472a. Some sections of this letter have become illegible with time and, I suspect, the ways in which it was handled before and after entering the archive. These passages may have been more legible in the late 1920s, when A. A. Sergeev translated the document into Russian, so I depended upon his text in reconstructing portions of the English text. (*Perepiska*, V, pp. 226-229)

472b. These passages in Letters No. 1686 and 1687 suggest that at this point Alexandra knew Nicholas had granted the long-demanded ministry responsible to the Duma (see Footnote 460), but that she did not know that the concession had made no impression and that her husband was forced to abdicate.

472c. A. A. Sergeev notes this document was published in issue no. 1 of *Ogonek*, 1923. (*Perepiska*, V, p. 227n)

473. Prince Ivan Dmitrievich Rataev was a lt.-col. in the guards and police commandant of the Winter Palace. M. Ivanov was obscure; Alexandra mentions him earlier, in Letter No. 846g. Vasily Vladimirovich Khvoshchinsky ("Khvotchinsky") was a lieutenant in the Guards Equipage<.

474. Sergeev notes that the sheets of postal paper upon which Alexandra wrote this and subsequent letters to her husband "were folded, evidently, into a package the size of which was not larger

than a vershok." (*Perepiska*, V, p. 229n) 1 *vershok* = 1.75 inches. My observations confirmed this information.

No. 1687/ Her No. 651.   [No place indicated] March. 2 1917.
Beloved, precious light of my Life,
    Gramotin and Solovev are going off with two letters. Hope that at least one of them can reach you to bring you news & get news. Its more than madening [sic] not being together—but soul & heart are more than ever [united]—nothing can tear us apart, tho they just wish this, thats why [they] wont let you see me until you have signed a paper of theirs about otv. min.[475] or constitution.[472b] The nightmare is that having no army behind you, you may be forced into it. But such a promise is "null" once in power again.[472b]—They meanly caught you like a mouse in the trap—unheard of in history.—Kills me the vileness & humiliation. These young men will tell you clearly the whole situation [here], wh. [is] too complicated to write, & I give only wee letters wh. can be burned or easier hidden. But God Almighty is above everything & loves his anointed of God & will save & bring you to your right again.[472b] I have absolute & <u>unflinching</u> faith in this & that keeps me up. Yr. little family is worthy of you, so brave & quiet. Now the eldest [and the] Cow [Anna Vyrubova] know everything. We had to hide it as they were very ill, such strong coughs, sick intensely bad & feeling terrible. And now bad general condition this morning O.[lga had a temperature of] 37.7, T.[atiana] 38.9, Anast.[asia] fell ill last, improved [from] 38.9 to 37.2 because of a powder they gave her for her headache & wh. took down her temp[erature]. Baby< asleep—yesterday 36.1, A.[nia]< 36.4 also recovering. All very weak & lie in the dark. Knowing nothing about you was the <u>worst</u> of all. This morning one awoke me with yr. wire & now its a balsam to the soul. Dear old Ivanov sat with me last night fr. 1 to 2½, he grasped the whole situation.[473] Groten behaves <u>very well</u>. Res.[in] alright [sic], continually come[s] to me about everything. We can get at no a.d.c., they are all busy, means they cant leave. I sent Linevich to town< about the order being here—he has never returned. Kirill< is daft, I think: he went to the Duma with the Ekip.[azh]<, stands for them, ours [i.e., the naval guard of the palace] have left us too (Ekip.), but officers returned, am just sending for them. Forgive such a wild letter. Apr.[akhsin<] & Res.[in] whole time disturb & my head goe's [sic] around. Lili< always with us & so sweet, sleeps upstairs. [Daughter] Marie with me. Al.[eksei] & she send prayers & love & only think of you. Lili wont return to [her son] Titi< so as not to leave us. Bless & kiss you without end—God is above all & will <u>never</u> forsake his own. Yr. very own <u>Wify</u>. [P.S.] You [will] read through the lines all & feel.

---

475. *Otvetstvennoe ministerstvo*, a "responsible ministry" in which the ministers would report to the Duma, not the tsar.

No. 1688/ Her No. 652. March 3rd 1917. - Beloved, soul of my soul, my own wee one—oh, how my heart bleeds for you—maddening knowing absolutely nothing except the vilest rumours wh. drive one wild. Wonder if the two youngsters [Gramotin and Solovev] reached you to-day with my letters. An officer's wife brings this.—Oh, for a line of life, no knowledge about you whatsoever, only heartrending things—& you, no doubt, hear the same. Won't tell anything in a letter. Is Nini's< husband [V. N. Voeikov] alive?—oh my, our 4 invalids go on suffering—only [daughter] Marie is up & about—calm & my helper growing thin as shows nothing of how she feels. [a]

We all go up & about as usual, each buries the anxiety inside— the heart hurts from pain for you & yr. utter solitude. I am afraid of writing much, as don't know if any letter can pass, if they won't search her on the way—to such a degree all are mad. In the evening I make my round with M.[arie] through the cellar to see all our men,—it does one good. A.[unt] Olga< and Helene< came to ask for news—very loving.—Ducky's< husband [Kirill<] abominable in town<, tho' pretends is working for Sovereign & Country. Ah, my angel, God is above all—I only live by my complete trust in him! He is our only hope. "God himself is kind and saves them",—[so it is written] on the large Image [icon]. [b]

We had a lovely moleben [prayer service] and akafist [acathistus] with the H.[oly] Virgin[, the icon which they] brought into their green bedroom—where they [the sick ones] all lay, did one such good—confided [sic] them & you into her Holy care. Then She passed through all the rooms & stopped in the Cow's [Anna Vyrubova's room] where I was then. Love, my love—it will go well, it must & I dont waver in my faith. Sweet angel, oh me loves you so—always together, night or day! I feel what you are going through—& yr. poor heart. God have mercy, give you strength & wisdom! He <u>wont</u> forsake you. He will help, recompense this mad sufferings & separation at such a time when one needs being together. Yesterday came a package for you with maps fr. headquarters, I have them safe & a list of promotion recompense fr. Belyaev<. Ah, whenever shall we be together again—utterly cut off in every way. Yet their illness perhaps is a saving, one cant move him. Dont fear for him, we'll all fight for our Sovereign; —and are at our places. Pauline well & calm tho' suffers beyond words,—lives in the house with her too, as do parents. Zhilik< is again well & faithful companion & playmate. Sig comes up & down[, he is] allowed to go. [c]

Blooming [the gardener] they have arrested & his two helps & red cap too & his aide who bows to the ground always. Lizochka behaves well. You understand I can't write properly—too much on my heart & soul. The family Benoiton kiss without end & suffer for Sweet Father. Lili & the Cow send love. Sunny blesses, prays, bears up by faith & her martyr's sake, she assists into <u>nothing</u> & has seen nobody of "those" & never asked to. So don't believe if one tells so. She is now only [a] mother with ill children. Can do nothing for fear of harming as has no news from her Sweetheart. Such sunny weather, no clouds—that means, trust & hope. All is pitch black around, but God is above all; we know not how he will help, but he will harken [sic] unto all prayers. Know nothing of the war, live cut off fr. the world. Always new madening [sic][rumors?]—the last that father [i.e., you] declined to keep the place he occupies for 23 years. One might loose [sic] one's reason—but we wont—we shall believe in a future of sunshine yet on the earth, remember that. [d]

Paul< just came—told me all. I <u>fully</u> understand yr. action [in abdicating], my own heroe [sic]! I <u>know</u> that could not sign [anything] against what you swore at yr. coronation. We know each other through & through—need no words —, as I live, we shall see you back on yr. throne, brought back by your people, to the glory of your reign. You have saved yr. son's reign & the country & yr. saintly purity & Judas Ruzsky [notwithstanding], you will be crowned by God on this earth—in yr. country. I hold you tight, tight in my arms & will never let them touch your shining soul. I kiss, kiss, kiss & bless you & will always understand you. Wify.[e]

No. 1689/ Telegram 3. Stavka> Tsarskoe Selo. 4 Mar 1917. 10.05> 11.58. To her majesty. Thanks, Darling. At last your telegram come [sic] during this night. Despairing being away. God bless you all. Love very tenderly. Niki

No. 1690. [Unnumbered]   [No place indicated] March 4th 1917.
Sweet, Beloved treasure,
   The lady leaves today instead of yesterday, so have occasion to write again. What relief it was to hear your precious voice [on the telephone], though one heard so badly & one listens now to all conversations! And yr. dear wire this morning—I wired to you yesterday evening about 9½ & this morning before one o'clock.[464] Baby< leaned over the bed & tell[s] me to kiss you. All 4 [sick ones] are lying in the green room in the dark, [daughter] Marie & I are writing, scarcely seeing anything with the curtains drawn. This morning only I read the manifest[o announcing your abdicatation in favor of your brother, Misha<] &, and then another fr. M.[isha, in which he refused the throne]. People are besides themselves with misery & adoration for my Angel. A movement is beginning among the troops. Fear nothing fr. Sunny[,i.e., me], she does not move & does not exist. Only I feel & foresee glorious sunshine ahead. [a]
   Am utterly disgusted with Ducky's< husband[, Kirill<—see Letters No. 1687a and 1688b]!! One shuts up people right & left,— officers of course. God knows what goes on—here rifles [i.e., soldiers] choose their own commanders & behave abominably to them, don't salute, smoke in the face of their officers. Don't want to write all that goes on, so hideous it is. N.P.< shut up at the [Guards] Equipage< in town!< Sailors came to fetch the others. The invalids upstairs & downstairs know nothing of yr. decision [to abdicate], fear to tell them, & also as yet unnecessary. Lili has been an angel & helped one being like iron & we have not once broken down. You my love my angel dear, cannot think of what you have & are going through—makes me mad! Oh, God! Of course, he will recompense 100fold for all of [your] sufferings. I wont write on that subject, one chut [?]—how one has humiliated you, sending these two brutes[, Shul'gin and Guchkov[470]] too—I did not know til [l] you told me [on the telephone this morning?] we of them had been [?]. I feel that the army will stand up ... [476] Revolution in Germany! W.[illiam] killed, [his] son wounded,[477] —one sees all over the freemasons in everything.— [b]
   Now An.[astasia, our daughter, has] temp. 38.6 & spots coming more out. Olga is spitting, the Cow [Anna Vyrubova] too. T.[atiana]'s ears [are] better. Sunbeam< [feels] better, cheery. How I wish you had them around you,—but they cannot move yet & I doubt one would let us pass anywhere. Gibbs saw Emma<, Nini< and their mother [Gedviga Eloiseovna Fredericks] in one room in an officers' hospital (english). Their rooms [apartment?] completely burned

down, Old Man [Count V. B. Fredericks] very ill. Red Hat [see Letter No. 1688d] still shut up. I am with you, love & adore you, kiss & embrace so tenderly, forever. God bless & keep you now & forever! Get somebody to bring a line—your plans more or less for the moment? God on high will help & a new krestopoklonnaya[478] [is] coming. Hold you tight, tight. Yr. own old   Wify. [P.S.] Only this morning we knew that all given over to M.[isha]< and that Baby [is] now safe[479]—such comfort! [c]

476. Dots indicating a break in thought are in the original text. Alexandra knew this letter might be intercepted by unfriendly parties, and she probably felt it wise to let her husband complete the thought: "loyal troops will restore you to power."

477. No such events were occurring in Germany. The empress was perhaps predicting all this as a result of the "Masonic movement," which she and other conservatives thought was driving events.

478. "Krestopoklonnaya" is the fourth week of Lent. See also Letter No. 874a.

479. Nicholas II abdicated in his brother's favor on Thursday, March 2/15, 1917. On March 3/16, Michael discussed the succession with Rodzyanko and several ministers of the new Provisional Government. Michael decided to accept the throne only if he were invited to do so by the forthcoming Constituent Assembly. Misha's "abdication" was in the newspapers on the morning of March 4/17, the date of this, Alexandra's last letter to her husband. Throughout the day, Alexandra "persisted in maintaining that Nicholas had only abdicated in order not to break his coronation oath by recognizing a constitutional regime. Count [P. C.] Benckendorff in the evening [of March 4] confirmed the news to her and she faced it with unconquered courage; but, he writes, 'as we went out I saw that she sat down at the table and burst into tears.' And to one of her ladies she said, 'Abdicated! And he all alone down there!'" (Pares, *Fall*, pp. 470-471) Two days before this, in the early morning hours of March 2/15, Nicholas wrote in his diary, "My thoughts and feelings are all the time there [with my family at Tsarskoe Selo], how hard it must be on poor Alix to go through all this by herself." (Pipes, *Russian Revolution*, p. 311)

No. 1691/ Telegram 5. Stavka> Tsarskoe Selo. 4 Mar 1917. 18.40> 19.55. To her majesty. Fond thanks [for] wire. Motherdear< arrived for two days, so kind lowing [sic] dine with her in train. Again snowstorm. Thoughts [and] prayers always together. Niki.[480]

480. "The Dowager Empress hastened from Kiev on hearing what had happened at Pskov, in order that she might be with her son in the hour of his trial. The ex-Tsar, in the Imperial train, had now returned to Mogilev." (Vulliamy, p. 320n)

No. 1692/ Telegram 9. Stavka> Tsarskoe Selo. 5 Mar 1917. 12.10> 22.28. To her majesty. Tender thanks. Motherdear< kisses you and children. Thinks much [of] Sunny [i.e., you]. Very cold. Seems calmer in town<. Hope invalids feeling better. Kiss all with devotion. Niki

No. 1693/ Telegram 12. Stavka> Tsarskoe Selo. 5 Mar 1917. 18.22> 12.24. To her majesty. Thanks for news. Old man [Fredericks] knows nothing about family. Could you not find out? Thoughts never leave you and children. God bless you. Sleep well. Fondest kisses. Niki

No. 1694/ Telegram 5 in Russian. Stavka> Tsarskoe Selo. 6 Mar 1917, 14.06> 7 Mar 1917. To her majesty. Tenderest thanks for many details atlast [sic]. Old man [Fredericks] and Son in Law [Voeikov] left for country place. Here quite

quiet. Am much with Motherdear<, who with me kisses you all most fondly.
Niki

Note. Nicholas Romanov was arrested at Mogilev on March 7, 1917, and brought to Tsarskoe Selo on March 9. While still at Mogilev, he sent one telegram and wrote two letters to the Empress Alexandra which have survived and are in the Central Archive of the Russian Federation. These texts follow; they have not heretofore been published in any language.

No. 1695/ Telegram 95 in Russian. [6 Mar 1917?], 19.35> [7 Mar 1917?]. From Kiev to her Majesty. Sandro< and I warmly thank [you] for dear telegram. Am writing with him. D.[yadya, i.e., U.(ncle)] Paul has arrived. Warmly embrace you. Niki.

No. 1696. [No place or date indicated. Much of this letter seems to be in a code that Nicholas improvised, hoping his wife would understand his meanings. The letter from Alexandra to which the fallen tsar refers may also have contained such a "code." This message begins on both sides of a card measuring four-and-a-half by three-and-three-eighths inches. The card features Nicholas's monogram and crown, all four edges are painted in gold. The message continues on one side of stationary with the imperial monogram and crown measuring 7¾ x 5 inches. The text is as follows:]

Darling Alex,
    Just a line or two to tell you that we found that letter of yours to Xenia delicious! We could not make out the words & expressions and laughed a good deal when it came out wrong. Really I miss you very much[.] [T]he ice looked so lonely when you left & the hills were astonished no one payed [sic] any attention to them. We played with Ella at badminton, but it was not quite the same. I have been to see the "Walkure" and "Sigfried [sic]." I find it lovely, what a pity we could' [sic] not come to see the Rheingold with you! So now good-bye.
Ever your loving Nicky

No. 1697. [Nicholas's last letter was written on stationery improvised from two sheets of paper containing someone else's handwriting in Russian. The text on these two sheets has been crossed out with vertical lines, three on each sheet. Someone (perhaps Nicholas) then glued the two sheets of paper together. Nicholas wrote his letter on the "clean side" of the document he made, and, when finished, folded the paper into quarters. Apparently Alexandra tore or cut away the top left-hand section, probably thinking its contents might compromise her husband and/or her with their jailers. (The bottom loop of a letter from a word written on the part which is gone spills down onto the portion of the letter which remains.) These theories would explain why the letter as we have it lacks a salutation, address or date, as well as why it begins abruptly, in the middle of a sentence.

Alexandra likewise tore away the bottom right-hand section of her husband's letter, possibly because it contained a "P.S." she did not want her enemies to see. At any rate, this section of the document is also missing, as is indicated on the following page. An envelope remains with this letter in the State Archive of the Russian Federation. Nicholas did not write anything on this envelope, but it contains several neat archival notations. The surviving text is as follows:]

... which is rather difficult under some circumstances, as he is producing strange noises followed by very bad smells. But now I am so accustomed to exercises, hearing the cannon shooting & gallopping [sic] in dense smoke, that this small circumstance does not trouble me much! I wish it were not winter to be able to go down the hills upon pullys once more. It is a great pity I could not stop on my way to Stuttgart to see the dear old goat for a minute. Now I close as Xenia is anxious to go on with her scribble. Another one of Pelly party.—Nicky.

Note. Nicholas Romanov returned to Tsarskoe Selo on March 9, 1917. The royal family set out for Tobol'sk in Siberia on August 14, 1917, arriving there on August 19. Nicholas and Alexandra were taken to Ekaterinburg on April 25, 1918. The six Romanovs, Dr. Botkin, Trupp the footman, Kharitonov the cook and Demidova the maid were killed in the basement of Ipat'ev's house on the night of July 16/17, 1918. In 1924, Ekaterinburg was renamed *Sverdlovsk* after the communist leader who was involved in the execution. The Ipat'ev house was demolished in 1977, when the U.N. announced its desire to include it on its list of historic protected buildings. The Soviet Union collapsed in 1991, and in 1992 the city was again known as *Ekaterinburg*, so named in honor of Catherine I, who reigned over Russia from 1727 to 1730. On July 16, 1993, several hundred monarchists gathered at the site of the Ipat'ev house to pay tribute to the murdered Romanovs. Surviving members of the family were on hand, including Georgy Mikhailovich Hohenzollern, the thirteen year-old pretender, who at that time lived in Spain. After the ceremony, "about 50 pro-monarchist Cossacks wearing pre-revolutionary uniforms tried unsuccessfully to topple a statue of ... Yuri Sverdlov several blocks from the execution site in the center of the Ural Mountains city." The following day, July 17, the monarchists planned to visit the pit from which the remains of five females and four males were excavated in 1991. "British scientists confirmed earlier this month that based on sophisticated genetic tests, the bones are almost certainly those of the czar, his wife Alexandra, and three of [their] five children. The other bodies were confirmed as three servants and the family doctor. The fate of the czar's youngest daughter, Anastasia, and his son, Alexei, is unknown." (*Murray [Kentucky] Ledger & Times*, July 21, 1993, page 8B) Nicholas II is dead, but the controversy surrounding his life and death continues.

Appendix I: Name and Term Identifier

This list identifies nicknames, abbreviations and irregular spellings of the names of people who appear at least five times in the "Nicky-Sunny" correspondence. For ranks in the army, navy, civil service, court and Church, see Appendix II: Table of Ranks as of 1914. Additional details concerning the people listed here will often be found in the Biographical Index. Frequently cited terms and places also appear in this "Identifier."

A.: either Anastasia, fourth oldest daughter of empress and emperor, or Anna Vyrubova

"Ago wee one": tsarevich Aleksei

"Aksel": A. E. von Pistol'kors

"Alek.": Alexander Petrovich, prince, oversaw sanitary-evacuation measures during war.

Alexandrovtsy: members of one of the empress's regs., the *Aleksandrovsky polk*

Alexeiev, Alexejev: M. V. Alekseev, head Gen. Staff and mil. planner at Stavka after Nicholas II replaced Nicholasha as c-in-c.

"Alia": Alexandra Pistolkors, former lady-in-waiting, wife of Aksel, sister of Anna Vyrubova.

Anastasia: youngest daughter of empress and emperor

Anastasia and Militsa: daughters of Nicholas I of Montenegro. Anastasia was married to "Nicholasha," Militsa was married to his brother, g.p. Peter Nicholaevich. See Footnote 1.

Andron.: M. M. Andronnikov, prince, homosexual, shady entrepreneur, influence peddler, ally of Rasputin and A. N. Khvostov.

"Ania," Anna: Anna Vyrubova, the empress's closest friend.

Ania's brother: S. A. Taneev

Anichkov Palace: located on Nevsky Prospect in Petrograd.

Anisia: Anisya Reshetnikova, follower of Rasputin, wife of Moscow merchant.

"Anpapa": Alexander III

Apraxin: P. N. Apraxin, Alexandra's private sec.

Aunt Alex, Alix: Alexandra, Danish princess, widow of King Edward VII.

Aunt Olga: Olga Constantinovna, daughter of g.p. Constantine Nicholaevich, widow of George I, king of Greece.

Axel P.: see Aksel

"B," "M-me. B.," "Becker," "Bekker": code words for menstruation.

"Baby," "Babykins," "Baby love," "Baby sweet": Aleksei, son of empress and emperor.

Balashov: N. P. Balashev, member State Council.

"Bariat.": Princess Maria Baryatinskaya, Alexandra's former lady-in-waiting.

"Becker," "Bekker": see "B"

Beletzky: S. P. Beletsky, became asst.-min. internal affairs and police director in 1911;
Dzhunkovsky replaced him, Jan. 1913; as ally of A. N. Khvostov returned to office
from Sept. 28, 1915 to Feb. 19, 1916.

Beliaiev: M. A. Belyaev, prominant gen., favored by the empress to follow Polivanov as
minister of war.

"Benk.," "Benkend.," "Benkendorf": P. C. Benckendorff, grand marshal of court; married to Maria Benckendorff.

"Betsy Shuv.": Countess Elizabeth Shuvalova

"big agoowee one": Nicholas II

"big girls:" two older daughters, Olga and Tatyana.

"Big Palace": In 1914 the large Catherine Palace at Tsarskoe Selo was converted into a
mil. hospital headed by Princess Gedroits, M.D. Alexandra, her daughters and Anna
Vyrubova served here as volunteer nurses. Known as the "bolshoi dvorets," it had
over 100 rooms. Alexandra could see the church at the hospital from her window in
the Alexander Palace. See Letter No. 1310b.

"black family," "black princesses": see Anastasia and Militsa

Bobr.: Count G. A. Bobrinsky, lt.-gen.; gov.-gen. when Galicia was occupied, then assigned to s.w. front.

Boris: Boris Vladimirovich, g.p., tsar's first cousin

Boysy, boyxy: one of Alexandra's pet names for her husband.

Butakov: probably A. I. Butakov, sr. naval lt. Guards Crew; killed, Dec. 14, 1914.

(Css.) Carlov, Carlow: Countess Natalya Karlova, wife of Georgy Georgevich, duke of
Mecklenburg-Strelitsk.

Costia: see Kostia

Coun. of the Em.: Council of the Empire or "State Council" (gosudarstvennyi sovet); see
Footnote 96.

cow: nickname for Alexandra's chubby friend, Anna Vyrubova.

"(My) Crimeans": members of the Crimean Cav. Reg. Which was named in honor of and
commanded by the reigning empress.

"crows": see Anastasia and Militsa

"D.": Dmitri Pavlovich

"Daisy": Margarita, Swedish princess, born British princess.

Den: Dmitry (Mitia) von Dehn, naval capt., Lili's< husband.

"Derev.": Derevenko, either the sailor attending the tsarevich or the physician with the
same name also in service to Aleksei.

"Djunk.": see "Dzhunk."

"Dm. Sherem.," "Dmitri Sh.": D. S. Sheremetev, col. Life Guards Horse Reg.

"Dmitri," "Dmitry P.": g.p. Dmitry Pavlovich, Nicholas's first cousin, brother of Maria
Pavlovna; Dmitry was "an elegant and perhaps decadent young man [who] wrote
verses and assisted at Rasputin's murder." (Vulliamy, p. 14n)

"Dona": Augusta-Victoria, wife of Kaiser Wilhelm II.

"Dr.," "Drent.": A. A. Drenteln, col. Preobrazhensky Reg. and later its commander; a.d.c
to Nicholas II.

Drina: see Trina

"Ducky": Victoria Fedorovna, wife of "Kirill"

Duvan: mayor of Evpatoriya, town on Crimea.

"Dzhunk.": V. F. Dzhunkovsky, asst.-min. internal affairs and police director, 1913-1915,
then field commander.

"Eberh.": A. A. Eberhard, commander, Russian Black Sea fleet.

"Echappar," "Eshappar": F. V. Dyubreil-Eshappar, former master of the household" of g.p. Georgy Michaelovich, member ministerial council of imp. court; died in Minsk, Nov. 1915.

Edigarov: see Endigarov

"Egor": Igor Constantinovich, son of Constantine Constantinovich.

Elagin: residence of Maria Fedorovna, Nicholas II's mother. Alexandra sometimes uses this name to refer to its occupant, the dowager empress herself.

"Elena": see "Helene"

"Elisavetgradtsi": members of the Guards Reg. named in honor of the Empress Elizabeth (reigned, 1740-1761).

"Ella": Alexandra's older sister, Elizabeth Fedorovna

"Emma," "Emma Fr.": Countess Emma Fredericks, lady-in-waiting, daughter of V. B. Fredericks.

Endigarov: D. S. Iedigarov, cav. capt. 1st grade

"eng.-mech.," "Engineer-mechanic": code words for menstruation

"Engal.,": P. N. Engalychev, gov.-gen. Warsaw

Equipage: see Guards Equipage

"Eriv.," "Erivanetz": member 13th Erivan Life Guard Grenadier Reg.

"Ernie": Grand Duke Ernst-Ludwig of Hesse, empress's brother

"Fat Orlov": V. N. Orlov, maj.-gen. His Maj.'s Suite, dir. tsar's inf. chancellery.

Father Alex.: Alexander Vasilev, imp. family's chaplain.

Feodorovsky Sobor: Fedorovsky Sobor, see "Pestchernyi Chapel"

"Feod.," Feodorov: S. P. Fedorov, imp. family's physician.

"(we) five": Alexandra and her four daughters

"5 treasures": the royal children, Olga, Tatyana, Maria, Anastasia and Aleksei

Fr., Fred., Freder., Freederikz: Count V. B. Fredericks, min. imp. court and appanages

(Css.) Fred.: Gedviga Fredericks, wife of B. V. Fredericks

G., Mr. G.: Pierre Gilliard, Swiss tutor of Aleksei

Galitzin: Prince N. D. Golitsyn, member Red Cross governing board, pres. committee to aid Russian pows. Chairman Council of Ministers, Jan. 1917, until fall of tsar's government in March 1917.

Gartvig, Alexandra: dir. empress's stores<

Gatchina: one of the Imperial Palaces, summer residence of Dowager Empress Maria Fedorovna; near Petrograd.

Ged., Gedroytz: Princess Vera Gedroits, surgeon, head, Tsarskoe Selo Hospital; instructed volunteer nurses.

Georgi, Georgie: g.p. Georgy Mikhailovich, lt.-gen.

Georgians: members of tsarevich's 14th Georgian Reg.

Georgie: see "Georgi"

"Georgie B.": young prince of Battenburg, British naval lt.

"girlies," "girls": four daughters, Olga, Tatyana, Maria, Anastasia

"Gor.," "Gorem.,": I. L. Goremykin, chairman, council of ministers, January 1914-January 1916.

Goutchkov: A. I. Guchkov, leader, Octobrist Party.

Gr., Greg.: Grigory Rasputin

"Greek Georgie & wife:" Prince George of Greece, Nicholas II's first cousin.

"Greek Nicky": see Nick

Guards Equipage: Russian marine companies (roty) were grouped in "equipages," each about 2,000 strong. The "Ship's Equipage" (gvardeisky ekipazh) represented the navy in the Imperial Guard; these men served on royal yachts, ships of the Baltic fleet, and during the winter as part of the Petrograd garrison. A special unit, the "Life Guards Ship's Co." (or the "Ship's Crew"), was stationed at Tsarskoe Selo. Under Kirill's<

command, it sided with the March Rev., an act which to the empress seemed a "bitter revelation of disloyalty and ingratitude." (Vulliamy, p. 23n.)

Hartwig, Hartwigs: see Alexandra Gartvig

"Helene": Elena Petrovna, Serbian princess, wife of "Little John."

Hitrovo: Margarita ("Rita") Khitrovo, lady-in-waiting to Alexandra.

Hohenfelsen: Princess Paley, wife of g.p. Paul Alexandrovich.

(the, our) hospital: see "Big Palace"

Igor: Igor Constantinovich, cav. capt., assigned to Stavka.

Inzhmekh: see "eng.-mech."

"Irina T.": Countess Irina Tolstaya.

"Irene": Irina, wife of Prince Henry of Prussia, Alexandra's sister.

"Irine": Irina Yusupova, wife of F. F. Yusupov, organizer of Rasputin's assassination.

"Isa," "Iza": Baroness Sophia Buxhoeveden, Alexandra's lady-in-waiting, author of important memoirs.

Ivan: I. A. Orlov, 1st lt., mil. aviator.

Izmailov officers: members of Life Guards Izmailovo Reg.

"Jagmin": Col. S. Yu. Yagmin

"Jakovlev": Yakovlev, managed g.p. Maria Nicholaevna's train.

"Janoushk.," "Janush.": see Yanoushkevitch

Jedigarov: see Endigarov

"Khan," "Khan-Nakhichevansky": Khan-Gussein Nakhichevansky, cav. gen., then field commander.

"Kira": Cyril Naryshkin, col., key assistant of Nicholas II.

Kirill: g.p. Cyril Vladimirovich, Nicholas's cousin; rear-ad., husband of "Ducky"; see also Guards Equipage.

Kniajevitch: N. A. Knyazhevich, maj.-gen., cav.

"Koj.": L. M. Kozhevnikov, sr. naval lt., Life Guards Ship's Co.

"Kostia": g.p. Constantine Constantinovich, inf. gen., insp.-gen. mil. schools; honorary pres. Academy of Sciences; also a poet.

"Kostia's boys": Georgy, Igor, Ioann and Oleg.

Kroshka: "little one," usually tsarevich Aleksei, sometimes Nicholas II.

"Kubl.": A. I. Kublitsky, sr. naval lt., Life Guards Ship's Co.

Kulomsin: A. A. Kulomzin, pres. State Council, active in wartime charities.

Kussov: B. V. Kusov, field commander.

Kutaissov: Col. C. P. Kutaisov

Kyra: see "Kira"

"Larka": Count I. I. Vorontsov-Dashkov, col. Hussar Life Guards Reg.

"Leo": probably nickname of Gustav Heinrichovich, valet of Alexandra.

"Lili," "Lilly D.": Julia Dehn, wife of K. A. Dehn.

"little admiral": C. D. Nilov, commander, imp. yacht *Standard.*

"little John": Prince Ioann Constantinovich, son of g.p. Constantine Constantinovich, cav. capt.

"Little Marie": see Marie, Marie P.

"little one": tsarevich Aleksei

"little ones": five children of empress and emperor

Lolo, Lolo D.: Olga Dolgorukaya, widow of A. S. Dolgoruky.

Louise: princess of Battenberg, relative of Alexandra.

M., Mordv.: Col. A. A. Mordvinov, a.d.c. to Nicholas II, friend of entire imp. family.

M. Den: see Mitia Den

"M-me. B.": see "B"

"Madelaine": Magdalina Zanotti, Alexandra's *kamer-frau.*

"Maksim," "Maximov.,": C. K. Maximovich, adj.-gen., cav. gen.; known and widely distrusted as an informant of the empress.

Marie: Maria (Russian spelling), third oldest daughter of the empress and emperor.

Marie, Marie P., Little Marie: Maria Pavlovna (the "Younger"), daughter of g.p. Paul Alexandrovich and sister of Dmitry Pavlovich. Served as a nurse during war, owned a train and a hospital at Pskov.

Marine of the Guard: see Guards Equipage

Mark., Markosov: V. V. Markozov, former officer in Alexandra's Life Guards Lancer Reg., active in her charities.

Martinov: A. I. Martynov, maj.-gen., cav.

"Masha," "Masha V.": Maria Vasilchikova, one of Alexandra's former ladies-in-waiting, apparently an Austrian agent.

Mavra: Elizabeth Mavrikievna, wife of Constantine Constantinovich.

"Max": Maximilian, prince of Baden.

Maximovitch, C. K.: see Maksim

"Mechanic": see "engineer-mechanic"

Mekk: V. V. von Mekk, sec. to Ella,< active in her wartime charities. (*Cf.* "Uncle Mekk.")

"Merica": Css. Maria Karlova, one of Alexandra's ladies-in-waiting.

"Miechen": Maria Pavlovna (the elder), widow of Nicholas's uncle Vladimir Alexandrovich; German princess who disliked the Hohenzollerns and was strongly pro-Russian.

Militsa, Militza: see Anastasia and Militsa

"Misha": g.p. Michael, brother of Nicholas II.

Mistchenko: P. I. Mishchenko, art. gen., field commander.

Mitia Den: Dmitry Vladimirovich von Dehn, naval capt., at Stavka, husband of "Lili."

Moscov. Vied.: *Moskovskie Vedomosti* (Moscow Gazette), a newspaper.

"Mr. G.": see "G"

"N," "Nicholasha" or "Nikolasha": g.p. Nicholas Nicholaevich, cousin of emperor, c.-in-c. Russian armies until Aug. 1915.

"N.M.," "Nikolay": g.p. Nicholas Michaelovich, grandson of Nicholas I; historian, liberal, warned emperor of the coming revolution.

Nast., Nastenka, Nastinka: Countess Anastasia Hendrikova, one of Alexandra's ladies-in-waiting.

Nat. Br.: Countess Natalya Brasova, wife of Misha<.

Nicky, "Greek Nicky": Prince Nicholas, son of King George I of Greece.

"Nijegorodtzy": members of Emperor's 17th Nizhegorodsky Dragoon Reg.

"Nini": Eugenia Voeikova, daughter of V. B. Fredericks, wife of V. N. Voeikov .

Nov. Vrem.: *Novoe Vremia* (New Times), conservative newspaper which usually followed the government's line and was often (though not always) its mouthpiece. The empress often read and quoted it— sometimes disapprovingly.

N.P., N.P.S.: N. P. Sablin, capt. 1st class, close friend of Nicholas and empress.

O.E., O. Evg., Olga E., Olga Evg.: Olga Byutsova, one of Alexandra's ladies-in-waiting.

"old Count V.": I. I. Vorontsov-Dashkov

"Old Madame Orlova": grandmother of Ivan Orlov

Olga: either eldest daughter of empress and emperor or g.p. Olga Alexandrovna, the tsar's younger sister and a volunteer nurse during war.

"Olga Evg.," "Olga Evgenievna": see O. Evg.

"Olga O": Olga Orlova, wife of "Fat Orlov."

"Onor": Eleonora, wife of Alexandra's brother Ernst-Ludwig.

(Pss.) Orlov: see Olga O.

Our Friend: Grigory Rasputin. The royal letters and telegrams also mention his wife
    Praskovaya, and their children, Dmitry, Maria and Varvara.

P.: see Paul

Palace, Palace Hospital: see "Big Palace"

Papa: Alexandra's father, Grand Duke Ludwig of Hesse.

Paul: g.p. Paul Alexandrovich, Nicholas II's last living uncle; married to Princess Paley.

Pavlovtsy: members of one of the tsar's regs., this named in honor of the emperor Paul
    (Pavel, reigned, 1796-1801).

Pestcherny Chapel: "Peshchernyi" is the Russian word for *crypt* or *cave*; this was a
    chapel located in the crypt of the Fedorovsky Sobor (Cathedral), a church at Tsarskoe
    Selo for which Alexandra had a special fondness.

Peter Vas., Peter Vass.: P. V. Petrov, administrator of mil. schools until assigned to tutor
    the tsarevich.

"Petia": Peter Alexandrovich, maj.-gen. His Maj.'s Suite, husband of tsar's sister Olga
    until their divorce in fall 1916.

"Petiusha": Peter Nicholaevich, Nicholasha's younger brother and husband of Militsa.

"(Mr.) Ph.," "Monsieur Philippe": Nizier Vachot Philippe, French mystic and healer who
    visited Russia and exerted strong influence on Alexandra and Nicholas before Ras-
    putin.

Pourtseladze: Othar Purtseladze, officer 13th Erivan Grenadier Reg.

"precious agoo wee one": the tsarevich

Preobr.: member of elite Preobrazhensky Life Guards Reg.

P-ss, Pss. G., the Princess: see Ged.

Putiatin: Prince M. S. Putyatin, maj.-gen., dir. imp. court.

P.V.P.: see Peter Vas.

ramolie: worn out, exhausted, from the French verb *ramollir*: to softenen, to make
    soft—as, in a humorous sense, "my brain!"

"Rebinder couple": N. A. Rebinder was marshal Kharkov nobility; elected to State Coun-
    cil. His wife, Elizabeth ("Liza") Rebinder, was admin. Kharkov Order of Red Cross
    Nurses.

Ressin: A. A. Resin, maj.-gen.

"Rita," "Rita H.": Margarita Khitrovo, a lady-in-waiting to Alexandra.

"Rod.": N. N. Rodionov, sr. naval lt., Life Guards Ship's Co.

"Rodz.": M. V. Rodzyanko, pres. Fourth Duma.

Rost., Rostoftzev: Count Ya. N. Rostovtsev, assistant to empress and active in several
    wartime charities.

Rostchakovsky: M. S. Roshchakovsky, former naval officer who served in
    Russo-Japanese War and was close to the court. During war took part in construction
    work on Murman coast.

Rouszky, Rouzsky, Russky: N. V. Ruzsky, important commander.

"Ruchlov": S. V. Rukhlov, min. communications, 1909 to Oct. 1915.

"Russin": A. I. Rusin, important naval commander.

Russkoe Slovo (Russian Word): a newspaper.

S.: see Anastasia and Militsa

Sandra G.: see Gartvig

"Sandra," "Sandra P.": Alexandra Petrovskaya, wife of Col. N. A. Petrovsky.

Sandra Schouvalov, Sandra Sh.: Countess Alexandra Shuvalova, widow of P. P. Shuva-
    lov.

"Sandro": Alexander Mikhailovich, g.p., son of g.p. Michael Nicholaevich, ad.; during
    war organized army aviation; husband of tsar's sister, Kseniya Alexandrovna.

"Sandro L.": A. G. Leuchtenberg (also Leikhtenberg), col. Hussar Life Guards Reg.,
    assigned to high command of armies on n. front during war.

"Saschka," "Sashka": Count A. I. Vorontsov-Dashkov, emperor's a.d.c. and col. Her Maj.'s Light Hussar Guards Reg.

Sch.: V. E. Schulenburg, count, col., active in wartime charities.

(M-lle) Schneider, Barbara: artist, admin. Female School of People's Art Named in Honor of Alexandra Fedorovna.

Schterbatov: N. B. Shcherbatov, prince, dir. state horse breeding farm, acting-min. internal affairs, June 5- Sept. 26, 1915.

Selenetzki: R. D. Zelenetsky, naval officer.

Sergei, Sergei M: g.p. Sergei Michaelovich, gen., art.-insp., brother of Nicholas Michaelovich.

Sergeiev: Ya. T. Sergeev, commanded Alexandra's 21st E. Siberian Reg.

"Shourik," "Shurik": Alexander Constantinovich Shvedov, officer in His Maj.'s convoy.

Shurik: see Shourik

Shvibzik: one of Alexandra's pet names for her daughter Anastasia.

(my, our) Siberians: members of 2nd and 8th W. Siberian and 21st E. Siberian Infantry Regs.

Siliaiev: Leo Zakharevich Silaev, a.d.c., col.

Siro-Boyarsky: A. V. Syroboyarsky, staff-capt. 9th art. brigade.

(all) six: Nicholas II's wife and five children.

S. M.: Sergei Michaelovich

Sonia: usually Sophia Ivanovna Dzhambakurian-Orbeliani, one of Alexandra's ladies-in-waiting; less often Sophia Dehn, wife of D. V. Dehn—in which cases she is so identified in the text.

Souchomlinov: Catherine Sukhomlinova, wife of V. A. Sukhomlinov.

Soukhomlinov: V. A. Sukhomlinov, min. war until June 13, 1915. Blamed for early shortages and poor organization of Russian army.

St.: see Sturmer

Stana: see Anastasia of Montenegro

Stavka: G.H.Q. Russian armies on western front.

Stcheglovitov: I. G. Shcheglovitov, min. justice, 1906 to July 1916, pres. State Council from Jan. 1, 1917.

Stch., Stcherb.: see Schterbatov

Stcherb., Stcherbatchev: D. G. Shcherbachev, adj.-gen., key inf. gen. throughout the war.

store: in Russian, *sklad,* a depot for Red Cross supplies financed by a wealthy, charitable person such as the empress.

Sunbeam: one of Alexandra's pet names for her son, occasionally also for her husband.

Sun Light: one of Alexandra's pet names for her husband.

"Sunny," "Sunshine": As a child Alexandra was known at the English court as "Sunshine"; "Sunny" was Nicholas's favorite nickname for his wife. Alexandra often called her husband "my Sunshine."

Synod: the "Most Holy Synod" (*Svyatteishy Vserossiisky Pravitelstvuyushchy Sinod)* was a board of bishops and churchmen that governed the Russian Orthodox Church. Peter created the Synod in 1721 to replace the patriarchate. The Synod was headed by a *director* ("Ober-Procurator") who was equivalent in rank to a minister, though much administrative work was in the hands of the *assistant-director.*

"Tail": A. N. Khvostov, min. internal affairs, Sept. 1915 to March 1916.

Taneev, S. A.: brother of Anna Vyrubova.

Taneyev: A. S. Taneev, father of Anna Vyrubova.

Tatiana: Tatyana (Russian spelling), second oldest daughter of the empress and emperor.

Tatiana, Tatiana K.: Tatyana Constantinovna, wife of Prince K. A. Bagration-Mukhransky.

Taube, G. N.: baron, ensign in Life Guards Ship's Co.

"Teter.": N. K. Teteryatnikov, valet of Nicholas II.
"Tino": Constantine I, king of Greece, 1913-17 and 1920-22
Tiny: tsarevich Aleksei
Titi: son of Julia and Karl Akimovich von Dehn
Toll: A. A. Tol, during war commanded 2nd Pavlovsky Hussar Reg.
Toria: Victoria-Alexandra-Olga-Maria, British princess, daughter of King Edward VII of Great Britain and Queen Alexandra.
"Tou-Tou": Maria, third oldest daughter of empress and emperor.
"town": Petrograd
(my) train: see D. N. Loman, Biographical Index.
Trepov, A. F.: replaced Rukhlov as min. communications, Oct. 30, 1915, also appointed chairman council of ministers on Nov. 10, 1916; dismissed from both positions, Dec. 27, 1916.
Trina: Catherine Schneider, "reader" to Alexandra; also gave lessons to the children.
"Tudels," "Tyudels,": Maria Tutelberg, second dresser to empress.
Tvertzi: member of Tver regiment; Tverets (sing.), Tvertsy (pl.), see Letter No. 888c.
Tyutcheva, Sophia: governess, dismissed in 1912 for opposing Rasputin.
"Uncle Mekk": N. K. von Mekk, active in Ella's< wartime charities, chairman board, Moscow-Kazan Railroad Co. (Cf. Mekk, V. V.)
"Uncle Willi": king of Greece, 1863-1913.
V: see "Voyeikov"
V. N.: see "Vl. Nik."
"Valia," "Valya": Prince V. A. Dolgorukov, attended tsar at Stavka.
Valuyev: F. M. Valuev, communications engineer and expert.
Vassiltchikov: Prince B. A. Vasilchikov, member supreme council to aid Russian pow families.
Vesselkin: M. M. Veselkin, rear-ad.
Vesselovsky: Maj.-Den. A. A. Veselovsky, infantry.
"Vicky": Victoria, queen of Sweden, wife of King Gustav.
Victoria: Alexandra's eldest sister, wife of Prince Louis of Battenburg.
Veliopolsky: Count S. I. Velepolsky, elected to State Council in 1916 by "landowners of the Polish Tsardom."
Vict. Erast.: see "Zabor."
Viltch., Viltchkovsky: S. N. Vilchkovsky, asst.-dir. imp. court, pres. Tsarskoe Selo Evacuation Committee, or his wife.
V. N., Vl. Nik, Vlad. Nik: V. N. Derevenko, one of imp. family's physicians.
Vojeik: see "Voyeikov"
Volzhin, A. N.: dir. Holy Synod, Oct. 1, 1915 to Aug. 7, 1916, then member State Council.
Voronov, P. A.: guards naval lt.
Vorontsov-Dashkov, I. Iv.: count, cav. gen. Not to be confused with "Saschka" or "Larka."
"Vosnesentsi": members of the Voznesentskii Guards Reg.
Voyeikov: V. N. Voeikov, maj.-gen. His Maj.'s Suite, palace commandant; known as a master of intrigue.
"wee ones": see "5 treasures"
Winter Palace: converted into a hospital in 1914; charitable committees also met here.
Witte, G. G. von: active in many wartime charities.
Xenia: g.p. Kseniya was the emperor's older sister; wife of Alexander Michaelovich.
Yanoushkevitch: N. N. Yanushkevich, chief of staff at Stavka in 1914.
Yedigarov: see "Endigarov"
"Yusik," "Yuzik": G. A. Rashpil, officer in His Majesty's convoy.

Zabor.: V. E. Zborovsky, *sotnik* in His Majesty's convoy.

Zeidler: G. F. Tseidler, M.D.

Zhilik: see G

"Zina": Zinaida Menshted, hairdresser, admirer of Rasputin from Smolensk.

(M-me.) Zizi: Elizabeth Naryshkina, widow of A. D. Naryshkin.

Znam., Znamenia, Znamenje: The Znamenskaya Church would be known in English as the "Church of the *Sign*." It was built at Tsarskoe Selo in 1747 to house a famous icon of the Virgin displaying Christ in her womb. (This is known as the "ikona Znamenskaya Bozhei Materi," the "Icon of the Sign of the Mother of God"). Mary is depicted in this image with outstretched arms, offering a *sign* of her son, Jesus Christ. Alexandra had a special love for this image, which was a guardian of the Romanov household and noted for miraculous healing. (Steinberg and Khrustalev, *Fall of Romanovs*, p. 67)

Appendix II: Table of Ranks as of 1914

The purpose of the following discussion is to clarify the titles and ranks referred to in the letters, telegrams and Biographical Index. Material for this discussion is drawn from L. E. Shepelev, "Chiny, zvaniya i tituly v Rossii" (Ranks, names and titles in Russia), *S.i.e.* (*Sovetskaya istoricheskaya entsiklopediya*), vol. XVI, pp. 52-59; S. M. Troitsky, "Tabel' o rangakh" (Table of Ranks), *S.i.e.*, vol. XIV, pp. 15-16; and Sergei G. Pushkarev, *Dictionary of Russian Historical Terms from the Eleventh Century to 1917*, edited by George Vernadsky and Ralph T. Fisher, Jr. (New Haven, Ct., Yale University Press, 1970).

The Table of Ranks was introduced by Peter the Great on January 24, 1722. It set forth a hierarchy of fourteen ranks with sub-gradations for all army and naval officers, court officials and civil servants in leadership positions. (Ordinary state clerks, copyists and secretaries stood below the fourteenth rank.) By the early 20th century, some of the original ranks had been abolished, new ranks had been created, and some titles had been assigned to different places within the hierarchy. The number of ranks, however, remained fixed at fourteen.

The number of people in the system grew over time. For example, between 1864 and 1897, the number of generals and admirals in active service rose from 351 to 1,212, staff officers from 2,630 to 6,282, company officers from 16,495 to 35,283. 43,720 officers were on active duty in 1897, only 52% of whom were hereditary noblemen. The army had 1,386 generals in 1902, 2,668 colonels in 1903.

In the years the Table of Ranks was in effect, 1722-1917, only eleven men reached the very highest rank of the civil service with the title of "chancellor," the last being A. M. Gorchakov in 1867. (I. L. Goremykin would have been a logical candidate for the honor and Rasputin supported his candidacy, but when he retired in 1916, the old man had to be content with the rank of *deistvitel'nyi tainyi sovetnik I-ogo klassa*.) With the exception of this highest rank, the number of civil servants in each rank expanded. For example, the number of *deistvitel'nye statskie sovetniki* increased from 674 in 1858 to 2,687 at the end of the nineteenth century. Excluding the Holy Synod, the State Council and military ranks, on January 1, 1897, there were 1,438 officials of the 1st-4th ranks, 50,082 of 5th-8th ranks, and 49,993 of 9th-14th ranks.

Court ranks and titles were more prestigious under the tsarist regime than their civil service equivalents. For this reason, many government officials who reached the 4th rank hoped next to attain court ranks. Such civil servants often petitioned for appointment "to the rank of *gofmeistr*." Successful applicants received the title, but not the pay or privileges of the higher rank, and they continued to serve in the civil sector. This willingness to grant court titles led to their proliferation. Whereas only nine officials held the rank of *ober-kamerger* during the entire eighteenth century, 16 were in service on January 1, 1898. 49 officials held the next six ranks during the eighteenth century, while at the later date 147 men held those ranks plus the rank of *ober-forshneider* created in 1856.

According to Peter the Great's vision, nobles and commoners would both begin service at the 14th rank and rise largely according to ability. But for more than a century after Peter's death, the most important factor was noble birth. Theoretically, promotions were based upon merit, but the time one served in each rank differed according to social background. This began to change in the mid-nineteenth century. Commoners were recruited into the civil service in growing numbers, while their noble colleagues were finding education and performance increasingly to be as important as "connections" and seniority in securing advancement. The Russian bureaucracy was becoming a professional institution. This process was capped by the introduction of uniform promotion standards in 1906. Civil and court officials were now to spend three years at the 14th, 12th, 10th and 9th ranks, four years from the 8th to the 6th, five years at the 5th, and 10 years at the 4th. Advancement to the three highest ranks still depended upon the emperor; in 1916 some 800 men were serving in those three ranks. Educational requirements for the 12th-8th ranks were also introduced in 1906. Three years were required of officers in each lower rank; army promotions above captain first grade depended upon vacancies.

The following relationship usually existed between government offices and the 14 classes in the Table of Ranks. Ministers held the second rank, assistant-ministers held the third rank. Directors of ministerial departments, provincial and town governors (the latter were known as *gradonachal'niki*) held the fourth rank. Assistant department directors and vice-governors held the fifth rank. Directors of department sections and institutions within the central bureaucracy held the sixth rank. Directors of bureaus within sections held the seventh rank.

Peter the Great hoped the Table of Ranks would foster an educated, working nobility open to new talent. Under Peter, the fourteenth (and lowest) rank gave commoners personal nobility; hereditary nobility (i.e., titles which could be inherited) came with the twelfth rank in the military, the eighth rank in the bureaucracy. A law of December 9, 1856, made it more difficult for commoners to gain both types of nobility. To gain personal nobility, an officer had to reach the twelfth rank; commoners in the civil service had to attain the ninth rank. Commoners became hereditary nobles with the fourth civil service rank and the sixth military rank.

Honorary titles were important in tsarist Russia. By royal decree, an official in the three highest ranks could be named "Senator," "member of the State Council," or could receive other high titles. The people so designated did not serve in the positions suggested. Lower-ranking officials might receive higher titles at retirement.

Military people formed "His Majesty's suite" and enjoyed the following titles. A member of ranks one through three, regardless of his actual assignment, was also "His Majesty's adjutant general" (*general-ad"iutant*); there were 60 of them in the early 20th century. A member of rank four in the army as a "major-general of His Majesty's suite," in the navy a "rear-admiral of His Majesty's suite;" he was also His Majesty's "aide-de-camp" (*fligel'ad"iutant*).

Those holding the honorary titles of *stats-sekretar' ego velichestva* or *dezhurnyi general- ad"iutant* had the right to made spoken representations to the emperor.

The court ranks for ladies were *ober-gofmeisterina, gofmeisterina, stats-dama, kamer-freilina, freilina ("fraulein")*. The first two ranks could be held only by ladies actually engaged in the duties of "*gofmeisterina*."

Written and verbal address to those holding ranks followed strict formulas. A *personal title* indicated rank or duty. For example, one addressed officers and officials as "general-leitenant," "admiral," "statskii sovetnik," "vice-governor," etc. *General titles* were as follows. A man holding the first two ranks was addressed as "vashe vysokopresvoskhoditel'stvo" ("Your High Excellency"); a man of rank three or four was "vashe prevoskhoditel'stvo" ("Your Excelleny"); a man of the fifth rank was "vashe vysokorodie" ("Your Great Honor"); a man who held rank six, seven or eight was "vashe vysokoblagorodie" ("Your High Honor"); an occupant of rank nine through fourteen was "vashe blagorodie" ("Your Honor").

Russians also used private titles indicating the origins of the person addressed. Thus the emperor was "vashe imperatorskoe velichestvo" ("Your Imperial Majesty") or "gosudar'" ("Sovereign"), a short but entirely respectful form of address. A grand prince (velikii knyaz') was "vashe imperatorskoe vysochestvo" ("Your Imperial Highness"). This group included the emperor's children and grandsons. A grand prince of the imperial family (velikii knyaz') more distant than a grandson of the emperor was "vashe vysochestvo" ("Your Highness"). The emperor's great-grandchildren and their male children as well as *svetleishie knyazya* (princes not related to the imperial family) were addressed as "vasha svetlost'" ("Your Radiance"). A *knyaginya* was a prince's wife, a *knyazhna* was a prince's unmarried daughter. Those of lower princely families and counts (*grafy*) were addressed as "vashe siyatel'stvo" ("Your Excellency"). Other nobles (*dvoryan'e*), including barons (*barona*), were addressed as "vashe blagorodie" ("Your Honor").

A Russian ruler before Peter the Great was known as *tsar'*, the Russian form of the Roman *caesar* ("emperor"). Russians took the title from Byzantium, viewing their ruler as the historic successor of the Byzantine emperor after Constantinople fell to the Turks in 1453. The tsar's wife was the *tsaritsa* (the term often appears in the West as "tsarina"), his son was a *tsarevich*, his daughter was a *tsarevna*. If a son (or brother) was the tsar's successor, he was referred to as the *tsetsarevich* or *naslednik* ("heir"). Although "tsar" has western roots, it is a Russian word with Muscovite associations. Peter the Great disliked this aspect of Russian tradition, and on October 22, 1721, he took the distinctively European title of *imperator*: "emperor." By Nicholas's time, however, "tsar" and "emperor" were used interchangeably. The emperor's wife was the *empress*.

Monastic leaders were divided into five ranks and addressed in the following ways. A metropolitan (*mitropolit*) and archbishop (*arkhiepiskop*) were addressed as "vashe vysokopreosvyashchenstvo" ("Your Eminence"); a bishop (*episkop*) was addressed as "vashe preosvyashchenstvo" ("Your Grace"); an archimandrite (*arkhimandrit*) and father superior (*igumen*) were addressed as "vashe vysokoprepodobie" ("Your Reverence"). The three higher monastic ranks were also known as "hierarchs" (*arkhieri*) and had the general title of "*vladyka*" (*vladiki*, pl.).

The parish clergy had four ranks: proto-hierach (*protoierei*) and hierarch (*ierei*); both were priests and were addressed as "vash vysokoprepodobie" ("Your Reverence); proto-deacon (*protod'yakon*) and deacon (*d'yakon*), and were addressed as "vashe prepodobie" ("Reverend").

The system of ranks and titles was abolished by a decree entitled "Concerning the Destruction of Estates and Civil Ranks" issued by the Central Executive Committee of the All-Russian Congress of Soviets and the Council of People's Commissars on November 10, 1917, only a few hours after the Bolsheviks seized power.

Words and abbreviations in parentheses in the following chart indicate how the Russian terms are rendered in English in the Index to these volumes.

FIRST RANK

Military
Army: general-fel'dmarshal (field marshall general)
Navy: general admiral (admiral general)

Civil Service
kantsler (chancellor)

Court
None

SECOND RANK

Military
Army: general ot infanterii (infantry general)
　　　general ot kavalerii (cavalry general)
　　　general ot artillerii (artillery general)
　　　inzener general (engineer general)
Navy: admiral

Civil Service
deistvitel'nyi taini sovetnik (d.t.s.)(actual privy counselor)

Court
ober-kamerger (high chamberlain)
ober-gofmarshal (high marshal of the imperial court)
ober-shtalmeister (high equerry)
ober-egermeister (high master of the hunt)
ober-gofmeister (high steward of the household)
ober-shenk (high confidant)
ober-tseremoniimeister (high master of ceremonies)
ober-forshneider (high forshneider)

Note.- The titles of court ranks do not indicate their duties. An *obertseremoniimeister*, for example, had nothing to do with "ceremonies," and an *ober-egermeister* did not deal with horses, at least not as a part of his service to the state.

THIRD RANK

Military
Army: general-leitenant (lieutenant general)
Navy: vitse-admiral (vice-admiral)

Civil Service
tainyi sovetnik (t.s.)(privy counselor)

Court
Gofmarshal (marshal of the imperial court)
Shtalmeister (equerry
egermeister (master of the hunt)
tseremoniimeister (master of ceremonies)

forshneider (high dignitary)

FOURTH RANK

Military
Army: none
Navy: none

Civil Service
deistvitel'nyi statskii sovetnik (d.s.s.)(actual state counselor)

Court
None

FIFTH RANK

Military
Army: none
Navy: none

Civil Service
statskii sovetnik (s.s.)(state counselor)

Court
Tseremoniimeister (master of ceremonies, fifth rank) was the lowest court rank.

SIXTH RANK

Military
Army: polkovnik (colonel)
Navy: kapitan I-ogo ranga (navy captain first grade)

Civil Service
kollezhskii sovetnik (k.s.)(collegial counselor)

SEVENTH RANK

Military
Army: podpolkovnik (lieutenant-colonel)
        voiskovoi starshina (equivalent Cossack rank; Cossack ranks are
            the same as army ranks unless otherwise specified)
Navy: kapitan II-ogo ranga (navy captain second grade)

Civil Service
nadvornyi sovetnik (n.s.)(court counselor)

EIGHTH RANK

Military
Army: kapitan (infantry captain first grade)
        rotmistr (equivalent cavalry rank; cavalry ranks are the same as
            army ranks unless otherwise specified)

essaul (equivalent Cossack rank)
Navy: none

Civil Servant
kollezhskii assesor (k.a.)(collegial assesor)

NINTH RANK

Military
Army: shtabs-kapitan (infantry captain second grade
            stabs-rotmistry (cavalry captain second grade)
            pod'esaul (equivalent Cossack rank)
Navy: leitenant (lieutenant)

Civil Service
tituliarnyi sovetnik (tl.s.)(titular counselor)

TENTH RANK

Military
Army: poruchik (first lieutenant)
            sotnik (equivalent Cossack rank)
Navy: michman (warrant officer)

Civil Service
kollezhskii sekretar' (k.sek.)(collegial secretary)

ELEVENTH RANK

Military
Army: none
Navy: none

Civil Service
korabel'nyi sekretar' (k.s.)(ship's secretary)

TWELFTH RANK

Military
Army: podporuchik (second lieutenant)
            kornet (cornet)(equivalent cavalry rank)
            khorunzhii (equivalent Cossack rank)
Navy: none

Civil Service
gubernskii sekretar' (g.s.)(gubernaya secretary)

THIRTEENTH RANK

Military
Army: praporshchik (third lieutenant)

Civil Service
provintsial'nyni sekretar' (p.s.)(provincial secretary)
senatskii registrator (s.r.)(senate registrar)
kabinetskii registrator (k.r.)(cabinet registrar)

FOURTEENTH RANK

Military
Army: none
Navy: none

Civil Service
kollezhskii registrator (kol.r.)(collegial registrar)

Bibliography

I. Published Editions of the Letters

Alexandra Fedorovna. *Letters of the Tsaritsa to the Tsar, 1914-1916*, with an Introduction by Sir Bernard Pares. London: Duckworth, 1923. These are the plates of the English texts as they appeared in the Berlin "Slovo" edition of 1922 (see below), though the absence of the footnotes in the Berlin edition make the London version less useful. Pares's 39-page "Introduction" is good, and the "Index" is of value in identifying characters Nicholas and Alexandra mention by nicknames, initials, etc.

_____. *Lettrés de l'impératrice Alexandra Fedorovna à l'empereur Nicolas II*, Preface and notes by J. W. Bienstock. Paris: Payot, 1927.

_____. *Die letzte Zarin, Ihre Briefe an Nikolaus II und ihre Tagebuchblatter von 1914 bis zur Ermordung*, edited and with an Introduction by Joachim Kuhn, translated by Viktor Bergmann. Berlin: Im Verlag Ullstein, 3rd ed., 1922. The selections from the letters of 1914-1916 occupy pp. 29-220. This edition is most useful for material from Alexandra's diary at Tobolsk and Ekaterinburg. The illustrations are good.

_____. *Pis'ma imperatritsy Aleksandry Fedorovny k imperatoru Nikolaiu Iioiu* (Letters of Alexandra Fedorovna to Emperor Nicholas II), in two volumes. Berlin: "Slovo," 1922. Volume One offers original English texts, Volume Two contains Russian translations with explanatory footnotes by V. D. Nabokov and a useful "Names Index" to the Russian texts. This is not a scholarly work: see valuable criticisms of it by A. A. Sergeev, "Zarubezhnoe izdanie," below.

Nicholas II. *The Letters of the Tsar to the Tsaritsa, 1914-1917*, translated by A. L. Hynes from the Official Edition of the Romanov Correspondence and now published for the first time in England, edited and with notes and index by C. E. Vulliamy with an Introduction by C. T. Hagberg Wright, LL.D. London: The Bodley Head, 1929.

Nicholas II and Alexandra Fedorovna. *Perepiska Nikolaia i Aleksandry Romanovykh* (Correspondence of Nicholas and Alexandra Romanov), III: *1914-1915 g.g.*; IV and V: *1916-1917 g.g.*, with an Introduction to each volume by M. N. Pokrovsky, prepared for publication by A. A. Sergeev, Moscow-Petrograd/ Lenin-

grad: Gosudarstvennoe izdatel'stvo, 1923, 1926, 1927; Tsent-arkhiv imprint.
Excellent scholarship; one only regrets the original English texts did not appear
along with the Russian translations. Volumes one and two were to cover the
pre-war correspondence; they have not appeared to date. The 65-page "Imennoi
Ukazatel'" in volume five was invaluable to me in compiling my own "Biographical Index."

II. Other Important Published Works

Buxhoeveden, Sophie. *The Life and Tragedy of Alexandra Feodorovna, Empress of Russia*. London: Longmans, Green, 1928.
Crawford, Rosemary, and Donald Crawford. *Michael and Natasha: the Life and Love of
Michael II, the Last of the Romanov Tsars*. Boston: Scribner's, 1997.
Curtiss, John Shelton. *Church and State in Russia, The Last Years of the Empire, 1900-
1917*. New York: Columbia, 1940.
de Jonge, Alex. *The Life and Times of Grigorii Rasputin*. New York: Coward, McCann
and Geoghegan, 1982.
Dupuy, R. Ernest and Trevor N. Dupuy. *The Harper Encyclopedia of Military History
from 3500 B.C. to the Present*. New York: Harper Collins, 4th ed., 1993.
Florinsky, Michael T. *End of the Russian Empire* (New Haven: Yale, 1931).
Fuhrmann, Joseph T. *Rasputin, A Life*. New York: Praeger, 1990).
Lincoln, W. Bruce. *Passage through Armageddon: The Russians in War and Revolution,
1914-1918*. New York: Simon and Schuster, 1986.
Marie, Grand Duchess of Russia (Maria Pavlovna Romanova). *Education of a Princess:
A Memoir*, translated under the editorial supervision of Russell Lord. New
York: Viking, 1931.
Massie, Robert K. *Nicholas and Alexandra*. New York: Atheneum, 1968, pp. 310-316,
provides an excellent discussion of the letters.
Oldenburg, S. S. *Last Tsar, Nicholas II: His Reign and his Russia*, in four volumes, trans.
Leonid I. Mihalap and Patrick J. Rollins. Gulf Breeze, Fla.: Academic Interna-
tional Press, 1975-1978.
Paléologue, Maurice. *An Ambassador's Memoirs*, in three volumes., trans. F. A. Holt.
New York: Hippocrene Books, 3rd ed., 1925.
Pares, Bernard. *The Fall of the Russian Monarchy, A Study of the Evidence*. New York:
Alfred A. Knopf, 1939; pp. 248-252, provide a useful discussion of the letters.
_____. "Rasputin and the Empress: Authors of the Russian Collapse," *Foreign Af-
fairs*, VI (1927-1928), pp. 140-154; Pares's scornful attitude towards Alexandra
and Rasputin lowers the tone of this sloppy little work, littered with inaccura-
cies. Its most useful feature is a "digest" of Alexandra's "suggestions" to her
husband from her letters of April 4, 1915, to December 17, 1916. This *is* a useful guide to 96 of Alexandra's letters. Pares's thesis is that Alexandra and Rasputin gave instructions that the tsar executed. The empress and "Father
Grigory" certainly had influence over church-state affairs. But Pares's case is
too simple. He does not indicate the times Nicholas ignored these "instructions"
or acted directly contrary to them; nor does Pares consider the possibility that
Nicholas often had his own reasons for doing as Alexandra-Rasputin advised,
reasons having nothing to do with those on the mind of his wife (or their
"Friend").
Pipes, Richard. *The Russian Revolution*. New York: Alfred A. Knopf, 1990.
The Romanov Family Album, Introductory text by Robert K. Massie, picture research and
descriptions by Marilyn Pfeifer Swezey, photographs assembled by Anna
Vyrubova (New York: Vendome Press, 1982), p. 12.

Sergeev, A. A. "Zarubezhnoe izdanie pisem byv. imp. Aleksandry Fedorovny (A Foreign Edition of the Letters of the Former Emp. Alexandra Fedorovna)," *Krasnyi arkhiv* (The Red Archive), No. 3 (1923), pp. 313-317. A fine work of scholarship, to be faulted only for brevity and sketchiness. For example, Sergeev fills in two "gaps" in Letters No. 56 and 139 (as they appear in the Berlin edition), but he only tells us that gaps exist in Letters No. 3, 18, 25, 27, 33, 39, 49, 53, 76, 77, 94, 99, 102, 107, 111, 112 (twice), 114, 115, 122, 144, 146, 148, 166, "and others" the gaps are not filled. Sergeev was working on his own edition of the letters at the time (see above).

Shchegolev, P. (ed.). *Padenie tsarskogo rezhima: Stenograficheskie otchety doprosov i pokazanii, dannykh v 1917 g. v Chrezvychainoi Sledstevennoimmissii Vremenogo Pravitel'stava* (Fall of the Tsarist Regime: Stenographic accounts of testimony and depositions given in 1917 to the Extraordinary Investigatory Commission of the Provisional Government), in seven volumes, Moscow and Leningrad: 1924-1927. An indispensable collection of documents; the "Imennoi Ukazatel'" has been valuable to me in compiling my own "Biographical Index."

Steinberg, Mark D., and Vladimir M. Khrustalev (eds.). *The Fall of the Romanovs: Political Dreams and Personal Struggles in a Time of Revolution*, Russian documents trans. Elizabeth Tucker. New Haven and London: Yale, 1995. The selection and presentation of documents is excellent, as are the editorial notes. Steinberg's Introduction, "Nicholas and Alexandra, an Intellectual Portrait," is almost remarkably insightful; its guardedly sympathetic tone is probably suggestive of what future mainstream scholarship on Nicholas II will resemble.

Sullivan, Michael John. *A Fatal Passion, The Story of Victoria Melita, the Uncrowned Last Empress of Russia*. New York: Random House, 1997. A well told story of the couple which figures so prominently in the Nicky-Sunny Correspondence as Kirill and "Ducky."

Yusupov, Prince Felix. *Lost Splendor*, trans. Ann Green and Nicholas Katkoff. London: Cape, 1953.

Biographical Index

Letters and telegrams are cited in this index by the number assigned by the editor to each document in the text; larger letters are divided into sections, each marked in brackets by a lowercase letter: [a], [b], [c], etc. "Fn." indicates a footnote of that number.

Ranks in the imperial army, navy, civil service, court and the Church; for example, lt.-gen., vice-ad., *tainyi sovetnik* (*t.s.*), *gofmeister, fraulein*, met., *igumen*, etc., are explained in Appendix I: Names and Terms Identifier, and in Appendix II: Table of Ranks as of 1914. Appendix I lists nicknames, abbreviations and irregular spellings of the names of people who appear at least five times in the "Nicky-Sunny" correspondence, along with such terms as *Alexandrovtsy* and *Coun. of the Emp.*, as well as such frequently cited places as *Anichkov*, "Big Palace," or *Znamenie*. Such names, terms and places are marked < the first time they appear in each letter or telegram.

Much of the information in this index comes from the marvelous "Imennoi Ukazatel'" (Name Index) in volume five of A. A. Sergeev's edition of the Nicky-Sunny *Perepiska*. Indeed, additional details concerning many of the people listed in this index may be found there. Obscure people not listed in this index may often be found in Sergeev's "Imennoi Ukazatel'."

Abortion, 393c

Actors. *See* Artists

Adlerberg, Alexander Alexandrovich ("Dudel"), retired inf. gen., 1296, 1616

Adlerberg, Catherine Nicholaevna, countess, former *fraulein*, wife of Count A. V. Adlerberg, 32d, 427c

Adrianov, Alexander Alexandrovich, maj.-gen., *gradonachal'nik* Moscow, 1908, until retired on June 11, 1915, 1452b (Fns. 362 and 364), 1456a, 1457, 1461a

Afrosimov, 116b, 119a, 556d

Agafangel, archb. Yaroslavl and Rostov, 447c, 450e

Air Force Men: Akimov, Boris Nicholaevich, ex-naval lt., senior nco reconnaissance aircraft command; killed, June 1916, 1123; **Mal'tsev**, col. in anti-aircraft battery, 1341a, 1373a; **Romanovsky**, 255a

Airplanes, Air Warfare, 10c, 18b, 19c, 24d, 32b, 62a, 187b, 225, 252b, 273b, 283a, 347c, 371e, 414f, 419c, 426b, 433a, 455e, 461c, 571f, 732a, 792a, 918c, 928c, 957b, 1295e,h, 1341a, 1352, 1560d (Fn. 401); *see also* Zeppelins

Albania, 755a

Barclay, Florence L., British writer, 918a (Fn. 246), 923a, 927, 929, Fn. 258, 977a,b, 978 (Fn. 269), 979, 980b, 982b, 985a, 989, 1004b, 1019 (Fn. 276), 1023, 1073 (Fn. 284), 1079b, 1143a, 1600e, 1607, 1611, 1616, 1620a, 1655b

Bark, Peter L'vovich, min. finance, 369c, 485k, 520a, 524c,d, 531c, 601a, 605g, 615b, 688b,c,d, 982b, 990b, 1008a, 1087a; relations with Rasputin, 312b, 513c

Baryatinskaya, Maria Viktorovna ("Marie"), princess, *fraulein* to Alexandra, 8, 295a; her sister, **Olga Viktorovna**, knyazhna, sister of shtal. Prince I. V. Baryatinsky, 295a, 323a, 329g

Baryatinskaya, Maria Vladimirovna, wife of kamerger Prince I. V. Baryatinsky, Alexandra's former *fraulein*, 193a, 295a, 323a, 329g, 333a, 596d

Batyushin, Nicholas Stepanovich, staff n.w. front, investigated Myasoedov and others, Fn. 367; 1625a (Fn. 419), 1655d, 1675a

Beatrice ("Aunt Beatrice"), Princess of Battenburg, younger daughter of Queen Victoria, Alexandra's aunt, widow of Prince Heinrich-Mavriky, 72c, 1089a

Beletsky, Stephen Petrovich, t.s., asst.-min. internal affairs and police director, 1911-Jan. 1913; returned to office as ally of A. N. Khvostov from Sept. 28, 1915 to Feb. 19, 1916, when he was dismissed in connection with plot to assassinate Rasputin; gov.-gen. Irkutsk until March 15, 1916, then senator, 496b,c,e; meets Alexandra, 534d, 538h; as assistant-min. interior and police director, 538b,f, 571e, 572a, 613c, 615b,g, 666a, 686a, 691b, 711d, Fn. 201, 751a, 756b; disgraced, dismissed, Fns. 220 and 232; 880c, 888a

Belgium, Belgians, 32b, 261a, 561f, 571d, 819c, 1670c, 1673c

Belyaev, Michael Alekseevich, gen., asst.-min. war, 531c, 615d, 634c, 738a, 746d, Fn. 237, 874c-e, 990a, 1461a, 1688b; Alexandra favors him as min. war, 1329, 1336f,g, 1345b, 1352, 1573b, 1651a; Nicholas's opinion, dismissed as asst.-min. war, 1334, 1336b, 1342; mission to Roumania, 1469b, 1474, 1479b, 1656a

Benckendorff, Alexander Constantinovich, amb. to London, Jan. 1902-July 1916, 18c, 443c

Benckendorff, Elena Dmitr'evna, countess, Naryshkin by birth, Rodzyanko's first wife, then wife of P. A. Benckendorff, 914a

Benckendorff, Paul Constantinovich ("Benk."), count, ober-gofmarshal, adj.-gen., guards cav. gen., 111, 140, 186b, 283b, 295b, 352c, 356d, 435d, 474e, 478k, 510c, 669a,d, 781b, 867b, 1054, 1057b, 1062a, 1083a, 1112, 1115, 1116a, 1141, 1147a, 1274, 1328, 1329, 1331, 1334, 1341a, 1356, 1380e, 1398, 1402a, 1426c, 1490, 1573a, 1606c, 1673c, 1686c, Fn. 478; his wife, **Maria Sergeevna**, 435d, 867b,c, 1270, 1410c, 1642b, 1686c

Bezobrazov, Vladimir Michaelovich, adj.-gen., cav. gen., commander Guards Corps from 1912 until dismissed for insubordination in July 1915; returned to front in Dec. as commander of special guards corps, 43a, 413i, 433a, 535b, 585c,d, 605c,i, 609c, 867c, 1002a, 1007a, 1008b; charged with recklessness, removed July 1916, 1295b-d,h, 1318, 1320, 1321, 1330, 1342, 1345b, 1346, 1349, 1352, 1355, 1407, 1673d

Bobrinsky, Aleksei Alexandrovich, count, member State Council, esteemed trustee Petrograd Board of Guardians, chairman board Russian-English Bank, ober-gofm., asst.-min. internal affairs March 25-July 21, 1916, then min. agriculture until Nov. 16, 1916; 1291a, 1317, 1325b, 1329, 1334, 1336e, 1418b, 1431, 1434g, 1437, 1439a,c, e,f, 1446, 1456b, 1533a (Fn. 384), 1542b; flatters Alexandra, 1430c; impresses Nicholas, 1436, 1443; dismissed, 1584, 1587c, 1591d, 1637a

Bobrinsky, Georgy Alexandrovich, count, adj.-gen., lt.-gen., made gov.-gen. when Galicia was first occupied, assigned to staff s.w. front after evacuation of "places held by right of war," 225, 248a, 252a, 295b

Boisman, col., 1675b,d,e, 1677b

Bolsheviks. *See* Revolutionaries

Bonch-Bruevich, Michael Dmitrievich, maj.-gen., quartermaster-gen. chief of staff n.-n.w. front under Ruzsky, then dismissed; supported Bolsheviks after November Revolution,

shtalm., envoy to Constantinople 1910-1915, ex-director staff for economic matters, min. foreign affairs, 159b, 827c

Byutsova, Olga Evgen'evna ("O. Evg.," "Olga Evg."), *fraulein* to Alexandra; married to G. N. Papafedorov (q.v.), 49e, 66c, 116c, 181, 333b, 572i, 723e, 766a, 767, 770a, 966c, 1336g, 1651c

Callwell, Sir Charles Edward, K.C.B., maj.-gen., retired 1909, directed War Office military operations first 17 months of war, then took part in special missions to allied armies, 753, 755a, 756b, 763b, 858a

Catherine, mother superior, 455e

Catherine II, the "Great," empress, 1762-96, 30a, 43a, 1434c

Caucasus, 38a, 62b, 84a,b, 867a, 1434a,b; fighting on this front, 719b, 724a, 728b, 738c, 751b, 789d, 798g, 803a, 804a, 845a, 932c, 936c, 1037, 1208, 1217, 1238, 1311b, 1322, 1325a, 1371, 1434a; zemstvoes, 1008b; *see also* Nicholas Nicholaevich, Turkey

Censorship, Fn. 108, 366c, 393b,d, 401g, 422c, 427d,f, 434, 435c, 444c, 460b,e, 463a, 466a, 481d,l, 485n, 1427 (Fn. 353c), 1625d; *see also* Pahlen

Central War Industries Committee, Fn. 209

Chagin, Ivan Ivanovich ("Johnny"), commander imp. yacht *Standard*; committed suicide, fall 1912, 255b, 1410d

Chebykin, Alexander Nesterovich, lt.-gen., served with guards inf.; ex-commander 3rd Life Guards Reg. and 1st brigade of 2nd Div., ex-maj.-gen. of His Maj.'s suite, *nachal'nik* of guards reserve brig., 723b, 1310b, 1313

Chelnokov, Michael Vasil'evich, *golova* of Moscow, 768a, 776, 1119e

Chichagov, probably Seraphim, archb. Tver', 644c

China, Chinamen, 1675b

Christopher ("Christo"), Greek prince, 914a, 926, 928b,d, 999, 1000a (Fn. 274)

Cinema, 229, 568b, 579a, 643, 732b, 742a, 744, 756b, 757, 763b, 836, 862, 867e, 873, 910, 1074, 1079a, 1109, 1143a, 1153, 1154b, 1160, 1161, 1164, 1205, 1211, 1272, 1276, 1315, 1343, 1373c, 1374, 1378, 1402b, 1408, 1432, 1511, 1521c, 1545, 1584, 1611, 1613b; war films, 1106-1107, 1111, 1150b, 1209, 1466, 1470, 1471

Conservatives, 892c; *see also* Octobrist Party, "Ultra-Right"

Constantine, archb. Mogilev, 732a; his wife, 1679

Constantine I ("Tino"), king of Greece, 1913-17 and 1920-22, Fn. 173; 593b, 928d, 1119g, 1242, 1274, 1338, 1447b, 1461c, 1501b, 1508b

Constantine Constantinovich ("Costia," "Kostia"), g.p., second cousin of Nicholas II, adj.-gen., inf. gen., insp.-gen. of military schools, honorary pres. Acad. Sciences, also a poet; died, June 1, 1915; 35, 69, 151a, 309b, 360a, 399a, 435g, 466f, 507f, 564h, 688c, 849e, 1081b, 1537b

Constantinople, 187a,b (Fn. 73), 1380b,c; Russian attack, Fn. 346; 1403, 1426a

"Coup from the right," Fn. 381; 1660 (Fn. 460)

Cyril, bish., 303a

Cyril Vladimirovich ("Kirill,"), g.p., son of Vladimir Alexandrovich, rear-ad. His Maj.'s Suite, commanded Life Guards Ship's Co. and naval battalion at front from Feb. 1915; supported March Rev.; husband of Victoria Fedorovna (q.v.), 18a, 64, 65, 116b, 119, 144, 196b, 255b, 257, 259, 420b, 421, 422e, 423, 430e, 435f, 444b, 450b, 572f, 575c, 603b, 681b, 723a,b, 741b, 746b, 759b, 763a, 798c,d, 843c, 846a,c, 851a, 860d, 863c, 867e, 869a, 870, 871a, 920b, 1068b, 1131b, 1143b, 1253, 1254, 1313, 1318, 1326, 1367a, 1398, 1410d, 1415a, 1418b, 1557, 1609a, 1638a, 1686c; during March Revolution, 1687, 1688b, 1690b

d'Amade, French general, 489

Louis-Hermann, prince of Hesse, relative of Alexandra, 807e

Ludendorff, Erich von, German general, Fns. 235, 290, 322

Ludwig, prince of Battenburg, husband of Princess Victoria of Hesse, Alexandra's brother-in-law, 807e, 819b, Fn. 247

Ludwig ("Papa"), Grand Duke of Hesse, Alexandra's father, 24e

Ludwig-Frantsisk ("Dickie," "Dicky"), prince of Battenburg, relative of Alexandra, 819b, 908a

L'vov, Georgy Evgeneevich, prince, headed All-Russian land union to aid the wounded and those injured in the war, member supreme council to aid Russian pow families, *glasnaya* of Moscow duma, first head of Provisional Government, 447d, 1625d, 1642d

Mackensen, August von, German field marshal, led 9th Army on eastern and Baltic fronts, 463j

Mail. *See* Spies and Espionage

Makarov, Alexander Alexandrovich, member State Council, senator, t.s., min. internal affairs, Sept. 1911-Dec. 1912; replaced A. A. Khvostov as min. justice, July 7, 1916, until Dec. 20, 1916, when he was replaced by N. A. Dobrovol'sky, 443f, 460c, 463d, 481m, 1049b, 1295g, 1305, 1456c, 1466, 1625a,b (Fns. 430 and 431); Rasputin opposes his return to office, 1043 (Fn. 280); Alexandra's opposition, 1246 (Fn. 324), 1283b, 1297, 1587c, 1595b, 1600d, 1606b, 1637c, 1642d, 1651e; considered as pres. State Council, 1644a, 1647a

Makary, met. Moscow, member Holy Synod, ally of Rasputin, 443f, 446, 447b, 510a, Fn. 174, 630c,d, 631, 634c, 843b, 1542e

Maklakov, Nicholas Alekseevich, gofin., member State Council, t.s., min. internal affairs and police director, 1912-June 5, 1915, ex-gov. Chernigov, 43a, 49e, 51, 98, 366c, 1673d; cultivates Alexandra to regain power, 874c,d, 888i,j, 892c; favored for State Council, 1642e

Maklakov, Vasily Alekseevich, member State Council, leader Kadet Party, 496b

Malama, Dmitry Yakovlevich, officer in Alexandra's Life Guards Lancer Reg., 72d, 76b, 79a, 116b, 733e, 892f

Malcolm, Sir Ian, K.C.M.G., British attaché to St.P. in 1896; rep. British Red Cross to Russia during war; Balfour's private sec. at Peace Conference in 1919, 524d, 550b, 571c, 629c, 634e, 888h

Malevsky-Malevich, Nicholas Andreevich, senator, gofin., Russian amb. to Tokyo, 1908-Feb. 13, 1916, 1119h

Mamantov, Vasily Il'ich, member State Council, egerm., director petitioners' chancellery, 196a, 730c, 737g, 1087b, 1305, 1378

Manasevich-Manuilov, Ivan Fedorovich, ex-agent in min. internal affairs; embezzlement charges against him were dismissed through Rasputin's intrigue, 1625a,b (Fn. 430), 1637b, 1647b

Manikovsky, Aleksei Alekseevich, art. gen., summer 1915 replaced Gen. D. D. Kuz'min-Karavaev as art. commander; dismissed and tried for treason, 882b, 1561b

Manukhin, Sergei Sergeevich, d.t.s., senator, member State Council, 336b, 340a

Manus, Ignatius Porfir'evich, honorary d.s.s., businessman, director Petrograd Carriage Factory, member board Siberian Trade Bank and S.W. Railroad Co., pres. Russian Transport and Insurance Co., "conductor of dubious transactions on the exchange. He was accused of being in close touch with enemy financiers, and it was rumoured, though perhaps with little foundation, that he paid large sums of money to Rasputin" (Vulliamy, p. 129n), 455e, 682b, 723b, 730c, 737a,e

Marchmont, A. W., British writer, 708b, 716b, 723e, 732a, 918a (Fn. 246)

March Revolution, 1917, signs of its approach, Fns. 463, 468, 469, 470; bakeries attacked, 1673a, 1675e; 1673c, 1675a, 1677b,d, 1680-1697

assigned to Stavka, 768b; **Raduta,** nurse in Anna Vyrubova's hospital, 1220; **Shevchuk,** nurse, 147; **Tseidler, German Fedorovich,** d.s.s., prof., 46a, 66a, 72d, 186b; **Varavka, Sergei Michaelovich,** honorary physician-in-ordinary to Stavka, 560c, 605b, 914a, 1473a; **Zander, Alexander L'vovich,** t.s., physician-in-ordinary to imp. court, 46b; **Zhuk,** attendant at Tsarskoe Selo hospital, 223b, 241, 413d, 601c, 613g, 728h, 746a, 888d, 992b, 1199b, 1677a, 1677d

Pil'ts, Alexander Ivanovich, d.s.s., gov. Mogilev; appointed asst.-min internal affairs on Feb. 14, 1916, on March 15 appointed gov. Irkutsk, 420a, 426d, 629a, 764b, 858a (Fns. 232, 233), 860e

Pistol'kors, Alexander Erikovich von ("Aksel'"), kamer-yunker of imp. court, assigned to state chancellery, devotee of Rasputin, 15, 384l, 496g, 746a, 1336a; his father, **Erik Augustinovich von,** lt.-gen, ex-husband of Olga Valerianovna Gogenfel'zen, 1341b; his wife, **Alexandra Alexandrovna ("Alia"),** Anna Vyrubova's sister, ex-*fraulein,* 38b, 43a, 58, 116a, 261b, 298, 329g, 360a, 363a, 419b, 455c, 463h, 571d, 590c, 880e, 1175, 1270, 1278, 1283b, 1336a, 1355, 1405a

Pitirim, ex-exarch of Georgia, made met. Petrograd, Nov. 23, 1916, member Holy Synod, close ally of Grigory Rasputin, 447d; appointed met. of Petrograd, 582d (Fn. 174), 601e; career in Petrograd, 666b, 669a, 737c, 746a, 749, 751a, 936d, 941d, 1000b, 1023c, 1055, 1186a,b, 1246b, 1257b, 1434b, 1439g, 1456e (Fn. 369), 1465c, 1476, 1477, 1587a, 1625a, 1637c (Fn. 435), 1651b; relations with Rasputin, 675b, 880b; influence with Alexandra, 737g, 920c; visit to Stavka displeases Nicholas, 756b, 760, 761 (Fn. 207); second visit, 1479a, 1480b

Platon, ex-archb. Aleutian islands and America, exarch of Georgia, member Holy Synod, ally of Nicholasha<, 1434b

Plautina, Maria Michaelovna, wife of N. S. Plautin, dismissed guards col., 427b, 450a, 455g

Plehn, Ivan Michaelovich, guards cav. col., assigned to g.p. Boris Vladimirovich, 1913-16, 860d, 1000a, 1007a

Plehve, Paul Adamovich, cav. gen., commanded n.w. front from Dec. 1915, outstanding officer but dismissed and appointed to State Council, Feb. 5, 1916, died, March 28, 1916, 792b,c,f, 803e, 804c, 811b, 820a,b, 827a, 892g, 894c

Ploto, German spy, 435g,h, 444a, 469j, 516a

Pochaev Monastery, 1096, 1098c

Pogulyaev, Sergei Sergeevich, rear-ad. His Maj.'s Suite from Feb. 29, 1916, then commanded 1st Division of Black Sea battleships, 880g, 888c, 1565b, 1570, 1600d; his wife, **Nadezhda Alexandrovna,** 627a

Poincaré, Raymond, Pres. French republic, ex-prime minister, 1461c

Poklevsky-Kozell, Stanislav Alfonsovich, kamerger, d.s.s., Russian envoy to Bucharest 1914-1917, 564i

Pokrovsky, Nicholas Nicholaevich, state controller, member State Council, t.s., Nov. 30, 1916 made min. foreign affairs, 892c, Fn. 423

Poland, 1434b; autonomy, 1255 (Fn. 326c), 1257, 1364, 1380c (Fn. 345), 1515a (Fn. 379), 1520 (Fn. 381), 1527a, 1651h

Polivanov, Aleksei Andreevich, inf. gen., head General Staff and asst.-min. war, then min. from June 13, 1915 until March 15, 1916; appointed min., 328a (Fn. 98); meets Alexandra, 354c, 366c, 371b; career as minister, 340a, 352a, 384d,f, 389i, 433f, 443d, 444c, 463a, 481g,m, 531c, 534d, 615d, 666a, 688b, 824a, 853b-d; Alexandra's hostility, 329d, 331, 373c, 746d, 781b, 846e, 874c, 888a, 892f, 1336g, 1352, 1642d; dismissed, 869b (Fn. 237), 882a,b, 884d, 888i; public sympathy for, 892b; later activities, 1430a, 1434a,f, 1439a, 1452c, 1469a, 1573b

Portugal, Portuguese, 1675b

Roshchakovsky, Michael Sergeevich, 579b,c (Fn. 242), 582a, 884a, 890, 891, 894a, 895, 956a, 963b; his wife, 963b

Rosseti-Solesko, Fedor Georgievich, Roumanian, ex-attaché to Berlin, son of G. K. Rosseti-Solesko, ex-envoy to Russia, 1453, 1456d

Rostislav Alexandrovich, prince, son of Alexander Michaelovich, 213, 426e

Rostovtsev, Yakov Nicholaevich ("Rost."), count, d.s.s., gofm., Alexandra's personal secretary, directed her chancellery and affairs of imp. children, member supreme council to aid Russian pow families, committee to aid Russian pows, and other charities, 66a, 82, 92a,b, 98, 140, 143, 169, 203, 343d, 366c, 435b, 447a, 463j, 493b, 534a, 550b, 560b, 601c, 634e, 669d, 781a, 846f, 877b, 1031, 1128, 1352, 1439i, 1456b, 1556c, 1625a

Roumania, 460b, 560c, 562, 563, 564a,i, 571f, 572i, 575b,c, 582b,c, 585b, 590b, 593b, 605f, 613d, 728b, 803a, Fn. 325, 1263, 1423, 1452a, 1453, 1474, 1508b, 1542e, 1547b, 1587a, 1644b, 1647b, 1648, 1652b, 1656a; enters war against Austria, 1326, 1329, 1337, 1466, 1469b; Germany declares war on her, 1341b, 1342; military action, 1353, 1367c (Fn. 342), 1373e, 1435, 1462, 1543b, 1620a, 1626, 1633g, 1637d; Nicholas's opinion, 1480b (*see also* Rosseti-Solesko)

Rubinstein, Dmitry L'vovich, director board Petro-Mar'evsky and Varvaroplessky Companies, involved in coal mining, insurance, stock exchange operations; friend of Rasputin, 455e, 688c; arrested for financial dealings, 1456c (Fn. 367), 1461a,d, 1470; freed, 1538c (Fn. 387), 1542e, 1552c

Rukhlov, Sergei Vasil'evich, stats-sekretar', member State Council, d.s.s., min. communications 1909 to Oct. 27, 1915, 186b, 187a, 190, 485f, 531b, 538c, 579c; Nicholas praises him, 1644a

Rusin, Alexander Ivanovich, ad., head naval General Staff, asst.-min. naval affairs, assigned to Stavka; travelled on special mission abroad, 413d, 507d, 853b, 1197, 1378

Russia, army, 62a, 65; Fn. 48; 159b, 187a,b, 211, 213; Fn. 83; 252b, 271, 426b, 461c, 686b, 714b; Fn. 235; 932c, 937a (Fn. 251), 1041, 1138, 1367c (Fn. 342), 1527d, 1543b (*see also* Brusilov offensive); army contingent sent to France, 957d, 1059c, 1075b, 1150b, 1313, 1587b; army demoralized, Fn. 386; navy, 30b, 32c, 43b, 162-164a, 172, 261b (Fn. 86), 262, 269, 271b,c, 389d, 406f, 460a, 466c, 469b, 552, 553a, 561b,c, 593b, 598a, 603b, 714b, 843c, 846a-c, 856a, 880f,g, 932c, 937a (Fn. 251), 1041, 1367a, 1378, 1499 (Fn. 376), 1673b; Russian pows, 46a, 200a, 268b, 373f, 376b-d, 422e, 425, 426e, 433e, 455f, 466b, 473, 474a,f, 485f, 538h, 571c,d, 579d, 582e, 615f, 714b, 737h, 856b, 874a, 888h, 957c, 1613a, 1675c; Russian nurses visiting Germany and Austria, 426g, 550b, 1043, 1049b, 1145, 1146a, 1237

Russkoe Znamya (*Russian Banner*), newspaper Union of Russian People, 1647c

Russky Invalid (*Russian Invalid*), newspaper min. war, 1652a

Ruzsky, Nicholas Vladimirovich, adj.-gen., inf. gen., member State Council and Military Council, commanded 3rd Army at outbreak of war, then c.-in-c. Russian armies n.w. and n. fronts, 10d, 17, 18b, 43a, 427e, 481f, 526b, 561e, 666a, 781b, 807e,g, 811b, 1452c, 1527b-e, 1538c, 1611; during March Revolution, Fn. 470, 1688e

Ryabushinsky, Paul Pavlovich, elected by industrialists to State Council in 1916, 481f,h

Rzhevsky, Boris Michaelovich, Fns. 220, 429

Sabler, Vladimir Karlovich, d.t.s., stats-sekretar', senator, member State Council, director Holy Synod, 1911 to July 5, 1915, 329f, 338a, 340a,c, 343a, 356b, 455a, 566c

Sablin, Nicholas Pavlovich ("N.P."), a.d.c., naval capt. 1st grade, senior officer on imp. yacht *Standard* 1912-1915, commanded naval battalion Life Guards Ship's Co. at Odessa in 1916, then *Standard*, 10, 15, 21a, 24b, 27a, 28, 46b, 49b,e, 57b, 62b, 66c, 50, 72d, 76c, 79b, 82, 84b,c, 92b, 116c, 119b, 123, 131, 133, 140, 143, 147, 151c, 153, 156c, 159b, 174, 181, 186b, 193b, 200a,c, 203, 214, 218b, 220, 223b, 227a, 231, 241, 248b, 249, 255b, 261b, 265, 298, 309b, 312b, 315a, 323c, 325d, 329g, 343l, 347d, 366g, 373d, 376i,

1655b; his son, **Sergei Alexandrovich ("Seriozha")**, tseremoniimeister imp. court, assigned to min. internal affairs, 15, 126, 131, 144, 328a, 443i, 590c, 593c, 613g, 1142, 1146b (?), 1150a, 1175, 1178e, 1300b

Tatars, 1439i, 1469b

Tatishchev, Dmitry Nicholaevich, maj.-gen., later lt.-gen., police director, 524e, 531c

Tatishchev, Il'ya Leonidovich, count, adj.-gen., lt.-gen., served in guards cav.; assigned to Kaiser Wilhelm II, 1905-1914, 187c, 728g, 732a, 1322

Tatishchev, Vladimir Sergeevich, count, d.s.s., director Association for Commerce and Industry in Iran and Central Asia, president United Bank, 605g, 688c,d,e

Tatyana Constantinovna ("Tatiana K."), knyaginya, older daughter of Constantine Constantinovich, widow of Prince C. A. Bagration-Mukhransky, 151b, 207a, 340b, 352a, 360a, 613h, 1000a (Fn. 274), 1031, 1081a

Tatyana Nicholaevna, second oldest daughter of Alexandra and Nicholas, 110, 764b, 877c, 1063b, 1067, 1068a, 1069, 1071, 1128a, 1238; wartime charity work, 30a, 41a, 62b, 67, 190, 1547b, 1630, 1633f; has measles, 1673c-1690; *see also* OTMA

Taube, Georgy Nicholaevich, baron, ensign in Life Guards Ship's Co., 303e, 846a, 860b, 966c, 1000a, 1137a, 1203, 1208, 1250a, 1295g, 1373a, 1395a

Telephone, 1549, 1550, 1552a, 1609b, 1647e, 1667a, 1690a; **telegraph-telephone**, 1667a; **telephonogram**, 1487b

Thailand. *See* Siam

Theater, Theater People. *See* Artists

Thomas, Albert, French minister who visited Stavka, 990a (Fn. 271)

Thornhill, British intelligence officer, Fn. 307

Timiryazev, Vasily Ivanovich, d.t.s., elected by industry to State Council in 1916, chairman Russian board of Foreign Trade Bank and also of Russian-English Chamber of Commerce, 329e

Tol', Alexander Alexandrovich ("Toll"), count, col. Alexandra's Life Guards Lancer Reg.; during war commanded 2nd Pavlovsky Hussar Reg., 393f, 601b, 613f, 1638c

Tolstaya, Irina Dmitr'evna ("Irina T."), countess, daughter of Count D. I. and Countess E. M. Tolstoi, 389c, 413d, 419b, 496i, 827b, 1380e

Tolstoi, Leo, 1616 (Fn. 425)

Torbi, Nadezhda Michaelovna ("Nadia"), countess, daughter of g.p. Michael Michaelovich, in 1916 married George, prince of Battenburg (q.v.), 950 (Fn. 259)

Trepov, Alexander Fedorovich, stats-sekretar', senator, egerm.; appointed min. communications, Oct. 30, 1915, chairman council ministers, Nov. 10, 1916, dismissed from both positions, Dec. 27, 1916, Rasputin foe; opposed by Rasputin, 564g; as min. communications, 612, 613c, 615a, 634b, 697c, 738a, 739, 741c, 892c, 977a, 1037, 1119e, 1126, 1154a, 1178c, 1184a, 1430a, 1521a; Fn. 384; 1542c, 1569; considered as chairman of council of ministers, 1574, 1577a; appointed, 1584; career, 1587a,c-f, 1591c,d, 1595, 1600b,d, 1606a,b, 1616, 1620b,c (Fn. 426), 1625b,d, 1627, 1636, 1637a,b,d, 1642a-d, 1647a, 1647c,d, 1651a,e,g; relations with Alexandra, 1583a, 1591b; relations with Nicholas, Fn. 416, 1609b, 1613b, 1621a, 1638b,c, 1644a; his son, 1595c; daughters, 323c, 325d, 496a

Trifon, vicar-b. Moscow, 340c

Tsushima Straits, Battle of, 1041 (Fn. 279)

Tumanov, Nicholas Evseevich, prince, engineer-gen., *nachal'nik* Dvinsk mil. region at beginning of war, in Sept. 1915 became *nachal'nik* Petrograd mil. region; June 1916 made communications dir. of armies on w. front, 309b, 481g, 510c, 853b; Rasputin praises him, 1098a

Turkey, the Turks, 38a, 43a,b, 153 (Fn. 53), 223a, 271b, 273a, 719b, 728f, 738c, 804a, 858a, 932c, 937 (Fn. 251), 1322, 1373a; expeditionary force demanded by Germany, 1263

committee, Tatyana's committee, and other charitable organizations, 169, 261a, 834a, 1085b, 1089b, 1154a, 1178h, 1183b, 1246b, 1395b

Witte, Sergei Yul'evich, ex-chairman council of ministers and min. finance, favored separate peace, hoped to return to office; died, 1915, 347a, 1595b; Nicholas's attitude, 178

Woman's legion, 261a

Worth, Paris dressmaker, 1063b

Wrangel, Peter Nicholaevich, baron, a.d.c., col., 1621b (Fn. 428)

Writers. *See* Artists

Yagmin, Stanislav Yul'evich, col. 17th Nizhegorodsky Dragoon Reg., during war replaced Col. Ofrosimov as reg. commander, 62a, 92b, 287b, 440c, 572g, 597, 598a, 766a, 770a

Yakovlev, ex-officer Alexandra's Life Guards Lancer Reg., managed Maria Nicholaevna's train, 406d, 593c, 856a, 860c, 1345a

Yanushkevich, Nicholas Nicholaevich, inf. gen., chief high command staff until Aug. 1915 when sent with Nicholasha to Caucasus as his assistant for military affairs, 18a,b, 187b, 315a, 345a,b, 393b, 422f, 435g,i, 867a, 874d, 1560d, 1570

Yudenich, Nicholas Nicholaevich, inf. gen., 858a (Fn. 232), 860e, 937a (Fn. 251)

Yur'evsky, Georgy Alexandrovich, prince, son of Alexander II from his marriage to E. M. Dolgorukaya, 673b

Yusupov, Felix Felixovich (the Elder), prince, Count Sumarokov-Elston, adj.-gen., lt.-gen., ex-commander Dowager Empress Maria Fedorovna's cav. reg., commander Moscow from May 5 to Sept. 3, 1915, when forced from post in connection with Moscow anti-German riots, father of F. F. Yusupov (the Younger)(q.v.), 323c, 345b, 373d, 414d, 422f, 427a,e, 433b, 434, 435c, 440g, 485i, 488, 490, 493a, 1325a, 1452b; his wife, **Zinaida Nicholaevna,** knyazhna, mother of F. F. Yusupov (the Younger)(q.v.), 422f, 426f, 427a, 440g, 485i, 1325a

Yusupov, Felix Felixovich (the Younger), prince, Count Sumarokov-Elston, organized assassination of Rasputin, exiled to estate in Kursk gubernaya whence he escaped to France, 207b, 323c, 358, 427e, 723e, 1333, 1336a; implicated in Rasputin's murder, 1655c,d, 1657, 1659, 1660; his wife, **Irina Alexandrovna ("Irina"),** countess, daughter of Alexander Michaelovich, 207b, 208-210, 213, 272, 273b, 276, 323c, 358, 376i, 343d (?), 426e, 1325, 1333, 1336a, 1380e, 1609a, 1655c, 1665b; their daughter, **Irina ("Little Irina"),** 207b, 210, 213, 1325

Zaionchkovsky, Nicholas Cheslavovich, t.s., asst.-director Holy Synod until Oct. 13, 1916, then senator, 1116 (Fn. 296), Fn. 339

Zamoisky, Adam Stanislavovich, count, cornet Life Guards Lancer Reg., ex-adj. to Nicholas Nicholaevich, made a.d.c., Feb. 13, 1916, 824a, 941g, 1257a, 1515b

Zanotti, Magdalina Frantsevna ("Madelaine"), kamer-frau of Alexandra, 159b, 196a, 766a, 807e, 923a, 1434f

Zborovsky, Victor Erastovich ("Zabor.", Vikt. Erast.), *sotnik* His Maj.'s convoy, 184 (Fn. 72), 413d, 609c, 634d, 637a, 640c, 644b, 918b, 1091a, 1093a, 1095b, 1097, 1123, 1124, 1127, 1128b, 1167b, 1204, 1208, 1220, 1573b

Zelenetsky, Rostislav Dmitrievich, officer Life Guards Ship's Co., ex-commander cruiser *Oleg* and imp. yacht *Standard*, naval capt. 1st-grade during war, then rear-ad.; made asst. to g.p. Cyril Vladimirovich who commanded naval detachments at front, 119a, 1107, 1313; replaced by Sablin as commander *Standard*, 1311b, 1318, 1410d, 1415b, 1418b, Fn. 448

Zemstvo, 596c, 598c, 992c, 1008b, 1178b; *see also* Union of Zemstvoes

Zeppelins, 433a, 770b; *see also* Airplanes

About the Author

JOSEPH T. FUHRMANN is Professor of History at Murray State University.
Praeger published his fifth book, *Rasputin, A Life*, in 1990.

ISBN 0-313-30511-0

EAN

9 780313 305115

90000>

HARDCOVER BAR CODE